Frank Moore

Anecdotes, Poetry and Incidents of the War

North and South from 1860 to 1865

Frank Moore

Anecdotes, Poetry and Incidents of the War
North and South from 1860 to 1865

ISBN/EAN: 9783337778323

Printed in Europe, USA, Canada, Australia, Japan

Cover: Foto ©ninafisch / pixelio.de

More available books at **www.hansebooks.com**

ANECDOTES,

POETRY AND INCIDENTS

OF THE WAR:

NORTH AND SOUTH.

1860—1865.

COLLECTED AND ARRANGED

BY FRANK MOORE,

EDITOR OF "THE REBELLION RECORD," "DIARY OF THE AMERICAN REVOLUTION," ETC., ETC.

———•◆◆•———

NEW YORK:

PRINTED FOR THE SUBSCRIBERS.

1866.

INTRODUCTORY NOTE.

In the preparation of this volume, it has been the design of the editor to preserve, as far as possible, the most notable anecdotes and incidents of the late war, and also such songs, ballads, and other pieces of versification, as have been well received, and are considered worthy of perpetuation by the reading public. Of course, many of the brilliant and heroic adventures that form an important part of the private and personal history of the great conflict, will not be found in these pages, for the simple and very proper reason, that the actors therein alone know them, and as yet they have not made them public. As it is the intention of the editor to prepare and publish a second series at a suitable time, should he find material sufficient for the purpose, it is important that the noble soldiers and sailors who have now returned from the field should forward to him such anecdotes and incidents as they may have knowledge of, that are not already included in this work. And should the reader discover any errors of fact in these pages, he will confer an obligation by advising of such errors, that they may be corrected in a future edition.

F. M.

New York, May, 1866.

ANECDOTES, POETRY, AND INCIDENTS.

ANECDOTE OF GENERAL GRANT.

The following was told by an officer of General Grant's staff : —

The hero and veteran, who was citizen, captain, colonel, brigadier and major-general within a space of nine months, though a rigid disciplinarian, and a perfect Ironsides in the discharge of his official duties, could enjoy a good joke, and is always ready to perpetrate one when an opportunity presents. Indeed, among his acquaintances, he is as much renowned for his eccentric humor as he is for his skill and bravery as a commander.

When Grant was a brigadier in South-east Missouri, he commanded an expedition against the rebels under Jeff. Thompson, in North-east Arkansas. The distance from the starting-point of the expedition to the supposed rendezvous of the rebels was about one hundred and ten miles, and the greater portion of the route lay through a howling wilderness. The imaginary suffering that our soldiers endured during the two first days of their march was enormous. It was impossible to steal or "confiscate" uncultivated real estate, and not a hog, or a chicken, or an ear of corn was anywhere to be seen. On the third day, however, affairs looked more hopeful, for a few small specks of ground, in a state of partial cultivation, were here and there visible. On that day, Lieutenant Wickfield, of an Indiana cavalry regiment, commanded the advance-guard, consisting of eight mounted men. About noon he came up to a small farm-house, from the outward appearance of which he judged that there might be something fit to eat inside. He halted his company, dismounted, and with two second lieutenants entered the dwelling. He knew that Grant's incipient fame had already gone out through all that country, and it occurred to him that by representing himself to be the general he might obtain the best the house afforded. So, assuming a very imperative demeanor, he accosted the inmates of the house, and told them he must have something for himself and staff to eat. They desired to know who he was, and he told them that he was Brigadier-General Grant. At the sound of that name they flew around with alarming alacrity, and served up about all they had in the house, taking great pains all the while to make loud professions of loyalty. The lieutenants ate as much as they could of the not over-sumptuous meal, but which was, nevertheless, good for that country, and demanded what was to pay. "Nothing." And they went on their way rejoicing.

In the mean time General Grant, who had halted his army a few miles further back for a brief resting-spell, came in sight of, and was rather favorably impressed with, the appearance of this same house. Riding up to the fence in front of the door, he desired to know if they would cook him a meal.

"No," said a female in a gruff voice ; "General Grant and his staff have just been here and eaten everything in the house except one pumpkin pie."

"Humph," murmured Grant; "what is your name ?"

"Selvidge," replied the woman.

Casting a half-dollar in at the door, he asked if she would keep that pie till he sent an officer for it, to which she replied that she would.

That evening, after the camping-ground had been selected, the various regiments were notified that there would be a grand parade at half-past six, for orders. Officers would see that their men all turned out, etc.

In five minutes the camp was in a perfect uproar, and filled with all sorts of rumors; some thought the enemy were upon them, it being so unusual to have parades when on a march.

At half-past six the parade was formed, ten columns deep, and nearly a quarter of a mile in length.

After the usual routine of ceremonies the Acting Assistant Adjutant-General read the following order :

HEAD-QUARTERS, ARMY IN THE FIELD.

SPECIAL ORDER No. ——.

Lieutenant Wickfield, of the —— Indiana cavalry, having on this day eaten everything in Mrs. Selvidge's house, at the crossing of the Ironton and Pocahontas and Black River and Cape Girardeau roads, except one pumpkin pie, Lieutenant Wickfield is hereby ordered to return with an escort of one hundred cavalry and eat that pie also.
U. S. GRANT,
Brigadier-General Commanding.

LITTLE EDDIE THE DRUMMER-BOY.

A REMINISCENCE OF WILSON'S CREEK.

A FEW days before our regiment received orders to join General Lyon, on his march to Wilson's Creek, the drummer of our company was taken sick and conveyed to the hospital, and on the evening preceding the day that we were to march, a negro was arrested within the lines of the camp, and brought before our captain, who asked him "what business he had within the lines?" He replied: "I know a drummer that you would like to enlist in your company, and I have come to tell you of it." He was immediately requested to inform the drummer that if he would enlist for our short term of service, he would be allowed extra pay, and to do this, he must be on the ground early in the morning. The negro was then passed beyond the guard.

On the following morning there appeared before the captain's quarters during the beating of the *réveille*, a good-looking, middle-aged woman, dressed in deep mourning, leading by the hand a sharp, sprightly-looking boy, apparently about twelve or thirteen years of age. Her story was soon told. She was from East Tennessee, where her husband had been killed by the rebels, and all their property destroyed. She had come to St. Louis in search of her sister, but not finding her, and being destitute of money, she thought if she could procure a situation for her boy as a drummer for the short time that we had to remain in the service, she could find employment for herself, and perhaps find her sister by the time we were discharged.

During the rehearsal of her story the little fellow kept his eyes intently fixed upon the countenance of the captain, who was about to express a determination not to take so small a boy, when he spoke out: "Don't be afraid, captain, I can drum." This was spoken with so much confidence, that the captain immediately observed, with a smile: "Well, well, sergeant, bring the drum, and order our fifer to come forward." In a few moments the drum was produced, and our fifer, a tall, round-shouldered, good-natured fellow, from the Dubuque mines, who stood, when erect, something over six feet in height, soon made his appearance.

Upon being introduced to his new comrade, he stooped down, with his hands resting upon his knees, that were thrown forward into an acute angle, and after peering into the little fellow's face a moment, he observed: "My little man, can you drum?" "Yes, sir," he replied, "I drummed for Captain Hill in Tennessee." Our fifer immediately commenced straightening himself upward until all the angles in his person had disappeared, when he placed his fife at his mouth, and played the "Flowers of Edinborough," one of the most difficult things to follow with the drum that could have been selected, and nobly did the little fellow follow him, showing himself to be a master of the drum. When the music ceased, our captain turned to the mother and observed: "Madam, I will take your boy. What is his name?" "Edward Lee," she replied; then placing her hand upon the captain's arm, she continued, "Captain, if he is not killed" — here her maternal feelings overcame her utterance, and she bent down over her boy and kissed him upon the forehead. As she arose, she observed: "Captain, you will bring him back with you, won't you?"

"Yes, yes," he replied, "we will be certain to bring him back with us. We shall be discharged in six weeks."

In an hour after, our company led the Iowa First out of camp, our drum and fife playing "The girl I left behind me." Eddie, as we called him, soon became a great favorite with all the men in the company. When any of the boys had returned from a horticultural excursion, Eddie's share of the peaches and melons was the first apportioned out. During our heavy and fatiguing march from Rolla to Springfield, it was often amusing to see our long-legged fifer wading through the mud with our little drummer mounted upon his back, and always in that position when fording streams.

During the fight at Wilson's Creek I was stationed with a part of our company on the right of Totten's battery, while the balance of our company, with a part of the Illinois regiment, was ordered down into a deep ravine upon our left, in which it was known a portion of the enemy was concealed, with whom they were soon engaged. The contest in the ravine continuing some time, Totten suddenly wheeled his battery upon the enemy in that quarter, when they soon retreated to the high ground behind their lines. In less than twenty minutes after, Totten had driven the enemy from the ravine, the word passed from man to man throughout the army, "Lyon is killed!" and soon after, hostilities having ceased upon both sides, the order came for our main force to fall back upon Springfield, while a part of the Iowa First and two companies of the Missouri regiment were to camp upon the ground and cover the retreat next morning. That night I was detailed for guard duty, my turn of guard closing with the morning call. When I went out with the officer as a relief, I found that my post was upon a high eminence that overlooked the deep ravine in which our men had engaged the enemy, until Totten's battery came to their assistance. It was a dreary, lonesome beat. The moon had gone down in the early part of the night, while the stars twinkled dimly through a hazy atmosphere, lighting up imperfectly the surrounding objects. Occasionally I would place my ear near the ground and listen for the sound of footsteps, but all was silent save the far-off howling of the wolf, that seemed to scent upon the evening air the banquet that we had been preparing for him. The hours passed slowly away, when at length the morning light began to streak along the eastern sky, making surrounding objects more plainly visible. Presently I heard a drum beat up the morning call. At first I thought it came from the camp of the enemy across the creek; but as I listened, I found that it came up from the deep ravine; for a few minutes it was silent, and then as it became more light I heard it again. I listened — the sound of the drum was familiar to me — and I knew that it was

Our drummer-boy from Tennessee
Beating for help the *réveille*.

I was about to desert my post to go to his assistance, when I discovered the officer of the guard approaching with two men. We all listened to the sound, and were satisfied that it was Eddie's drum. I asked permission to go to his assistance. The officer hesitated, saying that the orders were to march in twenty minutes. I promised to be back in that time, and he consented. I immediately started down the hill through the thick undergrowth, and upon reaching the valley I followed the sound of the drum, and soon found him seated upon the ground, his back leaning against the trunk of a fallen tree, while his drum hung upon a bush in front of him, reaching nearly to the ground. As soon as he discovered me he dropped his drumsticks and exclaimed, "O Corporal! I am so glad to see you. Give me a drink," reaching out his hand for my canteen, which was empty. I immediately turned to bring him some water from the brook that I could hear rippling through the bushes near by, when, thinking that I was about to leave him, he commenced crying, saying: "Don't leave me, Corporal — I can't walk." I was soon back with the water, when I discovered that both of his feet had been shot away by a cannon-ball. After satisfying his thirst, he looked up into my face and said: "You don't think I will die, Corporal, do you? This man said I would not — he said the surgeon could cure my feet." I now discovered a man lying in the grass near him. By his dress I recognized him as belonging to the enemy. It appeared that he had been shot through the bowels, and fallen near where Eddie lay. Knowing that he could not live, and seeing the condition of the boy, he had crawled to him, taken off his buckskin suspenders, and corded the little fellow's legs below the knee, and then laid down and died. While he was telling me these particulars, I heard the tramp of cavalry coming down the ravine, and in a moment a scout of the enemy was upon us, and I was taken prisoner. I requested the officer to take Eddie up in front of him, and he did so, carrying him with great tenderness and care. When we reached the camp of the enemy the little fellow was dead.

HOW TO CROSS A RIVER. — Colonel Weer, at the head of his division, arrived at White River, Arkansas, at night and found the stream impassable. The recent snow had gone off with a rain, raising the water very fast, and the whole army was hurrying by forced marches to cross the river before it rose, as it was so low as to be fordable; but, with all his haste, his forces were too slow. Colonel Weer ordered Captain Stock-

ton to cross his battery "as soon as possible." The captain asked, "Where are the boats?" Colonel Weer determined to beat Gens. Schofield and Herron, who marched upon two other roads, replied: "Make them, sir, the quickest way possible!" Captain Stockton took two wagon beds of his mule wagons, and covered them with tarpaulins, and making a cable out of prolongs, was crossing his battery within two hours! The next morning the rope across the stream broke, and all attempts to get across by swimming horses and tying it to mules' tails, failed, when Stockton drove a plug into a shell and fired it across! His lieutenant on the opposite shore, ran and picked it up, and all things went on swimmingly again. A trip with this boat was made and loaded in ten minutes! The boat was in constant use four days, and not a single accident happened.

A BRAVE WOMAN. — Captain Boight of Company H, Twenty-Third Kentucky Regiment, related the following anecdote of the war.

During the retreat of the army of Kirby Smith from Cumberland Gap, the regiment to which he belonged was in the van of the Federal army. One morning, when the regiment was about twenty-six miles east of the Wild Cat Mountains, they were surprised to see a file of ten men, all of them secesh, marching toward their lines, and a woman marching in their rear with a musket in her hands; on their coming within the Federal lines she coolly gave them up to the officer commanding as prisoners. In accounting for their capture, she said that her husband had joined a military company in the Federal service, and had left her alone to take care of the house, which lay between the two armies. Eleven secessionists had come into the house that morning and proceeded to make themselves perfectly at home, first killing all her chickens, and setting them to roast by the fire. They then proceeded to dispose of the things around the house, taking up the carpets, and constructing horse blankets out of them.

. They next perpetrated other atrocities of a destructive and objectionable character, which had the effect of making the lady of the house "furiously wild," as the captain expressed it, and she determined that such outrageous conduct should not go unpunished. She accordingly carried away their muskets to a place of safety, reserving two for her own use, and then going to the room in which they were regaling themselves on her defunct chickens, she informed them that they were her prisoners. One of them jumped up to seize her, when she levelled her gun at him and fired, causing him to bite the dust, which lay thickly strewed on the carpetless floor. Throwing away the now useless gun, she took the other in her hand and ordered the remaining ten to march toward the Union camp threatening to shoot the first who attempted to run away. Having a wholesome fear of sharing a similar fate to that of their companion, they went quietly along, and were accordingly handed over to the military authorities. On being laughed at for being taken prisoner by a woman, they said they had been wanting to get captured for some time past, and were heartily glad that they were prisoners at last. They were entirely sick of the war, they said, and did not care how, so that they got out of it.

UNDER THE WASHINGTON ELM.

CAMBRIDGE, APRIL 27, 1861.

BY OLIVER WENDELL HOLMES.

EIGHTY years have passed, and more,
 Since under the brave old tree
Our fathers gathered in arms, and swore
They would follow the sign their banners bore,
 And fight till the land was free.

Half of their work was done,
 Half is left to do—
Cambridge and Concord and Lexington!
When the battle is fought and won,
 What shall be told of you?

Hark! 'tis the south wind moans—
 Who are the martyrs down?—
Ah, the marrow was true in your children's bones,
That sprinkled with blood the cursed stones
 Of the murder-haunted town!

What if the storm-clouds blow?
 What if the green leaves fall?
Better the crashing tempest's throe,
Than the army of worms that gnawed below;
 Trample them one and all!

Then, when the battle is won,
 And the land from traitors free,
Our children shall tell of the strife begun
When Liberty's second April sun
 Was bright on our brave old tree!

FUN ON THE RAPPAHANNOCK:—A soldier of the Eighth Ohio regiment, writing from Falmouth, makes the following notes on the movements in that vicinity:—

"Everything seemed to be progressing finely until Tuesday night, when the "heavens opened" and the flood descended." "Eph" suggested that the flood gates must be entirely off their hinges, as his sleeping apartment suddenly became a bath house, and his bunk a bathing tub. Indeed our "brown stone front" came near being dissolved, and the "aristocratic" inmates drowned. The storm continued with very little cessation until Friday morning, and as every hour made the "soil" more *soft* than "sacred," the roads soon became blocked with an indescribable mass of artillery wagons, and "pontoons," hopelessly stuck in the mud. It was very evident that this "delay of the pontoons" was not attributable to a lack of energy on the part of Q. M. General Meigs, nor yet on account of a misunderstanding between Messrs. Generals Halleck

and Burnside. "Eph" thinks a greater General than any of these had something to do with it, and remarked that "it was undoubtedly on account of the same One to whom Victor Hugo ascribes Napoleon's failure to win the battle of Waterloo."

One thing is certain, the artillery and "pontoon" could move no more at present. The "meeting" was postponed, and after lying out in the mud and rain for three days and nights, the troops that had moved up the river came back, probably *believing* that it was "all for the best," but on account of the mud that obstructed their vision they failed to "see it." As we were to have crossed the river nearly opposite our camp, we did not leave our quarters, and had a good opportunity to witness the return of the muddy, straggling mass. The scene was anything but a pleasant one, yet there were many ludicrous incidents connected with it. "Eph" and three or four of the "boys" were standing near our mansion, looking at the floating mass of men, horses, mules, artillery, and wagons, when we observed a conglomeration of blue cloth and mud approaching. As it had on a gun, knapsack, haversack and canteen, we concluded it was a "straggler," and "Eph" hailed him with—

"Hallo! Earthen-ware! what regiment do *you* belong to?"

The figure never paused, but the earth; visible under the visor of a cap.moved, displaying a cavern from which issued the words:—

"Don't speak to *me!* I'm a spared monument! I've marched in mud, swam mud, drank mud, and slept in mud for three days and nights. My colonel and regiment were all drowned in mud. I'm the only man left, and I'm demoralized as ——"

"Eph" extracted the leather pontoons he wears from the rich soil in which he was standing, retreated "without loss" to the "sitting room," threw himself into the "easy" chair before the "coal grate," elevated his pontoons to the "mantel-piece," and remained in this position evidently meditating until we came in. After we had requested him to remove his muddy "pontoons" from the "furniture," he said:—

"That's the first *demoralized monument*, I ever saw. He was probably a *brother* of the Fire Zouave we saw over in Fredericksburg the other day, and I am inclined to believe most of his story." At this juncture some one called him out to look at the new balloon which was going up from near General Sumner's headquarters. On his return we asked him "what he supposed the professor saw that attracted him to such a dizzy height so often?" "Well," said "Eph," (at the same time setting one of his soiled "pontoons" down on our boots just polished for "inspection,") "I guess it ain't what he sees while he's up there so much as it is the *five thousand dollars* he sees every time he comes down."

To-day we rode down to the river to look at the enemy's fortifications, see their cannon and ask their pickets the price of cotton. At Falmouth we visited the ruins of an old bridge, on the end of which we had a picket to watch a gray-back" picket who was stationed at the opposite end, and whose duty was evidently to watch ours. All along the river we found the pickets of the opposing armies within easy hailing distance, and apparently quite friendly, but as conversation was not allowed, we asked no questions.

The hills back of Fredericksburg looked as though they were in possession of an enterprising oil company who were engaged in boring for "ile," but from the fact that the piles of fresh earth increased daily we suspected they had not "struck a vein." On our return we passed through the little hollow near General Sumner's headquarters, where a part of our hospitals were located during the battle of the 12th ult., and stopped to read some of the names appearing upon the little headboards that were planted in a regular row on one side. "Eph" made the discovery of several, that read "Private, Unknown," and one "Lieut., Unknown," whereupon he immediately seated himself upon a log, and crossing his "pontoons" — upon each of which he had strapped a "buzz saw" the two constituting what he calls his "spurs," and said : —

"Death is a rude customer to meet at *any* time and at any place ; he is not welcome even at home and among friends — but to think of a fellow dying as it were *alone*, with not even an old comrade or a familiar face near, and upon whose monument — a pine board two by three — appears the inscription ' Private or Lieutenant *Unknown*,' reminds me that I am not well and ought to be discharged." Here he looked pale, and we began to think he *was* unwell, but he continued : " I wonder if the one who wrote those epitaphs had an idea that when the Chief Bugler comes to sound the last 'reveille,' he *would* pause to learn whether the ashes that slumber beneath these pine boards ever wore straps or not ?" Here he paused again and looked at his old blouse, shrugged his shoulders, and concluded —

"When the epauletted general who *commands* and the soldier without straps who obeys, both stand before One in whose presence *all*

*   *   * ——' tinsel of time,
Must fade and die in the light of that region sublime,'

I wonder if they will remain Unknown ?"

"WHEN YOU IS ABOUT, WE IS." — During the passage of the national troops through Missouri, in pursuit of General Price, a crowd of negroes came out from a large house to see them, when the following colloquy took place " Boys, are you all for the Union ?" " Oh ! yes, massa, when you's about we is." " And when Price comes, you are secesh, are you ?" " Lor, yes, massa, we's good secesh then. Can't allow de white folks to git head niggers in dat way."

ARMY SPORTS. — The following extract is from the letter of a soldier in the army of the Potomac : — " I was accidentally a witness of a most interesting scene the other day, which occured close to the camp of the 141st New York regiment. It was a rabbit hunt, in which a whole company participated, and conducted it on strictly military principles. They first deployed as skirmishers, and each with a stick in his hand, moved in good order through a piece of land from which most of the wood had been taken ; heaps of branches and limbs scattered here and there, afforded excellent retreats for the game in question. As they marched along, each one beat every bush within reaching distance of his stick, until a rabbit was started. This was announced by a yell, that instantly put every one on the alert, and the scene that followed was exciting and ludicrous in the extreme ; the yell was caught up by every soldier, and a chase of the most vigorous description was the rapid result. The flankers strained every nerve to flank or surround the terrified creature, who, bewildered by the tumult on every side, would double at each point where a soldier opposed him, until his retreat was effectually cut off, and he was either caught alive or felled by a blow of a stick. Where the rabbit was an old one, he often escaped by fleeing to the cover, yet undisturbed by the axe, and the chase would have to be abandoned. I stood on a small hill for more than an hour, watching them, and the shouts of the men, the efforts of the quarry to escape, which was almost always in sight, the agile movements of the soldiers and the roars of laughter which followed when one less cautious or more excited than the others, tripped and fell his length in the bushes, while his companions either ran over him or around him, (never stopping) making altogether a most pleasing spectacle. Although ten blows hit a soldier where one hit the rabbit when he was surrounded, still the utmost good humor prevailed, and the fallen ones took the laugh of their comrades without the slightest sign of anger or ill feeling. Such little episodes in the life of a soldier are not only invaluable as regards his health and the important part they take in preventing a depressed state of mind, but furnish also a welcome change in the place of " hard tack," and salt beef, which comprise the staple articles of the soldier's food, for the company just mentioned caught eleven in less than two hours, which was about one half the number started."

SKEDADDLE.

The shades of night were falling fast,
As through a Southern village passed
A youth, who bore, not over nice,
A banner with the gay device,
        Skedaddle !

His hair was red, his toes beneath
Peeped, like an acorn from its sheath,
While with a frightened voice he sung
A burden strange to Yankee tongue,
        Skedaddle !

He saw no household fire where he
Might warm his toe or hominy ;
Beyond the Cordilleras shone,
And from his lips escaped a groan,
    Skedaddle!

" Oh ! stay," a cullered pusson said,
" An' on dis bossom res' your hed ! "
The octoroon she winked her eye,
But still he answered, with a sigh,
    Skedaddle!

" Beware McClellan, Buell, and Banks,
Beware of Halleck's deadly ranks ! "
This was the planter's last Good Night ;
The chap replied, far out of sight,
    Skedaddle!

At break of day, as several boys
From Maine, New York and Illinois
Were moving Southward, in the air
They heard these accents of despair,
    Skedaddle!

A chap was found and at his side
A bottle, showing how he died,
Still grasping in his hand of ice
That banner with the strange device,
    Skedaddle!

There in the twilight, thick and gray,
Considerably played out he lay ;
And through the vapor, gray and thick,
A voice fell like a rocket-stick,
    Skedaddle!

———

AN INCIDENT. — When the United States vessels were on their way to attack Fernandina, Florida, they picked up a contraband who had ventured to sea in a small boat to notify them that the rebels were deserting the place. While questioning the black, some of the officers of the Alabama remarked that he should have brought them newspapers to let them know what was going on. " I thought of dat," replied the contraband, " and fotched a Charleston paper wid me." With this he put his hand in his bosom and brought forth a paper, and with the air of a man who was rendering an important service, handed it to the circle of inquirers. They grasped it eagerly, but one glance induced a general burst of laughter, to the profound astonishment of poor Cuffee, who, it seems, could not read, and imagining that one paper was as good as another, had brought one dated 1822. It is a little odd that this paper, which had floated so long down the stream of time, contained *an article in favor of negro emancipation.*

———

POSTAL AFFAIRS. — THE following is the superscription of a letter that passed through the Louisville, Ky., post-office :

" Feds and Confeds, let this go free
Down to Nashville, Tennessee ;
This three-cent stamp will pay the cost
Until you find Sophia Yost.

" Postmasters North, or even South,
May open it and find the truth ;
I merely say my wife's got well,
And has a baby cross as ——, you know."

———

WHO FIRST ANSWERED THE PRESIDENT'S CALL ? — On the morning of the sixteenth of April, 1861, at nine o'clock, the Logan Guards received orders from Gov. Curtin to proceed immediately to Harrisburgh, and by nine o'clock that night they were ready to leave for that place with one hundred members. Through some mismanagement of the railroad company, they did not get off until the next morning at four o'clock. As a consequence, they arrived in Harrisburgh about six o'clock on the morning of the seventeenth, which was, at least *one hour before the arrival of any other company.* After the other companies arrived, they were all sworn in together ; and on the morning of the eighteenth the five companies left Harrisburgh for Washington city. During their passage through Baltimore, and their entrance into Washington, *the Logan Guards had the right, and were the first company to report themselves for duty to the Adjutant General.* The credit should fall on those who deserve it — the gallant Logan Guards, Capt. John B. Selheimer, of Lewiston, Mifflin County Pennsylvania.

———

TOUCHING FAREWELL ADDRESS. — Orpheus C. Kerr thus wrote, about the time General McClellan was relieved from the command of the army of the Potomac : —

But the whole body of the Mackerels, sane and insane alike, unite in a feeling of strong anguish blended with enthusiasm, at the removal of the beloved General of the Mackerel Brigade. He has been so much a father to them all, that they never expected to get a step farther while he was with them.

There's a piece of domestic philosophy for you, my boy.

When the General heard of his removal, my boy, he said that it was like divorcing a husband from a wife who had always supported him, and immediately let fly the following farewell address :

HEAD-QUARTERS OF ARMY OF ACCOMAC,
FOOT OF THE BLUE RIDGE.

MY CHILDREN : An order from the Honest Abe divorces us, and gives the command of all these attached beings to Major General Wobert Wobinson. [Heartrending and enthusiastic cheers.]

In parting with you I cannot express how much I love your dear bosoms. As an army, you have grown from youth to old age under my care. In you I never found doubt or coldness, nor anything else. The victories you have won under my command will live in the nation's work of fiction. The strategy we have achieved, the graves of many unripe Mackerels, the broken forms of those disabled by the emancipation proclamation — the strongest associations that can exist among men — still make it advisable that you should vote for me as President of the United States in 1865. Thus we shall ever be comrades in supporting the Constitution, and making the Constitution support us.

THE GENERAL OF THE MACKEREL BRIGADE.

[Green Seal.]

ADROIT SMUGGLING: — Some Irish women searched the market for a very large chicken, and on being shown one, asked if it would hold a pint flask. The dealer thought that it would, and the flask being produced, he satisfied them that it would. That was the chicken they wanted. The women finally admitted that they were going to cook the chicken, place the flask, after filling it with brandy, inside of it for stuffing, and send it to camp.

THERE'S LIFE IN THE OLD LAND YET!

BY JAS. R. RANDALL,

By blue Patapsco's billowy dash,
  The tyrant's war-shout comes,
Along with the cymbal's fitful clash,
  And the growl of his sullen drums,
We hear it! we heed it, with vengeful thrills,
  And we shall not forgive or forget ;
There's faith in the streams, there's hope in the hills,
  There's life in the old land yet!

Minions! we sleep, but we are not dead ;
  We are crushed, we are scourged, we are scarred ;
We crouch — 'tis to welcome the triumph tread
  Of the peerless BEAUREGARD.
Then woe to your vile, polluting horde
  When the Southern braves are met,
There's faith in the victor's stainless sword,
  There is life in the old land yet!

Bigots! ye quell not the valiant mind,
  With the clank of an iron chain,
The spirit of freedom sings in the wind,
  O'er *Merryman, Thomas,* and *Kane ;*
And we, though we smite not, and are not thralls,
  We are piling a gory debt ;
While down by McHenry's dungeon-walls,
  There's life in the old land yet !

Our women have hung their harps away,
  And they scowl on your brutal bands,
While the nimble poignard dares the day,
  In their dear defiant hands.
They will strip their tresses to string our bows,
  Ere the Northern sun is set ;
There's faith in their unrelenting woes,
  There's life in the old land yet!

There's life, though it throbbeth in silent veins,
  'Tis vocal without noise,
It gushed o'er Manassas' solemn plains,
  From the blood of the MARYLAND BOYS!
That blood shall cry aloud, and rise
  With an everlasting threat, —
By the death of the brave, by the God in the skies,
  There's life in the old land yet !

A HERO INDEED. — Colonel Edward E. Cross, thus described his experience at the battle of Fredericksburg : — " It came near being my last battle. As we were advancing to those fatal heights in line of battle, I was near my colors. A twelve-pounder shell, from the Washington battery, burst right in front of me. One fragment struck me just below the heart, making a bad wound. Another blew off my hat ; another (small bit) entered my mouth, and broke out three of my best jaw-teeth, while the gravel, bits of frozen earth, and minute fragments of shell covered my face with bruises.

" I fell insensible, and lay so for some time, when another fragment of shell, striking me on the left leg, below the knee, brought me to my senses. My mouth was full of blood, fragments of teeth and gravel, my breast-bone almost broken in, and I lay in mud two inches deep. My brave boys had gone along. I always told them never to stop for me. Dead and wounded lay thick around. One captain of French's division was gasping in death within a foot of my head, his bowels all torn out. The air was full of hissing bullets and bursting shells. Getting on my hands and knees, I looked for my flag. Thank God, there it fluttered right amid the smoke and fire of the front line. I could hear the cheers of my brave men. Twice the colors dropped, but were up in an instant. I tried to crawl along, but a shot came and struck the steel scabbard of my sabre, splitting it open, and knocking me down flat.

" Dizzy and faint, I had sense enough to lay myself out decently, 'feet to the foe.' Two lines passed over me, but soon they swayed back, trampling on the dead and dying. Halting about thirty yards in the rear, one line laid down and commenced firing. Imagine the situation. Right between two fires of bullets and shell — for our own artillery fire from over the river was mostly too short, and did great damage to our own troops. I lay on the field for hours, the most awful moments of my life. As the balls from our line hissed over me within a foot of my head, I covered my face with both hands, and counted rapidly from one to one hundred, expecting every moment my brains would spatter the ground. But they didn't.

" The guardian angels (if there be such personages) or my destiny saved me. The end of my days was reserved for another and I hope more fortunate occasion. For if I am to die on the battle-field, I pray that it may be with the cheers of victory in my ears. When it became dark some of my men found me and I was carried to the hospital."

And the prayer of the brave New Hampshire Colonel was answered, for he did " die with the cheers of victory in his ears," on the ever memorable field of Gettysburg.

ADVENTURES IN EAST TENNESSEE. — A rifleman belonging to the Southern army gives the following account of his experiences in the service: —

In the beginning of the American war I belonged to a regiment of mounted riflemen, and we were sent into Eastern Tennessee, where there was a good deal of bushwhacking about that time. We were picketed one day in a line about two miles long across country, and I was on the extreme left. I took my saddle off, holsters and all, and hung it on a branch of a peach-tree, and my carbine on another. We knew there were no Yankees near, and so I was kind o' off guard, eating peaches. By and by I saw a young woman coming down to where I was, on horseback. She wanted to know if there were many of the boys near, and if they would buy some milk of her if she took it down to them. I said I thought they would, and took about a quart myself; and as she hadn't much more, I emptied the water out of my canteen and took the rest. Says she, "If you'll come up to the house yonder, I've got something better than that; you may have some good peach brandy — some of your fellows might like a little." I said I'd go, and she says, "You needn't take your saddle or carbine, it's just a step, and they are safe enough here — there's nobody about." So I mounted bareback, and she led the way. When we passed the bars where she came in, she says, "You ride on a step, and I'll get down and put up the bars." I went on, and as she came up behind, she says pretty sharp, "Ride a little faster, if you please." I looked round and she had a revolver pointed straight at my head, and I saw that she knew how to use it. I had left everything behind me like a fool, and had to give in and obey orders. "That's the house if you please," she says, and showed me a house in the edge of the woods a quarter of a mile away. We got there, and she told me to get down and eat something, for she was going to give me a long ride — into the Yankee lines, about twenty miles away. Her father came out and abused me like a thief, and told me that he was going to have me sent into the Federal lines to be hung. It seems he had a son hung the week before by some of the Confederates, and was going to have his revenge out of me. I ate pretty well, for I thought I might need it before I got any more, and then the old fellow began to curse me and abuse me like anything. He said he would shoot me on the spot if it wasn't that he'd rather have me hung; and instead of giving me my own horse, he took the worst one he had in his stables, and they put me on that with my feet tied together under his belly. Luckily they didn't tie my hands, for they thought I had no arms, and couldn't help myself; but I always carried a small revolver in my shirt-bosom. The girl kept too sharp watch on me for me to use it. She never turned her revolver from me, and I knew that the first suspicious move I made I was a dead man. We went about ten miles in this way, when my old crow-bait gave out and wouldn't go any further. She wouldn't trust me afoot, and so had to give up her own horse; but she kept the bridle in her own hands, and walked ahead with one eye turned back on me, and the revolver cocked, with her finger on the trigger, so that I never had a chance to put my hand in my bosom. We finally came to a spring, and she asked me if I wanted to drink. I didn't feel much like drinking, but I said yes, and so she let me down. I put my head down to the water, and at the same time put my hand down to where the revolver was, and pulled it forward where I could put my hand on it easily; but she was on the watch, and I couldn't pull it out. I mounted again, and the first time she was off her guard a little, I fired and broke the arm she held the pistol in. "Now," says I, "it's my turn; you'll please get on that horse, and we'll go back." She didn't flinch or say a word, but got on the horse, and I tied her legs as they had mine, and we went back to the house. The old man he heard us come up to the door and looked out of the window. He turned as pale as a sheet and ran for his rifle. I knew what he was after, and pushed the door in before he was loaded. Says I, "You may put that shooting-iron down and come with me." He wasn't as brave as the girl, but it was no use to resist, and he knew it; so he came along. About half way back we met some of our fellows who had missed me, and come out to look me up. They took them both, and I don't know what they did with them, but I know very well what they would have done with me.

A RAINY DAY IN CAMP.

'Tis a cheerless, lonesome evening
    When the soaking, sodden ground
Will not echo to the footfall
    Of the sentinel's dull round.

God's blue star-spangled banner
    To-night is not unfurled,
Surely He has not deserted
    This weary, warring world.

I peer into the darkness,
    And the crowding fancies come;
The night wind blowing northward
    Carries all my heart towards home.

For I 'listed in this army
    Not exactly to my mind;
But my country called for helpers,
    And I could not stay behind.

Lo, I have had a sight of drilling,
    And have roughed it many ways,
And Death has nearly had me, —
    Still I think the service pays.

It's a blessed sort of feeling,
    Whether you live or die,
To know you've helped your country,
    And fought right loyally.

But I can't help thinking, sometimes
    When a wet day's leisure comes,
That I hear the old home voices
    Talking louder than the drums.

And that far familiar faces
  Press in at the tent door,
And the little children's footsteps
  Go pit-pat on the floor.

I can't help thinking, sometimes,
  Of all the parson reads
About that other soldier-life
  Which every true man leads.

And wife, soft-hearted creature,
  Seems a saying in mine ear,
" I'd rather have you in *those* ranks
  Than see you Brigadier."

I call myself a brave one,
  But in my heart I lie;
For my country and her honor
  I'm fiercely free to die,

But when the Lord who bought me,
  Asks for my service here,
To fight the good fight faithfully
  I'm skulking in the rear.

And yet I know that Captain
  All love and care to be;
He would not get impatient
  With a raw recruit like me.

And I know He'd not forget me,
  When the day of peace appears,
I should share with Him the victory
  Of all the volunteers.

And it's kind of cheerful thinking
  Beside the dull tent fire,
About that great promotion
  When He says " Come up higher."

And though 'tis dismal rainy,
  E'en now with thoughts of Him,
Camp-life looks extra cheery,
  And death a deal less grim.

For I seem to see him waiting
  Where a gathered Heaven greets
A great victorious army,
  Surging up the golden streets.

And I hear him read the roll-call,
  And my heart is all a flame
When the dear " Recording Angel "
  Writes down my happy name.

But my fire is dead white ashes,
  And the tent is chilling cold,
And I'm *playing win the battle*,
  When I've never been enrolled.

BEAU HACKETT AS A ZOUAVE. — Militia
companies have always been popular, but never
so much so as since the war broke out. Young
men with stay-at-home-and-take-care-of-the-wo-
men proclivities, are more than ever inclined to
join the Home Guards, in consequence of increased mortality in the army of the United
States, as shown by the newspaper statistics.

With a laudable ambition to support the Government, in any and every emergency, I have recently become a member of the War Department
myself. I joined the Ellsworth Zouaves, a remnant of what used to be a troupe of acrobats, who
distinguished themselves all the way from Chicago
to Washington, by turning double somersaults,
with muskets in their mouths and bayonets in
their hands.

There are no members of the Old Zouave battalion in the new one, but the new one retains
the name of Ellsworth because one of the members has a brother that once saw a picture of
Colonel Ellsworth's grandfather. The names
of organizations frequently have a more remote
origin than this, and many of them are about as
consistent and reasonable as a man claiming
relationship to the President of the United States
because he was born in Lincolnshire, or supposing he would be Governor if he married a gov-
erness, or trying to pass free at a circus as a representative of the press because he is a cheese-
maker.

I was put through a rigid course of examination before I could be made a Zouave, and I say
it with feelings of gratification and self-esteem,
that I was remarkably well posted in the catechism. My father was a hero of the revolution,
having been caught once in a water-wheel, and
whirled around rapidly a number of times.
Others of the family have also distinguished themselves as military men at different periods, but
their deeds of courage are too well known to
need repetition.

The following is a copy verbatim et literatim
et wordim of most of the questions propounded
to me, and the answers thereto, which my intimate acquaintance with the Army Regulations
and the report of the Committee on the Conduct
of the War enable me to answer readily and
accurately. My interrogator was a little man in
Federal blue, with gold leaves on his shoulders.
They called him Major, but he looked young
enough to be a minor. He led off with —

" How old are you, and what are your qualifications ? "

" Twenty-two and a strong stomach."

Then I requested him to fire his interrogations
singly, which he did :

" What is the first duty to be learned by a
soldier ? "

" How to draw his rations."

" What is the most difficult feat for a
to perform ? "

" Drawing his bounty."

" If you were in the rear rank of
during an action, and the man in
before you should be wounded ar
would you do ? "

" I would despatch myself
geon immediately. Some
ward and take the we
that is unnatural."

" If you were
saw cavalry adv
in the rear, w'

" Neithe
moveme

"If you were captured what line of conduct would you pursue?"

"I would treat my captors with the utmost civility."

"What are the duties of Home Guards?"

"Their duty is to see that they have no duties."

"What will you take?"

The latter question may have been answered with too much vehemence, and may have impressed listeners with the belief that I am in the habit of jumping at conclusions. Such, however, is not the case.

I am a Zouave; I am a Home Guard. I have been through all the manœuvres, and can right about face; I can also write about any other part of the body. I can do the hand-springs, and the tumbling, and the lay down and roll-overs, which are done with or without a musket. I have been drilled till the drill has become a bore. I have drilled in all the marches and leaps and vaults, and in the bayonet exercises, and in all the steps, — the common step, the quick step, the very quick step, and the double quick step, and the trot and the run; also in slow time and long time, which I never learned from my landlady nor my tailor. I can shoulder arms, and bear arms, and carry arms, (if they are not too heavy,) and reverse arms, and support arms, (ordinarily my arms support me,) and I can order arms better than I can pay for them after they are ordered. I can parry and tierce, and I can throw a hand-spring with a sword-bayonet in my hand without breaking the sword-bayonet in more than three pieces, and I can bite off a cartridge without breaking my teeth out.

Once, when an order was given to sling knapsacks, I slung mine out of the window, and when the order was given to unsling knapsacks, I went out and slung it back again quicker than anybody else could have done it. I have got a pretty knapsack too — there are letters on it. It is just the thing to sit down on in the time of an action, and is big enough for a breastwork in case of danger from bullets or anything of that sort. It's heavy, though, and I felt that there ʼas an immense responsibility resting on me the t time I shouldered it. I must have felt some- ʼlike Atlas did the first time he shouldered ʼrld. It was so heavy that, as a piece of strategy, I fell back the first time I ʼ onʼ; and as a piece of unmasterly ʼme near breaking my head against Major had promised to put saw- ʼvith soda-water, on the floor

ʼ a Major General's uni- ʼvery opportunity that ʼotion, in our corps, ʼMajor General of ʼzed at. I may ʼars before I ʼʼjor Gen- ʼʼase of ʼʼm-

success in the enterprise I have undertaken. I mean to strike the keynote of my campaign soon, and then look out for a sensation in military circles.

I haven't shaved my upper lip since yesterday afternoon. To-morrow will be the third day. I mean to grow a moustache that will be an object of admiration and envy. Mustachios are indispensable to the achievement of a Major General-ship. Mustachios are absolutely necessary to the achievement of anything that is useful.

In the event of a war between the United States and the Esquimaux, Chicago my residence will, in all likelihood, be one of the first cities attacked by the invading enemy, and every precaution should be taken to be fully prepared for them. Should such attack ever be made by the warlike and bloodthirsty Esquimaux, or any other of the great powers of the earth, and should it be my misfortune to be unable personally to command my forces, (for I have often observed that an invasion is productive of sickness,) I shall take care that my second officer is a man of sufficient capacity to defend the city as ably as I would do it myself. Should the worst come to the worst, I stand ready to sacrifice a substitute on the altar of my country.

BISHOP ROSECRANS. — As Bishop Rosecrans (brother of the General) was at dinner, the conversation reverted to the war.

"It would seem to me, Bishop, that you and your brother, the General, are engaged in very different callings," remarked a gentleman.

"Yes, it appears so," returned the Bishop. "And yet," he continued, "we are both fighting men. While the General is wielding the sword of flesh, I trust that I am using the sword of the Spirit. He is fighting the rebels, and I am fighting the spirits of darkness. There is this difference in the terms of our service: he is fighting with *Price*, while I am fighting without price."

INCIDENT OF FORT PILLOW. — When Commander Davis took possession of Fort Pillow after its evacuation by the Confederates the following letter was found lying on a table in the officers' quarters:

"FORT PILLOW, TENN.

To the first Yankee who reads this:

I present this table not as a manifestation of friendship, yet I entertain no personal animosity to him, but because I can't transport it. After six weeks' bombardment, without doing us any harm whatever, I know you will exult over the occupation of this place, but our evacuation will hurt you from another point with disastrous effect. Five millions white men fighting to be relieved from oppression will never be conquered by twenty millions actuated by malice and pecuniary gain, mark that. We have the science, energy and vigor, with the help of God, to extricate ourselves from this horrible and unnatural difficulty pressed upon us by the North; the day of retribution is approaching, and will fall upon you deadly as a bolt from heaven ; may your sojourn at this place be of few days and full of trouble."

SOLDIER WIT. — The Colonel of an Alabama regiment, was famous for having everything done up in military style. Once, while field officer of the day, and going his tour of inspection, he came on a sentinel from the eleventh Mississippi regiment sitting flat down on his post, with his gun taken entirely to pieces, when the following dialogue took place :

Colonel. "Don't you know that a sentinel while on duty, should always keep on his feet ?"

Sentinel (without looking up). "That's the way we used to do when the war first began ; but that's played out long ago."

Colonel (beginning to doubt if the man was on duty). Are you the sentinel here ?"

Sentinel. "Well, I'm a sort of a sentinel."

Colonel. "Well I'm a sort of officer of the day."

Sentinel. "Well, if you'll hold on till I sort of git my gun together, I'll give you a sort of salute."

SOUTH CAROLINA GENTLEMAN.

AIR — *The Fine Old English Gentleman.*

DOWN in a small Palmetto State the curious ones may find,
A ripping, tearing gentleman of an uncommon kind,
A staggering, swaggering sort of chap who takes his whiskey straight,
And frequently condemns his eyes to that ultimate vengeance which a clergyman of high standing has assured must be a sinner's fate ;
This South Carolina gentleman, one of the present time.

You trace his genealogy, and not far back you'll see,
A most undoubted Octoroon or mayhap a mustee,
And if you note the shaggy locks that cluster on his brow,
You'll find every other hair is varied with a kink that seldom denotes pure Caucasian blood, but on the contrary, betrays an admixture with a race not particular popular now :
This South Carolina gentleman, one of the present time.

He always wears a full dress coat, pre-Adamite in cut.
With waistcoat of the broadest style, through which his ruffles jut ;
Six breast-pins deck his horrid front, and on his fingers shine
Whole invoices of diamond rings which would hardly pass muster with the original Jacobs in Chatham street for jewels gen-u-ine ;
This South Carolina gentleman, one of the present time.

He chews tobacco by the pound and spits upon the floor,
If there is not a box of sand behind the nearest door ;
And when he takes his weekly spree, he clears a mighty track

Of everything that bears the shape of whiskey-skin, gin and sugar — brandy sour, peach, and honey, irrepressible cocktail, rum and gum, and luscious apple-jack,
This South Carolina gentleman, one of the present time.

He takes to euchre kindly, too, and plays an awful hand,
Especially when those he tricks his style don't understand,
And if he wins, why, then, he stops to pocket all the stakes,
But if he loses, then he says to the unfortunate stranger who had chanced to win, " It's my opinion you are a cursed Abolitionist, and if you don't leave South Carolina in one hour, you will be hung like a dog ;" but no offer to pay his losses he makes,
This South Carolina gentleman, one of the present time.

Of course he's all the time in debt to those who credit give,
Yet manages upon the best the market yields to live,
But if a Northern creditor asks him his bill to heed,
This honorable gentleman instantly draws his bowie-knives and a pistol, dons a blue cockade, and declares that in consequence of the repeated aggressions of the North, and its gross violations of the Constitution, he feels that it would utterly degrade him to pay any debt whatever, and that in fact he has at last determined to SECEDE,
This South Carolina gentleman, one of the present time.

TRUE SOLDIERS. — The following occurred on board the steamer Canada during her passage from Dubuque to St. Louis.

In the evening while many of the passengers were engaged in conversation, others whiling away their time at " euchre," while some more rude perhaps, with the ribald jest and ungentlemanly oath, were passing the evening away, a young man seated himself at one of the tables, and engaged in reading his Bible. Another, and still another took their places around this temporary altar, until nearly all of that little band of soldiers, numbering about twenty, were reading the Scriptures. An aged man took his station in their midst. He had a pious and venerable air, for his hoary locks proclaimed that many a winter had passed over his head. There, those farming boys, with that old man, formed a group, whose actions indeed were worthy of all commendation. The creaking machinery of the boat, the dirge-like music of the wind, was loud ; yet, above the clatter, all things else, we know those boys were heard in heaven, and that their prayers will be answered ! Their Bibles, precious gift of home, are sacred with them, and will shield them too, when the glittering *mail* of yore would fall. Parents and friends of home, fear not for such brave sons, who, relying on Heaven, are not ashamed nor afraid to praise God, and do battle for the Star-Spangled Banner.

These were soldiers of the regular army enlisted in Dubuque, by Captain Washington.

A SCOUT TO EAST TENNESSEE.

BY THE LOCHIEL CAVALRY.

At sunrise, on December 20th, 1862, ten companies of the Ninth Pennsylvania Cavalry — 460 men, under command of Major Russell, and eight companies of the Second Michigan — 300 men, under command of Col. Campbell, marched due east from Nicholasville, Ky., on a secret expedition, for which thirty days were allotted for those who should be so fortunate as to return. The orders were to move "light and easy," without tents, baggage or extra clothing; carry on your horse all *you* wanted, and two shoes and twenty nails for *him*. There were ten days' rations issued, which each trooper carried. Marching through the farms and by-paths to avoid all towns and villages, crossing the Kentucky river at an out of the way ford, and ascending Big Hill south of Richmond, we arrived at M'Kees, county town of Jackson county, Ky., containing six or eight houses, being the first village we had passed through. We were halted here one day, for a corn and provision train to come up that had pack-saddles in it. There were fifty mules packed here with two days' rations, and the wagons sent back to Lexington with half team force, leaving corn for our return, there being none in Jackson county.

December 24th.— The weather had been very fair and beautiful, except this last day, which was rainy and cold, and we marched out in the rain for Goose creek, near its junction with the Red Bird fork of Kentucky river. Halting in the meadow an hour to give the horses a bite of hay (the first they had for four days, and about all they ever got on the march), we were joined by the Seventh Ohio Cavalry — 240 men — from Winchester, Ky., under command of Major Reany. The whole force now numbered 1,000 men, and was under command of Brig. Gen. Carter, having on his staff Col. Carter, Col. Walker, Col. Garrett, Capt. Watkins, Capt. M'Nish, Capt. Easley and others, all acting as aids, assistants, or guides. We now ascertained we were sent to burn the bridges on the East Tennessee railroad, and were expected to foot it half the way over the successive steep and rugged mountain ranges of Kentucky, Virginia, and Tennessee, and recommended to cheerfully endure all the hardships and place ourselves on half rations to begin with. I will say for the soldiers that no man cavilled at it, or wanted to turn his back, but all went cheerfully forward, bearing their own burdens as best they might, without sleep, on half rations, food half cooked, and boots worn off their feet by tramping over the rocks to ease their own good horses, and trusting to Providence to keep down the wide and swift rivers that drain these wild mountains. There was to ford, on going and coming, the Cumberland, Powell's river, Wallen's river, the Clinch, North Holston, South Holston and the Watauga, the Holston and Clinch being navigable for steamboats when the waters are up. *Providentially* they *were* kept down for us. In three days after our exit they were in full flood, so that they could not even have been swum by our horses. From Goose creek we had only bridle-paths, and marched by file across a deep depression in the ridge to the Red Bird, up that and across it scores of times to its topmost spring.

December 27th.— Crossing the Kentucky Ridge, and down to the waters of the middle fork of Kentucky river, crossing and rising that, we came down to Straight creek and halted for half an hour to breathe, ere breasting the pine mountain that appeared to push its rocky side up like the wall of a house to near the clouds then lowering and dripping on our heads. The zig-zag paths up the face of this mountain turn and return on each other as often as a fox trail, and the toiling men and horses crawling up its side, looked, from the valley, like flies ascending and sticking to a wall. Its sandy eastern front was too steep to ride down, and there were several miles of arduous marching over the Pine Mountain ere we reached the Poor Fork at the Cumberland. Marched up its quicksand shores and beside the horizontal rock ledges that are natural fortresses, ready made to the hand of the men of Harlan county to defend themselves from invasion by way of Cumberland Gap or any other in the mountain range. Fording the Cumberland and Clover Fork and following up Martin's creek, we camped during the rainy night and slept by the fires for the last time for many days until our return into Kentucky again. Marching over a high ridge, the bold and beautiful Cumberland mountain rose 'majestically before us, and extended like a frowning barrier to right and left as far as the eye could reach without a perceptible break in the uniformity of its crest. Two-thirds of the way up the mountain was a level shoulder, as it were breaking the uniformity of its side and appearing as if there had been great waves running the length of the mountains, and thus arrested and changed to rock while in motion adding greatly to its beauty, while the softened rays of the declining sun shone in contrasted light and shadow on the gray rock waves, the green pines and the bare, brown poplars and oaks. Halting beside the little stream in the pleasant valley, an hour was spent in giving corn to the jaded horses, sending back the whole pack mule train, all inefficient horses and a few sick men to Lexington. At sunset, leading our horses for a two mile march up, and a one mile march down, we cheerfully addressed ourselves to the task of crossing the Cumberland mountain. We reached the summit in two hours, under the light of the full soft moon that silvered and beautified the scene, and passed over into the State of Virginia through Crank Gap, so called from its tortuous break in the horizontal rock crest of the Cumberland, some 200 feet deep and a quarter of a mile in width. This pass is more beautiful and picturesque than anything I have ever seen. It arrested the attention of every soldier and according to his temperament he viewed it to right and left in silent admiration at the wonderful works of God, or in rapturous comment as the soft moonlight silvered o'er and smoothed the ruggedness of each natural "frieze and coign of vantage" that was broken or rounded and carved, and overhung our winding path with all the softness of a summer Italian landscape by Claude Lorraine. Passing the crest we turned to the left and went down an easy grade on a projecting Sierra from the face of the mountain, with a precipice on each side. Reaching the end of that we turned short again to the left with our faces to the mountain and slipped down into chaos, pitching and sliding from rock to rock into a wild gorge. Looking directly up to the Kentucky heights was rock scenery of such savage character over our heads, as would have delighted the heart of Salvator Rosa. It would but have required a camp fire while our troops were filing and plunging down, and his pencil, to more than rival his scenes in the Appenines. The cliffs here were in shadow from the moon, and crested the whole northeastern face of the mountain in one rude unbroken strata, and projected like a threatening arm from Kentucky, raised to chastise any invader. It is not to be wondered that the white man had his superstitions in invading the western home of the Indian while climbing these cliffs from the east.

This Crank pass has the singular appearance of having fallen two hundred feet into some subterranean gulf, the pass being level for a quarter of a mile in width, winding over the mountains in a curve between the buttressed walls for more than half a mile, with the rocks torn sheer down from both sides, leaving the singular rock walls overhanging. The pass has the same kind of soil and trees on it that cap the rock battlements, and to soften the wild scene, were glassy glades around a dilapidated house, where some mountaineer had once built him a home, now abandoned. Below his house the sounds of falling water greeted our ears as we crossed the sunken pass, through an avenue of hemlocks and gigantic rhododendrons, intermingled with isolated rocks, moss covered by the falling waters, that were of such enormous sizes as would have made dwellings for the Genii or the Titans.

Turning with a sigh from all this wealth of natural beauty, thinking how much it would be endeared to us could the loved ones at home be at our side to appreciate it, and pondering on the thought of how far distant was the day when we could visit it with smiling peace waving her wing over the land, we looked the present toils and dangers fully in the face, and strode manfully on. Passing north up Poor Valley to avoid alarming Jonesville, we forded Powell's river and crossed Lee county during the night, reaching Wallen's Ridge at sunrise, where resting two hours, cooking our coffee and toasting our meat on long sticks or eating it raw (as many preferred), and feeding our horses with the corn we carried over the Cumberland we pushed on for Tennessee, crossing Powell's mountain. At

sunset we reached the broad and swift Clinch river; fording it, we halted at a very picturesque spot, where was a large old-time mansion and the only good flouring mill we had seen in our travels, with its very large wheel driven by the tumbling waters at a mountain brook poured on the top of it, glistening like silver in the soft twilight, while the river waters murmured by. Halting here for an hour for coffee, and to give to the horses a good feed of corn, which the mill and farm-house furnished, and was paid for in "greenbacks," though under the confederate iron rule the miller would not dare to use them, we pushed on through the mountain passes at Purchase Ridge and Copper Ridge for Estillville. We had captured many small squads of confederate soldiers and conscripts on our way, paroling them all. We this night captured several, under charge of a lieutenant, who were halting at a farm-house by the road-side. Before starting, orders were given that we were to report ourselves to inquirers along the road as confederate Georgia and Tennessee cavalry returning from a secret expedition, and every one along the road was deceived by it, as they thought we were purposely disguised in blue clothes. Passing Estillville, crossing Scott county, Virginia, and fording the north fork of the Holston at night, we reached Blountsville, Tennessee, at eight A. M. The Ninth Pennsylvania and Seventh Ohio were halted here an hour, and the Second Michigan were pressed forward six miles to Union Station, where the East Tennessee railroad crosses the south fork of Holston on an expensive bridge 1,000 feet long. Here, as we had understood from our prisoners of last night, were stationed three companies of the Sixty-second North Carolina confederate troops under Major McDowell. After all our marches, toils and trials, here was to be tested the complete surprise and success of our expedition, or we were to be met by the enemy, repulsed and driven back over the mountains without accomplishing our object. It was a moment for anxious thought on the part of General Carter, which was fully shared by each one in the expedition from highest to lowest. As it proved, the Almighty was pleased to bless our cause, for never was surprise more complete. We had outtravelled all certain information, but rumors of a coming host had preceded us like the mutterings of a thunder storm. Within eighty rods of the station Sergeant Whitemore, Co. A, commanding the Michigan Videttes, met six citizens riding up; they asking who our troops were, were answered First Georgia Cavalry. They were delighted, shook hands with the Sergeant and said, " The d — d Yankees were in Estillville, fifteen miles off, five thousand strong" — that " they had raised a hundred men besides the troop, and were going out into the country to raise more men to defend the post — that the Major was coming along right up and the Sergeant would meet him before he got to the bridge." Col. Carter came up to the citizens at that moment and passed them to the rear. The Sergeant told him he would go down to meet the Major. He said, "Yes, do so." The Sergeant moved forward to a sharp curve in the road and saw the Major and two citizens, at sixty rods' distance, talking to the sentinels at the bridge. He came back out of sight, dismounted three men and himself, sent the horses back to the column halted up the road, and secreted his men in a fence corner behind the road curve to await the Major's coming. When the Major and the two citizens came up, conversing about the "Yankees" to within five feet of the ambush, they were appalled by the sight of the bright revolving rifles close to their heads at full cock. The Sergeant said, "You are my prisoners." Involuntarily they halt, wheel their horses to flee, when a sharp halt! brought them to front face again. The Sergeant moved them up toward the column. Colonel Campbell had come to the point with Colonel Carter. Colonel Campbell addressed the Major, took his hand and told him *he had come to take his post,* and if he did not surrender unconditionally *he would take it at any rate;* saying also, "My men are posted to fire on you — you have not a moment to lose to avoid useless bloodshedding. The Major wrote a note to the Captain in command at the post and advised its surrender. It was sent down with a flag of truce and the place was surrendered at once; the rifles peering across the Holston from the hill commanding the camp being persuaders too potent to be gainsaid. The telegraph was instantly destroyed before an intimation of our presence could be conveyed and the railroad bridge fired. The two hundred prisoners (who appeared to be rejoiced) were placed under guard, and the Ninth Pennsylvanian and Seventh Ohio ordered forward from the Blountsville road. On their arriving, an expedition was ordered under Colonel Walker and Colonel Carter to capture and burn the bridge nine miles southwest across Watauga river, consisting of companies A, C, and D, the twelve rifles of Co. B, fifteen of Co. F, Ninth Pennsylvania Cavalry; companies A, and F, Second Michigan Cavalry, and two companies of the Seventh Ohio Cavalry. The balance of the troops were kept back by General Carter to destroy the county bridge, the turn-table, cars, ammunition, camp and commissary stores, and to follow us down to Watauga and defend our rear from the enemy's 800 troops at Bristol, fourteen miles by railway, and Humphrey Marshall's force at Abingdon, thirty miles off by railway. At five miles out the Watauga expedition heard a whistle. The troops were instantly dismounted and ambushed at both ends and besides a deep cut, a rail cut out with our axes in front, and men ambushed with orders to cut out a rail in her rear the instant the engine ran into the deep cut — all in less time than it takes me to write it. A locomotive and tender came in sight, ran into the cut, saw the rail out, reversed and backed out instanter, but not before the rail was up in their rear, and they were fully caged on the rifles peering over the bank. We had gotten a prize, having captured Col.

Love, of the Sixty-second North Carolina, a Major, a Captain and a telegraphic staff coming up to ascertain why the telegraph would not work. Five minutes sufficed to put a guard on the locomotive and run her down after us, and we were again on our way and on the alert. It had been raining slowly all day and now came on heavily. Nearing the rebel camp, Col. Carter, who knew all the ground, arranged the attack, Col. Walker assisting. Companies A and F, Second Michigan, dismounted on the right; the twelve rifles of Company A, Ninth Pennsylvania Cavalry, in the centre, and Company D, Seventh Ohio, with their rifles, on the left, were to surround the camp, the balance of the rifles being posted as rear guard and on the left of the road, and then it was to be summoned to surrender, to save useless bloodshed. Unfortunately there were some rebel soldiers on the ourtskirts of the camp chopping wood, six of whom were captured as the troops deployed, but two ran in and alarmed the camp. A shot was fired by some one on the left, and the attack became general. The rebels were under arms and the firing was very heavy on both sides for the numbers engaged, for ten minutes, when the Ninth Pennsylvania, followed by the Seventh Ohio, charged on the camp pistol in hand, and the enemy fled. Companies C and D and the balance of Company A, Ninth Pennsylvania Cavalry, had been formed in fours around the hill to charge with sabre should there be resistance. When the firing slacked they were ordered to charge, and did so, on the camp. Finding it almost abandoned, they galloped over the Watauga. Companies C and D filed left into a ploughed field to head off the retreating enemy. Company A kept the road, and at full charge came on them drawn up in two ranks by the roadside. Capt. Jones ordering them to throw down their arms at thirty paces, the rebels were so startled by the rush of horses and glancing of sabres that they all obeyed the order, but a half dozen, who came near losing their lives by not doing so. There were two lieutenants and seventy-two men who surrendered and saved much blood-shedding. They were making their way to a log house close at hand — a capital fortress — which we would have been compelled to have stormed at once. Companies C and D went down the road and overhauled sixteen more. The short, sharp action cost several lives. One man of Company D, Seventh Ohio, shot dead; one man of Company A, Second Michigan, mortally wounded in the abdomen, and two of the twelve men, Company A, Ninth Pennsylvania, wounded in the leg; one had to be amputated and the man left with the rebel wounded. Of the rebel forces, there were two killed and fifteen wounded. Our surgeon assisted in dressing their wounded, and two of our wounded men were left at the station, Col. Love and Lieut. Hill promising they should have the same care as their own men. The two Lieutenants, Hill and ——, of the Sixty-second North Carolina, fought their commands with great gallantry. What a pity that it should be exerted in so evil a cause as the disruption of their country.

Our prisoners were all paroled on the road, and here, amounting to near four hundred and fifty, inclusive of one Colonel, two Majors, two Captains and five Lieutenants. It was now dark. The telegraph was instantly destroyed, the camp and the bridge fired, the arms broken and put on the locomotive, and after the bridge had fallen, steam was drawn on the engine and she was run over the abutment on to the burning mass below with a great crash. In our haste to expedite these matters we lost a prize of another locomotive and train that came up in sight at the burning bridge, reversed her wheels and scudded down the road toward Knoxville. Jeff Davis himself *might* have been on the train. It is the only thing we have to reproach ourselves for during the expedition as being left undone, or half done. There were two hundred and fifty cavalry came up after dark to reinforce the infantry. Hearing of the fight they wheeled about and marched over into North Carolina, reporting there were thirty thousand of us at the railway. Our men were ordered to feed their horses on the rebel corn, and rest for a few hours; but there was no rest after the excitement of the day and night, and at one o'clock on the night of December 30th, we commenced our retreat, and by strategy to baffle the enemy that our scouts told us were massing to cut us off and pursue us. We felt confident they must be great adepts if they could outmanœuvre Gen. and Col. Carter and our guides. Our poor horses were sinking under the severe toil of marching, and it became a matter of prime military necessity to replenish the stock or leave straggling men on our retreat. Every man having a worn-out horse was sent out with a sergeant or corporal to trade off his horse at any farm-house right or left, day and night, leaving his own horse in exchange, it taking only *one* to make a horse-trade *Morgan fashion.* Some hundreds of horses were thus pressed into the service, but some six unwary men fell behind the column and were captured by the rebel troops that were following us at a safe distance for themselves in our rear. I find that the Richmond papers give us the credit of doing no marauding, nor injury to private property. Our scouts informed us that five hours after we left Watauga river the enemy had sixteen hundred infantry and four pieces of artillery brought up by railway from Jonesboro or Greenville, and put upon our trail. We laughed at the idea of footmen and field-pieces following up the paths we came across the farms and lanes and ravines. Our guides certainly must have been coon-hunting over that country all their lives at dark nights, to have guided us so unerringly. We got so that we left the horses to follow up in the dark, and although it felt sometimes as if both horse and saddle were going from under one and we going to perdition, we came out all right on the ravine bottom at last. Humphrey Marshall moved troops from Abingdon to Blountsville on our right, and troops

were moved from Rogersville to Kingsport to intercept us; but we passed between " Scylla" on the one hand and " Charybdis" on the other, and came out ahead of them all. While on our rout to Kingsport, a man by the roadside told me that the infantry and artillery stationed there had crossed our route six hours before marching to Blountsville, expecting to intercept us there. While on the high ridge above Kingsport we had a beautiful view of a snowy mountain, illumined by the setting sun. At fifty miles distance towered up the black mountain of North Carolina, six thousand nine hundred feet in the air, — the highest land in the old United States proper, standing like Saul a full head and shoulders over all his companions. It looked exceedingly rugged at that great distance, with its rude concave side towards us, seamed and furrowed by tremendous chasms from top to bottom. It had a crest of two or three miles in length, and is crescent-shaped on top, very steep on both ends, and towering so high above all others, seemed not to be a member of any chain of mountains that I could perceive in the distance. For an isolated mountain it was very picturesque in appearance, and was beautified by being covered with snow, while the surrounding landscape was dark. It looked a-rifted, inaccessible, and uninhabitable as the high Alps of Switzerland. Riding at night down the South Holston at Kingsport, — there a broad and beautiful stream fit for steamboating, — we were fired upon from over the river, the bullets whistling over our heads and striking the fence between our horses. I got tired at the one-sided arrangement and ordered some of my lads, who are adepts with their rifles, to try some long shots in the moonlight — dismounted; they never require a second bidding for that kind of work, and the popping from over the river was quickly ended. I cannot tell if there was " anybody hurt," but *we* came off clear. After fording the north Holston at its junction with the main stream, we marched on to a very fine and extensive farm, where the horses were fed and the men had their coffee. The night had become unusually nipping, and large fires with fence-rails were a great luxury to benumbed fingers and toes. The enemy would not let us rest in peace to enjoy our coffee, but kept popping at us from the hill-tops occasionally. There was quite a little skirmish back in town. Some of the cavalry following us up had the audacity after dark to attack Col. Carter, his orderly and a private, at a hotel in Kingsport, where he was acquainted, and had halted behind the column to appease his hunger. Some twenty or thirty shots were exchanged in the dark. The orderly got a ball through his hand, and our force of three were compelled to beat a retreat to camp across the North Fork. Our pickets dashed into the town, but the enemy had fled and all was quiet again. After resting three hours, we were in the saddle again at midnight, understanding there were some two hundred cavalry forward of us whom we desired to capture. Our advance came near their camp near

Clinch river, but they fled and our poor horses were too jaded to pursue them. The "bush-whackers" had quite a busy time, popping at us crossing Clinch river. Rested at night for a few hours on a limestone mountain, and exchanged a few long shots with the enemy to no purpose. Started at daybreak, without breakfast or horse-feed, on our last long day's march to the Cumberland mountain, crossing Powell's mountain, river, and valley. The "bushwhackers" here had an unusually busy day at it, even for them, lively as they are. But they are either miserable shots or have miserable guns, for they have not touched a man since we left the railroad, except Col. Carter's orderly, shot in the hand-to-hand fight; whereas two of the Michigan sharp-shooters "incontinently" rolled two of them down the rocks at about seven hundred yards. While I was fording Powell's river, they were darting in and out among the trees and rocky hill-tops, and throwing down some lead in a very spiteful way, but did no damage. I concluded, after crossing and seeing one fellow blazing away among the rocks, to try and cure him with a little *saltpetre*, as salt was scarce, and called two of my lads out of the ranks. One of them drew a *sight* on him, and he cut up some very ludicrous antics for a sane man. He flew round and scrabbled about among the rocks, and then made dart up the hill, rattling down the stones at an alarming rate; he bounced about it as if burnt with a hot iron, and not at all pleased with the *impression* made.

At Jonesville, Va., the rebels had quite a force. After our column had passed they engaged our rear guard of the Seventh Ohio, and we were all halted, the General sending back the rifles of Co. B, Ninth Pa. Cavalry, to deploy as skirmishers and engage them in the open field, and Co. D, Ninth Pa., with sabres. It was understood that they expected to engage our attention, so long as to enable a force to move around by Poor valley, occupy the mountain pass, engage our front, and have us between two fires. We were crossing at our old gap (only twenty miles from the Cumberland Gap), contrary to their expectations. There was some little firing on our front, and quite a brisk little skirmish in the rear. As usual they kept at too great a distance for their shooting and did no harm, but there were several rebels shot down by our rear guard and skirmishers, among whom were some Michigan rifles, when they concluded to draw off and let us go on our "winding way," which we did without further molestation. We had made a very severe day's march, with a little sprinkling of fighting, and nothing to eat since the night before for man or beast, and while we were at Jonesville, there was a very fair prospect of a regular mountain battle for the possession of the pass. I had been giddy from want of food and rest, while marching down to Watauga, but did not feel it much during the excitement of the homeward march. I slept on my horse during the bushwhacking of the day; and while waiting for the rear to scatter the ene-

my at Jonesville, one of my men said he was hungry. I had entirely forgotten that I had not eaten for twenty-four hours, and felt no symptoms of hunger, and told him that we might yet have a two days' fight up the cliffs of the Cumberland mountain without coffee, and I felt as if I would be able to stand it for three. We moved on to the foot of the mountain, and now there was the excitement to know whose horse would reach the top and whose would fail. They were all very carefully handled, but many a one of them failed, and the poor cavalryman would be seen breaking up his saddle with a rock and cutting up the leather with a knife to prevent secesh from using it. The poor horse wanted no quietus; he generally dropped dead in his efforts to scale a rock, and fell over out of the path, except one that made a convenient stepping-place for his more fortunate fellow horse. There must have been thirty horses fallen dead ascending the Cumberland. The men shouldered their blankets, gave one last look at their steed stiffening in the keen frosty night air, and clambered on over the rocks. When I reached the topmost crest I cried, "All hail, Kentucky!" and stretched out my arm as if to grasp and welcome a long lost friend. The excitement was over, and I felt faint and giddy. I scarcely know how I got down; and when I reached the little valley at the foot of the mountain, and had a fire of rails kindled, fatigue overpowered all the animal wants and ailments, and the moment I lay down upon the frozen earth, I was fast asleep, and so continued until well shaken after sunrise. Our horses had corn here, but we were on short rations. The ground was frozen hard, and all the shoes had been put on the horses' feet, and none short of Richmond or Nicholasville. There had been no kegs of shoes brought to McKees with the corn, and the prospects ahead were dark for the men who had limping horses whose feet were worn to the quick. I saw them cut up clothes and blankets and tie them on their feet, but it did no good; nothing but iron would answer on the frozen and rocky creek beds and gullies which formed our path. We had been signally favored by Providence with unfrozen roads in the enemy's country, but now they were telling on horse-flesh. Every day a score or more of men were compelled to drop their horses and shoulder their muskets. There was no murmuring; nor did I hear a whimper from any man who marched twenty or thirty miles in a day (all unused to walking as he was), with his boots worn and torn, and his feet on the rocks and frozen ground. Two days after our arrival on Kentucky soil, we encountered a storm, which raised all the Tennessee rivers and made them unfordable. Two days after our arrival here at Nicholasville, has come upon us the heaviest snow-storm for many years. I lift my hands in praise when I think of our escape from this storm among the mountains, and shudder at the thought of what would have been the condition of man and beast there without food or forage. We should have been compelled to adopt the plan Duroc proposed to Napoleon at Moscow: to slaughter, salt, and eat his horses to save his men. Our most arduous and hazardous march of five hundred miles to and fro in twenty days, over an almost impracticable mountain country in mid-winter, has been a complete success. Of one thousand men, there were only two killed, two wounded, and six missing — supposed to be captured.

I must relate a little incident of the march coming down the Red Bird, in a country where "corndodgers" are worth a dime. A part of one I have preserved as a curiosity, for its fossil-like appearance, to show what a soldier *can* subsist on when he is put to it. I think I must have it engraven for Harper or Frank Leslie, with all the finger-marks on it. The "corndodger" is an institution; and he is fitly named, as any one can tell who takes him in hand; for if he is mixed up as usual with water and no salt, and well baked and thrown at you, if you do not *dodge*, and he hits you, his name will be remembered for many a long day, I warrant it.

In the western counties of Kentucky saw-mills and grist-mills are known to but few inhabitants. The corn is broken into coarse grains with a pestle attached to a spring-pole, or grated on a piece of tin or iron punched out rough with a nail. The country is clear of wind-mills or sieves to clear it of husks; such superfluities have been played out, or rather they have never been played in; but hospitality has not been played out. I will relate an incident. The horse of one of my soldiers yielded up his life on the rugged paths this side of the Cumberland mountain. The soldier was making his way in the rear of the column over the rocks of the Red Bird, with his pistol at his belt and his trusty rifle, which had done him such good service at Watauga river (his "Betsy Ann," as he called it), on one shoulder and his blankets on the other, trudging along at sunset for the camp, miles ahead of him, and "whistling as he went for want of thought," when a native overtook him. "Stranger," said he, "you have a heavy load; give me your blankets" (and he took them off his shoulder). "You must come and stay with me to-night down to my house at the Big Rocks." So soldier, nothing loth, acquiesced, and they trudged through mud and over rocks, and in the bed of the creek for some miles, and arrived at his clay-chinked cabin, where were his "household gods" in form of a wife and a host of children, such as are to be found in every poor man's cabin in Kentucky. You will almost see the exact counterpart of the primer-book picture of John Rogers' wife, excepting there will be *ten, eleven,* or *twelve* children who can just peep over each others' heads in regular gradation beside "the one at the breast." The host says, "Mary Ann, can you get supper for this tired soldier?" "Yes," says the wife, "if you pound the corn," and she handed him four ears, he soon manipulated with his spring pole and pestle in the yard. The supper was soon prepared of the corn mixed with water (no salt, for they had none), and scraps of bacon

fried, and he ate on the principle of the Indian, "eat much, get strong!" The tired soldier, who had not seen the inside of a house for months, rested, after six days' march and no sleep, as only such men can rest when they know the pickets are posted and the guard mounted; he taking the Kentuckian for his guard. At sunrise he was wakened by the "thud, thud," of the *corn-grinding machine,* and presently the good dame invited him to sit at the table to the corndodgers, the bacon-scraps, and the corn-coffee, innocent of sugar or cream, so as to expedite him on his way before the children were up to have their remnants of clothes put on them. *After* he had eaten, *not before,* his host apologized for the lateness of his breakfast, saying that his corn was all eaten over night, and he had to go four miles to borrow some of his near neighbor for the soldier's breakfast. The soldier donning his load, having received no pay for more than four months, thanked him as he should have been thanked by a man ready and willing to pay, but having no money in his pocket, and with unwonted full stomach went on his way rejoicing to overtake his comrades.

Where indeed among the rich will such hospitality, such abnegation of *self* be found? or where among them the man that will contribute *such* a mite to his country? It is like the scriptural widow, who, out of her poverty "gave even all that she had." When we arrived at Big Hill we were met by a wagon train laden with rations and corn that had been sent for by Gen. Carter's messenger pressed on before us at Manchester, on our homeward route, to order the train forward to us. When the white-topped wagons were seen by our men, one universal shout went up as a glorification for the hard bread they knew them to contain. To men who had been roasting lumps of corn meal or of wheat flour in the ashes for days, the transition was great indeed, and ere dark the "slow enough" coffee was boiling, the bacon toasting on the sticks, and "there was a great feast of fat things" that night. Resting at Big Hill a few hours, with the cares and perplexities of the march off my shoulders, I had time to look back at the beauties of the place, which I had not done when we moved forward. Here is a table-land four hundred feet high, which was once the shore of the great lake of which the "blue grass region" is the bottom. The sand-stone strata of seventy feet crowning this table land has been washed into many singular and unique forms, each cliff so unlike the other that each would make a separate picture. In one place there is a genuine mountain, apart as it were. The water had washed entirely around it. The soft under strata giving way was only saved by the capping, which, covered with some earth and trees, once formed an island in the lake some distance from shore. Moving along for several miles these sand-stone cap rocks are seen in fantastic array succeeding each other, and you are astonished at the varied forms of them and at the sudden change in the form of each as you view it from another point. They are all well worth transferring to canvas, and as they have been somewhat noted in these wars, they should be placed with its illustrations. The quiet "blue grass region" possessed a great charm to our worn and anxious minds longing for rest, and the old walnut-trees near Richmond, covered with mistletoe until they looked like pine-trees, had a charm of still life in them that was very soothing, lulling the mind into dreams of the Druids and of that olden time when rushing, fiery modern wars were unknown.

THE VOICE OF THE NORTH.

BY JOHN G. WHITTIER.

Up the hill-side, down the glen,
Rouse the sleeping citizen:
Summon out the might of men!

Like a lion growling low —
Like a night-storm rising slow —
Like the tread of unseen foe —

It is coming — it is nigh!
Stand your homes and altars by,
On your own free threshold die.

Clang the bells in all your spires,
On the gray hills of your sires
Fling to heaven your signal-fires.

Oh! for God and duty stand,
Heart to heart, and hand to hand,
Round the old graves of the land.

Whoso shrinks or falters now,
Whoso to the yoke would bow,
Brand the craven on his brow.

Freedom's soil has only place
For a free and fearless race —
None for traitors false and base.

Perish party — perish clan;
Strike together while you can,
Like the strong arm of one man.

Like the angels' voice sublime,
Heard above a world of crime,
Crying for the end of Time.

With one heart and with one mouth,
Let the North speak to the South;
Speak the word befitting both.

CHRISTMAS AMONG THE FREEDMEN. — It is well understood that Christmas was the grand holiday of the slaves on the southern plantations. In some parts of the South, the colored people have this year, 1863, celebrated it with unusual zest. A correspondent writes home about one celebration by the soldiers of the Ninth Louisiana Regiment, corps d'Afrique, and tells how they met and gave expression to their feelings, on Christmas day — their first free Christmas. After prayer, and speeches were in order, one man, says the correspondent, spoke about as follows:

"*Fellow Soldiers of the Sebenth Regiment:* I is mighty glad to enjoy dis portunity for enjoying dis fust free Christmas in dis world what we live in. A year ago, where was we? We was down in de dark land of slavery. And now where are we? We are free men, and soldiers of the United States. And what have we to do? We have to fight de rebels so dat we never more be slaves. When de day of battle come what will we do? I speak for me, and I say for myself, I go and fight de rebels till de last man die. Yes, under de flags what was presented to us from New York, we fight till de last man die; and if I be de last man, what will I do? I hold up de flags, and if I die, den I go to my grave consified for doing my duty. De President of de United States is one great man what has done more good dan any oder man what ever was borned. I bless de Lord we fight for so good Commander. I have no more to say now and evermore — Amen."

CONSCRIPT QUAKERS. — An amusing incident occurred at the Provost Marshal's office at Gen. Lee's head-quarters at Orange Court House, Va. Four Quakers were brought in as conscripts from Loudon. They were ordered to fall in the ranks, in order to be marched to the command to which they were to be assigned. They refused, saying, "We will not fall in, but will follow whithersoever thou leadest." A few persuasive arguments, however, in the shape of thrusts with bayonets, changed their opinions, and they fell in and marched off to camp.

THE PRESIDENT AND THE PAYMASTER. — One of the numerous paymasters at Washington sought an introduction to Mr. Lincoln. He arrived at the White House quite opportunely, and was introduced to the President by the United States Marshal, with his blandest smile. While shaking hands with the President the paymaster remarked, "I have no official business with you, Mr. President, I only called to pay my compliments." "I understand," replied "honest Abe," "and from the complaints of the soldiers, I think that is all you do *pay*."

AN INCIDENT OF VICKSBURG. — A correspondent relates the following: — A wife who dwelt in the West, beyond the lakes, whose husband is an officer in the army, had not heard from him for some weeks. Two small boys were with him, — their only ones. While she sat at home, reading a paper, her eyes fell upon a notice of the death of her husband. All the tenderness of a mother's love, all the strength of a wife's devotion, nerved her to start immediately for her children, and clasp them to a widowed heart. Day after day passed; how slowly let a mother tell; how tedious let a widow speak who knows her idol broken in a distant land. Two weeks were past ere she reached Vicksburg.

Three days a sand bar! What torture! At last she reached the hoped-for city. As the boat neared the wharf one looked at the crowd, and saw her two boys upon ponies, and beside them the father and husband. One long, piercing cry of joy filled the air; the husband flew, rather than ran, and took the lifeless form in his arms. It was too much of joy for a heart overcharged with grief. The strings snapped and reason tottered for a time, to fall, in two days, to the sleep of death.

THE AMNESTY PROCLAMATION.—A few days after the publication of the President's Message and Proclamation, the fact of its promulgation having been made known to the rebel pickets, they manifested great curiosity to hear it; and one of our men consenting to read it to them, quite a party collected on the opposite bank to listen. While it was reading, the utmost silence and attention were preserved by the listening rebels, and after it was finished one of them called out: "Well, that sounds about right. We'll go back to camp and tell the boys about it." Papers are frequently exchanged by the pickets, but the rebels tell our men that their officers do not like them to get our papers of late as "there is nothing encouraging in them."

LETTERS TO SOLDIERS.—The army correspondent of the Atalanta "Intelligencer," relates the following incident to show how welcome a letter from home was to the soldier, and how depressing it was when those at home neglected to write to him:

"I witnessed an incident yesterday which goes far to show how welcome a letter is to the soldier, and how sad he feels, when those at home neglect to write to him. As I was riding to town I heard a man on horseback hail another in a wagon, and, going up, handed him a letter. Another man in the same wagon inquired if there was no letter for him, and the reply was 'none.' It was at that moment I noted the feeling between the two men by their changed countenances. The features of one lit up with pleasure, as he perused the epistle in his hand, — doubtless the letter of some dear wife or mother, — and as he read it, a smile of joy would illuminate his weather-beaten face. This was happiness. It was an oasis on the desert of his rough life of danger and suffering, and no doubt was welcomed by him as the dearest gift a relative could send. With the other the opposite effect was observed; as soon as the word 'none' had passed the lips of the man addressed, the look of anxiety with which the question was put faded away, and an appearance of extreme sorrow could have been seen plainly stamped on his features, while a feeling of envy at his fortunate comrade was very apparent. This was unhappiness. The song of hope that had illuminated his heart when he inquired if there was any letter for him had died away, and a feeling of loneliness and re-

gret at the neglect of those at home took possession of him. Happy are they who have homes and loved ones to hear from! While it is the cruelest of all neglect not to write to those relatives in the army; if it makes them sad and unhappy, how much more must those feel whose homes are in possession of the enemy, and they cannot hear from their relatives."

ABOU BEN BUTLER.

Abou Ben Butler (may his tribe increase!)
Awoke one night down by the old Belize,
And saw, outside the comfort of his room,
Making it warmer for the gathering gloom,
A black man shivering in the winter's cold.
Exceeding courage made Ben Butler bold,
And to the presence in the dark he said:
"What wantest thou?" The figure raised its head,
And with a look made of all sad accord
Answered: "The men who'll serve the purpose of the Lord."
"And am I one?" said Butler. "Nay, not so,"
Replied the black man. Butler spoke more low,
But cheerily still and said: "*As I am Ben,*
You'll not have cause to tell me that again."

The figure bowed and vanished. The next night
It came once more, environed strong in light,
And showed the names whom love of freedom blessed,
And lo! Ben Butler's name led all the rest.

ANECDOTE OF GENERAL SUMNER.—When a young man, he was a stage-driver among the Berkshire hills, in Massachusetts, and this is how he happened to get into the army: At a time in winter when the roads were dangerous, going down a steep hill, the stage slewed and turned over, but the horses kept on. One of the passengers pushed out the door on the upper side of the coach and climbed upon the box, and attempted to take the reins from Sumner's hands. "You let the reins alone or I'll throw you off!" said the driver, with determination. The passenger wisely abandoned his attempt at interference, and Sumner guided the team firmly till it was safe to stop them, dragging the overturned coach along, and so saved passengers and team. The passenger who attempted to take the reins was General Worth. He was so impressed with young Sumner's sterling qualities that he cultivated his acquaintance and induced him to join the army, and the cool and determined driver made an intrepid commander."

THE BIBLE ON THE BATTLE-FIELD. — Among the dead of one of the battle-fields before Richmond was a rebel soldier, who lay unburied several days after the conflict. Already the flesh had been eaten by the worms from his fingers, but underneath the skeleton hand lay an open copy of the Bible, and the fingers pressed upon those precious words of the twenty-third Psalm, "*Thy rod and thy staff they comfort me.*"

ENLISTED.

BY W. A. KENDALL.

" You've donned the peerless uniform
    Of good old Uncle Sam " —
Around my neck her arms she threw,
And to her breast my own she drew —
    With tears her fond eyes swam.

" You're dearer to me than I thought —
    Since in this steadfast hue
Your form was draped, its impress takes
A depth such as a hero's makes —
    All hail, my own true blue!

" Prouder am I to see you thus —
    Though it preludes good-by —
Than were you crowned perchance a king,
Whose name in action ne'er did ring,
    Whose soul gives fame the lie.

" Your stature seems to gain in height
    From your high motive's aim ;
And to such eminence my heart
Is lifted, I am strong to part —
    Oh ! to reserve were shame!

" Go, save our country ! she is first —
    Stand guard until you fall ;
Or till the danger overcome
Shall respite the alarum-drum —
    I will delay recall.

" Go, where along the lurid front
    The Union vanguards tramp !
Do your whole duty, danger spurn,
When Freedom's laurelled, then return —
    These arms shall be your camp !

" As I would ask, so you have done —
    ' God shield you ! ' is my charm :
Should you survive, redeem this kiss
And should you perish, one will miss
    From life its sweetest balm.

" These tears attest the grief I feel —
    God's and my own true blue !
For every one speed thou a shot ;
When *quietus* the foe has got,
    Valor for love may sue."

So spoke my own brave girl, and fled,
    Fearing her heart's dread pain
Would traitor prove unto her will,
And rising with rebellious thrill,
    Persuade me to remain.

To die for her were sweeter far
    Than loved by less to live ;
Such natures wear an aspect grand,
As with an unreserving hand
    They answer Duty's "give ! "

O woman ! how much patriot fire
    Thy breath has woke to flame !
How many heroes were not such
But for thy consecrating touch,
    None less than God can name !

A REMARKABLE PROPHECY.

THE vision or prophecy of Joseph Hoag, which is published below, is so remarkable in the accuracy of some of its details, that were its authenticity not attested by the most respectable and reliable living witnesses, we should hardly credit it. The predicted " civil war," through which we have just passed is not more singular than are several other features in the vision which have been verified.

Joseph Hoag was an eminent minister of the Gospel in the Society of Friends. At the date of his subjoined vision, in 1803, this Society was a unit, the division in it not having occurred until 1827 After the separation, Hoag affiliated with the orthodox branch, in which connection he continued until his death, at the age of forty-five. His ancestors were among the early settlers of New-England, and lived for several generations in the State of New Hampshire, although he was born in Duchess County, New York, but in early life removed to the home of his ancestors. In his services as a minister he travelled extensively throughout the United States, and he is well remembered by a large number of the old members of the Society of Friends in Philadelphia as a very gifted and spiritual-minded minister. Those who knew him best say that he was a man of great piety and very correct life and conversation from his youth ; also, that his spiritual perceptions were very deep and clear, so much so that he was often favored with a sense of the condition of other people without outward knowledge, and, in many instances, known to persons still living, foretold circumstances which occurred long afterward, and of which he could have had no knowledge when he predicted them. A journal of his life exists, in which the author says Hoag " was a man of good understanding, retentive memory, and a mind seasoned with grace. His conversation was truly instructive. He appeared most conspicuous in the gift of the ministry, and the spirit of prophecy." The following is Joseph Hoag's vision as transcribed by his daughter—who is still living—in the year 1805, since which time many duplicate MS. copies have been made and preserved by members of the Society, as a curious, interesting, and, as the sequel has shown, an amazingly premonitory document :

" In the year 1803, in the eighth or ninth month, I was one day alone in the field, and observed that the sun shone clear, but a mist eclipsed its brightness.

" As I reflected upon the singularity of the event, my mind was struck into a silence the most solemn I ever remembered to have witnessed, for all my faculties were low, and unusally brought into deep silence. I said to myself: ' What can all this mean ? I do not recollect ever before to have been sensible of such feelings.'

" And I heard a voice from heaven, saying: ' This which thou seest is a sign of the present coming times. I took the forefathers of this country from a land of oppression ; I planted them here among the people of the forest ; I sustained them and while they were humble I blessed them, and fed them, and they became a numerous people. But they have now become proud, and forgotten me, who nourished them, and protected them in the wilderness, and are running into every abomination and evil practice of which the old countries are guilty, and have taken quietude from the land, and suffered a dividing spirit to come among them — lift up thine eyes and behold.' And I saw them dividing in great heat. The division began in the churches on points of doctrine. It commenced in the Presbyterian Society, and went through the various religious denominations, and in its progress and close, its effects were the same. Those who dissented went off with high heads and taunting language, and those who kept to their original sentiments appeared exercised and sorrowful. And when the dividing spirit entered the Society of Friends, it raged in as high degree as in any I had noticed or before discovered; and, as before, those who separated went off with lofty looks, and taunting, censuring language. Those who kept their ancient principles retired by themselves. It next appeared in the Lodges of the Free Masons; it broke out in appearance like a volcano, inasmuch as it set the country in an uproar for a time.

"Then it entered politics throughout the United States, and did not stop until it produced a civil war. An abundance of blood was shed in the course of the combat; the Southern States lost their power, and slavery was annihilated from their borders. Then a monarchical power sprang up, took the government of the States, established a national religion, and made all societies tributary to support its expenses. I saw them take property from Friends. I was amazed at beholding all this, and I heard a voice proclaiming: 'This power shall not always stand, but with it I will chastise my Church until they return to the faithfulness of their forefathers; thou seest what is coming upon thy native country for their iniquities and the blood of Africa, the remembrance of which has come up before me.'

"This vision is yet for many days. I had no idea of writing it for many years, until it became such a burden, that, for my own relief, I have written it."

THE TRUE BALANCE. — Two councilmen of New Orleans were one evening in February, 1861, reeling down to the city hall steps discussing politics, as well as their cups and hiccups would permit them. One said solemnly, —

"The South's true balance must not be overthrown;" to which the other replied, —

"Confound the South's balance; try to keep your own."

AN IRISH REGULAR. — The following dialogue took place between Lieutenant A. C. C——d, late of the United States Texan army, and Pat Fletcher, one of the privates of the Second Cavalry, at Carlisle, then near Fort Bliss: —

Officer. — Well, Pat, ain't you going to follow the General (Twiggs)?

Pat. — If Gineral Scott ordhers us to folly him, sir, begor, Toby (Pat's horse) can gallop as well as the best of 'em.

Officer. — I mean, won't you leave the abolition army, and join the free South?

Pat. — Begor, I never enlisted in th' abolition army, and never will. I agreed to sarve Uncle Sam for five year, and the divil a pin mark was made in the contract, with my consint, ever since. When my time is up, if the army isn't the same as it is now, I won't join it agin.

Officer. — Pat, the "Second" (Cavalry) was eighteen months old when you and I joined. The man who raised our gallant regiment is now the Southern President; the man who so lately commanded it, is now a Southern General. Can you remain in it, when they are gone?

Pat. — Well, you see, the fact of the matther is, Lieut. C., I ain't much of a scholar; I can't argue the question with you; but what would my mother say, if I desarted my colors? Oh, the divil a give-in I'll ever give in, now, and that's the ind of it. I tried to run away once, a few weeks after enlistin', but a man wouldn't be missed thin. It's quite different now, Lieutenant, and I'm going not to disgrace naither iv my countries.

Officer. — Do you know that you will have to fire on green Irish colors, in the Southern ranks?

Pat. — And won't you have to fire on them colors, (pointing to the flag at Fort Bliss,) that yerself and five of us licked nineteen rangers under? Sure, it isn't a greater shame for an Irishman to fire on Irish colors, than for an American to fire on American colors. An' th' oath 'll be on my side, you know, Lieutenant.

Officer. — Confound the man that relies on Paddies, I say.

Pat. — The same compliments to desarters, your honor.

ANECDOTE OF ROGER A. PRYOR. — The following occurred during the attack on Fort Sumter in 1861. Roger A. Pryor, of Virginia, ex-member of Congress, was one of the second deputation that waited upon Major Anderson. He was the very embodiment of Southern chivalry. Literally dressed to kill, bristling with bowie-knives and revolvers, like a walking arsenal, he appeared to think himself individually capable of capturing the fort, without any extraneous assistance. Inside of the fort he seemed to think himself master of every thing — monarch of all he surveyed — and, in keeping with this pretension, seeing upon the table what appeared to be a glass of brandy, drank it without ceremony. Surgeon (afterward General Crawford, who had witnessed the feat, approached him and said: "Sir, what you have drank is poison — it was the iodide of potassium — *you are a dead man!*" The representative of chivalry instantly collapsed, bowie-knives, revolvers and all, and passed into the hands of Surgeon Crawford, who, by purgings, pumpings, and pukings, defeated his own prophecy in regard to his fate. Mr. Pryor left Fort Sumter a "wiser if not a better man."

TAKEN BY THE PIRATES.

The following letter is from a young Scotchman, who married a wife, and set sail from New York for Cardenas; the vessel was taken by a rebel piratical craft, and the party had the pleasure of a visit to Charleston, S. C. : —

MATANZAS, Nov. 11, 1861.

We sailed from New York on board the brig Betsy Ames, on October 5th. In all we were six passengers, beside Mrs. Bartlett, the wife of the captain. We were bound for Cardenas, and all went well until the morning of the 17th ult., when we observed a schooner making right for us. There was nothing suspicious about her at first sight, but about nine A. M. she fired at us, her shot falling short about a quarter of a mile. Captain Bartlett then ordered all sail to be made, but the breeze shortly after died away, and the now suspicious schooner made upon us, and fired another shot, which also fell a little short of our vessel. A third shot was fired, but we could not see in what direction it went. They fired a fourth shot, which passed close alongside our brig. This latter result caused our captain to take in sail and jog along more leisurely, till the schooner made up to us about twelve o'clock, M. Still, we could not tell what the little craft was, as she had no color flying.

When she came up to us, the captain of the schooner ordered our captain to take one of his boats and come on board with his papers, to which he responded, " My boats are unfit for service." The captain of the schooner then said, " I will come on board your brig, then," which he immediately did. He came in his own boat, with an officer and four men, when the captain and his officer went down into the cabin with our captain, and took possession of all his papers; then told him that he was a prisoner of the Confederate States of America.

While the officers were in the cabin, the men who were left in the boat sprang on deck and into the forehold, from which they took two barrels of potatoes, about two dozen cabbages, and a coil of rope, and put them into their boat.

When the officers came up on deck again, they ordered our crew to the boat, and thence to the privateer, which proved to be the Flying Sally, of Charleston, on board of which there were about sixty men and two pivot-guns. In a short time a prize crew was sent on board, and as our captain had his wife, they did not transfer him.

The prize crew were seven in all. The master was an old cooper, named Joseph Tully, who used to cooper both at Matanzas and Cardenas. He evidently knew nothing of seamanship.

About two o'clock we parted with the pirate schooner, and nothing particular occurred until the 24th, at daybreak, when we made land, but did not know where we were. Some of the crew said we were north of Charleston; but, as it turned out, we were south of North Edisto, where we ran aground and lost our false keel, but got off again, and went to sea. On the following day we saw no land, and on the evening of the 27th we made the land of St. Helena, almost the exact place where we were on the 25th. After tacking off and on all night, we were still in the same place. Then we beat up to the North Edisto Inlet.

While beating up we espied a schooner, which fact caused the crowd to take alarm, and, to a man, they rushed below, armed themselves with their swords, knives, and pistols, bagged their clothing and a few little valuables, then prepared for the boats, as they intended to beach the brig. They were apprehensive that the vessel sighted was a United States gunboat. When they came on deck, however, and took another observation, they discovered that it was only a little schooner. Then we made the inlet, when a boat's crew, armed to the teeth, came on board, and piloted us up to the anchorage, about forty miles inland. There they discharged their prizes, and the vessels were towed up to Charleston by tow-boats.

We arrived at Charleston at about three o'clock, P. M., on the 27th. Next morning the steamer General Clinch took us on board, with our baggage. I may also state, that the steamer Planter towed us up to this safe "pirates' village ground."

When we got into Charleston the prize captain took us to a private boarding-house, his agent having closed his office previous to our arrival.

Next morning we strolled about the city, and called upon the British Consul, who told us, strange as it may seem, that he could render us no assistance, as we had done wrong in taking our passage on board an American vessel, knowing that the *two countries* were at war; therefore, if the owners of the prize had the good feeling to pay our expenses, it was only to be expected from their generous character, but they could not be forced to do so. About twelve o'clock we were called upon to go to the marshal's office, and when we got there the marshal told us that we were prisoners. We were then sent to the city jail. The captain's wife, and the other lady of our company, did not accompany us to the jail. We remained in this limbo till half past eight o'clock, P. M., having been released at that time through the exertions of Her British Majesty's Consul, Mr. Bunce, who had been induced to act then only because an old English captain, who saw us in prison, went to him and prevailed upon him to use his influence in our behalf.

The next day we looked round to see if we could devise any means of getting away. The Spanish Consul informed us that the only schooner which was going for some time had been loaded, and had sailed already for Matanzas. However, we had the good fortune to meet Mr. Salas, the owner of two vessels which were ready for sea, and it appeared that Mr. Bunce had been to him to endeavor to procure us a passage; and as he could not assist us, Mr. Salas offered to take us to Matanzas on credit. That arrangement included the other British passengers, my wife, and myself. The other three passengers were Germans, having American passports, and could not be taken on board the schooner Jasper. The crew on board this craft declared her unseaworthy, after getting their advanced pay, and left. Mr. Salas had therefore to ship another crew, and we got ready for sea. As the bark Rowena was getting her name changed to the St. Helena of Charleston, S. C., having been loaded with a cargo of naval stores, awaiting a favorable opportunity to run the blockade, we waited and went out with her. So, on the night of the 2d inst., she was taken in tow by a steamer, and we followed her as closely as we could out past the United States vessels, and in half an hour were after her, and could see the lights of the United States ships quite distinctly, although none of them seemed to make any movement, and did not observe us. It was about ten o'clock, P. M., when we got clear of their lights. Then we thought ourselves safe on the sea once more. We arrived here safely on the night of Saturday, the 9th inst.

And now, when I think of the scenes I have passed through since I left New York, (the scenes of a honeymoon excursion,) what impressed me most was the almost death-like solemn appearance of Charleston, and the entire absence of anything like business. It appeared as if a Scotch fast day was being observed. At least one half of the stores have "To Let" posted upon the shut doors, and those which are occupied are all closed at noon every day, and every man has to turn out to drill, or be fined by the police the next day.

Another thing which struck me was the almost entire absence of "hard cash." One of my companions and I went into a bar-room to have a drink, and the only money we had to offer was Spanish. My friend offered a two dollar piece, but the bar-keeper was bewildered; he did not know its value, and asked us what it was worth. Being informed that it was worth two dollars twelve and a half cents in Cuba, he offered two dollars twenty-five cents in paper change. Then a crowd gathered around us, staring their eyes out of their heads, almost, at the novelty of the sight of gold, and many of them seemed really anxious to be the possessors. We saw no small change except pieces of paper, which certify that they are "good for five cents," "good for ten cents," and so on.

I must say that men, women, and children in Charleston seem united in the cause of secession. When they found that one of my fellow-passengers and myself were Scotchmen, they treated us very respectfully. Though our Consul did not at first seem to sympathize with us, still he exerted himself well on our behalf when he found that we were in prison. All seemed to have great respect for him in Charleston.

A PROPHECY. — The following, translated a few years since by a lady, who is an inmate of a religious institution in the vicinity of Washing-ton, has a peculiar interest. The original is in Latin, and bears marks of great antiquity. It is said to have been written by a recluse, some centuries since : —

> "Before thirteen united
> Shall be thrice what they are,
> The eagle shall be blighted
> By the lightning of war.
>
> When sixty is ended,
> And one takes its place,
> Then brothers offended
> Shall deal mutual disgrace.
>
> If white remain white,
> And black still be black,
> Once more they'll unite
> And bring happiness back.
>
> But whenever the Cross
> Stands aloft 'mong the Stars,
> They shall gain by their loss,
> And thus end all their wars."

OCCUPATION OF FORT SUMTER. — The following impressive incident occurred at Fort Sumter on Major Anderson taking possession of that place in December, 1860 : It is known that the American flag brought away from Fort Moultrie was raised at Sumter precisely at noon on the 27th of that month. It was a scene that will be a memorable reminiscence in the lives of those who witnessed it. A short time before noon, Major Anderson assembled the whole of his little force, with the workmen employed on the fort, around the foot of the flag-staff. The national ensign was attached to the cord, and Major Anderson, holding the end of the lines in his hand, knelt reverently down. The officers, soldiers, and men clustered around, many of them on their knees, all deeply impressed with the solemnity of the scene. The chaplain made an earnest prayer — such an appeal for support, encouragement, and mercy as one would make who felt that "man's extremity is God's opportunity." As the earnest, solemn words of the speaker ceased, and the men responded Amen with a fervency that perhaps they had never before experienced, Major Anderson drew the "Star-spangled Banner" up to the top of the staff, the band broke out with the national air of "Hail, Columbia!" and loud and exultant cheers, repeated again and again, were given by the officers, soldiers, and workmen. "If," said the narrator, "South Carolina had at that moment attacked the fort, there would have been no hesitation upon the part of any man within it about defending the flag."

INCIDENT OF THE WHITE HOUSE, VA. On the occupation of the White House, Va., by the soldiers of General McLellan, a small piece of paper, bearing the following inscription, was found pinned on the casing of an inner door: —

"Northern soldiers, who profess to reverence Washington, forbear to desecrate the house of his first married life, the property of his wife, now owned by her descendants.

"A granddaughter of Mrs. Washington."

Beneath the inscription was written the following:

"LADY: A Northern officer has protected your property in the sight of the enemy, and at the request of your overseer."

A FIGHTING CLERGYMAN. — Rev. B. C. Ward, pastor of a Congregational church in the village of Geneseo, Illinois, conceived it to be his duty to forsake the pulpit for the field. He received authority to raise a company of infantry, but proposed to enlist clergymen only. An appeal to his clerical brethren, published over his own signature, called upon "the fighting stock of the church militant" to prove to the world their willingness to "seal with their blood what they have talked in their pulpits," and closed with this extraordinary passage:

"Much as we have said and done to prove our loyalty, we have not yet resisted unto blood, striving against sin. Shall we now, at the call of Christ, come out from behind our velvet-cushioned barracks, whence we have so often hurled bold, indignant words at the giant iniquity of the age, and meet it face to face with the hot shot of rifled artillery, with the gleaming bayonet, or with clashing sabres in hand-to-hand encounter?"

THE LAST MAN OF BEAUFORT. — On the day the town of Beaufort, S. C., was entered by the national troops, all the inhabitants were found to have fled, except one white man, who, being too much intoxicated to join his compatriots in flight, had been forced to remain behind.

"'Tis the last man at Beaufort
    Left sitting alone;
All his valiant companions
    Had 'vamosed' and gone;
No secesh of his kindred
    To comfort is nigh,
And his liquor's expended,
    The bottle is dry!
We'll not leave thee, thou lone one,
    Or harshly condemn —
Since your friends have all 'mizzled,'
    You can't sleep with them;
And it's no joking matter
    To sleep with the dead;
So we'll take you back with us —
    Jim, lift up his head!
He muttered some words
    As they bore him away,
And the breeze thus repeated
    The words he did say:
'When the liquor's all out,
    And your friends they have flown,
O, who would inhabit
    This Beaufort alone?'"

J. M. LEARNED, of Oxfordville, New Hampshire, had three twins in the army. Two of them, twenty-three years old, were in the Massachusetts Fourteenth. The third, whose mate is a girl, was in the Fifth New Hampshire regiment.

A REMINISCENCE OF ABRAHAM LINCOLN. — When the convention was held in Chicago, which nominated Mr. Lincoln for the Presidency in 1860, a respectable gentleman in Massachusetts — not of Mr. Lincoln's party — was induced to take the opportunity, in company with several delegates and others interested in the objects of the convention, to go out to Chicago, and spend a few days in visiting that section of the country. In a very few minutes after the final balloting was had, and Mr. Lincoln was nominated, it happened that a train of cars started upon the Central Railroad, passing through Springfield, the place of Mr. Lincoln's residence, and Mr. R., the gentleman alluded to, took passage in the same. Arriving at Springfield, he put up at a public house, and loitering upon the front door steps, had the curiosity to inquire of the landlord where Mr. Lincoln lived. Whilst giving the necessary directions, the landlord suddenly remarked, "There is Mr. Lincoln now, coming down the sidewalk; that tall, crooked man, loosely walking this way; if you wish to see him you will have an opportunity by putting yourself in his track."

In a few moments the object of his curiosity reached the point our friend occupied, who advancing, ventured to accost him thus: "Is this Mr. Lincoln?" "That, sir, is my name." "My name is R., from Plymouth county, Massachusetts, and learning that you have to-day been made the public property of the United States, I have ventured to introduce myself with a view to a brief acquaintance, hoping you will pardon such a patriotic curiosity in a stranger." Mr. Lincoln received his salutations with cordiality, told him no apology was necessary for his introduction, and asked him to accompany him to his residence. He had just come from the telegraph office, where he had learned the fact of his nomination, and was on his return home when our friend met and accompanied him thither.

Arriving at Mr. Lincoln's residence, he was introduced to Mrs. Lincoln and the two boys, and entered into conversation in relation to the Lincoln family of the old colony — the Hingham General Lincoln of the Revolutionary army, and the two Worcester Lincolns, brothers, who were Governors of Massachusetts and Maine at one and the same time. In reply to Mr. R.'s inquiry whether Mr. Lincoln could trace his ancestry to either of those early families of his own name, Mr. Lincoln, with a characteristic facetiousness, replied that he could not say that he ever had an ancestor older than his father, and therefore had it not in his power to trace his genealogy to so patriotic a source as old General Lincoln of the Revolution — though he wished he could. After some further pleasant conversation, chiefly relating to the early history of the Pilgrim Fathers, with which he seemed familiar, Mr. R. desired the privilege of writing a letter to be despatched by the next mail. Mr. Lincoln very promptly and kindly provided him with the necessary means. As he began to write, Mr. Lincoln approached, and tapping him on the shoulder, expressed the hope that he was not a spy who had come thus early to report his faults to the public. "By no means, sir," protested Mr. R.; "I am writing home to my wife, who, I dare say, will hardly credit the fact that I am writing in your house." "O, sir," exclaimed Mr. Lincoln, "if your wife doubts your word, I will cheerfully indorse it, if you will give me permission;" and taking the pen from Mr. R., he wrote the following words, in a clear hand, upon the blank page of the letter:

"I am happy to say that your husband is at the present time a guest in my house, and in due time I trust you will greet his safe return to the bosom of his family.   A. LINCOLN."

This gave our friend an excellent autograph of Mr. Lincoln, besides bearing witness to his hospitable and cheerful spirit.

Whilst thus engaged in pleasant conversation, the cars arrived that brought from Chicago the committee of the convention appointed to notify Mr. Lincoln of his nomination. He received them at the door, and conducted them to seats in his parlor. Our friend, who related the interview to us, says that on the reception of this committee Mr. Lincoln appeared somewhat embarrassed, but soon resumed his wonted tranquillity and cheerfulness. At the proper time the chairman of the committee arose, and, with becoming dignity, informed Mr. Lincoln, that he and his fellows appeared in behalf of the convention now in session at Chicago, to inform him that he had that day been unanimously nominated to the office of President of the United States, and asked his permission to report to that body his acceptance of the nomination. Mr. Lincoln, with becoming modesty, but very handsomely, replied, that he felt his insufficiency for the vast responsibilities which must devolve upon that office under the impending circumstances of the times, but if God and his country called for his services in that direction, he should shrink from no duty that might be imposed upon him, and therefore he should not decline the nomination.

After this ceremony had passed, Mr. Lincoln remarked to the company, that as an appropriate conclusion to an interview so important and interesting as that which had just transpired, he supposed good manners would require that he should treat the committee with something to drink; and opening a door that led into a room in the rear, he called out, "Mary! Mary!" A girl responded to the call, whom Mr. Lincoln spoke a few words to in an under-tone; and, closing the door, returned again to converse with his guests. In a few minutes the maiden entered, bearing a large waiter, containing several glass tumblers, and a large pitcher in the midst, and placed it upon the centre-table. Mr. Lincoln arose, and gravely addressing the company, said, — "Gentlemen, we must pledge our mutual healths in the most healthy beverage which our God has given to man; it is the only beverage I have ever used or allowed in my family, and I cannot conscientiously depart from it on the present occasion; it is pure Adam's ale from the spring;" and taking a tumbler, he touched it to his lips and pledged them his highest respects in a cup of cold water. Of course, all his guests were constrained to admire his consistency, and to join in his example.

Mr. R., when he went to Chicago, had but little political sympathy with the Republican convention which nominated Mr. Lincoln; but when he saw, as he did see for himself, his sturdy adherence to a high moral principle, he returned an admirer of the man, and a zealous advocate of his election.

"ALL WE ASK IS TO BE LET ALONE."

BY H. H. BROWNELL.

As vonce I valked by a dismal swamp,
There sot an old cove in the dark and damp,
And at everybody as passed that road
A stick or a stone this old cove throwed.
And venever he flung his stick or his stone,
He'd set up a song of "Let me alone."

"Let me alone, for I loves to shy
These bits of things at the passers-by;
Let me alone, for I've got your tin,
And lots of other traps snugly in;
Let me alone — I am rigging a boat
To grab votever you've got afloat;
In a veek or so I expects to come,
And turn you out of your ouse and ome;
I'm a quiet old cove," says he, with a groan;
"All I axes, is, Let me alone."

Just then came along, on the self same vay,
Another old cove, and began for to say:
"Let you alone! That's comin' it strong!
You've ben let alone — a darned sight too long!
Of all the sarce that ever I heerd!
Put down that stick! (You may well look skeered.
Let go that stone! If you once show fight,
I'll knock you higher than ary kite.)

"You must have a lesson to stop your tricks,
And cure you of shying them stones and sticks;
And I'll have my hardware back, and my cash,
And knock your scow into tarnal smash;
And if ever I catches you round my ranch,
I'll string you up to the nearest branch.
The best you can do is to go to bed,
And keep a decent tongue in your head;
For I reckon, before you and I are done,
You'll wish you had let honest folks alone."

The old cove stopped, and the other old cove,
He sot quite still in his cypress grove,
And he looked at his stick, revolvin' slow,
Vether 'twere safe to shy it or no;
And he grumbled on, in an injured tone,
"All that I axed vos, *Let me alone.*"

THE MAN WHO WOULDN'T BE MADE A PRIS-
ONER. — During the last week in December, 1861,
while about a dozen oyster smacks were on their
way to the "banks" in Mississippi Sound, they
were surrounded by a number of launches from
the national ships : all were seized in the name of
the Government, and a guard put aboard each
to conduct them under the guns of the ships of
war. One of the smacks thus seized was the
"Clide," commanded and owned by Capt. King,
a man who had resided in New Orleans since
boyhood, and who was well known as a brave
and determined seaman by all of his acquaintances around the New Basin. A sergeant and
one soldier were placed aboard the "Clide," with
orders to steer for the New London, then
some twelve or eighteen miles off. The wind
was ahead, and the boat had to beat all the way.
The "Clide," somehow, strange to say, worked
badly; all the rest of the smacks were soon several miles ahead, and still the contrary wind was
blowing, and the lazy boat dragging slowly along.
So passed the greater part of the day, and at five
o'clock in the afternoon the fleet was yet several
miles off. The soldiers on board the "Clide"
grew hungry, and asked Capt. King if he had
anything to eat aboard. He politely told them
that there was plenty in the cabin — a sort of little hold in the after part of the craft, reached by
a narrow scuttle and two or three crooked steps.
The sergeant volunteered to go down and get the
victuals, directing the soldier to keep a sharp
watch while he did so. He started down the
steps with rifle in hand, Capt. King standing
near, officiously showing the way. As soon as
he had got into the cabin, and was about to stoop
and go forward, the hitherto polite and kind captain suddenly seized his rifle, and jerking it from
his hand, shot him dead on the spot. Not stopping to swap jack-knives, Capt. King jumped forward, and seizing the other soldier's gun before
he had time to recover from his fright and astonishment, commanded him to surrender. The
soldier saw there was no use to resist, gave up,
and was securely tied and laid in the hold.

Capt. King then set sail for Fort Pike, and as
if understanding the necessity for haste, the little
craft recovered from her languor, and sped over
the water at railroad speed. And it was well she
did, for the men on the other boats had heard
the musket shot, and suspecting something wrong
from seeing the "Clide" suddenly change her
course, made chase, one and all. The affair then
grew exciting, and for a while Capt. King's chances
for safety were rather squally; but his gallant
little craft was in earnest, and rushed on towards
the haven of safety as if she understood the whole
affair. Night soon came on, and darkness hiding
her from the view of her pursuers, enabled her to
get safely to Fort Pike, where Capt. King recited
his adventures, and excited the admiration of the
garrison. Leaving the fort the next morning, he
arrived in the New Basin with his prisoner and
dead sergeant, who were placed in the hands of
the military authorities. Besides his prisoner,
Capt. King captured a fine six-oared launch,

nearly new, one Minie rifle, one musket, three
bayonets, one sergeant's sword, and four cartridge
boxes filled with ammunition — quite a good day's
work for a simple oysterman.

———

GEN. CHEATHAM'S ESCAPE. — The following
story was told by Gen. Cheatham of the manner
in which he escaped capture at the battle of Belmont, Mo. : —

Just as the opposing armies were approaching
one another, Gen. Cheatham discovered a squadron of cavalry coming down a road near his
position. Uncertain as to which force it belonged,
accompanied only by an orderly, he rode up to
within a few yards of it, and inquired, —

"What cavalry is that ? "

"Illinois cavalry, sir," was the reply.

"O! Illinois cavalry. All right; just stand
where you are ! "

The cavalry obeyed the order, and unmolested
by them, who supposed he was one of the Federal officers, the general rode safely back, directly
under the guns of another Federal regiment,
which had by that time come up, but who, seeing
him coming from the direction of the cavalry,
also supposed that he was one of them. Some
of the national officers remembered the incident,
and agreed with the hero of it, that if they had
known who he was, it was very probable that
there would have been one general less that
night.

———

AN INCIDENT WITH A MORAL. — A chaplain in
one of the regiments on the Potomac narrates
the case of a sick soldier, which strikingly illustrates the reasoning of many men in the camp
and out of it. Some one had mentioned to the
soldier the case of the Vermonter who was sentenced to be shot for sleeping on his post. During
the evening following, the fever set in violently;
the sick man imagined he was the one sentenced
to be shot. The surgeon being called, the following conversation ensued : —

"Doctor, I am to be shot in the morning, and
wish you to send for the chaplain. I desire to
make all necessary preparations for my end."

"They shall not shoot you; I'll take care of
you. Whoever comes to take you from here, I
shall have them arrested and put under guard."

"Will you, dear doctor? Thank you, thank
you — well, then, you need not send for the
chaplain 'just yet.'"

———

THE SPOTTED HAND.

AN ANECDOTE OF JOHN C. CALHOUN.

ONE morning, at the breakfast table, when I,
an unobserved spectator, happened to be present,
Calhoun was observed to gaze frequently at his
right hand, and brush it with his left in a hurried
and nervous manner. He did this so often that
it excited attention. At length one of the per-

sons comprising the breakfast party — his name, I think, is Toombs, and he is a member of Congress from Georgia — took upon himself to ask the occasion of Mr. Calhoun's disquietude.

"Does your hand pain you?" he asked of Mr. Calhoun.

To this Mr. Calhoun replied, in rather a hurried manner, —

"Pshaw! it is nothing but a dream I had last night, and which makes me see perpetually a large black spot, like an ink blotch, upon the back of my right hand; an optical illusion, I suppose."

Of course these words excited the curiosity of the company, but no one ventured to beg the details of this singular dream, until Toombs asked quietly, —

"What was your dream like? I am not very superstitious about dreams; but sometimes they have a great deal of truth in them."

"But this was such a peculiarly absurd dream," said Mr. Calhoun, again brushing the back of his right hand; "however, if it does not intrude too much on the time of our friends, I will relate it to you."

Of course the company were profuse in their expressions of anxiety to know all about the dream, and Mr. Calhoun related it.

"At a late hour last night, as I was sitting in my room, engaged in writing, I was astonished by the entrance of a visitor, who, without a word, took a seat opposite me at my table. This surprised me, as I had given particular orders to the servant that I should on no account be disturbed. The manner in which the intruder entered, so perfectly self-possessed, taking his seat opposite me without a word, as though my room and all within it belonged to him, excited in me as much surprise as indignation. As I raised my head to look into his features, over the top of my shaded lamp, I discovered that he was wrapped in a thin cloak, which effectually concealed his face and features from my view; and as I raised my head, he spoke : —

"'What are you writing, senator from South Carolina?'

"I did not think of his impertinence at first, but answered him voluntarily, —

"'I am writing a plan for the dissolution of the American Union.'

"(You know, gentlemen, that I am expected to produce a plan of dissolution in the event of certain contingencies.) To this the intruder replied, in the coolest manner possible, —

"'Senator from South Carolina, will you allow me to look at your hand, your right hand?'

"He rose, the cloak fell, and I beheld his face. Gentlemen, the sight of that face struck me like a thunder-clap. It was the face of a dead man, whom extraordinary events had called back to life. The features were those of Gen. George Washington. He was dressed in the Revolutionary costume, such as you see in the Patent Office."

Here Mr. Calhoun paused, apparently agitated. His agitation, I need not tell you, was shared by the company. Toombs at length broke the embarrassing pause.

"Well, what was the issue of this scene?"

Mr. Calhoun resumed : —

"The intruder, as I have said, rose and asked to look at my right hand. As though I had not the power to refuse, I extended it. The truth is, I felt a strange thrill pervade me at his touch; he grasped it, and held it near the light, thus affording full time to examine every feature. It was the face of Washington. After holding my hand for a moment, he looked at me steadily, and said in a quiet way, —

"'And with this right hand, senator from South Carolina, you would sign your name to a paper declaring the Union dissolved?'

"I answered in the affirmative.

"'Yes,' I said, 'if a certain contingency arises, I will sign my name to the Declaration of Dissolution.'

"But at that moment a black blotch appeared on the back of my hand, which I seem to see now.

"'What is that?' said I, alarmed, I know not why, at the blotch on my hand.

"'That,' said he, dropping my hand, 'is the mark by which Benedict Arnold is known in the next world.'

"He said no more, gentlemen, but drew from beneath his cloak an object which he laid upon the table — laid upon the very paper on which I was writing. This object, gentlemen, was a skeleton.

"'There,' said he, 'there are the bones of Isaac Hayne, who was hung at Charleston by the British. He gave his life in order to establish the Union. When you put your name to a Declaration of Dissolution, why, you may as well have the bones of Isaac Hayne before you — he was a South Carolinian, and so are you. But there was no blotch on his right hand.'

"With these words the intruder left the room. I started back from the contact with the dead man's bones, and — awoke. Overcome by labor, I had fallen asleep, and had been dreaming. Was it not a singular dream?"

All the company answered in the affirmative, and Toombs muttered, "Singular, very singular," and at the same time looking curiously at the back of his right hand, while Mr. Calhoun placed his head between his hands, and seemed buried in thought.

A CONTRABAND REFRAIN,

MUCH IN VOGUE AT FORTRESS MONROE.

WAKE up, snakes, pelicans, and Sesh'ners!
    Don't yer hear 'um comin' —
        Comin' on de run?
Wake up, I tell yer! Git up, Jefferson!
    Bobolishion's comin' —
        Bob-o-lish-i-on.

ANECDOTE OF PRESIDENT LINCOLN. — The following is one of Mr. Lincoln's stories. These he told often in private conversation, rarely in his speeches.

"I once knew a good, sound churchman, whom we'll call Brown, who was on a committee to erect a bridge over a very dangerous and rapid river. Architect after architect failed, and at last Brown said he had a friend named Jones, who had built several bridges, and could build this. 'Let's have him in,' said the committee. In came Jones. 'Can you build this bridge, sir?' 'Yes,' replied Jones; 'I could build a bridge to the infernal regions, if necessary.' The sober committee were horrified; but when Jones retired, Brown thought it but fair to defend his friend. 'I know Jones so well,' said he, 'and he is so honest a man, and so good an architect, that, if he states soberly and positively that he can build a bridge to Hades — why, I believe it. But I have my doubts about the abutment on the infernal side.' So," Lincoln added, "when politicians said they could harmonize the Northern and Southern wings of the Democracy, why, I believed them. But I had my doubts about the abutment on the Southern side."

MR. WINTHROP, one of the Boston Union Committee, called on Senator Mason, in January, 1861, and, referring to his former visit to Massachusetts, remarked in the blandest tones: "I hope, Mr. Mason, we shall see you again at Bunker Hill." To which the senator stiffly jerked out the response: "Not unless I come as an ambassador, sir."

GENERAL ROUSSEAU AND A REBEL CLERGYMAN. — Rev. Frederick A. Ross had just been examined on a charge of treason, and convicted upon his own showing. Under charge of a guard he was about to leave the General's tent. Putting on a particularly sanctimonious expression of countenance, he took up his hat, turned to the General, and said: "Well, General, we must each do as we think best, and I hope we will both meet in heaven." The General replied: "Your getting to heaven, sir, will depend altogether upon your future conduct; before we can reasonably hope to meet in that region, you and I must become better men." The effect of this brief rejoinder was irresistible.

REBELS.

Rebels! 'tis a holy name!
  The name our fathers bore,
When battling in the cause of Right,
Against the tyrant in his might,
  In the dark days of yore.

Rebels! 'tis our family name!
  Our father, Washington,
Was the arch-rebel in the fight,
And gave the name to us — a right
  Of father unto son.

Rebels! 'tis our given name!
  Our mother, Liberty,
Received the title with her fame,
In days of grief, of fear and shame,
  When at her breast were we.

Rebels! 'tis our sealed name!
  A baptism of blood!
The war — ay, and the din of strife —
The fearful contest, life for life —
  The mingled crimson flood.

Rebels! 'tis a patriot's name!
  In struggles it was given;
We bore it then when tyrants raved,
And through their curses 'twas engraved
  On the doomsday book of heaven.

Rebels! 'tis our fighting name!
  For peace rules o'er the land,
Until they speak of craven woe —
Until our rights receive a blow,
  From foe's or brothers' hand.

Rebels! 'tis our dying name!
  For although life is dear,
Yet, freemen born and freemen bred,
We'd rather live as freemen dead,
  Than live in slavish fear.

Then call us Rebels if you will —
  We glory in the name;
For bending under unjust laws,
And swearing faith to an unjust cause,
  We count a greater shame.

AN EDITOR BEFORE THE CABINET. — The editor of the Chatauque (N. Y.) *Democrat* was spending his time in Washington, and writing home letters for publication. One of them, it was claimed, contained "contraband news," and the editor (if his statement may be believed) was summoned before the Cabinet to answer for the heinous offence. Here is his account of the affair:

"So many weeks had slipped away since my friends in Jamestown commenced sending the *Democrat* regularly to the members of the Cabinet and General McClellan, that the vision of a file of ferocious soldiers had departed from my imagination, when one morning the subscriber received a gilt-edged, jockey-club-scented note, requesting his distinguished presence at the White House at a certain hour. I had no doubt but the note was from Mrs. Lincoln, who, I supposed, wished to apologize for the blunder that she made in my not receiving her invitation to the White House ball.

"So, giving my boots an extra blacking, and my moustache an extra twist, I wended my way to the President's domicile. After disposing of hat, cane, &c., I was conducted into the room used for Cabinet meetings, and soon found myself in the presence of the President, Messrs. Seward, Stanton, and Welles. Mr. Seward, whom I had met at a dinner-party at General Risley's, in Fredonia, during the campaign of 1860, recognized me, and at once alluded to the excellence of General Risley's brandy, and proposed to Abe that he should send over to his cellar at the State Department, and get a nice article that he had there. I noticed three copies of the Chatauque *Democrat* spread out on the table, bearing certain initials, which for the sake of avoiding personalities I will not mention. I also noticed ominous black lines drawn around certain passages which I recognized as being part of my letter of several weeks ago. They looked like Mr. Benton's expunged resolutions on the Senate Journal.

Mr. Welles was so deeply engaged in reading a fourth copy, that he did not look up as I went in. It seems that the "mailing clerks" at Jamestown had neglected to furnish the Navy Department with a copy, and the Secretary was deeply absorbed in its perusal. Mr. Stanton was busy writing his recent order, thanking God and General Halleck for the victory and slaughter at Pittsburgh Landing, and paid no attention to my entrance.

Mr. Lincoln said: "A Cabinet meeting had been called at the request of General McClellan, to consider my offence in writing the letter conspicuously marked in the *Democrat* before us, and which had been kindly furnished several of their number by certain patriotic and high-toned gentlemen in Jamestown, N. Y. But they would have to delay a few minutes, to await the arrival of the Commodore from Yorktown, with despatches from General McClellan, who had telegraphed that the business must not go on till his despatches arrived."

During the interval, *me*, and Abe, and Seward, sauntered through the rooms, looking at the various objects of interest. On entering the library, we found that the messenger had returned from Seward's cellar, with some of the Secretary's best Auburn brand. The cork was drawn, and we sampled the fluid. We next visited the ladies' parlor, and were presented to "Mary," who came forward, and shook me cordially by the hand, and desired to know "how I flourished;" said "she never should forgive me for not attending her ball." She was greatly shocked to hear that there had been a failure to connect, about getting the card of invitation.

We were soon summoned to the council; the Commodore had arrived, bringing seventeen of General McClellan's staff, who had been delegated by him to transmit to the President his copy of the *Democrat*, which he had received at Fortress Monroe. On opening it, the same ominous inkmarks were drawn around the passages intended to be brought to the especial notice of the General. The staff-officers then withdrew, and the President proposed to proceed to business. At this juncture Mr. Welles looked up from the paper he had been so busily perusing, and inquired of the President: "If he had ever heard anything about the fight the *Democrat* spoke of, between the Monitor and the Merrimac, and the danger there was of the latter getting out and coming up the Potomac and bombarding Washington?" Mr. Lincoln said: "It was a fact." The Secretary

seemed greatly surprised, and said: "He must write to his brother-in-law in New York, to send round a vessel to Hampton Roads, to watch the Merrimac, and also to send him the *Weekly Post*, so that he could get the news." He chose the *Post*, because he had been in the habit, aforetime, of contributing essays for its columns. He also remarked that there was "much valuable and deeply interesting news in the *Democrat*," which was then only some four weeks old.

Mr. Stanton here proposed that the contraband article should be read, as he had been so busy of late, he had not read the copy sent him by his patriotic correspondents at Jamestown. So Mr. Seward read the article through carefully. When it was completed, Mr. Stanton brought his fist down on the table with the energy and vigor for which he is celebrated, and says he: "Them's my sentiments, by ——." The Secretary, contrary to the opinion of many who know him only by his short, pungent, pious, pithy, patriotic, and peculiar proclamations, profanes pretty profusely when excited. During the reading he had been fumbling his vest-pocket. Says he: "What's the price of that paper per annum?" I informed him that it was furnished to advance paying subscribers at one dollar. He handed me a gold dollar, and says he: "Send it along." Mr. Welles, who was just then absorbed in reading the account of the "embarkation" of the army from Alexandria, looked up and said: "He had thought of subscribing himself, but as Mr. Stanton had done so, he would have George send him the *Post*, and they could exchange."

The President now called for an opinion from the other members of the Cabinet, Mr. Stanton having *voted*, as I have before remarked. Mr. Seward, who was in a happy frame of mind, said that: "Perhaps it was impolitic to have written just such an article, as he was always opposed to the expression of any decided opinions, but he thought the editor of the *Democrat* knew good liquor when he smelt it, and in view of the fact that he hailed from Old Chatauque, whose inhabitants he remembered with pride, having once been a resident there, he voted that the article was not contraband, but that the writer must not do so again."

Mr. Welles said: "He did not know enough about the subject under consideration to give an opinion. He had been much interested in the perusal of the article, and had found some useful hints in it in regard to the danger to be apprehended from the Merrimac, which he thought he should act upon by next year—on the whole, he thought the good balanced the evil, and he was for calling it square."

It was the President's turn, now, to decide the matter. He always gets the opinion of his "constitutional advisers" all round, and then does as he has a mind to. Abe turned to me with a merry twinkle in his eye, and his lovely and expressive countenance seemed more seraphic than ever, and says he to me, says he: "Your letter on McClellan reminds me of a story that I heard in the days of John Tyler's Administration. There was an editor in Rhode Island, noted for his love of fun — it came to him irresistibly — and he couldn't help saying just what came into his mind. He was appointed Postmaster by Tyler. Some time after Tyler vetoed the Bank Bill, and came into disrepute with the Whigs, a conundrum went the rounds of the papers. It was as follows: 'Why is John Tyler like an ass?' This editor copied the conundrum, and could not resist the temptation to answer it, which he did as follows: 'Because he *is* an ass.' This piece of fun cost him his head, *but it was a fact.*

"On the whole," said Abe, "here's a dollar; send me your valuable paper for a year, and be careful in future how you disclose Government secrets that have been published in the Norfolk *Day Book* only two weeks."

I promised to be more discreet hereafter, pledging myself not to interfere further with General Thomas "or any other man" in his exclusive right to give the rebels the earliest information possible; also pledging myself to the best of my ability to aid the Government in its patriotic efforts to promote "loyal ignorance" among the masses of the Northern people.

"CALL ALL! CALL ALL!"

BY "GEORGIA."

Whoop! the Doodles have broken loose,
Roaring round like the very deuce!
Lice of Egypt, a hungry pack;
After 'em, boys, and drive 'em back.

Bull-dog, terrier, cur and fice,
Back to the beggarly land of ice,
Worry 'em, bite 'em, scratch and tear
Everybody and everywhere.

Old Kentucky is caved from under,
Tennessee is split asunder,
Alabama awaits attack,
And Georgia bristles up her back.

Old John Brown is dead and gone!
Still his spirit is marching on,
Lantern-jawed, and legs, my boys,
Long as an ape's from Illinois!

Want a weapon? Gather a brick!
Club or cudgel, or stone or stick,
Anything with a blade or butt!
Anything that can cleave or cut!

Anything heavy, or hard, or keen!
Any sort of slaying-machine!
Anything with a willing mind,
And the steady arm of a man, behind.

Want a weapon? Why, capture one!
Every Doodle has got a gun,
Belt and bayonet, bright and new:
Kill a Doodle and capture *two!*

Shoulder to shoulder, son and sire!
All, call all! to the feast of fire!
Mother and maiden, and child and slave
A common triumph or a single grave.

"ETHAN SPIKE" writes, that Hornby has "seceded," and that he consequently resigns his seat in the Maine Legislature. The following resolutions were passed at a public meeting of the new "sovereignty":

Resolved, That we are opposed to koercion, except when exercised by ourselves.

Resolved, That the okepation of the Baldwin lightus, by a State keeper, is a irritatin' circumstance, an' onless he is withdrawn, nour army be instructed to take possession of the same in the name of the taoun.

Resolved, That ef aour reasonable demands is not complied to, that we will take possession of, and hold *for aour own use,* the State's prison, and the insane assylum.

Resolved, That the haybius korpus act, taxes, an' the Main law be an' is suspended. Also an ordnance relating to weights and measures as used in the likker trade. Be it enacted, That henceforth and for ever, in this ere realm, *every quart pot shall hold a gallon.*

Ordered, that the forgoin' articles shall be the constitution of this suvrinty.

To THE OFFICERS OF THE NAVY. — Lieut. Craven, commanding the United States steamer Mohawk, which arrived at New York February 7, 1861, from Key West, published the following letter, addressed to the officers of the navy:

Basely unprincipled incendiaries have scattered throughout our land doctrines of a revolutionary character — doctrines calculated to inflame the minds of the excitable and thoughtless multitude — calculated to mislead the weak and wavering, and to lead on and incite to frenzy the needy adventurers — those wolves of the human race who rejoice in that anarchy and disorder which loosen the restraints of law, and afford them occasion for indulgence in license and rapine.

Sad indeed in the history of the world will be the day which witnesses the dismemberment of this Confederation — disastrous to the march of human freedom and civilization, the event which blots from the page of history our great and glorious nation of self-ruled men.

The oppressed of the earth, with hopeful hearts, have long regarded us as the exponents of "liberty, fraternity, equality." God avert from us the abasing acknowledgment that man is not capable of self-government. What a humiliating reflection, that man, in his passions, can be ruled only by the bayonet, by force — despotic force; his reasoning faculties gone, he sinks to the level of the brute; with no principle to guide him, he yields only to force.

Officers of the navy, be, as ever, loyal, brave, and true; our beloved country is convulsed with distracting troubles; our country is in danger; the great temple of liberty, founded by our fathers, and dedicated to the use of the human race, now reels and totters to its base; destruction threatens it; the machinations of designing men have brought it to the verge of ruin.

Officers of the navy, our country is in peril, and it behooves us, my friends, to consider well and earnestly what are our duties to the nation which has given us honored places among her sons; has enrolled us among her defenders; has "reposed special trust and confidence in our valor, patriotism, and fidelity."

There is no one among us, my friends, however humble his station, who has not, with laudable pride, enjoyed the honor of being a servant of his country; one of her defenders on the seas; one of the fostered sons of the favored arm of national defence. There can be no feeling more ennobling than that of him who bears arms in his country's defence; let us be slow to throw aside that armor; slow to abjure all allegiance, and never betray the trust reposed in us.

We have in a marked manner been the honored and cherished sons of our country; our countrymen have with exalted estimate valued the exploits of our heroic men, whose deeds have shed such lustre on our flag, and carried it in triumph and honor to all parts of the world; recollect, my friends, that each one of us is a sharer in all the glories won by naval valor; our great men have passed away, but they have left the honor of the navy, the honor of the flag, in our keeping. Some among us have had the fortune to do battle against our country's foes; all of us have had each our individual *rôle* in the great machinery by which the whole is moved; the fame of our flag belongs to us, and our duty is to rally to its support.

We must not forget that our initiation into the service of our country was by taking a solemn oath "to support the Constitution of the United States." That vow, my friends, is recorded on high; that vow was heard by Him who has said, "Render unto Cæsar the things which are Cæsar's." We must beware how we lightly treat so solemn an oath; it cannot be thrown off; we cannot ignore the claims of our country; we may, it is true, cease to serve, but we cannot, dare not, offend the Most High by turning our arms against those laws which we have sworn to sustain; nor can we be too guarded, lest by any act of ours a single stain is brought upon our bright escutcheon.

Let us not be deceived by the vain and idle sophistries of those deluded men who would tell us that the United States are only bound together by a weak alliance, to be shaken off at pleasure by any one, without even so much notice of the abrogation as common decency has established as customary among the civilized nations of the earth. Let us discard from our minds the illusions of those who would in fact persuade us that we never had any nationality. If their arguments are correctly based, we have never indeed been one nation. We are mere pretenders, who have, without shadow of right, adopted a national style and law by which to impose upon mankind.

Let us not listen to the reasoning of those who would seduce us from our allegiance by special pleading and abstract questions of State sovereignty. "Remember your oath"—"Remember!" What have we to do with States? What indeed have you to do with States, those of you who, by virtue of your national office, are disfranchised by the laws of the States in which you reside?

The Union is our country; the Union is our State; the Constitution is our law. A great trust devolves on us. Let not the poisonous bane of revolution have any spread among our ranks. Let us show ourselves ever worthy of the confidence of our countrymen. We are not partisans. We must not listen to treason in any shape or form. We cannot abjure our duties without being guilty of treason; and by no train of reasoning can acts against the Government be styled by any other name than treason.

The fame of our proudly-waving flag belongs to us, and whatever be the fate of that honored emblem of our country,—that honored badge of our power,—whatever be its fate, my friends, let us beware that it suffer no stain through the navy.

T. AUGS. CRAVEN,
Lieutenant commanding U. S. steamer "Mohawk."

A DARING EXPLOIT.—During the month of December, 1861, a squad of some half dozen left Col. Shackleford's regiment, at Calhoun, Ky., on Green River, to bring back three soldiers who had gone to Todd County. While on their route, after night, they came upon some rebel cavalry, and our men seeing that resistance would be useless, took to the woods. One of them, named Wilkins, was separated from his companions, and in winding about through the woods, came several times in close proximity to rebel squads, but succeeded in eluding them. He at last overtook three of them, and seeing that his chances were desperate, he determined to join them, and pass himself off as one of their number. By keeping a little in the rear, he watched a favorable opportunity, when he drew his revolver, and firing rapidly, killed one, badly wounded another, and caused the third to take to flight. Wilkins succeeded in making his escape, and returned to camp at Calhoun, where a gentleman arrived the next day from Elkton, and stated that the rebel cavalry reported that the country was overrun with Federal troops, and that they had been forced to retreat before a superior force. The camp at Calhoun contained plenty of such pluck in the regiments under Cols. Shackleford, Jackson, Hawkins, and Burbridge.

AN INCIDENT that carries its own comment is related by a visitor on his way to one of the patriot camps in the Old Dominion. Seated by the roadside was a soldier, his musket in one hand, and a volume in the other, which he was reading with deep interest. He was clad roughly but comfortably, and bore the evidences of having seen hard service. As the party approached, he rose to his feet, advanced into the road, and exclaimed, "Halt! Let me see your pass." After carefully inspecting the strangers and their pass, he quietly told them to move on, and resumed his seat and his book. One of the party glanced at the volume, and found that it was a beautiful copy of Tennyson's Poems.

A HEROINE IN BALTIMORE. — The band of the Sixth Regiment that left Boston in April, 1861, consisted of twenty-four persons, who, together with their musical instruments, occupied a car by themselves from Philadelphia to Baltimore. By some accident, the musicians' car got switched off at the Canton Depot, so that, instead of being the first, it was left in the rear of all the others, and after the attack had been made by the mob upon the soldiers, they came upon the car in which the band was still sitting, wholly unarmed, and incapable of making any defence. The infuriated demons approached them howling and yelling, and poured in upon them a shower of stones, broken iron, and other missiles, wounding some severely, and demolishing their instruments. Some of the miscreants jumped upon the roof of the car, and with a bar of iron beat a hole through it, while others were calling for powder to blow them all up in a heap. Finding that it would be sure destruction to remain longer in the car, the poor fellows jumped out to meet their fiendish assailants hand to hand. They were saluted with a shower of stones, but took to their heels, fighting their way through the crowd, and running at random, without knowing in what direction to go for assistance or shelter. As they were hurrying along, a rough-looking man suddenly jumped in front of their leader, and exclaimed, "This way, boys! this way!" It was the first friendly voice they had heard since entering Baltimore, and they stopped to ask no questions, but followed their guide, who took them up a narrow court, where they found an open door, into which they rushed, being met inside by a powerful-looking woman, who grasped each one by the hand, and directed them upstairs. The last of their band was knocked senseless just as he was entering the door, by a stone, which struck him on the head; but the woman who had welcomed them immediately caught up their fallen comrade, and carried him in her arms up the stairs.

"You are perfectly safe here, boys," said the Amazon, who directly proceeded to wash and bind up their wounds.

After having done this, she procured them food, and then told them to strip off their uniforms, and put on the clothes she had brought them, a motley assortment of baize jackets, ragged coats, and old trousers. Thus equipped, they were enabled to go out in search of their companions, without danger of attack from the Plug Uglies and Blood Tubs, who had given them so rough a reception.

They then learned the particulars of the attack upon the soldiers, and of their escape, and saw lying at the station the two men who had been killed, and the others who had been wounded. One of their own band was missing, and he has not yet been found, and it is uncertain whether he was killed or not. On going back to the house where they were so humanely treated, they found that their clothes had been carefully tied up, and with their battered instruments, had been sent to the depot of the Philadelphia Railroad, where they were advised to go themselves. They did not long hesitate, but started in the next train, and arrived at Philadelphia just in time to meet the Eighth Regiment of Massachusetts Volunteers, under the command of Gen. Butler, who told them to hurry back to the Old Bay State to show their battered faces and broken limbs, and that they should yet come back, and play Hail Columbia in the streets of Baltimore, where they had been so inhumanly assaulted.

The noble-hearted woman who rescued these men is a well-known character in Baltimore, and according to all the usages of Christian society, is an outcast and a polluted being; but she is a true heroine, nevertheless, and entitled to the grateful consideration of the country. When Gov. Hicks had put himself at the head of the rabble rout of miscreants, and Winter Davis had fled in dismay, and the men of wealth and official dignity had hid themselves in their terror, and the police were powerless to protect the handful of unarmed strangers who were struggling with the infuriated mob, this degraded woman took them under her protection, dressed their wounds, fed them at her own cost, and sent them back in safety to their homes. As she is too notorious in Baltimore not to be perfectly well known by what we have already told of her, it will not be exposing her to any persecution to mention her name. Ann Manley is the name by which she is known in the city of Blood Tubs, and the loyal men of the North, when they march again through its streets, should remember her for her humanity to their countrymen.

THE MODERN GILPIN.

A BALLAD OF BULL RUN.

WILL RUSSELL was a writer rare,
  Of genius and renown,
A war-trained correspondent he
  From famous London town.

On Indian and Crimean coasts
  He wrote of guns and drums,
And now as through our land he posts,
  To Washington he comes.

Will Russell said to chosen friend,
  "Though four months I have been
In search of some great Yankee fight,
  No skrimmage have I seen.

To-morrow's sun will see a fight
  On Bull Run's banks, they say;
So there, my friend, we'll early go,
  All in a *two-'oss shay.*

I'll also take a saddle-horse
  To bear the battle's brunt,
Whereon in my Crimean style,
  I'll see the fight *in front*.

And I will don the coolest of
  My Himalayan suits —
My belt, felt hat, revolver, and
  My old East Indian boots.

Fresh stores of pens I'll surely need,
  And foolscap, too, I think ;
And in one holster snugly thrust
  A pint of Dovell's ink.

While in the bottom of the gig
  We'll stow the choice Bordeaux,
And eke this bottle of *cold tea* —
  To cool us off, you know !

And for that, in this heathen land,
  The grub is all a sham,
I've here wrapped up some sausage, too,
  And sandwiches of 'am.

Experience on Crimean shores
  Has taught me how to forage,
And how these creature comforts tend
  To keep up martial courage."

Smack ! went his lips at thought thereof,
  Off rolled the Yankee gig,
Before the shouts and rolling whites
  Of starers, small and big !

Like clouds of dust his spirits rise,
  While merry cracks the whip ;
The led-horse pranced and " bobbed around "
  Like porpoise round a ship.

The Long Bridge planks jumped up and down
  In sympathetic jig —
They little thought he would return
  Minus the " creaking gig."

That rotten Rubicon is passed,
  And likewise frowning " Runyon " —
Its outline marked with many a black
  Columbiad on its trunnion.

Past fields where just the day before
  The harvest-scythe was sweeping,
They rushed where soon its human sheaves
  Death's sickle would be reaping !

As rise the distant cannon's tones,
  So mounts his martial ardor,
His thoughts half on the work " in front " —
  Half on his meagre larder.

At length he's there at Centreville !
  In sight and sound of what
He came so far to see and sketch,
  Where rained the shell and shot !

But ere he ventures, careful soul !
  To reach that scene of death,
He seeks a cool and shady place
  " To give his horses breath."

Then forth he draws the precious stores, —
  Cold tea, Bordeaux, and 'am, —
'Mid cannon-shots and bottle-pops,
  Enjoys his lunch and dram.

The dubious issue of the fight
  Contents him with his seat,
Until a courier from the field
  Reports the foe's retreat !

Up sprang Will Russell from the charms
  Of tea and 'am so vile —
His toilet for " the front " prepares
  In his Crimean style.

" My 'oss ! my 'oss ! quick, bring it me !
  What would the *Thunderer* say,
If they should end this Bull Run fight,
  While I lunch in my *shay ?*"

His " Indian " sack hangs down and hides
  Each short and sturdy limb ;
His hat o'erhangs his jolly form
  With amplitude of brim.

Beneath its shade, his round, red face
  Flames like St. George's banner ;
While from its rim, in *havelock* style,
  A buff and red bandanna !

In guise like this, he grandly mounts
  And starts in warlike trot,
That *did not* turn to gallop as
  He neared the deadly spot.

But lo ! a motley frightened crowd
  Before him doth appear,
Of such as ever follow camps,
  All hurrying to the rear.

And pushing through this heaving mass
  Of human breakers, soon
He found himself 'mid reeling ranks,
  Battalion and platoon !

But 'mid that frightened crowd, he says
  He only kept his wits,
And puffs, and scolds, and wonders, too,
  What trouble " gave them fits !"

" I do declare ! What means all this ?
  What has your vict'ry nipped ?
Why run you so ? " — the sole reply
  Was panted forth, " We're whipped !"

" Dear me ! I fain would get in front !
  How would the people stare,
If Fame should ask my whereabouts,
  And echo say, ' *the rear !* '

" You cravens, stand ! *why* do you run ?
  Return to the assault ! "
Bang ! bang ! — a shell bursts o'er his head —
  Will Russell calls a halt !

" Aw ! that *was* near ! no further need
  For me to make researches —
I'll simply book what I have seen,
  Behind yon grove of birches."

Bang ! bang ! " Aw ! there's another shell !
  And one that is a screamer ;
And, let me think — I must leave now,
  To write by Wednesday's steamer !

And though my steed has come to-day
  Full thirty miles and better,
Needs must he now to take me back
  To mail my battle-letter."

He turns his horse! both are afloat
  On the retreating wave!
But as he struggles back, he scoffs
  In words — not accents brave.

To clear the road and let him pass,
  He hails each runaway;
But their respect for *rank*, alas!
  Is broke and done away!

Wagon and cart, and man and beast,
  All in the turnpike jammed;
Mess pork and hams, and shot and grain, —
  No thoroughfare so damned!

The dainty stores that fed "the staff"
  Mixed with the private's fare!
Sad waste! "O, what, my countrymen,
  A falling off was there!"

The teamsters "cut and ran," and left;
  No *traces* you could find;
While those afoot from horsemen feared
  A dreadful "cut behind!"

"The Cavalry!" at that dread sound
  Will's courage was bereft him;
Although he tried, by valiant words,
  To show it had not left him.

And eke before his mental eye
  The dreadful vision rose,
Of that warm suit the Southern press
  Had threatened him for clothes!

"That threat! when 'tis so 'orrid 'ot —
  Beyond East Indian weather!
How my too solid flesh would melt
  In suit of tar and feather!"

His anxious looks, yet valiant words,
  Make many jeer and hoot him,
While every random shot he fears
  Is some attempt to shoot him.

While thus he trembles for his life,
  By coward taunt and curse,
So, to his eye, each ambulance
  Seems an untimely hearse!

At each artillery "thud" he hears,
  Up close his legs he tucks,
Then down upon his saddle bow
  His anxious visage ducks!

And eke behind his Indian sack
  Swells in balloon-like manner,
While flaps and flies around his neck
  The buff and red bandanna!

Again he's back at Centreville,
  In search of friend and gig;
"They are not here! nor 'am, nor tea —
  They're just the things to prig.

O for a glass of wine, or slice
  Of those fine wasted 'ams! —
But though there's plenty on the road,
  They're no longer Uncle Sam's!

So now for Washington, my steed!
  It is no use to whine;
You brought me here to see a fight,
  Now take me back to dine!"

A sudden squad of fugitives
  Here through the village fled,
And Bill's great fancy for the front
  Soon placed him at their head.

But as he leads the flying herd
  Adown a hill's decline,
Behold, across the road drawn up
  A regiment in line!

"What brings you here?" the Colonel shouts.
  "Back! back! I say: I'll shoot
The coward that across my ranks
  Would dare to place his foot!"

The herd recoils, save Russell wild,
  Who, fumbling in his vest:
"But, sir — you know! — I'm English! Come!
  You must not me arrest!

I have a pass — aw! here it is!
  'Tis signed by General Scott —
Don't keep me here!" "Pass this man up!"
  Replied the Colonel, hot.

Nor time lost Will, as off he dashed,
  In sudden bolt that snapped
A loop of sack and havelock both,
  That now far rearward flapped!

At Fairfax Court House next he stops,
  To breathe his horse and sup;
But here his rest by Boniface
  Is quickly broken up.

Quoth he, "They fear Virginia's horse?
  Well may they, stranger, when
These mountain riders number now
  Full twenty thousand men!"

"Good 'eavens! no? — but do they though?"
  Our startled hero cries.
Then off again, though cruel need,
  To Washington he flies!

Night finds him bravely spurring on
  Past wood, and grove, and thicket,
With brave words frequent cheering up
  Each watchful, anxious picket.

"What news? What news?" they all do shout.
  Says Russell in reply:
"It is no rout! the army's safe!
  Keep up your heart — don't fly!"

"Stop! stop! Bill Russell! tell us why,"
  Loud after him they bawl,
"If all is safe, you run so fast,
  Or why you run at all?"

Yet on *he* flies; up hill, down dale,
  In very ghost-like manner;
While ever rearward flaps and flies
  The buff and red bandanna!

The night wanes on, the moon is up,
  And soon our correspondent,
Though near his goal, with new-born fears
  Grew suddenly despondent.

"The guards are set upon the bridge;
  Dear me, what fate is mine!
They'll hail me soon, and I may die
  And give no countersign!"

His fears are vain — that vet'ran name
  Is good, as you'll agree,
(As has been often said before,)
  To pass him through, *Scott* free.

At last he's safe upon the bridge!
  He sees the lights of town,
Mirrored in broad Potomac's tide,
  Hang brightly dripping down!

Then droops his head, then droops his steed,
  In sympathetic manner;
Then droops his sack, then droops also
  The buff and red bandanna!

Can this be he that o'er these planks
  At morning dashed so trig?
Revisiting beneath the moon
  In such a dismal rig!

The bridge is passed! and he again
  Resumes his martial port,
And swells, and puffs, and comforts all
  With words of valiant sort.

But sudden from the rising clouds
  A vivid lightning flash!
"The foe!" he cries, and fearful lists
  To hear the cannon's crash!

He's off again! up Fourteenth Street!
  Once more, like ghostly banner,
Behind him dimly flaps and flies
  The buff and red bandanna!

His rooms are reached, he bolts his door,
  When lo! before his eyes,
A midnight supper ready spread,
  To which he instant flies.

No time, by doffing hat or dress,
  To balk his famished jaws!
But, Cassius-like, he "plunges in,
  Accoutred as he was!"

Sausage, and cheese, and 'am again,
  With draughts of wine between;
Down that vast throat of British gauge,
  In quick procession seen!

What grunts of bliss beneath that hat
  O'er this unlooked-for manna!
While as he munched still rose and fell
  The buff and red bandanna!

At last he's full! but quickly now
  His brain is all astir;
To forge fit bolts of caustic for
  His chief, the *Thunderer!*

His pen is drawn, and o'er his sheet
  Fast its vocation plies,
In telling what he *thought* he saw —
  Wherein his genius *lies!*

But soon the inspiration's o'er!
  With wine and sausage pressed,
His eyelids close, his burly head
  Down drops upon his breast.

Hark to the thunders of his snore!
  In deep, bassoon-like manner!
While with each swell still rose and fell
  The buff and red bandanna!

Rest, Russell, rest! thy race is o'er;
  And well you won it, too;
For no such time was ever made
  Since days of Waterloo!

Now let us sing, in jolly ring,
  Great Russell's martial spree —
When next he goes to see a fight,
  May he *get there* to see!

Ye poets! who may sing some day,
  In strains, rich, racy, full,
The race from Bull Run, don't forget
  The run of Mr. Bull.

INCIDENTS OF BULL RUN. — At the battle, when the order came from the headquarters for the retreat, word was passed down the line to the New York Zouaves. "Do not!" exclaimed a score of the "pet lambs" in a breath. "Do not!" "We are ordered to retreat," said the commander. "Wot'n thunder's *that?*" responded one of the hard-heads, who evidently did not comprehend the word exactly. "Go back — retire," continued the commander. "Go back — *where?*" "Leave the field." "*Leave?* Why, that ain't what we come for. We're here to fight," insisted the boys. "We came here with 1,040 men," said the commander. "There are now 600 left. Fall back, boys!" and the "lambs" sulkily retired, evidently displeased with the order.

Two of the New Hampshire Second were leaving the field, through the woods, when they were suddenly confronted by five rebels, who ordered them to "*halt!* or we fire." The Granite boys saw their dilemma, but the foremost of them presented his musket, and answered, "Halt *you*, or *we* fire!" and, at the word, both discharged their pieces. The rebel fell, his assailant was unharmed. Seizing his companion's musket, he brought it to his shoulder, and said to the other, "Fire!" Both fired their guns at once, and two more rebels fell. The others fled. The leader's name was Hanford, from Dover, N. H.

As the Maine troops were leaving the field of battle, a soldier stepped up to one of the officers of the Fifth regiment, and requested him to lend him a knife. The officer took out a common pocket-knife, and handed it to the soldier, who sat down at the side of the road, pulled up the leg of his trousers, and deliberately dug a musket-ball out of his leg, jumped up, and resumed his march.

When the news of the repulse reached the camp meeting at Desplaines, Ill., Rev. Henry Cox, who was preaching at the time the intelligence was received, remarked, on closing his sermon, "Brethren, we had better adjourn this camp meeting, and go home and drill."

ADVENTURE OF A SPY. — I have lately returned from the South; but my exact whereabouts in that region, for obvious reasons, it would not be politic to state. Suspected of being a Northerner, it was often my advantage to court obscurity. Known as a spy, a "short shrift" and a ready rope would have prevented the blotting of this paper. Hanging, disguised, on the outskirts of a camp, mixing with its idlers, laughing at their jokes, examining their arms, counting their numbers, endeavoring to discover the plans of their leaders, listening to this party and pursuing that, joining in the chorus of a rebel song, betting on rebel success, cursing Abolitionism, reviling Lincoln, traducing Scott, extolling Gen. Beauregard, despising Northern fighters, laughing at their tactics and sneering at their weapons, praising the beauty of Southern belles and decrying that of Northern, calling New York a den of cutthroats, and New Orleans a paradise of immaculate chivalry, is but a small portion of the practice of my profession as a spy. This may not seem honorable nor desirable. As to the honor, let the country that benefits by the investigations and warnings of the spy be judge ; and the danger, often incurred, is more serious and personal than that of the battle-field, which may, perhaps, detract from its desirability.

It was a dark night. Not a star on the glimmer. I had collected my quotum of intelligence, and was on the move for the Northern lines. I was approaching the banks of a stream whose waters I had to cross, and had then some miles to traverse before I could reach the pickets of our gallant troops. A feeling of uneasiness began to creep over me ; I was on the outskirt of a wood fringing the dark waters at my feet, whose presence could scarcely be detected but for their sullen murmurs as they rushed through the gloom. The wind sighed in gentle accordance. I walked forty or fifty yards along the bank. I then crept on all-fours along the ground, and groped with my hands. I paused — I groped again — my breath thickened, perspiration oozed from me at every pore, and I was prostrated with horror ! I had missed my landmark, and knew not where I was. Below or above, beneath the shelter of the bank, lay the skiff I had hidden ten days before, when I commenced my operations among the followers of Jeff. Davis.

As I stood gasping for breath, with all the unmistakable proofs of my calling about me, the sudden cry of a bird or plunging of a fish would act like magnetism on my frame, not wont to shudder at a shadow. No matter how pressing the danger may be, if a man sees an opportunity for escape, he breathes with freedom. But let him be surrounded by darkness, impenetrable at two yards' distance, within rifle's length of concealed foes, for what knowledge he has to the contrary ; knowing, too, with painful accuracy, the detection of his presence would reward him with a sudden and violent death, and if he breathes no faster, and feels his limbs as free and his spirits as light as when taking a favorite promenade, he is more fitted for a hero than I am.

In the agony of that moment — in the sudden and utter helplessness I felt to discover my true bearings — I was about to let myself gently into the stream, and breast its current, for life or death. There was no alternative. The Northern pickets must be reached in safety before the morning broke, or I should soon swing between heaven and earth, from some green limb of the black forest in which I stood.

At that moment the low, sullen bay of a bloodhound struck my ear. The sound was reviving — the fearful stillness broken. The uncertain dread flew before the certain danger. I was standing to my middle in the shallow bed of the river, just beneath the jutting banks. After a pause of a few seconds I began to creep mechanically and stealthily down the stream, followed, as I knew from the rustling of the grass and frequent breaking of twigs, by the insatiable brute ; although, by certain uneasy growls, I felt assured he was at fault. Something struck against my breast. I could not prevent a slight cry from escaping me, as, stretching out my hand, I grasped the gunwale of a boat moored beneath the bank. Between surprise and joy I felt half choked. In an instant I had scrambled on board, and began to search for the painter in the bow, in order to cast her from her fastenings.

Suddenly a bright ray of moonlight — the first gleam of hope in that black night — fell directly on the spot, revealing the silvery stream, my own skiff, (hidden there ten days before,) lighting the deep shadows of the verging wood, and, on the log half buried in the bank, and from which I had that instant cast the line that had bound me to it, the supple form of the crouching bloodhound, his red eyes gleaming in the moonlight, jaws distended, and poising for the spring. With one dart the light skiff was yards out in the stream, and the savage after it. With an oar I aimed a blow at his head, which, however, he eluded with ease. In the effort thus made the boat careened over towards my antagonist, who made a desperate effort to get his forepaws over the side, at the same time seizing the gunwale with his teeth.

Now or never was my time to get rid of the accursed brute. I drew my revolver, and placed the muzzle between his eyes, but hesitated to fire, for that one report might bring on me a volley from the shore. Meantime the strength of the dog careened the frail craft so much that the water rushed over the side, threatening to swamp her. I changed my tactics, threw my revolver into the bottom of the skiff, and grasping my "bowie," keen as a Malay creese, and glittering, as I released it from the sheath, like a moonbeam on the stream. In an instant I had severed the sinewy throat of the hound, cutting through brawn and muscle to the nape of the neck. The tenacious wretch gave a wild, convulsive leap half out of the water, then sank, and was gone.

Five minutes' pulling landed me on the other side of the river, and in an hour after, without further accident, I was among friends, encompassed by the Northern lines. That night I related at headquarters the intelligence I had gathered.

_____

A FIDDLER. — When Wright's Georgia regiment was drawn up in line of battle, to go into its first fight in North Carolina, Wright, (afterwards a Major-General,) in passing in front of his regiment, observed a tall, gaunt fellow, with a violin case strapped to his back. Wright asked him "what he was going to do with his fiddle?" The rude soldier had never heard of Mirabeau's dying exclamation, but he almost quoted it when he said, he wanted to "die to the sound of Betsy," this being the term of endearment which he applied to his violin.

After the fight was over, the fiddling soldier did not answer at roll-call. He was found, with a broken leg, at the root of a tree, to which he had crawled, quietly sawing the strings of "Betsy."

THE STORY OF BALL'S BLUFF.

BY AN OFFICER WHO TOOK PART IN IT.

THE history of the battle of Ball's Bluff has never been published. No event of the war since the assault upon Fort Sumter created a like sensation; and the cause of the disaster, the name of the persons culpable, or the plans and purposes of the officers who ordered the movement, have not officially or certainly been made known. The report of General Stone, in command, was not satisfactory to the country, and Congress called upon the War Department for the facts. Major-General McClellan, who, it was known, ordered the movement, refused to furnish the facts. The insulted Congress repeated its demand, and received a second time the same answer. A joint committee of both Houses of Congress was appointed to inquire into the "conduct of the present war," especially, as was remarked in the debate, "as regards the battle of Ball's Bluff." That committee has as yet made no report.* General Stone, by order of the President, was arrested and imprisoned upon several charges involving disloyalty, and "for misconduct at the battle of Ball's Bluff." After a confinement of six months he was discharged without trial, and the cherished expectations of the public for the facts so long withheld were again disappointed.

Ball's Bluff, so called from Mr. Ball, a farmer living in the vicinity, is a bold embankment, of one hundred feet elevation, on the Virginia shore of the Potomac, three miles from Leesburg northwesterly, and an equal distance from Edwards' Ferry in a southern direction. Poolsville, Md., lies opposite, five miles, and by the road running easterly, Washington is distant thirty-four miles. From the river's edge to the summit, the Bluff is covered with trees and bushes, which, joining with the woods on either side, enclose above, in the form of a half circle, an open natural clearing of seven acres. In the middle of the Potomac, in front of the Bluff, lies Harrison's Island, a fertile strip of land two hundred yards wide and four

miles long. At a distance of half a mile north of the Bluff is Smoot's Mill, situated upon a gentle slope of the bank; and near to it a road leads from the river, by an easy ascent, to the Leesburg turnpike, which, running southerly to Drainesville, passes near to Edwards' Ferry. On the day of the battle General McCall, with twenty-four thousand men, was in that turnpike, nine miles from Ball's Bluff, and General Gorman, with fourteen hundred men was at Edwards' Ferry, on the Virginia side. The whole distance from Ball's Bluff to the Maryland side of the Potomac, across Harrison's Island, is not six hundred yards.

On Sunday night, Oct. 20, 1861, in obedience to orders of General Stone, Colonel Devens, of the Fifteenth Mass. Volunteers, proceeded, with three hundred men, from camp at Poolsville to a point opposite Ball's Bluff and Harrison's Island, and in three small boats crossed to the Virginia shore, arriving at the summit just before daylight. The landing-place was soft and mucky, and the ascent winding and difficult. At the same time four companies of the First Minnesota Volunteers crossed the river at Edwards' Ferry. No enemy was encountered at either place, and his pickets had not been seen for two days. Whatever knowledge of the topography of our country our forces possessed had been acquired by distant observation from Maryland, and no guide accompanied them.

At daybreak Colonel Devens led his troops over the open field, and through the woods towards and within one mile of Leesburg, where, in scattered small numbers, he descried rebels, and after exchanging several volleys with them at long range, fell back to the woods. Here being attacked, he repulsed the enemy with small loss on both sides, and then retired to the Bluff, where he was joined by the remainder of his regiment, and by Colonel Lee with one hundred men of the Twentieth Mass. Volunteers, making in all seven hundred and twenty Federal troops across the river. The day was fair.

At the same time, eight o'clock, A. M., Colonel Baker arrived from his camp near Poolsville on the Maryland side, opposite, where he found the first battalion of the California regiment, six hundred and eighty officers and men, Lieutenant-Colonel Wistar commanding. He was informed of an order from General Stone, then at Edwards' Ferry, that in the event of heavy firing in front, the California battalion should cross and reinforce Colonel Devens. Upon inquiring as to the means of transportation, and learning that they consisted of two frail scows, each capable of carrying twenty-five men, and the river deep and rapid, Colonel Baker rode in haste to Edwards' Ferry that he might have better assurance of an order so extraordinary. Meanwhile several dead and wounded arrived from the Bluff, where firing was growing more frequent, and three companies of the California regiment crossed to Harrison's Island. Colonel Baker returned from Edwards' Ferry at eleven o'clock, bearing a written order from General Stone to reinforce or retire Colonel Devens, "in his discretion." The returned wounded

---

* This paper was written in July, 1862. The report of the War Committee, published in March, 1863, corroborates all its statements. The late restoration of Gen. Stone to active duty is a vindication and acquittal of misconduct charged upon him, and places the responsibility upon another.

reported the enemy in force, pressing Colonel Devens. How could seven hundred men be safely retired in two small boats under the fire of a bloodthirsty and superior enemy? Shall they be left to their fate, or will he reinforce them and share their peril? Colonel Baker was not long in determining upon his course of duty.

A larger scow, discovered in the canal running parallel to the river, was with great labor dragged across the tow-path and launched in the channel. Placing Captain Ritman in charge of the transportation of the troops, and directing that they should cross as rapidly as possible, with his staff composed of Assistant Adjutant-General Harvey and Captain Young, Brigade Quartermaster, Colonel Baker embarked for the Island, where, on the western side, he found three hundred men awaiting their chance to go over to the Virginia shore. Impressed with the grave responsibility of his position, Colonel Baker was silently remarking the two small boats plying with their heavy freight of reinforcements, when his attention was called to an officer of one of the Massachusetts regiments standing on the Virginia shore, who cried out, " We can see three regiments of the enemy coming down from Leesburg." Colonel Baker responded, "All right; be of good cheer — there will be the more for us to whip " — and immediately crossed the river. On reaching the summit, and assuming command, he found the Massachusetts troops drawn up on the right of the field in good order, quietly awaiting a nearer attack of the enemy, who, though silent, with the exception of occasional shots, were known to be in large force in the woods in the front and on the right. It was three o'clock before all of the California battalion had crossed and climbed the Bluff, which, joined to two companies of the Tammany regiment, made with the Massachusetts troops, our whole force seventeen hundred. An order was received from General Stone advising Colonel Baker that the enemy was four thousand strong, and that he might count upon General Gorman coming to his reinforcement from Edwards' Ferry, on the left. He decided, therefore, not to advance, but await the arrival of the promised aid, formed his line of battle by placing Colonel Devens and his command on the right at the border of the woods, resting upon and making a right angle with the centre, composed of two companies of Twentieth Mass. and two companies of the Tammany regiment; the California battalion forming the left and touching the woods bounding the plateau to the south. The ground, sloping from a point distant thirty yards from the edge of the cliff, afforded a fair cover for men lying upon their faces, from the increasing fire of the enemy in the woods. At three o'clock Colonel Coggswell of the Tammany regiment arrived upon the field, and being received by Colonel Baker with much enthusiasm, was placed in command of the artillery, consisting of one six-pounder and two mountain howitzers, then in charge of Lieutenant Bramhall, of the Ninth New York State Militia. The pieces were drawn into the open field, twenty yards in advance of the centre of the line of battle. Colonel

Baker, with his staff on foot, — there were no mounted officers on the field, — traversed several times the whole line of forces under his command, addressing pleasant words to officers and men, and setting them an example of coolness, courage, and confidence. From the Maryland shore frequent shells came flying over the river and bluff, bursting harmlessly far in the rear of the enemy, who seemed patiently to defer his attack until we crossed in greater numbers.

At precisely four o'clock loud yells preceded a flashing line of fire in the woods, and the report of a thousand rifles announced the opening of the engagement with part of the enemy, several of whom had climbed into the trees, that they might have a better aim at our recumbent men. For nearly an hour showers of bullets and buck-shot continued to pour upon our devoted line; but considering the nearness of the enemy, the casualties were not very great. On our part the cannon alone for the first half hour responded with thundering voice, clearly telling General Stone and the Union forces at Edwards' Ferry of the hot engagement near them; and flying farther, reached the ears of General McCall and his division, which, by order of Major-General McClellan, was returning to its camp at Drainesville. Six thousand troops had, during the afternoon, assembled at the crossing-place opposite the Bluff, but by reason of the small means of transportation, were obliged to remain there regarding in helplessness and rage the unequal contest. A rope had been stretched across the channel to the island, which aided much in the passage of the boats; but from the Virginia side there was no rope, and the solitary leaky scow was poled over and back slowly. By five o'clock nearly two thousand men had ascended the Bluff, and engaged in most part in returning the fire of the enemy. Notwithstanding the discouraging aspect of matters, our troops generally exhibited good feeling, determined courage, and obedience to command. The wounded and some dead were carried by their comrades down the hill, who, after placing them in the boat, returned to the field. The enemy was several times driven back with great loss by discharges of the cannon, which, after the artillery men had been killed or wounded, was loaded and fired by Colonel Coggswell, Lieutenant Bramhall, and other officers. A volley of musketry from the thick forest on the left attracted our attention, and Colonel Baker, thinking it came from the expected and promised reinforcement from Edwards' Ferry, ordered a company of the California men to advance cautiously, and discover if they were friends or foes.

The officer commanding the company, having called out, " Who are you ? " received for answer, " Confederates ! " and another volley following immediately, many of our men were killed and wounded. Colonel Baker fell dead, struck with three balls. Five or six rebels ran from the woods towards his body, lying ten yards in advance of the line of battle, when Captain Bieral, of the California regiment, with a dozen of his men, dashed forward, and driving the others back, rescued the corpse and sword, which were immediately carried from the field by Captain Young, who had but a moment before been ordered by Colonel Baker to go to General Stone, and report the state of the engagement, and ask for reinforcements. At the same time Lieutenant Colonel Wistar and Lieutenant Bramhall, being severely wounded, were helped down the hill, and with Colonel Baker's body, safely reached the island. At the last discharge of the cannon it recoiled even to the edge of the cliff, and falling over, was inextricably lost in the rock and jungle. Later the two howitzers, which had not been fired during the engagement, were thrown over the bank, and they with the cannon were afterwards recovered by the enemy. By seniority Colonel Coggswell assumed command, and regarding the battle as hopelessly lost, and there being no retreat by the river, he determined to fight his way to Edwards' Ferry. By his order the Fifteenth Massachusetts moved across the field from the right to the left of the line, where the two companies of the Tammany regiment had already moved. While making the proper arrangements for retreat, a rebel officer misled our troops by approaching them and giving a command to charge upon a large body of the enemy who now occupied our late position on the right. Rushing forward *en masse*, our men received a destructive fire, and the line being broken, general confusion ensued for a few moments. Re-forming in line, several volleys were exchanged with the enemy, who were now near, in sight, in front, with considerable loss on both sides; but. night coming on, and no one knowing the road to Edwards' Ferry, Colonel Coggswell abandoned his plan of retreat to that point, and gave an order to fall back to the river's bank, below the Bluff, leaving two companies above to hold the enemy in check. At this moment, the only boat in the channel was seen to go down, overloaded with wounded and fugitives ; and thus disappeared the only means of escape, except by swimming. The enemy soon occupied the heights, and poured down a fatal fire upon the crowded mass below. Three times bodies of our men climbed to the summit, and after delivering their fire, returned to their helpless comrades below. Throwing their arms and clothing into the river, many swam over the island, while others, aided by the increasing darkness, crept along the bank above and below the Bluff, and on logs, and in a small skiff which by good fortune was found, escaped.

There was no formal surrender, but a sullen submission to adverse fate. The colors, heavily weighed with stones, were cast into the stream. At eight o'clock all firing and noise had ceased, save the moans of the wounded, and the shrieks of the drowning in their vain attempts to swim to the island. At midnight twenty-two commissioned officers and seven hundred and ten men were prisoners of war, on their march to Leesburg.

Never was a conquered army less subdued in spirit. Astounded, bewildered, indignant, there was no feeling of shame, for never did soldiers conduct themselves with more courage. Each man felt that something had gone wrong. "Some one had blundered," or may be worse, and silently marching under the rebel guard, each sought in his own mind, or in whispering voices of his companions, for an explanation of the disaster.

The enemy's force engaged is not known, but is stated in the report of Colonel Evans, who commanded them, at twenty-six hundred. It is believed that there were full four thousand. His loss was not less than four hundred, mostly killed. On our side the casualties cannot be precisely stated, as many were missing whose death by drowning or killed on the field could not be ascertained. The total loss was one hundred and fifty killed, two hundred wounded, and seven hundred and ten taken prisoners.

Such is the narrative of the affair at Ball's Bluff, as told by those who were engaged in it, but had no part in its planning, and are still ignorant of its purpose. As stated, all attempts to discover the object of sending across the Potomac at that point a small force, while Generals McCall and Smith, with over twenty thousand men, were already on the Virginia side, within nine miles of Leesburg, have not been successful. In vain is the inquiry repeated, "Why was Ball's Bluff chosen as a crossing-place, while, at a distance of one half mile above it, the land slopes to the river bank, and an easy ascent and open country would have placed our force on equal footing with the enemy? Why was not transportation provided in advance, adequate for a successful withdrawal of Colonels Devens and Lee and their commands, or for throwing over a large force for their support?" The movement was not unpremeditated, and there was no want of boats or material for pontoons and bridges in the vicinity of Harrison's Island. An army of ten thousand men had been lying idle at Poolsville for months, expecting at some time to cross the river. The canal leading to Washington offered excellent facilities for furnishing the necessary means for crossing, and three frail scows, made of inch plank, and one skiff, were all that our army found there on the day of the battle.

Why were not the promised reinforcements sent to our aid from Edwards' Ferry? During the engagement fourteen hundred troops, under the command of General Gorman, awaited on the Virginia shore, at Edwards' Ferry, an order to march to our aid ; and in his report General Gorman says, that at the moment Colonel Baker fell, General Stone sent an order for them to throw up intrenchments ! There was no enemy between Edwards' Ferry and the battle-field, and we may fairly suppose that one hundred men coming up and attacking them on their flank would have changed the fortunes of that day. That night General McClellan, at Washington, having learned of the disastrous result of the expedition he had ordered, despatched an order to General Banks, at Darnstown, Md., twelve miles from Ball's Bluff, to march his division to the Potomac, at the same points, which, during the day, had been occupied by eight thousand of our troops, vainly demanding transportation to their commands over the river! Generals McCall and Smith, at Drainesville, Va., received no orders. Two days afterwards, all of the Federal forces returned to their respective camps; and thus concludes the affair of Ball's Bluff.

ON THE SHORES OF TENNESSEE.

"MOVE my arm-chair, faithful Pompey,
  In the sunshine bright and strong,
For this world is fading, Pompey —
  Massa won't be with you long;
And I fain would hear the south wind
  Bring once more the sound to me
Of the wavelets softly breaking
  On the shores of Tennessee.

"Mournful though the ripples murmur,
  As they still the story tell,
How no vessels float the banner
  That I've loved so long and well,
I shall listen to their music,
  Dreaming that again I see
Stars and Stripes on sloop and shallop,
  Sailing up the Tennessee.

"And, Pompey, while old Massa's waiting
  For death's last despatch to come,
If that exiled starry banner
  Should come proudly sailing home,
You shall greet it, slave no longer —
  Voice and hand shall both be free
That shout and point to Union colors,
  On the waves of Tennessee.'

"Massa's berry kind to Pompey;
  But ole darky's happy here,
Where he's tended corn and cotton
  For 'ese many a long-gone year.
Over yonder Missis sleeping —
  No one tends her grave like me;
Mebbe she would miss the flowers
  She used to love in Tennessee.

"'Pears like she was watching, Massa,
  If Pompey should beside him stay;
Mebbe she'd remember better
  How for him she used to pray;
Telling him that way up yonder
  White as snow his soul would be,
If he served the Lord of heaven
  While he lived in Tennessee."

Silently the tears were rolling
  Down the poor old dusky face,
As he stepped behind his master,
  In his long-accustomed place.
Then a silence fell around them,
  As they gazed on rock and tree,
Pictured in the placid waters
  Of the rolling Tennessee; —

Master, dreaming of the battle
  Where he fought by Marion's side,
When he bid the haughty Tarleton
  Stoop his lordly crest of pride;
Man, remembering how you sleeper
  Once he held upon his knee,
Ere she loved the gallant soldier,
  Ralph Vervair, of Tennessee.

Still the south wind fondly lingers
  'Mid the veteran's silvery hair;
Still the bondman, close beside him,
  Stands behind the old arm-chair.
With his dark-hued hand uplifted,
  Shading eyes, he bends to see
Where the woodland, boldly jutting,
  Turns aside the Tennessee.

Thus he watches cloud-born shadows
  Glide from tree to mountain crest,
Softly creeping, aye and ever,
  To the river's yielding breast.
Ha! above the foliage yonder
  Something flutters wild and free!
"Massa! Massa! Hallelujah!
  The flag's come back to Tennessee!"

"Pompey, hold me on your shoulder,
  Help me stand on foot once more,
That I may salute the colors
  As they pass my cabin door.
Here's the paper signed that frees you;
  Give a freeman's shout with me —
'God and Union!' be our watchword
  Evermore in Tennessee."

Then the trembling voice grew fainter,
  And the limbs refused to stand;
One prayer to Jesus — and the soldier
  Glided to that better land.
When the flag went down the river,
  Man and master both were free,
While the ring-dove's note was mingled
  With the rippling Tennessee.

INCIDENTS OF ROANOKE ISLAND. — Colonel Russell, of the Tenth Connecticut regiment, fell dead from his horse at the head of his regiment, while marching against the enemy. Strange as it may appear, not a scratch was found upon his body when examined, and his death must have come from the wind of a cannon ball, or from excitement.

Lieutenant-Colonel De Monteil, who volunteered in the assault upon the rebel battery, received his death wound while heading the advance, and while in the act of shouting: "Come on, boys! we'll show them how to fight!"

In the course of the action a shell burst on the United States gunboat Hetzel, and set her magazine on fire. Lieutenant Franklin, her executive officer, ordered the men to the magazine to extinguish the fire; but seeing that they hesitated, he took the hose in his own hands, and sprang down and extinguished the flames before they reached the powder.

A similar occurrence took place on board the Ceres, from the bursting of a gun, when Acting-Master Diarmaid sprang into the magazine and extinguished the fire.

A shell entered the coal-bunks of another of the steamers, setting them on fire. The flames were subdued after much difficulty, with but little damage to the vessel.

EXPLOITS OF CAPT. CARPENTER, OF THE "JESSIE SCOUTS."

THE secret history of any military campaign would be of absorbing interest; much more the secret story of our war. In all camps there are men whose occupation it is to gain for the commanding general information of the enemy's force, positions, and movements. Much depends on this; and the most successful generals have always been the best informed.

In our own service, during the present war, the spy service has been performed by different classes of men. Some of our commanders have had the wit and fortune to secure the services of men whose hearts were full of zeal for the Union and of hatred for the slave aristocracy and their rebellion. Such men, when they have also the activity, presence of mind, ingenuity, and courage needed for this office, are the best that can be got. Such, we have reason to know, are the company known as the "Jessie Scouts," who first served under Gen. Fremont in Missouri, afterwards in Tennessee under Grant, McClernand, and others, and again in Virginia under Fremont, Milroy, &c.

There is another class, hirelings, who serve not for the sake of the cause, but for the sake of the reward. Such men, too, are valuable; but a great commander seeks rather to use men who, from devotion to a principle, or else by reason of some personal wrong, are animated by enmity to the opposite side.

Our spy system has not always been well conducted, else Stuart's "raids" would not have become famous; else Jackson could not have made his march down the Valley; else Corinth could not have been secretly evacuated by Beauregard, nor Yorktown by Johnson, nor Winchester before the first battle of Bull Run, by the same officer. If we had an efficient spy service, Gen. McClellan would have known that after the battle of Fair Oaks, Richmond lay in his power; and Patterson would have held Johnson in check, or else followed him pell-mell into the first battle-field of Bull Run, and saved the day.

There is a story told of that first campaign in Virginia which does not redound to the credit of our military authorities. Some weeks before Bull Run, Patterson, it is said, sent a man as spy into Winchester. The fellow rode there, examined thoroughly the rebel camp, works, and forces, and returned with a full report. He was sent to Washington to get his pay, and when he got there, received from the officer under Gen. Scott, who attended to his case, the sum of twenty-five dollars, which did not pay the expenses of his journey. It is added that he swore he would go over to the enemy; probably he did. If spies and scouts were treated thus in our first Virginia campaign, no wonder Johnson got away from Patterson.

Probably no man in this war has lived through as many exciting and desperate adventures as Capt. Carpenter, who was leader of the "Jessie Scouts." He was originally one of "John Brown's men," and participated in the attack on Harper's Ferry, where he escaped by crawling through a long culvert, or covered drain, which led from the famous engine-house to the river. The Captain does not love the slave lords; he has notions about the crime of claiming ownership in men which to some would seem extreme, and he certainly thinks almost anything good enough for a man-selling aristocrat who rebels against the Union.

The writer of this passed a few quiet hours with Capt. Carpenter lately, while the latter was an invalid from a severe wound received last fall in Western Virginia. Some of the campaigning stories then heard will interest the reader, and will attract the sympathy of all who admire daring, skill, and invention — especially where, as in this case, all these faculties are sharpened and vivified by a single-hearted and fiery devotion to liberty and the Union. Capt. Carpenter boasts, in a quiet way, that no army for which he has scouted has ever suffered from a "raid" in its rear, or has ever been surprised. He has an idea that such things cannot be done where trustworthy and zealous scouts are employed.

"Did you ever see Price?" he was asked.

He replied, "Several times."

Once he drove a team in Price's army two days, at the end of which time, unluckily, the team and wagon, and a negro who happened to be in it, ran away, "and curiously enough, never stopped till we got into our own lines," said the Captain, with a twinkle in his eye.

"The black man is working for himself now in Iowa, and I sold the mules to pay my expenses."

Once he rode down to the rebel pickets at Wilson's Creek, dressed as a woman, to deliver a letter to a supposititious brother in Price's army. He bears witness to the politeness of the rebel officer who escorted the lady half back to our lines. This trip was made because "the General" wanted to know precisely the position of a part of the rebel lines.

"After the surrender of Lexington," said the Captain, "Gen. Fremont suspected that the telegraph operators between Hannibal and St. Joseph were disloyal, and had given information to the enemy, and I was ordered to make an investigation. The fact was, however, the rebels had 'tapped' the wire. A woman in St. Louis told me. She asked me if I knew a rebel spy in town. I asked who he was and what he did; and she replied that he had a telegraph apparatus on the Hannibal and St. Joseph Railroad, and had told her so. He was to see her and take her to a theatre that evening.

"I told her I would give her fifty dollars if she would say, when he came, that she was sick, and would not go. She agreed, and I arranged that she should introduce me to him as a rebel spy from Pillow's camp, which she did. I immediately gained his confidence. We drank wine together, and the fool told me everything. Soon he left the city, and I took one of my men with me, and off we started after him.

"We found him on the Grand River, near the railroad, just where he had said. He had a hut in the brush, where the telegraphing operations were carried on. There were two men — my man and another. We crept up to them, and on a survey, came to the conclusion that as we might not be able to capture them, the best way was to shoot them. I shot my man, but Hale only wounded his. We rushed up. He made fight. I had to despatch him with my pistol. We got the telegraph instruments, with twenty-two hundred feet of silk wire, two horses, blankets, and sixty-five dollars in money. There were also two daguerreotypes.

"I went into Price's camp when Mulligan was at Lexington. I had a double-barrelled shot-gun with both locks broken, and rode into the camp with numbers of country people who were flocking to join Price. I rode around freely, talking secession, and very soon saw how things were going. I could see plainly that Mulligan was in a tight place, and I started off for St. Louis as soon as possible, and gave the information that Mulligan must surrender. Twelve hours after, news came that he had surrendered.

"Fremont did all he could to help Mulligan, but the telegraph 'tapper' (who was afterwards killed) got a despatch which was sent by Fremont for Sturgis to move across the river to the support of Mulligan; and the rebels, having possession of our plans, moved against Sturgis, and compelled him to fall back.

"Henry Hale, one of the best scouts in the country, left Leavenworth, while Mulligan was before Lexington, with despatches. As he rode along, men from every direction were going to join Price. He saw one old secessionist with a little shot-gun, and thought it would be a nice thing to drive off the fellow, and take his horse into Lexington. So he engaged the man in conversation, and getting an opportunity, put his revolver to the secessionist's head, ordered him to tie his gun to the saddle, to dismount, and finally to skedaddle.' The old man made tracks rapidly, glad to escape with his life. Hale took the horse by the bridle, and rode on whistling 'Yankee Doodle.' He had ridden a mile or two, when at a turn of the road, he was suddenly ordered to halt. The old secessionist had procured another gun, and got ahead of him. The gun was squarely aimed at Hale's head. 'Get off that horse,' cried the secessionist. Hale got down. 'Tie that revolver to the saddle.' He obeyed. 'Pull off your pants.' Hale did it. 'Skedaddle!' an order which Hale at once carried into effect, merely saying, 'Well, Captain, I thought my shirt would come next — good-bye.' The secessionist went off with the two horses, whistling 'Dixie;' while Hale marched seven miles into Lexington, with only his coat and shirt on. His coat contained his despatches. He will never be permitted to forget that seven miles' march.

"I burned Randolph, Mo. The town was a rebel depot, where their supplies were gathered. The country people came in every day with provisions, and these provisions and other goods were conveyed to the enemy. I went over with twenty-two men, and routed two hundred and fifty. It was a year ago on the 10th or 12th of September. I divided my men, and had them approach from different directions. I made them all officers, and up we went, every man of us shouting out orders as though each had a regiment at his back.

"The rebels were frightened. They ran in all directions, but we killed several of them. One of my men was badly wounded, and I was wounded also. I tackled one fellow with a sabre. He fought savagely, but I killed him after he had given me a thrust over the eye that might have finished me. He had been a soldier in the regular army, but deserted, and went over to the rebels. He belonged to the First United States Dragoons. We took seventeen prisoners. Of course we could not, with our small force, hold the town; so we set fire to the rebel stores, and destroyed them.

"I was captured back of Paducah — Lieutenant Robb and I; and we were placed under guard, to stay all night. There were thirteen guardsmen in all; but ten of them went to a party, and got drunk. The others got some whiskey, too. Robb and I concluded to rebel. We managed to seize their revolvers. Robb tapped one, that came at us first, over the head and stunned him, and before the others could come to his assistance we shot them. Then we made off. We went by Fort Donelson, clear across the country, and told Zollicoffer that we were spies, and had despatches for Breckinridge. We had forged despatches for the purpose, and thus passed. As we had just come from the rebels, we knew enough to deceive the old fellow, who treated us with great kindness, told us to be careful of the Yankees, gave us horses through his lines, and good horses, and in three hours and a half we were inside our lines.

"At Platte City I made a speech to the rebels in favor of Jeff. Davis, which was very successful; but in the afternoon a fellow in town recognized me, and had me seized. They put me under guard, in a house; but the same night I got out, got on a horse which fell in my way, and rode out till I ran in the dark against two rebel videttes. They stopped me; I explained to them that I was hurrying off to bring up some recruits who were wanted; but the men were obstinate, and would not let me go without a pass. So I proposed to one to go in with me to headquarters, and I would get him my pass. He consented; we walked our horses along the road. My case was desperate; if they caught me they would hang me. I talked to the man in the dark till we were some distance in, then suddenly pulled out my knife, and with one stab slew him.

"I waited a while, then rode back to where the other vidette remained, and handed him a piece of an old letter, saying, 'There's the pass.' He must go to the smouldering fire in the wood near by to examine it, and as he did so I knocked him over, and rode off.

"I rode into Jeff. Thompson's camp, half naked,

as a crazy man, shouting and whooping so that the whole camp was aroused. No better way to get in occurred to me just then. General Thompson is much of a gentleman. He caused a surgeon to examine me, who reported that I had lost my senses from a blow on the temple, the mark of which was still fresh. He said I was quite harmless, and the General proposed to send me into the Yankee lines, because they could take care of such a poor fellow better than he.

"I lay down under a wagon, near the General's tent, when it came dark, and listened to hear what I could hear. About midnight a messenger rode in, on a fine horse, and tied it near me. When he got into the tent, and no one was looking, I got on the horse, and, having the best road in my mind, rode out as hard as I could drive, the pickets firing at me, but without effect; and I got safely in to make my report.

"I went into Fort Henry two days before the attack on it, and brought General Grant an accurate account of the position and number of the rebel forces and defences. I have General Grant's letter certifying to that.

"Also I went into Fort Donelson, while our troops lay at Fort Henry. I went in there in Confederate uniform; and I have General McClernand's letter to show that I brought him information which proved to be accurate. On my way out a cavalry force passed me, while I lay by the roadside; and its commander told one of his men to leave a fine flag, which he feared would be torn on the way. The flag was stuck into the road, that a returning rebel picket might carry it in. But I got it, wrapped it around my body, and rode into Fort Henry with it."

SOUTHERN MATHEMATICS. — General D. H. Hill, who was captured at Roanoke Island, is rather a remarkable character. He has written one or two theological works of some note. He is also a mathematician. The youthful rebels are allowed to regale themselves at school with Hill's Elements of Algebra, a work which is conceived in the true spirit of a gallant Southron. One would think it rather difficult to give mathematical instruction such a form as to imbue pupils with contempt and hatred for the North. But Hill has attempted the work, and has displayed no little ingenuity in the effort. He has framed problems beginning in the following style:

" A *Yankee* mixes a certain quantity of wooden nutmegs, which cost him one fourth cent apiece, with a quantity of real nutmegs, worth four cents apiece," etc.

" A *Northern* railroad is assessed one hundred and twenty thousand dollars damages for contusions and broken limbs caused by a collision of cars."

" The years in which the Governors of Massachusetts and Connecticut send treasonable messages to their respective legislatures, is expressed by four digits."

" The field of battle of Buena Vista is six and a half miles from Saltillo. Two Indiana volunteers ran away from the field of battle at the same time."

A BRAVE FELLOW. — In the Fort Henry gunboat fight, in the explosion on the Essex, one of the seamen was shockingly scalded. His clothing was at once removed, linseed oil and flour applied to his parboiled flesh, and he was carefully wrapped in blankets and placed in bed. A few moments after came the news that the rebel flag was struck, and the fort surrendered. In his enthusiasm he sprang out of his berth, ran up on deck, and waved his blanket in the air, huzzaing for the Stars and Stripes. The poor fellow, after the first excitement was over, was assisted below, and in the night he died, full of rejoicing to the last at the triumph of the old flag.

A REBEL SONG. — The following "song," composed by some enthusiastic rebel soldier, was found in Fort Bartow, Roanoke Island. It is written on a half-sheet of foolscap paper:

Sir William was king georges son to the north the waryers race was run he wore A star all on his breast to show you a sign of the waryers dress, come young ladies will you list and go, come young ladies will you list and go. A new silk dress you shall put on, to follow up the music fife and drum, the drum shall beat and the fife shall play, the drum shall beat and the fife shall play its A merry lives we'l march away.

new york.s A pretty place,; and so is philadelphia the streets are lined with doll. bills and pretty girls a plenty.

Come my love com go with me, for I am a roveing dandy, I,ll take you home I'll treat you well, I'll feed you on sweet candy, where coffee grows on white oak stump and the rivers flow with brandy, and little hills are lin'd with gold and the girls are sweet as candy.

RELIGIOUS MUSIC AMONG THE SOLDIERS. — A letter from Hatteras Inlet, N. C., says: The New England troops excel in the musical faculty, and in every regiment from Massachusetts, Connecticut, or New Hampshire, music teachers or good singers abound, and many an otherwise tedious evening has thus been beguiled by the elevating influence of music. In this respect, no regiment, perhaps, is more favored than the Massachusetts Twenty-third, composed chiefly of Salem, Marblehead, Danvers, and Boston men. Many of the officers were members of the best musical societies, and leaders or pillars in their church choirs at home. Could their friends have looked in upon us on board of the Highlander, during many of the boisterous nights we have been anchored in this Sound, while the storm howled without, they might have heard:

" Perhaps Dundee's wild, warbling measures rise, Or plaintive Martyrs, worthy of the name, Or noble Elgin beat the heavenward flame."

On board of the Huzza, which carries the left wing of the Twenty-third, they have their full share of sweet singers, and a very excellent band of music, under the lead of Henry C. Brown, of Boston. In the centre of the fleet, which covers an area of some two miles of the bay, is anchored the S. R. Spaulding, the present flag-ship of Gen. Burnside. From her high deck he can easily survey the entire fleet, and observe all that is going on. On the deck of one or two vessels near us are gathered quiet groups of soldiers, and the sublime strains of "Old Hundred," which float across the waters, human voices mingling with the bands, testify that they are engaged in religious worship. To many of these brave and earnest men it will be, perhaps, their last Sabbath on earth.

INCIDENTS OF THE PAINTVILLE BATTLE. — A body of the enemy was posted on a commanding hill, and it became necessary to dislodge them. The Fourteenth Kentucky volunteered for the service, as they knew the nature of the ground. Said Col. Garfield: "Go in, boys; give them —— *Hail Columbia!*"

The hill was cleared, and soon the reserve of the brigade came in at a double-quick. As soon as he saw them, Col. Garfield pulled off his coat, and flung it up in the air, where it lodged in a tree, out of reach. The men threw up their caps with a wild shout, and rushed at the enemy, Col. Garfield, *in his shirt-sleeves,* leading the way.

As the Federal troops reached the top of the hill, a rebel officer shouted in surprise: "Why, how many of you are there?" "Twenty-five thousand men, —— you!" yelled a Kentucky Union officer, rushing at the rebel. In an instant the rebels broke and ran in utter confusion.

Several instances of personal daring and coolness were related. A member of Capt. Bushnell's company, in the Forty-second, was about to bite a cartridge, when a musket-ball struck the cartridge from his fingers. Coolly facing the direction from which the shot came, he took out another cartridge, and exclaimed: "You can't do that again, old fellow."

MARYLAND.

BY J. R. RANDALL.

THE despot's heel is on thy shore,
  Maryland!
His torch is at thy temple door,
  Maryland!
Avenge the patriotic gore
That flooded the streets of Baltimore,
And be the battle queen of yore,
  Maryland! My Maryland!

Hark to thy wandering son's appeal,
  Maryland!
My mother State! to thee I kneel,
  Maryland!
For life and death, for woe and weal,
Thy peerless chivalry reveal,
And gird thy beauteous limbs with steel,
  Maryland! My Maryland!

Thou wilt not cower in the dust,
  Maryland!
Thy beaming sword shall never rust,
  Maryland!
Remember Carroll's sacred trust,
Remember Howard's warlike thrust,
And all thy slumberers with the just,
  Maryland! My Maryland!

Come! 'tis the red dawn of the day,
  Maryland!
Come! with thy panoplied array,
  Maryland!
With Ringgold's spirit for the fray,
With Watson's blood at Monterey,
With fearless Lowe and dashing May,
  Maryland! My Maryland!

Come! for thy shield is bright and strong,
  Maryland!
Come! for thy dalliance does thee wrong,
  Maryland!
Come! to thine own heroic throng,
That stalks with Liberty along,
And give a new *Key* to thy song,
  Maryland! My Maryland!

Dear Mother! burst the tyrant's chain,
  Maryland!
Virginia should not call in vain,
  Maryland!
She meets her sisters on the plain —
"*Sic semper,*" 'tis the proud refrain,
That baffles minions back amain,
  Maryland!
Arise in majesty again,
  Maryland! My Maryland!

I see the blush upon thy cheek,
  Maryland!
But thou wast ever bravely meek,
  Maryland!
But lo! there surges forth a shriek
From hill to hill, from creek to creek —
Potomac calls to Chesapeake,
  Maryland! My Maryland!

Thou wilt not yield the Vandal toll,
  Maryland!
Thou wilt not crook to his control,
  Maryland!
Better the fire upon thee roll,
Better the blade, the shot, the bowl,
Than crucifixion of the soul,
  Maryland! My Maryland!

I hear the distant thunder hum,
  Maryland!
The Old Line's bugle, fife, and drum,
  Maryland!
She is not dead, nor deaf, nor dumb —
Huzza! she spurns the Northern scum!
She breathes — she burns! she'll come! she'll come!
  Maryland! My Maryland!

A RACE FOR LIFE. — A soldier from Rhode Island, while on picket-guard, was rushed upon by a party of rebel cavalry. He instantly fired his piece at the foremost, and ran. The way before him was an open field, about fifty rods across, the other side being hemmed in by an old, rotten, log fence, and, still beyond, a sort of chaparral of brier bushes and underbrush. To this retreat the soldier started, on quadruple quick, with half a dozen horsemen after him. Fortunately for the soldier, the rains had made the field quite muddy, and the horses slumped through the turf so badly that they could not lessen the distance between them and the fugitive. All this time the rebels were keeping up a roar of *pistolry*, one of the balls passing through the soldier's hat, and another went clean through his cartridge box and lodged in his coat. Still on ran the hero, and still on splashed the horsemen. The picket at last reached the fence, and with one bound landed on the top, intending to give a long spring ahead; but the fence was frail, and crumbled beneath his weight. It so chanced that a hog had rooted out a gutter at this place, and was lying snoring therein. At the cracking of the fence, his swine-ship evacuated his hole, and scampered, barking, into the underbrush. As luck would have it, the soldier fell in that hole, muddy as it was, and the fence rattled down upon him. This was no more than fairly done, when up came the horsemen, and, hearing the rustling of leaves, and not doubting it was their prey, dashed through the gap in the fence, and, seeing a path in the brush, they put through it after the hog, and were soon out of sight. When the sound of their footsteps died away, the picket returned to camp and reported. The next day one of these rebel horsemen was taken prisoner. When our hero saw him he recognized him at once, and sung out:

"I say, old fellow, did you catch that hog yesterday?"

"We did that," retorted the prisoner, "*but it wasn't the one we were after.*"

A SHARP RIDE. — A correspondent with General Grant's army gives the following amusing account of a cotton broker in the neighborhood of Lagrange, Tennessee. He says:

The experience of a Mr. Cones, who was captured near Lagrange, was relieved by some flashes of humor which may be an apology for the very emphatic language which was used by the actors.

Cones, in company with two or three other buyers, had bought some cotton out at Moscow, twelve miles from Lagrange, just before our army marched from the latter place, and as General Quinby's division had just removed from there, they thought the sooner they got the cotton into Lagrange the better; consequently four of them, besides the drivers of the teams, started out after it. Cones was the only one of the four who was not armed and was not on horseback, he riding in one of the teams. They succeeded in getting the cotton, and hurried back until they came in sight of the Union pickets at Lagrange, and then Cones' three friends, thinking the mules were out of danger, left him, and rode on into town.

Only two or three minutes after they had left, and as the wagons went down into a hollow, out of sight of the picket-guards, five guerrillas dashed out of the wood and were alongside in an instant. "Halt!" Every one of the teams halted as though they had run against a stone wall. The next instant the muzzle of a revolver was at the ear of every one of them, Cones included, who was riding on the cotton.

"Are you armed?" said the guerrilla, who held his pistol at Cones' head.

"No, sir."

"Then get down and unhitch them mules, and turn 'em around devilish quick!"

It was done in the time *specified*.

Guerrilla. — "Have you a match? I want to touch off this cotton."

Cones. — "No, sir. I am glad to say I haven't."

Guerrilla. — "Then git on to that mule, quick."

In an instant, Cones was mounted on what he says was "a wonderful sharp-backed mule."

Guerrilla (giving the mule a terrific slash with the wagon whip). — "Now, lick them mules up! Make 'em go! Give 'em thunder!"

And away they went at a pace which, to Cones on his razor-back mule, he thought must split him in two before many miles, three guerrillas behind lashing the mule at every jump. Five miles or more they went at this pace, and not another word had been spoken by any one, when they turned out of the main road into an old and unfrequented road, that wound its zigzag through one of the densely-wooded creek bottoms. "Halt!" said the guerrilla, and he who gave the command commenced hurriedly to relieve himself of some of his accoutrements, as though he was about to go to work in earnest at some devilish deed. The place was lonely and fitting to such murderous intents, and Cones says he felt a cold sort of chill run down the full length of even his long legs.

Guerrilla (drawing the cork out of his canteen) — "You look a pretty good feller. Let's take a drink; and for fear you might think it's pizen, I'll drink first!"

And suiting the action to his words, he placed the canteen to his lips, and turned his face up in the position of one making astronomical observations. After a long pull, he passed the canteen over to Cones, who thought it 'mightn't be pizen,' and imbibed.

Guerrilla. — "Now, lick up them mules; give 'em thunder! Hurry up!"

At each injunction he emphasized on the rear of the flying mules with his whip.

They bivouacked in a thicket that night, but early the next morning began their journey at the same pace, and toward evening of that day they galloped into a rude-looking camp, which turned out to be the nest of Richardson and his guerrilla band, within a few miles of Fort Pillow. In a few minutes Cones was marched up before Colonel Richardson. After a number of questions as to what was his business, whether he had served against the Confederate States, &c., Richardson said:

"Well, sir. I'll parole you."

At the mention of "parole," the guerrilla who had been the most prominent in the capture, and had invited Cones "to drink," began to remonstrate.

4

Guerrilla. — "Why, Colonel, you ain't a goin' to parole that infernal cotton-buyer, are you?"

Richardson. — "Well, I've got to parole him or shoot him; and (turning to Cones inquiringly) you'd rather be paroled than shot, hadn't you?"

Cones. — "Yes, but I don't want to take another ride on that mule."

The parole was soon written, and much to his astonishment, without being robbed of his money and watch, he was told that he was at liberty to walk back to Lagrange, forty miles. In an hour afterward he started, and soon after leaving the camp he was startled again by the command "Halt!" He halted, and out started the guerrilla who had been most prominent in his capture, and had gone away sulky because the Colonel would not shoot "that infernal cotton-buyer," instead of paroling him.

Cones was unarmed, and began to have serious apprehensions of what was to follow, when the guerrilla said: "Old feller, let's take a drink!" Cones' heart felt lighter immediately. So did the canteen.

During the next three days he footed it back to Lagrange, but he never after looked at a lean, sharp-backed mule without a shudder.

CAMP ANECDOTE. — The Sergeant of the picket-guard being stationed near Pohick Church, Va., had his attention drawn to the tinkling of a cow-bell in the bushes. With visions of new milk running through his head, he examined carefully, and to his intense astonishment made the discovery that as he advanced the cow-bell retreated. The Sergeant made a double quick retrograde movement, and immediately reported the affair to Colonel Hays. The Colonel secreted a squad of men in the woods, and the Sergeant again made himself conspicuous. He brushed about among the bushes, and the cow-bell approached. The squad soon had the satisfaction of seeing — not the cow, but a "Secesher" with a cow-bell hung to his neck, and a six shooter in his belt. When he got within easy range, and in sight of the squad, the Sergeant hailed him:

"I say, old fellow, would you rather go to the devil or to Washington?"

The squad at the same time rushed forward.

"To Washington, I reckon," drawled the rebel. "I ain't clothed for a warm climate."

And he accordingly delivered himself up.

A JOKE ON A REBEL EDITOR. — The editor of the *Rebel Banner*, published at Murfreesboro' until Bragg's retreat to Shelbyville, and afterwards hailing from the latter town, tells the following good story:

On Wednesday, the 31st of December, 1863, we went to the battle-field in search of glory and items.

While following up the charge of General McCown's division, we met a body of prisoners moving to the rear, and at once struck up a conversation with them. Unfortunately, we were dressed in cerulean habiliments, and, upon attempting to leave, were ordered by the guard to remain where we were. With a smile of ineffable contempt, we drew from our pocket a pass; but what was our chagrin when we were accosted with, "I say, my boy, none of us can read; but that thar trick's too old; and I'll tell you another thing, yer infernal blue-bellied Yankee, if you try any more of them dodges, I'll souse this thing into yer gizzard."

Think of that, O ye tribe of brother quill-drivers? The editor of this paper, the leading journal of the South, to be called a Yankee, and to be accredited with possessing an azure abdomen.

GENERAL ROUSSEAU relates the following incident of Shiloh:

Two days after the battle I walked into the hospital tent on the ground where the fiercest contest had taken place, and where many of our men and those of the enemy had fallen. The hospital was exclusively for the wounded rebels, and they were laid thickly around. Many of them were Kentuckians, of Breckinridge's command. As I stepped into the tent, and spoke to some one, I was addressed by a voice, the childish tone of which arrested my attention: "That's General Rousseau! General, I knew your son Dickey. Where is Dick? I knew him very well." Turning to him, I saw stretched on the ground a handsome boy about sixteen years of age. His face was a bright one, but the hectic glow and flush on the cheeks, his restless manner, and his grasping and catching his breath as he spoke, alarmed me. I knelt by his side and pressed his fevered brow with my hand, and would have taken the child into my arms, if I could. "And who are you, my son?" said I. "Why, I am Eddy McFadden, from Louisville," was the reply. "I know you, General, and I know your son Dick. I've played with him. Where is Dick?" I thought of my own dear boy, of what might have befallen him; that he, too, deluded by villains, might, like this poor boy, have been mortally wounded, among strangers, and left to die. My heart bled for the poor child; for he was a child; my manhood gave way, and burning tears attested, in spite of me, my intense suffering. I asked him of his father. He had no father. His mother. He had no mother. Brothers and sisters. "I have a brother," said he. "I never knew what soldiering was. I was but a boy, and they got me off down here." He was shot through the shoulder and lungs. I asked him what he needed. He said he was cold and the ground was hard. I had no tent nor blankets; our baggage was all in the rear at Savannah. But I sent the poor boy my saddle-blanket, and returned the next morning with lemons for him and the rest; but his brother, in the Second Kentucky regiment, had taken him over to his regiment to nurse him. I never saw the child again. He died in a day or two. Peace to his ashes. I never think of this incident that I do not fill up as if he were my own child.

THE DEAD DRUMMER BOY.

'Midst tangled roots that lined the wild ravine,
  Where the fierce fight raged hottest through the
    day,
And where the dead in scattered heaps were seen,
Amid the darkling forest's shade and sheen,
    Speechless in death he lay.

The setting sun, which glanced athwart the place
  In slanting lines, like amber-tinted rain,
Fell sidewise on the drummer's upturned face,
Where Death had left his gory finger's trace
    In one bright crimson stain.

The silken fringes of his once bright eye
  Lay like a shadow on his cheek so fair;
His lips were parted by a long-drawn sigh,
That with his soul had mounted to the sky
    On some wild martial air.

No more his hand the fierce tattoo shall beat,
  The shrill reveille, or the long roll's call,
Or sound the charges, when, in smoke and heat
Of fiery onset, foe with foe shall meet,
    And gallant men shall fall.

Yet may be in some happy home, that one,
  A mother, reading from the list of dead,
Shall chance to view the name of her dead son,
And move her lips to say, "God's will be done!"
    And bow in grief her head.

But more than this what tongue shall tell his story?
  Perhaps his boyish longings were for fame.
He lived, he died; and so *memento mori*.
Enough if on the page of War and Glory
    Some hand has writ his name.

THE BADGE OF THE FIFTEENTH ARMY CORPS.
— The troops from the army of the Potomac, sent to join the army of the Cumberland, carried with them various ornamental habits and customs that were new to the Western soldiers. Among them was the corps badge, which designated the corps to which officers and men were attached. For instance, the badge of the Eleventh Corps is a crescent, that of the Twelfth a star. The badge is made of any material, — gold, silver, or red flannel, — and is worn conspicuously on some part of the clothing. The Western corps had no such badge. How an Irishman explained the matter is thus told: A soldier came by the headquarters of Gen. Butterfield, — a tired, weather-beaten straggler. He was one of those who made Sherman's march from Memphis to Chattanooga, thence to Knoxville, and was now returning in the terrible cold of that returning march, thinly clad, one foot covered with a badly worn army shoe, the other with a piece of raw hide bound with strings about a sockless foot — both feet cut and bleeding. "Arms at will," he trudged past the headquarters' guard, intent only upon overtaking his regiment.

"Halt," said a sentinel with a bright piece, clean uniform, and white gloves. "What do you belong to?"

"Eighth Misshoory, sure."

"What division?"

"Morgan L. Smith's, av coorse."

"What brigade?"

"Giles Smith's Second Brigade of the Second Division."

"But what army corps?"

"The Fifteenth, you fool. I am one of the heroes of Vicksburg. Anything more, Mr. Sentinel?"

"Where is your badge?"

"My badge, is it? What is that?"

"Do you see this star on my cap? That is the badge of the Twelfth Corps. That crescent on my partner's cap is the badge of the Eleventh Corps."

"I see now. That's how yez Potomick fellers gits home uv dark nights. Ye takes the moon and shtars with ye."

"But what is the badge of your corps?"

Making a round about, and slapping his cartridge-box, our soldier replied, "D'ye see that? A cartridge-box, with a U. S. on a brash plate, and forty rounds in the cartridge-box, and sixty rounds in our pockets. That's the badge of the Fifteenth, that came from Vicksburg to help ye fight Chattanoogy."

SLAVE'S PRAYER. — A Virginia slave, who had heard of the President's promise concerning the proclamation to be issued on the 1st of January, then only a few days in the future, was heard praying, and with great earnestness and a deeply affected heart, thus:

"O God Almighty! keep the engine of the rebellion going till New Year's! Good Lord! pray, don't let off the steam; Lord, don't reverse the engine; don't back up; Lord, don't put on the brakes! But pray, good Lord, put on more steam! Make it go a mile a minute! Yes, Lord, pray make it go sixty miles an hour! ('Amen!' 'Do, good Lord!' responded the brethren and sisters.) Lord, don't let the express train of rebellion smash up till the 1st of January! Don't let the rebels back down, but harden their hearts as hard as Pharaoh's, and keep all hands going, till the train reaches the Depot of Emancipation!"

HOW THE VETERAN MAKES HIMSELF COMFORTABLE. — An army letter gives the following description of the manner in which a veteran soldier makes himself comfortable in camp:

"It is a trite remark that a man never knows how much he can do without until he tries it, but it is more to my present purpose to say that he never knows with how little he can make himself comfortable until he makes the experiment. Nobody possesses this invaluable knowledge so much as a veteran. Put a recruit into a forest of pine trees, with his shelter tent, and if he have nobody but recruits about him, ten to one you will find him under his shelter tent three weeks from that time.

"Not so with the veteran. If he be camped in the pine forest, give him an old axe, a boot-leg, a mud-puddle, a board or two, and a handful of nails, and he builds him a house, and a house, too, comfortable and commodious, and not wanting in architectural beauty. First he fells his trees, then cuts and notches his logs, and lays them together to the required height. His roof he puts on, giving it a great slope, and thatching it with the green of the pine trees.

"He has been careful to leave window spaces, and tacking pieces of his shelter tent over these, he has provided light, but he keeps out the nipping air of winter. Then with his board he makes the door, and the boot-leg supplying the hinges, it soon swings into its place. Then he fills the spaces between the logs with soft earth from his mud-puddle, and his house is done, except the chimney, and the forest and the mud-puddle soon provide that, for his chimney is nothing but a pile of sticks, plentifully plastered without and within with mud. Then with his old axe he manufactures out of pine logs a full assortment of furniture, — bedstead, chairs, table, wardrobe, and generally adds a mantel. Then, with a bright fire upon his hearth, he is prepared to laugh at winter, and generally does."

A COMMITTEE of the Louisiana State Convention, appointed to prepare a flag and seal for that State, thus expressed their opinion of that Pelican which had so long been the cherished emblem of Louisiana: "On consultation, and especially with those descended from the ancient colonists of the country, the Committee found that what has been considered the symbol of Louisiana, commands neither their favor nor their affection. The pelican is in form unsightly, in habits filthy, in nature cowardly." The Committee also learned from Audubon, to their amazement, that the story of the pelican's feeding its young with its own blood is, in expressive phrase, "gammon." Therefore they did not commend this water-fowl as a fit subject for their flag, but rather as one of loathing and contumely.

UNION IN TENNESSEE. — A traveller, passing through one of the counties of Tennessee on horseback, stopped at a modest cottage on the roadside, and asked for shelter, as it was quite dark and raining. The "head of the family" came to the door, and accosted the traveller with, —

"What do you want?"

"I want to stay all night," was the reply.

"What are yer?"

This interrogatory was not fully understood by the traveller, and he asked an explanation.

"I mean, what's yer politics?" rejoined the former. "Air yer fur this Union, or agin it?"

This was a poser, as the traveller was not certain whether the "man of the house" was a Union man or a secessionist, and he was anxious to "tie up" for the night; so he made up his mind, and said, —

"My friend, I am for the Union."

"Stranger, you kin kum in."

TO CANAAN!

A SONG OF THE SIX HUNDRED THOUSAND.[*]

BY OLIVER WENDELL HOLMES.

WHERE are you going, soldiers,
  With banner, gun, and sword?
We're marching South to Canaan
  To battle for the Lord!
What Captain leads your armies
  Along the rebel coasts?
The Mighty One of Israel,
  His name is Lord of Hosts!
    To Canaan, to Canaan,
      The Lord has led us forth,
    To blow before the heathen walls
      The trumpets of the North!

What flag is this you carry
  Along the sea and shore?
The same our grandsires lifted up,
  The same our fathers bore!
In many a battle's tempest
  It shed the crimson rain:
What God has woven in his loom
  Let no man rend in twain!
    To Canaan, to Canaan,
      The Lord has led us forth,
    To plant upon the rebel towers
      The banners of the North!

What troop is this that follows,
  All armed with picks and spades?
These are the swarthy bondsmen,
  The iron-skin brigades!
They'll pile up Freedom's breastwork,
  They'll scoop out rebels' graves;
Who then will be their owner,
  And march them off for slaves?
    To Canaan, to Canaan,
      The Lord has led us forth,
    To strike upon the captive's chain
      The hammers of the North!

What song is this you're singing?
  The same that Israel sung
When Moses led the mighty choir,
  And Miriam's timbrel rung!
To Canaan! to Canaan!
  The priests and maidens cried;
To Canaan! to Canaan!
  The people's voice replied.
    To Canaan, to Canaan,
      The Lord has led us forth,
    To thunder through its adder-dens
      The anthems of the North!

When Canaan's hosts are scattered,
  And all her walls lie flat,
What follows next in order?
  —— The Lord will see to that!

[*] See Num. i. 45, 46.

We'll break the tyrant's sceptre,
We'll build the people's throne —
When half the world is Freedom's,
Then all the world's our own !
To Canaan, to Canaan,
The Lord has led us forth,
To sweep the rebel threshing-floors,
A whirlwind from the North !

THE SECRET SERVICE.

"GENERAL ORDERS No. . — Captain Carter, —th Indiana Volunteers, is hereby relieved from his command indefinitely, and will report at these headquarters immediately.

By order of Major-General ROSECRANS.
Lieut. Col. C. GODDARD, A. A. G.
(Current Series.) "

The above order was read upon dress parade to the gallant old —th, in January, 1863. The cotton fields and cedar thickets of "Stone River" were as yet scarcely dry from the loyal blood which had there been given up to freedom's cause. The regiment was struck dumb, so to speak, and the captain most of all. What could such an order mean? Surely, none deserved censure less than Captain Carter. He was the idol of the regiment — a perfect specimen of manly strength; bold and fearless in battle, perfect master of the "sword" and "gloves," kind and gentle-hearted, always found upon the side of the weak. He had been frequently spoken of by his superiors for his gallantry. These thoughts passed through the minds of some after this order was read, but none could give a sufficient reason why he should be thus relieved; for, said they, does not the order imply disgrace? But these mutterings were not heard at headquarters, and were of no avail. The Captain retired to his tent, relieved himself of his accoutrements, called his servant Tom, and set out for headquarters, with none but his sable companion.

General Rosecrans was quartered in Judge Ready's house, and had a private suit of rooms on the second floor, with windows opening upon a veranda. He was sitting before a bright fire on the evening our story opens, in undress uniform, with nothing but the buttons to betoken rank. An orderly entered and announced Captain Carter. The General arose quickly, and advanced to meet him, with that easy, smiling look, that put the Captain's fears at rest. The General took him by the hand, while his countenance assumed a more thoughtful look, or rather settled in repose, and said:

"This is Captain Carter, of the —th Indiana?"

"It is, sir," replied the Captain.

"You received a peremptory order this evening to report forthwith."

"I did, sir, and have done so."

"Yes, yes; take a seat, Captain. I am in want of a man of some experience, Captain, who has not only a 'hand to do and a heart to dare,' but also has judgment to guide and direct both. General Thomas, after quietly looking through

his command, has picked on you; and I have such confidence in the 'grizzled old hero' that I have summoned you here for secret service. Are you willing to undertake it, with all its risks?"

"Anything, General, for our country's good."

"Very well, sir; you will remain here to-night. Any of your effects you may need, send for by the orderly at the door. During the night I will inform you what your duties will be."

General Bragg's headquarters were at Tullahoma. The two armies were lying in a semicircle, the rebel right resting on the Cumberland at Hartsville, above Nashville, their left resting at the "shoals" below.

General Van Dorn commanded the left, with headquarters at Spring Hill. Our right rested at Franklin, which is nearly on a direct line between Spring Hill and Nashville. This much by way of explanation.

One morning in February, 1863, two persons were making their way on horseback from Shelbyville to Spring Hill. The first of these was dressed in Quaker garb, and bestrode a light-built, dapple bay stallion, whose small, sinewy limbs, broad chest, and open nostrils betokened both speed and bottom. Horse and rider were ill-matched, but seemed to have a perfect understanding.

The other person was a negro, dressed like his master, broad brim, white neck-tie and all, mounted on a stout roadster. They were fast approaching a vidette post; were shortly halted by a cavalryman; they drew rein and dismounted.

"Is thee a man of war?" asked the Quaker.

"Don't know; reckon, tho', I mought be. But what's your business, Quaker?"

"Does thee know a Mr. Van Dorn about here?"

"Well, I reckon I does; but he'll mister ye if you call him that."

"Well, I have business with him, and I desire admittance into thy camps."

"All right, old fellow; wait till I call the corporal."

General Van Dorn was examining some maps and charts, when an orderly entered and announced that a Quaker desired to see him.

"Admit him," said the General.

"Is thee Mr. Van Dorn, whom carnal men call General?"

"What is your business with me, sir?" asked the General, without answering the question.

"I am sent, friend Van Dorn, by my society, to administer comforts and consolation to these men of war, and would ask permission to bring such things as they may need or my means may supply."

"Have you any recommendations?"

"Yes, verily;" and the Quaker produced a bundle of papers, and commenced assorting them out. "Here is one from friend Quakenbush, and here —"

"Never mind," said the General, while the corners of his mouth commenced to jerk; "here, Mr. —"

"Thurston," suggested the Quaker.

"Mr. Thurston, here is a pass through the lines at will for such articles as you may see proper to bring. This is all, sir?"

"May I ask, friend, how far it is to those ungodly men who are persecuting our people with fire and sword, whom the carnal men call the Yankees?"

"Yes, sir. About fourteen miles. See that you give them a wide berth, for they have a curious way of burning men of your persuasion."

"Yes, verily will I;" and with this the Quaker retired.

"Queer character, that," remarked the General to himself; "but it takes all kinds to make a world."

The Quaker passed out among the camps, meeting a smile here, and a rough jest there; but they seemed not to ruffle the placidity of his countenance, though the negro's eyes flashed, who followed a few steps in the rear. The Quaker seemed to have a good supply of tracts and religious papers, which he scattered freely, with a word of gentle admonition to the card-players, and a hint of the world to come to all. He was particular in his inquiries for the sick, and even visited all the forts and fortifications, and made particular inquiries in and about them for the sick, writing a letter for one, furnishing a stamp to another; so that at the close of the day he had visited all, and made a memorandum of what was needed, and was preparing to leave camp when a Lieutenant came and accosted him with, "I say, stranger, haven't we met before?"

"Nay, verily," replied the Quaker, "I go not about where carnal men do battle."

"No! Well, I must have seen you at some place, but I don't recollect where. Likely I'm mistaken."

"Very like, friend; good day to you."

"Massa, did ye see dat debbil's eyes brighten up towards the last? Tells ye, sure, we'd better be trablin."

"Yes, Sam, I saw it, and my recollection is better than his, for I took him prisoner at Stone River, though he escaped soon after. We will pass out as soon as possible."

Not long after, the Quaker and his colored companion were galloping over the smooth pike. As they approached a house, they slackened their speed, but when out of sight, they again increased it. Thus they pushed on till after dark, when they came to a by-road, into which they rode some miles, and finally drew rein at a little log-cabin, to which, after reconnoitring a little, the negro advanced, and knocked, and a voice from the inside bade him enter, which he did, followed by his master.

That night a despatch went to Gen. Bragg, which read:

"Look out for a Quaker, followed by a nigger. He is a spy. Arrest him.

"Gen. Van Dorn."

The next day a negro rode into Murfreesboro', and passed on to Gen. Rosecrans' headquarters, and presenting a pass, was admitted to his private apartments, and handed the General a paper which read: "2 overcoats and 6 hats, 37 shirts, 3200 tracts, 2000 for the unconverted at Spring Hill."

Gen. Rosecrans was eagerly looking over the document when Gen. Thomas was announced. The latter was cordially met by Gen. Rosecrans, who immediately handed him the paper he had just received.

"This is all cipher to me, General," said Gen. Thomas.

"I suppose so," said the former, who had been writing. "Well, here is something more intelligible: 'Two forts of six guns each; thirty-seven additional guns; 3200 troops, 2000 of which are cavalry, at Spring Hill.'"

"Humph! Some of Capt. Carter's ingenuity," said Gen. Thomas.

"Yes, he is doing his work nobly, so far. I only hope no harm may come to him."

"Well, General," said Thomas, "Col. B——, of the —th Indiana, was asking me to-day why the Captain was relieved of his command; of course I knew nothing about it."

"That was right," said Rosecrans; "the effectiveness of the 'secret service' would be greatly impaired by having the names of those engaged in it made known. I enjoined the utmost secrecy upon the Captain, and kept him here that night that he might not be questioned too closely by his comrades. We will hear from him by ten o'clock to-morrow."

"Where do you reside?" asked Gen. Bragg.

"I live near Brandyville, General, and came down to see if something can't be done to keep these infernal Yankees from our section. They was down there yesterday, and took off over two thousand bushels of corn, and nearly all the wheat in the country."

The speaker was a middle-aged man of rather good features, but his countenance betokened the too free use of Confederate whiskey.

"What did you say your name was, Colonel?"

"Ashcroft, sir."

"Yes, yes, I have heard of your family. You have done nobly for our cause, from report."

"We have tried to do our duty, General, and what little I have left you are welcome to, but I don't want the Yankees to get it. I sent down by Gen. Wheeler's command, the other day, a hundred bushels of meal as a gift."

"I wish we had more like you," said Bragg. "Let me fill your glass again, Colonel. I wish I had something better to offer you."

"Permit me, General, to send to my portmanteau for a bottle of wine."

"Yes, sah."

"Rare vintage, this, General. It's one of a lot I got North before the war."

"Excellent," says Bragg. "I would like to have a supply. By the way, Colonel, did you see anything of a Quaker-like personage on the road this morning?"

"Riding a bay horse, with a nigger following?"

"The same."

"Why, yes. He came to my plantation last night. I insisted on his staying all night, but he was in a hurry, and could not stop."

"He was a Yankee spy," said Bragg.

"The devil! and to think I gave the rascal his supper!"

"Well, well, never mind, Colonel; we'll pick him up yet. I'm going to make a feint on the enemy's flanks to-morrow with my cavalry, and we'll probably get him. He has information that would be valuable to the enemy. I look for a couple of officers back in a few days, that I sent up to Franklin to find out the enemy's strength. If they bring me a correct report, I'll match Rosecrans, with all his low cunning. Besides this, Colonel, I'm looking for some Georgia and Alabama troops up shortly, and if the cowardly Dutchman don't run, I'll make another Stone River for him."

"Good for you, General. Don't leave even one of the cussed mudsills on our soil. But it's getting late, and I must try and get some supplies before I go back. Will you accommodate me with a pass?"

"Certainly, and here is a bill of protection for your person and property. No thanks; good day to you."

"Golly, Massa Cap'n, you's bin talkin' to de ole debbil hissef."

"Hush! not so loud, Tom. I've got one more to visit, and then we'll be off, and take a straight shoot up Hoover's Gap."

"Cap'n, Cap'n! dey's a regiment ob dese dirty rebels just started up de Manchester road, dat's going up from Hoober's Gap, for I heard de Kernel say so."

"All right, Tom; we'll take the Shelbyville road, and run the risk of meeting Van Dorn. Go out through the 'abatis,' the same way we came in with the horses, and I'll meet you in half an hour by that old house."

"Missus, dey's a gentleman dat got a frow off his hoss out here, and would like to stop awhile wid ye, if ye please, Missus."

"Very well; I'll send a boy out to help him in. — Are you much hurt, sir?"

"No, madam, I think not; my horse got frightened at some object in the road, and threw me heavily on my right shoulder. A night's rest, madam, will enable me to pursue my journey, I think."

Our hero found, upon examination, that there were no bones broken, and yet the bruise was severe enough to make him covet a night's rest, in preference to passing it on the saddle. So without more ado, he submitted to his hostess's desire to bathe the bruised shoulder, and prepare him a comfortable bed by the fire.

During the night he was awakened by the loud clatter of horses' roofs, followed immediately by a loud "hilloa."

During the conversation which occurred outside, he heard the name of Van Dorn mentioned, and the thought that they might meet was anything but comfortable to him just at that time; but he resolved to trust to luck, and if that failed, he would try what virtue there was in "right angles, horizontals," &c. Presently the door opened, and an officer entered, dressed in the height of Confederate style, — gilt buttons, gold lace, and all, — a glance at which showed that he bore the rank of Lieutenant-General. The conversation that ensued informed our hero that he had the honor of occupying the same room with Gen. Hardee. He had as yet feigned sleep. He heard the General ask the lady if she knew who he was, and her reply was, that she did not. Then followed the story of his getting thrown, and so on. He was anxious to establish his reputation with the General as a *sound secesh*, and a little ruse occurred to him, which he resolved to practise even to the extent of making himself ridiculous, suddenly bawling out, as if asleep, —

"Run, Tom; the infernal Yankees are coming; put all the horses in the back pasture; take away every nigger with you."

"Ha, ha!" laughed the General; "he's all right. I'll bet on him. But you see, madam, there is a spy in our lines that we are anxious to catch, and he has, so far, eluded us, and if we meet a stranger, we are anxious to find out his standing. I'm satisfied with this one, for a man will tell the truth when he's asleep."

"Your supper's ready, sah."

"And I'm ready for it," replied the General, and left the room.

Our hero moved, grunted, and finally turned over, and found his hostess still in the room, and behind her he saw Tom making motions for him to come out.

The lady asked if he felt comfortable, had he slept well, &c., to all of which he replied in the affirmative; upon which she left the room, and he followed soon after, and found Tom waiting for him.

"Massa, dese debbils has 'sprised' us, and we'd better be a leabin. I'se got a 'nigh shoot' from de niggahs, dat we can cut across to Manchester and up fru de gap from heah."

"All right, Tom; where's the horses?"

"I'se got um, Massa, out below here."

"Here's for them, then, Tom; come on quickly."

It is needless to follow them further; suffice it to say they reached our lines the following evening, and reported to Gen. Rosecrans.

The following order explains itself: —

SPECIAL FIELD ORDER, No. —.

Capt. Carter (—th Ind. Vols.) is hereby ordered to return to his command, and is recommended for promotion. By order

W. S. ROSECRANS, *Maj.-Gen.*

Lieut.-Col. C. GODDARD, *A. A. G.*

SOLDIERS' AID SOCIETIES.

To the quiet nooks of home,
To the public halls so wide,
The women, all loyal, hurrying come,
And sit down side by side,

To fight for their native land,
　With womanly weapons girt,
For dagger a needle, scissors for brand,
　While they sing the song of the shirt.

O women with sons so dear,
　O tender, loving wives,
It is not money you work for now,
　But the saving of precious lives.
'Tis roused for the battle we feel —
　O for a thousand experts,
Armed with tiny darts of steel,
　To conquer thousands of shirts!

Stitch — stitch — stitch
　Under the sheltering roof,
Come to the rescue, poor and rich,
　Nor stay from the work aloof;
To the men who are shedding their blood,
　To the brave, devoted band,
Whose action is honor, whose cause is good,
　We pledge our strong right hand.

Work — work — work,
　With earnest heart and soul —
Work — work — work,
　To keep the Union whole.
And 'tis O for the land of the brave,
　Where treason and cowardice lurk,
Where there's all to lose or all to save,
　That we're doing this Christian work.

Brothers are fighting abroad,
　Sisters will help them here,
Husbands and wives with one accord
　Serving the cause so dear.
Stand by our colors to-day —
　Keep to the Union true —
Under our flag while yet we may
　Hurrah for the Red, White, and Blue.

A MAN OF NERVE. — A venerable judge related the following anecdote:

The morning following the battle of Yorktown, I had the curiosity to attend the wounded. Among others whose limbs were so much injured as to require amputation, was a musician, who had received a musket ball in his knee. As usual in such a case, preparations were made to prevent the possibility of his moving. Says the sufferer, "Now, what would you be at?" "My lad, I'm going to take off your leg, and it is necessary that you should be lashed down." "I'll consent to no such thing. You may pluck my heart from my bosom, but you'll not confine me. Is there a violin in the camp? if so, bring it to me." A violin was furnished, and tuning it, he said, "Now, Doctor, begin." And he continued to play until the operation, which lasted about forty minutes, was completed, without missing a note or moving a muscle.

ADVENTURES OF A DESPATCH BEARER. — The following account of the adventures of Lamar Fontaine, who acted as a despatch bearer for the Southern forces around Vicksburg, was written by the father of young Fontaine:

Lamar is almost continually in the saddle, and employed in very hazardous enterprises. His last feat of arms was the most daring he has yet performed.

He left my house, under orders from Gen. Johnston, to bear a verbal despatch to Gen. Pemberton, in Vicksburg, and to carry a supply of percussion caps to our troops in that besieged city. I parted with him, hardly hoping ever to see him again alive, for I knew that Vicksburg was closely invested on all sides. The enemy's lines of circumvallation extend from Snyder's Bluff, on the Yazoo, to Warrenton, on the Mississippi, and the rivers and their opposite shores are filled and lined with their forces.

He was well mounted, but was burdened with forty pounds of percussion caps, besides his blanket and crutches. He has no use of his broken leg, and cannot walk a step without a crutch; and in mounting his horse he has to lift it over the saddle with his right hand. But he accomplishes this operation with much dexterity, and without assistance. I loaned him a very fine sabre, with wooden scabbard, to prevent rattling, and a very reliable revolver, which has never missed fire when loaded by me.

The family were called together for prayers, and we prayed fervently that the God of our fathers would shield him from all danger, and enable him to fulfil his mission to Vicksburg successfully, and give him a safe return to us all. I then exhorted him to remember that, if it was the will of God for him to live and serve his country, all the Yankees owned by LINCOLN could not kill him; but if it was the divine will that he should die, he would be in as much danger at home as in Vicksburg, and death would certainly find him, no matter where he might be. I charged him to use his best endeavors to kill every one of the jackals who should attempt to stop his course, or come within reach of his sword or pistol.

He crossed Big Black River that night, and the next day got between their lines and the division of their army, which was at Mechanicsburg. He hid his horse in a ravine, and ensconced himself in a fallen tree, overlooking the road, during that day. From his hiding-place he witnessed the retreat of the Yankees, who passed him in considerable haste and confusion. After their columns had gone by, and the night had made it safe for him to move, he continued his route in the direction of Snyder's Bluff. As he entered the telegraphic road from Yazoo City to Vicksburg, he was hailed by a picket, but dashed by him. A volley was fired at him by the Yankees. He escaped unhurt; but a Minie ball wounded his horse mortally. The spirited animal, however, carried him safely to the bank of the Yazoo River, where he died, and left him afoot. He lost one of his crutches in making his escape. This was jerked from him by the limb of a tree, and he had no time to pick it up.

With the assistance of one crutch, he carried his baggage, and groped along the Yazoo, until he providentially discovered a small log canoe, tied by a rope, within his reach. He pressed this into his service, and paddled down the river, until he met three Yankee gunboats coming up to Yazoo City. He avoided them by running under some willows overhanging the water, and lying concealed until they passed. Soon afterwards he floated by Snyder's Bluff, which was illuminated, and alive with Yankees and negroes, participating in the amusement of a grand ball of mixed races. He lay flat in his canoe, which was nothing but a hollow log, and could hardly be distinguished from a piece of drift-wood, and glided safely through the gunboats, transports, and barges of the amalgamationists. He reached the back-water of the Mississippi before day, and in the darkness missed the outlet of the Yazoo, and got into what is called "Old River." After searching in vain for a pass into the Mississippi, day dawned, and he discovered his mistake. He was forced to conceal his boat and himself, and lie by for another day. He had been two days and nights without food, and began to suffer the pangs of hunger.

At night he paddled back into the Yazoo, and descended it to the Mississippi, passing forty or fifty of the Yankee transports. Only one man hailed him, from the stern of a steamboat, and asked him where he was going. He replied that he was going to his fishing lines. In the bend above Vicksburg, he floated by the mortar fleet, lying flat in his canoe. The mortars were in full blast, bombarding the city. The next morning he tied a white handkerchief to his paddle, raised himself up in the midst of our picket boats at Vicksburg, and gave a loud huzza for JEFF. DAVIS and the Southern Confederacy, amid the *vivas* of our sailors, who gave him a joyful reception, and assisted him to Gen. Pemberton's headquarters.

After resting a day and night in the city, he started out with a despatch from Gen. Pemberton to Gen. Johnston. He embarked on his same canoe, and soon reached the enemy's fleet below the city. He avoided their picket-boats on both shores, and floated near their gunboats. He passed so near one of these, that through an open port-hole he could see men playing cards, and hear them converse. At Diamond Place he landed, and bade adieu to his faithful "dug-out." After hobbling through the bottom to the hills, he reached the residence of a man who had been robbed by the savages of all his mules and horses, except an old worthless gelding and a half-broken colt. He gave him the choice of them, and he mounted the colt, but found that he travelled badly. Providentially he came upon a very fine horse in the bottom, tied by a blind bridle, without a saddle. As a basket and old bag were lying near him, he inferred that a negro had left him there, and that a Yankee camp was not far distant. He exchanged bridles, saddled the horse and mounted him, after turning loose the colt.

After riding so as to avoid the supposed position of the Yankees, he encountered one of the thieves, who was returning to it from a successful plundering excursion. He was loaded with chickens and a bucket of honey. He commenced catechising Lamar in the true Yankee style, who concluded it best to satisfy his curiosity by sending him where he could know all that the devil could teach him. With a pistol bullet through his forehead, he left him, with his honey and poultry lying in the path, to excite the conjectures of his fellow-thieves.

He approached with much caution the next settlement. There he hired a guide, for fifty dollars, to pilot him to Hankerson's ferry on Big Black River, which he wished to reach near that point, without following any road. The fellow he hired proved to be a traitor. When he got near the ferry, Lamar sent him ahead to ascertain whether any Yankees were in the vicinity. The conversation and manners of the man had excited his suspicions, and as soon as he left him he concealed himself, but remained where he could watch his return. He remained much longer than be expected; but returned and reported that the way was open, and that no Yankees were near the ferry. After paying him, he took the precaution to avoid the ferry, and to approach the river above it, instead of following the guide's directions. By this he flanked a force of the Yankees posted to intercept him; but as he entered the road near the river bank, one of them, who seemed to be on the right flank of a long line of sentinels, suddenly rose up within ten feet of him, and ordered him to halt. He replied with a pistol shot, which killed the sentinel dead, and, wheeling his horse, galloped through the bottom up the river; but the Yankees sent a shower of balls after him, two of which wounded his right hand, injuring four of his fingers. One grazed his right leg, cutting two holes through his pantaloons, and another cut through one side of my sword scabbard, spoiling its beauty, but leaving a mark which makes me prize it more highly. Seven bullets struck the horse, which reeled under him, but had strength and speed to bear him a mile from his pursuers before he fell and died. Lamar than divided his clothes and arms into packages, and swam Big Black River safely. He did not walk far before a patriotic lady supplied him with the only horse she had — a stray one, which came to her house after the Yankees had carried off all the animals belonging to the place. On this he reached Raymond at two o'clock in the morning, changed his horse for a fresh one, carried his despatch to Jackson that morning, and rejoiced us all by an unexpected visit the same day.

A WEDDING PARTY BROUGHT TO GRIEF. — A correspondent of a Southern paper, after narrating "the outrages committed by Averill and his band," concludes his letter with the following amusing yet unfortunate incident:

"Few tragedies are without their comic and grotesque interludes. And Averill's devastating march had its farce. On the very top of Price's or Eleven Mile Mountain, as it is sometimes called, dwells a widow woman, with a considerable family, including several grandchildren. She seems to defy the elements of the most tempestuous height I know of. Up to this elevated position, where everything may be supposed to be pure and nice from its thorough ventilation, a romantic justice of the peace had carried his affections, and fixed them on a fair daughter of the widow. His aspirations met with the highest favor, and on the very night of Averill's advent their mutual loves culminated in a wedding feast, celebrated amidst the wild shrieking and howlings of the tempest on the mountain. The festivity had progressed to the fourth degree with uncommon energy. The gentler sex were paying their respects to the supper table, and some of the more vigorous of the mountaineers were employing their time with a powerful jig. A famous Boniface from the valley below had thrown off coat, jacket, and shoes, and was spreading himself. Indeed, the dance promised to rival that of Tam O'Shanter, beheld in Kirk Alloway — the locality and surroundings, and the tempest, all favored a scene of no small dramatic effect. But just then — O, untimely event! — the Yankees obtruded upon the scene, and dissipated all its joys, and terminated for the night all its physical recreations. They ate up all the supper — took some thirty horses, ridden up by the guests from the 'valley below' — and carried off as prisoners the male portion of the guests, including the hero of the dance, and, worst of all, the bridegroom besides! To the inexpressible mortification of the prisoners, they saw one of the ladies of the wedding party kiss a Yankee for a cupful of coffee, which he had offered to any one of them who would bestow such a mark of favor on him. The prisoners were marched off, and detained a day or two before they were permitted to return, on foot."

Thus ended the comedy of the terrible mountain raid of Averill — a warning to wedding parties on the border to look out for Yankees.

THE DEAD BROUGHT TO LIFE AGAIN. — The following remarkable incident occurred in Dodgeville, Wisconsin:

When the war first broke out, a young man who resided in the above village joined a company commanded by Captain Tom Allen, which was afterwards incorporated in the Second regiment of Wisconsin Volunteers, and was present at the terrible and disastrous battle of Bull Run. The intelligence came back to his family at Dodgeville that he was slain upon the battle-field, and his body left to be cared for by the enemy. The news nearly killed his affectionate mother, and she, with the remainder of those relatives who had been nearly related to him, wore mourning for him who had poured out his blood and sacrificed his young life for his country. This gnawing grief had preyed upon these loving hearts for many months, until they had learned to view it with a species of resignation. What could then depict their unspeakable astonishment and joy, when he walked into the house, hearty and well!

His story is briefly told thus: He had been left severely wounded, with many others, upon the battle-field. After the engagement was over, and his friends had retreated in confusion, a company of secessionists came where they were lying, and actually bayoneted his wounded companions before his eyes. They even went so far as to stab the bodies of senseless corpses, lest there be some spark of life left in them! A man came to where he was lying on the ground, and raised his ensanguined weapon for the fatal thrust, which he fully expected would end his mortal carreer. He closed his eyes, fairly sick with the horrid emotion, and waited to receive his fate. His enemy hesitated. He lowered his musket, and finally raised him carefully up, and gave him water from his canteen. He was afterwards removed to the hospitals of Richmond, where he received careful treatment, and at last was exchanged and allowed to return home.

ANECDOTE OF COMMODORE FOOTE. — He attended a Presbyterian church. A large congregation was in attendance, but the preacher did not make his appearance. A general impatience beginning to manifest itself, the Commodore sought the elder of the church, and urged him to perform the services. The elder refusing, the Commodore, on the impulse of the moment, took the pulpit, read a chapter in the Bible, prayed, and delivered a short discourse from the text: "Let not your hearts be troubled. Ye believe in God: believe also in me." The congregation was delighted. On coming down from the pulpit, the minister, who had arrived just after the prayer, approached and tendered his thanks; but the Commodore rebuked him for his tardiness of duty, and reproached him for his neglect to take the pulpit immediately on his arrival. This incident is illustrative of the Commodore's energetic, earnest character and sincere piety.

NEGRO PATRIOTISM. — I sat in my tent-door thoughtfully, but very thoughtlessly humming "Dixie." I had not observed "Charles," a servant, or "contraband," here, who sat just within the tent.

"We stop a-singin' dat song now, massa!" said he, interrupting me.

"Why?" I inquired.

Charles was confused for a moment, but I pressed the question.

"Well," he replied hesitatingly, "it don't b'long to my perfession, sir; dat's all, I s'pose. — I don't wish I was in Dixie, I'se sure!" continued he. "None o' de niggers does; you may bet your soul o' dat!"

"Where is Dixie, Charles?"

"'S Norfolk — dat's whar 'tis," was the indignant reply. "Kills de niggers in Dixie, jist like sheep, a-working in de batteries!"

The idea of our contest is fully appreciated by the colored people. The representations at the North, that the slaves do not understand the cause for which the Federal army are moving upon the South, are utterly false. I have seen here and in Hampton scores of the fugitives, and conversed with them; and I have never found one who did not perfectly understand the issue of the war, and hang with terrible anxiety upon its success or failure.

I was particularly struck with this at Hampton, when the battle of Great Bethel was progressing. They crowded together in little squads about the streets, listening to the reports of the cannon in the distance, or the accounts of those who came in from the field. Many of them were almost insane with anxiety, and expressed themselves extravagantly.

"If the 'Unioners' get the fight," I said, "what will it do for you?"

"*Den we'll be free!*" answered all who stood near me, almost in one breath.

"But if they lose the battle?"

"O, den it be worser for us dan ebber," they said, shaking their heads mournfully, and in their simplicity believing that all the issue of the war hung upon the result of that day. — *Letter from Fort Monroe.*

LIFE IN EASTERN TENNESSEE. — A traveller in East Tennessee gives the following graphic pictures of life in that region:

"In Dry Valley lived the Methodist preacher named Dugan, (of Brownlow notoriety,) weighing some two hundred and fifty pounds, that these devils incarnate arrested for his loyalty to the Government, making him walk some ten miles through the hot sun, and riding in his buggy themselves. The poor old man fainted time and again on the journey, but there was no relenting with them. They told him they would sweat the Lincoln fever out of him. They robbed him of all he had, and imprisoned him; but he managed in some way to escape, and is now preaching again at his old stand. What rendered the crime more heinous was the fact that his enemies (some of them) were those with whom he had taken sweet counsel in the house of God, and with whom he had knelt around the altar of prayer. What can be more appropriate to this persecuted class of men than those lines of Captain Grisham, of the 10th East Tennessee cavalry:

'They struggled, fell; their life-blood stained
  The cruel murderer's hand;
 They clasped their country's flag, and cried,
  "God and our native land!"
Let angels spread their wings above;
  Let flowers forever bloom;
Let bays, green bays, spring forth to mark
  The martyr's sacred tomb.'

"At early dawn we left our kind friend and his family, and rode on towards Athens. It was a lonesome ride, resembling very much some of the bluff roads on the Illinois River. We passed only one house the whole distance, and that was a miserable log house situated in a clump of pines. As we rode past the house, we were astonished at the number of tow-head children at the woodpile — the tallest of whom was not over three feet in height. We commenced counting, two, four, six, eight; and to the question asked the oldest, 'Are you all here?' 'O no,' says he, 'the two little ones are in the house.' They hurrahed for Old Abe, and we rode on. We travelled this lonesome road a few miles farther, and came at last to the crest of the hill, some five hundred feet, directly overlooking the valley. There it lay at our feet, extending north as far as the eye could reach, and at least three miles in width — dotted with neat farm-houses, and just below us Mouse Creek Station, with its dozen or more neat white cottages, and one large brick mansion. A couplet in that beautiful hymn by Heber, as I surveyed this beautiful valley, ran through my head continually:

'Where every prospect pleases,
  And only man is vile.'

"We passed on through this valley, and, night overtaking us nine miles south of Loudon, we called at a fine farm-house, and requested permission to tarry, which was readily granted. To the question, 'Are you Union or rebel?' the answer was, 'Both.' 'Well,' says I, 'that is a new state of things, which I do not understand.' This was the house of a widow lady, and her story was a simple statement of facts, which we listened to very attentively. When she had finished her story, she drew one long, deep sigh, and retired. I pitied the poor woman from the bottom of my heart. She said she had two sons in the rebel army, and one in the Union. Her son now at home had fled to the mountains to avoid conscription. Her two daughters now at home, young ladies, eighteen and twenty years of age, were divided, one Union and one rebel. For herself, she had nothing to say — the divisions in her family had made her prematurely gray, (holding up a lock of hair,) and the only wish she had was, that the war might speedily end in some way; and when I asked the usual question, the Union girl stepped into the other room, and returned with a beautiful silk Union flag. If a rebel officer should stay there next week, the rebel girl, no doubt, would bring out just as neat a rebel flag. Such is life in Eastern Tennessee."

HOW ROGER A. PRYOR WAS CAPTURED AND ESCAPED. — Brig. Gen. Roger A. Pryor, during the battle between Gen. Pope and the Confederates, near Manasses, in August, 1862, had the misfortune to be taken a prisoner, but the corresponding good fortune to escape.

He had started off on foot to call up two or three regiments for reënforcements, and on his return found his command moved from the position in which he had left it. Thinking it had gone ahead, he too went on, wondering all the time where his men were, until he suddenly encountered two Yankee soldiers, sitting at the foot of a hay-rick. His uniform being covered by a Mexican poncho, they did not observe that he was not one of their own men; nor was there any mark visible upon his person to indicate that he was an officer.

They accordingly familiarly inquired how everything was going on in front. He replied, "Very well," and in the conversation which ensued, learned that he was a mile and a half within the Federal lines. They asked him numerous questions, under some of which he began to quake and grow uneasy, fearing his inability, good lawyer though he is, to cope successfully with a cross-examination of such a dangerous character. He accordingly began to look about him to discover some means of escape. There was apparently none. He observed standing near him, however, the two muskets of the men, one of them with a bayonet, and the other without.

The colloquy had not proceeded much further before one of them, looking at him keenly, asked him to what regiment, brigade, and division he belonged; and as Pryor hesitated and stammered out his reply, the Yankee sprang to his feet and exclaimed: " You are a —— rebel, and my prisoner." In an instant, the General, who is a powerful man and as active as a squirrel, seized the gun with the bayonet, and, before his antagonist could turn, ran him through the body twice. The other now jumped to his feet, apparently as if to escape, but he also received from Pryor a lunge that left him helpless on the field. Throwing down the musket, the General moved rapidly away in the direction from whence he came, and after dodging Federal stragglers for an hour or two, had the satisfaction of finally regaining his command.

Anxious to know the fate of the two men whom he had so summarily disposed of, he sent one of his aids the next day to examine the hospitals in that neighborhood, and ascertain, if possible, whether any men were present wounded with a bayonet. The aid returned with the information that he had found one so injured. Whereupon Pryor mounted his horse, and went in person to see him. The man was asleep when he entered the hospital, but the surgeon awoke him, and the General asked if he recognized him. "Yes, sir, I do," was the reply. " You're the man who stuck me." The wounded man was not less surprised when he learned that the author of his misery was the redoubtable Roger A. Pryor.

JAMES GARRABRANT, a member of Co. D., 13th New Jersey regiment, while fighting, at a battle on the Rappahannock, saw a daguerreotype fall from the pocket of a dead rebel. Impelled by curiosity, he picked it up and placed it in the breast pocket of his blouse. Soon he was struck by a bullet and fell. His brother, who was near him, picked him up, supposing him to be killed. Upon examination, the ball was found to have pierced his clothing, gone through the front of the daguerreotype, shivered the glass, and indented deeply the metal plate upon which the likeness was, which, however, it failed to penetrate, thus saving the young man's life, as it lay right over his heart. The wooden back of the picture was shivered to splinters by the concussion. The bullet was shown us with the picture, fitting neatly into the indentation of the plate. There can be no doubt that the force of the ball was destroyed by the gradual yielding of the soft copper plate. Had the material been more rigid, the ball would probably have gone through. The likeness is that of a young and not unattractive looking female; and it may well be imagined that our gallant soldier prizes the " counterfeit presentment " of the southern damsel as the saviour of his life.

SKETCHES IN THE HOSPITALS. — One evening I found a lately-emptied bed occupied by a large, fair man, with a fine face and the serenest eyes I ever met. One of the earlier comers had often spoken of a friend who had remained behind, that those apparently worse wounded than himself might reach a shelter first. It seemed a David and Jonathan sort of friendship. The man fretted for his mate, and was never tired of praising John, his courage, sobriety, self-denial, and unfailing kindliness of heart, always winding up with : " He's an out and out fine feller, ma'am, you see if he ain't." I had some curiosity to behold this piece of excellence, and when he came, watched him for a night or two before I made friends with him; for, to tell the truth, I was afraid of the stately-looking man, whose bed had to be lengthened to accommodate his commanding stature, who seldom spoke, uttered no complaint, asked no sympathy, but tranquilly observed all that went on about him, and as he lay high upon his pillows, no picture of dying statesman or warrior was ever fuller of real dignity than this Virginia blacksmith.

A most attractive face he had, framed in brown hair and beard, comely-featured and full of vigor, as yet unsubdued by pain, thoughtful and often beautifully mild while watching the afflictions of others, as if entirely forgetful of his own. His mouth was firm and grave, with plenty of will and courage in its lines, but a smile could make it as sweet as any woman's; and his eyes were child's eyes, looking one fairly in the face, with a clear, straightforward glance, which promised well for such as placed their faith in him. He seemed to cling to life as if it were rich in duties and delights, and he had learned the secret of content. The only time I saw his composure disturbed was when my surgeon brought another to examine John, who scrutinized their faces with an anxious look, asking of the elder : " Do you think I shall pull through, sir? " " I hope so, my man." And as the two passed on, John's eyes followed him with an intentness which would have won a clearer answer from them, had they seen it. A momentary shadow flitted over his face; then came the usual serenity, as if, in that brief eclipse, he had acknowledged the existence of some hard possibility, and, asking nothing, yet hoping all things, left the issue in God's hand, with that submission which is of true piety.

The next night, as I went my rounds with Dr. P——, I happened to ask which man in the room probably suffered most, and to my great surprise he glanced at John.

" Every breath he draws is like a stab ; for

the ball pierced the left lung, broke a rib, and did no end of damage here and there; so the poor lad can find neither forgetfulness nor ease, because he must lie on his wounded back or suffocate. It will be a hard struggle, and a long one, for he possesses great vitality; but even his temperate life can't save him. I wish it could."

"You don't mean he must die, doctor!"

"Bless you, there is not the slightest hope for him, and you'd better tell him so before long. Women have a way of doing such things comfortably; so I leave it to you. He won't last more than a day or two, at farthest."

I could have sat down on the spot and cried heartily if I had not learned the propriety of bottling up one's tears for leisure moments. Such an end seemed very hard for such a man, when half a dozen worn-out, worthless bodies round him were gathering up the remnants of wasted lives to linger on for years, perhaps burdens to others, daily reproaches to themselves. The army needed men like John, earnest, brave, and faithful, fighting for liberty and justice with both heart and hand, a true soldier of the Lord. I could not give him up so soon, or think with any patience of so excellent a nature robbed of its fulfilment, and blundered into eternity by the rashness or stupidity of those at whose hands so many lives may be required. It was an easy thing for Dr. P——— to say, "Tell him he must die," but a cruel, hard thing to do, and by no means as "comfortable" as he politely suggested. I had not the heart to do it then, and privately indulged the hope that some change for the better might take place, in spite of gloomy prophecies, so rendering my task unnecessary.

After that night, an hour of each evening that remained to him was devoted to his ease or pleasure. He could not talk much, for breath was precious, and he spoke in whispers, but from occasional conversations I gleaned scraps of private history which added to the affection and respect I felt for him. Once he asked me to write a letter, and as I settled pen and paper, I said with an irrepressible glimmer of female curiosity: "Shall it be addressed to mother or wife, John?"

"Neither, ma'am; I've got no wife, and will write to mother myself when I get better. Did you think I was married because of this?" he asked, touching a plain gold ring which he wore, and often turned thoughtfully on his finger when he lay alone.

"Partly that, but more from a settled sort of look you have, a look young men seldom get until they marry."

"I didn't know that, but I'm not so very wrong, ma'am, — thirty in May, — and have been what you might call settled this ten years, for mother's a widow. I'm the oldest child she has, and it wouldn't do for me to marry till Lizzie has a home of her own, and Laurie has learned his trade; for we're not rich, and I must be father to the children, and husband to the dear old woman, if I can."

"No doubt you are both, John; yet how came you to go to the war, if you felt so? Wasn't enlisting as bad as marrying?"

"No, ma'am, not as I see it; for one is helping my neighbor, the other pleasing myself. I went because I couldn't help it. I didn't want the glory or the pay. I wanted the right thing done, and the people said the men who were in earnest ought to fight. I was in earnest, the Lord knows, but I held off as long as I could, not knowing which was my duty. Mother saw the case, gave me her ring to keep me steady, and said, 'Go.' I went."

A short story and a simple one; but the man and the mother were portrayed better than pages of fine writing could have done it.

"Do you ever regret that you came, when you lie here suffering so much?"

"Never, ma'am. I haven't helped a great deal, but I've shown I was willing to give my life, and perhaps I've got to; but I don't blame anybody, and if it was to do over again, I'd do it. I'm a little so ry I wasn't wounded in front. It looks cowardly to be hit in the back; but I obeyed orders, and it don't matter much in the end, I know."

Poor John! it did not matter now, except that a shot in front might have spared the long agony in store for him. He seemed to read the thought that troubled me, as he spoke so hopefully when there was no hope, for he suddenly added:

"This is my first battle — do they think it's going to be my last?"

"I'm afraid they do, John."

It was the hardest question I had ever been called upon to answer; doubly hard with those clear eyes fixed upon mine, forcing a truthful answer by their own truth. He seemed a little startled at first, pondered over the hateful fact a moment, then shook his head with a glance at the broad chest and muscular limbs stretched out before him.

"I'm not afraid, but it's difficult to believe all at once. I'm so strong it does not seem possible for such a little wound to kill me."

"Shall I write to your mother now?" I asked, thinking that these sudden tidings might change all plans and purposes; but they did not; for the man received the order from the Divine Commander to march, with the same unquestioning obedience with which the soldier had received that of the human one, doubtless remembering that the first led him to life, the last to death.

"No, ma'am: to Laurie, just the same; he'll break it to her best, and I'll add a line to her myself, when you get done."

So I wrote the letter which he dictated, finding it better than any I had sent, for, though here and there a little ungrammatical or inelegant, each sentence came to me briefly worded, but most expressive, full of excellent counsel to the boy, tenderly bequeathing "mother and Lizzie" to his care, and bidding him good by in words the sadder for their simplicity. He added a few lines with steady hand, and, as I sealed it, said, with a patient sort of sigh, "I hope the answer will come in time for me to see it;" then, turning away his face, laid the flowers against his lips, as if he would hide some quiver of emotion at the thought of such a sudden sundering of all the dear home ties.

These things had happened two days before. Now, John was dying, and the letter had not come. I had been summoned to many death beds in my life, but to none that made my heart ache as it did then, since my mother called me to watch the departure of a spirit akin to this, in its gentleness and patient strength. As I went in, John stretched out both hands.

"I knew you'd come! I guess I'm moving on, ma'am."

He was, and so rapidly, that even while he spoke, over his face I saw the gray veil falling that no human hand can lift. I sat down by him, wiped the drops from his forehead, stirred the air about him with the slow wave of a fan, and waited to help him die. He stood in sore need of help, and I could do so little; for, as the doctor had foretold, the strong body rebelled against death, and fought every inch of the way, forcing him to draw each breath with a spasm, and clench his hands with an imploring look, as if he asked, "How long must I endure this, and be still?" For hours he suffered dumbly, without a moment's respite or a moment's murmuring. His limbs grew cold, his face damp, his lips white, and again and again he tore the covering off his breast, as if the lightest weight added to his agony; yet, through it all, his eyes never lost their perfect serenity, and the man's soul seemed to sit therein, undaunted by the ills that vexed his flesh.

One by one the men woke, and round the room appeared a circle of pale faces and watchful eyes, full of awe and pity; for, though a stranger, John was beloved by all. Each man there had wondered at his patience, respected his piety, admired his fortitude, and now lamented his hard death; for the influence of an upright nature had made itself deeply felt even in one little week. Presently Jonathan, who so loved this comely David, came creeping from his bed for a last look and word. The kind soul was full of trouble, as the choke in his voice, the grasp of his hand, betrayed; but there were no tears, and the farewell of the friends was the more touching for its brevity.

"Old boy, how are you?" faltered the one.

"Most through, thank Heaven!" whispered the other.

"Can I say or do anything for you anywheres?"

"Take my things home, and tell them that I did my best."

"I will! I will!"

"Good by, Ned."

"Good by, John, good by!"

They kissed each other tenderly as women, and so parted; for poor Ned could not stay to see his comrade die. For a little while there was no sound in the room but the drip of water from a pump or two, and John's distressful gasps as he slowly breathed his life away. I thought him

nearly gone, and had laid down the fan, believing its help no longer needed, when suddenly he rose up in his bed, and cried out with a bitter cry that broke the silence, sharply startling every one with its agonized appeal. "For God's sake, give me air!"

It was the only cry pain or death had wrung from him, the only boon he had asked, and none of us could grant it, for all the airs that blow were useless now. Dan flung up the window; the first red streak of dawn was warming the gray east, a herald of the coming sun. John saw it, and with the love of light that lingers in us to the end, seemed to read in it a sign of hope; for over his whole face broke that mysterious expression, brighter than any smile, which often comes to eyes that look their last. He laid himself down gently, and stretching out his strong right arm, as if to grasp and bring the blessed air to his lips in fuller flow, lapsed into a merciful unconsciousness, which assured us that for him suffering was forever past.

As we stood looking at him, the ward master handed me a letter, saying it had been forgotten the night before. It was John's letter, come just an hour too late to gladden the eyes that had looked and longed for it so eagerly — yet he had it; for after I had cut some brown locks for his mother, and taken off the ring to send her, telling how well the talisman had done its work, I kissed this good son for her sake, and laid the letter in his hand, still folded as when I drew my own away.

A BABY ON THE BATTLE-FIELD. — At the battle of the Hatchie, when the conflict was waging fiercest, upon advancing, midway between the contending forces, we found — what do you think? Not a masked battery — not an insidious trap, inviting but to destroy — not any terrible engine of death — but a sweet little blue-eyed BABY. Sweet little thing, as I saw it there, hugging the cold earth, its only bed — the little tear on its cheek, —

"That nature bade it weep, turned
An ice-drop sparkling in the morning beam." —

Unalarmed 'mid the awful confusion of that fearful battle, with the missiles of death flying thick about it and crowding close upon its young existence, yet unhurt, it seemed a wonderful verification of the Divine declaration: "Out of the mouths of babes and sucklings I will ordain wisdom." That little "child of war," as it lay in its miraculous safety, seemed to say to me these words of profound instruction: "My helplessness and innocence appealed to God, and he preserved me in the midst of this wrecking carnage. If you will make your plaint to Heaven, God will preserve your poor bleeding country."

Little child of destiny, born 'mid the flash of musketry, the thunder of cannon, and the clash of arms, I will watch your course through life, and witness whether an existence so auspiciously begun will pass by the masses unnoticed, and end without leaving a name "damned to everlasting

fame!" Who would suppose that in the wild, fierce battle of the Hatchie, when the field was strewn with the dead, and the shrieks of the wounded rent the heavens with agony, a great army would pause in the thickest of the conflict to save a harmless, a helpless child? Yet the brave Fourteenth, that never yet has quailed in battle, did pause, and an officer of the regiment ordered "our little baby" carried to headquarters and tenderly cared for.

I remember having read, somewhere in Grecian history, a story something like the one I have related. A little child was found on the battlefield, and by an infuriated soldiery trampled in the dust. After the battle the victorious general, in an address to his army, said: "But for the blood of a *little child* that mars it, our victory would be complete." Thank God, the blood of no *little child* mars our victory.

The next day after the battle "our babe" was brought before the Fourteenth, and unanimously adopted "Child of the Regiment." Three or four days later, strange as it may seem, a poor, heart-stricken, poverty-pinched mother came searching the battle-field in quest of her child. My dear reader, imagine if you can the wild exclamations of thanksgiving that burst from that poor woman's heart, when informed that her child had been rescued, and with a mother's tenderness cared for. I saw the mother receive her child, heard her brief prayer for the soldiers who saved it, and, with the blessings of a thousand men following her and hers, she took away

"Our little baby—
Little blue-eyed, laughing baby."

A NEW WAY TO ATTACK FORT PICKENS. — A Southern paper put forth the following proposition:

"Let General Bragg detail a few thousand of his ten thousand to the work of catching snakes, and as soon as they have collected several cartloads of these interesting reptiles, let tin or sheet-iron shell or canisters be charged with them — the enclosure being cylindrical and of size to fit the largest mortar, and so made that it will break to pieces, and liberate its contents upon falling within the fort. We would warn those who charge the shells to put only the same species into each, as if the different snakes were mixed they would sting each other to death before having a chance to operate on Billy Wilson's Zouaves. The corners and interstices in each shell might be filled up with a few quarts of tarantulas, scorpions, centipedes, and lizards, however, to make close work, as the snakes would pack loosely."

A CAPTAIN'S STRATEGY. — On the passage of the steamer Fitzhugh up the Mississippi River, her officers were informed that they would probably meet with trouble from a company of guerrillas stationed at Curlew, Kentucky, and were advised to be on their guard. There was not a gun

on board, but the master managed to procure a piece of timber about five feet long and a foot in diameter, which, with a little paint, he managed so as to make resemble a cannon, covered it with a tarpaulin, and mounted it on a pair of trucks, and, thus armed, prepared to meet the enemy. Arriving at Curlew, they found fifty guerrillas drawn up in line, who incontinently demanded their surrender. Those on the boat said nothing, but brought up from the hold a number of small pieces of limestone sewed up in canvas bags to represent ammunition, and carefully laid them alongside the gun. The harmless bit of wood was then turned towards the rascals, and the tarpaulin was about to be removed, when the doughty warriors took to their heels, and ran as if the Old Nick was after them. At Battery Rock, on the Illinois shore, another party, numbering about forty, who had crossed over the night previous in an old flatboat, essayed the same undertaking; but these, too, were put to flight by this mighty piece of ordnance.

A UNION WOMAN. — The following incident is told concerning the independent and successful stand taken by a woman in New Orleans, on behalf of the Union. She and her husband — a Mississippi steamboat captain — occupied the middle front room of the lowest range of sleeping apartments in the St. Charles Hotel, at the time when the city was to be illuminated in honor of secession. She refused to allow the illuminating candles to be fixed in the windows of her room, and the proprietors remonstrated in vain — she finally ordering them to leave the room, of which she claimed, while its occupant, to have entire control. The rest of the story is thus told:

"Determined not to be outdone in a matter of such grave importance, the captain, who was not in the room during the above proceedings, was next found and appealed to. He heard their case; said his wife had reported him correctly on the Union question; nevertheless, he would go with them to the room and see if the matter could be amicably arranged. The captain's disposition to yield was not to be seconded by his better half. The proprietors next proposed to vacate the best chamber in her favor, in some other part of the house, if that would be satisfactory; but the lady's 'No!' was still as peremptory as ever. Her point was gained, and the St. Charles was doomed to have a dark front chamber. Pleased with this triumph, Mrs. —— devised the following manœuvre to make the most of her victory. Summoning a servant, she sent him out to procure for her an American flag, which, at dusk, she suspended from her window. When evening came, the streets, animated by a merry throng, were illuminated; but, alas! the St. Charles was disfigured by its sombre chamber, when suddenly a succession of lamps, suspended on both sides of the flag, revealing the Stars and Stripes, were lit up, and the ensign of *the Union* waved from the centre of a hotel illuminated in honor of its overthrow! The effect was, to give the impression that the whole house was thus paying homage to the American flag; and what is more significant, is the fact that the latter was greeted by the passing crowd with vociferous applause. So much for the firmness of a true Union woman."

PETER APPLE, of Oakland, Marion County, Indiana, was recruited for the Eleventh regiment of that State, and took part in the attempt to storm one of the Vicksburg batteries. The rebel fire was so destructive, that the Union forces recoiled. Apple, the "raw recruit," "didn't see" the backward movement, and kept going ahead, until he came right up to one of the rebel guns, caught a gunner by the collar, and brought him within our lines, saying: "Boys, why didn't you come on? Every fellow might have got one."

REMINISCENCES OF SHILOH. — An eye-witness gives the following pictures of the battle-field of Shiloh:

"On that peaceful Sunday morning of April 6, 1862, the sun was rising with splendor. I had walked out to enjoy the fresh air, and, returning by my friend Lieut. D's tent, I called upon him. Said he, 'H., take a cup of coffee; I have found some milk.' 'Don't care if I do,' said I. 'I always write home on Sunday morning, and like to do it over a good cup of coffee.' 'Yes, I mean to write to my little wife,' said D. 'I expect to resign soon. Don't you want a pair of new shoulder-straps, H., and bran new pair of gauntlets?' I told D. I would take them; and in a moment left his tent, after making him promise to take tea with me.

"But how were things at tea time? D. was mangled and dead, lying by the roadside, at the hospital by the Landing, with hundreds of others, and I had passed the most momentous day of my life — had participated (I am since told creditably) in one of the greatest battles, exceeding in fury, courage, waste, stupendousness, and gallantry, the wildest dreams of my youth. Should your happy city, on some bright Sunday morning, be sunk, with all its life, by an earthquake, and the cold waves rolling over it in eternal solitude before night, the change could be no more unexpected, nor could it come upon you with more bewildering and stunning suddenness and awfulness. On the evening of the 5th, the 18th Wisconsin infantry arrived, and were assigned to General Prentiss's division, on the front. Said Colonel ——, who had preceded them, looking for the General's quarters, 'Here they come — the bully boys — they weigh just 166 pounds apiece. Just left home six days ago.' The 18th Wisconsin cooked their first suppers in the field that night at nine o'clock, and wrapped themselves in their blankets, to be awakened by the roar of battle, and receive, thus early, their bloody baptism. Before they had been on the field one day, their magnificent corps was deci-

mated, most of the officers killed — the proud and exultant Colonel among the dead.

"I saw an intelligent looking man with his whole diaphragm torn off. He was holding up nearly all of his viscera with both hands and arms. His face expressed a longing for assistance and an apprehension of fatality.

"On going to the field the second day, our regiment strode on in line over wounded, dying, and dead. My office detaching me from the lines, I had an opportunity to notice incidents about the field. The regiment halted amidst a a gory, ghastly scene. I heard a voice calling, 'Ho, friend! ho! for God's sake, come here.' I went to a gory pile of dead human forms in every kind of stiff contortion; I saw one arm raised, beckoning me. I found there a rebel, covered with clotted blood, pillowing his head on the dead body of a comrade. Both were red from head to foot. The dead man's brains had gushed out in a reddish and grayish mass over his face. The live one had lain across him all that horrible, long night in the storm. The first thing he said to me was, 'Give me some water. Send me a surgeon — won't you! O God! What made you come down here to fight us? We never would have come up there.' And then he affectionately put one arm over the form, and laid his bloody face against the cold, clammy, bloody face of his dead friend. I filled his canteen nearly — reserving some for myself — knowing I might be in the same sad condition. I told him we had no surgeon in our regiment, and that we would have to suffer, if wounded, the same as he; that other regiments were coming, and to call on them for a surgeon; that they were humane. 'Forward!' shouted the Colonel; and 'Forward!' was repeated by the officers. I left him.

"The above recalls to mind one of the hardest principles in warfare — where your sympathy and humanity are appealed to, and from sense of expediency you are forbidden to exercise it. After our regiment had been nearly annihilated, and were compelled to retreat under a galling fire, a boy was supporting his dying brother on one arm, and trying to drag him from the field and the advancing foe. He looked at me imploringly, and said: 'Captain, help him — won't you? Do, Captain; he'll live.' I said: 'He's shot through the head; don't you see? and can't live — he's dying now.' 'O, no, he ain't, Captain. Don't leave me.' I was forced to reply: 'The rebels won't hurt him. Lay him down and come, or both you and I will be lost.' The rush of bullets and the yells of the approaching demons hurried me away — leaving the young soldier over his dying brother.

"Nearly every rebel's face turned black immediately after death. Union men's faces retained the natural pallor two or three days.

"I ate my dinner on Monday within six paces of a rebel in four pieces. Both legs were blown off. His pelvis was the third piece, and his head and chest were the fourth piece. Those four pieces occupied a space of twelve feet square. I saw five dead rebels in a row, with their heads knocked off by a round shot. Myself and other amateur anatomists, when the regiment was resting temporarily on arms, would leave to examine the internal structure of man. We would examine brains, heart, stomach, layers of muscles, structure of bones, &c., for there was every form of mutilation. At home I used to wince at the sight of a wound or of a corpse; but here, in one day, I learned to be among the scenes I am describing without emotion — as perfectly cool as I am now. My friend, Adjutant ——, and myself, on the second night, looking in the dark for a place to lie down, he said, 'Let's lie down here. Here's some fellows sleeping.' We slept in quiet until dawn revealed that we had passed a night among sprawling, stiffened, ghastly corpses.

"I saw one of our dead soldiers with his mouth crammed full of cartridges until the cheeks were bulged out. Several protruded from his mouth. This was done by the rebels.

"On the third day most of our time was employed in burying the dead. Shallow pits were dug, which would soon fill with water. Into these we threw our comrades with a heavy splash, or a dump against solid bottom. Many a hopeful, promising youth thus indecently ended his career.

"Some of our boys were disposed to kick the secesh into these pits. One fell in with a heavy dump on his face. The more humane proposed to turn him over. 'O, that'll do,' said a Union Missourian, 'for when he scratches, he'll scratch nearer hell.' This is a hard story, I know, but I want you to see real war.

"I stood in one place in the woods near the spot of the engagement of the 57th Illinois, and counted eighty-one dead rebels. There I saw one tree, seven inches in diameter, with thirty-one bullet holes. Such had been death's storm. Near the scenes of the last of the fighting, where the rebels precipitately retreated, I saw one grave containing one hundred and thirty-seven dead rebels, and one side of it another grave containing forty-one dead Federals. Several other trenches were in view from that spot.

"One dead and uniformed officer lay covered with a little housing of rails. On it was a fly-leaf of a memorandum-book with the pencil-writing: '*Federals, respect my father's corpse.*' Many of our boys wanted to cut off his buttons and gold cord; but our Colonel had the body religiously guarded.

"Many of our regiments were paid off just previously to the battle, and our dead comrades were robbed of thousands of dollars. The rebels were surprised and abashed at the apparent wealth of our army. They attired themselves in our uniforms, and rifled from officers' trunks tens of thousands of dollars worth of fine clothing, toilet articles, and interesting souvenirs of every man's trunk. They made themselves stupid and drunk over our fine victuals and wines. They seem to have gone mad with the lust of plunder.

"To show how complete and successful was the advance of the enemy, their advance guard lay in the woods on the 5th, witnessing our parades and reviews. One of our returned paroled prisoners, a mule-driver, who was captured two days before the battle, has told me that he was taken through their whole army, which was camped three miles from ours, the night before the attack.

"A resident here told me that on the retreat of the rebel army from Shiloh, it was utterly routed and demoralized.

"After the battle was over, we, formerly citizens who had never seen or heard the hiss of bullet, gathered the mangled corpses of those we had known at home and joked with the day before — friends who were as full of life, hope, and ambition as ourselves — and buried them in blankets, or sent them home in boxes, with as little concern as possible, and went immediately to joking and preparing to fight again. What spirit or principle was it that in one day gave us all the indifference and stoicism of veterans?

"Two women, laundresses in the 16th Wisconsin, running to the rear when the attack was commenced, were killed.

"My poor friend Carson, — the scout, — after having fought, and worked, and slaved from the beginning of the war, unrequited, comparatively, and after having passed hundreds of hair-breadth escapes, and through this wild battle, was killed by almost the last shot. A round shot took off his whole face and fore part of his head. Poor Carson! We all remember your patriotism, your courage, your devotion. We will cheer, all we can, the bereaved and dear ones you have left.

"Surgeons on the field would halt officers and order them to strip off their white shirts for bandages. Many an officer, halted on the field, tore off his accoutrements and uniform to provide the necessary bandages."

GENERAL KELLEY AND A SECESSION GIRL. — When the General was in quest of guerrillas in Western Virginia, he captured a young woman named Sallie Dusky, two brothers of whom were Captains in the rebel army. The General, feeling confident that the girl knew the hiding-places of the guerrillas, had a private conversation with her, and during the interview, having failed to get much satisfaction, he told her, if she would make a clean breast of it, he would give her the chances for a husband of all the young officers in his staff. This failed to bring the information, and Sallie was taken away in charge of Captain Baggs. As she moved away from the General's presence, she asked the Captain if the General was really in earnest in making the last proposition. Baggs assured her that the General was sincere, and that he would have lived up to his promise. The girl assumed a kind of thoughtful manner, and after a short time replied: "Well, I believe I'd about as lief have the old man (meaning the General himself) as any of 'em."

5

ORIGIN OF "SKEDADDLE." — A correspondent says: The word "skedaddle" is not derived from the Greek verb *Skedao*, to scatter, as has been recently asserted by certain learned etymologists. The root of "*Skedaddle*" is found in the Gaelic, Celtic, and the ancient British or Welsh language. In Gaelic, "*Sgiotadh*" is the present participle from the verb "*Sgiot*," and signifies "*scattering*," the act of scattering. In the Irish, which is, properly speaking, the Gaelic, "*Sgadad*" signifies "*flight*," and "*Uile*," or "*Ol*," all, or entirely — "*all flight*." In the Welsh we have "*Ysguduo*," or "*Ysgudaw*," to scud about. So, also, in the Scandinavian languages; in the Swedish we have "*Skuddo*," to throw or put out; "*Sceotan*," Saxon, to flee or haste away; in a general sense, to be driven, or to flee with haste. "*Skedaddle*" might be derived more naturally from "*Skud*," or "*Scud*," and "*Daddle*," than from the Greek "*Skedao*."

A TOUCHING INCIDENT. — The war has given birth to many gems of poetry, patriotic, humorous, and pathetic, illustrative of the times. The following was suggested by an affecting scene in one of the army hospitals. A brave lad of sixteen years, belonging to a New England regiment, mortally wounded at Fredericksburg, and sent to the Patent Office Hospital in Washington, was anxiously looking for the coming of his mother. As his last hour approached, and his sight grew dim, he mistook a sympathetic lady who was wiping the cold, clammy perspiration from his forehead, for the expected one, and with a smile of joy lighting up his pale face, he whispered tenderly, "Is that mother?" "Then," says the writer, "drawing her towards him with all his feeble strength, he nestled his head in her arms like a sleeping infant, and thus died with the sweet word *mother* on his quivering lips."

"IS THAT MOTHER?"

Is that mother bending o'er me,
  As she sang my cradle hymn —
Kneeling there in tears before me?
  Say? — my sight is growing dim.

Comes she from the old home lowly,
  Out among the northern hills,
To her pet boy dying slowly
  Of war's battle wounds and ills?

Mother! O, we bravely battled —
  Battled till the day was done;
While the leaden hail storm rattled —
  Man to man and gun to gun.

But we failed — and I'm dying —
  Dying in my boyhood's years,
There — no weeping — self-denying,
  Noble deaths demand no tears.

Fold your arms again around me;
  Press again my aching head;
Sing the lullaby you sang me —
  Kiss me, mother, ere I'm dead.

AN INCIDENT. — On Sunday, the 29th of July, 1862, a large number of Union officers attended the Old School Presbyterian Church of the Rev. Dr. W. H. Mitchell, at Florence, Alabama. So many of them were present that they constituted a majority of the congregation. After the usual opening hymn, the minister asked the congregation to unite in prayer, when, to their utter astonishment, the reverend traitor prayed for Jeff. Davis, for the success of the Confederate arms, and for the attainment of the independence of the Confederate people. The Union men were greatly indignant at this gross insult, but remained standing until the prayer was concluded, when they all left the church. After he had commenced his sermon, Colonel Harlan returned to the church, walked up to the pulpit, arrested the preacher, and delivered him, in compliance with the orders of General Thomas, to a detachment of cavalry, which immediately conveyed him as a prisoner to Tuscumbia.

AN OLD BIBLE CAPTURED IN BATTLE. — Mr. H. Jallonack, of Syracuse, N. Y., exhibited to the editor of the *Journal* of that city a valuable relic — a Protestant Bible printed in German text two hundred and twenty-five years ago — the imprint bearing date 1637. The book was in an excellent state of preservation, the printing perfectly legible, the binding sound and substantial, and the fastening a brass clasp. The following receipt shows how the volume came into Mr. Jallonack's possession: —

NEW YORK, August 21, 1862.

Received of Mr. H. Jallonack one hundred and fifty dollars for a copy of one of the first Protestant Bibles published in the Netherlands, 1637, with the Proclamation of the King of the Netherlands. This was taken from a descendant Hollander at the battle before Richmond, in the rebel service, by a private of the Irish Brigade.

JOSEPH HEIME, M. D., 4 Houston Street.

A REBEL soldier, after burying a Federal who had been killed during one of those sanguinary engagements which terminated in the retreat of the Union army from before Richmond, fixed a shingle over the grave, bearing this inscription:

"The Yankee hosts with blood-stained hands
  Came southward to divide our lands.
  This narrow and contracted spot
  Is all that this poor Yankee got!"

INCIDENTS OF FORT PICKENS. — The following is given by an officer on board the United States steamer Richmond, after the bombardment of Fort Pickens:

I went, by invitation of Lieut. ——, of the Engineers, to visit the Fort. Took a circuit first of the covered way, then of the parapet and ramparts. All around the Fort, inside and out, were marks of the enemy's shot and shell. On the glacis, here and there, are deep grooves, ending in a large hole, where the shot had plumped into it, and where there had been shell which had burst. The hole was a great excavation, into which you could drive an ox-cart. Where the projectiles have struck the standing walls, they have clipped off patches of the brick-work (it is a brick and not a stone fort) perhaps eight or ten feet deep, and, where they struck the corners, larger portions have been removed; but in no case has any part of the fortifications received an injury tending in the least to weaken it, and this after two days' heavy firing. The only man who was killed outright during the two days' action, was an artilleryman, who was passing into the casemates with some bread from the bake-house. A shell exploded at the other side of the area, and one piece, flying a distance of some two or three hundred feet, passed through his body, under his arms. He walked a few steps and fell dead. There were many almost miraculous escapes. A shell was heard coming towards a gun on the parapet, and the men dodged under their bomb-proofs. The shell hit fair on top of the bomb-proof, went through, and dropped into a pail of water beside the officer, where it exploded. When the men came out again to resume their work, all they saw of the officer was his heels sticking out of a pile of rubbish. After digging him out, they stood amazed to see that he was not even *hurt*. He rose up, shook the sand from his hair and clothes, and coolly said: "Come, come! what are you standing there gaping at? Load that gun there." At it they went again, as if nothing had happened. Another officer, who had charge of a battery of mortars, had no less than seventeen shells strike within ten yards of him. I saw the ground ploughed up in every direction, and yet not a man was hurt. About twenty of the men, who had been relieved from their guns, were sitting smoking and watching the firing in a corner protected from shot by the walls, when half of a huge shell struck and buried itself right in the middle of the group, without disturbing them in the least. "What's that?" asked one. "The devil knows, and he won't tell," indifferently responded another, and went on smoking. A ten-inch columbiad came rolling towards a group, the fuze whizzing and smoking. "Wonder if that'll hit us?" "Guess not; we're too near it!" Crack went the shell! flying in every direction, but fortunately injuring none of them. The rebel powder was poor; as also their shot, except that portion which they succeeded in stealing before the rebellion broke out. Their practice, however, was said to be good—how could it have been otherwise? Uncle Sam taught them at his unparalleled school at West Point, but with little thought that the teaching would be thus employed.

DISTURBING AN ORATOR.—When the Union lines advanced towards Corinth, a battery was planted on an eminence commanding a considerable portion of the country, but completely shrouded from view by a dense thicket. Scouts were sent out to discover the exact position of the rebels, and were but a short distance in advance, to give a signal as to the direction to fire, if any were discovered.

One of the rebel commanders, unaware of the presence of the nationals, called around him a brigade, and commenced addressing them in something like the following strain:

"Sons of the South: We are here to defend our homes, our wives and daughters, against the horde of Vandals who have come here to possess the first and violate the last. Here upon this sacred soil, we have assembled to drive back the Northern invaders—drive them into the Tennessee. Will you follow me? If we cannot hold this place we can defend no spot of our Confederacy. Shall we drive the invaders back, and strike to death the men who would desecrate our homes? Is there a man so base among those who hear me as to retreat from the contemptible foe before us? I will never blanch before their fire, nor——"

At this interesting period the signal was given, and six shells fell in the vicinity of the gallant officer and his men, who suddenly forgot their fiery resolves, and fled in confusion to their breastworks.

———

THE "HOME GUARDS."—Rev. Mr. ——, a man about six feet four in his stockings, and of proportions worthy a grenadier, and whose heart is as stout as his frame, a thorough Union man, and in for the war until all treason is thoroughly crushed out, was recently conducting a religious conference meeting, when a brother arose to speak, who, after alluding to his hopes and fears in a religious point of view, branched out in reference to the state of the country, saying that so great was his devotion to the Stars and Stripes, that he had enlisted; and, after a few further patriotic remarks, begged an interest in the prayers of the church, that he might be protected by Divine Providence on the field of battle, and that should he fall a victim to the bullets of the enemy, he might be prepared for the change.

Such a speech at any time would thrill with patriotic fervor the brave heart of the worthy minister, and he consequently spoke a few words of encouragement to the hero, when the wife of the enlisting brother volunteered her experience, in the course of which, alluding to her husband's enlistment, she expressed a willingness to give him up, even unto death, in the service of his country.

In a few moments after, the meeting came to an end, when the minister, all anxiety for the welfare of the patriot volunteer, proceeded to make some inquiries in reference to his regiment, commencing with the very natural question as to its name and number, when he received the startling reply:

"I've jined the HOME GUARDS!"

OLD DICK, THE DRUMMER. — Dick, a venerable darky in uniform, was arrested at Richmond for carrying a huge bowie-knife. He was on his return home to Danville from a campaign against the Yankees, and the Mayor discharged him after confiscating the knife.

He occupied the position of chief drummer for the Eighteenth Virginia regiment, and was highly esteemed by the regiment, not only as a musician, but as a brave and gallant old man. He is a hero of two wars, and in several instances rendered good service to the country. When the war with Mexico broke out, he enlisted as musician for a South Carolina regiment, and followed it through the war, and was present when the glorious Gen. Butler fell. The war being successfully terminated, he returned home to his usual avocations. Upon the breaking out of the rebellion, though old and gray, he was among the first to respond to Virginia's call for volunteers, and was regularly mustered into service with the Eighteenth regiment.

In the memorable battle of the 21st July, 1861, he deserted his drum, and, with musket in hand, followed the regiment throughout the battle. Several days after the battle, while strolling through the woods, he discovered the hiding-place of what he thought a Yankee, and on reporting it, went down with several of the regiment, and captured three of the enemy — one of them Col. Wood, of the Fourteenth Brooklyn. In every scene of danger or of difficulty, Old Dick accompanied the regiment with bowie-knife by his side and musket in hand. When on picket duty at Mason's Hill, in sight of the enemy, he would go beyond the picket lines to get a fair crack at the Yankee pickets. In fine, Old Dick is a gentleman and true patriot, and it is wrong that his knife, around which clung so many proud associations to him, should have been taken from him. He valued it above all things except his musket. It is true, the law may have required its confiscation, as setting a bad example to darkies in civil life; but under the circumstances, it does seem hard to have subjected the old man not only to the loss of his bowie-knife, but the mortification attendant on a suspicion of evil designs.

JOE PARSONS, A MARYLAND BRAVE. — A correspondent, writing from the hospitals of Alexandria, Va., relates the following anecdote: Joe enlisted in the First Maryland regiment, and was plainly a "rough" originally. As we passed along the hall we first saw him crouched near an open window, lustily singing, "I'am a bold soldier boy;" and observing the broad bandage over his eyes, I said: "What's your name, my good fellow?" "Joe, sir," he answered, "Joe Parsons." "And what is the matter with you?" "Blind, sir, blind as a bat." "In battle?" "Yes, at Antietam; both eyes shot out at one clip." Poor Joe was in the front, at Antietam Creek, and a Minie ball had passed directly through his eyes, across his face, destroying his sight forever. He was but twenty years old, but he was as happy as a lark! "It is dreadful," I said. "I'm very thankful I'm alive, sir. It might ha' been worse, yer see," he continued. And then he told us his story.

"I was hit," he said, "and it knocked me down. I lay there all night, and the next day the fight was renewed. I could stand the pain, yer see, but the balls was flyin' all round, and I wanted to get away. I couldn't see nothin', though. So I waited and listened; and at last I heard a feller groanin' beyond me. 'Hello!' says I. 'Hello yourself,' says he. 'Who be yer?' says I — 'a rebel?' 'You're a Yankee,' says he. 'So I am,' says I; 'what's the matter with yer?' 'My leg's smashed,' says he. 'Can't yer walk?' 'No.' 'Can yer see?' 'Yes.' 'Well,' says I, 'you're a —— rebel, but will you do me a little favor?' 'I will,' says he, 'ef I ken.' Then I says: 'Well, ole butternut, I can't see nothin.' 'My eyes is knocked out; but I ken walk. Come over yere. Let's git out o' this. You p'int the way, an' I'll tote yer off the field on my back.' 'Bully for you,' says he. And so we managed to git together. We shook hands on it. I took a wink out o' his canteen, and he got on to my shoulders.

"I did the walkin' for both, an' he did the navigatin'. An' ef he didn't make me carry him straight into a rebel colonel's tent, a mile away, I'm a liar! Hows'ever, the colonel came up, an' says he, 'Whar d'yer come from? who be yer?' I told him. He said I was done for, and couldn't do no more shoot'n; an' he sent me over to our lines. So, after three days, I came down here with the wounded boys, where we're doin' pretty well, all things considered." "But you will never see the light again, my poor fellow," I suggested, sympathetically. "That's so," he answered, glibly, "but I can't help it, you notice. I did my dooty — got shot, pop in the eye — an' that's my misfort'n, not my fault — as the old man said of his blind hoss. But — 'I'm a bold soldier boy,'" he continued, cheerily renewing his song; and we left him in his singular merriment. Poor, sightless, unlucky, but stout-hearted Joe Parsons!

PARTING WORDS TO THE YANKEES. — The following document was found in one of the dwellings at Yorktown, Va.:

To the Future Yankee Occupants of this Place

We have retired to the country for a short time to recruit our health. We find that with your two hundred thousand men you are too modest to visit this place, and we give you an opportunity to satisfy your curiosity with regard to our defences, assuring you that we will call upon you soon.

We hope a few days' residence in a house once occupied by men will induce enough courage in your gallant hearts to enable you to come within at least two miles of white men hereafter. Be sure to have on hand a supply of "pork'n beans" when we return; also, some codfish and "apple sass." When we learn to relish such diet we may become like you — Puritanical, selfish, thieving, God-forgotten, devil-worshipping, devil-belonging, African-loving, blue-bellied Yankees. Advise father Abraham to keep his Scotch cloak on hand, to keep soberer, and your wise Congress to hunt up two thousand five hundred millions of specie to pay the debt you have incurred in winning the contempt of every live man. We have on hand a few tools which we devote to the special duty of loosening the links of your steel shirts. Couldn't you get a few iron-clad men to do your fighting? Are you not horribly afraid that we will shoot you below the shirts? When are you coming to Richmond? Couldn't you go up the river with us? There is one score which we will yet settle with you to the death. Your fiend-like treatment of old men and helpless women reads you out of the pale of civilized warfare, and if rifles are true and knives keen, we will rid some of you of your beastly inclinations.

When you arise as high in the scale of created beings as a Brazilian monkey, we will allow you sometimes to associate with our negroes; but until then Southern soil will be too hot for the sons of the Pilgrims. The only dealing we will have with you is, henceforth, war to the knife. We despise you as heartily as we can whip you easily on any equal field.

Most heartily at your service, whenever you offer a fight.   J. TRAVISO SCOTT,
       Company A, Sixth Georgia Volunteers.

AN ELEGY. — The following lines were written by a soldier in the hospital at New Haven, Conn., who lost his leg in the battle of Fair Oaks:

L-E-G ON MY LEG.

Good leg, thou wast a faithful friend,
    And truly hast thy duty done;
I thank thee most that to the end
    Thou didst not let this body run.

Strange paradox! that in the fight
    Where I of thee was thus bereft,
I lost my left leg for "the Right,"
    And yet the right's the one that's left!

But while the sturdy stump remains,
    I may be able yet to patch it,
For even now I've taken pains
    To make an L-E-G to match it.

THE REBEL RETREAT FROM MILL SPRING. — In the course of a notice of Capt. C. C. Spiller, the following particulars of the rebel retreat from Mill Spring occur:

The Noble Ellis was at Gainsboro'; three ineffectual attempts had been made to take her up the river to where our army was. Finally Capt. Spiller was ordered to bring the boat; it was executed. Before the fight, he asked permission to lead his company; but Gen. Zollicoffer ordered him to remain at the river, in charge of operations there. The battle was fought, and our army driven back to the river, where a successful and skilful crossing alone could have saved it from utter ruin. Spiller was the man for the post — the world could not have furnished a better. The crossing began at three o'clock P. M. One of the enemy's batteries opened on the boat, and the fire was incessant until dark. The steamer was run all night. At four o'clock in the morning, when two thousand five hundred men were yet to cross, the captain and pilot left. It was understood that the engineer would leave her the next trip, and Spiller sent for Dick Fields, then one of his cavalry company, but formerly an engineer on one of his Tennessee river boats. Spiller knew Dick — together they had braved danger before that on the water. Sure enough, the engineer and deck-hands quit the boat, Dick took his place, and the boat was manned from the company. At daylight the work was done, and the last man was over. During the night the enemy had placed a Parrott gun in position, and at the earliest dawn the firing began. The first shell fell short but a few yards; the third passed through the chimney, and exploded over the wheel, scattering its fragments in every direction. Now that the troops were over, and all the horses that could be saved were saved, the torch was applied to the Noble Ellis. Spiller's company were near by; they had been ordered to fall back out of range of the enemy's fire, but they would not; their captain, whom they loved, was at his post, and they would not leave him. As the flames spread over the boat, and told that the army had crossed, and that all chance of pursuit was gone, the gallant Spiller, at the head of his troops, moved away to aid the retreating forces. But three of his men left him.

A SOUTHERN SCENE.

"O MAMMY. have you heard the news?"
    Thus spake a Southern child,
As in the nurse's aged face
    She upward glanced and smiled.

"What news you mean, my little one?
    It must be mighty fine,
To make my darlin's face so red,
    Her sunny blue eyes shine."

"Why, Abr'am Lincoln, don't you know,
    The Yankee President,
Whose ugly picture once we saw,
    When up to town we went?

"Well, he is goin' to free you all,
    And make you rich and grand,
And you'll be dressed in silk and gold,
    Like the proudest in the land.

"A gilded coach shall carry you
    Where'er you wish to ride;
And, mammy, all your work shall be
    Forever laid aside."

The eager speaker paused for breath,
    And then the old nurse said,
While closer to her swarthy cheek
    She pressed the golden head:

"My little missus, stop and res' —
  You' talkin' mighty fas';
Jes' look up dere, and tell me what
  You see in yonder glass?

"You sees old mammy's wrinkly face,
  As black as any coal;
And underneath her handkerchief
  Whole heaps of knotty wool.

"My darlin's face is red and white,
  Her skin is soff and fine,
And on her pretty little head
  De yallur ringlets shine.

"My chile, who made dis difference
  'Twixt mammy and 'twixt you?
You reads de dear Lord's blessed book,
  And you can tell me true.

"De dear Lord said it must be so;
  And, honey, I, for one,
Wid tankful heart will always say,
  His holy will be done.

"I tanks Mas' Linkum all de same,
  But when I wants for free,
I'll ask de Lord of glory,
  Not poor buckra man like he.

"And as for gilded carriages,
  Dey's notin' 'tall to see;
My massa's coach, what carries him,
  Is good enough for me.

"And, honey, when your mammy wants
  To change her homespun dress,
She'll pray, like dear old missus,
  To be clothed with righteousness.

"My work's been done dis many a day,
  And now I takes my ease,
A waitin' for de Master's call,
  Jes' when de Master please.

"And when at las' de time's done come,
  And poor old mammy dies,
Your own dear mother's soff white hand
  Shall close these tired old eyes.

"De dear Lord Jesus soon will call
  Old mammy home to him,
And he can wash my guilty soul
  From ebery spot of sin.

"And at his feet I shall lie down,
  Who died and rose for me;
And den, and not till den, my chile,
  Your mammy will be free.

"Come, little missus, say your prayers;
  Let old Mas' Linkum 'lone;
The debil knows who b'longs to him,
  And he'll take care of his own."

THE CAPTURE OF SMITHFIELD, VA. — The rebels having retired from Norfolk, Virginia, in May, 1862, General Mansfield sent his Aid-de-Camp, Drake De Kay, to reconnoitre the various rivers and creeks setting in from the James River.

Captain De Kay started with a sail-boat and eight men, and examined the Nansemond River and Chuckatuck Creek, and then proceeded to Smithfield Creek. This being narrow and tortuous, with high banks, he hoisted the rebel flag, and ran up some five miles to the town of Smithfield. This town is situated on a hill, stretching back from the river, contains some one thousand two hundred inhabitants, is very prettily laid out, has several handsome churches, and fine "old family" homesteads.

The people are all rank secesh — hardly a man, woman, or child to be seen in the streets who does not scowl at the Yankees. The negroes, even, did not speak to us, as their masters had forbidden it, and beaten them severely for doing so. The whole negro population would run away, were it not that every boat has been broken up.

Upon arriving at the town the rebel flag was pulled down on board the sail-boat, and the United States ensign run up, to the horror of the citizens, who had come down to congratulate the (as they supposed) escaped rebel boat. Captain De Kay proceeded on shore with his body-guard, sent for the Mayor and authorities, who called a meeting of the citizens. At this meeting a resolution was read setting forth "that the citizens would surrender as the conquered to the conquerors, and that they were and always would remain true and loyal citizens of the Confederate States of America."

Thereupon Captain De Kay seized and imprisoned the Mayor, Aldermen, and Committee — no resistance being made by their fellow-citizens, from the fear of a supposed gunboat outside the bar of the creek!

The authorities, left to themselves, and wisely removed from all excitement, began now to see the error of their ways. Visions of Fortress Monroe dungeons in the foreground, and handsomely constructed gallows, with patent drops, in the background, worked upon their imaginations, so that, one by one, and stoutly contesting point after point, they came down at last to Captain De Kay's simple propositions, which were:

1. To surrender the town and all public property to the United States forces unconditionally.

2. To hoist the American flag officially over the Town Hall, and to protect it there.

3. To, each and all, take the oath of allegiance to the United States of America.

To this they came at last, and after the oath the Mayor (a bitter secesh) nailed up with his own hand the glorious Stars and Stripes.

Lying opposite the town was a fine schooner, the Beauregard, with a full cargo of soft coal for the Merrimac. A prize crew (one man) was put on board, and some contrabands to work her, and she was sent to Fortress Monroe — the first prize vessel taken on James River.

Thus Smithfield was captured by eight men. The "supposed gunboat in the offing" never appeared!

A PASS FOR A REBEL. — The following incident illustrates the character of the secessionists, and the vigorous policy pursued by General McCook in Kentucky:

A man named Buz Rowe, living near Bacon Creek, was early afflicted with the secession fever, and when the rebels occupied that portion of Kentucky, the sickness assumed a malignant form. It was his practice to lie around a tavern at Bacon Creek Station, drink whiskey, swagger, blow about Southern rights, and insult Union men. When the Union troops advanced to Nevin, and the rebels fell back to Green River, Buz changed his tune. He was not disposed to take up arms in behalf of the cause he represented. In fact, to secure peace and safety at home, he expressed his willingness to "take the oath."

On being lectured by Union men, he stated that he was only going through the form to prevent being troubled at home, and that when he could do good for the rebel cause he would not regard the obligation in the least. It was some time before Buz could get a Union man to go to the camp with him; but finally, in company with such, he called on General McCook, and asked for the privilege of taking the oath and obtaining a pass. The General knew his man, and addressing the Union man who accompanied him, said:

"Administer the oath to *him* — a ready traitor to his country! What regard do you suppose he would have for the solemn obligations of an oath? A man, sir, who would betray his country has no respect for his oath."

Buz turned pale. The truth cut him deep, and he began to see that his time had come.

The General absolutely refused to have the oath administered, or to grant a pass. He could not get out of camp without some sort of a document, and he besought the interference of those whom he had so greatly abused when they were without protection. At last General McCook agreed to pass him out of camp, and gave him a document which read something in this way:

"To the guards and pickets:

"The bearer is a traitor to his country. Pass him; but, in doing so, mark him well, and if you see him hereafter prowling about our lines, shoot him at once."

This pass the brawling rebel had to show to the whole line of guards and pickets, who, all marked him well before they let him pass.

A BRILLIANT EXPLOIT. — One of the coolest and most extraordinary exploits of the war is thus described in a letter by Brigadier-General E. B. Brown, dated Springfield, Mo. After a preliminary description of an engagement with the rebels, eighteen miles from Newtonia, General Brown proceeds:

"The General (Schofield) sent Lieutenant Blodgett, attended by an orderly, with orders to Colonel Hall, Fourth Missouri cavalry, to move to the left, and attack in that direction. The route of the Lieutenant was across a point of woods, in which, while passing, he suddenly found himself facing about forty rebels drawn up in irregular line. Without a moment's hesitation, he and the orderly drew their pistols and charged.

At the same time, tempering bravery with mercy, and not feeling any desire to shed blood needlessly, he drew out his handkerchief, and waved it in token of his willingness to surround and capture the whole rebel force rather than shoot them down.

"The cool impudence of the act nonplused the foe, and perhaps thinking there was a large force in the rear, eight of them threw down their arms and surrendered, and the balance 'skedaddled.' It is difficult to say which I admired most in the Lieutenant, his bravery in making the charge against such odds, when to have hesitated a moment was certain death, or his presence of mind and coolness in offering them their lives. The Orderly, too, deserves more than a passing notice. His name is Peter Basnett, and he was at one time Sheriff of Brown County, Wis. The Lieutenant and Orderly were well matched — both quiet and determined men. I am glad of having an opportunity of bearing testimony to the bravery and soldierly conduct of Lieutenant Weils H. Blodgett. I hope the Governor will reward him as he deserves."

AN INCIDENT OF MILL SPRING. — After the battle, when the Minnesota regiment returned to its quarters at Camp Hamilton, they marched past the Colonel's marquee with banners flying, and their splendid band playing "Hail Columbia." Standing in front of the tent were Dr. Cliff, Zollicoffer's Brigade Surgeon, Lieut. Col. Carter, of the Twentieth Tennessee (rebel) regiment, and several Union officers. "Hail Columbia" affected both the rebel officers to tears — they wept like children — and Carter remarked that, although compelled to fight against the old flag, he loved it still.

A NATIONAL HYMN.

BY PARK BENJAMIN.

GREAT God! to whom our nation's woes,
Our dire distress, our angry foes,
In all their awful gloom are known,
We bow to thee, and thee alone.

We pray thee, mitigate this strife,
Attended by such waste of life,
Such wounds and anguish, groans and tears,
That fill our inmost hearts with fears.

O, darkly now the tempest rolls
Wide o'er our desolated souls;
Yet, beaten downward to the dust,
In thy forgiveness still we trust.

We trust to thy protecting power
In this, our country's saddest hour,
And pray that thou wilt spread thy shield
Above us in the camp and field.

O God of battles, let thy might
Protect our armies in the fight —
Till they shall win the victory,
And set the hapless bondmen free; —

Till, guided by thy glorious hand,
Those armies reunite the land,
And North and South alike shall raise
To God their peaceful hymns of praise.

INCIDENT OF THE HOSPITAL. — I was conversing not long since with a returned volunteer.

I was in the hospital, as nurse, for a long time, said he, and assisted in taking off limbs, and dressing all sorts of wounds; but the hardest thing I ever did was to take my thumb off a man's leg.

Ah! said I; how was that? Then he told me. It was a young man who had a severe wound in the thigh. The ball passed completely through, and amputation was necessary. The limb was cut off close up to the body, the arteries taken up, and he seemed to be doing well. Subsequently one of the small arteries sloughed off. An incision was made, and it was again taken up. "It is well it was not the main artery," said the surgeon, as he performed the operation; "he might have bled to death before we could have taken it up." But Charley got on finely, and was a favorite with us all.

I was passing through the wards one night about midnight, when suddenly, as I was passing Charley's bed he spoke to me. "H——, my leg is bleeding again." I threw back the clothes, and the blood spirted in the air. The main artery had opened afresh!

Fortunately, I knew just what to do; and in an instant I had pressed my thumb on the place, and stopped the bleeding. It was so close to the body that there was barely room for my thumb; but I succeeded in keeping it there, and rousing one of the convalescents, sent him for the surgeon, who came in on the run. "I am so thankful, H——," said he as he saw me, "that you were up and knew what to do, for he must have bled to death before I could have got here."

But on examination of the case he looked exceedingly serious, and sent out for other surgeons. All came who were within reach, and a consultation was held over the poor fellow. One conclusion was reached by all. There was no place to work save the spot where my thumb pressed; they could not work under my thumb, and if I moved he would bleed to death before the artery could be taken up. There was no way to save his life.

Poor Charley! He was very calm when they told him, and requested that his brother, who was in the same hospital, might be called up. He came and sat down by the bedside, and for three hours I stood, and by the pressure of my thumb, kept up the life in Charley while the brothers had their last conversation on earth. It was a strange place for me to be in, to feel that I held the life of a fellow-mortal in my hands, as it were, and stranger yet, to feel that an act of mine must cause that life to depart. Loving the poor fellow as I did, it was a hard thought, but there was no alternative.

The last words were spoken. Charley had arranged all his business affairs, and sent tender messages to absent ones, who little dreamed how near their loved one stood to the grave. The tears filled my eyes more than once as I listened to those parting words. All were said, and he turned to me. "Now, H——, I guess you had better take off your thumb." "O Charley! how can I?" I said. "But it must be, you know," he replied, cheerfully: "I thank you very much for your kindness, and now good by."

He turned away his head. I raised my thumb. Once more the crimson life-current gushed forth. In three minutes poor Charley was dead.

A HOME SCENE. — A member of one of the Charleston companies, on leave of absence in the city, received a summons to appear at his post on Sullivan's Island on one of the nights when the air was rife with the most startling rumors of the coming of an overwhelming fleet. With cheerful promptitude the brave soldier prepared to obey the imperative call. He was a husband, and the father of a blue-eyed little girl, who had just begun to put words together. After the preparation for the camp had been made, the soldier nerved himself for the good by. Those present thought that the wife felt the parting less than the husband. Lively words flowed fast, and her fair face was as bright and calm as a morning in May. Her heart seemed to be full of gladness.

She cheered him with pleasant earnestness to show himself a man, and running on in a gleeful strain, admonished him *not* to come back if he were shot in the back. With incredible fortitude she bade her child tell papa good by, and say to him that she would not own him her father if he proved to be a coward. The echo of the soldier's footfall through the corridor had hardly died away, when a ghastly pallor was seen spreading over the lady's face. In a voice weak and husky she begged a friend to take her child, and before she could be supported she fell from her chair prostrate on the floor.

By a tremendous effort the noble woman had controlled her feelings; but nature could bear no longer, and she fainted. The swoon was deep, and it was some time before consciousness returned. At length she opened her eyes languidly, and looked around upon the sympathizing group, and in a tremulous tone inquired "if she had fainted before her husband left the room."

THE FEAST OF DOUGHNUTS. — The ladies of Augusta, Me., distributed over fifty bushels of doughnuts to the Third Volunteer regiment of Maine, previous to their departure for the seat of war in 1861. A procession of ladies, headed by music, passed between double lines of troops, who presented arms, and were afterwards drawn up in hollow square to receive the welcome *dough*-nation.

Never before was seen such an aggregate of doughnuts since the world began. The circumambient air was redolent of doughnuts. Every breeze sighed doughnuts — everybody talked of doughnuts. The display of doughnuts beggared description. There was the molasses doughnut and the sugar doughnut — the long doughnut and the short doughnut — the round doughnut and the square doughnut — the rectangular doughnut and the triangular doughnut — the single twisted doughnut and the double twisted doughnut — the "light riz" doughnut and the hard-kneaded doughnut — the straight solid doughnut and the circular doughnut, with a hole in the centre. There were doughnuts of all imaginary kinds, qualities, shapes, and dimensions. It was emphatically a feast of doughnuts, if not a flow of soul.

LIEUT. GREBLE AT GREAT BETHEL. — As soon as the confusion arising from the mistake (the cross firing) was over, Gen. Pierce ordered the troops to advance. No scouts were thrown out, nor were troops aware of the vicinity of the enemy's batteries until they came within their fire. Lieut. Greble was ordered to unlimber his gun. He advanced, firing his gun alternately, until he came within two hundred yards of the masked battery of the rebels.

Soon after the firing commenced, he was left alone with his original command of eleven men, in an open road, the volunteers having retreated before the telling fire of the rifled cannon.

He worked his guns until he had silenced all those of the enemy, except one rifled cannon.

The Zouaves made a demonstration, and only desired permission to storm the fort, but no general officer was seen from the commencement of the action, and fifteen hundred troops were kept lying on the ground for an hour and forty minutes, waiting for a commander.

Lieut. Greble stood the brunt of the action for two hours; he was begged by several officers to retreat, but he refused. Lieut. Butler asked him at least to take the same care of himself that the rest did, and dodge. He replied, "I never dodge, and when I hear the notes of the bugle calling a retreat, I shall retreat, and not before." The enemy made a sortie. Lieut. Greble said to Capt. Bartlett, who was standing alongside of him, "Now, Charley, I have something to fire at, just see how I will make them scamper." He immediately loaded with grape, and fired, when the enemy at once retreated behind their intrenchment.

Seeing himself left entirely alone, with five men at his own gun, he turned to Corporal Peoples, and said, "All he could do would be useless — limber up the gun and take it away." At this moment a shot struck him on the left temple. He immediately fell, and his only exclamation was, "O, my gun!" The same ball went through the body of another man, and took the leg off a third.

Throughout the firing he had sighted every gun himself, and examined the effect of every shot with his glass. It was remarked by his own men, that every ball was placed in the very spot that he aimed for. The men say that he exhibited the same coolness that he would on parade.

The enemy did not come out again until the Federal troops had been withdrawn a half hour. Lieut. Greble did not spike his gun, but kept it charged in preparing to withdraw his command. The Sergeant spiked it after the Lieutenant was killed.

A HUMOROUS INCIDENT. — One of the Justices of the Police Court, in Boston, Mass., who had seen much service in the Volunteer Militia, was holding court, when a company of Volunteers passed the court-house, marching to the immortal tune of the "Star Spangled Banner." The spectators sprang to their feet, responsive to the understood order of "Forward, to the door!" Running feet shuffled in the entry. Boom! boom! sounded the band. "O, long may it wave!" screamed a patriotic urchin outside the window. "*First Regiment, take the witness stand!*" thundered the Court, which must have imagined itself on the *green field*, at the head of its command.

THE OTHER "ABOU-BEN-ADHEM." — The following ingenious and witty parody of a poem universally known, is from a feminine pen. The tart and somewhat malicious allusions to "Rye" refer, we suppose, to President Buchanan's letter to some Western friends, acknowledging, with thanks, the receipt of some excellent rye whiskey:

James B-Uchanan — may his tribe *decrease* —
Awoke one night from a strange dream of peace,
And saw, within the curtains of his bed,
Making his t'other eye to squint with dread —
Old *Jackson*, writing in a book of gold.
Exceeding Rye had made Buchanan bold,
And to the stern Ex-President he said :
"Wha — what writ'st thou ?" The spirit shook
   his head,
The while he answered, with the voice of old:
"The names of those who ne'er their country sold!"
"And is *mine* one ?" asked J. B. "*Nary !*" cried
The General, with a frown. Buchanan sighed,
And groaned, and turned himself upon his bed,
And took another "nip" of "rye," then said :
"Well, ere thou lay thy record on the shelf,
Write me at least as one who *sold himself !*
'Democs' and 'Rye' so long my spirits were,
That when the 'Crisis' came — I wasn't there !"
The General wrote, and vanished ; the next night
He came again, in more appalling plight,
And showed those names that all *true men detest*,
And lo! Buchanan's name *led all* the rest !

YOUNG HART THE GUIDE. — Rich Mountain is famous as the scene where the first decisive battle was fought in West Virginia, between Gen. McClellan and Gen. Garnett.

Rich Mountain range, as it is sometimes called, is in Randolph County, sixty miles from Glenville, one hundred miles from Parkersburg, and twelve miles from Beverly, the county seat of Randolph County. It is long, narrow, and high ; and, except the summit, whereon is Mr. Hart's farm, it is covered with timber densely, save a narrow strip on one side, which is thickly covered with laurel. The Parkersburg and Staunton Pike winds round the mountain, and passes, by the heads of ravines, directly over its top. The soil is black and rich, differing from that of all adjacent mountains, and it is from this circumstance that its name is derived.

The topographical formation of the mountain top is admirably adapted for the erection of strong military defences ; and on this account Gen. Garnett had selected it as a stronghold for his army. He had erected formidable fortifications, rendering an attack fatal to the assailing party, on the *road* leading up the mountain, which was deemed the only route by which the enemy could possibly reach his position. Gen. McClellan was advancing with an army of five thousand men from Clarksburg, on the Parkersburg and Staunton Turnpike, intending to attack Garnett early in the morning where his works crossed the road, not deeming any *other* route up the mountain practicable. Had he carried his plan into execution, subsequent examination showed that no earthly power could have saved him and his army from certain defeat. The mountain was steep in front of the fortifications ; reconnoisance, except in force, was impossible ; and McClellan had determined to risk a battle directly on the road, where Garnett, without McClellan's knowledge, had rendered his defences impervious to any power that man could bring against him.

Mr. Hart, whose farm is on the mountain, was a Union man, knew the ground occupied by Garnett, and had carefully examined his fortifications on the road coming up the mountain. Hearing that McClellan was advancing, and fearing that he might attempt to scale the works at the road, he sent his little son, Joseph Hart, in the night, to meet McClellan and inform him of the situation of affairs on the mountain. Joseph, being but a boy, got through the rebel lines without difficulty, and travelling the rest of the night and part of the following day, reached the advanced guard of the Union army, informed them of the object of his coming, and was taken, under guard, to the General's quarters. Young as he was, the Federal commander looked upon him with suspicion. He questioned him closely. Joseph related in simple language all his father had told him of Garnett's position, the number of his force, the character of his works, and the impossibility of successfully attacking him on the mountain in the direction he proposed. The General listened attentively to his simple story, occasionally interrupting him with : " Tell the truth, my boy." At each interruption Joseph earnestly but quietly would reply : " I *am* telling you the truth, General." " But," says the latter, " do you know, if you are not, you will be shot as a spy ? " " I am *willing* to be shot if all I say is not true," gently responded Joseph. " Well," says the General, after being satisfied of the entire honesty of his little visitor, " if I cannot go up the mountain by the road, in what way am I to go up ? " Joseph, who now saw that he was believed, from the manner of his interrogator, said there was a way up the *other* side, leaving the turnpike just at the foot, and going round the base to where the laurel was. There was no road there, and the mountain was very steep ; but *he* had been up there : there were but few trees standing, and none fallen down to be in the way. The laurel was very thick up the side of the mountain, and the top matted together so closely that a man could walk on the tops. The last statement of Joseph once more awakened a slight suspicion of Gen. McClellan, who said sharply, " Do you say men can walk on the *tops* of the laurel ? " " Yes sir," said Joseph. " Do you think my army can go up the mountain, over the tops of the laurel ? " " No, sir," promptly answered Joseph ; " but *I* have done so, and a man *might*, if he would walk slowly and had nothing to carry." " But, my boy, don't you see, I have a great many men, and horses, and cannon to take up, and how do you think we could get up over that laurel ? " " The trees are small ; they are so small you can cut them down, without making any noise, with knives and hatchets ; and they will not know on the top of the mountain what you are doing or when you are coming," promptly and respectfully answered Joseph, who was now really to be the leader of the little army that was to decide the political destiny of West Virginia.

The Federal commander was satisfied with this ; and although he had marched all day, and intended that night to take the easy way up the mountain by the road, he immediately changed his plan of attack, and suddenly the army of the Union were moving away in the direction pointed out by Joseph Hart. When they came to the foot of the mountain, they left the smooth and easy track of the turnpike, and with difficulty wound round the broad base of the mountain, through ravines and ugly gorges, to the point indicated by the little guide. Here the army halted. McClellan and some of his staff, with Joseph, proceeded to examine the nature of the ground, and the superincumbent laurel covering the mountain from its base to its summit. All was precisely as Joseph had described it in the chief's tent on the Staunton Pike ; and the quick eye of the hero of Rich Mountain saw at a glance the feasibility of the attack. It was past midnight when the army reached the foot of the mountain. Though floating clouds hid the stars, the night was not entirely dark, and more than a thousand knives and hatchets were soon busy clearing away the marvellous laurel. Silence reigned throughout the lines, save the sharp click of the small blades and the rustle of the falling laurel. Before daybreak the narrow and precipitous way was cleared, and the work of ascending commenced. The horses were tied at the foot of the mountain. The artillery horses were taken from the carriages. One by one the cannon were taken up the rough and steep side of the mountain by hand, and left within a short distance of the top, in such a situation as to be readily moved forward when the moment of attack should arrive. The main army then commenced the march up by companies, many falling down, but suddenly recovering their places. The ascent was a slow and tedious one. The way was winding and a full mile. But before daybreak all was ready, and the Yankee cannon were booming upon and over the enemy's works, nearly in his rear, at an unexpected moment, and from an entirely unexpected quarter. They were *thunder* struck, as well as struck by shell and canister. They did the best they could by a feeble resistance, and fled precipitately down the mountain, pursued by the Federals to Cheat River, where the brave Garnett was killed. Two hundred fell on the mountain, and are buried by the side of the turnpike, with no other sign of the field of interment than a long indentation made by the sinking down of the earth in the line where the bodies lie.

A COURAGEOUS WOMAN. — A good story is told of the courageous conduct of the wife of Capt. McGilvery, master of the ship Mary Goodell, which was captured by a rebel privateer, and subsequently released, and arrived at Portland. Mrs. McGilvery was on the voyage with her husband, and when the ship was boarded by the pirates, she was asked by them for a supply of small stores for their use, as they were rather short. She immediately replied that she had nothing but arsenic, and would gladly give them a supply, but that they could have nothing else from her. Seeing the national flag near at hand, they started to secure it, when she sprang forward, and grasping the flag, threw it into a chest, and placing herself over it, declared they should not have it unless they took her with it. Finding the lady rather too spunky for them, they retired without further molesting her.

THE GREAT BELL ROLAND. *

BY THEODORE TILTON.

(Suggested by the President's first call for Volunteers.)

I.

Toll! Roland, toll!
In old St. Bavon's tower,
At midnight hour,
The great bell Roland spoke!
All souls that slept in Ghent awoke!
What meant the thunder-stroke?
Why trembled wife and maid?
Why caught each man his blade?
Why echoed every street
With tramp of thronging feet?
   All flying to the city's wall!
   It was the warning call
That Freedom stood in peril of a foe!
   And even timid hearts grew bold
   Whenever Roland tolled,
   And every hand a sword could hold!
      So acted men
      Like patriots then
   Three hundred years ago!

* The famous bell Roland, of Ghent, was an object of great affection to the people, because it rang to arm them when Liberty was in danger.

II.

Toll! Roland, toll!
Bell never yet was hung,
Between whose lips there swung
So grand a tongue!
   If men be patriots still,
   At thy first sound
   True hearts will bound,
   Great souls will thrill!
Then toll and strike the test
Through each man's breast,
Till loyal hearts shall stand confest, —
And may God's wrath smite all the rest!

III.

Toll! Roland, toll!
Not now in old St. Bavon's tower —
Not now at midnight hour —
Not now from River Scheldt to Zuyder Zee —
   But here, — this side the sea! —
   Toll here, in broad, bright day! —
   For not by night awaits
   A noble foe without the gates,
But perjured friends within betray,
And do the deed at noon!
   Toll! Roland, toll!
Thy sound is not too soon!
To arms! Ring out the leader's call!
Re-echo it from East to West
Till every hero's breast
Shall swell beneath a soldier's crest!
   Toll! Roland, toll!
Till cottager from cottage wall
Snatch pouch and powder-horn and gun!
The sire bequeathed them to the son
When only half their work was done!
   Toll! Roland, toll!
Till swords from scabbards leap!
   Toll! Roland, toll!
What tears can widows weep
Less bitter than when brave men fall!
   Toll! Roland, toll!
In shadowed hut and hall
Shall lie the soldier's pall,
And hearts shall break while graves are filled!
   Amen! so God hath willed!
And may His grace anoint us all!

IV.

Toll! Roland, toll!
The Dragon on thy tower
Stands sentry to this hour,
And Freedom so stands safe in Ghent,
And merrier bells now ring,
And in the land's serene content,
Men shout, "God save the King!"
   Until the skies are rent!
So let it be!
A kingly king is he
Who keeps his people free!
   Toll! Roland, toll!
Ring out across the sea!
No longer They, but We,
Have now such need of thee!
   Toll! Roland, toll!
Nor ever may thy throat
Keep dumb its warning note,
Till Freedom's perils be outbraved!
   Toll! Roland, toll!

Till Freedom's flag, wherever waved,
Shall shadow not a man enslaved!
   Toll! Roland, toll!
From northern lake to southern strand!
   Toll! Roland, toll!
Till friend and foe, at thy command,
Once more shall clasp each other's hand,
And shout, one-voiced, " God save the land! "
And love the land that God hath saved!
   Toll! Roland, toll!

HORSES AT BULL RUN. — One of the guns of Sherman's battery was rescued from capture by the rebels, and brought off the field by two horses that had been shot through by Minie musket-balls. When the order, " Forward," was given, they resolutely straightened out, and absolutely brought off the gun.

At the commencement of the battle, Lieut. Hasbrouck, of the West Point battery, was riding a little sorrel horse. In a short time he was shot three times, and from loss of blood became too weak for further service. He was stripped of bridle and saddle, and turned loose, as his owner supposed, to die. In the heat of the contest nothing more was thought of the little sorrel, nor was he seen again until the remnant of the battery was far towards Washington on the retreat. It paused at Centreville, and while resting there, Lieut. Hasbrouck was delighted to be joined by his faithful horse, which, by a strong instinct, had obeyed the bugle call to retreat, and had found his true position with the battery, which is more than most of the human mass engaged on the field could boast of doing. He went safely into Washington, recovered of his wounds, ready for another fight.

INCIDENTS OF THE PENINSULA. — At the battle of Hanover Court House, Va., two sergeants met in the woods; each drew his knife, and the two bodies were found together, each with a knife buried in to the hilt. Some men had a cool way of disposing of prisoners. One, an officer of the Massachusetts Ninth, well known in Boston as a professor of muscular Christianity, better known as "the child of the regiment," while rushing through the woods at the head of his company, came upon a rebel. Seizing the "grayback" by the collar, he threw him over his shoulder, with, " Pick him up, somebody." A little Yankee, marching down by the side of a fence which skirted the woods, came upon a strapping secesh, who attempted to seize and pull him over the rails; but the little one had too much science. A blow with the butt of a musket levelled secesh to the ground, and made him a prisoner.

'CUTENESS OF A CONTRABAND SCOUT. — A private letter from West Point, Va., narrates an exciting adventure which befell a negro scout in the employ of the Union forces, and his shrewdness in escaping from the rebels. His name was Claiborne, and he was a full-blooded African,

with big lips, flat nose, &c. He lived in the vicinity all his life, and was therefore familiar with the country, which rendered him a very valuable scout. On Claiborne's last trip inside the enemy's lines, after scouting around as much as he wished, he picked up eight chickens and started for camp. His road led past the house of a secesh doctor named Roberts, who knew him, and who ordered him to stop, which, of course, Claiborne had no idea of doing, and kept on, when the doctor fired on him, and gave chase, shouting at the top of his voice. The negro was making good time towards camp, when all at once he was confronted by a whole regiment of rebel soldiers, who ordered him to halt. For a moment the scout was dumbfounded, and thought his hour had come; but the next he sung out:

" The Yankees are coming! the Yankees are coming! "

" Where? where? " inquired the rebels.

" Just up in front of Dr. Roberts' house, in a piece of woods," returned Sambo. " Dr. R. sent me down to tell you to come up quick, or they'll kill the whole of us."

" Come in, come into camp," said the soldiers.

" No, no," says the 'cute African, " I have got to go down and tell the cavalry pickets, and can't wait a second." So off he sprang with a bound, running for dear life, the rebs, discovering the ruse, chasing him for three miles, and he running six, when he got safely into camp, but minus his chickens, which he dropped at the first fire.

AN AFFECTING INCIDENT. — An incident is related which affords a striking but sad illustration of the effects of civil war. The lady in question has resided with an only daughter for many years in Alexandria. About nine months since, a mutual friend introduced a young gentleman of Richmond to the family. The young people soon became intimately acquainted, and, quite naturally, fell in love. The parents on both sides consenting, the parties were betrothed, and the marriage day was fixed for the 4th of July. In the mean time, however, the Virginians were called upon to decide on which side they would stand. The ladies declared themselves on the side of the Government, but the gentleman joined the forces of his State. No opportunity was afforded for the interchange of sentiments between the young folks, or anything settled as to their future movements. Matters thus remained till the 4th of July, when, exactly within an hour of the time originally fixed for the marriage, intelligence was received at the residence of the ladies that the young man had been shot by a sentry two days before, while attempting to desert and join his bride. His betrothed did not shed a tear, but, standing erect, smiled, and then remarking to her mother, " I am going to desert too," fell to the floor, while the blood bubbled from her lips, as her soul passed back to Him who gave it.

A DRAFT AT SAVANNAH, GA. — A correspondent at Charleston furnished the following description of the scene which ensued on the occasion of a draft for four hundred men in Savannah, to complete a requisition for troops, the requisite number not having volunteered. Fifteen hundred of the business men and mechanics of the city were drawn up in a hollow square on the parade-ground, all in a high state of excitement, when the following proceedings took place:

"The Colonel now takes his place in the centre, and from the back of a magnificent horse, in a few well-timed remarks, calls for volunteers. He said it was a shame that a Georgian should submit to be drafted, and dishonorable to a citizen of Savannah to be forced into the service of his country. He appealed to their patriotism, their pluck, and their — pelf. He told them of good clothes, good living, and fifty dollars bounty; and on the strength of these considerations, invited everybody to walk three paces in front. Nobody did it. An ugly pause ensued, worse than a dead silence between the ticking of a conversation. The Colonel thought he might not have been heard or understood, and repeated his catalogue of persuasions. At this point one of the sides of the square opened, and in marched a company of about forty stalwart Irishmen, whom their Captain, in a loud and exultant tone, announced as the Mitchell Guards. 'We volunteer, Colonel, in a body.' The Colonel was delighted. He proposed 'three cheers for the Mitchell Guards,' and the crowd indulged not inordinately in the pulmonary exercise. The requisite number did not seem to be forthcoming, however, and the Colonel made another little speech, winding up with an invitation to the black drummer and fifer to perambulate the quadrangle and play Dixie; which they did, but they came as they went — solitary and alone; not the ghost of a volunteer being anywhere visible in the Ethiopian wake. The Colonel looked as blank as if he was getting desperate, and a draft seemed indispensable.

As a dernier resort the Colonel directed all who had excuses to advance to the centre, and submit them for examination. Did you ever see a crowd run away from a falling building or a fire, or towards a dog-fight, or a street-show? If you have, you can form some idea of the tempestuous nature of the wave that swept towards the little table in the centre of the square, around which were gathered the four grave gentlemen who were to examine the documents. It was a scene, which, as an uninterested outsider, one could only hold his sides and laugh at. Hats were crushed, ribs punched, corns smashed, and clothes torn. Every hand held its magical bit of paper, from the begrimed digits of the individual just from a stable or a foundery, to the dainty gloved extremity of the dry goods clerk, just from his counter. Young and old, rich and poor, neat and nasty, Americans, Englishmen, Irishmen, Germans, Frenchmen, Italians, Israelites, and Gentiles, all went to make up the motley mass. What a pretty lot of sick and disabled individuals there were, to be sure! Swelled arms, limping legs, spine diseases, bad eyes, corns, toothaches, constitutional debility in the bread-basket, eruptive diseases, deafness, rheumatism, not well generally — these, and a thousand other complaints, were represented as variously and heterogeneously as by any procession of pilgrims that ever visited the Holy Land.

"And so the day progressed, nearly ten hours being consumed in the endeavor to secure a draft. This afternoon the absentees were gathered together, and the efforts renewed, when, strange to say, every man who found the liability imminent of his being forced to enlist, protested that he was just on the point of doing so, and willingly put his name to the roll."

SOUTHERN WOMEN. — A gentleman from Charleston says that everything there (Jan. 7, 1861,) betokens active preparations for fight. Last Sunday, he says, not a lady was at the church he attended. They were all at home making cartridges and cylinders, and scraping lint. The thousand negroes busy in building batteries, so far from inclining to insurrection, were grinning from ear to ear at the prospect of shooting the Yankees. Extravagant reports were current as to the hostile designs of the Federal Government, such as that the Macedonian was on her way with five hundred troops.

A MODEL BODY-GUARD. — "Brick" Pomeroy, of the La Crosse Wisconsin, on being invited to assist in forming a body-guard for President Lincoln, after due consideration decided to "go in," provided the following basis could be adopted and rigidly adhered to throughout the war:

The company shall be entirely composed of colonels, who shall draw pay and rations in advance.

Every man shall have a commission, two servants, and white kids.

Each man shall be mounted in a covered buggy, drawn by two white stallions.

Under the seat of each buggy shall be a cupboard, containing cold chicken, pounded ice, and champagne, a la members of Congress and military officers at Bull Run.

Each man shall have plenty of cards and red chips to play poker with.

The only side-arms to be opera-glasses, champagne glasses, and gold-headed canes.

The duty of the company shall be to take observations of battle, and on no account shall it be allowed to approach nearer than ten miles to the seat of war.

Behind each buggy shall be an ambulance, so arranged as to be converted into a first-class boarding-house in the daytime, and a sumptuous sleeping and dressing room at night.

The regimental band must be composed of

pianos and guitars, played by young ladies, who shall never play a quickstep except in case of retreat.

Reveille shall not be sounded till late breakfast time, and not then if any one of the regiment has a headache.

In case of a forced march into an enemy's country, two miles a week shall be the maximum, and no marches shall be made except the country abound in game, or if any member of the regiment object.

Kid gloves, gold toothpicks, cologne, hairdressing, silk underclothes, cosmetics, and all other rations, to be furnished by the Government.

Each member of the regiment shall be allowed a reporter for some New York paper, who shall draw a salary of two hundred dollars a week, for puffs, from the incidental fund.

Every member shall be in command, and when one is promoted, all are to be.

Commissions never to be revoked.

THE FIGHT AT BIG BETHEL. — The following account of the battle of Big Bethel was given by a Confederate soldier, who participated in the defence: "An engagement lasting four hours took place yesterday, June 10, between five regiments of the troops from Old Point, and 1100 Confederate troops, consisting of Virginians and North Carolinians under Gen. Magruder, at Bethel Church, York County. Before telling you of the battle, I will give you some circumstances preceding it. About two weeks ago, a party of three hundred Yankees came up from Hampton, and occupied Bethel Church, which position they held a day or two, and then retired, leaving written on the walls of the church several inscriptions, such as 'Death to the Traitors,' 'Down with the Rebels,' &c. To nearly all these the names of the writers were defiantly signed, and all of the penmen signed themselves as from New York, except one, who was from Boston, Mass., U. S. To these excursions into the interior, of which this was the boldest, Gen. Magruder determined to put a stop, and accordingly filled the place, after the Yankees left, with a few companies of his own troops. In addition to this, he determined to carry the war into the enemy's country, and on Wednesday last, Stanard's battery of the Howitzer Battalion was ordered down to the church, where it was soon joined by a portion of Brown's battery of the same corps. The North Carolina regiment, under Col. Hill, was also there, making in all about 1100 men, and seven howitzer guns. On Saturday last the first excursion of considerable importance was made. A detachment of 200 infantry and a howitzer gun under Major Randolph, and one of 70 infantry and another howitzer under Major Lane, of the North Carolina regiment, started different routes to cut off a party which had left Hampton. The party was seen and fired at by Major Randolph's detachment, but made such fast time that they escaped. The troops under Major Lane

passed within sight of Hampton, and as they turned up the road to return to Bethel, encountered the Yankees, numbering about 90, who were intrenched behind a fence in the field, protected by a high bank. Our advance guard fired on them, and in another moment the North Carolinians were dashing over the fence in regular French (not New York) Zouave style, firing at them in real squirrel-hunting style. The Yankees fled for their lives after firing for about three minutes without effect, leaving behind them three dead and a prisoner. The fellow was a stout, ugly fellow, from Troy, N. Y. He said he had nothing against the South, but somebody must be soldiers, and he thought he had as well enlist. None of our men were hurt. This bold excursion, under the very guns of the enemy, determined the authorities at Old Point to put a stop to it, and clear us out from Bethel. This determination was conveyed to us from persons who came from the neighborhood of the enemy. On Monday morning, 600 infantry and two guns, under Gen. Magruder, left the camp and proceeded towards Hampton, but after advancing a mile or two, received information that the Yankees were coming in large force. We then retired, and after reaching camp the guns were placed in battery, and the infantry took their places behind their breastwork. Everybody was cool, and all were anxious to give the invaders a good reception. About nine o'clock, the glittering bayonets of the enemy appeared on the hill opposite, and above them waved the Star-spangled Banner. The moment the head of the column advanced far enough to show one or two companies, the Parrott gun of the Howitzer-Battery opened on them, throwing a shell right into their midst. Their ranks broke in confusion, and the column, or as much of it as we could see, retreated behind two small farm-houses. From their position a fire was opened on us, which was replied to by our battery, which commanded the route of their approach. Our firing was excellent, and the shells scattered in all directions when they burst. They could hardly approach the guns which they were firing for the shells which came from our battery. Within our encampment fell a perfect hail-storm of canister-shot, bullets, and balls. Remarkable to say, not one of our men was killed inside of our encampment. Several horses were slain by the shells and bullets. Finding that bombardment would not answer, the enemy, about eleven o'clock, tried to carry the position by assault, but met a terrible repulse at the hands of the infantry as he tried to scale the breastworks. The men disregarded sometimes the defences erected for them, and, leaping on the embankment, stood and fired at the Yankees, cutting them down as they came up. One company of the New York 7th Regiment, under Capt. Winthrop, attempted to take the redoubt on the left. The marsh they crossed was strewn with their bodies. Their Captain, a fine-looking man, reached the fence, and, leaping on a log, waved his sword, crying, 'Come on, boys; one charge, and the day is ours!' The words were his last, for a Carolina rifle ended his life the next moment, and his men fled in terror back. At the redoubt on the right, a company of about 300 New York Zouaves charged one of our guns, but could not stand the fire of the infantry, and retreated precipitately. During these charges the main body of the enemy on the hill were attempting to concentrate for a general assault, but the shells from the Howitzer Battery prevented them. As one regiment would give up the effort, another would be marched to the position, but with no better success, for a shell would scatter them like chaff. The men did not seem able to stand fire at all. About one o'clock their guns were silenced, and a few moments after, their infantry retreated precipitately down the road to Hampton. Our cavalry, numbering three companies, went in pursuit, and harassed them down to the edge of Hampton. As they retreated many of the wounded fell along the road and died, and the whole road to Hampton was strewn with haversacks, overcoats, canteens, muskets, &c., which the men had thrown off in their retreat. After the battle, I visited the position they held. The houses behind which they had been hid had been burned by our troops. Around the yard were the dead bodies of the men who had been killed by our cannon, mangled in the most frightful manner by the shells. The uniforms on the bodies were very different, and many of them are like those of the Virginia soldiery. A little farther on we came to the point to which they had carried some of their wounded, who had since died. The gay-looking uniforms of the New York Zouaves contrasted greatly with the pale, fixed faces of their dead owners. Going to the swamp, through which they attempted to pass to assault our lines, presented another bloody scene. Bodies dotted the black morass from one end to the other. I saw one boyish, delicate-looking fellow lying on the mud, with a bullet-hole through his breast. One hand was pressed on the wound, from which his life-blood had poured, and the other was clinched in the grass that grew near him. Lying on the ground was a Testament which had fallen from his pocket, dabbled with blood. On opening the cover, I found the printed inscription : 'Presented to the Defenders of their Country by the New York Bible Society.' A United States flag was also stamped on the title-page. Among the haversacks picked up along the route were many letters from the Northern States, asking if they liked the Southern farms, and if the Southern barbarians had been whipped out yet. The force of the enemy brought against us was 4000, according to the statement of the six prisoners we took. Ours was 1100. Their loss in killed and wounded must be nearly 200. Our loss is one killed and three wounded. The fatal case was that of a North Carolinian who volunteered to fire one of the houses behind which they were stationed. He started from the breastwork to accomplish it, but was shot in the head. He died this morning in the hospital. The wounded are Harry Shook, of Richmond, of Brown's battery, shot in the wrist ; John Werth, of Richmond, of the same battery, shot in the leg, and Lieut. Hudnall, of the same battery, shot in the foot. None of the wounds are serious. The Louisiana regiment arrived about one hour after the fight was over."

INCIDENT OF WAR. — One of the most interesting incidents of the battle of Bull Run, says a Southern journal, is presented in the case of Willie P. Mangum, Jr., son of Ex-Senator Mangum, of North Carolina. This young man was attached to Col. Fisher's regiment, and owes the preservation of his life to a copy of the Bible presented him by his sister. He had the good book in his left coat-pocket. It was struck by a ball near the edge, but the book changed the direction of the bullet, and it glanced off, inflicting a severe, but not dangerous flesh wound. The book was saturated with blood, but the advice written on a fly-leaf by the sister who gave it was perfectly legible.

OLD HANNAH. — "When I was in Jefferson, in the fall of 1862," said Robert Collyer, " I found the hospitals in the most fearful condition you can imagine. I cannot stop to tell you all the scenes I saw ; it is enough to say that one poor fellow had lain there sick on the boards, and seen five men carried away dead, one after another, from his side. He was worn to a skeleton, worn through, so that great sores were all over his back, and filthy beyond description.

"One day, a little before my visit, old Hannah, a black woman, who had some washing to do for a doctor, went down the ward to hunt him up. She saw this dying man, and had compassion on him, and said, ' O, doctor, let me bring this man to my bed, to keep him off the floor.'

"The doctor said, 'The man is dying ; he will be dead to-morrow.' To-morrow came, and old Hannah could not rest. She went to see the man, and he was still alive. Then she got some help, took her bed, put the man on it, and carried him boldly to her shanty ; then she washed him all over, as a woman washes a baby, and fed him with a spoon, and fought death, hand to hand, day and night, and beat him back, and saved the soldier's life.

"The day before I went to Jefferson, the man had gone on a furlough to his home in Indiana. He besought Hannah to go with him, but she could not spare time ; there was all that washing to do. She went with him to the steamboat, got him fixed just to her mind, and then kissed him, and the man lifted up his voice, as she left, and wept like a child. I say we have grown noble in our suffering."

A LOYAL PIGEON. — The following is a true and singularly remarkable story of a pigeon captured by Mr. Tinker, a teamster of the Forty-second New York Volunteers, while the regiment was encamped at Kalorama Heights, Va. Mr. Tinker made a pet of him, and kept him in camp until they started for Poolesville. Strange to say, the pigeon followed on with the train, occasionally flying away at a great distance, but always returning, and, when weary, would alight on some wagon of the train.

At night he was sure to come home, and, watching his opportunity, would select a position, and quietly go to roost in Tinker's wagon. Many of the men in the regiment took a fancy to him, and he soon became a general favorite. From Poolesville he followed to Washington, and down to the dock, where Tinker took him on board the steamer; so he went to Fortress Monroe, thence to Yorktown, where he was accustomed to make flights over and beyond the enemy's works, but was always sure to return at evening, to roost and receive his food in Tinker's wagon. From thence he went all through the Peninsular campaign, afterwards to Antietam, and Harper's Ferry, witnessing all the battles fought by his regiment.

By this time he had gained so much favor, that a friend offered twenty-five dollars to purchase him; but Tinker would not sell him at any price, and soon after sent him home as a present to some friend. It might be interesting to trace the future movements of this remarkable specimen of the feathered tribe, but none will doubt his instinctive loyalty, and attachment to the old Tammany regiment.

Any of the brave Forty-second boys, who read this history of their favorite, will attest the truth of these statements, and be pleased to see him honored by this history of his wanderings. Such devotion to the Stars and Stripes is a fair illustration of the character of the Tammany regiment in the field, and worthy of imitation by those who have more than instinct to guide them.

SOUTHERN IDEAS OF NORTHERN BRAVERY. — The Chinese and the Yankees are exceedingly alike, and we have always thought that they were much more nearly related than the Japanese and the almond-eyed people of the Flowery Kingdom.

When a Chinaman prepares for war — measuring his enemy's courage by his own — he attempts to work upon his fears. He puts on a hideous mask, arms himself with a huge shield, upon which he paints some unearthly monster; and, when thus accoutred, he goes forth in cold sweat to encounter the enemy. As soon as he beholds his adversary, he utters a fearful roar, broadsides his shield, and if his opponent does not at once take to his heels, John Chinaman always does.

The wars of New England have always been conducted upon the Chinese plan. To hear their orators, and read their newspapers, one would suppose that he was looking at a Chinaman clothed with all the pomp and circumstance of mask, shield, and stink-pot. The Yankee orators are only equalled by the Yankee editors in deeds of valor. Let war be breathed, and the first swear to a man that they are ready and anxious to exterminate creation, whilst the latter, not content, like Alexander, to sigh for more worlds to conquer, threaten to destroy the laws of gravity, and lay violent hands upon the whole planetary system. Yet, these war mandarins are all members of the Peace Society, and would no more think of resenting a blow on the cheek, the seduction of a wife, or the dishonor of a daughter, than they would of flying. We have not forgotten how all Massachusetts collected in Boston when Anthony Burns was to be delivered to his Virginia master, and swore that it should not be done. A single file of soldiers, however, marched the fugitive from State Street to the lower end of Long Wharf, through miles of streets packed with valorous fanatics, who did nothing but sing old Puritan hymns, with a most hideous and barbarous disregard to metre. — *Richmond Examiner.*

INCIDENTS OF THE FORT DONELSON FIGHT. — Immediately after the surrender, Capt. T. I. Newsham (Gen. Smith's Assistant Adjutant General) rode up to the headquarters of Gen. Buckner, where he was introduced to the rebel commander. Capt. Newsham was mounted on a splendid white charger. Buckner, noticing the horse, inquired if he was the individual who rode that horse during the battle the day previous. Capt. N. replied yes. "Then," said Buckner, "you certainly bear a charmed life. You attracted my attention during the entire day. I ordered and saw our most experienced gunners fire at you six times from a six-pounder rifled gun, and noticed other gunners aiming at you also." Capt. Newsham informed me that two rifled ten-pound solid shots passed close by his back, between it and his horse's rump. Several passed above his head, the wind of which was felt by him. Another passed so near to his face that he felt the gust of the concussion of the air. Several others passed between his body and his horse's head, and a charge of grape passed under his horse without injuring him. The skin of his horse, however, was barked in several places, but the animal was not disabled.

When Capt. N. was riding into the fort, he discovered a very remarkable looking gun lying near the breastworks. Near by was a rebel who had it in charge. The Captain told the rebel he would take it in charge, when the rebel told him that it was the property of his Captain, named Naughton. Capt. Newsham replied that it would be safer in his hands than in those of the rebels, and giving the rebel his name, and telling him he would be responsible for it, he rode on. The gun referred to is most remarkable; it is a Turkish arm, the stock of which is of a peculiar shape, and very bulky. The bands of the piece are of pure silver, inlaid with figured gold and ivory. The barrel is of Damascus steel, three-quarters of an inch bore, and rifled. The gun is said to have cost eleven hundred dollars. The owner of it, Capt. Naughton, upon learning who had possession of it, Capt. Newsham having been described to him, said that Capt. N. was welcome to keep it; adding, at the same time, that he had taken deliberate aim at him with it eleven times, and had seldom before been known to miss his mark. Quite as much astonishment may be felt at the miraculous escape of General Smith, as he never for a moment screened himself from the continuous fire of the rebel cannon and musketry. It is said of him, that he was never seen to dodge a shot during the entire fight, while all the officers around him kept ducking their heads whenever the enemy's cannon belched forth their fearful messengers, but rode majestically along his lines and among his men, where ball, and shot, and shell fell like showers of hail around him, as though some revelation had given him assurance of safety.

At one time, while swinging his sword above his head, a ten-pound solid shot passed between his arm and head, another passed in such close proximity to his head as to raise his cap, and a spent grapeshot struck him in the stomach. There were fourteen mounted men, his staff, and orderlies, attending upon Gen. Smith, and, strange to relate, not one of them was hit, although men were struck down by shot and shell between their horses and on all sides of them. Gen. Smith showed himself a true soldier in sharing the same hardships with his men, as on the night of the battle, and preceding the surrender, he slept by the side of a log, wrapped in his blankets, without any tent to cover him from the inclemency of the weather, his feet towards his camp-fire, with the cold so intense that his blankets caught fire at his feet and burned into his boots before he felt the heat.

The following is a statement of a very remarkable and praiseworthy case of a young man attached to the Thirty-first regiment of Illinois volunteers (Colonel John A. Logan). He received a musket-shot wound in the right thigh, the ball passing through the intervening flesh, and lodging in the left thigh. The boy repaired to the rear, and applied to the doctor to dress his wound. He, however, manifested a peculiar reserve in the matter, requesting the doctor to keep his misfortune a secret from his comrades and officers.

He then asked the surgeon if he would dress his wound at once in order that he might be enabled to return to the fight. The surgeon told him that he was not in a condition to admit of his return, and that he had better go to the hospital; but the young brave insisted upon going back, offering as an argument in favor of it the fact that he had fired twenty-two rounds after receiving his wound, and he was confident he could fire as many more after his wound should be dressed. The surgeon found he could not prevent his returning to the field; so he attended to his wants, and the young soldier went off to rejoin his comrades in their struggle, and remained, dealing out his ammunition to good account until the day was over, as if nothing had happened to him. Several days after, he returned to the doctor to have his wound re-dressed, and continued to pay him daily visits in his leisure hours, attending to duty in the mean time.

A case in some particulars not dissimilar to the above is related of a boy about eleven years old, whose father, a volunteer, had been taken prisoner by the rebels some time before. The boy smuggled himself on board one of the transports at Cincinnati, laden with troops for this point. On the field, the morning of the great fight, he joined the Seventy-eighth Ohio, and being questioned by one of the officers, he told him of his father having been taken prisoner, and, having no mother, he had no one to care for him, and he wanted to fight his father's captors. The officer tried to get him to turn back, but he was not to be denied. So he succeeded in obtaining a musket, and went into the thickest of the battle. He finally by degrees crept up within a short distance of the rebel intrenchments, and posted himself behind a tree, from which he kept firing as often as he could see a head to fire at. He was soon discovered by the enemy's sharpshooters, who endeavored to drive him away from his position, as he kept picking them off very frequently. One of the rebels, who was outside of the work, got sight on the boy with his rifle, but before he got his piece off, the little warrior fired, and down went Mr. Rebel. As the rebel had a fine Minie rifle, the boy ran out and picked it up, taking time to get pouch and balls, together with his knapsack, while the bullets were flying on all sides of him; and then he retreated to his wooden breastwork, where he renewed his fire, and with a little better success.; and, after being in the fight all day, he returned to the Seventy-eighth at night with his prizes. This story might appear incredible for one so young to be the hero, but it is vouched for by a number of officers and men who saw the boy on the field and in the position mentioned, and many saw him shoot the rebel referred to, besides several others.

Another case, very similar to the last, is that of one of Birge's sharpshooters, who succeeded in getting within speaking distance of the fort, where he planted himself behind a stump, and by his unerring aim, succeeded in keeping one of their guns silent during the whole day. As fast as the men appeared to man it, they were let down by a shot from his rifle. Every effort was made to dislodge him from his death-dealing position, but without effect. He kept it until the rebels, finding it to be certain death to attempt to man the gun, completely abandoned it. This case has been presented to General Grant, and will doubtless receive, as it should, special mention.

A surprising case of escape from instantaneous death is presented by one of the surgeons who was on the field during the day. A private in the Eighteenth Illinois regiment was struck in the thigh by a twelve-pound round shell, which buried itself in the thigh, but did not explode. It was cut out on the field by Dr. Davis, surgeon of the Eighteenth Illinois regiment. The limb was, of course, terribly shattered, rendering amputation necessary.

An instance of unprecedented endurance and patience occurred at the hospital on the right wing. The columns having been forced back,

6

the hospital, which was a little up from the road, had come within range of the rebels' fire, and was fast becoming an unpleasant position, but no damage was done to it. Just about this time, a poor fellow came sauntering leisurely along, with the lower part of his arm dangling from the part above the elbow, it having been struck with a grape-shot. Meeting the surgeon in the house, who was busily attending to other wounded, he inquired how long it would be before he could attend to him, and was told, in a few minutes. "All right," said the wounded man, and then walked outside and watched the progress of the battle for a short time, and then returned and waited the surgeon's opportunity to attend to him. The arm was amputated without a murmur from the unfortunate man. After the stump was bound up, the young man put his good hand into his pocket and took out a piece of tobacco, from which he took a chew, then walking over to the fire, he leaned his well arm against the mantel-piece, and rested his head against his arm, and kept squirting tobacco-juice into the fire, whilst his eyes were cast into the flames, all with the most astonishing composure, as though he was indulging in some pleasant reverie. He remained in this position for some time, then walked off, and went out of sight near where the fighting was going on.

A young man came strolling down to the transport with one arm amputated; and in the well hand he held three chickens, which he had captured. A steward of one of the boats stepped up to him, and asked him if he wanted to sell the chickens. He looked at the chickens for a little while, and replied, "Well, no. I had so much trouble in catching the d—d things, I believe I'll eat 'em myself;" and off he went with his *fowl* prisoners.

Orderly-Sergeant Charles A. Bedard, Company H. of the immortal Eleventh Illinois, was killed in the morning fight of the 15th inst. He was a brother of Frank W. Bedard, of the St. Charles Hotel, at Cairo. His bravery and coolness on the field during a most terrific fire from the enemy are spoken of in the most praiseworthy terms by officers and men. His only attention during the severest of the fight appeared to be in keeping his men in line, and preventing disorder in the ranks, moving along in the face of the foe, watching with jealous care his men in charge, as on he pushed, loading, firing, and reloading his piece.

THE PICKET GUARD.

BY MRS. HOWLAND.

"ALL quiet along the Potomac," they say,
"Except now and then a stray picket
Is shot, as he walks on his beat to and fro,
By a rifleman in the thicket.
'Tis nothing — a private or two, now and then,
Will not count in the news of the battle;
Not an officer lost — only one of the men,
Moaning out, all alone, the death-rattle."

All quiet along the Potomac to-night,
Where the soldiers lie peacefully dreaming;
Their tents, in the rays of the clear autumn moon,
Or the light of the watch-fires, are gleaming.
A tremulous sigh, as the gentle night wind
Through the forest leaves softly is creeping;
While stars up above, with their glittering eyes,
Keep guard — for the army is sleeping.

There's only the sound of the lone sentry's tread,
As he tramps from the rock to the fountain,
And thinks of the two in the low trundle-bed,
Far away in the cot on the mountain.
His musket falls slack — his face, dark and grim,
Grows gentle with memories tender,
As he mutters a prayer for the children asleep —
For their mother — may Heaven defend her!

The moon seems to shine just as brightly as then,
That night, when the love yet unspoken
Leaped up to his lips — when low, murmured vows
Were pledged to be ever unbroken.
Then drawing his sleeve roughly over his eyes,
He dashes off tears that are welling,
And gathers his gun closer up to its place,
As if to keep down the heart-swelling.

He passes the fountain, the blasted pine tree —
The footstep is lagging and weary;
Yet onward he goes, through the broad belt of light,
Towards the shades of the forest so dreary.
Hark! was it the night-wind that rustled the leaves?
Was it moonlight so wondrously flashing?
It looked like a rifle — "Ha! MARY, good-by!"
And the life-blood is ebbing and plashing.

All quiet along the Potomac to-night —
No sound save the rush of the river;
While soft falls the dew on the face of the dead —
The picket's off duty forever.

THE TONE OF BULLETS. — A soldier, writing from one of the camps on the Potomac, thus alluded to the peculiar music made by bullets passing through the air: "It is a very good place to exercise the mind, with the enemy's picket rattling close at hand. A musical ear can study the different tones of the bullets as they skim through the air. I caught the pitch of a large-sized Minie yesterday — it was a swell from E flat to F, and as it passed into the distance and lost its velocity, receded to D — a very pretty change. One of the most startling sounds is that produced by the Hotchkiss shell. It comes like the shriek of a demon, and the bravest old soldiers feel like ducking when they hear it. It is no more destructive than some other missiles, but there is a good deal in mere sound to work upon men's fears.

"The tremendous scream is caused by a ragged edge of lead, which is left on the shell. In favorable positions of light, the phenomenon can sometimes be seen, as you stand directly behind a gun, of the clinging of the air to the ball. The ball seems to gather up the atmosphere, and carry it along, as the earth carries its atmosphere through space. Men are frequently killed by the wind of a cannon-shot. There is a law which causes the atmosphere to cling to the earth, or which presses upon it with a force, at the surface, of fifteen pounds to the square inch; does the same law, or a modification, pertain to cannon-balls in flight? I do not remember of meeting with a discussion of the subject in any published work. It is certainly an interesting philosophic question."

AN INCIDENT OF ROMNEY.—While the National forces were standing under the enemy's fire, on the day of the battle at Romney, Va., and the shot and shell were flying in every direction around us, a little incident occurred which is worthy of notice.

Capt. Butterfield, of the Eighth Ohio regiment, (being one of the ranking Captains,) acted as Major upon that occasion, and was obliged to ride an old sorrel horse, which had been used as a team horse, and required both spurs and whip, which the Captain had provided himself with, the latter cut from a tree, and about five feet long. It was found that our small six-pound guns would not reach the enemy's battery, and Col. Mason ordered Capt. B. to bring forward a brass twelve-pounder, which was in the rear. Off sped the old sorrel and his brave rider, and in a few moments up came the gun. Its position was assigned, and made ready for the match, but the Captain came dashing back in front of the gun, and the smell of powder, or something else, had made the old sorrel almost unmanageable, for in trying to wheel him from the front of the gun, the more the Captain applied the whip and spur, the more the old sorrel would not go. This kept the gunners in terrible suspense, for much depended on that shot. Finally, the Captain finding his efforts to move his steed fruitless, he sang out, at the top of his voice, "Never mind the old horse; blaze away;" and, sure enough, they did blaze away, and it proved a good shot, for it caused the rebels to limber up their battery, and take to their heels. At that moment, orders came to charge, and off dashed the old sorsel, frightened at the discharge of the gun, which had scorched his tail, and mingled in the charge. He was lost to view until he arrived in the town, where he was brought to a halt, and the Captain, standing in his stirrups. with his cap flying, cheered for the glorious victory that had been achieved.

A DYING SOLDIER PRAYS FOR THE PRESIDENT.—Never, until we stood by the grave of the Green Mountain boy, did we realize how much stranger is truth than fiction. A private was court-martialed for sleeping on his post out near Chain Bridge, on the Upper Potomac. He was convicted; his sentence was death; the finding was approved of by the General, and the day fixed for his execution. He was a youth of more than ordinary intelligence; he did not beg for pardon, but was willing to meet his fate.

The time drew near; the stern necessity of war required that an example should be made of some one; his was an aggravated case. But the case reached the ears of the President; he resolved to save him; he signed a pardon and sent it out; the day came. "Suppose," thought the President, "my pardon has not reached him." The telegraph was called into requisition; an answer did not come promptly. "Bring up my carriage," he ordered. It came; and soon the important state papers were dropped, and through the hot broiling sun and dusty roads he rode to the camp, about ten miles, and saw that the soldier was saved!

He had, doubtless, forgotten the incident, but the soldier did not. When the Third Vermont charged upon the rifle-pits, the enemy poured a volley upon them. The first man who fell, with six bullets in his body, was William Scott, of Company K. His comrades caught him up, and as his life-blood ebbed away, he raised to heaven, amid the din of war, the cries of the dying, and the shouts of the enemy, a prayer for the President, and as he died he remarked to his comrade that he had shown he was no coward, and not afraid to die.

He was interred, in the presence of his regiment, in a little grove, about two miles to the rear of the rebel fort, in the centre of a group of holly and vines; a few cherry trees, in full bloom, are scattered around the edge. In digging his grave a skull and bones were found, and metal buttons, showing that the identical spot had been used in the revolutionary war for our fathers who fell in the same cause. The chaplain narrated the circumstance to the boys, who stood around with uncovered heads. He prayed for the President, and paid the most glowing tribute to his noble heart that we ever heard. The tears started to their eyes as the clods of earth were thrown upon him in his narrow grave, where he lay shrouded in his coat and blanket.

The men separated; in a few minutes all were engaged in something around the camp, as though nothing had happened unusual; but that scene will live upon their memories while life lasts; the calm look of Scott's face, the seeming look of satisfaction he felt, still lingered; and could the President have seen him, he would have felt that his act of mercy had been wisely bestowed.

ADVENTURES OF TWO HOOSIER SOLDIERS.—A couple of boys, of the Twenty-sixth Indiana regiment, Marshall Storey and William Waters, were sent with despatches to Independence, Mo., distant from Sedalia ninety miles. They were dressed as citizens, without arms or papers that would detect them if captured or examined. The despatches were snugly secreted in their hats and boots. Their route was directly through the country infested by the bands of jayhawkers under the famous guerrilla chief Quantrell. The boys made their way without molestation, until within about twenty miles of Independence, when, passing through the brush, they were halted by five shot-gun armed rebels, who ordered them off their horses and demanded their business. The boys said they were hunting for a horse which had been stolen by some home-guards, and, as they had learned, taken through that part of the country. They protested that they were secesh of the right stripe, and lived six miles north of Booneville. They were, however, searched. Finding nothing but a few fishing-hooks, which Marsh had in his vest-pocket, and which the rebels appropriated, they were allowed to go on their way. The boys, thinking all safe now, pushed on ; but in crossing a neck of woods about five miles farther on, they were again called to a halt by a band of seven men, armed in the regular jayhawking style, who were some fifty yards from them. Marsh, whose wit is ready on all occasions, whispered to his companion that he would " play crazy." Waters should be his brother, taking him home from St. Louis. Marsh has a peculiar way of drawing one eye down, which makes him look rather comical. This, with the slobber running down his dusty whiskers, and his long hair hanging over his forehead, enabled him to play the game successfully. As soon as they came near, he jumped off his horse and ran towards them, and Waters yelled out : " Don't mind him ; he's crazy ; he don't know what he's doing." Marsh looked very foolishly at their clothes, guns, horses, &c. He became particularly fond of a pretty black pony, which he concluded he must have instead of the poor old horse he had been riding, and even got on the pony and started off. This tickled all the rebels except the owner of the pony, who caught him and jerked him off. Marsh, to carry on the joke, gathered a stick of wood and made fight. This caused the others to yell with laughter. Waters came to his rescue, and told them not to provoke him, as it made him worse. In the mean time, Waters had been searched from head to foot, but with no better success than rewarded the first hand. Waters tried to get Marsh on his horse ; but no, he must have the pony, which he almost fought for. Finally, one of the band came forward and assisted Waters. Marsh very reluctantly left pony and rebels. As soon as they were out of sight, they put spurs to their nags, and reached Independence, after a ride, including the two stops, of four hours.

A PATRIOTIC BLACKSMITH. — Before the departure of the 14th New York regiment for the war, a man, who carried on a blacksmith shop in connection with two of his sons, went to the headquarters, and concluded to enlist. He said that he could leave the blacksmith business in the hands of the boys. He couldn't stand it any longer, and go he must. He was enlisted.

Next day down comes the oldest of the boys. The blacksmith's business "wasn't very drivin'," and he guessed John could take care of it." "Well," said the old man, "go it." And the oldest son went it. But the following day John made his appearance. He felt lonesome, and had

shut up the shop. The father remonstrated, but the boy would enlist, and enlist he did. Now the old gentleman had two more sons, who "worked the farm" near Flushing, Long Island. The military fever seems to have run in the family ; for no sooner had the father and two older brothers enlisted, than the younger sons came in for a like purpose. The *paterfamilias* was a man of few words, but he said that he "wouldn't stand this anyhow." The blacksmith business might go to — some other place, but the farm must be looked after. So the boys were sent home. Presently one of them reappeared. They had concluded that one could manage the farm, and had tossed up who should go with the Fourteenth, and he had won the chance.

This arrangement was finally agreed to. But on the day of departure the last boy of the family was on hand to join, and on foot for marching. The old man was somewhat puzzled to know what arrangement could have been made which would allow all of the family to go : but the explanation of the boy solved the difficulty. "Father," said he, with a confidential chuckle in the old man's ear, "I've let the farm on shares !" The whole family, father and four sons, went with the Fourteenth regiment.

A SENTIMENTAL YOUNG LADY in Northern Georgia indited the following to some of her admirers in the —— " Ridgeament : "

" 'Tis hard for youens to sleep in camp;
    'Tis hard for youens to fight;
    'Tis hard for youens through snow to tramp ;
    In snow to sleep at night ;
But harder for weans from youens to part,
Since youens have stolen weans hearts."

INCIDENTS IN THE BATTLE OF WILDCAT. — The hill upon which it took place is a round, lofty elevation, a third of a mile from our camp, surrounded by deeply-wooded ravines, and cleared for the space of about two acres on top. To take and hold this, Col. Coburn, with half his regiment, dashed off through the bushes in a trot from the camp, like boys starting out on a turkey hunt. In ten minutes they could be seen on the high summit taking places. Very shortly they were fired on ; the fact is, it was a scramble between Coburn's men and Zollicoffer's which should get on the hill first, approaching from opposite directions. When the firing had fairly commenced, at intervals in the roar could be heard, in the camp, the shrill, wild voices of Coburn, and Durham, his adjutant, crying out, " Give them hell, boys ! " " Dose them with cold lead ! " " Shoot the hounds ! " " Load up, load up, for God's sake ! " " Give it to old Gollywhopper ! " Then the boys would cheer and yell till the glens re-echoed.

Capt. Dille, during the fight, in rushing around and helping on the cause, ran astride a brier bush, the nethermost part of his unmentionables was torn, and a flag of white cotton was seen flaunting in the air. One of the boys said, " Captain, it can't be said of you that you never turned tail on the enemy." By the way, the Captain is a heroic fellow, and did, as the boys say, "a big job of fighting." He has a queer old fellow in his company named John Memherter, a crack marksman, with a big goggle, rolling eye. John would take his tree, fire, and then move on a little. At one time he was peeping over a stump taking aim, when a ball struck the stump a few inches from the top at the opposite side, which knocked bark and splinters in his eyes. "Bully for Jake!" says John. This is now a cant phrase in the camp. "Bully for Jake" can be heard at all hours.

When Major Ward, of the Seventeenth Ohio, came over the hill with a part of the regiment, Col. Coburn took him down the hillside in front of the Kentuckians in a somewhat exposed place. Some one asked the Colonel why he put him there. "Well," said he, "I eyed him, and he looked like an old bull-dog; so I put him down where he could wool the hounds." The Major, you know, never before had a compliment paid to his homely, sturdy face, being rather hard-favored. Next day some of the boys got the joke on him by telling him they had heard his beauty complimented. He asked for the compliment, got it, and dryly remarked, "that it was rather an equivocal recommendation of his pretty face."

Almost every officer fought gun in hand, except Cols. Coburn and Woodford, who were armed with navies. Capt. Hauser, Adj. Durham, Capt. Dille, Lieuts. Maze and Scott, more than the men themselves, blazed away at the rebels. What could not men do with such examples set them. When part of the Kentucky boys fled, Capt. Alexander screamed out to the men, "Boys, if you are such damned cowards as to run, I'll stay and die." Instantly a boy scarce sixteen years old turned back, ran up to the Captain's side, saying, "Yes, Cap, and I'll stay and die with you." He did stay, and others followed his example. In the afternoon, when the fighting had ceased, General Schoepff came over to the hill, and taking Cols. Coburn and Woodford by the hand in the presence of the boys, thanked them for saving the hill, for it saved Camp Wildcat, and prevented a retreat of our whole force to the other side of the river. Just then a shower of balls whizzed around, and one knocking the dirt in his eyes, the General quietly rubbed it out, and looked around as unconcerned as if at dress parade. He is a noble-looking man, a Hungarian patriot, one of Gen. Bem's officers, who spent three years in Turkey with him drilling their army.

Just before the enemy made their charges, there could be seen two regiments in a neighboring field. One of the boys said to Col. Coburn, "We'll have to retreat." Another sturdy little fellow stepped up and swore he was not of the running kind, and he'd stay and fight anyhow. He got three cheers; so the boys concluded to stay, and did stay about there all that day and night. Such pluck makes one man equal to four. The boys captured an orderly sergeant's book, love

letters, a diary, &c., giving details up to the hour of battle. The utmost confidence in victory was expressed.

Since the battle, some of our boys were out looking at a grave of one of the secesh; he had not been well buried, and one hand stuck out. "He's reaching for his land warrant," says one.

When Col. Coburn and Capt. Dille were rallying the flying Kentuckians, the former found a crowd sheltered behind one stump: he cried out, "Pile out, pile out, boys; it don't take seventeen men to guard a black stump." It was electric; they after this fought like men.

THE IRISH WIT ALWAYS READY. — It is now known that the surrender of Lexington was rendered a necessity by the want of ammunition, as well as by the want of water. A few of the companies had one or two rounds left, but the majority had fired their last bullet. After the surrender, an officer was detailed by Price to collect the ammunition, and place it in safe charge. The officer, addressing Adjutant Cosgrove, asked him to have the ammunition surrendered. Cosgrove called up a dozen men, one after the other, and exhibiting the empty cartridge-boxes, said to the astonished rebel officer, "I believe, sir, we gave you all the ammunition we had before we had stopped fighting. Had there been any more, upon my word, you should have had it, sir. But I will inquire, and if by accident there is a cartridge left, I will let you know." The rebel officer turned away, reflecting upon the glorious victory of having captured men who had fired their last shot.

An Irishman, from Battle Creek, Michigan, was at Bull Run battle, and was somewhat startled when the head of his companion on the left hand was knocked off by a cannon-ball. A few moments after, however, a spent ball broke the fingers of his comrade on the other side. The latter threw down his gun and yelled with pain, when the Irishman rushed to him, exclaiming, "Blasht your soul, you ould woman, shtop cryin'; you make more noise about it than the man that losht his head!"

A WIFE ON THE BATTLE-FIELD. — The following extract from a letter, dated at Corinth, on the 6th of October, 1862, vividly portrays the fearful emotions and anxious thoughts which torture the mind of an observer during the progress of battle, and narrates but one of the many harrowing scenes of war:

"O, my friend! how can I tell you of the tortures that have nearly crazed me, for the last three days? Pen is powerless to trace, words weak to convey one tithe of the misery I have endured. I thought myself strong before. I have seen so much of suffering that I thought my nerves had grown steady, and I could bear anything; but to-day I am weak and trembling, like a frightened child.

"But do not wonder at it. My dear husband lies besides me, wounded unto death, perhaps. I have lost all hope of saving him, though I thank God for the privilege of being this moment beside him. And, besides this, all around me the sufferers lie moaning in agony. There has been little time to tend them, poor fellows. True, the surgeons are busy all the time, but all the wounded have not yet been brought in, and it seems as if the time will never come when our brave men shall have been made comfortable as circumstances may permit. It is awful to look around me. I can see every imaginable form of suffering, and yet am helpless to aid them any of consequence.

"Since night before last I have not left my husband's side for a moment, except to get such things as I required, or to hand some poor fellow a cup of water. Even as I write, my heart throbs achingly to hear the deep groans and sharp cries about me. F—— is sleeping, but I dare not close my eyes, lest he should die while I sleep. And it is to keep awake, and in a manner relieve my overburdened heart, that I am now writing you under such sad circumstances.

"On the morning of the third instant the fight began. The attack was made on Gen. McArthur's division, and we could plainly hear the roar of the artillery here, as it is about two miles and a half distant only from this place. O, the fearful agony of that awful, awful day! I had seen F—— a moment early in the morning, but it was only a moment, when he bade me good-by, saying, hurriedly, as he tore himself away: 'Pray for me, my wife, and if I fall, God protect you!' There was something in his look and tone which struck a chill to my heart, and every moment after I knew the fight had begun, I felt as if he had indeed fallen. I cannot tell how long it was before I heard that Oglesby's brigade was engaged, but it seemed an age to me. After that my agony was nearly intolerable. I never had a thought of fear for myself; I was thinking only of F——. Then I got the word that he had been hotly pursued by the rebels, and had fallen back.

"Late in the afternoon I succeeded in gaining a little intelligible information. Poor Gen. Hackleman was shot through the neck, while giving a command, and fell mortally wounded. He died between ten and eleven o'clock the same night, I have since learned. Up to the time of receiving the wound he had acted with the greatest bravery and enthusiasm, tempered by a coolness that made every action effective. When dusk at last put an end to the first day's conflict, I learned that Gen. Oglesby had been dangerously wounded, but could gain no intelligence of my husband. I could not bear the suspense. Dark as it was, and hopeless as it seemed to search for him then, I started out to the battle-field.

"O, *how* shall I describe the search of that night? It looked like madness. It *was* madness. But all night long I staggered amongst bleeding corpses, over dead horses, trampled limbs, shattered artillery—everything that goes to make up the horrors of a battle-field when the conflict is over. They were removing the wounded all night. O, think how awful to stumble over the dead, and hear the cries of the wounded and dying, alone, and in the night-time. I had to start off alone, else they would not have let me go.

"As you may suppose, I could not find him, either amongst the living or the dead. But the next morning, just after sunrise, I came to a little clump of timbers, where a horse had fallen—his head shot off, and his body half covering a man whom I supposed dead. His face was to the ground; but, as I stooped to look closer, I perceived a slight movement of the body, then heard a faint moan. I stooped and turned the face upward. The head and face were both covered with blood, but when I turned it to the light, I knew it in spite of its disfiguration. O God! the agony of that moment sickened me almost to suffocation. With a strength I thought impossible in me, I drew him, crushed and bleeding, from beneath the carcass of our poor old horse, whom we had both so loved and petted, and dipping my handkerchief in a little pool of water amongst the bushes, bathed his face, and pressed some moisture between his parched, swollen lips. He was utterly senseless, and there was a dreadful wound in his head. Both limbs were crushed hopelessly beneath his horse. He was utterly beyond the reach of human skill to save, but as soon as possible I had him conveyed to the hospital. I have nursed him ever since—hopelessly, and with a heart breaking with grief. O, how many wives, how many mothers, are to-day mourning the dead and dying, even as I mourn my dying! He has not opened his eyes to look at me, or spoken to me, since he fell. O, could he but speak to me once before he dies, I should give him up with more resignation. But to die thus—without a look or word! O, my heart is breaking!" ———

THE GUERRILLAS.

BY S. TEAKLE WALLIS.

Awake and to horse, my brothers!
  For the dawn is glimmering gray,
And hark! in the crackling brushwood
  There are feet that tread this way.

"Who cometh?" "A friend." "What tidings?"
  "O God! I sicken to tell;
For the earth seems earth no longer,
  And its sights are sights of hell!

"From the far-off conquered cities
  Comes a voice of stifled wail,
And the shrieks and moans of the houseless
  Ring out like a dirge on the gale.

"I've seen from the smoking village
  Our mothers and daughters fly;
I've seen where the little children
  Sank down in the furrows to die.

"On the banks of the battle-stained river
  I stood as the moonlight shone,
And it glared on the face of my brother
  As the sad wave swept him on.

"Where my home was glad are ashes,
And horrors and shame had been there,
For I found on the fallen lintel
This tress of my wife's torn hair !.

"They are turning the slaves upon us,
And with more than the fiend's worst art
Have uncovered the fire of the savage
That slept in his untaught heart!

"The ties to our hearths that bound him,
They have rent with curses away,
And maddened him, with their madness,
To be almost as brutal as they.

"With halter, and torch, and Bible,
And hymns to the sound of the drum,
They preach the gospel of murder,
And pray for lust's kingdom to come.

"To saddle ! to saddle ! my brothers !
Look up to the rising sun, .
And ask of the God who shines there
Whether deeds like these shall be done.

"Wherever the Vandal cometh
Press home to his heart with your steel,
And when at his bosom you cannot,
Like the serpent, go strike at his heel.

"Through thicket and wood go hunt him,
Creep up to his camp-fire side,
And let ten of his corpses blacken,
Where one of our brothers hath died.

'In his fainting foot-sore marches,
In his flight from the stricken fray,
In the snare of the lonely ambush,
The debts we owe him pay.

"In God's hand alone is vengeance,
But he strikes with the hands of men,
And his blight would wither our manhood
If we smite not the smiter again.

"By the graves where our fathers slumber,
By the shrines where our mothers prayed,
By our homes, and hopes, and freedom,
Let every man swear on his blade,

"That he will not sheath nor stay it,
Till from point to hilt it glow
With the flush of Almighty vengeance
In the blood of the felon foe."

They swore — and the answering sunlight
Leaped red from their lifted swords,
And the hate in their hearts made echo
To the wrath in their burning words.

There's weeping in all New England,
And by Schuylkill's banks a knell,
And the widows there, and the orphans,
How the oath was kept can tell.

THE SPIRIT OF '76. — While the Senate of Maryland were in session in the State House, at Annapolis, a number of soldiers entered the ante-room, and inquired if the Senate Chamber was not the place where Gen. Washington once stood. An employee of the House answered that it was, and showed one of them, as near as he could, the spot where Washington stood when he resigned his commission. The young man reverently approached the spot, and standing for several minutes apparently fixed to the place, hastily turned and left the chamber, exclaiming, that he could stand it no longer, for he "felt his Fourth of July rising too fast."

THE CRUISE OF THE ALABAMA.

NARRATED BY HER OFFICERS.

It was the 13th of August, 1862, that we left Liverpool in the chartered steamer Bahama, to the Western Isles, where we were to meet the Alabama, which had gone out before us to receive her armament, officers, and crew, for service. Our party consisted chiefly of the former officers of the Sumter — the gallant little vessel which created so much terror amongst the Yankee bottoms on the American coast, and although pursued by all the Federal fleet, crossed the Atlantic in winter with safety, and found a harbor refuge under the guns of Gibraltar. There, however, she was blockaded, and was sold on account of the Confederate States Government. She was re-purchased privately, and her hull was taken over to England, where she was to be refitted, and is now, no doubt, afloat again under another name, but still bearing proudly the Southern flag. Her officers followed their captain, ready to obey his orders, for all admired him as a skilful seaman, a good tactician, an excellent diplomatist, and a brave man. They spent a short time in England, when the Alabama, or 290, as she was then named, was purchased, and Capt. Semmes at once prepared to take command of her, under commission from President Davis, with the object of doing as much damage as possible to the enemy's commerce on the sea.

At Porta Praya, in the Island of Terceira, (Azores,) we found our ship taking in guns, ammunition, &c., which had been brought to this place by chartered vessels. The Alabama pleased us all. She is a fine ship of 1040 tons; the length of keel, 210 feet; breadth of beam, 32 feet; depth of hold, 17 feet 3 inches; has two engines combined of 300 horse power, and three furnaces, each below the water line; the diameter of her propeller is 14 feet, with two blades 3 feet in width and 21 feet pitch; and is capable of running 14 knots. She mounts eight guns — one rifled 7-inch Blakeley's patent, and one 8-inch shell or solid-shot gun, (pivots,) and six 32-pounders of forty-two hundred weight, (broadsides.) Her motto is: *Aide toi et Dieu t'aidera.* The officers numbered twenty, and the crew at this time only eighty — and the terms which the latter insisted upon on engaging called forth the remark from Capt. Semmes, that the modern sailor has greatly changed in character; for he now stickles for pay like a sharper, and seems to have lost his former love of adventure and recklessness. The ordinary seamen get as much as £4 10 per month; petty officers, £5 to £6; firemen, £7. All the officers held commissions from the Confederate States Government, and receive pay according to the regular scale, varying from £150 to £800 per annum.

On the 24th of August, the command of the Alabama was formally handed over by Capt. Bullock (who had brought her out from Liverpool) to Capt. Semmes; and the "Stars and Bars" were flung to the wind amid the cheers of all hands. The Captain called all the crew and explained to them the risks and dangers they would have to undergo, and the inducement of prize money; furthermore, he said he did not intend to rush headlong into battle with a whole fleet of the enemy, but that he did not intend to run away if he met with any, and that he would give battle to the last, so that he expected every man to do his duty. He did not wish to deceive or entice any one to go, and they were free to judge for themselves, either to stay in the Alabama or return with the Bahama to Liverpool. This speech had a good effect, and was loudly cheered, and very few left with the Bahama, which then parted company with us.

After leaving Terceira, several days were devoted to putting our ship in order and drilling the crew, who were mostly good seamen, but unacquainted with naval discipline. On the 5th September we caught our first prize, the Ockmulgee, off the Azores, and continued to cruise in that vicinity for about ten days, capturing and destroying several ships of the enemy. From the Azores we proceeded to the Banks of Newfoundland, and cruised thence in the direction of New York, capturing and destroying several other valuable ships. Among our seizures were the Starlight, on board of which we found some despatches for Secretary Seward; the Tonawanda, bound from New York to Liverpool, with seventy-five passengers, forty of whom were women; and the T. B. Wales, from Calcutta, with an American consul and his lady on board. We provided for them as well as possible — two of the ward-room officers giving up their rooms for them. The consul, however, got so troublesome and intermeddling, that Capt. Semmes had to tell him that he was only tolerated there on account of his lady; but if he again spoke to the men or his crew, he would be put in double irons and tied to the gun rack — which threat had its intended effect on the Yankee. The fate of the vessels captured was to be destroyed by fire, and the night effect of this spectacle at sea was sometimes very striking. One of the doomed vessels, the Levi Starbuck, was set on fire at six o'clock in the evening, and was one of the grandest sights ever witnessed by us. After the decks took fire, the flame sprang to the rigging, running from yard to yard, until it reached the royal truck, leaving half the canvas-head burnt away, and forming one mass of glittering stars; in a few minutes afterwards the powder charges exploded, tearing the vessel into a thousand pieces.

When within about 250 miles of New York, finding we had but four days' coal on board, Capt. Semmes bore off for the island of Martinique, where he had ordered a coal ship to rendezvous. On the way we captured and destroyed two very valuable ships. We reached Martinique on the 18th November, where we were received with enthusiasm by the inhabitants; but finding that our coal ship had been there a week or ten days, and that the object of her visit was well known, Capt. Semmes sent her out to sea again, appointing a new rendezvous. It was well that he did so, for she had not been gone twenty-four hours when the United States frigate San Jacinto arrived. Immediately she was seen, all our hands were called to quarters, ready for action, thinking the enemy would put his threat into force, of running into us, wherever he found us; but, as usual, it turned out to be their mode of gaining a victory. The San Jacinto kept moving in and out so long, that the Governor of the island boarded her, and ordered her either to come to anchor or proceed to sea, three miles clear of the land, which she obeyed, and lay to, blockading the port. Capt. Semmes determined to go out and fight her; but was advised against this by the French officer, who came on board of us, who said she was too heavy, as she carried twelve eight-inch broadside guns, and two eleven-inch pivots, with a crew of two hundred and fifty men. The Governor said that if we desired to take in coals, we must get under the guns of his fort, and he would protect us against Admiral Wilkes and his fleet; but as the bark with coals was sent off the day before, we concluded it was best to go to sea. So at eight o'clock that night we got ready for action, and steamed out of harbor, without any molestation from the enemy, who was keeping watch and ward a marine league off. We coaled at the Island of Blanquille, on the coast of Venezuela, the new rendezvous appointed; and here we found a United States whaling schooner, but forbore to capture her, because of the claim of Venezuela to the barren little island — a claim as barren as the island, for there was no settled population on it, and, of course, no vestige of government. There were only two or three fishermen's huts on the place; and we put ashore, with the brand of infamy, a seaman named Forest, who had deserted from the Sumter, and was captured on board one of our prizes; he was found guilty of inciting the crew to mutiny.

Desiring to strike a blow at the enemy, the Alabama, after coaling, sailed for the east end of Cuba, in the track of the California steamers. On our way we captured and destroyed a bark from Boston for Aux Cayes; on the 7th of November, after lying off Cape Maise for several days, we captured the U. S. steamer Ariel — unfortunately outward, instead of homeward bound. She was brought to by a shot which struck her mizzenmast. She had on board $8000 in United States treasury notes, and $1500 in silver; and as there was no certificate or other papers on board claiming it as neutral property, it was taken possession of as prize of war. There were one hundred and forty marines on board, with six officers, all of whom were disarmed and paroled, as was also Commander Saston, U. S. A., who was on board. As this ship had some seven hundred passengers and crew, many of whom were women and children, and it was alike impossible to take her into a neutral port, or to receive the passengers in the Alabama, there was no alternative but to release her under a ransom bond of $250,000; and as we parted company, the passengers gave three cheers for Capt. Semmes.

After this the Alabama hove to on the north side of Jamaica, to repair some damage which had happened to one of our engines, and then set out for the Accas Island, Gulf of Mexico, where we refilled with coal, and calked and repaired ship. Here some of our men erected on the island an epitaph in black, "To the memory of Abe Lincoln, who died January, 1861, of negro fever of the head," with a card on which was written, in Spanish, instructions to those who visit the island to forward the board to the nearest United States Consul.

On board the Ariel we found some New York papers containing accounts of an intended expedition by Gen. Banks, which we concluded was destined for Texas, and we presumed would rendezvous at Galveston. As it was said that the expedition was to consist of twenty thousand men, we knew a large number of transports would be required: many of these vessels would have to lie outside the bar, and we determined upon making a night attack upon forty or fifty of them, laden with troops, sink and set on fire many of them, and escape before our vessel could be pursued by a superior force. As it afterwards turned out, we found the expedition of Gen. Banks took another direction, and landed at New Orleans.

After coaling at Accas, however, the Alabama set sail for Galveston, and arrived there on the 11th January, and before nightfall made out the enemy's fleet lying off the bar, consisting of five ships of war. One of their steamers we observed to get under weigh, and come in our direction. Captain Semmes ordered steam to be got up, but kept sail on our vessel as a decoy, to entice the enemy's ship sufficiently far from the fleet to give battle. We wore ship, and stood away from the bar, permitting the enemy to approach by slow degrees. When she was sufficiently near we took in all sail, and wearing short round, ran up within hail. It was now dark, about nine o'clock. The enemy hailed: "What ship is that?" We replied: "Her Majesty's steamer Petrel." The reply was, "I'll send a boat on board."

We now hailed in turn, to know what the enemy was, and when we received the reply that she was the United States steamer Hatteras, we again hailed and informed him that we were the Confederate steamer Alabama; and at the same time Capt. Semmes directed the First Lieutenant to open fire on him. This fire was promptly returned, and a brisk action ensued, which lasted, however, only thirteen minutes, as at the end of that time the enemy fired an off-gun, and showed

a light; and on being hailed to know if he surrendered, he said he did, and was in a sinking condition. We immediately despatched boats to his assistance, and had just time to rescue the crew, when the ship went down. The casualties were slight on both sides, although the action was fought at a distance of one hundred and fifty to four hundred yards. Our shot all told on his hull, about the water-line, and hence the small number of killed and wounded on the part of the enemy — two of the former, and three of the latter. We had none killed, and only one wounded, although the Alabama received several shot-holes, doing no material damage. The Hatteras mounted eight guns, and had a crew of eighteen officers and one hundred and eight men. The Alabama had also eight guns, with a small captured piece, (a twenty-four-pounder, too light to be of any service,) and a crew of one hundred and ten men, exclusive of officers. Four of the Hatteras' guns were thirty-two pounders, the same calibre as our broadside guns, but our pivot guns were heavier than theirs. This was the only disparity between the two ships. The U. S. frigate Brooklyn and another steamer came out in pursuit soon after the action commenced, but missed us in the darkness of the night. The Alabama then proceeded to Kingston, Jamaica, where the prisoners were landed on the 20th January, and we repaired damages and coaled, and on the 25th proceed again to sea.

We touched at the Island of St. Domingo, on the 28th, to land two enemy's crews we had captured; sailed again next day for the Equator, and remained for some days at the Island of Fernando de Noronha. From thence we put into Bahia, where we landed more prisoners. The Government at this place demanded explanations of our proceedings at Fernando de Noronha, as the American Consul represented that we had made captures there in Brazilian waters; but as we clearly showed that no vessel had been taken within a prescribed distance from the island, the authorities were satisfied, and we were allowed to remain ten days, refitting. Meanwhile, the Castor, a coal ship, ostensibly bound for Shanghai, entered the port, and we commenced coaling from her. The American Consul again protested, and wrote to the President of Bahia, stating that the Castor had on board guns and sailors for the Confederates. The President next day forwarded this complaint to the English Consul at Bahia, inviting him to accompany the custom-house officers on board the Castor, to see whether the complaint had any foundation. The English Consul returned the following reply:

"The denunciation of the American Consul is devoid of foundation. The facts he has put forward are quite inexact. The opinion he expresses is entirely illusive. The English Consul has been on board the Castor; has ascertained that she does not carry arms; that her crew consists only of the men upon the ship's books; and that the only real fact of those alleged is her delivery of coal — a proceeding which it is the sole aim of the American Consul to prevent. The Consul is ready to be present at the visit proposed by the President. The Captain of the Castor is perfectly willing to permit such visit, but the Consul, in any case, protests against every act assuming the character of the right of search or of requisition by the Consul of the United States. He (the English Consul) entertains grave doubts of the American Consul's right, owing to the mere supply of coal, to raise any claim against an English ship, belonging to a neutral nation, at anchor in the harbor of Bahia, a neutral port. The neutrality resulting from the independent exercise of its right by a state cannot obstruct commercial relations, and a belligerent power is not entitled to demand their cessation in a neutral port between its opponent and the subjects of a neutral nation. Toleration by the President of the province of the supply of coal, by an English ship, to the Confederate cruisers in this port, cannot (without infringing common sense and international law) be considered a hostile act, contrary to the strict neutrality of Brazil."

The proposed visit on board the Castor took place, accompanied by interrogation of Captain and crew. The result showed no proof whatever of the allegations, although it seemed pretty clear that the cargo of coal had no other original destination than the Confederate privateers. The Captain of the Alabama, indeed, admitted the fact, plainly declaring that he had a perfect right to purchase coal in England, and to provide for its discharge taking place out of a neutral ship, within a neutral port. Capt. Semmes, at the same time, requested the President's authorization to continue taking in his coal. The President replied that the coal must be put on shore and sent to the market, where Capt. Semmes could buy as much as he pleased. He added that his instructions forbade him to allow the delivery of any kind of goods coming direct from another country, where the sale had taken place abroad. Under these circumstances, Captain Semmes directed the coal ship to meet him at Saldanha Bay, Cape of Good Hope. — and we left Bahia. On our passage to the Cape, we captured the S. Gildensleeve, the Justina, Jabez Snow, Amazonian, Talisman, Conrad, A. F. Schmidt, and Express — all valuable prizes except the Justina, which, being a Baltimore ship, was ransomed, and a number of the crews of the other vessels were transferred to her. The Amazonian attempted to elude us, but we gave chase, and while five miles distant from her, fired our rifle-gun, with a reduced charge of 7 lbs. powder and a 100-pound shot, at an extreme elevation, which crossed her bows, and she soon clewed her courses and hove to.

The Conrad, which we captured, was a fine bark, and we fitted her out as a tender to the Alabama. The vessel was named the Tuscaloosa, and commissioned at sea on the 21st June. The command was given to Lieut. Lowe, an excellent officer, with fifteen men; she was provided with two brass rifled twelve-pounders, pistols, rifles, and ammunition, and having provisions for three months, was ordered to cruise in the direction of the Cape. We then made for Saldanha Bay, where we anchored and repaired ship, expecting to meet the coal vessel; but nothing could be seen of her, and we supposed she must have met with some mishap.*

From Saldanha Bay we came round to Table Bay, and spied the American bark Sea Bride, standing into port, outside of all headlands, and at a distance from the main land. As we approached her, our officers were directed by the Captain to make observation of the distance; and all agreed that the capture was made from two to three miles outside of the marine league.

The total number of our captures has been fifty-six ships, by which we estimate the damage to the enemy to be not less than four million dollars, to say nothing of the indirect results of the cruise in the way of loss of freights, high war insurance, and numerous sales of enemy's ships, to put them under neutral flags. In no instance, however, have we destroyed a ship where the proof was complete that the cargo was neutral, though there have been some awkward attempts on the part of unscrupulous merchants to cover property, — but when such were destroyed the proof of the fraud was apparent on the papers.

The following is a complete list of her captures:

Ockmulgee,	Chastalaire,
Starlight,	Palmetto,
Ocean Rover,	Golden Eagle,
Alert,	Olive Jane,
Weathergauge,	Washington,
Altamaha,	Betha Thager,
Benjamin Tucker,	J. A. Parker,
Courser,	Punjaub,
Virginia,	Morning Star,
Elisha Dunbar,	Kingfisher,
Brilliant,	Charles Hill,
Emily Farnum,	Nora,
Wave Crest,	Louisa Hatch,
Dunquerque,	Lafayette,
Manchester,	Kate Corey,
Tonawanda,	Nye,
Lamplighter,	Dorcas Price,
Lafayette,	Lelah,
Crenshaw,	Union Jack,
Lauretta,	S. Gildensleeve,
Baron De Castine,	J. Snow,
Levi Starbuck,	Justina,
T. B. Wales,	Amazonian,

* If the Castor was the vessel expected, it is very probable that some mishap occurred to her; for by late Rio papers we learn that after the Alabama left, the Federal steam frigate Mohican put in at Bahia, and a report was immediately circulated that she intended to seize the Castor. The Captain of the English vessel attempted to leave the port without having complied with the forms required by the customs. He was brought to by the guns of the forts, and put back, and went through the accustomed formalities preparatory to setting sail anew. Before the Castor was outside the harbor, the Mohican got up steam and went in pursuit. Perceiving himself chased, the Captain of the Castor determined not to leave the port, but to place himself under the protection of Brazilian ships until the arrival of an English man-of-war. Thereupon the Mohican left Bahia to look after the Confederate privateers.

Martha,
Union,
Ariel, mail steamer,
U. S. gunb't Hatteras,
Golden Rule,

Talisman,
Conrad,
A. F. Schmidt,
Express,
Sea Bride.

The Alabama had the usual quota of wits and fun-makers among her crew. An Irish fiddler on board is the life of the forecastle. When the men are off duty he sets them dancing to his lighter strains, or, dividing them into Northerners and Southerners, like a true Irishman, he gets up a sham fight to the spirit-stirring strains of a march, in which fight the Northerners are, of course, invariably beaten. Another sailor, Frank Townshend, is no mean poet, as will be seen from the verses which here follow. He had sung the exploits of their beloved ship to his messmates in rude and vigorous strains.

THE FIGHT OF THE "HATTERAS" AND "ALABAMA."

Off Galveston, the Yankee fleet secure at anchor
  lay,
Preparing for a heavy fight they were to have next
  day;
Down came the Alabama, like an eagle o'er the
  wave,
And soon their gunboat Hatteras had found a watery grave.

'Twas in the month of January; the day was bright
  and clear;
The Alabama she bore down; no Yankee did we
  fear:
Their Commodore he spied us; to take us long he
  burned;
So he sent the smartest boat he had, but she never
  back returned!

The sun had sunk far in the West when down to
  us she came;
Our Captain quickly hailed her, and asked them
  for her name;
Then spoke our First Lieutenant, — for her name
  had roused his ire, —
"This is the Alabama — now, Alabamas, fire."

Then flew a rattling broadside, that made her timbers shake;
And through the holes made in her side the angry
  waves did break;
We then blew up her engine, that she could steam
  no more —
They fired a gun to leeward, and so the fight was
  o'er.

So thirteen minutes passed away before they gave
  in beat;
A boat had left the Yankee's side, and pulled in for
  their fleet;
The rest we took on board of us, as prisoners to
  stay;
Then stopped and saw their ship go down, and then
  we bore away.

And now, to give our foes their due, they fought
  with all their might;
But yet they could not conquer us, for God defends the right;

One at a time the ships they have to fight us they
  may come,
And rest assured that our good ship from them will
  never run.

THE "STARS AND BARS."

See yonder bright flag, as it floats on the breeze;
It is feared by its foes, though young on the seas;
As a bird on the ocean, 'tis met all alone,
But a deed of dishonor it never has known.
In defending its rights, much blood has been shed;
As an emblem of this, see its borders all red.
Then look at the centre, the blue and the white —
An assurance our cause is true, just, and right.
O, long may it float o'er the ocean's dark breast,
Till sun, moon, and stars sink forever to rest;
And its gallant defenders forever prove true;
With this wish, flag of freedom, I'll bid thee adieu!
With this wish, flag of freedom, I'll bid thee adieu!

THE SOUTH, BOYS.

Hark, hark! there's a sound in the West,
  That's wafted far over the sea;
'Tis the voice of the brave, though oppressed,
  That are struggling hard to be free.
Basely wronged they have been by a brother,
  Who sought to oppress in his might;
But the South, boys, the South, boys, forever!
  'Tis the cause that we all know is right.

To shake off the yoke of a tyrant,
  Their forefathers fought side by side;
And ere they could claim Freedom's Charter,
  Many hundreds of brave men had died;
But the Eagle, that then soared so proudly,
  Can now scarcely look on the light;
But the South, boys, the South, boys, forever!
  'Tis the cause that we all know is right.

A Tableau. — A correspondent describes a tableau, given at Murfreesboro', Tenn., for the benefit of the soldiers, on the 22d of January, 1862, as follows:

"We should not do justice to the tableau, unless we were to describe the first scene. A young gentleman, representing King Cotton, sat upon a throne resembling a bale of cotton. Down on one side of the throne sat a representative of the ebon race, with a basket of cotton. The king held a cotton cloth as a sceptre, and one of his feet rested on a globe. Around him stood young ladies dressed in white, with scarfs of red and white looped on the shoulder with blue. On their heads they wore appropriate crowns. These represented the Confederate States. Missouri and Kentucky were guarded by armed soldiers.

"While we were gazing on this picture, a dark-haired maiden, robed in black, with brow encircled by a cypress-wreath, and her delicate wrists bound with clanking chains, came on and knelt before his majesty. He extended his sceptre, and she arose. He waved his wand again, and an armed soldier appeared with a scarf and crown, like those worn by her sister States. He unchained this gentle girl at the bidding of his monarch, changed her crown of mourning for one of joy and liberty, and threw the Confederate flag across her, raised the flag over her, and led her forward; then Kentucky advanced, took her by the hand, and led her into the ranks. Need we tell you whom this maiden of sable garments was intended to represent? We leave that to be understood. If your readers cannot divine, it is owing to our description, and not to the scene. The ceremony was performed in pantomime.

"We will gratify the pride of the F. F. V.'s by saying that their representative had inscribed on her crown, '*Mater Heroum*.' After this attempt to praise you, dear *Express*, you will surely pardon us if we tell you that North Carolina wore on her brow a white crown, on which was the word 'Bethel.' Both of these States were represented by their own daughters."

A STRANGE SCENE for a Sabbath day is presented to a visitor, who will stand on one of the hills back of Alexandria, and look around him. Thousands of camps dot the hillsides, which are whitened by whole villages of them as far as the eye can extend. Frowning fortifications crown every hill, while innumerable roads and paths cross from one to the other, intersecting at all angles. The valleys are filled with soldiers, who are strolling about for wood, water, and various other purposes. Here and there horsemen are seen galloping from camp to camp. Guards are stationed in every direction, pacing regularly to and fro, and a strange activity, yet military precision, marks the whole. The ruin and desolation, as well as the "pomp, pride, and circumstance of glorious war," are the distinguishing features of the whole scene.

Yonder, amid all this strange sight, is a funeral procession. In front, mounted on a splendid charger, rides the chaplain. He is followed by a full band of music, from which come the saddening, yet thrilling and solemn tones of a dirge, whose reverberations startle many a warrior from his toil, to look on the solemn procession as it passes. Following these is the ambulance with the remains, escorted by a few companions of the deceased. Another soldier has gone to rest, far from home and friends. Who is he? "Only a private!" "Henry Sleeper, Company H, 13th New Hampshire, died November 15, 1862," will be the simple record on his regimental rolls, and on the rude board, placed on the sacred soil where sleeps the brave, and then he will be forgotten. Fond friends in the distant home will weep for a time, almost broken-hearted, and then he will be remembered only by the wife or mother, who will, in after years, tell of the loved one who lost his life in suppressing the great Southern rebellion. Virginia will, indeed, be "sacred soil" to many an aching heart all over our land — sacred as the resting-place of the flower of thousands of families. — *Nov. 1862.*

A YOUNG PATRIOT. — The following was written by a young Bostonian, who was engaged in mercantile business at the place from which he dates his letter:

NEW YORK, July 29, 1862.

My Dear Father and Mother: I wrote you a day or two ago on passing events. Now I write on the subject that lies nearest my heart. The country calls for men, and we must have them! Recruiting lags, and we are in danger of a draft. It is now useless to say there are enough men without me. It is not the fact. I want to volunteer; and had I a hundred lives I would now place them at the disposal of the Government, for it needs all the young men who can be spared, and I am one who can. Let me calmly state the case to you. First, if the rebellion succeeds, we shall have the disintegration of our country to look upon. We shall not have North and South alone, but after that, State will separate from State, county from county, and then it may be every man for himself. Then will commence a series of wars none of us could see the end of. The stronger State will make war on the weaker, and the successful military commander would assume power. We should have military despotism and anarchy alternately. If we succeed, all will be peace, and we shall enjoy the freedom of institutions, and the perfect liberty we have hitherto enjoyed.

Then you must acknowledge the power to do, or not to do, lies with ourselves. We have the men, but they must come forward. Money we have, and we must use it. The South are terribly in earnest. The North *are fast asleep*, compared with them. We are fighting for life, for our old institutions, for nationality, for all we hold most dear. The South are endeavoring to destroy all these, and to prevent them *we must have men*. We *must* conquer. We *can* if we use our means. If the South conquer, I don't want to live in this country any longer. Now I acknowledge that a father's and a mother's love is one of the greatest blessings a young man can enjoy, next to the favor of God himself; but that love descends to selfishness when it restrains a young man from his manifest duty. The love for parents, and fear of their displeasure if they disobey them, are what hold many hundred young men from joining our noble army.

Let all such restrictions be removed, and our ranks will swell with twice the rapidity they are now doing. My duty is to go — yours to let me go. The duties of the country at large are patience, steadfastness, hope, and prayer. A very fine preacher here says: "Pray for your dying son, but pray for your country more than ten thousand sons." The love of money must be put down. What good is money going to do us if we have no country to live in? I don't want a living if I have not a country. Hoping, praying, trusting, you will accede to my wishes, I await an answer. My name is on the militia rolls; so I am subject to draft; and sooner than have me go with drafted men here, I know you will let me go in a Massachusetts regiment. I have written this letter after weeks of deliberation, and in no sudden burst of enthusiasm.

INCIDENTS OF A FIGHT WITH MOSBY.

FAIRFAX COURT HOUSE, June 2, 1863. — The sun glistens on a twelve-pound brass howitzer, which, with its limber, occupies a position directly in front of Gen. Stahl's headquarters. The story of the gun is this : Made in the year 1859, it was used by the Union troops at Ball's Bluff, where it fell into the hands of the rebels, and since that time has done service in the rebel army. After Mosby had been whipped several times by Stahl's cavalry, this gun was furnished him to redeem his laurels. On Friday night last, Mosby, with about one hundred and seventy-five men and the howitzer, camped at Greenwich. Early on Saturday they made a hurried march toward the Orange and Alexandria Railroad, which they struck about one and a half miles this side of Catlett's Station. Here they concealed themselves in the woods, placed the howitzer in position, and awaited the arrival of the train from Alexandria, carrying forage and stores to Bealeton. As the cars came opposite the ambuscade, a rail, adroitly displaced, caused the locomotive to run off the track. At this moment a ball from the gun went through the boiler, and another pierced the smoke-stack. The guard upon the train were scared by hearing artillery, and beat a hasty retreat, leaving the train at the disposition of the rebels. Had any resistance been offered, it is believed that the train could have been saved, and all the rebels captured. As it was, the guerrillas destroyed the cars, ten in number, and then, anticipating a visit from Stahl's cavalry, made off in the direction of Auburn. Meanwhile, Col. Mann, of the Seventh Michigan cavalry, who was in command of the portion of Stahl's cavalry at Bristow, hearing the firing, started with portions of the Fifth New York, First Vermont, and Seventh Michigan, to learn the cause. Taking the precaution to send the Fifth New York, Capt. A. H. Hasbrouck commanding, across the country to Auburn, to intercept the retreat, he followed up the railroad until the sight of the burning train told that portion of the story. Leaving the burning train, Col. Mann followed the track of the retreating foe, and soon heard the sound of cannon towards Greenwich, indicating that Capt. Hasbrouck, with the Fifth New York, had either intercepted or come up with the enemy. As it afterwards proved, they had come upon their rear, and had been fired upon from the howitzer. Owing to the nature of the ground, the Fifth New York was unable to deploy, so as to operate effectively, and the enemy again started on the run, closely followed by Capt. Hasbrouck and his command. Col. Mann pressed on to reach the scene of the firing. Learning the particulars of their escape, he divided his force, sending Lieut.-Col. Preston, with part of the First Vermont cavalry, to reënforce the Fifth New York, and with the balance he

struck across the country, again hoping to intercept them.

Finding themselves so hotly pressed, the enemy, when near Grapewood Farm, about two miles from Greenwich, took position at the head of a short, narrow lane, with high fences on either side, placing the howitzer so as to command the lane, strongly supported by his whole force. The advance of the Fifth New York, about twenty-five men, under Lieut. Elmer Barker, coming up, the Lieutenant determined to charge the gun, fearing, if he halted, the rebels would again run away. Gallantly riding up the narrow lane, with almost certain death before them, these brave men, bravely led by Lieut. Barker, dashed with a yell towards the gun. When within about fifty yards, the rebels opened fire with grape upon them. The result was, three men were killed and seven wounded. The rebels immediately charged, led by Mosby himself. Lieut. Barker, twice wounded in the leg, continued with his handful of men to contest every inch of the ground, and himself crossed sabres with Mosby. But numbers told, and several of the Fifth New York were made prisoners. This gallant fight of Lieut. Barker afforded Col. Preston an opportunity to come up with the First Vermont. Lieut. Hazleton was in advance, with about seventy-five men, and charged bravely up the lane, the few boys of the Fifth New York, who were left, joining the Vermonters. Again and again the gun dealt destruction through the ranks, but nothing could check their impetuosity, and the brave fellows rode over the gun, sabring the gunners, and captured the piece. Serg. Carey, of the First Vermont, was shot dead by the side of the gun ; his brother, a corporal in the same regiment, although his arm was shattered, struck down the gunner as he applied the match for the last time. Mosby and his men fought desperately to recover the gun, but in vain.

Meanwhile, Col. Preston had charged across the fields upon their flank, and the enemy fled in all directions, taking refuge in the thickets, with which they are so familiar. One party attempted to take away the limber, but it was speedily captured and brought in. The long chase in the hot sun, the desperate fight, and the jaded condition of the horses, prevented further pursuit, which, with the enemy so widely scattered, and with their knowledge of every by-path and thicket, would have been almost fruitless. Capt. B. S. Haskins, an Englishman, and formerly a Captain in the Forty-Fourth royal infantry, who was with Mosby, was so badly wounded that he has since died. Lieut. Capman, formerly of the regular army, who was in charge of the gun, was also dangerously wounded and paroled on the field, as he could not be removed. Our loss was four killed and fifteen wounded. The rebels had six killed, twenty wounded, and lost ten prisoners. All the Fifth New York who were taken by the rebels were recaptured.

The result of this fight is more disastrous to the rebels than the previous engagements. The

Southern Confederacy will not be apt to trust Mr. Mosby with other guns if he cannot take better care of them than he has of this one. The enemy was beaten by about the same force, in a position chosen by themselves, and defended by a howitzer. Their killed and wounded outnumber ours, and the howitzer is ready to be turned against them at the earliest opportunity. The conduct of officers and men is highly commended by Col. Mann in his official report to Gen. Stahl, and the gallantry of the charge of the Fifth New York and the First Vermont is deserving mention.

SOUTHRONS, HEAR YOUR COUNTRY CALL YOU.

BY ALBERT PIKE.

Southrons! hear your country call you!
Up! lest worse than death befall you!
    To arms! To arms! To arms, in Dixie!
Lo! all the beacon-fires are lighted —
Let all hearts be now united!
    To arms! To arms! To arms, in Dixie!
      Advance the flag of Dixie!
      Hurrah! hurrah!
For Dixie's land we take our stand,
    And live or die for Dixie!
      To arms! To arms!
    And conquer peace for Dixie!
      To arms! To arms!
    And conquer peace for Dixie!

Hear the Northern thunders mutter!
Northern flags in South wind flutter!
    To arms! &c.
      Advance the flag of Dixie! &c.

Fear no danger! Shun no labor!
Lift up rifle, pike, and sabre!
    To arms! &c.
Shoulder pressing close to shoulder,
Let the odds make each heart bolder!
    To arms! &c.
      Advance the flag of Dixie! &c.

How the South's great heart rejoices
At your cannons' ringing voices!
    To arms! &c.
For faith betrayed, and pledges broken,
Wrongs inflicted, insults spoken,
    To arms! &c.
      Advance the flag of Dixie! &c.

Strong as lions, swift as eagles,
Back to their kennels hunt these beagles!
    To arms! &c.
Cut the unequal words asunder!
Let them then each other plunder!
    To arms! &c.
      Advance the flag of Dixie! &c.

Swear upon your country's altar
Never to submit or falter!
    To arms! &c.
Till the spoilers are defeated,
Till the Lord's work is completed,
    To arms! &c.
      Advance the flag of Dixie! &c.

Halt not, till our Federation
Secures among earth's powers its station!
    To arms! &c.
Then at peace, and crowned with glory,
Hear your children tell the story!
    To arms! &c.
      Advance the flag of Dixie! &c.

If the loved ones weep in sadness,
Victory soon shall bring them gladness.
    To arms! &c.
Exultant pride soon banish sorrow;
Smiles chase tears away to-morrow.
    To arms! &c.
      Advance the flag of Dixie! &c.

SPARROWGRASS' proposition, that the Home Guard should not leave home except in case of invasion, is equal to the old story of the Bungtown Riflemen, an Ohio military company, whose by-laws consisted of two sections, namely:

"*Article First.* — This company shall be known as the Bungtown Riflemen.

"*Article Second.* — In case of war this company shall immediately disband."

INCIDENTS OF THE WAR. — A correspondent relates the following incidents:

"The Platte Valley steamer was brought to by the guns of the St. Louis arsenal, with a load of traitors and contrabands. The first shot, a blank cartridge, produced no effect. The next was a shell, which was made to explode a little beyond the boat; and this also was disregarded. The third, a large ball, passed just above her deck, between the chimneys and the wheel-house, and had the effect to set the bell ringing and the whistle screaming, which signals of acquiescence were continued till the boat reached the landing. 'Why, sir,' said the Captain to the gunner,' did you mean to sink me?' 'Certainly,' was the cool reply; 'I am ordered to fire one harmless shot at least; I gave you the benefit of two, and aimed a third at your engine, but the gun was ranged a little too high. I did not want to hit your boilers, and scald you all to death; but the next time I shall sink you at the second shot!' 'For God's sake, don't trouble yourself,' replied the Captain; '*just send a small boy down to tap a drum* whenever you want me, and I'll come to at once.'

"Major Rawlings tells an anecdote, in the same vein, of a prominent lawyer of St. Louis. 'Major,' said he, lately, 'I'm a choleric man, and I find it won't do. I'm getting to have a profound respect for Minie bullets. Won't you do me the favor to get me one? and whenever I find my temper rising against the Dutch, I will put my hand in my pocket, and *feel a bullet,* and that will cool me off!' The Major got the bullet for him, and the effect seems to be equal to the expectation. Certainly it is better to have one in the pocket than in the body, if the effect on one's loyalty is just the same.

"Some one inquired of Col. Boernstein how long he should remain. 'I don't know,' he replied with a French shrug of the shoulder; 'perhaps a year; so long as the Governor chooses to stay away. I am Governor now, you see, till he comes back!' His notions of freedom of speech and the press he expressed freely, like this: 'All people zall speak vot dey tink, write vot dey pleazhe, and be free to do any tink dey pleazhe — only dey zall speak and write no treason!'" — *National Intelligencer.*

ONE OF THE ARMY OF MARTYRS.

The telegraph announces the death of William Fuller, of Needham, a private in the 18th regiment of Massachusetts Volunteers. The tidings afflicted me much. I knew that he joined the army from deliberate convictions of duty, and with the belief that it was to be a war for freedom; and I earnestly desired that he should live to see the glorious result he anticipated. He was an ardent republican, and worked zealously for Fremont in the campaign of '56. He was a working man, and the enslavement of working men excited generous indignation in his breast. He was among the first three years' men that joined the army. Late in September, 1861, when he had been some time in Virginia, he wrote to me: "I enlisted purely from principle; to do what I could to save the free institutions of the country. We are hard at work, making intrenchments and cutting roads through the woods to Munson's Hill. We have to endure many privations and hardships; but these I will not dwell upon. I am willing to sacrifice the comforts of home, and even life itself, if the desired end can be accomplished by this war."

A month later, he wrote: "Before I came here, I was often told that I should not think so badly of slavery, if I had been in the Slave States. But I must say I have not yet seen any beauty in the system. When I do, I will inform you. While on picket duty, I often meet with slaves, and have opportunities of conversing with them. I said to one, who came into camp the other day, 'How have you been treated, Robert?' 'Pretty well, sar.' 'Have you been well fed and clothed?' 'Pretty well, till dis year. Massa hab no money to spare dis year.' 'Were you contented?' 'No, sar.' 'You say you were pretty well treated, and pretty well supplied with food and clothes; why wasn't you contented then?' 'Cause I wanted to be free, sar.' 'But what could you do to support yourself and your wife and children, if you were all free?' His face brightened, and you could see his eyes sparkle, as he replied, 'I'd hire a little hut, and hab a little garden, and keep a pig and a cow, and I'd work out by the day, and save money. I could save money. I've laid up eight dollars this summer; but if I couldn't lay up a cent, I should like to be free. I should *feel* better.' 'Can you read and write?' 'No, sar. But massa's mighty fraid to have us touch a paper; they say Massa Lincoln is going to free all the slaves.' 'Where did you hear that?' 'We used to hear massa say so, last fall,

before Massa Lincoln was President.' 'Did you ever hear of John Brown?' 'Yes, indeed, sar. There was great times down here when he come to Harper's Ferry. The folks was all skeered to death. They went from all round here to see him hung.' 'Do you think he was a good man?' 'Yes, sar, a mighty fine man.'

"All the slaves I have met with talk in much the same way. I could fill pages with similar conversations. It is a false notion that slaves are contented if they are not beaten, and have enough to eat. Liberty is just as sweet to them as it is to us. I can say, from the bottom of my heart, may we never come to any terms with the rebels till this blot of slavery is wiped out. I, for one, would be willing to stay here ten years, and endure any amount of hardship, if at the end I could see America truly free. If the war could only accomplish this object, it seems as if I could say, 'Now let thy servant depart in peace.'"

At the close of November, 1861, he wrote: "I have been watching the tide of public opinion, and I rejoice to see that the sentiments of Sumner, Wilson, and Fremont are fast gaining ground. Emancipation! Blessed word! I have prayed for it; I came here to fight for it; I am ready to die for it. When I first came here, they said I was as bad as a secessionist; and when I indorsed all Charles Sumner said at Worcester, they told me if I had such views I ought to have staid at home. But I stood my ground firmly, and spoke the honest convictions of my heart; for I know that Mr. Sumner is right, and that the right will conquer at last. I have sometimes feared it might not be in my day; but I now feel that the tide is setting strongly in the right direction. A great change has been wrought within a few months. I feel a stronger interest in the subject than ever, since I have seen the poor slaves and talked with them. No one that inquires of them can have a doubt that they are longing for their freedom. I know that they are expecting us to free them, and are ready at a word to help us. We have the power to do it; why do we delay? The day *will* come when the Stars and Stripes will wave over a country truly free; that it may come soon, is the earnest prayer of a poor soldier."

In January, 1862, he wrote: "The other day, in going out to the line of our pickets, which is near to the rebels, I passed by a house where a fine-looking colored lad, of seventeen, was holding a horse. He told me his master was in the rebel army. He had taken all his money away with him; but his mistress, who was a Union woman, made heaps of money by selling victuals to the United States soldiers, cooked by his mother, who was one of her slaves. He said that his mistress had a pass to go to the line of our pickets whenever she liked, and that she wanted to take him with her, to work for a man near our outposts. I advised him not to go, lest it should prove a trap. When I passed the house a fortnight later, I saw the same lad chopping wood, with a book peeping from his pocket. I asked him what he did with it. He said he wanted very much to learn to read, and that a little boy of six years was teaching him. What a picture it would make — that poor slave learning his letters of a little child six years old! I wish I were an artist, that I might paint it. In the course of our short conversation, the lad told me he had found out why his mistress wanted him to go to our outposts to work for a man. She and her husband had agreed upon a meeting near the lines, and he wanted to take this young slave to work for the rebel army. So much for this woman's pretended Union sentiments! The trouble is, too much confidence is placed in the loyal professions of these people. I am not surprised that you are sometimes despondent concerning the prospects of the country. I am also. O, what a chance is offered us to make this a really free country — a fitting home for the oppressed of all nations! Will this glorious opportunity be lost? If so, who will be accountable? It surely will not be the poor soldiers, who, at their country's call, have left home and families — all that was near and dear to them. I have taken some pains to find out the sentiments of those around me, and, almost to a man, they say we can never have permanent peace till slavery is abolished. Here are two hundred thousand men ready to go forth, at the *word*, to victory or death, and I believe they are generally desirous to see, Freedom to All, inscribed upon their banners. I will not believe that the glorious opportunity is to slip by us. Surely God will not permit it. He hears the prayers of the poor slaves, and of those who have been working and praying for them for years. I still pray on, and hope on. I want to do much; but how can I do more than I am doing? I must perform my duty, and wait for the wheels of Government to move. They seem to move so slowly, that I long to put my shoulder to the wheels and push them along.

"From appearances, I judge we shall have a battle soon. When the time for action comes I shall try to do my duty, God helping me. I have written my views to you fully, that if it should be my lot to fall in battle, you may know with what feelings I go into the conflict. The extermination of slavery, and freedom for all, through the whole length and breadth of the land, is the idea that nerves my arm. May God give me strength! May victory be ours! And through our efforts may the millions now in bondage be able to proclaim to the world, 'Once we were Slaves, but now we are all Free Men!'"

The expected battle was indefinitely postponed, as we all know; and the soldiers waited patiently for the slow wheels to move. The last of July, 1862, six months later, after the seven days' battle before Richmond, followed by a retreat of the United States army, Mr. Fuller wrote: "We have been so hurried that I have had no time to collect my thoughts until now. I was at Savage's Station on Saturday, after the fight at Gaines' Mill. All day I assisted in the care of the wounded, some two thousand in number. May I never see such dreadful sights again! And to think they had to be left to the mercy of the

rebels! O, it was too painful! But they were all patient — not a murmur or complaint. What a 'lesson it taught me'!

"Now we have a little rest; and as I sit near the banks of James River, my mind is busy with reflections concerning the last five months. I need not speak of the great sacrifices of life and property, of the recent bloody battles and the defeat of our army: you know it all. The thought ever present to my mind is, What have we accomplished by all our toil, and hardship, suffering, and death? Is freedom any nearer at hand? Is the nation even so strong as it was five months ago? What are our prospects for the future? The men are disheartened. It must be confessed that something is wrong somewhere. Who is responsible for this defeat? The people ought to know. The poor soldiers ought to know. Let the truth be made known!

"It is my firm conviction that if President Lincoln had proclaimed emancipation at the beginning of the war, the end would be much nearer than it now is, and there would have been far less expenditure of blood and treasure. Emancipation is a strong word, but it *must* come to that before we can have peace. I know I am not competent to advise the President; but these are my honest convictions, confirmed day by day, the more I see of this accursed system of slavery, which is the cause of all our trouble. I am teaching some slaves in our camp; that is, they *were* slaves, but I pray to God they may never be so again."

The next I heard from Mr. Fuller was that he was wounded in the last battle at Bull Run. In answer to my inquiries, he informed me, by another hand, that he had been badly wounded in the shoulder, but was doing well. He added, "My consolation is, that I have done what I could."

A week afterwards, they told he was dead. I thought of him as I last saw him, a healthy, young man, full of life and hope. He had few advantages for education in his youth, but his remarks evinced good intelligence and a generous heart. He left a wife and young children and went into the army, not from the mere contagion of public excitement, but from convictions of duty, after deliberate reflection.

He was "only a private;" his name is unknown to fame; but I honor his memory, as a brave man, a true patriot, and, better still, a friend to the whole human race, of all nations and colors. It fills my soul with sadness to think of the last words he wrote to me: "Something is wrong, somewhere. The poor soldiers ought to know."

Alas, thousands of poor, weary soldiers have doubtless gazed on the rivers and hills of Virginia, while they asked themselves, despondingly, "What has been accomplished by all our privations, toils and sufferings?" Thousands of brave young souls have passed away with heroic patience, saying, "My consolation is, that I have done what I could."   L. MARIA CHILD.

LYON.

Sing, bird, on green Missouri's plain,
    The saddest song of sorrow ;
Drop tears, O clouds, in gentlest rain
Ye from the winds can borrow ;
Breathe out, ye winds, your softest sigh,
    Weep, flowers, in dewy splendor,
For him who knew well how to die,
    But never to surrender.

Up rose serene the August sun
    Upon that day of glory ;
Up curled from musket and from gun
    The war-cloud gray and hoary ;
It gathered like a funeral pall,
    Now broken and now blended,
Where rang the buffalo's angry call,
    And rank with rank contended.

Four thousand men, as brave and true
    As e'er went forth in daring,
Upon the foe that morning threw
    The strength of their despairing.
They feared not death — men bless the field
    That patriot soldiers die on —
Fair freedom's cause was sword and shield,
    And at their head was Lyon !

Their leader's troubled soul looked forth
    From eyes of troubled brightness ;
Sad soul ! the burden of the North
    Had pressed out all its lightness.
He gazed upon the unequal fight,
    His ranks all rent and gory,
And felt the shadows close like night
    Round his career of glory.

"General, come, lead us !" loud the cry
    From a brave band was ringing —
"Lead us, and we will stop, or die,
    That battery's awful singing."
He spurred to where his heroes stood,
    Twice wounded, — no wound knowing, —
The fire of battle in his blood .
    And on his forehead glowing.

O, cursed for aye that traitor's hand,
    And cursed that aim so deadly,
Which smote the bravest of the land,
    And dyed his bosom redly !
Serene he lay while past him pressed
    The battle's furious billow,
As calmly as a babe may rest
    Upon its mother's pillow.

So Lyon died ! and well may flowers
    His place of burial cover,
For never had this land of ours
    A more devoted lover.
Living, his country was his bride ;
    His life he gave her, dying ;
Life, fortune, love — he nought denied
    To her and to her sighing.

Rest, Patriot, in thy hillside grave,
    Beside her form who bore thee !
Long may the land thou diedst to save
    Her bannered stars wave o'er thee !
Upon her history's brightest page,
    And on Fame's glowing portal,
She'll write thy grand, heroic page,
    And grave thy name immortal !

7

BEFORE THE BATTLE OF BETHEL. — Just as we halted to start to the rear on hearing firing, said Adjutant Stevens of the First Vermont, a rebel scoundrel came out of a house and deliberately fired his gun at us. The ball passed so close to me that I heard it whiz — on its way going through the coat and pants, and just grazing the skin of, Orderly Sergeant Sweet, of the Woodstock company. The rascal was secured, and is a prisoner ; and what was done, by way of stern entertainment, to one of the F. F. V.'s, you will hear if I ever live to return. I then, as the firing to the rear had ceased, with revolver in hand, accompanied by Fifer, approached the fellow's house, having some expectation of an ounce of lead being deposited in my tall body without asking my permission. By this time all our troops were out of sight in the woods, by a turn in the road, and I was alone with Fifer, when some negroes came from the house, having less fear of two men than of two thousand. On inquiry, the slaves told me that Adjutant Whiting, whom we had just taken prisoner, was the owner, that he belonged to the secession army, and that no white folks were in the house, all having left. Without the ceremony of ringing, I entered and surveyed the premises, and found a most elegantly furnished house. I took a hasty survey in search of arms, but, finding none, left the house, and started to overtake our column. On reaching the bend in the road, I took a survey of the rear, to "see what I might see," and discovered a single soldier coming towards me, and waited for him to come up. I found it was Clark, of the Bradford company. Before he reached me, I observed a horseman coming at full speed towards me. On reaching the house, he turned in, which induced me to think him a secessionist. I ordered Clark to cover him with his rifle, and revolver in hand, ordered him to dismount and surrender. He cried out, "Who are you ?" Answer, "Vermont !" "Then raise your piece, Vermont ; I am Col. Duryea, of the Zouaves ;" and so it was. His gay-looking red boys just appeared turning the corner of the road, coming towards us. He asked me the cause of the firing in the rear, and whose premises we were on. I told him he knew the first as well as I did, but as to the last, could give full information ; that the house belonged to one Adjutant Whiting, who, just before, had sent a bullet whizzing by me, and shot one of my boys, and that my greatest pleasure would be to burn the rascal's house in payment. "Your wish will be gratified at once," said the Colonel. "I am ordered by Gen. Butler to burn every house whose occupant or owner fires upon our troops. Burn it." He leaped from his horse, and I upon the steps, and by that time three Zouaves were with me. I ordered them to try the door with the butts of their guns — down went the door, and in went we. A well-packed travelling bag lay upon a mahogany table. I tore it open with the hopes of finding a revolver, but did not. The first thing I took out was a white linen coat : I laid it on the table, and Col. Duryea put a lighted match to it. Other clothing was added to the pile, and soon we had a rousing fire. Before leaving, I went into the large parlor in the right wing of the house — it was perfectly splendid. A large room with a tapestry carpet, a nice piano, a fine library of miscellaneous books, rich sofas, elegant chairs, with superior needle-work wrought bottoms, whatnots in the corners, loaded with articles of luxury, taste, and refinement, and upon a mahogany centre-table lay a Bible and a lady's portrait. The last two articles I took, and have them now in my possession. I also took a decanter of most excellent old brandy from the sideboard, and left the burning house. By this time the Zouave regiment had come up. I joined them, and in a short time came up with our rear guard, and saw a sight, the like of which I wish never to see again — viz.: nine of Col. Townsend's Albany regiment stretched on the floor of a house, where they had just been carried, and eight of them mortally wounded, by *our own men*. O, the sight was dreadful. I cried like a boy, and so did many others. I immediately thought of my decanter of brandy, took a tin cup from a soldier and poured into it the brandy, and filled it (the cup) with water from a canteen, and from one poor boy to another I passed and poured into their pale and quivering lips the invigorating fluid, and with my hand wiped the sweat-drops of death from their foreheads. O, how gratefully the poor fellows looked at me as they saw, by my uniform, that the usually stern officer and commander had become to them the kind and tender-hearted woman, by doing for them the woman's holy duty. One strong fellow, wounded in the head, and bloody as a butcher's floor, soon rallied, and was able to converse with me. I asked him if he knew the poor fellows around him. He said yes, and pointing to one, he said, " That man stood at my side — he was my section man — I saw his gun fly out of his hands, being struck by a grape shot, and a moment after we both tumbled to the ground together." I went out and picked up an Enfield rifle, nearly cut in two by a ball; said he, " That is his gun." I saw its owner die, and brought the gun with me back to my camp, and have it in my possession.

MUSIC OF THE PORT ROYAL NEGROES. — The editor of *Dwight's Journal of Music* published a letter from Miss Lucy McKim, of Philadelphia, accompanying a specimen of the songs in vogue among the negroes about Port Royal. Miss McKim accompanied her father thither on a recent visit, and wrote as follows :

It is difficult to express the entire character of these negro ballads by mere musical notes and signs. The odd turns made in the throat, and the curious rhythmic effect produced by single voices chiming in at different irregular intervals, seem almost as impossible to place on score as the singing of birds or the tones of an Æolian harp. The airs, however, can be reached. They are too decided not to be easily understood, and their striking originality would catch the ear of

any musician. Besides this, they are valuable as an expression of the character and life of the race which is playing such a conspicuous part in our history. The wild, sad strains tell, as the sufferers themselves never could, of crushed hopes, keen sorrow, and a dull, daily misery which covered them as hopelessly as the fog from the rice-swamps. On the other hand, the words breathe a trusting faith in rest in the future — in " Canaan's fair and happy land," to which their eyes seem constantly turned.

A complaint might be made against these songs on the score of monotony. It is true there is a great deal of repetition of the music, but that is to accommodate the leader, who, if he be a good one, is always an improvisator. For instance, on one occasion, the name of each of our party who was present was dexterously introduced.

As the same songs are sung at every sort of work, of course the *tempo* is not always alike. On the water, the oars dip " Poor Rosy " to an even andante ; a stout boy and girl at the hominy-mill will make the same " Poor Rosy " fly, to keep up with the whirling stone ; and in the evening, after the day's work is done, " Heab'n shall a be my home " peals up slowly and mournfully from the distant quarters. One woman — a respectable house-servant, who had lost all but one of her twenty-two children — said to me :
" P'shaw ! don't har to dese yar chil'en, missis. Dey jest rattles it off; dey don't know how for sing it. I likes ' Poor Rosy ' better dan all de songs, but it can't be sung widout a full heart and a troubled sperrit ! "

All the songs make good barcarolles. Whittier " builded better than he knew," when he wrote his " Song of the Negro Boatman." It seemed wonderfully applicable as we were being rowed across Hilton Head Harbor among United States gunboats — the Wabash and the Vermont towering on either side. I thought the crew *must* strike up :

> " And massa tink it day ob doom,
> And we ob jubilee."

Perhaps the grandest singing we heard was at the Baptist Church, on St. Helena Island, when a congregation of three hundred men and women joined in a hymn :

> " Roll, Jordan, roll, Jordan !
> Roll, Jordan, roll ! "

It swelled forth like a triumphal anthem. That same hymn was sung by thousands of negroes on the Fourth of July last, when they marched in procession under the Stars and Stripes, cheering them for the first time as the " flag of *our* country." A friend, writing from there, says that the chorus was indescribably grand — " that the whole woods and world seemed joining in that rolling sound."

There is much more in this new and curious music of which it is a temptation to write, but I must remember that it can speak for itself better than any one for it.

"STONEWALL JACKSON'S WAY.'

Come, stack arms, men ! Pile on the rails,
　Stir up the camp-fire bright;
No matter if the canteen fails,
　We'll make a roaring night.
Here Shenandoah brawls along,
There burly Blue Ridge echoes strong,
To swell the brigade's rousing song
　Of "Stonewall Jackson's way."

We see him now — the old slouched hat
　Cocked o'er his eye askew,
The shrewd, dry smile, the speech so pat,
　So calm, so blunt, so true.
The "Blue-Light Elder" knows 'em well;
Says he, "That's Banks — he's fond of shell;
Lord save his soul ! we'll give him " — well,
　That's "Stonewall Jackson's way."

Silence ! ground arms ! kneel, all ! caps off !
　Old Blue-Light's going to pray.
Strangle the fool that dares to scoff !
　Attention ! it's his way.
Appealing from his native sod,
In *forma pauperis* to God —
"Lay bare thine arm, stretch forth thy rod !
　Amen ! " That's "Stonewall's way."

He's in the saddle now. Fall in !
　Steady, the whole brigade !
Hill's at the ford, cut off — we'll win
　His way out, ball and blade !
What matter if our shoes are worn ?
What matter if our feet are torn ?
"Quick-step ! we're with him before dawn !"
　That's "Stonewall Jackson's way."

The sun's bright lances rout the mists
　Of morning, and, by George !
Here's Longstreet struggling in the lists,
　Hemmed in an ugly gorge.
Pope and his Yankees, whipped before,
"Bay'nets and grape !" near Stonewall roar;
"Charge, Stuart ! Pay off Ashby's score!"
　Is "Stonewall Jackson's way."

Ah, maiden, wait, and watch, and yearn
　For news of Stonewall's band !
Ah, widow, read, with eyes that burn,
　That ring upon thy hand !
Ah, wife, sew on, pray on, hope on !
　Thy life shall not be all forlorn.
The foe had better ne'er been born
　That gets in "Stonewall's way."

Who raised the Flag at Yorktown? — To the Twenty-second Massachusetts regiment, Col. Gove, and to the Twenty-second alone, belongs the glory of first planting the American flag on the works at Yorktown: of the truth of the statement there is and can be no question. The following brief account can be relied upon:

The day before the evacuation, Saturday, May 3d, the Twenty-second regiment received orders to march to a position within one thousand yards of the enemy's works. Spades were furnished each man. We were then deployed on a line six feet apart, and the order came : "Dig for your lives." Considering that we were completely exposed to a direct fire in front, and to a cross-fire from a water-battery stationed on the opposite side of the river, you may readily believe we hastened to obey orders. Fortunately, the enemy did not at once open fire, and our boys had a chance to do some little digging before the storm of ball and shell commenced ; but long before the pits were fully completed, their guns were played upon us. Up to twelve o'clock, the enemy had fired one hundred and seventy-five shell and shot, and though none of our regiment were killed or wounded, there were many narrow escapes.

Lieut. Stiles, commanding second company sharpshooters, in the absence of Capt. Wentworth, barely escaped being struck by a shell. In order to be able to give his men due notice when to dodge at the flash, he bravely and fearlessly exposed himself. In another case, one of the men was entirely buried by a shell striking the earth in front of the pit, and had actually to be dug out by his comrades.

During the whole day our boys kept themselves busy, while the sharpshooters took every chance offered. When evening came, we were ordered back to camp ; but before we had got fairly settled, the rebels commenced shelling us again. A piece of a shell struck the Adjutant's tent, and buried itself a foot and a half in the ground. The Adjutant and one of the surgeons were in the tent at the time. At twelve o'clock our siege guns commenced operations, and the enemy ceased firing. The next morning at five o'clock, the Twenty-second were ordered to go on picket duty in front of the enemy's lines.

The regiment, having taken their position, soon discovered that the works were evacuated, and at once marched forward and took possession. There being no colors allowed with a regiment on picket duty, Col. Gove immediately sent to his camp for the American flag, and with his own hands planted it on the works at Yorktown. At this time there were no other regiments, or parts of regiments, present under their proper officers; there were simply only a few stragglers, who followed after the Twenty-second. Col. Gove raised the flag, and was within ten feet of the concealed shell, which exploded and wounded seven of our men.

A Talk with a Rebel Picket in Mississippi. — A private of the Sixth Ohio regiment gave the following lively sketch of campaigning life :

I must record a little adventure, pleasing and interesting, I had day before yesterday near Corinth. My last spoke about the continued firing between pickets. To such an extent was it carried, so incessant the firing day and night, that nothing short of a battle would alarm the camp, whereas a single gun should be the signal for the long-roll. But within the last three or four days a change for the better has taken place.

On Monday our regiment was sent to the fortifications. It is the custom for the various battalions to take their turn in staying at the breastworks for twenty-four hours, forming a sort of reserve picket; and from each regiment so stationed two companies are sent to the outposts. It fell to our lot to go out. The company we relieved informed us that the rebels were disposed to be friendly; and with instructions from the field-officer not to fire unless fired upon, or the enemy attempted to advance, we set to work to watch the movements of our neighbors. The enemy's pickets were in the edge of a wood about two hundred yards from us, and my post — one of the best for observation — similarly situated in another wood, with a level between us. For some time we looked closely without being able to see any of them, as they were disposed to be shy. We, on the contrary, exposed ourselves to their view, which had the effect of making them bolder; and occasionally a rebel passed from one tree to another and levelled a field-glass at us.

I waved a handkerchief, which was answered from the other side, and tacitly understood to mean no firing. An hour later one of our Southern friends waved a handkerchief and shouted: "Meet me half-way." "All right;" and arming myself with a newspaper profusely illustrated with pictures incidental to the capture of New Orleans, I started out. A rebel surgeon of the Third Tennessee was the individual who met me. He was dressed in a citizen's suit of black, with military buttons, and the rank of captain designated, not by shoulder-straps, but by marks on the collar. After shaking hands and exchanging the customary salutations, we proceeded to talk about the war. He was at Fort Donelson, and made his escape the night before the surrender; spoke of the battle of Shiloh, at which he assisted; said it was their intention to have made the attack on Saturday instead of Sunday, but on account of a misunderstanding between their generals the plan failed. The number of deserters from his side appeared to have a prominent place in his mind, which he vainly endeavored to conceal. "Do you have many deserters from your ranks?" he commenced. I told him of only two cases which had come under my notice for more than a year, taking care to add that they ran home. He wanted to know if many of their men came over to us. I answered rather equivocally: "A few." "How many?"

Fearful now that if I told him the great number that actually did come to us, the rebel leaders would increase their vigilance, I merely said that I had seen six, the number I had personally beheld. "I guess they go the other way," he replied, thereby acknowledging they suffered much from desertion. Mr. Tennessee wanted to know why we did not make the attack; they were anxiously waiting for us, and confident of victory. I said that they could not be more eager for the battle, or more sure of success, than ourselves; that to us everything appeared to be ready; but we were not supposed to know Gen. Halleck's plans.

We talked together some fifteen minutes, both of us very wary about giving contraband information. He was a gentlemanly, well-educated man, apparently under thirty years of age, and from Maury County, Tennessee. I gave him the pictorial, and asked for a Memphis paper. He had none, but promised to send me over one, if he could procure it during the day. Before parting, I remarked that it would be well to make some agreement about picket firing, and learned that they had received orders precisely like ours.

Gen. Garfield, who had the supervision of the outposts, called me in; so we again shook hands and separated, leaving many things unsaid that we would like to have spoken about. Garfield questioned me closely as to our conversation, and seemed satisfied that it was all right. However, being fearful that the rebels might learn something from us if such intercourse was allowed, he ordered us not to go out again, but to let any rebel that wished it to come over all the way. I had reason to regret this very much, as in the afternoon my friend, the doctor, came half way with the promised paper. We gave him to understand that it was against our orders to leave the post, and if he would come all the way we would do him no harm. He said he had a very late paper, but could not be induced to come farther than the neutral ground, and returned, much to our disappointment.

After the interview of the morning all apprehension of danger from bullets from either side was at an end, and the sentinels on both sides paced their beats without so much as thinking to seek cover.

OUR COUNTRY'S CALL.

BY WILLIAM CULLEN BRYANT.

Lay down the axe, fling by the spade;
  Leave in its track the toiling plough;
The rifle and the bayonet blade
  For arms like yours were fitter now;
And let the hands that ply the pen
  Quit the light task, and learn to wield
The horseman's crooked brand, and rein
  The charger on the battle-field.

Our country calls; away! away!
  To where the blood-stream blots the green;
Strike to defend the gentlest sway
  That Time in all his course has seen.
See, from a thousand coverts — see
  Spring the armed foes that haunt her track;
They rush to smite her down, and we
  Must beat the banded traitors back.

Ho! sturdy as the oaks ye cleave,
  And moved as soon to fear and flight,
Men of the glade and forest! leave
  Your woodcraft for the field of fight.
The arms that wield the axe must pour
  An iron tempest on the foe;
His serried ranks shall reel before
  The arm that lays the panther low.

And ye who breast the mountain storm,
　By grassy steep or highland lake,
Come, for the land ye love to form
　A bulwark that no foe can break.
Stand, like your own gray cliffs that mock
　The whirlwind, stand in her defence :
The blast as soon shall move the rock
　As rushing squadrons bear ye thence.

And ye, whose homes are by her grand,
　Swift rivers, rising far away,
Come from the depth of her green land,
　As mighty in your march as they,
As terrible as when the rains
　Have swelled them over bank and bourn,
With sudden floods to drown the plains
　And sweep along the woods uptorn.

And ye who throng, beside the deep,
　Her ports and hamlets of the strand,
In number like the waves that leap
　On his long, murmuring marge of sand,
Come, like that deep, when o'er his brim
　He rises, all his floods to pour,
And flings the proudest barks that swim,
　A helpless wreck, against his shore.

Few, few were they whose swords, of old,
　Won the fair land in which we dwell ;
But we are many, we who hold
　The grim resolve to guard it well.
Strike, for that broad and goodly land,
　Blow after blow, till men shall see
That Might and Right move hand in hand,
　And glorious must their triumph be.

THE CRUISE OF THE FLORIDA.

MAFFIT'S ACCOUNT OF HIS ADVENTURES. —
Arriving in Brest, by way of Quimper and
Chateaulin, the first thing I heard on getting on
board the steamer which navigates the picturesque
little river Elorn from the latter place to Brest,
was the arrival of the Confederate States cruiser
Florida ; and on crossing the glorious Rade de
Brest for the mouth of the harbor, I had no
difficulty in making out this now celebrated
vessel, as she lay at anchor among some of the
giants of the French navy — a long, low, black,
rakish-looking craft, not over smart in appearance,
yet useful, every inch of her — a pygmy among
these monsters, and yet a formidable pygmy, even
to the unpractised eye, the Palmetto flag flying
proudly from her mizzen. We happened to have
a French Vice-Admiral, a Russian Vice-Admiral,
and a Senator of the Empire on board ; and you
may imagine there was an infinity of gossip, but
no reliable information.

When we landed at the Cale in the harbor, the
crowd which usually assembles to welcome or
pester new comers was full of "La Floride" and
her doings. "Elle a," cried an enthusiastic
commissionaire to me, "elle a, Monsieur, je vous
assure sur ma parole d'honneur, près deux millions
de livres sterling à bord, tout en or, je vous
assure." "Eh! mon Dieu! c'est beaucoup!"
cried a smart little mousse from the Turenne. I

could not help agreeing with the mousse that the
sum was certainly a great deal.

That evening (aided by my fellow-traveller,
Mr. Henry Tupper, Vice-Consul of France in
Guernsey, and one of the jurats of that island)
I found some of the officers of the Florida at the
Hotel de Nantes, (Rue d'Aiguillon.) Lieut.
Lingard Hoole (a young man, who apparently
did not number more than 23 years) received us
courteously, and gave us his card to assure us
admission on board. He stated, however, that
his superior officer, Capt. Maffit, was generally to
be found on board his vessel, and would be glad
to see us. The frankness, courtesy, and total
absence of boasting manifested by this young
officer, impressed us most favorably.

All next day it blew a gale of wind in the
Rade, and we could not find a boat to venture
out. To-day, however, the weather was most
propitious, and early morning found us alongside
of the Florida. We sent our cards to Capt.
Maffit, and were immediately admitted on board,
the captain himself coming to the top of the
companion to receive us. Directly Capt. Maffit
understood that we were British subjects, he
invited us below into his little cabin, and when I
told him that there were many people in England
who regarded his career with great interest, he
entered very freely into a recital of his adventures.

I will here subjoin a copy of some notes which
Capt. Maffit subsequently handed to me, relative
to the career of the Florida, promising, at the
same time, a continuation, which has not yet
arrived. They are as follows :

"The C. S. steamer Florida, Commander J. N.
Maffit. This steamer was built in Liverpool, and
sent to Nassau in April, 1862 ; was put in the
Admiralty Court ; cleared on the 6th of August,
when her present commander took charge with
18 men ; went to sea ; met her tender, and received guns, &c. On the 16th of August the
yellow fever appeared on board, and Capt. Maffit
had to perform surgeon's duty, until necessity
forced the vessel into Cardenas. There she lost
nearly all her crew, her paymaster, and third
engineer. She ran the blockade off Havana, in
and out, and on the 4th of September appeared
off Mobile. The entire blockading fleet put after
her. Capt. Maffit was brought up from a bed of
sickness (yellow fever) to take her in. For 2
hours and 48 minutes she was under a close fire.
All the crew were sent below, and the officers
only remained on deck, for she had but 11 men
on duty, and her guns were not furnished with
rammers, quoins, beds, or sights ; in fact, she
was almost helpless. Three heavy shots struck
her hull. One shell struck her amidships, and
passed through, killing one man and wounding
seven. Her standing rigging was shot away,
and some 1500 shrapnel shot struck her hull
and masts."

So far the notes which Capt. Maffit has as yet
found time to send me. Of the Captain himself,
I may say that he is a slight, middle-sized, well-
knit man, of about forty-two ; a merry-looking
man, with a ready, determined air, full of life

and business; apparently the sort of man who is equally ready for a fight or a jollification, and whose preference for the latter would by no means interfere with his creditable conduct of the former. His plainly furnished little state-room looked as business-like as a merchant's office. The round table in the centre was strewn with books and innumerable manuscripts, and on the shelves were formidable looking rows of account books, charts, &c. I may observe of the cabin, as of every part of the Florida, that none of it appears to have been built for ornament — all for use. "You see," said the Captain, pointing to the heaps of papers, letters on files, account books, &c., which literally littered the table, — "you see I've no sinecure of it. Since my paymaster died, I've had to be my own paymaster. There's a young man named Davis (no relation to our President) who does paymaster's duty; but he's not yet quite up to the work."

Capt. Maffit forthwith began an animated recital of his career and adventures. He is forty-two years old, and is the oldest officer on board. All the officers were born in the Confederate States, and most of them were officers in the United States Navy before the outbreak of the war. The oldest of the officers is not more than twenty-three. The men are more mixed. There are about one hundred able seamen on board the Florida, and about thirteen officers. Four fine fellows are from the neighborhood of Brest. Capt. Maffit says that he has hardly ever taken a prize but what some of the crew of the prize have come forward to say, "Should like to serve with you, sir." Generally speaking, he has to refuse; but sometimes, when he sees a very likely fellow, he takes him on.

Capt. Maffit was a Lieutenant of the United States Navy before the outbreak, and in that capacity distinguished himself greatly. In 1858, he commanded the brig Dolphin, when he captured the slaver Echo, with four hundred slaves on board, and took her into Charleston. For this feat his health was drank at a public dinner at Liverpool; and it is a curious fact, for those who maintain that the civil war in America is founded upon the slave question, that the commander of this important Confederate cruiser, should be the very man who has distinguished himself actively against the slave trade. In 1859, Capt. Maffit commanded the United States steamer Crusader, and captured four slavers.

The Captain had a great deal to say about his successful feat at Mobile. In his opinion, it has been the greatest naval feat of modern times. He dwelt long and warmly upon the incidents of the affair, and pointed proudly to the marks of shrapnel, which are numerous enough, upon the masts and smoke-stacks. The Florida was struck with three heavy shots on the occasion, and one can easily perceive in the side of the ship where the mischief caused by the 11-inch shell has been repaired. The Florida made no endeavor to reply to the fire which she received, the sea running too high to admit of steady aim, and her small crew being too much occupied in the management of the ship. The Captain showed us a water-color sketch (very well drawn by one of the midshipmen) of the Florida running the blockade. It would not have disgraced a professional artist.

The only broadside which the Florida has fired in anger was against the Ericsson, an armed merchantman, which she encountered some forty miles from New York. The Ericsson, a very large vessel, did not reply, but made the best of her way off, and succeeded in escaping. When they ventured within forty miles of New York, they did not know that the arrival of the Tacony, one of their 'outfits,' had put the New Yorkers on their guard, and they soon found that there were about seventy armed vessels out searching for them, and so were glad to retreat. "We never seek a fight," said Capt. Maffit, "and we don't avoid one. You see, we've only two vessels against fifteen hundred; so we should stand a poor chance. Our object is merely to destroy their commerce, so as to bring about a peace. We have taken altogether seventy-two prizes, and estimate the value at about fifteen million dollars. The Jacob Bell alone was worth two million one hundred thousand dollars." The Captain exhibited a book in which all the prizes were regularly entered, and all particulars relating thereto. He explained that their mode of procedure was to burn and destroy the property of the Northern States wherever they found it. I asked if they took gold and precious articles, and the reply was, "Pretty quick, when we get them."

The papers of the burned prizes are all kept, and a valuation is made before the destruction of the vessels, in the expectation that when peace is restored, the Confederate Government will make an appropriation of money equivalent to the claims of the captors. In consequence of this arrangement there is very little actual treasure on board the Florida; the officers and crew are working mainly on the faith of the future independence and solvency of the Confederacy. "Any way," said Capt. Maffit, "we have cost the Government very little, for we've lived on the enemy; O, yes, we've served them out beautifully." In reply to some questions as to the method of capture, the Captain said, "We only make war with the United States Government, and we respect little property. We treat prisoners of war with the greatest respect. Most of those whom we have captured have spoken well of us. To be sure, we have met with some ungrateful rascals; but you meet with those all the world over. The best prize we took was the Anglo-Saxon, which we took in the English Channel, the other day, in mid channel, about sixty miles from Cork. She had coal on board, and we burned her.

"The pilot was a saucy fellow, and maintained that he was on his piloting ground. He insisted on being landed in an English port; but we could not do that. I brought him and twenty-four men here, (to Brest,) and sent them to the English Consul. If the pilot has any just claim upon us, it will be settled by the Confederate Government. That's not my business. My business is to take care of the ship."

When the Florida came into Brest, she had been at sea eight months without spending more than four entire days in port. Before entering the port of Brest, she had not been more than twenty-four hours in any one port, although she had visited Nassau, Bermuda, Pernambuco, and Sierra (Brazil). "Yes, indeed, sir," said the Captain, "two hundred and forty-five days upon solid junk, without repairs or provisions." During all this time, they have only lost fifteen men, including those who were killed and wounded at Mobile, the paymaster, (who died of consumption,) and one officer who was accidentally drowned. They have come into Brest to repair the engines, which are somewhat out of order, the shaft being quite out of line. The Emperor has given orders that the Florida is to be admitted into the port for all necessary repairs, and is to be supplied with everything she may require except munitions of war.

In the course of conversation, Capt. Maffit gave me an account of what he called the "outfits" of the Florida. These have been three in number. The Clarence was captured off Pernambuco on the 5th of May, and Lieut. Reed was put on board with twenty men and one gun. These were afterwards changed to the Tacony, a better vessel, which was captured shortly after, and (to borrow Capt. Maffit's expression) "she captured right and left." Finally, she took the revenue cutter off Portland harbor. The other "fit-out" was the Lapwing, on board of which Lieut. Avrett was put to cruise on the equator. He made several captures, and has now returned to his ship.

Capt. Maffit showed us over his ship, which was in pretty good order, considering the eight months' almost interrupted cruise, and he presented us both with a photographic picture of her, which was taken at Bermuda. The Florida mounts only eight guns — six 48-pounders of the Blakeley pattern, made at Low Moor, and stern and bow chasers.

On taking our leave, I asked Capt. Maffit whether he expected to be intercepted on leaving Brest, pointing at the same time to the Goulet, the narrow passage which affords the only ingress and egress to and from the Rade. "Well," replied he, "I expect there will be seven or eight of them out there before long, but I'm not afraid. I've run eight blockades already, and it'll go hard but I'll run the ninth."

BATTLE-HYMN OF THE REPUBLIC.

BY MRS. JULIA WARD HOWE.

MINE eyes have seen the glory of the coming of the Lord:
He is trampling out the vintage where the grapes of wrath are stored;
He hath loosed the fateful lightning of his terrible swift sword:
      His truth is marching on.

I have seen him in the watch-fires of a hundred circling camps;
They have builded him an altar in the evening dews and damps;
I have read his righteous sentence by the dim and flaring lamps:
      His day is marching on.

I have read a fiery gospel writ in burnished rows of steel:
"As ye deal with my contemners, so with you my grace shall deal;
Let the Hero, born of woman, crush the serpent with his heel,
      Since God is marching on."

He has sounded forth the trumpet that shall never call retreat;
He is sifting out the hearts of men before his judgment seat;
O, be swift, my soul, to answer him! be jubilant, my feet!
      Our God is marching on.

In the beauty of the lilies Christ was born across the sea,
With a glory in his bosom that transfigures you and me:
As he died to make men holy, let us die to make men free,
      While God is marching on.

INCIDENTS OF VICKSBURG. — In the action which occurred on the twenty-ninth day of December, 1862, but two divisions — those of Morgan's and Steele's — were generally and closely engaged. A portion of Smith's division made some advance under a terrible fire, in which the gallant Sixth Missouri were most actively engaged. This regiment crossed the levee, which had been occupied by the enemy as an earthwork, and was still, after being crossed, commanded by the enemy's cannon. It, however, led to an advance upon Smith's line, but without any positive advantage to us. From certain points on the new line thus made, Vicksburg could be seen. The movements of the rebel troops in the city, and some portions of Vicksburg, were clearly and fairly in view. It was tempting to look straight in upon the beleaguered city, and still know that its occupation was improbable, if not impossible. But so it was, and the Union troops lay down upon their arms on the night of the twenty-ninth with anxious hearts and high hopes that something might occur to make it practicable. The night of the twenty-ninth passed, and the morning dawned without any new development being made, except that the enemy assumed a threatening position with their artillery. It was evidently his intention to shell the camp. It having rained incessantly during the night, and the men having been exposed to it all, it was deemed advisable to place them in such a position that they would not be exposed to the enemy's cannon, and where they could examine their ammunition and clean their rusted arms, preparatory to further operations.

In the mean time, the front was to be held firmly, and heavier artillery was to be placed in position behind earth-works. The threatening preparations in front deterred the enemy from shelling the camps, and put him on his guard, for offensive operations on our part. Wednesday was occupied by both armies, in the presence of each other, throwing up new works, digging new pits, preparing for operations offensive and defensive. During the afternoon of Tuesday, the cries of our wounded could be heard, and an impromptu effort was made to recover them by a flag of truce. Being irregular, and perhaps not authorized, and occasional skirmishes still going on, the flag was fired on by the enemy. The wounded and dead of Thayer's and Blair's brigades had to lie there and await the tedious process of official communication. This is one of the most horrible pictures which a battle-field presents, but frequently is unavoidable. It seems to have been so in this instance. While a tear here and there was dropped for the dying and the dead, still the great purpose of the expedition was not accomplished, and generally our army looked forward to watch future movements.

Wednesday morning came, and still no change from Tuesday. The front was kept up by Smith's and Morgan's divisions, while Steele's division lay along Chickasaw Bayou, ready to meet the enemy if they should make a deployment in that direction. Everything was quiet on the line, and this being a favorable opportunity, a flag of truce was sent to the enemy for the purpose of recovering and attending to our dead and wounded. The flag was duly recognized, the message was received and was answered, allowing us four hours to bury our dead. The cessation of hostilities consequent to the removal of the dead and wounded, gave the sharpshooters and pickets an opportunity to converse with each other. The conversation was opened by our pickets, by asking: "How far is it to Vicksburg?"

Rebel Picket. — So far that you'll never git thar.

Federal. — How many men you got?

Rebel. — Enough to clean you out.

One rebel, who seemed to be somewhat of a stumper, said that "Banks had been whipped out at Port Hudson, that Memphis had been retaken, and that the Yankees would not take Vicksburg till hell froze over." A thousand questions were asked, and all answered in the same defiant way.

While this interesting parley was going on, the wounded and dead were removed. In a very short time the field was cleared, and everything was again quiet on the lines.

The camps were soon astir again; orderlies and aids were galloping to and from the various division and brigade headquarters; of course it could be interpreted to mean nothing else than further orders. The critical and trying position of our army lent an additional interest to orders. They were important, for Steele's division was ordered to make a night assault on Haines' Bluff, while the other division commanders were to hold their fronts firm and advance, if they could, while Steele was storming the enemy's works at Haines' Bluff. The movement preparatory to this was, for Steele to mask his division from the enemy's lookouts by marching down Chickasaw Bayou to the river, put his troops on board the transports, and steam quietly up the Yazoo, and before daylight debark his troops under the enemy's guns at Haines' Bluff. In this matter the gunboat and mortar fleets were to play an important part. The river was lined with torpedoes, and it was necessary to clear it out before the transports could go up. This being accomplished, they were to take a position further up the river from the point of debarkation, and engage the batteries, while the troops should advance to the Bluffs. During the day, the boilers of the steamboats designated for the hazardous business were protected by bales of hay and otherwise. Pilots and river men were shaky, and anxiously inquired what it meant. No information was imparted, as the whole plan was to be kept strictly secret.

———

A BRAVE DRUMMER-BOY. — Orion P. Howe, of Waukegan, Illinois, drummer-boy to the Fifty-fifth Volunteers of that State, was appointed to fill a vacancy in the Naval School at Newport. The following extract from a letter, written by Major-General Sherman to Secretary Stanton, detailing an incident which transpired during the assault upon the rebel works at Vicksburg, on May 19th, doubtless secured the boy's promotion:

"When the assault at Vicksburg was at its height on the 19th of May, and I was in front near the road which formed my line of attack, this young lad came up to me wounded and bleeding, with a good, healthy boy's cry: 'Gen. Sherman, send some cartridges to Col. Malmborg; the men are nearly all out.' 'What is the matter, my boy?' 'They shot me in the leg, sir, but I can go to the hospital. Send the cartridges right away.' Even where we stood, the shot fell thick, and I told him to go to the rear at once, I would attend to the cartridges, and off he limped. Just before he disappeared on the hill, he turned and called as loud as he could: 'Calibre 54.' I have not seen the lad since, and his Colonel, Malmborg, on inquiry, gives me his address as above, and says he is a bright, intelligent boy, with a fair preliminary education.

"What arrested my attention then was, and what renews my memory of the fact now is, that one so young, carrying a musket-ball wound through his leg, should have found his way to me on that fatal spot, and delivered his message, not forgetting the very important part even of the calibre of his musket, 54, which you know is an unusual one.

"I'll warrant that the boy has in him the elements of a man, and I commend him to the Government as one worthy the fostering care of some one of its national institutions."

COL. ELLSWORTH'S LAST SPEECH.—"Boys, no doubt you felt surprised on hearing my orders to be in readiness at a moment's notice, but I will explain all as far as I am allowed. Yesterday forenoon I understood that a movement was to be made against Alexandria. Of course, I was on the *qui vive*. I went to see Gen. Mansfield, the commander at Washington, and told him that I should consider it as a personal affront if he would not allow us to have the right of the line, which is our due, as the first volunteer regiment sworn in for the war. All that I can tell you is to prepare yourselves for a nice little sail, and, at the end of it, a skirmish. Go to your tents, lie down, and take your rest till two o'clock, when the boat will arrive, and we go forward to victory or death. When we reach the place of destination, act as men; do nothing to shame the regiment; show the enemy that you are men, as well as soldiers, and that you will treat them with kindness until they force you to use violence. I want to kill them with kindness. Go to your tents, and do as I tell you."

ADVENTURES IN THE SOUTH.—Lieut. F. Perry and private William P. Pugh, of the Third West Tennessee cavalry were out on recruiting service, and were captured on the 7th of October, 1863, after a skirmish with Faulkner's and Wilson's partisans, near Como, some sixty miles from Paducah. Mr. Pugh had previously been captured by, and had made his escape from, the same parties; and being a Tennessean, was subjected to some severities. His captors declared he should not again escape, and exercised unusual vigilance in conducting their prisoners southward.

They were forced to walk from the place of capture to Gadsden, Alabama, on the Coosa River, and were conveyed thence by boat to Rome, Georgia, where they took cars for Atlanta, and, subsequently, for Richmond. Thirty miles east of Raleigh, North Carolina, they jumped from the cars, made their way to Washington, where they were received inside the Federal lines, and thence sent north to join their comrades, who still supposed them in Libby Prison.

They suffered great privations on the march from Como to Gadsden, particularly after crossing the Tennessee River. In the Tuscumbia Valley they were three days without anything to eat, their captors stating that the Yankees had been there and destroyed all supplies. At Decatur they paid twenty-five cents an ear for corn, which was their sole sustenance the greater part of the march. They were compelled to make forced marches by by-roads, and through an unfrequented country, as Sherman was at Tuscumbia, and the rebels anticipated that he would turn south, and advance in the direction of Gadsden. Several times the prisoners heard his cannon, and fondly hoped for rescue. There was great scarcity of provisions wherever they went, and Confederate money was at an enormous discount. At Decatur, a woman offered a chicken-pie for sale, for which she wanted one dollar in silver or greenbacks. She refused to sell it for Confederate money, though ten dollars were offered. At Gadsden, the prisoners found a considerable number of rebel conscripts, who, whenever their officers and guards were not by, told them they were Union men, and would escape on the first opportunity. They generally manifested their sympathy for the boys by slipping a roll of Confederate bills into their hands, and saying they were sorry there was not more of it.

Here the prisoners found Confederate Lieutenants and other subordinate officers engaged in selling pies to Yankee prisoners. These pies were made of sweet potatoes, without sugar or shortening in the crust, and were peddled in baskets, after the fashion we see at railroad stations. A Colonel of an Alabama regiment, at Gadsden, sent a sack of corn, which he tried to sell them for greenbacks. Everywhere there was a demand for Uncle Sam's money, which was hoarded as carefully as silver and gold, and kept out of circulation.

At Rome the prisoners saw a considerable body of Georgia State militia. They were mostly boys under sixteen, and old men over forty-five, badly clothed, and poorly disciplined, but well armed. Mr. Perry, who was placed on his parole of honor, says that at Augusta, Georgia, he saw an immense pile of cotton, covering an area of perhaps one acre, and piled higher than any building in Cincinnati. There were also considerable quantities at Atlanta, but none that he saw at Rome.

They were detained at Atlanta some ten days, before starting for Richmond. At Columbia, South Carolina, they found that Charleston money was absolutely valueless; nobody would take it; the reason being assigned that the city might at any day fall into Federal hands, and then the currency would be worth nothing. Between Atlanta and Raleigh they saw no organized bodies of Confederate troops, and very little material out of which to make them. The resources of the country, in that respect, seemed to have been thoroughly exhausted.

When they left Raleigh for Richmond, a plan of escape was arranged between Messrs. Perry, Pugh, and John Carr, of the First Missouri Artillery, who was formerly chief clerk, at Corinth, for Gen. Carr. About three o'clock in the morning, being about thirty miles from Raleigh, on the Weldon road, the three leaped from the car, and plunged into the forest. They made as near south-east as they could, guided by the stars and the course of the clouds, concealing themselves by day.

They did not venture near any settlement or plantation, till forced to do so by excessive hunger, and one night ventured to arouse the inmates of a negro cabin, who were very inquisitive, and would not commit themselves until satisfied they were real Yankees, which was decided by an old negro, who felt Mr. Perry's cavalry jacket, and declared it was too fine for a rebel's. Then they were treated with great hospitality, and feasted on corn bread and "possum," and subjected to a great deal of questioning.

Among other things, the patriarch of the cabin wanted to know whether they "hab seen Mr. Linkum," and under the impression that they had left his presence but a short time, affectionately inquired after his health. "An' dere's anodder man," said the darkey, "dey call him Mr. Britain—hab you seen him?" The Yankees were puzzled. "Ole massa," said the darkey, explaining, "call him Mr. Great Britain, an' says he's on his side, an' some says he's on yourn." The Yankees "took," said they knew him, and that he was well; and having satisfied the curiosity of their hospitable entertainers and their own hunger, took up their march for Washington.

They met no Confederate soldiers until within some five miles of Washington, and there they narrowly escaped capture, running into their pickets twice, and being fired on once, at which time they lost sight of Carr, whom they supposed to have been killed or captured, and they heard no more of him. They arrived at Washington almost naked, foot-sore, and exhausted, having been ten days wandering about the country.

ON BOARD THE CUMBERLAND.

March 7, 1862.

BY GEORGE H. BOKER.

"STAND to your guns, men!" Morris cried.
　Small need to pass the word;
Our men at quarters ranged themselves
　Before the drum was heard.

And then began the sailors' jests:
　"What thing is that, I say?"
"A long-shore meeting-house adrift
　Is standing down the bay!"

A frown came over Morris' face;
　The strange, dark craft he knew;
"That is the iron Merrimac,
　Manned by a rebel crew.

"So shot your guns, and point them straight;
　Before this day goes by,
We'll try of what her metal's made."
　A cheer was our reply.

"Remember, boys, this flag of ours
　Has seldom left its place;
And where it falls, the deck it strikes
　Is covered with disgrace.

"I ask but this: or sink or swim,
　Or live or nobly die,
My last sight upon earth may be
　To see that ensign fly!"

Meanwhile, the shapeless iron mass
　Came moving o'er the wave,
As gloomy as a passing hearse,
　As silent as the grave.

Her ports were closed; from stem to stern
　No sign of life appeared.
We wondered, questioned, strained our eyes,
　Joked—everything but feared.

She reached our range. Our broadside rang,
　Our heavy pivots roared;
And shot and shell, a fire of hell,
　Against her sides we poured.

God's mercy! from her sloping roof
　The iron tempest glanced,
As hail bounds from a cottage-thatch,
　And round her leaped and danced.

Or when against her dusky hull
　We struck a fair, full blow,
The mighty, solid iron globes
　Were crumbled up like snow.

On, on, with fast increasing speed,
　The silent monster came,
Though all our starboard battery
　Was one long line of flame.

She heeded not; no gun she fired;
　Straight on our bow she bore;
Through riving plank and crashing frame
　Her furious way she tore.

Alas! our beautiful keen bow,
　That in the fiercest blast
So gently folded back the seas,
　They hardly felt we passed!

Alas! alas! my Cumberland,
　That ne'er knew grief before,
To be so gored, to feel so deep
　The tusk of that sea-boar!

Once more she backward drew a space,
　Once more our side she rent;
Then, in the wantonness of hate,
　Her broadside through us sent.

The dead and dying round us lay,
　But our foemen lay abeam;
Her open port-holes maddened us;
　We fired with shout and scream.

We felt our vessel settling fast,
　We knew our time was brief;
"The pumps! the pumps!" But they who pumped,
　And fought not, wept with grief.

"O, keep us but an hour afloat!
　O, give us only time
To be the instruments of Heaven
　Against the traitors' crime!"

From captain down to powder-boy
　No hand was idle then!
Two soldiers, but by chance aboard,
　Fought on like sailor-men.

And when a gun's crew lost a hand,
　Some bold marine stepped out,
And jerked his braided jacket off,
　And hauled the gun about.

Our forward magazine was drowned;
　And up from the sick bay
Crawled out the wounded, red with blood,
　And round us gasping lay.

Yes, cheering, calling us by name,
　Struggling with failing breath,
To keep their shipmates at the post
　Where glory strove with death.

With decks afloat, and powder gone,
The last broadside we gave
From the guns' heated iron lips
Burst out beneath the wave.

So sponges, rammers, and handspikes —
As men-of-war's-men should —
We placed within their proper racks,
And at our quarters stood.

"Up to the spar-deck! save yourselves!"
Cried Selfridge. "Up, my men!
God grant that some of you may live
To fight yon ship again!"

We turned — we did not like to go;
Yet staying seemed but vain,
Knee-deep in water; so we left;
Some swore, some groaned with pain.

We reached the deck. There Randall stood:
"Another turn, men — so!"
Calmly he aimed his pivot-gun:
"Now, Tenny, let her go!"

It did our sore hearts good to hear
The song our pivot sang,
As rushing on, from wave to wave,
The whirring bomb-shell sprang.

Brave Randall leaped upon the gun,
And waved his cap in sport;
"Well done! well aimed! I saw that shell
Go through an open port."

It was our last, our deadliest shot;
The deck was overflown;
The poor ship staggered, lurched to port,
And gave a living groan.

Down, down, as headlong through the waves
Our gallant vessel rushed,
A thousand gurgling watery sounds
Around my senses gushed.

Then I remember little more.
One look to heaven I gave,
Where, like an angel's wing, I saw
Our spotless ensign wave.

I tried to cheer. I cannot say
Whether I swam or sank;
A blue mist closed around my eyes,
And everything was blank.

When I awoke, a soldier lad,
All dripping from the sea,
With two great tears upon his cheeks,
Was bending over me.

I tried to speak. He understood
The wish I could not speak.
He turned me. There, thank God! the flag
Still fluttered at the peak!

And there, while thread shall hang to thread,
O, let that ensign fly!
The noblest constellation set
Against our northern sky.

A sign that we who live may claim
The peerage of the brave;
A monument that needs no scroll
For those beneath the wave!

A YANKEE IN DIXIE.

BY CORPORAL PURDUM.

I WILL endeavor to give a short account of what I saw and heard while in the hands of the rebels, beginning with my capture when I was first introduced to the inside of the great Southern humbug.

It was on the evening of the 20th of September, 1863, that myself, in company with a number of others from the 33d and other regiments, was taken prisoner by a part of Longstreet's corps. We were taken a short distance to the rear of their first line, and camped for the night. The rebs used us very well at first, and were very civil and polite. At daylight on Monday morning we commenced our pilgrimage south in the direction of Ringgold, where we arrived about 2 o'clock P. M., and were brought up in front of the Provost Marshal, surrounded by his numerous clerks, and our names were taken, which business occupied about two hours. This being done we were started forward again, bound for Tunnel Hill Station, which place we arrived at about 9 o'clock at night, and were turned into a field to remain the rest of the night. We were very tired and hungry, having marched twenty-two miles and had no rations. We lay down to rest ourselves and get some sleep, but were called up at 2 o'clock to draw some rations, (if it could be called such.) They consisted of a little meal and bacon, which was so strong the boys said it could almost walk alone. After disposing of our meal as best we could, some making mush in tin cups, some ash cakes, and some who were fortunate enough to get ovens, made something resembling bread. They then brought us up in line, preparatory to taking our rubber blankets, knapsacks, and canteens from us; but as soon as the boys found out what was to be done, we commenced to tear everything to pieces that we could not sell; so they got but few things from us; and by the time they were done the place had the appearance of an old deserted camp, as strips of blankets, knapsacks, and broken canteens were strewn all over the ground, for we were determined that the rebs should not be benefited by them. Here we expected to get on the cars, but were disappointed, and started on foot for Dalton, seven miles distant from Tunnel Hill; and the road being very dusty, and we not being in the best of humor after having our things taken from us, we struck out almost on a double-quick in order to tire out the guards, and several times we were stopped for them to rest and get to their places.

On this trip I stopped at a house to get some bread, and had to pay one dollar for *three small biscuits*; but the money being of but little value, I paid it with a good grace, and went on my way, rejoicing that my lot was not permanently cast in the land of cotton and starvation. On arriving at Dalton we again drew rations of flour and meat, and after getting our supper — or rather partaking of a mixture of dough, flour, and tainted bacon — we were marched through the town, as we thought, to get on the cars; but I guess it was done in order that the citizens might satisfy their curiosity by seeing the "Yankees," as we were taken back to the same place and kept till morning. Then they put us on the cars and started for Atlanta. On the way we were subject to a great many insults, not only from the men, but the women. They came out as we passed, and threw clubs and stones at us, and did everything they could to express their hatred of the "Yankees;" but they soon got tired, for the boys were not in the humor to be outdone by these so-called *Southern ladies*, and paid them back in their own coin, till they would go back into their houses or silently look on and wonder at the impudence the "Yankees" had to *insult them*.

Arriving at Atlanta we were met by crowds of men, women, and children, both white and black, and of all ages, from old grayheaded men and women down to the little urchins that could scarcely walk — all gazing with the greatest eagerness to get a sight of us, to see if we did really look like human beings. Many appeared surprised at seeing us, and I could hear them saying, "*Is them Yankees?*" One old woman came running out and asked me if we were really Yankees. I told her we were, "but as we had come from the West, and were younger ones than those in the East, our horns had not yet appeared." This answer seemed to satisfy her, for she went off and said no more about Yankees. In every direction we saw the young negroes and white children running about hollowing, "Yanks, Yanks!" and the scene was quite amusing to behold.

Leaving the depot we were taken to the rear of the town and put in a lot which had the appearance of having been used for a hog lot, and left to spend the night as best we could, which was none the pleasantest, I can assure you. The next day we were formed into companies of one hundred each, our names again taken, and we marched into the barracks to spend the night. Here they took our woollen blankets and pocket knives from us, but they got but few of the latter, for we concealed them. There we got five days' rations of hard bread and meat, which was to last us till we got to Richmond.

After leaving Atlanta we made but few stops till we got to Richmond. We passed through Augusta, formerly the capital of Georgia. It had the appearance of once being a beautiful and prosperous city; it is situated in a fine country on the west side of the Savannah River, though like all other towns of the South, it is behind the cities of the North *about a half century* IN CIVILIZATION. The next place of any importance we came to was Columbia, the capital of South Carolina, which is near the centre of the State, but in a very poor country and among hills, so that a person, to view the place, must go through it. Leaving this specimen of Southern cities, we went south till we came to Branchville, forty-five miles from Charleston. Here we struck the Raleigh and North Carolina Railroad, and were soon in North Carolina. Arriving at Raleigh, the capital, we went into camp for a while.

There are a great many Union people in Raleigh, but they have to be very cautious, as they are closely watched by the military authorities. North Carolina is a better country than either South Carolina or Georgia; it looks more like the North; but in South Carolina the soil is the poorest that I have seen in any place. In some parts of the State they have tried to raise grain, but it has been almost a complete failure. What little corn I saw was very poor, it being so thin over the field that I could almost count the stalks as we passed in the cars. Their farming implements are of a very poor quality. They break up their ground with a small plough with one horse or mule attached. What grain they raise is not enough for home consumption, let alone to supply an army with bread and meat. The principal timber through the South is pine, which grows in great abundance. On arriving in sight of Richmond, we got off the cars and were taken to Bell Island on the morning of the 31st of September, being just ten days on the way; the distance we travelled over being 850 miles. The island is situated in James River, at the foot of the falls, and opposite the upper part of the city. That part of the island we were on is a very low sand bar, over which the chilly air comes from the river, and almost every night and morning we were enveloped in a dense fog. Here we were exposed to all kinds of weather, without any shelter from the cold rains and chilly winds. Our rations here consisted of a small piece of bread and a few mouthfuls of meat or soup, over which we would hold a consultation to determine what it was made of, and came to the conclusion that it was intended for bean soup, although the greater portion of the ingredients were sand and bugs. But we must eat it or do without anything, and as the bugs were well cooked and the sand well settled to the bottom of the vessel, we managed to eat it without any great inconvenience. In this way we lived for five days, when we were taken over into the city, and took up lodgings in a large tobacco warehouse, opposite Libby Prison, and in the lower part of the city. In this building they crowded eleven hundred of us. I was fortunate enough to get up in the third story, and it was much more comfortable than either of the others. We were so crowded that we had scarcely room to lie down without getting on top of each other. Here I remained about forty days. We were not allowed to go out of the house except to get rations. In this way I managed to get out twice while there. When first put in we got about one half rations, which I thought was doing well; but it soon got less, until we were scarcely able to keep from starving. On the day after we were put in the prison the Provost Marshal came in and took our names for the third time since being captured, and told us that if all those who had any greenbacks would give them up to him, he would return them when we went away. All who did not give them up would be searched, and if any money was found it would be confiscated. By this means a great many of the boys were induced to give up their money, thinking that we should go away in a few days, and then they would get it back again. But some were not to be fooled in that way, but were determined to keep their money if possible; so they went to work to conceal it, which was done in various ways, some by sewing it in their clothes, others by putting it in their tobacco, and some would take the buttons of their blouses apart, put a bill in, and then fix it together to look as if it had never been touched. In this last-mentioned way I kept ten dollars, and gave two to the Marshal. After getting all they could in this way, they commenced to search us, but finding that they were not getting enough to pay them for the trouble, they soon quit it, and issued us some rations, as we had not had any for thirty-six hours, and were getting pretty hungry! The guards were strictly forbidden to sell anything to us, but they would do almost anything to get our greenbacks, and at night would smuggle in bread to those who had any money; and in this way I managed to get bread for four of us for several days by being economical. For a one dollar greenback we could get eight or ten loaves of bread, but for one of Confederate money, sometimes we could get two loaves. Others would not have it at all, said they had their pockets full of it. After we had been there about two weeks some of the men came so near starving that they would trade off their clothes for bread — their shoes and socks, and some even traded their shirts, and any little thing they could find; and some days the door would present the appearance of a toy shop. There were handkerchiefs, pocket knives, finger rings, combs, buttons, spoons, knives and forks, and everything a soldier could find about his person was offered for bread. "*Bread!*" "*Bread!*" was the cry, and indeed it was a sorrowful sight to see men of all grades of society, from the college professor down to the ignorant and unlettered, all brought to the verge of starvation by the inhuman barbarity of their captors. In passing around the room I could see men once stout and hearty made helpless as infants, their cheeks of a pale death color, their eyes sunken and the light that once sparkled in them gone, and their skeleton-like forms all saying plainly that unless soon aided their time was short for this world. The sight was enough to draw pity from the hardest of hearts, unless they were so steeped in crime that nothing could affect them. The anguish and suffering here endured can never be told. Future history will fail in its endeavors to picture the noble heroism here displayed by men when they were suffering all the misery possible for man to endure, yet true to their country's cause, and would rather die than sacrifice their honor and patriotism, by turning traitor to their country. Almost every day there were from eight to ten taken to the hospital, there to linger on for weeks, and perhaps months, before receiving any benefit by the change, if indeed they ever recovered.

But there was still another evil to contend against; and that was the vermin, which got so numerous that we could in no way rid ourselves of them; and when a person once got down and

was unable to help himself, there was danger of his actually being *killed by the lice*. It makes me shudder now while I think of it. What a terrible condition we were then in! but how much worse must it have become by this time, as it has been near six weeks since I left! But I will not dwell longer on so horrible a scene. After having used what little money I had, and trading my knife and haversack for bread, and seeing what there was in store for me if I remained longer in that place, I resolved to effect my escape or die in the attempt, as it was death any how if I remained there. I mentioned it to my comrades, but they did not approve of it. But not minding what they said, and finding a young fellow from Pennsylvania who was as anxious to get away as myself, we went to work to contrive some means of escape, which was no easy job, for we were closely guarded on all sides. The house we were in is a four-story building; and by going on the upper floor we could get a view of a good part of the city, and there we marked out the course we would pursue if successful in getting out. We were to go directly east for about four or five miles, and then incline more to the south, so as to come to our lines at Williamsburg, Va. We tried several plans, but could not succeed. One was to tear off some plank at the rear of the building where they had been nailed up to the window, then lay them over on to the fence near by, and get into a lot. We worked at it several nights until we were detected, and had to abandon it. But not in the least discouraged we went at something else. After examining the house all through we could find no place but what was closely guarded. So we came to the conclusion that the only way left was to go out at the door past the guard; and as there had been several of the rebs in cleaning up the house, or rather having it done, we thought it a good time. Without saying anything to the boys as to what we were about to undertake for fear we might not be successful, as they had been making sport at our not having succeeded before, we went down to the lower floor to get ready for the trial of our new plan. Whichever got out first was to go to a small hill, about three squares from the prison, and wait for the other. Just about dusk, I got a rebel suit from one of our boys, without much trouble. My partner had got his a few days before. After rigging ourselves in rebel costume, I told my comrade that we would wait till after the relief came on at seven o'clock before going out, and in the mean time look around for a little sport.

Well, we walked round through the house, and all the boys took us to be rebels, which was just what we wanted. One of them took me to one side, and wanted me to try to get him out of the prison; he said that he had been conscripted, and did not want to fight against the South, had never been in a battle, nor fired a gun at the *Southern people*. I told him that I would see about it, and left him. Some of the boys wanted us to bring them in some bread. I told them that the guard would not let us trade with them, but I would try to get some if he would let me bring it in. Seven o'clock came, and I started out, passed the first guard without saying a word, came to the one on the street; he halted me, and asked where I belonged; I told him I was Police Sergeant, and had been in having the prisoners clean up the house. He did not like to let me pass, but I finally got off, and went directly to the place agreed upon for us to meet. Getting up on the bank, I concealed myself where I could see down the street.

When my partner started, the guard would not let him pass; so he had to go back into the house. But he was determined on being out, so he got the boys to attract the guard's attention at the window, and he went back to where some boards had been taken off, and where the guard had been stationed, and crawled out and got away safe. He came directly to where I had been waiting an hour and a half, and was nearly frozen. I will not attempt to describe our feelings at once more finding ourselves free, at least for the present. But we still had dangers to encounter, being in a strange country, without a guide, and our enemies all around us. But we were resolved to push ahead as best we could; so shaping our course in an eastern direction, we struck out, guided by the stars. We crossed the fields and woods till we came to the fortifications, which were not very formidable. These we passed very cautiously. Coming to a house we tried to rouse the inmates, which we supposed to be negroes, but we could not get them to answer us, and we started on. We soon came to a road which ran in the right direction, and we followed it till about two o'clock, when we got so tired, and being so weak, that we had to stop and rest. Going into an old stable, we lay down; but it was too cold for us there. So we got up and went to a house close by, and found an old crippled negro by herself. We went in and warmed, and remained till daylight. Then we found we had travelled ten miles during the night, and were on the right road. This we followed all day, occasionally meeting some citizens and some few soldiers. But being dressed in rebel clothes, they did not molest us. At noon, we stopped at a small cabin to get something to eat, and found a woman whose husband was in the army. Here we got some bread and milk, and learned a great deal about the road. We came to the Chickahominy River, twenty miles from Richmond. This we crossed on some logs where the long bridges had been, but were destroyed at the time McClellan advanced on Richmond.

Soon after crossing the river we met a man whom at first sight we took to be a rebel soldier; but we were mistaken. He came up and began to question us pretty closely. He asked where we belonged; we told him, in Richmond, to the 19th Virginia Battalion, which was guarding prisoners at Richmond. He then wanted to know where we were going. We said, "Home on furlough." He looked at us a while, and began to laugh, saying, we need not try to fool him; that we were escaped prisoners, trying to get to the Federal lines. This we stoutly denied. So, finding that he could get nothing from us, he told us that we had better turn back to Richmond, that we never could get past the pickets. We told him that when our furlough was out we would go back, and not before. So he rode off and left us. We did not stop long to consider what we should do, but started off as fast as we could walk for about five miles, when we found a negro. From him we found out where the pickets were stationed, and how to get around them. He also told us where to find a free negro's house, and as we were pretty tired, we concluded to go and stay all night. He put us in the house that the owner had left in his charge, made us a good fire, and got some corn bread for us to eat. We got a pretty good rest, and daylight found us again on the road. We had gone but a short distance, when, just ahead of us, we saw a squad of cavalry coming. There was no time to lose; so, bounding into the woods, we ran as fast as we could for about half a mile; but finding they were not following us, we ceased running. After that we did not venture on the road, but kept in the woods all the time, occasionally going to a negro cabin to find the way; and we always found them willing to aid us in any way that they could. Night coming on, and as we could not well travel in the woods after night, we looked around for a place to stop. We found a large house near by, and concealing ourselves in the bushes, we watched to see if there were any white folks living in it, but could not see any; so, after it got dark, we went to it, and found no one but a negro and his family. They gave us some sweet potatoes for supper, and some blankets to keep us warm, and we did very well that night. We were out bright and early the next morning. We had to be more cautious now, as we were among the scouts. The negroes showed us by-paths through the woods, which we followed all day. We saw several scouts, but managed to evade them.

Our road was very rough, and we made slow progress. We missed our way, and travelled about three miles before finding it out, then had to go back and start anew. We had to go through woods and across swamps almost impassable. We finally came to the place we had been told to go; got permission to stay over night, a first rate supper and good bed. Upon inquiry we found that we were within seven miles of the Union pickets, and that there was no more danger, so we felt at home. In the morning, after partaking of a good breakfast, our host went with us about two miles, and set us on the main road. We here thanked him for his assistance, and bade him good by.

We went forward with light hearts that morning, thinking that we were soon to be in the midst of friends. We soon came in sight of the pickets posted on a hill. They saw us coming, and came out to meet us, thinking we were rebel deserters. We soon told our story, and were warmly received and well provided for.

THE NEW BALLAD OF LORD LOVELL.*

Lord Lovell he sat in St. Charles's Hotel,
In St. Charles's Hotel sat he,
As fine a case of a Southern swell
As ever you'd wish to see — see — see,
As ever you'd wish to see.

Lord Lovell the town had vowed to defend ;
A-waving his sword on high,
He swore that his last ounce of powder he'd spend,
And in the last ditch he'd die.

He swore by black and he swore by blue,
He swore by the stars and bars,
That never he'd fly from a Yankee crew
While he was a son of Mars.

He had fifty thousand gallant men,
Fifty thousand men had he,
Who had all sworn with him that they'd never surren—
Der to any tarnation Yankee.

He had forts that no Yankee alive could take ;
He had iron-clad boats a score,
And batteries all around the Lake
And along the river-shore.

Sir Farragut came with a mighty fleet,
With a mighty fleet came he,
And Lord Lovell instanter began to retreat
Before the first boat he could see.

His fifty thousand gallant men
Dwindled down to thousands six .
They heard a distant cannon, and then
Commenced a-cutting their sticks.

"O ! tarry, Lord Lovell ! " Sir Farragut cried,
"O ! tarry, Lord Lovell ! " said he ;
"I rather think not," Lord Lovell replied,
"For I'm in a great hurry.

"I like the drinks at St. Charles's Hotel,
But I never could bear strong Porter,
Especially when its served on the shell,
Or mixed in an iron mortar."

"I reckon you're right," Sir Farragut said,
"I reckon you're right," said he,
"For if my Porter should fly to your head,
A terrible smash there'd be."

O ! a wonder it was to see them run,
A wonderful thing to see ;
And the Yankees sailed up without shooting a gun,
And captured their great citic.

Lord Lovell kept running all day and night,
Lord Lovell a-running kept he,
For he swore he couldn't abide the sight
Of the gun of a live Yankee.

When Lord Lovell's life was brought to a close
By a sharp-shooting Yankee gunner,
From his head there sprouted a red, red nose,
From his feet — a Scarlet Runner.

* Mansfield Lovell, who commanded the rebel forces at New Orleans, and who, on the approach of the national fleet and army to that place, "led his forces out of the town."

CAPTURE OF NEW ORLEANS — WHAT JU-DITH SAW. — Allow me to describe how I spent the day, at the time of the first arrival of the Federal fleet at this city. The first day that the fleet arrived, I and my sister, and a great many others, were wending our way to the levee. On our way we met a gentleman acquaintance of ours, who asked us if we were going to get some sugar. I felt quite indignant; but as I was in an amiable mood then, I forgave him with all my heart, as I had no wish to be angry only with those hateful secessionists, who were destroying all the sugar and cotton, and burning the ships and steamboats that had been left standing. If I had had the power over those that proposed it, I would have taken them all, women and men, and placed them in the burning ships, and there let them remain until secession and secessionists were consumed by the flames. I would have shown them no mercy. "Be merciful unto him that showeth mercy." The next persons we met were a lady and gentleman — the lady appearing to be quite delighted at the sight of the cotton and ships burning. There were a great many others who had come to see the fleet — some with joyful hearts, once again to behold that time-honored flag, as it was unfurled to the breeze ; others came for curiosity, and others with feelings of hate burning in their hearts, because they knew they were conquered, or would be in a short time. They foolishly depended upon some traitors to drive out the enemy when they came ; but the cowards made good their escape when they heard that the fleet had arrived, leaving their dupes to take care of themselves the best way they could, telling them how vain is the help of man in an unjust cause. We were often stopped in our progress by the burning of the wharves and piles of cotton. We had gone a good distance, when right before us lay piles of cotton burning. We had our choice, either to return back the way we came, or jump across the cotton-piles. At last we came to the conclusion that we would do the jumping ; so we selected a pile that we thought had been well burned out, and my sister made the first leap ; and as soon as she was over she exclaimed, "O my! but that was hot!" and told me that I had better find some other place to jump ; but I wanted to have some experience in jumping cotton-piles ; so over I went. When I was over I exclaimed with my sister — "O my ! but that was hot ! " and looking round to see what could have caused such heat, we saw the piles of cotton that we had jumped across burning. What appeared to have been all ashes to us, we found out by experience was a little too hot to be only ashes. We shook our dresses well, so as to make sure that there were no sparks on them, and went on our way rejoicing ; but we made up our minds that the next time we jumped cotton-piles, we would look before we leaped.

In looking at the ship burning, there was a young lady standing before us, who seemed quite unconscious about her dress burning, until told by us. Then there was another old lady, who was so absorbed in looking at the fleet, that she did not take notice of where she stood; and, being at the edge of the wharf, where it had been burned, the plank gave way, and she was precipitated into the river. Fortunately, she caught hold of another portion of the wharf, and two men assisted her out. No harm was done, but she was pretty much scared. Nothing of importance happened to us, until we noticed that one of the gunboats was coming towards our side of the river, (for the fleet was in the middle of the river.) I and my sister ran to see where it would land, so that we could get a good view. It landed near the St. Mary's Market; so we took our position before the gunboat. As we were running along, three women, who were behind us, made some remarks, one of which I overheard: she said that all persons who seemed glad to see the Yankees ought to be punished. I turned round and told them if they did not like it, why did they not remain at home. They looked at me, as much as to say I was not worth answering, and we passed on. While we were standing before the gunboat, we waved our handkerchiefs towards the men on the boat, when one of the officers lifted his cap and bowed. This attracted the attention of the three women, who had come up to us, when the eldest of them touched my sister on the shoulder, and said, "Do you mean to say that you are waving your handkerchief at them?" pointing to the men on the gunboat. My sister said it was none of her business, and I said: "Certainly." Then she said: "You had better go to them." I said I would if the boat came near enough, so that I could get in. The two younger ones called us rebels, and giving us a disdainful look, passed out of sight. You may be assured I was quite surprised on being addressed so unexpectedly; but for all that, we were ready to answer them or any other person. While the gunboat was leaving the wharf, we still continued waving our pocket handkerchiefs and bidding them good by. A man said to my sister: "Give me the handkerchief, and I will wave it for you." My sister thanked him, and said she could wave it herself. She knew it was his intention to throw it into the river. As we came farther on, we noticed two young girls, one of them waving a small Confederate flag, and calling out to them — "Go back, you dirty Yankee devils; go back where you came from." I asked, "Where are the dirty (not Yankee, but) secession devils?" and echo answered, there; and looking around I saw that it was those two young girls, the one still holding the flag and calling them names, and the other one assisting her. At last we left them, and returned home about six in the evening. We passed through Annunciation Square, which but a short while ago had been filled with tents and traitors, but now vacant. Only here and there could be seen some poor woman picking up some wood and bottles that were left by the brave defenders of the Confederacy, in their hurry to escape from the conquerors. From thence we passed up home.

CONTRABAND NEGROES. — Gen. Ashley, member of Congress from Ohio, gave the following account of the reception of the "contraband" slaves at Fortress Monroe:

"You will have heard, by the time this reaches you, of the manner in which Gen. Butler disposed of Col. Mallory, who came into the fort under a flag of truce, to claim three of his loyal slaves, who had fled from his kind and hospitable roof, and taken shelter in Fortress Monroe among strangers. Who will say that Gen. Butler, so far as he went, was not right? This Col. Mallory had met Gen. Butler in the Charleston and Baltimore Conventions, and with that impudence and assumption characteristic of the oligarchy, he comes into Gen. Butler's camp, and, though engaged in open treason against the Government, demands that he shall enforce the Fugitive Slave law upon the soil of Virginia with United States soldiers, and return him his happy and contented slaves.

"Gen. Butler says, 'You hold that negro slaves are property, and that Virginia is no longer a part of the United States?'

"The Colonel answered, 'I do, sir.'

"Gen. Butler then said, 'You are a lawyer, sir, and I want to know if you claim that the Fugitive Slave act of the United States is binding on a foreign nation; and if a foreign nation uses this kind of property to destroy the lives and property of citizens of the United States, if that species of property ought not to be regarded as contraband?'

"This was too much for the Colonel, and he knocked under and withdrew.

"This was but the beginning at Fort Monroe, and is but the beginning of a question which this Administration must meet and determine, viz., 'What shall be done with the slaves who refuse to fight against the Government of the United States, and escape from the traitors, and come into our camps for protection?' If the Administration meets this question as it ought, well; if not, it will prove its overthrow. It is a question of more magnitude and importance than the rebellion itself; and woe to the public man or the party who proves false to the demands of humanity and justice.

"On Sunday, eight more stout, able-bodied men came in. Gen. Butler said to me, 'As you went to see John Brown hung, and have some claim to control Virginia volunteers, I authorize you to see who and what those colored men are, and decide what is to be done with them.' He added, 'You had better examine them separately, and take down in writing the material part of their answers.'

"Before doing so, I went out to the fence where the slaves were standing, surrounded by about two hundred volunteers. I asked the colored men a few questions, and was about to go into the house to call them in separately, as suggested by the General, when one of the slaves said, 'Massa, what's you gwine to do wid us?'

"I told him that I did not know, but that we would not hurt them.

"'O, we knows dat,' quickly responded another; 'we knows you's our friends. What we wants to know is, whether you's gwine to send us back.'

"I answered that I had no authority over them, and no power to do anything, but that my opinion was 'it would be some time before their masters would see them again.' I said this in a low, conversational tone of voice, without noticing that all the volunteers were eagerly listening; but no sooner had the words fallen from my lips, than a hundred voices shouted, 'Good! good!' and some in laughter and some in tears clapped their hands and gave three rousing cheers, which brought out the officers and General, who supposed I had been making a speech to the troops.

"This little incident tells me more plainly than ever, that what I said last winter in the House is true, when I declared that 'the logic of events told me unmistakably that slavery must die.'

"If I had the time, and you the space, I would give in their own words the material portion of the answers of the most intelligent slaves. There is one thing certain; every slave in the United States understands this rebellion, its causes and consequences, far better than ever I supposed. I asked one old man, who said he was a Methodist class-leader, to tell me frankly whether this matter was well understood by all the slaves, and he answered me that it was, and that he had 'prayed for it for many, many long years.'

"He said that their masters and all talked about it, and he added, 'Lor' bless you, honey — we don give it up last September dat de North's too much for us;' meaning, of course, that Mr. Lincoln's election was conceded even there by the slave masters, and was understood and hoped for by all the slaves. I asked the same man how many more would probably come into the fort. He said, 'A good many; and if we's not sent back, you'll see 'em 'fore to-morrow night.'

"I asked why so, and he said, 'Dey'll understan. if we's not sent back, dat we're 'mong our friends; for if de slaveholder sees us, we gets sent right back.' And sure enough, on Monday about forty or fifty more, of all ages, colors, and sexes, came into camp, and the guard was bound to arrest them."

CARTE DE VISITE.

"'Twas a terrible fight," the soldier said;
  "Our Colonel was one of the first to fall,
  Shot dead on the field by a rifle-ball —
A braver heart than his never bled."

A group for the painter's art were they:
  The soldier with scarred and sunburnt face,
  A fair-haired girl, full of youth and grace,
And her aged mother, wrinkled and gray.

These three in porch, where the sunlight came
  Through the tangled leaves of the jasmine-vine,
  Spilling itself like a golden wine,
And flecking the doorway with rings of flame.

The soldier had stopped to rest by the way,
  For the air was sultry with summer-heat;
  The road was like ashes under the feet,
And a weary distance before him lay.

"Yes, a terrible fight; our ensign was shot
  As the order to charge was given the men,
  When one from the ranks seized our colors, and
    then
He, too, fell dead on the self-same spot.

"A handsome boy was this last: his hair
  Clustered in curls round his noble brow;
  I can almost fancy I see him now,
With the scarlet stain on his face so fair."

"What was his name? — have you never heard? —
  Where was he from, this youth who fell?
  And your regiment, stranger, which was it? tell!"
"Our regiment? It was the Twenty-third."

The color fled from the young girl's cheek,
  Leaving it white as the face of the dead;
  The mother lifted her eyes and said:
"Pity my daughter — in mercy speak!"

"I never knew aught of this gallant youth,"
  The soldier answered; "not even his name,
  Or from what part of our State he came:
As God is above, I speak the truth!

"But when we buried our dead that night,
  I took from his breast this picture — see!
  It is as like him as like can be:
Hold it this way, towards the light."

One glance, and a look, half-sad, half-wild,
  Passed over her face, which grew more pale,
  Then a passionate, hopeless, heart-broken wail,
And the mother bent low o'er the prostrate child.

EXPERIENCES OF CAPT. WILKINS. — Capt. Wilkins, of Gen. Williams' staff, who was captured at the battle of Chancellorsville, gave the following account of his experience with the Confederates. At the time the Eleventh corps was routed he was despatched with important orders from his chief:

"On galloping to convey the orders referred to, Capt. Wilkins found that two regiments had already gained their positions. He communicated the orders to their Colonels, and passed on to convey them also to Gen. Kuger, commanding the Third brigade, who was considerably nearer the enemy. Soon after leaving the embankments he passed a double line of skirmishers, and saw, to his astonishment, that they wore gray coats. Up to this moment he had no idea the enemy were so near. It was now about eight o'clock in the evening, and owing to the darkness and the fact of his riding with such speed directly towards them, the skirmishers evidently mistook him for one of their own officers, and allowed him to pass. At this moment he saw the distinguishing flag of the First brigade of Williams' division (every brigade in the Army of the Potomac carries a distinguishing flag of bright colors) to the left, and still farther on. He rode towards it, expecting to deliver the orders to the commander of the brigade. On reaching it he discovered that it had just been captured by a Georgia regiment, and was then in the possession of the enemy, by whom he was surrounded. He threw himself upon the neck of his horse, and endeavored to escape by leaping the abatis; but he found that the rebels were on every side of him. His horse was shot under him, a blow from a musket dislocated his knee, and he was dragged to the ground in a nearly insensible condition.

He was placed in charge of a guard, who took him a short distance to the rear and to the plank road, where he met Gen. Jackson and staff. Jackson had at this time formed a column of attack on the plank road, with the design of flanking our army and obtaining possession of United States Ford. The column consisted of upwards of 15,000 men, massed in columns of sections, having three batteries of artillery on the flank. Jackson was sitting on his horse, at the head of the column, surrounded by his staff. He wore a new suit of gray uniform, and was a spare man, with a weather-beaten face, and a bright, grayish-blue eye. He had a peculiarly sad and gloomy expression of countenance, as though he already saw a premonition of his fate. It was but fifteen minutes later that he was mortally wounded. As they came into his presence the guard announced, 'A captured Yankee officer.' Capt. Wilkins asked if it was Maj.-Gen. Thomas J. Jackson. On being answered in the affirmative, he raised his hat. Gen. Jackson said: 'A regular army officer, I suppose; your officers do not usually salute ours.' Capt. Wilkins replied: 'No, I am not; I salute you out of respect to you as a gallant officer.' He then asked his name and rank. On being told, he further inquired what corps and commanders were opposed in front. Capt. Wilkins replied that as an officer, he could not return a truthful answer to such questions. Jackson then turned to the guard and ordered them to search him. He then had in the breast-pocket of his coat Hooker's confidential orders to corps commanders, giving a plan in part of the campaign, the countersigns of the field for a week in advance, and the field returns, giving the effective strength of the Twelfth corps on the preceding day.

Fortunately, before the guard could carry the orders into execution, a terrific raking fire was opened on Jackson's column by twenty pieces of artillery, commanded by Capt. Best, from an eminence on the plank road. The first eight or ten shots flew over the heads of the column. The men and gunners dismounted, leaving their horses and guns. Our artillery soon got the range with more precision, and the shell and round shot ricocheted and ploughed through this dense mass of the enemy with terrific effect. Shells were continually bursting, and the screams and groans of the wounded and dying could be heard on every side. As an instance of the terrible effect of this fire, one of the guard was struck by a solid shot just below the hips, sweeping off both his legs. A battery came dashing up; but when they got into the vortex of the fire,

the gunners fled, deserting their guns, and could not be made to man them. An officer, splendidly mounted and equipped, attempted in a most gallant manner to rally them. A ball struck him on the neck, completely severing his head from his body, and leaving his spinal column standing. His body rolled to the ground, and the horse galloped to the rear. One of the shells struck a caisson full of artillery ammunition, which, exploding, ascended in a crater of variously colored flame, and showered down on the heads of the men below a mass of fragments of shot and shell. The loss inflicted by this fire must have been terrible, placing considerably over one thousand men *hors du combat*, and effectually breaking up the contemplated attack of the column.

An officer of Jackson's staff subsequently stated that it was about fifteen minutes after this that Gen. Jackson with staff advanced to the front to reconnoitre our position, having accomplished which he returned by a different path towards his own men, who, mistaking his approach for that of a party of our cavalry, fired upon him, killing and wounding four of his staff, and wounding Jackson once in the right arm and twice in the left arm and hand.

While Capt. Wilkins was being taken to the rear he devoted his attention to disposing of the important papers which he had on his person. He dared not take them from his pocket to attempt to tear them up, but cautiously placed his hand in his pocket, and worked the papers into a ball, and as they were passing along, got them into his bosom, and finally into his arm-pit under his arm, where he carried them all that night. The next morning the guard halted to get their breakfasts, and a soldier was trying to kindle a fire to cook some coffee which they had taken from our men. The wood was damp, and the fire refused to burn. The soldier swore at it until his patience gave out, when Capt. Wilkins asked him if he would not like some kindlings, and handed him the important papers. The soldier took them, and, not dreaming of their importance, used them to kindle the fire."

TRUMPET SONG.

OLIVER WENDELL HOLMES.

The battle-drum's loud rattle is rending the air;
The troopers all are mounted, their sabres are bare;
The guns are unlimbered, the bayonets shine;
Hark! hark! 'tis the trumpet-call! wheel into
   line!
  Ta, ra! ta, ta, ta!
  Trum, trum! tra, ra, ra, ra!
  Beat drums and blow trumpets!
  Hurrah, boys, hurrah!

March onward, soldiers, onward; the strife is begun;
Loud bellowing rolls the boom of the black-throated
   gun;
The rifles are cracking, the torn banners toss,
The sabres are clashing, the bayonets cross,
  Ta, ra, &c.

Down with the leaguing liars, the traitors to their
    trust,
Who trampled the fair charter of Freedom in dust;
They falter — they waver — they scatter — they
    run —
The field is our own, and the battle is won!
      Ta, ra, &c.

God save our mighty people and prosper our cause!
We're fighting for our nation, our land, and our
    laws!
Though tyrants may hate us, their threats we defy,
And drum-beat and trumpet shall peal our reply!
      Ta, ra! ta, ta, ta!
    Beat drums and blow trumpets!
    Trum, trum, tra, ra, ra, ra!
    Hurrah, boys, hurrah!

LIEUT. McNEILL's EXPLOIT. — After the surprise and capture of New Creek, Va., by Gen.
Rosser, Maj.-Gen. Crook, of the Yankee army,
was assigned to the command of the department
in which that station is embraced. Maj.-Gen.
Kelley, who previously commanded the department, still remained in Cumberland, having his
headquarters at one of the hotels in the town.
Gen. Crook established his headquarters in the
same town, at the other principal hotel. As
soon as this state of affairs became known to
Lieut. Jesse C. McNeill, upon whom has devolved
the command of McNeill's Rangers since the
death of his father, the lamented old Captain, he
resolved to risk an attempt to surprise and bring
off those two Generals.

Having posted himself thoroughly in regard to
the situation of affairs in and around Cumberland, the night of Monday, 20th inst., he, with
sixty trusty men, crossed Knobby Mountain to
the North Branch of the Potomac. Reaching
this stream, at a point below the first picket post
that overlooked the selected route of ingress into
Cumberland, he crossed, and in a few minutes the
Yankees on duty were relieved. "Your countersign," demanded Lieut. McNeill, to a burly Dutchman, with such accompaniments as seemed to impress the fellow with the notion that to divulge
it was a matter of self-preservation. "Bool's
Kaah," (meaning "Bull's Gap,") was the quick
response.

Then on briskly down the county road towards
town, near five miles distant, he moved. As the
little band struck what is known as the old pike,
soon, "Halt! who comes there?" rings out on the
air. "Friends, with countersign," is the response.
"Dismount, one, advance, and give the countersign," is the picket's next order to the Lieutenant.

Having lately had his ankle crushed, the Lieutenant was not in a condition to obey; and so
urging his horse forward, he quickly heard from
the astonished picket, "Don't shoot; I surrender."

On they rushed, and the reserves were gathered in. The first picket captured was cavalry,
the next infantry. The former were brought
along; the latter were disarmed, their guns

smashed, and they were paroled to remain where
they were until morning; were told that the town
was surrounded, and it would be impossible for
them to escape.

Entering town on the west side, they passed
another picket on the right bank of the North
Branch. By this picket they were not halted.
Crossing Will's Creek, (which flows through the
town,) at the Iron Bridge, coolly and deliberately
up Baltimore Street they ride, some whistling,
some laughing and talking, as if they were Yankees, at home among friends.

To and fro, on the street, by the gas-light, are
seen walking Yankee guards. "Helloa, boys!
whose command is that?" "Scouts from New
Creek," is the response.

Presently here they are, between two and three
o'clock in the morning, in front of the St. Nicholas Hotel, Kelley's headquarters. Down spring,
quietly and calmly, the men who, by previous arrangement, are to visit Kelley's room. They enter the hall, and having procured a light, they
enter the General's room. The General, aroused
by the knock, resting on one elbow, "You know
me, General, I suppose," says Joseph W. Kuy-
kendall, who had charge of this party. "I do,"
said the General. "You are ———," giving his
name. "General, you had me once; it is my
honor to have you now. You are a prisoner."
"But," says the General, "whom am I surrendering to?" "To me, sir," was the emphatic
response. "No place or time for ceremony; so
you will dress quickly." The order was obeyed.

While this was going on at the St. Nicholas,
another scene was transpiring at the Revere
House. Thither went promptly a portion of the
men, as per arrangement, under Lieut. Welton.
Reaching it they halt—five men, in charge of
Joseph L. Vandiver, dismount, and "Halt!" is
the greeting of the sentinel, standing in front of
the entrance. "Friends, with countersign, bearing important despatches for Gen. Crook," is
Vandiver's answer. "Advance, one," &c. In a
moment, Vandiver had the sentinel's gun, and
ordered him to stand aside under guard. The
door is rapped at — a voice from within asks,
"Who is you? I don't know you." "Open the
door; I must see Gen. Crook." The door is
opened, and there stands a small darkey. "Is
Gen. Crook in?" "Yes, sir." "Show me his
room." "I'm afeerd to; but I will, if you don't
tell on me." Crook's room is reached; a rap
given. "Come in." In obedience to the invitation, a tall and stalwart form, with light in one
hand, and pistol undisplayed in the other, stands
erect, cool and deliberate, before the General.
"Gen. Crook, I presume," says Vandiver. "I
am, sir." "I am Gen. Rosser, sir; you are in
my power; you have two minutes to dress in."
Then the General rubbed his eyes, as if he thought
he dreamed. "Come, General, there are your
clothes; you can either put them on, or go as
you are." The General quickly arose and dressed

The prisoner and his captors make their exit
to their vigilant comrades without. The General is made to mount behind Vandiver. Off

they start, soon rejoin the St. Nicholas party with their prize, and then they all commence to "evacuate" the city quietly, coolly, and in good order. Reaching Will's Creek Bridge, they turned to the left, and proceeded down the tow-path.

On the opposite side of the canal, encamped on the hills around the town, are many of Crook's and Kelley's soldiers, who dream not of the surprise the morning shall bring them; the sentinels too, as unconscious as their slumbering comrades of the proximity of a foe. A few are awake, and with curiosity aroused by the sound of horsemen moving, as it were, in midnight review before them, inquire, "Whose command?" "Scouts going out," is the careless response. At length, they are about five miles below the town, where they intend to recross to "Old Virginia." A "Halt" greets the advance. "Friends, with countersign." The picket gives the usual command. "Bull's Gap," says McNeill; "no time to dismount; are in a hurry; the enemy are reported close; we are sent out by Gen. Crook to watch his movements." "Go on, then; cold night, boys, to be out." "Yes, pretty cold." "Give the Johnnies h—l, boys." "O, yes, we are the boys to do that;" are some of the words interchanged, as McNeill and his boys file past the unsuspecting Yankees. A moment or two more, and McNeill is in Virginia!

"McGregor is on his native heath,
With McGregor's clan around him."

On he pushes briskly, without any report of Yankees pursuing in the rear, to which a strict watch is kept. Romney, twenty-seven miles from Cumberland, is reached; the rear-guard report about sixty Yankees in sight, with some of whom they exchanged a few shots, but the Yankees exhibited no disposition to push on very fast. At about two o'clock in the day, McNeill is seen near Moorefield, moving up the South Branch of the Potomac, while up the pike, on the opposite side, move the Yankees, about two hundred strong, their horses the worse for having galloped from New Creek Station, some thirty-five miles off, from which point they started about eight o'clock in the morning, as we afterwards learned. Tuesday night, McNeill camped on the South Fork of the South Branch, with his prisoners all safe, but, like their captors, all tired. The next morning, five hundred Yankee cavalry entered Moorefield; a large force was also reliably reported to Lieut. McNeill, going up Lost River, to intercept him; but they didn't, as the Generals reached this city Sunday morning, about two o'clock, in charge of Lieut. J. S. Welton, who rendered prompt, active, and efficient service in effecting the capture.

It is proper to say, that the entrance into Gen. Kelley's room was through his Adjutant-General's apartment. An eye was kept to this gentleman, and he was brought off with four headquarter colors. His name is Major Melvin.

To have entered Cumberland, a city of eight or nine thousand inhabitants, (a majority of whom are bitterly hostile,) with, according to our best information, seven or eight thousand troops encamped in and around, is very strong evidence that Lieut. Jesse C. McNeill is a chip of the old block, a worthy son of his gallant old sire, Capt. John Hanson McNeill, who, and his eldest son, have already laid their lives upon their country's altar.

Gen. Early, immediately on the receipt of the news of his exploit, advanced the gallant young officer to the rank of Captain in McNeill's Rangers.

ROLL CALL.

BY N. G. SHEPHERD.

"CORPORAL GREEN!" the Orderly cried;
  "Here!" was the answer, loud and clear,
  From the lips of a soldier, who stood near;
And "Here!" was the word the next replied.

"Cyrus Drew!"—then a silence fell—
  This time no answer followed the call;
  Only his rear man had seen him fall,
Killed or wounded, he could not tell.

There they stood, in the falling light,
  These men of battle, with grave, dark looks,
  As plain to be read as open books,
While slowly gathered the shades of night.

The fern on the hill-sides was splashed with blood,
  And down in the corn, where the poppies grew,
  Were redder stains than the poppies knew,
And crimson-dyed as the river's flood.

For the foe had crossed from the other side,
  That day, in the face of a murderous fire,
  That swept them down in its terrible ire;
And their life-blood went to color the tide.

"Herbert Cline!" At the call there came
  Two stalwart soldiers into the line,
  Bearing between them this Herbert Cline,
Wounded and bleeding, to answer his name.

"Ezra Kerr!"—and a voice answered, "Here!"
  "Hiram Kerr!" but no man replied:
  They were brothers, these two: the sad wind sighed,
And a shudder crept through the cornfield near.

"Ephraim Deane!"—then a soldier spoke;
  "Deane carried our regiment's colors," he said,
  "When our ensign was shot; I left him dead,
Just after the enemy wavered and broke.

"Close to the road-side his body lies;
  I paused a moment, and gave him to drink;
  He murmured his mother's name, I think,
And Death came with it and closed his eyes."

'Twas a victory—yes; but it cost us dear;
  For that company's roll, when called at night,
  Of a hundred men who went into the fight,
Numbered but twenty that answered, "Here!"

THE SCHOOLS OF FERNANDINA. — A correspondent writing from Fernandina, Fla., says:—The colored schools, which have been in successful operation here, closed for a vacation of two months. The progress made by the pupils more than equals the expectations of the most sanguine friends of the race. The children have evinced an aptitude to learn, and a capacity fully equal to white children at the North, and in all the better characteristics they are in no way behind them. . . . . None who have witnessed the grateful expressions of fathers and mothers, and the daily tributes of flowers, and other evidences of affection of the children for their teachers, will ever question the natural susceptibility of this people to cultivation, and a prompt response to the ordinary appliances which make mankind respectable. Corporeal punishment has been so rare that I question whether, during the entire term, among three hundred children, there have been more than half a dozen cases; and I have never seen uneducated children anywhere exhibit more sensibility to the dishonor of a banishment from school, or other similar infliction, than these children of slavery.

Some of the girls and boys had committed pieces, which were properly spoken; and one little ebony, only eight years old, showed extraordinary aptness at declamation in a little piece he had learned. True, he was in rags, and his skin was coal-black, but a more intelligent and happy face I never saw. If permitted, that boy will yet shame many a "pale-face" by his superior intellectual power.

At the close of the exercises, a little book or primer was presented to each scholar as a present for their attendance and good conduct; and it was pleasing to see with what eagerness and satisfaction each received this first testimonial of scholarship. Nearly three hundred presents were distributed, which were furnished principally through the liberality of Hon. Joseph Hoxie, of New York, who had visited the schools a few months since, and whose judicious selections were universally commended, and his generosity fully appreciated. These children will never forget this occasion.

Among the songs by the school, interspersed throughout the exercises, — and *every* child sings in these schools, — was the following, which, aside from its intrinsic merit and affecting pathos, was particularly interesting from the fact that just before the rebellion, a congregation of slaves attending a public baptism on Sunday, at Savannah, were arrested, imprisoned, and punished with thirty-nine lashes each, for singing the song of spiritual freedom — now a crime, since slavery has become a "divine institution."

SLAVE SONG.

My mother! how long! Mothers! how long!
    mothers! how long!
Will sinners suffer here?
Chorus. — It won't be long! It won't be long! It
    won't be long!
That sinners 'll suffer here!

We'll walk de golden streets! we'll walk de golden
    streets! we'll walk de golden streets!
Where pleasures never die!
Chorus. — It won't be long! &c.

My brother! do sing! my brother! do sing! my
    brother! do sing!
De praises ob de Lord!
Chorus. — It won't be long! &c.

We'll *soon* be free! we'll *soon* be free! we'll *soon*
    be free!
De Lord will call us home!
Chorus. — My brother! do sing! my brother! do
    sing! my brother! do sing!
De praises ob de Lord!

And these verses, so expressive and pathetic, are added to almost indefinitely, in the same style, by the interested singers. Now, where this and the hundred kindred songs sung by the slaves came from, or who amidst the darkness of slavery inditeth them, I cannot of course say; but it is easy to determine the source of the inspiration. In patient faith and enduring hope these "songs of Zion" have been sung by generations of these bondmen, as the only relief for bleeding hearts and lacerated bodies; and now God comes in judgment to requite the nation for the wrongs inflicted upon his oppressed and suffering poor.

Another interesting and significant event connected with the people here, occurred on Monday. The women called a meeting at the church, to consider the propriety of presenting Col. Littlefield's regiment, now enlisting here, a stand of colors. Like the great dinner and celebration on the Fourth, all was arranged by the colored women, and fifty dollars were contributed on the spot, by these poor fugitives, from the hard earnings of their brief freedom — contributed to purchase an American flag to be borne by their colored brethren — the flag which had been to them till now the emblem of oppression! They cherish no feelings of malignity for the wrongs which have been inflicted, but hail the new era of freedom with joy, and rally to the country's standard with pride and satisfaction, now that the country is prepared to respect their humanity and protect their rights. Among the contributors was one slave woman, who has five sons and a husband in the army, while she remains at home to care for younger children.

Ned Simons, an old negro belonging to the Dungenness estate of Gen. Nathan Greene, on Cumberland Island, and who was left by the rebel inheritor, Nightingale, on his evacuation of the place, died here last week, at the house of the lady teachers of the schools, who have kindly cared for him since their arrival here. Ned was over one hundred years old, and remembered Gen. Washington well, and was one of the number who assisted in carrying him through the streets of Savannah on his last visit to that place. Old Ned took a lively interest in the affairs of the nation, and rejoiced in the prospect of the freedom of his race. He was deeply interested in the cause of education, and, though partially blind with age, he desired himself to learn to read. On being asked why he wished to learn, when he could not expect to live much longer, he replied, "As the tree falls, so it will lay;" his attainments on earth would contribute to higher attainments on high; and the ladies yielded to his request, and during the last months of his life, he, with much labor and effort, acquired a knowledge of his letters and syllables. Poor old Ned! After a long life of unrequited toil and slavery, he has "gone where the good negroes go;" where no slave-driver will ever follow; where he can sing "de praises ob de Lord" in freedom and safety.

INCIDENT OF FREDERICKSBURG. — While the Union cavalry were on the retreat, one of the men heard the clattering of a horse's hoofs close in his rear, and supposing he was pursued by a rebel, put spurs to his horse and increased his pace, without looking behind him. After travelling at a rapid rate for some distance, our man turned his head, and discovered that the pursuing horse was riderless. The sudden shock of satisfaction was so great that he fell from his horse, and both horses went cantering over the fields without riders, and the Union cavalryman took possession of his unexpected prize.

A SPARTAN GIRL. — A young daughter of Baltimore wrote thus to a schoolmate and friend in Charleston:

BALTIMORE, May 16, 1861.

You must pardon me for intruding upon you an expression of my Southern sentiments. I so often think and speak of you with the rest of your friends, and I envy your living in the bosom of a home which we are denied. You cannot see as well as we how miserably our happiness, our liberty, our homes, have been sold by traitors, who would risk all this to be pampered minions of an Abe Lincoln and his party.

I can scarcely control myself while I am writing you. I am boiling over with indignation. I once prayed for peace; but now, next to begging the blessing of God, I pray — "Hurrah for Jeff Davis and the Southern Confederacy!" and, woman as I am, if I knew the way, I would walk out of Maryland, until my foot rested upon more Southern soil. You are happy indeed, and have nothing to contend with in comparison with us poor Baltimorians, or, I should have said, Marylanders; for here there are hearts that beat as warm to the South, as ever throbbed at the guns of Charleston. We are not conquered, and *never will be*; and God grant that before long the flag of secession may wave over our city and State. Then we can run to the embraces of friends whom we love, though we know them not. It is sufficient we are all for the same cause — Southern rights.

It would amuse you exceedingly if you could hear the women talk. Some offer themselves as escorts to the gentlemen, who find it difficult to get out of the city; others are almost ready to hang old Hicks, and, but for the men, I believe they would; others, and I among the number, are ready to shoulder our muskets to defend the just and holy cause of the South, in case the men fail.

In the event of Maryland doing anything that would seem hostile to the South, do you, and beg your friends to, keep one sympathizing thought for those who are with you in spirit; for

    "'Tis home where'er the heart is."

How I would love to be able to talk to you about old and new times!

INCIDENTS OF BULL RUN. — In the thickest of the contest, a secession Colonel of cavalry was knocked out of his saddle by a ball from one of our riflemen. "There goes old Baker, of the Georgia First!" shouted one of our boys, in hearing of his chaplain. "Who?" queried the parson. "Col. Baker, of the rebel ranks, has just gone to his long home." "Ah, well," replied the chaplain, quietly, "the longer I live, the less cause I have to find fault with the inscrutable acts of Divine Providence." An unlucky private in one of the New York regiments was wounded in this fight, and his father arrived at the hospital just as the surgeon was removing the ball from the back of his shoulder. The boy lay with his face downwards on the pallet. "Ah, my poor son," said the father, mournfully, "I'm very sorry for you. But it's a bad place to be hit in — thus, *in the back*." The sufferer turned over, bared his breast, and pointing to the opening above the armpit, exclaimed, "Father, here's where the ball went in!"

One of the Zouaves was struck by a cannon shot, which tore through his thigh, close to his body, nearly severing the limb from the trunk. As he fell, he drew his photograph from his breast, and said to his nearest comrade, "Take this to my wife. Tell her I died like a soldier, faithful to my country's cause, and the good old flag. Good by!" and he died where he fell.

An artillery-man lay on the ground, nearly exhausted from loss of blood, and too weak to get out of the way of the tramping troops and horses that flitted about him. A mounted horseman came towards him, when he raised the bleeding stumps of both his arms, and cried out, "Don't tread on me, Cap'n! See! both hands are gone." The trooper leaped over him, a shell broke near by, and the crashing fragments put the sufferer quickly out of his misery.

A rebel — one of the Georgia regiments — lay with a fearful shot-wound in his side, which tore out several of his ribs. The life-blood of the poor fellow was fast oozing out, when one of our troops came dashing forward, from out of the melée, and fell, sharply wounded, close beside him. The Georgian recognized his uniform, though he was fatally hurt, and feebly held out his hand. "We came into this battle," he said, "enemies. Let us die friends. Farewell." He spoke no more, but his companion in disaster took the extended hand, and escaped to relate this touching fact.

One of our riflemen had his piece carried away by a ball, which struck it out of his hands just as his company was in the act of advancing to storm one of the smaller rebel batteries. Unharmed, he sprang forward, and threw himself down on his face, under the enemy's guns. A Zouave lay there, wounded and bleeding, out of the way of the murderous fire. "Lay close—lay close, old boy," said the latter to the new comer; "the boys 'll take this old furnace 'n a minute, and then we'll git up an' give the rebels fits ag'in." Three minutes afterwards the battery was carried, and the two soldiers were in the thickest of the fight again.

A member of the Second Connecticut regiment wrote as follows:

While at a halt it was my lot to witness a very painful scene. I captured a prisoner, (a German,) belonging to the Eighth South Carolina regiment, and took him to Major Colburn for instructions as to how to dispose of him. The prisoner requested one privilege as his last, which the Major very humanely granted. He said his brother lay a short distance off, in a dying condition, and he wished to see him. I bade him lead the way, and I followed.

He took me to an old log hut but a few rods from where our regiment was halted. On the north side, in the shade, we found the wounded man. The prisoner spoke to him — he opened his eyes — the film of death had already overspread them, and the tide of life was fast ebbing. He was covered with blood, and the swarms of flies and mosquitoes, which were fattening upon his life's blood, indicated that he had lain there for some time. They clasped hands together, muttered a few words in the German language, supplicating the Throne of Grace for their families at home, kissed, and bade each other a final adieu; the prisoner remarking, as I took him by the arm to lead him away, for the column was moving, "Brother, you are dying, and I am a prisoner." The man was shot with a musket ball in the back, just over the hip; from which fact I inferred that he was on the retreat when the deadly ball overtook him.

JACKSON.

BY HARRY FLASH.

Not 'midst the lightning of the stormy fight,
Not in the rush upon the Vandal foe,
Did kingly Death, with his resistless might,
　　Lay the Great Leader low.

His warrior soul its earthly shackles broke
In the full sunshine of a peaceful town;
When all the storm was hushed, the trusty oak
　　That propped our cause went down.

Though his alone the blood that flecks the ground,
Recording all his grand, heroic deeds,
Freedom herself is writhing with the wound,
　　And all the country bleeds.

He entered not the nation's Promised Land
At the red belching of the cannon's mouth,
But broke the House of Bondage with his hand,
　　The Moses of the South!

O, gracious God! not gainless is the loss;
A glorious sunbeam gilds thy sternest frown;
And while his country staggers with the cross,
　　He rises with the crown!

INCIDENTS OF THE BATTLE OF PEA-RIDGE. — One of the Ninth Missouri was so enraged, on the second day of the battle, at seeing his brother, a member of the same regiment, horribly butchered and scalped, that he swore vengeance against the Indians, and for the remainder of the day devoted his attention entirely to them, concealing himself behind trees, and fighting in their fashion. An excellent marksman, he would often creep along the ground to obtain a better range; and then woe to the savage who exposed any part of his body. When he had shot an Indian, he would shout with delicious joy: "There goes another red-skin to ——. Hurrah for the Stars and Stripes, and —— all Indians!" Though ever following the wily foe, and though fired upon again and again, he received not a scratch; and on his return to camp, after nightfall, bore with him nine scalps of aboriginal warriors, slain by his own hand to avenge his brother's death.

A German soldier, in the Thirty-fifth Illinois, met with two very narrow escapes in fifteen minutes, while Gen. Carr's division was contending so vigorously against the enemy in Cross-Timber Hollow. He wore earrings for the benefit of his eyes, and a musket-ball cut one of them in two, (the broken segments still remaining,) and passed into the shoulder of the Second Lieutenant of the company. Ten minutes after, during a temporary lull in the strife, while the German was relating the story of his escape, a bullet whistled by, carrying the other ring with it, and abrading the skin of his ear, without doing further harm. Such are the vagaries of fate, and the mysterious shiftings on the battle-field between life and death.

One of the Texas soldiers was advancing with his bayonet upon a Lieutenant of the Ninth Iowa, whose sword had been broken. The officer saw his intention, avoided the thrust, fell down at his foeman's feet, caught hold of his legs, threw him heavily to the ground, and before he could rise, drew a long knife from his adversary's belt, and buried it in his bosom. The Texan, with dying grasp, seized the Lieutenant by the hair, and sank down lifeless, bathing the brown leaves with his blood. So firm was the hold of the nerveless hand, that it was necessary to cut the hair from the head of the officer before he could be freed from the corpse of the foe.

Presentiments on the battle-field often prove prophetic. Here is an instance: While Col. Osterhaus was gallantly attacking the centre of the enemy, on the second day, a Sergeant of the Twelfth Missouri requested the Captain of his company to send his wife's portrait, which he had taken from his bosom, to her address in St. Louis, with his dying declaration that he thought of her in his last moments. "What is that for?" asked the Captain. "You are not wounded — are you?" "No," answered the Sergeant; "but I know I shall be killed to-day. I have been in battle before, but I never felt as I do now. A moment ago I became convinced my time had come; but how, I cannot tell. Will you gratify my request? Remember, I speak to you as a dying man." "Certainly, my brave fellow; but you will live to a good old age with your wife. Do not grow melancholy over a fancy or a dream." "You will see," was the response. The picture changed hands. The Sergeant stepped forward to the front of the column, and the Captain perceived him no more. At the camp-fire that evening the officer inquired for the Sergeant. He was not present. He had been killed three hours before by a grape-shot from one of the enemy's batteries.

While the fight was raging about Miser's farm-house, on the ridge, on Friday morning, a soldier, belonging to the Twenty-fifth Missouri, and a member of a Mississippi company, became separated from their commands, and found each other climbing the same fence. The rebel had one of those long knives made of a file, which the South has so extensively paraded, but so rarely used, and the Missourian had one also, having picked it up on the field. The rebel challenged his enemy to a fair, open combat with the knife, intending to bully him, no doubt; and the challenge was promptly accepted. The two removed their coats, rolled up their sleeves, and began. The Mississippian had more skill, but his opponent more strength, and consequently the latter could not strike his enemy, while he received several cuts on the head and breast.

The blood began trickling down the Unionist's face, and, running into his eyes, almost blinded him. The Union man became desperate, for he saw the secessionist was unhurt. He made a feint; the rebel leaned forward to arrest the blow, but employing too much energy, he could not recover himself at once. The Missourian perceived his advantage, and knew he could not lose it. In five seconds more it would be too late. His enemy, glaring at him like a wild beast, was on the eve of striking again. Another feint; another dodge on the rebel's part; and then the blade of the Missourian, hurled through the air, fell with tremendous force upon the Mississippian's neck. The blood spirted from the throat, and the head fell over, almost entirely severed from the body. Ghastly sight! too ghastly even for the doer of the deed! He fainted at the spectacle, weakened by the loss of his own blood, and was soon after butchered by a Seminole, who saw him sink to the earth.

On Saturday morning, a body of three or four hundred Indians was discovered on the north side of Sugar Creek, below the curve of a hill, firing from thick clusters of post-oaks into three or four companies of Arkansas soldiers, marching in McCulloch's division towards the upper part of the ridge. The Major of the battalion, seeing this, hallooed out to them that they were firing upon their own friends, and placed his white handkerchief on his sword, and waved it in the air.

The Indians either did not see, or did not care for, the flag of truce, but poured two volleys into the Arkansans, killing, among others, the Major himself. The presumption then was, that the Cherokees had turned traitors; and the secession soldiers were immediately ordered to charge upon them. They did so, and for an hour a terrible fight ensued among the oaks between them and their late savage allies, in which it is stated some two hundred and fifty were killed and wounded on both sides. The Indians suffered severely, as they were driven from their hiding-places, and shot and butchered without mercy. A person who witnessed this part of the fight says it was the most bloody and desperate that occurred on the field, being conducted with the most reckless and brutal energy by the two parties, of whom it would be difficult to say which was the most barbarous. On the dead savages were found, in some instances, two or three scalps fastened to their belts by thongs of leather.

AN ENERGETIC WOMAN. — A correspondent writing from Jasper county, Mississippi, gave the following:

Mrs. Simmons, a widow lady of Jasper county, Mississippi, made, during one year of the war, (1863,) 500 bushels of corn, 100 bushels of potatoes, with peas and pinders enough to fatten her hogs. She did the ploughing herself, and did it with an old wind-broken pony. Her two little daughters, aged twelve and fourteen years, did the hoeing. She also made 100 pounds of tobacco. After her crop was finished, she did weaving enough to buy her salt, and a pair of cards, and had some money left.

INCIDENTS OF BULL RUN. — A Southern writer, in recounting the incidents of the battle of Bull Run, says:

Our regiment by this time had come in reach of the enemy's cannon. The balls fell before and behind us, but no damage was done. We now threw our knapsacks away to engage in a hand-to-hand fight. We ran to the point at which the fire seemed to be most severe. Advancing in front of the cannon, we got within musket-shot of our enemy, and fell to the ground, having a slight mound to protect us. Had we been standing, scarcely one would have been left. Twice did the cannon-balls throw dirt upon me, and musket-balls whistled by the hundred within a few inches of my head. Several of our regiment (18th Virginia) were killed, but the exact number I know not. Young Hatchett was wounded, but not seriously, the ball entering his leg. Men would raise their heads a few inches from the ground to peep, and several times were shot in that position. Men fell on my right and left. We remained about ten minutes receiving the enemy's fire, and were not allowed to return fire. The command to fire came at last. We rose and fired with deadly effect upon our foes. We rushed forward to the top of the hill, and fired again;

also a third time. Now, for the first time, the foe began to retire in a run, and in great disorder. I think that a great majority of the regiment upon which we fired were killed. No boasting, — God forbid! to him all praise is due. At our approach the enemy left an excellent rifled battery, manned by regulars, in our hands. They fought until all their horses were killed, and nearly every man. We were now left victors of the field, and started in pursuit of the foe. We followed them a mile or so, and were then brought back within a mile of Manassas, marching at night a distance of six or seven miles. The fight lasted eight hours — from nine to five. I cannot describe the horrors of the fight. Noise and confusion of many kinds prevailed — the firing of cannon, the discharge of musketry, the whizzing of balls, the bursting of bombs, the roar of artillery, the tramp of horses, the advance of infantry, the shouts of the conquering, the groans of the dying, the shrieks of the wounded, large numbers of the dead lying upon the ground, the carrying of the wounded by scores, and all enveloped in a dark cloud of smoke, — all go to make one vast spectacle of horrors such as I never wish to see again, or hear. Many were the dead and wounded over which I was forced to pass, both of our men and of our foes. O, how I wanted to aid them, but could not! The fight was desperate. The enemy succeeded in carrying off hundreds of their dead, but left many behind. Our cavalry, who pursued them in the direction of Centreville, report the road strewn with dead and wounded.

Our enemies are not cowards. Many men were found with bayonets in them, some side by side, each with his bayonet in the other. Our enemy is said to have run generally when we advanced with the bayonet. Certainly this was the worst of the fight. Gen. Beauregard, who commanded in person, told us that he would depend principally upon the bayonet. Gen. B. cheered us as we advanced, and our loud cheers in return were said to have frightened the enemy.

THE BOY SOLDIER. — When the Tenth Indiana was recruited in the fall of 1861, they took for their drummer a little fellow, named Johnny McLaughlin, whose parents reside at Lafayette, Indiana. He was then a little over ten years of age, and beat his tattoo at the head of the regiment for several months of active service.

At Donelson and at Shiloh, when the drumbeats were drowned in the deeper roar of battle, Johnny laid down his sticks, and taking the musket and cartridge box from a dead soldier, went out to the front, and fought as bravely as the stoutest soldier in the regiment. Escaping unhurt in each of these engagements, he was enamoured of soldier life, and sought a transfer from the infantry to Col. Jacob's Kentucky cavalry. Being favorably impressed with the spirit and zeal of the young warrior, Col. Jacob put him into his best company, and mounted him on a good horse. At the engagement at Richmond, which soon followed, in the summer of 1862, he fought with as much coolness and skill as any of his company, handling his sabre, revolver, and revolving rifle with the address of a veteran.

In October following, he was in another battle, at Perryville, where he received his first wound, a ball passing through the leg above the knee.

In this engagement Col. Jacob, with a part of his command, was temporarily separated from the greater part of the regiment, and while thus cut off was attacked by a largely superior force of the enemy, led by a Major. Col. Jacob was deliberating for a moment on the demand to surrender, when the little hero drew his pistol and shot the Major in the mouth, killing him instantly. A few moments of confusion and delay followed in the rebel regiment, during which Col. Jacob and his men escaped.

A few weeks after, he was engaged in a skirmish with some of John Morgan's men, who were raiding through Kentucky, and the fighting was severe.

Johnny was set upon by a strapping fellow, who gave him a pretty severe cut on the leg with his sabre, and knocked him off his horse. A moment after, another rebel seized him by the collar, and exclaimed: "We've got one d—d little Yankee, anyhow." The little Yankee did not see it in that light, however, and quickly drawing his pistol, shot his captor dead, and a moment after the rebels were routed, and he escaped capture.

As he was going back to Indiana on furlough to give his wound time to heal, he was stopped at one point by a provost guard, and his pass demanded.

"O," said he, "the Colonel didn't give me one, but just told me to go along with the rest. But," added the little soldier, showing his wound, "here's a pass the rebs gave me; ain't that good enough for a little fellow like me?" The guard thought it was.

His wound proved quite serious, and, much to his surprise, and against his wishes, he received his discharge in consequence of this and his extreme youthfulness. Not relishing civil life as long as the hostilities lasted, he applied at a recruiting office, but the condition of his leg excluded him.

Nothing daunted, however, he sought and obtained an interview with the President, who on hearing the story of the boyish veteran, gave a special order for his enlistment.

He had now made up his mind to follow the life of a soldier, and joined the regular army of the United States as a bugler in the cavalry service, and makes as fine-looking, neat, and obedient a little dragoon as there is in the army.

JOAN OF ARC IN THE WEST. — At a flag-raising at North Plato, Kane County, Illinois, after the Stars and Stripes had been duly hoisted, the assembly adjourned to the village church, where some speeches were made by patriotic gentlemen, and an opportunity was offered for young men to come forward and enlist, the company at Plato not being quite full. Not a man went up! This aroused the patriotism as well as the "dander" of the village schoolmistress, who, with many other ladies, was present, and she walked boldly forward to the secretary's desk, and headed the muster-roll with a name rendered illustrious as having been affixed to the Declaration of Independence, with the prenomen Mary. She was followed by another lady, and lo, and behold! the Plato company was not long in filling its ranks! The muster-roll, bearing the names of the spirited young vivandieres, has been sent to headquarters, and the company accepted by the "powers that be." After that day four flag-raisings came off in that portion of Kane county, and "Mary" and "May" — the soldier girls — in uniforms of white, red, and blue, attended all of them, at the request of the officers, marching, as pioneers, at the head of their company. The Captain said he could not get along without them; and after the flag had been sent up, he allowed them to fire each three guns in honor of the Union, the Stars and Stripes. Much of the success of the recruiting service, and the patriotic fire in old Kane, was attributed to the gallant conduct and bright eyes of these young ladies.

THE CONFEDERATE PRIMER.

At Nashville's fall
We sinned all.

At Number Ten
We sinned again.

Thy purse to mend,
Old Floyd attend.

Abe Lincoln bold
Our ports doth hold.

Jeff Davis tells a lie,
And so must you and I.

Isham did mourn
His case forlorn.

Brave Pillow's flight
Is out of sight.

Buell doth play
And after slay.

Yon oak will be the gallows-tree
Of Richmond's fallen majesty.

A LITERARY SOLDIER. — Adam Badeau, a literary man and journalist of New York, volunteered, at Port Royal, to act in any capacity which might prove useful, when Gen. Sherman contemplated an advance upon Savannah, in January, 1862. He was immediately appointed volunteer Aid on Gen. Sherman's staff, and served in this capacity, without either rank or pay, till Gen. Sherman was relieved. The preparations for the siege of Fort Pulaski having then been completed, he volunteered and served as Aid to Gen. Gillmore, who commanded the United States forces during the bombardment of that work. He, with Gen. Gillmore, was the first to enter Fort Pulaski, being sent forward to meet the rebel officer who approached on Gen. Gillmore's landing, after the flag of the fort was struck. The rebel was Capt. Simms, late editor of the Savannah *Republican*. Capt. Simms' first words were civil: "I trust, sir, you will pardon the delay that has occurred in receiving you; we thought you would land at the other wharf." After this, Capt. Simms wished to conduct Mr. Badeau to the commandant of the fort, but Badeau requested Simms rather to go to Gen. Gillmore. This was acceded to, and after a few words of parley, the three, accompanied also by Col. Rust of a Maine regiment, entered the fort; they were received at the portcullis by Col. Olmstead, the commandant, who conducted them first to his quarters, and afterwards to inspect the works, pointing out the havoc which had been made by the National batteries. In an interview of an hour's duration between the two commanders, the terms of the capitulation were arranged. Gen. Gillmore and Col. Rust returned to Tybee Island, and Mr. Badeau was left to introduce a second party of National officers sent to receive the swords of the rebels. The ceremony of surrender took place in one of the casemates (used by Col. Olmstead for his own quarters) at about dark. Five National officers, besides Badeau, were present: Maj. Halpine, Adj.-Gen. for Gen. Hunter, Capt. S. H. Pelouze, Capt. Ely, Lieut. O'Rorke, and Lieut. Irwin of the Wabash. Each rebel, as he laid his sword on the table, announced his name and rank. The Colonel said, "I yield my sword, but I trust I have not disgraced it;" others made remarks less felicitous. After the ceremony, the National officers were invited to supper by these prisoners, and then returned to Tybee Island. Badeau, however, remained all night in Fort Pulaski, sleeping in the room with three rebel officers, and even sharing the bed of one of the hospitable prisoners. No Union troops arrived in the fort until about midnight, so that his sojourn among those who had so lately been his enemies, had a dash of romance about it. He was treated, however, with the greatest courtesy, the rebels apologizing for the fare he was offered by saying: "You see to what you have reduced us." Hominy, molasses, hard bread, and pork were served for supper and breakfast; for variety, sweet oil was used instead of molasses. The conversation was animated, and often touched on politics.

Immediately afterwards, Mr. Badeau was recommended to the President, by Gen. Hunter, for a captaincy, and made bearer of despatches to the Government, announcing the fall of Pulaski. He had also the honor of being mentioned in Gen. Gillmore's formal report of the operations. The President accordingly at once appointed him an additional Aid to Maj.-Gen. Halleck, with the rank of Captain in the regular army.

Capt. Badeau was assigned to duty with his old chief, Brig.-Gen. Sherman, served under him during the siege of Corinth, and in the subsequent pursuit of Beauregard in Mississippi. He was afterwards ordered to the Department of the Gulf, but now (1865) occupies a position on the staff of Lieut.-Gen. Grant.

MINNESOTIANS AT FREDERICKSBURG. — The following incident in the terrible battle at Fredericksburg was related by Col. Morgan: Maj.-Gen. Howard, who commanded the extreme right, ordered a strong line of pickets to be formed, as a line of battle, by Col. Morgan, in command of heavy detachments from five regiments, with the Minnesota First, as usual, on the extreme right, and most exposed place. The morning dawned — the rebels opened with shot and shell, ploughing up the ground and covering the line with heaps of earth. It was a very hot place, and three of the regiments broke, and run like sheep. Gens. Howard and Sully (Sully, their old Colonel, whom they loved dearly) were watching them. "There," said Maj.-Gen. Howard, — "there, they don't stand fire — *see them run.*" "Not a bit of it," says Gen. Sully; "my old Minnesota don't run." Gen. Howard fixed his glass on them.

"No — no — no, sir; they — your old regiment don't flinch a hair — they don't run." Sully, raising himself up to his full height, exclaimed, in his soft language, "Who in —— ever supposed they would run? They are not of the running breed." Gen. Howard complimented them as the most reliable, the bravest regiment in the division, if not in the army.

ANECDOTE OF STONEWALL JACKSON. — At a council of generals early in the war, one remarked that Major —— was wounded, and would not be able to perform a duty that it was proposed to assign him. "Wounded!" said Jackson. "If it really is so, I think it must have been by an accidental discharge of his duty."

A SOLDIER WITH THE RIGHT SPIRIT. — Henry W. Camp, Adjutant of the Tenth Connecticut volunteers, was made prisoner by the rebels at Morris Island, off Charleston, in July, 1863. After ten months' confinement in the jails of Charleston, Columbia, and Richmond, he reached his home in Hartford on the 7th of May, being released on parole. In five days the news reached him of his exchange; and though he had a leave of twenty days, he started at once for his regiment in Butler's department, above Norfolk, on the James. On reaching Bermuda Hundreds he learned that the Tenth Connecticut had gone to the front, and was then probably engaged with the enemy. Pressing forward as speedily as possible, he met the retreating column of the Eighteenth corps falling back from the attack of Beauregard. They told him that the road by which he could reach his regiment was already in possession of the enemy, and that an attempt to proceed under the circumstances would only throw him again into a rebel prison. Nothing daunted, however, he kept on, and about ten o'clock in the morning reached

his regiment just as it was coming out of one brisk skirmish, and was about advancing to another attack.

Within fifteen minutes he was at his place, under fire, and bearing himself gallantly, as always. His conduct excited the warmest admiration on the part of the regiment. Notwithstanding the engrossing excitement of the battle, officers and men hailed his return with cheer upon cheer in the very face of the enemy, and with the Minie balls flying thickly around them.

Col. Plaisted, commanding the brigade, joined in the greeting given to the beloved officer whose conduct was so praiseworthy, and even Gen. Terry, the division commander, swung his hat in the general cheering, and rode forward to welcome in person the returning adjutant to his old command.

How much richer in true honor and pleasure that manly greeting by the regiment in battle line and under fire, than all the flattery and delight that a prolonged furlough in his native city could have afforded him!

SPIRIT OF THE WOMEN OF VIRGINIA. — A lady of Clarke County, Virginia, whose husband had been during two years in Yankee prisons, and in exile from his home, and whose son (an only child, in his 18th year) was then in some Northern Bastile, as a prisoner of war, wrote to her husband as follows: "If it were possible, I should like you to be at home; but I do not want you or O. ever to give up the struggle for liberty and our rights. If your salary fails to pay your board, go at something else for the Confederacy; I will try and contrive a way to clothe you. I would love to be with you; but do not expect it now, in these times. I wish O. was at home — I mean in his company; but I would rather he would be held a prisoner for the war, than have him at home dodging his duty, as some do. I am proud to think every man in my little family is in the army. If I have but two, they are at their post of duty."

HOW GEN. BANKS' ARMY WAS SAVED. — Charley H. Greenleaf, of the Fifth New York cavalry, made the following statement in a letter to his parents: "You have probably heard of the three days' fighting from Strasburg and Front Royal to Martinsburg. Our company and company B were ordered to Front Royal, in the mountains, twelve miles from Strasburg, last Friday, and when we got within two miles of our destination we heard cannonading. The Major ordered the baggage to stop, and our two companies dashed on, and found several companies of our infantry and two pieces of artillery engaged with several thousand of the enemy. Just as we arrived on the field, Col. Parem, who had command of our forces, rode up to me, and ordered me to take one man and the two fastest horses in our company, and ride for dear life to Gen. Banks' headquarters in Strasburg for reenforcements. The direct road to Strasburg was occupied by the enemy; so I was obliged to ride round by another, seventeen miles. I rode the seventeen miles in fifty-five minutes. Gen. Banks didn't seem to think it very serious, but ordered one regiment of infantry and two pieces of artillery off. I asked Gen. Banks for a fresh horse to rejoin my company, and he gave me the best horse that I ever rode, and I started back. I came out on the Front Royal turnpike, about two miles this side of where I left our men. Saw two men standing in the road, and their horses standing by the fence. I supposed they were our pickets. They didn't halt me; so I asked them if they were pickets. They said, "No." Says I, "Who are you?" "We are part of Gen. Jackson's staff." I supposed that they were only joking. I laughed, and asked them where Jackson was. They said he was in the advance. I left them and rode to Front Royal, till I overtook a soldier, and asked him what regiment he belonged to. He said he belonged to the Eighth Louisiana. I asked how large a force they had, and the reply was, "Twenty thousand." I turned back and drew my revolver, expecting either a desperate fight or a Southern jail; but the officers in the road didn't stop me, and I was lucky enough not to meet any of their pickets. But if it was not a narrow escape, then I don't know what is. When I got out of the enemy's lines I rode as fast as the horse could carry me to Gen. Banks, and reported what I had seen and heard. He said I had saved the army. In less than an hour the whole army was in motion towards Winchester. After I left Front Royal to take the first despatch to Strasburg, our two companies of cavalry, who were covering the retreat of infantry and baggage, were attacked on three sides by about 3000 of the enemy's cavalry. Our boys fought like devils, till nearly half of them were killed or wounded, and then retreated to Winchester. Capt. White, William Watson, Henry Appleby, and nine or ten men of our company, are killed or taken. William Marshall is all right, except a slight sabre wound in the shoulder. We had a battle at Winchester, got licked, and retreated. Our company and company E were ordered to cover a Parrott gun battery and bring up the rear. We rode all the way from Winchester to Martinsburg with cannon shot and shell flying around us faster than it did at Bull Run. We crossed the Potomac last night. It was so dark that we couldn't find the ford, and had to swim our horses across. We have got our batteries in position on this side, and the rear of the army is crossing."

IN STATU QUO. — "Joe," said a soldier to a comrade, who was reading the morning paper, "where the devil's Statu Quo? I see this paper says our army's in Statu Quo."

"Dunno!" replied Joe — "reckon she must be the east fork of the Chickamorgy!"

BRAVERY OF CAPT. W. N. GREEN. — Among the interesting incidents of the battle of Chancellorsville, that of the capture of the colors of the Twelfth regiment Georgia Volunteers, during the battle of Sunday, May 3, 1863, by Capt. William N. Green, commanding the color company of the One Hundred and Second regiment N. Y. S. V., is worthy of commemoration.

After several days' severe fighting between the United States forces, under Gen. Hooker, and the Confederate forces, under Gen. Lee, the morning of Sunday, May 3, 1863, found the One Hundred and Second regiment N. Y. S. V., forming a portion of the Twelfth Army Corps, lying in the trenches on the extreme left of the Federal forces.

The battle commenced at five A. M., and the One Hundred and Second were for several hours subjected to a heavy fire from a battery of the rebels, situated on their right flank; at ten A. M., the enemy's infantry attacked the brigade of which the One Hundred and Second N. Y. S. V. was a part, and succeeded in driving the regiment, which was on the right of the One Hundred and Second, away in confusion; advancing up the trenches, the enemy charged the One Hundred and Second, and were repulsed. Soon after, the One Hundred and Second was charged upon by the Twelfth regiment Georgia Volunteers, and immediately the men of each regiment were engaged in hand-to-hand conflicts.

The company of the One Hundred and Second N. Y. S. V., which Capt. Green commanded, was especially singled out by the enemy for a fierce struggle, as they had charge of the National colors; the Captain commanding the Twelfth regiment Georgia Volunteers rushed forward at the head of his men, and made a jump right at Capt. Green, calling out to him, "Surrender!" to which Capt. Green replied, "Not yet;" then seizing the rebel Captain by the throat with his left hand, he flung him violently to the ground, by tripping him up, and wrenched his sword from his grasp. Capt. Green was then seized from behind by an ambulance-sergeant of the rebels, who, putting his knee in the middle of his back, flung him on the ground. Capt. Green sprung to his feet, and putting both swords (his own and the rebel Captain's) into his left hand, he knocked the ambulance-sergeant down with his right hand.

Capt. Green then sprang forward some six feet, and grasped with his right hand the flagstaff of the rebel battle-flag, which the color-sergeant was holding, and said to the color-bearer, "Give me that flag," at the same time pulling the flag-staff away from the Sergeant; he then tore the flag from the flag-staff, and flung the staff over the parapet, putting the flag inside the breast of his fatigue-jacket. Capt. Green then went to two rebel privates, who were a few feet off, and commanded them to give up their muskets, which they did. Taking the muskets, he gave them to some of his own company to carry off, and taking the equipments of the two privates, he flung them into a puddle of water near by; then going to the rebel Captain, he pulled him up off of the ground, and putting him, together with the ambulance-sergeant, the color-sergeant, and the two privates, under charge of two of his

COM. JOHN RODGERS

company, sent them to the rear, to be placed in custody under the provost guard.

Thus, in the short space of five minutes, Capt. Green disarmed one Captain, one ambulance-sergeant, and two privates of the Twelfth Georgia volunteers, besides taking their color-sergeant, with his colors, and sending the whole of them, five in number, as prisoners, under guard, to the rear.

The rebel flag was one of the Confederate battle-flags, made of coarse red serge cloth, about four and a half feet square, having a blue Saint Andrew's cross running from each corner; three white stars were in each limb of the cross, and one star in the centre, making thirteen stars in all. The flag was sent to Gen. Hooker by his order: the sword was presented to Capt. Green by his brigade commander, for his good conduct during the battle.

BATTLE ANTHEM.

BY JOHN NEAL.

Up, Christian warrior, up! I hear
  The trumpet of the North
    Sounding the charge!
  Fathers and sons!—to horse!
  Fling the old standard forth,
    Blazing and large!

And now I hear the heavy tramp
  Of nations on the march,
    Silent as death!
  A slowly-gathering host,
  Like clouds o'er yonder arch,
    Holding their breath!

Our great blue sky is overcast;
  And stars are dropping out,
    Through smoke and flame,
  Hail-stones, and coals of fire!
  Now comes the battle-shout!
    Jehovah's name!

And now the rebel pomp! To prayer!
  Look to your stirrups, men!
    Yonder rides death!
  Now with a whirlwind sweep!
  Empty their saddles, when
    Hot comes their breath!

As through the midnight forest tears,
  With trumpeting and fire,
    A thunder-blast,
  So, reapers! tear your way
Through yonder camp, until you hear,
  " it is enough! Put up thy sword!
    O angel of the Lord!
    My wrath is past!"

AN INCIDENT OF THE WILDERNESS. — The following account of the exploits and sufferings of Maj. William B. Darlington, of the Eighteenth Pennsylvania cavalry, gives some idea of the hazards, as well as the glories, of war:

On the 5th of May, 1864, the day preceding the great engagements of the 6th and 7th, there was heavy skirmishing by the cavalry of the two armies, that of the enemy being commanded by Wade Hampton. Maj. Darlington, with his regiment, was ordered to hold a certain position in Gen. Wilson's line, for forty-five minutes, while the remainder of the force was retiring to more advantageous ground. He obeyed the order, with a grace of five minutes, and then, attempting to retire, found his line of retreat commanded by an entire brigade of rebel cavalry commanded by Rosser. The Major drew up his men in the proper formation and charged.

This was met by a counter-charge on the part of the enemy, and hard fighting followed, the greater part of the Union force, however, accomplishing their purpose.

But, when leading the first charge, Maj. Darlington received a ball in the right leg, which shattered the thigh bone, and brought him to the ground. Here he lay, the enemy and his own men charging backward and forward over him; but, strange to say, he received no other injury.

On that battle-field he lay for three days and nights, without food or attendance of any kind. As this part of the field was left in the temporary possession of the enemy, after the battle which raged on the two following days, he was found and carried to Hampton's headquarters, where the amputation of his leg was performed by the chief surgeon of the division.

The operation was performed with skill, and he received as good treatment as the limited resources of the rebels would permit. He was then conveyed to a farm-house, some three miles from the scene of the action, and there he lay five weeks, slowly recovering.

When Sheridan made his famous raid, in the latter part of June, Maj. Darlington was found at the farm-house, and being laid in an ambulance, kept with the column for eight days, until he reached West Point. Gen. Sheridan and his men showed him the utmost kindness, especially in providing for him palatable and nutritious food, of which he was greatly in need.

He had been officially reported as killed; and few constitutions could have survived the loss of blood, the hardship and exposure, followed by amputation, from which he was now rapidly recovering.

A NARROW ESCAPE. — An army correspondent gives the following narrative of the manner in which a Confederate soldier in Mississippi escaped the clutches of the Yankees: "While dwelling upon the subject of ladies, and the purifying influence of ladies' society, I will take occasion to mention, for the benefit of the fastidious, an adventure of two nice and accomplished young ladies, together with a young gentleman well versed in gallantry. Not long since, *mon cher* M., of this brigade, while in the vicinity of the Federal encampments, took occasion to put up for the night at the house of an old acquaintance, where he had often called to enjoy a pleasant repast with the young ladies. During the night, the Federals, learning his whereabouts, approached the house, creating a bluster every-where, save in our young hero's apartment. He soundly slept, and continued to sleep, as if on 'beds of roses,' unconscious of approaching danger, until the young ladies, panic-stricken on his account, rushed, *en dishabille*, into his room, and awoke him from his slumbers.

"But the Federals had advanced too far for him to make his escape in the front, and there was no window or door in the rear. How then was his escape to be effected? Reader, the young ladies instituted a plan unprecedented in the history of military operations. When the old lady discovered he could not escape by running, she rushed in, crying, 'Girls! we must do something — the Federals are already in the passage.' No sooner said than done. The young ladies leaped in bed with our young hero, one on each side, completely concealing his head, and thereby causing the search of the Federals to be fruitless. They looked into every nook, and under every bed in the house, not excepting the one occupied by the hero; but the young Confederate scout was no-where to be found. How much better than to have suffered him to be murdered or imprisoned for years in a felon's cell! So we say; but the mystery to us is, why they did not think of look-ing in the bed, as well as under it."

HEROISM OF MISS SCHWARTZ.

HEADQUARTERS DISTRICT OF CENTRAL MO.,
JEFFERSON CITY, August 9, 1863.

GENERAL ORDERS No. 42. — On the night of the 6th instant, a party of bushwhackers, some three in number, visited the house of a Mr. Schwartz, about twelve miles from Jefferson City, in Cole County, and on demanding admittance they were refused by Miss Schwartz, a young lady of fifteen. They replied they would come in, at the same time trying to break down the door. While this was going on, the other inmates of the house, namely, Mr. Schwartz, John Wise, Capt. Golden, Government horse-dealer, and a young man in his employ, all left, taking with them (as they supposed) all the arms and ammunition. In their hasty retreat they left behind a revolver, which Miss Schwartz appropriated to her own use. She went to the door, and on opening it presented the pistol to the leader of the gang, telling them to "come on if they wanted to, and that some of them should fall, or she would." They threatened to kill her if she did not leave the door. She replied: "The first one who takes one step towards this door dies, for this is the home of my parents, and my brothers and sisters, and I am able to and shall defend it." Seeing that she was determined in her purpose, after holding a consultation together, they left.

Here is an instance of true courage; a young girl of fifteen years of age, after all the inmates of the house, even her father, had fled, leaving her alone to her fate, with a courage worthy of a Joan of Arc, boldly defended her native home against three bloodthirsty and cowardly ruffians, and by her coolness and heroic daring, succeeded in turning them from their hellish designs.

It is with feelings of no ordinary pride and pleasure the Commanding General announces this act to the citizens and soldiers in his district. On the other hand, those miserable cowards who deserted this brave girl in the hour of danger, flying from the house, leaving her to her fate, are unworthy the name of men, deserve the scorn and contempt of the community at large, and whose society should be shunned by every one who has the least spark of honor or bravery within them.

By order of　　　　Brig.-Gen. BROWN.

RUFUS BROCKWAY. — A correspondent of a Wisconsin paper had his attention arrested by the appearance of a rather oldish man among a company of recruits for the Seventeenth (Irish) Wisconsin regiment, who were on board the cars, on the way to camp, who gave his name, as follows:

"My name is Rufus Brockway, and I am in the seventieth year of my age. I am a Yankee, from the State of New Hampshire; was a volunteer in the last war with England for nearly three years. I have served under Gens. Izard, McNeil, and Macomb, being transferred from one command to another, as the circumstances then required. I was at the battle of Plattsburg, at the battle of French Creek in Canada, and at the battle of Chateaugay, on the 14th day of October, 1813, and was present at the surrender of McDonough.

"I was now a farmer, in the town of Beaver Dam, Dodge County, and, with my son, the owner of three hundred acres of land; my son was a volunteer in the Federal army at the battle of Bull Run, had his nose badly barked, and his hips broken in, and disabled for life, by a charge of the rebel cavalry, and now I am going to see if the rebels can bark the old man's nose.

"I tell you," said the old man, "if England pitches in, you'll see a great many old men like me turning out; but the greatest of my fears is, that I shall not be permitted to take an active part in the present war."

A SOLDIER in one of the Union hospitals, who had lost one of his arms, was rejoicing over the fact. Said he: "My grandfather lost a leg in the Revolutionary war, and our family have been bragging over it ever since. That story is an old one, and now I am going to be the hero of the family."

INCIDENT OF LIBERTYTOWN, MD. — Early in the spring of 1862, four young men of the city of Frederick went to the good old town of Liberty, and while passing the Stars and Stripes floating from a pole at the west end of the town, took occasion to *curse* that time-honored emblem, and say something about taking it down. Hearing, however, that they would be called to account for their rebellious acts, they loaded their pistols before leaving the hotel, and said what they would do if attacked. Now comes the "fun." About five o'clock the carriage is seen coming up the hill, and when nearly opposite the flag, two of the citizens walked out into the middle of the street and gave the command, "*Halt*," which was promptly obeyed. The next command was: "Salute that flag." After an excuse or two about a "bad cold," and "how salute it," they gave a weak "cheer." The answer was: "That won't do: a little louder!" and the second time their voices were raised considerably; but, "Louder yet," was commanded; and the third time they gave a mighty good proof of strong lungs. They were then ordered to *curse secessionism*, and they did so; after which they were allowed to pass on, wiser, if not better men.

CAMP ANECDOTES. — A soldier writing home from Fort Slocum, near Washington, gave the following anecdotes of life in camp: While in Florida we had an Irishman named Murphy, who was very much afflicted with the prevalent camp malady known as "Spring Fever." In order to escape duty, he reported himself to his Orderly Sergeant as sick, and in due time was taken to the doctor. Being asked the nature of his disease, he complained of a very *heavy lightness* in the head. "Why," replied the doctor, "that is a paradox;" and giving him a light dose of "ipecac," he returned him to duty. Mick left the tent in high dudgeon, exclaiming, "The devil take a doctor who will put a man on duty with a paradox in his head."

Another fellow, by the name of G——, tried to play the "old soldier" on the same doctor, and also got a dose of "ipecac." He did not get far from the tent before he began to "heave Jonah." Cursing the doctor, he went back and said he wanted some other medicine, as the first did not stay on his stomach. The doctor gave him another dose of the same, slightly colored, and G—— went off perfectly satisfied. He did not get far before he realized that he had another Jonah. About this time he "appreciated," and was content to do duty.

The other evening, one of our bold Lieutenants went up to a "pizen shop" on the hill, and was returning to camp with a little heavier load than the regulations require, when he lost his way, and came through a field but lately cleared. Just as the sentry gave the usual challenge — "Who comes there?" — Charley struck his shin against a fallen tree, and feeling more expressive than poetical, he cried out lustily, "The devil." "Corporal of the guard, post number six, double-quick," called out the sentry, adding, "Mine Got in Himmel, here comes ter tivel!"

While on Staten Island, previous to embarking for the South, one of the captains was severely injured by a block of wood falling from one of the third tier of casemates and striking him on the head. The next morning, a New Jersey Dutchman, one of his company, called to inquire after his health. "Good morning, Captain," says the Dutchman; "how are you getting along?"

Being assured that the Captain was out of danger, the Dutchman said: "I heard something drop, and I thought it was a Lieutenant had fallen from the top of the fort, and was knocked all to pieces; and I didn't think it worth while to pick the pieces up till the coroner came."

One of our Lieutenants, who boasts of eighteen years' service in the "reg'lar army," has been very much troubled by the privates coming into his quarters. To put a stop to this, he has displayed a large notice in front of his tent. It is, as near as I can copy it, *verbatim et literatim*, as follows:

Notis
No 1 aloud in here excep on bisnes,
By order of
Lt. H—— F——
Ferst leutenant.

A few days ago one of our boys played a rather small game to get on guard as "supernumerary" — who only have to stand on post while any of the men may have to leave for some necessary reason; at other times he can stay in the guard tents out of the storm. The rest of the boys did not like it much, and agreed among themselves to repay him. As soon, therefore, as their "relief" came on, one of them called out, "Corporal of the guard; post number three wants to be relieved," and the supernumerary had to take his place. As soon as number three returned and took his place, number five called to be relieved; and so they kept the poor fellow travelling from one post to another all night. Since then he has gone by the name of "Supernumerary."

A SONG.

BY FITZGREENE HALLECK.

Hark! a bugle's echo comes;
Hark! a fife is singing;
Hark! the roll of far off drums
Through the air is ringing!

Nearer the bugle's echo comes,
Nearer the fife is singing;
Near and more near the roll of drums
Through the air is ringing.

War! it is thy music proud,
Wakening the brave-hearted;
Memories — hopes — a glorious crowd,
At its call have started.

Memories of our sires of old,
Who, oppression-driven,
High their rainbow flag unrolled
To the sun and sky of heaven.

Memories of the true and brave,
Who, at Honor's bidding,
Stepped, their country's life to save,
To war as to their wedding.

Memories of many a battle plain,
Where their life-blood flowing,
Made green the grass, and gold the grain,
Above their grave-mounds growing.

Hopes — that the children of their prayers,
    With them in valor vying,
May do as noble deeds as theirs,
    In living and in dying, —

And make, for children yet to come,
    The land of their bequeathing
The imperial and the peerless home
    Of happiest beings breathing.

For this the warrior-path we tread,
    The battle-path of duty,
And change, for field and forest bed,
    Our bowers of love and beauty.

Music! bid thy minstrels play
    No tunes of grief or sorrow,
Let them cheer the living brave to-day;
    They may wail the dead to-morrow.

A PATRIOTIC BOY. — The following is one of
the most remarkable letters we ever read from a
boy. The writer was only fifteen years old, and
his appeals to his mother for liberty to join the
army are most striking. No one, whose whole
soul was not fully in the matter, could make
such ardent appeals. One sentence will be noticed by parents — the one in which he says that
nothing, save the dissent of his mother, could
keep him away from the field of strife. His
mother's assent was finally obtained, though she
hesitated for some time, as her boy was in a favorable situation, with excellent prospects for the
future. He left for the South in the Eighth regiment Connecticut volunteers, in the capacity of
a drummer boy. Here is his letter:

WATERBURY, May, 1861.

Dear Mother: I have not written you for some
time, as I have had nothing to write. I want to
ask a very important question. May I go to the
war? I do not expect to go as a volunteer, but
as an officer's servant. When I say "officer's
servant," I don't mean that I shall be at the beck
and call of the whole company, but I shall arrange the tent, and go on errands for the officer,
and for him alone. My heart is in the work. If
I assist an officer, there can be another man in
the ranks. I shall be in little or no danger, because I shall not probably stand in the ranks.
But what if I am in danger? I shall not die until my time comes; and if I am appointed to die
in the "service of my country," I shall be there,
and no earthly power can keep me away. What
if I do die in my country's service? Who is not
willing to die in battle, if, by so doing, he can
perpetuate the freedom and liberty of this Nation through all time? Gen. Scott says that more
die at home, out of the same number that go to
war, than are killed in battle. Be patriotic,
mother, and let me go; don't think that enough
will go without me; no such thing should enter
your mind; but have true patriotism, and be
willing to sacrifice all you have, if need be, to let
the "Star-spangled Banner in triumph wave
o'er the land of the free and the home of the
brave."

Mother, I *cannot* be happy to stay where I am,
at this time of my country's peril. Please write,
and tell me I may go, when I can get an opportunity. If you say no, I fear I shall go mad.
Mother, I should do that. My heart goes as fast
as my pen, and if you should say *no!* I should not
be worth a cent to anybody.

I never was so uneasy in my life as at present,
and it should be the last thing I should think of
— that is, to give up going to war at this "glorious period." Mother, don't fear for me in any
way. I shall keep right side up with care, and
abstain from the use of all intoxicating liquors,
profane language, and tobacco in every form. I
will keep a journal of daily occurrences, and
send to you in the form of letters, which please
keep with great care. Nothing would, or will,
keep me away from war, neither argument, persuasion, or force, nor anything but a dislike to
disobey you. Please don't procrastinate, but say
"you will," "it's right," and "go ahead." I
ought to be in the garden at work, but it has
"no charms for me." My mind is so worked up
that I'd rather take a flogging that would make me
raw all over, than give up the *hopes* and *desires*
I have so long cherished. It is not for any pecuniary benefit which I may derive, for I only
spoke of that to let you see I could provide for
myself when once installed into the army; but
there is a deeper feeling which stirs up my whole
frame, that tells me "go and prosper." I have
only six cents in my pocket-book; it will take
three to pay for this letter, and two to pay for
a letter to cousin; so if you want me to write
again, please send a stamp. I do not think it
necessary to write any more until I am in the
army. Please don't put me off. Write all the
news, and don't miss a mail.

A GOOD ANECDOTE is told of a lad on one of
the Union gunboats. The vessel was just going
into action, and our soldier was upon his knees,
when an officer sneeringly asked him if he was
afraid?

"No, I was praying," was the response.

"Well, what were you praying for?"

"Praying," said the soldier, "that the enemy's
bullets may be distributed the same way as the
prize money is, *principally among the officers.*"

GEN. LANDER AND THE BIBLE. — One day a
staff officer caught him with a Bible in his hand,
and said:

"General, do you ever search the Scriptures?"

Gen. Lander replied: "My mother gave me a
Bible, which I have always carried with me. Once
in the Rocky Mountains I had only fifteen pounds
of flour. We used to collect grasshoppers at four
o'clock in the day, to catch some fish for our supper at night. It was during the Mormon war,
and my men desired to turn back. I was then
searching for a route for the wagon road. 'I will
turn back if the Bible says so,' said I, 'and we

will take it as an inspiration.' I opened the book at the following passage:

" ' Go on, and search the mountain, and the gates of the city shall not be shut against you.' "

All concurred in the definite statement of the passage, and the heroic explorer once more led his men into the wild country of the Indians.

INCIDENT OF ANTIETAM.—At the battle of Antietam, as one of the regiments was for the second time going into the conflict, a soldier staggered. It was from no wound, but in the group of dying and dead, through which they were passing, he saw his father, of another regiment, lying dead. There, too, was a wounded man who knew them both, who pointed to the father's corpse, and then upwards, saying only, "It is all right with him." Onward went the son, by his father's corpse, to do his duty in the line, which, with bayonets fixed, advanced upon the enemy. When the battle was over, he came back, and with other help, buried his father. From his person he took the only thing he had, a Bible, given to the father years before, when he was an apprentice.

HOMESICK IN THE HOSPITAL. — A correspondent, writing from the general hospital at Nashville, Tenn., says : "Perhaps the greatest fault military surgeons are apt to fall into, is to be too military in their treatment of their patients. A soldier, when he enters a hospital as a patient, is no longer a soldier, but a patient, and should be treated as such, and not as a soldier. In civil life, we all know how tenderly the sick are treated, and in the great majority of cases, how beneficent to them is our medication. And, ordinarily, too, when a man is stricken down, even, with a formidable disease, there are good constitutional efforts in his system to carry him through his illness. This is seldom the case with our hospital patients. In their sickness we have generally to contend with a broken-down or exhausted constitution, and often the babe in the cradle is not entitled to more tender and skilful treatment to save its flickering life, than the now sick and broken-down soldier. Through want of a uniform understanding on the part of our military, and even some of our medical officers on this very point, many lives are sacrificed. There is in this city the 'convalescent camp.' I don't believe our convalescent soldiers have any fear of any more dreadful doom than to be consigned to this place. When they get well of their diseases, they beg hard for some other destination than this camp. They will cheerfully go front, or to their regiments, or any other place, than the dreaded 'convalescent camp.' I think the reason for the odium this place has for the convalescent soldier, is the one above stated. They are treated as soldiers, and not as convalescents.

"Soon after I got into this hospital, a very sick boy was brought into my ward from the 'convalescent camp.' He had been prematurely sent to that place when recovering from pneumonia. It was apprehended that the rebels were going to make a raid on Nashville. This boy, with other convalescent soldiers, was put on duty by lying in the trenches for one night. Here was a very feeble patient, with but one healthy lung, to act as soldier. The exposure brought on pneumonia of the well lung. In this critical condition he was brought into my ward. Soon after, a most touching nostalgic delirium set in. He wanted to go home. He taxed his delirious mind in all conceivable ways, to consummate the object in view. He begged, coaxed, reasoned, and at times would wildly cry out, 'I will go home.' A short time before he died, he sprang out of his bunk, and with a sheet around him, ran through the ward, crying, 'I'll go now, and no power on earth shall stay me.' The attendants put him back in bed, and not many hours after his heavenly Father took his spirit from earth, we will humbly hope, to that pure and blissful state, 'where the wicked cease from troubling and the weary are at rest.'

"On one inspection occasion, a Sergeant, who had been wounded in the head, was pointed out to the surgeon in charge, as being considered well enough for the 'convalescent camp.' 'Don't send him,' says the doctor, with noble consideration for the patient, and, with a smile, added, ' They are in the habit there of cutting off almost everything that is wounded ; if you send the man there, they may conclude to cut his head off.' To save the gallant soldier's head, it was decided not to send him to the 'convalescent camp.' Another case of homesickness I am reminded of. A poor boy, from the front, was brought into this ward, with the camp dysentery. A more attenuated living being I had never seen. Home, with him, too, was the absorbing subject of his thoughts. 'I want to see my mother,' was his constant utterance. Often he wept like a child to go home. I put him off from time to time, endeavoring to feed and stimulate him, to bring him into a condition fit to be sent home. One morning, coming into the ward. I found his bed empty. ' What! poor Jimmy dead ?' I asked of the ward master. 'No,' he answered, 'Jimmy started for home, under the care of our female nurse.' Here was a case where a resolute and conscientious woman voluntarily took charge of a helpless boy, to take him to his home, a thousand miles away, solely because she felt that she could thereby save his life. She succeeded in getting him home alive, and we have heard he is now getting along well.

"Homesickness is one of the most frequent, difficult, and annoying complications we have in the treatment of hospital patients. When a soldier gets sick, he wishes himself at home. It is well for the surgeon to gratify this feeling, when the patient is in a fit condition to go. And when the case is such that it is not for the patient's benefit to leave the hospital, and he cannot control himself to submit to circumstances, he is, in a medical point of view, exceedingly difficult to manage. It is thus that nostalgia has helped to send many a lamented soldier to his grave.

"Great is the variety of wounds in a military hospital. One remarkable fact connected with wounds is, that a man's life is not alway jeopardized in proportion to the number of wounds he may have received. One from a slight wound may die. Another may be fearfully mutilated, and yet get well. After the battle of Chickamauga, we received two patients in this hospital, who afforded a striking illustration of this. I asked one of them where he was wounded. 'All over,' he answered. I directed the nurse to divest him of his clothes, and found his word pretty much verified. This warrior was perforated by more than half a dozen balls, and yet he got well. Another one had a slight wound on the left knee, caused by a buckshot. The little missile was extracted, and after he had suffered most severely for two months he died."

A FAITHFUL DOG. — The widow of Lieut. Pheff, of Illinois, was enabled to find her husband's grave, at Pittsburg Landing, by seeing a dog which had accompanied the Lieutenant to the war. The dog approached her with the most intense manifestations of joy, and immediately indicated to her, as well as he was able, his desire that she should follow him. She did so, and he led the way to a distant part of the field, and stopped before a single grave. She caused it to be opened, and there found the body of her dead husband. It appears from the statements of some of the soldiers, that when Lieut. Pheff fell, his dog was by his side, and thus remained, licking his wounds, until he was taken from the field and buried. He then took his station by the grave, and nothing could induce him to abandon it, but for a sufficient length of time each day to satisfy his hunger, until, by some means, he was made aware of the presence of his mistress. Thus he watched for twelve days by the grave of his slain master.

DECEMBER IN VIRGINIA.

CONTRABAND *loquitur.*

DE leaves hab blown away,
  De trees am black an bare,
De day am cold an damp,
  De rain am in de air.
De wailin win's hab struck
  De strings ob Nature's lyre;
De brooks am swollen deep,
  De roads am mud an mire.
De horses yank de team,
  De wheels am stickin thar;
De Yankee massa yell —
  De Lord! how he do swar!
De oafs dat he do take,
  De nigger dismember;
De Dutch, De Deuce, De Debbil,
De — all tings dat am ebil —
  DE-CEMBER!

FREEDMEN'S BUREAUS. — An ancient colored woman appeared at the office of the Freedmen's Bureau, at Chattanooga, Tenn., and asked if that was the place where they kept the freedmen's bureaus. The clerk was momentarily nonplused, but instantly recovering his gravity, blandly replied in the affirmative. Dinah, with an air of mystery, and speaking in a confidential whisper, said: "I have come for my bureau; now give me a pretty large one, with a glass top; I have a wash-stand at home, but it is too small to put my fixins' in."

A WONDERFUL OLD SOLDIER. — The Thirty-seventh regiment of Iowa, doing duty in St. Louis, in 1862, was a regiment of exempts — few, if any, of its members being under forty-five years of age, and many of them over eighty. "Take them all together," says a correspondent, "they are a band of hardy veterans, whom the exigencies of the situation have fired with a zealous patriotism well worthy of imitation by younger men. But the most remarkable member of this regiment is a private of company H, named Curtis King, whose history and description are truly curious. He is over eighty-one years of age, six feet two inches in height, of brawny and stalwart frame, baring his bosom to the cold winds of winter without endangering his health, and moving in his round of duties with the celerity of a youth of eighteen. Owing to his great age, and the fact of his being blind of an eye, he found great difficulty, when the regiment was forming, in getting permission to enlist, two or three companies refusing to take him; but he was at length successful, and since the regiment has been on duty he has proved one of the most efficient men in it. He is, and has been from his youth, a Democrat of the old Jackson school, and even now indulges industrious invective against the Abolitionists. He was born in Culpepper County, Va., and claims to be a lineal descendant of Pocahontas; and this statement is verified by his physiognomy, which betrays the characteristics of an Indian. He has been twice married, (first when only nineteen years of age,) and is the father of twenty-one children, one of which was, two weeks since, only fifteen months old when it died. He claims to be able to repeat every word of the Bible from the beginning of Genesis to the end of Revelation, and can *neither read nor write* — a daughter having read the book to him, his wonderful memory allowing him to retain it after committing it to memory. The daughter commenced her reading to him at five years of age, he being then twenty-six. In 1815 he emigrated to Ohio, resided there some twenty-five years, and then removed to Wapello County, Iowa, where his home now is, and where he enlisted. Mr. King's family is somewhat celebrated for longevity, his mother having lived to the age of 103, and one grandfather to 105 years.

The history of this country is familiar to him, and his citations of historical points and the connection with them of great men who flourished during the latter part of the last century, are wonderfully accurate — remembering, as he does, Washington, Jefferson, Randolph, and the Adamses, &c. He has often seen Washington, and remarked as a characteristic of the "Father of his

Country," that he never saw him smile; that he seemed to have little sympathy in the enjoyments of other men. The father of Mr. King was a soldier of the Revolution.

About twenty of Mr. K.'s grandsons and some four or five great-grandsons are now in the United States service, and the old man indulges a laudable pride in the fact that not one of his family is disloyal. Eleven of his grandsons responded to the first call of the President for volunteers. One of his daughters, who resides in Ohio, weighs 325 pounds. He himself never took a dose of medicine from a doctor, nor did any one of his family while they remained under his control, he being what is called a "root doctor," and having done the physicking for his own people by the use of herb and root teas; his "practice," too, was successful.

The opinion of this aged veteran upon the war, though he gives it in a somewhat homely and antique figure of speech, is not to be ignored as devoid of good foundation. When asked his ideas as to the result of the struggle, he replied: "Well, I think the longest pole will knock the persimmon. It may take a long time; but the North has got the most men and the most money, and it is bound to come out first best in the end. And," he continued, "if the young men will do as I intend to do, the rebellion will be put down, for I am in for the war, or as long as I last." The cheerful and contented disposition of this old man might well be taken for an example by younger soldiers, to say nothing of his strict observance of discipline, or the efficiency and value of such men to the service.

NEGRO SCHOOLS AT NEWBERN. — "I have just visited a negro school," said a letter writer. "I never had such hard work to control my risibles in my life. There sat along the sides of the room, all in one class, little girls of five years, and men of forty — each equally advanced in their studies. Of course their curiosity was excited to see the stranger. So, occasionally they looked up, which called forth from the old man in charge, the admonition, "Confine yersels to yer buks. Sam, keep yer eyes on yer knowledge buks. Miss Susan, stop dat, or I'll give yer de cowskin 'cross yer legs," and other equally gentle corrections. I heard them read; and as they were standing up in rows, without regard to height or age, reading in concert, interspersed with the old man's scowls over his big brass spectacles, and his threatenings with the cowskin, I could not resist any involuntary smile."

TWINKLEY TWINKLE. — A war correspondent of a New Orleans paper wrote thus from Jackson, Tenn.:

"An officer of my acquaintance, who is inordinately fond of 'fritters,' just dropped into a dwelling at Jackson a day or two since, where this delicacy was smoking hot upon the table, and very politely asked to share the meal with the landlady. She graciously complied, and asked him to be seated. 'Will you take the "twinkley twinkle," or on the "dab"?' My friend was entirely ignorant of the meaning of these terms, but at a venture chose the former. He was soon enlightened. The ancient female dipped her not over clean fingers into a tumbler of molasses standing beside her, and allowing the drippings to fall on the delicacy, presented it to him as 'twinkley twinkle.' 'On the dab,' was a spoonful of treacle upon the centre of the fritter."

GEN. ROSECRANS indulges occasionally in a witticism. A lady called upon him for the purpose of procuring a pass, which was declined very politely. Tears came to the lady's eyes as she remarked that her uncle was very ill, and might not recover. "Very sorry, indeed, madam," replied the General. "My uncle has been indisposed for some time. As soon as Uncle Sam recovers a little, you shall have a pass to go where you please."

ANECDOTE OF GEN. BUTLER. — It will be remembered that the little Count Mejan once frantically appealed to the Emperor Napoleon to send an armed force to protect the grog-shop-keepers of New Orleans from an "unconstitutional" tax Gen. Butler had levied upon them. The Emperor was so puzzled to know what his consul had to do with the American Constitution, and on what principles he made himself the champion of whiskey-venders in an American city, that he called the Count home to explain.

It will be seen, from what follows, that Gen. Butler's tyranny did not stop at taxing grog-shops. It seems that after the expulsion of the rebels and their allies, the Thugs, from New Orleans, the dead walls of that city were suddenly covered with conspicuous bills containing the following sentence:

"Get your shirts at Moody's, 207 Canal Street."

A planter, a secessionist, came to town some months after Butler had taken the reins in his hands, and marvelled much at the cleanliness and good order he found prevailing; also he was surprised at this notice, which everywhere stared him in the face.

"Get your shirts at Moody's?" said he to an acquaintance he met in the street; "what does this mean? I see it everywhere posted up. What does it mean?"

"O," was the reply, "that is another of the outrageous acts of this fellow Butler. This is one of the orders of which you hear so much. Don't you see? he has ordered us to get our shirts at Moody's, and we have to do so. It is, of course, suspected that he is a silent partner in the concern, and pockets the profits."

The poor planter listened with eyes and mouth open and replied:

"I don't need any shirts just now, and it's a great piece of tyranny; but this Butler enforces his orders so savagely that it is better to give in at once," and accordingly he went to "Moody's" and purchased half a dozen shirts, — on compulsion.

BEYOND THE POTOMAC.

BY PAUL H. HAYNE.

They slept on the fields which their valor had won,
But arose with the first early blush of the sun,
For they knew that a great deed remained to be done,
    When they passed o'er the River!

They rose with the sun, and caught life from his
    light —
Those giants of courage, those Anaks in fight —
And they laughed out aloud in the joy of their might,
    Marching swift for the River!

On! on! like the rushing of storms through the
    hills —
On! on! with a tramp that is firm as their wills —
And the one heart of thousands grows buoyant and
    thrills
    At the thought of the River!

O, the sheen of their swords! the fierce gleam of
    their eyes!
It seemed as on earth a new sunlight would rise,
And king-like flash up to the sun in the skies,
    O'er the path to the River.

But their banners, shot-scarred, and all darkened
    with gore,
On a strong wind of morning streamed wildly before,
Like the wings of death-angels swept fast to the
    shore,
    The green shore of the River.

As they march — from the hill-side, the hamlet, the
    stream —
Gaunt throngs, whom the foeman had manacled,
    teem,
Like men just aroused from some terrible dream,
    To pass o'er the River.

They behold the broad banners, blood-darkened,
    yet fair,
And a moment dissolves the last spell of despair,
While a peal as of victory swells on the air,
    Rolling out to the River.

And that cry, with a thousand strange echoings
    spread,
Till the ashes of heroes seemed stirred in their bed,
And the deep voice of passion surged up from the
    dead —
    Ay! press on to the River!

On! on! like the rushing of storms through the hills,
On! on! with a tramp that is firm as their wills,
And the one heart of thousands grows buoyant and
    thrills
    As they pause by the River.

Then the wan face of Maryland, haggard and worn,
At that sight lost the touch of its aspect forlorn,
And she turned on the foeman, full statured in scorn,
    Pointing stern to the River.

And Potomac flowed calm, scarcely heaving her
    breast,
With her low-lying billows all bright in the West,
For the hand of the Lord lulled the waters to rest
    Of the fair rolling River.

Passed! passed! the glad thousands march safe
    through the tide.
(Hark, Despot! and hear the wild knell of your
    pride,
Ringing weird-like and wild, pealing up from the
    side
    Of the calm flowing River!)

'Neath a blow swift and mighty the Tyrant shall
    fall;
Vain! vain! to his God swells a desolate call,
For his grave has been hollowed, and woven his
    pall,
    Since they passed o'er the River!

Value of Free Schools. — Gen. Negley
sent out a foraging expedition from Nashville,
with orders to the commander to visit every habitation, mill, barn, and out-house, and seize upon
everything fit for consumption by man and beast.
During the expedition a squad made a break for
a free school-house.

"Don't disturb anything there!" cried one of
the officers. "If there had been a few more such
institutions in the South, there would have been
no rebellion."

Brother against Brother. — A writer in
Philadelphia relates the following: "In one of
our beautiful suburban cemeteries was employed
a venerable man. For a number of years past
he has prepared the last resting-place for those
called from among us. Though poor, he raised
four gallant boys, giving to each of them a moderate education and a good trade. The two elder
went five years ago to New Orleans, where prosperity attended their industry.

The two younger brothers remained with their
father. George and Frederick were their names.
The latter is but seventeen years of age. When
the war broke out, both left their employments
and enlisted. The elder brothers had constantly
written home, and frequent presents accompanied
their letters. At the battle of Fredericksburg, in
the very front of the line, at the church upon the
rifle pits at the back of the town, were the two
boys Frederick and George. A sortie was made
by the rebel riflemen upon the retreating Federals,
and among those who dropped were the two boys,
the youngest sons of the old gravedigger. A
minie ball had pierced the bodies of each.

The rebel soldiers, whose weapons had done the
deed, were clad in rags of linsey. They ran with
alacrity to secure the clothing, the canteens, and
perhaps the money, of the men whom they had
laid low. The foremost one reached the body of
his dead enemy, turned it over — for the face was
downward — and to his horror beheld the corpse
of his youngest brother, his woollen shirt stained
with a stream of blood that oozed from a bullet
hole above the heart. Our informant, a chaplain
of the army, could tell us nothing of the other
rebel brother. But this one made his way into
the Union lines, and is now in the hospital at
Alexandria a hopeless maniac. We learn that in
their childhood this youngling of the flock had

been the especial charge of the eldest brother. When he left for New Orleans it was in the expectation of entering business to which he could bring up the boy. That boy he lived to shoot down with his own hands. Unless the remaining rebel brother survive, the family are now extinct. The father died of a broken heart, and was buried last Sunday. This is a simple statement of fact. It is doubtless one of ten thousand never to be written."

ADVENTURES IN VIRGINIA. — A correspondent writing from the camp of the Fourth Virginia brigade, on the 11th of November, 1863, relates the following: "Instances of courage and daring on the part of private soldiers in our army are of no rare occurrence, and consequently are often passed by unnoticed and unrewarded. But the bold acts of some will impress themselves upon the notice of the officers in command, and elicit their admiration. Such was the case with four privates who received the credit which they merited for the part they acted in the late affair on the Rappahannock. When the enemy had taken our redoubts beyond the river, orders were given to burn the pontoon bridge; it was fired, but failed to burn, and before combustible material could be gathered to fire it again, the enemy had reached the north side, and placed a heavy guard there to fire upon any party attempting to destroy it. The bridge remained unburned until about 12 o'clock at night, when volunteers were called for to renew the effort to fire it; at the same time, all were told that the work was a dangerous one, and none were desired to undertake it, except those who were perfectly willing. Four privates of Gen. Pegram's brigade (formerly Gen. Smith's) volunteered, and successfully fired and destroyed the bridge. They were not fired upon, but the danger was encountered, and their quiet and cool demeanor was all that prevented them from being discovered. Had the enemy heard the least noise, the bridge would have been swept by a volley of musketry. The names of the privates are Peter Berton, company E, 18th Virginia; Thomas Berton, company E, 18th Virginia; James F. Fristoe, company G, 49th Virginia; and Sandy Cooper, company A, 49th Virginia — Lieut. Buck, 18th Virginia, commanding. In connection with the above, I would mention an incident that occurred at Culpepper Court House, in which a lady acted the part of a heroine. In September last, when the Yankee army advanced on that town, it was the scene of quite a brisk fight — especially was the artillery firing heavy. During the fight, one of our wounded heroes, who was between the fire of friend and foe, was seen by a lady, whose tender sympathies were deeply aroused in his behalf; and having resolved to save him, she rushed from her house, regardless of her own safety, between the combatants, amidst shot and shell, raised him, bleeding, from the dust, and had almost succeeded in gaining a place of safety, when (our forces having fallen back) a Yankee officer rode up, and being struck by her patriotism, dismounted, and assisted her in carrying her wounded countryman into the house. Well

was it for the suffering hero, that his dangerous position was witnessed by Miss Belle Norris, whose courage was equal to her patriotism; for, in a few moments, being unable to move, he would have been crushed by the enemy's cavalry, charging over the road. Long may she — one of the many patriotic ladies of the town of Culpepper — live to receive the heartfelt thanks of grateful soldiers for the many acts of kindness they have received at her hands.   MILES.

AN EXCITING ADVENTURE. — Corporals Hamilton and Vaneman, of the 1st Virginia infantry, stationed at North Mountain, on the Baltimore and Ohio Railroad, got permission to visit some friends, in the Virginia regiments encamped about Winchester. They started from Martinsburg in a stage coach. The coach contained five gentlemen and three ladies, among them Gen. Cluseret's Adjutant-General, a Lieutenant on Gen. Milroy's staff, and a Mr. Greer, from Wheeling. Shortly after leaving Martinsburg, the coach was upset, and the whole party were piled up in a miscellaneous heap on the road-side. The coach was soon righted, and after proceeding a few miles farther, two of the ladies got out. When near Bunker Hill, the coach was stopped by a gang of rebel cavalry, dressed in the uniform of Federal soldiers. The rebels cursed the occupants of the coach, and told them to get down and surrender, or they would blow out their brains, and of course the passengers surrendered. The rebels ransacked the trunks and valises. They permitted Mr. Greer and the young lady to go unharmed, but ordered the rest to unhitch the coach horses; and while this was being done, the Lieutenant of Gen. Milroy's staff crawled in, and concealed himself between the body of the coach and the coupling pole. The rest of the prisoners were hurried off in the direction of Front Royal. The stage horses, not being "used to much feed," were very thin and angular, and the boys thought it a very severe "rail ride" into Dixie. Upon reaching a small town called Middlebourne, the prisoners and their captors were charged upon by a body of Union cavalry, under command of the Lieutenant who had concealed himself under the coach. The rebels were completely routed. About fifty shots were exchanged. The Major commanding the rebels was wounded, as was the Lieutenant commanding the rescuing party. Two or three of the rebels were killed, and more than half of them were captured and taken to Winchester with the released prisoners.

The Lieutenant, who had concealed himself under the coach, as soon as the rebels were out of sight, borrowed a horse from a farmer, and started post haste for Winchester. Gen. Milroy immediately despatched thirty of the 1st New York cavalry towards Middlebourne in command of his Lieutenant, and fifteen to the point of departure from the main pike. The detachment sent to Middlebourne got there before the rebels, and lay in wait for them with the above result. The two Corporals returned to their regiment at North Mountain.

DISCOVERING A FRIEND. — During the autumn of 1862, a general rally was made by the women of Princeton, Iowa, and vicinity, to prepare a large amount of bandages, lint, &c., for the use of wounded soldiers. Among the donations made, were several rolls of bandages prepared by Mrs. Field, into which she placed a card bearing her name and address. A few days ago, she received a letter from a Lieutenant at Fayetteville, Ark., stating that after the dreadful battle of Prairie Grove, as he was assisting to dress the wound of Willie F. B. Culbertson, of this place, and who has since died, and was unrolling the bandage, a card dropped out, which Willie at once recognized, with delight, to be from an acquaintance of his own town. It was a strange circumstance, that a gift, after passing so far, and through so many hands, should at last be used on one of the donor's own neighbors; but it may be only one of the thousands of instances in which the noble women of the North shall see, after this struggle is closed, the fruit of their labors, like "bread cast upon the waters," after many days. The kindness that the brave defenders of our nation has and will receive from their mothers, wives, sisters, and friends at home, is, no doubt, received with grateful hearts while living, and will not be forgotten, though they be, like Willie, "far beyond the rolling river," where the strife of battle is never known.

SERGEANT PLUNKETT. — In the battle of Fredericksburg, the color-bearer of the Twenty-first Massachusetts regiment fell mortally wounded, when Serg. Plunkett seized the standard, bore it to the front, and there held his ground until both arms were shot away by a shell. He was carried to the hospital, and subsequently was taken to Washington, the whole regiment turning out to escort him to the station. So brave a man deserved so marked an honor.

A MOHAMMEDAN COLONEL. — A well-known Colonel in the Union service, who had been injured several times in various actions during the war, received, at the battle of Fort Fisher, a wound which was considered fatal. As usual in such cases, the chaplain approached him, and was about offering words of consolation, when the wounded Colonel interrupted him with, "Pass on. I'm a Mohammedan."

AN OBSERVING NEGRO. — A fine-looking negro went into the Union lines on the Potomac, and reported himself for work.

"Where are you from?" asked the officer on duty.

"Culpepper Court House, sar."

"What's the news down there?"

"Nothing, massa, 'cept dar's a man down dar lost a mighty good and valuable nigger dis morning, and I reckon he dun lose more afore night."

SERGEANT JOHN MURKLAND. — When the gallant Capt. Simonds, of the Fifteenth Massachusetts regiment, fell at the battle of Antietam, Lieut.-Col. Kimball took the dying man's sword off, and, handing to Serg. Murkland, said: "I want you to take this sword, and lead this company; will you do it?" He answered gallantly, "I will do so — anywhere you may order." This noble answer, made in the face of death and danger, won for him a Captain's commission.

GENERAL HAYES' LATEST THOUGHTS. — It may be interesting to know the state of Gen. Hayes' thoughts and feelings just before entering upon that desperate conflict in the Wilderness, where he lost his life. In a letter written upon the morning on which the march commenced, he says:

"This morning was beautiful, for

'Lightly and brightly shone the sun,
As if the morn was a jocund one.'

"Although we were anticipating to march at eight o'clock, it might have been an appropriate harbinger of the day of the regeneration of mankind; but it only brought to remembrance, through the throats of many bugles, that duty enjoined upon each one, perhaps, before the setting sun, to lay down a life for his country."

A SOLDIER in the field sent the following appeal to the boys to volunteer:

I've left my home and all my friends,
And crossed the mountains craggy,
To fight the foe and traitor bands,
And left my own dear Maggie.

But now old Jeff is doomed to fall;
The traitor dogs do yelp;
But why leave us to do it all?
Why don't you come and help?

A STARTLING EPISODE. — The following account of a very strange adventure was given by a letter writer under whose observation it occurred:

During the month of August, in 1861, while our Iowa regiment was stationed at Rolla, in Missouri, our company was detached from the regiment, and sent to guard the railroad bridge at the Mozeille Mills, which, it was rumored, the guerrillas of that neighborhood were preparing to destroy.

We had been upon the ground but a few days, when there appeared in camp, early one morning, a very old, decrepit mule, which made direct for the door of a stable that adjoined the Captain's quarters, from which it appeared he had recently been stolen by a guerrilla and carried away, as a pack animal. Upon approaching the mule, a letter was discovered, secured to the throat-latch of the bridle, which, being addressed to the Captain, was immediately handed into his quarters. Upon opening the letter, its contents (written in the delicate handwriting of a female) consisted of the following singular announcement: "The Temple of Jerusalem was destroyed on the first Friday before the full moon." The Captain professed to understand it, and said: "The guerrillas will attack the bridge to-night," and immediately ordered the company to be mustered, and informed them of the imminence of an attack, which might be looked for at any moment. Ammunition was ordered to be distributed, the guards were doubled, pickets thrown out, and every precaution taken to guard against surprise. At the close of the day a drizzling rain set in, which continued until the next morning, causing the night to be intensely dark.

Three picket stations had been thrown out into the country about half a mile from the opposite end of the bridge, where the main guard was posted behind a pile of railroad ties. It was our lot to be one of the six that composed the midnight guard at this station. We had been upon our post about an hour, when one of the men observed, "I hear footsteps." We listened, and presently heard the footsteps of several persons approaching us, apparently with great caution, through a dense undergrowth that skirted the opposite side of the road. The darkness of the night was so great that we could not see them even when they were within forty feet of us; but we could distinctly hear one of them observe, in a petulant, but suppressed tone, "Jim, hold up that gun of yours; that's twice you've stuck that bayonet in me." At this moment we opened upon them with all our guns. There was no gun fired in return, but we could distinctly hear them for some time rushing with receding steps through the thicket, in the direction of a cornfield, in which stood a log cabin, occupied by a woman and two children, the husband and father of whom was a Union soldier in one of the Missouri regiments. The firing of our guns, which overshot the enemy, had aroused the entire command, and brought in the picket guard, when the log cabin alluded to was discovered to be on fire. Believing it to be the incendiary work of these guerrillas, the Captain immediately ordered a command of twenty men to double-quick through to the house, and endeavor to rescue the family if in danger. Upon reaching the vicinity of the opening that surrounded the cabin, we discovered that a quantity of hay had been placed against the door and fired; and near the building a party of eight or nine guerrillas, armed with guns, were grouped together, apparently listening to some speaker. Our party, which had divided at the edge of the cornfield, with the view of surrounding the cabin, now rushed in upon them, and succeeded in capturing three of their number.

We had arrived too late to render any assistance to the inmates of the cabin, which had already sunk down into a smouldering heap, beneath which the mother and her children had perished. After securing our prisoners with a portion of a clothes line, hanging from a branch of a tree, they were conducted to camp, where the Captain immediately summoned a drum-head court-martial to try them upon the charge of murder, assuring them that if they were found guilty they would be shot at sunrise, as a warning to their guerrilla comrades. One of the party, a short, thick fellow, with a bushy head of red hair, and bloated expression of countenance, when asked by the court-martial "if he had anything to say," sneeringly turned away, refusing to make any answer. The second prisoner, a tall, slender person, of dark complexion, with one eye concealed beneath a handkerchief that was tied diagonally around his head, while his face was scratched and scarred with fresh wounds, apparently the result of some bacchanalian brawl with his comrades, observed, "This shooting a feller, arter he's a prisoner, for fighting for the freedom of Missouri, and ag'in the abolitioners, ain't accorden to law." Here a member of the court-martial asked him "if the murdering of a helpless woman and her children, at the midnight hour, by burning them to death while sleeping, was fighting for the freedom of Missouri." The fellow turned away from this question with a dejected look, muttering that "her husband was a damned abolitioner." The third person was a young man, or boy, apparently about sixteen years old. From his dialect, and the nationality of expression on his countenance, it was easy to discern that he was of Irish descent. He was well dressed, and appeared to be greatly distressed at his situation as a prisoner. He observed, with much alarm expressed on his countenance, that he was an Irish boy, and that he had been in the United States but ten weeks, and had taken no part in the war; that the man who had burned the house had called upon him that evening, and asked him to join them in a coon hunt, and it was not until they were fired upon at the bridge, that he was aware of the character and object of the party. He would have left them then, but the night was dark, and he did not know the way home.

Here one of the court arose, and informed him that his story partook of the character of all guerrilla pleas of innocence, and that it availed him nothing. He had been caught with others in the very act of committing this cruel and unfeeling murder, and it only remained for him to say that the court found all of them guilty of murder, and sentenced them to be shot at nine o'clock the next morning.

The prisoners were then ordered to the guard-house — a log dwelling — and placed in the cellar beneath the building. The remainder of the night was devoted to the making of the coffins and the digging of a grave of sufficient dimensions to hold them side by side. When the morning returned, the rain had ceased — the clouds had passed away, and soon the sun arose with a warm and genial glow. All nature seemed refreshed with the murky shower of the night — while all around, the blades of grass, the lilac bushes, and forest leaves, drooped under the sparkling rain-drops that glittered on their folds; and the birds carolled wild and loud their morning matins. All felt that it was a day to live, and not to die in. The drum was beat at early dawn, mustering the company under arms, to witness the punishment; and a detail of twelve men was made, as executioners, under the command of a corporal. As the time drew near for the execution, it was discovered that two of the prisoners had made their escape by forcing a passage through the partition wall of the cellar, into the cellar of an adjoining house.

The boy, however, was still a prisoner, and all were determined that he should be made an example of. Accordingly, about eight o'clock, he was brought out, to be conducted to the place of execution. Upon seeing the soldiers drawn up to receive him, he commenced wringing his hands, crying and calling to the Captain, saying, "O, Captain, I am not guilty. Do not let them kill me. Don't, Captain; you can save me. I will give you my watch — my sister will give you money. O God! O Holy Mother! O Captain, speak to them quick; they are taking me away!" With a soldier upon each side of him, he was now led by the arms towards the place of execution, still calling upon the Captain to save him. When he discovered the coffin and grave that had been prepared for him, he gave a wild, frantic scream, and then for the first time seemed to realize that in a few minutes he would be no more among the living; for in a moment after he became calm, when, turning to the officer of the guard, he requested him to ask the Captain if he would give him time to write to his mother in Ireland. The Captain, who was standing upon one side of the hollow square of soldiers that surrounded the prisoner, hearing his request, immediately answered, "Yes; let him have writing materials," — which were immediately brought, when he kneeled down, placing the paper upon the coffin lid, and as his pen dashed off the words, "Dear Mother," tears fell upon the paper, which, in brushing away with his coat sleeve, erased the words he had written; when, springing to his feet, he commenced wringing his hands, saying: "I cannot write, I cannot write; O soldier, will you write for me?" addressing the Corporal of the guard.

At that moment, there arose upon the stillness of the scene the wild, piercing scream of a female, as she burst through the ranks of the soldiers, and swept out upon the hollow square, in the direction of the prisoner. It was an Irish girl, apparently about eighteen years old, without bonnet or shoes, her dress bespotted with mud, and her long, dark hair streaming in the wind, as she rushed forward with a wild, heart-rending scream, saying, "He is my brother; he is my brother." In a moment she had crossed the square, and clasping her brother in her arms, she continued, with an agonizing scream, "O soldiers! O Holy Mother! gentlemen! for the love of Jesus, do not kill him. He is innocent — he is my brother!" I never wish to look upon a scene like that again; and many a hardy hunter, from Iowa's border, while gazing on it, felt the involuntary tear course down his manly cheek. But we were surrounded by murderers and assassins. The hand that had received pay from the soldier for a draught of water had been known to strike him in the back with a dagger as he turned away; and our officers had determined to make an example of the first murderer that fell into our hands. The girl at length was ordered to be removed. When two soldiers advanced and unloosed her grasp upon her brother, her screams, her appeals to all for mercy, were terrible. They had dragged her but a short distance from him, when, looking back, and seeing a black handkerchief already tied over his eyes, with one wild, frantic scream, she flung the soldiers from her, and, bounding back to her brother, tore the handkerchief from his eyes, and again enfolded him in her arms. As the soldiers were again removing her, the coat sleeve of one of them was torn during the struggles, and her eye fell upon a breast-pin that he had fastened upon his shirt sleeve, perhaps for concealment and safety. In an instant all her physical powers were relaxed, and in a calm, subdued, and confident tone of voice, she observed, as she pointed to the pin, "Soldiers, let me make one more effort for my brother." The soldiers, startled at the strangeness of her manner, unloosed their grasp upon her, and in a moment she bounded away to her brother, shielding his body again with her person at the very moment that the guns were descending to receive the word "fire." Turning her back to her brother, and facing the file of soldiers, she stood forth a stately woman. There was no scream, no tear, no agonizing expression, but, calm and erect, she swept the field with her eye, and then advancing three steps, she gave the grand hailing signal of the Master Mason. None but Masons among those soldiers observed it, and there were many of them in that command, who now stood mute with astonishment at the strange and mysterious spectacle before them. There was a grouping of the officers for a few minutes, when the Captain came forward, and in a loud voice said, that "owing to the distress and interference of the young woman, the execution would be postponed until nine o'clock next day." The guard was then ordered to be doubled, and a strict watch kept over the prisoner during the night.

Notwithstanding this precaution, it was discovered in the morning, that both the boy and his sister had made their escape; in what way they accomplished it has been a mystery with the company from that time to this. During the early part of the evening, there was a meeting of the Masonic members of the company at the Captain's quarters, where the girl was examined, and found to have passed all the degrees in Masonry, to that of a Master Mason. Where or how she had acquired these degrees she declined to say.

INCIDENT OF FORT WAGNER. — A correspondent of the *Southern Presbyterian*, in a narrative of the "last days of Battery Wagner," thus writes:

In one case, a squad of six men was ordered to repair a parapet, which the enemy had cut down, and were still at work upon. They started out, and almost instantly a shell burst among them, killing one and wounding four; the remaining man picked up his sand-bag, and walked up to the breach without a moment's hesitation. The next squad was called, and went up to the work in just the same manner. A ten-inch columbiad, loaded, was dismounted by the enemy's shot, fell over, and pointed directly at a magazine, its carriage took fire, and the officers who ran up to it, tried in vain to extinguish the fire, by shovelling sand upon it. They called for volunteers, but the cannonade was too furious. Many shrank; it was not a command, but an invitation. At last, one gallant fellow rushed up, joined the officers in their work, got the fire under, and came down, thank God, in perfect safety.

THE BELGIAN MUSKETS. — An Illinois Colonel felt it his duty to praise these double-acting arms. Said he, "In platoon firing with the Belgian musket, I can tell what I cannot with any other arm, and that is, how many pieces have been fired."

"How can you tell that?"

"O, *I count the men on the ground.* It never deceives me. It is 'fire and *fall back*,' *flat.*

"One of these Belgian muskets will kick like a mule, and burst with the greatest facility. Several soldiers in our Illinois regiments have been killed in this way. The bayonet, too, is a novelty—a soft-iron affair, apparently designed to coil round the enemy, as it is introduced, thus taking him prisoner."

GRATITUDE ON THE BATTLE-FIELD. — In the terrible engagement at Fort Donelson, an Orderly Sergeant, seeing a rebel point a rifle at the Captain of his company, threw himself before his beloved officer, received the bullet in his breast, and fell dead in the arms of the man he had saved. The brave fellow had been reared and very generously treated by the Captain's father, and had declared, when enlisting, that he would be happy to die to save the life of his benefactor's son. The affection shown each other by Damon and Pythias did not exceed that of this nameless soldier.

THE REV. DR. MOORE, of Richmond, Va., delivered a lecture in that city on the origin and meaning of words, in which many curious facts were developed, among which were that the word *Davis* means, "God with us," and that *Lincoln*, when subjected to etymological analysis, means, "On the verge of a precipice."

INCIDENTS OF BALL'S BLUFF. — A soldier, who was in this battle, relates the following incidents:

A young man, named Greenhall, of the California regiment, missing, secreted himself, with three comrades, in some underbrush. Greenhall was an excellent marksman, and picked off seven of the enemy who had got between him and the river. One of them, he thinks, was an officer. The rest then briefly vacated the spot, and, with his comrades, Greenhall managed to make his way back to our lines.

The number of those killed while recrossing in the boats must have been quite large. In one of the boats, a Philadelphian, name unknown, and two men of the Tammany regiment, were pulling at the oars. They were compelled to stand upright, and their shoulders were used as *rests* by their comrades, who kept up a continuous fire. Singular to say, the boat had reached the middle of the stream before one of the oarsmen was struck. They finally fell simultaneously. Their places were instantly supplied; the boat, however, turned with the current, drifted, as they thought, out of danger. In less than fifteen minutes, however, a terrific fire was poured into it from the skulking enemy, and, filling slowly, it began to sink. The scene then presented was fearful beyond conception. A shriek of horror went up from the crew. Men clutched each other in despair, and went down together. Voices that strove to shout for help were drowned in the rushing waters, and died away in gurgles.

Among the rebels was one prominent individual, who wore a red handkerchief tied round his head, but was utterly hatless, coatless, and reckless, standing out in advance of his line. He loaded, and deliberately fired at our men for nearly an hour before he was struck down. He was shot by a member of the Tammany regiment, who, almost at the same moment, was pierced by a rebel musket ball.

Another rebel was observed to be ensconced on the top of a tree, and seldom fired without inflicting a death-wound. Capt. Keffer, of company K, directed one of his men to shoot him. An instant after, the rebel fell from his perch, and went crashing like a log through branch and foliage. Several other adjacent trees were observed to be vacated before much time had elapsed.

After the battle, one of our men was found stark dead in the hollow of a log! The manner of his death is supposed to have been as follows: At the commencement of the battle, while a general confusion prevailed, he probably crept into the log (which lay near the bank) for the purpose of "picking off the enemy." This shelter was very much decayed and worm-eaten, and was speedily pierced by a rifle-ball. When dragged out, his musket was found to have been recently discharged. The rifle-ball had entered his breast, and passed through the left lung.

In the panic that ensued upon the discovery that the rebels had been reënforced, and could not be driven from their cover, many scenes, that might have seemed ludicrous in many other junctures, occurred upon the hill-side. It was not uncommon for frantic men to leap the whole distance of the bluff, and plant their feet on their comrades' backs. A lusty loyalist, who had pounced upon a prisoner, slipped at the top of the bluff, but still keeping a desperate hold upon his prey, the two rolled to the bottom in a firm embrace!

There was in the California regiment a gray-haired private from our city. He had fought hard all day, and had been twice wounded, the last shot carrying away his trigger-finger. He stood upon the banks of the stream, divesting himself of his surplus clothing, when a burly fellow, belonging to a New York regiment, leaped upon him, knocking the breath out of the old man's body. In the hurry and excitement consequent upon the fight, Unionists and rebels frequently fell into each other's lines, and began to fire at their own columns. In this way several of our soldiers were captured.

A man named Stokes, who was among the list of prisoners, seeing no chance of escape, lay down in an open field among a number of the dead, as though he were really *hors de combat.* At length a rebel sharpshooter, stumbling upon his body, selected it as an excellent one for a foot-rest. Poor Stokes was in tribulation, but held his peace. At length, the rebel, having made a very successful shot, sprang up and danced around for joy, well nigh kneading his footstool into a jelly! "Stop! for God's sake!" shouted Stokes. The sharpshooter drew back, perfectly thunderstruck; then, divining the true state of affairs, he shouted out, "You sneaking Yankee cuss, git up here!" The ejaculation brought a score of rebels to the spot, and Stokes, when last seen, was going off under a guard, with a very crest-fallen face.

The most deadly contest of the day occurred between a member of the Massachusetts Fifteenth and Eighth Virginia regiments. The latter, as is well known, were at the time retreating, with the Fifteenth hotly pursuing. The rebel rear was brought up by a most determined fellow, who turned repeatedly, and discharged his musket in our ranks. Animated by the same personal daring, a Union soldier rushed beyond the head of his column, firing continually. After the pursuit had continued for some distance, it being feared that our men were to be drawn into a trap, they were ordered to retire. The order was obeyed by all save the volunteer, who had led the advance, and before many minutes, he was seen struggling with the laggard Virginian, whose own column had gone ahead. Three barrels of a revolver were discharged at the rebel without seeming effect, and the Virginian, rushing upon his assailant with a huge knife, was about to stab him. His knee was on the other's breast, and the loyalist had shut his eyes. The knife, however, fell from the other's grasp, and he reeled over, lifeless. All three of the pistol shots had actually taken effect upon him, yet such was his overmastering brute ferocity, that for some instants his wounds were without effect.

It is related of Sewall Randall, of company D, California regiment, that the night before the engagement he had a singular dream. Next morning, so vivid was the impression left on his memory, that he related it to a companion, and added a belief that it was an unfavorable omen. Neither ridicule nor reason could move him from this strange conviction; and when the advance had been made, he went into action as though he had received his death-warrant. He had crossed the river, but had barely reached the top of the opposite bluff, when he fell, shot through the side. He lingered for some time in great agony, but before death his pain was somewhat abated.

THE DYING SOLDIER. — It was the evening after a great battle. All day long the din of strife had echoed far, and thickly strewn lay the shattered forms of those so lately erect and exultant in the flush and strength of manhood. Among the many who bowed to the conqueror Death that night was a youth in the freshness of mature life. The strong limbs lay listless, and the dark hair was matted with gore on the pale, broad forehead. His eyes were closed. As one who ministered to the sufferer bent over him, he at first thought him dead; but the white lips moved, and slowly, in weak tones, he repeated:

> "Now I lay me down to sleep;
> I pray the Lord my soul to keep;
> If I should die before I wake,
> I pray the Lord my soul to take;
> And this I ask for Jesus' sake."

As he finished, he opened his eyes, and meeting the pitying gaze of a brother soldier, he exclaimed, "My mother taught me that when I was a little boy, and I have said it every night since I can remember. Before the morning dawns, I believe God will take my soul for 'Jesus' sake;' but before I die I want to send a message to my mother."

He was carried to a temporary hospital, and a letter was written to his mother, which he dictated, full of Christian faith and filial love. He was calm and peaceful. Just as the sun arose his spirit went home, his last articulate words being:

> "I pray the Lord my soul to take;
> And this I ask for Jesus' sake."

So died William B———, of the Massachusetts volunteers. The prayer of childhood was the prayer of manhood. He learned it at his mother's knee, in his far distant Northern home, and he whispered it in dying, when his young life ebbed away on a Southern battle-field. It was his nightly petition in life, and the angel who bore his spirit home to heaven, bore the sweet prayer his soul loved so well.

God bless the saintly words, alike loved and repeated by high and low, rich and poor, wise and ignorant, old and young, only second to our Lord's prayer in beauty and simplicity. Happy the soul that can repeat it with the holy fervor of our dying soldier.

BELMONT AFTER THE FIGHT. — John Seaton, Captain of company B, in the Twenty-second Illinois regiment, relates the following incidents:

"The day after the battle, Col. Hart was in command of the party that went down with a flag of truce to bury the dead, and take up the wounded that still lay on the battle-field. Of my company, there went Lieut. Morgan, Corporal B. B. Gould, privates T. C. Young, J. W. Young, and Phil. Sackett. They relate some very affecting scenes they witnessed upon the battle-field, one of which was the finding of the body of Lieut.-Col. Wentz by his wife. There lay the corpse on that blood-stained field, ghastly in the embrace of death. She stands gazing at it fixedly, and motionless as though rooted to the spot; presently her eyes fill with tears, and she breaks out in a low, agonizing cry: 'Poor — poor — soul — is it gone?' and falls prostrate upon his body. Then it was that stout and hard-featured men wept. Every rebel officer took out his pocket handkerchief to wipe away the tears that came trickling down their cheeks. One of them remarked, 'I'd give ten thousand dollars to recall that man to life.' And the 'boys' say they believe he *meant* it. They found many poor fellows badly wounded that had lain there since the battle. The rebels had been around during the night, and given them water, and other necessaries, and had taken a great many into the hospitals.

"I believe we did meet the flower of the Southern army, for they fought bravely, and their arms were all superior to ours. Every piece I saw was rifled, and had all the latest improvements; and there were a great many Sharp's six-shooting rifles. Their officers' uniforms were splendid and gorgeous, but the men's clothes were nearly all of a brownish gray, coarse, homespun jeans. In the early part of the fight, two men of company C brought a long, lean prisoner to me. He was about six feet two inches, and belonged to the Second Tennessee regiment. He was very much scared. I asked him how many men we were fighting; he raised his hands above his head, and spoke in that peculiar style so much in vogue in the rural districts of Slave States, where they see so much of the 'nigger.' 'To God, stranger, I can't tell; this ground was jist kivered with men this mornin'; swar me in, stranger; I'll take the oath right now; I'll fight for you; only please don't kill me." I told him he should not be hurt, if he behaved himself, and tied him, commanding him to lie down and remain there till I came back, and then left him. I saw him no more that day, but some one else brought him along before night.

THE NEGRO SERGEANT OF PADUCAH. — A negro Sergeant in charge of the fort at Paducah, where the Confederates, under Col. Thompson, tried to storm it, was conspicuous for his gallantry. He did not always use military terms, but his words answered as well. "Hurry, boys! load afore the smoke clears," — and before the advancing column of the enemy had gained many steps, a terrific discharge of spherical case or other shot staggered them back, and thus the horrid butchery visited on Fort Pillow was averted from Paducah.

SPRING AT THE CAPITAL.

BY MRS. PAUL AKERS.

THE poplar drops beside the way
Its tasselled plumes of silver gray;
The chestnut pouts its great brown buds, impatient for the laggard May.

The honeysuckles lace the wall;
The hyacinths grow fair and tall;
And mellow sun, and pleasant wind, and odorous bees are over all.

Down-looking in this snow-white bud,
How distant seems the war's red flood!
How far remote the streaming wounds, the sickening scent of human blood!

Nor Nature does not recognize
This strife that rends the earth and skies;
No war-dreams vex the winter sleep of clover-heads and daisy eyes.

She holds her even way the same,
Though navies sink or cities flame;
A snow-drop is a snow-drop still, despite the nation's joy or shame.

When blood her grassy altar wets,
She sends the pitying violets
To heal the outrage with their bloom, and cover it with soft regrets.

O crocuses, with rain-wet eyes,
O tender-lipped anemones,
What do you know of agony, and death, and blood-won victories!

No shudder breaks your sunshine trance,
Though near you rolls, with slow advance,
Clouding your shining leaves with dust, the anguish-laden ambulance.

Yonder a white encampment hums;
The clash of martial music comes;
And now your startled stems are all a-tremble with the jar of drums.

Whether it lessen or increase,
Or whether trumpets shout or cease,
Still deep within your tranquil hearts the happy bees are humming, "Peace!"

O flowers, the soul that faints or grieves,
New comfort from your lips receives;
Sweet confidence and patient faith are hidden in your healing leaves.

Help us to trust, still on and on,
That this dark night will soon be gone,
And that these battle-stains are but the blood-red trouble of the dawn —

Dawn of a broader, whiter day
Than ever blessed us with its ray —
A dawn beneath whose purer light all guilt and wrong shall fade away.

Then shall our nation break its bands,
And silencing the envious lands,
Stand in the searching light unshamed, with spotless robe, and clean, white hands.

CAPT. REID, of the Fifteenth Iowa regiment, relates the following incident of the march from Vicksburg to Meridian: "An amusing circumstance occurred at Jackson, which I heard related, but did not witness, but wished, when I heard of it, I had had a dead-head ticket to the show. A house was on fire, and an elderly lady wished to save from the wreck a large old-fashioned mirror, which was up stairs. Being unable to manage it herself, she called upon a soldier, who kindly consented to assist her; and going up, shouldered the mirror, and with it on his back, had nearly reached the bottom of the long flight of stairs, when, seeing a chicken, of which a party were in pursuit, he became so excited, and so far forgot himself and the precious burden with which he was loaded, that he gave one long bound for the chicken, dashing the mirror on the floor, and breaking it into a thousand pieces. The lady stood still, and raising up both hands, gazed at the young scapegrace as he ran in mute wonder and astonishment. Poor woman! Like the milkmaid in Webster's old spelling book, her castles built in the air vanished like a noonday dream."

A SHELL burst near an Irishman in the trenches, when, surveying the fragments, he exclaimed: "Be jabers! them's the fellows to teckle yer ear!"

AN INCIDENT AT GETTYSBURG. — A surgeon of the Virginia army relates the following incident: "As I was pushing my way through a crowd of idle spectators, at the Second Corps hospital, Gettysburg, one of our wounded, from a North Carolina regiment, called to me in a feeble voice. I went to him, and he said: 'You are a Confederate surgeon — are you not?' I answered him, 'Yes; what can I do for you?' He caught me nervously by the arm; and in a manner very striking and very eloquent, he uttered: 'What do you think, doctor? I am wounded and dying in defence of my country, and these people are trying to persuade me to take the oath of allegiance to theirs!'

"The crowd around him scattered as if a bomb had fallen into their midst, whilst I, overcome by the fervent eloquence of his words, could only bow in silence over the gallant fellow, upon whose brow the damp shadow of death was already gathering."

CRUELTIES OF THE WAR. — Before the rebellion, there resided in Carter County, Tennessee, two families named Hetherley and Tipton, who were on the most intimate and friendly terms. When the troubles came upon the country, the male members of the Hetherley family organized a Federal company for home protection, while the Tipton boys espoused the rebel cause, and joined the Confederate army in Virginia. After an absence of a year, the elder Tipton returned to his native county with a Lieutenant's commission, and a squad of soldiers, and immediately set to work to clear the neighborhood of all the Unionists. Tipton was brutal and unscrupulous in the course he pursued towards his former friends. Learning that one of the Hetherleys was lurking in the vicinity, and failing, after a thorough search, to discover his whereabouts, he took Hetherley's widowed mother from her house in the night, carried her to an adjoining wood, and putting a rope around her neck, threatened that if she did not instantly reveal her son's hiding-place, he would hang her. This she refused to do, and Tipton, as good as his word, had her suspended to a tree until life was nearly extinct. When she came to, he assured her that unless she told where her son was concealed, he would surely kill her. But the old lady was not to be intimidated, and again and again was she strung up, when Tipton, convinced that he could not wring her secret from her, left her lying on the ground more dead than alive. Hetherley heard of the outrage perpetrated upon his mother, and sent word to Tipton to look out, for the avenger was on his track. That very night, as Tipton was making preparations to leave the country, he was surprised at his father's house by Hetherley's company, and taken to the mountains. Here he was compelled to pay the penalty of death for his cruelties. Hetherley, maddened at the cruelties inflicted upon his helpless old mother, had him stripped and bound, made him kneel upon a coffin and take the oath of allegiance to the Federal Government, and then compelled the negro servant to blow his brains out with a revolver.

A GIRL WORTH HAVING. — "One of our fair countrywomen," says a correspondent, "the daughter of a rich and independent farmer of Rockingham, was married, the other day, to a gentleman who may congratulate himself upon having secured a prize worth having. She was what we should call 'an independent girl,' sure enough. Her bridal outfit was all made with her own hands, from her beautiful straw hat down to the handsome gaiters upon her feet! Her own delicate hands spun and wove the material of which her wedding dress and travelling cloak were made; so that she had nothing upon her person, when she was married, which was not made by herself! Nor was she compelled by necessity or poverty to make this exhibition of her independence. She did it for the purpose of showing to the world how independent Southern girls are. If this noble girl were not wedded, we should be tempted to publish her name in this connection, so that our bachelor readers might see who of our girls are most to be desired. If she were yet single, and we were to publish her name, her pa's house would be at once thronged with gallant gentlemen seeking the hand of a woman of such priceless value." — Richmond Sentinel.

THE CAPTAIN AND THE CHAPLAIN. — A correspondent with the army of the Cumberland tells the following: —

On the morning of our arrival at Strawberry Plains, a Captain on Gen. Sheridan's staff descried a man dressed in a semi-military garb, common to sutlers and other army followers, riding leisurely along in a dilapidated carriage, drawn by a span of mules. The most remarkable feature about the individual in the carriage, was a Bardolphian proboscis of magnificent proportions and gorgeous colors, at once suggestive of luscious tods and invigorating cordials. The Captain, fatigued and thirsty, taking his cue from the other's illuminated frontispiece, rode close beside him, and asked, in a confidential tone, if he couldn't give him a "suck." "No, sir," was the reply; "I am not a wet nurse." "O, but I mean a drink of whiskey; the fact is, I'm devilish dry." "No, sir, I cannot; I never use intoxicating beverages of any description; therefore, have none." "But," persisted the Captain, "have you no friends or acquaintances that you could recommend me to. I'm hankering mightily after a nip." "No, sir; I do not frequent the society of intemperate men." "Well," said the Captain, looking hard at him of the fiery visage and rum-blossomed nose, "perhaps we have both mistaken your calling; are you not a sutler?" "Sutler? no, sir," returned the now exasperated occupant of the carriage. "I am a follower of the Lord Jesus Christ; the chaplain of the —— Ohio cavalry, and a——." The Captain stopped not to hear more, but putting spurs to his horse, left in a twinkling.

———

SCOUTS AND SPIES. — There is a description of invaluable service, says Benj. F. Taylor in his entertaining letters, requiring the coolest courage, and the clearest head and the quickest wit of any soldierly duty, but which, from its nature, seldom appears in print. I refer, of course, to the achievements of the scout. He passes the enemy's lines, sits at his camp fire, penetrates even into the presence of the commanding General; he seems a Tennesseean, a Georgian, an Irishman, a German — anything indeed but what he really is; if he falls, no friendly heart can ever know where; his grave is nameless. I might name a soldier from Illinois who has thus gained information of the greatest moment, and whose dangers and daring would make a chapter of romance.

Women not invariably any "better than they should be" have always been employed to persuade information out of unsuspecting, but not unsuspected persons, and they bring a degree of tact and shrewdness into play that hirsute humanity can never hope to equal. Many a wasp has been caught with their honey of hypocrisy. Take an illustration: A subordinate Federal officer in a certain city within this department had been long suspected of disloyalty, but no proof to warrant his arrest could be obtained, and so, as a dernier resort, a woman was set at him. She smiled her way into his confidence, and became his "next best friend;" but finding that ears were of no use, — for he could not be induced to say one word of matters pertaining to his office, — she changed her plan of attack, and turned a couple of curious,

and, as I am told, beautiful eyes upon him. Not unfrequently he would ride out of town into the country, be absent three or four hours, and return. For all the hours of the twenty-four, but just these, she could account. Within them, then, lay the mischief, if mischief there was; and she began to watch if he made any preparations for these excursions. None. He loaded his old-fashioned pistol, drew on his gloves, lighted a cigar, bade her a loving good by — "only that, and nothing more." Was he deep and she dull? Time would show. At last, she observed that he put an unusual charge into the pistol, one day, and all at once she grew curious in pistols. Would he show her some day how to charge a pistol, how to fire a pistol, how to be a dead shot? And just at that minute she was athirst, and would he bring her a lemonade? She was left toying with the weapon, and he went for the drink as requested. The instant the door closed behind him, she drew the charge, for she knew as much of pistols as he, and substituted another. She was not a minute too soon, for back he came, took the pistol, and rode away. No sooner had he gone than she set about an examination of the charge, and it proved to be plans and details of Federal forces and movements, snugly rolled together. The mischief *was* in the pistol, then, though none but a woman would have thought of it; and so it was that he carried information to his rebel friends with rural proclivities. The woman's purpose was gained, and when the officer returned, his "next best friend" had vanished like an Arab or a vision, and he had hardly time to turn about before he was under arrest. Admiring the adroitness of the achievement, we cannot help regretting that a woman performed it. The memory of a man's mother is sacred, and he feels that whoever wears her form unworthily, and debases woman's graceful gifts, profanes it.

———

A FRIGHTENED CONTRABAND. — An army correspondent on the Rappahannock related the following:

An amusing incident occurred in camp a night or two since. A portly young contraband, from Charleston, S. C., who escaped from his rebel master at Antietam, and was for a while quartered subsequently in Washington, was engaged by one of our junior staff officers as his body servant, and brought down here to his quarters to attend him. It chanced that the officer had served his country gallantly at Sharpsburg, where he lost a leg, below the knee, the absence of which had been made up by an artificial limb, which the Captain wore with so easy a grace that few persons who met him suspected his misfortune — his sable attendant being among the blissfully ignorant as to the existence of the fact.

The Captain had been "out to dine," and returned in excellent spirits to his tent. Upon retiring, he called his darky servant to assist him in pulling off his riding boots.

"Now, Jimmy, look sharp," said the Captain. "I'm a little — ic — flimsy, Jimmy, t'night. Look sharp, an' — ic — pull steady."

"Ise allers keerful, Cap'n," says Jimmy, drawing off one long, wet boot, with considerable difficulty, and standing it aside.

"Now, mind your eye, Jim! The other—ie—a little tight;" and black Jimmy chuckled and showed his shining ivories, as he reflected, perhaps, that his master was quite as "tight" as he deemed his boot to be.

"Easy, now—that's it. Pull away!" continued the Captain, good-naturedly, and enjoying the prospective joke, while he loosened the straps about his waist which held his cork leg up—"*now* you've got it! Yip—*there* you are! O Lord! O Lord! O *Lord!*" screamed the Captain, as contraband, cork leg, riding boot, and ligatures tumbled across the tent in a heap, and the one-legged officer fell back on his pallet, convulsed with spasmodic laughter. At this moment the door opened and a Lieutenant entered.

"G'way fum me, g'way fum me—lemmy be! lemmy be! I ain't done nuffin," yelled the contraband, lustily, and rushing to the door, really *supposing he had pulled his master's leg clean off.* "Lemmy go! I didn't do nuffin—g'way! g'way!" And Jimmy put for the woods in his desperation, since which he hasn't been seen or heard from, though his Captain has diligently sought for him far and near.

AN INCIDENT.—The following occurred while arrangements for an exchange of prisoners were being completed near the Union lines at Decatur, Ala.: Sergeant Miller of the Ninth Illinois infantry, who had been taken prisoner during the fight at Moulton, and who had been exchanged one week before, was along with the squad of national troops who had gone out to effect the exchange. When taken prisoner, a rebel soldier demanded of him his pocket-book and "greenbacks." He had, of course, to surrender it. Before he was exchanged, he had made the remark in the presence of several rebels, that he would shoot the man who took his pocket-book the first time he could get his eyes upon him. When we met that soldier was there. He immediately recognized Sergeant Miller, took him aside, and gave him his pocket-book and money, with the exception of five dollars, which he had loaned to some one. This he promised to get and send in to him the first chance.

AN ESCAPE FROM RICHMOND.—John Bray, of the First New Jersey cavalry, thus describes his escape from Richmond captivity:

"On Sunday morning I made my final attempt to escape. Arranging necessary preliminaries with a comrade, I passed down stairs with the detail sent for provisions, wearing my blanket, and keeping as much as possible under cover of those whom I was about to leave. Reaching the yard, which was filled with rebel soldiers, I suddenly, upon a favorable opportunity, slipped the blanket from my shoulders to those of my chum, and stepping quickly into the throng, stood, to all appearance, a rebel, having precisely their uniform, and looking as dirty and ragged as the worst among them. But I was not yet free. The point now was to get out of the yard. To do this it was necessary to pass the sentinels at the gates, all of which were thus guarded. My wits, however, difficult as I knew my enterprise to be, did not desert me. With an air of unconcern, whistling the "Bonnie Blue Flag," I sauntered towards the nearest gate, paused a moment as I neared it to laugh with the rest at some joke of one of the guard; then, abstractedly, and with deliberate pace, as if passing in and out had been such a customary affair with me as to make any formal recognition of the sentinels unnecessary, I passed out. That my heart throbbed painfully under my waistcoat, and that I expected every moment to hear the dread summons, "Halt!" you need not be told. An age of feeling was crowded into that moment. But I passed out unchallenged. Whether it was that my nonchalant air put the sentinels off their guard, or that they were for the moment absorbed in the joke at which all the soldiers were laughing, I cannot tell; nor does it matter. I was free; the whole world was before me; and my whole being was aglow with that thought. I had still dangers, it was true, to encounter, but the worst was past, and I felt equal to any that might lie before."

LOYAL TENNESSEE WOMEN.—It is a singular and remarkable circumstance that loyal sentiment in the South is found inseparably connected with a broken and mountainous surface.

The low and fertile bottoms were everywhere committed to slavery, and hence to disunion. Nowhere was this more aptly illustrated than in Tennessee.

East Tennessee was loyal by an overwhelming majority. There was a strong Union sentiment in Northern Georgia and Northern Alabama. So also in Western Tennessee, as there is a line of high and sharp hills just west of the Tennessee River, there may be found a decided attachment to the old flag.

Wherever in such communities there is genuine loyalty, its displays have been magnanimous and decided; and the traditions of those communities abound in incidents of fidelity and devotion, under circumstances where such displays were by no means sentimental or free from danger.

The following incident will show the devotion and loyalty of two plain women living in an obscure county of Tennessee:—

The Twenty-seventh Iowa regiment had taken cars at Corinth, and were travelling in the direction of Jackson. It was the summer of 1862, when Jackson contained the headquarters of Gen. Grant. The train started, and was proceeding at a high rate of speed, every square foot where a man could sit or stand being covered with a soldier.

Just before reaching a railroad bridge the engineer saw a couple of lanterns being waved in the distance directly on the track. He stopped the locomotive, and sent men ahead to ascertain the cause of the alarm. They found the lanterns held by two women, who explained how a crew of guerrillas in that vicinity had been informed that a train thus loaded with Union soldiers was expected, and had fired the bridge at eight o'clock that evening, and allowed the main timbers to burn so that the bridge would break under the weight of the train, and then put out the fire. These noble women had heard of the act, and walked ten miles through the mud at midnight, carrying their lanterns, and taking their station on the track, where they had patiently waited for hours, with the determination of thwarting the dastardly plan of the villains. The officers of the regiment, thus saved from a terrible accident through the heroism of these women, begged of them to accept some present as a proof of their gratitude; but they would have nothing, saying they did it for their country, and wanted no pay. A party of soldiers was detailed to escort them to their homes. How far is such conduct above all human praise or the rewards that man can bestow!

INCIDENTS OF WEBB'S CROSS-ROADS.—While the body of Zollicoffer lay upon the ground in front of a Minnesota tent, surrounded by soldiers, an excited officer rode up, exclaiming to the men: "What in h—l are you doing here? Why are you not at the stretchers, bringing in the wounded?" "This is Zollicoffer," said a soldier. "I know that," replied the officer; "he is dead, and could not have been sent to h—l by a better man, for Col. Fry shot him; leave him, and go to your work."

When the two Parrott guns were planted on the hill at Brown's house, overlooking the enemy's camp, the peculiar whir-r-r of the shells was new to our astonished darky, who, with hat off and eyes protruding, exclaimed to his sable companion: "Gosh, mighty, Sam, don't dat go howlin' trou de wilderness?"

In nearly a direct line with the course we had marched from the battle-field to the rebel works, is a bold elevation about three fourths of a mile this side of said works, on which one of our batteries was immediately planted, and commenced throwing shot and shell into their camp. Several regiments had lain down upon the ground to rest from the fatigue of their march; and as the rebels answered but feebly with two guns, their shot passed over the heads of our men. As the intervals grew longer and longer, watching the shot became a matter of amusement with them.— "Secesh ball! Secesh ball!" they would cry out, while half a dozen would start and run after it, others calling out: "Run harder, or you won't overtake it." While this amusement was going on, a rabbit sprang out of a bush between the lines, when the cry, "Secesh ball! Secesh ball!" arose, and the boys took after it with better success, for they caught it.

Upon the high ground last referred to, the rebels made a brief stand half an hour before we reached it, but were driven off by a few shots from Stannard's battery. One of these six-pound shots struck a poplar tree, about two feet in diameter, directly in the centre, and some twenty feet from the General, passing entirely through the tree, tearing off splinters eight or ten feet long, and passing on "trou de wilderness." Another shot struck a tree seven or eight inches in diameter, directly beside the other, but lower down, cutting it off nearly as square as though it had been done with a saw.

Being among the first who entered the rebel fortifications, I discovered a barrel, which proved to contain apple-brandy. Pulling out the corn-cob from the bung-hole, I turned it up and filled a canteen. While doing this, one of Bob McCook's skirmishers came in, and says: "Vat you gets there?" I replied that it appeared to be pretty fair apple-brandy; upon which the Dutchman ran to the door, calling out, furiously: "Hans! Heinrich! schnapps! See! come arous!" Upon which a dozen Dutchmen came in, and the brandy which was not spilled upon the ground was soon transferred to their canteens. I said: "Boys, you had better look out; this is a doctor's shop, and there may be strychnine in that brandy." They paused a moment to look at each other, when one of them exclaimed, "Py Got, Hans, I tells you vat I do; I trinks some, and if it don't kill me, den you trinks;" upon which he took a long and hearty pull at his canteen, and smacking his lips a moment, said, "All right, Hans! *go ahead!*"

DIRGE FOR A SOLDIER.

IN MEMORY OF GEN. PHILIP KEARNY.

BY GEORGE H. BOKER.

CLOSE his eyes; his work is done!
  What to him is friend or foeman,
Rise of moon, or set of sun,
  Hand of man, or kiss of woman?
    Lay him low, lay him low,
    In the clover or the snow!
    What cares he? he cannot know:
    Lay him low!

As man may, he fought his fight,
  Proved his truth by his endeavor;
Let him sleep in solemn night,
  Sleep forever and forever.
    Lay him low, lay him low,
    In the clover or the snow!
    What cares he? he cannot know:
    Lay him low!

Fold him in his country's stars,
  Roll the drum and fire the volley!
What to him are all our wars,
  What but death bemocking folly?
    Lay him low, lay him low,
    In the clover or the snow!
    What cares he? he cannot know:
    Lay him low!

Leave him to God's watching eye,
  Trust him to the hand that made him.
Mortal love weeps idly by:
  God alone has power to aid him.
    Lay him low, lay him low,
    In the clover or the snow!
    What cares he? he cannot know:
    Lay him low!

THE BEDFORD BOY "ALEX."— At the battle of Winchester a young soldier was detailed for duty in guarding army property. He stood to his post until about the time his regiment made its famous charge, when he "made a break" for that regiment, joined it, and helped in the two desperate charges that decided the day. The young soldier was brought before a court-martial, and he came up with tears streaming down his face, and between sobs said: "You may shoot me if you must, but 'dad' told me, on leaving home, that when there was any fighting going on I must be in the thickest, and I was. Now, if you want your 'stuff' guarded when there is a fight, somebody besides me must do it." The boy "Alex," of Bedford, was let off on that plea, and after ever proved one of the best soldiers in his regiment.

THE LIFE AND DEATH OF A PATRIOT SOLDIER.— A surgeon in one of the military hospitals at Alexandria, writes in a private note: "Our wounded men bear their sufferings nobly; I have hardly heard a word of complaint from one of them. A soldier from the 'stern and rock-bound coast' of Maine — a victim of the slaughter at Fredericksburg — lay in this hospital, his life ebbing away from a fatal wound. He had a father, brothers, sisters, a wife, a little boy of two or three years of age, on whom his heart seemed set. Half an hour before he ceased to breathe, I stood by his side, holding his hand. He was in the full exercise of his intellectual faculties, and was aware that he had but a very brief time to live. He was asked if he had any message to leave for his dear ones at home, whom he loved so well. 'Tell them,' said he, 'how I died — they know how I lived!'"

CALLING ON PRESIDENT LINCOLN. — An officer under the Government called at the Executive Mansion, accompanied by a clerical friend. "Mr. President," said he, "allow me to present to you my friend, the Rev. M. F., of ——. Mr. F. has expressed a desire to see you, and have some conversation with you, and I am happy to be the means of introducing him." The President shook hands with Mr. F., and desiring him to be seated, took a seat himself. Then,— his countenance having assumed an expression of patient waiting, — he said, "I am now ready to hear what you have to say." "O, bless you, sir," said Mr. F., "I have nothing special to say. I merely called to pay my respects to you, and, as one of the million, to assure you of my hearty sympathy and support." "My dear sir," said the President, rising promptly, his face showing instant relief, and with both hands grasping that of his visitor, "I am very glad to see you; I am very glad to see you, indeed. I thought you had come to preach to me!"

A TENNESSEE HERO. — There are many names in Tennessee, and particularly in the eastern portion of that State, which the loyal people will not let die. They will be read and thought of in the far future as the present generation look back at the demigods of the Revolution. A letter from Cincinnati, of recent date, gives some account of one of those noble-hearted Tennesseeans; and as the story came from the lips of a dying man, it is probably truthful. The writer states that among the rebel prisoners at Camp Dennison, Ohio, was one named Neil, who, when asked how he came to be a rebel, stated that the secessionists scared him into it.

He had been a postmaster in Van Buren County, Tennessee, and a Union man. The rebels held three elections in that county, but got hardly a solitary vote in Neil's precinct. Enraged at this, they imported a force of soldiers, and began to lynch unarmed Unionists. This style of procedure made some converts, but it was withstood. Among the victims Neil spoke of — and as he knew that he was dying, he reminded his hearers of his obligation to speak the simple truth — was the martyr patriot whose history he thus recited:

There was in Van Buren County an old Methodist preacher of a great deal of ability, named Cavender. He was from the first a most determined Union man; and as his influence in the county was great, they determined to make an example of him, and get him out of the way. So they took him out of his house, put a rope around his neck, set him upon a horse, and led him into a forest. They then told him that unless he would publicly renounce his Unionism, they would hang him. Cavender replied, "God gave me my breath to bear witness to his truth; and when I must turn it to the work of lies and crime, it is well enough to yield it up to Him who gave it."

They then asked him if he had any parting request. He said " he had no hope that they would attend to anything he might ask." They said they would. He then desired that they would take his body to his daughter, with the request that she would lay it beside the remains of his wife. They then said, "It's time to go to your prayers." He replied, "I am not one of the sort who has to wait until a rope is round his neck to pray." Then they said, "Come, old man, no nonsense; if you don't swear to stand by the Confederacy, you'll have to hang," at the same time tying the rope to a branch.

The old man said, "Hang away." One then gave a blow with a will to the horse upon which Cavender sat; the horse sprang forward, and the faithful servant of God and his country passed into eternity. You will remember that they said they would fulfil his last request. Well, they tore the flesh off his bones and threw it to the hogs; his heart was cut out, and lay in a public place till it rotted. Can it be wondered if few are strong enough to resist their only legitimate arguments for rebellion?

A LIEUTENANT was promenading in full uniform one day, and approaching a volunteer on sentry, who challenged him with, "Halt! Who comes there?" The Lieutenant, with contempt in every lineament of his face, expressed his ire with an indignant, "Ass!" The sentry's reply, apt and quick, came, "Advance, ass, and give the countersign."

"A GRISWOLD FOR AN ALABAMA." — There is a beautiful thought in the address of the ladies of England in reply to Mrs. Stowe: "You have sent us the Griswold for the Alabama." Not "a Roland for an Oliver," not tit for tat, but good for evil. Let it pass into a saying in our mother tongue, "A Griswold for an Alabama," when good is returned for evil.*

EMMA SANSOM OF CHEROKEE. — The following is the story of her exploit, as related by Gen. Forrest to a party of his friends at Chattanooga:

Our readers have doubtless seen one or two short versions of the romantic part played by the above-named indomitable girl, in the great raid of Gen. Forrest from Murfreesboro', Tenn., to Rome, Ga., in pursuit of Streight's cavalry; but never the story as related by the General himself. The romantic and heroic conduct of Miss Sansom will long live in the memory of the survivors of this war; and we are pleased in this connection to add, by late action of the Legislature of our State, she has been granted a valuable donation of land, as a token of appreciation for the undaunted bravery and fearless patriotism she evinced on the occasion referred to. The editor of the *Southern Confederacy* remembers the story, as related by Gen. Forrest, shortly after the capture of Streight and his command, and says:

He had been pursuing the enemy all day, and was close upon their heels, when the pursuit was effectually checked by the destruction, by the enemy, of a bridge over a deep creek, which, for the time, separated pursuer and pursued. The country was exceedingly wild and rugged, and the banks of the creek too steep for passage on horseback. Gen. Forrest rode up to a modest little farm-house on the road-side, and seeing a young maiden standing upon the little stoop in front of the dwelling, he accosted her, and inquired if there was any ford or passage for his men across the creek, above or below the destroyed bridge. The young girl proceeded to direct him with animated gesture, and cheeks flushed with excitement, and almost breathless in her eagerness to aid the noble cause of the gallant Confederate General.

It was a scene for a painter — the Southern girl, her cheeks glowing, and her bright eyes flashing; while her mother, attracted by the colloquy, stood holding the door, and gazing upon the cavalcade over her venerable spectacles, the cavalry chieftain resting his legs carelessly over the saddle pommel, his staff drawn up around him, and his weather-worn veterans scattered in groups about the road, and some of them actually

nodding in their saddles from excessive fatigue. After some further inquiry, Gen. Forrest asked the young lady if she would not mount behind him, and show him the way to the ford. She hesitated, and turned her mother an inquiring look. The mother, with a delicacy becoming a prudent parent, rather seemed to object to her going with the soldiers. "Mother," she said, "I am not afraid to trust myself with as brave a man as Gen. Forrest."

"But, my dear, folks will talk about you." "Let them talk," responded the heroic girl; "I must go." And with that she lightly sprang upon the roots of a fallen tree. Forrest drew his mettled charger near her; she grasped the hero fearlessly about the waist, and sprang up behind him; and away they went — over brake and bramble, through the glade, and on towards the ford. The route was a difficult one, even for as experienced a rider as Forrest; but his fair young companion and guide held her seat, like an experienced horsewoman, and without the slightest evidence of fear. At length they drew near to the ford. Upon the high ridge above, the quick eye of Forrest descried the Yankee sharpshooters, dodging from tree to tree; and pretty soon an angry minie whistled by his ear.

"What was that, Gen. Forrest?" asked the maiden.

"Bullets," he replied; "are you afraid?" She replied in the negative, and they proceeded on. At length it became necessary, from the density of the undergrowth and snags, to dismount; and Forrest hitched his horse, and the girl preceded him, leading the way herself — remarking that the Yankees would not fire upon her; and they might fire, if he went first. To this Forrest objected, not wishing to screen himself behind the brave girl; and taking the lead himself, the two proceeded on to the ford, under the fire of the Yankee rear-guard. Having discovered the route, he returned, brought up his axe-men, and cleared out a road, and safely crossed his whole column.

Upon taking leave of his fair young guide, the General asked if there was anything he might do for her, in return for her invaluable services. She told him that the Yankees on ahead had her brother prisoner, and if Gen. Forrest would only release him, she should be more than repaid. The General took out his watch, and examined it. It was just five minutes to eleven. "To-morrow," he said, "at five minutes to eleven o'clock, your brother shall be returned to you." And so the sequel proved. Streight, with his whole command, was captured at ten the next morning. Young Sansom was released, and despatched on the fleetest horse in the command, to return to his heroic sister, whose courage and presence of mind had contributed so much to the success of one of the most remarkable cavalry pursuits and captures known in the world's history.

SERGEANT CARNEY. — The story of this heroic preserver of the American flag, in the assault on Fort Wagner, in July, 1863, is as follows:

---

* During the war the ship George Griswold was sent to England with a cargo for her starving poor.

When the Sergeant arrived to within about one hundred yards of the fort, — he was with the first battalion, which was in the advance of the storming column, — he received the regimental colors, and pressed forward to the front rank, near the Colonel, who was leading the men over the ditch. He says, as they ascended the wall of the fort, the ranks were full; but as soon as they reached the top, "they melted away" before the enemy's fire, "almost instantly." He received a severe wound in the thigh, but fell only upon his knee. He planted the flag upon the parapet, lay down on the outer slope, that he might get as much shelter as possible, and there remained for over half an hour, till the Second brigade came up. He kept the colors flying until the second conflict was ended. When our forces retired, he followed, creeping on one knee, still holding up the flag. It was thus that Sergeant Carney came from the field — having held the emblem of liberty over the walls of Fort Wagner during the sanguinary conflict of the two brigades — and having received two very severe wounds, one in the thigh, and one in the head. Still he refused to give up his sacred trust until he found an officer of his regiment.

When he entered the field hospital, where his wounded comrades were being brought in, they cheered him and the colors. Though nearly exhausted with the loss of blood, he said, "Boys, the old flag never touched the ground."

A DARING EXPLOIT. — During a scout of the Tenth Michigan cavalry, in Platt Valley, Tenn., a detachment of the First Tennessee Confederate cavalry was discovered. Having ascertained their number, company D dismounted, and advanced as skirmishers, firing several volleys. The enemy were followed about four miles, when the pursuit was given up. Before the main body of the enemy had been discovered, John M. Gibson, company A, was acting as one of the advance videttes on foot. A horseman rode into the road, a few rods in advance of him, in our uniform, and, riding up, drew a revolver, and informed John he was a prisoner. "Give up your gun." "Well," says John, "I suppose I will have to do it," and, in bringing his repeater from his shoulder, he threw a ball into the barrel, cocked his piece, and shot his captor through the heart, took his horse, and saddle, and revolver, and took them to the company.

A "PRESSED" TEXAN. — A soldier belonging to the army of Gen. Dick Taylor, who was captured after the battle at Pleasant Hill, La., on being carried into the national camp, stated that he was born in Indiana.

"How did you come to be in a Texas regiment?"

"Pressed in."

"Why didn't you run away before you were conscripted?"

"Tried to, but they caught me. They hunted me with dogs, sir. When I was put into the ranks, I told them I would do my common duty, and that I would never kill a Union soldier. Before I was taken to-day, I was sent out to skirmish on the left, and I know where every ball I fired struck — in the trees, sir — and all the while the Sixteenth Indiana boys, born in my own State, were firing at me like ——. Three of their bullets came so near me, that I thought each time I was to be a dead man. But now, I thank the Lord, I'm all right. You couldn't give me a little coffee, could you?"

Mrs. Browning has immortalized a similar incident in verse; but her young Italian, forced into the Austrian service, was no more of a hero than the homely Hoosier who played his part so well at "Crump's Corner."

WORSHIP OF THE NEGROES. — A correspondent at Port Royal, S. C., gives an interesting account of the religious meetings of negroes, in which singing is the favorite exercise. They have a great variety of sacred songs, which they sing and shout at the top of their voices, and never grow weary. A favorite melody is, "Roll, Jordan, roll:"

"Little children sitting on the tree of life,
    To hear when Jordan roll;
    O, roll, Jordan, roll; roll, Jordan, roll;
We march the angel march; O, march the angel march;
On! my soul is rising heavenward, to hear when Jordan roll.
    O my brother! sitting on the tree of life,
    To hear when Jordan roll, &c.
    Sister Mary sitting on the tree of life,
    To hear when Jordan roll, &c."

The verses vary only in the recitative. If Mr. Jones is a visitor, he will hear, "Mr. Jones is sitting on the tree of life." All of the persons present are introduced to the tree of life — Nancy, James, and Sancho. There is no pause; before the last roll is ended, the one giving the recitative places another brother or sister on the tree, and then Jordan rolls again. It is a continuous refrain, till all have had their turn upon the tree.

A weird plantation refrain, in a minor key, is, "Down in the Lonesome Valley." This has also a recitative and chorus:

"My sister, don't you want to get religion?
    Go down in the lonesome valley,
    Go down in the lonesome valley,
    Go down in the lonesome valley, my Lord,
    To meet my Jesus there."

As the song goes on the enthusiasm rises. They sing louder and stronger. The one giving the recitative leads off with more vigor, and the chorus rolls with an increasing volume. They beat time at first with their feet, then with their hands. William cannot sit still. He rises, begins a shuffle with his feet, jerking his arms. Ann, a short, thick-set, pure-blooded black woman, wearing a checked gingham dress, and an apron which was once a window curtain, can no longer keep her seat. She claps her hands, makes a short, quick jerk of her body on the unaccented part of the measure, keeping exact time. Catharine and Sancho catch the inspiration. We push the centre table aside to give them room. They go round in a circle, singing, shuffling, jerking, shouting louder and louder. Those upon the seats respond more vigorously, keeping time with feet and hands. William seems in a trance; his eyes are fixed, yet he goes on into a double shuffle. Every joint in his body seems to be hung on wires. Feet, legs, arms, head, body, jerk like a dancing dandy Jack. Sancho enters into the praise with his whole heart, clasping his hands, looking upward and outward upon the crowd as if they were his children, and he a patriarch. His countenance beams with joy. He is all but carried away with the excitement of the moment. So it goes on till nature is exhausted. When the meeting breaks up, the singers go through the ceremony of shaking hands all round, keeping time to the tune, "There's a meeting here to-night."

THE BATTLE AT PADUCAH. — When the refusal of Col. Hicks was communicated to Gen. Forrest, a general charge was ordered, and away the whole line dashed upon the works. The fort is a small, low earth-work, surrounded by a shallow ditch. The fierce onslaught was met by a sheet of flame from the fort, which made many of the assailants bite the dust, but it stayed them not — on they came, yelling like demons, many of them crossing the ditch, and were killed upon the walls of the fort, before, broken and repulsed, the thinned ranks of the enemy sullenly retired.

The sharpshooters in the houses which commanded the fort kept up an incessant fire upon the garrison, while the volleys from the main body were almost continual. Four or five times during the afternoon and evening was the attack renewed, and each time successfully repulsed, until the whole ground between the fort and the town was covered with the slain and wounded. The artillery of the fort was by no means idle during this time, but was dividing its attention between the attacking party and the houses which contained the sharpshooters, whom they finally dislodged, and destroyed the buildings to prevent their again being made hiding-places for rebel soldiers. The final charge was made at seven o'clock, after which Forrest retired beyond gun-shot, and took refuge in the city among the buildings.

A number of citizens went into the fort, and fought bravely during the whole engagement. One took his family to a place of safety, when he took his place with the soldiers behind the ramparts. In the early part of the action, a ball severely wounded him in the arm, but he refused to give up so long as a rebel was in sight, and continued to fight until the enemy retired. After the second repulse, one of the Kentucky cavalrymen rushed out of the fort, and found the body of his brother, who had been killed in the first charge.

Many of the citizens could not cross the river before the battle commenced. Of these, several ladies sought refuge under the bluff, out of range of shot. A rebel sharpshooter, knowing that the Federals would not harm the ladies, sought refuge in the crowd, and from behind his new-fashioned breastwork, opened fire upon one of the gun-boats. This was borne as long as possible, until a shot was sent into the bank a few feet above their heads, when the women ran shrieking for other shelter, and Mr. Reb. did the tallest running on record.

In Broadway, a crowd of women collected; behind them stood a rank of rebels, who kept up an incessant fire upon the boats. Several shells were sent over their heads, but the women stood their ground, protecting the scoundrels behind them. Finally a shot fell in their midst, killing one young woman, and wounding several rebels.

Little respect was paid to a man's sentiments — sympathizers' stores suffered about equally with Union men's. Immense booty was obtained and carried off — the amount of loss can hardly be estimated. There is one instance, however, which occurred, in which they showed some little regard for a friend — nearly every horse and mule in the city was taken, except a few belonging to the Government — it was believed that those belonged to a strong rebel sympathizer, and on that account the horses were not taken.

Firing from the gun-boats and the fort and the rebel artillery continued at intervals until near midnight on Friday, after which all became quiet, and scarce a shot was heard till after the retreat of Forrest, which occurred on Saturday, between two and three o'clock in the afternoon. The enemy retired towards Mayfield, tearing up the railroad track in his rear. A large number of houses were set on fire, both by shells and by the rebels. The first destroyed were some buildings occupied by the Government, — set in flames by the rebels, — others followed in quick succession, until probably fifteen or twenty houses of various descriptions were burned to the ground.

When the battle was over, it was found that the ammunition, both in the fort and on the gun-boats, was nearly expended. Little or no provision was in the fort, and the men sadly wanted food after their arduous labors. As soon as the news of the battle reached this city, reënforcements were despatched to Paducah, as well as ammunition and provisions. When the provisions arrived, Col. Hicks sent a full supply to the suffering citizens, and had it distributed among the hungry crowd of women and children on the Illinois shore.

The rebel Brig.-Gen. Thompson was shot through the head, while on his horse near the fort, during the fight. After falling to the ground, a shell struck him in the abdomen, and blew him to pieces. His spinal column was found several feet from his mangled body.

Towards evening the ammunition in the fort became well nigh exhausted. When this was discovered, Col. Hicks ordered that, should ammunition run out, the works should be defended with the bayonet as long as a man remained alive.

FORAGING. — A member of a Wisconsin regiment related the following : Our boys sometimes come great tricks over the secesh planters for the purpose of securing a prize from their hen-roosts, garden, &c. The biggest thing of the season, in this line of business, happened a few weeks since. Some of the boys had been roving around the country on a kind of "reconnoissance," and among other matters of interest, they discovered, in the garden of a certain farm-house, three or four bee-hives, containing a large amount of most delicious honey. On consultation, it was determined that that honey should be "confiscated," and contribute to sweeten the sugary teeth of the brave sons of Mars who captured it. Their plans were laid, and the expedition was to come off on a certain night. The night proved favorable to their design — so dark that nothing but a "stack of black cats" could excel it in the intenseness of its darkness. The party of ten or twelve started from camp, and after a number of amusing adventures, reached their destination. But all the danger was yet to come. The house was protected by two guards. To overcome this difficulty, they had to resort to strategy. They placed guards of their own at each door, and notified the occupants of the house that they were under arrest on some terrible charge, and at the same time admonished them to keep quiet, and to stay within doors, and that an officer would soon be around to make the search. In the mean time the balance of the party were scampering off with their prizes, — all made secure, — the self-constituted guard withdrew, and it was not till the next morning that the frightened rebels found out the sad havoc that had been made amongst their potatoes, honey, and barn-yard fowls by the "rascally Yankees."

"EIN FESTE BURG IST UNSER GOTT."

(Luther's Hymn.)

BY JOHN G. WHITTIER.

WE wait beneath the furnace blast
The pangs of transformation ;
Not painlessly doth God recast
And mould anew the nation.
    Hot burns the fire
    Where wrongs expire ;
    Nor spares the hand
    That from the land
Uproots the ancient evil.

The hand-breadth cloud the sages feared
Its bloody rain is dropping ;
The poison plant the fathers spared
All else is overtopping.
    East, West, South, North,
    It curses the earth :
    All justice dies,
    And fraud and lies
Live only in its shadow.

What gives the wheat field blades of steel ?
What points the rebel cannon ?
What sets the roaring rabble's heel
On the old star-spangled pennon ?
    What breaks the oath
    Of the men of the South ?
    What whets the knife
    For the Union's life ? —
Hark to the answer : — SLAVERY !

Then waste no blows on lesser foes,
In strife unworthy freemen.
God lifts to-day the veil, and shows
The features of the demon !
    O North and South,
    Its victims both,
    Can ye not cry,
    " Let Slavery die ! "
And Union find in freedom ?

What though the cast-out spirit tear
The nation in his going ?
We who have shared the guilt, must share
The pang of his o'erthrowing !
    Whate'er the loss,
    Whate'er the cross,
    Shall they complain
    Of present pain,
Who trust in God's hereafter ?

For who that leans on His right arm
Was ever yet forsaken ?
What righteous cause can suffer harm,
If He its part has taken ?
    Though wild and loud,
    And dark the cloud,
    Behind its folds
    His hand upholds
The calm sky of to-morrow !

Above the maddening cry for blood,
Above the wild war-drumming,
Let Freedom's voice be heard, with good
The evil overcoming.
    Give prayer and purse
    To stay The Curse,
    Whose wrong we share,
    Whose shame we bear,
Whose end shall gladden heaven !

In vain the bells of war shall ring
Of triumphs and revenges,
While still is spared the evil thing
That severs and estranges.
    But blest the ear
    That yet shall hear
    The jubilant bell
    That rings the knell
Of Slavery forever !

Then let the selfish lip be dumb,
And hushed the breath of sighing ;
Before the joy of peace must come
The pains of purifying.
    God give us grace,
    Each in his place
    To bear his lot,
    And, murmuring not,
Endure, and wait, and labor !

THE ESCAPE FROM THE LIBBY. — The following is the account given by the Union officers, who succeeded in reaching the Federal lines, after their escape from Richmond, in February, 1864:

Over two months previous to the consummation of their plan, the officers confined in Libby Prison conceived the idea of effecting their own exchange; and after the matter had been seriously discussed by some seven or eight of them, they undertook to dig for a distance towards a sewer running into the basin. This they proposed doing by commencing at a point in the cellar, near a chimney. This cellar was immediately under the hospital, and was the receptacle for refuse straw, thrown from the beds when they were changed, and for other refuse matter. Above the hospital was a room for officers, and above that yet another room. The chimney ran through all these rooms; and the prisoners who were in the secret, improvised a rope, and night after night let working parties down, who successfully prosecuted their excavating operations.

The dirt was hid under the straw and other refuse matter in the cellar, and it was trampled down so as not to present too great a bulk. When the working party had got to a considerable distance under ground, it was found difficult to haul the dirt back by hand, and a spittoon, which had been furnished by the officers in one of the rooms, was made to serve the purpose of a cart. A string was attached to it, and it was run in the tunnel, and as soon as filled was drawn out, and the dirt deposited under the straw. But, after hard work, and digging, with finger-nails, knives, and chisels, a number of feet, the working party found themselves stopped by piles driven into the ground. These were at least a foot in diameter. But they were not discouraged. Penknives, or any other articles that would cut, were called for; and, after chipping, chipping, chipping for a long time, the piles were severed, and the tunnellers commenced again, and in a few moments reached the sewer.

But here an unexpected obstacle met their farther progress. The stench from the sewers and the flow of filthy water was so great that one of the party fainted, and was dragged out more dead than alive, and the project in that direction had to be abandoned. The failure was communicated to a few others besides those who had first thought of escape, and then a party of seventeen, after viewing the premises and surroundings, concluded to tunnel under Carey Street. On the opposite side of this street from the prison was a sort of carriage-house, or out-house, and the project was to dig under the street and emerge from under or near the house. There was a high fence around it, and the guard was outside of this fence. The prisoners then commenced to dig at the other side of the chimney; and after a few handfuls of dirt had been removed, they found themselves stopped by a stone wall, which proved afterwards to be three feet thick. The party were by no means daunted, and with penknives and pocket-knives they commenced operations upon the stone and mortar.

After nineteen days' and nights' hard work, they again struck the earth beyond the wall and pushed their work forward. Here, too, (after they had got some distance under ground,) the friendly spittoon was brought into requisition, and the dirt was hauled out in small quantities. After digging for some days, the question arose whether they had not reached the point aimed at; and in order, if possible, to test the matter, Capt. Gallagher, of the Second Ohio regiment, pretended that he had a box in the carriage-house over the way, and desired to search it out. This carriage-house, it is proper to state, was used as a receptacle for boxes and goods sent to prisoners from the North, and the recipients were often allowed to go, under guard, across the street to secure their property. Capt. Gallagher was granted permission to go there, and as he walked across, under guard, he, as well as he could, paced off the distance, and concluded that the street was about fifty feet wide.

On the 6th or 7th of February the working party supposed they had gone a sufficient distance, and commenced to dig upward. When near the surface they heard the rebel guards talking above them, and discovered they were some two or three feet yet outside the fence.

The displacing of a stone made considerable noise, and one of the sentinels called to his comrade and asked him what the noise meant. The guards, after listening a few minutes, concluded that nothing was wrong, and returned to their beats. This hole was stopped up by inserting into the crevice a pair of old pantaloons filled with straw, and by bolstering the whole up with boards, which they secured from the floors, &c., of the prison.

The tunnel was then continued some six or seven feet more; and when the working party supposed they were about ready to emerge to daylight, others in the prison were informed that there was a way now open for escape. One hundred and nine of the prisoners decided to make the attempt to get away. Others refused, fearing the consequences if they were recaptured; and others yet (among whom were Gen. Neal Dow) declined to make the attempt, because (as they said) they did not desire to have their Government back down from its enunciated policy of exchange. Col. Rose, of New York, Col. Kendrick, of Tenn., Capt. Jones, Lieut. Bradford, and others, informed Gen. Dow that they could not see how making their escape would affect the policy of exchange. Their principle was, that it was their personal right to escape if they could, and their duty to their Government to make the attempt.

About half past eight o'clock on the evening of the 9th, the prisoners started out, Col. Rose, of New York, leading the van. Before starting, the prisoners had divided themselves into squads of two, three, and four, and each squad was to take a different route, and, after they were out, were to push for the Union lines as fast as possible. It was the understanding that the working party was to have an hour's start of the other prisoners, and, consequently, the rope ladder in the cellar was drawn out. Before the expiration of the hour, however, the other prisoners became impatient, and were let down through the chimney successfully into the cellar.

Col. W. P. Kendrick, of West Tennessee, Capt. D. J. Jones, of the First Kentucky cavalry, and Lieut. R. Y. Bradford, of the Second West Tennessee, were detailed as a rear-guard, or, rather, to go out last; and from a window Col. K. and his companions could see the fugitives walk out of a gate at the other end of the enclosure of the carriage-house, and fearlessly move off. The aperture was so narrow that but one man could get through at a time, and each squad carried with them provisions in a haversack. At midnight a false alarm was created, and the prisoners made considerable noise in getting to their respective quarters. Providentially, however, the guard suspected nothing wrong, and in a few moments the exodus was again commenced. Col. Kendrick and his companions looked with some trepidation upon the movements of the fugitives, as some of them, exercising but little discretion, moved boldly out on the enclosure into the glare of the gas-light. Many of them were, however, in citizens' dress; and as all the rebel guards wear the United States uniform, but little suspicion could be excited, even if the fugitives had been accosted by a guard.

Between one and two o'clock the lamps were extinguished in the streets, and then the exit was more safely accomplished. There were many officers who desired to leave, who were so weak and feeble that they were dragged through the tunnel by main force, and carried to places of safety, until such time as they would be able to move on their journey. At half past two o'clock, Capt. Jones, Col. Kendrick, and Lieut. Bradford passed out in the order in which they are named; and as Col. K. emerged from the hole, he heard the guard within a few feet of him sing out, "Post No. 7, half past two in the morning, and all's well." Col. K. says he could hardly resist the temptation of saying, "Not so well as you think, except for the Yanks." Lieut. Bradford was intrusted with the provisions for this squad; and in getting through he was obliged to leave his haversack behind him, as he could not get through with it upon him.

Once out, they proceeded up the street, keeping in the shade of the buildings, and passed eastwardly through the city.

A description of the route pursued by this party, and of the tribulations through which they passed, will give some idea of the rough time they all had of it. Col. Kendrick had, before leaving the prison, mapped out his course, and concluded that the best route to take was the one towards Norfolk, or Fortress Monroe, as there were fewer rebel pickets in that direction. They therefore kept the York River Railroad to the left, and moved towards the Chickahominy River. They passed through Boar Swamp, and crossed the road leading to Bottom Bridge. Sometimes they waded through mud and water almost up to their necks,

and kept the Bottom Bridge road to their left, although at times they could see and hear the cars travelling over the York River Road.

While passing through the swamp near the Chickahominy, Col. Kendrick sprained his ankle and fell. Fortunate, too, was that fall for him and his party; for while he was lying there, one of them chanced to look up, and saw, in a direct line with them, a swamp bridge; and in the dim outline they could perceive that parties with muskets were passing over the bridge. They therefore moved some distance to the south; and after passing through more of the swamp, reached the Chickahominy about four miles below Bottom Bridge. Here, now, was a difficulty. The river was only twenty feet wide, but it was very deep, and the refugees were worn out and fatigued. Chancing, however, to look up, Lieut. Bradford saw that two trees had fallen on either side of the river, and that their branches were interlocked. By crawling up one tree and down the other, the fugitives reached the east bank of the Chickahominy; and Col. Kendrick could not help remarking that he believed Providence was on their side, else they would not have met that natural bridge.

They subsequently learned from a friendly negro that had they crossed the bridge they had seen, they would assuredly have been recaptured, for Capt. Turner, the keeper of Libby Prison, had been out and posted guards there, and in fact had alarmed the whole country, and got the people up as a vigilance committee to capture the escaped prisoners.

After crossing over this natural bridge, they lay down on the ground and slept until sunrise on the morning of the 11th, when they continued on their way, keeping eastwardly as near as they could. Up to this time they had had nothing to eat, and were almost famished. About noon of the 11th they met several negroes, who gave them information as to the whereabouts of the rebel pickets, and furnished them with food.

Acting under the advice of these friendly negroes, they remained quietly in the woods until darkness had set in, when they were furnished with a comfortable supper by the negroes, and after dark proceeded on their way, the negroes (who everywhere showed their friendship for the fugitives) having first directed them how to avoid the rebel pickets. That night they passed a camp of rebels, and could plainly see the smoke and camp fires. But their wearied feet gave out, and they were compelled to stop and rest, having only marched five miles that day.

They started again at daylight on the 13th, and after moving a while through the woods, they saw a negro woman working in a field, and called her to them, and from her received directions, and were told that the rebel pickets had been about there looking for the fugitives from Libby. Here they lay low again, and resumed their journey when darkness set in, and marched five miles, but halted until the morning of the 14th, when the journey was resumed.

At one point they met a negro in the field, and

she told them that her mistress was a secesh woman, and that she had a son in the rebel army. The party, however, were exceedingly hungry, and they determined to secure some food. This they did by boldly approaching the house and informing the mistress that they were fugitives from Norfolk, who had been driven out by Butler; and the secesh sympathies of the woman were at once aroused, and she gave them of her substance, and started them on their way, with directions how to avoid the Yankee soldiers, who occasionally scouted in that vicinity. This information was exceedingly valuable to the refugees, for by it they discovered the whereabouts of the Union forces.

When about fifteen miles from Williamsburg, the party came upon the main road, and found the tracks of a large body of cavalry. A piece of paper found by Capt. Jones, satisfied him that they were Union cavalry; but his companions were suspicious, and avoided the road, and moved forward; and at the "Burnt Ordinary," (about ten miles from Williamsburg,) awaited the return of the cavalry that had moved up the road; and from behind a fence corner, where they were secreted, the fugitives saw the flag of the Union, supported by a squadron of cavalry, which proved to be a detachment of Col. Spear's Eleventh Pennsylvania regiment, sent out for the purpose of picking up escaped prisoners. Col. Kendrick says his feelings at seeing the old flag were indescribable.

The party rode into Williamsburg with the cavalry, where they were quartered for the night, and where they found eleven others who had escaped safely.

A WEDDING ON HORSEBACK. — The following occurred at Battle Creek, on the Chattanooga Railroad, in March, 1864: A pair of lovers bethought themselves of getting married, and having procured a license, they set out on horseback. They soon came up to a parson "setting" on a fence, — it seems he did something occasionally at farming, — and requested him to "solemnize the sacred rites of matrimony at once." The parson finally assented, and he "setting" on the fence, and they on their horses, the "sacred rite" was "solemnized," after which they went on their way rejoicing.

A HERO INDEED. — A good deal of interest was felt at the time when the Confederate officers, prisoners on board the "Maple Leaf," captured that steamer, and made their escape to Currituck, in North Carolina. A correspondent furnishes the following instances of heroism connected with the affair, the hero of which is "a poor old man bowed down with age and poverty." The writer says:

"A few days after their escape, a squad of Federal cavalry, in scouring the country to arrest them, came upon the subject of this notice — Dempsey Kight by name — in the highway. A small tin bucket, which the old fisherman was carrying in his hand, attracted their attention.

They halted, and asked him if he had not been feeding the escaped rebel officers. Too proud to utter a falsehood, he unhesitatingly answered in the affirmative. Whereupon they demanded of him to reveal the place of their concealment, and with threats and blows sought to wrest it from him. But the principle of honor was too strong in the old man's bosom, and to all their importunities he yielded not — their brutality he could not resist. They swore they would have the secret, or that he should die. With this intention, they hurried him aboard a gun-boat, and again tendered him the alternatives of death or of compliance with their wishes. He answered that he was convinced that they intended to hang him, but that he was resolved to die before he "would tell where those officers were." Immediately they suspended him by the neck until life was nearly extinct. They then cut him down, and after reviving him, they repeated the same question, and received the same answer. Again his body hung in the air, and when his life was far more spent than before, they again unloosed the halter, receiving, as before, the same firm denial. Exasperated to fury, they told him that this was his only chance, and that they would not cut him down again. Sustained in this hour of sore trial by his sense of honor, which was stronger than his fear of death, the old man replied that he was convinced of his approaching end, yet he deemed death preferable to dishonor, and that he was ready to meet his fate. Again, and for the third time, his aged frame quivered in the agonies of death, and when he had ceased to struggle, they once more released him. Applying powerful stimulants, they succeeded in restoring him, when, with a determination worthy of the elder Brutus, he drew forth a knife, and attempted, by cutting his own throat, to free himself from his persecutors. By violence they forced his knife from him, when, by a mighty effort, he dashed the fiends aside, and plunged into the boiling surf to drown himself. With boat-hooks they fished him up, and baffled by his unyielding will, they permitted him to go ashore. This is a true statement of this infamous transaction. Dempsey Kight still lives, and plies his humble calling as a fisherman, and that he is one of God's noblemen none will gainsay."

INCIDENTS OF THE FIGHT AT BEAUFORT. — On almost every vessel, after the fight, the men were called aft, and publicly thanked by their respective Captains. On the ship "Bienville," particular mention was made, and special thanks returned, in presence of the ship's company, to William Henry Steele, a boy not fourteen years old, who conducted himself with distinguished bravery. He is a powder boy, and not only never flinched or dodged a shot, but when two men were killed at his gun, he did not turn pale, or cease for an instant his duties, but handed the cartridge he had in hand to the gunner, stepped carefully over the bodies, and hastened below for more ammunition.

The case of Thomas Jackson, coxswain of the "Wabash," deserves notice. He was struck by a shot, or a splinter, which so nearly cut his leg off as to leave it hanging but by a small portion of the muscle and skin. Partially rising, and leaning painfully against a gun, Jackson glanced at his mangled limb, and in an instant perceived its hopeless condition. Feeling behind his back in his belt, where seamen always carry their knives, he drew his sheath-knife from its leather scabbard, and deliberately began to saw away at his leg; but the knife was dull, and he could not cut the limb off. As he was borne below by his mates, and afterwards, he asked continually how the fight was going, and kept saying, "I hope we'll win it; I hope we'll win." In two hours he died, his last words being a wish for our victory in this battle, and a word of thanks that he had been able to do something for the honor of the "dear old flag."

The enthusiasm of the soldiers for the blue-jackets, after the action, literally knew no bounds. Whenever a boat's crew of men-of-war's-men came alongside a transport, there was a rush to the side to catch a nearer view of the gallant sailors, and, if possible, to clasp a tarry hand; and whenever they appeared, the cheers were frantically loud, and long drawn out, and the brave Jacks were as happy and proud as men can be.

THE TYPO WARRIORS. — The typos of the Thirteenth Illinois regiment of volunteers amused themselves at Camp Rolla, Mo., by printing a paper entitled "Our Regiment." A correspondent thus made his shot:

HEADQUARTERS HEAVY MUD INFANTRY, }
CAMP ROLLA, July 17, 1861. }

To the Editor of Our Regiment:

Heavy? Yes, sir! Bound to shoot rebels. This is the report. Chicago boy, the undersigned. I'm always boasting of Chicago. I'm full of fight. Although fighting is not my *forte*, I do not think I would stand being knocked down. I joined this August body in April, and we May March daily, for we are getting stronger weekly. I may say in good season, if we Spring upon the enemy he is sure to Fall, for our Summer-saults will be a dose that will prove "the Winter of his discontent." He will have to evacuate. We won't strike light, for the South is no match for us. When the country called all hands to arms, I thought it a proud legacy to leave posterity that I joined a division for the Union. I set my name down, and there it stands. Nice uniform. Had my hair cut with a knife and fork. Red hair, yellow jacket, blue shirt, white hat, plantation shoes, pink trousers, bell buttons on behind, where I never saw them before. Left the city under encouraging circumstances. Toothache, nail in my shoe, forgot my rations, something in my eye. Chap in rear file rasping my skins. Got out of step and hurt my instep. While marching, washwoman handed me a bill. Had no money,

and she had no sense — wanted to know where our quarters were. Asked her who gave the order to charge. Bad boy on sidewalk crying out, "Pay the poor woman." Loaded the little sun-of-a-gun with abuse, and he went off. Arrived at Camp Rolla all right, nobody being left. Intentions to sleep in tents, but were intensely disappointed, as we slept on the grass, which, after all, served as well to all intents and purposes. Placed minute-men on watch, who moved all hands every second, until we really thought it time to strike. Took my turn in going round. Shot a cow and calf. "'Tis meet to be here." Fighting, you see, for the public weal, places our lives at stake. Took the hindquarters into headquarters. Pork in various shapes for rations heretofore. Not Jew-dishes. Serg. Hinmann would like to have some mutton. Told me to stir up, get a horse and find a saddle. Serg. Hinmann's drilling is a complete bore, and he thinks he augurs well on the whole. Marches us around in a body, until he almost wears out our soles. Makes our squad run so we will be fully able to sail in when we have the enemy at bay. Of course we have our fine times. Had some light reading sent me by a Sexton: "Annual Report of Rose-Hill," "Ghost Stories," and his business circular, with price list of coffins, &c. I should like to overtake that undertaker. Serg. Hinmann speaks disparagingly of our literary tastes. Says the only thing red in the camp is my nose — my nasal "organ." I mention it because it's a military move to right about face. Music by the band. I must come to a full stop now for a period. Flip flap.

Yours, jolly and con-tent-ed,
G. N. L. SCOTTY.

A SERGEANT HALTS A WHOLE REBEL REGIMENT. — Among the beauties of the war in Western Virginia was the "mixed-up" way in which the combatants manœuvre among the mountains. Here is an instance where a single loyal soldier halted an entire rebel regiment:

Serg. Carter, of Tippecanoe, Ohio, was upon the post first attacked by the enemy. The advance-guard of the Second Virginia, (rebel,) consisting of twelve men, came suddenly upon him and his three companions. The bright moonlight revealed the flashing bayonets of the advancing regiment. He was surrounded and separated from his reserve. With great presence of mind he stepped out and challenged: "Halt! Who goes there?" The advance-guard, supposing they had come upon a scouting party of their own men, answered, "Friends, with the countersign." At his order, "Advance, one, and give the countersign," they hesitated. He repeated the order peremptorily, "Advance and give the countersign or I'll blow you through." They answered, without advancing, "Mississippi." "Where do you belong?" he demanded. "To the Second Virginia regiment." "Where are you going?" "Along the ridge." They then in turn questioned him, — "Who are you?" "That's my own business," he answered, and taking deliberate aim, he shot down his questioner.

He called for his boys to follow him, and sprung down a ledge of rock, while a full volley went over his head. He heard his companions summoned to surrender, and the order given to the Major to advance with the regiment. Several started in pursuit of him. He had to descend the hill on the side towards the enemy's camp. While he eluded his pursuers, he found himself in a new danger. He had got within the enemy's camp pickets! He had, while running, torn the U. S. from his cartridge box, and covered his belt plate with his cap box, and torn the strips from his pantaloons. He was challenged by their sentinels while making his way out, and answered, giving the countersign, "'Mississippi,' Second Virginia regiment." They asked him what he was doing there. He said that the boys had gone off on a scout after the Yankees, that he had been detained in camp, and in trying to find them he had got bewildered.

As he passed through, to prevent further questioning, he said, "Our boys are up on the ridge; which is the best way up?" They answered, "Bear to the left, and you'll find it easier to climb." Soon again his pursuers were after him, as he expressed it, "breaking brush" behind him; this time with a hound on his trail. He made his way to a brook, and running down the shallow stream, threw the dog off the scent, and, as the day was dawning, he suddenly came upon four pickets, who brought their arms to a ready, and challenged him. He gave the countersign, "Mississippi," and claimed to belong to the Second Virginia regiment. His cap box had slipped from his belt plate. They asked him where he got that belt. He told them he had captured it that night from a Yankee. They told him to advance, and, as he approached, he recognized their accoutrements, and knew that he was among his own men, a picket guard from the First Kentucky.

He was taken before Col. Enyart, and dismissed to his regiment. His motive in halting a whole column of the enemy was to give intimation to the reserve of their advance, that they might open upon them on their left flank, and so, perhaps, arrest their progress.

SURGEON RAT. — We have heard and read a great many stories about the rat; but in all our experience, we never before had one brought before us in the character of a surgeon. At one of our large hospitals, an operation was successfully performed upon an invalid soldier, by a common rat; which the surgeon in charge had himself delayed for a time, with the hope of causing less suffering to the patient. This patient was suffering from the effects of a fracture of the frontal bone of the skull, a piece of which projected outwards to some length; and the healing of the fleshy parts depended upon its removal. The bone was so firmly fixed, however, as, in the opinion of the surgeon, would cause unnecessary pain in its forcible removal; and such remedies were applied as would assist nature in eventually ejecting it. A soothing poultice was placed upon the part a night or two ago, a hole being made through the application for the insertion of the projecting bone. The patient was soon asleep in his bed, but during the night was aroused by the sting of pain, and awoke, to discover a rat making off with the piece of bone in his mouth. He struck at and hit the rat, but did not hurt him. The rat had probably been drawn to the bed of the soldier by the scent of the poultice, which was pleasant to his olfactories; but on reaching it, his keen appetite, no doubt, caused him to relish, in a large degree, the juicy bone so convenient to his teeth. He, therefore, seized, and drew it from its position, and was made to scamper off by the patient, whom he had aroused with pain. It was a skilful operation, quickly performed, and will result beneficially to the invalid. — *Petersburg Express.*

EXPERIENCES WITH REBEL PRISONERS. — "Strange as it may seem," says a soldier, "we made some very pleasant acquaintances among the prisoners we were sent to guard, some of whom we had helped to capture, and cared for when wounded on the field. One rebel — Maj. McKnight, of the rebel Gen. Loring's staff — was an especial favorite. He was a poet, musician, and joker, and used to run 'from grave to gay, from lively to severe,' on almost all matters. I append a little morceau of his, under his *nom de plume* of Asa Hartz, entitled

MY LOVE AND I.

BY ASA HARTZ.

My love reposes on a rosewood frame;
    A bunk have I;
A couch of feathery down fills up the same;
    Mine's straw, but dry;
She sinks to rest at night with scarce a sigh;
With waking eyes I watch the hours creep by.

My love her daily dinner takes in state,
    And so do I;
The richest viands flank her silver plate;
    Coarse grub have I;
Pure wines she sips at ease, her thirst to slake;
I pump my drink from Erie's limpid lake.

My love has all the world at will to roam;
    Three acres I;
She goes abroad, or quiet sits at home;
    So cannot I.
Bright angels watch around her couch at night;
A Yank, with loaded gun, keeps me in sight.

A thousand weary miles now stretch between
    My love and I.
To her this wintry night, cold, calm, serene,
    I waft a sigh,
And hope with all my earnestness of soul,
To-morrow's mail may bring me my parole.

There's hope ahead! we'll one day meet again,
    My love and I.
We'll wipe away all tears of sorrow then;
    Her love-lit eye
Will all my many troubles then beguile,
And keep this wayward reb from Johnson's Isle.

ADVENTURES OF A UNION OFFICER. — The experiences of Col. De Villiers, of the Eleventh Ohio regiment, who was captured with others, in Western Virginia, in 1861, and conveyed to Richmond, and who afterwards made his escape, is thus detailed:

"Arrived at Richmond, they were taken to a tobacco warehouse, where they found forty other prisoners. In the room there was neither table nor bed. They were kept without food; no breakfast given them the next morning after their arrival — and when, finally, a little bread was brought them, it was thrown upon the floor as to a dog; and the quantity so small, that every man must make double-quick in grabbing it, or he got none, and was compelled to beg from the others. But there were rich officers, who could *buy* something to eat; for if the rebels did not love the Northerners, they loved their gold. But to shorten, he got the brain fever in prison, and was removed to the hospital; and here the Colonel took occasion to affirm, that the kindness which had been spoken of, as practised by the physicians, was not from rebels, but from our own surgeons.

"Being by profession a physician, Col. De V., when he had sufficiently recovered, was asked by the hospital doctor to assist, which he consented to do; and he was thus permitted to enjoy more liberty. By good fortune, one day the commanding General gave the physicians liberty to go into the city several times. They wore, as a distinguished body, a red ribbon, or badge, fixed in their button-hole. When he encountered the sentinel, he was challenged, and forbidden to pass on the ground of being a prisoner; the order of the General did not include him. Now, as they called him a French Yankee, he thought he would play them a Yankee trick; so he wrote a note stating that he was included. When he returned to the hospital, the rebel physician said he had been practising deceit, and must consequently go back among the prisoners. He was again incarcerated and put in irons. He soon made up his mind, however, to escape from there, or die. He was asked to take an oath by the rebels; but, said he, 'I have taken an oath as a naturalized citizen of the United States, and I will never take another to conflict with it.' He had been tempted by the offer of position, but he abhorred the enemies of this Union, and could never forget that he came here for Liberty's sake. He told Col. Woodruff of his determination to escape, for his time had come. Col. W. wished him well, and hoped that he would escape. He set about it, and devised a lie, and stole; for which he felt assured he would be forgiven. He stole the coat and hat of a secession officer, and in that garb passed the guard.

"Col. De Villiers, while Brigade Inspector at Camp Dennison, Ohio, learned a lesson from the soldiers who wanted to go to Cincinnati. They were in the habit of lying in the bushes to hear the countersign, and having obtained it, passed the guard. Without the countersign he could not get out of the gate, even with his full uniform.

So he lay for about two hours behind the guardhouse, (in the night, as should have been stated,) until he was happy by hearing it. The guard called at his approach, 'Who comes there?' 'A friend, with the countersign.' He passed the guard, the gate was opened, and he was once more free. He made his way to Manassas Junction, which is nothing but a swamp. About six miles from Richmond, he was encountered by a guard, and to his challenge replied, 'A friend, without the countersign.' [He had the precaution to lay the double-barrel shot gun, which he contrived to get before he escaped from Richmond, down, before he approached this guard. He had, besides, a revolver and a bowie knife.]

"Approaching, they asked him where he was from and whither he was going. He replied from Richmond to Petersburg. They then asked why he did not take the railroad, and he said he missed the cars. They then took him in custody, and marched one on each side of him upon a narrow bridge crossing a stream near at hand. The situation was desperate, but he was determined never to go back to Richmond alive; so when he got to about the middle of the bridge, he struck to the right and left, knocking one of the guards on one side and the other on the other side, and giving them both a good swim. Hence he made his way towards Petersburg, subsisting for three days upon nothing but a few raw beans, 'which was not very good for his digestion.'

"Upon this tramp, for a distance of sixty-five miles, he carried his skiff for crossing rivers (a pine board) upon his shoulder. During his travels he was several times shot at. When he got in the neighborhood of Magruder's forces, his hardest time began. He tried to pass sentinels several times, and at one time was twice shot at in quick succession. He shot too. He did not know whether he hit the two sentinels or not, but they never answered. But the whole brigade was aroused, and he took to the James River in what he called his skiff, viz., his pine-board companion. He landed on the other side in a swamp, recrossing again near Jamestown, where he lost his gun. He had cast away his officer's coat, and what remained of his suit was rusty enough. So he took an open course, and resolved to ask for work; but like the poor men in the South, when they ask for work, they are told to go into the service. Even the ladies do not look upon a young man unless he is in the service; viewed from this test, there were more patriots in the South than in the North; they were all soldiers, old and young.

"He hired with a German blacksmith, at $1.50 per week, having concluded to remain a while, and learn something of the condition of the rebel forces. He staid a fortnight, observing all the rebel movements. At the expiration of this time, he got tired of blacksmithing, and wanted to go home. He found a good German Union man, to whom he told his story, without reservation, just as if he was telling it here to-night. This was of great service to him; he led him for nine days, the Colonel having adopted another Yankee trick, and made a blind man of himself; he couldn't see, and the German was his guide. Dropping the Yankee French, he became a French subject, and wanted to go back to France, because he could not get any work to do here; and so he told Gen. Huger, when he got into his command. This General promised to send him to Fortress Monroe with a flag of truce. The next flag of truce that was sent he accompanied, blind still, and led by his faithful German Union man.

"He contrived, unobserved, to tell the Captain of the flag party that he was a prisoner, a Union officer, and had assumed blindness as a disguise, and that he should take him; but the young officer said he could not understand it, and said he would inform Gen. Wool. He did so, and Wool, being an old soldier, comprehended the matter at once, immediately sending another boat out to bring him; but it was too late, for the rebel officer said it was not worth while waiting on the Yankees, and hastened off. Having lost his German guide, Gen. Huger himself led him (the poor old blind man) with unaffected sympathy, to the hotel, and he assured him that he should go with the next flag of truce which was sent; and he further took the trouble of writing a special letter to Gen. Wool about the 'old French blind man who wanted to go home.' Col. De Villiers remarked that Gen. Huger evinced true kindness towards him.

"With the flag, there were, besides, a number of ladies, who 'left the South for the purpose of going North to do business.' Though he was blind, he could see the glances they exchanged; and though old and somewhat deaf, he could hear the officers tell the ladies to learn all they could, and come back with the information — wishing them much success. 'It is surprising what fine spies they make!'

"When he got into safe quarters, he threw off his disguise, his decrepitude — saw and was strong — observing, without surprise himself, the astonishment of the ladies at the change."

FIRST EXPERIENCE IN BATTLE. — A Union soldier, who was in the battle of Piketon, Kentucky, gives the following graphic description of his sensations during the fight:

"And now for my share in the battle. I was riding along, somewhat carelessly, when crack! crack! went their rifles, and down fell our men. Crack! crack! crack! they came. Off I jumped from my horse, when along came the Major, and gave me his horse to hold; but I soon hitched them both to a tree down by the river, and sprung again up the bank, when whiz! went a bullet past my face, about three inches from it, and made me draw back in a hurry, I can assure you. I looked up the hill, but could see no one for the smoke, which was plenty; so I levelled in the direction of the enemy and fired — loaded again and fired. I got my rifle in readiness again! Ah! that ball was pretty close. Here comes another — buzz, buzz — (you can hear their whiz for fully a hundred yards as they come) —

get out of the way. But where is it to go to? Whew! that was close. But, great God! it has gone through a man's shoulder within a few yards of me! He falls! some of his comrades pick him up.

"Now a horseman comes past in a hurry. He is right opposite me — when whiz. crack! a ball strikes his horse in the fore-shoulder. Off tumbles the man; down falls the horse, stiffened out and dead. If the bullet had gone through the animal, it would doubtless have struck me.

"Here come a dozen more. How they whiz as they go past! 'Load and fire!' 'Load and fire!' is the order — and load and fire it is. My notice was especially drawn to a very fine-looking man, who stood close to me, and he truly acted like a hero — loading and firing just as if he was on parade, when whiz! whiz! comes a bullet. My God, how close! It almost stunned me. When I looked towards my soldier, I saw his comrades lifting him up. He was shot through the breast, and died in less than half an hour. O the horrors of war! Vengeance on the heads of those who initiate it.

"I directed my attention up the hill; a little puff of smoke was dying away. 'Boys,' says I to the squad of his fellows, 'you see that smoke; aim for it; a rebel's in its rear.' I raised my Enfield, and glanced through its sights, when I for a moment caught sight of a man through the bushes and smoke there. Crack went our guns, and all was over.

"We crossed to the place afterwards, and found musket-balls, and one Enfield rifle-ball — mine, as mine was the only rifle-ball fired. They all went through him, either of which would have killed him — mine through his breast. Thank God, I have done my duty for the poor fellow who fell beside me."

A GALLANT LIEUTENANT. — During the battle near Spottsylvania Court-House, Va., on the 14th of May, 1864, Maj.-Gen. Wright's brigade was ordered to charge the Union works. In doing so, the Third Georgia regiment passed through a heavy fire of minie balls, losing seventy-eight men in killed and wounded. The color-bearer of the regiment, being wounded, planted the colors in the ground, and retired to the rear. At this moment the skirmish line was ordered to halt, which was understood by many as an order for the regiment to halt, which they did. Perceiving that a crisis was at hand, Lieut. R. G. Hyman sprang forward, seized the colors from amid a pile of slain, and waving them in the face of the foe, called upon the old Third to rally to it, which they did, with a yell, and the Yankee breastworks were taken. Lieut. Hyman was at least fifty yards in advance of the regiment all the time. — *Folsom's Georgia Record.*

CAPT. GILLINGHAM'S ADVENTURE. — On the 23d of August, 1863, Captain Ned Gillingham, of the Thirteenth New York cavalry, with an escort of eight Sergeants, whilst going from camp, near Centreville, as bearer of despatches to Washington, was met on the road near Allandale, about two o'clock P. M., by a detachment of the Second Massachusetts cavalry, the Sergeant of the latter asking Capt. Gillingham if they need apprehend any danger; to which Capt. Gillingham replied : "So far, we have not met with any obstruction." Capt. Gillingham had scarcely gone over four hundred yards, when he was met by a party of Mosby's cavalry, consisting of about one hundred men, by whom he was ordered, under fire, to halt. Capt. Gillingham, taking them for our own troops, (as they were dressed similarly to his own men,) replied : "Hold up firing — you are fools — you are firing on Government troops ; " to which the Captain of said troops replied : " Surrender there, you Yankee ——." Capt. Gillingham replied he could not see the joke. Then, turning to Sergeant Long, Orderly of company B, and to Sergeant Burnham, ordered them to draw their sabres and follow him. A general conflict ensued, in which sabres and pistols were freely used, resulting in the wounding of Orderly Sergeant Long and Sergeant Zeagle, both of company B, who, with four other Sergeants, were all taken prisoners. Capt. Ned Gillingham and Serg. Burnham effected their escape, the former having been wounded in the arm, and the latter in the hip, as well as having their horses shot. Obtaining horses on the road, they reached Washington about six o'clock P. M.

THE WOUNDED SOLDIER.

The following beautiful and touching lines were written by Lieut. John McKee, of company K, 74th Ohio regiment, who was accidentally drowned at Cincinnati, on his way home :

Among the pines that overlook
  Stone River's rocky bed,
Ohio knows full many a son
  There numbered with the dead.

'Tis hard to die 'mid scenes of strife,
  No friend or kindred near,
To wipe the death damp from the brow,
  Or shed affection's tear.

To soothe the sufferer, in his pain,
  With words of holy cheer,
Or bend the knee, in earnest prayer,
  For the dying volunteer.

That day, when all along our lines
  Rained showers of shot and shell,
Thus many a brave young soldier died —
  Thus many a hero fell.

When night closed o'er this bloody scene,
  Returning o'er the ground,
I heard the piteous moans of one
  Laid low by mortal wound.

'Twas by the ford we crossed that day —
  The ground so dearly bought —
Where Miller led his stalwart men,
  And gallant Moody fought.

The wounded soldier's cheek was wan,
  And beamless was his eye ;
I knew before another morn
  The wounded man must die.

I built a fire of cedar rails, —
  The air was cold and damp, —
And filled his canteen from the spring,
  Below the river's bank.

And then I sat me down to ask
  If he would wish to send
A last request or parting word
  To mother, sister, friend.

"I have some word," the boy replied,
  " My friends would love to hear ;
'Twould fill my sister's soul with joy,
  My mother's heart would cheer.

" Tell them I died a soldier's death,
  Upon the battle-field,
But lived to know the day was ours,
  And see the rebels yield ; —

"That ere I died their colors fell,
  Their columns broke, and then
I heard the wild, victorious shouts
  Of Negley's valiant men.

" But most of all I'd have them know,
  That with my latest breath
I spoke of Him I loved in life :
  'Twas joy and peace in death.

" Tell sister I have read with care —
  For holy ties endeared —
The Bible mother gave to me
  Before I volunteered.

"I'm very tired with talking now ;
  Please raise my head some higher,
And fold my blanket closely down,
  And build a larger fire.

" The air is very cold to-night."
  I raised his head with care ;
He closed his eyes as if to sleep,
  But clasped his hands in prayer.

In silent converse with his God
  The wounded hero lay ;
It seemed to him communion sweet,
  No agony to pray.

He smiled as does the gentle child
  When angels whisper near ;
No anguish worked upon his brow,
  Nor blanched his cheek with fear.

I saw that death was coming fast ;
  His mind was all in prayer ;
I asked him for his regiment,
  And where his comrades were.

" My Captain's dead," the boy replied,
  In accents low and mild ;
" I've heard my mother speak of him
  When I was but a child."

I knew his mind was wandering,
  That he was thinking then
Of him who gave his life to save
  His faithful, valiant men.

And thus he died that stormy night,
No friend or kindred near
To wipe the death damp from his brow,
Or shed affection's tear.

Thus I have known the love of God
Joy, peace, and comfort yield
To one who fell with mortal wound
On the bloody battle-field.

And should you wander o'er the ground
Where fell so many brave,
Among the cedars on the hill
There lies his lonely grave.

The flowers will soon light up with smiles
Stone River's rocky shore ;
His spirit knows a brighter clime,
Where flowers bloom evermore.

And mild-eyed Peace may visit soon
Stone River's rocky shore,
But Murfrees' chiming Sabbath bells
Will never wake him more.

ANECDOTE OF GEN. WYMAN. — A correspondent accompanying the Union forces in their march from Jefferson City to Rolla, Mo., in 1861, relates the following: "After leaving camp at Union Hollow, a rugged part of the mountains beyond Springfield, an incident occurred worthy of preservation. Gen. Wyman had issued orders that no man should go in advance of his company. About five miles from camp the General met two of the boys of the Illinois Thirteenth, waiting the approach of their company. Those who know the General, know, when he does not like anything, how roughly he can reprimand a soldier. The General addressed the boys in one of his very roughest styles:

"'Boys, why —— are you in advance of your company this morning?'

"One of the men, taking off his hat, addressed the General in the following style :

"'General, about two and a half miles from here are the graves of my mother and sisters, and I thought it was likely this was the last time I should be permitted to visit them, and I got permission of the Captain to go this morning to visit them, and I am here waiting for them to come up.'

"This was too much for the General. Said he, 'My boy, that was right. I have always loved you, but that makes me love you twice as well as I ever did.' At this point, tears choked the words of the noble soldier, and one might have seen one whole-souled man weeping under the effects of paternal affection. Some time after this, they joined our staff, and rode with us, and while riding with me, he narrated to me the incident, and again gave vent to tears. Said he, 'I am not ashamed of tears under such circumstances.'"

A THRILLING EVENT.—On Thursday, Sept. 10, 1863, while General Forrest was at Lafayette, Ga., he was ordered to Ringgold for the purpose of checking the enemy, reported to be marching in large force in that direction. Picking up about four hundred of his command, he marched off with all the promptitude of his ardent and enthusiastic nature. Here he found Vancleve's corps, consisting of seventeen thousand infantry and cavalry. Skirmishing immediately commenced, General Forrest fighting them at every step, as he slowly fell back. For two days did the unequal conflict continue, and notwithstanding the disparity of numbers, the loss on either side was about the same. General Forrest retired to Tunnel Hill about four o'clock, and in an hour the enemy was in sight, when one of the most gallant and thrilling incidents of the war occurred. The enemy's advancing column marched on, — right on, — and the cloud of dust and the huge paraphernalia which they displayed made them look indeed "terrible as an army with banners." On reaching the apex of the hill, a short pause was perceptible ; but skirmishers being thrown out on the right and left, on they came. In every ambush, behind every knoll, and house, and tree, could be seen a blue-coat, slyly, cautiously sneaking up like a hungry wolf in search of its prey. General Forrest levelled his trusty gun at the nearest one. The smoke from his gun seemed only to exasperate the infuriated foe, and to inspire them with anxiety either to capture or destroy the small but defiant squad of Confederates, and for this purpose a hundred guns opened upon them, while a dozen Yankees rushed across the railroad for the purpose of getting still closer. As they crossed the track, General Forrest looked still farther up, and he saw a couple of Confederate soldiers coming down the road, unaware of the approach of the enemy, and the immediate danger that surrounded them. The impudence of the Yankees that had crossed the railroad, and were seen crawling in the woods, together with the peril that surrounded the two Confederate soldiers approaching, was more than General Forrest could stand. Hastily calling to his side five of his escort, he told them that his imperilled soldiers must be rescued, and that the insolent squad that had crossed the road must be captured. With coolness and self-possession, but with a loud and cheering shout, he ordered his little squad to the charge. In the midst of the iron hail that rained upon them, they rushed on. Every man forgot his own danger. The soldier stooped over his musket, or leaned upon his horse, absorbed in the scene. Dressed in a huge duster, General Forrest, as he dashed on in his fierce purpose, looked infernal. There was a sudden pause ; then their heads were curtained in by the wreathing smoke of their own guns. The Yankees were seen retreating back across the road, and the Confederate soldiers rescued from death. From the hill-side a volley of musketry was now poured upon the small squad. Having accomplished their purpose, they turned to retreat, but three of the seven were wounded. A ball struck General Forrest near the spine, within an inch of the wound he received at Shiloh, inflicting a painful but not dangerous wound ; while two of his escort were wounded — one in the back of the head, the other in the arm. — *Marietta Rebel.*

DEATH OF A YOUNG WOMAN ON THE BATTLE-FIELD OF CHICKAMAUGA. — The case of a young woman in Willoughby Street, Brooklyn, brings to mind the story of the unfortunate Maid of Orleans, who was "burnt by wicked Bedford for a witch." It well illustrates the Solomonic proverb that "there is nothing new under the sun." The superstitions of the days of Joan of Arc still flourish.

Early in 1863, when disaster everywhere overtook the Union arms, and our gallant sons were falling fast under that marvellous sword of rebellion, a young lady, scarce nineteen, just from school, conceived the idea that she was destined by Providence to lead our arms to victory, and our nation through successful war. It was at first thought by her parents that her mind was weakened simply by reading accounts of continued reverses to our arms, and they treated her as they would a sick child. This only had the effect of making her more demonstrative, and her enthusiastic declarations and apparent sincerity gave the family great anxiety. Dr. B—— was consulted, the minister was spoken to, friends advised, family meetings held, interviews with the young lady by her former companions in the academy were frequent, but nothing could shake the feeling which had possessed her.

It was finally resolved to take her to Michigan. A maiden aunt accompanied the fair enthusiast, and for a few weeks Ann Arbor became their home. The stern command of her aunt alone prevented her from making her way to Washington to solicit an interview with the President for the purpose of getting command of the United States army. Finally it was found necessary to restrain her from seeing any but her own family, and her private parlor became her prison. To a high-spirited girl, this would be unendurable at any time, but to a young lady filled with such a hallucination, it was worse than death. She resolved to elude her friends, and succeeded, leaving them clandestinely; and although the most distinguished detectives of the East and the West were employed to find her whereabouts, it was unavailing. None could even conjecture the hiding-place. This was in April, 1863. She was mourned as lost. The habiliments of mourning were donned by her grief-stricken parents, and a suicide's grave was assumed to be hers. But it was not so. The infatuated girl, finding no sympathy with her friends, resolved to enter the army disguised as a drummer boy, dreaming, poor girl, that her destiny would be worked out by such a mode. She joined the drum corps of a Michigan regiment at Detroit, her sex known only to herself, and succeeded in getting with her regiment to the army of the Cumberland. How the poor girl survived the hardships of the Kentucky campaign, where strong men fell in numbers, must forever remain a mystery. The regiment to which she was attached had a place in the

division of the gallant Van Cleve, and during the bloody battle of Sunday, the fair girl fell, pierced in the left side by a minie ball ; and when borne to the surgeon's tent, her sex was discovered. She was told by the surgeon that her wound was mortal, and advised to give her name, that her family might be informed of her fate. This she finally, though reluctantly, consented to do, and the Colonel of the regiment, although suffering himself from a painful wound, became interested in her behalf, and prevailed upon her to let him send a despatch to her father. This she directed in the following manner :

"Mr. ——, No — Willoughby Street, Brooklyn : Forgive your dying daughter. I have but a few moments to live. My native soil drinks my blood. I expected to deliver my country, but the Fates would not have it so. I am content to die. Pray, pa, forgive me. Tell ma to kiss my daguerreotype.   EMILY.

"P. S. Give my old watch to little Eph." (The youngest brother of the dying girl.)

The poor girl was buried on the field on which she fell in the service of her country, which she fondly hoped to save.

THE HERO OF SUGAR PINE.

"O, TELL me, Sergeant of Battery B,
  O hero of Sugar Pine,
Some glorious deed of the battle-field,
  Some wonderful feat of thine ; —

"Some skilful move when the fearful game
  Of battle and life was played
On yon grimy field, whose broken squares
  In scarlet and black are laid."

"Ah ! stranger, here at my gun all day
  I fought till my final round
Was spent, and I had but powder left,
  And never a shot to be found.

"So I trained my gun on a rebel piece ;
  So true was my range and aim,
A shot from his cannon entered mine,
  And finished the load of the same !"

"Enough ! O Sergeant of Battery B,
  O hero of Sugar Pine !
Alas ! I fear that thy cannon's throat
  Can swallow much more than mine !"

A THRILLING INCIDENT. — A. Z. Reeve, of the Iowa army, gives the following in a letter from Germantown, Tenn., March 12, 1863 :

"We have been here about six weeks, protecting the railroad. Col. Richardson, a rebel guerrilla, has been hovering in the vicinity for some time, capturing forage parties and tearing up the road whenever opportunity offered. When pursued, he retreats to the swamps, and his command, dispersing in small squads, generally evade all attempts to discover them. To make the matter worse, they frequently dress in Federal uniform. On the morning of the 9th of this month, our regiment and the Fourth Illinois cavalry started out with a guide for the retreat of the guerrillas. Before we reached the rebel camp, the Sixth Illinois cavalry, with flying artillery attached, attacked the rebels from the opposite side, killed twenty-five of them, took some prisoners, and burned the camp and garrison equipage. In their headlong stampede, the rebels came well nigh running into our hands. While in hot pursuit, we came to the residence of one Robert C. Forbes, who, intrenching himself in the house, commenced firing on our flankers as they approached. The flankers then charged on the house, effected an entrance, and discovered that Forbes had taken shelter in an upper chamber. The desperate man was called upon to surrender, but refused. He had already killed one member of the Fourth Illinois cavalry, and had wounded another. He also had received a wound in the right arm, which disabled him to such an extent that he could not load his gun. His wound was received by a shot fired up through the floor. Still the desperate man refused to yield. As a last resort the house was set on fire. This compelled the man to come down, but he still obstinately refused to surrender. He was immediately surrounded by the exasperated soldiers, who refrained from shooting him on account of the certainty of shooting their comrades. Meanwhile the old man clubbed his gun, and although his arm was badly lacerated and bleeding, he ferociously kept the soldiers at bay. At length one of the officers ordered the soldiers opposite to him to get away, and give him a chance " to shoot the old secession scoundrel."

At these words the gun dropped from the old man's hands, and he earnestly inquired :

"Is it possible? Have I been fighting Union soldiers all this time?"

"Of course we are Union men," replied the officer.

"My God! why didn't I know this before?" said the old man in a voice of agony; "I am a Union man, too. I thought I was fighting Richardson's guerrillas!"

The soldiers did not believe him at first, but in brief time he proved to them beyond all dispute that there was no counterfeit Unionism about him. He had been an incorruptible patriot during the war. At the outbreak of the rebellion he had been arrested by Confederate authority, and placed in chains. His crime consisted in telling the rebels that they were traitors, and deserved hanging. When Gen. Hurlbut passed through this part of the country, the old man joined him, but came back occasionally to see his family. He was on a brief furlough from the Federal army when the raid was made on his house. Richardson had sworn vengeance against him, and he had resolved never to be taken alive. Owing to the fact that the guerrillas were in the habit of prowling about in Federal uniform, the old man was led to mistake our soldiers for rebels.

The explanation came too late to save the house. It was consumed with all its contents. There was not a quilt left to defend the mother and children from the cold. They had fled from the burning building just in time to save their lives. It was a sad spectacle. The old man begged to be taken along with us. He told his wife to get to the Federal lines as soon as possible. A braver and a truer man to his country does not exist than Robert C. Forbes. I gave the mother and children ten dollars in greenbacks and my blankets. The other soldiers contributed to relieve the distresses of the family. Many sympathizing tears were shed by us all. I have not witnessed a scene so affecting since my enlistment.

YANKEEISM ON THE FIELD. — A correspondent gives the following, which, whether exactly true or not, is a good story :

At the battle of the Rappahannock Station, after the Fifth Maine had gained possession of the works in their front, and were busy taking a whole brigade of Johnnies to the rear, Col. Edwards, who was one of the first to reach the rifle-pits, took a few men from company G, and pressed on in quest of more prisoners, supposing some might be trying to get away in the darkness of the night. Following the line of fortifications down towards the river, he saw before him a long line of troops in the rifle-pits. Finding that he was in a tight fix, he determined to put on a bold face.

"Where is the officer in command of these troops?" demanded the gallant Colonel.

"Here," answered the Colonel who was commanding the rebel brigade; "and who are you, sir?"

"My name is Col. Edwards, of the Fifth Maine, and I demand of you to surrender your command."

"I will confer with my officers first," replied the rebel officer.

"Not a moment will I allow, sir," said Col. Edwards. "Don't you see my columns advancing?" (pointing to a large body of men marching over the hill, but who were rebel prisoners being marched to the rear.) " Your forces on the right have all been captured, and your retreat is cut off;" and as the rebel commander hesitated, he continued : " Forward! Fifth Maine and Twenty-first New York!"

"I surrender, sir," said the rebel commander, quickly. "Will you allow me the courtesy of retaining a sword that has never been dishonored?"

"Yes, sir," replied Col. E., " but I will take the swords of those officers," pointing to the Colonels by his side.

They were handed to him.

"Now order your men to lay down their arms, and pass to the rear with this guard."

They obeyed, and a whole brigade of Louisianians, the famous Fifth and Sixth Tigers being among them, permitted themselves to be disarmed and marched to the rear as prisoners of war, by Col. Edwards and less than a dozen of his regiment.

A CHALLENGE. — The following is a copy of a challenge, which appears to have been prepared by a member of the Pillow Guards: —

MEMPHIS, TENN., June 3.

Pillow Guards of Memphis to Prentiss Guards of Cairo:

We have enlisted under the stars and bars of the Confederate States for the purpose of defending Southern rights and vindicating Southern honor. But more especially we have been selected and sworn in for the purpose of guarding the person of our gallant Gen. Pillow. Understanding that you occupy a like position with reference to Prentiss, the commandant at Cairo, we challenge you to meet us at any time, at any place, in any number, and with any arms or equipments which you may select. We wish to meet no others till we have met and conquered you and your General. Make your own terms, only let us know when and where, and be certain you will meet the bravest guard the world has ever known.

The signatures of the challenging party are omitted in the copy in possession of your correspondent, but on the back is indorsed the following, viz.:

JUNE 17, 1861.

Prentiss Guards to Pillow Guards:

We accept no challenge from traitors, but hang them. If we ever meet, you shall suffer the fate of traitors. JOSEPH D. WALKER,
Captain Company.

———

A BRAVE EXPLOIT. — During the last year of the war, Kentucky was infested with roving squads of armed men, sometimes calling themselves Confederate cavalry. But in general they were little better than robbers, who took advantage of the disorders of the time to ply their nefarious business; and when called to account, would demand the treatment usually given to prisoners of war. Many old neighborhood feuds were thus revenged, and numerous deeds of blood and shame, which were attempted to be explained as only the disorders incident to civil war.

In December, 1864, a small number of Union soldiers were stationed at Caseyville, on the Ohio River, with instructions to ferret out and punish all guerrilla bands infesting the neighborhood. Major Shook commanded the force, and about the 15th of December he sent out Capt. Peck with a squad of men to hunt for Lyon, a troublesome guerrilla in that region. Three of his men — Lieut. Bogard, Serg. Richards, and Corp. Doughtey — rode some two miles in advance of the scouting party, and they saw a group of men in blue overcoats before them in the road. Riding straight up to them, one of the men inquired what command they belonged to. Lieut. B. replied, "To Major Shook's command, at Caseyville." Capt. Stedman, in command of the rebels, then ordered the three men to surrender.

"That's played out," coolly replied Serg. Richards; and drawing his pistol shot Stedman, so that he died next morning. Lieut. Bogard and Corp. Doughtey then fired on two other men,

and brought them both to the ground. As Lieut. B. was wounded, the Union party now fell back a few yards, when the Lieutenant fell from his horse. His companions, instead of continuing the retreat, now turned their horses and charged upon the hostile party, routing them, and bringing off the bodies of the three who had fallen. The other two besides Stedman proved to be George Henry and Capt. Woodfolk.

Woodfolk and Stedman were both notorious guerrillas and daring men — the latter having once been employed in the office of the Richmond Examiner, and having on his person a large quantity of Confederate money.

Woodfolk had once before been captured, brought to Louisville, and condemned to be shot, but by some means had made his escape. Besides killing these three, the party captured four horses, seven pistols, two guns, and seven cavalry equipments complete.

———

LITTLE JOHNNY CLEM. — Of course you remember the story of Little Johnny Clem, the motherless atom of a drummer boy, "aged ten," who strayed away from Newark, Ohio; and the first we knew of him, though small enough to live in a drum, was beating the long roll for the Twenty-second Michigan. At Chickamauga he filled the office of "marker," carrying the guidon whereby they form the lines — a duty having its counterpart in the surveyor's more peaceful calling; in the flag-man, who flutters the red signal along the metes and bounds. On the Sunday of the battle, the little fellow's occupation gone, he picked up a gun that had fallen from some dying hand, provided himself with ammunition, and began putting in the periods quite on his own account, blazing away close to the ground, like a fire-fly in the grass. Late in the waning day, the waif left almost alone in the whirl of the battle, a rebel Colonel dashed up, and looking down at him, ordered him to surrender. "Surrender!" he shouted, "you little d—d son of a —!" The words were hardly out of his mouth, when Johnny brought his piece to "order arms," and as his hand slipped down to the hammer, he pressed it back, swung up the gun to the position of "charge bayonet;" and as the officer raised his sabre to strike the piece aside, the glancing barrel lifted into range, and the proud Colonel tumbled from his horse, his lips fresh-stained with the syllable of vile reproach he had flung on a mother's grave in the hearing of her child!

A few swift moments ticked on by musket-shots, and the tiny gunner was swept up at a rebel swoop, and borne away a prisoner. Soldiers, bigger but not better, were taken with him, only to be washed back again by a surge of Federal troopers, and the prisoner of thirty minutes was again John Clem "of ours;" and Gen. Rosecrans made him a Sergeant, and the stripes of rank covered him all over, like a mouse in a harness; and the daughter of Mr. Secretary Chase presented him a silver medal, appropriately inscribed, which he worthily wears — a royal order of honor — upon his left breast.

A SINGULAR INCIDENT. — A soldier, writing from his camp near Fredericksburg, narrated the following, which occurred while he was on picket duty with his company : —

It was Christmas day and after partaking of a Christmas dinner of salt junk and hard tack, our attention was attracted by a rebel picket who hailed us from the opposite side of the river.

"I say, Yank, if a fellow goes over there, will you let him come back again ? "

Receiving an affirmative answer, he proceeded to test the truth of it by paddling himself across the river. He was decidedly the cleanest specimen of a rebel I had seen. In answer to a question, he said he belonged to the Georgia Legion. One of our boys remarked, " I met quite a number of your boys at South Mountain."

"Yes, I suppose so — if you were there," said the rebel, while his face grew very sad. " We left many of our boys there. My brother, poor Will, was killed there. It was a hot place for a while, and we had to leave it in a hurry."

"That's so, Georgia; your fellows fought well there, and had all the advantage, but the old Keystone boys were pressing you hard. By the way, I have a likeness here (taking it out of his pocket), that I picked up on the battle-field the next morning, and I have carried it ever since." He handed it to the rebel, who, on looking at it pressed it to his lips exclaiming, " My mother ! my mother ! "

He exhibited considerable emotion at the recovery of the picture, but on the recovery of his composure he said that his brother had it in his possession, and must have lost it in the fight. He then asked the name of the one to whom he was indebted for the lost likeness of his mother, remarking, " There may be better times soon, and we may know each other better."

He had taken from his pocket a small pocket-bible in which to write the address, when Alex ——, who had taken no part in the conversation, fairly yelled, " I know that book ; I lost it at Bull Run ! "

"Thar's whar I got it, Mr. Yank," said the rebel, and he handed it to Alex.

"I am much obliged to you, Georgia Legion ; I would not part with it for all the Southern Confederacy."

I was a little curious to know something further of the book, so I asked Alex to let me see it. He passed it to me. I opened it, and on the fly-leaf was written in a neat hand, " My Christmas Gift, to Alex ——, Dec. 25th, 1860. Ella." " Well, Alex," said I, " it is not often one has the same gift presented to him a second time."

"True, Captain ; and if I could but see the giver of that to-day, there's but one other gift I would want."

"What's that, Alex ? "

"This rebellion played out, and my discharge in my pocket."

The boys had all been busy talking to our rebel friend, who, seeing a horseman approaching in the direction of his post, bid us a hasty good-by, and made a quick trip across the Rappahannock. Night came on, and those not on duty lay down on the frozen ground to dream of other Christmas nights, when we knew not of war.

———

AN INCIDENT OF ANTIETAM. — During the battle, Corporal William Roach, of Co. K, Eighty-first Pennsylvania, shot a color-sergeant, ran forward of the company, took his cap, and, placing it upon the end of his bayonet, twirled it about, and cried out to his companions, " That is the way to do it," but a member of another company in the meantime had seized the colors and carried them off in triumph. This act was done under a heavy fire of musketry, in as cool a manner and with as much deliberation, as if the regiment had been on parade.

———

FIGHTING AT CLOSE QUARTERS. — At the battle of Hanover Court-House, Va., two sergeants met in the woods: each drew his knife, and the two bodies were found together, each with a knife buried in it to the hilt. Some men had a cool way of disposing of prisoners. One, an officer of the Massachusetts Ninth, well known in Boston as a professor of muscular Christianity, better known as " the child of the regiment," while rushing through the woods at the head of his company, came upon a rebel. Seizing the "gray buck" by the collar, he threw him over his shoulder with " Pick him up, somebody." A little Yankee, marching down by the side of a fence which skirted the woods, came upon a strapping secesh, who attempted to seize and pull him over the rails, but the little one had too much science. A blow with the butt of a musket levelled secesh to the ground and made him a prisoner.

———

INCIDENTS OF MORGAN'S RAID. — The Morgan raid is ended — the great marauder captured and safely quartered in the Ohio Penitentiary ; the brave militia, who responded so nobly to the governor's call to rally and drive the invaders from our soil, have returned to their homes, and the narration of adventures is now the order. As every incident connected with the raid is of interest, I propose to relate my experience with the raiders, how they looked, and what they said.*

About an hour before the expedition under Colonel Runkle left, I received from Surgeon Scott a peremptory order to report forthwith for duty on his staff. Reported accordingly at the railroad depot, where Dr. Scott was already waiting with sundry ominous looking mahogany boxes, baskets of bandages, lint and other articles necessary in the care of sick and wounded. For an hour we waited at the depot, while in the dim starlight, companies and regiments of armed men marched and countermarched, forwarded and halted, and at last about midnight, all were safely stowed away in the cars, and the long train moved off amid enthusiastic cheers.

Arrived at Hamden about two o'clock. From

* From the "Sciota Gazette."

11

there we could distinctly see the light of the burning depot at Jackson — evidence unmistakable that we were in the vicinity of "the enemy." Our forces, numbering about 2,000, were unloaded and got in marching order, and about daylight the column began to move toward Berlin, distant six miles, where it was thought the rebels would pass on their way east from Jackson. Reached a position about half a mile from Berlin about six o'clock A. M., when a report was brought in that the rebs were still in Jackson, and would probably soon be in our vicinity. For a short time there was a little excitement along our column, but this soon died away, and it grew dull and tiresome, lying there by the roadside waiting for something to turn up. An hour passed away, and yet no rebels in sight or hearing; so, borrowing a couple of horses that our men had "pressed" into the service, Dr. J. D. Miller and myself organized ourselves into an independent scouting party and set out to gather what information we could about the enemy.

The morning was pleasant, the air pure and bracing, and the excitement just sufficient to render the ride delightful. Learning that a number of scouts had gone out on the Jackson road, we decided to strike south from Berlin to the road leading from Jackson to Gallipolis, which we thought it probable the rebels would take. All along the road the houses were apparently deserted; the doors were closed, the window-blinds down, and neither man, woman, child nor horse was to be seen. At one house we could see, through a broken window-pane, the breakfast-table standing with the morning meal apparently untouched. The family had probably heard the news of Morgan's approach, and without waiting for his appearance had made a precipitate retreat. At another, where all was quiet and apparently deserted, on looking back after we had passed, we saw a terrified looking face peeping timidly out from behind a window-blind. The people along that road were evidently enjoying a tremendous scare.

At length we arrived at the little village of Winchester, on the road leading from Jackson to Gallipolis, and eight miles from the former. It is a pretty hard place, and I'll wager an old hat that its voters are pretty nearly unanimous for Vallandigham. We had the luck to be mistaken here for a couple of Morgan's men, which I can only account for from the fact that my companion, Dr. J. D. M., is an ardent Vallandighammer. I haven't much doubt, however, but that we fared better than if we had been known as Union scouts. We inquired of a mild-looking old man, if he could tell us where we could get something to eat. He directed us up the street to a little eight-by-ten grocery; we rode up and found the door locked and the windows barred. After sundry vigorous knocks, we got an answer from the proprietor inside, who cautiously unlocked the door, when the following colloquy took place:

"Have you any bread?"

"No, sir."

"Any pies?"

"No, sir."

"Any crackers?"

"Yes, a few."

"Any cheese?"

"Not a bit."

"Well, give us some crackers, then;" and with trembling hand he weighed out a pound or so, that might have been a part of the stores in Noah's ark. In the meanwhile a crowd of a dozen or so of rather variegated specimens of humanity gathered around, all eager to learn the news. We ate our crackers and departed toward Jackson, distant eight miles, keeping a sharp lookout from every hill-top for the rebels. We met one young man who advised us not to go any further on that road; he had been chased by about twenty-five of Morgan's men.

"How near did they get to you?" I asked.

"Within about two miles."

The young man was evidently a little frightened.

We rode on rapidly about a mile further, when leaving the main road we made a circuit of a mile or so through the fields toward the top of a high hill, from which we had been told we could see into Jackson. On the hill-side we tied our horses to a fence where they were, as we thought well concealed by the brier and other bushes. Walking up to the top of the hill, we found a number of citizens there, eagerly watching the movements of the rebels, who could be seen from our position riding through the streets of the town, about a mile distant. In a short time they began to move out on the road we had travelled, and which passed within half a mile of our position on the hill. Securing the services of a young man to carry a dispatch back to Colonel Runkle, I left Dr. J. D. and the citizens on the hill, and went down to a house by the roadside where I could have a better view of the rebels and see how they were mounted, armed, &c.

I had been there but a few minutes when two of the raiders, who were about a quarter of a mile in advance of the main body, came along. Riding up to where I was standing, they inquired the distance to Gallipolis; what was the nearest point to the river; whether there was any Union troops about there, &c. I answered their questions so as to leave them rather more in the dark than before, and turning questioner asked them how many men they had.

"How many do you think we have?"

"There are various reports about your number," I replied.

"Well, what is your opinion?"

"I don't think you have more than four or five thousand."

"Yes, we have over twelve thousand," one of them replied.

"You haven't half that number," I answered.

"Well we have enough any how to ride through your state without any trouble," said they.

"You're not through yet," I replied as they moved along.

Shortly the main body came up, and I began to count them. They rode along rather slowly, several of them stopping a few minutes to inquire about the road, the nearest route to the river, &c, but I managed to keep an accurate count until about five hundred had passed, while one of them rode up with the request:

"Will you be so good as to bring me a drink of water?"

He was *very* polite for a rebel and a horse-thief to boot and if it had not been for the company he was in would have passed for a gentleman. I can't say I liked his polite request, but as it was backed by a pair of revolvers and a carbine, I concluded that it might be promotive of my longevity to comply, so without stopping to argue the matter, I merely remarked,

"Well sir, I don't like to wait on a rebel, but as you are a pretty good-looking man, I guess I can get you a drink."

Next came a man apparently fifty years of age riding in a buggy with a boy not more than fourteen or fifteen. "Will you please give me a cup of water for my sick boy?" he asked. The boy was evidently quite sick. He was leaning heavily against his father, who supported him as well as he could with his left arm. I handed him the cup which he took with a trembling hand, thanking me very kindly for it, his eyes speaking more thanks than his lips. He was a fine looking boy, but what a training was it that he was receiving! His father I could see felt very anxious about his condition, and to my remark that "that was a hard business for a boy, especially a sick one," he replied, "Yes, and I wish we were out of it." My conversation with them was cut short by a fellow with a face that ought to have hung him long ago, who rode up to the fence and sung out,

"Here, stranger give *me* a drink."

I took another look at his face, and then at the pair of revolvers in his belt, and concluded that I had better get rid of *him* as soon as possible; so I gave him a drink and he went on without so much as saying "Thank you."

By this time quite a number had gathered around the place where I was standing, some wanting water, others bread, others pies, or anything else they could get to eat; while others appeared more anxious to learn the nearest road to the river. I told them to go to the well and help themselves to water, and a number of them rode in, while others dismounted, tied their horses to the fence and walked in. Their applications for food were not very successful; all they got was a cold biscuit and two cold potatoes, — the ladies at the house assuring them that they had nothing else prepared. One of the ladies was the mother and the other the wife of Lieut. Col. Dove of the Second (Union) Virginia Cavalry. Col. D. had returned home wounded, a few days before; but, on hearing of the approach of the raiders, had been taken to some place of concealment. The ladies, of course, were unconditional Unionists, and not at all disposed to furnish supplies for such a band of rebel marauders. One fellow rode up and inquired of Mrs. D. if there was a saddle about the place that he could get. She told him there was not.

"I'll see if I can't find one," he said, as he rode over to the barn on the opposite side of the road.

He didn't find a saddle, but there was a good buggy in the barn, to which he harnessed his horse, and driving out into the road, took his place in the ranks and went on, apparently very well pleased with the change in his mode of travelling.

"What do you think of rebels now?" inquired a rather jolly-looking young man, as they rode by.

"Rather a hard-looking set," I answered.

"Well, I haven't seen a good-looking Yankee, since I've been north of the river," he replied; at which the squad he was with felt called upon to indulge in a laugh.

Another stopped and dismounted near where I was standing to arrange something about his saddle. His horse was small, poor and nearly worn out.

"If I got my horses as you do," I remarked to him, "I'd ride a better one than that."

"We can't always get such as we want," said he; "and they don't raise any good horses through here."

Another came riding up on what had been one of the finest horses they had — a large and elegantly built iron gray — but very much worn down. The rebel said he had ridden him ever since they crossed the river — said he wanted a fresh horse, and asked if I had one I'd like to trade. Told him I didn't know but I had.

"Where?"

"Across there."

"How far?"

"About forty or fifty miles."

"I guess I'll not go to-day," he said, as he started off.

I asked another why they didn't go to Chillicothe the day before?

"Were they looking for us there?"

"I believe some people were."

"Well, we're going on through two or three more States, and we'll call as we return," he replied.

"Provided Hobson isn't in your way," I said.

"Hobson wont trouble us," he answered. "All we know about him is what we see in the daily papers."

I thought, but didn't say, that it was probable they would have the honor of a more intimate acquaintance ere many days.

But enough of what they said. A few words about how they looked.

Personally a majority of them would have been fine-looking men, if they had been washed and respectably dressed; but they were covered with dust and all looked tired and worn down. Many went nodding along half asleep. A hundred or more wore veils, most of which looked new, and I presume had been taken from the stores in Jackson; others had handkerchiefs over their faces to shield them from the dust. I noticed an intelligent looking contraband wearing a fine blue veil, which he raised very gracefully, as he rode up to a rebel, whom he accosted as "massa." Scarcely any two were dressed alike. Their clothing was made of butternut jeans, tweed, cassimere, linen, cloth, and almost everything ever used for men's wear. A few — perhaps a dozen — wore blue blouses and pants, such as are worn by United States soldiers.

A large number of them had various articles of dry goods, — bolts of calico and muslin, pieces of silks and satins, cassimeres, and broadcloths, — tied on behind their saddles. Some had two or three pairs of new boots and shoes hanging about them. I don't think the stock of dry goods left in Jackson could have been very large or varied.

They were not well armed, as has been reported. A few had carbines, many had double-barrel shot guns, some muskets, a small number had revolving rifles, and nearly all had revolving pistols. There were not, I think, a dozen sabres in the whole division. They had three pieces of artillery, — brass six-pounders, — but not a single caisson, so that all the ammunition for these must have been carried in the boxes of the gun-carriages, which would have held but a small supply.

Their only wagon-train consisted of five light two-horse wagons. In four of these they had sick men; in the other, carpet-sacks, valises, a few trunks, &c, which I took to be the officers' baggage.

They did not ride in any regular order, but two, three, four and sometimes eight abreast, just as it happened. The officers wore no badges, or anything that would distinguish them from privates. The last two men in the division rode up to where I was standing, and entered into conversation. One was perhaps twenty years of age, the other about twenty-five, and both appeared to be intelligent and well-informed. I learned from them that their division was under command of Col. Bushrod Johnson; that John Morgan and Basil Duke were both with the division that took the Berlin road from Jackson (and with which our boys fought the famous "battle of Berlin Heights.") They admitted that they were very tired, but felt confident they could get safely out of the State. I told them, in the course of the conversation, that I was from Chillicothe, when they said they knew some of our citizens, and, naming them, inquired if I was acquainted with them. Answering in the affirmative, they gave me some friendly messages for their Chillicothe friends and rode on. The name of the elder was George Logan, that of the younger, Lloyd Malone. I did not tell them that one of their friends was a Major in one of our militia regiments, and about that time was up at Berlin engaging their leader, John Morgan. I have since learned that Malone was until recently, a strong Unionist, and it was only after long continued importunity by his father that he was induced to espouse the rebel cause.

I think the number of men in that division was about 2,500, and comprised something more than half of Morgan's entire force.

As soon as they had all passed, I started up the hill, intending to get my horse and ride back to head-quarters as speedily as possible and report to Col. Runkle. I had not gone far when I met a badly frightened individual making fast time down the hill. I managed to bring him to a halt, and learned from him that a squad of the rebels had just passed that way and taken our horses, saddles and bridles, leaving in their stead, two of their worn-down horses, and one mule, but no saddle or bridle. They were better horse-thieves than I gave them credit for being, or they never would have found our horses, away up there among the brier-bushes. Arriving at the top of the hill, I stopped a short time to consider "the situation." My companion, J. D. M., after a liberal application of Jackson county free soil to his hands and face, borrowed an old coat and an old hat, and thus disguised, ventured, with the citizens who had collected on the hill, to go out to the roadside at a point half a mile or so beyond the house to which I had gone. I have heard, but don't vouch for the truth of the report, that the doctor, in order to insure his personal safety and conciliate the rebs, assured a number of them that he was an ardent Vallandighammer.

I waited a short time for his return to the place we had left our horses, but he did not come, and I started alone on my way back to camp. He soon afterward returned, however, and secured the horses the rebels had left in place of ours, went to Jackson, and there got a conveyance to head-quarters, where he arrived about ten o'clock that night.

The rebels did not make anything by that trade — the horses they left, as soon as they recover from their fatigue, will be worth more than those they took.

My march back to camp was not a very pleasant one. To save distance, I took across hills and fields and through the woods. The mercury must have been about ninety, and those Jackson hills are high and steep and rough. I tried at several farm-houses to "press" a horse into service, but always found that Morgan's men had been there just before me. I heard, as I neared Berlin, some exciting stories about the terrific "battle of Berlin Heights" — how there had been heavy cannonading all day, and how our gallant militia had "fought like demons." Arrived at head-quarters about four P. M., and made my report to Col. Runkle, well satisfied with my day's scouting.

APOCALYPSE.

"All hail to the Stars and Stripes!"

LUTHER C. LADD. *

Straight to his heart the bullet crushed,
Down from his breast the red blood gushed,
And o'er his face a glory rushed.

A sudden spasm rent his frame,
And in his ear there went and came
A sound as of devouring flame.

Which in a moment ceased, and then
The great light clasped his brows again,
So that they shone like Stephen's, when

* Killed at Baltimore, Md., April 19, 1861.

Saul stood apart a little space,
And shook with shuddering awe to trace
God's splendors settling o'er his face.

Thus, like a king, erect in pride,
Raising his hands to heaven, he cried,
"All hail the Stars and Stripes!" and died.

Died grandly; but before he fell,
(O, blessedness ineffable!)
Vision apocalyptical

Was granted to him, and his eyes,
All radiant with glad surprise,
Looked forward through the centuries,

And saw the seeds that sages cast
In the world's soil in cycles past,
Spring up and blossom at the last;

Saw how the souls of men had grown,
And where the scythes of Truth had mown
Clear space for Liberty's white throne;

Saw how, by Sorrow tried and proved,
The last dark stains had been removed
Forever from the land he loved;

Saw Treason crushed, and freedom crowned,
And clamorous faction gagged and bound,
Gasping its life out on the ground;

While over all his country's slopes
Walked swarming troops of cheerful hopes,
Which evermore to broader scopes

Increased with power that comprehends
The world's weal in its own, and bends
Self-needs to large, unselfish ends.

Saw how, throughout the vast extents
Of earth's most populous continents,
She dropped such rare heart-affluence,

That, from beyond the farthest seas,
The wondering people thronged to seize
Her proffered pure benignities;

And how of all her trebled host
Of widening empires, none could boast
Whose strength or love was uppermost,

Because they grew so equal there
Beneath the flag, which debonnaire,
Waved joyous in the golden air: —

Wherefore the martyr gazing clear
Beyond the gloomy atmosphere
Which shuts us in with doubt and fear, —

He, marking how her high increase
Ran greatening in perpetual lease
Through balmy years of odorous Peace

Greeted in one transcendent cry
Of intense passionate ecstacy,
The sight that thrilled him utterly, —

Saluting with most proud disdain
Of murder and of mortal pain,
The vision which shall be again;

So, lifted with prophetic pride,
Raised conquering hands to heaven and cried,
"All hail the Stars and Stripes," and died.

CLARENCE BUTLER.

MR. LINCOLN'S KIND-HEARTEDNESS. — A correspondent referring to the second capture by the rebels of Benjamin Shultz, a member of the eighth New Jersey Regiment, mentions the following: —

An incident connected with Mr. Shultz illustrates the kind-heartedness of Mr. Lincoln. On his return from his former imprisonment, on parole, young Shultz was sent to Camp Parole, at Alexandria. Having had no furlough since the war, efforts were made, without success, to get him liberty to pay a brief visit to his friends; but having faith in the warm-heartedness of the President, the young soldier's widowed mother wrote to Mr. Lincoln, stating that he had been in nearly every battle fought by the Army of the Potomac, had never asked a furlough; was now a paroled prisoner, and in consequence unable to perform active duties; that two of his brothers had also served in the army, and asking that he be allowed to visit home, that she might see him once more. Her trust in the President was not unfounded. He immediately caused a furlough to be granted to her son, who, shortly before he was exchanged, visited his family to their great surprise and joy.

———

"THE SPIRIT OF '76." — The lad — for he was but a stripling, though he had seen hard service — lay stretched out on the seat of the car. Another lad, of less than twenty summers, with his arm in a sling, came and took a seat behind him, gazing upon him with mournful interest. Looking up to me, for I was accompanying the sick boy to his home, he asked:

"Is he a soldier?"

"Yes."

"Of what regiment?"

"The thirteenth Illinois Cavalry. Are you a soldier?"

"Yes."

"Where do you belong?" In the one-hundred and fifth Regiment of Illinois Volunteers."

"The one-hundred and fifth Regiment! That sounds well. Illinois is doing nobly."

"I did belong to the eleventh Illinois Infantry."

"Then how came you in the one-hundred and fifth?"

"I was wounded at the battle of Fort Donelson so that I was pronounced unfit for service and discharged. But I recovered from my wound, and when they commenced raising this regiment in my neighborhood, I again enlisted.

Hitherto the sick boy had been perfectly still; now he slowly turned over, looked up with glistening eyes, stretched forth his hand with the slow movement of a sick man to the top of the seat and without saying a word eagerly grasped the hand of the new recruit. The patriotism that glowed in those wan features and prompted those slow, tremulous movements, like electricity ran through every heart. The twice-enlisted youth, as soon as he saw his intention, delighted at the appreciation and reflection of his own spirit, grasped the outstretched hand, exclaiming "*Bully for you!*"

Words cannot describe the effect upon the passengers as they saw those hands clasped in token of mutual esteem for love of country; a mutual pledge that each was ready to give his life, his all, for that country. They felt that the spirit of '76 still survived.

ANECDOTES OF STONEWALL JACKSON. — A Yankee captain, captured in the battles beyond Richmond, was brought to some brigadier's head-quarters. Being fatigued, he laid down under a tree to rest. Pretty soon Gen. Lee and staff rode up. The Yankee asked who he was, and when told, praised his soldierly appearance in extravagant terms. Not long after Jackson and his staff rode up. When told that that was Jackson, the Yankee bounced to his feet in great excitement, showing that he was much more anxious to see Old Stonewall than Lee. He gazed at him a long time. "And that's Stonewall Jackson?" "Yes." "Waal, I swan he ain't much for looks;" and with that he laid down and went to sleep.

During the same battles, a straggler who had built a nice fire in the old field and was enjoying it all to himself, observed what he took to be a squad of cavalry. The man in front seemed to be reeling in his saddle. The straggler ran out to him and said, "Look here, old fellow, you are mighty happy. Where do you get your liquor from? Give me some, I'm as dry as a powder-horn." Imagine his feelings when he found it was Jackson—the most ungraceful rider in the army, and who naturally sways from side to side.

THE MARRIAGE IN CAMP. — Six bold riflemen clad in blue, with scarlet doublets over the left shoulder, bearing blazing torches; six glittering Zouaves, with brilliant trappings, sparkling in the light; and then the hollow square, where march the bridegroom and bride; then seven rows of six groomsmen in a row, all armed *cap-a-pie*, with burnished weapons, flashing back the lustre of the Zouave uniform; and all around the grand regiment darkening the white tent-folds, as their ruddy faces are but half disclosed between the red and yellow glare of the fires, and the soft, silver light of the May-moon. (This is all you will bear in mind, out on the broad, open air. The encampment occupies a conically-shaped hill-top, flanked around the rear crescent by a wood of fan-leaved maples sprinkled with blossoming dogberries, and looking out at the cone upon the river-swards below. The plain is full of mounds and ridges, save where it bulges in the centre to a circular elevation perfectly flat, around which, like façades about a court-yard, are arrayed the spiral tents, illuminated in honor of the coming nuptials.) The bride is the daughter of the regiment; the to-be-husband a favorite sergeant. Marching thus, preceded by two files of sixes, and followed by the glittering rows of groomsmen, the little cortège has moved out of the great tent on the edge of the circle, and comes slowly, amid the bold strains of the grand "Mid-summer-Night's Dream," towards the regimental chaplain.

You have seen the colored prints of Jenny Lind on the back of the music of "*Vive la France.*" You have noted the light-flowing hair, the soft Swiss eye, the military bodice, the coquettish red skirt, and the pretty buskined feet and ankles underneath. The print is not unlike the bride. She was fair-haired, blue eyed, rosy-cheeked, darkened in their hue by exposure to the sun, in just the dress worn by *les filles du regiment.* She was formed in that athletic mould which distinguishes the Amazon from her opposite extreme of frailty. You could not doubt her capacity to undergo the fatigues and hardships of a campaign, but your mind did not suggest to your eye those grosser and more masculine qualities which, whilst girting the woman with strength, disrobe her of the purer, more effeminate traits of body. You saw before you a young girl, apparently about eighteen years of age, with clear, courageous eye, quiverless lip, and soldierly tread, a veritable daughter of the regiment. You have seen Caroline Richings and good old Peter (St. Peter!) march over the stage as the corporal and *la fille.* Well, this girl, barring the light flaxen hair, would remind you of the latter drilling a squad of grenadiers.

The bridegroom was of the same sanguine, Germanic temperament as the bride. As he marched, full six-feet in height, with long, light-colored beard, high cheek-bones, aquiline nose, piercing, deeply-studded blue eye, broad shoulders, long arms, sturdy legs, feet and hands of a laborious development, cocked hat with blue plume, dark blue frock, with bright scarlet blanket, tartan fashion over the shoulder, small sword, you would have taken him for a hero of Sir Walter. Faith, had Sir Walter seen him, he himself would have taken him. In default, however, of Sir Walter, I make bold to appropriate him as a hero on the present occasion. Indeed, he was a hero, and looked it, every inch of him, leading that self-sacrificing girl up to the regimental chaplain, with his robe, and surplice, and great book, amid the stare of a thousand anxious eyes, to the music of glorious old Mendelssohn, and the beating of a thousand earnest hearts!

The music ceased; a silence as calm as the silent moon held the strange, wild place; the fires seemed to sparkle less noisily in reverence; and a little white cloud paused in its course across the sky to look down on the group below; the clear voice of the preacher sounded above the suppressed breathing of the spectators, and the vague burning of the fagot heaps; a few short words, a few heartfelt prayers, the formal legal ceremonial and the happy "Amen." It was done. The pair were man and wife. In rain or sunshine, joy or sorrow, for weal or woe, bone of one bone, and flesh of one flesh, forever and ever, amen!

SPLITTING THE DIFFERENCE.—As soon as the West Virginia State bill passed Congress, Mr. Carlisle, true to his purpose, went at once to the President.

"Now, Mr. Lincoln," said he, "you must veto that bill."

"Well," said the honest president, with just the least bit in the world of humor, "I'll tell you what I'll do. I'll split the difference and *say nothing about it.*"

HEROIC CONDUCT OF TWO LADIES.—The conduct of two young ladies at Danville, on the occasion of the arrival of the rebels at that place was equal to Spartan courage. For many months a beautiful specimen of the national flag had floated from the residence of Mrs. Taylor, an estimable widow lady, and when the rebels took possession of Danville, it was but natural that they should seek to remove the hated emblem. A squad of half-a-dozen men was sent to Mrs. Taylor's residence, to take possession of the flag, but they were confronted at the door of the residence by Miss Maria and Miss Mattie Taylor, the two accomplished and charming daughters of the patriotic widow, the young ladies announcing their determination to defend the cherished banner. The chivalrous half-dozen returned to their commander and reported that it would require a force equal to a full company to capture the flag, and a company was accordingly dispatched to make the capture. Arriving in front of Mrs. Taylor's residence, the commander of the company demanded the surrender of the flag; but the two young ladies again made their appearance, bearing the flag between them, each armed with a revolver. In response to the demand for the flag, the ladies informed their persecutors that they would never surrender it to rebels, and, drawing their pistols, vowed that they would shoot the first rebel that polluted the sacred emblem with his foul touch. The company of rebels retired, leaving the ladies in quiet possession of their flag.

YANKEE VANDALS.

AIR—"*Gay and Happy.*"

THE Northern Abolition vandals,
Who have come to free the slave,
Will meet their doom in "Old Virginny,"
Where they all will get a grave.

CHORUS.

So let the Yankees say what they will,
We'll love and fight for Dixie still,
Love and fight for, love and fight for,
We'll love and fight for Dixie still.

They started for Manassas Junction,
With an army full of fight,
But they caught a Southern tartar,
And they took a bully flight.
So let the Yankees, etc.

"Old Fuss and Feathers" could not save them,
All their boasting was in vain,

Before the Southern steel they cowered,
And their bodies strewed the plain.
So let the Yankees, etc.

The "Maryland Line" was there as ever,
With their battle-shout and blade,
They shed new lustre on their mother,
When that final charge they made.
So let the Yankees, etc.

Old Abe may make another effort,
For to take his onward way,
But his legions then as ever,
Will be forced to run away.
So let the Yankees, etc.

Brave Jeff and glorious Beauregard,
With dashing Johnston, noble, true,
Will meet their hireling hosts again,
And scatter them like morning dew.
So let the Yankees, etc.

When the Hessian horde is driven,
O'er Potomac's classic flood,
The pulses of a new-born freedom
Then will stir old Maryland's blood.
So let the Yankees, etc.

From the lofty Alleghanies,
To old Worcester's sea-washed shore,
Her sons will come to greet the victors,
There in good old Baltimore.
So let the Yankees, etc.

Then with voices light and gladsome,
We will swell the choral strain,
Telling that our dear old mother,
Glorious Maryland's free again.
So let the Yankees, etc.

Then we'll crown our warrior chieftains,
Who have led us in the fight,
And have brought the South in triumph
Through dread danger's troubled night.
So let the Yankees, etc.

And the brave who nobly perished,
Struggling in the bloody fray,
We'll weave a wreath of fadeless laurel,
For their glorious memory.
So let the Yankees, etc.

O'er their graves the southern maidens,
From sea-shore to mountain grot,
Will plant the smiling rose of beauty,
And the sweet forget-me-not.
So let the Yankees, etc.

STORY OF THE ONE-ARMED.—A soldier in the general hospital at Fredericksburg, a day or two after the battle in December, 1862, wrote as follows:—Having lost my *right arm* on last Saturday, on that fatal "inclined plane" in front of Fredericksburg, I am obliged to employ an amanuensis to relieve my brain, which under the stimulus of some reactionary fever, must find legitimate work, or it will go off into all sorts of phantasies, or, perhaps, fall into a melancholy mood not at all productive of "healing by first intention," as the doctors call a speedy cure. I don't know what I can do better than to set down some of my experiences, which, I doubt not, are unfortunately or fortunately, as the case may be, similar to those of hundreds of my fellow-victims. It matters not to what particular regiment I belong, seeing that it is a Philadelphia regiment, and not altogether unknown to fame. Strange as it may seem, my recollections of Saturday, until four o'clock in the afternoon, are confused and indistinct. I remember well enough of being roused before daylight, from a very profound sleep upon the sidewalk in Fredericksburg by the sudden boom of cannon, and that, at short intervals, the firing continued till after sunrise, when the crash of small-arms began to betoken close quarters, and the air seemed to groan in unison as in the agony of an elemental dissolution.

Column after column of marching men went past in all the buoyancy of high hope, courage in their hearts, and determination in every lineament of their faces. Following every regiment were the litter-bearers, with their ready stretchers jauntily slung upon their shoulders; and I remember well of calculating in my own mind the chances of each man for an exit from the front upon one of those humane inventions.

By and by the litter-bearers returned, burdened with mangled, bleeding men, and from the great numbers carried off I calculated the stubbornness of the resistance to our advance to Richmond. I was not excited; I was not fearful; I was simply apathetic, while awaiting the order to advance. At last it came — clear and distinct, but not loud, the words came : — "Attention, Battalion!" Instantly the line closed with a steady straight front, and every man stood erect with suspended breath for the next command. Nor did we wait long. "Battalion right face, forward, quick, march!" and we were off.

Forward we went until we cleared the streets of the town and arrived opposite the batteries on the hill on our left, when at the command, "By the left flank, march!" we changed our direction to the front, and faced the fire before us, advanced to the lines of the brigade that preceded us from town ; but soon the smoke obscured the view of everything, save the flashes of the batteries before us, and the sparkle of the musketry in the dim sulphurous twilight of the battle, until the receding lines, in falling back, produced a mingled mass of retreating and advancing men. "Steady men, — forward!" rang out the voice of our commander; and disentangled from the retreating fugitives, we steadily bore on until we neared the batteries, and, with a cheer we sprang forward, but that instant a line of fire leaped out from behind a stone wall close in our front, and — I don't remember anything more about it. My next recollections were of a confused and mixed character; one moment I would seem perfectly conscious of something, the next of nothing. Then I would imagine I was at home, and half asleep, while all the house was astir with some past or anticipated catastrophe with which I was in some way connected. All

was dark, and a great load seemed to press me down and glue me to the ground in spite of all my efforts to rise.

I could hear voices, but none familiar and but one that seemed spoken by human kind, or had a human chord of sympathy in it. Then I felt something force open my jaws, and some fluid trickle into my throat, which I managed to swallow to prevent strangling, and it still trickled down, and I still painfully swallowed, hoping, praying that it would stop ; but it did not until I recognized that it was some strong spirit that I was taking and that I was becoming more able to swallow it. All this time I could hear the kind voice encouraging me, also some cold unsympathizing voices ; but I could not distinguish what they said. Only by the tone could I tell the sympathetic from the unsympathetic. At last I distinguished the words, in part, of one who said, " It's no use working with him. He's dying now." Quietly, but oh, so earnestly and sympathizingly the kind voice replied, " No, doctor, he is not dying ; he is coming to life ; he will live if we don't give him up ; this hurt of his head wont amount to anything if we can get him warmed up ; don't you see he has been nearly frozen to death, while faint from loss of blood ; but he is coming on finely, and by and by you can take off his arm, and the man may get well. Who knows but he has a mother or a sister to love him, and thank you or me some day for a son or brother saved."

Yes, I was saved ; I understood it all now ; I remembered the battle and my state, its doubtless consequence, and, for the sake of that dear mother and sister so strangely invoked, with an effort I succeeded in opening my eyes once more to the light of the sun on earth. At first the light confused me, but soon I could distinguish three surgeons beside me, looking at me with some curiosity, if not interest. On the opposite side, as I lay on the ground, in a large tent, kneeled a *woman*, who, with her left hand, supported my head, while with her right she held a spoon, with which, at short intervals, she dipped the warm fluid from a cup held by a mere boy-soldier, who seemed her special attendant.

I tried to speak, but could not, and she merely shook her head to discourage my efforts, and, turning to her attendant, said : — "Now, Johnny, the beef soup," and in a minute the soup was substituted for the toddy, and I gradually felt life and the love of it returning. After further effort to look about me, I saw that there was a basin of water beside me, with a sponge in it, and from the blood on the lady's hands, I inferred what I afterwards learned to be the truth, that she had been engaged in washing the blood from my head and face, when she discovered that what had seemed on a superficial view to be a most desperate wound of the head, including the skull, was but a mere scalp wound, which bled profusely, and doubtless made a most unpromising case for surgery at first view — a view very natural indeed, taking into consideration the state of my stupor. Gradually I recovered strength, until after sufficient reaction, my shattered arm was amputated, and I am doing as well as could be expected. I was, it seems, struck both in the head and arm by pieces of the same projectile, whatever it may have been, and lay senseless on the field till late in the night, when I was found by some humane litter-bearers, and carried to the city; and then, before being dressed, was put into an ambulance and carried over here, where, among the hundreds similarly brought, I was necessarily obliged to await my turn and thank God when my turn did come I fell into good hands — a woman's hands at that. In that place even in the roar and din and carnage of battle, was found a woman with a heart to dare danger and sympathize with the battle-struck-en, and sense and skill and *experience* enough to make her a treasure beyond all price. May the choicest blessings of Heaven be hers in all time to come! I have since observed her in her ministrations here, and she does indeed, seem gifted in a most wonderful degree for scenes like this, or else a hard school of suffering has made her the strange woman she is. To the wounded she is all sympathy and kindness, but let any one not a patient attempt familiarity, even in jest, and her black eyes flash such an indignant rebuke as is hardly equalled by her cool cutting rejoinder. More than one shoulder-strapped puppy has had occasion to rue the time he intruded his remarks upon her. I have learned that she has been in the army ever since the war broke out, nursing the sick and wounded, and "ever in front." Hospitals in the rear are no place for her.

Dr. McDonald, of the Seventy-ninth New York Volunteers, the Surgeon in charge here, has placed her in charge of the supplies and stores, and most efficiently does she deal them out. Many a "poor wounded soldier" would lack his timely stimulant, soup or delicacies, if she did not pass through the tents at all hours of the day and night, for they say she seldom sleeps. Dr. McDonald has known her long as the matron of the One Hundredth Pennsylvania, or as it is better known the Roundhead Regiment which has been in South Carolina with the Seventy-ninth New York Regiment, and is still with it in the same division and he informs me that, on on that fatal day of Gen. Benham's defeat, on James Island, she performed incredible labors just as she does here. And yet she has never been a *paid nurse*. She is a member of her regiment," she says, "and it is only because it does not require her services that she works for others.

For all the labors, and privations, and sufferings of her campaigning life she receives no pay; she draws her rations as a private soldier, and the private soldiers who know her almost worship her.

I overheard one say to-day, that he would kill, as he would kill a dog, the man who would dare insult her, even in thought; and I believe it. War produces great developments of character, and Miss Nellie M. Chase is a most notable instance of it. She is not yet twenty-four years old,

but in experience as a nurse or hospital matron, on the battle-field, I think she has no living equal. She may not thank me for this notice of her great services: I don't think she will, for she dislikes notoriety, and never mingles in the "society of the army," nor permits intimacies nor attentions from any but those who have adopted her and protected her. But the world has a right to know its heroines, as well as its heroes, and hers is a name that must at least be known as widely as that of the veteran regiment of which she is a member.

But gratitude for life preserved, has led me from my way, and I return to it to state my further experience of "wounded and in general hospital," as the next tri-monthly report of my regiment will have me accounted for. We are placed in large "hospital tents," in a secluded valley near Falmouth Station, and receive all the care and attention that such accommodations admit; but, without doubt a "cold snap" would soon "reduce the number of inmates" to less than a moiety of their present "muster."

The brain that would work, or do mischief, an hour ago, grows weary now, and I must wait another time to tell the further story of the —
ONE-ARMED.

THE WOODS OF TENNESSEE.

The whip-poor-will is calling
From its perch on splintered limb,
And the plaintive notes are echoing
Through the aisles of the forest dim;
The slanting threads of starlight
Are silvering shrub and tree,
And the spot where the loved are sleeping,
In the woods of Tennessee.

The leaves are gently rustling,
But they're stained with a tinge of red —
For they proved to many a soldier
Their last and lonely bed.
As they prayed in mortal agony
To God to set them free,
Death touched them with his finger
In the woods of Tennessee.

In the list of the killed and wounded,
Ah, me! alas! we saw
The name of our noble brother,
Who went to the Southern war.
He fell in the tide of battle
On the banks of the old "Hatchie,"
And rests 'neath the wild grape arbors
In the woods of Tennessee.

There's many still forms lying
In their forgotten graves,
On the green slope of the hill-sides,
Along Potomac's waves;
But the memory will be ever sweet
Of him so dear to me,
On his country's altar offered,
In the woods of Tennessee.

A BATTLE IN THE AIR. — During the heat of the battle of Chickamauga, an owl, alarmed at the unusual tempests of sounds, was frightened from his usual haunts. Two or three crows spied him at once, and made pursuit, and a battle ensued.

The contest was observed by an Irishman of the Tenth Tennessee, which was at the time hotly engaged. Pat ceased firing, dropped the breach of his gun to the ground and exclaimed in astonishment, "Moses, what a country! The very birds in the air are fighting."

READING THE LISTS.— At the door of the Chronicle Office in Washington was a bulletin board, on which proof-slips of important telegrams were posted.

Passing the other day, said a correspondent, I found an old man there alone. Tall, erect, firm of mouth, tender of eye, nervous of nostril, of speech quick — he looked fifty or sixty years of age, and like a master mechanic. He stood close to the board slowly rolling a lead pencil down the list of killed and intently following it with his eye. He turned as he heard my step. "Young man, let me use your eyes a minute." "Certainly, sir," I answered. "I've lost my glasses — I've got a boy in the army — we first heard he was wounded and then we heard he was killed — help me." He told me the name of the regiment — the twelfth New Jersey. I ran down the half column of "dead." "Not there," I said. "Ah!"— sharp and reserved, but there was a long relieving breath thereafter. Then I began the columns of "wounded." Down the first one — down the second one — slowly, a little nervously, for I heard the labored breathing of the firm-mouthed old man close at my side, and through his dress and bearing was looking into his Newark home. Three or four inches down the third column I found the name. He knew I had found it before I took my finger from the paper. "Well?" — The boy is a hero if he is like his father. "In the arm and in Judiciary Square Hospital," was my answer. I left him at the gate of the square. Next day I called at the hospital. The old man met me at the door. "All right; left arm just above the elbow: I've got him a furlough, and we go home to-morrow morning." I shall not soon forget the proud tone in his voice as he said that "all right."

MAN'S LIFE TO HIMSELF. —I noticed upon the hurricane-deck, said a letter-writer, an elderly darkey with a very philosophical and retrospective cast of countenance, squatted upon his bundle toasting his shins against the chimney, and apparently plunged in a state of deep meditation. Finding upon inquiry that he belonged to the Ninth Illinois, one of the most gallantly behaved and heavily losing regiments at the Fort Donelson battle, and part of which was aboard, I began to interrogate him upon the subject. His philosophy was so much in the Falstaffian vein that I will give his views in his own words, as near as my memory serves me.

"Were you in the fight?"

"Had a little taste of it, sa."

"Stood your ground, did you?"

"No, sa, I runs."

"Run at the first fire, did you?"

"Yes, — sa, and I would have run soona, had I knoad it war coming."

"Why, that wasn't very creditable to your courage."

"Dat isn't in my line, sa — cookin's my profeshun."

"Well but have you no regard for your reputation?"

"Reputation's nofin by the side of life."

"Do you consider your life worth more than other people's."

"It's worth more to me sa."

"Then you must value it very highly!"

"Yes, sa, I does — more dan all dis world — more dan a million ob dollas sa, for what would that be wuth to a man with the bref out of him? Self preserbashum am the first law wid me."

"But why should you act upon a different rule from other men?"

"Because different men set different values upon dar lives — mine is not in the market."

"But if you lost it, you would have the satisfaction of knowing that you died for your country."

"What satisfaction would dat be to me when de power of feelin' was gone?"

"Then patriotism and honor are nothing to you?"

"Nuffin whatever, sa, — I regard them as among de vanities."

"If our soldiers were like you, traitors might have broken up the government without resistance."

"Yes, sa, dar would have been no help for it. I would'nt put my head in de scale, 'gainst no gobernment dat eber existed, for no gobernment could replace de loss to me."

"Do you think any of your company would have missed you if you had been killed?"

"May be not, sa — a dead white man ain't much to dese sogers, let lone a dead nigga — but I'd a miss myself, and dat was de pint wid me."

It is safe to say that the dusky corpse of that African will never darken the field of carnage.

INCIDENT OF ANTIETAM. — In a small clump of woods near the battle field, the body of a dead Union soldier in a partially upright position, was found resting against a tree.

The expression of the man's countenance was perfectly natural — in fact he appeared as if he was only asleep. Alongside of him was an old and worn Bible, which the poor fellow, knowing his time had come, was reading, and in this way, a soldier and Christian he died; and now, with thousands of others, his grave is unknown.

SOLDIER MORALS.—General Sherman seemed to understand that a "hungry soldier has no morale or morals;" for when he caught a lad in blue in his wagon one night abstracting therefrom a large sugar-cured ham, he asked him kindly and without show of anger, "Have you no meat?" "None," said the soldier; "the regiment is one day behind on rations, and the commissary doesn't want to make extra issues." "Take the ham then," said Sherman as he resumed his cigar, "and whenever you need any more come to me and *ask* for them."

THE MEETING ON THE BORDER.

THE civil war had just begun,
   And caused much consternation,
While O. P. Morton governed one
   Great State of this great nation,
       So it did.

Magoffin governed old Kentuck,
   And Dennison Ohio;
And no three humans had more pluck
   Than this puissant trio,
       So they hadn't.

Magoffin was the leading man:
   He telegraphed to Perry,
And writ, by post, to Dennison,
   To meet him in a hurry,
       So he did.

And Dennison and Morton too,
   Believed they had good reason
To fear Magoffin sought to do
   Some hellish act of treason,
       So they did.

But they concluded it was best
   To do as he demanded,
So they would have a chance to test
   The question, "Is he candid?"
       So they did.

And Morton, with some trusty chaps,
   Went up to see "Meguffin;"
At 6 A. M. they took their traps,
   And off they went a-puffin',
       So they did.

Magoffin 4 A. M. did fix,
   By post and by the wire;
But when the hour had come — why nix
   Comehraus was he — Beriah,
       So he was.

And then could you have heard them swear!
   Them chaps along with Perry;
They cussed, and stamped, and pulled their hair,
   For they were angry — very,
       So they were.

And when they found that they were sold,
   And saw no chance for fighting,
They took a train that they controlled,
   And home they went a-kiting,
       So they did.

At 2 A. M. the scamp *did* come,
   But didn't let them know it;
And so, at three, they started home,
   And *when* they start, they "go it,"
       So they do.

No matter what they find to do,
   'Tis done with all their power;
What other men will do in two,
   They'll do in just one hour,
       So they will.

And now if they could mix his "todd,"
   They'd put some pizen stuff in,
And serve their country and their God,
   By killing off "Meguffin,"
       So they would.

And serve the devil, too, as well,
   By sending him, a traitor,
To roast eternally in hell,
   As Pat would roast a tater,
       So they would.

Just give them chaps a half a chance —
   Let them but lay a hand on
A traitor, and he'll have to dance,
   With atmosphere to stand on,
       So he will.

But those who love old Uncle Sam,
   THEY love and in their greeting
They show it, and in every palm,
   You feel the heart a beating,
       So you do.

For patriots are brothers all —
   Alike our flag they cherish;
With it, aloft, they bear the scroll;
   "Let every traitor perish,"
       So they do.

STONEWALL JACKSON. — Thomas Jefferson Jackson was a psychological event. With him it was but one splendid leap from bed to battery, from the stagnations of a sickly fancy to the inspirations of a robust and exclusive fame. The energies that slept in the sluggish, dull cadet — in the uninteresting, morose professor, — the querulous, tedious hypochondriac — the formal and severe elder — the odd and awkward man — not walking, "only getting along," and talking to himself — awoke with a bound of joy at the call of the trumpets, at the waving of the banners, once more to exult with the bayonets, as at Contreras; among the batteries, as at Cherubusco and Chepultepec. Nor any the less ready, if the trumpet were the trumpet of the Spirit, and the banner the banner of the Lord. The modern covenanter, who, debating all day, and praying all night, dashed into the smoke of the argument with his loyal father-in-law, to convert him to secession, and the inspired rebel, who, praying all night, and fighting all day, repelled, rocklike, the shock of the Union charge at Bull Run, were the same — and both were most like that Richard Cameron, who cried, three times above the din and dust of his last fight, "Lord, spare the green and take the ripe!" — that Richard Cameron, under whose head, as placid as John the Baptist's, and as bloody — under whose reeking hands, no more to fight with Bible or with sword, some admiring enemy had inscribed, "Here hang the remains of one who lived praying and preaching, and died praying and fighting!" And so of the man, who, praying, smote Shields at Cross Keys and Port Republic, taking revenge for Winchester; who, praying, drove Banks pell-mell out of the Valley and across the Potomac; who, praying, stormed Harper's Ferry with a *feu d'enfer*; and, still watching and praying, thundered in our rear at Richmond and Bull Run the second, at Fredericksburg and Chancellorsville. Of this muscular Christian his admiring foes competed in phrascologies of generous praise, "forgetting his fatal error to applaud the greatness of his soul." They recounted with genial iteration the separate virtues of the man—his courage, his patience, his sincerity, his devotion, his singleness of purpose, his self-abnegation, his just obedience, and his faith in God; of the Christian, the simplicity of his every word and act, his perfect truthfulness, his mildness and his mercy, his religious enthusiasm, his continual prayerfulness, his almost superstitious observance of the Sabbath, his iron rule of duty, and "first, last, and all the time," his faith in God; of the soldier, his intrepidity, his modesty, his magnanimity, his fury in the fight, and his generosity in victory, his stable bearing in reverse, his tenderness toward his own wounded and the wounded of the enemy—how he shared the privations of his men, setting them examples of endurance and devotion; his calmness "among the shrieking shells and the death-lights of the battle;" the absolute fearlessness of his demeanor, as of one who knew what his men hoped, that the Almighty would not sound his recall until his work was done; of the General—his celerity, his ubiquity, his momentum, his forced marches, his "thundering in the rear," his indomitable will, the magic of his personal influence, and "how his cause did hang upon his heart." We have been told (still by his enemies), of his splendid originality, his military genius, as bold as it was modest. "Every time we have been seriously threatened," writes a loyal chaplain, "he did it —no one else has done it. The first time I saw his face my heart sank within me. His moral brain is grand."

We have heard on every hand that the men idolized him, not so much for what he did, as for how he did it. He thought as little of the glory as of the danger, and his impulse sprang less from patriotism than from piety. An eminent Northern divine, a representative man in the ranks of the rebel enemies, has defined Jackson's motive as a "solemn feeling of obligation to his Maker who he thought had called him to this mission." He was sublimely impersonal — incapable of pride, insensible to praise, unconscious of criticism — "serving God," as he supposed, and going straight on. The applause that took the form of cheers embarrassed him absurdly; and when the captured garrison at Harper's Ferry greeted him with that spontaneous burst with which the heart of the true soldier salutes the soldier of true heart, his confusion was only exceeded by his surprise. He afterward expressed to his prisoners his sense of the extraordinary compliment in the eloquent language of *double rations*.

His religious character, and in equal degree with his military qualities, impressed itself upon his command; not an officer or private of the old Stonewall Brigade but shut down "the soldier's safety-valve" (as some rough definer has styled hard swearing) within the hearing of his General. His supplication before battle to the God of battles, for inspiration and strength — his thanks, when the day was won or lost, for victory or preservation; his "camp-meetings" among his men; the almost invariable formula with which he introduced his brief and plain dispatches, "By the blessing of Almighty God we have had a success," — these were traits not less characteristic of this rebel General Jackson than the famous "By the Eternal!" of his loyal and self-sufficient namesake. So likewise, were the "Very good, very good — it's all right!" with which he received his death-warrant from the lips of his agonized wife; and, before that, his, "Don't tell the troops I'm wounded." That must have been a touching smile with which in his dying hour he indulged himself for once, in a comrade-like expression of a soldier's satisfaction, "The men who may live through this war will be proud to say, 'I was one of the Stonewall Brigade!'"

And apropos of "Stonewall." A correspondent, over the signature of "Altamont," contributed to The Tribune a sketch of the vigorous rebel, in some respects fresher and fuller than any that had appeared before, and therein his soubriquet was traced back, not to the stone bridge at Bull Run, nor to the "There stands Jackson like a stone wall," of Gen. Bee, or to the stone fences of Winchester Heights; but to Jackson's original "Stonewall Brigade," so called because principally recruited in a stone-wall country — the valley counties of Jefferson, Clarke, Frederick, Page, and Warren; and the writer showed that the brigade had borne this name before the first battle of Bull Run, and of course before the affair of Winchester Heights, and that the brigade had lent its name to its stout leader, not derived it from him. Since his death this sketch has been reproduced in many papers, but the light it threw on the "Stonewall" question has been everywhere ignored; nevertheless, Stonewall Jackson, in his last hours, was careful to explain to some members of his staff who hung upon his parting words, that the honorable title belonged to his men, not to him; it was not personal and figurative like "Old Hickory," as the newspapers persist in making it — but the local designation of a corps.

The Rebels say he was a "fearful loss;" that they would have given Richmond for him, even their victories of Chancellorsville and the Wilderness; but that his work was done. "He helped to build a nation, and all that now remains to do is to dedicate it to God and to honor." So in Richmond he lay in state, wrapped in the new "National flag," that on the morrow was given, for the first time, to the breeze over the "National Capitol." That same flag was afterward presented to his wife by the "President of the Confederate States of America."!

The personal peculiarities of Jackson were all on the side of modesty. We have all heard or read, again and again, how he shunned observation, and how difficult it was for a stranger to single him out from among his men by his appearance or his manner, for his appearance was far from imposing, and his manner that of a plain man minding his own business. On horseback, he by no means looked the hero of a tableau. On his earlier fields and marches he had been blessed with a "charger" that happily resembled its rider—"a plain horse, that went straight ahead, and minded its own business; but one day it got shot under him, and then his friends presented him with a more ornamental beast, a mare that took on airs, and threw him; so he exchanged her, in disgust, for a less visionary and artistic quadruped — still a horse, but never such a congenial spirit as that original "Ole Virginny" of his, that never tired, and whose everlasting long-legged, swinging walk was the very thing to make marches with. "He's in the saddle now," sang those limber rebels, from the song of their corps:

"He's in the saddle now! fall in!
    Steady the whole brigade!
Hill's at the ford, cut off; we'll win
    His way out, ball and blade.
What matter if our shoes are worn?
What matter if our feet are torn?
Quick step! We're with him before morn!
    That's Stonewall Jackson's way."

Jackson had never seen his home since the war broke out; nor would he, he declared, until it was over — "unless the war itself should take him thither." He firmly declined the luxury of "hospitable mansions" along the line of his march; nor after his occupation of Winchester could he, without much difficulty, be induced to pass a night in the house of any old friend in Frederick, Clarke, or Jefferson. He preferred to sleep among his men. It was one of these valley friends of his who miscarried so absurdly in an attempt to cajole him out of his imperturbable reticence. The gentleman, at whose house Jackson had been induced to make a brief visit in passing, was eagerly curious to learn what the next movement of the ubiquitous rebel would be; so he boldly claimed his confidence on the score of ancient friendship. After a few minutes of well-affected concern and reflection the grim joker button-holed his bore. "My stanch old friend," said he with mysterious deliberation, "can — you — keep — a secret?"

"Ah, General!"

"So can I."

The love and admiration he at all times evinced for Lee resembled the devotion with which Turner Ashby had followed *him*. Replying to the remarks of a friend about his own peculiar military ideas and habits, and his proneness "to do his marching and fighting his own way," he said "We are blessed with at least one General whom I would cheerfully follow blindfold, whose most dubious strategy I would execute without question or hesitation, and that General is Robert E. Lee." The anecdote is authentic. But Jackson had the sagacity to perceive very early that his military genius was essentially local and partisan — that it was as an executive officer exclusively that he was remarkable — and that kaleidoscopic and subtle combinations must be left to the Lees and Johnstons of the Rebel army.

When the question of Secession, Union, or "Armed Neutrality," went before the people of Virginia, Stonewall Jackson voted the Union ticket; but when the State went out he went out with her. From first to last he had no patience (if such a phrase can be true of such a man) with the intemperate expressions of bitter sectional hate that continually affronted his ear; and he was blunt in his admonition to the women of Winchester—when he again left the checkered fortunes of that town to our advancing troops — "not to forget themselves." "My child," he would say to some immoderate rebel in crinoline, "you and I have no right to our hates: personal rancor is the lowest expression of patriotism and a sin beside. We must leave these things to God."

Immediately on the heels of the battle of Antietam, and almost within gun-shot of McClellan's 100,000 men, Stonewall Jackson with a force not exceeding 7,000, destroyed thirty miles of Baltimore and Ohio Railroad track, from seven miles west of Harper's Ferry to the North Mountain. He actually obliterated the road, so that when the road-masters with their gangs went to work to restore it, it was only by the charred and twisted debris that the track could be traced. Every tie was burned, every rail bent—nothing remained to be done but to cart off the bare ballast. The General took off his coat, and, with a cross-tie for a fulcrum and a rail for a lever, helped to demolish the "permanent way;" and with his own hands he assisted in bending the heated rails around the trunks of trees.

All this while McClellan, with his splendid army, lay all around him, and might, with but a small show of energy, and less of strategy, have brought the guns that were yet warm from Antietam to bear on the slouched hat of the renowned rebel as he was in the act of prying out his first rail; nor was Jackson at any time more than fifteen miles off from our little Napoleon.

When we reflect that Gen. McClellan had been a practical railroad man, that the dust of the track was yet on his boots, and that of all our generals he should have had the most lively appreciation of the vital importance of such a great military thorough-fare as the Baltimore and Ohio Road to the plans of the Government, and to the operations of his own army; when we recollect with what force and importunity he had urged these considerations upon the War Department, we can only wonder why he left Jackson to the undisturbed enjoyment of his railroad exercises. Was it lack of energy merely?

Though in no respect a railroad man, neither practically nor theoretically, Jackson's attentions to the Baltimore and Ohio line were unremitting and full of solicitude—so much so, that when, on the occasion I have just recalled, the task of rail-stripping and twisting, and the burning was done, he walked over the whole thirty miles of his work to see that it was good. He looked upon that road with the eye of military genius, and the great part it must play in the warlike machinery of the Government was plain to him; therefore he took more pains to destroy it once, than Gen. McClellan had taken to save it from many assaults; and but for the Jacksonian sagacity, and energy that from the beginning of the war has presided over the very life of the road, to guard and guide it, the valor of the rebel must have triumphed.

An intelligent Union chaplain has said, " if any man whom this war has developed resembles Napoleon, it is Stonewall Jackson." Bating the qualified exaggeration of the remark it is not without reason. Like Napoleon, Jackson had daring originality, and like him he taught his enemy that if they would beat him they must imitate him. He adopted and adapted in the East the whole system of raid which Morgan had made so redoubtable in the West; and not only the Stuarts, Mosebys, Imbodens, Jenkinses, Joneses and Wilders, are of his making, but in a certain sense the Stonemans, Griersons, Kilpatricks, and Davises also.

HOMESPUN DRESS. — The accompanying song was taken from a letter of a Southern girl to her lover in Lee's army, which letter was obtained from a mail captured on Sherman's march through Northern Alabama. The materials of which the dress alluded to is made are of cotton and wool, and woven on the hand-loom, so commonly seen in the houses at the South. The scrap of a dress, enclosed in the letter as a sample, was of a gray color with a stripe of crimson and green — quite pretty and creditable to the lady who made it.

The lines are not a false indication of the universal sentiment of the women of the South, who by the encouragement they have extended to the soldiers and the sacrifices they have made, have exercised an influence which has proved of the greatest importance to the rebels, and have shown what can be accomplished by united effort on the part of the gentle sex.

HOMESPUN DRESS.

Air — "*Bonny Blue Flag.*"

Oh yes! I am a Southern girl, and glory in the name,
And boast it with far greater pride than glittering wealth or fame;
I envy not the Northern girl her robes of beauty rare,
Though diamonds deck her snowy neck and pearls bedeck her hair.
Chorus — Hurrah! hurrah! for the Sunny South so dear,
    Three cheers for the homespun dress the Southern ladies wear.

This homespun dress is plain, I know, my hat's palmetto too,
But then it shows what Southern girls for Southern rights will do —
We scorn to wear a dress of silk, a bit of Northern lace,
We make our homespun dresses up and wear them with much grace.
Chorus — Hurrah! etc.

Now Northern goods are out of date, and since Old Abe's blockade,
We Southern girls are quite content with goods ourselves have made —
We sent the brave from out our land to battle with the foe,
And we will lend a helping hand — we love the South you know.
Chorus — Hurrah! etc.

Our land it is a glorious land, and ours a glorious cause,
Then, three cheers for the homespun dress and for the Southern boys;
We sent our sweethearts to the war, but, dear girls, never mind,
The soldier never will forget the girl he left behind.
Chorus — Hurrah! etc.

A soldier is the lad for me — a brave heart I adore,
And when the Sunny South is free, and fighting is no more,
I then will choose a lover brave from out that glorious band,
The soldier-boy that I love best shall have my heart and hand.
Chorus — Hurrah! etc.

And now, young men, a word to you, if you would win the fair,
Go to the field where honor calls, and win your ladies there;
Remember that our brightest smiles are for the true and brave,
And that our tears are for the one that fills a soldier's grave.
Chorus — Hurrah, etc.

GEORGE MORSE, THE NORTH WOODS GUIDE. — George Morse, the well known North Woods Guide, was killed in the terrible battle near the James river. Born in the woods, he was never contented out of them. Although friends, who appreciated his good qualities, often tried to induce him to change his mode of life, and to apply himself to some of the ordinary pursuits of civilization, he could never long keep away from the woods and waters of our Northern wilderness. He was lost in towns, while he knew every river and mountain and lake of the vast forest reaching from the Mohawk to the St. Lawrence. He was our beau ideal of a woodsman — of exhaustless endurance — with an eye like the eagle's — equally fearless and gentle — proud of his wife and children — temperate in all things and the best shot in the state. As a guide, he was invaluable — quiet, attentive, unobtrusive and kind-hearted — anticipating every want — always watchful and never at fault. "We ne'er shall look upon his like again."

He was an enthusiastic lover of the Union, and

joined the Herkimer regiment (the Thirty-fourth) soon after it took the field. His habits of life rendered him invaluable as a scout, and he was employed as such whenever unusual skill was necessary to accomplish the result desired. His adventures while thus employed, would fill a volume. Scores of rebels were made to bite the dust by his trusty rifle. And yet cruelty constituted no part of his composition. As an illustration: While scouting near Ball's Bluff, on the Potomac, he approached to within a few yards of the dwelling of a rebel spy, who, with his wife, was at the moment drinking tea near the open door of the house, which was surrounded by rebel troops. The capture or death of the spy was an ambition with him. Nothing laid so near his heart; (for he had caused the death of two Union scouts a few days before) and he was buoyant with exultation when he had him thus within short range. But the wife sat in a direct line of her husband, and it was impossible to shoot the one without hitting the other. The temptation was very great, but George Morse could not peril the life of a woman even to kill a spy; and, heavy-hearted, he retired, trusting to the chances of another day.

With the best intentions in the world, he could never tie himself down to camp life or to the soldier's drill. His colonel knew this, and making him a sergeant, allowed him to do as he pleased; and the whole regiment acquiesced. As a reward they were often feasted upon rebel spoils, gathered by our lamented friend as an amusement. It was an almost every-day occurrence to see him marching into camp with eatable burthens, heavy as himself, upon his shoulders; and when any sick soldier coveted some delicacy unattainable in camp it was only necessary to "tell George Morse" to ensure it.

Those who knew him can fancy his efficiency in battle. He never fought in the ranks. He was own captain and general. He never wasted powder or ball; and every other man in the army may have been fatigued, but he was not. We can imagine him in the retreat, leaping or crawling, from tree to tree, within short range of the enemy's advance, loading and firing with the rapidity of lightning, but with the red man's caution, and bringing down his game at every shot. When he fell, one of the most effective men in that entire host of heroes fell; and tears will be shed in forest huts and in city palaces when it is announced that George Morse is dead.

INDIAN STRATEGY. — One of the Fourteenth New York Artillery — a Seneca Indian, undertook on a wager, to bring in alive a rebel sharpshooter who was perched in a tree in front of the Union lines at Petersburg, considerably in advance of his own. His manner of accomplishing this was as ingenious as successful. Procuring a quantity of pine boughs, he enveloped himself with them from head to foot, attaching them securely to a branch, which he lashed lengthwise of his body. When completed, he was indistinguishable to a casual observer from the surrounding foliage, and resembled a tree as closely as it was possible for his really artistic efforts to render him. Thus prepared, and with musket in hand, concealed likewise, he stole by almost imperceptible movements to beneath the tree where the sharpshooter was lodged. Here he patiently waited until his prey had emptied his piece at one of our men, when he suddenly brought his musket to bear on the "reb," giving him no time to reload. The sharpshooter was taken at a disadvantage. To the demand to come down he readily assented, when the Indian triumphantly marched him a prisoner into camp and won his wager.

INCIDENT OF STURGIS'S EXPEDITION. — The main body of Sturgis's command halted at Salem, and a detachment of 300 men were sent out to reconnoitre the road to Ripley, a little town about twenty miles south-west of Corinth, Miss. When within a few miles of that place the advance guard of the detachment came upon and captured a squad of half-a-dozen rebel cavalry without firing a gun. As is customary, the prisoners were closely examined with a view to eliciting such information of the enemy's whereabouts and intentions as they might be able to give.

A gaunt, stringy-haired man, who seemed to be the leader of the rebel party, was conducted to the officer in command of our advance.

"What regiment do you belong to?" asked the officer.

"I wont tell," was the pointed reply of the rebel.

"How far is it to Ripley?" was the next question."

"Don't know," answered the man, sullenly.

"Who is your commander?"

"Wont tell."

"How far off is the command to which you belong?" still inquired the persevering Federal, pretending not to notice the crusty demeanor of his prisoner.

Here the rebel informed him, in terms that would not be altogether comely in print, that he would see him in a much hotter region than Mississippi before he would tell him anything at all.

"Very well," said the officer, drawing and cocking a revolver; "I will send you there to wait for me."

"You may shoot me if you want to," said the plucky Confederate, "but you will be sorry for it."

"Why?"

"Because there is a hundred men over yonder in the woods, and if they hear you shoot they will come up and murder every man of you."

"Well," said the officer, "since you have told me just what I wanted to find out, I guess I won't shoot you;" and in thirty minutes the whole hundred men were prisoners also.

An Incident in the Cars. — In a car on a railroad which runs into New York, a scene occurred which will never be forgotten by the witnesses of it. A person dressed as a gentleman, speaking to a friend across the car, said, "Well, I hope the war may last six months longer. If it does, I shall have made enough to retire from business. In the last six months I've made a hundred thousand dollars — six months more and I shall have enough."

A lady sat behind the speaker, and necessarily heard his remark; but when he was done she tapped him on the shoulder, and said to him: "Sir, I had two sons — one was killed at the battle of Fredericksburg, the other was killed at the battle of Murfreesboro."

She was silent a moment, and so were all around who heard her. Then, overcome by her indignation, she suddenly slapped the speculator, first on one cheek, and then on the other, and before the fellow could say a word, the passengers sitting near, who had witnessed the whole affair, seized him, and pushed him hurriedly out of the car, as one not fit to ride with decent people.

Capture of the Greyhound. — Pollard, in his observations in the North, gives the following account of the capture and the events preceding it.

On the night of the 9th of May, 1864, the Greyhound was lying off Fort Fisher, the signalmen blinking at each other with their lights in sliding boxes. It was necessary to get a dispensation from the fort for the Greyhound to pass out to sea, as no less than three fugitive conscripts — "stowaways" — had been found aboard of her. Two of them were discovered on searching the vessel at Wilmington. But lower down the stream the vessel is overhauled again, and goes through the process of the *fumigation* of her hold to discover improper passengers. In the case of the Greyhound, to the intense disgust of the captain, and execrations of the crew, the process brought to light an unhappy stowaway, who was recognized as a liquor-dealer of Wilmington, and made no secret of his design to flee the conscription. After the threat, and apparently serious preparations, to throw him overboard, the "stowaway" was, no doubt, relieved to find himself taken ashore to the comparative mercies of the enrolling officer.

At last we are off. The moon is down; the steward has had orders to kill the geese and shut up the dog; the captain has put on a suit of dark clothes; every light is extinguished, every word spoken in a whisper, and the turn of the propeller of the Greyhound sounds like the beat of a human heart. There is an excitement in these circumstances. The low, white-gray vessel glides furtively through the water, and you catch the whispered commands of the captain: "stead-ey," and then the more intense and energetic whisper, "Black smoke, by G—; cut off your smoke." Every eye is strained into the shadows of the night. But how utterly useless

did all this precaution and vigilance appear on the Greyhound; for after two hours of suspense we were out of the blockade lines, and had seen nothing but the caps of the waves. A blockade for blockheads, surely, I thought as I composed myself to sleep, dismissing entirely from my mind all terrors of the Yankee.

It was about two o'clock the next day, and the Greyhound was about one hundred and fifty miles out at sea, when the lookout reported a steamer astern of us. The day was hazy, and when the vessel was first descried, she could not have been more than five or six miles astern of us. For a few moments there was a sharp suspense; perhaps the steamer had not seen us; every one listened with breathless anxiety, as the tall fellow at the mast-head reported the discoveries he was making, through his glasses, of the suspicious vessel. "He is bearing towards a bark, sir;" and for a few moments hope mounted in our hearts that we might not have been observed, and might yet escape into the misty obscurity of the sea. In vain. "He is a side-wheel steamer, and is bearing directly for us, sir."

"Give her her way," shouted the captain in response; and there was a tumultuous rush of the crew to the engine-room, and the black smoke curling above the smoke-stack, and the white foam in our wake told plainly enough that the startled Greyhound was making desperate speed.

But she was evidently no match for the Yankee. We were being rapidly overhauled, and in something more than an hour from the beginning of the chase, a shell from the Yankee vessel, the "Connecticut," was whistling over our bows. The crew became unruly; but captain "Henry," revolver in hand, ordered back the man to the wheel, declaring "he was master of the vessel yet." The mate reported that a very small crew appeared to be aboard the Yankee. "Then we will fight for it," said the spunky captain. But the madness of such a resolution became soon manifest; for as the Connecticut overhauled us more closely, her decks and wheel-houses were seen to be black with men, and a shell which grazed our engine, warned us that we were at the mercy of the enemy. But for that peculiar nuisance of blockade-runners — women passengers — the Greyhound might have been burnt, and the last duty performed in the face of the rapacious enemy.

Dizzy, and disgusted with sea-sickness; never supposing that a vessel which had passed out of the asserted lines of blockade without seeing a blockader, without being pursued from those lines, and already far out on the sacred highway of the ocean, and flying the British ensign, could be the subject of piratical seizure; never dreaming that a simple confederate passenger could be the victim of *kidnapping* on the high seas, outside of all military and territorial lines, I had but a dim appreciation of the exciting scenes on the Greyhound in the chase. Papers, memoranda, packages of Confederate bonds, were ruthlessly tossed into the purser's bag to be consumed by the flames in the engine-room; the contents of trunks were wildly scattered over the decks; the white waves danced with ambrotypes, souvenirs, and the torn fragments of the large package of letters, missives of friendship, records of affection, which had been entrusted to me, and which I at last unwillingly gave to the sea.

Here, at last, close alongside of us, in the bright day, was the black, guilty thing, while from her sides were pushing out boats, with well-dressed crews in lustrous uniforms, and officers in the picturesqueness of gold and blue — a brave sight for grimy confederates! The Greyhound was no sooner boarded, than an ensign, who had his hair parted in the middle, and his hands encased in lavender-colored kids, came up to me and asked me with a very joyous air how many bales of cotton were on board the vessel. I afterwards understood that, from my disconsolate looks, he had taken me to be the owner of the cotton, and was probably desirous, by his amiable question, to give a sly pinch to my misery.

HO! YANKEE BOYS THROUGHOUT THE WEST.

BY R. TOMPKINS.

Ho! Yankee boys throughout the West,
  Hear ye the traitor's shout,
"We'll build the Union up again,
  And leave New England out!"
And shall we join the rabble cry,
  At tyranny's command ?
Traduce the homes our childhood loved,
  Betray our father land ?
        CHORUS.
And shall we join the rabble cry,
  At tyranny's command ?
Traduce the homes our childhood loved,
  Betray our father land ?

Forget the days we rambled o'er
  Our free New England hills :
Forget the joyous hours we passed,
  Beside her shining rills ;
Forget the cheerful fires, whose smoke
  Upon her free air curls ?
Forget the hearths where cluster round
  New England's peerless girls ?
        CHORUS. — Forget the cheerful, &c.

What! look with alien eyes upon
  The land where Hancock died,
And in a vile and impious tone
  The pilgrims' faith deride ?
Shall Lexington and Bunker Hill,
  Be named by us in scorn,
Because a revolution there
  In Freedom's name was born ?
        CHORUS. — Shall Lexington, &c.

No! By the blood of heroes shed
  On Bunker's gory height ;
No! by the mem'ry of the dead,
  Who dared old England's might —
The flag that floats o'er Plymouth rock
  Shall wave o'er Sumter's wall ;
These States shall all together stand,
  Or all together fall.
        CHORUS. — The flag, &c.
12

We've met a boasting cavalier —
  Proud lord of whips and chains,
Within our nation's council halls
  And conquered him with brains ;
And now, if he will have it so,
  We'll make the Southron feel
The pilgrims' sons, wherever found,
  Can handle lead and steel.
        CHORUS. — And now, if he, &c.

The torch that burned at Lexington,
  Lit by our patriot sires,
Shall yet illume the southern skies
  With freedom's holy fires ;
And Yankee schools shall dot the plains,
  And Yankee churches rise,
Till truth and light dissolve each chain
  And slavery groans and dies.
        CHORUS. — And Yankee schools, &c.

THE DEATH OF GENERAL STEVENS. — The army was retreating from Centreville. The battle was fought against a rebel force that had penetrated five miles nearer Washington than our rear and was moving to strike upon the flank. Gen. Stevens' division, the advance of Reno's corps, was on the left of the road taken by the trains, and intercepted the enemy. He saw that the rebels must be beaten back at once, or during the night they would stampede the wagons, and probably so disconcert our retreat that the last divisions would fall a prey to their main force. He decided to attack immediately, at the same time sending back for support. Having made his dispositions, he led the attack on foot at the head the Eighty-eighth (Highlanders). Soon meeting a withering fire and the color-sergeant, Sandy Campbell, a grizzled old Scotchman, being wounded, they faltered. One of the color-guard took up the flag, when the General snatched it from him. The wounded Highlander at his feet cried, "For God's sake, General, don't you take the colors; they'll shoot you if you do!" The answer was, "Give me the colors! If they don't follow now, they never will;" and he sprang forward, crying, "We are all Highlanders; follow. Highlanders; forward, my Highlanders!" The Highlanders did follow their Scottish chief, but while sweeping forward a ball struck him on his right temple. He died instantly. An hour afterwards, when taken up, his hands were still clinched around the flag-staff.

A moment after seizing the colors, his son, Captain Hazzard Stevens, fell wounded, and cried to his father that he was hurt. With but a glance back, that Roman father said: "I cannot attend to you now, Hazzard. Corporal Thompson, see to my boy."

ANECDOTE OF PRESIDENT LINCOLN. — Judge Baldwin, of California, an old and highly respectable and sedate gentleman, called on General Halleck, and, presuming upon a familiar acquaintance in California a few years since, solicited a pass outside of the lines to see a brother in Virginia, not thinking that he would meet with a refusal, as both his brother and himself were good

Union men. " We have been deceived too often," said General Halleck, " and I regret I can't grant it." Judge B. then went to Stanton, and was very briefly disposed of with the same result. Finally he obtained an interview with Mr. Lincoln, and stated his case. " Have you applied to General Halleck ? " inquired the President. " And met with a flat refusal," said Judge B. " Then you must see Stanton," continued the President. " I have, and with the same result," was the reply. " Well, then," said the President with a smile of good humor, " I can do nothing, for you must know *that I have very little influence with this Administration!*"

SHERMAN'S LOVE OF MUSIC. — A correspondent with Sherman's army recorded this incident.

Memorable the music " that mocked the moon " of November of the soil of Georgia ; sometimes a triumphant march, sometimes a glorious waltz, again an old air stirring the heart alike to recollection and to hope. Floating out from throats of brass to the ears of soldiers in their blankets and generals within their tents, these tunes hallowed the eves to all who listened.

Sitting before his tent in the glow of a camp fire one evening, General Sherman let his cigar go out to listen to an air that a distant band was playing. The musicians ceased at last. The general turned to one of his officers :

" Send an orderly to ask that band to play that tune again."

A little while, and the band received the word. The tune was "The Blue Juniata," with exquisite variations. The band played it again, even more beautifully than before. Again it ceased, and then, off to the right, nearly a quarter of a mile away, the voices of some soldiers took it up with words. The band, and still another band, played a low accompaniment. Camp after camp began singing ; the music of " The Blue Juniata " became, for a few minutes, the oratorio of half an army.

AN INCIDENT BY THE WAY. — On my last trip toward Huntsville we found the track torn up, and the cross-ties still burning. Nearly half a mile was destroyed — for the iron had been heated till it was bent and useless. Guerrillas were seen at a distance. Pickets were thrown out, and the negroes and white laborers went to work. As it was getting dark, the fences were soon made into huge fires to enable the workmen to see. Suddenly a " butternut " laborer came running along the line.

" The rebels ! The rebels ! "

" How many ? " asked the captain.

" Oh ! the world is full of them ! " he shouted, without stopping a second.

" The situation " had quite a serious aspect, — a small party of us, enclosed by woods, with thick undergrowth, great fires to show our position, and no knowledge of the whereabouts of Granger's command. But " the rebels " proved to be our own men — an Indiana cavalry regiment that was hunting a mounted gang of guerrillas. One of

their men had been tortured and then murdered a few days before, and these boys declared that their rule of action was death to all traitors, and to take no prisoners.

In a few hours — with really wonderful speed — the break was repaired, and we went slowly on our way. These rapid repairs have caused the Georgians to invent a new military maxim : " The Yankees carry their railroads with them."

On these car-tops one often hears tales of deeds of heroism by privates that somehow seldom get into print.

On my last trip down, I was speaking to an officer about the hospitals. A soldier who sat next to me said he had been a steward in one of them several months. I asked him if the soldiers, when they were sick, persisted in the continuous swearing which characterizes the army.

" No, sir," he said, " they are like little children then ; they return to their father's house."

I saw that I had come in contact with a man worth talking to, and had a long conversation with him. Only a few scraps of it can be given now :

" Oh," he said, " they are so grateful for the smallest favors ! I have heard them say so softly, ' thank you, sir,' for every little thing I did for them, that I was almost ashamed. I thought I had seen brave men in battle, but I never knew what bravery was till I went to the hospital. They often told me to fix them out."

" What is that ? "

" Well, they would see that the doctor gave them up, and they would ask me about it. I would tell them the truth. I told one man that, and he asked how long ? I said, not over twenty minutes. He did not show any fear — they never do. He put up his hand *so*, and closed his eyes with his own fingers, and then stretched himself out, and crossed his arms over his breast. ' Now, fix me,' he said. I pinned the toes of his stockings together ; that was the way we laid corpses out ; and he died in a few minutes. His face looked as pleasant as if he was asleep and smiling. Many's the time the boys have fixed themselves that way before they died."

I asked him another question :

" Yes," he said, " the soldiers when they are dying almost always speak of some woman. When they are married men, it's oftenest about their wives. If they are not married, it is mostly their mothers and sisters — oftenest a mother."

I saw that the soldier had a Bible in his pocket.

" When I left my company," he said, " I thought nothing of the swearing ; but when I came back to it from the hospital, it seemed awful."

Yet such is the power of the influence of association that my good friend — really and not sham pious friend — when I afterward spoke of the insurgents, got indignant at the contemplation of their conduct, and called them the d—d rebels !

REPRIEVED AT LAST. — A correspondent writing from Norfolk, Va., on the eighteenth of April, 1864 says: A scene of very thrilling interest transpired here on Wednesday last, in reference to a soldier of the Tenth N. Hampshire who had been condemned to be shot on charge of desertion. The facts were briefly these. The soldier, a young man of 24 years of age, was a native of Virginia. With other young men who had loved the old flag, he had been conscripted and forced into the rebel army. During the siege of Washington, N. C., a year since, he served in the Eighteenth Virginia one of the regiments that attempted to take that town. When, however, the rebel army withdrew without accomplishing its object, he with six other Virginians, and three East Tennesseans, deserted and came into our lines. I remember them distinctly and had a number of conversations with them while they were kept under guard. They all took the oath of allegiance at length, and enlisted in the Union service, except the one named above. He desired to go north and was permitted to do so. When the last calls for troops were made he found himself at Portsmouth, N. H., and was finally induced, by the large bounty and love of military life, to enlist in the Tenth regiment of that state. The regiment came out here and was stationed some eight or ten miles from this city. He desired, it seems, to visit the city, and frequently applied to his captain for a pass, but was as frequently refused. In an evil hour, he resolved to get a suit of citizen's clothes and come to the city without a pass. A man living on the borders of the camp furnished him the suit, and thus attired he started for the city. He had only just come into the road when he met his Lt. Col. and Captain, and was challenged, disarmed, arrested and finally tried by court martial for desertion and condemned to be shot. He was absent from camp only six hours all told, and affirmed to the last that he never dreamed of deserting. His sentence was read to him on Tuesday, and on Wednesday at 12 o'clock, he was to be shot. He was overwhelmed with amazement and fear, not having once conceived so fatal an issue to his case. From that time till he was led out of his prison to be executed, one or more chaplains were with him a large part of the time, to offer him the spiritual counsel and comfort that he needed. He, in the end, became calm, and looked on death with composure, forgave all who had sought his life, and left messages for his friends.

In the mean time efforts were made to obtain his reprieve, but up to nine o'clock on Wednesday morning, nothing had been effected, and the prisoner was taken from his cell, and started for the field, where his coffin and grave, and troops drawn up in hollow around them, awaited his coming. But on the way the hoped-for reprieve, for seven days, overtook him. The train was stopped and the commander of the escort read him the unexpected paper. In a moment he turned deadly pale, and then threw his arms around the neck of the guard, who sat in front of him, and wept aloud. It was a scene I never shall forget. Strong men wept like children, in the great joy that had well-nigh killed the prisoner.

AN INCIDENT OF BRISTOE.—A correspondent of a southern paper writing from Cook's brigade of the Confederate Army, relates the following incident:—" I will now give you an incident in the battle at Bristoe, which I can assure you is strictly true, as the officer who *saw* it, and told me about it, is a man of undoubted veracity. There was a man of Company A. Twenty-seventh North Carolina troops, named George P. Piner, who went into the fight, with a small Testament in his breast pocket. A ball struck the book, and penetrated as far as the fifth chapter of Matthew, twenty-first and twenty-second verses. It merely blackened that passage, glanced off, and left the man uninjured. The verses read: " Ye have heard that it was said by them of old time, Thou shalt not kill, and whosoever shall kill, shall be in danger of the judgment, and whosoever is angry with his brother without cause shall be in danger of judgment." The man said, *that* Yankee ball was like the devil,—it had to turn its course when met by scriptural opposition.

There was a man also of the same company and regiment, named J. H. Parker, who discovered a Yankee sharp-shooter behind an old chimney. He ran up to him, and bayoneted the Yankee through the body, killing him instantly. Parker was killed himself shortly afterwards.

TEAMSTERS' CONUNDRUMS. — Army teamsters are proverbial for the scientific volubility with which they swear. A teamster with the Cumberland army, not long ago got stuck in the mud and he let fly a stream of profane epithets that would have astonished " our army in Flanders," even. A chaplain passing at the time was greatly shocked.

" My friend," said he to the teamster, " do you know who died for sinners ? "

" D——n your conundrums. Don't you see I'm stuck in the mud ? "

HOW TO CLEAN A WELL. — A gentleman in Atlanta, Georgia, whom we will call Mack, had a well pretty much filled up with rubbish and trash of different kinds, which he wanted cleaned out. He spoke to a freedman about the job, and in a very confidential way intimated that there was a treasure hid in that well he was anxious to exhume. He imposed profound secrecy upon his sable help, and sent him off in search of another one of his hue who could be trusted. The upshot of the matter was that about one hundred negroes soon knew that an iron safe belonging to the express company, and which contained almost an invaluable amount of gold, had been precipitated into this well when the city was evacuated. The affair was speedily brought to the ears of the Provost Marshal and Mack on going to see about his well one morning, found it guarded by a strong provost guard, who forbade any one coming on the premises. Mack protested against any such proceeding, and persisted that everything on that lot, in the well and out of it, was his individual property. The Assistant Provost Marshal gave him an official wink, and intimated that 'all was right.' Mack thought if it was not, it would be in the end.

A strong posse of freedmen was sent down into the well to work. Bucketful after bucketful of rubbish and mud was drawn out; but no treasure as yet made its appearance. Occasionally the officer of the guard went down on a prospecting tour. In punching about with his bayonet he hit upon something that had the true metallic sound. They had the treasure now sure. Again the negroes went to work, and after laboring some hours succeeded in bringing out the top of an old tin-plate stove. At last the firm bottom of the well was reached, but no iron safe. Mack said he thought the safe was about ten feet further down. Whatever may have been the provost marshal's opinion on the subject, he concluded he had not time to prosecute the search further, and withdrew his forces, leaving Mack in possession of a thoroughly cleansed well, and at liberty to hunt up the safe if he wanted to. Mack didn't want to.

How Thieves were treated in the Ninth Corps. — Brigadier General Potter, commanding the Ninth Corps, riding along with his orderly in East Tennessee, saw a man running with something in his hand, followed by a woman crying out after him. Stopping him, he found he had stolen some article, and asked him his corps. "Ninth Corps," "Very well," said the General; and he ordered his orderly to tie him up to a tree, and give him a good strapping, with a stirrup strap. Amid his howls it came out that he belonged to the Fourth Corps. "Very well," said the General. "I am commander of the Ninth Corps; if you belong to it, all right; if not you'll know how we treat fellows that steal in the Ninth Corps."

Waifs and Estrays. — After the retreat of Shelby's force from Boonville, Mo. a small bundle of papers was picked up on the street, left there by some systematic and sentimental Confederate in his hasty flight. First among this bundle was the log-book, containing a succinct diary of events, belonging to a rebel soldier. The leaves of the diary were composed of heavily ruled, coarse blue foolscap, and the cover made of wall-paper. It contained a chronology of daily events, of which the following is a specimen:

the 12 came to clinton
the 13 came to fort hutson and went boord the boat
an started up the river.
14 still going up the river.
15 going up the river.
16 arrived at trinity on Black river.
17 awaiting at trinity for a Boat.
18 left Trinity.
19 got to monro.
20 crost the anames line.
21 come to camden.

A few pages further on was a specimen of keeping accounts:

G Harden Detter
for work 26 days $26
for cofoy too Pounds $14

Several pages of correspondence occurred after the writer arrived in Polk county, Missouri.

The writer wrote to his friend, that " wee hav plenty of corn bred and pore beefe to eat and sasafrass tee to drink," and concluded, hopefully, thus:

"come wee will, come I hope wee will come in peace and can enjoy our lives as wee yewst to do bee fore the wore broke out."

It will be seen by the following, that Pegasus accompanied Shelby in his raid, and was ridden by William H. Landreth:

HEART-RENDING BOAT BALLAD.

1. father father bild Me a Boat
and pot it on the oason that I may float
her father was welthy he bilt her a Boat
an pot it on the oason that She Mite float
She Stepte on the Boat She cride out Goy
Now Il find my sweet salar Boy.

2. She handent Bin Sailen far on the Main
She Spide three Ships come in from Spain
She hailed each captain as he drew ni
An of him She did in quire of her swee Salar Boy.

3. Capttain Captain tell me trew
if my sweet william is in your crew
Il tell you far lady Il tell you My Dear
your Sweet William is not hear.

4. At the head of rockeyilent as we past By
Will was taken Sick an thare did die
She stove her boat a gants a rock
I thaut in my Soal her heart was Break
She rong her hand She toar her hair
Jest like a lady in dis pair.

5. go bring me a Cher for to set on
a pen and ink for to set it down
at the end or ever line she dropt a tire
at the end of ever virs it was o My dire.

6. go dig my grave booth Wide an deep
poot a marvel Stone at my head an feet
an on my breast you may carv a dove
too let the world no that I dide for love.

WM. H. LANDRETH.

THE NEW RIVER SHOOR — A BALLAD.

1. at the foot of yon Montain wher fountain do flow,
there is music to entertain me whar Plesent wind blow;
thare I spide a fair Damsel, a girl I a doar,
as she was a Walking on the new river Shoar.

2. I ask her rite kinley could She fancy Me,
all tho my fourtun is not grat that's noth She Sho,
your Beuty is a nouf and it is you I a doar,
an it is you I will Mary on the new river Shoar.

3. as soon as her old father, this same come too her,
he swear he Wood de Prive mee of my Deares Dear.
he Sent me a way Wher loud canon do roar,
an left my Dear trulove on the new river shoar.

4. She rote Me a letter an in this letter these lines,
and in this letter these Words you May find:
Come Back My dear dewell for it you I a doar,
an it is you I Will Mary on the new river Shoar.

5. I Prused this letter I Prused it moast Sad,
thare was non in that company culd Make My hart glad,
I drew out My Brawd Soard an onward did go,
to meet My dear tru love on the new river shoar.

6. as Son as her old father, tis same came to hear,
he Swar he wood de Prive Me of my derest der.
he rased him a army fooul twenty or Moar,
to fite a yong Soalger on the new river Shoar.

7. I Drew out My Brawd Soard an Waverd it round,
there is no yous, My little army, that you all kno,
to fight a yong Soalg on the new river Shoar.

8. So hard is the Coquest of all women kind,
they all Ways hav ruld, they all Ways confined;
they hav children to Squall an husban to scold,
Makes Many yong lases look Wethered and old.
W. H. L.

ONE OF THE PICTURES OF WAR. — A correspondent relates the following interview of a Federal foraging party with a Tennessee farmer:

At another place we called on the owner, a man of over sixty years, well saved, yet evidently much cast down and disheartened. He was polite, and answered all questions studiously. On being asked what he had to spare, he answered, "Not much; indeed, nothing." His wife and four children, standing beside him, said not a word, but the countenance of the whole group showed that the old man told the truth. "Indeed, I have nothing," said he; "what, with one army and another campaigning through this part of Tennessee, they have stripped me of all I could spare and more too."

"Have you no horses or mules?" asked the officer.

"Yes," answered the man, "I have one more mule, which is entirely broken down; it was left by a trooper, who took my last horse in its stead."

"No beef-cattle?" was the next question.

"No, not one," was the answer.

"Any hogs?"

"Yes, sir; I have four pigs, which I had intended for my winter's supply of meat."

"Any negroes?" asked the officer.

"No, not one; my servants all left me two or three months ago. I have not one on the place. I have to chop all my wood, and my wife and daughters do the in-doors, what they can."

"Any corn or wheat?"

"No wheat, and only two or three barrels of corn," was the reply.

"Let's see your mule," said the officer. It was brought up, and was as the old man said.

"Show me those pigs," was the next demand.

When the old man heard this, he could hardly speak; his hopes were almost at an end. He showed the pigs, however; they were no more than such a family would need, nor as much.

The officer then kindly said: "You may keep all these things; they will help you and can be of little good to us," and gave the old man a "safeguard," which might save his property from our troops. Three years before, this man owned a large, well-stocked plantation; had cattle and hogs in plenty, with servants to come at his call, and corn to sell or keep. Now, he was sincerely thankful, and much moved that we spared him his four little shoats, his pittance of corn, and his old mare-mule with which he hoped to make a small crop next spring. The war has been at his very door; he had seen it in all relations, and knew that it was vigorously prosecuted.

THE LITTLE GIRL'S KINDNESS TO THE SOLDIERS. — "After the battle of Sharpsburg, we passed over a line of railroad in Central Georgia. The disabled soldiers from Gen. Lee's armies were returning to their homes. At every station the wives and daughters of the farmers came on the cars, and distributed food and wines and bandages among the sick and wounded.

"We shall never forget how very like an angel was a little girl, — how blushingly and modestly she went to a great rude, bearded soldier, who had carved a crutch from a rough plank to replace a lost leg; how this little girl asked him if he was hungry, — and how he ate like a famished wolf! She asked if his wound was painful, and in a voice of soft, mellow accents, 'Can I do nothing more for you? I am sorry that you are so badly hurt; have you a little daughter, and wont she cry when she sees you?'

"The rude soldier's heart was touched, and tears of love and gratitude filled his eyes. He only answered, 'I have three little children; God grant they may be such angels as you.'

"With an evident effort he repressed a desire to kiss the fair brow of the pretty little girl. He took her little hand between both his own, and bade her 'good-by, — God bless you!' The child will always be a better woman because of these lessons of practical charity stamped ineffaceably upon her young heart." — Southern paper.

HOW BRAVE MEN SUFFER AND DIE. — "If anybody thinks," says B. F. Taylor, in his account of the battle of Chicamauga, "that when men are stricken upon the field they fill the air with cries and groans, till it shivers with such evidence of agony, he greatly errs. An arm is shattered, a leg carried away, a bullet pierces the breast, and the soldier sinks down silently upon the ground, or creeps away if he can, without a murmur or complaint; falls as the sparrow falls, speechlessly; and like that sparrow, I earnestly believe, not without a Father. The horse gives out his fearful utterance of almost human suffering, but the mangled rider is dumb. The crash of musketry, the crack of rifles, the roar of guns, the shriek of shells, the rebel whoop, the Federal cheer, and that indescribable undertone of rumbling, grinding, splintering sound, make up the voices of the battle-field."

AN INCIDENT OF SHILOH. — During the battle of Shiloh an officer hurriedly rode up to an aid and inquired for Grant. "That's him with the field-glass," said the aid.

Wheeling his horse about, the officer furiously rode up to the General, and touching his cap, thus addressed him, —

"Sheneral, I vants to make one report; Schwartz's battery is took."

"Ah!" says the General, "how was that?"

"Vell, you see, Sheneral, de sheshenists come up in front of us, and de sheshenists flanked us, and de sheshenists come in de rear of us, and Schwartz's battery was took."

"Well, sir," says the General, "you of course spiked the guns."

"Vat," exclaimed the Dutchman, in astonishment, "schpike dem guns, schpike dem new guns! — no, it would schpoil hem!"

"Well," said the General, sharply, "What did you do?"

"Do? vy, we took dem back again!"

COOLNESS ON THE FIELD. — A lad of fifteen years of age, belonging to the Fifth Wisconsin, whose name is Douglas, and resides at Beaver Dam, was in the battle of Williamsburg, and got his gun wet so that it could not fire. During the hottest of the fight, and whilst the regiment was falling back, he deliberately sat down, took out his screw-driver, unscrewed the tube from his gun, dried it out, put it back, capped it, got up and put into the field as if nothing unusual was going on.

A GENUINE NOBLEMAN. — Returning home from Philadelphia, we had for a fellow-passenger a poor, broken, emaciated Massachusetts soldier, too weak to sit erect, and so far gone in physical constitution as to give little hope for aught else than his possible arrival at his home in Boston with the breath of life not extinct. He was accompanied by a kind matron, who, though no relation of the sufferer, was a Massachusetts woman, and had in the pity of her soul volunteered to attend his passage home to die. It was a piteous sight, and but a type of many hundreds we have seen the past year. Of course an object of such interest awakened the tenderest sympathies of all beholders. We proffered such aid as we could, and on arrival at the wharf in New-York attempted negotiations with various carriers for a passage for the invalid up to the New-Haven cars. As the boy was destitute of money, as well as broken down in health, we tried to so far touch the pity of some of the hack-drivers as to get him conveyed at an honest price. While chaffering with the crowd, up stepped a frank and honest-looking driver, who,

listening to the narration, at once responded, "I'll take the poor fellow up there for nothing. I carried just such a one up last night, but I guess I shant lose nothing." No, thought we, my dear fellow, such true nobility of nature shall not result in loss to you if we can help it, so we demanded his card, and here it is.

WILLIAM RYDER,
Proprietor of Carriages Nos. 28 & 46.
Stable 96 Lawrence St.
New York.

QUAKER GUNS. — When General Sills's division left Frankfort, Ky., the last thing they did was to remove the two monster cannon from their position on the hills over South Frankfort. Some Union men of Frankfort, during the night, went over to the spot and planted two empty beer-kegs in the place of the cannon, and covered them with a tarpaulin. All next day a lot of Morgan's cavalry were scouting around the kegs, but dared not enter Frankfort for fear of being charged upon. On Wednesday night "our forces" abandoned the kegs, when, as we learn, they made a bold and daring charge on the "tarpaulin beer-keg battery," and captured it without the loss of a man. The captain acknowledged that he had been "sold by the Yanks," and it was not until then that they were aware of the fact that Gen. Sills's whole corps had left Frankfort. Then, as they have always done, they pounced upon an unprotected city. But Gen. Dumont's forces soon let them know that it was not the "battle of the kegs" when they attacked them. It was these men and the two empty beer kegs that kept the rebels from burning all the bridges around Frankfort.

ONE OF THE VIRGINIA RESERVES. — Pollard, in his observations in the North, relates the following: —

General Butler followed up his little story by an amusing account of an interview he had had with a certain gentleman of Richmond — one of the "Virginia Reserves" — who had strayed into his lines. I must confess his laughter was a little contagious as he gave the details of the interview. The unfortunate individual had come into his lines by some mistake, bewildered as to the points of the compass. His appearance was rather unmilitary, as General B. described it; a suit of black, wet and glued to his skin, a stove-pipe hat, and what seems to have attracted most at headquarters, as a curiosity of Richmond — "a black satin vest."

"Who are you?" thundered General Butler.

"Sir," said the unfortunate individual, with the air of importance in misery, "I am one of the Virginia Reserves."

"Alluding only to the oddity of his appearance," said General Butler, I remarked: "and how many more are there like you, Mr. M——?"

"I will answer all proper questions," replied the unfortunate individual; "but, sir, General Butler, do not expect me to inform you as to *our military resources!*"

The General seems to have thought the old gentleman a little stilted, and explained to me that he only wanted to have a little fun out of him. So, with what I can imagine to have been the growl of an ogre, he remarked: "Ah, ha, Mr. M——; so, so, Mr. M——; we have another name than that of soldiers for persons in your dress; yes, sir, another name: we call them SPIES!" At the mention of this dreadful word the unfortunate proprietor of the satin vest went off into protest — pledging "his honor," "his sacred honor," "his honor, which no man, General Butler, had ever doubted;" that he was "a soldier."

THE CUMBERLAND.

HENRY W. LONGFELLOW.

At anchor in Hampton Roads we lay,
  On board the Cumberland sloop-of-war;
And at times from the fortress across the bay
  The alarm of drums swept past,
    Or a bugle blast
  From the camp on shore.

Then far away to the south uprose
  A little feather of snow-white smoke,
And we knew that the iron ship of our foes
  Was steadily steering its course,
    To try the force
  Of our ribs of oak.

Down upon us heavily runs
  Silent and sullen, the floating fort;
Then comes a puff of smoke from her guns,
  And leaps the terrible death,
    With fiery breath,
  From each open port.

We are not idle, but send her straight
  Defiance back in a full broadside!
As hail rebounds from a roof of slate,
  Rebounds our heavier hail
    From each iron scale
  Of the monster's hide.

"Strike your flag!" the rebel cries,
  In his arrogant old plantation strain,
"Never!" our gallant Morris replies;
  "It is better to sink than to yield!"
    And the whole air pealed
  With the cheers of our men.

Then, like a kraken huge and black,
  She crushed our ribs in her iron grasp!
Down went the Cumberland all a wrack,
  With a sudden shudder of death,
    And the cannon's breath
  For her dying gasp.

Next morn, as the sun rose over the bay,
  Still floated our flag at the mainmast-head,
Lord, how beautiful was Thy day!
  Every waft of the air
    Was a whisper of prayer,
  Or a dirge for the dead.

Ho! brave hearts that went down in the seas,
  Ye are at peace in the troubled stream,
Ho! brave land! with hearts like these,
  Thy flag that is rent in twain,
    Shall be one again,
  And without a seam.

CAPTAIN WILLIAMS' ESCAPE. — T. J. Williams, Captain in the Twenty-Third regiment of Kentucky Volunteers gives the following account of his remarkable escape from the prison at Macon, Georgia: — I was captured May 27, 1864, at the battle of New Hope Church, or Dallas, Georgia; June 1st, I arrived at Macon, Georgia, and was placed in the stockade, or "pen" where I found twelve or fourteen hundred officers, taken at different periods of the war. Among them Captain John A. Arthur, Eighth Kentucky Cavalry, and when the war began, connected with the "Daily Times"; also, Captain Paul and Lieutenant David Locke, of Newport, and Lieutenant Neimyer, of Covington, who were all in good health. The stockade embraced about two acres; the fence was about twelve feet high, and twelve feet from the outer fence was another about six feet high, which was called "the dead line," the sentinels having instructions to shoot any one touching this line. June 11, an officer, whose name I do not remember, and who was bathing at least fifteen feet from this line, was shot and killed by one of the guard, who received a furlough as a reward for his inhumanity.

On the evening of June 4, I escaped from the stockade by getting between the coupling-pole and bed of the sutler's wagon, and in this manner rode by the guard, but was detected after getting beyond all the guards. For this offence I was sent to the Macon jail with an order "place him (me) in close confinement," and feed me on corn-bread and water until further orders. The further orders never came to hand.

Shortly after being placed in jail I managed to procure the impression of the cell keys on a piece of dough made out of some wheat bread I obtained for the occasion, and with the assistance of a file, I succeeded in manufacturing, out of teaspoons, keys to fit all the locks.

JUNE 30. — I had everything in readiness to release all the prisoners, but was betrayed by an inmate of the jail.

After this attempt I was placed in a cell with Captain Whitlock, Aid to General Logan, Sergeant Gillespie, First Kentucky Cavalry, and George Manning, Twenty-Fourth Massachusetts Infantry.

JULY 4. — We made a Declaration of Independence, and came near gaining our freedom in the following manner:

During the day one of our number feigned sickness. At night when the doors were opened for the purpose of changing water, our sick man stole into an empty cell and his place in our cell was filled with a stuffed pair of pants and shirt. The ruse not being detected, the man on the outside with the assistance of the teaspoon keys, opened our doors, and by two o'clock in the morning of July 5, we were nearly through the wall; we were however detected shortly afterward, and again locked up. The jailer thinking I was the one to blame for the damage done, threatened me with a chain round my neck, and one around each ankle, should I make another attempt to escape.

JULY 22.—By another ruse, we again succeeded in getting out of our cell. By 2 o'clock we had an opening nearly large enough to pass through. Being in the third story of the jail, we required a rope, with which to reach the ground, and made it by tearing our blankets up for the purpose, and a very strong cable was the result of our labor. Fifteen minutes, and we would be outside of the gloomy walls. But again we were doomed to disappointment, and were again locked up, and after this attempt a guard of soldiers was placed around the jail to make sure of us.

JULY 26.— Captain Whitlock and myself concluded to attempt the passage of the guards disguised as one of the negro attendants of the jail. Accordingly, we made a fire on the cell floor by splitting some fine kindling of pine wood, burned some cork which we were fortunate in procuring, and by 6 o'clock that evening were ready for the experiment, myself to attempt it first. When the doors were opened for the purpose of changing the water, I placed one bucket on my head and another in my right hand, and passed within two feet of the guard without detection. I was in the act of passing out of the yard-gate when recognized, and the attention of the guard called to me by a deserter from the Army of the Potomac. I was again placed in my cell, and passed the night sadly. It appeared to me that I was not to succeed in making my escape, no matter how often I attempted it. But I concluded to "try again."

JULY 30.— Our plans were interrupted by being placed in the cars "for Charleston, South Carolina," but Stoneman came to the rescue. The authorities, learning that the road had been cut, removed us from the cars to the stockade. Stoneman fought the rebels all day within our hearing, and toward evening drove the rebels within three-fourths of a mile of the city. His shells struck several buildings in the centre of the city, creating quite a panic. Hopes of being released by Stoneman created the warmest feeling among our prisoners, but we were doomed to disappointment, as our troops were compelled by the overwhelming force brought against them, to fall back, and two days later Stoneman himself was brought in a prisoner.

JULY 31.— Captain Whitlock, myself, and eight others were returned to jail as "dangerous characters." August 3, another plan was concocted. Myself and another were to smuggle ourselves into a cell on the outside of the door which closed at the end of the entry, and which it was necessary to open in order to allow the escape of all the prisoners. Another prisoner was to remain outside his cell, and co-operate with us from the inside. This he failed to do, and for fear of detection next morning, myself and partner resolved to escape that night.

The prisoners of the cell in which we had managed to smuggle ourselves, not having made any attempt to escape, the jailer was in the habit of only locking the inside door upon them. Any one having a key could open this door from the inside; I had altered a key to fit it. About nine o'clock, we opened the door, and after passing out closed and locked it again. I was to pass the guard first, get over the fence, and make a signal to my comrade. I stole gently down to the large outer door where I could observe the guard passing and repassing. We had hoped to catch the guard asleep, but after watching until three o'clock in the morning, they were still on the alert. I resolved to attempt the passage when he was pacing his beat with his back toward me, and was in the act of making the leap, when the command "Halt! who comes there?" rang out upon the air. I drew back and discovered the relief-guard approaching; the guard was relieved, and five minutes later I gave a leap, and thinking the guard had noticed me, and was about to fire, threw myself upon the ground; I lay here some ten minutes, the guard passing within twelve feet of me. Finding that he had not noticed me I made my way to the fence and scaled it in safety. I made the signal agreed upon, waited an hour and a half, and thinking my friend would not risk the running of the guard, started on my journey, reaching the city limits just at daylight.

Sometime before my escape I contrived to get hold of a confederate uniform, upon which I sewed two bars which indicated, in the rebel army, a first lieutenant. Five miles from the city I obtained a first-rate breakfast, for which they refused pay, thinking that I was what I represented myself to be, "Lieutenant J. R. Brown, Fourth Louisiana Battalion Volunteer Infantry." During the forenoon I lost myself, and at noon found myself only nine miles from Macon. I took dinner at an old planter's; living at this house was a young man who had been in the army — he proved very inquisitive; he asked me the names of our officers, engagements in which we had taken part, &c., all of which I was able to answer correctly, being in possession of the complete history of the regiment, which I obtained from a confederate soldier in prison. The old gentleman was not so suspicious, but on the contrary was very sociable, asking me if I was a married man, and drawing my attention to the fact that he had four daughters, all unmarried, &c. Before I left, the young man was satisfied that I was a loyal southerner, and the old gentleman refused to take any pay from a "soldier." I thanked him, and bade them all good-by.

That night I had to pay five dollars in Confederate money, for supper. I engaged a bed, and had a good sound sleep only twelve miles from Macon. I also learned that two hundred of Wheeler's men were in camp only two miles off. Next morning I started early, and passed about one hundred wounded men on furlough going down to the station to take the cars for home. I approved of the policy of allowing wounded men to go home, &c. They wanted to know whether I was on furlough or not. I replied that I was just out of the hospital, and then *en route* to see a friend three miles from Forsythe; I passed on. Near Forsythe I passed a squad of Wheeler's men, in search of the camp of which I had heard the night previous. I gave them directions where to find the camp, after which they asked me what command I belonged to, &c. I gave them the same old tale, which satisfied them and passed on.

At the edge of Forsythe, I passed three hospital camps, and experienced no trouble in doing so. Two miles beyond the town I asked permission from an old planter, who was returning home, to ride with him in his buggy, which he granted. Seven and a-half miles from town, we came to this gentleman's home. I thanked him for his kindness and passed on.

I learned from a negro the names of parties living on the opposite side of the Omulgee River, which I had to cross that evening, and meeting any one, I generally satisfied their curiosity by telling them that I was just going down to Mr. Bradford's or "any other man's" name that I happened to know in advance.

At the river I found three cavalrymen (Wheeler's), on duty, "looking after Yanks." Stoneman's men at this time were scattered all over this part of the country, and made it more difficult to escape than under other circumstances.

The old ferryman was very inquisitive. I think I satisfied him by giving him a larger bill than he could change, and telling him to keep the change until my return on the following day. I asked the guards if they were "looking out for Yanks," to which they replied, "Yes." I told them what command I belonged to, &c., and passed on. Five miles from this place I encountered my hardest customer. He had been an officer in the rebel Eastern army, but resigned early in the war. He suspected me at first sight, and the following dialogue ensued between us:

Reb. — "What command do you belong to?"

Yank. — "Fourth Louisiana Battalion."

Reb. — "Give me the names of officers commanding your regiment, brigade and division."

Yank. — "Lieut. Colonel John McHenry, formerly commanded the regiment. He was wounded in the arm and thigh at the battle of Resaca, since which time Major Bowie has commanded. Colonel Gibson commands the brigade, and Major General Stewart the division."

Reb. — "Where is Col. McHenry at now?"

Yank. — "He is in the hospital at Columbus, Georgia."

Reb. — "Have you any papers to vouch for the truth of your statements?"

Yank. — "I have not."

Reb. — "How is it that you are without passes?"

Yank. — "It is not necessary for an officer to have papers in going so short a distance."

Reb. — "You may be all right, but I want to be satisfied. I fitted myself out for the purpose of scouting for Yanks, and we are picking them up every day. How far have you come to-day?"

Yank. — "From Forsythe. I came over to see my friend Joe Smith, the miller, who lives three miles down the river to the left of the road as you come from Macon. I am now going to Mr. Sanderson Middlebrook's, on private business for a friend in the hospital at Forsythe."

Reb. — "How long have you been in Forsythe?"

Yank. — "Over two months. I was wounded at Resaca; after recovering from my wound, I was taken with erysipelas."

Reb. — "You can give the names of citizens of Forsythe if you have been there two months."

Yank. — "No, sir, I cannot. I suffered severely, and was afterward so sick that I did not leave camp, and consequently did not form any acquaintances."

Reb. — "Describe the camp and buildings surrounding it."

I described quite a number of buildings I had noticed in coming through.

Reb. — "Can you describe no others?"

Yank. — "No, sir."

Reb. — "You have omitted the most conspicuous building in the camp. Can you not describe it?"

Yank. — "No, sir."

Reb. — "Well, sir, I will have to take you to camp at Graball, where there are officers better able to decide the matter."

Yank. — "My friend, if you do your duty you do well; but when you go beyond that, it is unbearable. I am a confederate officer, and expect to be treated as such. I have given you enough proof to satisfy any reasonable man; and if you were an old soldier you would have been satisfied with half the questions answered by me. I have to be in Forsythe on Monday next, in order to go to the front. If I go with you, I will have to come back to-morrow to Middlebrook's, and then I cannot reach Forsythe in time."

Reb. — "Well, come and go back to Mr. Smith's and stay all night."

Yank. — "I cannot go there, for the same reason that I cannot go to camp."

Reb. — "Well, sir, if you will describe Mr. Smith's house, I will be satisfied that you are all right."

It struck the rebel that if I was one, I could describe the house. That if I was a Yankee, I had not been to Mr. Smith's, — which was three miles off the road, — and consequently could not describe it. I knew that if I did not describe it I would have to go to camp with him, so I determined to make the attempt. In order to gain time, I pretended not to understand him.

I knew that there were no brick buildings in that part of the country, and that it must be either a frame or a log house. Mr. Smith being a miller, I concluded that it must be a frame. After asking him what he said, I told him that I could describe it; and commenced to do so. I told him that it was a two-story frame house, of pretty good size.

He replied that I was right, and that he was thoroughly satisfied ; asked my pardon for detaining me so long ; shook hands, and we parted. After this I resolved to travel at night, only.

At Hillsboro I was compelled to lie over three days, until General Iverson's brigade of Wheeler's command, got out of my way — narrowly escaping capture, twice, by pickets or scouts of this command. One of Stoneman's raiders was captured at this place, driven into the woods, and brutally murdered by his captors. Near Monticello I was chased by blood-hounds, but having procured an article which destroys the scent before leaving Macon, I escaped from them and their savage masters. The dogs having lost the scent, myself and negro guide — whom I engaged to take me around the town — went into a negro house and took supper. While there we were informed that three Yankees had been caught a short distance from town, and a negro, caught with them, had been shot. My guide, upon hearing this, made an excuse to go out, and never afterward returned. Shortly afterward I started on again. There being but one road for me to take, and fearing my pursuers might cross over and lie in wait for me, I concluded to lie over that night. I came to an old cotton-gin in the end of which was a window, but no visible means of getting up. After hunting around awhile, I found a pine pole, which I placed against the end of the building, and, by dint of pretty good climbing reached the window and got in. Here I lay all next day, sometimes gazing at the soldiers passing along the road, not more than fifty yards distant, and sometimes sleeping. At night I got down, went back to the negro house of the night before and took supper.

At Madison, three more of Stoneman's cavalry were captured and murdered in cold blood.

Near Lawrenceville, hearing that our army had been driven across the Chattahoochie river, and was retiring on Chattanooga, and deeming it best to change my direction, I resolved to enter the house of a rich widow lady, engage supper, and endeavor to obtain sight of a map.

I got supper, and also saw a map, from which I added some new points on my lead-pencil map. While in the house, the old lady asked me what I thought about the war. I replied that if the people of other States did as well as those of Georgia they would be successful. She replied that she thought they were a subjugated people. This was before the fall of Atlanta. While I stayed near Lawrenceville, large numbers of rebels passed by — some going home, others making for the mountains. They said there was no use staying at Atlanta and being killed up; that they were whipped anyhow.

The morning of August 25th found me six miles from the Chattahoochie river, and twenty-seven miles from Marietta.

That night I reached the river at a place know as Mackeyfield's Bridge. I found that the bridge had been destroyed by our cavalry in their retreat, and I was compelled to swim it, which I did at twelve o'clock at night. I passed through Roswell at daylight, and concluded to travel that day until I reached our lines at Marietta. I met quite a large number of citizens, to whom I represented myself as having been paroled by Stoneman, in front of Macon, with the understanding that I was to send out a Federal Lieutenant in my stead, and that if I failed to do so I was to report at Marietta as prisoner of war. Several of them advised me not to report, but "I couldn't think of breaking my parole." Five miles from Marietta I took breakfast at an old lady's house ; she told me of the cruel treatment received at the hands of the Yankees, &c. She mentioned one case, I remember, in which she had traded butter and milk for flour and coffee, and afterward the flour and coffee were taken from her by the Yankees.

I reached our lines at Marietta that day, August 26th, at ten o'clock, A. M., after a tedious and dangerous journey of twenty-two days, having travelled a distance of one hundred and sixty miles, all but thirteen miles on foot. None but those who have experienced it, can imagine the intense feeling of joy that overwhelms one upon again beholding the old flag, after a period of suffering in Southern dungeons.

DRAGOON'S SONG.

CLASH, clash goes the sabre against my steed's side,
Kling, kling go the rowels as onward I ride ;
And all my bright harness is living and speaks,
And under my horse-shoe the frosty ground creaks ;
I wave my buff glove to the girl whom I love,
Then join my dark squadron, and forward I move.

The foe all secure, has laid down by his gun ;
I'll open his eyelids before the bright sun ;
I burst on his pickets — they scatter, they fly ;
Too late they awaken — 'tis only to die.
Now the torch to their camp ; I'll make it a lamp,
As back to my quarters so slowly I tramp.

Kiss, kiss me my darling ; your lover is here,
Nay, kiss off the smoke-stains ; keep back that bright tear ;
Keep back that bright tear till the day when I come,
To the low wailing fife and deep muffled drum,
With a bullet half through the bosom so true,
To die, as I ought for my country and you.

GEORGE H. BOKER.

SOUTHERN OPINIONS. — At every movement of General Sherman's army, he captured more or less of the confederates, and occasionally a few came forward and voluntarily gave themselves up. One of them being asked what he thought of the Union forces and General Sherman, replied in the following rather extravagant but at the same time truthful style : " Sherman gits on a hill, flops his wings and crows; then yells out, ' Attention! creation! by kingdoms, right wheel! march!' and then we git."

Some of the prisoners, with an air of curiosity

JOHN SEDGWICK

worthy of a 'Yank,' inquire where the boys get those guns which they load on Sunday and fire all the week.

THE OCCUPATION OF WILMINGTON.—

The reception accorded to the soldiers of the Republic by the inhabitants of Wilmington, N. C. was a great and pleasing surprise to the officers and men.

The inhabitants, male and female, came from their houses into the streets, waving their hats and handkerchiefs as greetings of welcome. "We have been looking for you for a long time," said one. "You have got here at last," exclaimed another. "God bless you." And many like expressions. American flags were brought out and suspended over doors and from windows. One old lady expressed herself very glad to see Gen. Terry and his staff, for, said the ancient dame, "when I first seed you I thought you were Confederate officers come looking up tobacco." The colored people seemed beside themselves with joy; they sang and jumped, and shouted for joy.

The sight of the colored troops filled the measure of their ecstatic joy. The men danced in jubilation, the women screamed and went into hysterics, then and there, on the sidewalks. And their sable brethren in arms marched past, proud and erect, singing their "John Brown" hymn, where it was never sung before. Some of the larger houses were closed and abandoned; the people inhabiting these dwellings were affiliated with treason and rebellion. To their imagination, and their guilty consciences prompted the imaginings, our soldiers were not deliverers, but the avenging agents of the government which they had wantonly and without cause outraged and insulted.

Even from some of the finest mansions came forth the inmates with smiles of welcome for the defenders of the Union. What houses were closed or abandoned were of the first class. The middle class are nearly all loyal and four years' experience of secession has convinced even many of the slave-holding aristocracy that they committed a grave mistake, as well as a great crime, when they attempted to sever the bands of our common Union.

LOOKING ALIKE.—

The following incident illustrates how desirous the volunteers are to obey orders, and the good result of their efforts:

I suppose you will see that I have written mother's letter with a pencil, and yours with pen and ink. It is because we have just had a lot of pen-holders and pens given us by the government. We have also had a box and a half of shoe-blacking given to each man. You will remember that in my last letter I stated that G. F., one of the privates, had no shoes. When the Colonel gave us the blacking he said he wanted us to look as much alike as possible. So G. F. went to work and blacked his feet and polished them; and when the Colonel came along on dress parade, he asked F. why he did that. He replied, "To look as much alike as possible."— The Colonel burst out laughing, and went, after parade, to the store and bought him a pair of shoes with his own money.

GEN. HARDEE AND THE STRAGGLER.—

While on a forced march in some of the army movements in Mississippi, Gen. Hardee came up with a straggler who had fallen some distance in the rear of his command. The General ordered him forward, when the soldier replied that he was weak and broken down, not having had even half rations for several days.

"That's hard," replied the General, "but you must push forward, my good fellow, and join your command, or the provost guard will take you in hand."

The soldier halted, and, looking up at the General, asked:

"Aint you Gen. Hardee?"

"Yes," replied the General.

"Didn't you write Hardee's Tactics?"

"Yes."

"Well, General, I've studied them tactics, and know 'em by heart. You've got an order thar to double column at half distance, aint you?"

"Well," asked the General, "what has that order to do with your case?"

"I'm a good soldier, General, and obey all that is possible to be obeyed: but if you can show me an order in your tactics, or anybody else's tactics, to double distance on half rations, then I'll give in."

The General, with a hearty laugh, admitted that there were no tactics to meet the case, and putting spurs to his horse, rode forward.

HOW A LIEUTENANT ESCAPED.—

The following incident is connected with the flight at Sommerville, during the raid of Forrest through Tennessee:—Lieut. McIntyre, Ninth Illinois Cavalry, who was sent by Gen. Grierson with dispatches from Newcastle, eight miles east of Sommerville and twelve miles north of the La Grange, finding himself suddenly surrounded, threw away his arms and crawled under a house. From there he crept to a cotton gin near by. In the gin was a large pile of cotton seeds. The lieutenant dug a hole in it, crawled in, pulled a large basket over his head, and was thus completely ensconced, save his legs, over which he drew sufficient to conceal them, some of the seed. No sooner had he hid, than a surgeon of the Seventh Illinois also came rushing into the gin, pursued by ten rebels. He had just time to conceal himself between some boards in the loft, when the rebels came rushing up, and began to search for him. They had not seen the lieutenant enter the gin, but they were certain the surgeon was there. They put a guard at every avenue of escape, at each door and window, and then commenced the search. They went all through the building upstairs, tried upon the plank beneath which lay the surgeon, but did not find him. They peeped into every knot-hole but in vain.

Not long after it was ascertained that Forrest had returned South, and the various columns of infantry, cavalry and artillery were accordingly ordered back and went into camp.

AN INCIDENT OF SPOTTSYLVANIA. — During the lull in the strife, I rode back to the Second corps' hospitals to see the wounded.

"How goes it, boys?" was the question.

"All right," said one.

"Pretty rough," said another.

"They niver will get through the Second corps," said a Hibernian.

The lull had become a storm. How fearfully rolled the musketry! It is utterly useless to attempt a description or comparison. It was volley after volley, surge after surge, roll after roll.

Maurice Collins, of the Twelfth Massachusetts, was brought in with an ugly wound through his shoulder. He was a Catholic, and the priest was showing him the crucifix.

"Will it be mortal?" he asked.

"Perhaps not, if you will lie still and keep quiet; but you may have to lose your arm."

"Well, I am willing to give my arm to my country," was the reply of one, who, though born in the ever green isle, while loving the harp and shamrock, adores the stars and stripes of his adopted country.

THE FLORIDA'S CRUISE.

BY A FORETOP-MAN OF THE C. S. S. FLORIDA.

Air — *Red, White, and Blue* (Southern edition).

ONE evening, off Mobile, the Yanks they all knew
That the wind from the north'ard most bitterly blew;
They also all knew, and they thought they were sure,
They'd block'd in the Florida, safe and secure.
  Huzza! huzza, for the Florida's crew!
  We'll range with bold Maffitt the world through
    and through.

Nine cruisers they had, and they lay off the bar,
Their long line to seaward extending so far,
And Preble, he said, as he shut his eyes tight:
I'm sure they're all hammock'd this bitter cold night.

Bold Maffitt commanded, a man of great fame,
He sail'd in the Dolphin — you've heard of the same;
He call'd us all aft, and these words he did say:
I'm bound to run out, boys, up anchor, away!

Our hull was well whitewash'd, our sails were all
    stow'd,
Our steam was chock up, and the fresh wind it
    blow'd;
As we crawl'd along by them, the Yanks gave a
    shout —
We dropp'd all our canvas and open'd her out.

You'd have thought them all mad, if you'd heard
    the curs'd racket
They made upon seeing our flash little packet;

Their boatswains did pipe, and the blue lights did
    play,
And the great Drummond light — it turn'd night into
    day.

The Cuyler, a boat that's unrival'd for speed,
Quick let slip her cables, and quickly indeed
She thought for to catch us and keep us in play,
Till her larger companions could get under way.

She chas'd and she chas'd, till at dawning of day
From her backers she thought she was too far away,
So she gave up the chase and reported, no doubt,
That she'd sunk us and burnt us somewhere there-
    about.

So when we were out, boys, all on the salt sea,
We brought the Estelle to, right under our lee,
And burnt her and sunk her with all her fine gear,
And straight sail'd for Havana the bold privateer.

'Twas there we recruited and took in some stores,
Then kiss'd the senoras and sail'd from their shores,
And on leaving their waters, by way of a joke,
With two Yankee brigs, boys, we made a great smoke.

Our hull was well wash'd with the limestone so white,
Which sailors all know is not quite Christianlike,
So to paint her all ship-shape we went to Green Keys,
Where the Sonoma came foaming, the Rebel to seize.

We put on all sail and up steam right away,
And for forty-eight hours she made us some play,
When our coal being dusty and choking the flue,
Our steam it slack'd down, and nearer she drew.

Oh, ho! cried our captain, I see what's your game!
Clear away the stern pivot, the Bulldog by name,
And two smaller dogs to keep him companie,
For very sharp teeth have these dogs of the sea.

The Sonoma came up, until nearly in range,
When her engines gave out! — now wasn't that
    strange?
— I don't know the truth, but it's my firm belief
She didn't like the looks of the Florida's teeth.

She gave up the chase and returned to Key West,
And told her flag captain that she done her best;
But the story went round, and it grew rather strong,
And the public acknowledg'd that something was
    wrong.

We went on a cruising and soon did espy
A fine, lofty clipper, bound home from Shanghai;
We burnt her and sunk her i' th' midst of the sea,
And drank to Old Jeff in the best of Bohea!

We next found a ship with a quakerish name:
A wolf in sheep's clothing oft plays a deep game, —
For the hold of that beautiful, mild, peaceful Star
Was full of saltpetre, to make powder for war.

Of course the best nature could never stand that,
Saltpetre for Boston's a little too fat,
So we burnt her and sunk her, she made a great
    blaze,
She's a star now gone down, and we've put out her
    rays.

We next took a schooner well laden with bread;
What the devil got into Old Uncle Abe's head?

To send us such biscuit is such a fine thing,
It sets us all laughing, as we sit and sing.

We next took the Lapwing, right stuff in her hold,
And that was black diamonds that people call coal;
With that in our bunkers we'll tell Uncle Sam,
That we think his gunboats are not worth a damn.

The Mary Jane Colcord to Cape Town was bound,
We bade her heave to though and swing her yards
round,
And to Davy Jones' locker without more delay
We sent her afire, and so sailed on our way.
　　Huzza! huzza, for the Florida's crew!
　　We'll range with bold Maffitt the world through
　　　and through.

FRENCH DELANEY. — Near Falls Church,
Virginia, there lived before the war a wealthy
and highly-respected family of the name of Delaney. When the war broke out one of the
sons joined Mosby's band, and a daughter became
a volunteer nurse in a rebel hospital. Both became celebrated in their way. The son was
young, daring and adventurous, the pride of the
female sex for thirty miles around the place of his
nativity. He was soon the dread of Union soldiers and Union men of Virginia.

Not a stray soldier from picket escaped him,
not a Union farmer, but trembled at his name.
The vicinity of Dranesville, Chantilly, Falls
Church and Vienna can attest to his notoriety and
achievement. The father of a rebellious son and
daughter sternly maintained his loyalty and fidelity to the Union. At the opening of the war he
immediately offered his services to the Federal
Government, and was promoted to the rank of
colonel in the volunteer service.

Early one day a scouting party, consisting of
detachments from the Thirteenth New York and
Second Massachusetts Cavalry, under the command of Lieutenant E. B. Lyell, started from
Falls Church in pursuit of guerillas, reported to
be in the neighborhood of Chantilly and Herndon
station. On the morning following their departure, the troops were quietly drinking their coffee
within half a mile of the station, five of the advance guard posted on the road; suddenly, as if
rising from the earth, came galloping at full speed,
five men fully armed and equipped.

A volley from the advanced guard caused a momentary pause; the next minute the guerillas
turned and fled, the advance starting in pursuit,
an exciting chase ensuing for half a mile. A second volley was fired by the pursuers; but still the
rebels kept onward in their course till they arrived
near the pine woods, when they dashed in and
the men dared not follow. A stray horse was
seen to gallop from the woods without a rider!
A man was shot! Where was he?

The neighborhood was searched, and, in an adjoining house, stretched on a bed, pale and breathing hard, was found a wounded man, a young lady
fanning him tenderly. The officer in command
asked him, "Do you belong to the regular Confederate army, and what regiment?" He replied;
"I belong to Mosby's command." He stated

that he had always used the Union men well
when he had taken them prisoners, and begged
that a surgeon be sent; with which request Lieutenant Lyell promptly complied. The surgeon
came too late, for two nights afterwards the notorious Frenchy Delaney breathed his last, Colonel Delaney arriving just in time to take a last
farewell.

Curious to relate, Colonel Delaney was tak-
en prisoner to Richmond, and his own son was
present at the capture. The news of his fate flew
fast; on arriving at Dranesville, the officer in
charge was accosted by the fair damsels of rebeldom, in terms like this: "Now, have you really
shot Frenchy Delaney? Well, now, that is too
bad; I hope he wont die." "Yes," replied Lyell, "and very soon you will have no rebel
beaux to marry? you will have to take up with
Union men." "We will," was the answer, "but
we will convert them." "Perhaps," said the
Lieutenant, "we shall convert you." The maidens smiled incredulously, and Lyell left for his
command.

REMINISCENCES OF GENERAL SUMNER. —
When the history of this war is faithfully written,
Sumner's name will be one of the brightest in
that noble army which has illustrated the discipline and valor of Northern troops on so many
bloody fields, but which, through a leader infirm
of purpose, never yet gathered the ripe fruits of
victory. At Fair Oaks and Malvern Hill he decided the fate of the day; and through the whole
Peninsular campaign he was in the hottest, deadliest of the fighting.

He had the true soldierly temperament. Not
only was his whole heart in the war, but if it is
possible for any man to love fighting, to feel what
the ancients called "the rapture of the strike,"
Sumner was that man. He snuffed the battle
afar off. He went into it with a boyish enthusiasm. Our generals usually expose themselves
not too little but too much. If they participated
less in the peril, they might often economize the
lives of their men more and yet achieve the same
results. But in this soldiery imprudence Sumner
eclipsed them all. The chronic wonder of his
friends was that he ever came out of battle
alive; but at last they began to believe with him,
that he was invincible. He would get bullets in
his hat, his coat, his boots, his saddle, his horse,
sometimes have his person scratched, but always
escaped without serious injury. His soldiers
used to tell, with great relish, the story that in the
Mexican war a bullet which struck him square in
the forehead fell flattened to the ground without
breaking the skin, as the hunter's ball glances
from the forehead of the buffalo. It was this
anecdote which won for him the soubriquet of
"Old Bull Sumner." He desired, when his time
should come, to fall in battle; but it illustrates
the fortunes of war that the officer who for forty
years had thus courted death should at last die
peacefully in his bed, surrounded by his family.

At Fair Oaks, when his troops were staggering under a pitiless storm of bullets, Sumner came galloping along up and down the advance line, more exposed than any private in the ranks. "What regiment is this?" he asked. "The fifteenth Massachusetts," replied a hundred voices. "I, too, am from Massachusetts; three cheers for our old Bay State!" And, swinging his hat, the general led off, and every soldier joined in three thundering cheers. The enemy looked on in wonder at the strange episode, but was driven back by the fierce charge which followed.

This was no unusual scene; it was the way Sumner fought his battles. Staff officers will tell you by the hour, how, when the guns began to pound, his mild eye would light up with flashes of fire; how he would take out his artificial teeth, which became troublesome during the excitement of battle, and place them carefully in his pocket; raise his spectacles from his eyes and rest them upon the forehead, that he might see clearly objects at a distance; give his orders to his subordinates, and then gallop headlong into the thick of the fight.

How many soldiers, as they read and talk of his death, recall the erect form, the snowy hair streaming in the wind, the frank face of that wonderful old man, who,

> "In worst extremes,
> And on the perilous edge of battle
> When it raged,"

would ride along their front lines, when they were falling like grass before the mower, encouraging the fearful, and shouting through the smoke, "Steady, men, steady! Don't be excited. When you have been soldiers as long as I, you will learn that this is nothing. Stand firm and do your duty!"

For a man of sixty-four, his health was marvellous. His long, temperate life in the pure air of the great plains and the mountains — a region of which he was enthusiastically fond — retained in his vigorous frame the elasticity of boyhood. Upon a march he usually quite wore out his staff with hard riding. When he left the field a short time previous to his death there were few officers as nimble and agile as he; few who could spring upon a horse more easily, or ride with more grace and endurance.

There was no straining for dramatic effect about Sumner. He never advertised his exploits. He sometimes displayed heroism which would illustrate the brightest pages of history; but he did it unostentatiously, unconsciously. It was the act of a soldier quietly performing a soldier's duty.

At Fair Oaks, on Saturday evening, after Casey and Heintzelman had suffered greatly, and been driven three or four miles, Sumner crossed the Chickahominy at an unexpected point, and attacking the enemy vigorously in flank and rear, turned the tide of battle. On Sunday morning the fight was renewed; many a gallant officer fell. Gen. Howard lost his arm at the head of his brigade, and our triumph was gained at a heavy cost; but Sumner held his advantage.

During a lull in the battle, McClellan crossed the river, remained long enough to write his famous despatch censuring Casey's men, and then succeeded in returning upon a log over the swelling stream. Our bridges were swept away; our army was thus cut in twain; and Sumner, with his three shattered corps, was left without hope of reinforcements. The weakened half of our army was at the mercy of the enemy's entire force.

On that Sunday night, after making his dispositions to receive an attack, Sumner sent for Gen. Sedgwick, who commanded his Second Division, — one of his special friends and most trusty soldiers. "Sedgwick," said he, "you perceive the situation. The enemy will probably precipitate himself upon us at daylight. Reinforcements are impossible; he can overwhelm and destroy us. But at this most critical period the country cannot afford to have us defeated. The enemy may win a victory; but we must make it a victory that shall ruin him. There is just one thing for us to do: we must stand here and die like men! Impress it upon your officers that we must do this to the last man — to the last man! We may not meet again; but we will at least die like soldiers."

And so Sumner wrung the hand of his lieutenant and bade him farewell. Morning came; the rebels failing to discover our perilous condition, did not renew the attack; in a day or two new bridges were built, and the sacrifice was averted. But Sumner was the man to carry out his resolution to the letter.

After Fair Oaks, he retained possession of a house on our old line of battle; and the headquarters' tents were brought up and pitched there. They were within range of a rebel battery which awoke the General and his staff every morning, by dropping shot and shell all about them for two or three hours. Sumner implored permission to capture or drive away that battery, but was refused, on the ground that it might bring on a general engagement. He chafed and stormed: "It is the most disgraceful thing of my life," he said," that this should be permitted;" but McClellan, whose prudence never forsook him, was inexorable. Sumner was begged to remove his head-quarters to a safer position, but he persisted in staying there for fourteen days, and at last only withdrew upon a peremptory order from his superior.

The experience of that fortnight shows how much iron and lead may fly about men's ears without harming them. During the whole bombardment only two persons at the head-quarters were injured. The surgeon of a Rhode Island battery was slightly wounded in the head by a piece of shell which flew into his tent; and a private, who laid down behind a log for protection, was instantly killed by a shell knocking a splinter from the log, which fractured his skull. There were many hairbreadth escapes; but not another man received a scratch.

During the artillery fighting, the day before Antietam, Sumner lay upon the grass under the shade trees, in front of the brick house which served for General Head-quarters. A few yards distant, in an open field, a party of staff officers and civilians were suddenly startled by a stray shell from the enemy, which dropped about a hundred feet from them. It was followed by another which fell still nearer, and the group broke up and scattered with great alacrity. "Why," remarked Sumner, with a peculiar smile, "the shells excite a good deal of commotion among those young gentlemen!" The idea which seemed to amuse him was that anybody should be disconcerted by shells.

At Fredericksburg, by the express order of Burnside, Sumner remained on this side of the river during the fighting. The precaution probably saved his life. Had he ridden with his usual rashness out on that fiery front, he had never returned to tell what he saw. Still, he chafed sadly under the restriction. As the sun went down on that day of glorious but fruitless endeavor, he paced to and fro in front of the Lacey House with one arm thrown around the neck of his son, his face haggard with sorrow and anxiety, and his eyes straining eagerly for the arrival of each successive messenger.

He was a man of high ambition. Once, hearing Gen. Howard remark that he did not aspire to the command of a corps, he exclaimed: "General, you surprise me. I would command the world, if I could!" But it was the ambition of a soldier and a patriot. He gave to his superiors not merely lip-service, but zealous, hearty, untiring co-operation. It was a point of honor with him, even when he believed them mistaken or incompetent, never to breathe a word to their disparagement.

He was sometimes called arbitrary; but he had great love for his soldiers, especially his old companions in arms. One of his officers tell a laughable story of applying to him for a ten days' furlough, when the rule against them was imperative. Sumner peremptorily refused it. But the officer sat down beside him, and began to talk about the Peninsula campaign, the battles in which he had done his duty, immediately under Sumner' eye; and it was not many minutes before the General granted his petition. "If he had only waited," said the narrator, "until I reminded him of some scenes at Antietam, I am sure he would have given me twenty days instead of ten."

He possessed great kindness of heart: he was intrinsically a gentleman — an example which some of our Major-Generals might study to advantage. His intercourse with women and children was characterized by peculiar chivalry and gentleness. There was much about him to revive the old ideal of the soldier — terrible in battle, but with a heart open and tender as a child's.

To his youngest son — a captain upon his staff — he was bound by ties of unusual affection. "Sammy" was his constant companion; in private he leaned upon him, caressed him, and consulted him upon the most trivial matters. It was a touching bond which united the gray, war-worn veteran to the child of his old age.

THE CAPTAIN'S WIFE.

BY THEODORE TILTON.

WE gathered roses, Blanche and I, for little Madge,
  one morning, —
"I am a soldier's wife," said Blanche, "and dread
  a soldier's fate!" —
Her voice a little trembled then, as under some fore-
  warning, —
A soldier galloped up the lane, and halted at the
  gate.

"Which house is Malcolm Blake's?" he cried, — "a
  letter for his sister!"
And when I thanked him, Blanche inquired, "But
  none for me, his wife?"
The soldier played with Madge's curls, and stooping
  over, kissed her:
"Your father was my captain, child; — I loved
  him as my life!"

Then suddenly he galloped off, and left the rest unspoken;
I burst the seal, and Blanche exclaimed — "What
  makes you tremble so?"
What answer did I dare to speak? — how ought the
  news be broken?
I could not shield her from the stroke, yet tried to
  ease the blow.

"A battle in the swamps," I said, — "our men were
  brave, but lost it;"
And pausing there, — "the note," I said, "is not
  in Malcolm's hand."
And first a flush went through her face, and then a
  shadow crossed it, —
"Read quick, dear May, — read all, I pray, and
  let me understand!"

I did not read it as it stood, but tempered so the
  phrases
As not at first to hint the worst, — held back the
  fatal word,
And half re-told his gallant charge, his shouts, his
  comrades' praises, —
When, like a statue carved in stone, she neither
  spoke nor stirred!

Oh! never yet a woman's heart was frozen so com-
  pletely! —
So unbaptized with helping tears! — so passionless
  and dumb!
Spell-bound she stood, and motionless — till little
  Madge spoke sweetly:
"Dear mother, is the battle done? — and will my
  father come?"

I laid my finger on her lips, and set the child to playing;
Poor Blanche! the winter in her cheek was snowy,
  like her name!
What could she do but kneel and pray? — and linger
  at her praying?
O Christ, when other heroes die, moan other wives
  the same?

Must other women's hearts yet break, to keep the
  cause from failing?
God pity our brave lovers then, who face the battle's blaze!
And pity wives in widowhood! — But is it unavailing?
O Lord, give Freedom first, then Peace, — and
  unto Thee be praise!

AN INCIDENT OF THE BATTLE FIELD. — A writer in the "Congregationalist" tells this: —

Returning, we saw a newly opened grave. It was for a Michigan boy of eighteen, who had been shot down by the side of his father, who was a private in the same company. The father sat beside the grave, carving his boy's name upon a rude head-board. It was his first-born. I took him by the hand, and gave him all my heart; offered a prayer, which brother Holmes followed with appropriate words. There was no coffin, but a few pieces of board were laid in the bottom of the grave, between the body and the bare ground.

"Wrap him in this blanket," said the father; "it is one his sister sent him. Ah! me, how will they bear it at home? What will his poor mother do? She must have a lock of his hair!"

I stooped to cut the lock with my penknife, when a soldier came forward with a pair of scissors from his little "housewife." My heart blessed the Sabbath-school child who had made that timely gift. And so, having rendered the last offices of faith and affection, we laid the brave boy in his grave, while the cannon was still roaring the doom of others, young and brave, whom we had just left on the field.

A STORY OF GENERAL GRANT. — A visitor to the army called upon him one morning, and found the General sitting in his tent smoking, and talking to one of his staff-officers. The stranger approached the chieftain, and inquired of him as follows: —

"General, if you flank Lee, and get between him and Richmond, will you not 'uncover Washington,' and leave it a prey to the enemy?"

General Grant, discharging a cloud of smoke, with a "silver lining," from his mouth, indifferently replied, "Yes, I reckon so."

Stranger, encouraged by the reply he thus received, propounded question number two, —

"General, do you not think Lee can detach sufficient force from his army to reinforce Beauregard and overwhelm Butler?"

"Not a doubt of it," replied the General.

Stranger, becoming fortified by his success, propounded question number three, as follows, —

"General, is there not danger that Johnston may come up and reinforce Lee, so that the latter will swing around and cut your communications and seize your supplies?"

"Very likely," was the cool reply of the General, as he knocked the ashes from the end of his cigar with his little finger.

Stranger, horrified at the awful fate about to befall General Grant and the army, made his exit and hastened to Washington to communicate the "news."

REMINISCENCE OF FORT DONELSON. — On Saturday night before the surrender, a council of war was called. Pillow, Floyd, Buckner, and a number of brigadiers composed this body.

There was much confusion and exciting debate for a while. Some thought it necessary to surrender, and some did not. It was midnight, and no definite understanding was come to. General Floyd, seeing this, dismissed the council, requesting Pillow and Buckner to remain. The three sat down gloomily by the fire to ponder over the sad aspect of affairs. A long silence ensued.

"Well, gentlemen," said Floyd, "I see you are still divided, and as I have the casting vote, I will settle the matter at once. I favor a surrender myself, provided the duty does not devolve upon me. I cannot surrender, because the United States Government have indicted me for treason, and the probability is that if they were to get me they would hang me. So you see the thing is impossible. I transfer the command to you, General."

"Well, gentlemen, it remains with us to decide this matter, and we must do it at once. It is now midnight, and if we retreat we haven't got a minute to lose."

"I say retreat," said Pillow.

"I say surrender! We have shed enough blood already to no purpose," said Buckner.

"Well, gentlemen," said Pillow, "I'm in the same fix as yourself. The Yankees have got me indicted for shipping guns and munitions of war to the Confederate Government. So you see I can't surrender either; they would hang me as quick as they would you, and if you are excusable I guess I am too. So I transfer my right of command to you, General Buckner."

General Buckner bowed, but said nothing. At that moment a noise was heard without. The door opened, and the courier announced an officer who desired admittance. He was ordered to show him in, and the next moment Colonel Forrest, all splashed with mud and water, with high topped boots and an old slouched hat, made his appearance. He walked to the fireplace and seated himself without saying a word. After a few moments Floyd said:

"Well, Colonel, have you anything important to communicate that you come here at this late hour, or has your curiosity led you to pay us this visit in order to find out what we have decided upon?"

"Both," replied Forrest, dryly; then rising from his chair, he said:

"But is it possible, gentlemen, as I have already heard whispered this night, that you intend to surrender?"

"Yes," was the reply. "We have just arrived at that conclusion."

"But," said Forrest, "there is no occasion for it, gentlemen; the whole army can easily escape without the loss of a man; not an hour ago I crossed the river on my horse where it was not waist deep. I crossed it going on horseback, and waded it coming back. It is free from Yankee pickets also, and there is no danger to be feared."

"Yes; but, Colonel," said General Floyd, "my scouts have reconnoitred the entire river, and an officer who arrived not half an hour ago told me that he had tested the river everywhere, and no spot had he found that was fordable."

"I don't care, General, if he did," said Forrest; "he told you a d—d lie, as I am ready to swear that I waded the river not half an hour ago, as my wet clothes will testify. And now, gentlemen, as it is getting late, it is high time you should be acting. Will you take my advice and make your escape?"

"No," was the reply, "it is too late."

"I have one request to make," said Forrest; "I have a fine regiment of cavalry here, and I want permission to take it out. Grant me this much, and I'm off." ·

General Buckner nodded his head, when Forrest bolted out of the house, took his command, crossed the river, at the aforesaid place, and made his escape without the loss of a man.

A GOOD MARKSMAN. — The effectiveness of the batteries is proverbial. While advancing on Resaca, when Sweeney's division was on the right and in reserve, Captain Arndt's Michigan battery was wheeled into position.

"Do you see that house?" said the captain, addressing one of his gunners, and pointing to a building a mile away.

"I do, captain," was the response.

"Can you hit it?"

"Yes, sir."

The piece was levelled, the lanyard drawn, and the chimney of the house fell with a crash!

AMUSING INCIDENT. — Charles Gates, a minor son wished to enlist, but his aged parents objected to it. One morning he was sent to drive the cows to pasture, on his way to work, taking his dinner with him. But at night he did not come back, because he had run away and enlisted. He remained through the three years without a furlough, and returned with the regiment unharmed by rebel bullets. He arrived in the old pasture at home one night just at "cow-time," and leisurely drove up the same old cows as if he hadn't been away for three years. His "reception" was a joyful one, none the less so because his coming was a complete surprise.

A BURIAL AT SEA. — A correspondent at Nassau, N. P. wrote as follows: — "A melancholy incident occurred upon the steamship Fannie, while being chased by a Yankee man-of-war. One of the passengers on board, Captain Frank Du Barry, late chief of ordnance on Gen. Beauregard's staff, C. S. A., died. Preparations had to be completed for his burial, which took place amid all the excitement of the chase. A burial at sea is a ceremony at all times full of solemnity, but it is when coupled with such events as this that war assumes its most repulsive aspect. In that frail little steamer, quivering with her efforts to escape the relentless fate bearing down on her with frowning guns, and the ferocity of a

13

tiger, while every living heart on board was throbbing with anxiety for safety, they were suddenly called upon to render the last and most solemn rites known to our existence. No time then to stop in mid-ocean, while words that consigned "dust to dust," "ashes to ashes," went up in presence of the grim destroyer, but still dashing onward through the waves — a short and hurried service, a heavy splash, and a body sank to its eternal resting-place in the broad ocean's bosom, while all that was dear to it in life sped from it on its way like the arrow from the bow."

THE SOLDIER BIRD. — One day in the spring of 1861, Chief Sky, a Chippewa Indian, living in the northern wilds of Wisconsin, captured an eagle's nest. To make sure of his prize he cut the tree down, and caught the eaglets as they were sliding from the nest to run and hide in the grass. One died. He took the other home, and built it a nest in a tree close by his wigwam. The eaglet was as big as a hen, covered with soft brown down. The red children were delighted with their new pet; and as soon as it got acquainted, it liked to sit down in the grass and see them play with the dogs. But Chief Sky was poor, and he had to sell it to a white man for a bushel of corn. The white man brought it to Eau Claire, a little village alive with white men going to the war. "Here's a recruit," said the man. "An eagle, an eagle!" shouted the soldiers, "let him enlist;" and sure enough, he was sworn into the service with ribbons round his neck, red, white, and blue.

On a perch surmounted by stars and stripes, the company took him to Madison, the capital of the state. As they marched into camp Randall, with colors flying, drums beating, and the people cheering, the eagle seized the flag in his beak and spread his wings, his bright eye kindling with the spirit of the scene. Shouts rent the air; "The bird of Columbia! the eagle of freedom forever!" The state made him a new perch, the boys named him "Old Abe," and the regiment, the Eighth Wisconsin, was henceforth called "the Eagle regiment." On the march it was carried at the head of the company, and everywhere was greeted with delight. At St. Louis, a gentleman offered five hundred dollars for it, and another his farm. No, no, the boys had no notion of parting with their bird. It was above all price, — an emblem of battle and of victory. Besides it interested their minds, and made them think less of hardships and of home.

I cannot tell you all the droll adventures of the bird through its three years of service, its flights in the air, its fights with the guinea hens, and its race with the darkies. When the regiment was in summer quarters at Clear Creek in Dixie, it was allowed to run at large, and every morning went to the river half a mile off, where it splashed and played in the water to its heart's content, faithfully returning to camp when it had enough. Old Abe's favorite place of resort was the sutler's tent, where a live chicken found no quarter in his presence. But rations got low, and for two days Abe had nothing to eat. Hard-tack he objected to, fasting was disagreeable, and Tom, his bearer, could not get beyond the pickets to a farmyard. At last, pushing his way to the colonel's tent, he pleaded for poor Abe. The colonel gave him a pass, and Tom got him an excellent dinner.

One day a rebel farmer asked Tom to come and show the eagle to his children. Satisfying the curiosity of the family, Tom sat him down in the barnyard. Oh what a screeching and scattering among the fowls; for what should Abe do but pounce upon one and gobble up another, to the great disgust of the farmer, who declared that was not in the bargain. Abe, however, thought there was no harm in confiscating, nor did Tom.

Abe was in twenty battles, besides many skirmishes. He was at the seige of Vicksburg, the storming of Corinth, and marched with Sherman up the Red river. The whiz of bullets and the scream of shells were his delight. As the battle grew hot and hotter, he would flap his wings and mingle his wildest notes with the noise around him. He was very fond of music, especially Yankee Doodle and Old John Brown. Upon parade he always gave heed to "Attention." With his eye on the commander, he would listen and obey orders, noting time accurately. After parade he would put off his soldierly air, flap his wings, and make himself at home. The rebels called him "Yankee Buzzard," "Old Owl," and other hard names; but his eagle nature was quite above noticing it.

The rebel General Price gave orders to his men to be sure and capture the eagle of the Eighth Wisconsin; he would rather have it than a dozen battle flags. But for all that he scarcely lost a feather; only one from his right wing. His tail-feathers were once cropped by a bullet.

At last the great rebellion came to an end, and the brave Wisconsin Eighth, with their live eagle and torn and riddled flags, were welcomed back to Madison. They went out a thousand strong, and returned a little band, scarred and toil-worn, having fought and won.

And what of the soldier bird? In the name of his gallant veterans, Capt. Wolf presented him to the state. Governor Lewis accepted the illustrious gift, and ample quarters are provided for him in the beautiful State-house grounds, where may be long live to tell us

"What heroes from the woodland sprang,
When through the fresh awakened land
The thrilling cry of freedom rang."

Nor is the end yet. At the great fair in Chicago an enterprising gentleman, invited "Abe" to attend. He had colored photographs of the old hero struck off, and sold $16,700 worth for the benefit of poor and sick soldiers. Has not the American eagle done its part?   K.

A STORY OF PRESIDENT LINCOLN. — "Mr. President," said a friend to him, "there isn't much left of Hood's army, is there?"

"Well, no, Medill; I think Hood's army is about in the fix of Bill Sykes' dog, down in Sangamon county. Did you ever hear it?"

Of course, the answer was, "Never."

"Well, Bill Sykes had a long, *yaller* dog, that was forever getting into the neighbors' meat-houses and chicken-coops. They had tried to kill it a hundred times, but the dog was always too smart for them. Finally, one of them got a bladder of a coon, and filled it up with powder, tying the neck around a piece of punk. When he saw the dog coming he fired this punk, split open a hot biscuit and put the bladder in, then buttered all nicely and threw it out. The dog swallowed it at a gulp. Pretty soon there was an explosion. The head of the dog lit on the porch, the fore-legs caught astraddle the fence, the hind-legs fell in the ditch, and the rest of the dog lay around loose. Pretty soon Bill Sykes came along, and the neighbor said : 'Bill, I guess there aint much of that dog of your'n left.' 'Well, no,' said Bill; 'I see plenty of pieces, but I guess that dog, *as a dog*, aint of much more account.' Just so, Medill, there may be fragments of Hood's army around, but I guess that dog, *as a dog*, aint of much more account."

SHERMAN'S IN SAVANNAH.

LIKE the tribes of Israel,
  Fed on quails and manna,
Sherman and his glorious band
Journeyed through the rebel land,
Fed from Heaven's all bounteous hand,
  Marching on Savannah.

As the moving pillar shone
  Streamed the starry banner,
All the day in rosy light,
Beaming glory all the night,
Till it swooped in eagle flight
  Down on doomed Savannah.

Glory be to God on high!
  Shout the loud hosanna!
Treason's wilderness is past,
Canaan's shore is won at last;
Peal a nation's trumpet-blast, —
  Sherman's in Savannah!

LIFE IN SOUTHERN PRISONS. — During the expedition of Col. Streight through Georgia in the spring of 1863, Capt. T. M. Anderson of Company D, Fifty-first Regiment, of Indiana, was captured by the confederates and imprisoned at Richmond, from whence he escaped in company with Lieutenant Skelton, of the Seventeenth Iowa Regiment, and, reached the Union lines in safety, after much suffering. The following is his account of his experiences : —

I was taken prisoner on the third day of May, 1863, near Rome, Ga., with Col. Streight's command. We were all paroled and sent to Richmond with the expectation of going through to our lines ; but judge of our surprise when we were thrust into Libby Prison, and our paroles taken from us. We entered Libby on the sixteenth day of May, and from that day I was not on the ground until I made my escape.

From the day that I entered until I succeeded in getting away, did I watch my opportunity. I soon became satisfied that to get out of any of the upper rooms was an impossibility, and the only room that there was any prospect of getting out of was the hospital room in the east end of the building, which is as low as the street on the north side, but the second floor on the south side. Well, I had to get into this hospital before I could hope to escape; consequently, I was taken suddenly very sick. Of course I was carried to the hospital, where all sick men are taken. I kept my bed three or four days; was visited by the surgeon (a mullet-headed fellow, that didn't know beans), regularly, every day. He left me a large dose of medicine, which I found did me a great deal of good, in my vest-pocket. After several days of feigned sickness, I set to work to find a companion to go with me; and, as fortune favored me, I found the man, Lieut. Skelton, of the Seventeenth Iowa Regiment, who had long had the same opinion that I had, that he would get away from there if possible.

We soon commenced our arrangements, and worked very slowly, and everything being ready on the eleventh of this month, we resolved to make the attempt. During the day we went down into the basement story, which is used as a cook-room for the hospital, and cut a small door open into the south-east corner of the room. This we opened with a large beef-cleaver, by drawing the spikes and nails and by cutting off the cross-bars. As we had to work very cautiously and silently, it took us some time to do this, but it was accomplished ere dark. The hour of ten o'clock was the hour we set to make the break. We prepared crackers and dried beef enough to last us through, and then dressed ourselves in citizens' clothes (which we had received from home), and then everything was ready. We watched the sentinels very closely, and just as the hour of ten was called they all turned and walked to the west, and at that moment we opened the door, and like lightning we crossed the guard-line, and when the guards faced about we were walking coolly and briskly down the street.

We kept down Canal street some two squares, and then turned up Main street. We then thought that the boldest step was safest, so we went through the city on Main street, then through Rockets, a little town adjoining Richmond on the east. After passing through Rockets we came to the Williamsburg road. This we kept for about a mile, when we came in sight of their batteries and forts, and we knew that pickets were on the road; so, to avoid the batteries and pickets, we took a by-path leading off to the right and down into a deep ravine, and in this we passed between their forts out into the country. The night was dark, and consequently it was very difficult travelling. We made about seven miles that night, and came to the Williamsburg road again just at daybreak. We filed into a thick clump of cedar bushes and lay down for the day. It was raining very hard, and it was chilling cold; *but we were* FREE; what cared we for cold rains when we were breathing the air of freedom! All day Saturday we were in the bushes. The rebel drums we could plainly hear on all sides of us, guns firing, and soldiers were passing and re-passing; and at one time five rebs passed so near us that I thought we should surely be discovered, but they did not see us, and we, of course, did not hail them. We had been surmising all day about our whereabouts, but could not find out our exact locality, so we concluded to hail the first darkey that passed. We watched the road closely, and about sundown I heard a wagon coming. Lieutenant Skelton said he would go out and stop it if it was driven by a negro. He crawled close to the road-side and awaited the coming of the wagon, when he jumped out and told the negro-driver to halt.

The boy stopped his team, and out came a white man to know what he wanted. He instantly saw our danger, and being ready for any emergency cried out: "Say, Mister, I have lost a black boy, and have tracked him out into this neighborhood, but here I lost him. Have you heard or seen anything of a boy about twenty years old, five feet five and very black? My name is Calloway and if you hear anything of my boy you will do me a grand kindness by having him put in irons. Good day, sir." The man promised to do his best, and believing every word, drove on. Just at dark we again set forward on the Williamsburg road leading to Bottom's bridge, over the Chickahominy river. There is a force of about 400 men at the bridge. We travelled some three miles, and fearing we would run into their pickets if we went further, we turned into the woods again. It had been raining some time, and consequently was as dark as Egypt in the woods. We could not go any further, so laid down for the night again. We could not sleep, for we were by this time as wet as if we had been in the river. Day at last dawned, and ere it was quite light we were on our way. We had only left Richmond some ten miles behind us up to Sunday morning. We now by the aid of a small pocket compass, laid out our course directly north, and kept it for several hours. We then turned directly east, toward the Chickahominy river, and soon found ourselves in one of the most dense swamps that it was ever my fortune to get into, but in this swamp we knew we could travel with safety. On we went through under-brush and briers, through water over our boots several inches, and all of that day did we travel through that miry swamp.

We crossed the Chickahominy about a half an hour by sun, and again fortune favored us, for at the very point where we first struck the river there was a large tree blown across the stream. On this we crossed about three miles north of Bottom's bridge. Being very weary, we did not go more than a mile from the river where we halted for the night in the woods. We were now close to the main travelled road running from Bottom's bridge, parallel with the river up to Savage's, and we could hear cavalry passing along this road all night. We did not sleep any, for again it rained and it was a cold night, but almost everything has an ending, and so it was with that Sunday night, but I thought it was forty-eight hours long. After feasting on our dried beef and hard tack we set forward and soon came to this road, and just as we were in the act of crossing the fence we spied a rebel scout coming up the road. He had seen us and we dared not run, for then he would be sure to suspicion us, so we stood our ground prepared to club him if he said anything.

He came up and we looked at him boldly and impudently, and without uttering a word. He passed on, never looking back to see where we went. We quickly crossed the road and entered the woods, and if we didn't do some tall walking then for about ten miles, I wouldn't be here to say so. On we went, keeping our course directly east, allowing nothing to turn us from it but farm-houses, all of which we were very careful to go around; but through swamps, over hills and hollows we went. About ten o'clock A. M. on Monday, as we were going through the woods we suddenly came in sight of a farm-house, and a negro girl raking leaves close by. I thought likely she could tell us where we were, so I went up and spoke to her. All that she could tell was that we were, in New Kent County. I then asked her whether her master was a secesh, and whether he was at home or not. She said he was both. I then told her that we were Yankees, trying to get home, and that she must not tell her master that she had seen any one all of which she readily promised.

She said, "I am looking for Mr. Bradley (which was her master's name) every minute, and you had better run." Again we made good time, and soon came to one of the most intricate swamps I ever saw. It was about two hundred yards wide, and as far as we could see to the right or left it was the same. There were little tufts of grass growing up all over it, some three or four feet apart, and out of these there were little sprouts growing. We had to pull ourselves from one of the bunches of grass to another, and I feel justified in saying that the quicksand and mire was six feet deep in many places, but in about an hour, and after getting very wet, we succeeded in getting over, and then we turned around, pulled off our hats, and yelled, "Good by, Mr. Bradley." During all of our day's travel that was a by-word with us, but on we pushed, exerting ourselves to the utmost to put as many miles between us and Richmond as possible.

That night we came within three miles of Dyuscuna Creek, and about twenty-two miles from Williamsburg. We were now in a negro settlement, and stopped for the night. We engaged a negro guide to conduct us to Dyuscuna Creek bridge the next morning, and an hour before daylight we were on our way, arriving at the bridge just at sun-up. We here partook sparingly of our beef and crackers, and then set forward. We had not gone more than a mile before we saw two horsemen coming down the

road toward us. We thought that it was perfectly safe to travel the road by daylight then, as we had heard that our troops had been at the bridge late the evening before; so when these horsemen came in sight we quickly jumped into the bushes to await their coming. I saw they were colored men, and felt no hesitancy in coming out to the road and speaking to them. They said, in answer to my inquiries, that there were rebel scouts on that road every day. I then told them that we were Yankee prisoners from Richmond trying to get within our lines. Their faces instantly brightened, and they told us to go back in the woods, and remain there until night or we would be picked up. We knew it to be good advice, so we backed into the bushes again.

One of the darkies lived only a few miles from us, and the other near Chickahominy Church, some eight miles directly on our route. This darkey told us that he would pass there on his way back home in the evening, and said he would show us the way home if we would wait. We remained in the bushes all that day, which was Tuesday, and true to his promise the darkey made his appearance late in the evening. He instructed us how to get round a large plantation that was close by and reach his friend's house. We accordingly set forth, and in about an hour arrived safely at the house. The old darkies gave us our supper, and kept a strict watch for intruders while we were eating. When it became sufficiently dark our guide harnessed his horse and put him to his cart, putting on the cover and tying it down very tight all round.

We then ensconced ourselves very snugly in the back part of the cart, while the darkey almost filled the front part, and away we went, driving like the wind sometimes. When about half way we came to a picket post. Mr. Darkey told us to lay down and be mute, whereupon he gave his horses the reins and whip and we went past that picket like a whirlwind. If there were any pickets there, they saw nothing but the outlines of a cart, for we were out of sight ere they could halt us. We reached the church about nine o'clock, and after giving us another supper the darkey piloted us for three miles on the road to Williamsburg and then left us. We were now about eight miles from our lines, on a plain road leading to them. We had some fears of meeting with some of the rebel scouts on the road, for our guide told us they were on the road day and night. So we moved briskly but very cautiously. The road was not the mainly-travelled one leading to Williamsburg, but we came into it when within about two miles of the town.

We thought if we met any scouts at all it would be at the junction of these two roads, so we approached the main road very slowly but found no one there. Then we thought ourselves safe. So on we went toward town, not knowing at what unfortunate moment we might come in contact with a party of rebel scouts, and have all our hopes dashed to the ground. We had gone about two miles and walking very fast, when suddenly and unexpectedly the stillness of the night was broken by a gruff voice calling out, "Halt." We did not wait for a second challenge, but came to a dead halt instantly, not knowing whether we were near our own pickets or a couple of rebs, for we could see that there were two. "Who comes there?" was the next challenge. I answered "friends." He then told me to advance and give the countersign. Not liking to go up blindly, I asked "To whom I should advance;" and without answering my question, he asked "To whom are you friends?" That was the hardest question I ever had to answer. I knew not what to say, but in a moment answered, "We are friends to the North." "Come up," said he; "we are Union pickets."

I thought those were the sweetest words that I ever heard. We threw up our hats high in the air, and went with such a yell that the sentries thought us crazy. When inside our pickets we turned and said, "Good-by, Mr. Bradley." We soon explained our boisterous conduct to the pickets, who were looking on with amazement, and then everything was all right. My pen here fails, dear *Tribune*, to express our happiness; but to know and feel that we were under the protection of Uncle Sam, and standing on the ground over which that dear flag was triumphantly floating, under whose folds both of us had fought on many battle-fields, was inexpressible. We were conducted to the quarters of the Lieutenant of the Guard, and there remained until morning. It was at two o'clock, A. M. when we crossed the lines. We had walked nearly seventy-five miles through swamps, woods, and briers, and consequently our feet were nearly used up.

I had cut my boots off my feet the night before, for my feet were wet from the first night of starting, and my boots had contracted to my feet and were punishing me severely, so on Wednesday morning we were without boots or socks, our feet swollen and bruised, even bleeding, and it was with the utmost difficulty that I could walk. Yet we were two of the happiest boys, I suppose, in America at that time. What cared we then whether we had any feet at all or not, for we had our liberty. We took breakfast with Major Wheeling of the Fourth N. Y Cavalry, and Provost Marshal of the District. He treated us with the greatest kindness, and after breakfast sent us in his buggy to Col. Forrest's quarters with a letter of introduction to that officer.

Col. West received us kindly, and gave us stockings and slippers, and in the evening sent us to Yorktown, where we arrived on the night of the great fire and magazine explosion. We had been ordered to report to Gen. Butler at Fortress Monroe, and at Yorktown were furnished transportation by Gen. —— to the fort, with a letter of introduction to Gen. Butler. Immediately on our arrival we went to the General's head-quarters and were shown to his room, in rather a sorry plight to be sure — clothes torn in many places by the briers, and slip-shod, with sore feet. The old General eyed us very closely when we entered. His military eye

ran all over us in a moment. After saluting him, he asked, "Do you wish to see me on business?" Whereupon we gave him our letter from Col. West. After glancing over it he changed instantly. It was not the rigid General Butler of a moment before, for now he grasped our hands, shaking them warmly. After asking us many questions concerning our prisoners, he placed us in the care of the gentlemanly Capt. Puffer, one of his A. D. C's. with orders to furnish us with clothing, transportation and everything else that we needed, which was all faithfully attended to by that officer.

HOW GENERAL McPHERSON WAS KILLED.

A soldier who was near the General at the time he was shot gives the following particulars of the occurrence and the actions of the confederates which preceded it: — "I entered the woods to behold a wounded man whose name is George Reynolds, of the Fifteenth Iowa Fourth Division, Seventeenth Army Corps, and a short distance from him lay General James B. McPherson, suffering intense agony from a fatal wound, a Minie ball having entered the right breast, passed near the heart, and came out near the left side.

I then took my position close to his side and requested him to drink a little cold water I had secured a short time before, and asked the privilege to bathe his temples; to which interrogatories I could elicit no reply, only a faint nod of the head. Occasionally returning to consciousness he would ask me for his hat, which by search I found had been stolen from him, as also his belt. I had not been in this situation over five minutes when a rebel straggler came up, to whom I remarked, "You are a prisoner, are you not?" To which he replied, "No, sir-ee!" and then asked me, "Can you walk? Come along," etc. I gave a negative answer and exhibited a very sore and bandaged leg, all besmeared with blood, which had troubled me of late, and was thus successful in making him believe I was severely wounded.

This was the work of a few moments; when four more rebels came up, and simultaneously two more of our stragglers passed near by. They were taken with the previously mentioned. They then extracted the papers which were in plain view from the General's pocket, took his watch and marine glass, but did not search the remainder of his pockets, nor ask any questions in reference to whom he was nor did we inform them. They acted with civility, considering it a battle-field. They then ordered the wounded man and myself to follow them. We told them we were not able, and if they took us they would have to carry us, etc.; when to my glad astonishment they absconded with their three prisoners, with the aforementioned articles, leaving their two supposed cripples with the General. All this time the rebel shot and shell were crashing with fearful rapidity all around us, in every direction. Several balls lighted within a few feet of the General, scattering the dirt all over him in a complete shower. While the rebels were taking from the General the articles previously mentioned, he sat up and again asked for his hat, which I believe, were the last words he spoke, for his agony was most intense.

After the rebels had gone, it was agreed that I should go in search of an ambulance, while my solitary wounded companion remained with the General. My companion believing that our men were still in front fighting as well as rear, I proceeded in the direction of Atlanta, as near as I can judge, about three-eighths of a mile, when I saw rebel skirmishers not far distant in my front, as also their works; the brush being rather thin, it was difficult to escape; but by creeping back where the brush was more dense, I then ran as best I could until I got back again to the General, when my companion informed me he had just died, but said nothing after I left him. During this interval the woods were thoroughly riddled, and every moment I expected to meet the General's sad fate; but Providence spared me.

A straggler who said he belonged to the Third or Fourth Division, Pioneer Corps, came up and was requested to act as witness. He, it seems, committed the theft.

The first thing we examined was the contents of the wallet, and on opening it saw the gold chains and gold piece, or medal; opening another apartment, we saw a roll of bills, which our new comer instantly grabbed, as he said, to ascertain the contents. Unfolding them, as near as I can recollect, I saw the aforementioned bills. As soon as his eye caught sight of the large bills, he separated them from the smaller ones, and then made the following diabolical proposition, to wit: — Boys, let us equally divide the spoils and say nothing about it. We positively and in the strongest terms refused to be accomplices in such an infernal scheme. He then kept possession of all the large bills, leaving only eight dollars, and ran as fast as his legs could carry him in a westerly course toward the wagon trains.

I looked upon him as a wretch like Judas of old, and could have wished that in his escape he had met with the same fate as he of whom sacred writ informs us, "He burst asunder and all his bowels gushed out." Leaving the guilty culprit with the fruits of his dastardly act, I would remark that fearing capture every moment, and the importance of the General's rescue, was the reason of our not continuing a critical examination of the remaining contents, and making all speed, we proceeded in the direction I entered the woods an hour or more before. Emerging from the woods we bore to the south-west, in which direction we saw wagon-trains and ambulances.

The first ambulance to which we made known our mission refused to go. Proceeding further, we came to two more, when we requested the foremost one to go with us, and seeing three officers riding up toward us, we explained to them our object, when they informed us they were part of his staff and were very anxious to get him. So taking the first ambulance, we piloted them to the spot, and then a most thrilling scene took place that I shall never forget. Looking down

the woods from the ambulance, I saw the rebel skirmishers steadily advancing, and thinking the staff officers were not fully aware of the danger we were all in (as I had intentionally refrained from describing the danger to them previously), I jumped from the ambulance, and to my surprise, confronted an armed rebel.

Seeing we were in desperate circumstances, I rushed to inform the staff officers, who were now carrying his body out of the woods, and I informed them that the rebels were now closing in around us, and the necessity of all who had revolvers being ready to use them. I believe they all drew them, and I endeavored as best I could to assist in carrying his body to the ambulance. We got him in as best we could, under such exciting circumstances (for I was afraid every moment a cannon ball or shell would crush the ambulance or kill the mules), and whirling swiftly around, we drove off at a perfect gallop, with rebel shot and shell and Minie balls hurled in a perfect storm after us. But, fortunately, no one was hurt.

So great was the danger that we had to drive with fearful rapidity nearly three-fourths of a mile before we could properly and comfortably adjust the General's body. I only remember the name of one of these staff officers, and that is Lieutenant Colonel Strong. There was also a Captain and First Lieutenant. I would remark that the officers acted with determined bravery; in fact, all did, and the coolness of my wounded companion was really sublime amidst severe suffering from his arm.

After the rescue we drove to Gen. Sherman's head-quarters. The body was taken out and carried into the house to be examined. Gen. Sherman seemed deeply affected by the sight. My wounded companion was then taken to the nearest hospital of the Twenty-third Corps, by order of the Medical Director. He was wounded by a Minie ball through the left arm just above the elbow. He went through all the exciting circumstances from the time he was wounded to the time he was taken to the hospital before he had it dressed, which must have been nearly five hours. The General was wounded about half-past 12 p. m., and rescued from the rebels about 3 p. m. He lived about one hour after he was wounded.

THE MOCKING BIRD OF RESACA. — A correspondent in Georgia, wrote as follows: — I find in an Atlanta paper the following extravaganza upon a mocking bird at Resaca. It calls to my mind a fact that I had forgotten. At the first advance upon Resaca, on the 9th of May, I remember observing at dusk an unusual number of birds, and as night fell, just as the troops were withdrawing, a grand chorus of whip-poor-wills rang through the forest. Perhaps Resaca has been a favorite home for the songsters of the woods.

"Waverley," the correspondent, who was an eye-witness and participator in the late battles in North Georgia, relates the following pretty incident of the battle of Resaca :

" In the hottest part of the battle of Sunday, a shell came screaming through the air from the works in front of our left. It paused above a point where General Johnston and General Polk were standing, whistled like a top above them, and before exploding whistled half-a-dozen notes clear as a fife to the drum-like rattle of musketry. The din had scarce died away, and the fragments fallen to the ground, when the attention of the party was directed to one of the upper boughs of a tall pine, where a mocking-bird had begun to imitate the whistle of the shell. Neither the roar of cannon, nor the rain of balls could drive this brave bird from its lofty perch. It sat above the battle-field like a little god of war, its blythe tones warbling over the din of arms—

" In profuse strains of unpremeditated art,"

and its stout heart as free as though it swelled to the breezy winds of peace in the summer woods. Thou Touchstone of the battle-field, mocking the very air of death and pouring out a cheery canticle for the slain, who are happy in dying for the land they love, thou art the true type of the great Confederate heart. Be it like thine, as bold and free. May it swell as it is pressed, and grow strong as it hurls back the vandal and invader. May it stand upon its own door-sill, as that gallant bird stood upon the bough of the pine, and trill a chant of defiance in the face of danger, and though despair span its bony fingers about its throat, may its armies take a lesson from thy pluck, thou valiant mocking-bird, and sing in the breach and shout on the hills, to the music of Minie ball and shrapnell, never doubting, never daunted, defying the power of the world, and obedient only to the God of the universe. For he who dies in the front dies in the love of the Lord, and there is not a sentiment truer for the soldier than that the brave who perish in the cause of liberty are thrice blessed above the lazy sons of peace.

" Not man nor monarch half so proud,
As he whose flag becomes his shroud."

A TOUCHING INCIDENT OF THE WAR. — An interesting anecdote is related of Franklin, who, it is alleged, in order to test the parental instinct existing between mother and child, introduced himself as a belated traveller to his mother's house after an absence of many years. Her house being filled with more illustrious guests than the unknown stranger, she refused him shelter, and would have turned him from her door. Hence he concluded that this so-called parental instinct was a pleasant delusive belief, not susceptible of proof.

The opposite of this occurred in Washington. In one of the fierce engagements with the rebels near Mechanicsville, a young lieutenant of a Rhode Island battery had his right foot so shattered by a fragment of shell that, on reaching Washington after one of those horrible ambulance rides, and a journey of a week's duration, he was obliged to undergo amputation of the leg. He telegraphed home hundreds of miles away that all was going well, and with a soldier's fortitude composed himself to bear his sufferings alone.

Unknown to him, however, his mother, one of those dear reserves of the army, hastened up to join the main force. She reached the city at midnight, and the nurses would have kept her from him until morning. One sat by his side fanning him as he slept, her hand on the feeble fluctuating pulsations which foreboded sad results. But what woman's heart could resist the pleadings of a mother then ? In the darkness she was finally allowed to glide in and take the place at his side. She touched his pulse as the nurse had done ; not a word had been spoken ; but the sleeping boy opened his eyes and said, " That feels like my mother's hand ; who is this beside me ? It is my mother ; turn up the gas and let me see mother ! "

The two dear faces met in one long, joyful sobbing embrace, and the fondness pent up in each heart sobbed and panted, and wept forth its expression.

The gallant fellow, just twenty-one, his leg amputated on the last day of his three years' service, underwent operation after operation, and at last, when death drew nigh, and he was told by tearful friends that it only remained to make him comfortable, said, " he had looked death in the face too many times to be afraid now," and died as gallantly as did the men of the Cumberland.

YE LONDONNE TIMES CORRESPONDENTE HIS BULLE RUNNE LETTRRE.

" BULLE RUNNE, July ye twenty-firste ;
Welle, here am I, alle righte,
And just returned from wytnessinge
Ye famouse Bulle Runne fighte.

" There was no fighte, there was no Bulle,
Unlesse itte mighte bee mee ;
And I the onlie manne to runne,
At leaste thatte I could see.

" I satte me on a dystante hylle,
Fulle fyfteene myles awaye,
Thatte I mighte see ye soldierees kille,
Iffe anie came mye waye.

" I hadde a branne newe telescope,
And a bottelle of olde Porte,
Wytthe sandewytches, inne case I founde
Ye provenderre ranne shorte.

" Ande soone I sawe a monstrouse crowde
Fulle fyfteene myles awaye,
And cannones there were roaringe loude,
And muskettes inne fulle playe.

" I satte mee there fromme earlie dawne
Untille ye settynge sunne,
And thenne I thoughte thatte certaynellie
Ye battelle muste bee done.

" I sawe no fighte, butte I muste write
  As iffe I sawe itte alle,
Thoughe reallie I do believe,
  Therre was no fighte atte alle.

" And thysse itte is mye judgemente,
  Afterre carefulle studie mayde,
Thatte one syde is a cowarde,
  And ye otherre is afrayde.

" I wisshe you woulde lette mee come home —
  I'm tyred of alle thysse bustle ;
I wysshe no more ye worlde to roame,
  Youres truly, BILLIE RUSSELLE."

INCIDENTS OF KENESAW. — It was an imposing scene ! A rebel regiment, their bayonets glistening in the slanting rays of the setting sun, were having a dress-parade on the summit of the Kenesaw Mountain. Below were their rifle-pits, and their *camarades d'armes* occupying them.

A courier dashed up ; he hands the adjutant a document. It is an order from Johnston, announcing to the troops that Sherman had brought his army so far south that his line of supplies was longer than he could hold ; that he was too far from his base — just where their commanding general wished to get him ; that a part of their army would hold the railroad, thirty miles north of the Etoway, and that the great railroad bridge at Alatoona, had been completely destroyed ; that in a few days Sherman would be out of supplies because he could bring no more trains through by the railroad. They were urged to maintain a bold front, and in a few days the Yankees would be forced to retreat. Breathless silence evinces the attention which every word of the order receives, as the adjutant reads. Cheers are about to be given, when hark ! loud whistles from Sherman's cars, at Big Shanty, interrupt them. The number of whistles increase. Alatoona, Ackworth, and Big Shanty depots resound with them. Supplies have arrived. The effect can easily be imagined. The illustration was so apt — the commentary so appropriate — that it was appreciated at the instant. " Bully for the base of supplies !" " Bully for the long line !" " Three cheers for the big bridge !" " Here's your Yankee cars !" " There's Sherman's rations !" Bedlam was loose along their line for a short time.

There is a tree in front of General Harrow's Fourth Division, Fifteenth Army Corps, Sherman's army, which is called the fatal tree. Eight men were shot, one after another, as soon as they advanced to the ill-fated tree to take a secure position behind its huge trunk. Seven men were shot, when a board was placed there with the word "dangerous" chalked upon it. The rebels shot the guide-post into fragments, and a sergeant took his place behind the unsuspecting tree. In less than two minutes two Minie balls pierced the sergeant's body, and he fell, the eighth martyr beneath the shadow of the tree of death.

A FAIR DIVISION. — One of those biting cold mornings, while the armies of Meade and Lee were staring at each other across the little rivulet known as Mine Run, when moments appeared to be hours, and hours days, so near at hand seemed the deadly strife, a solitary sheep leisurely walked along the run on the rebel side. A rebel vidette fired and killed the sheep, and droping his gun, advanced to remove the prize. In an instant he was covered by a gun in the hands of a Union vidette, who said, " Divide is the word or you are a dead Johnny." This proposition was assented to, and there, between the two skirmish lines, Mr. Rebel skinned the sheep, took one half, and moved back to his post, when his challenger, in turn dropping his gun, crossed the run, got the other half of the sheep, and again assumed the duties of his post amid the cheers of his comrades, who expected to help him eat it. Of the hundreds of hostile men arrayed against each other on either bank of that run, not one dared to violate the truce intuitively agreed upon by these two soldiers.

A ROMANCE OF THE WAR. — The following simple and unvarnished story has hardly a parallel in the page of fiction. Its strict truth is beyond question :

Near Murfreesboro, June 28, 1864. — The original of the following letter is in my possession. The events so graphically narrated transpired in Overton County, Tennessee. I knew Dr. Sadler from a small boy. The men who murdered him were noted guerillas, and killed him for no personal grudge, but on account of his sentiments. I have no personal acquaintance with the young lady ; but have the highest authority for stating that she is a pure, high-minded girl, the daughter of a plain farmer in moderate circumstances. It only remains to state that Petect was killed January 30, and Gordenhire February 4, 1864, so that the vengeance they invoked has overtaken all three of the murderers of M. G. Sadler.

JOHN W. BOWEN.

MARTIN'S CREEK, April 30, 1864.

Major Clift, — According to promise I now attempt to give you a statement of the reasons why I killed Turner, and a brief history of the affair. Dr. Sadler had, for two years previous to his death, seemed equally as near and dear to me as a brother, and for several months nearer than any person, — my parents not excepted. If he had not, I never would have done what I did, promise to be his.

The men who killed him had threatened his life often because he was a Union man ; they said he should not live ; and after taking the oath they arrested him, but Lieutenant Oakley released him at pa's gate. He stayed at pa's till bed-time, and I warned him of the danger he was in ; told him I had heard his life threatened that day, and that I felt confident he would be killed if he did not leave the neighborhood, and stay off until these men became reconciled.

He promised to go; said he had some business at Carthage, and would leave the neighborhood that night, or by daylight next morning, and we felt assured he had gone. But for some unaccountable reason he did not leave. About 3 o'clock, P. M., next day, news came to me, at Mr. Johnson's, where I had gone with my brother, that Dr. Sadler was killed. I had met Peteet, Gordenhire, and Turner on the road, and told my brother there that they were searching for Dr. Sadler to kill him. Sure enough they went to the house where he was, and, strange to me, after his warning, he permitted them to come in. They met him apparently perfectly friendly, and said they had come to get some brandy from Mr. Yelton, which they obtained, and immediately after drinking, they all three drew their pistols and commenced firing at Sadler. He drew his, but it was snatched away from him. He then drew his knife, which was also taken from him. He then ran round the house and up a stairway, escaping out of their sight. They followed, however, and searched till they found him, and brought him down and laid him on a bed, mortally wounded. He requested some of his people to send for Dr. Dillin to dress his wounds. It is strange to me, why, but Sadler's friends had all left the room, when Turner went up, and put his pistol against his temples, and shot him through the head. They all rejoiced like demons, and stood by till he had made his last struggle. They then pulled his eyes open, and asked him in a loud voice if he was dead. They then took his horse and saddle, and pistols, and robbed him of all his money, and otherwise insulted and abused his remains.

Now, for this, I resolved to have revenge. Peteet and Gordenhire being dead, I determined to kill Turner, and to seek an early opportunity of doing it. But I kept that resolution to myself, knowing that if I did not I would be prevented. I went prepared, but never could get to see him.

On the Thursday before I killed him, I learned he was preparing to leave for Louisiana, and I determined he should not escape if I could prevent it. I arose that morning, and fixed my pistols so that they would be sure fire, and determined to hunt him all that day. Then, sitting down, I wrote a few lines; so that, if I fell, my friends might know where to look for my remains. I took my knitting, as if I were going to spend the day with a neighbor living on the road toward Turner's. It rained very severely, making the roads muddy, so that I became fatigued, and concluded to go back and ride the next day, on Saturday. But ma rode my horse on Saturday, and left me to keep house. We had company Sunday P. M., so that I could not leave; but the company left about noon, and I started again in search of Turner. I went to his house, about two-and-a-half miles from pa's. I found no one at home, and therefore sat down to await his return. After waiting perhaps one-and-a-half hours, a man came to see Turner, and not finding him, he said he supposed he and his wife had gone to Mrs. Christian's, his sister-in-law, who lived about one-half mile distant.

I concluded to go there and see, fearing the man would tell him I was waiting for him, and he would escape me. I found him there, and a number of other persons, including his wife, and her father and mother. Most of them left when I entered the house. I asked Mrs. Christian if Turner was gone. She pointed to him at the gate, just leaving. I looked at the clock, and it was 4-30 o'clock, P. M. I then walked out into the yard, and, as Turner was starting, called to him to stop. He turned, and saw I was preparing to shoot him; he started to run. I fired at the distance of about twelve paces, and missed. I fired again as quick as possible, and hit him in the back of the head, and he fell on his face and knees. I fired again and hit him in the back, and he fell on his right side. I fired twice more, only one of these shots taking effect. By this time I was within five steps of him, and stood and watched him till he was dead, and then turned round and walked toward the house, and met Mrs. Christian and her sister, his wife, coming out. They asked me what I did that for. My response was, "You know what that man did the 13th of December last, — murdered a dear friend of mine. I have been determined to do this deed ever since, and I never shall regret it." They said no more to me, but commenced hallooing and blowing a horn. I got my horse out and started home, where I shall stay or leave when I choose, going where I please, and saying what I please. L. J. W.

GENERAL SUMNER AT ANTIETAM. — A story is told of the veteran Sumner at the battle of Antietam. His son, young Captain Sumner, a youth of twenty-one, was on his staff. The old man calmly stood, amidst a storm of shot and shells, and turned to send him through a doubly raging fire, upon a mission of duty. He might never see his boy again, but his country claimed his life, and, as he looked upon his young brow, he grasped his hand, encircled him in his arms, and fondly kissed him. "Good-by, Sammy," "Good-by, father," and the youth, mounting his horse, rode gayly on the message. He returned unharmed, and again his hand was grasped with a cordial "How d'ye do, Sammy?" answered by a grasp of equal affection. The scene was touching to those around.

INCIDENT OF LOOKOUT MOUNTAIN. — It was near sundown when General T. J. Wood, whose conduct all through the three days' battle marked him as one of the ablest leaders of the national armies, rode along the lines of his superb division. Loud shouts of enthusiasm everywhere greeted his appearance, until at last his feelings, no longer controllable, broke out in a speech:

"'Brave men!' said he, 'you were ordered to go forward and take the rifle-pits at the foot of these hills; you did so; and then, by the Eternal! without orders, you pushed forward and took all the enemy's works on top! Here is a fine chance for having you all court-martialled! and I myself will appear as the principal witness against you, unless you promise me one thing.'

" ' What is it? what is it?' laughingly inquired his men.

" ' It is,' resumed the General, ' that as you are now in possession of these works, you will continue against all opposition of Bragg, Johnston, Jeff. Davis and the devil, steadfastly to hold them!'

" At the conclusion of this speech, the enthusiasm of the soldiers knew no bounds. They left the ranks and crowded round their General. ' We promise! we promise!' they cried. And, amid such exclamations as, ' Of course we'll hold them!' ' Let any one try to take them from us!' ' Bully for you!' ' Three cheers for old Wood,' the gallant officer rode off the field."

"I FIGHTS MIT SIGEL!"

BY GRANT P. ROBINSON.

I MET him again, he was trudging along,
  His knapsack with chickens was swelling;
He'd " Blenkered " these dainties, and thought it no
    wrong,
  From some secessionist's dwelling.
" What regiment's yours? and under whose flag
  Do you fight?" said I, touching his shoulder;
Turning slowly around he smilingly said,
  For the thought made him stronger and bolder;
        " I fights mit Sigel."

The next time I saw him his knapsack was gone,
  His cap and canteen were missing,
Shell, shrapnell, and grape, and the swift rifle-ball
  Around him and o'er him were hissing.
How are you, my friend, and where have you been,
  And for what and for whom are you fighting?
He said, as a shell from the enemy's gun
  Sent his arm and his musket a "kiting,"
        " I fights mit Sigel."

And once more I saw him and knelt by his side,
  His life-blood was rapidly flowing;
I whispered of home, wife, children, and friends,
  The bright land to which he was going;
And have you no word for the dear ones at home,
  The " wee one," the father or mother?
" Yaw! yaw!" said he, " tell them! oh! tell them
    I fights "—
  Poor fellow! he thought of no other—
        " I fights mit Sigel."

We scraped out a grave, and he dreamlessly sleeps
  On the banks of the Shenandoah River;
His home and his kindred alike are unknown,
  His reward in the hands of the Giver.
We placed a rough board at the head of his grave,
  " And we left him alone in his glory,"
But on it we marked ere we turned from the spot,
  The little we knew of his story—
        " I fights mit Sigel."

ARMY SIGNALS. — This most interesting and useful arm of the military service is perhaps, less heard of by the public than any other; and its

invaluable labors, as well as its frequent imminent perils, are alike unrecorded, and, therefore, unappreciated. The signal officer who would bring late and full news to the commanding General must undergo not a little fatigue and hardship. He must climb high trees to watch the enemy; he must penetrate through tangled thickets and forests, in search of eligible stations; he must climb the sides of steep and rugged mountains, and his bright and showy flag never fails to attract the rebel sharpshooter's fire when he is in reach, which he must often be to secure a good post, or observe the enemy.

When once a station is established, his flag must never droop by day nor his torch grow dim by night, till he has orders from his chief to abandon his post for a new one. And yet so great is the mystery with which he must enshroud his art, so profoundly secret must he keep the weighty messages and orders confided to him, and so silent are his operations, that the world and even the army know little about him. He alone is proof against the wiles of those "universal walking interrogation-points," the correspondents, though he, above all others, is the man whom they would delight to be permitted to "use." But he has his reward for all this. In the clear upper air where he dwells, he sees, as with a hawk's eye, the whole great drama played out beneath him; he sees the long lines of men deployed through the valleys, and knows where they go, and why; his eyes feast upon the field of battle, where the columns of attack rush impetuously down a wooded slope, across an open field, and up into another piece of wood, and all is clear to him and intelligible, while, to others who must grovel on the ground, there is nothing but an exasperating muddle.

Signal stations are of two kinds; reflecting stations and stations of observation; the former for transmitting dispatches, the latter for watching the enemy and communicating the results to the commander. Both are constructed on the same principles, and employ the same instruments. The latter are few and simple. The flag is made of different colors, to contrast with the line of the background, white, black, or red. The one usually employed is but four feet square; for the largest distances it is made six feet square, and mounted on a third joint of staff to give it wider range. The marine glass is used for scanning the horizon rapidly, and making general observations; the telescope for reading signals at a great distance, and observing fixed points minutely. Besides these there is a certain mysterious pasteboard disc, stamped with a circle of figures, and a sliding interior one of letters corresponding to each. This is the key and clew of the whole matter, and to the uninitiated is, of course, impenetrable.

When a message is about to be sent, the flagman takes his station upon some elevated object, and "calls" the station with which he desires to communicate by waving the flag or torch slowly to and fro. The operator, seated at the glass, watches closely the distant flag, and as soon as it responds by dipping, he is ready to send his dispatch. Holding the written message before him, he calls out to the flagman certain numbers, each figure or combination of figures standing for a letter. The flagman indicates each separate figure by an ingenious combination of a few very simple motions. For instance, one stroke of the flag from a perpendicular to a right horizontal, indicates one figure; a stroke to the left horizontal, indicates another; a stroke executing a half circle, another, &c. After each motion indicating a figure, the flag returns always to a perpendicular. There are a few syllables which are indicated by a single stroke of the flag; otherwise the word must be spelled out letter by letter. Experienced signal officers, however, employ many abreviations by omitting vowels, &c., so that scarcely a single word, unless a very unused one, is spelled out in full.

When a message is being received, the operator sits at the glass, with the flagman near to record it. This the operator then interprets, for not even the General himself is in the secret, and by supplying the omitted vowels, &c., makes out an intelligible piece of the king's English.

The rapidity with which all this is executed by experienced operators is astonishing. The flag is kept in such rapid motion that the eye of the inexpert can scarcely follow, and his wonder is increased by being told that the reader, of whom he cannot see the slightest indication with his naked eye, is ten or twelve miles away. An ordinary message of a few lines is despatched in ten minutes; a whole page of foolscap occupies about thirty minutes in its transmission. Officers who have long worked together, and are intimately acquainted with each other's abbreviations and peculiar expressions, can improve upon even this speed.

The distance also through which signals can be transmitted, without an intermediate station, is surprising. Captain Leonard, chief signal officer of the Fourth Corps, sent despatches regularly from Ringgold to Summerville, on Lookout Mountain, a distance of eighteen miles. Lieut. William Reynolds, formerly of the Tenth Corps, signalled from the deck of a gunboat twenty miles into Port Royal harbor. N. Daniels was sent by the Secretary of War, to Maryland Heights to give information of the enemy's movements, and he succeeded in sending messages rapidly over the extraordinary distance of twenty-four miles —from the Heights to Sugar-loaf Mountain —four miles from Frederick. But these instances required remarkably favorable conditions of the atmosphere, locality, &c. Ordinarily, messages were not sent a greater distance than six or eight miles.

AN ANECDOTE OF THE WILDERNESS. — In the battles of the Wilderness, the Twentieth Massachusetts regiment was in the thick of the fight, and one color-bearer after another was shot down almost as fast as the men could be replaced. But such was the eagerness to keep the flag aloft

that at one time, two men, — Irishmen — caught hold of the standard at once, as it was about to fall, and struggled for it. Just then a shot struck the staff, cutting it in two, and leaving one man with the flag, and the other with the broken stick. "Bedad!" said the man with the short end of the staff, "the rebels have decided for us this time!" and went to loading and firing again, as coolly as if nothing had happened.

AN INCIDENT OF ROCKY FACE. — Brigadier General Morgan related the following incident that occurred on his line of operations. While his brigade occupied the gap, between Oak Knob and Rocky Face, a corporal of Company I, Sixtieth Illinois, broke from the line, and under cover of projecting ledges got up within twenty feet of a squad of rebels on the summit. Taking shelter from the sharpshooters, he called out:

"I say, rebs, don't you want to hear Old Abe's amnesty proclamation read?"

"Yes! yes!" was the unanimous cry; "give us the ape's proclamation."

"Attention!" commanded the corporal, and in a clear and resonant voice, he read the amnesty proclamation to the rebels, beneath the cannon planted by rebel hands to destroy the fabric of government established by our fathers. When he arrived at those passages of the proclamation where the negro was referred to, he was interrupted by cries of "None of your d—d abolitionism — look out for rocks!" And down over his hiding-place descended a shower of stones and rocks. Having finished the reading, the corporal asked:

"Well, rebs, how do you like the terms? Will you hear it again?"

"Not to-day, you bloody Yank. Now crawl down in a hurry and we wont fire," was the response; and the daring corporal descended and rejoined his command, which had distinctly heard all that passed.

THE DEATH AND BURIAL OF GEN. J. E. B. STUART. — No incident of mortality since the fall of the great Jackson, has occasioned more painful regret than this, said the Richmond Examiner of May 13, 1864. Major J. E. B. Stuart, the model of Virginia cavaliers and dashing chieftain, whose name was a terror to the enemy, and familiar as a household word in two continents, is dead, struck down by a bullet from the dastardly foe, and the whole Confederacy mourns him. He breathed out his gallant spirit resignedly, and in the full possession of all his remarkable faculties of mind and body at twenty-two minutes to eight o'clock, Thursday night, at the residence of Dr. Brewer, a relative, on Grace street, in the presence of Drs. Brewer, Garnett, Gibson, and Fontaine of the General's staff, Rev. Messrs. Peterkin and Keppler, and a circle of sorrow-stricken comrades and friends.

We learn from the physicians in attendance upon the General that his condition during the day was very changeable, with occasional delirium, and other unmistakable symptoms of speedy dissolution. In the moments of delirium the General's mind wandered, and like the immortal Jackson, (whose spirit, we trust, his has joined), in the lapse of reason his faculties were busied with the details of his command. He reviewed, in broken sentences, all his glorious campaigns around McClellan's rear on the Peninsula, beyond the Potomac, and upon the Rapidan, quoting from his orders and issuing new ones to his couriers, with a last injunction to " make haste."

About noon Thursday, President Davis visited his bedside, and spent some fifteen minutes in the dying chamber of his favorite chieftain. The President, taking his hand, said, " General, how do you feel ? " He replied, " Easy, but willing to die, if God and my country think I have fulfilled my destiny and done my duty." As evening approached the General's delirium increased and his mind again wandered to the battle-fields over which he had fought, then off to wife and children, and off again to the front. A telegraphic message had been sent for his wife, who was in the country, with the injunction to make all haste as the General was dangerously wounded. Some thoughtless, but unauthorized person, thinking probably to spare his wife pain, altered the dispatch to " slightly wounded," and it was thus she received it, and did not make that haste which she otherwise would have done to reach his side.

As evening wore on the paroxysms of pain increased, and mortification set in rapidly. Though suffering the greatest agony at times, the General was calm, and applied to the wound, with his own hand, the ice intended to relieve the pain. During the evening he asked Dr. Brewer how long he thought he could live, and whether it was possible for him to survive through the night. The doctor, knowing he did not desire to be buoyed by false hopes, told him frankly that death, the last enemy, was rapidly approaching. The General nodded, and said, " I am resigned if it be God's will; but I would like to live to see my wife. But God's will be done." Several times he roused up and asked if she had come.

To the doctor, who sat holding his wrist, and counting the fleeting, weakening pulse, he remarked, " Doctor, I suppose I am going fast now. It will soon be over. But God's will be done. I hope I have fulfilled my destiny to my country and my duty to my God."

At half-past seven o'clock it was evident to the physicians that death was setting its clammy seal upon the brave, open brow of the General, and they told him so — asked if he had any last messages to give. The General, with a mind perfectly clear and possessed, then made disposition of his staff and personal effects. To Mrs. General R. E. Lee he directed that the golden spurs be given as a dying memento of his love and esteem of her husband. To his staff officers he gave his horses. So particular was he in small things, even in the dying hour, that he emphatically exhibited and illustrated the ruling passion strong in death. To one of his staff, who was a heavy-built man, he said, " You had better take the

larger horse ; he will carry you better." Other mementos he disposed of in a similar manner. To his young son, he left his glorious sword.

His worldly matters closed, the eternal interests of his soul engaged his mind. Turning to the Rev. Mr. Peterkin, of the Episcopal Church, and of which he was an exemplary member, he asked him to sing the hymn commencing :

> " Rock of ages cleft for me,
> Let me hide myself in thee,"

he joining with all the voice his strength would permit. He then joined in prayer with the ministers. To the doctor he again said, " I am going fast now ; I am resigned ; God's will be done." Thus died General J. E. B. Stuart.

His wife reached the house of death and mourning about 10 o'clock on Thursday night, one hour and a half after dissolution, and was, of course, plunged into the greatest grief by the announcement that death had intervened between the announcement of the wounding of the General and her arrival.

The funeral services preliminary to the consignment to the grave of the remains of General Stuart, were conducted yesterday afternoon in St. James' Episcopal church, corner of Marshall and Fifth streets, Rev. Dr. Peterkin, rector. The *cortege* reached the church about five o'clock without music or military escort, the Public Guard being absent on duty. The church was already crowded with citizens. The metallic case, containing the corpse, was borne into the church and up the center aisle to the altar, the organ pealing a solemn funeral dirge and anthem by the choir.

Among the pall-bearers we noticed Brigadier-General John H. Winder, General George W. Randolph, General Joseph R. Anderson, Brigadier-General Lawton, and Commodore Forrest.

Among the congregation appeared President Davis, General Bragg, General Ransom, and other civil and military officials in Richmond. A portion of the funeral services, according to the Episcopal Church, was read by Rev. Dr. Peterkin, assisted by other ministers, concluding with singing and prayer.

The body was then borne forth to the hearse in waiting, decorated with black plumes, and drawn by four white horses. The organ pealed its slow, solemn music as the body was borne to the entrance, and while the *cortege* was forming, the congregation standing by with heads uncovered. Several carriages in the line were occupied by the members of the deceased General's staff, and relatives. From the church the *cortege* moved to Hollywood Cemetery, where the remains were deposited in a vault; the concluding portion of the service read by Dr. Minnigerode, of St. Paul's Church, — and all that was mortal of the dead hero was shut in from the gaze of men.

Dr. Brewer, the brother-in-law of Gen. Stuart, has furnished us with some particulars obtained from the General's own lips, of the manner in which he came by his wound.

He had formed a line of skirmishers near the Yellow Tavern, when, seeing a brigade preparing to charge on his left, Gen. Stuart and his staff dashed down the line to form troops to repel the charge. About this time the Yankees came thundering down upon the General and his small escort. Twelve shots were fired at the General at short range, the Yankees evidently recognizing his well-known person. The General wheeled upon them with the natural bravery which had always characterized him, and discharged six shots at his assailants. The last of the shots fired at him struck the General in the left side of the stomach. He did not fall, knowing he would be captured if he did, and, nerving himself in his seat, wheeled his horse's head and rode for the protection of his lines. Before he reached them his wound overcame him, and he fell, or was helped from his saddle by one of his ever-faithful troopers, and carried to a place of security. Subsequently, he was brought to Richmond in an ambulance. The immediate cause of death was mortification of the stomach, induced by the flow of blood from the kidneys and intestines into the cavity of the stomach.

General Stuart was about thirty-five years of age. He leaves a widow and two children. His oldest offspring, a sprightly boy, died a year ago while he was battling for his country on the Rappahannock. When telegraphed that his child was dying he sent the reply, "I must leave my child in the hands of God; my country needs me here; I cannot come."

Thus has passed away, amid the exciting scenes of this revolution, one of the bravest and most dashing cavaliers that the "Old Dominion" has ever given birth to. Long will her sons recount the story of his achievements, and mourn his untimely departure. Like the hero of the old song,—

"Of all our knights he was the flower,
  Compagnon de la Marjolaine;
Of all our knights he was the flower,
  Always gay."

HOME LIFE IN THE SOUTH.—"There are many little things in which our daily life is changed," said the wife of a Confederate officer, —"many luxuries cut off from the table which we have forgotten to miss. Our mode of procuring necessaries is very different and far more complicated. The condition of our currency has brought about many curious results; for instance, I have just procured leather, for our negro-shoes, by exchanging tallow for it, of which we had a quantity from some fine beeves, fattened and killed upon the place.

"I am now bargaining, with a factory up the country, to exchange pork and lard, with them, for blocks of yarn, to weave negro clothes; and not only negro-clothing I have woven, I am now dyeing thread to weave homespun for myself and daughters. I am ravelling up, or having ravelled, all the old scraps of fine worsteds and dark silks, to spin thread for gloves, for the General and self, which gloves I am to knit. These home-knit gloves and these homespun dresses will look much neater and nicer than you would suppose. My daughters and I being in want of under garments, I sent a quantity of lard to the Macon factory, and received in return fine unbleached calico,—a pound of lard paying for a yard of cloth. They will not sell their cloth for money. This unbleached calico my daughters and self are now making up for ourselves. You see some foresight is necessary to provide for the necessaries of life.

"If I were to describe the cutting and altering of old things to make new, which now perpetually go on, I should far outstep the limits of a letter, —perhaps I have done so already,—but I thought this sketch would amuse you, and give you some idea of our Confederate ways and means of living and doing. At Christmas I sent presents to my relations in Savannah, and instead of the elegant trifles I used to give at that season, I bestowed as follows: several bushels of meal, peas, bacon, lard, eggs, sausages, soap (home-made), rope, string, and a coarse basket! all which articles, I am assured, were most warmly welcomed, and more acceptable than jewels and silks would have been. To all of this we are so familiarized that we laugh at these changes in our ways of life, and keep our regrets for graver things.

"The photographs of your children I was so happy to see. You would have smiled to have heard my daughters divining the present fashion from the style of dress in the likenesses. You must know that, amid all the woes of the Southern Confederacy, her women still feel their utter ignorance of the fashions, whenever they have a new dress to make up or an old one to renovate. I imagine that when our intercourse with the rest of mankind is revived we shall present a singular aspect; but what we shall have lost in external appearance I trust we shall have gained in sublimer virtues and more important qualities."

THE LAST WORDS OF COLONEL STONE.—Much has been said — but not too much — in praise of Col. Newton Stone, late commander of the Vermont Second, who fell in the second day's fight in the Wilderness. He was first wounded in the leg, and conveyed to the rear; and, after having his wound dressed, requested to be placed upon his horse, which was done; when he immediately rode to the front and took his position at the head of his regiment, amid the cheers of his men, whom he addressed briefly as follows, —

"Well, boys, this is rough work; but I have done as I told you I wished you to do, not to leave for a slight wound, but remain just as long as you could do any good; I am here to do as long as I can." He then rode along the line, speaking a word of good cheer to every company, and, as he halted to address Company B, a rifle-ball pierced his head, and he fell from his horse a corpse. At that moment, the regiment was forced back and the body of their Colonel was captured, but was immediately re-taken.

"PICCIOLA."

It was a sergeant old and gray,
  Well singed and bronzed from siege and pillage,
Went tramping in an army's wake,
  Along the turnpike of the village.

For days and nights the winding host
  Had through the little place been marching,
And ever loud the rustics cheered,
  Till ev'ry throat was hoarse and parching.

The squire and farmer, maid and dame,
  All took the sight's electric stirring,
And hats were waved, and staves were sung,
  And 'kerchiefs white were countless whirling.

They only saw a gallant show
  Of heroes stalwart under banners,
And in the fierce heroic glow
  'Twas theirs to yield but wild hosannas.

The sergeant heard the shrill hurrahs,
  Where he behind in step was keeping;
But glancing down beside the road
  He saw a little maid sit weeping.

"And how is this?" he gruffly said,
  A moment pausing to regard her;
"Why weepest thou, my little chit?"
  And then she only cried the harder.

"And how is this my little chit,"
  The sturdy trooper straight repeated,
"When all the village cheers us on,
  That you, in tears, apart are seated?"

"We march two hundred thousand strong!
  And that's a sight my baby beauty,
To quicken silence into song,
  And glorify the soldier's duty."

"It's very, very grand, I know,"
  The little maid gave soft replying;
"And father, mother, brother, too,
  All say 'hurrah' while I am crying."

"But think — O, Mr. Soldier, think,
  How many little sisters' brothers
Are going all away to fight,
  Who may be *killed* as well as others!"

"Why, bless thee, child," the sergeant said,
  His brawny hand her curls caressing,
"'Tis left for little ones like you
  To find that war's not all a blessing."

And, "bless thee!" once again he cried;
  Then cleared his throat and looked indignant,
And marched away with wrinkled brow
  To stop the straggling tear benignant.

And still the ringing shouts went up
  From doorway, thatch, and fields of tillage;
The pall behind the standard seen
  By one alone, of all the village.

The oak and cedar bend and writhe
  When roars the wind through gap and braken;
But 'tis the tenderest reed of all
  That trembles first when earth is shaken.

THE CRUELTIES OF WAR. — In the month of January, 1863, at Laurel, N. C., near the Tennessee border, all the salt was seized for distribution by Confederate Commissioners. Salt was selling at seventy-five to one hundred dollars a sack. The Commissioners declared that the "Tories" should have none, and positively refused to give Union men their portion of the quantity to be distributed in that vicinity. This palpable injustice roused the Union men, they assembled together and determined to seize their proportion of the salt by force. They did so, taking at Marshall, N. C., what they deemed to be their share, and which had been withheld from them, simply because they adhered with unconquerable devotion to the government of their fathers.

Immediately afterward the Sixty-fifth N. C. regiment, under command of Lieut. Col. Jas. Keith, was ordered to Laurel, to arrest the offenders.

L. M. Allen was Colonel of the regiment, but had been suspended for six months for crime and drunkenness. Many of the men engaged in the salt seizure left their homes. Those who did not participate in it became the sufferers. Among those arrested were Joseph Wood, about sixty years of age; Day Shelton, sixty; James Shelton, fifty; Roddy Shelton, forty-five; Ellison King, forty; Halen Moore, forty; Wade Moore, thirty-five; Isaiah Shelton, fifteen; Wm. Shelton, twelve; James Medcalf, ten; Jasper Channel, fourteen; Sam Shelton, nineteen, and his brother aged seventeen, sons of Lifus Shelton, — in all thirteen men and boys. Nearly all of them declared they were innocent, and had taken no part in appropriating the salt. They begged for a trial, asserting that they could prove their innocence.

Col. Allen who was with his troops, but not in command, told them they should have a trial but that they would be taken to Tennessee for that purpose. They bid farewell to their wives, daughters and sisters, directing them to procure the witnesses and bring them to the Court in Tennessee, where they supposed their trial would take place. Alas! how little they dreamed what a fate awaited them! The poor fellows had proceeded but a few miles when they were turned from the road into a gorge in the mountain, and halted. Without any warning of what was to be done with them, five of them were ordered to kneel down. Ten paces in front of these five a file of soldiers were placed with loaded muskets. The terrible reality flashed upon the minds of the doomed patriots.

Old man Wood (sixty years of age,) cried out: "For God's sake men, you are not going to shoot us? If you are going to murder us, give us at least time to pray." Col. Allen was reminded of his promise to give them a trial. They were informed that Allen had no authority; that Keith was in command; and that there was no time for praying. — The order was given to fire; the old man and boys put their hands to their faces and rent the air with agonizing cries of despair; the soldiers wavered and hesitated to obey the command. Keith said, if they did not fire instantly, he would make them change places with the prisoners.—The soldiers raised their guns, the victims shuddered convulsively, the word fire was given and the five men fell pierced with rebel bullets. Old man Wood and Shelton were shot in the head, and their brains scattered upon the ground, and they died, without a struggle. The other three lived only a few minutes.

Five others were ordered to kneel, among them little Billy Shelton, a mere child, only twelve years old. He implored the men not to shoot him in the face.—"You have killed my father and brothers," said he, "you have shot my father in the face; do not shoot me in the face." He covered his face with his hands. The soldiers received the order to fire, and five more fell. Poor little Billy was wounded in both arms. He ran to an officer, clasped him around the legs, and besought him to spare his life. "You have killed my old father and my three brothers; you have shot me in both arms—I forgive you all this—I can get well. Let me go home to my mother and sisters." What a heart of adamant the man must have had who could disregard such an appeal! The little boy was dragged back to the place of execution; again the terrible word, "fire!" was given, and he fell dead, eight balls having entered his body. The remaining three were murdered in the same manner. Those in whom life was not entirely extinct, the heartless officers dispatched with their pistols. A hole was then dug, and the thirteen bodies were pitched into it.

The grave was scarcely large enough; some of the bodies lay about the ground. A wretch, named Sergeant N. B. D. Jay, a Virginian, but attached to a Tennessee company of the Sixty-fifth North Carolina regiment, jumped upon the bleeding bodies, and said to some of the men: "Pat Juba for me while I dance the damned scoundrels down to and through hell." The grave was covered lightly with earth, and the next day when the wives and families of the murdered men heard of their fate, searched for, and found their grave, the hogs had rooted up one man's body, and eaten his head off. Oh, heavens! what must have been the agony of their wives and children on beholding that sight!—When the awful reality burst upon them, what great drops of affliction must have oozed from their bleeding hearts! Yet all this was done in the cause of freedom! "O Liberty! what crimes are committed in thy name!"

Captain Moorley, in charge of a cavalry force, and Col. Thomas, in command of a number of Indians, accompanied Keith's men. These proceeded to Tennessee; Keith's men returned to Laurel, and were instructed to say that the cavalry had taken the prisoners with them to be tried, in accordance with the pledge of Col. Allen. In their progress through the country, many Union men were known to have been killed and scalped by the Indians. Upon the return of Keith and his men to Laurel they began systematically to torture the women of loyal men, to force them to tell where their fathers and husbands could be found, and what part each had taken in the salt raid. The women refused to divulge anything. They were then whipped with hickory switches—many of them till the blood coursed in streams down their persons to the ground; and the men who did this were called soldiers! Mrs. Sarah Shelton, wife of Ezra Shelton, who escaped from the town, and Mrs. Mary Shelton, wife of Lifus Shelton, were whipped and hung by the neck till they were almost dead; but would give no information. Martha White, an idiotic girl, was beaten and tied by the neck all day to a tree. Old Mrs. Unus Riddle, aged *eighty-five* years, was whipped, hung, and robbed of a considerable amount of money. Many others were treated with the same barbarity. And the men who did this were called soldiers! The daughters of William Shelton, a man of wealth and highly respectable, were requested by some of the officers to play and sing for them. They played and sang a few National airs.; Keith learned of it, and ordered that the ladies be placed under arrest and sent to the guardhouse, where they remained all night.

Old Mrs. Sallie Moore, seventy years of age, was whipped with hickory rods till the blood ran in streams down her back to the ground; and the perpetrators of this were clothed in the habiliments of rebellion, and bore the name of soldiers!

One woman, who had an infant five or six weeks old, was tied in the snow to a tree, her child placed in the doorway in her sight, and, as she knew about the seizure of the salt, both herself and her child were allowed to perish. Sergeant N. B. D. Jay, of Capt. Reynolds' company, and Lieut. R. M. Deever assisted their men in the execution of the hellish outrages. Houses were burned and torn down. All kinds of property were destroyed or carried off. All the women and children of the Union men who were shot, and of those who escaped, were ordered to General Alfred E. Jackson's headquarters at Jonesboro,' to be sent through the lines by way of Knoxville. When the first of them arrived at this place, the officer in charge applied to Gen. Donelson (formerly Speaker of the House of Representatives at Nashville) to know by which route they should be sent from there, whether by Cumberland Gap or Nashville. Gen. Donelson immediately directed them to be released and sent home, saying that such a thing was unknown in civilized countries. They were then sent home, and all the refugees met on the road were also turned back.

On the 13th of February, 1863, a squad of soldiers were sent to conscript James McCollum, of Green county, Tennessee, a very respectable, industrious man thirty or thirty-five years of age. They found him feeding his cattle. When he saw some of them he ran to the back of his barn, and, without halting or attempting to arrest him, one of them shot him through the neck, killing him instantly. His three little children, who saw it, ran to the house and told their mother; she came out wringing her hands in anguish, and screaming with terror and dismay.

The soldiers were sitting upon the fence. They laughed at her agony, and said they had only killed "a damned Tory." The murdered man was highly esteemed by his neighbors, and was a firm Union man.

In April last, two rebel soldiers named Wood and Ignole went to the house of Mrs. Ruth Ann Rhea, living on the waters of Lick Creek county, to conscript her son. The old lady was partially deranged; she commanded the soldiers to leave her house, and raised a stick to strike one of them. He told her if she struck him, he would run her through with his bayonet; she gave the blow, and he shot her through the breast.

In the same month, Jesse Price, an old man sixty years of age, two sons and two nephews, were arrested in Johnson county, Tennessee, bordering on Virginia, by Col. Fouke's cavalry, composed of Tennessee and North Carolina men. They were taken to Ash county, North Carolina, to be tried for disloyalty to Jefferson Davis & Co. The old man had been previously arrested, taken to Knoxville, tried and acquitted.

When the five prisoners arrived in Ash county, a groggery keeper proposed to treat Fouke's men to eight gallons of brandy if they would hang the old man, his sons and nephews, without trial. The bargain was struck, and the five unfortunate men were hanged without further ceremony. The brandy was furnished, and some of it drank before the tragedy, — the rest afterward.

And it is upon the graves of such martyrs, upon the basis of such damning acts of barbarity, that the independence of a Southern Confederacy is to be established? The blood of these murdered men, women, and children, appeals to heaven against such a consummation. Read this bloody record of inhuman fiendish slaughter, ye snivelling *sympathizers*, and ask yourselves if the vengeance of a just God must not, sooner or later, blast the hopes and schemes of such enemies of their race. Is it possible that an inexorable idol, demanding such rivers of innocent blood, can be long worshipped in the light of the nineteenth century? Forbid it God! Forbid it, all ye mighty hosts of heaven! Christianity cries out against it. American honor demands that the monstrosity be cast into flames and destroyed forever.

All the blessed memories of the past; all the glorious anticipations of the future, call upon the noble patriots of the Union to avenge the blood of these martyrs to the cause of freedom and nationality. — *Memphis Bulletin.*

GENERAL RENO'S LAST WORDS. — When General Reno fell, Gen Sturges was within a few yards of him. He was in command of the division formerly commanded by Reno, increased by several new regiments, and the men had just distinguished themselves in driving the rebels from the summit of the Blue Ridge. These generals were bosom friends; had been classmates at West Point, and graduated together. When Reno fell, Sturges ran to his assistance, had him picked up, and said: "Jesse, are you badly wounded?" To which he replied, "Yes, Sam, I am a dead man." General Sturges had him placed upon a litter and carried to the rear, where he died in an hour. His last words, before leaving the battle-field were, "Boys, I can be with you no longer in body, but I am with you in spirit."

THE SOUTHERN CROSS.

FLING wide each fold, brave flag unrolled
  In all thy breadth and length!
Float out unfurled, and show the world
  A new-born nation's strength.
Thou dost not wave all bright and brave
  In holiday attire;
'Mid cannon chimes a thousand times
  Baptized in blood and fire.

No silken toy to flaunt in joy,
  When careless shouts are heard:
Where thou art borne all scathed and torn,
  A nation's heart is stirred.
Where half-clad groups of toil-worn troops,
  Are marching to the wars,
What grateful tears and heartfelt cheers
  Salute thy cross of stars!

Thou ne'er hast seen the pomp and sheen,
  The pageant of a court;
Or masquerade of war's parade,
  When fields are fought in sport;
But thou know'st well the battle yell
  From which thy foemen reel,
When down the steeps resistless leaps
  A sea of Southern steel.

Thou know'st the storm of balls that swarm
  In dense and hurtling fight,
When thy crossed bars, a blaze of stars,
  Plunge headlong through the fight;
Where thou'rt unfurled are thickest hurled
  The thunderbolts of war;
And thou art met with loudest threat
  Of cannon from afar.

For thee is told the merchant's gold;
  The planter's harvests fall:
Thine is the gain of hand and brain,
  And the heart's wealth of all.
For thee each heart has borne to part
  With what it holds most dear;
Through all the land no woman's hand
  Has staid one volunteer.

Though from thy birth outlawed on earth,
  By older nations spurned,
Their full-grown fame may dread the name
  Thy infancy has earned.
For thou dost flood the land with blood,
  And sweep the seas with fire;
And all the earth applauds the worth
  Of deeds thou dost inspire!

Thy stainless field shall empire wield,
  Supreme from sea to sea,
And proudly shine the honored sign
  Of peoples yet to be.
When thou shalt grace the hard-won place
  The nations grudge thee now,
No land shall show to friend or foe
  A nobler flag than thou.

GRANT AND THE POLITICIAN. — A certain western Colonel in Major-General Grant's army, took advantage of a sick-furlough to canvass for a nomination to Congress. On application for an extension of his furlough, Gen. Grant wrote on back of it, as follows:

"If Col. —— is able to travel over his district to electioneer for Congress, he is able to be with his regiment, and he is hereby ordered to join it immediately, or be dismissed from the service."

ABRAHAM LINCOLN'S FIRST SPEECH. — President Lincoln made his maiden speech in Sangamon county, at Pappysville (or Richland) in the year 1832. He was then a Whig, and was a candidate for the legislature of this State. The speech was sharp and sensible. To understand why it was so short, the following facts will show: First, Mr. Lincoln was a young man, say twenty-two years of age, and timid. Secondly, his friends and opponents, in the joint discussion had rolled the sun nearly down. Mr. Lincoln saw that it was not a proper time to discuss the questions fully, and hence he cut his remarks short. Probably the other candidate had wholly exhausted the subjects under discussion. The time, according to W. H. Herndon's informant — who has kindly furnished this valuable reminiscence for us — was 1832, it may have been 1834. The President lived at that time with James A. Herndon, at Salem, Sangamon county, who heard the speech, talked about it, and knows the report to be correct. The speech which was characteristic of the man, was as follows:

"GENTLEMEN, FELLOW-CITIZENS: I presume you all know who I am. I am humble Abraham Lincoln. I have been solicited by many friends to become a candidate for the legislature. My politics are short and sweet, like an *old woman's dance.* I am in favor of a National Bank. I am in favor of the internal improvement system, and a high protective tariff. These are my sentiments and political principles. If elected, I shall be thankful; if not, it will be all the same."

THE BATTLE-FIELD OF GETTYSBURG. — I have just returned from a visit to Gettysburg and if you choose to accompany me in a long ramble over the field and hear what a participant in the battle has to say, well and good. In the main, "I tell the story as 'twas told to me;" but it is hard to say anything new upon a theme already hackneyed. You newspaper people have, I know, what most people have, a horror of — long articles; therefore, "for fear your readers should grow skittish," you have my full permission to abbreviate, expunge, or omit, at your pleasure. Assuming this article, then, to have escaped the fate of your waste-paper basket, start with me on this fine November morning, out on the Emmettsburg road. For our companion and guide we have Captain. A. F. Cavada, a gallant

and accomplished young officer, who served all through, from Yorktown to Petersburg, and for nearly two years on the staff of Major General Humphreys.

About a mile out we halt. The Captain *loquitur.* "Now I begin to feel at home. Let me take an observation, as these fences were not here then. All right. I've got it now. Do you see that big walnut on the ridge over there? That was Gen. Humphrey's headquarters on the morning of Thursday, July 2d. Almost worn out with hard marching, I was aroused from my weary bivouac at daylight, and ordered to post Col. Tilghman's regiment — the Twenty-sixth Pennsylvania — on picket along here. Later in the the day, right of our division, Carr's brigade, held this brick house. Further down was posted Turnbull's battery. There, below that barn, stood Lieut. Seeley's and still further toward our left the batteries of Birney's division, under Livingston, Smith, Randolph, Clark, and Winslow. I mention them all, for never were guns handled more beautifully. All suffered fearfully — Seeley's especially. He had hardly a man or horse left standing, and was himself severely wounded. He was a gallant officer, and had risen from the ranks. Now go with me into that orchard. I want to find a certain apple-tree which served as a rendezvous during the day for us staff officers and our orderlies. At one period, standing under it, with Captains Humphreys and McClellan, a shell exploded in the tree, killing three of our poor orderlies, besides striking my horse." We found the tree — its limbs were shattered, and the top entirely gone.

"About 2 o'clock the whole Third Corps moved out in line-of-battle over the open ground, and a more magnificent spectacle of 'living valor rolling on the foe,' I never witnessed. Away over on that bare spot of rising ground the rebels had planted two batteries, with which they enfiladed our whole line, fairly sweeping it from left to right. Lord! how they pitched it into us! Longstreet's infantry debouched from those woods, and in a short time all around where we are standing — to the right, left and in front — along this road, through that peach orchard, away down toward Round Top, for hours the battle raged. General Sickles was wounded near that large barn. How well I remember this spot of ground. It was here, behind that stone-fence, that I had been ordered to post Colonel Burling's brigade. On my way back, I passed the One Hundred and Fourteenth Pennsylvania Regiment, then commanded by my brother, Lieut. Col. F. F. Cavada. It had just been ordered to an advanced position beyond the road. I rode up and shook hands with him. 'Good-by, Fred, look out for yourself; you are going into a hot place, and are sure to catch it.' So it turned out. The One Hundred and fourteenth, in connection with the Sixty-eighth Pennsylvania, Col. Trippin, had a bloody fight of it, and lost heavily. My brother and his brigade commander, Gen. Graham, were both taken prisoners, the latter severely wounded. I never saw the rebels fight with such diabolical

14

fury. The most murderous fire — canister, shrapnel, and musketry — was poured into their faces as it were, but nothing stopped them. The Third Corps, those heroes of Chancellorsville, and other bloody fields, led by Birney, Humphreys, De Trobriand, Ward, Graham and Carr — never fought more heroically."

A word of criticism here. At one period of the battle, Birney, being hard pressed called upon Gen. Sykes, in command of the Fifth Corps, for assistance. Sykes had *been ordered* to support the Third if called upon, but he returned for answer that he "would be up in time — that his men were tired and were making coffee!" They *did* come up in *about an hour*, and, says Gen. Warren, in his testimony, "the troops under General Sykes arrived barely in time to save Round Top, and they had a very desperate fight to hold it." And again of the operations next day. "When the repulse took place, Gen. Meade intended to move forward and assault the enemy in turn. He ordered an advance of the Fifth Corps, but it was *carried on so slowly* that it did not amount to much, if anything." Gen. George Sykes is a brave man, but entirely "too slow," so at least Gen. Grant seemed to think, for in the subsequent reorganization of the Army of the Potomac, the services of "Tardy George," No. 2, were dispensed with. The Fifth, as a corps, has a glorious record, and never failed to fight bravely when properly handled.

To resume the captain's narrative. "As the afternoon wore on the pressure became greater and greater, until at last our whole corps, with the exception of Carr's brigade and a few other regiments, was hurled down the slope, broken and discomfited, the rebels following in hot pursuit. Our losses were frightful. In our division, of 5,000 men, our loss was nearly 2,000." "Well, Captain, you saw most of the heavy fighting done by this army, tell me, were you ever in a *hotter* place than this?" "Never but once — and that reminds me of a little story. In the attack upon the enemy's position at the first Fredericksburg, our division was ordered to storm the heights. As we were preparing to move, Gen. Humphreys — always a very *polite man* — turned round to his staff, and in his blandest manner remarked, 'Young gentlemen, I intend to lead this assault, and shall be happy to have the pleasure of your company.' Of course, the invitation was too polite to be declined. *That* was the roughest place I ever was in, and I can't conceive, even to this day, how any of us ever got back alive. Our division lost nearly 1,100 men in about fifteen minutes. In this clump of bushes my horse received a second wound, and fell dead under me. I managed to scramble over the ridge, where our men were being rallied, and soon after the sun went down and the rebels were beaten back beyond the road.

"Capt. Chester, of our military family, was seen to go down in the melée and after night-fall a party started out in search of him. We found him near that large flat rock, alive, but grievously wounded. His horse and faithful orderly both lay dead beside him, and across his legs a rebel soldier, whom he had killed with his revolver, while in the act of plundering him of his watch. He was taken up tenderly, and conveyed to the hospital on Rock Creek where he died next day.

"With heavy hearts we now set about the task of burying such of our poor fellows as were within reach. Always the saddest of a soldier's duties, it was peculiarly so upon this occasion, for all felt that the rising sun would bring with it a repetition of this day's horrors, and that, perhaps, at this hour to-morrow, some comrade might be performing this same sad office for us.

"'Few and short were the prayers we said,
    And we spoke not a word of sorrow,
As we steadfastly gazed on the face of the dead,
    And bitterly thought on *the morrow.*'"

In the course of the day we paid a visit to Mr. Sherfey's house, where we were most hospitably received. This house stands about the centre of the field and is riddled from garret to basement. Traces of the conflict are to be seen on every side, including the last resting-place of many poor Southerners. Mr. Sherfey's barn was burnt during the fight, and some of the wounded who sought refuge there perished in the flames. "These," said Mrs. Sherfey, producing some tin cans, "contain peaches that were growing in our orchard over there at the time of the battle. These are *my* trophies." In the front garden grows the beautiful shrub known as the "burning bush," luxuriant with its crop of bright red berries, typical of the blood shed at its roots. "Take some of the berries with you and plant them," said the kind old lady; "they will grow anywhere, and will be pleasant mementos of Gettysburg."

We next made our way to Little Round Top, where we had the pleasure of meeting Colonel Batchelder. This gentleman is engaged in collecting the details of the battle, and will, no doubt, produce a book of equal interest with his great map. I was sorry to hear him say that he intends designating this as "Weed's Hill," in honor of the general who fell on its top. Honor the memory of the brave man in some other way, Colonel, but don't seek to change this name. As "Little Round Top," it has already passed into history, and so it will be known forever. There are few finer views of the whole field than from this point, and here took place the closest and most sanguinary fighting of Thursday. In front and to the right the Fifth Corps had a heavy thing of it. On the height fought two of the noblest soldiers of the army, Vincent and Rice. The former laid down his life here, the latter at Spottsylvania the year after. All the little stone walls thrown up between the huge boulders are still here. In fact, nothing is changed. Would that this could be said of other parts of the field. Inscriptions upon the rocks mark the spots where Vincent and Hazlett fell. Here, too, at the early age of twenty-five, fell that accomplished soldier Col. O'Rourke, of the One Hundred and Fortieth New York. Graduating at the head of his class, two years before, he was at once assigned to duty in the field, and soon became distinguished for his reckless and impetuous courage. He was struck while mounted upon a rock gallantly animating his men. Fortunately, the extreme left was held by that splendid regiment the Twentieth Maine, then under the command of Col. Chamberlain, afterwards one of Sheridan's heroes of the Five Forks. Firing away their last cartridge, Chamberlain ordered his regiment to charge down the hill, and succeeded in clearing its sides with the bayonet. The remarkable ledge of rocks known as the "Devil's Den," directly opposite Round Top, was occupied by the enemy's sharpshooters, one of whom had a safe position within the cleft and picked off our men with fatal accuracy. The face of the boulder behind which he lay is covered with marks of the minies sent at him. One even "went for him" clean through the crevice, but missed. He was finally dislodged by a charge and escaped through an opening to the rear. Seven muskets, it is said, were found in his hiding place. There is *room enough for fifty.* On the slope in front of his den lie bleaching the bones of rebel dead, washed out by the rains. The scene of Crawford's charge, with our superb Pennsylvania Reserves, was to the right and in front of Little Round Top. Brigadier General Zook and Colonel Jeffards — the latter of the Fourth Michigan — were killed in the field beyond. Colonel Jeffards was killed by a bayonet-thrust, while gallantly holding up with his own hands the colors of his regiment. Near that ploughed field, charging at the head of his brave "Bucktails," fell our Chester county neighbor, Col. Frederick Taylor. No death in the whole army was more sincerely mourned.

"Many the ways that lead to death, but few
    Grandly; and one alone is glory's gate,
Standing wherever free men dare their fate,
Determined, as *thou wert,* to die — or do!"

We now proceed along the line held by us on Friday, Colonel B. politely acting as guide. In that little grove, close to our lines, fell the rebel General Barksdale on Thursday. This violent, brawling rebel started in search of "*his rights,*" and this little pile of stones here marks the spot where he is presumed to have *found them.* It is said that he was *drunk* when he started on the charge, and this may account for his headlong, reckless bravery. True or not, "the story's still extant." Here in the thickest of the fight, exposing himself like a common soldier, the gallant Hancock received his wound. That advanced line of works was held by the Vermont brigade. It was commanded by Gen. Stannard, who subsequently gave an arm to the cause on the James. A pile of knapsacks, just as they were unslung, still lie mouldering here, — on one the inscription "Sixteenth Vermont" is still visible. Even now the *debris* of battle — hats, shoes, cartridge-boxes, bayonet-scabbards, canteens, &c. — lie scattered all over the field. Next we come to the position held by the "Phil-

adelphia Brigade," composed of the Sixty-ninth — "Paddy Owens' regulars;" the Seventy-second, Baxter's Zouaves, and that splendid fighting regiment, the Seventy-first, or California, commanded originally by the lamented Baker, and subsequently by our fellow-townsmen, Colonels John Markoe and R. Penn Smith. This brigade — veteran fighters, every man of them — was led upon this occasion by a gallant New Yorker, Brigadier-General Webb, and nobly was the honor of both cities sustained. Would that I had it in my power to particularize all the organizations conspicuous for courage and conduct in this great battle, but that would be to mention almost every regiment, battery and squadron engaged. From here we have an excellent view of Seminary Ridge, the line of woods whence the rebels issued and the beautiful level fields over which they swept in their grand charge. This certainly is the most magnificent battle-field in the world. The heights of La Belle Alliance and Mont Saint Jean in some respects resemble our Cemetery and Seminary Ridges, with the same gentle, undulating valley intervening; but at Waterloo the principal road runs at right angles, while here, parallel with the position. Speaking of the bombardment which preceded the charge, that experienced soldier, General Hancock, says: "It was the most terrific cannonade I ever witnessed, and the most prolonged." A rebel eye-witness describing it, says: "I have never yet heard such tremendous artillery firing. The very earth shook beneath our feet, and the hills and rocks seemed to reel like a drunken man. For one hour and a half this most terrific firing was continued, during which time the shrieking of shells, the crash of falling timber, the fragments of rock flying through the air, shattered from the cliffs by solid-shot; the heavy mutterings from the valley between the opposing armies, the splash of bursting shrapnel, and the neighing of wounded artillery horses, made the same terribly grand and sublime." After this came the charge. Our eighty guns, planted on the crest from Cemetery Hill to Round Top, "volley'd and thundered," and, when the infantry joined in the chorus, so terrible was the fire that tore through them that the rebel columns presented the extraordinary spectacle of ten thousand men playing at "leap-frog!" In spite of every effort, the flower of Lee's veterans, directed by tried leaders such as Garnett, Armstead, Kemper, Wright, Posey and Mahone, failed in carrying our position, although at one or two points they charged up to, and even *over* it. "What other than *Southern* troops would have made that charge?" Ay, sir, but what other than *Northern* would have met and repulsed it? *Northern* endurance, upon this occasion was too much for *Southern* impetuosity and dash. "There swung the *pine* against the *palm.*" In the bloody ruck hundreds of their best officers went down. It was the turning point of the grand drama, and with the sun, on that third day of July, went down the sun of "the Confederacy" forever! Although known as "Pickett's charge," Gen. Graham, whom I met here yesterday, informs me that Pickett himself was not in it. He describes him as a coarse, brutal fellow, and says he treated him with the greatest inhumanity after the battle, whilst wounded, and a prisoner in his hands. The rebel corps commanders either did did not expose themselves as freely as our own, or they had better luck, for none were hit, whilst we lost one, Reynolds, killed; and two, Hancock and Sickels, wounded. The story told in *Blackwood*, by Col. Freemantle, of the British army, who was present may help to explain it. He says, that carried away by excitement, he rushed up to Longstreet, who was sitting on a fence "quietly whitterling a stick," whilst watching the charge, and said. "Gen. Longstreet, isn't this splendid; I wouldn't have missed it for the world?" "The d—l you wouldn't," replied Longstreet; "why, don't you see we are getting licked like h—l!" We now crossed the Baltimore pike, calling on our way at the small frame building, on the Taneytown road, used as the head-quarters of Gen. Meade on Friday. This will always be a point of great interest. The house is sadly shattered, and the poor widow who owns it complains bitterly of her losses. "When I *comes* home, my house was all over blood; the 'sogers' took away all my coverlits and quilts, two tons of hay, they *spiled* my spring, my apple-trees and every *ding*." She says a couple of hundred dollars would be a great help to her, and thinks she should get it from *someveres*." Sure enough, why *shouldn't* the poor woman get it? In the garden of a cottage in the little village of Waterloo the visitor is shown the monument erected over the Marquis of Anglesea's leg, and the poor peasant has made quite a little fortune by exhibiting the boot cut from the leg, and the table upon which the amputation was performed. This hint might not be thrown away upon a more enterprising person, but I doubt if this poor, old, frowsy German woman will ever profit by it. To the right of Cemetery Hill was stationed the battery so furiously assaulted by Hays' brigade of Louisiana Tigers. The lunettes and traverses remain undisturbed and grass-grown.

The little eminence in front was held, and with distinguished honor, by that conscientious and patriotic soldier, Brigadier-Gen. Wadsworth. The works thrown up by our men on Culp's Hill are still to be seen, except such portion of the timber as is being removed by the owner of the ground. Only think of the meanness of the man who is pulling to pieces these monuments, and converting the timber into fence-rails and cordwood! The effect of the furious fire poured upon Ewell's swarming columns is visible enough. Hardly a rock or a tree in front of these works has escaped. Many of the trees are covered and scarred with bullets as high as fifty feet from the ground. There was "wild," as well as deadly shooting here on that fearful Thursday night and early Friday morning. Along this rough, rocky hill fought our own Geary, and that distinguished Rhode Islander, Brigadier General Green. Five months after, at the desperate midnight battle of Wahatchie, in Lookout Valley, this indomitable fighting officer only added to the laurels already gained at Antietam, and Gettysburg. An inscription on a tree close by tells the story of a large mound in the ravine below: "To the right lie buried forty-five rebels!" From here we struck across to the scene of the first day's fight. In the following communication to Governor Curtin, General Cutler tells us how the battle opened: "I owe a duty to one of your regiments, the Fifty-sixth, and its brave commander, Colonel J. W. Hofmann. It was my fortune to be in the advance on the morning of July 1st. The atmosphere being a little thick, I took out my glass to examine the enemy, being a few paces in front of Colonel H., he turned to me and inquired, 'Is that the enemy?' My reply was 'Yes.' Turning to his men, he commanded, 'Ready—right oblique—aim—fire!' and the battle of Gettysburg was opened. The fire was followed by other regiments instantly, still, that battle on the soil of Pennsylvania was opened by her own sons, and it is just that it should become a matter of history." Here is the ground fought over by our brave cavalrymen, under Pleasanton, Buford, Kilpatrick, Farnsworth, Merrit, Custer and Gregg. Never, in any preceding campaign, had the cavalry of this army rendered such distinguished and invaluable service. To meet the enemy was to overthrow them, until, at last, it was only with the greatest difficulty that Stuart could get his men to stand at all. The next point reached was the scene of the bloody, though unavailing struggle of the First and Eleventh Corps. The marks of battle still abound, but the interest centres in the spot where Reynolds was killed. The General was nearly up with the skirmish line — no place, say military men, for a corps commander; "but *that* was just like John Reynolds;" and he had just despatched several of his aids, Capts. Baird, Rosengarten and Riddle, on some special duties, and was himself watching the deployment of a brigade of Wisconsin troops, when the fatal bullet, fired by a sharpshooter, struck him in the neck and he fell off his horse dead. Poor Reynolds!

"There have been tears and breaking hearts for thee."

We now stand in the National Cemetery, on Cemetery Hill. Who can stand unmoved in this silent city of the dead. Here repose the precious offerings laid upon the altar of the country by the loyal States. Ordinarily the filling up of a cemetery is slow work — the work of years. *Three days sufficed to fill this!* And what is the reward of those brave men for their weeks of weary marching, and days and nights of fearful fighting? "Two paces of the vilest earth!" Here they lie, "those unnamed demi-gods" of the rank and file. "Unknown!" "unknown!" the only epitaph of hundreds. Yes, here they lie "massed" with beautiful military precision, rank upon rank, as if awaiting the order to appear in review before the Great Commander-in-chief of us all!

> "Up many a fortress wall
> They charged — those boys in blue ;
> 'Mid surging smoke and volleying ball
> The bravest were the first to fall —
> To fall for me and you ! "

Who can ever forget those terrible days of July, that period of agonizing suspense ?
And when the news *did* come, oh, how that sad catalogue pulled upon the heart-strings ! Reynolds, Zook, Farnsworth, Card, Weed, Jeffards, Taylor, Arrowsmith, O'Rourke, Lowery, Cross, Hazlett, Vincent, Devereaux, Willard, Adams, Miller.

> "Period of honor as of woes,
> What bright careers 'twas thine to close !
> Mark'd on thy roll of blood what names,
> To *Freedom's* memory, and to Fame's
> Laid there their last immortal claims ! "

So ends my story of Gettysburg.

G. J. GROSS.

———

FRANKLIN W. SMITH, a Boston contractor, was tried by court-martial, and found guilty of pocketing a thousand or two dollars out of a contract with the Navy department for supplies. The report of the court-martial was sent to President Lincoln for his examination, who returned it with this characteristic indorsement :
"*Whereas*, Franklin W. Smith, had transactions with the United States Navy Department to a million and a quarter of dollars, and had the chance to steal a quarter of a million ; and *whereas*, he was charged with stealing only ten thousand dollars, and from the final revision of the testimony it is only claimed that he stole one hundred dollars, I don't believe he stole anything at all.
"*Therefore*, the records of the court-martial, together with the finding and sentence, are disapproved, declared null and void, and the defendant is fully discharged.

A. LINCOLN."

———

THE STARS AND BARS.

> 'Tis sixty-two ! — and sixty-one,
> With the old Union, now is gone,
> Recking with bloody wars —
> Gone with that ensign, once so prized,
> The Stars and Stripes, now so despised —
> Struck for the stars and bars.
>
> The burden once of patriot's song,
> Now badge of tyranny and wrong,
> For us no more it waves ;
> We claim the stars — the stripes we yield,
> We give *them* up on every field,
> Where fight the Southern braves.
>
> Our motto this, "God and our right,"
> For sacred liberty we fight —
> Not for the lust of power ;

> Compelled by wrongs the sword t' unsheath,
> We'll fight, be free, or cease to breathe —
> We'll die before we cower.
>
> By all the blood our fathers shed,
> We will from tyranny be freed —
> We will not conquered be ;
> Like them, no higher power we own
> But God's — we bow to him alone —
> We will, we will be free !
>
> For homes and altars we contend,
> Assured that God will us defend —
> He makes our cause his own ;
> Not of our gallant patriot host,
> Not of brave leaders do we boast —
> We trust in God alone.
>
> Sumter, and Bethel, and Bull Run
> Witnessed fierce battles fought and won,
> By aid of Power Divine ;
> We met the foe, who us defied,
> In all his pomp, in all his pride,
> Shouting, "Manasseh's mine ! "
>
> It was not thine, thou boasting foe !
> We laid thy vandal legions low —
> We made them bite the sod ;
> At Lexington the braggart yields,
> Leesburgh, Belmont, and other fields ;—
> Still help us, mighty God !
>
> Thou smiledst on the patriot seven —
> Thou smilest on the brave eleven
> Free, independent States ;
> Their number thou wilt soon increase,
> And bless them with a lasting peace,
> Within their happy gates.
>
> No more shall violence be heard,
> Wasting, destruction no more feared
> In all this Southern land ;
> "Praise," she her gates devoutly calls,
> "Salvation," her Heaven-guarded walls —
> What shall her power withstand ?
>
> "The little one," by heavenly aid,
> "A thousand is — the strong one made,
> "A nation — oh ! how strong ! "
> Jehovah, who the right befriends,
> Jehovah, who our flag defends,
> Is hastening it along !

———

INCIDENT OF THE MORGAN RAID. — When Gen. John Morgan's band was within four miles of Jasper, Pike county, Ohio, they captured a number of citizens, among them a school-teacher, by the name of Joseph McDougal, aged forty-seven. The captured men were marched on the double-quick to the village of Jasper, allowed a few moments' rest, and then double-quicked two and a half miles to Piketon, and there, with others captured, formed into line for parole.
Before the oath was administered, however, Captain Mitchell, of one of Morgan's companies, ordered Mr. McDougal to step out of the ranks. After a little parley, this Mitchell ordered two

soldiers to march McDougal to the Sciota river, a short distance off. Here he was placed in a canoe, facing Mitchell and his two men; and, at a signal from Mitchell, two shots were fired at the prisoner; one ball taking effect just below the right eye, the other in his left breast, near his heart. Death followed instantaneously. The wretches left their victim in the canoe. Prisoners who were with Mr. McDougal represent him as a gentle but brave-hearted man, the flag of his country being sacred to him above all earthly symbols.

WHIPPED AND DEMORALIZED, BUT NOT SCATTERED. — A soldier of Bates' division of the confederate army, after the command had run two days from Nashville, had thrown away his gun and accoutrements, and alone in the woods, sat down and commenced thinking — the first chance he had for such a thing. Rolling up his sleeves, and looking at his legs and general physique, he thus gave vent to his feelings. "I am whipped, badly whipped, and somewhat demoralized, but no man can say I am scattered."

ANECDOTE OF GENERAL BROOKS. — A soldier in the Fourth Vermont Regiment relates the following incident of the battle of Sharpsburg: —

We marched through a cornfield, and the men lay down with Ayres's battery, which is connected with our brigade, and took position. The enemy saw us, and poured in a perfect hurricane of canister, grape, and shell, but did but little damage. Then old Ayers opened, and for three hours I could not hear myself think. The air was full of bursting shells and whistling balls, mingled with the roar of artillery and the sharp crack of the sharpshooters' rifles. General Brooks would not lie down as his men did, but stood up in plain sight. I told the boys he would get hit before night, and so he did; a ball struck him in the cheek and knocked out two teeth, but did no other injury. I have told you before how short and gruff he is. When he was struck, one of the men who was close beside him, asked him if he was wounded. "No, sir; had a tooth pulled," said the old man; and he never left the field until after dark.

FRENCH NOTIONS OF AMERICAN GEOGRAPHY. — We translate from the "Almanach du Magazin Pittoresque," the following paragraph contained in an abstract of events of the war in the United States: —

May 23. — The Federal troops assembled at Harper's Ferry, cross the Potomac, and after a first engagement occupy Alexandria.

May 27. — The Federals commanded by Gen. Banks, experienced a first reverse. They recross the Potomac, and fall back upon Williamsburg.

May 30 and 31. — A great battle is fought near Richmond; on the first day the advantage remains with the Confederates; on the second day they experience considerable loss, and abandon Corinth.

After seven days of bloody fighting near Richmond (June 23 to 29), 95,000 Federals, commanded by McClellan, retire before the Confederate army, which, with re-enforcements brought by Gens. Beauregard and Jackson, have been increased to 185,000 men. They take position on the James River, 17 miles from Charleston.

On the cover of the book it is stated that " the Central Committee of Primary Instruction in the City of Paris has placed the 'Magazin Pittoresque' on the list of books proper to be given as prizes in the public schools."

MARCH ALONG.

GEORGE H. BOKER.

SOLDIERS are we from the mountain and valley,
  Soldiers are we from the hill and the plain;
Under the flag of our fathers we rally;
  Death, for its sake, is but living again.
    Then march along, gay and strong,
    March to battle with a song
    March, march along!

We have a history told of our nation,
  We have a name that must never go down;
Heroes achieved it through toil and privation;
  Bear it on, bright with its ancient renown!
    Then march along, etc.

Who that shall dare say the flag waving o'er us,
  Which floated in glory from Texas to Maine,
Must fall, where our ancestors bore it before us,
  Writes his own fate on the roll of the slain.
    Then march along, etc.

Look at it, traitors, and blush to behold it!
  Quail as it flashes its stars in the sun!
Think you a hand in the nation will fold it,
  While there's a hand that can level a gun?
    Then march along, etc.

Carry it onward, till victory earn it
  The rights it once owned in the land of the free;
Then, in God's name, in our fury we'll turn it
  Full on the treachery over the sea!
    Then march along, etc.

England shall feel what a vengeance the liar
  Stores in the bosom he aims to deceive;
England shall feel how God's truth can inspire;
  England shall feel it, but only to grieve.
    Then march along, etc.

Peace shall unite us again and forever,
  Though thousands lie cold in the graves of these wars;
Those who survive them shall never prove, never,
  False to the flag of the stripes and the stars!
    Then march along, gay and strong,
    March to battle with a song!
    March, march along!

ILLINOIS AT THE BATTLE OF GETTYSBURG.

—The part borne in this terrible struggle by the troops of Illinois, is thus described by Colonel William Gamble, who commanded the Eighth Cavalry from that state:—

On the afternoon of the 30th of June the first cavalry brigade of Buford's division, commanded by Col. W. Gamble, of the Eighth Illinois cavalry, arrived at Gettysburg,—the Eighth Illinois cavalry in front. Col. Gamble received orders to pass through the town on the Cashtown road and select the most eligible line of battle beyond the Seminary that could be found, encamp the brigade and send forward one or two squadrons to find the enemy, and remain on picket to watch the movements of the enemy. These orders were promptly carried out. The squadrons for advanced picket duty were taken from the Eighth Illinois cavalry, who advanced three miles further, found the enemy, remained in front until seven o'clock the next morning, when the enemy commenced advancing in three divisions under Gen. A. P. Hill, and with shell and musketry drove in the squadrons mentioned, and the Eighth Illinois cavalry had the honor of being first fired on by the enemy and of returning their fire.

The advance of the enemy was immediately reported to General Meade, the infantry advance being eight miles in our rear were ordered up to support the cavalry.

The cavalry of Buford's Division was ordered to fight the enemy. I dismounted part of the Eighth Illinois, Eighth New York, and Third Indiana cavalry, in all about 900 men, and ordered them to the front to keep back the enemy as long as possible till our infantry came up to our support. Devin's brigade of New York cavalry was on our right and Merrit's brigade of regular cavalry was on our left. We had to fight the whole Army Corps of Gen. A. P. Hill, 25,000 strong, for three and a half hours, from 7 till $10\frac{1}{2}$ A. M., to hold the original line of battle selected by me according to previous orders.

Tidball's horse battery, A, Second U. S. artillery, was attached to my brigade that day.

The cavalry above mentioned fought Hill's corps for three and a half hours, on the morning of the 1st of July, and held the original line of battle selected beyond the Seminary, until our infantry came up, with a loss of one hundred and eleven officers and men, killed, wounded, and missing, and fifty-six cavalry horses killed, thirteen artillery horses killed, and fifteen artillerymen killed and wounded. Nothing of this is mentioned in the newspapers or dispatches, but the above are absolute facts, under my own observation.

An hour before dark the rebels outflanked our left; this brigade of cavalry was again ordered to the front, dismounted and fought the rebels on Seminary Ridge, and saved a whole division of our infantry from being surrounded and captured. Nothing of this either is mentioned in the newspapers or dispatches, yet these facts occurred, with the loss of some of our best officers and men.

WHITTIER AND THE ALABAMA PLANTER.

—He met with an Alabama planter in Boston, who expressed a desire to converse with him, and an interview took place, during which there was a free interchange of views. The planter frankly acknowledged that there was in the South a strong feeling of hate toward the North and Northern men, and they were determined to fight. He explained how this feeling was fostered by the politicians of the South, and how the feelings of the North were represented there, and stated that almost his sole object in coming to Boston was to ascertain for himself whether the facts were as they had been represented. He was evidently surprised to find the anti-slavery poet "so mild mannered a man," and confessed that, generally, he did not perceive that the feeling of the North toward the South was so bitter and unfriendly as he had been led to expect. He had experienced nothing but civility and courtesy, and admitted that Southerners generally received the same treatment.

Finally, Whittier, after attending him to some of the desirable places of resort, told him that, as he was now here, he might as well see the worst of the anti-slavery phase of Northern fanaticism, as the fashionable phrase is, and proposed to visit Garrison. The planter consented, and so they turned their steps to the *Liberator* office, where they found Garrison, Wendell Phillips, and Fred. Douglass, and there they enjoyed a "precious season of conversation." Would it not have been a sight worth seeing—that conclave in the *Liberator* office, with Garrison, Whittier, Phillips, Douglass, and the Alabama planter in the foreground? The planter went to his home a wiser, and perhaps a sadder man, than he came, and protested that all he could do, while mourning for the condition of the country, was to *pray* over it. Would that more of the Southern people might come and see for themselves how basely the North had been belied!

THE UNION MEN OF ALABAMA.

—The following account of the condition and persecutions of the Union men of North Alabama, and of the efforts of our troops, particularly the Fifty-first Indiana regiment, commanded by Col. A. D. Streight, to relieve them, is from the pen of the chaplain of that regiment.

CAMP NEAR DECATUR, July 16.

The subject on which I wish to write, is the condition and suffering of the mountaineers in Northern and Central Alabama. There is a vast valley of rich soil extending from beyond Tuscumbia west to Huntsville in the east. In this valley the great planters live. Here is their great cotton-growing region and the wealth of the state.

These mountains are peopled with quite another class of inhabitants, shorn of highfalutin aristocracy—a plain, candid, industrious people. Now these poor classes, deprived of culture, as they climb the mountains, pass through the gorges, and roam over the plains, think for themselves.

It came to pass in the course of human events, when Jeff Davis wished these honest-hearted men to assist him in carrying out his great, grand, and overwhelming scheme of unnatural rebellion against the government they cherished, they said no. Things went on without opposition only as they opposed its course to destruction at the ballot-box. Here they met the enemies of their country every time, and almost with a unanimous voice did they declare against secession in every form. When the affairs of the state had assumed a malignant form, and were far on the road to ruin and wild desperation, they only expostulated; but when the abominable, uncivil, anti-republican conscript act passed, and was being enforced by an unfeeling, heartless band of ruffians; when confusion, dire confusion, had come upon them, turning brother against brother, and father against son; when squalid poverty stared them in the face and desperation was ensuing, caused by their being driven from home to seek a place of safety in the mountains, in caverns, in dens, — they opened their eyes to gaze upon the painful sight of liberty gone, constitution prostrated, home gone, and with it quietude and honor. To escape despotism and these heartless ruffians, men left their homes and fled to the mountains. Some made for the Union army, coming through the mountain pathways for twenty, forty, sixty, and some even ninety miles, having a complete line of friends to help them extending from Decatur to near Montgomery — the best underground railroad ever heard of or ever established.

Old men and young men came asking and praying the army to assist them, demanding protection from the old flag, and asking to live and to fight under the old Constitution, declaring they only owed allegiance to the old government, and it was the only one they would fight for.

Their piteous cries moved our colonel, A. D. Streight, who asked for a leave of absence for four days, that his regiment might visit the mountains, pry into the caverns, and ascertain more positively the true condition of those loyal persecuted men. Accordingly, early Saturday morning, July 12th, with the Fourteenth Cavalry, and a sufficient number of our Alabamians for pilots, the Fifty-first crossed the river, and set out for the mountain regions. On we moved across the valley, while the sun poured his rays upon us — not an Indiana sun, but the sun away down in Alabama. Now this sun was shining much hotter than the sun shines any day in Indiana. Col. Streight steered us for Col. Davis's, who lived twenty-five miles out from Decatur, at a pass in the mountains called Davis's Gap.

We arrived at Col. Davis's at dark, and merciful heavens, what did we there behold! An elderly lady came to the door, who was between sixty and seventy years old. She was asked does Col. Davis live here? She answered he did. Is he at home? She answered he is not. Said Col. Streight, "we are Union troops; have heard of your suffering, and have come to relieve you." She still hesitated. "Do you believe me?" She said she would dislike to dispute his word, but a young lady came to the door and asked, "have you any of the Alabama boys with you?" They were called up from the rear. While coming, the young lady remarked, "We have been so often deceived by guerillas, that we"— The boys came. "Is that you, John?" Instantly she sprang into his arms, threw her arms around him, while she exclaimed: "Thank God, we are safe." "Now," answered the elderly lady, "I can have the old man here in a few minutes." "Where is he?" "Just back in the mountains." What! an old man of seventy-three years, resident of the same farm for more than forty-four years, known by all men as a quiet peaceable, and pious man — to be driven from his home, to have to seek refuge in the mountains, in the caverns, and dismal, secluded retreats, where the eyes of only the wild beasts had gazed! Yes, it is this old gentleman who had been driven from home, simply because he loved his country.

The night passed away without any strange occurrences and morning came on. We started out, three companies strong, to scour the country round, to, if possible, find the wounded man, but after searching, inquiring after, and tracing him till he abandoned his horse, we came to the conclusion that further search would be fruitless, fearing the rascals had pursued and murdered him. He may, there is a slight probability he will, come up yet. They stole his horse and accoutrements. While this search was going on, companies were sent out in almost every direction to scour the surrounding country. When we all meet, in the evening, some have arrested prominent secessionists, who have saddles, some have pantaloons taken from artillerymen they had previously murdered several miles away, and others horses. Sunday evening found us with over fifty recruits. They came to us all day Monday like doves to the windows. Monday evening we had speaking exercises, in which Col. Streight, Adjutant Ramsay, and Chris. Sheets took part. The speeches of the colonel and adjutant were such as they should have delivered, but that of Sheets was a strange tune coming from an Alabamian. Sheets represented Winson county in the Convention when Alabama is said to have seceded. He was prominent among the very few in that Convention who would not and did not sign the ordinance of secession.

Sheets is a young man of fine promise and makes a splendid speech. He declared to his downtrodden countrymen that the time had come for them to act, and act they must, either in an army they had no sympathy with, and in a cause for which they could have no reasonable hope of success — must thus fight an enemy they loved and for a cause they hated; or, on the other hand, join the army of the United States, fight in a cause they loved, among their friends, contend against a foe to God and man, one they hated, and one that must be put down before peace, quietude and prosperity could again prevail. He advised them to join that army and be men, and fight the Southern Confederacy to hell and back again. Said he, "To-morrow morning I am going to the Union army. I am going to expose this fiendish villany before the world. They shall hear from me. I have slept in the mountains, in caves and caverns, till I am become musty; my health and manhood are failing me. I will stay here no longer till I am enabled to dwell in quiet at home."

Tuesday morning came — the morning we had set, and were compelled by our time being out to return to camp, thirty-one or thirty-two miles away. At about seven o'clock a company of about twenty men were seen approaching our lines, being led by a woman. They entered amid great applause. She told her story in her peculiar way, with her own peculiar gestures, the tears streaming from her eyes. Said she, " I knew I could pass those guerrillas, and find my husband and son," who had fled for their lives some thirty-four miles back in the mountains. The lady, not in good health, and fifty-five years old, had ridden a poor old horse over the mountains, tracing the mountain pathways through the gorges and around the precipices, sixty-four miles, counting the distance to and from her friends, and had made the trip in thirty hours, hunting her friends and cooking their breakfast in the time. These acts (for there are many such) should be known. Such heroines from the mountains have manifested more devotion for their country and friends than any of our Revolutionary mothers, whose acts of patriotism are held in everlasting remembrance. When the historian tells of noble deeds of daring and devotion to country, Anna Campbell, of Morgan County, Alabama, should stand first on the scroll of fame. It is no use to talk — when this old lady related her simple tale, there were but few who were not affected. Adjutant Ramsay wept, and it is said that even Colonel Streight shed tears. I know I did. I felt it was noble to weep on such occasions.

I visited an old patriot of eighty-four years. He was blind, so that he had not left his home in seven years — a peaceful, quiet old man, ripening for a better land, for he was devotedly pious. Now, simply because this old gentleman had raised his family well, so that they were all for the Union, and none of them in the Southern army, these fiends incarnate were thirsting for his blood, and had threatened him with hanging; for they had taken one of his neighbors not less virtuous, and only ten years younger.

Time came for us to leave, and our boys, having divided their rations with the Alabama recruits, were on less than half rations. This was the hottest day of the season, and there were no ambulances in which to carry the weak. But there could be no falling out, for we must pass through a hostile country. The men were formed into a long line, for we had about one hundred and fifty recruits from the mountains. And now comes the most touching scene of the expedition. We had left our families when it was heart-rending to part with the loved ones; but what was that to the parting here? We left our wives in the bosom of a sympathizing community; but these poor men must now leave their families in the midst of an unfeeling, heartless set — a community who would turn their wives out, or burn their houses over their heads, or destroy their scanty means of subsistence, and, may be, as they have done several times before, outrage their persons. The wives bade their husbands farewell, bidding them go, and they would take care of themselves as best they could. Mothers wept when they bade their sons good by, with their blessings on them. Forward! was the command — a wild shriek — and we move from scenes of sufferings such as we have never before seen.

MR. LINCOLN "GOOD ON THE CHOP." — During one of the last visits that the martyred President made to James River, a short time before the capture of Richmond, he spent some time in walking around among the hospitals, and in visiting various fatigue parties at work in putting up cabins and other buildings.

He came upon one squad who were cutting logs for a house; and, chatting a moment with the hardy woodsmen, asked one of them to let him see his axe. Mr. Lincoln grasped the helve with the easy air of one perfectly familiar with the tool, and remarked that he "used to be good on the chop."

The President then let in on a big log, making the chips fly, and making as smooth a cut as the best lumberman in Maine could do.

Meantime the men crowded around to see the work; and, as he handed back the axe, and walked away with a pleasant joke, the choppers gave him three as hearty cheers as he ever heard in the whole of his political career.

BAPTISM OF THE BIG GUN. — Father Mooney, on the occasion of the baptizing of one of the big guns mounted at Fort Corcoran in June, 1861, made the following remarks:

"Gentlemen: It is with more than ordinary pleasure I come forward to perform a ceremony which is not only pleasing to us all, but highly honorable — I may say, a welcome prerogative to me on this auspicious occasion — and that is, the christening of the noble gun on Fort Corcoran. In the kind providence of God, it has been for me, as a priest, during the last nine years, to baptize many a fine blue-eyed babe; but never had I brought before me such a large, quiet, healthy, and promising fellow as the one now before me. Indeed, I may remark, it has often occurred, when pouring the baptismal water on the child's head, he opened his little eyes, and got a little more of the baptismal water than he wished; but, on this occasion, this noble son of a great father has his mouth open, evidently indicating that he is anxious to speak, which I have no doubt he soon will, in a thundering voice, to the joy of his friends and terror of his enemies. I need not tell you that a most appropriate name has been selected by our esteemed Colonel, and one that will be welcomed by you all; and that is the honorable name of the gallant commander of our brigade, Colonel Hunter. Therefore, the great gun shall hereafter answer to its name — the Hunter Gun. Now, parents anxiously listen to the first lispings of the infant's lips, and the mother's heart swells with joy when she catches the first utterance of her cherished babe, in the words, 'mamma, mamma!' but here I shall guarantee to you that this promising boy will speak for the first time, in loud, clear accents, those endearing words, 'papa, papa, papa! — *patria mia, patria mia!*' and, in name as in effect, he will hunt traitors from this fort, while the echo of his voice will be as sweet music, inviting the children of Columbia to share the comforts of his father's home; and thus may he soon speak, to the glory of the Stars and Stripes, honor to the name that he bears, and lasting credit to the Sixty-ninth New York."

SCENES AT VICKSBURG. — "As I was riding by a small, religious-looking church, cruciform in shape — all churches do not look sacred — but this, in a grove of magnolia trees, with a small spire surmounted with the emblem of faith, gothic windows, and everything that tends to make it a place of worship, and inspire one with love for Him who holds the wind in the palm of His hand, who careth for the bird and feedeth the young lambs upon the hills, —

"I halted at the gateway, and noticed that the doors were open. After dismounting and climbing a hill, I stood upon a level with the church. Could it be? I could not realize until I walked to the door and looked in. Not a vestige of floor, not a remnant of a pew — altar gone. Even the string-pieces that supported the floor were gone. A few negroes sat in the corners cooking meat, while the smoke arose in reluctant wreaths, as though hesitating at the desecration. A beautiful marble font lay broken upon the ground, while the bowl was used for ordinary ablutions and the washing of dishes.

"I asked *how* this had been done. 'Why,' said they, 'rebel cavalry used to camp in it, and they burned all the seats and the pulpit; we only burned the floor.'

"I had a superstitious fear about entering it to look in the small side rooms, one of which had given forth sounds of praise, and in the other the sacred vestments of the priest were kept. The organ had long since vanished; the vestments were gone. Desecration and desolation sat here in silence — mournful reminder of a curse too deep for words, that Fate had uttered against the people who conceived this thing. What a fit comment on the rebellion! Churches desecrated, and graveyards defiled.

"In a cemetery there are graves opened by curious, impious hands. One grave has the body of a celebrated duellist who was killed in Arkansas, opposite Memphis, embalmed. He looks like one sleeping. There are skulls that seem to laugh at the chaos which perplexes us, and

fresh faces sleeping under glass that look as though they were in eternal sleep.

"Infants, with their white caps, looking like cherubs asleep, through the glass of metallic cases, awake not nor arise at the tread of the stranger.

"The fences were burned by the rebels, and the passing of hurrying feet and the tread of animals have worn off many of the graves until the occupants are exposed." — *Letter of Sept.* 1863.

A BATTLE WITHIN A BATTLE. — An officer of the Second Connecticut regiment, in a letter to his family, says: "The coolest thing I ever heard of happened at the battle of Fair Oaks. Right in the hottest of the battle, two of the Second's boys got at loggerheads with each other, threw down their muskets, and fell to at fisticuffs — had it out, picked up their arms, and pitched into the rebels again. I have heard of a wheel within a wheel; but a battle within a battle is certainly something new."

A YOUNG HERO. — A correspondent at Cincinnati gives the following touching incident of the hospital: "The eyes of a youth but twenty-one years of age, by name W. N. Bullard, of company A, Eighth Illinois regiment, were closed in death yesterday morning, at the Marine Hospital in this city, by the tender hands of that noble-hearted and faithful woman, Mrs. Caldwell, who has been unwearied in her personal attention to the sick and wounded since the establishment of the Marine as a military hospital for its present purpose. Young Bullard was shot in the breast at Fort Donelson. The ball, a minie, tore his breast open, and lacerated an artery. He bled internally as well as externally. At every gasp, as his end drew near, the blood spirted from his breast. He expired at nine o'clock. Early in the day, when he became fully aware that he could not live long, he showed that he clung to life, and was loath to leave it; but he cried: 'If I could only see my mother — if I could only see my mother before I die, I should be better satisfied.' He was conscious to the last moment, almost, and after reminding Mrs. Caldwell that there were several letters for his mother in his portfolio, she breathed words of consolation to him: 'You die in a glorious cause — you die for your country.' 'Yes,' replied he, 'I am proud to die for my country.'"

AN OLD WOMAN'S WELCOME TO THE FLAG. — A correspondent at Monticello, Kentucky, speaking of the manner in which the people received the national troops in the advance on that place, says, "One old lady, a mile beyond this place, said, as she saw the columns rushing on after the rebels, 'When I seed that old flag comin', I jist throwed my old bonnet on the ground and stomped it.'"

"RICHMUN ON THE JEEMS."

A soldier, filled with Bourbon, lay puking in the
    street,
From battle-field es-ca-ped, with swiftly running
    feet;
He'd fallen from too much "strychnine," and
    drowned all gallant schemes,
And got as far as possible from Richmun on the
    Jeems!

And one there lay beside him — his comrade in the
    flight;
They had been boon companions, and frequently
    got tight;
And side by side they lay there, indulging maudlin
    dreams,
Far from the Libby Prison and Richmun on the
    Jeems!

One said: " Old feller, tell me, what think you of
    this war,
Made by the boastin' rebels, our prosperous peace
    to mar?
Are Lee and Stonewall Jackson such thunderation
    teams,
As to keep us out of Richmun, ole Richmun on the
    Jeems?

" Say, do you think that Hooker — they call him
    ' Fightin' Joe ' —
Who 'for the war committee run down McClellan
    so, —
Will he cross the Rappyhannick, and carry out his
    schemes,
And take us down to Richmun, upon the River
    Jeems?

" Why, when I left old Kaintuck, just eighteen
    months ago,
My mam and sister Ruby both said I shouldn't go;
But I ax'd 'em both, and Susan, to think of me in
    dreams, —
For I'se bound to go to Richmun, old Richmun on
    the Jeems!

" You know, through tribulation, we marched on,
    night and day,
Through woods, and mud, and dusty roads, and
    fightin' in the fray;
By smoke-houses and chicken-coops, and where the
    b'iler steems,
Which cooked our hard-earned rations tow'rd Rich-
    mun on the Jeems.

" And now we're going homeward — me and the
    other scamp —
Yet far from old Kentucky we are obleeged to
    tramp;
And him who's out of postage stamps, there's no-
    body esteems,
E'en though he's been in Richmun, and seed the
    River Jeems!

" To hell with old Phiginny, and all her sacred sile!
She's made a heap of trouble, and kept it up awhile;
And if she's helped herself right much, 'tis like to
    them sunbeams
The niggers squeeze from cucumbers, in Richmun
    on the Jeems! "

And then his boon companion convulsively turned
    o'er,
And, grunting an affirmative, straightway began to
    snore,
Oblivious to war's alarms or love's delightful
    themes,
Or to the fact that Richmun still stands upon the
    Jeems!

Grow on, thou " sour apple-tree," where Jeffy is to
    hang!
Rejoice, ye running contrabands, for this is your
    chebang!
No more you'll stem tobacco, thresh wheat, or drive
    the teams
Of rebels round the city — old Richmun on the
    Jeems!

INCIDENT OF WEST POINT. — James E. Montgomery gives the following narrative of his experience at the battle of West Point, Virginia,
which was fought in May, 1862: " My own escape
is wonderful, and, indeed, almost miraculous, and
I forgot not to thank God for his watchfulness
over me. It was about one o'clock P. M. when
I received an order from General Newton to go
forward into the woods to ascertain whether the
rebels were falling back, and whether a certain
regiment of ours held its position there. I went
forward at once, as fast as my well-tried horse
could carry me, and upon entering the woods
moved cautiously until I reached a barricade,
when, hearing voices beside me, I plunged into the
woods, thinking, of course, it was one of our regiments, Thirty-first New York, and was surprised
to find that I had gone right into a perfect nest
of the Hampton Legion, from South Carolina,
who were lying behind trees, standing behind
bushes, and kneeling behind stumps, like bees. I
at once perceived my mistake, and knew that
nothing but the most consummate coolness would
save me. I therefore saluted them, and they,
taking me for a rebel officer, asked me how far
General Hampton was then. I answered without hesitation, and with rather more assurance
than I thought I possessed, ' I left him about ten
rods below here;' and added, ' Now, boys, the
General expects you to do your duty to-day.' I
then turned my horse slowly to lull suspicion, and
was congratulating myself on the probable success
of my ruse, when, seeing the U. S. on my cap,
they yelled out, ' That's a d—d Yankee son of a
b—! Give him h—!' On hearing this, I dashed
the spurs into my horse, threw my head over his
neck, and made for the road. A perfect volley of
minie balls passed over and around me — killed
my horse, who rolled over, carrying me with him,
and left me down. Knowing that apparently
nothing but time would save me, I lay with my
head back in a ditch as I fell, and appeared *dead*
for some ten minutes. I did not move a muscle
or a feature, although the scoundrels were swarming around me, and threatening to ' end me.' I
remained in this way until they came up to me,
took away my pistol, and commenced general
plundering; and as they fingered away, I could

not suppress a smile; and then rising, I said, 'Well, men, I yield as a prisoner of war.' They said, 'You have been shamming, you d—d Yankee scoundrel, have you?' 'Certainly,' said I; 'everything is fair in war.' They then commenced to abuse me, as a d—d Yankee this, and a d—d Yankee that; when I turned upon them, and said, 'I have yielded as a prisoner of war; I demand to be used as such. We in the North know how to treat dogs better than you do men; now lead me to your commanding officer.' They gave me another volley of abuse, at which I merely smiled, and then a shell, fired by our artillery to the place where I was seen to enter, burst like the wind amongst us — skinning my nose, and scattering the rebel rascals like chaff. They seized their muskets, pointed two of them at me, and told me to 'come along, you d—d Yankee!' I still talked with them to gain time, when another shell bursting amongst us, they moved on farther, calling to me to 'come on,' while I said, 'Go ahead, lead the way, quick.' I then saw a favorable moment, and preferring freedom to a Southern prison, I made one bound into the woods, and went back as fast as one leg would carry me. I felt very much exhausted, and was carried to the rear by some men and placed under a tree, when, with whiskey and care, I soon felt stronger, although my leg was stiff. They wished me to go in an ambulance to hospital, but I politely declined; and calling for an extra horse, I was lifted on his back, and returned to the field, and reported to General Newton for duty. He kindly told me that I had distinguished myself enough this day, and requested me to keep quiet."

THE FOURTEENTH TENNESSEE. — This regiment, when the prospects of the Confederacy opened so brilliant in 1861, left Clarksville, Tenn., with nine hundred and sixty men. They were of the best families, and the pride of Montgomery County. Young men, of fine education, surrounded with superior comforts, and who were marked for high positions in civil community, left their homes, pleasant associations, and all the endearments of the fireside — left the legal bar, the counting-room, and the hall of princely home on the plantation, to go into the Confederate ranks, and exterminate the cowardly legions of a tyrannical North. Wily statesmen appealed to the chivalry of Southern hearts to break the bonds of Union, throw off a despotism, and strike for liberty, independence, and the firesides of home. Ambitious fathers pointed to future glories of a Confederacy, and by acts, if not words, urged the son to go in defence of the Southern cause. Mothers kissed the parting boy oft without a tear, and with a burning appeal to die nobly on the battle-field, saw him depart from the childhood home. And girls, just budding into womanhood, the fairy schoolmates and early friends of the young men, cheered them on to deeds of valor and glory. All was wild enthusiasm. Popular frenzy ruled the hour, and he who refused to volunteer was coldly sneered at, and turned from as a coward, and unworthy the name of Southron. Every household that boasted a son was robbed of its idol. The ranks swelled rapidly, faces were missed from every corner, and from every home. And as the hurricane sweeps the stately forest before it, leaving sad destruction in its track, so were the youth swept from their homes, and wildly cheered on to the battle-fields, a sacrifice to the shrine of Ambition.

Wildly, enthusiastically, they left their homes without one solid thought as to the true responsibilities of the undertaking. Their march to camp was more like going to the transient joys of a ball-room or festival, than to the cold realities of the battle-field. They then thought the war would be of short duration — that the Northern States would quail before the imposing array of the military and warlike South. They calculated without the cost. They dreamed not that they would be sent from the States to protect the capital of the Confederacy, and participate in the sanguinary battles on the bloody fields of Virginia, while the homes they volunteered to defend, were left unprotected, and occupied by Federal troops.

Two years and a half have flown. A sad change has come over the prospect of the Confederacy. The Fourteenth Tennessee has met a terrible fate. Ever thrown into the front, it has fought in all the bloody contests of Virginia. The fickle Goddess of Fortune failed to smile upon the regiment. Each battle thinned their ranks; and when night closed over each day's fearful fight they counted their numbers, and knew that carnage had reigned with an unsparing hand. Steadily they have met the shock of battle, and O, how many hearts at home have been saddened by the results! The bright star of their destiny has gradually faded; and at the late fierce battle of Gettysburg, the orb, dimmed in lustre, sank behind the red storm-cloud of battle, on the field of disaster and blood. The regiment went into the fight with sixty men, all told, and in a desperate charge, where Federal cannon and volleys of musketry swept the rugged plain, the remaining sixty men of the once nine hundred and sixty were felled to the ground, dead, dying, wounded, and left in the hands of the enemy. We are told that in this charge only three men out of the sixty escaped; all the rest were killed or wounded.

Thus the band that once was the pride of the city of Clarksville has fallen. The rugged plains of Virginia are stained with their blood, and every battle-field furnishes a grave for some of the fallen. A gloom rests over the city; the hopes and affections of the people were wrapped in the regiment. The idols have fallen, and a void is left within their hearts. Their forms sleep in a common grave, far from the scenes of home. Fathers, mothers, brothers and sisters now realize the terrible sacrifice that has been made; and to know the victims were cheered on to the destiny, is a fact no less grievous than true. Their pulses are now numbered with sorrow; and turning to the past, a vivid picture is drawn — a noble boy passing from the threshold of his home, going to the field of battle with almost a smile on his face, passing out into night and darkness forever!

The early scenes of childhood and manhood are treasured, and form a bright past to the picture; but eternal night obscures the future. The pride of the household is fallen — fallen in a strange land, on a field where carnage held high revel. They only know that he is dead — mortal knows not where the form sleeps — the soldier's "sleep that knows no waking." Strange hands have gathered the dead, and heaped the bodies together in one rude and common burial. Friends may visit the battle-ground in search of the lost loved, but return bewildered with the sickening scene, where a wilderness of trenches form a common grave for thousands of friend and foe.

Yes, the sacrifice has been made; the heart is robbed of its idol; death has claimed the victim, and we know not where the loved one sleeps. He died with a ghastly wound, writhed in pain; no mother soothed his brow; no sister held the refreshing draught to his lips — rolled his glassy eyes heavenward; no father knelt in prayer; but alone — his ears filled with the roar of cannon, the rattle of musketry and the groans of fellow-wounded — his lips parted, and parched in death agony; and death and blood everywhere meeting the cold stare of his fading eyesight, the icy chill steals over his body — one struggle — one gasp, and the soul is freed from the "prison-house of pain"! The sacrifice is complete: ambition is satisfied, and turns to gloat with fiendish delight over new victims.

Ah! what a terrible responsibility rests upon those that inaugurated this unholy war, and who have sacrificed so many lives for the accomplishment of their desires. May the pale shadows of their victims haunt their day dreams, and appear in ghostly form in all their night visions. May the cold stare of their accusing eyes haunt them continually, stagger their brain with wild fancies, and demons ever howl their guilt in their ears.

LEONARD GRENEWALD. — The destruction of the pontoon bridge and train at Falling Waters, in July, 1863, was one of the most daring exploits of the war, and the credit of it belongs mainly to Leonard Grenewald, chief of the Gray Eagle Scouts, and formerly of the Jessie Scouts. During previous trips, he had ascertained the strength of the ground and location of the bridge, and finally obtained from General French a detail of two hundred men from the First Virginia and Thirteenth and Fourteenth New York cavalry, under Major Foley and Lieutenant Dawson, to undertake its destruction. They arrived at the Potomac in the morning, just at daylight, and found the character of the bridge to be part trestle work, with pontoons in the centre, which were carefully floated out every evening, and taken to the Virginia shore, rendering the bridge useless for the night. Lieutenant Dawson and Grenewald then swam the river, and brought back several pontoons, with which they ferried over some

forty of the detachment, being all that were willing to go. Arriving on the southern side, they surprised the rebel camp, fired a volley into the sleeping rebels, and created an utter stampede. They captured about twenty rebels, including one officer. Then, destroying the camp, some stores, and four wagons of ammunition, they took all the pontoons over the river, and either burned or cut them to pieces. The balance of the bridge was destroyed, and the party came off without the loss of a man. Grenewald desired to perform the same thing at Williamsport, but his party declined to back him up. He was one of the most daring and reliable of scouts, and performed great service.

SHERMAN'S FLANK MOVEMENTS. — General Sherman's strategy in flanking the rebels out of their strong positions puzzled the natives a good deal. A young woman said it was not fair to fight the Southern soldiers "on end." She then went on to say, that the day before General Bragg had formed "two streaks of fight" in their door-yard with "walking soldiers," and General Wheeler formed "one streak of fight with critter soldiers" — meaning cavalry — behind the house, but that Joe Hooker had come up and flanked Bragg, and made him fall back, which he did in such a hurry, that he "upset dad's ash-hopper plant," which cost two dollars and fifty cents in Atlanta; and "dad was a-goin' to sue Bragg for waste."

THE DEATH OF GENERAL LYTLE. — A soldier of Chickamauga relates the following: "The noble General died as a soldier loves to die, with his brave men around him, steadily fighting vastly superior numbers. A moment before he received the fatal wound, he said: 'Brave Wisconsin boys, I am proud of you!' and with renewed vigor they poured in their fire, though their numbers were rapidly decreasing. And he was justly proud of them, for I never saw men stand up to their work so steadily and coolly, and I am glad to have the privilege of saying it to you, their old commander. How your heart would have swelled, and your eyes kindled, if you had seen them go in and stay, until unsupported on both flanks they were compelled to fall back, and not then until poor Lytle had been carried away from their immediate vicinity, where he had been sitting on his horse, encouraging them by his cheering words."

THE SPIRIT OF KENTUCKY. — The Cleveland *Plaindealer* related the following incident, which transpired in the Kentucky Legislature:

"A venerable farmer, from a neighboring county, one of that kind for whom Kentucky has an instinctive veneration, appeared in the Legislative Hall, uncovered his snowy locks, and sat down. At the first lull in the debate, he rose slowly, and said he had a word to say, but was aware it was out of order for him to speak before the Legislature while in session. His dignified and venerable appearance arrested attention, and 'Go on,' 'Go on,' from several voices, seemed to keep him on his feet. Again expressing his diffidence at speaking, out of propriety — 'Hear! hear!' resounded generally over the room. The members' curiosity, as well as respect, for the appearance and manner of the man was up, and silence followed the 'Hear! hear!' when the old hero delivered the following eloquent, but laconic speech:

"'Gentlemen: I am delegated by my county to inform you, that if you hold a secret session here, as you threaten to do, not one stone of this Capitol will rest upon another twenty-four hours after. Good day!' and he left."

STORY OF A NORTH CAROLINA NEGRO. — A slave related this story to a member of the Twenty-seventh Massachusetts regiment, while at Newbern:

"I was owned up the country [the western part of the State] by a man who had a large plantation, and four or five hundred slaves. I was well used, every way, by him, and one day he told me to carry a letter to a man in Raleigh. I knew this man was a speculator in slaves, and I was suspicious that all was not right; but I could not believe my master would deceive me; so I started. On my way, I met a free colored man that I was acquainted with, and he could read. I told him where I was going, and for what. He asked to see the letter. It was not sealed, and he took it out and read it to me. It was a bill of sale, and I was one of the lot; and we were sold to go to Alabama. My master had taken this way to deliver me, rather than have a 'scene,' as it is termed; and this speculator was to seize me upon my appearance, and send me South. I had rather have died than gone; so, after thinking it over, and consulting my colored friend, I, with his help, got a couple of knives and a good rifle, a few clothes and some provisions, and took to the bush [woods and swamps], where I could defy pursuit. There I lived and suffered *seven years*, relying upon my trusty rifle for food, and got so expert that I could kill a coon or bear at forty rods every time. [Bears are, and were, somewhat numerous here in the swamp.]

"I heard when the war broke out, and heard when Burnside took Newbern; so I made tracks for the Union people, and when I came in here, I went straight to Burnside's headquarters, and told him my story. He told me to take off my coat, which was nothing but rags, and he gave me one of his own coats, and called me a brave fellow."

MORGAN'S ESCAPE. — The following incident is connected with the remarkable escape of Morgan from his Northern imprisonment:

Having made application to two respectable citizens of Clayton, Rabun County, Georgia, for a night's lodgings, and been refused because they thought he was an impostor, and recognized him, Mr. N—— invited him to his house, where he spent the night. Meantime, it had been currently reported in the village and vicinity, that an impostor, pretending to be John Morgan, was at the house of Mr. N——. Next morning about twenty of the "Home Guards" assembled, and, under the direction of their efficient Captain, arrested him. He quietly submitted, and assured them that, if he failed to prove his identity, he would accompany them to Atlanta. About this time, one or two gentlemen, who had seen him, recognized him, and some facts were developed which satisfied the Home Guards that they had captured the veritable John H. Morgan! Of course, he was at once released. Before leaving, he addressed the crowd briefly, commending, in the highest terms, the vigilance they displayed; advised them to arrest all persons who could not give a satisfactory account of themselves; and closed with the playful remark that twenty men had accomplished, in Rabun, what it required forty thousand in Ohio to do!

The crowd gave nine cheers for Morgan, and he proceeded on his way to Walhalla.

DEATH OF A BERDAN SHARPSHOOTER. — A correspondent of a Southern paper says:

"A gentleman informs us of the death of one of McClellan's sharpshooters, on the Peninsula, under circumstances which possess interest sufficient to give them to the public. Several of our men, it seems, were killed while going to a spring near by, but by whom no one could imagine. It was at last determined to stop this inhuman game, if possible, even at the cost of killing the hireling himself, who was thus in cold blood butchering our men. So a sharp lookout was kept for this sharpshooter, and the next time he fired the smoke of his rifle revealed the locality of his pit.

"That night a pit was dug by the Confederate soldiers, commanding the position of the Yankee sharpshooter, and arrangements made to get rid of the annoying creature. For this purpose a young Kentuckian was placed in our pit, with a trusty rifle, and provisions enough to last him until the next night. Next morning early a man was despatched, as usual, with two buckets to go to the spring. He had proceeded about two hundred yards, when the Yankee marksman elevated himself, and placing his rifle to his shoulder, was about to pull trigger; but the Kentuckian was too quick for him, for he pulled his trigger first, and simultaneously therewith the Yankee fell.

"Upon repairing to the spot, which the Kentuckian did immediately, he discovered a riflepit, and a sturdy Yankee in it, in the last agonies of expiring nature. The pit was provided with a cushioned chair, pipes and tobacco, liquors and provisions. But the rifle which had been used was really a valuable prize. It was of most superb manufacture, and supplied with the latest invention — an improved telescopic sight upon its end. The pit had been dug at night, and its occupant had been provisioned at night; so, but for a sharp lookout for the smoke of his gun, there is no saying how long this Yankee vandal would have enjoyed the luxury of killing Southern men, without even a chance of losing his own worthless life."

AN INCIDENT OF THE BATTLE OF THE FORTS. — Captain Boggs, of the Varuna, tells a story of a brave boy who was on board his vessel, during the bombardment of the forts on the Mississippi River. The lad, who answers to the name of Oscar, is but thirteen years of age, but he has an old head on his shoulders, and is alert and energetic. During the hottest of the fire he was busily engaged in passing ammunition to the gunners, and narrowly escaped death when one of the terrific broadsides of the Varuna's rebel antagonist was poured in. Covered with dirt, and begrimed with powder, he was met by Captain Boggs, who asked "where he was going in such a hurry?" "To get a passing-box, sir; the other one was smashed by a ball!" And so, throughout the fight, the brave lad held his place and did his duty.

When the Varuna went down, Captain Boggs missed his boy, and thought he was among the victims of the battle. But a few minutes afterwards he saw the lad swimming gallantly towards the wreck. Clambering on board of Captain Boggs' boat, he threw his hand up to his forehead, giving the usual salute, and uttering only the words, "All right, sir; I report myself on board," and passed coolly to his station.

BLACK TOM.

HUNTED by his rebel master
  Over many a hill and glade,
Black Tom, with his wife and children,
  Found his way to our brigade.

Tom had sense, and truth, and courage,
  Often tried where danger rose —
Once our flag his strong arm rescued
  From the grasp of rebel foes.

One day Tom was marching with us
  Through the forest as our guide,
When a ball from traitor's rifle
  Broke his arm and pierced his side.

On a litter white men bore him
  Through the forest drear and damp,
Laid him, dying, where our banners
  Brightly fluttered o'er our camp.

Pointing to his wife and children,
  While he suffered racking pain,
Said he to our soldiers round him,
  "Don't let them be slaves again!"

"No, by Heaven!" outspoke a soldier, —
  And *that* oath was not profane, —
"Our brigade will still protect them —
  They shall ne'er be slaves again."

Over old Tom's dusky features
  Came and staid a joyous ray;
And with saddened friends around him,
  His free spirit passed away.

INCIDENTS OF CHATTANOOGA. — "Captain Harris, of the Nineteenth Indiana battery, stood by his guns, after being twice wounded; and when he became weak from loss of blood, he made his men support him while he sighted the guns.

"A man, by the name of Brock, in the Eleventh Ohio regiment, was wounded through the neck and lower jaw, at Perryville. He had not been in the engagement over ten minutes, on Sunday, when a ball struck him in the same place, taking the same course with the other, making a horrible wound.

"George Kizer, of the Seventy-fifth Indiana regiment, company F, was killed on the field. Before he was killed he had requested his messmate to send his photograph, with some other things, to his mother, in case he was killed; but there is not often a chance to attend to such things on the field. On Saturday night the rebels thought we were evacuating the place, and they threw forward their right to attack us. They soon found out their mistake. They were scooped in no time. We took thirty prisoners, and killed and wounded as many more. On one of the dead rebs the Indiana boys found Kizer's knapsack, with his likeness and all his things, which the boys have now sent to his mother. I saw the likeness myself, and the boys were positive in the identity.

"At one of our pickets and posts a sharpshooter had annoyed the men for some time, and no one could find his whereabouts. At last one of the men thought he saw a small cedar tree move. The boys laughed at him, but he blazed away, and down came the bush. On examination they found that a rebel had stuck cedar boughs in his boots and belt, so that he looked just like a small tree a little way off." — *From a correspondent.*

DIANA SMITH, THE HEROINE OF THE NORTH-WEST. — She was born and raised in the County of Jackson, Virginia. Her father is a consistent member of the Methodist Episcopal Church, and was leading a quiet, peaceful, and useful life, until his country was invaded, when he called his countrymen to arms, and raised the first company of guerrillas, which he commanded until last fall, when, by fraud and treachery, he was captured, and ever since has been confined in a loathsome dungeon at Camp Chase, Ohio, without hope of delivery, unless our government should interpose and procure his release.

Diana, his only daughter, a beautiful girl, has been tenderly raised and well educated. She is also a member of the Methodist Episcopal Church, and has always been regarded as very pious and exemplary. She is descended from a race of unflinching nerve, and satisfied with nothing less than freedom, as unrestrained as the pure air of their mountain home.

Her devotion to the cause of Southern rights, in which her father had nobly engaged, has caused her, too, to feel the oppressor's power. Although a tender and delicate flower, upon whose cheek the bloom of sixteen summers yet lingers, she has been five times captured by the Yankees, and marched sometimes on foot, in *manacles*, a prisoner — once a considerable distance into Ohio, at which time she made her escape. She was never released, but in each instance managed to escape from her guard. She, too, has seen service; she was in several battles in which her father engaged the enemy. She has seen blood flow like water. Her trusty rifle has made more than one of the vile Yankees bite the dust. She left her home in company with the Moccason Rangers, Captain Kesler, and came through the enemy's lines in safety, and is now at the Blue Sulphur Springs.

She was accompanied by Miss Duskie, who has also earned the proud distinction of a heroine. On one occasion this fearless girl, surrounded by fifty Yankees and Union men, rushed through their ranks with a daring that struck terror to their craven hearts. With her rifle lashed across her shoulders, she swam the west fork of the Kanawha River, and made her way to the Mountain Rangers, preferring to trust her safety to those brave spirits, well knowing that her sex would entitle her to protection from these brave mountaineers. These young ladies have lain in the mountains for months, with no bed but the earth, and no covering but the canopy of heaven. They have shared the soldier's rough fare, his dangers, his hopes, and his joys.

The great crime with which these daring young ladies are charged by the enemy, is cooking, washing, mending and making clothes, and buying powder for the soldiers. We are informed that they are both ladies of the first rank at home, and are every way worthy of the highest place in any society where virtue, integrity, and sterling principle give position. — *Southern paper.*

GALLANTRY OF YOUNG SHALER. — A correspondent gives an account of the gallant conduct of Henry Shaler, of Indianapolis, Indiana, at the battle of Gettysburg, written by a son of Daniel Noble to his mother. Young Shaler more than equalled the mythical performance of the Irishman who "surrounded" a half dozen of the enemy, and captured them. His parents live on South Alabama Street, in Indianapolis, Indiana. They are Germans. Young Noble says : " Harry is a brick ; he did more, that is, he took more prisoners, in the battle of Gettysburg, than any other man in the army. He took in all twenty-five men — one lieutenant and eighteen men at one time. He took them by strategy that *was* strategy ; he 'surrounded them,' and they had to give up. On the morning of the fourth he went out with his poncho over his shoulders, so that the rebs couldn't see his coat ; so they thought he was one of their own men. He went up, and told them to lay down their arms, and come and help carry some wounded off the field. They did so. When he got them away from their arms, he rode up to the lieutenant, and told him to give up his sword. The lieutenant refused at first ; but Harry drew his pepper-box, and, like Crockett's

coon, the lieutenant came down without a shot. Harry then took them all into camp. He took a captain and five men at another time, making twenty-five in all, which is doing pretty well for a little Dutchman ; and he deserves to be remembered for it."

CHICKAMAUGA, OR THE RIVER OF DEATH. — In the spring of 1858, while seeking the benefit of a change of climate and relaxation from laborious duties, I met the late Colonel Whiteside at Chattanooga. Among the many interesting traditions associated with various localities in this beautiful region of country, he related one in explanation of the meaning of the word " Chickamauga," and how it came to be applied to the two small streams which bear this name. A tribe of Cherokees occupied this region ; and when the small-pox was first communicated to the Indians of this continent, it appeared in this tribe, and made frightful havoc among them. It was the custom of the Indians, at the height of the disease, to go by scores, and jump into the river to allay the tormenting symptoms. This of course increased the mortality, and the name " Chickamauga," or " River of Death," was applied to the two streams, which they have borne ever since. The remnant of the tribe was also afterwards called the " Chickamauga tribe." We hope General Bragg will call his great victory the Battle of Chickamauga, and not " Peavine Creek," or " Crawfish Springs," as is suggested in Rosecrans' despatch. He has certainly *crawfished* out of Georgia, but we prefer " Chickamauga," or " River of Death." — *Southern correspondent.*

AN INTERESTING INCIDENT. — In the freshman class at Harvard was a Washington, from Virginia, the nearest relative of the General, bearing the name of George, and born on the 22d of February. He was a youth of excellent principles, a communicant in the Episcopal Church, and respected and beloved by his classmates. On the breaking out of difficulties, he left Cambridge, — not for any sympathy with secession, for he was strongly against it in all his feelings, — but because he thought it his duty to be near his mother, a widow, whose estate lay in the threatened portion of the border. Soon afterwards others of his class left college to join the Massachusetts regiments.

A few days after the battle of Winchester, one of these young men, Lieutenant Crowninshield, of the Massachusetts Second regiment, was walking through the wards of the hospital, then filled with rebel officers and soldiers, and heard his familiar college nickname, " Crowny, Crowny," called by a feeble voice from one of the beds. He went to it, and there — pale, faint, shot through the lungs by a musket ball — lay his classmate, young Washington. It is needless to say, that everything possible was done for him. The mother was allowed to take her son home for maternal care.

CHARGE OF THE MULE BRIGADE.

ON the night of October 28, 1863, when Gen. Geary's division of the Twelfth corps repulsed the attacking forces of Longstreet at Wauhatchie, Tenn., a number of mules, affrighted by the noise of battle, dashed into the ranks of Hampton's Legion, causing much dismay among the rebels, and compelling many of them to fall back, under a supposed charge of cavalry.

Capt. Thomas H. Elliott, of Gen. Geary's staff, gives the following rendition of the incident, which he gleaned from an interior contemporary. Its authorship is not known:

I.

Half a mile, half a mile,
Half a mile onward,
Right towards the Georgia troops,
Broke the two hundred.
"Forward, the Mule Brigade,"
"Charge for the Rebs!" they neighed;
Straight for the Georgia troops
Broke the two hundred.

II.

"Forward, the Mule Brigade!"
Was there a mule dismayed?
Not when the long ears felt
All their ropes sundered;
Theirs not to make reply;
Theirs not to reason why;
Theirs but to make them fly.
On! to the Georgia troops,
Broke the two hundred.

III.

Mules to the right of them,
Mules to the left of them,
Mules behind them,
Pawed, brayed, and thundered.
Breaking their own confines,
Breaking through Longstreet's lines,
Into the Georgia troops
Stormed the two hundred.

IV.

Wild all their eyes did glare,
Whisked all their tails in air,
Scattering the chivalry there,
While all the world wondered.
Not a mule back bestraddled,
Yet how they all skedaddled!
Fled every Georgian.
Unsabred, unsaddled,
Scattered and sundered,
How they were routed there
By the two hundred!

V.

Mules to the right of them,
Mules to the left of them,
Mules behind them
Pawed, brayed, and thundered;
Followed by hoof and head,
Full many a hero fled,
Fain in the last ditch dead,
Back from an "ass's jaw,"
All that was left of them,
Left by the two hundred.

VI.

When can their glory fade?
O! the wild charge they made!
All the world wondered.
Honor the charge they made,
Honor the Mule Brigade,
Long-eared two hundred.

AN INCIDENT UNDER A FLAG OF TRUCE. — Lieut.-Commander H. A. Adams, Jr., United States Navy, arrived at New Orleans, having been relieved of the command of the United States forces in Mississippi Sound by Lieut.-Commander Green. He recently sent his boat on shore, and desired the officer in charge to say that if any military officer received the flag, he would be glad to see him on board to arrange the business of the truce. As the boat returned, he saw an officer, who recognized him, but he could not make out who he was. When the boat came alongside, he went to the gangway to receive the stranger, and even helped him over the rail on deck, when he immediately found himself clasped in the arms of his own brother, one in command of the Confederate forces on shore, the other in command of the United States forces afloat. The meeting, under such circumstances, was, as you may imagine, a very painful one. After the business was over, and a brotherly chat had, they parted — the Confederate saying, as he got into the boat, "Whatever happens, Hal, recollect one thing — we will always be brothers."

GENERAL GRANT OBEYS ORDERS. — General Grant was walking the dock at City Point, absorbed in thought, and with the inevitable cigar in his mouth, when a negro guard touched his arm, saying, "No smoking on the dock, sir." "Are these your orders?" asked the General, looking up. "Yes, sir," replied the negro, courteously, but decidedly. "Very good orders," said Grant, throwing his cigar into the water.

A JUVENILE WARRIOR OF EXPERIENCE. — The town of Swanzey, in New Hampshire, is the home of George B. Mattoon, a young man only eighteen years old, who served three years in the Union army, had been in forty-three battles and twenty-seven skirmishes, had two horses shot under him, and during the whole time did not receive a single injury, nor was he absent from duty a single day.

A CONTRABAND. — A soldier gives the following sketch of the appearance and peculiarities of one of the slaves met with by his regiment while marching South:

"As I went into the yard I saw standing in the midst of the men an aged contraband, whose woolly pate was profusely mottled with gray, and a gray, woolly fringe around the base of his ebon face, gave him a most singular appearance. His enormous mouth, thick lips, and flattened nose of purely African stamp, and retreating fore-head, very low in height, would convey an idea of almost idiotic intellect within. As I approached, his lower jaw slowly moved downwards, and then upwards, like the first movements of the arm of a ponderous steam engine, and then from the expansive reservoir of his throat came forth a *sound*, and he began to sing a hymn. There was not much melody in his music, but he seemed to enjoy it as well as an Ole Bull or Paganini would their own performance. He was dressed in the cast-off uniform, overcoat, and pants of some rebel soldier; and the coat half dropping from one shoulder, in a careless style, plainly indicated an innate '*cuffee*.' He finished his hymn, and some one asked him if he wouldn't *pray*. The old man paused for a moment, and then said:

"'De good book say dat when we worship God we mus do it wid de speret and de troof, and I doesn't like for see sich tings treated lightly. Now, if ye'll all be quiet, and not larf, and pay attention, I'll do de bes I ken.'

"Having promised good behavior, the old man knelt down. As he was kneeling, some one asked him to pray for the war to close. He commenced his prayer with an eloquence of language and propriety of expression absolutely astonishing, and I could hardly believe that in that apparently demented cranium could be stored an intellect which displayed itself in a manner indicating that nature had given it a power and utterance far above many of those who were looking upon the possessor as they would on a monkey or parrot, or some other natural curiosity. There was an expression in his prayer which, in connection with the request to pray for the soldiers, was peculiarly noticeable. He prayed:

"'O Massa Lord God A'mity! have mercy on all sogers, an em's gwine to war. O Lord! batter all dere big guns inter prowsheers, and dere swords inter prune hooks, and make peace come quick.'

"This expression seemed an isolated one in his prayer, as having less propriety of expression than any other one. At the close of his prayer, he was asked where his master was, and replied:

"'O, he's done gone dis four months; he wouldn't jine *Mr. Linkum's* company, so he had to leave, and go off way down Souf.'

"''Twould be a snug chance for him if he was at home here now — wouldn't it?' some one asked.

"'Golly, massa, 'deed 'twould, I reckon,' laughed the sable chattel. 'He'd ben dead an buried up in de grave long time go, if he hadn't run off.'

"He was asked if many soldiers came there, and replied that they came every day, in the morning, and that they had been there that morning on horseback. He was asked what they were, and replied, —

"'Can't tell, massa, 'deed I can't; some say't dey's scessongers, but 'pon my soul an body, massa, I can't tell one from t'other — 'deed I can't. But I'se on Mr. *Linkum's* side — 'deed I is.'

"He was then asked to preach, and finally consented, and commenced, taking for his subject the characters of Nicodemus and Hezekiah, and commenced in a manner displaying an astonishing depth of knowledge of Scripture history, and drawing logical deductions with a style of language and beauty of expression that need not be ashamed of as worthy the efforts of many an extemporaneous preacher in the most enlightened portions of civilized community in the free States.

"As I listened, I thought what, but for the accursed, soul-destroying influence of slavery, which binds its victims in shackles of ignorance, might not this man have been. Possessed of an intellect of uncommon wealth and vigor, though clothed in rags, and bound by the rankling shackles of an unjust oppression, which forbids it to *wish* even to rise to seek its own level among humanity, it breaks the bonds with the force which nature alone imparts, and rises, unaided by the acquirements of art, above the common herd around. To what eminence might it not have attained if cultivated and trained by the aids which the times now afford the free man?"

THE TAKING OF POTOSI, MO.

THE Union men of Washington County having been threatened with extermination, and some of them having been driven from Potosi, the county seat, complaint was made to Gen. Lyon, of the St. Louis Arsenal, and that brave and gallant officer determined to give the Union men in that section of the country protection. Accordingly an expedition was planned, and put under the command of Capt. Coles, of company A, Fifth regiment of United States volunteers. At ten o'clock P. M., Tuesday, May 14, 1861, Capt. Cole's command, consisting of some one hundred and fifty men, left the arsenal on a special train for their destination. They arrived at Potosi at three o'clock, A. M., on Wednesday, and immediately threw a chain of sentinels around the entire town. Guards were then stationed around the dwellings of the most prominent secessionists, and shortly after daylight, some one hundred and fifty men found themselves prisoners, and were marched off to the Court House. Here the prisoners were formed in line, and by the assistance of a gentleman who had been driven out of Potosi, who knew all the inhabitants of the place, the Union men were recognized, and released, amounting to over half of those taken prisoners. Some fifty of the secessionists were also released, on parole of honor, after subscribing to the usual oath *not to take up arms against the United States*, and nine of the leaders were marched off to the cars. The guard then made a descent on a secession lead manufactory, and captured near four hundred pigs of that very useful article in time of war, which belonged to a man who had been furnishing lead to the Southern rebels. The man's name is John Dean, and he is now a prisoner at the arsenal. It appears he was not satisfied to simply sell the lead to the enemy, in defiance of the authority of the Government, but was engaged with his own team in hauling it to near the Arkansas line, where the traitors could get possession of it without danger. The guard captured several pistols, rifles, shot guns, and a quantity of secession uniforms, most of them unfinished, and some uniform cloth.

After being furnished with breakfast and dinner, and very handsomely treated by the Union men of Potosi, and invited to stay a month in that place, at their expense, the command started for home. On their way back, the train made a halt at De Soto, in Jefferson County, where there was to be a grand secession "love-feast" and flag-raising. Here they found a company of secession cavalry drilling for the occasion, which took to their heels as soon as they got a sight of the United States troops. In their flight, the cavalry left some thirty of their horses, which were captured by the troops, and placed under guard. The pole — one hundred feet high — on which the rebels were going to fly the secession flag was soon graced with the Stars and Stripes, amid the wildest enthusiasm of the Union men and Government troops. The next move was to capture the rebel flag, which was known to be in town; and for this agreeable duty, Captain Cole detailed a guard of six men, under command of Serg. Walker, accompanied by Dr. Franklin, Surgeon of the Fifth Regiment. The guard surrounded the house supposed to contain the flag, and Dr. Franklin and Serg. Walker entered. After searching in vain for some time, the Doctor thought he observed the lady of the house sitting in rather an uneasy position, and he very politely asked her to rise. At first the lady hesitated, but finding the Doctor's persuasive sauvity irresistible, she rose slowly, and lo! the blood-red stripe of the rebel ensign appeared below the lady's hoops. The Doctor, bowing a graceful "beg pardon, madam," stooped, and quietly catching hold of the gaudy color, carefully delivered the lady of a secession flag, thirty feet long, and nine feet wide. The Doctor bore off his prize in triumph to the camp, where the troops greeted him with wild shouts, and characterized his feat as the crowning glory of the occasion. Here the troops captured another rebel leader, and after placing thirty men, under Lieut. Murphy, to guard the Union flag and the thirty horses, Capt. Cole's command started on their way. At Victoria, the train stopped a moment, when another secessionist came up hurrahing for Jeff Davis; and quick as thought the ardent rebel was surrounded by a half dozen bayonets, and marched into the cars a prisoner of war, and the train moved on. They arrived at the arsenal about six and a half o'clock P. M., where a crowd of soldiers and visitors awaited them. The spoils were unloaded, and the prisoners marched to safe and comfortable quarters. Gen. Lyon received them in the spirit of a true soldier, and the troops gave three cheers for Gen. Lyon, three for Col. Blair, and three for the Stars and Stripes, and then caught the secession flag, and tore it into shreds in a twinkling.

NOT YET.

BY WILLIAM CULLEN BRYANT.

O country, marvel of the earth!
    O realm to sudden greatness grown!
The age that gloried in thy birth,
    Shall it behold thee overthrown?
Shall traitors lay that greatness low?
No! Land of Hope and Blessing, No!

And we who wear thy glorious name,
    Shall we, like cravens, stand apart,
When those whom thou hast trusted aim
    The death-blow at thy generous heart?
Forth goes the battle-cry, and lo!
Hosts rise in harness, shouting, No!

And they who founded in our land
    The power that rules from sea to sea,
Bled they in vain, or vainly planned
    To leave their country great and free?
Their sleeping ashes from below
Send up the thrilling murmur, No!

Knit they the gentle ties which long
    These sister States were proud to wear,
And forged the kindly links so strong,
    For idle hands in sport to tear —
For scornful hands aside to throw?
No! by our fathers' memory, No!

Our humming marts, our iron ways,
    Our wind-tossed woods on mountain crest,
The hoarse Atlantic, with his bays,
    The calm, broad Ocean of the West,
And Mississippi's torrent-flow,
And loud Niagara, answer, No!

Not yet the hour is nigh when they
    Who deep in Eld's dim twilight sit,
Earth's ancient kings, shall rise and say,
    "Proud country, welcome to the pit!
So soon art thou, like us, brought low!"
No! sullen group of shadows, No!

For now, behold, the arm that gave
    The victory in our fathers' day,
Strong as of old to guard and save, —
    That mighty arm which none can stay, —
On clouds above, and fields below,
Writes, in men's sight, the answer, No!

INCIDENTS OF CARRICK'S FORD. — In one of the Indiana regiments that took part in the fight at Carrick's Ford, was a Methodist preacher, said to be one of the very best shots of his regiment. During the battle, he was particularly conspicuous for the zeal with which he kept up a constant fire. The Fourteenth Ohio regiment, in the thick of the fight, fired an average of eleven rounds to every man, but this parson managed to get in a great deal more than that average. He fired carefully, with perfect coolness, and always after a steady aim, and the boys declare that every time, as he took down his gun, after firing, he added, "And may the Lord have mercy on your soul!" Evidently he thought the *body* not worth praying for after the aim he had so carefully taken.

Per contra: One of Steedmen's men (in the

Fourteenth Ohio) was from Cheesedom, and didn't like the irreverent tone adopted by the Southern chivalry in speaking of the "d—d Yankees." He took deliberate aim, but, unlike the parson, after every fire he added the invariable formula, "Blast your secession souls, how do you like the Yankees?"

Another, an Englishman, was wounded. Steedman noticed him limping, and called out, "Jack, are you wounded?" "Yes, I'm 'it." "Where are you hit, Jack?" "O, I'm 'it in the 'ip, but I — (in great anxiety lest Steedman should send him to the hospital) but it don't 'urt me. I'm only 'it in the 'ip; it don't 'urt me;" and away he blazed with another load, adding, "Confound you, I guess I paid you off that time."

CLOSE QUARTERS. — At the battle of Charleston, Mo., in August, 1861, Lieut.-Col. Ransom, of the Eleventh Illinois regiment, was urging his men to the charge, when a man rode up, and called out, "What do you mean? You are killing our own men." Ransom replied, "I know what I am doing. Who are you?" The reply was, "I am for Jeff Davis." Ransom replied, "You are the man I am after;" and instantly two pistols were drawn. The rebel fired first, taking effect in Col. Ransom's arm, near the shoulder. The Colonel fired, killing his antagonist instantly.

AS BRAVE AS A LION. — At the fight at Scarytown, Va., the soldier John Haven was wounded. He was a handsome, intelligent young man, as brave as a lion, and the pet of the company. Poor fellow! his right hip was shot away just as he was passing a ball to his gun. When his Captain saw him fall, he ran and picked him up, and conveyed him in his own arms to a place of safety. "Never mind me, Captain," he cried; "but don't let that flag go down!"

THE MARCH OF THE SEVENTH REGIMENT.

BY FITZ JAMES O'BRIEN.

THE CAPITOL, WASHINGTON, }
Saturday, April 27, 1861. }

WE are here. Those three words sum up as much as Napier's "Peccavi," when he took Scinde, and we all feel somewhat as Mr. Cæsar Augustus must have felt when he had crossed the Rubicon.

It is almost unnecessary for me to detail to you the events of the day on which we left New York. The scene at the armory on Friday was one to be commemorated. For the first time since its formation, the Seventh regiment left its native city on active service. All day long, from an early hour in the morning, young men in uniforms or civilian's dress, might have been seen hurrying up and down Broadway, with anomalous-looking bundles under their arms. Dandies, who were the pride of club windows, were not above

brown paper parcels; military tailors were stormed and taken with considerable loss — to the pocket. Delmonico, calm and serene, superintended sandwiches which were destined for the canteen. People in the streets looked with a sort of regretful admiration at the gray uniforms hurrying by. Hardware stores were ransacked of revolvers. A feverish excitement throbbed through the city — the beating of that big Northern pulse, so slow, so sure, and so steady.

At three P. M., we mustered at the Armory, against which there beat a surge of human beings likes waves against a rock. Within, all was commotion. Fitting of belts, wild lamentations over uniforms expected, but not arrived; hearty exchanges of comradeships between members of different companies, who felt that they were about to depart on a mission which might end in death. Here and there flickered Spring bonnets, which enclosed charming faces, as the calyx enfolds the flower; and, let me tell you, that on the faces of many of those dear blossoms there hung drops of mournful dew. At last the regiment was formed in companies, and we marched. Was there ever such an ovation? When Trajan returned conqueror, dragging barbaric kings at his chariot-wheels, Rome vomited its people into the streets, and that glorious column, that will be ever immortal, was raised. But what greeted the Emperor at his outset? The marble walls of Broadway were never before rent with such cheers as greeted us when we passed. The faces of the buildings were so thick with people, that it seemed as if an army of black ants were marching, after their resistless fashion, through the city, and had scaled the houses. Handkerchiefs fluttered in the air like myriads of white butterflies. An avenue of brave, honest faces smiled upon us as we passed, and sent a sunshine into our hearts that lives there still. In a prominent position stood Maj. Anderson, who saluted us, and was welcomed as such a man should be welcomed. And so on to the ferry.

Swift through New Jersey — against which no sneer be uttered evermore. All along the track shouting crowds, hoarse and valorous, sent to us, as we passed, their hopes and wishes. When we stopped at the different stations, rough hands came in through the windows, apparently unconnected with any one in particular until you shook them, and then the subtle, magnetic thrill told that there were bold hearts beating at the end. This continued until night closed, and, indeed, until after midnight.

Within the cars the sight was strange. A thousand young men, the flower of the North, in whose welfare a million of friends and relatives were interested, were rushing along to conjectured hostilities with the same smiling faces that they would wear going to a "German" party in Fifth Avenue. It was more like a festivity than a march. Those fine old songs, the choruses of which were familiar to all, were sung with sweet voice. We were assured many times, in melodious accents, that "the whiskey bottle was empty on the shelf," and several individuals of that prominent, but not respectable class known as "bummers," were invited to "meet us on Canaan's happy shore." The brave old Harvard song of "Upi dee" was started, and, shameful to say, Mr. Longfellow's "Excelsior" seemed naturally to adapt itself to the tune. I do not think that "the pious monks of St. Bernard" would have been edified, had they heard themselves alluded to in that profane music.

Our arrival at Philadelphia took place at four o'clock. We slept in the cars, awaiting orders from our Colonel; but at daylight hunger — and it may be thirst — becoming imperious, we sallied out, and roamed about that cheerless neighborhood that surrounds the depot. Close by there was a small wooden shanty — let us say an Irish palace — which was presently filled by arid soldiers. The prog in the larder of this sumptuous residence was, I regret to say, limited. I did not even see the traditional pig about, although heaven knows he would have been appropriate enough. Finding that we were likely to remain for some time in the city — although under the impression that we were to go straight through to Baltimore — we wandered away from the Desert of the Depot and descended on civilized quarters. The superintendent of the Deaf and Dumb Asylum was a man for the emergency. He provided a handsome breakfast for all such members of the Seventh as chose to partake of it, and we commanded beefsteak on our fingers, and ordered tea by sign-manual. Great numbers of our regiment, being luxurious dogs, went down to the Continental and Girard hotels, where they campaigned on marble floors, and bivouacked on velvet couches. They are such delicate fellows, the Seventh regiment! Farther on you will see what those delicate hands have done.

We, of course, were entirely ignorant of our route, or how we were going. The general feeling of the regiment was in favor of pushing our way coûte qui coûte straight through Baltimore. Rumors came along that the city was in arms. The Massachusetts troops had to fight their way through, killing eighteen and losing two men. This seemed only to stimulate our boys, and the universal word was Baltimore. But as it turned out afterwards, we were under a wise direction, and the policy of our Colonel, to whom we perhaps are altogether indebted for bringing us safely here, was, I presume, to avoid all unnecessary collision, and bring his regiment intact into Washington. The rails were reported to have been torn up for forty miles about Baltimore, and as we were summoned for the defence of the Capital, it follows, according to reason, that if we could get there without loss we would better fulfil our duty. As it happened afterwards, we had to run through more peril than Baltimore could have offered.

There seemed but little enthusiasm in Philadelphia. A city that washes every morning with soap and water is not easily roused into excitement. The Quaker placidity still prevails, and when you add to this the majestic stolidity of the German element, it is not wonderful that the

Capital of the Keystone State should not be uproarious. Still let me do Philadelphia justice. I understand that the people were out in large numbers to see us enter, but our delay disappointed them, and they went home. During our stay a lethargic decorum prevailed. The prim beavers of the citizens were glossy and self-possessed. We came and went without a reception or demonstration.

There was one peculiar difference that I noticed existing between the Massachusetts regiments that we met in Philadelphia and our men. The Massachusetts men — to whom all honor be given for the splendid manner in which they afterwards acted in a most trying situation — presented a singular moral contrast to the members of the Seventh. They were earnest, grim, determined. Badly equipped, haggard, unshorn, they yet had a manhood in their look that hardships could not kill. They were evidently thinking all the time of the contest into which they were about to enter. Their gray, eager eyes seemed to be looking for the heights of Virginia. With us it was somewhat different. Our men were gay and careless, confident of being at any moment capable of performing, and more than performing, their duty. They looked battle in the face with a smile, and were ready to hob-nob with an enemy, and kill him afterwards. The one was courage in the rough; the other was courage burnished. The steel was the same in both, but the last was a little more polished.

On April 20, at 4:20 P. M., we left the Philadelphia dock, on board the steamer Boston. The regiment was in entire ignorance of its destination. Some said we were going back to New York, at which suggestion there was a howl of indignation. Others presumed that we were going to steam up the Potomac — a course which was not much approved of, inasmuch as we were cooped up in a kind of river steamer that a shot from the fort at Alexandria might sink at any moment. We, however, — to make use of a familiar expression, — "went it blind," and faces did not smile the less because our object was unknown.

It was on board of this steamer that "Joe" came out. You, of course, don't know who "Joe" is. Well, you may rest contented, because he will always remain "Joe" to you. I may, without transgression, however, give you his typograph. I will put him in position, level the lens, and — here he is. Imagine a well-built young fellow, about twenty-one, with mercury instead of blood in his veins, ever on the move, with a sort of quaint, joyous humor seething from him, as if he was always at boiling point. Joe's two specialties, like a winnowing machine that I once saw, are work and chaff. During the evening, on board the steamer, he distributed himself generally about, with a merry word and a joke for every one. What number of bad puns he made, or what horrible conundrums he made, my exhausted and horrified memory refuses to recall; suffice it to say, that laughter and good-humor followed in his wake, as the white foam smiles astern of some sharp little cutter going before the wind.

The first evening, April 20, on board the Boston, passed delightfully. We were all in first-rate spirits, and the calm, sweet evenings that stole on us as we approached the South, diffused a soft and gentle influence over us. The scene on board the ship was exceedingly picturesque. Fellows fumbling in haversacks for rations, or extracting sandwiches from reluctant canteens; guards pacing up and down with drawn bayonets; knapsacks piled in corners, bristling heaps of muskets, with sharp, shining teeth, crowded into every available nook; picturesque groups of men lolling on deck, pipe or cigar in mouth, indulging in the *dolce far niente*, as if they were on the blue shores of Capri, rather than on their way to battle; unbuttoned jackets, crossed legs, heads leaning on knapsacks, blue uniforms everywhere, with here and there a glint of officer's red lighting up the foreground — all formed a scene that such painters as the English Warren would have revelled in.

I regret to say that all was not rose-colored. The steamer that the Colonel chartered had to get ready at three or four hours' notice, he having changed his plans, in consequence of the tearing up of the rails around Baltimore. The result was, that she was imperfectly provisioned. As the appetites of the men began to develop, the resources of the vessel began to appear. In the first place, she was far too small to accommodate a thousand men, and we were obliged to sleep in all sorts of impossible attitudes. There is an ingenious device known to carpenters as "dovetailing;" and we were so thick that we had positively to dovetail, only that there was very little of the dove about it; for when perambulating soldiers stepped on the faces and stomachs of the sleepers, as they lay on deck, the greeting that they received had but little flavor of the olive branch.

Notwithstanding that we found very soon that the commissariat was in a bad way, the men were as jolly as sandboys. I never saw a more good-humored set of men in my life. Fellows who would at Delmonico's have sent back a *turban de volaille aux truffes*, because the truffles were tough, here cheerfully took their places in file between decks, tin plates and tin cups in hand, in order to get an insufficient piece of beef and a vision of coffee. But it was all merrily done. The scant fare was seasoned with hilarity; and here I say to those people in New York who have sneered at the Seventh regiment as being dandies, and guilty of the unpardonable crimes of cleanliness and kid gloves, that they would cease to scoff, and remain to bless, had they beheld the square, honest, genial way in which these military Brummells roughed it. Farther on, you will see what they did in the way of endurance and activity.

April 21 was Sunday — a glorious, cloudless day. We had steamed all night, and about ten o'clock were in the vicinity of Chesapeake Bay. At eleven o'clock A. M. we had service read by our chaplain, and at one P. M. we were seven miles from the coast. The day was calm and delicious. In spite of our troubles with regard to food — troubles, be it understood, entirely unavoidable — we drank in with delight the serenity of the scene. A hazy tent of blue hung over our heads. On one side the dim thread of shore hemmed in the sea. Flights of loons and ducks skimmed along the ocean, rising lazily, and spattering the waves with their wings, as they flew against the wind, until they rose into air, and, wheeling, swept into calmer feeding grounds. Now and then the calm of the hour was broken with the heavy tramp of men, and the metallic voice of the Corporal of the Guard relieving his comrades. At five o'clock P. M. we passed a light-ship, and hailed her, our object being to discover whether any United States vessels were in the neighborhood, waiting to convoy us up the Potomac River. We had heard that the forts at Alexandria were ready to open upon us if we attempted to pass up, and our steamer was of such a build, that, had a shell or shot struck it, we would have been burned or drowned. It therefore behooved us to be cautious. The answers we got from the light-ship and other vessels that we hailed in this spot were unsatisfactory, and although the feelings of the men were unanimous in wishing to force the Potomac, wiser counsels, as it proved, were behind us, and we kept on. About this time a curious phenomenon occurred. Some men in the regiment, who have fine voices, — and their name is legion, — had been singing, with all that delicious effect that music at sea produces, several of the finest psalms in our liturgy. The ocean softens, and delicately repeats sound; and those airs, trembling and sliding along the almost unrippled surface of the sea, were so melodious, that if the Southern Cerberi had heard them, they would have slumbered at the gates of their own hell. While we were singing, the moon swung clear into air, and round her white disk was seen three circles, clear and distinct — *red, white, and blue!* The omen was caught by common instinct, and a thousand cheers went up to that heaven that seemed in its visible signs to manifest its approval of the cause in which we were about to fight. All this time we were entirely ignorant of where we were going. The officers kept all secret, and our conjectures drifted like a drifting boat. On the morning of the 22d we were in sight of Annapolis, off which the Constitution was lying, and there found the Eighth regiment of Massachusetts volunteers on board the Maryland. They were aground, owing, it is supposed, to the treachery of the Captain, whom they put in irons, and wanted to hang. I regret to say that they did not do it. During the greater portion of that forenoon we were occupied in trying to get the Maryland off the sandbar on which she was grounded. From our decks we could see the men in file trying to rock her, so as to facilitate our tugging. These men were without water and without food, were well conducted and uncomplaining, and behaved, in all respects, like heroes. They were under the command of Col. Butler, and I regret that that gentleman did not care more for the comforts of men whose subsequent pluck proved that nothing was too good for them. During the endeavors to get the Maryland afloat, we had some idle time on our hands, and your humble servant employed some of it in "composing" a Seventh regiment song, which is now in rehearsal by the vocalists of the corps:

THE SEVENTH.

Air — "Gilla Machree."

I.

Och ! we're the boys
That hearts desthroys
Wid making love and fighting ;
We take a fort,
The girls we court,
But most the last delight in.
To fire a gun,
Or raise some fun,
To us is no endeavor ;
So let us hear
One hearty cheer —
The Seventh's lads forever !
CHORUS. — For we're the boys
That hearts desthroys,
Wid making love and fighting ;
We take a fort,
The girls we court,
But most the last delight in.

II.

There's handsome Joe,
Whose constant flow
Of merriment unfailing,
Upon the tramp,
Or in the camp,
Will keep our hearts from ailing.
And B—— and Chat,
Who might have sat
For Pythias and Damon,
Och ! whin they get
Their heavy wet,
They get as high as Haman.
CHORUS. — For we're the boys
That hearts desthroys, &c.

III.

Like Jove above,
We're fond of love,
But fonder still of victuals ;
Wid turtle steaks,
An' codfish cakes,
We always fills our kittles.
To dhrown aich dish,
We dhrinks like fish,
And Mumm's the word we utther ;
An' thin we swill
Our Léoville,
That oils our throats like butther.
CHORUS. — For we're the boys
That hearts desthroys, &c.

IV.

We make from hay
A splindid tay,
From beans a gorgeous coffee ;
Our crame is prime,
With chalk and lime —
In fact, 'tis quite a throphy.

Our chickens roast,
Wid butthered toast,
I'm sure would timpt St. Pether.
Now, you'll declare
Our bill of fare
It couldn't be complether.
CHORUS. — For we're the boys
That hearts desthroys, &c.

V.

Now, silence all,
While I recall
A memory sweet and tender ;
The maids and wives
That light our lives
With deep, enduring splendor.—
We'll give no cheer
For those so dear,
But in our hearts we'll bless them,
And pray to-night
That angels bright
May watch them and caress them.
CHORUS. — For we're the boys
That hearts desthroys,
Wid making love and fighting ;
We take a fort,
The girls we court,
But most the last delight in.

On the afternoon of the 22d we landed at the Annapolis dock, after having spent hours in trying to relieve the Maryland. For the first time in his life, your correspondent was put to work to roll flour-barrels. He was intrusted with the honorable and onerous duty of transporting stores from the steamer to the dock. Later still, he descended to the position of mess servant, when, in company with gentlemen well known in Broadway for immaculate kids, he had the honor of attending on his company with buckets of cooked meat and crackers ; the only difference between him and Co. and the ordinary waiter being, that the former were civil.

After this, I had the pleasing duty of performing three hours of guard duty on the dock, with a view to protect the baggage and stores. It was monotonous — being my first guard — but not unpleasant. The moon rose calm and white. A long dock next to the one on which I was stationed, stretched away into the bay, resting on its numerous piles, until it looked in the clear moonlight like a centipede. All was still and calm, until at certain periods the guard challenged persons attempting to pass. There was a holy influence in the hour, and somehow the hot fever of anxiety that had been over us for days seemed to pass away under the touch of the magnetic fingers of the night.

We were quartered in the buildings belonging to the Naval School at Annapolis. I had a bunking-place in what is there called a fort, which is a rickety structure, that a lucifer match would set on fire, but furnished with imposing guns. I suppose it was merely built to practise the cadets, because as a defence it is worthless. The same evening boats were sent off from the yard, and towards nightfall the Massachusetts men landed, fagged, hungry, thirsty, but indomitable. At an early hour there was a universal snore through the Naval School of Annapolis.

The two days that we remained at Annapolis were welcome. We had been without a fair night's sleep since we left New York, and even the hard quarters we had there were a luxury compared to the dirty decks of the Boston. Besides, there were natural attractions. The grounds are very prettily laid out, and in the course of my experience, I never saw a handsomer or better bred set of young men than the cadets. They number about ——, only twenty having left the school owing to political conviction. The remainder are sound Union fellows, eager to prove their devotion to the flag. After spending a delightful time in the Navy School, resting and amusing ourselves, our repose was disturbed, at nine P. M., April 23, by rockets being thrown up in the bay. The men were scattered all over the grounds; some in bed, others walking or smoking, all more or less undressed. The rockets being of a suspicious character, it was conjectured that a Southern fleet was outside, and our drummer beat the roll-call to arms. From the stroke of the drum, until the time that every man, fully equipped and in fighting order, was in the ranks, was exactly, by watch, *seven minutes*. It is needless to say anything about such celerity—it speaks for itself. The alarm, however, proved to be false, the vessels in the offing proving to be laden with the Seventy-first and other New York regiments; so that, after an unpremeditated trial of our readiness for action, we were permitted to retire to our virtuous couches, which means, permit me to say, a blanket on the floor, with a military overcoat over you, and a nasal concert all around you, that in noise and number outvies Musard's celebrated *concerts monstres*.

On the morning of the 24th of April we started on what afterwards proved to be one of the hardest marches on record. The secessionists of Annapolis and the surrounding district had threatened to cut us off in our march, and even went so far as to say that they would attack our quarters. This, of course, was the drunken Southern ebullition. A civilian told me that he met in the streets of Annapolis two cavalry soldiers who came to cut our throats without delay, but as each brave warrior was endeavoring to hold the other up, my friend did not apprehend much danger.

A curious revulsion of feeling took place at Annapolis, and indeed all through Maryland, after our arrival.

The admirable good conduct which characterizes the regiment, the open liberality which it displays in all pecuniary transactions, and the courteous demeanor which it exhibits to all classes, took the narrow-minded population of this excessively wretched town by surprise. They were prepared for pillage. They thought we were going to sack the place. They found, instead, that we were prepared and willing to pay liberal prices for everything, and that even patriotic presentations were steadily refused. While we were

in the Navy School, of course all sorts of rumors as to our operations were floating about. It surprised me that no one suggested that we were to go off in a balloon; however, all surmises were put to an end by our receiving orders, the evening of the 23d, to assemble in marching order next morning. The dawn saw us up. Knapsacks, with our blankets and overcoats strapped on them, were piled on the green. A brief and insufficient breakfast was taken, our canteens filled with vinegar and water, cartridges distributed to each man, and after mustering and loading, we started on our first march through a hostile country.

Gen. Scott has stated, as I have been informed, that the march that we performed from Annapolis to the Junction is one of the most remarkable on record. I know that I felt it the most fatiguing, and some of our officers have told me that it was the most perilous. We marched the first eight miles under a burning sun, in heavy marching order, in less than three hours; and it is well known that, placing all elementary considerations out of the way, marching on a railroad track is the most harassing. We started at about eight o'clock A. M., and for the first time saw the town of Annapolis, which, without any disrespect to that place, I may say, looked very much as if some celestial schoolboy, with a box of toys under his arm, had dropped a few houses and men as he was going home from school, and that the accidental settlement was called Annapolis. Through the town we marched, the people unsympathizing, but afraid. They saw the Seventh for the first time, and for the first time they realized the men that they had threatened.

The tracks had been torn up between Annapolis and the Junction, and here it was that the wonderful qualities of the Massachusetts Eighth regiment came out. The locomotives had been taken to pieces by the inhabitants, in order to prevent our travel. In steps a Massachusetts volunteer, looks at the piecemeal engine, takes up a flange, and says coolly, "I made this engine, and I can put it together again." Engineers were wanted when the engine was ready. Nineteen stepped out of the ranks. The rails were torn up. Practical railroad makers out of the regiment laid them again; and all this, mind you, without care or food. These brave boys, I say, were starving while they were doing this good work. What their Colonel was doing, I can't say. As we marched along the track that they had laid, they greeted us with ranks of smiling but hungry faces. One boy told me, with a laugh on his young lips, that he had not eaten anything for thirty hours. There was not, thank God, a haversack in our regiment that was not emptied into the hands of these ill-treated heroes, nor a flask that was not at their disposal. I am glad to pay them tribute here, and mentally doff my cap.

Our march lay through an arid, sandy, tobacco-growing country. The sun poured on our heads like hot lava. The sixth and second companies were sent on for skirmishing duty, under the command of Capts. Clarke and Nevers, the latter commanding as senior officer. A car, on which was placed a howitzer, loaded with grape and canister, headed the column, manned by the engineer and artillery corps, commanded by Lieut. Bunting. This was the rallying point of the skirmishing party, on which, in case of difficulty, they could fall back. In the centre of the column came the cars laden with medical stores, and bearing our sick and wounded, while the extreme rear was brought up with a second howitzer, loaded also with grape and canister. The engineer corps, of course, had to do the forwarding work. New York dandies, sir — but they built bridges, laid rails, and headed the regiment through that terrible march. After marching about eight miles, during which time several men caved in from exhaustion, and one young gentleman was sunstruck and sent back to New York, we halted, and instantly, with the Divine instinct which characterizes the hungry soldier, proceeded to forage. The worst of it was, there was no foraging to be done. The only house within reach was inhabited by a lethargic person, who, like most Southern men, had no idea of gaining money by labor. We offered him extravagant prices to get us fresh water, and it was with the utmost reluctance we could get him to obtain us a few pailfuls. Over the mantel-piece of his miserable shanty I saw — a curious coincidence — the portrait of Col. Duryea, of our regiment.

After a brief rest of about an hour, we again commenced our march; a march which lasted until the next morning — a march than which in history, nothing but those marches in which defeated troops have fled from the enemy, can equal. Our Colonel, it seems, determined to march by railroad, in preference to the common road, inasmuch as he had obtained such secret information as led him to suppose that we were waited for on the latter route. Events justified his judgment. There were cavalry troops posted in defiles to cut us off. They could not have done it, of course, but they could have harassed us severely. As we went along the railroad we threw out skirmishing parties from the second and sixth companies, to keep the road clear. I know not if I can describe that night's march. I have dim recollections of deep cuts through which we passed, gloomy and treacherous-looking, with the moon shining full on our muskets, while the banks were wrapped in shade, and we each moment expecting to see the flash and hear the crack of the rifle of the Southern guerrilla. The tree frogs and lizards made mournful music as we passed. The soil on which we travelled was soft and heavy. The sleepers lying at intervals across the track made the march terribly fatiguing. On all sides dark, lonely pine woods stretched away, and high over the hooting of owls or the plaintive petition of the whip-poor-will rose the bass commands of Halt! Forward, march! — and when we came to any ticklish spot, the word would run from the head of the column along the line, "Holes," "Bridge — pass it along," &c.

As the night wore on, the monotony of the march became oppressive. Owing to our having to explore every inch of the way, we did not make more than a mile or a mile and a half an hour. We ran out of stimulants, and almost out of water. Most of us had had no sleep for four nights, and as the night advanced our march was almost a stagger. This was not so much fatigue as want of excitement. Our fellows were spoiling for a fight, and when a dropping shot was heard in the distance, it was wonderful to see how the languid legs straightened, and the column braced itself for action. If we had had even the smallest kind of a skirmish, the men would have been able to walk to Washington. As it was, we went sleepily on. I myself fell asleep walking in the ranks. Numbers, I find, followed my example; but never before was there shown such indomitable pluck and perseverance as the Seventh showed during that march of twenty miles. The country that we passed through seemed to have been entirely deserted. The inhabitants, who were going to kill us when they thought we daren't come through, now vamosed their respective ranches, and we saw them not. Houses were empty. The population retired into the interior, burying their money, and carrying their families along with them. They, it seems, were under the impression that we came to ravage and pillage, and they fled as the Gauls must have fled when Attila and his Huns came down on them from the north. As we did at Annapolis, we did in Maryland State. We left an impression that cannot be forgotten. Every thing was paid for. No discourtesy was offered to any inhabitant, and the sobriety of the regiment should be an example to others.

ADVENTURE OF CAPTAIN STRONG. — The following account of the adventure of Captain W. E. Strong, of the Second regiment of Wisconsin volunteers, was given by that officer in an official report to Maj. Larrabee, dated at Camp Advance, September 7, 1861:

"In pursuance of your order of yesterday, I proceeded to examine the woods to the right of our exterior line, for the purpose of satisfying yourself whether the line should be extended. The last picket was stationed about four hundred yards from the river — being our outpost on our right exterior line — leaving a dense thicket of pine undergrowth between it and the river. From my means of observation up to that time, I had concluded that our pickets were not sufficiently advanced in that direction, as this space was wholly unoccupied. At least I thought the ground should be examined; and in this you were pleased to fully concur.

"You desired me to make a minute examination of the ground, and be ready to report when you should return, at three o'clock P. M. of that day. Accordingly, after dinner I passed along the line until I reached the extreme outpost on the right, which consisted of Lieut. Dodge, Corp. Manderson, and three privates, and then proceeded along over very rough and densely wooded ground to the river. I soon ascertained that these physical obstacles were so great that no body of troops could, in this direction, turn our right flank, and there was no necessity of extending our pickets. I then concluded to return; and for the purpose of avoiding the dense undergrowth, I turned back on a line about a hundred rods in advance of the direction of our line of pickets. As I was passing through a thicket, I was surrounded by six rebel soldiers — four infantry and two cavalry. The footmen were poorly dressed and badly armed. Seeing I was caught, I thought it best to surrender at once. So I said, 'Gentlemen, you have me.' I was asked various questions as to who I was, where I was going, what regiment I belonged to, &c., all of which I refused to answer. One of the footmen said, 'Let's hang the d—d Yankee scoundrel,' and pointed to a convenient limb. Another man said, 'No; let's take him to the camp, and then hang him.' One of the cavalrymen, who seemed to be leader, said, 'We'll take him to camp.' They then marched me through an open place — two in front, two in the rear, and a cavalryman on each side of me. I was armed with two revolvers and my sword.

"After going some twenty rods, the Sergeant on my right, noticing my pistols, ordered me to give them up, together with my sword. I said, 'Certainly, gentlemen,' and immediately halted. As I stopped, they all filed past me, and of course were in front. We were at this time in an open part of the woods, but about sixty yards to the rear was a thicket of undergrowth. Thus everything was in my favor; I was quick of foot, and a passable shot; yet the design of escape was not formed until I brought my pistol pouches round to the front part of my body, and my hands touched the stocks. The grasping of the pistols suggested the thought of cocking them as I drew them out. This I did; and the moment I got command of them, I shot down two footmen nearest me — about sixty feet off — one with each hand. I immediately turned and ran towards the thicket in the rear. The confusion of my captors was apparently so great, that I had nearly reached cover before shots were fired at me. One ball passed through my left cheek, passing out of my mouth. Another one, a musket-ball, passed through my canteen. Immediately upon this volley the two cavalrymen separated — one on my left and the other on my right — to cut off my retreat. The remaining two footmen charged directly towards me; I turned, when the horsemen got up, and fired three or four shots, but the balls flew wild. I ran on, got over a small knoll, and nearly regained one of our pickets, when I was headed off by both the mounted men. The Sergeant called out to me to halt and surrender; I gave no reply, but fired and ran in the opposite direction. He pursued and overtook me; I turned, took good aim, pulled the trigger, but the cap snapped. At this time his carbine was unslung, and he was holding it with both hands on the left side of his horse. He fired at my breast without raising the piece to his shoulder, and the shot passed from the right side of my coat, through it and my shirt, to the left, just grazing the skin; the piece was so near as to burn the cloth out the size of one's hand. I was, however, uninjured at this time, save the shot through my cheek. I then fired at him again, and brought him to the ground, hanging by his foot in the left stirrup, and the horse galloping towards the camp. I saw no more of the other horseman, nor of the footmen, but running on soon came to our own pickets uninjured, save the shot through my cheek, but otherwise much exhausted from my exertions."

THE POWER OF SLAVE LABOR. — The following curious passage appears in a sermon preached by Rev. William O. Prentiss, at three different times, twice by request repeated, in South Carolina, in 1860:

"Three hundred and fifty thousand white men directing the labor of less than four millions of African slaves, have furnished the material, out of which has been reared this colossal fabric, and it begins to topple to its fall at the first bright promise that their sustaining aid shall be withdrawn. If further proof be required that the labor to which I have alluded, has built up these vast, these important interests, consult the statistics of our country; study figures which no human ingenuity can torture into the indorsement of a lie. History shows that the country makes no palpable improvement until the grand staple of the earth's necessities begins to be reared here, and that its advances are exactly proportioned to the amount and value of the African slave labor employed by us. The whole commerce of the civilized world is based upon this labor; it feeds the hungry, it clothes the naked, it employs the idler, it supports tottering thrones and starving paupers; kings in their diadems, and beggars in their rags, all cry aloud to the god who feeds them, 'Give us this day our daily cotton.'"

STONEWALL JACKSON AT BULL RUN. — A Southern correspondent, who was present at the first battle of Bull Run, relates the following:

"General Jackson's brigade had been lying for hours sustaining with unflinching courage a most terrific fire. The general had his horse shot under him, and a finger of the left hand shot off; but, cool as a cucumber, he still urged his 'boys' to be steady; and steady they were, when they charged and butchered the Fire Zouaves and other regiments right and left. The General has a way of holding his head up very straight; and his almost invariable response to any remark is, 'Very well,' whilst his chin seems trying to get up towards the top of his head. The writer remembers, in the midst of the fight, to have seen the General rallying his men, while his chin seemed to stick out farther, and his 'Very wells' seemed to sound more euphoniously than ever; and when the writer wished to pour a little whiskey upon the shattered finger, he was told that it was 'of no consequence;' and away went the General, with a battery following him, to take position in some advantageous spot. If any one was ever entitled to a sobriquet, the General certainly deserved that of *cool*."

ANECDOTE OF GENERAL WADSWORTH. — The following is one of the most beautiful and pathetic stories of the war:

Paymaster Rochester, feeling his lips to be unsealed by the death of General Wadsworth, tells that he always paid him from his entry into the service ; and that when the General called on him for money, on the eve of starting to the Mississippi Valley, on a special mission connected with the arming and organization of the slaves of that region, he casually remarked to him, that when he got to New Orleans he would find there Paymaster Vedder, to whom he would recommend him, as a gentlemanly officer, to apply for any moneys he might need. " No, sir," said General Wadsworth; " I shall not apply to Maj. Vedder. While I am in the service I shall be paid only by you. And my reason for that is, that I wish my account with the Government to be kept with one paymaster only ; for it is my purpose, at the close of the war, to call on you for an accurate statement of all the money I have received from the United States. The amount, whatever it is, I shall give to some permanent institution founded for the relief of disabled soldiers. This is the least invidious way in which I can refuse pay for fighting for my country in her hour of danger."

GENERAL LYON'S MEMORY. — A soldier of Gen. Herron's division wrote from Springfield, Mo., as follows :

" Gen. Lyon's memory is cherished by the soldiers here as something holy. The Union men think that no man ever lived like him. The Third division visited the battle-field of Wilson's Creek on Thanksgiving Day, and each man placed a stone on the spot where Lyon fell, so that there now stands a monument some ten feet high, built by eight thousand soldiers, to point the out to the visitor of this classic ground the place where the hero died."

AN AFFECTING INCIDENT. — The State Military Agent of Michigan, at Nashville, L. B. Willard, relates the following affecting incident :

" As I was passing by the post hospital, my attention was arrested by the singing, in a rather loud tone, of ' Rally round the flag, boys,' by one of the patients inside. While listening to the beautiful music of that popular song, I observed to a nurse standing in the doorway, that the person singing must be in a very merry mood, and could not be very sick. ' You are mistaken, sir,' said he ; ' the poor fellow engaged in singing that good old song is now grappling with death — has been dying all day. I am his nurse,' he continued, ' and the scene so affected me that I was obliged to leave the room. He is just about breathing his last.' I stepped into the ward, and, true enough, the brave man was near his end. His eyes were already fixed in death. He was struggling with all his remaining strength against the grim monster, while at the same time there gushed forth from his patriotic soul, incoherently, the words, ' Rally round the flag, boys,' which

had so often cheered him through his weary march, and braced him up when entering the field of blood in defence of his country. Finally he sank away into his death-slumber, and joined his Maker's command, that is marching onward to that far-off, better land. The last audible sound that escaped his lips was, ' Rally, boys ; rally once again !' As his eyes were closing, some dozen of his comrades joined in a solemn yet beautiful hymn, appropriate to the occasion. Take it altogether, this was one of the most affecting scenes I have ever witnessed in a hospital. It drew tears copiously from near one hundred of us. It occurred in the large ward, which occupies the entire body of the church on Cherry Street. The deceased was an Illinoisan, and had been wounded in one of the recent skirmishes."

A REMARKABLE ESCAPE. — Maj. K. V. Whaley, member of Congress from Wayne County, Va., was captured at Guyandotte by H. Clay Pate, at the time of the massacre in that town, and carried to the vicinity of Chapmansville, two days' journey distant. The prisoner and his captors stopped at a house near Chapmansville. Night coming on, Maj. Whaley, after hanging up his coat and hat by the fire to dry, went to bed with Capt. Wicher. In this room there were eight men, one of whom acted as a guard. About three o'clock in the morning Maj. Whaley awoke, and finding the guard nodding in front of the fire, and all the rest in deep slumber, determined to effect an escape. Leaving his bed as quietly as possible, he approached the guard, and, ascertaining that he was asleep, took Capt. Wicher's hat, picked up his own shoes, raised the latch of the door, and, seeing all clear outside, ran with all his might about two hundred yards down the Guyandotte River. Here he put on his shoes, and looked about for some drift wood upon which to cross the stream ; but, finding none, concluded to swim the river, which he did with considerable ease. He then proceeded down the river about a mile and a half, and commenced to ascend a mountain, the summit of which he reached just at daybreak, and just as Wicher was firing his guns as a signal of the escape. The firing was answered from all directions. Maj. Whaley, knowing it would be fatal to attempt to travel in daylight, sought a thicket of red oak brush, in which he found a sort of path. To and fro over this path he walked all day. A bleak wind was blowing ; and being wet through, and having no coat, he was compelled to walk rapidly in order to save his life. When night came on he started down the Guyandotte Valley, tracing the foot of the hills, a distance of two miles, when he came upon a camp of about one hundred cavalry ; and, knowing it would be folly to attempt to pass, retreated again to the mountains. The next day he took a circuit upon the top of the hills, to try and trace the valley and keep off the river, which he supposed would be guarded.

At last he came upon Hart's Creek, and supposed himself to be in the vicinity of a Union settlement, at the head of Twelve Pole. He went up Hart's Creek, and inquired of an old lady named Adkins, who, with her son and son-in-law, were in the house, asking her to direct him to Kyer's Creek, which he knew to be one of the branches of Twelve Pole. Young Adkins finally agreed to show him the creek for two dollars; and when they started, the Major observed that the son-in-law, Thompson, started in another direction. The Major suspected that Thompson knew him, and feared pursuit; so he hurried young Adkins along a good deal faster than that young gentleman desired to move. Arriving at the creek, the Major, having been robbed of all his money at Guyandotte on the night of the fight, could not comply with his contract with Adkins, but gave him twenty-five cents, all the money he had, and a new pair of soldier's shoes, taking in exchange the guide's old moccasons. The Major struck down the creek, along a very narrow road, passing two houses, at one of which he saw a little girl, but had not gone a great distance before he heard the tramp of the cavalry coming in pursuit. The Major was about turning a bend in the road, and had barely time to jump over a fence, and lie flat upon his belly, when along dashed a company, led by the fellow Thompson, before mentioned. The Major was lying not six feet from where his pursuers passed, and could see their eyes peering anxiously forward in search of him.

After the pursuers passed, he crawled up a ravine, and spent another twelve hours, exposed to the hardest kind of a rain, accompanied by the fiercest lightning and the loudest thunder.

[The Major afterwards learned that the little girl whom he had seen had informed his pursuers that he had just gone around the bend in the road; and in their anxiety to gain the bend and capture him, they never thought of looking to the right nor to the left.]

Being exceedingly weak and feeble, in consequence of having gone three days without food, the Major determined to approach a house a short distance ahead, and ask for something to eat. He was answered by the man of the house, a Union man, who recognized the Major almost at once, and warned him not to remain a minute if he wanted to escape, as the cavalry had been there hunting for him. The Major offered the man five hundred dollars to conduct him to the Queen Settlement, and to the house of Absalom Queen. The man, although avowing himself a good Union man, refused the offer, stating that he would be killed by his cannibal neighbors if discovered. He, however, gave the Major a blanket to throw over his shivering shoulders, and directed him to the house of Queen.

The Major plodded on, and at last reached the house of Queen, where he found a Home Guard of twenty-five men, who had assembled to keep the rebels from driving off the cattle from the Union settlement. Here was the first place he got anything to eat after making his escape. Queen and eleven of his men accompanied the Major, travelling only at night.

The party reached the mouth of Big Sandy on Sunday at twelve o'clock, and there was great rejoicing all along the Ohio River, firing of cannon, &c.

Absalom Queen was a brave soldier in the war of 1812, and as true and loyal a man as lives. There were about two hundred Union men in the settlement in which he resided, one hundred of whom, through his individual influence, joined Col. Zeigler's Fifth Virginia regiment.

KENTUCKY! O KENTUCKY!

John Morgan's foot is on thy shore,
    Kentucky! O Kentucky!
His hand is on thy stable door,
    Kentucky! O Kentucky!
You'll see your good gray mare no more;
He'll ride her till her back is sore,
And leave her at some stranger's door,
    Kentucky! O Kentucky!

For feeding John you're paying dear,
    Kentucky! O Kentucky!
His very name now makes you fear,
    Kentucky! O Kentucky!
In every valley, far and near,
He's gobbled every horse and steer;
You'll rue his raids for many a year,
    Kentucky! O Kentucky!

Yet you have many a traitorous fool,
    Kentucky! O Kentucky!
Who still will be the rebel's tool,
    Kentucky! O Kentucky!
They'll learn to yield to Abra'm's rule
In none but Johnny's costly school,
At cost of every animule,
    Kentucky! O Kentucky!

SCENES IN THE WAR. — Dick Boughton, of the Second Kansas regiment, in a letter to his sister, gives the following incidents:

"It would be singular if, in a four or five months' arduous campaign, I should not be occasionally in a tight place, as well as the witness of some painful scenes. While the Kansas Second were stopping at St. Joseph, on their way home, in September, two persons were arrested, and placed under guard in one of the hotels in that city. On the evening of their arrest, and the following day, it chanced to be my turn at guard duty; and I was one of the two placed at the door to guard the prisoners. Our instructions were to keep a sharp lookout, as one of them was a desperate character, arrested under the grave charge of shooting a Union man, and would probably attempt to get away. On the following morning the mother of one of the prisoners, hearing of the arrest of her son, came up to the room in great distress. She told her story amid tears and sobs, persisting in saying that her son was a good Union man; that he never carried any weapons, and had none when arrested, &c., &c. Poor woman! she was under the impression that her son was about to be strung up to the nearest tree, without ceremony, by the Second Kansas boys, whose ferocity she had heard tell so much about. After her first burst of grief had subsided into comparative silence, I told her that, if what she said were true, she need have no fears for the safety of her son; and added that, when relieved from my post, I would see our Major, who would inquire into the matter; and I could assure her that he would ask only to know the circumstances of her son's arrest, without stopping to query upon opinions and sentiments. That evening he was honorably released, and I had the satisfaction of taking mother and son by the hand, and receiving their gratulation.

"The case of the other prisoner was more serious and painful to me; and I give it, not as one worthy of being singled out as especially sad, but only as one of many circumstances of an equally painful nature, with which the soldier in active service in this terrible war has become reluctantly familiar. While still dwelling pleasantly upon the consolation my words had given the old lady in the morning, a light footstep was heard on the stairs, and presently a young lady made her appearance in the hall leading to our room. Her countenance was so pale and sad, with traces of tears, that it would have drawn pity from a heart of stone. Her step was so feeble and uncertain that I involuntarily took her by the arm as she approached, and supported her into the presence of her husband. They embraced each other for some moments, the silence only broken by convulsive sobs. Presently the wife, making a strong effort to be calm, spoke:

"'Our child — our little Willie!'

"The husband knew too well the terrible purport of her words. At the time of the arrest, their only child lay ill in its mother's arms, its little spirit hovering upon the verge of another world. When she could sufficiently command her emotions, she added:

"'Before he died, he rose in my arms, and called for you, Charles — yes, he called for pa! O Charles, Charles! you could not come to us then.' She again sank upon her husband's bosom in uncontrollable anguish. Their tears mingled freely; and I found the moisture collecting in my own eyes in inconvenient quantities as the 'second relief' stationed themselves at our post, thus relieving us for a time. When we left the city, the prisoner pleaded very hard to be allowed to go with us; and I shall not soon forget his look of despair when it became necessary for our Major, despite his pleadings, to deliver him over to the command then stationed at that place.

"At the hazard of being tedious, dear sister, I will relate a little circumstance which happened while guarding these same prisoners. We had just got fairly settled at our posts after the arrest, when the officer of the guard came around, full of importance, and talking loudly, as if he wished to be considered Lord Mogul, Gen. Jackson, or some other distinguished individual.

"'See here, guards; keep an eye on that tall fellow there; he's a d—d secesh. If he undertakes to get away, run your bayonet through him. We'll attend to his case directly;' and he took especial care that the prisoner should hear his remarks. I did not wish to conceal my resentment at such language upon such an occasion; for I felt that he who used it disgraced the badge of distinction which rested upon his shoulders. It so chanced that a young lady, whose husband, a young lawyer, was off to the secession army, often passed by our door in going to and from her room, which was near. She often paused in her vibrations to express her sentiments on the secession question, which she did with great freedom, and with more unction at times than was compatible with her ladyship. I suppose somebody of sensitive nerves must have informed our officer of the guard that the lady was growing troublesome with her much talking. So when he came round again, he addressed himself to me in a voice full of authority, with:

"'If that woman comes around here with any more of her gab, just put her in that room there, and lock her in.' Sister, you know I am the coolest boy out, and can retain my linen with a grace under almost any circumstances; but just at that moment I felt more savage than my words would indicate, as I very coolly returned in substance that I hoped I never should so far disgrace my manhood as to offer violence to a woman for any sentiments she might utter.

"'Obey my orders, sir,' was sung out with a pomp and emphasis intended to carry terror along with them, but which aroused in me feelings wickedly opposed to anything like fear. 'You'll please excuse me, sir,' I immediately responded, with just enough of tartness and accent to add impudence to disobedience. He then advanced towards me in a rage, saying something about putting me under guard, and reaching out his hand as if to take me by the collar.

"'Hands off, if you please,' said I, as I brushed his hand aside with a spiteful movement. He passionately seized his pistol hanging at his side. I saw his thumb upon the hammer as he drew it forth, thundering out as he did so:

"'I'll shoot you down like —'

"I finished the sentence for him, as, springing forward with an activity that astonished myself, I planted a blow just over his left eye, which sent him reeling backwards towards the stairway; and he seized the baluster to save himself. His pistol fell from his hand, and rattled down the stairs behind. This ended the interesting scene, for he flung up his arms, and crying like a child, begged me not to strike again.

"I was now left to the pleasant contemplation of my situation, and the penalty attached to striking an officer; but my fellow-guard, when questioned, placed the matter in so favorable a light for me that I was not even arrested."

ATTACK ON THE IRONSIDES. — One of the most daring and gallant naval exploits of the war, distinguished by the greatest coolness, presence of mind, and intrepidity of the brave men associated in the enterprise, was performed Monday night, October 6, 1863. This was no less than an attempt to blow up the United States steamer New Ironsides, lying off Morris Island. Though not fully meeting the expectations of those who conceived the plan, and those who carried it into execution, it called forth unbounded admiration for the brilliant heroism of the actors in their dangerous but patriotic and self-sacrificing undertaking.

The torpedo steamer David, with a crew of four volunteers, consisting of Lieut. Wm. T. Glassell, J. H. Toombs, chief engineer, and James Sullivan, fireman of the gunboat Chicora, with J. W. Cannon, assistant pilot of the gunboat Palmetto State, left South Atlantic Wharf between six and seven o'clock in the evening, for the purpose of running out to the Ironsides, exploding a torpedo under that vessel near amidships, and if possible blow her up. The weather, being dark and hazy, favored the enterprise. The boat, with its gallant little crew, proceeded down the harbor, skirting along the shoals on the inside of the channel, until nearly abreast of their formidable antagonist, the New Ironsides.

They remained in this position for a short time, circling around on the large shoal near the anchorage of the object of their visit. Lieut. Glassell, with a double-barrelled gun, sat in front of Pilot Cannon, who had charge of the helm. Chief Engineer Toombs was at the engine, with the brave and undaunted Sullivan, the volunteer fireman, when something like the following conversation ensued:

Lieut. Glassell. "It is now nine o'clock. Shall we strike her?"

Pilot Cannon. "That is what we came for. I am ready."

Engineer Toombs. "Let us go at her then, and do our best."

Sullivan, fireman. "I am with you all, and waiting. Go ahead."

The boat was now put bow on, and aimed directly for the Ironsides. As the little steamer darted forward, the lookout on the Ironsides hailed them with: "Take care there; you will run into us. What steamer is that?" Lieut. Glassell replied by discharging one barrel at the Yankee sentinel, and tendering the gun to Pilot Cannon, told him there was another Yankee, pointing to one with his body half over the bulwarks, and asked Cannon to take care of him with the other barrel.

The next moment they had struck the Ironsides, and exploded the torpedo about fifteen feet from the keel, on the starboard side. An immense volume of water was thrown up, covering the little boat, and going through the smoke-stack, entered the furnace, completely extinguishing the fires.

In addition to this, pieces of the ballast had fallen into the works of the engine, rendering it unmanageable at that time. Volley after volley of musketry from the crew of the Ironsides and from the launches began to pour in upon them.

Lieut. Glassell gave the order to back, but it was found impossible. In this condition, with no shelter, and no hope of escape, they thought it best to surrender, and hailed the enemy to that effect. The Yankees, however, paid no attention to the call. It was then proposed to put on their life-preservers, jump overboard, and endeavor to swim to the shore. All but Pilot Cannon consented. The latter, being unable to swim, said he would stay and take his chances in the boat. Lieut. Glassell, Engineer Toombs, and Sullivan the fireman, left the boat, the first two having on life-preservers, and the latter supporting himself on one of the hatches thrown to him by the pilot. Engineer Toombs, becoming embarrassed with his clothing in the water, got back to the boat, and was assisted in by Cannon.

The boat was then rapidly drifting from the Ironsides. He now fortunately found a match, and lighting a torch, crept back to the engine, discovered and removed the cause of its not working, and soon got it in order. Engineer Toombs and Cannon reached their wharf in the city about midnight, fatigued, and presenting a worn-out appearance, but rejoicing at their fortunate and narrow escape.

CAVALRY SONG.

BY ELBRIDGE JEFFERSON CUTLER.

The squadron is forming, the war-bugles play.
To saddle, brave comrades, stout hearts for a fray!
Our Captain is mounted — strike spurs, and away!

No breeze shakes the blossoms or tosses the grain;
But the wind of our speed floats the galloper's mane,
As he feels the bold rider's firm hand on the rein.

Lo! dim in the starlight their white tents appear!
Ride softly! ride slowly! the onset is near!
More slowly! more softly! the sentry may hear!

Now fall on the rebel — a tempest of flame!
Strike down the false banner whose triumph were shame!
Strike, strike for the true flag, for freedom and fame!

Hurrah! sheathe your swords! the carnage is done.
All red with our valor, we welcome the sun.
Up, up with the stars! we have won! we have won!

The End of the Alabama. — A Confederate soldier gives the following account of the sinking of that famous vessel and his subsequent adventures:

"I was with Semmes everywhere he went, in the naval brigade, and in blockade running, and was on the Alabama all the time he commanded her. I was with him when she sank, and was picked up when he was, by the Deerhound. A sharp fight it was, I assure you, but it wasn't altogether the eleven-inch guns of the Kearsarge that did the business. We never had a chance of success, and our men knew it; and then we had no gunners to compare with the Kearsarge's.

"Our gunners fired by routine, and when they had a gun loaded, fired it off blind. They never changed the elevation of their guns all through the fight, and the Kearsarge was working up all the time, taking advantage of every time she was hid by the smoke to work a little nearer, and then her gunners took aim for every shot. We never tried to board the Kearsarge, but, on the contrary, tried our best to get away, from the time the fight commenced.

"We knew very well that if we got in range of her Dahlgren howitzers she would sink us in ten minutes.

"Semmes never supposed he could whip the Kearsarge when he went out to fight her. He was bullied into it, and took good care to leave all his valuables on shore, and had a life-preserver on through the fight. I saw him put it on, and I thought if it was wise in him, it wouldn't be foolish in me to do the same. When Semmes saw that the ship was going down, he told us all to swim who could, and was one of the first to jump into the water, and we all made for the Deerhound.

"I was a long way ahead of Semmes, and when I came up to the Deerhound's boat, they asked me if I was Semmes, before they would take me in. They would not take me in till I told them I was an officer on the Alabama, and as soon as they had Semmes aboard they made tracks as fast as they knew how, and left everybody else to be drowned or picked up by the Kearsage."

GEN. BUTLER AND THE "PERFECTIONISTS." —In Norfolk there was a society called "Perfectionists," and in their behalf some ten or twelve of them addressed a letter to the Commanding General of that department, setting forth their objections to swearing allegiance to any earthly government. The subject was disposed of by Gen. Butler in the following characteristic manner:

HEADQUARTERS OF EIGHTEENTH ARMY CORPS,
FORT MONROE, VA., January 13, 1864.

J. F. Dozier, E. H. Beaseley, and others:

GENTLEMEN : I have read your petition to Gen. Barnes, setting forth your objections to swearing allegiance to any earthly government.

The first reason which you set forth is that "all human governments are a necessary evil, and are continued in existence only by the permission of Jehovah until the time arrives for the establishment of his kingdom, and in the establishment of which all others will be subdued unto it, thus fulfilling that declaration in the eighth of Daniel, fourteenth verse," &c.

You therein establish to your own satisfaction three points:

First. That government, although an evil, is a necessary one. Second. That for a time it is permitted to exist by the wisdom of Jehovah. Third. That the time at which a period is to be put to its existence is not come.

Therefore you ought to swear allegiance to the government of the United States :

First. Because, though an evil, you admit it to be necessary. Second. Although an evil, you admit that it is permitted by the wisdom of Jehovah, and that it is not for his creatures to question the wisdom of his acts. Third. You only claim to be excused when Jehovah's government is substituted, which period, you admit, has not yet arrived.

Your obedient servant,
BENJ. F. BUTLER.

FIVE DAYS A PRISONER. — Lieutenant Charles O. Phillips was captured, with his orderly, on the morning of the 3d of April, 1865, during the advance on Richmond, and while under orders from General Weitzel, upon whose staff he was serving. "I was taken to General Geary," said he, "and questioned closely by him; he finally concluded by telling me I was 'a d—d intelligent staff officer,' because I could not tell him the strength of our corps, who commanded it, nor even what troops were entering the city when I was captured.

"The first day's march was twenty-eight miles on foot, with nothing to eat. I tried to escape that night, but was caught. The second day we marched twenty-three miles, and the rebels promised to feed us at night, but did not. The third day we marched twenty-six miles, Sheridan after us. He took a train of three hundred wagons, with stores, and destroyed the whole. At night (the third) I found so much fault that they gave me two ears of corn to eat. This night I got permission to go to the river and bathe, my feet being very sore and chafed badly. I made arrangements with the guard to desert, but was caught, when the provost marshal told me he would shoot me if I attempted to escape again, at which I suggested whether it might not be as well to shoot me as to starve me to death.

"The next day we marched twenty-five miles, and at four P. M. Sheridan was very close to us. I was so completely exhausted that I thought life was not worth much; so down I sat in the road, my orderly doing likewise, determined not to march farther without rest. The Captain threatened to shoot me again, and I told him to act his pleasure, as Uncle Sam knew how, and had as many of their men as they had of ours. He finally chose what he thought was his best and most reliable man to leave as guard over myself and orderly, giving him instructions to keep us within their lines at all hazards. Soon I got on the right side of Johnny, and made arrangements to desert with him, whenever an opportunity could be gained.

"At dusk we found ourselves in a little pine grove with rebels all around us. The bright moon plagued me considerably, and I feared my plan for escape would not result favorably; but anything, I thought, was preferable to my present condition. At a time when no one was watching us, I succeeded in concealing myself with my two comrades in a deep ravine, under a large cedar. Soon I heard voices, and looking out carefully, I saw a lieutenant and several men pass along. Creeping out, I followed them, and saw the officer post his men on picket surrounding the ravine. I then followed him to his reserve, ascertained at the next relief that the positions of the men were not changed each time, and then returned to our hiding-place to communicate the good news to the orderly and the Johnny. The latter began to be a little shaky, and I a little doubtful. It was a long time to wait till the moon went down, and finally the guard fell asleep. He had previously agreed to let us go, and he would return to his company, I demanding that he should wait till we had started. Seeing him asleep, I changed my tactics, quietly took his rifle, &c., gently shook him by the shoulder, and informed him that during his short nap affairs had changed. He was now my prisoner, and would do precisely as I said, or his brains were worthless. He looked very much surprised, but saw there was no help for him.

"At half past four A. M. it was a little cloudy, and I quietly informed Johnny that he was to take the lead, on his hands and knees, my orderly would go next, and myself with Johnny's musket in the rear. In this way we escaped through the enemy's picket line, and reached our friends in safety at half past six o'clock on the morning of the seventh. I turned the rebel guard over to Major Stevens, provost marshal of this (Twenty-fifth) corps, and he immediately took the oath, thanking me for bringing him over."

CAPTAIN CUSHING'S EXPLOIT. — One pleasant night, while the blockading fleet lay off Wilmington, young Cushing, of the gunboat Monticello, took a first cutter, with fifteen men and two officers (Acting Ensign Jones and Acting Master's Mate Howard), and succeeded in passing the forts off the west bar at Wilmington, and started up the Cape Fear River. After a narrow escape of being run over by one of the rebel steamers plying the river, he passed the second line of batteries, and continued his course until Old Brunswick was reached, where the rebels had a heavy battery, when he was hailed and fired upon, but succeeded in passing unscathed, by feigning to pass down the river, and crossing to the friendly cover of the opposite bank. He then continued his course up the river. By this artifice the rebels were deceived, and signalized to the forts to intercept him as he came down the river, which they supposed was the direction taken.

At half past two the next morning the Captain had reached a point seven miles distant from Wilmington, where he caused the boat to be hauled on the banks, and concealed from view by bushes and marsh grass. Day had now dawned, and it became necessary to select a place of concealment, which was found in the brush on the banks.

Soon after daylight, the rebel steamers, blockade runners, and transports could be seen by the party plying up and down the river; and, in fact, the flagship of the rebel Commodore Lynch

passed by, pennant flying, the distinguished gentleman unconscious of the fact that a rifle in a steady hand could, and would, but for obvious reasons, have given him his quietus. Two blockade steamers, of the first class, passed up, and one down, during the first twenty-four hours. When night had fairly set in, the Captain prepared to launch his boat, when two boats rounded the point; and, as he supposed, having discovered his position, they designed to attack him; but it proved to be a returned fishing party. The entire party were captured — eight in number. Compelling them to act in the capacity of guides, he proceeded to examine all the fortifications, river obstructions, and other objects of interest within three miles of Wilmington. Here he was compelled to pass through a creek, running through a cypress swamp, for several hours, through grass eight feet high, and immense cypress trees on each side, whose shadow cast a dark gloom, only exceeded by darkness.

By two o'clock that morning a road was reached, which proved to be a branch of the main road to Wilmington, and joining it at a point two miles distant. The party were here divided, ten being left to hold this road; and the Captain, taking the remaining eight men, took position at the junction of the roads, one of which was the main. Several prisoners were here captured, but none of importance. At about eleven o'clock in the morning, the rebel courier, with the mails from Fort Fisher and lower batteries, en route to Wilmington, whose approach was awaited, came duly along, and he, with his entire mail, was captured.

On examination, this proved to be a prize of value, there being upwards of two hundred documents, private and official, and many of great importance. The party, having thus far labored successfully, experienced the necessity for refreshment for the inner man, and accordingly Master's Mate Howard garbed himself in the courier's clothes, and mounting the same worthy's horse, proceeded two miles to a store, and purchased a supply of provisions, with which he safely returned. The prices the mate thought exorbitant, but did not feel disposed, in his liberal mood, to haggle or beat down.

Shortly after, more prisoners were captured, and all that was now required to add to the éclat of the achievement was to capture the courier and mail from Wilmington, whose advent was looked for at five P. M. The impatience of the party may be imagined, when it is stated that the mail would contain the day's papers issued at Wilmington at one P. M., and our nomadic friends were anxious to obtain the latest news early.

The courier arrived slightly in advance of time; but one of the sailors, having moved incautiously across the road, was seen by him, and taking alarm, he took to his heels at full speed. Capt. Cushing, like Paul Duval No. 2, awaited him on the road, with pistol cocked, put spurs to his horse, and pursued for about three miles. But the courier speeded on like a whirlwind, and the

Captain, being rather farther from his base than he thought prudent, took to his line of retreat, and fell back in rapid, but good order.

The telegraph wire leading to Wilmington was then cut for several hundred yards, and the party, with prisoners and spoils, rejoined the squad left with the boat, and proceeding down the creek, reached the river about dark. The prisoners impeding the speed of the boats, measures were taken to dispose of them by depriving one of the fishing boats of oars and sails, and setting it adrift in the middle of the river, thus rendering it impossible for them to give the alarm until the tide floated them on some friendly bank. But while putting this plan into execution, a steamer approached rapidly, and detection was only avoided by the party leaping into the water, and holding on to the gunwales of the boat. The steamer passing, the prisoners and boat were sent adrift.

Nothing of interest occurred on the route down the river, until at a point between the batteries at Brunswick and Fort Fisher, when a boat was discovered making rapidly towards the shore. After an exciting chase she was overtaken, and her occupants, consisting of six persons, four of whom were soldiers, were taken on board, and the boat cut adrift. From them information was obtained that the rebels were on the *qui vive*, having boats posted at the narrow entrance between the forts to intercept the return. To understand the position of the party, it should be known that they were but three hundred yards distant from two forts, and this on a moonlight night. Capt. Cushing, on learning the rebels' designs, resolved to take a desperate chance of fighting his way through, supposing that in case there were but one or two boats, he might, by giving a broadside, escape in the confusion. On arriving at the mouth of the harbor, he perceived, as he imagined, one large boat, which, wonderfully prolific, soon gave birth to three more, which were afterwards increased in number by five from the opposite bank.

This completely blocked up the narrow entrance to the harbor. The helm was put hard aport to gain distance, and, seeing a large sailboat filled with troops (seventy-five musketeers), it was decided that the only hope lay in outmanœuvring them. The rebels, providentially, did not, during this interval, fire a shot, no doubt anticipating the certain capture of all. There being another means of entrance into the harbor (the west bar), the only possible hope was in impressing the rebels with the opinion that he would attempt that, the only remaining chance of escape. Accordingly, apparently making for this point, the rebel boats were drawn together in pursuit, when, rapidly changing his direction, the Captain brought his boat back to the other entrance (the east bar), and, deeply loaded as she was (twenty-six in the boat), forced her into the breakers. The rebels, evidently foiled, dared not venture to follow, and the guns of the batteries, which were pointed to rake the channel, were unprepared to inflict damage.

Capt. Cushing arrived safely with his prisoners and the mail, having performed one of the most hazardous and daring feats of the war, and obtained information of great value to the service.

A COMPLIMENT. — "We have heard of an incident which lately took place at a review of the army of the Potomac," says a correspondent of a Southern paper, "which should send a thrill of pleasure through the breast of every man, woman, and child in Florida. At the time when the Florida corps was passing, Gen. Hill turned to Gen. Lee, saying: 'That is the remnant of the gallant Florida brigade.' Gen. Lee immediately took off his hat, and remained uncovered until the Florida brigade passed. It was a compliment which we do not remember ever to have seen paid by our gallant commander of the Potomac to any other corps. Gen. Lee never pays a compliment to any person or party of men without it is deserved."

AN EDITOR, announcing that he had been drafted, discoursed as follows:

"Why should we mourn conscripted friends,
    Or shake at draft's alarms?
'Tis but the voice that Abr'am sends
    To make us shoulder arms."

THE YANKEE SOLDIER. — Major Clark Wright obtained considerable prominence as a scout and soldier. He moved from Ohio to Polk County, Missouri, in 1858, and buying a large amount of prairie, commenced the business of stock raising. He was just before married to a woman of more than ordinary intelligence and determination, who proved herself eminently fitted for the duties which their new life imposed upon them. He prospered greatly, and in a short time had erected a house, furnished in the best style possible, had two young children, an amiable wife, a good home, and was adding rapidly to an original fortune.

In the winter of 1860, when the roar of secession came up from South Carolina, he heard it in common with others of his neighbors; but while avowing himself in favor of sustaining the Union, he determined to attend strictly to his own business. He had no hesitation in expressing his sentiments of loyalty to the Government, but he did it quietly, and with a view not to give offence. Soon after, at a Baptist meeting near his residence, a few of the brethren, after refreshing their spiritual appetites in the sanctuary, took his case into consideration, and unanimously determined that he should be made to leave the country, appointing a committee of three to inform him of their decision.

One of the party, although an ardent secessionist, happened to be a personal friend of Wright, and hastening away, informed him of the meeting, and that the committee would wait on him the next day. Wright thanked his kind friend, and then, like a dutiful husband, laid the case before his wife, and asked her advice. She pondered a few moments, and then asked if he had done anything to warrant such a proceeding. Nothing. "Then let us fight!" was the reply; and to fight was the conclusion. Wright was plentifully supplied with revolvers; he took two, and his wife another, loaded them carefully, and awaited further developments.

Monday afternoon three men rode up and inquired for Mr. Wright. He walked out, with the butt of a revolver sticking warily from his pocket, and inquired their wishes. The revolver seemed to upset their ideas. They answered nothing in particular, and proceeded to converse upon everything in general, but never alluded to their errand. Finally, after a half hour had passed, and the men still talked on without coming to their mission, Wright grew impatient, and asked if they had any special business; if not, he had a pressing engagement, and would like to be excused. Well, they had a little business, said one, with considerable hesitation, as he glanced at the revolver butt.

"Stop!" said Wright; "before you tell it, I wish to say a word. I *know* your business, and I just promised my wife, on my honor as a man, that I would blow h—l out of the first man who told me of it, and by the eternal God I'll do it! Now tell me your errand!" and as he concluded he pulled out his revolver and cocked it. The fellow glanced a moment at the deadly-looking pistol, and took in the stalwart form of Wright, who was glaring at him with murder in his eye, and concluded to postpone the announcement. The three rode away, and reported the reception to their principals.

The next Sunday, after another refreshing season, the brethren again met, and took action upon the contumacy of Mr. Wright. The Captain of a company of secessionists was present, and after due deliberation, it was determined that, upon the next Thursday, he should take his command, proceed to Wright's, and summarily eject him from the sacred soil of Missouri. Wright's friend was again present, and he soon communicated the state of affairs to Mr. W., with a suggestion that it would save trouble and bloodshed if he got away before the day appointed.

Wright lived in a portion of the country remote from the church and the residence of those who were endeavoring to drive him out, and he determined, if possible, to prepare a surprise for the worthy Captain and his gallant force. To this end he bought a barrel of whiskey, another of crackers, a few cheeses, and some other provisions, and then mounting a black boy upon a swift horse, sent him around the country, inviting his friends to come and see him, and bring their arms. By Wednesday night he had gathered a force of about three hundred men, to whom he communicated the condition of things, and asked their assistance. They promised to back him to the death. The next day they concealed themselves in a cornfield, back of the house, and awaited the development of events.

A little after noon, the Captain and some eighty men rode up to the place, and inquired for Mr. Wright. That gentleman immediately made his appearance, when the Captain informed him that, being satisfied of his Abolitionism, they had come to eject him from the State.

"Won't you give me two days to settle up my affairs?" asked Wright.

"Two days be ——! I'll give you just five minutes to pack up your traps and leave!"

"But I can't get ready in five minutes! I have a fine property here, a happy home, and if you drive me off, you make me a beggar. I have done nothing. If I go, my wife and children must starve!"

"To —— with your beggars! You must travel!"

"Give me two hours!"

"I'll give you just five minutes, not a second longer! If you ain't out by that time (here the gallant soldier swore a most fearful oath), I'll blow out your cursed Abolition heart!"

"Well, if I must, I must!" and Wright turned towards the house, as if in despair, gave a preconcerted whistle, and almost instantly after, the concealed forces rushed out, and surrounded the astounded Captain and his braves.

"Ah, Captain!" said Wright, as he turned imploringly towards him, "won't you grant me two days, — two hours, at least, — my brave friend — only two hours in which to prepare myself and family for beggary and starvation — now do — won't you?"

The Captain could give no reply, but sat upon his horse, shaking as if ague-smitten.

"Don't kill me!" he at length found voice to say.

"Kill you! No, you black-livered coward, I won't dirty my hands with any such filthy work. If I kill you, I'll have one of my niggers do it! Get down from that horse!"

The gallant Captain obeyed, imploring only for life. The result of the matter was, that the whole company dismounted, laid down their arms, and then, as they filed out, were sworn to preserve their allegiance inviolate to the United States. An hour after, Mr. Wright had organized a force of two hundred and forty men for the war, and by acclamation was elected Captain. The next Sunday, he started with his command to join the national troops under Lyon, stopping long enough on his way to surround the Hardshell Church, at which had been inaugurated all his miseries. After the service was over, he administered the oath of allegiance to every one present, including the Reverend Pecksniff who officiated, and then left them to plot treason and worship God in their own peculiarly pious and harmonious manner.

He soon after became Maj. Wright, and continued in command of the crowd he enlisted at the beginning.

UNION MEN AT THE SOUTH. — An Illinois soldier, who was captured at Shiloh, gives the following incident of his visit to Memphis, then in the hands of the Confederates :

"A little good talking, mixed with the requisite amount of 'cheek,' secured to Serg. Eddy, well known among the Chicago typos, and myself, the privilege of a walk around town in company with a couple of German home guards, who carried two of Fremont's 'needle gun' for our protection. Our first stopping-place was the 'Appeal' office, where we found eight or ten 'comps,' and a score or so of 'secesh' flags — all hands intensely bitter against the North, 'secesh' all over, and every man of them born outside of Dixie. One of them — I forget his name, but shall never forget the man — asked:

"'Do you find as much Union sentiment as you expected?'

"I answered that I felt sure that such sentiment everywhere existed.

"'You are mistaken,' said he; 'there is not to-day a Union man in Memphis — not one.'

"Glancing at the guards, I saw evident signs of nervousness and anger, and thinking that perhaps, in the heat of debate, we had said too much, and should have a difficulty with them, my friend and I made preparations to leave. Scarcely had the door closed behind us, when one of the guards brought his piece down with a thump on the iron step, exclaiming:

"'Dare ish no Union sentiment here, eh? O, no! We are all tamd "secesh"! You comes mit me, I shows you. We all lay down our lives for dis Suturn Confederacy. O, yes! We be glad to.'

"We followed the guard to the outskirts of the town, and entered a blacksmith's shop, where, working at the forge, we recognized a couple of Chicago boys — they, too, belonged to the home guard. A sharp lookout was kept at the front and back doors; presently the coast was announced clear, and then you should have seen us making good time over back fences and through alleys, until we reached the abiding-place of our guide — entering, a buxom German girl placed chairs for us to be seated.

"'Frau,' said the guard, as soon as he had recovered sufficient breath to speak. 'Frau, here is a couple of tamd Yankees; you show dem we is good "secesh," eh.' 'Yes, I show dem;' and the 'Frau' placed a table in the centre of the room, and then disappeared. Presently the hissing of the tea-kettle is heard, and in a few minutes coffee which cost one dollar and twenty-five cents per pound, bread made from flour costing twenty dollars per barrel, and sausages from meat proportionately high, were served up to us. Our haversacks were filled, and then 'Frau' grumbled because we would not accept more. They were poor, and we could not rob them. While we were eating, the guards amused themselves by taking the main-springs out of their gun-locks, and burning them in the stove. As we shook hands at our prison-house door, they whispered, 'We are all tam "secesh."' We made arrangements with these men for a disguise to escape, but before they were again on duty, the 'show' was started for a new place."

SONG OF THE CROAKER.

BY HORATIO ALGER, JR.

An old frog lived in a dismal swamp,
  In a dismal kind of way;
And all that he did, whatever befell,
  Was to croak the livelong day.
    Croak, croak, croak,
  When darkness filled the air,
    And croak, croak, croak,
  When the skies were bright and fair.

"Good Master Frog, a battle is fought,
  And the foeman's power is broke;"
But he only turned a greener hue,
  And answered with a croak.
    Croak, croak, croak,
  When the clouds are dark and dun,
    And croak, croak, croak,
  In the blaze of the noontide sun.

"Good Master Frog, the forces of Right
  Are driving the hosts of Wrong;"
But he gives his head an ominous shake,
  And croaks out, "*Nous verrons!*"
    Croak, croak, croak,
  Till the heart is full of gloom,
    And croak, croak, croak,
  Till the world seems but a tomb.

To poison the cup of life
  By always dreading the worst,
Is to make of the earth a dungeon damp,
  And the happiest life accursed.
    Croak, croak, croak,
  When the noontide sun rides high,
    And croak, croak, croak,
  Lest the night come by and by.

Farewell to the dismal frog:
  Let him croak as loud as he may,
He cannot blot the sun from heaven,
  Nor hinder the march of day,
    Though he croak, croak, croak,
  Till the heart is full of gloom,
    And croak, croak, croak,
  Till the world seems but a tomb.

A PHILADELPHIA WELCOME. — A soldier of the Fourth New Hampshire regiment gives his experience in Philadelphia as follows:

"We arrived in the city at five o'clock on Sunday morning, Sept. 29, 1861, and the regiment was welcomed in a manner better appreciated than described. Within five or six rods of the ferry are three or four hundred wash-bowls, with pipes of warm and cold water to supply them. Here a scene followed, which reminded me that 'cleanliness is next to godliness.' Then we were marched to a building literally filled with nice bread, hot coffee, cold meats, pickles, cheese, and sour krout, and invited to partake of a Quaker's hospitality. After eating we were informed that stationery and every convenience for writing was at our disposal, and not a few accepted the kind privilege of writing home. No pay would be received for postage stamps, which were furnished as freely as water.

"As the good old matrons, with their three-cornered handkerchiefs and nicely ironed caps, glided among us, attending to our every want, inquiring after our health, wishing us God speed, &c., many an eye was moistened, and emotions awakened, which, perhaps, had been sleeping in many for years. And as the Quaker girls shook our hands, and even kissed some of the Yankee boys, I know our New Hampshire girls will not be jealous if we say, and truthfully too, that for the time being we forgot them at home. Although it is said that on one or two occasions 'the Quakers didn't come out,' it is true they *come out* to meet every regiment that passes through their city in a manner that no other city can boast of."

A DARING ADVENTURE. — It was late in the summer of 1864. The veteran and heroic army of Sherman in May that wonderful series of battles and marches which lasted while the rebellion continued, and which were the fatal and finishing blows by which the rebellion was crushed. By degrees, and after marking every mountain pass and almost every mile with blood, the rebel army had been pushed back and dislodged from one position after another, till now they had settled sullenly around the doomed city of Atlanta. The cautious and able Johnson was displaced in favor of the madcap and brainless fighter, Hood, who, in the language of the insurgent chief, "was determined to strike one manly blow for Atlanta." While the antagonists lay thus at bay, and Sherman was perfecting the details of that splendid manœuvre by which the stronghold became ours, a youthful soldier in the Union army, by the name of Ira B. Tuttle, with four of his men, performed a feat of military daring, which equals the exploits of Morgan, or any of the famous raiders of the war. The small village of Villa Rica lies about twenty-seven miles south by west of Atlanta, and about ten miles south of Dallas; near it is another little village, not inappropriately called Dark Corner.

In this village of Villa Rica the rebel General had established a principal magazine of supplies. As the greater part of his force lay between that point and the enemy, he regarded the point as entirely safe, and had left no guard on the spot, but only a Lieutenant-Colonel, a Captain, and three issuing Sergeants, to deliver the subsistence stores to the army wagons as they came for them. Rebel camps were, in fact, all around them, in front and in rear, not more than a mile distant. Tuttle and his four men, in their scouting adventures, had penetrated very near the place, and resolved on making a bold dash upon it, thus running an immense risk; while, on the other hand, they might inflict on the enemy a great loss, and make good their escape. Putting spurs to their horses, they rode directly up to the largest building, where fifty thousand bushels of corn and a large amount of bacon were stored. The officers and enlisted men at the magazine were taken wholly by surprise, not even having side arms. Tuttle made them mount their horses, while he and his men fired the buildings, and five wagons loaded with bacon for the army. As soon as the flames were well started, he ordered his five prisoners to ride on in front, while he with his four men rode behind, with hands on their pistol hilts.

As they rode away with their prisoners, the smoke of the burning storehouses had been seen at the rebel camp a mile distant, and men were seen rushing to save them, if possible. But it was too late. The material was highly combustible, the weather hot and dry, and water distant. While the astonished rebels were running towards the fire, in the vain hope of "saving their bacon," Tuttle and his brave companions, who had the fear of Andersonville before their eyes, put spurs to their horses, and drove their five prisoners before them into the Union camp.

CLARA BARTON. — The following is an extract of a letter from Brigade Surgeon James L. Dunn:

"The Sanitary Commission, together with three or four noble, self-sacrificing women, have furnished everything that could be required. I will tell you of one of these women, a Miss Barton, the daughter of Judge Barton, of Boston, Mass. I first met her at the battle of Cedar Mountain, where she appeared in front of the hospital at twelve o'clock at night, with a four mule team loaded with everything needed, and at a time when we were entirely out of dressings of every kind; she supplied us with everything; and while the shells were bursting in every direction, took her course to the hospital on our right, where she found everything wanting again. After doing everything she could on the field, she returned to Culpepper, where she staid dealing out shirts to the naked wounded, and preparing soup, and seeing it prepared, in all the hospitals. I thought that night if Heaven ever sent out an angel, she must be one, her assistance was so timely. Well, we began our retreat up the Rappahannock. I thought no more of our lady friend, only that she had gone back to Washington. We arrived on the disastrous field of Bull Run; and while the battle was raging the fiercest on Friday, who should drive up in front of our hospital but this same woman, with her mules almost dead, having made forced marches from Washington to the army. She was again a welcome visitor to both the wounded and the surgeons.

"The battle was over, our wounded removed on Sunday, and we were ordered to Fairfax Station; we had hardly got there before the battle of Chantilly commenced, and soon the wounded began to come in. Here we had nothing but our instruments — not even a bottle of wine. When the cars whistled up to the station, the first person on the platform was Miss Barton, to again supply us with bandages, brandy, wine, prepared soup, jellies, meal, and every article that could be thought of. She staid there until the last wounded soldier was placed on the cars, and then bade us good by and left.

"I wrote you at the time how we got to Alexandria that night and next morning. Our soldiers had no time to rest after reaching Washington, but were ordered to Maryland by forced marches. Several days of hard marching brought us to Frederick, and the battle of South Mountain followed. The next day our army stood face to face with the whole force. The rattle of one hundred and fifty thousand muskets, and the fearful thunder of over two hundred cannon, told us that the great battle of Antietam had commenced. I was in a hospital in the afternoon, for it was then only that the wounded began to come in.

"We had expended every bandage, torn up every sheet in the house, and everything we could find, when who should drive up but our old friend Miss Barton, with a team loaded down with dressings of every kind, and everything we could ask for. She distributed her articles to the different hospitals, worked all night making soup, all the next day and night; and when I left, four days after the battle, I left her there ministering to the wounded and the dying. When I returned to the field hospital last week, she was still at work, supplying them with delicacies of every kind, and administering to their wants — all of which she does out of her own private fortune. Now, what do you think of Miss Barton? In my feeble estimation, Gen. McClellan, with all his laurels, sinks into insignificance beside the true heroine of the age — *the angel of the battle-field.*"

A PRIVATE in battery F, Fourth U. S. artillery, wrote the following epitaph for John B. Floyd :

Floyd has died, and few have sobbed,
Since, had he lived, all had been robbed :
He's paid Dame Nature's debt, 'tis said,
The only one he ever paid.
Some doubt that he resigned his breath,
But vow he has cheated even death.
If he is buried, O, then, ye dead, beware !
Look to your swaddlings, of your shrouds take care,
Lest Floyd should to your coffins make his way,
And steal the linen from your mouldering clay.

SONGS UPON THE BATTLE-FIELD. — A brave and godly Captain in one of our Western regiments told us his story as we were taking him to the hospital. He was shot through both thighs with a rifle-bullet — a wound from which he could not recover. While lying on the field he suffered intense agony from thirst. He supported his head upon his hand, and the rain from heaven was falling around him. In a little while a little pool of water formed under his elbow, and he thought if he could only get to that puddle he might quench his thirst. He tried to get into a position to suck up a mouthful of muddy water, but he was unable to reach within a foot of it. Said he, "I never felt so much the loss of any earthly blessing. By and by night fell, and the stars shone out clear and beautiful above the dark field, and I began to

think of that great God who had given his Son to die a death of agony for me, and that he was up there — up above the scene of suffering, and above those glorious stars ; and I felt that I was going home to meet him, and praise him there ; and I felt that I ought to praise God, even wounded and on the battle-field. I could not help singing that beautiful hymn :

' When I can read my title clear
    To mansions in the skies,
I'll bid farewell to every fear,
    And dry my weeping eyes.'

"And," said he, "there was a Christian brother in the brush near me. I could not see him, but I could hear him. He took up the strain, and beyond him another and another caught it up, all over the terrible battle-field of Shiloh. That night the echo was resounding, and we made the field of battle ring with the hymns of praise to God."

THE DRUMMER BOY OF THE RAPPAHANNOCK. — Recently, a bright boy, with dark eyes and ruddy cheeks, gave a brief history of his adventures at the battle of Fredericksburg. He was neatly dressed in a military suit of gray cloth, and carried in his hands a pair of drumsticks ; his drum was destroyed by the fragment of a shell immediately after his landing on the river bank, in that hurricane of sulphury fire and iron hail on the 12th of December, 1862.

The reader will distinctly remember that for several days a curtain of thick fog rose up from the waters of the Rappahannock, completely hiding from view the artillery that crowned the opposite hills, and the infantry that crowded the sheltering ravines; but the preparation for the great fight, so hopefully commenced, was continued amid the thunder of cannon and the volcanic eruptions of exploding batteries.

The hazardous work of laying the pontoon bridges was frequently interrupted by the murderous fire of rebel sharpshooters, concealed in the stores and dwelling-houses on the bank of the river. To dislodge these men, and drive them out of their hiding-places, seemed an impossible task. At a given signal our batteries opened with a terrific fire upon the city, crashing through the walls of houses and public buildings, not sparing even the churches, in which treason had been taught as paramount to Christianity. In this storm of shot and shell, which ploughed the streets and set the buildings on fire, the sharpshooters survived, like salamanders in the flames, and continued to pour a deadly fire upon our engineers and bridge builders.

In this dilemma it became evident that the bridges could not be laid except by a bold dash. Volunteers were called for to cross in small boats; forthwith, hundreds stepped forward and offered their services. One hundred men were chosen, and at once started for the boats. Robert Henry Hendershot, the hero of our sketch, was then a member of the Eighth Michigan, acting as a drummer. Seeing a part of the Michigan Seventh preparing to cross the river, he ran ahead and leaped into the boat. One of the officers ordered him out, saying he would be shot. The boy replied that he didn't care, he was willing to die for his country. When he (the boy) found that the Captain would not permit him to remain in the boat, he begged the privilege of pushing the boat off, and the request was granted. Whereupon, instead of remaining on shore, he clung to the stern of the boat, and, submerged to the waist in water, he crossed the Rappahannock. Soon as he landed, a fragment of a shell struck his old drum and knocked it to pieces. Picking up a musket, he went in search of rebel relics, and obtained a secesh flag, a clock, a knife, and a bone ring. On opening a back door in one of the rebel houses, he found a rebel wounded in the hand, and ordered him to surrender. He did so, and was taken by the boy soldier to the Seventh Michigan. When the drummer boy recrossed the river from Fredericksburg, General Burnside said to him, in the presence of the army, " Boy, I glory in your spunk; if you keep on this way a few more years, you will be in my place."

At the battle of Murfreesboro', where the Union forces were taken by surprise, before daylight in the morning, after beating the long roll, and pulling the fifer out of bed to assist him, he threw aside his drum, and seizing a gun, fired sixteen rounds at the enemy from the window of the court-house in which his regiment was quartered; but the nationals were compelled to surrender, and they were all taken prisoners, but were immediately paroled, and afterwards sent to Camp Chase, Ohio.

THE BONNIE BLUE FLAG.

We are a band of brothers, and natives to the soil,
Fighting for the property we gained by honest toil;
And when our rights were threatened, the cry rose
near and far,
Hurrah for the bonnie Blue Flag that bears the
single star!

CHORUS.

Hurrah! hurrah! for the bonnie Blue Flag
That bears the single star.

As long as the Union was faithful to her trust,
Like friends and like brothers, kind were we and
just;
But now, when Northern treachery attempts our
rights to mar,
We hoist on high the bonnie Blue Flag that bears
the single star.

First, gallant South Carolina nobly made the stand;
Then came Alabama, who took her by the hand;
Next quickly Mississippi, Georgia and Florida —
All raised the flag, the bonnie Blue Flag that bears
a single star.

Ye men of valor, gather round the banner of the
right;
Texas and fair Louisiana join us in the fight.
Davis, our loved President, and Stephens, statesmen
are;
Now rally round the bonnie Blue Flag that bears a
single star.

And here's to brave Virginia! The Old Dominion
State
With the young Confederacy at length has linked
her fate.
Impelled by her example, now other States prepare
To hoist on high the bonnie Blue Flag that bears a
single star.

Then here's to our Confederacy; strong we are and
brave:
Like patriots of old we'll fight, our heritage to save;
And rather than submit to shame, to die we would
prefer;
So cheer for the bonnie Blue Flag that bears a single
star.

Then cheer, boys, cheer; raise the joyous shout,
For Arkansas and North Carolina now have both
gone out;
And let another rousing cheer for Tennessee be given.
The single star of the bonnie Blue Flag has grown
to be eleven!

THE PRIVATE SOLDIER. — Under this head the Jackson Mississippi Crisis pays the following tribute to the private soldier:

Justice has never been done him. His virtuous merit and unobtrusive patriotism have never been justly estimated. We do not speak of the regular soldier, who makes the army his trade for twelve dollars per month. We do not include the coward, who skulks; nor the vulgarian, who can perpetrate acts of meanness; nor the laggard, who must be forced to fight for his home and country. These are not the subjects of our comment. We speak of the great body of citizen soldiery who constitute the provisional army of the Confederacy, and who, at the sound of a trumpet and drum, marched out with rifle or musket to fight — to repel their country's invaders, or perish on that soil which their fathers bequeathed, with the glorious boon of civil liberty. These are the gallant men of whom we write, and these have saved the country; these have made a breastwork of their manly bosoms to shield the sacred precinct of altar-place and fireside. Among these private soldiers are to be found men of culture, men of gentle training, men of intellect, men of social position, men of character at home, men endeared to a domestic circle of refinement and elegance, men of wealth, men who gave tone and character to the society in which they moved, and men who for conscience' sake have made a living sacrifice of property, home, comfort, and are ready to add crimson life to the holy offering. Many of these, if they could have surrendered honor and a sense of independence, could have remained in possession of all these elegances and comforts. But they felt like the Roman who said, " Put honor in one hand and death in the other, and I will look on both indifferently." Without rank, without title, without anticipated distinction, animated only by the highest and noblest sentiments which can influence our common nature, the private labors, and toils, and marches, and fights; endures hunger and thirst, and fatigue; through watchings, and weariness, and sleepless nights, and cheerless, laborious days, he holds up before him the one glorious prize — "Freedom to my country ;" "Independence and my home !" If we can suppose the intervention of less worthy motive, the officer, and not the private, is the man whose merit must commingle such alloy. The officer may become renowned — the private never reckons upon that ; the officer may live in history — the private looks to no such record ; the officer may attract the public gaze — the private does not look for such recognition ; the officer has a salary — the private only a monthly stipend, the amount of which he has been accustomed to pay to some field laborer on his rich domains ; the officer may escape harm in battle by reason of distance — the private must face the storm of death ; the officer moves on horseback — the private on foot ; the officer carries a sword, the emblem of authority, and does not fight — the privates carries his musket, and does all the fighting. The battle has been fought — the victory won ; and Lee, or Longstreet, or others, have achieved a glorious success ; but that success was attained by the private soldier, at the cost of patriot blood, of shattered bones, and torn and mangled muscle and nerves ! We do not mean to under-estimate the officer, or disparage his courage, or his patriotism. We draw the parallel for another purpose, and that is, to show, if other than the highest human motive prompts the soldier to action, it is the officer, and not the private, who is not liable to feel its influence.

We have often felt pained and annoyed at the flippant reference to the privates, while the unreasoning speaker seemed to regard the officers as the prime and meritorious agents of all that is done. Why, in those ranks is an amount of intellect which would instruct and astonish a statesman. In those ranks the merit of every officer and every action is settled unappealably. In those ranks there is public virtue and capacity enough to construct a government, and administer its civil and military offices. The opinion of these men will guide the historian, and fix the merit of generals and statesmen. The opinion of these men will be, and ought to be, omnipotent with the people and government of the Confederacy. Heaven bless these brave, heroic men ! Our heart warms to them. Our admiration of their devotion and heroism is without limit. Their devotion to principle amounts to moral sublimity. We feel their sufferings, and share their hopes, and desire to be identified in our day and generation with such a host of spirits, tried and true, who bend the knee to none but God, and render homage only to worth and merit.

MARKED ARTICLES. — Some of the marks which were fastened on the blankets, shirts, &c., sent to the Sanitary Commission for the soldiers, show the thought and feeling at home. Thus — on a home-spun blanket, worn but washed as clean as snow, was pinned a bit of paper, which said : "This blanket was carried by Milly Al-

drich (who is ninety-three years old), down hill and up hill, one and a half miles, to be given to some soldier."

On a bed-quilt was pinned a card, saying : "My son is in the army. Whoever is made warm by this quilt, which I have worked on for six days and most all of six nights, let him remember his own mother's love."

On another blanket was this : "This blanket was used by a soldier in the war of 1812 — may it keep some soldier warm in this war against traitors."

On a pillow was written : "This pillow belonged to my little boy, who died resting on it ; it is a precious treasure to me, but I give it for the soldiers."

On a pair of woollen socks was written : "These stockings were knit by a little girl five years old, and she is going to knit some more, for mother says it will help some poor soldier."

On a box of beautiful lint was this mark : "Made in a sick room, where the sunlight has not entered for nine years, but where God has entered, and where two sons have bid their mother good by as they have gone out to the war."

On a bundle containing bandages was written : "This is a poor gift, but it is all I had ; I have given my husband and my boy, and only wish I had more to give, but I haven't."

On some eye-shades were marked : "Made by one who is blind. O, how I long to see the *dear Old Flag* that you are all fighting under !"

TO PRESIDENT LINCOLN.

PROUDEST of all earth's thrones
  Is his who rules by a free people's choice ;
Who, 'midst fierce party strife and battle groans,
Hears, ever rising in harmonious tones,
  A grateful people's voice.

Steadfast in thee we trust,
  Tried as no man was ever tried before ;
God made thee merciful — God keep thee just ;
Be true ! — and triumph over all thou must.
  God bless thee evermore !

A SOLDIER'S STORY. — "Not long since," said a soldier, "a lot of us — I am a H. P., 'high private,' now — were quartered in several wooden tenements, and in the inner room of one lay the *corpus* of a young secesh officer awaiting burial. The news soon spread to a village not far off, and down came a sentimental, not bad-looking specimen of a Virginia dame.

"'Let me kiss him for his mother !' she cried, as I interrupted her progress. 'Do let me kiss him for his mother !'

"'Kiss whom ?'

"'The dear little Lieutenant, the one who lies dead within. I never saw him, but, O'——

"I led her through a room in which Lieut. ——, of Philadelphia, lay stretched out in an upturned trough, fast asleep. Supposing him to be the article sought for, she rushed up, exclaiming, 'Let me kiss him for his mother,' and approached her lips to his forehead. What was her amazement, when the 'corpse' clasped his arms around her, and exclaimed, 'Never mind the old lady, miss; go it on your own account. I haven't the slightest objection.'"

EXPERIENCE OF A WOUNDED SOLDIER. — The following extract gives the experience of one shot in battle:

"I remember no acute sensation of pain, not even any distinct shot, only an instantaneous consciousness of having been struck; then my breath came hard and labored, with a croup-like sound, and with a dull, aching feeling in my right shoulder; my arm fell powerless at my side, and the Enfield dropped from my grasp. I threw my left hand up to my throat, and withdrew it covered with the warm, bright-red blood. The end had come at last! But, thank God, it was death in battle. Only let me get back out of that deathly storm, and breathe away the few minutes that were left me of life in some place of comparative rest and security. It all rushed into my mind in an instant. I turned and staggered away to the rear. A comrade brushed by me, shot through the hand, who, a moment before, was firing away close at my side. I saw feeble reënforcements moving up, and I recollect a thrill of joy even then, as I thought that the tide of battle might yet be turned, and those rebel masses beaten back, broken, foiled, disheartened.

"But my work was done. I was growing faint and weak, although not yet half way out of range of fire. A narrow space between two massive bowlders, over which rested lengthwise the trunk of a fallen tree, offered refuge and hope of safety from further danger. I crawled into it, and lay down to die. I counted the minutes before I must bleed to death. I had no more hope of seeing the new year on the morrow than I now have of outliving the next century. Thank God, death did not seem so dreadful, now that it was come. And then the sacrifice was not all in vain, falling thus in God's own holy cause of freedom. But home and friends! O, the rush of thought then!

"Let the veil be drawn here. The temple of memory has its holy place, into which only one's own soul may, once in a great season, solemnly enter.

"And so I lay there, with my head pillowed on my blanket, while the battle swelled again around and over me — bullets glancing from the sides of stone that sheltered me, or sinking into the log above me, and shot and shell crashing through the tree-tops, and falling all about me. Two shells, I remember, struck scarcely ten feet from me, and in their explosion covered me with dirt and splinters; but that was all. Still I lived on. I smile now as I think of it, how I kept raising my left hand to see if the finger nails were growing white and purple, as they do when one bleeds to death, and wondering to find them still warm and ruddy. Hemorrhage must have ceased almost, and the instincts of existence said, 'Live!'

Then came the agony of waiting for removal from the field. How I longed and looked for some familiar face, as our men twice charged up into that wood, directly over me! But they belonged to another division, and had other work to do than bearing off the wounded."

COULDN'T UNDERSTAND IT. — A war-beaten veteran of Longstreet's corps made a funny remark to a prominent politician who conversed with him while coming in from the front. Said he, "I do not understand this; Lee has won a big victory over Grant on the Rapidan, and told us so, and that night we retreated. Then he won another in the Wilderness, and told us so, and we retreated to Spottsylvania. Then he won another tre-*men*-jus victory, and I got tuk prisoner; but I reckon he has retreated ag'in. Now, when he *used* to lick them, the Yanks fell back and claimed a victory, and we understood it. Now Lee claims victories, and keeps a fallin' back, and I *can't understand it*."

A NO-SIDER. — A correspondent tells the following story of one of the farmers in the vicinity of Culpepper, whose possessions lay in a district where both armies foraged. The old chap, one day, while surveying ruefully the streaks in the soil where his fences once stood, remarked with much feeling:

"I hain't took no sides in this yer rebellion, but I'll be dog-gorned if both sides hain't took me."

A WHITE HOUSE ANECDOTE. — An old farmer, from the West, who knew President Lincoln in days by-gone, called to pay his respects at the Presidential mansion. Slapping the Chief Magistrate upon the back, he exclaimed: "Well, old hoss, how are you?" Old Abe, being thoroughly democratic in his ideas, and withal relishing a joke, responded: "So I'm an old hoss—am I? What kind of a hoss, pray?" "Why, an old draft hoss, to be sure," was the rejoinder.

BARBARITIES OF THE SIOUX.

MRS. HURD'S NARRATIVE.

On the 2d of June, 1862, Mr. Phineas B. Hurd, with another man, left home, at the north end of Sheteck Lake, Minnesota, on a trip to Dacotah Territory, to be absent a month, taking a span of horses and wagon, and such other outfit as would be required upon such an expedition, leaving Mrs. Hurd alone with her two children and a Mr. Voight, who had charge of the farm. On the morning of the 20th of August, about five o'clock, while Mrs. Hurd was milking, some twenty Indians rode up to the house and dismounted. Mrs. Hurd discovered among the horses one of their own that was taken away by Mr. Hurd. Mrs. H. got into the house before the Indians, who

MAJ. GEN. W.T. SHERMAN

entered and began smoking, as was their custom. Five of these she knew, one being a half-breed who could speak English. Her children were in bed, and, at the time of the entrance of the Indians, asleep. The youngest, about a year old, awoke and cried, when Mr. Voight took it up and carried it into the front yard, when one of the Indians stepped to the door and shot him through the body. He fell dead with the child in his arms. At this signal some ten or fifteen more Indians and squaws rushed into the house, — they having been concealed near by, — and commenced an indiscriminate destruction of everything in the house, breaking open trunks, destroying furniture, cutting open feather beds, and scattering the contents about the house and yard.

Mrs. Hurd, in her uncommon energy and industry as a pioneer housewife, had, with a good stock of cows, begun to make butter and cheese, and had on hand at the time about two hundred pounds of butter and twenty-three cheeses. These the Indians threw into the yard and destroyed. While this destruction was going on, Mrs. Hurd was told that her life would be spared on the condition that she would give no alarm, and leave the settlement by an unfrequented path or trail, leading directly east across the prairie, in the direction of New Ulm, and was ordered to take her children and commence her march. Upon pleading for her children's clothes, they having on only their right clothes, she was hurried off, being refused even her sun-bonnet or shawl. She took the youngest in her arms, and led the other, a little boy of a little over three years, by the hand; and being escorted by seven Indians on horseback, she turned her back on her once prosperous and happy home. The distance across the prairie, in the direction which she was sent, was sixty or seventy miles to a habitation. The Indians went out with her three miles, and before taking leave of her, repeated the condition of her release, and told her that all the whites were to be killed, but that she might go to her mother. Thus was she left with her two children almost naked, herself bareheaded, without food or raiment, not even a blanket to shelter herself and children from the cold dews of the night or storm.

After the Indians left her, three miles from her home, on the prairie, "we took our way," said Mrs. Hurd, "through the unfrequented road or trail into which the Indians had conducted us. It was clear, and the sun shone with more than usual brightness. The dew on the grass was heavy. My little boy, William Henry, being barefooted and thinly clad, shivered with the cold, and pressing close to me, entreated me to return to our home. He did not know of the death of Mr. Voight, as I kept him from the sight of the corpse. He did not understand why I insisted upon going on, enduring the pain and cold of so cheerless a walk. He cried pitifully at first, but after a time, pressing my hand, he trudged manfully along by my side. The little one rested in my arms, unconscious of our situation. Two guns were fired when I was a short distance out, which told the death of my neighbor, Mr. Cook. I knew well

the fearful meaning. There was death behind, and all the horrors of starvation before me. But there was no alternative. For my children, anything except death at the hands of the merciless savage; even starvation on the prairies seemed preferable to this.

"About ten o'clock in the forenoon a thunderstorm suddenly arose. It was of unusual violence; the wind was not high, but the lightning, thunder, and rain were most terrible. The violence of the storm was expended in about three hours, but the rain continued to fall slowly until night, and at intervals continued until morning. During the storm I lost the trail, and walked on, not knowing whether I was right or wrong. Water covered the lower portions of the prairie, and it was with difficulty that I could find a place to rest when night came on. At last I came to a sand-hill or knoll; on the top of this I sat down to rest for the night. I laid my children down, and leaned over them to protect them from the rain and chilling blast. Hungry, weary, and wet, William fell asleep, and continued so until morning. The younger one worried much; the night wore away slowly, and the morning at last came, inviting us to renewed efforts. As soon as I could see, I took my little ones and moved on. About seven o'clock I heard guns, and for the first time became conscious that I had lost my way, and was still in the vicinity of the lake. I changed my course, avoiding the direction in which I heard the guns, and pressed on with increased energy. No trail was visible. As for myself, I was not conscious of hunger; but it was harassing to the mother's heart to listen to the cries of my precious boy for his usual beverage of milk, and his constant complaints of hunger. But there was no remedy. The entire day was misty, and the grass wet. Our clothes were not dry during the day. Towards night William grew sick, and vomited, until it seemed impossible for him longer to keep up. The youngest child still nursed, and did not seem to suffer materially.

"About dark on the second day I struck a road, and knew at once where I was, and to my horror found I was only four miles from home. Thus had two days and one night been passed, travelling, probably, in a circle. I felt almost exhausted, and my journey but just begun; but as discouraging as this misfortune might be, as the shades of night again closed around me, the sight of a known object was a pleasure to me. I was no longer lost upon the vast prairies.

"It was now that I felt for the first time it would be better to die at once; that it would be a satisfaction to die here, and end our weary journey on this travelled road, over which we had passed in our happier days. I could not bear to lie down with my little ones on the unknown and trackless waste over which we had been wandering. But this feeling was but for a moment. I took courage and started on the road to New Ulm. When it became quite dark I halted for the night; that night I passed, as before, without sleep.

"In the morning early I started on. It was

foggy, and the grass wet; the road, being but little travelled, was grown up with grass. William was so sick that morning that he could not walk much of the time; so I was obliged to carry both. I was now sensibly reduced in strength, and felt approaching hunger. My boy no longer asked for food, but was thirsty, and drank frequently from the pools by the wayside. I could no longer carry both my children at the same time, but took one on at a distance of a quarter or half a mile, laid it in the grass, and returned for the other. In this way I travelled twelve miles, to a place called Dutch Charlie's, sixteen miles from Lake Sheteck. I arrived there about sunset, having been sustained in my weary journey by the sweet hope of relief. My toils seemed almost at an end, as I approached the house, with a heart full of joyous expectations; but what were my consternation and despair when I found it empty! Every article of food and clothing was removed! My heart seemed to die within me, and I sank down in despair. The cries of my child aroused me from my almost unconscious state, and I began my search for food. The house had not been plundered by the Indians, but abandoned by its owner. I had promised my boy food when we arrived here, and when none could be found he cried most bitterly. But I did not shed a tear, nor am I conscious of having done so during all this journey. I found some green corn, which I endeavored to eat, but my stomach rejected it. I found some carrots and onions growing in the garden, which I ate raw, having no fire. My oldest child continued vomiting. I offered him some carrot, but he could not eat it.

"That night we staid in a cornfield, and the next morning at daylight I renewed my search for food. To my great joy I found the remains of a spoiled ham. Here, I may say, my good fortune began. There was no more than a pound of it, and that much decayed. This I saved for my boy, feeding it to him in very small quantities; his vomiting ceased, and he revived rapidly. I gathered more carrots and onions, and with this store of provisions, at about eight o'clock on the morning of the third day, I again set forth on my weary road for the residence of Mr. Brown, twenty-five miles distant. This distance I reached in two days. Under the effects of the food I was able to give my boy, he gained strength, and was able to walk all of the last day. When within about three miles of the residence of Mr. Brown, two of our old neighbors, from Lake Sheteck settlement, overtook us under the escort of the mail carrier. Both of them had been wounded by the Indians and left for dead in the attack on the settlement. Thomas Ireland, one of the party, had been hit with eight balls, and, strange to say, was still able to walk, and had done so most of the way. Mrs. Estleck, the other person under escort, was utterly unable to walk, having been shot in the foot, once in the side, and once in the arm. Her husband had been killed, and her son, about ten years old, wounded. The mail carrier had overtaken this party after the fight with the Indians at the Lake, and placing Mrs. Estleck

in her sulky, he was leading his horse. As the little party came in sight I took them to be Indians, and felt that after all my toil and suffering I must die, with my children, by the hands of the savage. I feared to look around, but kept on my way until overtaken, when my joy was so great at seeing my friends alive, I sank to the earth insensible.

"This was a little before sunset, and we all arrived at the residence of Mr. Brown that week. This house was also deserted and empty, but being fastened up, we thought they might come back. Our company being too weak and destitute to proceed, we took possession of the house, and remained ten days. There we found potatoes and green corn. The mail carrier, accompanied by Mr. Ireland, lame as he was, proceeded on the next morning to New Ulm, where they found there had been a battle with the Indians, and one hundred and ninety-two houses burned. A party of twelve men were immediately sent with a wagon to our relief. It was now that we learned the fate of Mr. Brown and family — all had been murdered! We also learned of the general outbreak, and massacre of all the more remote settlements, and the sad, sickening thought was now fully confirmed in my mind, that my husband was dead! my fatherless children and myself made beggars!"

Mrs. Hurd had resided at the Lake three years, and was well acquainted with many of the Indians — could speak their language, and had always treated them with much friendship. It is to this fact that she attributed their mercy in saving her life. But who can bring back to her the murdered husband — the beauty, loveliness, and enjoyment that surrounded her on the morning of the 20th of August, 1862, or blot from her memory those awful, dreary nights of watching, alone upon the broad prairie, in the storm and in the tempest, amid thunderings and lightning? Or who can contemplate that mother's feelings as her sick and helpless child cried for bread, and there was none to give, or as she bore the one along the almost trackless waste, and laid it down amid the prairie grass, and then returned for her other offspring?

The Mantuan bard has touched a universal chord of human sympathy in his deep-toned description of the flight of his hero from the burning city of Troy, bearing his "good father," Anchises, on his back, and leading "the little Ascanius" by the hand, who, ever and anon falling in the rear, would "follow with unequal step." The heroine of Lake Sheteck bore her two Ascanii in her arms, but unequal to the double burden, was compelled to deposit half of her precious cargo in the prairie grass, and returning for the other, to repeat for the third time her painful steps over the same. This process, repeated at the end of each quarter or half mile, extended the fearful duration of her terrible flight through the lonely and uninhabited prairie.

The force of nature could go no farther, and maternal love has no stronger exemplification. But for the plentiful showers of refreshing rain, sent by a merciful Providence, these poor wanderers would have fainted by the way, and the touching story of the heroine of Shetcck Lake would have been forever shrouded in mystery.

AN INCIDENT AT CHATTANOOGA. — At one point there was a lull in the battle. At least, it had gone scattering and thundering down the line, and the boys were as much "at ease" as boys can be on whom at any moment the storm may roll back again. To be sure, occasional shots, and now and then a cometary shell, kept them alive; but one of the boys ran down to a little spring, and to the woods where the enemy lay, for water. He had just stopped and swung down his canteen — "tick," and a minie ball struck it at an angle, and bounded away. He looked around an instant, discovered nobody, thought it was a chance shot — a piece of lead, you know, that goes at a killing rate without malice prepense; and so, nowise infirm of purpose, he bent to get the water. Ping! a second bullet cut the cord of his canteen, and the boy "get the idea" — a sharpshooter was after him, and he went on the right-about, on the double-quick, to the ranks. A soldier from another part of the line made a pilgrimage to the spring, was struck, and fell by its brink. But where was the marksman? Two or three boys ran out to draw his fire while others watched. Crack went the unseen piece again, and some keen-eyed fellow spied the smoke roll out from a little cedar. This was the spot, then. The reb had made him a hawk's nest, — in choice Indian, a Chattanooga in the tree, — and drawing the green covert around him, was taking a quiet hand at "steeple-shooting" at long range.

A big blue-eyed German, tall enough to look into the third generation, and a sharpshooter withal, volunteered to dislodge him. Dropping into a little run-way that neared the tree diagonally, he turned upon his back, and worked himself cautiously along; reaching a point perilously close, he whipped over, took aim as he lay, and God and his true right hand "gave him good deliverance." Away flew the bullet, a minute elapsed, the volume of the cedar parted, and "like a big frog," as the boys described it, out leaped a grayback — the hawk's nest was empty, and a dead rebel lay under the tree. It was neatly done by the German. May he live to tell the story a thousand times to his moon-faced grandchildren!

A SOUTHERN GIRL thus wrote to her cousin, who was a prisoner at Camp Morton, Indianapolis:

"I will be for Jeffdavise till the tenisce river freazes over, and then be for him, and scratch on the ice

Jeffdavise rides a white horse,
Lincoln rides a mule,
Jeffdavise is a gentleman,
And Lincoln is a fule."

THE SHARPSHOOTER'S LAMENT ON THE BANKS OF THE POTOMAC.

"THE sunlight is yellow and pleasant;
What darkens your spirit, Jem True?"
"Ay, Sergeant, it's bright for the present,
And I know it looks mean to be blue,
Squattin' here, like a draggle-tailed pheasant;
But what's a poor fellow to do?

"Nary shot since I left the 'peraries,'
And 'listed in sarch o' big game.
It's a rule that must work by contraries,
That inveigled me on till I came
To this ground without even canaries
Or chippies to warrant an aim.

"Misfortin' comes crowdin' misfortin',
And between 'em old Jem is nigh beat,
For here comes the news of the sportin'
As has come to them chaps on the fleet;
And, bless yer, they're greenies for courtin'
The shrews of grim death as they'll meet.

"Why, there isn't one cove in a dozen,
For all they're stout as you'll see,
As distinguishes well 'twixt the buzzin'
Of a bullet and that of a bee;
And among 'em there's Billy, my cousin —
He shakes 'on a rest' like a flea.

"And Toby, though brave as a lion,
His intentions his in'ards confound;
When to jerkin' the trigger he's nigh on,
The vartigo bobs him around;
And that bully old sinner, O'Ryan,
He's cross-eyed, and shoots at the ground.

"While here's the old boy as can jingle
Any button as shines on a breast,
With a pill as can operate single
At eight hundred yards and 'no rest;'
He's left for his cusses to mingle,
Like a eagle what's glued to his nest.

"'Twas only last night, when on duty,
A sightin' them pickets o' theirs,
That I drew a true bead on a 'beauty,'
With a greasy old coon on his ears.
'O beautiful varmint! I'll shoot ye,'
I whispered aloud unawares.

"'No, you won't,' says my comrade, old Dan'l;
'The orders keep pickets from harm.'
'Well, I'll rip up them stripes of red flannel
What so sarcily shine on his arm,'
I pleaded; but 'No,' says old Dan'l,
'The orders keep pickets from harm.'

"Sech orders my heart's disappointin' —
'Twasn't sech as inveigled me in
To clap my mark down to the writin'
The recruiter said glories would win.
O, when fellers is gathered for fightin',
Say, why can't the scrimmage begin?

"O, I'm sick of this lazy black river,
Where forever we're likely to stay.
Why, the Capital's saved, if it ever
Will be, and it can't run away!
Can't we leave it a spell? are we never
To sport in these diggins here — say?

"Must a cove as can ring up his twenty
  At twelve hundred yards on a 'string,'
Get his hand out when varmints is plenty,
  Like a watch-works what hasn't no spring?
Must a screamer be mum when he's sent t'ye
  In voice for his sweetest to sing?

"I cares not for fierce adversaries,
  If for fighting we wasn't so slow.
O Sergeant! it's waitin' that varies
  The misery that hangs on me so.
I longs for my darlin' 'peraries,'
  And that's why my feelin's is low."

COLONEL WILLICH'S VICTORY. — Chaplain Ganter, of the Fifteenth Ohio regiment, gives the following account of the fight that took place near Camp George Wood, Kentucky, on the 17th of December, 1861:

"The noted Texas Rangers have been for some time dodging, sneaking, dashing about us in a desperate manner. Sunday last we had a skirmish with them in which Colonel Willich had two men wounded and one sergeant taken prisoner. Yesterday (Tuesday, 17th,) Colonel Willich sent over one or two companies to watch them. About noon the trumpeter came to the bank on the opposite side of the river and blew the signal for reënforcements. Immediately four or five companies (of Colonel Willich's regiment) crossed the river at double-quick (across the bridge which they had just completed). They ran in eagerness to fight, stimulated to rage, to revenge their wounded comrades of Sunday last. When they crossed the river they deployed as skirmishers and double-quicked it over fences, through the woods, when all at once one of their men cried halt, and seeing a horse in the woods near by, he fired, and the horse fell. Immediately a yell echoed through the woods, and about one hundred and fifty Rangers issued forth, and came within ten feet of the muzzles of the guns of our men. Here they halted, and did not stir or budge one inch until each one of their number had fired fourteen shots, being armed with a pair of revolvers and double shot gun apiece. But while this was going on our men were not idle. Rangers dropped — Rangers yelled, groaned, and cursed — horses Rangerless, riderless, were galloping in all directions. When the Rangers had performed their shooting in a cool, careless way, they just as coolly turned round and retired. They had no sooner disappeared, and our men were once more advancing — than another company of Rangers galloped up, and performed the same remarkable fourteen-shot feat in the same cool, determined manner, and were met by the same sturdy, brave German square. Once more Rangers and Germans mingled dying groans — when at length, after the Rangers had gone through this exact programme several times, three or four hundred of them made one grand rush, with the evident intention of breaking the German *currere*, or square. They came up with the same dash, and fired their shots with the same apparent neglect of life — some were literally lifted from their horses on the point of the bayonet — some were knocked off with butts of the guns. It became a hand-to-hand fight — Rangers retreating and Germans following up. Lieutenant Saxe at this point of the fight was somewhat in advance. He was surrounded by Rangers — they asked him to surrender — but instead of replying he rushed at the man who made this request, but before he reached the object of his attack dropped dead in his tracks, receiving five bullets in the chest and about twenty buckshot in the abdomen. Then the struggle became fiercer and hotter, when all at once the Germans found themselves in a net. On the right came the firing from concealed infantry; on the left the boom of cannon from a masked battery startled the heroes. Seven hundred cavalry at once came into view in front. We could see the whole affair from the high bluff on this side of Green River. Reënforcements were hurried across — Cotter's batteries opened from our bluff — Germans slowly, but unwillingly, retired to the woods, and just by chance, the merest in the world, escaped from a dreadful slaughter. The Forty-ninth Ohio and Thirty-ninth Indiana formed in line of battle, and double-quicked it over the field; but the enemy had retired. Now let me give you the results and objects of this fight; and what I tell you may be relied upon, especially with regard to numbers. Our loss was eleven killed, twenty-one wounded, and five missing (when I say wounded, I mean severely). Among the killed was one officer, Lieutenant Saxe, a Jew, an old country soldier, and a brave man. The loss of the enemy (I am giving you the lowest figures) was thirty-three killed; wounded we cannot positively tell, for they were all carried off the field. Colonel Terry, their brave and celebrated Colonel of Rangers, was killed. And now with regard to numbers engaged: We had about five hundred men (all of Colonel Willich's command) actually engaged at one time or another. They had seven hundred Rangers, one regiment of infantry (six hundred men), and four cannon. The fight: well, you may judge from my description, that there was 'no discount' on that from either side. The Germans acknowledge that they never saw 'Regular Cavalry' in the old country wars, surpass the Rangers in daring, bravery, and apparent insensibility to danger and death. They describe them as swarthy complexioned, a mixture of creoles, trappers, desperadoes, with long hair and shaggy whiskers, and even when lying wounded upon the ground exhibiting the fierceness of a wounded tiger. I visited all the wounded to-day. Number one has his ear shot off, number two is minus the bridge of his nose, four or five wounded in the arms, four or five in the legs, four in the chest, one in the abdomen, another has a quantity of buckshot in his side. I saw the latter gentleman as the doctor was cutting out the shot. He remarked 'tat dey didn't shoot mit buckshot in de old country,' but he hoped the rebels would 'shoot buckshot all de times.' They all took great pleasure in explaining their wounds, and most of them did not wince under the doctor's dressing. One poor fellow comforted himself with the reflection that if he had to lose his leg he would join the cavalry. This morning I went to see the dead; they were laid out in the field, neatly dressed; graves were dug on the top of a knoll, in a semicircle. The regiment formed around them. The Colonel made a speech, and then remarked, ' that as their brave comrades had fallen in the struggle for human rights and liberty, and were now on their journey to immortality, they would give them three cheers;' and cheer they did, and then the band played the Marseilles Hymn, and the soldiers marched around the graves, each throwing a handful of earth into each of the graves. No salutes were fired on account of the close proximity of the hospital."

A SQUAD of Indiana volunteers, out scouting, came across a female in a log cabin in the mountains. After the usual salutations, one of them asked her, "Well, old lady, are you a secesh?" "No," was the answer. "Are you Union?" "No." "What are you, then?" "A Baptist, an' always have been." The Hoosiers let down.

A SINGULAR SPECTACLE IN BATTLE. — At the battle of Stone River, while the men were lying behind a crest, waiting, a brace of frantic wild turkeys, so paralyzed with fright that they were incapable of flying, ran between the lines, and endeavored to hide among the men. But the frenzy among the turkeys was not so touching as the exquisite fright of the birds and rabbits. When the roar of battle rushed through the cedar thickets, flocks of little birds fluttered and circled above the field in a state of utter bewilderment, and scores of rabbits fled for protection to the men lying down in line on the left, nestling under their coats, and creeping under their legs in a state of utter distraction. They hopped over the field like toads, and as perfectly tamed by fright as household pets. Many officers witnessed it, remarking it as one of the most curious spectacles ever seen upon a battle-field.

TIME TO LEAVE. — One of the "contrabands," who found his way to Boston with returning troops, related his experience on the battle-field as follows : " Ye see, massa, I was drivin' an ambulance, when a musket-ball come and kill my horse; and den, pretty soon, the shell come along, and he blow my wagon all to pieces — and *den I got off* !"

SOL. MEREDITH. — A pleasant story is told by a correspondent, of Colonel Sol. Meredith, of Wayne County, Indiana, commanding the Nineteenth Indiana, on the Potomac.

At the Lewinsville skirmish, the Colonel was at the head of his men, as they were formed in line of battle, under the fire of the enemy. As the shells exploded over them, his boys would involuntarily duck their heads. The Colonel saw their motions, and in a pleasant way exhorted them, as he rode along the line, to hold up their heads and act like men. He turned to speak to one of his officers, and at that moment an eighteen-pounder shell burst within a few yards of him, scattering the fragments in all directions. Instinctively, he jerked his head almost to the saddle-bow, while his horse squatted with fear. "Boys," said he, as he raised up and reined his steed, "you MAY dodge the large ones!" A laugh ran along the line at his expense, and after that no more was said about the impropriety of dodging shells.

"MOST THAR." — During the march of McClellan's army up the Peninsula, from Yorktown, a tall Vermont soldier got separated from his regiment, and was trudging along through the mud, endeavoring to overtake it. Finally, coming to a crossing, he was puzzled as to which road he should take; but on seeing one of the "natives," his countenance lighted up at the prospect of obtaining the desired information, and he inquired, " Where does this road lead to?" "To hell!" was the surly answer of the "native." " Well," drawled the Vermonter, "judging by the lay of the land, and the appearance of the inhabitants, I kalkerlate I'm most thar."

AN EASY CAPTURE. — Captain Wood, of the Fourth Rhode Island regiment, was sailing around alone, a day or two after the occupancy of Carolina City, N. C., and seeing a suspicious schooner coming down towards the fort, he sailed alongside, and the following colloquy ensued :

" What kept you so long?" queried the Captain.

" Well, bad weather, &c., &c.," responded the unsuspicious Skipper, adding, "have the Yankees got down this way yet?"

" O, no! They're up towards Newbern, I hear."

The Captain ingratiated himself, and told them his "nice new clothes" were the uniform of Branch's men (rebels), who now were encamped at Carolina City.

He learned their cargo was salt, &c.: they had a mail, despatches, money, &c., for Colonel White, and finally, under pretext of seeing the " General" at the depot, got them to make fast to the railroad pier. The Skipper introduced Mr. ——, who piloted lots of vessels through our blockade, and two other men. The Captain chatted, and drew them unsuspiciously into the depot, where, fortunately, General Parke was, and introduced the four to the General.

" Well ! I'm blowed if that ain't the smartest Yankee trick yet ! Well, I'll have to gin in," was the Skipper's ejaculation.

BEAUREGARD'S ADVICE. — Beauregard, on a visit to the "Response" battalion, after shaking hands with the " boys," addressed them as follows :

"Boys, be patient. The spider is patient; it

takes him a long time to weave his web, but he never fails to catch his fly. We must imitate the spider; our web is nearly complete. In a few days you will have work to do. My advice to you is, to keep cool; don't be in too great a hurry; take your time when the fight comes, which I think will be in a few days; load and shoot slow, and aim low. Follow this, and history will have another victory to record for you."

After another warm shake of the hands, and a cordial "God bless you," the General left, amid the wildest applause.

A SCOTCH TRAVELLER, on a visit to the United States, furnished the following anecdote of General Grant:

"The day before Grant attacked Fort Donelson, the troops had had a march of twenty miles, part of it during a bitter cold night. Grant called a council of war, to consider whether they should attack the fort at once, or should give the troops a day or two's rest. The officers were in favor of resting. Grant said nothing till they had all given their opinion; then he said: 'There is a deserter come in this morning—let us see him, and hear what he has to say.' When he came in, Grant looked into his knapsack. 'Where are you from?' 'Fort Donelson.' 'Six days' rations in your knapsack, have you not, my man?' 'Yes, sir.' 'When were they served out?' 'Yesterday morning.' 'Were the same rations served out to all the troops?' 'Yes, sir.' 'Gentlemen,' said Grant, 'troops do not have six days' rations served out to them in a fort if they mean to stay there. These men mean to retreat—not to fight. We will attack at once.'"

ANECDOTES OF GENERAL BUFORD. — Major-General Buford, than whom probably no commander was so devotedly loved by those around him, was offered a Major-General's commission in the rebel army, when in Utah. He crushed the communication in his hand, and declared that he would live and die under the flag of the Union. A few hours before his death, and while suffering from delirium, he roundly scolded his negro servant; but, recovering himself temporarily, he called the negro to his bedside, and said to him: "Edward, I hear I have been scolding you. I did not know what I was saying. You have been a faithful servant, Edward." The poor negro sat down and wept as though his heart was broken. When General Buford received his commission as Major-General, he exclaimed: "Now I wish that I could live." His last intelligible words, uttered during an attack of delirium, were : "Put guards on all the roads, and don't let the men run back to the rear." This was an illustration of the ruling passion strong in death, for no trait in General Buford's character was more conspicuous than his dislike to see men skulking or hanging on the rear.

VERSES.

Supposed to be written by General John Morgan, on surveying his solitary abode in his cell, in the Ohio Penitentiary at Columbus.

I AM monarch of all I survey;
  My right there is none to dispute;
Naked walls, a stone floor, a tin tray,
  Iron spoon, checkered pants, and clean suit.

I am out of Jeff. Davis's reach,
  I must finish my journey in stone,
Never hear a big secession speech—
  I start at the sound of my own.

O solitude! strange are the fancies
  Of those who see charms in thy face;
Better dwell in the midst of the Yankees,
  Than reign in this horrible place.

Ye steeds that have made me your sport,
  Convey to this desolate cell
Some cordial, endearing report
  Of the thefts I have practised so well.

Horse-stealing, bridge-burning, and fight,
  Divinely bestowed upon man;
O, had I the wings of a kite,
  How soon would I taste you again!

My sorrows I then might assuage
  In the work of destruction and raiding;
Might laugh at the wisdom of age,
  Nor feel the least pang of upbraiding.

Rebellion! what music untold
  Resides in that heavenly word!
It helps me to silver and gold,
  And all that the earth can afford.

But the sweet sound of burning and plunder
  These prison-walls never yet heard,
Never echoed the chivalry's thunder,
  Nor mocked at the Union's grand bird.

How fleet is a glance of the mind
  Compared with the speed of my flight!
But Shackelford came up behind,
  So I found 'twas no use to fight.

The Buckeyes that gave me a race
  My form with indifference see;
They are so light of foot on the chase,
  Their coolness is shocking to me.

When I think of my dear native land,
  I confess that I wish I was there;
Confound these hard stone walls at hand,
  And my bald pate, all shaven of hair.

My friends, do they now and then send
  A wish or a thought after me?
Like Burbeck, that quick-coming friend?
  For a friend in need truly was he.

But the sea-fowl is gone to her rest,
  The beast is laid down in his lair;
Yet not like John Morgan unblest,
  As I to my straw-bed repair.

HOW FORT SUMTER WAS PROVISIONED. — The traitor Floyd took great pains to put the United States forts in Charleston harbor into the hands of the South Carolinians, without expense of men or money. For this purpose he refused the constant entreaties of Colonel John L. Gardner, the officer in command at Fort Moultrie, for troops. Just at the time the danger was becoming imminent, he sent, instead of soldiers for defence, a body of laborers, who, under the direction of an engineer, were ordered to repair the fort in such a way and at such a time as to render the fort defenceless against the seceders. These laborers were to be fed from the supplies at the fort. This made it necessary to purchase provisions in Charleston from week to week, so that, in the event of a siege, the garrison would be starved out in a few days. By desperate efforts the repairs were finished in such a way that the forty-five men in the fort could make some defence; but being dependent on Charleston for food, the South Carolinians and Floyd well knew that the fort was completely in their power whenever they should see fit to cut off supplies from the city.

In this dilemma Colonel Gardner practised the piece of strategy which finally enabled Anderson to hold the fort and make his defence. Colonel G. wrote to an old friend, the chief of the commissary department, to send him provisions for one hundred men for six months; at the same time significantly hinting to him that he could obey this requisition in the ordinary discretionary routine of his duty without consulting with the Secretary of War. He added also the further request that the transport should be ordered to land her cargo at Fort Moultrie immediately on her arrival in the harbor, and before she should go to Charleston. The patriotic commissary officer, Colonel Taylor, the brother of the late President Taylor, understood the hint conveyed, and the reason for it, and took the responsibility of acting on Colonel Gardner's requisition. The provisions were thus safely landed at Fort Moultrie, the traitor Secretary being not a whit the wiser for the operation. These were the provisions which were gradually carried over to Fort Sumter in the engineer's boats, and supported Major Anderson and his gallant command during the memorable siege. Floyd, not knowing the ruse that had been played upon him by Colonel Gardner, expected every day that hunger would do the business for the little garrison, which he intended to hand over, bound hand and foot, to the enemy.

While these matters were going on, Floyd sent down a young officer to look after the carrying out of his plans, and to represent to Colonel G., by various indirect processes, the Secretary's idea of an officer's duty in command at Fort Moultrie. Colonel Gardner had reported to the Secretary that, though he had but one man for each great gun, he was determined to defend the place to the utmost against whatever force should be sent against it. Floyd's spy found Colonel Gardner's men at work day and night adding to the defences of the place. He found even the brick quarters within the fort loopholed for a stand with musketry, in case of an escalade by a sudden rush of a large number of men. All this was evidently directly the opposite of the Secretary's policy, as represented in various indirect ways by the officer whom he had sent. He was shown all the preparations for a desperate defence, which Colonel Gardner had made, and was told that they would be used against any force which should march from Charleston, as soon as they came within range of the guns. He was, moreover, requested to tell the Secretary all that he had seen and heard. The consequence was, that the commandant, disposed to do his duty *too well*, was suspended, and an officer of Kentucky birth, who had married in Georgia, was put in command.

From Major Anderson's birth and connections Floyd evidently supposed that he had obtained a pliant tool for his purposes. A few days' observation convinced Major Anderson that he had been sent there to sacrifice his honor, and that he could save it only by carrying out the desperate measures of defence already begun by Colonel Gardner. The retreat to Fort Sumter, its repair, its siege, and bombardment were the natural sequel. All these events, so important already in history, turned upon the *ruse* by which Colonel Gardner's requisition for provisions was met by Colonel Taylor and kept secret from Floyd. This is a scrap of history well worth remembering, and is given on the best of authority.

———

BUCK TRAVIS' CAPTURE. — In the early days of the rebellion, ere the keen edge of Southern chivalry was blunted by contact with the mudsills of the North, Buck Travis raised a regiment among the young bloods of Henry County, in West Tennessee. The regiment was organized by the election of Travis as Colonel, and the celebrated J. D. C. Atkins as Lieutenant-Colonel. Travis lost no time in putting himself at the head of his gallant band, and "starting forth on martial deeds intent," they approached Union City, Tennessee, just at the time when Pillow was transferring military stores, ordnance, &c., to Columbus, Kentucky. They arrived at the depot simultaneously with a train from the South, bearing several pieces of artillery. These, by some strange mistake, were at once seized by Travis as Lincoln guns, and a telegram was immediately sent to Atkins, who had remained behind at Paris, announcing the brilliant achievement. The despatch was handed to him on the Square, surrounded by a crowd of citizens. He glanced at its contents, and looked around for the most eligible site for a rostrum. Discovering a pile of boxes on the corner, he made for them, followed by the eager crowd. Mounting the box, he lifted his voice and announced the glorious intelligence. "My countrymen!" he said, "this is a proud day for Henry County and for the State. I am proud to announce to you that your gallant sons, under the lead of the indomitable Travis, have already wreathed their brows with an imperishable fame. The murderous artillery with which the tyrant Lincoln sought to enslave our people, has been wrested from the tyrant's hands, and —" Here another despatch was handed to the speaker, and he was heard to remark, with an oath, "Buck always was a d—d fool. Boys, them was our guns, after all."

STONEWALL JACKSON ADMINISTERS THE SACRAMENT. — On the morning of a battle near Harper's Ferry, after a sermon by one of his chaplains, Stonewall Jackson, who was an elder in the Presbyterian Church, administered the sacrament to the church members in his army. He invited all Christians to participate in the ceremony. A Baptist, the straitest of his sect, thoroughly imbued with the idea of close communion, was seen to hesitate; but the occasion, and the man who presided, overcame his scruples; and thus it has happened that the prospect of a fight and the eloquence of Jackson made a Baptist forget that baptism is the door into the church. In all Jackson's army an oath was rarely uttered. A religious enthusiasm pervaded it, which made every man a hero. Conscious of the justice of his cause, and imbued with the strongest convictions of patriotism, his men were irresistible. In this incident we have an explanation of General Jackson's invincibility; and we are thus enabled to understand why his men were heroes, and why they endured without a murmur the severest hardships to which any troops were subjected during the war.

ADVENTURES AT BULL RUN.

BY EDWIN S. BARRETT.

This narrative of personal adventures before and at the battle of Bull Run commences with the night preceding the action: "On Saturday evening, the 20th of July, I heard we were to start at half past two the following morning, and our line was to be in readiness at that early hour. We had occupied the camp at Centreville since Thursday night. Wrapping my blanket around me, at ten o'clock I stretched myself upon the bare ground to sleep. The night was cool, and at twelve o'clock I awoke, feeling very cold, and, unable to sleep more, I anxiously waited to hear the signal to prepare. At two o'clock one drum sounded through the camp, and was repeated through the numerous camps around us, and in half an hour forty thousand men stood ready to battle for the Union.

"The Fifth Massachusetts regiment, which I accompanied, was in the division under Colonel Heintzelman, acting Major General, and our regiment was third in the column. The First Minnesota, under Colonel Gorman, led, followed by the Massachusetts Eleventh, Colonel Clarke; then the Fifth, Colonel Lawrence, with the regular cavalry, and a battery of artillery leading the advance. We waited, in marching order, from half past two o'clock until after six before the order was given to advance, and then we learned that Colonel Hunter, with eight regiments, including Governor Sprague's command, had preceded us, and we were to follow. General McDowell and staff now headed our division.

"Mounted on a secession horse, which I had captured two days previously, I followed in the rear of the regiment, in company with Quartermaster Billings and Surgeon Hurd. From Centreville we took the extreme northern road, leaving the Warrenton road on our left, which General Tyler had taken with his division. Passing through a forest of heavy oak timber, some three or four miles in length, we emerged into the open country, with a wide intervale on our left. and the Blue Ridge Mountains distinctly visible on our right. We had heard an occasional cannon shot during the morning, but not until ten o'clock was there any sound of a general engagement. The heavy cannonading on our left and in front caused the march to be hastened, and our men could hardly be restrained, so eager were they for the fight. About a mile and a half before we reached the field, the men began to throw away their blankets, haversacks, and all unnecessary appendages — the different regiments trying to throw them into a pile, or as near together as possible, without halting. I tied my horse near the hospital headquarters, and hastened to the head of the column, which advanced in double-quick time till they came within reach of the enemy's guns. The fight was raging on our left and in front, as our division came on to the field. I could see that the enemy's batteries were posted on a long ridge, with woods extending on either flank, and separated from us by a valley. It was now about half past eleven o'clock. General McDowell ordered one brigade, under Colonel Franklin, consisting of the First Minnesota, Eleventh and Fifth Massachusetts, and a Pennsylvania regiment, to advance down the hill and take a position in the valley, on a slight elevation directly in front of the rebel batteries. I followed on some distance, but the shot rattled about me, and I halted near General McDowell and staff, while the brigade swept past me and down the hill. I watched for some time the colors of the Fifth with intense interest. The regiment reached the valley, and deploying to the right on to a slight knoll, fell flat on their faces, while the shot from the rebel batteries mostly passed over their heads. A battery swept past me to take a position. I followed it along some distance, when the Major galloped back to me, and called out, 'Friend, tell Captain F. to hurry up my supports.' I did not know Captain F., but hastened back and met an orderly, of whom I inquired where he was. He pointed him out to me, near a regiment of infantry. I rushed up to him and gave my message. He replied, 'They are coming right along.' And on double-quick the regiment followed after the battery. The rifle-cannon shot, shells, and bullets, struck all around me, and men were falling in every direction. Seeing a high persimmon tree standing alone, a short distance down the hill, I determined to climb it. The top of it was dead, and about thirty feet from the ground. From this elevation I had an unobstructed view of the whole line, and I could see into the enemy's intrenchments, where the men looked like so many bees in a hive; and I could plainly see their officers riding about, and their different columns moving hither and thither. Their batteries on the right and left were masked with trees so completely, that I could not distinguish them except by the flash from their guns; and a battery in a cornfield, on our extreme left, was so completely concealed by the cornstalks placed so naturally about it, that our men came suddenly upon it, never dreaming of one so near. The cannon balls struck the ground continually close to the tree, and bounded along for a quarter of a mile to the rear. I felt that I was above the range of these, but the rifle balls whistled about my head, striking the tree in a way anything but pleasant. Just after I had reached the top of the tree, a New Hampshire regiment, close at my left, had succeeded in driving the rebels from the woods in front, and, with three cheers, they fell back into line. When the line was formed, three cheers were given for Colonel Marston, who had fought gallantly and received two severe wounds. Sherman's battery then commenced firing, on my right, within thirty rods of me, and at the first discharge the men cheered, and watched the effect of the shell, which exploded inside the enemy's intrenchments. The men cheered again, to see that they got the range so quickly, and continued to fire with great rapidity, while the enemy returned the fire with equal vigor and precision, the cannonading being kept up incessantly for an hour.

"The shot and shell from this battery must have done the rebels great damage, as every shot took effect within their intrenchments. Still men and horses kept falling near our guns, and the infantry lines were parted in many places by their cannon balls. The valley for nearly one half a mile in front of the enemy's works was filled with our infantry, extending to some patches of woods on our right. Our batteries were placed on various eminences on the flank and rear, shifting their positions from time to time. The fire from our lines in this valley was terrific, and as they kept slowly advancing, firing, retreating to load, and then advancing again, it was a sight which no words could describe. For three long hours we poured into their intrenchments this terrible fire, and whenever the enemy showed themselves on the flanks they were driven back with great slaughter. During all this time our men were subjected to a cross-fire from the enemy's infantry stationed in the woods on our left. At one time the 'Stars and Stripes' were waved in these woods, and men dressed much like our own called out not to fire that way. Our men gradually drew up towards the flag, when immediately the secession flag was thrown out, and the rebels poured a volley into our men so unexpectedly that they were for the time driven back, but we soon regained the ground.

"General McDowell now ordered a battery forward to take a position near a house on our right; the Fire Zouaves were ordered to support it. The position appeared to me, from my look-out, like a strong one, as it was on a hill on a level with the rebel batteries. Our battery started, the horses running at the top of their speed, and shortly began to ascend the eminence, the Zouaves following closely; but scarcely had the battery halted and fired, before the enemy opened upon them from new masked batteries, and a terrific fire of musketry from the woods, and our artillery were driven back, many of their men and horses being killed. The Zouaves stood their ground manfully, firing in lines and then falling on their faces to load. Their ranks were becoming dreadfully thinned, yet they would not yield an inch; when suddenly out dashed the Black Horse Cavalry, and charged furiously, with uplifted sabres, upon them. The Zouaves gallantly resisted this furious onset without flinching, and after firing their muskets — too sorely pressed to load — would fight furiously with their bayonets, or any weapon they could seize, and in some instances drag the riders from their saddles, stabbing them with their knives, and mounting their splendid black horses, gallop over the field. Never, since the famous charge of the Light Brigade, was a cavalry corps more cut to pieces. There is a bitter animosity existing between the Black Horse Cavalry and Ellsworth's Zouaves. A great many of the cavalry are citizens of Alexandria and Fairfax County, and they resolved to kill every Zouave they could lay their hands upon, to avenge the death of Jackson; and the Zouaves were equally determined to avenge the murder of Ellsworth; so no quarter was expected by them.

"I had now been in the tree some two hours, and all this time a continuous stream of wounded were being carried past me to the rear. The soldiers would cross their muskets, place their wounded companions across, and slowly carry them past; another soldier would have a wounded man with his arm around his neck, slowly walking back; and then two men would be bearing a mortally wounded comrade in their arms, who was in convulsions and writhing in his last agonies. These were to me the most affecting scenes I witnessed, and I could hardly keep back the tears, while I could look upon the dead unmoved. Picking a couple of persimmons as a remembrance, I descended the tree, startling two soldiers leaning against it, by requesting them to move their guns so that I could get down. They looked up in astonishment at hearing a voice, and no doubt their first thought was that I might be a rebel spy; but the 'U. S.' on my belt, and my anxious inquiries after their regiment, soon reassured them.

"Leaving the tree, I went along over the field to the left, the bullets whistling about me, and the cannon balls ploughing up the ground in every direction, when I came across two of our men with a prisoner, who said he belonged to a South Carolina regiment. I asked him some questions, but he was dogged and silent, and did not appear to be disposed to reply to my inquiries. The shot fell so thick, and shells bursting around me, I hardly knew which way to turn. A musket ball whizzed past my ear, so near that I felt the heat, and for a moment thought I was hit. The ground was strewed with broken guns, swords, cartridge-boxes, blankets, haversacks, gun-carriages, to-

17

gether with all the paraphernalia of warfare, mingled with the dead and wounded men. I saw here a horse, and his rider under him, both killed by the same cannon ball. Seeing a small white house still towards the left, with a well near it, I started for some water, and getting over a wall, I discovered lying beside it a number of our dead with their haversacks drawn over their faces. I lifted the cover from their faces, thinking, perhaps, I might come across some of my friends; but they were all strangers, or so disfigured that I could not recognize them. I went to the well for a drink, and as I drew near the house, I heard loud groans; and such a scene as was there presented, in that little house of two rooms, and on the grass around it, was enough to appall the stoutest heart.

"The rooms were crowded, and I could not get in; but all around on the grass were men mortally wounded. I should think there were at least forty on that greensward within twenty rods of the house, and such wounds — some with both legs shot off; some with a thigh shot away; some with both legs broken; others with horrid flesh wounds made from shells. I saw one man with a wound in his back large enough to put in my fist; he was fast bleeding to death. They lay so thick around me, that I could hardly step between them, and every step was in blood. As I walked among them, some besought me to kill them, and put an end to their agony; some were just gasping, and some had died since they had been brought there, and the dying convulsions of these strong men were agonizing in the extreme. Some were calling for the surgeon, but the hospital was more than a mile off, and there were but two surgeons here.

"I left the house, and bore off to the right, towards some low pine woods, about a hundred rods distant, and scattered along were the dead bodies of our men. On reaching the wood, I found the ground literally covered with the corpses of the enemy, and I counted, in the space of about ten rods square, forty-seven dead rebels and ten mortally wounded, and scattered all through the woods, still farther back, were any number more. I talked with several of the wounded, and they told me they belonged to the Eighth Georgia regiment, Colonel Bartow, and had arrived at Manassas, from Winchester, the day before, where they had been with General Johnston. They told me their whole regiment was posted in this pine wood. One young man told me he was from Macon, and that his father was a merchant. I asked another where he was from. He replied, defiantly, 'I am for disunion — opposed to you.' This man had both thighs broken.

"I heard one of our soldiers ask a wounded Georgian if their orders were to kill our wounded. He answered, 'No.' Our soldiers carried water to these wounded men, and as they lay there writhing in agony, a cup of water was put within their reach. The convulsions of one of these was awful to look upon. He appeared to have been shot in the lungs, as he vomited blood in large quantities, and in his struggles for breath, would throw himself clear from the ground. I noticed among this heap of bodies an officer dressed in light blue uniform, with green stripes on his pants, — a fine-looking man, — whom I took to be a captain. I also saw one of our soldiers take sixty dollars from the body of a dead Georgian, and their knives, revolvers, &c., were appropriated in the same way. This I looked upon as legitimate plunder for the soldiers, but as a citizen, I forbore to take anything from the field.

"I think the fight in this wood must have been fiercer than in any part of the field, except it may be on our right, where the Zouaves were. This wood was near the enemy's right, and where the fight commenced in the morning with Hunter's division, and as Heintzelman's division came into action, the rebels were giving way at this point, under the galling fire of Colonel Marston's regiment, while the Rhode Island troops and some New York regiments had driven back their extreme right. Passing through these pine woods, I still bore to the right, towards our centre, and crossed a cleared space, and came to some heavy wood, on the edge of which I perceived a number of dead scattered about, and seeing several wounded men, I went up to one of them, and found he was a rebel belonging to an Alabama regiment. He told me he joined the regiment the 13th of April. He pointed to a dead horse close to us, and said, 'There is my Colonel's horse, and I suppose you have taken him prisoner.'

"Most of these rebels had gray suits, with black trimmings — very similar to the uniforms of some of our men. Scattered all through this wood were our men and the Alabamians, dead and wounded mingled together. I noticed a splendid bay horse nibbling the leaves from a tree, and was thinking what a fine animal he was, when I saw that one fore leg was shot off, clean as though cut by a knife, and bleeding a stream. Until this time I supposed that everything was being swept before us, as the fire from the batteries had been nearly silenced on their right, and only an occasional discharge was heard. On the enemy's left, the firing was not nearly as vigorous as half an hour previous. I came out of the woods, and to my utter astonishment, saw our whole body retreating in utter confusion and disorder — no lines, no companies, no regiments, could be distinguished. I stood still a few moments, unable to comprehend the extraordinary spectacle.

"I heard my name called, and turning round, a Lieutenant of the Massachusetts Fifth came towards me. 'My God, Ed.! what are you here for?' he exclaimed. Without replying, I asked if the Fifth had suffered much. He said it had, and that the Colonel was dangerously wounded. I waited to find others of my friends, but the whole line was drifting back through the valley. I fell in with them, and went slowly up the hill, occasionally halting and looking back. I stopped on the brow of a hill while the volume drifted by, and I can compare it to nothing more than a drove of cattle, so entirely broken and disorganized were our lines. The enemy had nearly ceased firing from the batteries on their right and centre, but still, on our extreme right, beyond a patch of woods, the fight was going on, and their cannonading was kept up with vigor.

"The line where the main battle was fought was a half to three quarters of a mile in length, the ground uneven and broken by knolls and patches of wood. At no time did we have a fair chance at the enemy in the open field. They kept behind their intrenchments, or under cover of the woods. Our comparatively slight loss may be attributed to the fact that the great body of our troops were posted in the valley in front of the enemy's batteries, but by keeping as close to the ground as possible, the enemy's shot passed over their heads, while the cross fire of infantry from their flanks caused us the most damage.

"I did not leave the hill until the enemy's infantry came out from their intrenchments, and slowly moved forward, their guns glistening in the sun; but they showed no disposition to charge, and only advanced a short distance. Had they precipitated their columns upon our panic-stricken army, the slaughter would have been dreadful, for so thorough was the panic, that no power on earth could have stopped the retreat, and made our men turn and fight. They were exhausted with twelve hours' marching and fighting, having had little to eat, their mouths parched with thirst, and no water in their canteens — what could be expected of them then? Our men did fight like heroes, and only retreated when they had no officers to control and command them.

"I found my horse tied to the tree where I left him in the morning. Mounting him, I rode up to the hospital headquarters, and stopped some time watching the ambulances bringing their loads of wounded, fearing I might discover a friend or acquaintance. As these loads of wounded men were brought up, blood flowed from the ambulances like water from an ice cart, and their mutilated limbs protruding from the rear had no semblance of humanity.

"I left these scenes of blood and carnage, and fell into this retreating mass of disorderly and confused soldiery. Then commenced my retreat. None who dragged their weary limbs through the long hours of that night will ever forget it. Officers of regiments placed themselves in front of a body of their men, and besought them to halt and form, for if they did not make a stand, their retreat would be cut off. But they might as well have asked the wind to cease blowing. The men heeded them not, but pressed on in retreat. The regiments two or three miles to our rear, which had not been in action, exhorted our men to halt, as we drifted by, but all to no purpose. No power *could* stop them. The various regiments tried to collect as many as possible by calling out the number of their regiment and their State. In some instances, they collected together two or three hundred men.

"At a narrow place in the road the baggage wagons and artillery got jammed together in a dead lock, and in trying to get through I was hemmed in so completely that for fifteen minutes I could not move in either direction, and in this way I became separated from a remnant of the Fifth, and did not see them again till I reached Centreville. I finally extricated myself by breaking down a rail fence, and driving my horse over it, struck across a large cornfield, thus cutting off considerable distance and reaching the road at a point where it entered the oak forest. Shortly after entering the woods the column in front of me suddenly broke and ran into the woods on the left; the panic spread past me, and soldiers ran pell-mell into the woods, leaving me alone on my horse. I was afraid that in their fright they might shoot me, and I shouted lustily, 'False alarm.'

"Turning my horse about, not a man could I see; but soon a soldier thrust his head from behind a large oak. I asked him what the matter was. He replied, 'The enemy are in front.' Somewhat provoked at the scare, I made some reflection on his courage, and shouted again still louder, 'False alarm," which was soon taken up along the road, and in five minutes we were going along as before. This was between five and six o'clock in the afternoon. Shortly after I overtook two soldiers helping along a disabled Lieutenant; they asked me to take him up behind me, to which I readily assented, although my horse was already encumbered with a pair of saddle-bags and several blankets. The poor man groaned as they lifted him up behind me. I was fearful he might fall off, and I told him to put both arms around me and hold on tight. Leaning his head upon my shoulder, we started on.

"He soon felt better, gave me his name, and informed me that he was a First Lieutenant of the Marines, and belonged in Connecticut. He stated that they had in the fight four companies, of eighty men each, and that Lieutenant Hitchcock (a very dear friend) was killed by his side. A cavalry officer, with his arm in a sling, came riding along, and drawing up near to me, I asked him if he was much hurt. He replied, that he had received a rifle ball through the fleshy part of his arm. He also told me that during the fight he had two horses shot under him, and the one on which he was then riding he caught on the field. I questioned him as to the cause of our disaster, and he answered, that our light troops and light batteries could make no headway against the heavy guns of the enemy, strongly intrenched. I asked him how the enemy's works could have been carried; with characteristic faith in his branch of the service, he replied, 'By allowing the cavalry to charge, supported by infantry.' He also informed me that we had about one thousand cavalry in the field during the battle.

"As we continued our retreat through the wood, the men, overcome with weariness, dropped by the roadside, and immediately fell asleep: some, completely exhausted, begged to be carried, the wagons being already overloaded with those unable to walk; and some shrewd ones quietly bargained with the driver of an ordnance wagon for a seat by his side. Passing out through this wood, we came in sight of the hills of Centreville. I noticed that the column mostly left the road, and bore off through an open field, leaving the bridge we had crossed in the morning some distance on our right. I could not account for this deviation from the morning's course, and I left the main body and continued along some distance farther, determined to keep the main road, as I knew of no other way to cross the creek, except by the bridge we had crossed in the morning; but coming up to a line of broken-down wagons, it occurred to me that the bridge might be blocked up, as I recollected the passage was quite narrow. I then started off to the left, across a level field, but upon looking back I perceived that the wagons still continued on towards the bridge; in fact, there was no other way for them to cross. I followed the crowd of soldiers through the field and into some low woods.

"Here they scattered in every direction, as there was no path, and each one was compelled to choose his own route. I picked my way among the tangled underbrush till I came to the creek; the bank down to the water was very steep, and I feared my horse could not carry us both down safely; so, dismounting, I led him slowly down, and then, mounting, I drove into the stream. The bottom was soft and miry, and my horse sunk in to his belly. I began to think that we should all be soon floundering in the stream; then urging him to his utmost strength, we reached the opposite bank in safety. Twice my gallant horse started up the bank and fell back. After crossing this creek I came into a cornfield, and soon struck a road leading into Centreville, which village I soon reached, and there my companion met with his captain, and he then dismounted. Never was a man more grateful for a favor than was this Lieutenant. With tears in his eyes, he thanked me a thousand times, and, wringing my hands, walked away with his friends.

"From Centreville I could see the disordered army winding along for some two miles; a portion of the men, and all the wagons and artillery, took the road over the bridge, while another portion came in nearly the direction I had taken. It was now nearly eight o'clock, and as it grew darker, our retreating army kept the main road over the bridge. About two miles from Centreville, on the southern road, was a rebel battery, where the fight had taken place the Thursday previous. This battery commanded the bridge above mentioned. Suddenly a cannon shot was fired from the battery and struck our column, crowding across this narrow bridge. The utmost consternation was created by this fire. In their haste, wagons and gun-carriages were crowded together and overturned; the drivers cut their horses loose, who galloped they scarcely knew whither. Our men plunged into the stream, waist deep, and were scattered in every direction, and some who were seen up to this time have not been heard of since.

"The enemy still fired from the battery, but did not dare to sally out, as they were kept in check by our reserve on the heights of Centreville. I reached our camp that we had left in the morning a little after eight o'clock, and found that a few of the Fifth had arrived before me. It was then expected we should encamp for the night; but about nine o'clock we received orders to march to Alexandria. We had already travelled from ten to twelve miles, and now our weary soldiers were ordered to march twenty-five or thirty miles farther.

"Slowly the fragment of our regiment fell into line and began this dreadful night march. I took a sick man behind me and followed in the rear of our regiment, and crossing a field to the main road we fell in with the drifting mass. A friend of mine from the Fifth, who could hardly walk, approached me. I offered him my horse if he would hold the sick man who was groaning at every step. To this he readily assented; so I dismounted. I saw no more of my horse till morning, but trudged along all night without once sitting down to rest, only occasionally stopping to get water.

"I felt comparatively fresh when compared with my companions. The dust was intolerable, and, not having any canteen, I suffered exceedingly from thirst. Men dropped down along the road by scores; some, completely exhausted, pleaded piteously to be helped along; some took hold of the rear of the wagons, which was considerable support to them, and many a horse had two men on his back, with another helped along by his tail; in fact, a horse carrying but one was an exception. I assisted one fine fellow along for a long distance, who told me he was taken with bleeding at the lungs while on the field; he was very weak, and in vain I tried to find an opportunity for him to ride, but he bore up manfully through the night, and I saw him the next day in Washington.

"After passing Fairfax Court House some of the regiments, or such a portion as could be collected together, bivouacked for the night, but the men were so scattered that I doubt if half a regiment halted at any one spot. I still walked on, never once resting, fearing if I did I should feel worse when I again started. Towards morning my feet began to be blistered, and the cords of my legs worked like rusty wires, giving me great pain at every step. Gladly did I hail the first faint streak of light in the east.

"At daylight we were within five miles of Alexandria. About this time we came to where the Washington road branches off from the main road to Alexandria, and here our column divided. I continued on towards Alexandria, and in about an hour came in sight of Shuter's hill. I then felt my journey was nearly accomplished, but the last two miles seemed endless.

"I stopped at a small house just back of Fort Ellsworth, and asked the old negro woman for some breakfast. Two Zouaves were there when I entered, and soon four more came in. She knew them all, as they had paid her frequent visits while encamped in that neighborhood. She gladly got us the best she had, and these six Zouaves and myself, nearly famished as we were, sat down to that breakfast of fried pork, hoe cake, and coffee, served to us by this old slave woman, with greater delight than ever a king seated himself at a banquet.

"The Zouaves each had their story of the battle to relate, but the charge of the Black Horse Cavalry was their especial theme. One of them, pulling a large Colt's pistol from his pocket, said, 'There, I gave that fellow h—l, and he wasn't the only one either.' I coveted this pistol, and soon bargained for it, and now have it in my possession; one barrel only had been fired. The Zouaves gradually dropped off, and after paying the slave woman for the meal, I started over the hill to the camp of the Fifth, where I arrived about half past eight o'clock, and found that my horse with his riders had arrived safely some time before."

A PSALM OF LIFE.

As chanted by Gideon J. Pillow and his boys on retreating from Lafayette, Georgia, June 24, 1864.

TELL me not, in boastful twaddle,
Yankees five by one "Confed"
Are unnerved and made skedaddle,
With coat-tail as high as head.

"Feds" will fight — a bold defender
Is each member of their ranks ;
That they readily surrender,
Can't be spoken of the "Yanks."

'Twas enjoyment, and not sorrow,
That we hoped to reap to-day ;
Certain that before the morrow
We should march the Yanks away.

Without bloodshed, without battle,
In their bivouac so nice,
We would pen them like dumb cattle,
Gobble all up in a trice.

But their bullets now remind us
We should all be making tracks,
And, departing, leave behind us —
Far behind — those deadly "cracks."

Deadly, and perhaps some other
Fell shots may increase our slain ;
Many a fallen, war-wrecked brother
Never can take aim again.

'Stride our horses let's be jumping,
While our hearts we thought so brave,
Like unmuffled drums, are thumping,
And our knees are like to cave.

Trust no shelter, howe'er pleasant !
Let the Yankees bury our dead !
Run ! run ! in this dreadful present,
Bullets whizzing overhead !

Let us, too, continue going,
Spur our "plugs" to fastest gait :
For the blue-coats are pursuing,
And we've had "enough" of late.

A BRAVE IRISHMAN. — One of the Indiana regiments was fiercely attacked by a whole brigade, in one of the battles in Mississippi. The Indianians, unable to withstand such great odds, were compelled to fall back about thirty or forty yards, losing, to the utter mortification of the officers and men, their flag, which remained in the hands of the enemy. Suddenly, a tall Irishman, a private in the color company, rushed from the ranks across the vacant ground, attacked the squad of rebels who had possession of the conquered flag, with his musket felled several to the ground, snatched the flag from them, and returned safely back to his regiment. The bold fellow was, of course, immediately surrounded by his jubilant comrades, and greatly praised for his gallantry. His Captain appointed him to a sergeantcy on the spot ; but the hero cut everything short by the reply, "O, never mind, Captain, — say no more about it. I dropped my whiskey flask among the rebels, and fetched that back, and I thought I might just as well bring the flag along !"

"IT IS MY MOTHER !" — An interesting anecdote, though of doubtful authenticity, is related of Franklin, who, it is alleged, in order to test the parental instinct existing between mother and child, introduced himself as a belated traveller to his mother's house after an absence of many years. Her house being filled with more illustrious guests than the unknown stranger, she refused him shelter, and would have turned him from her door. Hence, he concluded that this so-called parental instinct was a pleasant delusive belief, not susceptible of proof.

The opposite of this lately occurred in Washington. In one of the fierce engagements with the rebels near Mechanicsville, in May, 1864, a young Lieutenant of a Rhode Island battery had his right foot so shattered by a fragment of shell that, on reaching Washington, after one of those horrible ambulance rides, and a journey of a week's duration, he was obliged to undergo amputation of the leg. He telegraphed home, hundreds of miles away, that all was going well, and with a soldier's fortitude composed himself to bear his sufferings alone.

Unknown to him, however, his mother, one of those dear reserves of the army, hastened up to join the main force. She reached the city at midnight, and the nurses would have kept her from him until morning. One sat by his side fanning him as he slept, her hand on the feeble, fluctuating pulsations which foreboded sad results. But what woman's heart could resist the pleadings of a mother then ? In the darkness she was finally allowed to glide in and take the place at his side. She touched his pulse as the nurse had done ; not a word had been spoken, but the sleeping boy opened his eyes and said, "That feels like my mother's hand ; who is this beside me ? It *is* my mother ; turn up the gas and let me see mother !"

The two dear faces met in one long, joyful, sobbing embrace, and the fondness pent up in each heart sobbed and panted, and wept forth its expression.

The gallant fellow, just twenty-one, his leg amputated on the last day of his three years' service, underwent operation after operation; and at last, when death drew nigh, and he was told by tearful friends that it only remained to make him comfortable, said he had "looked death in the face too many times to be afraid now," and died as gallantly as did the men of the Cumberland.

THE FLIGHT FROM BULL RUN. — A correspondent gives the following account of the panic and flight at the battle of Bull Run : "I was near the rear of the movement, with the brave Captain Alexander, who endeavored, by the most gallant but unavailable exertions, to check the onward tumult. It was difficult to believe in the reality of our sudden reverse. 'What does it all mean?' I asked Alexander. 'It means defeat,' was his reply. 'We are beaten; it is a shameful, a cowardly retreat! Hold up, men!' he shouted; 'don't be such infernal cowards!' and he rode backwards and forwards, placing his horse across the road, and vainly trying to rally the running troops. The teams and wagons confused and dismembered every corps. We were now cut off from the advance body by the enemy's infantry, who had rushed on the slope just left by us, surrounded the guns and sutlers' wagons, and were apparently pressing up against us. 'It's no use, Alexander,' I said; 'you must leave with the rest.' 'I'll be d—d if I will,' was the sullen reply; and the splendid fellow rode back to make his way as best he could. Meantime, I saw officers with leaves and eagles on their shoulder-straps, Majors and Colonels, who had deserted their commands, pass me, galloping as if for dear life. No enemy pursued just then ; but I suppose all were afraid that his guns would be trained down the long, narrow avenue, and mow the retreating thousands, and batter to pieces army wagons and everything else which crowded it. Only one field-officer, so far as my observation extended, seemed to have remembered his duty. Lieutenant-Colonel Speidel, a foreigner, attached to a Connecticut regiment, strove against the current for a league. I positively declare that, with the two exceptions mentioned, all efforts made to check the panic before Centreville was reached, were confined to *civilians*. I saw a man in citizen's dress, who had thrown off his coat, seize a musket, and was trying to rally the soldiers who came by at the point of the bayonet. In reply to a request for his name, he said it was Washburne, and I learned he was the member by that name from Illinois. The Hon. Mr. Kellogg made a similar effort. Both these Congressmen bravely stood their ground till the last moment, and were serviceable at Centreville in assisting the halt there ultimately made. And other civilians did what they could.

"But what a scene! and how terrific the onset of that tumultuous retreat! For three miles, hosts of Federal troops — all detached from their regiments, all mingled in one disorderly rout — were fleeing along the road, but mostly through the lots on either side. Army wagons, sutlers' teams, and private carriages, choked the passage, tumbling against each other, amid clouds of dust, and sickening sights and sounds. Hacks, containing unlucky spectators of the late affray, were smashed like glass, and the occupants were lost sight of in the debris. Horses, flying wildly from the battle-field, many of them in death agony, galloped at random forward, joining in the stampede. Those on foot, who could catch them, rode them bareback, as much to save themselves from being run over, as to make quicker time. Wounded men, lying along the banks, — the few neither left on the field nor taken to the captured hospitals, — appealed, with raised hands, to those who rode horses, begging to be lifted behind, but few regarded such petitions. Then the artillery — such as was saved — came thundering along, smashing and overpowering everything. The regular cavalry (I record it to their shame) joined in the mêlée, adding to its terrors, for they rode down footmen without mercy. One of the great guns was overturned, and lay amid the ruins of a caisson. As I passed it, I saw an artilleryman running between the ponderous fore and after wheels of his gun-carriage, hanging on with both hands, and vainly striving to jump upon the ordnance. The drivers were spurring the horses ; he could not cling much longer, and a more agonized expression never fixed the features of a drowning man. The carriage bounded from the roughness of a steep hill leading to a creek ; he lost his hold, fell, and in an instant the great wheels had crushed the life out of him. Who ever saw such a flight? Could the retreat at Borodino have exceeded it in confusion and tumult? I think not. It did not slack in the least until Centreville was reached. There the sight of the reserve — Miles' brigade — formed in order on the hill, seemed somewhat to reassure the van. But still the teams and foot soldiers pushed on, passing their own camps, and heading swiftly for the distant Potomac, until, for ten miles, the road over which the grand army had so lately passed southward, gay with unstained banners, and flushed with surety of strength, was covered with the fragments of its retreating forces, shattered and panic-stricken in a single day. From the branch route, the trains attached to Hunter's division had caught the contagion of the flight, and poured into its already swollen current another turbid freshet of confusion and dismay. Who ever saw a more shameful abandonment of munitions, gathered at such vast expense? The teamsters, many of them, cut the traces of their horses, and galloped from the wagons. Others threw out their loads to accelerate their flight, and grain, picks, and shovels, and provisions of every kind, lay trampled in the dust for leagues. Thousands of muskets strewed the route, and when some of us succeeded in rallying a body of fugitives, and forming them in a line across the road, hardly one but had thrown away his arms. If the enemy had brought up his artillery, and served it upon the retreating train, or had intercepted our progress with five hundred of his cavalry, he might have captured enough supplies for a week's feast of thanksgiving. As it was, enough was left behind to tell the story of the panic. The rout of the Federal army seemed complete."

INCIDENTS OF SHILOH. — Early on Monday morning, General Nelson despatched an orderly from a cavalry company to the river with a message. The General waited in vain for an answer, and the day wore away without hearing from the messenger. General Nelson was furious, and directed, the following day, a search to be made for the orderly. He was, after some trouble, found, and taken immediately to headquarters. He was called upon for an account, and said, in a brief, off-hand manner, that when he got to the river, he found several thousand skulkers, and six hundred of these agreed to go into action if they could find a leader. The young cavalryman promptly offered himself, and as promptly led the men into the hottest of the fight. He reported to General Crittenden, was assigned a position which he maintained all day, losing from his impromptu command ten men killed and fifty wounded. The General was so well pleased with the young man and his gallant conduct, that he immediately sent his name to General Buell, and instead of being a private, he is now a commissioned officer.

A begrimed individual, face several shades blacker than the ace of spades, and continually deepening in color from a contact with powder, hurriedly ran up to Captain Pick Russell and asked for a few rounds of cartridges. "Give me some, for God's sake, Captain; right down here I have a bully place, and every time I fire, down goes a secesher." He was accommodated, and while the Captain was filling his cartridge-box, the fellow was loading his piece. After being supplied, he dashed to the left and disappeared in the woods. A roar of musketry in the direction he took was kept up all day, but whether he escaped or not has not been ascertained.

A GALLANT BAND. — A soldier gives the following account of one of the most brilliant exhibitions of bravery and daring that occurred during the war:

"When the advance of the rebel cavalry arrived at Manassas Junction, on the evening of the 26th of August, 1862, about fifty stragglers belonging to different regiments in Pope's and McClellan's commands gathered around the railroad depot, with loaded muskets, uncertain whether to run or stay by and try to defend the place. Among the number was one Samuel Condé, a member of the Eleventh New York battery, who for the previous two months had been on duty at General Pope's headquarters, and was then on his way to Washington. Finding there was no commissioned officer to take command, and that the rebels were close upon us, this brave young man seized a musket, and calling upon his comrades to rally and follow him, he posted his little company at a short distance from the railroad, near an old rebel fortification, and awaited with fixed bayonets the approach of the enemy. The first that appeared was a squadron of cavalry, who dashed up furiously towards the depot. No sooner had they passed us than our little band, led by their new commander, charged with a shout at the enemy, scattering them in all directions. On reaching the depot, we were surrounded by a whole regiment of rebel infantry, who commanded us to surrender. 'Never,' shouted our brave leader, and with the words 'come on, boys,' we dashed through their ranks, only to find ourselves still further surrounded by a large force of cavalry. Here, for a moment, we faltered; but hearing our leader still urging us on, we pushed forward through a heavy volley of musketry, and soon passed the enemy's lines with the loss of more than half of our little band, including our brave commander. Finding it folly to remain longer in that vicinity, we took to the woods, and arrived at Fairfax Station early the next morning. It would be impossible for me to give the names of any of this little band, for we were all strangers to each other, and I can only bear testimony to the fearless bravery of our leader, who, I fear, has fallen a victim to a rebel bullet, hoping that, if this ever meets the eye of any of his friends, they may have the gratification of knowing that he died a hero."

THE CLOTHES-LINE TELEGRAPH. — In the early part of 1863, when the Union army was encamped at Falmouth, and picketing the banks of the Rappahannock, the utmost tact and ingenuity were displayed, by the scouts and videttes, in gaining a knowledge of contemplated movements on either side; and here, as at various other times, the shrewdness of the African camp attendants was very remarkable.

One circumstance in particular shows how quick the race are in learning the art of communicating by signals.

There came into the Union lines a negro from a farm on the other side of the river, known by the name of Dabney, who was found to possess a remarkably clear knowledge of the topography of the whole region; and he was employed as cook and body servant at headquarters. When he first saw our system of army telegraphs, the idea interested him intensely, and he begged the operators to explain the signs to him. They did so, and found that he could understand and remember the meaning of the various movements as well as any of his brethren of paler hue.

Not long after, his wife, who had come with him, expressed a great anxiety to be allowed to go over to the other side as servant to a "secesh woman," whom General Hooker was about sending over to her friends. The request was granted, and Dabney's wife went across the Rappahannock, and in a few days was duly installed as laundress at the headquarters of a prominent rebel General. Dabney, her husband, on the north bank, was soon found to be wonderfully well informed as to all the rebel plans. Within an hour of the time that a movement of any kind was projected, or even discussed, among the rebel generals, Hooker knew all about it. He knew which corps was moving, or about to move, in what direction, how long they had been on the march, and in what force; and all this knowledge came through Dabney, and his reports always turned out to be true.

Yet Dabney was never absent, and never talked with the scouts, and seemed to be always taken up with his duties as cook and groom about headquarters.

How he obtained his information remained for some time a puzzle to the Union officers. At length, upon much solicitation, he unfolded his marvellous secret to one of our officers.

Taking him to a point where a clear view could be obtained of Fredericksburg, he pointed out a little cabin in the suburbs near the river bank, and asked him if he saw that clothes-line with clothes hanging on it to dry "Well," said he, "that clothes-line tells me in half an hour just what goes on at Lee's headquarters. You see my wife over there; she washes for the officers, and cooks, and waits around, and as soon as she hears about any movement or anything going on, she comes down and moves the clothes on that line so I can understand it in a minute. That there gray shirt is Longstreet; and when she takes it off, it means he's gone down about Richmond. That white shirt means Hill; and when she moves it up to the west end of the line, Hill's corps has moved up stream. That red one is Stonewall. He's down on the right now, and if he moves, she will move that red shirt."

One morning Dabney came in and reported a movement over there. "But," says he, "it don't amount to any thing. They're just making believe."

An officer went out to look at the clothes line telegraph through his field-glass. There had been quite a shifting over there among the army flannels. "But how do you know but there is something in it?"

"Do you see those two blankets pinned together at the bottom?" said Dabney. "Yes, but what of it?" said the officer. "Why, that's her way of making a fish-trap; and when she pins the clothes together that way, it means that Lee is only trying to draw us into his fish-trap."

As long as the two armies lay watching each other on opposite banks of the stream, Dabney, with his clothes-line telegraph, continued to be one of the promptest and most reliable of General Hooker's scouts.

ARKANSAS TACTICS. — An Arkansas Colonel had the following order for mounting his men:

First order. — Prepare fer tur git onto yer creeters!

Second order. — GIT!

THE OLD SERGEANT.

BY FORCEYTHE WILLSON.

THE carrier cannot sing to-day the ballads
　　With which he used to go
Rhyming the grand rounds of the Happy New
　　　　Years
　　That are now beneath the snow ; —

For the same awful and portentous shadow
　　That overcast the earth,
And smote the land last year with desolation,
　　Still darkens every hearth.

And the carrier hears Beethoven's mighty dead-
　　　　march
　　Come up from every mart,
And he hears and feels it breathing in his bosom,
　　And beating in his heart.

And to-day, like a scarred and weather-beaten vet-
　　　　eran,
　　Again he comes along,
To tell the story of the Old Year's struggles,
　　In another New Year's song.

And the song is his, but not so with the story;
　　For the story, you must know
Was told in prose to Assistant-Surgeon Austin,
　　By a soldier of Shiloh ; —

By Robert Burton, who was brought up on the
　　　　Adams
　　With his death-wound in his side,
And who told the story to the Assistant-Surgeon
　　On the same night that he died.

But the singer feels it will better suit the ballad,
　　If all should deem it right,
To sing the story as if what it speaks of
　　Had happened but last night.

"Come a little nearer, Doctor — Thank you! let
　　me take the cup!
Draw your chair up ! — draw it closer — just an-
　　other little sup!
May be you may think I'm better, but I'm pretty
　　well used up —
Doctor, you've done all you could do, but I'm just
　　a going up.

"Feel my pulse, sir, if you want to, but it is no use
　　to try."
"Never say that," said the Surgeon, as he smoth-
　　ered down a sigh;
"It will never do, old comrade, for a soldier to say
　　die !"
"What you say will make no difference, Doctor,
　　when you come to die.

"Doctor, what has been the matter?"　"You were
　　very faint, they say;
You must try to get to sleep now."　"Doctor, have
　　I been away?"
"No, my venerable comrade."　"Doctor, will you
　　please to stay?
There is something I must tell you, and you won't
　　have long to stay !

"I have got my marching orders, and am ready now
　　to go;
Doctor, did you say I fainted? — but it couldn't
　　have been so —

For as sure as I'm a Sergeant and was wounded at
    Shiloh,
I've this very night been back there — on the old
    field of Shiloh !

"You may think it all delusion — all the sickness
    of the brain :
If you do, you are mistaken, and mistaken to my pain ;
For upon my dying honor, as I hope to live again,
I have just been back to Shiloh and all over it again !

"This is all that I remember ; the last time the
    Lighter came,
And the lights had all been lowered, and the noises
    much the same,
He had not been gone five minutes before something
    called my name —
' ORDERLY - SERGEANT - ROBERT - BURTON !' — just
    that way it called my name.

"Then I thought, who could have called me so dis-
    tinctly and so slow —
It can't be the Lighter, surely ; he could not have
    spoken so ;
And I tried to answer, ' Here, sir !' but I couldn't
    make it go,
For I couldn't move a muscle, and I couldn't make
    it go !

"Then I thought it all a nightmare — all a humbug
    and a bore !
It is just another *grapevine*, and it won't come any
    more ;
But it came, sir, notwithstanding, just the same
    words as before,
' ORDERLY - SERGEANT - ROBERT - BURTON !' more
    distinctly than before !

' That is all that I remember, till a sudden burst of
    light,
And I stood beside the river, where we stood that
    Sunday night,
Waiting to be ferried over to the dark bluffs oppo-
    site,
When the river seemed perdition, and all hell seemed
    opposite !

"And the same old palpitation came again with all
    its power,
And I heard a bugle sounding, as from heaven or a
    tower ;
And the same mysterious voice said : ' IT IS — THE
    ELEVENTH HOUR !
ORDERLY-SERGEANT — ROBERT BURTON — IT IS
    THE ELEVENTH HOUR !'

"Dr. Austin ! — what *day* is this ?" — "It is
    Wednesday night, you know."
"Yes ! To-morrow will be New Year's, and a right
    good time below !
What *time* is it, Dr. Austin ?" — "Nearly twelve."
    — "Then don't you go !
Can it be that all this happened — all this — not an
    hour ago !

"There was where the gunboats opened on the dark,
    rebellious host,
And where Webster semicircled his last guns upon
    the coast —
There were still the two log-houses, just the same,
    or else their ghost —
And the same old transport came and took me over
    — or its ghost !

"And the whole field lay before me, all deserted far
    and wide —
There was where they fell on Prentiss — there
    McClernand met the tide ;
There was where stern Sherman rallied, and where
    Hurlbut's heroes died —
Lower down, where Wallace charged them, and
    kept charging till he died !

"There was where Lew Wallace showed them he
    was of the *cannie* kin —
There was where old Nelson thundered, and where
    Rousseau waded in —
There McCook ' sent them to breakfast,' and we all
    began to win —
There was where the grape-shot took me just as we
    began to win.

"Now a shroud of snow and silence over everything
    was spread ;
And but for this old, blue mantle, and the old hat
    on my head,
I should not have even doubted, to this moment, I
    was dead ;
For my footsteps were as silent as the snow upon
    the dead !

"Death and silence ! Death and silence ! starry
    silence overhead !
And behold a mighty tower, as if builded to the
    dead,
To the heaven of the heavens lifted up its mighty
    head !
Till the Stars and Stripes of heaven all seemed
    waving from its head !

"Round and mighty-based, it towered — up into
    the infinite !
And I knew no mortal mason could have built a
    shaft so bright ;
For it shone like solid sunshine ; and a winding
    stair of light
Wound around it and around it till it wound clear
    out of sight !

"And, behold, as I approached it with a rapt and
    dazzled stare —
Thinking that I saw old comrades just ascending the
    great stair —
Suddenly the solemn challenge broke, of, ' Halt !'
    and ' Who goes there ? '
' I'm a friend,' I said, ' if you are.' — ' Then ad-
    vance, sir, to the stair !'

"I advanced — that sentry, Doctor, was Elijah Bal-
    lantyne —
First of all to fall on Monday, after we had formed
    the line !
' Welcome ! my old Sergeant, welcome ! Welcome
    by that countersign !'
And he pointed to the scar there under this old
    cloak of mine !

"As he grasped my hand, I shuddered — thinking
    only of the grave —
But he smiled, and pointed upward, with a bright
    and bloodless glaive —
' That's the way, sir, to headquarters.' — ' What
    headquarters ? ' — ' Of the brave !'
' But the great tower ? ' — ' That was builded of the
    great deeds of the brave !'

"Then a sudden shame came o'er me at his uniform
   of light —
At my own so old and tattered, and at his so new
   and bright:
'Ah!' said he, 'you have forgotten the new uniform to-night!
Hurry back, for you must be here at just twelve
   o'clock to-night!'

"And the next thing I remember, you were sitting
   there, and I —
Doctor! it is hard to leave you — Hark! God bless
   you all! Good by!
Doctor! please to give my musket and my knapsack, when I die,
To my son — my son that's coming — he won't get
   here till I die!

"Tell him his old father blessed him as he never
   did before —
And to carry that old musket —" Hark! a knock
   is at the door! —
"Till the Union" — see! it opens! — "Father!
   father! speak once more!" —
"Bless you!" gasped the old, gray Sergeant, and
   he lay and said no more!

When the Surgeon gave the heir-son the old Sergeant's last advice —
And his musket and his knapsack — how the fire
   flashed in his eyes! —
He is on the march this morning, and will march
   on till he dies —
He will save this bleeding country, or will fight
   until he dies! *

PRESIDENT LINCOLN'S TRIBUTE TO THE LOY-
AL WOMEN OF AMERICA. — At the close of the
Patent Office Fair in Washington, Mr. Lincoln,
in answer to loud and continuous calls, made the
following remarks:

"Ladies and Gentlemen: I appear, to say but
a word. This extraordinary war in which we are
engaged falls heavily upon all classes of people,
but the most heavily upon the soldier. For it has
been said, 'All that a man hath will he give for
his life;' and while all contribute of their substance, the soldier puts his life at stake, and often
yields it up in his country's cause. The highest
merit, then, is due to the soldier.

"In this extraordinary war extraordinary developments have manifested themselves, such as
have not been seen in former wars; and among
these manifestations nothing has been more remarkable than these Fairs for the relief of suffering soldiers and their families. And the chief
agents in these Fairs are the women of America.

"I am not accustomed to the use of language
of eulogy; I have never studied the art of paying
compliments to women; but I must say, that if
all that has been said by orators and poets since
the creation of the world in praise of woman were
applied to the women of America, it would not do
them justice for their conduct during this war. I
will close by saying, God bless the women of
America."

* This very remarkable poem was distributed on
the first day of the year, 1863, by the carriers of the
Louisville Journal.

THE LOYAL VIRGINIA GIRL, AND HOW SHE
SAVED THE WAR MAPS FOR THE UNION SCOUTS.
— During the winter of 1861-2, when McClellan's grand army lay along the Potomac, and before it had been decided to try an advance by
the Peninsula, it became a matter of the utmost
importance to the Union Generals to obtain accurate and thorough maps of all North-eastern
Virginia, the region destined to be the theatre
of movements so important.

With that view, a number of intelligent and
scientific scouts, armed with minute pocket com-
passes and small boxes of drawing materials,
fearlessly pushed their way through the lines,
and as they were apparently rambling about
among the hills and through the woods as non-
belligerents and in the dress of citizens, were
collecting and tracing down on maps a very
complete topographical history of all they saw.

Southern surveyors and draughtsmen were engaged in the same work, and as they had every
facility in their operations, and were directed by
an engineer no less skilful than Beauregard,
their maps were of inestimable value to the Federal officers, and for the service of preserving
and delivering them to the Union scouts, we are
indebted to the coolness, presence of mind, and
loyalty of Miss ——, a Virginia girl of fourteen.

The topographical corps sent out by Beauregard had established their headquarters at her
father's house, and were there busy in plotting
down their surveys, when this girl, who was
watching at the window, gave the alarm, "The
blue-coats are coming down the road." Without
stopping to save a paper, they all rushed the
other way, out at the back door, and hid in the
woods adjacent. The little squad of Union
scouts rode quickly down the road, but mistrust-
ing some mischief, soon turned back, and rode
away.

Meantime this young girl had gathered up all
the maps into one great roll, and taken it into
the attic, and hid it in a hole in the chimney.

In time the alarm subsided, and the topogra-
phers came cautiously back from the bushes, but,
to their great astonishment and chagrin, found
not a vestige of their work.

They inquired of the girl what had become of
their maps.

"O," said she, "do you think I was stupid
enough to let them Yanks get hold of them?
No, indeed. When I saw them riding down the
road, those maps were going up the chimney!"

"Good for you!" was the reply. "We'll have
them all to draw over again, but that's better
than for those confounded blue-coats to get
them."

Considering the situation somewhat perilous,
they withdrew; and a day or two after, a Union
scout came in, and found a prompt welcome.

He requested her to watch at the window for
him, while he pulled out a secret roll of paper,
and commenced to map out the country through
which he had been wandering.

"So it's maps that you are making too. I
think I can give you some that I reckon you
never saw before." So saying, she ran up stairs,

and brought down the roll from the hole in the chimney, and told him how she saved them, and how entirely satisfied the other party had been that their maps had *gone up the chimney* in a very different sense.

"DIDN'T SEE IT."—A correspondent gives the following instance of Vermont pluck: "In Kilpatrick's last 'On to Richmond' was a soldier boy by the name of Edwin A. Porter, whose mother lives in Wells, Vt. In one of the skirmishes, he rode up fearlessly to a squad of rebels. The officer demanded of him to surrender. He replied, coolly, 'Don't see it;' and suiting his actions to his words, he instantly drew his sabre, with which he cleft the head of the officer, at the same instant wheeling his horse to join his company, the rebels firing a volley at him, of which shower the lad carried off in his person four bullets, joining his company, G. He kept his saddle for more than one hour, and is now doing well."

THE AMERICAN FLAG IN NASHVILLE. — The following letter, on the joy of seeing the American flag in Nashville, was written by a young lady:

"Rejoice with me, dear grandma! The glorious Star-spangled Banner of the United States is again floating above us! O, how we have hoped for, longed for, prayed for this joyous day! I am wild, crazed almost, with delight. I am still fearful that I shall awake, and find our deliverance, our freedom, is all a dream. I cannot believe that it is a positive fact, it has come upon us so unexpectedly, this successful move of the Union army. Grandma, I cannot write connectedly at all. Forgive me all faults of composition, for I can see the Stars and Stripes of my ever-loved floating from the State House — the first time my eyes have been gladdened by such a sight for nearly a year. So great is my ecstasy, I cannot sit still — I cannot keep my eyes on the paper — indeed, I cannot do anything but sing, whistle, or hum 'Yankee Doodle,' 'Hail Columbia,' 'The Star-spangled Banner,' and feast my eyes on those victorious colors.

"O grandma! you cannot imagine our happiness at this sudden change in the aspect of public affairs. The morning that Fort Donelson surrendered, there seemed to be such an intense feeling of bitterness here against the Union men! The papers (how little did they imagine that *that* would be their last issue!) came out on that Sunday morning with maledictions and threats the most inhuman against them, saying that if such a *fiendish villain* remained in our midst, he must and should be dealt with instantly as a traitor of the deepest dye.

"We have had so much to bear since I wrote you! My father and brother have been taunted, sneered and hissed at, threatened by every one, until endurance was becoming impossible. But *nothing* (I am *so* proud to say it, and thank God for it), nothing could make them play the hypo-

crite. They believed the Federal cause was just and right, and they would, in spite of our prayers and tears, express their opinions openly, and denounce secession boldly. We have been warned, since Zollicoffer's death, that there was imminent danger here for them; and the hatred towards Union men was becoming so intense that both ma and I have been in an agony of suspense. We could not leave home, as we never did, without being insulted. I have had to sit quietly by, and hear my father and brother denounced as traitors. My temper is quick, and the curb that I have been obliged to keep upon it has been a galling one — indeed, sometimes I have thought all that was gentle and womanly in me was turned into bitterness and hate.

"For my idolized brother I have felt more keenly than for anything else. He is naturally sensitive, and of such delicacy of feeling that he has suffered deeply. Being drafted, he procured a substitute; and, though displaying so much moral courage, he has been hissed at as a coward ever since, until he would vow to escape and join the Federal army, and several times endeavored to do so; but pa, discovering his plans, prevented him from it, by showing him the ruin he would bring upon us all by such a step. The cloud was lowering over us, growing darker and darker day by day, and I thought the silver lining never would appear; but *it is here!* — even now beaming upon us so brightly that we can scarcely credit the reality.

"Can you wonder that, in the state of feeling I was in that Sunday morning, dear grandma, when Tom knocked at the door, and called out to me that Fort Donelson was surrendered, and the Federal army would soon be in Nashville, I became perfectly frantic with joy?

"I ran screaming over the house, knocking down chairs and tables, clapping my hands, and shouting for the 'Union,' until the children were terrified, and ma and pa thought I was delirious! I rushed into the parlor and thundered 'Yankee Doodle' on the piano in such a manner as I had never done before. I caught little Johnny up in my arms, and held him over the porch railing up stairs until he hurrahed for the Star-spangled Banner, Seward, Lincoln, and McClellan! The little fellow thought his sister was going to kill him, she looked so wild, and would not come near me again for several days.

"Just in the midst of these rejoicings, intelligence came that Johnston's army from Bowling Green had evacuated the place, and was even then passing on the turnpike to Nashville. Could it be possible? Yes, indeed! There they were retreating most valiantly. Grandma, you never saw such a frightened set of men! They could not get over the river fast enough! I never bade the Southern army 'God-speed' but that once, and then I did it with my whole heart. May their present advance be successful even to the Gulf of Mexico itself!

"If you could have seen Breckinridge! the meanest, the most downfallen looking specimen of humanity imaginable. The army did not stop in Nashville *one day*, but went on as swiftly as possible. The citizens here were mortified and exasperated to the quick by this surrender. Floyd remained in Nashville a few days after his *brave* escape from Fort Donelson. After the army had gone, and the city had sent commissioners to surrender, he had both bridges destroyed, though he could give no reason for it, and though it was against the prayers and protestations of the citizens. He is a wicked wretch. Is it wrong to wish that he may soon meet the fate he deserves?

"It was not until a week after Donelson's fall that the Federals came in. We, whose *all* depended upon their speedy arrival, had begun to think that they were not coming, after all, and *our* freedom was not yet at hand; but on a Sunday afternoon, my brother came in, the picture of happiness, with the intelligence that Buell would be here in a few days; that he had ridden up and met his advanced guard, and that now at last we could rejoice. Buell came in at night. The troops were in perfect discipline, and completely amazed the poor duped people here by their orderly behavior. For the people believed that the soldiers would not stop till they had *murdered the women and eaten the children;* but when it was seen that they took nothing *without pay*, the people were rejoiced to *sell*, for money of any kind has long been a marvellous sight here.

"But O, grandma, I have not told you what did *me* more good than anything else — the *panic* here on the 16th. Away flew the citizens without stopping for anything! The brave city regiments who on the 15th took their stand on the square with Andrew Ewing at their head, and vowed to die there, fighting even against myriads of the 'barbarians,' should they ever reach Nashville, heard at twelve o'clock on the 16th of the surrender of Donelson, and at eight o'clock in the evening of that same day, not *one* of the gallant determined braves was to be found within miles of Nashville. Didn't I clap my hands and shriek for joy when it was told on Monday that not one editor remained in our city! that their wicked threats had been published for the last time here?

"The town is almost deserted, so many families have left their homes, and fled, panic-stricken, away. It is so distressing to think of the sufferings they have brought upon themselves so needlessly. The Federals have interfered with no one whatever, and have behaved much better than the rebel army. The Governor and Legislature left the very day Donelson surrendered. May they never return!

"Grandma, you will think me a heartless girl to write thus, and I know it is wrong, but you would excuse me if you knew what we had to contend with. I speak the truth when I say that, notwithstanding our former social position and popularity here, there is not now one family of all our friends who would cross our threshold, or bid us welcome to theirs. My noble uncle is always an exception. He and pa have stood firmly together, enduring the tempest, and nothing now should ever divide us. Mr. ——, too, has never faltered in his allegiance. When the death of his only son was told him, his exclamation was, 'Would to God he had died in a nobler cause!'

"But I tremble when I think of the possibility of a reverse — that the Confederates should ever get back here. Then *our* doom is spoken — either flight — beggary — or, remaining, death.

"O that the United States troops would push onward rapidly, and make an end to the rebellion while the Confederates are quaking with fear and dismay. Give them no time to rally.

"Now that the railroad and telegraph will soon be opened, we will be again in a civilized country; and surely we have cause to rejoice, for we have been living in utter darkness a long, weary time. If you could see my father it would do you good. He looks happy again! The gloomy, sad brow of two weeks ago is once more smoothed with content! Three cheers for the sight of the old banner!"

"DABNEY," THE COLORED SCOUT. — He was emphatically what the old Southern advertisements used to call a "smart, likely negro fellow;" and after he had left his secesh master, who lived on the south bank of the Rappahannock, above Fredericksburg, General Hooker found his minute and reliable knowledge of the country and the character of its inhabitants of great importance to him.

On one occasion, just before the battle of Chancellorsville, a scouting party had come in, who reported a certain locality entirely free of the enemy; they had talked with Mr. D——, a farmer, who said there were no Southerners anywhere near him, and had not been for several days. Dabney heard the report of the scouts, and warned the General not to believe a word of what they heard Mr. D—— say.

"You must take him just contrariwise from what he talks," said Dabney. "If he says there are no rebs there, you may be sure there are plenty of them all about, and got their big guns all ready."

But considerable faith was attached to what the scouts had reported, and a force was sent to feel in that neighborhood, and see what there might be there.

Dabney went at the head of the column as pilot, though all the time protesting that, instead of taking that man at his word, they should be prepared for the worst. Dabney was well mounted, and felt no little pride as he moved along, at the head of a powerful column, over roads which he had so often trod with the dejected air and clouded spirit of a slave.

"I know that man very well," he kept saying. "He's my ole mass'r, and he's a man you have to take just contrary to what he says."

Soon the head of the column approached the locality; and, sure enough, the rebels were there in force, and opened with a storm of grape and canister. The Union force soon got guns in position, and a brisk skirmish was going on, in the midst of which Dabney's fine horse fell under him, pierced by a grape-shot. But he was not to be dismounted as easily as that, and while the fight was quite lively, and his old master was fully occupied with the stirring scene, Dabney slipped down to the river, swam across, went to the stables, and taking the finest horse there, mounted him, dashed down to the river, swam him across, and came back to the Union lines, all the time under fire, saying, as he rode up, " I told you you couldn't depend on what that man said about the rebs not being there; but never mind, it has given me a chance to 'fiscate a mighty fine horse."

After that adventure, as he was finely mounted, and his knowledge of the inhabitants was shown to be reliable, he was constantly employed as a pilot to the scouting parties.

PADDY ON SAMBO AS A SOLDIER.

BY PRIVATE MILES O'REILLY.

AIR: *"The Low-Backed Car."*

SOME tell us 'tis a burning shame
  To make the naygurs fight,
An' that the thrade of bein' kilt
  Belongs but to the white;
But as for me, upon my sowl!
  So liberal are we here,
I'll let Sambo be murdered in place of myself
  On every day in the year!
    On every day in the year, boys,
      And every hour in the day,
    The right to be kilt I'll divide wid him,
      An' divil a word I'll say.

In battle's wild commotion
  I shouldn't at all object
If Sambo's body should stop a ball
  That was comin' for me direct;
And the prod of a Southern bagnet,
  So liberal are we here,
I'll resign, and let Sambo take it,
  On every day in the year!
    On every day in the year, boys,
      And wid none of your nasty pride,
    All my right in a Southern bagnet prod
      Wid Sambo I'll divide.

The men who object to Sambo
  Should take his place and fight;
And it's better to have a naygur's hue
  Than a liver that's wake an' white.
Though Sambo's black as the ace of spades,
  His finger a thrigger can pull,
And his eye runs straight on the barrel-sights
  From under his thatch of wool!
    So hear me all, boys, darlings, —
      Don't think I'm tippin' you chaff, —
    The right to be kilt I'll divide wid him,
      And give him the largest half!

INCIDENTS OF BULL RUN. — The famous Sixty-ninth Irish regiment, sixteen hundred strong, who had so much of the hard digging to perform, claimed the honor of a share in the hard fighting, and led the van of Tyler's attack, followed by the Seventy-ninth (Highlanders) and Thirteenth New York and Second Wisconsin.

It was a brave sight — that rush of the Sixty-ninth into the death-struggle! With such cheers as those which won the battles in the Peninsula, with a quick step at first, and then a double quick, and at last a run, they dashed forward, and along the edge of the extended forest. Coats and knapsacks were thrown to either side, that nothing might impede their work; but we knew that no guns would slip from the hands of those determined fellows, even if dying agonies were needed to close them with a firmer grasp. As the line swept along, Meagher galloped towards the head, crying, "Come on, boys! you've got your chance at last!"

Colonel Bartow's horse had been shot from under him. It was observed that the forces with which his movement was to be supported had not come up. But it was enough that he had been ordered to storm the battery; so, placing himself at the head of the Seventh Regiment, he again led the charge, this time on foot, and gallantly encouraging his men as they rushed on. The first discharge from the enemy's guns killed the regimental color-bearer. Bartow immediately seized the flag, and again putting himself in the front, dashed on, flag in hand, his voice ringing clear over the battle-fields, and saying, " On, my boys! we will die rather than yield or retreat." And on the brave boys *did* go, and faster flew the enemy's bullets. The fire was awful. Not less than four thousand muskets were pouring their fatal contents upon them, while the battery itself was dealing death on every side.

The gallant Eighth regiment, which had already passed through the distressing ordeal, again rallied, determined to stand by their chivalric Colonel to the last. The more furious the fire, the quicker became the advancing step of the two regiments. At last, and just when they were nearing the goal of their hopes, and almost in the arms of victory, the brave and noble Bartow was shot down, the ball striking him in the left breast, just above the heart. Colonel Bartow died soon after he was borne from the field. His last words, as repeated to me, were: "They have killed me, my brave boys, but never give up the ship — we'll whip them yet." And so we did!

THE ONE HUNDRED AND FIFTH RHODE ISLAND. — One of the Rhode Island boys out on picket near Yorktown, Va., found himself in close proximity to one of the enemy's pickets, and, after exchanging a few shots without availing anything, they mutually agreed to cease and go to dinner. " What regiment do you belong to? " asked our inquisitive Yankee friend of his neighbor. " The Seventeenth Georgia " was the response; "and what regiment do you belong to?" asked Secesh. "The *One Hundred and Fifth* Rhode Island," answered our Yankee friend. Secesh gave a long, low whistle, and — evaporated.

ANECDOTE OF PRESIDENT LINCOLN. — A lieutenant, whom debts compelled to leave his fatherland and service, succeeded in being admitted to the late President Lincoln, and, by reason of his commendable and winning deportment and intelligent appearance, was promised a lieutenant's commission in a cavalry regiment. He was so enraptured with his success, that he deemed it a duty to inform the President that he belonged to one of the oldest noble houses in Germany. "O, never mind that," said Mr. Lincoln; "you will not find that to be an obstacle to your advancement."

PATRIOTISM. — Orpheus C. Kerr says: "Patriotism, my boy, is a very beautiful thing. The surgeon of a Western regiment has analyzed a very nice case of it, and says it is peculiar to the hemisphere. He says it first breaks out in the mouth, and from thence extends to the heart, causing the heart to swell. He says it goes on raging until it reaches the pocket, when it suddenly disappears, leaving the patient very constitutional and conservative."

TO AND FROM LIBBY PRISON.

BY JOHN F. HILL.

For the satisfaction of the friends,[*] I shall give a brief statement of our capture, prison life, and of the escape of three of our members from the Danville prison, with an account of their safe arrival within our Union lines.

The post my regiment was assigned to, at the great battle of Chickamauga, on the 20th of September, 1863, was one which it required great coolness and bravery on our part to hold against the heavy masses that were from time to time hurled against us. It was past the middle of the day when we were brought into action. We had been held back in the forenoon on the reserve, and, when we went into the fight, the original line had become broken, and was falling back in considerable confusion. The rebels came charging down upon us, but our boys stood the fire nobly. We would be compelled at times to fall back, but we would rally again, and regain the ground we had lost. We had orders to hold the ground to the last possible moment, so as to allow our line of battle to fall back and re-form. For over five hours we kept three times our number at bay, fighting them from behind trees and logs, and lying down on the ground. Our ammunition began to fail at last, and we had to resort to the cartridge-boxes of the slain for more. Half of our men had been killed, wounded, or fallen back to the rear. Darkness was coming on; still we despaired not. General Granger had been on the ground, and promised to send us reënforcements.

A column of infantry was seen at our right, coming directly towards us, but it was so dark that we could not discern who they were. At the distance of one hundred yards our men commenced firing into them, when our Colonel or-

[*] Written especially for the Eighty-ninth Ohio regiment, and published in the Scioto Gazette.

dered us to cease firing, for they were friends. At the distance of fifty yards our Colonel hailed them, asking who they were, and they replied, "Friends;" but in a moment we saw who they were; for they were rebels coming at charge bayonet. Our Colonel hallooed out, "I know who you are." Their rebel commander demanded with an oath, "Do you never intend to surrender?" to which Colonel Carlton asked, "Is there a possibility of an escape?" to which the rebel commander replied: "None, for we have our lines thrown entirely around you." Without further ceremony we soon found ourselves divested of guns and cartridge-boxes, and under guard by our victors — the Fifty-Fourth Virginia infantry. Out of three hundred and thirty of our regiment that went into the fight, only one hundred and seventy were captured, the remainder having been either killed, wounded, or straggled back to the rear, early enough in the day to make good their escape. Of commissioned officers they got a good sprinkle, including Colonel Carlton, Lieutenant-Colonel Glenn, Captains Day, Barrett, Adams, Gatch, and Glenn; Lieutenants Edmonson, Harrison, Scott, Baird, and Fairfield, and Assistant-Surgeon Purdum.

We were taken directly to the rear that night, and passed directly over the battle-ground of Saturday. Here we noticed that none of the dead had been interred, or even the wounded attended to; and many a poor fellow cried piteously to us for help. There they had been lying for thirty-six hours, suffering from painful wounds, in a hot sun, parching up for want of water; and the woods were in several places on fire, threatening them with the most horrible death.

We found our captors very kind and gentlemanly to us, doing everything in their power to make us feel happy and contented with our lot. We acknowledged to them that they were victors; but they said they had nothing to boast of, for they had bought us at a dear price of life and blood.

They hurried us that night to General Buckner's headquarters, where we rested about an hour, and then were sent on farther to the rear, and it must have been two o'clock Monday morning, when they permitted us to lie down and sleep till sunrise. We were then marched to Tunnel Hill. There we were robbed of our knapsacks, gum blankets, and canteens. The next day they marched us to Dalton, where, on the morning of the 23d, we took the cars to Atlanta, Ga. There the authorities and citizens were very saucy and insulting to us, calling us by all kinds of names and asking us: "When is old Rosy coming again to Georgia? and how we liked Chickamauga." But our boys would give them half-a-dozen for six, and ask them when old Lee was going up into Pennsylvania again, or how they liked Gettysburg, &c. There they robbed us again of our woollen blankets, and also, by an order from Howell Cobb, Provost Marshal, they took all of our penknives, in retaliation, they said, for the way the North had served John Morgan and his men.

There we were put aboard the cars again, and after six days' and nights' travel, found ourselves in the rebel capital, and shortly afterwards inmates of one of the Libby prisons, known as the warehouse of Crew & Pemberton, tobacconists. The building was a substantial brick, four stories high. In this they thrust twenty-one hundred of us. There were seven rooms of about forty by one hundred feet, with three hundred men to each room. There, almost crowded to death, commenced a life that will be forever impressed upon our minds; and I am fearful that some of us will have the effects of that prison life so impressed into our systems that it will hurry us to our graves. The horrors of those prisons I will leave for future historians to paint; but I will attempt, in my plain and simple style, to bring a few items to the public gaze — now while humanity, charity, and Christianity are the boast of the great Southern Confederacy.

The first day after we had been thrust into this modern bastile, a rebel officer by the name of Captain Turner came in and had us all drawn up into lines, and there we had to stand under guard. He then proceeded to tell us that we had to give up all our greenbacks. He said that he had a book there in which he would enter our names, company, and regiment, and the amount, and that when we left the prison, exchanged or paroled, we would have all our money refunded to us; and moreover, if we refused to give our money up thus voluntarily, we should be searched, and all moneys and valuables found about us would be confiscated. We saw the dilemma we were in, and concluded that we would take the matter as easy as possible, swearing vengeance would be ours some day. The boys were thus robbed of several thousand dollars, and I have not the least idea that they will ever see one cent of it again.

We were also robbed of almost everything else we had, save the clothes on our backs, and they were poor and thin, for we had worn them for the last eight months (not having drawn our winter suits yet). Some had no shirts, others no blouses, some barefooted, others bareheaded, and our pants all full of holes. With this thin clothing, and no blankets, we were compelled to stretch ourselves upon the hard floor to sleep and rest, and that too in rooms where there was not the least spark of fire. You may have some idea of our suffering at that season of the year; but your imaginations can never realize the true state of things. To say we slept would only be in imagination, for I am confident of myself that I never enjoyed a nap of over half an hour's duration at one time during my whole stay in prison. And when we slept, it was nothing but a doze, filled with pleasant dreams of home and friends, of well-spread tables and inviting victuals. I have often awoke, catching myself in the very act of feeling for the bed covering; and then imagine my feelings, when I found myself disappointed and compelled to lie there shivering. Our bones would become so sore that we were compelled to be turning from side to side the

whole night long. Through the coldness of the room, and the hardness of the floor, we would often be compelled to get up in the night and walk up and down the room to keep ourselves warm. And I have seen at the hour of midnight one third of the men in the room pacing the floors to and fro, so as to pass off the long, weary hours of the night. How many a poor sufferer in after life will trace back the cause of his disease to seeds sown in this cold, desolate prison!

But the darkest part of my story remains yet to be told. Man may suffer with cold, pass through incredible hardships, endure fatigue, and never murmur — but let hunger prey upon his vitals, and he becomes mad, frantic, and raving. He loses all patience, humanity, and sympathy for others, and will then stoop to acts which he would at other times have shunned with disdain.

At first, our daily allowance was one half pound of bread per day, and two ounces of tainted beef, and that without salt. I do not remember of our ever getting any fresh meat all the time we were there. It generally was so bad that we could smell it as soon as it was brought into the room. At times we had some bacon issued to us, and it was strong, old, and maggot-eaten, looking like a honey-comb, it having been saved and cured with ashes and saltpetre, and the meat then had a slimy look, like soft soap. At last we got some kind of meat we could not fairly account for. It was neither beef, pork, mutton, veal, nor venison. It was a tough, lean, black-looking kind of flesh; and it was the decided opinion of all that it was *mule meat*. Hard as it was, we were very thankful to get even that. From off this mingled lot of corrupted flesh they would furnish us a pint of soup. No, I will not class it with that much-favored dish — it was mere dish slop.

You may ask if we relished this, and that without salt. Yes, the crumbs that fall from your table, and the slop of your swill-tubs, could be eaten there without asking any questions. At last, meat was entirely "*played out*," and then for two days we got one gill of rice, and then one day we got two sweet potatoes, and then at last had nothing but bread alone, and that from half a pound had been also reduced to a small corn "dodger," about the size of a saucer, and hard enough to knock a negro down, and so strong with alum — instead of salt — as to fairly burn our throats. We became so starved at last that we fell upon some bran that we found in a cellar under our prison. Of this we helped ourselves freely. We generally managed it so as to keep a good supply of this stuff on hand. We took the dry bran and put it in our tin cups, and then poured enough water upon it to mix it into a dough, and of this we ate freely; and to satisfy hunger we thought it answered remarkably well. It looked distressing to see us eating this weak diet with our fingers, relishing it as if it was food supplied from a king's table.

We were also compelled by starvation to sell the guards all of our jewelry, including our watches, gold pens and holders, finger-rings, and pocket-books; and some even sold the shoes from off their feet, for a small pittance to keep soul and body together. Starvation caused us to resort to a great many means to procure the necessaries of life; and although we were closely confined, and strictly guarded, we often played off some pretty sharp jokes and tricks on the Southern Confederacy.

Some of the boys, that had smuggled some money through, would take one-dollar bills (greenbacks), and have them altered to tens. These they would take, after night, and pass off on the guards for bread and tobacco. And I know of one instance where one of our new copper cents was passed off for a two and a half gold dollar piece. This may look too much like roguery; but what will not a man do before he will starve? All of our trading had to be done after dark, for the guards were not allowed to speak to us. They even had orders to shoot us, if we even put our heads out of the windows. But after dark, when there was no rebel officer near, we could approach the guard, and trade freely; but ere this time, their trading times are over, for their resources have long ago failed.

There is one joke that we played off on the rebel authorities that I must not forget to mention. It looks like a gigantic thing, but it can be well vouched for by hundreds of prisoners. It was nothing less than stealing a great quantity of sugar and salt in the rebel capital. We had a large cellar under our prison, and it was strongly locked and bolted; and we soon mistrusted that there might be something under there that we could use to advantage. So we went to work and cut a hole through the lower floor, and let ourselves down into the cellar after night. And, lo! there we found it filled with sugar and salt. We made daily draws upon it for a week, until the authorities found it out, when they cut off our supplies by removing their commissariat. You may judge we lived upon the "fat of the land" for one week, if we did suffer for it afterwards. The joke was a good one, and the rebels felt completely sold over it. By a statement, shortly afterwards, in the "*Dispatch*," they called us "gray rats, that had dug a hole into their cellar, and carried off over nine thousand pounds of sugar, and thirty-five hundred pounds of salt." Upon this I need add no comments, for every one will say, "Well done."

We had no regular prison rules, only what we made of our own. We drew rations only once a day; sometimes that would be at nine o'clock A. M., and then sometimes not until eight o'clock at night. That was indeed a long time to fast, but we had to bear it all with patience. We would always be so hungry that we would devour it all at one meal, and then be compelled to go twenty-four hours without tasting another mouthful of food.

Amidst all our suffering we had also another enemy to contend against — that was the vermin. We soon became so covered with these living creatures that it took several hours of our daily life to rid ourselves of them. It was to me an undesired job, but I had to do it, or be literally eaten up alive. This may look, in some people's eyes, like laziness or negligence on our part to get so, but I will defy any person to be put a few weeks in prison without getting so infested.

It always appeared to me that the rebel authorities tried to make our sojourn with them as miserable as they possibly could. They would agree to no terms of a parole or exchange. It appeared as if they intended to keep us there for the purpose of punishing us, and to kill us all inch by inch. We never could receive a civil answer from the authorities to any question we might ask them. When we would ask them for bread, they would threaten to give us lead. Every sentence would be accompanied with an oath and epithets of abuse, calling us invaders, negro stealers, &c., saying we were getting better treatment than we deserved. Of the soldiers that guarded us, we have no complaint to make. They treated us with a great deal of humanity and respect. They would run great risks to try to accommodate us, and often made themselves liable to the severest punishment in trying to smuggle us in a little bread, tobacco, or some newspapers.

I talked with a great many of them, who said they were tired of the war, and that they had not the least hope of success. And a great many told me that they knew they were fighting on the wrong side, and contrary to their own principles; they had not gone voluntarily, having been conscripted; and they said if they ever got near enough to some of our armies, they were going across the lines. I can truthfully say, that one third of the soldiers that guarded us were good Union men, but had been dragged into the rebel ranks, and were too fearful to make an attempt to escape. They knew their doom, if caught attempting to escape to our lines, would be death. The guards acknowledged also to us, that they were also in nearly a starving condition. They drew the same quality of rations that we did, only a little more. The inhabitants of Richmond showed signs of being in a starving condition.

In the month of October there were two bread riots in the city. The women collected together in masses, and proceeding to the rebel commissaries, burst open the doors, and helped themselves. There is no doubt that there are thousands of helpless families in the South in as bad a condition as our own Union prisoners.

A rebel soldier's pay is only one hundred and thirty-two dollars per year; now on this small sum, how is he to support a family, where everything is selling at such extravagant prices? Flour at one hundred dollars per barrel, corn ten dollars per bushel, pork two dollars per pound, calico twelve dollars per yard, and cotton five dollars, and wool ten dollars per pound. Imagine, ye Northern sympathizers, the fruits that follow a rebellious people, and you will soon come to the conclusion that the way of the transgressor is hard. Of the two most horrible prisons in Richmond, we are so fortunate as to know but little. One is Belle Island, said to be a dreary, sandy, bleak place. On it are generally put our Eastern troops, whom the rebels have a greater hatred for than Western troops. The suffering on that island it is impossible for me to picture. If you could see some of those miserable prisoners there, in their tattered clothing, and with dejected countenances, on a cold, bleak morning in November, hovering over some smouldering embers, it would melt the hardest heart with compassion. Castle Thunder is also another prison of considerable note. There they put their own deserters and criminals, and also our own incorrigible "Yankees" that they cannot so easily manage in the Libby prisons. The treatment and fare in Castle Thunder are said to be worse than were ever known in any half-civilized nation on the globe. There are said to be men within that prison who have not a particle of clothing, and have for their beds piles of saw-dust, in which they nestle down together like hogs. They are there denied all privileges of comfort — no lights, or water to wash with, just only a little food, barely to sustain nature.

They had also three large hospitals filled with our sick soldiers. These were said to be most horrible places. The accommodations and treatment were nothing better than what we received at the prisons. Hundreds upon hundreds have died in these filthy pens, who would this day have been living if they had been under the hands of humane nurses, and at a place where they could have received good healthy nourishment and proper remedies. We had a surgeon, who made a call once a day at our rooms, would make a short examination of our sick, but would generally go off without giving them any medicine, making the excuse that he had none of the proper kind. A man would have to get almost helpless before they would remove him to the hospital, and probably when he got there he would not survive more than a day or so, and then he would pass away from his troubles here to his final rest.

The number of Union prisoners in Richmond, at the date of November 13, was about thirteen thousand; something near one thousand of these were officers, and they were confined in what is known as Old Libby, the same building they used when the rebellion broke out. To Belle Island all of the prisoners from the Potomac are sent. They number now about five thousand, and some of them have been there ever since the battle of Gettysburg.

Our Western troops are all put in large tobacco factories, which could be made comfortable if they would only give them good clothes and blankets, and furnish them with plenty of fuel.

At times great excitement would prevail in the city. Every time General Meade would make a movement towards the rebel capital, we would notice it by a great bustle on the streets. And at times I thought they were fearful, also, of the prisoners, for it had more than once been whispered around that we were all going to make a general outbreak, fire the city, and make our escape. The thing could have been once easily done if we could only have had a little help from outside.

There were few troops in the city. We were guarded principally by artillerymen from the fortifications.

As for the rebel currency, it is nothing but mere trash; the whole country is overflowing with it. The rich are putting it all off on the poor, buying up their stock and grain at extravagant prices; so that when their rotten Confederacy goes down, the poor class will have the worthless pictures on hand, and they will only be worth about two cents per pound (the price of rags), and the rich will have all the produce. But I think they will not have their own way much longer. Uncle Sam will soon go down amongst them; and I judge then the whole drama will be changed, the oppressed and downtrodden will arise and shake off their shackles, and be made once more to rejoice under our old banner of freedom.

Friday, November 13. — This morning we were aroused an hour before daylight, by the guards, with orders to prepare to move immediately. Great hilarity existed among the boys, and we were making great calculations on a speedy trip around to the North, where we would get plenty to eat, and meet once again with the loved ones at home. But our bright hopes were soon blasted, and we were made to feel more despairing, when we learned that our removal was to another prison. They issued to us that morning a small loaf of corn bread, weighing about ten ounces. We all considered that it was intended for our breakfast; so we ate it all, they promising us that they were going to take us to a place where we would get plenty to eat, and that there would be a supper ready for us on our arrival that evening at Danville, N. C., our destined place. The sun was just peeping up from behind the eastern fortifications of the capital of Rebeldom when we bade adieu to the Libby prisons, and soon found ourselves safely stored away in box cars, and rolling along at the speed of eleven miles per hour. We arrived safe at Danville that night, by eight o'clock P. M., and were soon incarcerated in another "Tobacco Prison." Danville is south-west of Richmond, distance one hundred and forty miles, and is located on the south bank of Dan River, a tributary of the Roanoke. It contains about twelve or fifteen hundred inhabitants, with some pretty snug buildings, and is in one of the best tobacco regions in the State. It also is the terminus of the Richmond and Danville Railroad. Our prison there was another brick building, forty by sixty feet, and three stories high; and our train load of seven hundred prisoners filled the building full enough to be comfortable. But to our disappointment (and not much either, for we had lost all faith in their promises), we had to lie down to sleep without anything to eat. But such things we had got so used to that we acquiesced without a murmur.

Saturday, November 14. — Daylight came, but nothing to eat. Noon came, but still no food. Night came, and nothing yet. No wonder we looked up some desperate effort to better

18

our condition. Thoughts had been in my head, from the time I had been in Libby one week, to make my escape if the thing was in any way possible; I had even felt sorry that I had let so many opportunities slip, when they were bringing us to Richmond, which I could have done a hundred times, from the carelessness of our guards. While in Richmond, it was continually upon my mind, but the thing looked like an impossibility there. Probably I could have got out of the prison, but I never could get out of the city, and pass their line of pickets and fortifications. We also thought of making the attempt when we run down on the cars to Danville, but before dark set in they came around and locked us all safe up in the cars. The first thing I did on that morning, when I got up, was to take a general survey of the place, and see what the prospect was for making an escape. I saw things looked pretty favorable; and I soon found an accomplice in the Sergeant-Major of the Nineteenth Regulars, a brave and dashing young man.

We two put our heads together, and laid a scheme for making a general outbreak, by bursting open all three of our prison doors, overpowering the guards, capturing the town, destroying the railroad bridge across Dan River, cutting the telegraph, destroying all the commissary stores, securing all the arms and horses that we could, and then making all speed for the mountains. The whole thing could have been easily effected, for we were seven hundred strong in the building, and there were seven hundred more expected about eight o'clock that night, and that, then, would make a considerable force. The rebels had not more than one hundred soldiers there, and no more troops nearer than Richmond, and they had only nine on duty at a time. When night came, it set in dark and rainy, and guards that were not on duty were rambling about the town. We had selected the time when the cars would come in to make the move. We were to divide into three squads. One was to capture the guards as quietly as possible, and then go to their headquarters and pick up all there, and then break out into the town, and take and destroy everything valuable. We had assigned for this four hundred men. Then two hundred more were to make for the railroad bridge, and burn it, and then one hundred were to go to the telegraph office and demolish it. We were then to burn the entire train, depot buildings, &c.; and then, as soon as we could mount and arm seventy-five or one hundred men, we were to start them off to the East Tennessee and Virginia Railroad to cut the telegraph, and destroy the track by burning some bridges at and near Salem, in Roanoke County, a distance of sixty miles, which they could make in twelve hours; and then for them to go on and notify our forces in Western Virginia to come to our assistance, and meet us in the mountains.

After having everything completed, we set to work to talk with the men, and to enlist every one in the enterprise. We labored hard and faithfully that day among the men, and could only get sixty men out of seven hundred to go into it. They said they would not go out if we threw the doors wide open. They were so weak and feeble from their sufferings for want of clothes and food that they could never reach our lines, and were certain we would be captured; and then they judged we would all have to fare harder than ever. This might have been the case, but I viewed it in a different light; for to remain there much longer would be death, and it could not be worse than death to make the attempt. So when we found out that we could not effect a general stampede, we concluded that it would be the best policy to get out as secretly as possible, and get as far away as we could before the authorities would find it out. After dark we went to work and cut a hole through the fence. It was a pine board one inch thick and one foot broad; we cut it off about eighteen inches from the ground. It was done with an old table knife that had been broken off two inches short. It was not more than the work of half an hour, and all was ready; but we waited so as to let the people in town settle down. About half past seven o'clock we commenced going out in small squads of three and four men. We had to pass within ten feet of one of their guards, but he did not appear to pay any attention to us. I should judge he was a good Union man, or well bribed, and how it turned out with him I have never learned. A little before eight o'clock three of us, Sergeant Solomon Stookey, Corporal Henry Thompson, and myself, all being members of the same company, started, and in a moment were through the orifice and once more in free air.

We knew we had undertaken a very hazardous enterprise — but it was life or death. We had not tasted any food for thirty-six hours, and were almost frantic with hunger. As soon as we found ourselves safely out, we made for the banks of the river, distant about fifty yards. By the time we reached the river we heard the guards crying the rounds of the night, and when it came to the guard that we passed, we distinctly heard him halloo out, "Post number nine, eight o'clock, and all's well." I could not help laughing to myself, and thought, "Old soldier, you did not tell the truth that time."

We hurried up the river bank on a fast run, but as it was raining and the ground slippery, I fell down almost every rod, being weak and exhausted; but my two comrades would hurry me along. About half a mile from the prison we came to a small meadow, and found in it a persimmon tree; we pitched into it and ate over one pint of the fruit apiece, and I thought they did us a great deal of good by giving us strength. We could have eaten a great many more, but I urged the boys on, for we were not yet out of sight of the lights of the town. I had been selected as the guide, and it was my intention to take a north-west course, as anything between north and west would bring us into our lines at some place in Western Virginia.

My first object was to get across Dan River as quick as possible, for I knew our escape would be found out, and they would hotly pursue us, and that all ferries would soon be guarded for the purpose of recapturing us. We made up the river as fast as we could travel, reaching what is known as Wilson's Ferry. There the Danville Pike crosses, going to the Blue Ridge. There we worked for two hours, trying to break the locks or draw the staple, but could not effect anything. We felt a great interest in getting the boat loose for the purpose of crossing, and also of setting the ferry boat afloat so as to retard our pursuers. Finding all our efforts fruitless, we abandoned it and moved up the river about three miles, and as it was raining very hard and dark, we became so exhausted that we could not proceed any farther. We lay down in a pine thicket to rest, but there was no rest for us. We were so famished, and the weather so wet and cold, that hope almost fled. There was Dan River we must cross early in the morning if we had to swim. Delay would be dangerous. The whole thing kept my mind excited so that I could not rest.

Sunday, November 15. — We felt very blue this morning, but by daylight we were up and off. We proceeded right up the banks of the river, gathering some raw corn and turnips to subsist on. We had not gone very far until we found a canoe tied up to a tree, and half full of water. We went to work and soon had it baled out, and with a piece of a root for a paddle, we managed to get across, the canoe turning around some half a dozen times in the middle of the stream. As soon as we were safely across, we "broke for timber," but had not proceeded far, when, as we were going out of a ravine to the top of a hill, we espied three armed men in advance of us. Two of them were on horseback, and they had a kind of an ugly look. We ordered a retreat, and fell back half a mile unobserved by them, hid ourselves in some thick undergrowth, considering that it would not be best to travel in the daylight. We lay by the balance of the day and slept some, and as soon as it began to get dark started again. We took our direction through bush and woods and over fields until about nine o'clock, when it became so dark that we could not see how to travel, and as I used the moon and stars for my guide, we were obliged to halt and camp. In doing so we gathered a few leaves into a fence corner; into this we nestled down and tried to sleep, but no sleep closed our eyelids that night. Everything was wet and cold, and we did nothing but lie there and shiver. God forbid that I should ever pass through such another night. Death would then have been a welcome visitor. I then despaired, and told my two partners we never could make it. Here we were three days without anything to eat, save a little raw corn and turnips, and that was doing us more harm than good. O, ye rich and opulent of the North, when you lie down on downy beds, do you think what the poor soldier has to pass through at times to save your country, your home, and your wealth?

Monday, November 16. — We arose this morning in despair; we did not care which way the scale turned. We had lost all energy to push forward, and the only thing that engrossed our mind was something to eat. We looked around and espied a small cabin at a short distance in a small clearing. We took it to be a negro hut, and we would make a venture to it, let the consequences be what they would. It was agreed that but one should make the venture, and if all was not safe the other two could escape. It was put upon me to make that venture. I proceeded to the house, caring but little what the consequences might be, so that I got something to eat. When I came to the yard, a white woman came out; it frightened me a little, but I thought I would go ahead, let what might follow. I told her not to be alarmed, that I was a "Yankee," and had escaped from a Confederate prison, and was making an effort to reach my home in Ohio. She looked suspiciously at me for a while; but after talking a few moments, she believed my story. I then told her I was famishing for something to eat. She then bade me come in, and said she would do the best she could, although she knew she was running a great risk, for if the rebel authorities should find it out they would severely punish her for harboring and assisting their enemy. I then told her of my two comrades, and she bade me call them in, and said we were welcome to the best she had. We enjoyed ourselves around a warm, blazing fire, for it was the first we had seen or felt for eight weeks. Mrs. Corban (for that was the good woman's name) went to work and hastily prepared us a good warm breakfast of stewed chicken, butter, cabbage, coffee (Confederate), and corn bread. You need not ask us whether we did justice to the smoking dishes before us. There is one thing certain, we had very grateful hearts. At the table Mrs. Corban informed us who she was. She said she was as good a Union woman as we ever saw, and that she had a husband, who was in the rebel army at that time, but was as good a Union man as was ever in Ohio. But he, like thousands more of his unfortunate class, had been conscripted, but was going to cross the lines at the first favorable opportunity.

After breakfast she took us to a deep forest, where a couple of deserters were hid. We found them in their hermit home, and she left us with them there, while she went off to find a good Union man to help us, one who had some knowledge of the country, so as to get us on safely without falling into the hands of the enemy. She returned late in the evening, bringing with her a nice dinner of beef, potatoes, corn bread, and pumpkin pies, and also the good intelligence that she had found a man by the name of Yates, an overseer on a plantation, who was true Union, and willing to do all in his power to make us comfortable and to assist us on our journey. How devoted and true is a loyal woman to the cause of our country! Such heroines are not rare, and that, too, in the very heart of the Southern Confederacy. Noble woman! As we were parting, she went into the house and brought us the best quilt she had, and gave it to us.

Now consider one moment: that woman was poor, and she had five helpless children, her husband in the rebel ranks; most of her subsistence she had to draw weekly from the Confederate Government, and you may plainly see why we call her a heroine. Do not such people — laying aside the great interest of our country — demand protection? Can we not bravely fight for such, and redeem them from the thraldom of tyrants? After dark the two deserters (who were Union also) piloted us to the house of Mr. Yates. We found him a thorough Union man, who was glad to receive us, and gave us a hearty supper and a warm bed under his hospitable roof. He was one of those bold, dashing men who did not care what he said; and he remarked to us that the Confederate authorities were more afraid of him than he was of them. Of his being a Union man, almost every man knew it, and yet he remained unmolested. About midnight three more of our runaway boys came to his house and craved his hospitality, which he freely gave by treating them the same as he did us. This is another proof of the loyalty of the downtrodden people of the South. What would have been that man's fate if the rebels had caught us all in his house? Was there any doubt of true loyalty there?

Tuesday, November 17. — Long before daylight we were up and had our breakfasts, and then our good friend advised us that it would not be safe for us to remain at his house that day, for probably the rebel soldiers would be there and search his house for some of us. He then took us to a nice pine thicket adjacent to his house, where we passed the day quietly. At noon his son brought us our dinner, and after dark the old gentleman came, bringing us our supper and one day's rations. Then we learned for the first time that sixty of our men had actually effected their escape, and that the whole country was swarming with cavalry in hot pursuit, and that six of our boys had been captured that day in front of his door. I could not pity them much, for they were too foolhardy and careless in attempting to travel in the daylight, and that, too, upon a public highway; and moreover to let one man capture the whole of them!

We ate our supper, and bade our good friend adieu; and as the shades of night were closing in, we set out again to the "land of promise," with a determination to go through now or die in the attempt. I set out as guide about one hundred yards in advance of my two comrades. On that night, through woods and over fields, and wading one considerable stream, we travelled about twelve miles in a proper direction, when the moon went down and it became dark. We travelled on, but I soon found I was making a circle, as I had lost my way; so after midnight, we raked together some leaves and slept till morning.

Wednesday, November 18. — We ate our breakfast at a widow woman's by the name of Smith, who was true and loyal. We slept in the woods near by all day, and as soon as it was dark we were off. This night we took through woods and fields again, keeping our course, and by two o'clock in the morning were across what is known as Turkey Mountain, and entered a poor man's house by the name of Carder, who allowed us to sleep on the floor in front of the fire. He would not believe we were Yankees, but took us to be rebel detectives, and I could not exactly find him out.

Thursday, November 19. — Mr. Carder was not able to give us our breakfast; so we had to go on half a mile to a Mrs. Reynolds, who was as good a Union woman as any in Old Virginia. She hastily prepared us a warm meal; and as she was in the kitchen cooking it, a rebel soldier came into the sitting-room where we were. He immediately asked us if we were not runaway Yankee prisoners. We answered in the affirmative. He then said he took us to be such, for he had heard of our escape from Danville, and two of our boys had been along there the day before; and as they were somewhat astray, he piloted them a couple of miles; but he had not more than left them before they were recaptured by some rebel cavalry. He then advised us not to attempt to get any farther, for it was impossible for us to get through, as the cavalry and citizens had turned out to the number of five hundred, and were ranging the country all around for us. He said it would go easier with us if we would voluntarily give ourselves up to him, and he would take us to where we would be well treated and get plenty to eat. We gave him to understand we did not put much faith in his promises, and also we did not intend to surrender ourselves to one man. Here our conversation was interrupted by breakfast being ready. At the table Mrs. Reynolds informed us that the rebel soldier was her brother, but for us to pay no attention to him, and advised us to go ahead at all hazards. She deeply sympathized with us in our perilous undertaking, but wished us God speed.

After breakfast, the rebel soldier volunteered his services to pilot us to some secluded spot, where we might rest in safety through the day. I politely thanked him. I had undertaken that job myself, and I did not wish his assistance. I saw what he was fishing after, for there was three thousand dollars reward for each of us, and he was after Confederate legal tender. We left him very unceremoniously, and broke for a chain of small hills and mountains. That cursed imp of rebeldom caused me a great amount of uneasiness, and we travelled nearly the whole day, so as to get as far away as possible. By sundown we were over another small mountain called Snow Creek, at the foot of which we entered a man's house and got our supper. He was good Union, although he had a son in the rebel ranks. He informed us then that we were in Franklin County, and within fifteen miles of the county seat (Rocky Mound). He said that it was directly on our road to the Blue Ridge, but advised us to leave it to the right or left, as it was not safe for us to go through, as there were two companies of cavalry always stationed there. We thanked him for his information, and proceeded on, crossing another small mountain called Chestnut Ridge, and then for the first time took the road. When we thought we were near Rocky Mound, and had come to a fork in the road, we aimed to take the road that would not take us through that place. But we took the wrong road, and directly we crossed a river on a bridge, and found ourselves right in the heart of a considerable sized town. It was too late to back out; so we moved on as noiselessly as cats. We looked every moment for some one to halt us; but, thank God, we went through undisturbed. We learned next day that we had actually come through Rocky Mound. We travelled on that night, crossing Grassy Mountain and Blackwater River, wading it, and turned into a house for breakfast just at daylight.

Friday, November 20. — We felt very sore, having walked thirty-five or forty miles in the last twenty-four hours, and not having slept any. There was none but a woman and children in the house, and she took us to be rebel deserters, and we said nothing to the contrary. We ate our breakfast, and then went into a thicket and slept sweetly all day. At dark we went to a house near by, where we got our supper. There we were taken for rebel deserters again, and the old man let on to be a rebel himself; but I have since thought him to be a good stanch Union man. But he was fearful of us. We were soon off again, and took the main road, and by midnight reached the Blue Ridge. There we passed some splendid natural scenery; but we did not waste much time in stopping to admire it. This night we were pursued by a wildcat or catamount for over three miles. The mischievous little creature gave us a great deal of uneasiness, for we had no arms to defend ourselves. We then proceeded safely, and about three o'clock it set in to rain, and we were compelled to stop and take shelter under some pine bushes.

Saturday, November 21. — It rained all day. This morning we had to go without any thing to eat. All the houses looked too fine for us to make a venture. We got into an old barn, and hid ourselves in some hay, so as to see and not be seen. We noticed through the day several rebel soldiers pass the road, but we felt safe. In the afternoon, as it was raining so hard that there was no travel, we ventured out, and went back from the road a mile, and found a house where we got some bread and beef, and also learned that we were within three miles of the East Tennessee Railroad. We proceeded on cautiously through the rain, and got within half a mile of the railroad, and then waited for the shades of night, so as to pursue our way. As soon as it was dark enough, we proceeded on, and every place was a sea of water and pretty cold. We crossed Roanoke River by wading, and the railroad half a mile south of what is known as Lick Spring Station. We then proceeded up the valley parallel to the railroad, and through one of the finest and the most fertile and well improved sections that I had seen in the Confederacy. The plantations were large, and appeared in the highest state of cultivation. After going up the valley about eight miles, we were compelled by hunger

to enter a small cabin for something to eat. We then learned that we were in Roanoke County, within a mile or so of the county seat, Salem; and were advised to flank the town, as it was not safe for us to pass through, and also to avoid the road over Salem Mountain (a spur of the Alleghanies), as it was constantly watched, night and day, to catch rebel deserters who were making for the Union lines. We also learned that Salem was one of the hottest nests of secession in the whole valley, that it was their principal depot for army stores, and that there was at that time on hand an abundance of corn, flour, meat, &c. But since our visit there I have learned that General Averill has been in there and damaged their hive, to their great discomfiture.

We proceeded on that night, making direct to the mountain. We soon reached its foot, and began our weary ascent, through brush, and over ledges of rocks, and climbing places almost perpendicular; and the night was as dark as pitch, besides being wet and cold. Our lot was then a trying one, so much so that we at last became completely bewildered. We called a halt and camped for the night, building a large fire out of dry chestnut, and contrived to dry ourselves, but slept none.

Sunday, November 22. — As soon as it was light enough, we fell back about half a mile, and found a house in which we had a very welcome breakfast set before us by a good old Quakeress, who appeared as if she could not do enough for us. After eating and thanking the good woman, we made for the top of Salem Mountain, which we reached after a two hours' walk, climbing nearly the whole way by pulling ourselves up by the bushes. We built a fire, and spent the day in returning thanks to Almighty God for his protection in our perilous undertaking. We slept some through the day, but always kept one out on guard while the other two would sleep. From our refuge we could see all around for miles. It was a beautiful sight; we could see directly down into the rebel town of Salem, and see the people promenading the streets. Little dreamt they that they were watched by Yankees; but, as for us, we felt secure, for I felt as if a kind Providence had a hand in our escape. We began our descent an hour before sundown, and dark found us again in the road making pretty good headway for Yankeedom.

Our course led about ten miles up that valley (Catawba). This was also very fertile, and, in travelling along the road, we had to pass near some very fine houses. All these we endeavored to avoid by taking across the fields. And, as a general thing, we never went near a house but what a dozen dogs would come baying out after us, and they would keep up their yelping as far as we could hear. I often remarked to my comrades that I could never have any more friendship for the canine creatures. That night a man chased us for nearly two miles with his dogs. We would have stood and given battle, but we did not want to leave any tracks behind. We crossed another small mountain known as Catawba, and came into Craig Valley. After midnight it became cloudy, and, as our road led up Craig Creek, and we had to wade it in several places, and it turned cold, and as we were wet and very much fatigued, we began to look around for some place to sleep and rest. But, as every place was wet and muddy, we could do no better than to chase some pigs from their bed, and, for the time being, take military possession of their snug and comfortable quarters — comfortable, if we did rise up covered with creepers. But we were willing to do or pass through anything to regain our freedom.

Monday, November 23. — We rose feeling pretty well, except our empty stomachs; but we soon found a nice warm breakfast at the house of a Mrs. Brillhart. While at the table, she informed us of a band of deserters which was near by, who, she thought, would do all in their power to aid and assist us in getting through. We got the direction, and found their headquarters about noon. We were cordially received, and treated with the best they had. The news of our arrival spread fast, and by dark not less than twenty persons came in to see us. They thought it was a great curiosity to see "live Yankees" in their midst. We found them all true Union men in principle, and would be so in action, if it was not for the iron rule of tyrants that keeps them down.

There we found deserters from the rebel ranks who had been there, hid in the mountains, for over eighteen months. We were assigned a room that night in the stable loft, and received visitors until nearly midnight. I was heartily glad when they quit coming, for I needed some rest. I slept that night as sweetly, and felt as safe, as if I had been at home. I knew I was among friends, and that not a few.

Tuesday, November 24. — We arose in great glee. A Squire Somebody had sent us a bottle of home-made liquor, which we did not object to, as we thought a little refreshment would not go amiss, if it did cost six dollars a pint. Visitors came flocking in all day, and I was getting fearful, lest the thing was getting too public, and might arouse suspicion. We coaxed four deserters to fix up and go along with us, for we knew they would be excellent pilots, from their knowledge of the country.

We also found that they had been running deserters from that place across to our lines. And for doing this, they had established a route with a number of posts on it — a kind of an underground railroad. And besides this, they had a secret organization, with its grips, signs, and passwords; and for a person to be a member, he had to sign an obligation, and take a solemn oath, the punishment for violation of which was death.

Under an old shed near by, we were all three of us initiated into this mystic lodge; and thereafter we could tell our friends at first sight; and it was a great help to us during the balance of our sojourn in Dixie. We found there men of all ages — from the beardless youth to the gray-headed old man — praying day and night that the Yankees might come and take possession of their country. They had felt the gall and bitterness of secession — they knew its aim — the subjugation of the poor, and to lift up the rich into despotic chairs. O ye butternuts of the North, who voted for exiles, and outlaws, and friends of secession, if you could but half feel the fruits of disunion, how soon you would change your principles! We spent one happy day in the Confederacy. They brought us in great baskets of provisions. It appeared as if they could not do enough for us; and when we went to start, they filled our haversacks to overflowing, and gave us also fifteen dollars in money (Confederate). Everything being in readiness, and with many adieus and God speed you well, from both men and women, we started off, accompanied by the four deserters and about twenty of the citizens, who went with us a couple of miles. Such true types of Unionism are hardly found here in our midst — certainly no better.

The deserters went ahead as our guides. We were soon across Craig Mountain, and in the Sinking Creek Valley, and were proceeding along, as we thought, in all security. As we were going down a small creek, which led out to a public road, we had not more than got out into the road, when all in an instant we heard the words, "Halt, halt, halt!" coming from a sentinel not over twenty-five yards in front of us. We then saw, to the right of the road, eight or ten camp fires, and saw in an instant our danger. We made off at full speed, and ran on for a mile until we were completely exhausted. The sentinel never fired at us, nor made the alarm in camp. I have always thought that he did not suspect who we were. It was a narrow escape, and also a lesson of caution.

After getting over our fright, we made off again, over fields and through woods, wading Sinking Creek, and then over Sinking Creek Mountain, through the brush; then across John's Creek Valley, and wading John's Creek, which was very deep and cold, and made the top of John's Creek Mountain by daylight.

Wednesday, November 25. — We took a good day's rest, and were off again at dark, down across a large valley, thence over Peter's Mountain; the last and highest of the Alleghanies. This night was very cold, and we suffered, for our clothes were so thin, and my shoes were now about gone; and I was compelled to tear up some of my other clothes to keep my feet safe, for I knew our success depended upon them. We stopped that night about midnight at the house of a Mr. Smith, at the west foot of Peter's Mountain. This was a post on our route, and as the next one was twenty-five miles ahead, we wanted to take a whole night for it. Mr. Smith gave us a very hospitable reception, but informed us that it would be impossible for us to get through, as General Averill had been pitching into the rebels at Lewisburg, and had scattered them all along down the Greenbrier country, — and we also had in our pathway the two bushwhacking companies, commanded by William and Philip Thurman, who were doing great mischief, taking their spite out on the Union men in the country for their defeat at Lewisburg.

His tales were so horrible that we could not persuade the rebel deserters to come another foot with us; they started back immediately that night. Their courage failed them after coming forty miles with us, and we were then within eighty miles of our lines.

Thursday, November 26. — After a good nap on the floor, and a warm breakfast before daybreak, we went into a thicket and lay concealed there all day in perfect security. Mr. Smith went ahead that day several miles to learn the true state of things, as to the safety of our going forward, and returned at night with the news, that it might be barely possible. At night, after a hearty supper, we set forward to make Greenbrier River before daylight, with a recommendation to a Mr. L. Guinn, our next post. That night's travel took us directly through Monroe County, and our road led through Uniontown, the county seat, and as that was another hot secesh hold we were told to flank it. We came in sight of the town about ten o'clock. As there were a great many lights there, we struck off to the left, and by so doing got upon the wrong road, but did not find our mistake until we had gone eight miles. We then altered our course, and made Greenbrier a little before daylight. I entered a cabin, and inquired for a man by the name of L. Guinn. I was informed that a man by the name of Layton Guinn lived a mile down the river. Without stopping to ask whether he was Union or not, we started down the river to Mr. Guinn's. We soon came in sight of the house, and as it was Sergeant Stookey's turn to make the venture, the other two of us lay hid. Sergeant Stookey went up to the yard fence, as it was breaking day. The folks of the house were up. He hallooed, and a man came out. Stookey asked him "if Mr. Guinn lived there," to which the man replied, that was his name, and residence, but he had only got home the night before, for he belonged to one of Thurman's independent companies — a kind of genteel name for bushwhackers. Stookey soon saw the difficulty he was in, but gathered up courage and played off. He immediately replied that he was the very man he "wanted to find, for he wanted to enlist in one of them independent companies," and probably now he could get some information how to get to them. This appeared to please the man, and he immediately asked, "Who are you? a deserter? What regiment, Twenty-second, Forty-fifth, or Sixtieth Virginia?" Stookey answered him that he used to belong to the army, but as his regiment was a long way off, he thought he would try one of his companies for a while. To this Mr. Guinn proceeded to inform him where the two companies were. One was at such a ferry on New River, and had scouts scattered here and there, &c., the other one was up on Muddy Creek, with directions how to go to it, where to cross the river, and what roads to take, &c. Just the very kind of information we so greatly desired. He then invited Stookey to come in and get his breakfast. Stookey politely thanked him, as he had plenty in his haversack; so he bade him good morning, and hastily rejoined us. After this news, we set our wits to work to make the best of it. We had struck the wrong man, and to make any more ventures we thought would not be safe, and we must manage to get across Greenbrier the best we could. We made immediately for the river, and went down it a mile, to a place where there were no houses in sight. There we built a fire. We were compelled to do so, for it was a very cold night, and I had my feet and fingers partially frost-bitten. After we had thawed out a little, and eaten the last mouthful in our haversacks, we began to look for some way to cross the river. In a pile of drift-wood there was an old canoe. This we got out and launched, and all three of us got into it, and began to paddle over, but were not more than one third over when the little, frail thing upset, and threw us into the water. It was a cold baptism, and we swam back, dripping with wet and trembling with cold. We rebuilt our fire, wrung and dried our clothes, and in two hours were ready to try it again. This time Stookey went over in the canoe alone, and Thompson and myself went down about half a mile to a riffle, stripped, and waded. It was a bitter pill, but there was no alternative. After being safely over we made for the Snell Mountains, whose summit we reached a little after dark. A bed was soon made out of some leaves, in which we snugly slept all night.

Saturday, November 27. — Hunger drove us this morning to a cabin for something to eat. We met, as usual, with a good Union man. We were now aiming for New River, and he advised us to keep along the top of the Snell Mountains, and that they would take us there in fourteen miles. We started off, but as it was raining and sleeting we made poor headway, stopping at several houses, and keeping ourselves well posted as to the dangers of the country.

By the middle of the afternoon we had reached the residence of Mr. Thomas Richmond, one of the best Union men in the country, and a man of wealth. He advised us to go no farther in daylight, but told us to stay with him until midnight, when he would go with us as far as New River; then he thought we should be safe. We passed our time very much at home at Mr. Richmond's, who was a whole-souled gentleman. He interested us by giving an account of his family and connections, which were very numerous, and good Union. But they had suffered severely from the hands of the bushwhackers. His brother, who owned a ferry on New River, had been shot dead in his own yard, and his two sons taken thirty miles off and shot. He also had one brother who had been in Castle Thunder for over two years, and he did not know whether he was alive or not. Besides, a great many of the family had to flee to the North, leaving all of their possessions behind. It would make any one shudder to listen to his tales of the sufferings of the loyal people. He told me there would be a great many old grudges to settle after this war was over, between them and the treacherous and murderous rebel bushwhackers of the country.

Sunday, November 29.—This was the third Sabbath we had passed in making our escape from Rebeldom. By three o'clock we were up, had our breakfast, and were off, Mr. Richmond acting as our guide. By daylight we were at New River, at what is known as Richmond's Ferry. There Mr. Richmond parted with us. We proceeded down on the right hand bank of the river for ten miles, and then got a man to take us across in his canoe, and then down the left bank, travelling pretty briskly until dark, when we stopped with a man by the name of Samuel Kincade, who turned out to be a notorious bushwhacker. When we entered the house he took us to be men of his own order. He proceeded to tell us about the success of the freebooters in that part of the country, &c. He was getting under pretty good headway, when Sergeant Stookey told him he had better be careful how he was talking, for we were Yankees. This put the old fellow "on nettles;" he was restless all night, and was not very communicative thereafter.

Monday, November 30. — We were up pretty early, and our old rebel host appeared rather cool. He charged us a dollar apiece for our lodging—the first and only man that took a cent from us. They generally would rather give us something than take anything from us. If we had had any kind of weapons we would have marched this Mr. Kincaid into Fayetteville that day. We left him deeply absorbed in thought as to who we actually were.

We walked very rapidly for ten miles down the river, and then took off across the country for Fayetteville. The nearer we got to our lines, the more uneasy I felt, to think, after coming so far, and through so many hardships, and then that we might be "gobbled up" in sight of our haven of rest. We also knew our doom would be death if we fell into the hands of the bushwhackers. At last I thought we could not travel fast enough, I was so impatient to get through.

About three o'clock P. M., as we made a bend in the road, we espied off ahead of us a blue overcoat; it was a picket post. Can I describe our feelings at that time? I am not capable of the task. I only refer you to the indescribable joy of Pilgrim when he crossed the River Jordan. At the post we met some of the boys from the Ninety-first Ohio infantry. After they learned who we were, they were overjoyed to see us. A courier was sent in immediately to Colonel White, commander of the post at Fayetteville. An order was sent out to have us brought in. You may imagine we had not a very prepossessing appearance. Our clothes were hanging all in tatters and rags. I was nearly barefooted, and my feet were so bruised and sore that I could but just hobble along. We also looked dirty and mangy, and our countenances had a sallow, haggard look. Indeed, we were hard-looking specimens of humanity. Colonel White very hospitably received us, and furnished us with new suits of clothes. And the noble and generous boys of the Twelfth Ohio volunteers, shall we ever forget them? They took us in as strangers, and fed us; and not satisfied with doing that, they gave us thirty dollars in money. Brave, generous fellows: may your future be a bright and happy one. We now felt ourselves at home; we had run the blockade; we had for once, as common soldiers, out-generalled the rebels, and made good our escape. We were sixteen days and nights making the trip of two hundred and fifty miles, over a dozen mountains, wading streams of all sizes, suffering from cold, and all manner of hardships. Always in danger, scarcely saw a moment that we felt safe, making ventures all the time for something to eat. We entered twenty-two houses; nineteen of them were Union. We ate nineteen meals in houses, and slept three nights in houses. To the good loyal people of the country, and the All-wise Creator, that rules the nations, we owe our success.

We remained at Fayetteville two days, and then proceeded with letters to General Scammon, at Charleston, West Virginia. He very cordially received us, and sent us on, with passes, through the lines of his department.

ISHMAEL DAY. — This determined old hero gives the following account of the attack on his flag, at his house in Baltimore County, Maryland, on Monday, July 11, 1864:

"On Sunday evening, the 10th, I heard that Dulaney's Valley was filled with rebels, stealing horses and cattle; did not believe it, but thought they were Federal troops pressing horses. About sundown, the same day, I heard the rebels were on the Harford Pike, about a mile distant, the people living thereon being much excited. I went to bed, leaving my lamp dimly burning all night, and arose early on Monday morning, and ran up the glorious old Stars and Stripes rather earlier than usual. I then sat down in my front porch, and was soon accompanied by Mrs. Day. About six o'clock A. M. my little colored girl told her mistress that she heard soldiers up the road hurrahing. I still thought they were our troops. In a few minutes my wife said she heard the sound of horses' feet coming down the road; and looking up the road, said, 'There they are,' two of them coming in full tilt. A little while after, they were before the door, and I moved down on the lower step to see if there were any more near; and seeing none, resumed my seat. By this time the foremost one had dismounted, seized hold of the bottom of the flag, jerked it down, and broke the rope, cursing and calling it a 'damned old rag.' I then coolly asked him, 'What do you mean? What are you about?' and, without waiting a reply, ran immediately up stairs, seized one of my two guns, already loaded in my bed-room, and shot the foremost one of them, out of the second story window, which was already up, while he was in the act of folding up the flag for his departure. He then raised his hands and fell back, exclaiming, 'I am shot.' I then seized the other gun, ran down stairs, when I was met by Mrs. D. crying, imploring me not to shoot again, or they would kill me. I, however, pressed out into the yard to take a shot at the other; but he was among the missing, having clapped spurs to his horse on the fall of his companion, which I regretted very much, as he did not give me an opportunity of giving him his bitters also; and seeing none of the squad at the time, I walked up to the wounded man, and said, 'You rebel rascal, I will now finish you,' and cocked the gun for that purpose, but he asked for mercy, and surrendered; and knowing that he had received the whole charge, I was satisfied that he could not live, and, therefore, did not shoot him again. By this time I heard the whole troop coming down the road; I returned to my bed-room, got my six-barrelled revolver, and with the loaded gun started for my hiding-place, about two hundred and fifty yards north-east of my house, and hardly had done so before they were all at the house, and fired all my buildings, except a small corn and hen-house. Everything was burnt, including all my personal property, and thirty-five dollars in money, which was either taken by the rebels or consumed by the fire; after which I went to one of my nearest neighbors to get my breakfast, and went to a second one to get dinner, and was conveyed to Baltimore on the same day. On Thursday after, I had my name enrolled in the Company of the Aged Guard of 1862, commanded by Captain Child, for the defence of Baltimore; and on the same day obtained a guard from headquarters to bring in the wounded rebel, whom I took to West's Hospital, where he has since died."

THE PATRIOT ISHMAEL DAY.
BY W. H. HAYWARD.

COME forth, my muse, now don't refuse;
  Assist me, in this lay,
To sing of one — " My Maryland's " son —
  The patriot Ishmael Day.

One Monday morn, at early dawn,
  The hour when good men pray,
A rebel host, with threats and boast,
  Came on to scare old Day.

He soon had word — the noise he heard
  In the distance far away —
That Gilmore's men were coming then
  To capture Ishmael Day.

"That's what's the matter — O, what a clatter!
  I'll keep them awhile at bay,
Till I hoist my flag, of which I brag,"
  Said the brave old Ishmael Day.

On rushed the crowd with curses loud,
  Begrimed with dust and gray;
"My flag I'll nail to the garden pale,
  And die by it," said Day.

The thieving horde came down the road —
  They had no time to stay.
"Our flag is here — touch it who dare!"
  Shouted old Ishmael Day.

A trooper rushed, with whiskey flushed,
  Swore he'd take that rag away.
"Let any man dare try that plan,
  I'll shoot him," says old Day.

He feared the cock of his old flint-lock
  Might miss, so this prayer did say:
That a load of duck-shot might pepper him hot
  By the hands of Ishmael Day.

On the raider came — old Day was game;
  Reb swore that flag shouldn't stay;
With a curse and a frown, cried, "Down with it,
  down!"
  Bang! blazed away Ishmael Day.

Flint-lock he could trust, for down in the dust
  The traitorous rebel lay,
Crying, "Spare my life, I'm tired of this strife."
  "So am I," said Ishmael Day.

Now let each loyal heart in our cause take a part,
  Do his duty, watch, fight, and pray;
Shoulder his gun, stand by, never run,
  And imitate Ishmael Day.

Then we boldly say, a few men like Day,
  With guns, ammunition at hand,
We need not be afraid of Gilmore's next raid
  On the soil of " My Maryland."

I now close my song, for fear it's too long;
  On this subject I could much more say;
Let us all shout hosanna to the Star-spangled
  Banner,
  And hurrah for brave Ishmael Day.

INCIDENT OF WILLIAMSBURG. — During the battle, one of the Louisiana Tigers went up to one of the wounded Union soldiers, who played dead for fear of being bayoneted, and commenced searching his pockets, when a Tennessee soldier came up, and saying to him, "Will you rob a dead man?" shot him dead on the spot. Another rebel came up to a wounded soldier, and was in the act of bayoneting him, when another rebel came up, and knocked the fellow down with his musket, and gave the soldier a drink from his canteen. In bringing in a boat load of wounded rebels from Williamsburg, a rebel swore that he would kill every Yankee he saw, if he could, and threw a large knife at one of the doctors, injuring him slightly, when the doctor drew his revolver and shot him through the heart.

THE GLORY OF PHILADELPHIA. — An accomplished and brilliant woman gives the following account of that noble institution in Philadelphia, the Volunteer Refreshment Saloon, in a letter dated October, 1861:
"On Thursday last I spent a day, that, if I live, I hope many a time to describe to my grand-nieces and nephews. Emily and I were sitting knitting by our cheery glass door, through which a warm October sun was pouring a flood of red, and yellow, and purple light, when we heard two cannons fired. It was a signal that soldiers were to pass through the city. By the same impulse, Emily and I both proposed that we should go down and see them land, and be entertained at the Volunteer Refreshment Saloon. Off we started, on the spur of the moment, went down to

Helen's a recruiting — got her to join us — took the cars, and soon found ourselves at the corner of Prince and Front Streets, where the Refreshment Saloon stands.

"When we entered, we were met by a dapper, smart little man — a real handsome fellow — looking very much like ———, such beautiful features and bright eyes. He belonged to the class of mechanics, but, with our American facility, had picked up most excellent manners and address. We asked whether we had properly interpreted the signal of firing the cannons, and if a regiment were shortly expected. It appeared we had made a mistake, the firing we heard being in another direction, where they were trying the range of a new piece. However, a regiment was expected in the afternoon, and two during the evening. Our dapper friend invited us to look over the establishment. But let me stop a minute to give you some little account of what the Volunteer Refreshment Saloon is. When the war first broke out, and thousands and tens of thousands of soldiers were passing through our city daily, we found there was great deficiency of means of providing an immediate meal for them. Sometimes they would have to wait for hours, sometimes go away hungry. In Southwark, some dozen or so of the women joined heads and purses, and put up a little street corner refreshment place, just boards propped up against the sides of the houses, where they served hot coffee and other things, as they could afford it, free of charge to the soldiers, as they landed at the foot of Prime Street to proceed to the Baltimore depot. The thanks and blessings of the weary and hungry soldiers, who went away refreshed, incited these patriotic women to renewed efforts, and the thing has taken form and system. I will describe it to you as our little friend showed it to us, with many a bow and flourish, last Thursday. We entered a long, low room, rather poor-looking, and with marks of partitions having been knocked away to make it. In it were ranged, along the whole length, five long tables, about breast high, so that the soldiers might conveniently stand and eat. These were neatly spread with a white cloth, and set with plates, tin cups, castors, &c. At the upper end of the room were two rather handsomely laid tables for the officers. In this room they make a spread for five hundred at one time. The scrupulous cleanliness and neatness of the whole strike you. From the eating-room we went into the larder and cooking-room. In the larder we saw abundance of ham, corned beef, fresh mutton and beef, cheese, pickles, cold slaw, and most beautiful butter and bread, sweet potatoes, tomatoes — in short, all the vegetables of the season. Everything the very best of its kind. Up stairs is a retiring room, where they take any sick or wounded. There are comfortable lounges all around it, and in the middle a table with writing materials, and envelopes all ready stamped, if any one wants to despatch a letter. There is a bed or two, if any become sick and want to be nursed a day or two before rejoining their company. Now, remember this thing is wholly the work of the *middle class Southwark women*. There are now about twenty men and twenty-five women who are actively employed in it. Only one person is a paid employee. All the others' labor is voluntary. The young man, who was our guide, said that he had been at work since three o'clock in the night, and did not expect to get any rest until after midnight, as they had three thousand men to give supper to. It works on this wise: they take turns among themselves for one man and one woman to remain all day on the spot. When they receive a despatch that a regiment is coming, a cannon is fired as a signal, and within half an hour every member is bound to make his appearance, or send a substitute, never mind what hour of day or night it is. Well! we were so interested and stirred up by the sight of so much patriotism, that we determined to return in the evening, and see a thousand New Hampshire boys take their supper. When we were going out, I said to our bright and hearty little guide, 'Now you people must remember all you are doing, and write it down, for it will make an interesting page in history one day.' 'Why, miss, that is just what I'm thinking myself. When one thing or another happens, I say to myself, I'll remember that, and maybe when I'm an old man, and they're making books about it, I can help them to a thing or two.' Then he went on to tell two or three incidents of some poor little boys in the neighborhood who set to work picking and selling chips till they had five dollars to give for the soldiers; and of a little five-year old boy, whose mother had given him a ten-cent piece for the Fourth of July. *Five* he laid out in irresistible fire-crackers, the other five he came and offered to feed the soldiers. The committee laid by that five-cent piece, and intend to keep it.

"In the afternoon, Doctor and Sallie, Matty, Emily, and myself, made a party, and went down there again. What a hive it was, to be sure! Nice young girls, and plump, hearty *materfamilias* bustling about with meat and cheese, and all good things, a real tempting meal. And O! the coffee: the delicious aroma almost brought tears to the eyes of us outsiders, who had to content ourselves with the smell alone.

"By and by, after a half hour's waiting, a signal gun was fired, and the cry, 'They come! They come!' went forth from mouth to mouth. Sarah, I can't give you any idea of the intense excitement and enthusiasm of that moment — the tapping of the drum; the tramp, tramp, tramp; the ringing order, "Halt;" and then they began filing in, company by company, in perfect quiet and order, ranging themselves along the table, till the great room was one dense mass of soldiers; unless you were here, and had caught the enthusiasm of our war spirit, you cannot know how the sight of a thousand armed men moves one. I wanted to embrace the whole regiment. I wanted to put my hands on their heads and bless them. I wanted to beat the drum, and sing, 'Hail Columbia.' I wanted to turn myself inside out, generally, and not being able to do any of these things,

I shed some tears on my bonnet strings, much to their detriment, and rushed off and gave five dollars, that I don't know how I can possibly spare. Sarah, they were a magnificent looking set of men. Never tell me the Yankees are an ugly race, after seeing those five hundred handsome New Hampshire boys. They were mostly farmers, and scarcely a small man among them. You never saw so quiet and orderly a meal; no indecent haste or snatching, no raised voice or word of swearing; perfect courtesy to the women, in most cases turning to thank them before leaving. They were supplied with newspapers, while eating, and it was remarkable to see how many made haste to finish and have a few minutes to read their papers. I do not believe there was ever such an intelligent army in the world as ours. Our farmers, our mechanics, the very bone and sinew of our nation, are going forth, intelligently and determinedly, to fight the cause of freedom against slavery, liberty against tyranny, civilization against barbarism.

"Let me wind up my rather long description by saying that these people have fed one hundred and twenty thousand soldiers, and that it takes one hundred dollars to each thousand, and supported entirely by voluntary subscription. One more remark and I have done. I never wished more heartily than at that blessed moment to be a mother, and then I wished for six big sons, that I might send them all to fight their country's battles. I even gave vent to the sentiment in a way that shocked some of my auditory. I had been looking long and admiringly at a very handsome six-foot youth, an officer. He was very like —— ——, only even handsomer, with a clear, pure, truthful face. He ate with a hearty, manly appetite, and when risen from the table, shook hands with two or three common-looking Southwark dames, in a respectful, courteous way, just as gracefully as —— —— would have done it, saying, 'I thank you, ladies; I thank you for your hospitality.' I could not help exclaiming, 'I wish that boy were my son.' I am glad that I am living history. It is a fine thing to read it, but a far better thing to *live* history. I am going to do everything I can, and connect myself as much as possible with what I believe to be a great *era* in our history. I should be disappointed to die before I saw it through. They are going to open the Girard House as a hospital here, and if I can possibly get —— —— to accede to it, and I can make satisfactory arrangements, I shall go as a volunteer nurse. In Baltimore the nurses have a uniform, — a black or brown merino dress, tight sleeves, no hoops, tiny linen collar and cuffs, and a white tarleton cap. Wouldn't that be 'cute'? Imagine me flying around with a little tarleton cap on, reading and doing the sentimental part of the nursing — soothing their brows — and grapes — and jelly — and talking about their mothers, and so on.

"What do you think! —— ——; —— the elegant; —— of the club, and red mustache, has been doing. Forgive me ——, if I have ever done thee any injustice, even in my thoughts. I do revere thee now. Seriously, —— has been doing the work of a hero. You know he has a gem of a little house up in —— Place, so elegantly furnished, where he watches over his little children like a mother. Well, —— could not leave his little brood to go to the war; so all summer long he has sought out sick and wounded soldiers, taken them to his house, and there nursed them. All his beds have been filled, and during the summer he has nursed about a hundred men. There, who will say that war does not develop fine virtues? You have heard, of course, that I am taking care of my country's toes, corns, and bunions, in the way of knitting stockings. I have sent ninety pairs to the Quartermaster, four knit by my own fingers. I have one hundred and ten pairs out, in process of being knit. I am going to accomplish four hundred before I begin anything else. Helen is employed in collecting luxuries for the hospitals — jellies, farina, gelatin, &c. She will despatch a large box to-morrow, and still expects enough material for another. So you see we are all, according to our ability, spending and being spent for our dear old mother country.

. . . . .

"One word more for our country, and I have done. We are at our wits' ends for blankets. With five hundred thousand men under arms in the Northern States, it is no easy thing to provide them all with blankets; and as this is no wool-growing country, there is no store or supply to fall back upon. Government has put forth stirring appeals to the loyal women to come to the rescue, and give or sell their hoards of household blankets to the army: you may be sure this was generously responded to; and yet there is great and pressing need. Many women I know have cut up their drugget and half worn ingrain carpets, bound them, and sent them off. I do believe the generosity of this people, now and here, has no parallel in history. Helen sent two pairs of good bed blankets, and my sisters out at Darley (you know their limited means) sent ten — almost all they possessed. I mean to send some drugget. I can't well send my only two pairs of blankets, as they are old rose relics. If the need continues, however, I shall make the sacrifice. You understand it is no little economy in Government. It is because there is not enough wool in the country. Money cannot get them; so they must be got for love. Now, my darling, you can perhaps perceive what my hobby is now. If you were here, you would be *death on patriotism* too. Dr. Boardman's church is the very head of all good works for the country; you would find it would cost as much labor and money to keep up with them, as travelling among the Alps does. . . . Do you know, Sarah, it is *fashionable* here to be traitorous; not exactly to say, I am a secessionist, but to call one's self a 'peace man' — an anti-administration man — just as in the days of the Revolution it was fashionable to be Tories. It is the legitimate offspring of the spirit of trade, whose cry is, 'Give us prosperity; only give us prosperity in our day, and *après nous le déluge.*' It is willing that the South should pull our noses, and that all nations under heaven should spit in our faces for cowards, rather than have wealth and trade, ease and comfort, interfered with. It is only in the great cities, and among the wealthy, that you meet this demoralization. Throughout the country, and among the great middle classes, patriotism is warm and earnest. . . . We had a stirring talk last night at —— ——, on the times. We there all believed that the North was too backward about facing the subject of slavery. We have been in the habit so long of protecting it, and of so hating the word *Abolitionist*, that now we are afraid to face the great question that Providence is thrusting upon us. We are willing to kill our white brethren, if need be, burn their cities, and yet are squeamish about their slave property. We acknowledge it to be an evil, and a burden to the land; and yet, in this time of great uprooting and regeneration, we are *afraid* to say this thing shall be purged away. Mr. —— said he believed there was a special Providence in our panic at Bull Run; that if we had been victorious, and taken Richmond, and patched a hasty peace, we would have shirked the whole question — skinned over the cancer that would have broken out again. W—— said that he thought Providence had taken the whole matter out of the hands of man, and by showing the world the necessity of growing cotton elsewhere, had given the death-blow to slavery. When the American cotton King is deposed, Cuffee is free."

COLONEL MONTGOMERY'S ESCAPE. — The following story of the escape of Colonel Montgomery from the Confederate authorities at Vicksburg, was given by him at the Union League Rooms at Washington, in April, 1864: —

"One year ago last November I was in jail in Vicksburg, condemned to be shot. I escaped one day; I ran home to my wife and little ones. It was about noon; a train would leave the city at three o'clock. I told my wife to pack up our trunks, and we must go. She packed them, and sent them to the depot by a negro, and then followed with our little girl, and boy, while I went around outside the town, met the train going through a cut, jumped aboard, and all went well till we got to Holly Springs. I must go to Memphis, fifty miles, and no railroad, and most of the way through rebel pickets. I must get a pass and a conveyance if I could. I went to the General's office; he was away, but his Adjutant was there, and said it was of no use to ask for a pass; if I was Jefferson Davis' son, and had my mother with me, I could not be passed in that direction. I talked with him about other things; I asked him down to take a drink. He drank, and I talked. I told him how many adjutants I had known, and what smart men they were, and that I thought him the smartest of all, and was sure, when his merits were known, he would be at the head of all the adjutants in the Confederacy. The General came at last, and the Adjutant begged him to grant a pass to this *very particular* friend

of his, to take his wife and children to Memphis and *return*. I was particular about the return. He gave the pass, but it did not cover a conveyance, and there was none to be had. Then the telegraph brought news of my escape, and orders to have me sent back to be shot. The Adjutant had the order, and he told me to *git*. Do you know what *git* means? Well, I tell you, in such a case it means to — *git!* The Adjutant had indorsed me as his friend; he was afraid he had his foot in, so he wanted me to *git*, and I *did*. My wife made a bundle of what clothes the children must have. I put it on my back, took my little boy by the hand, she took the little girl, and we started on foot for Memphis. It was a day of scorching heat; the thermometer above 90°; the burning sand six inches deep; my little ones both barefooted; my little boy with no hat; and my wife with only thin-soled slippers on, worth about forty cents, but for which I paid ten dollars hard cash. There was no getting out of that burning sun and burning sand; and, as we went on, O my God! the screams of those little children! the red, fiery streaks ran up their white ankles; every step was agony, and every breath. We dragged them on. Every moment we expected to hear the couriers behind, coming for me. My wife and little girl were before me, the little boy was too young to keep up with them. At every rise of ground my wife would turn and look to see if a messenger were coming for me. One time, as she stood so, my little boy reached her, his poor feet all red and blistered, his curls matted to his head with perspiration, with both hands clinging to her dress, and his dusty, tearful face lifted to hers, he cried out, 'O mamma, can't you see our home now?'

"So we went on all one day. At night we stopped at an overseer's house, where we were permitted to stay. They were poor, but kind. A bed was made on the floor for us, but the agony the children suffered was so great they could not sleep, exhausted as they were. We bound their little feet in cloths, and I sat by all night to keep them wet with cold water; then they could sleep. If in my stupor and exhaustion I chanced to forget myself, their shrieks quickly wakened me again. In the morning we had to start; there was no staying here. Those poor little feet, burnt all day and soaked all night, looked as if they had been parboiled; yet blistered as they were, swollen till shapeless, and streaked with red and purple and blue, they must go into that burning sand again. O my God! my God! those cries! will thine avenging angel gather up the tears that bedewed that fiery path, tears from those helpless little ones in their awful agony! [He covered his face with his hand an instant, and then resumed.] But we dragged them on! I don't know how it happened that I did not notice when the little hand slipped from mine, but, from whatever distraction of mind I was in, I was startled by a shriek that is ringing in my ears yet, and looking back I saw my little boy lying in the sand in the road behind me. He could not walk another step, and thought I had left him to die. I put my pack over on one shoulder, and laid him across the other with his burning cheek to mine, and his hot breath fanning my face. His mother and sister had gone on, and were sitting on the grass under a tree waiting for us. Little Freddy saw them, and said:

"'Papa, do mamma and sister see our home now?'

"I said, 'Yes.'

"'Well,' said he, 'if Ponto sees them, he'll know I'm coming, and he'll run past them, and I'll call him, and get on his back, and ride home, and then you won't have to carry me — will you, papa?' Ponto was a great dog we had at home.

"I laid the child down on the grass beside his mother; she told me then that she could go no farther. There we were. Presently my wife saw a cloud of dust in the distance. I saw it too.

"'It is the courier coming for you,' she said. 'He will take you from us; and what will become of you? what will become of us?'

"I looked and saw that the man was in a small buggy — just room enough for him and me — no provision for my family. My poor wife was on her knees. Her face was white as marble, and cold. She was trying to pray, but she only repeated over and over again, 'O my God! O my God!' Not another word would come. I put my hand on her shoulder, and said, 'My dear, there is but *one* man, and no *one man* takes me from you to-day!'

"The man in the buggy drove up. He stopped and looked at us. Said he, 'I see you are travelling.' 'No, sir,' said I; 'travelling and I have quit.' 'Well, you don't live hereabouts.' 'No.' 'What is your name?' 'Montgomery.'

"He looked at the feet of my little ones, lying on the grass. 'Have those children got the small pox?' 'No.' 'The measles?' 'No.' 'Well, what have they got?' 'My dear sir, they have got just as near nothing as it is possible for a human being to get.' I found he was the rebel mail carrier. I showed him my pass, and asked what he would charge to take my wife and children through the lines. He said, 'Fifty dollars in gold.' My wife and her mother had saved fifty dollars in gold, and fifty cents in silver, all of which I had, and it was all. I put my wife in the seat beside him, the little boy in her lap, the little girl at her feet, my bundle under the seat, gave the man the fifty dollars in gold, put the fifty cents in my pocket, and they drove off. I followed. When I came to a picket, I showed my pass, and asked about the buggy. The answer was always, 'Yes; the mail carrier, with a woman and two children, went by about an hour and a half ago, and reported a man coming with a pass covering the woman and children. All right.' I went on. At last I asked, 'How many more picket stations are there?' 'Only one.' 'How far is it?' 'Three miles.' 'That is the last?' 'Yes.' I had on such boots as the slaves wear. I had paid thirty dollars for them, and I made them earn every cent of the money in that three miles. I came in sight of

the picket so soon that I was frightened. I thought of the telegraph wires. What might they not have told before this? Who knew but that man held my life in his hands? There was no help for it. I walked up to him as he sat on his horse, and handed up my pass, and asked about the buggy. Yes, it had gone by an hour and a half ago. But why did the man not give me back my pass? Would he never be done reading it? — or, instead of giving it back, would he level his pistol and shoot me? There I stood, on the border of Rebeldom. The United States was before me — the free, glorious United States, and wife and little ones; and what was behind? O God! would the man never be done reading that little scrap of writing? That flag, our flag was before me, and freedom. My heart beat so loud I was afraid the man would hear it. I tried to stir. Was he reaching down his hand to shoot me? No; it was only to give back the pass, as he said, 'All right!' and I was a free man again — free, and in the United States, and under the flag of stars! I was not long in getting to St. Louis with my family. We walked the streets of that city barefooted. There was a political meeting that night — a republican one. I happened in. The chances are that something was said. The next morning the copperhead paper stated that there was such a meeting, and that it was entertained by the blatant ravings of a southern renegade. That meant me. Since then, I have been in many of your Northern cities and States, and without a pass. Here is the difference: at the South you cannot turn round, cross the street, kiss your wife, or go to market, without a pass. Here, where Abraham Lincoln tyrannizes like a military despot, — where he usurps all the people's rights and puts them in his pocket, — every one can go where he pleases, like sheep without a shepherd. Jeff Davis takes better care of the liberties of his people!

"Now I must say a word about that little wife of mine. I am going to take her home to die! [Here the tears almost choked his utterance; but he crushed them back, and went on. His simple, touching narrative had already brought tears to many eyes, and there was scarcely a dry one in that crowded room.] Yes, I am going to take her home to die! The doctors have told us she cannot live long, and she wants to die and be buried among her own people; so we are going. The ladies of one of your Northern cities have given her a beautiful silk flag — a flag with all the stripes and all the stars upon it. We will take that with us, and if our old home is standing, the flag shall float above it. If it is not standing, then we will plant the flag upon its ruins, or over the place where it once was; and as we sit beneath its folds, we will think, with tears of gratitude, of all the kindness of these free and happy Northern people to the wandering, homeless refugees."

A WHITE SOLDIER, at the camp of the Fifteenth regiment of colored troops, in Nashville, Tenn., while deprecating the employment of negroes as soldiers, boasted that he could make the grand rounds on the colored boys, and capture a musket or bayonet. Accordingly, he approached a sable guard, drew him into conversation, and kindly requested to see his musket, which the guard refused. He then wished to look at his bayonet, but the guard stood on his orders. He then tried intimidation, and, pretending to be insulted, assumed a fighting attitude; but the guard ordered him to retire or he would shoot. The foolish fellow advanced, and was promptly shot, and the loss of an arm was the penalty of his imprudence.

HUMORS OF THE CAMP. — A soldier at the headquarters of the artillery brigade of the Fifth corps, at Culpepper, Va., gives the following account of the amusements in camp:

"Almost the only diversion the soldiers have nowadays, is derived from the new recruits, constantly arriving. They are the butt of all jokes, and the easy prey of all sells and tricks. No class of men enjoy fun more heartily than the soldiers. They squeeze sport out of everything, and seem to have acquired the faculty of ascertaining, intuitively, where most of it is to be found. On drill, a new recruit is always sure to get his toes exactly where a 'Vet.' wishes to put the butt of his musket, as he 'orders arms;' and if there is a mud-puddle within a yard of him, he is sure to 'dress' into it. Captain Reynolds, of Battery 'S,' First New York artillery, has got a large number of new recruits, and some of the jokes that the Veterans play on them are very amusing. The recruits are constantly sighing over departed luxuries, and are very easily duped into any sell, where the inner man is concerned. A mischievous 'Vet.' got a whole squad of them out in line the other day, when it was raining quite hard, to receive their ration of 'warm bread.' One fellow, greener than the rest, was sent to the Captain's quarters for his 'ticket for *butter*.' Another one went to the Company Clerk with a two-quart pail for his 'three days' ration of *maple sugar*.' Some of them have very funny ideas of discipline in the army. In a newly arrived squad, a few days since, was one of these, who thought he would ingratiate himself with the Captain by making him a call in the evening. Accordingly, he rapped at the door, walked in, took off his hat, made a very low bow, and replaced his hat on his head.

"'Well, what do *you* want?' said the Captain.

"'O, nothing,' says the fellow, at the same time seating himself in a chair opposite the Captain. 'I thought I would come down and have a little chat with you.'

"'O, that's it,' said the Captain. 'Well, that isn't the way they do in the army. When a soldier comes into an officer's quarters, he takes off his hat and stands at "attention," with his heels together, his toes at an angle of forty-five degrees, hands at his side, and eyes to the "front." He does not take a seat unless *asked* to, and

when he has done his business, salutes the officer, makes an "about face," and — *leaves*.'

"The fellow did not wait for further instructions, but took his departure, having received his first lesson in the 'school of the soldier.'"

In repartee and fun our soldiers are not behind any class of men living, and they have a most keen appreciation of the ludicrous and sarcastic. Chapman tells a good story:

"A few days ago, two soldiers were sentenced, for some trivial offence, to ten days in the guardhouse; but they were taken out occasionally to do police duty about camp. Doing police duty, you must know, is not in the army what it is in the city; but consists in going about under guard and cleaning up the camp. These soldiers were put to cleaning away the mud from the front of the Colonel's quarters. They were from a New York city regiment, and to judge from their dialect, might have been named Mose and Sykesy. At any rate, I shall call them so in the recital. They had worked well, and finally seated themselves on a log to await the arrival of the Sergeant of the Guard to relieve them, when the following conversation took place:

"Mose — 'Say, Sykesy, what you going to do when yer three years up? Goin' to be a Vet.? Say.'

"Sykesy — 'Not if I know myself, I ain't; no! I'm goin' to be a citizen, I am. I'm goin' back to New York, and am goin' to lay off and take comfort, bum around the engine-house, and run wid der machine.'

"Mose — 'Well, I tell yer what I'm agoin' to do. I've jest been thinkin' the matter all over, and got the whole thing fixed. In the first place, I'm goin' home to New York, and as soon as I get my discharge, I'm goin' to take a good bath, and get this Virginia sacred soil off me. Then I'm goin' to have my head shampooed, my hair cut and combed forward and 'iled, and then I'm goin' to some up-town clothing store, and buy me a suit of togs. I'm agoin' to get a gallus suit, too — black breeches, red shirt, black silk choker, stove-pipe hat, with black bombazine around it, and a pair of them shiny butes. Then I'm goin' up to Delmonico's place, and am goin' for to order der best dinner he can get up. I'm goin' to have all he has on his dinner ticket, you can bet. What? No! I guess I won't have a gay old dinner, much; for I'll be a citizen then, and won't have to break my teeth off gnawin' hard tack. After I've had my dinner, I will call for a bottle of wine and a cigar, and all the New York papers, and then I'll jest set down, perch my feet up on the table, drink my wine, smoke my cigar, read the news, and wonder why the devil the army of the Potomac don't move.'"

SCENES IN THE HOSPITAL. — The editor of The American Wesleyan relates the following as a portion of his experience among the wounded in the hospitals:

"Not long since I was called to witness the

following, which I will call ' *The Dying Soldier's Dream of Childhood.*'

"He was brought in mortally wounded, although by a false feeling of kindness one or two of the surgeons told him his wound was severe, but not dangerous. I thought it my duty to undeceive him; and so, sitting down beside his lowly pallet, and taking his hand in mine while I brushed back the dark curls from his high, open brow, I tried to lead him easily into such a channel of conversation as I desired. I had not conversed long with him when he suddenly inquired what I thought of his prospects of recovery. Rather avoiding for the time giving a direct answer, I inquired how he felt himself in regard to that matter. He answered with considerable hesitation, that the surgeons told him he would get along nicely; but that he himself felt afraid that he would never recover. I noticed, too, that his lips quivered, and he drew a long, deep sigh. Then he turned his youthful, open face full upon me; he sighed again; there was a choking, fluttering sensation which told the intensity of his feelings, and he said, 'If I was only at home!' Poor boy! Many a hill, and valley, and mountain gorge, and broad river, lay between him and his home! And the loving ones there were all unconscious of his deep distress; and even before his name would appear in the list of killed and wounded of some daily paper, he would already be 'where the wicked cease from troubling, and the weary are at rest.' I spoke to him of the tender sympathy of the infinite Father, of the all-sufficient Savior, who was wounded for our transgressions and bruised for our iniquities, and how that a full and free salvation was offered to all through the death and sufferings of the Lord Jesus. I could not get him to say much, and so, after praying with him, I left him for a time. In a few hours I called to see him again, and in the course of conversation endeavored to press home the momentous truths of salvation. At last he opened his mind freely, told me he thought he was once a Christian, that he sought an interest in Christ when a boy, and felt happy in the belief that he loved the Savior — that his happiest hours were spent in the Sunday school, and that he used to take delight in prayer and reading the Scriptures. 'I remember, too,' said he, 'how my father prayed — O Chaplain! I had a good father — he's in heaven now — how he prayed for *me*, that I might always be good. I remember the night that he died — and how happy he was, and how he sung "On Jordan's stormy banks I stand," and how he put his hand on my head and told me to serve God and meet him in heaven. O, if I was as good as my father was, it would be better with me now! I have forgotten my promises, I have turned my back on Christ. What shall I do? what shall I do? I'm dying — I know I'm dying, and I am afraid to die! O Jesus, have mercy on me a sinner!'

"I did not interrupt him till he had given full and free vent to his feelings, and then tried to point him to the all-sufficient Savior.

"' Do you think God will have mercy on my poor soul?' he exclaimed in such a piteous tone of voice and with such genuine earnestness, that my own feelings nearly overcame me, and I could barely say, 'Yes, dear brother, God is ready *now* to bless you, to forgive you all your sins, and make you happy in the enjoyment of his love.'

"' But I have neglected prayer and backslidden from God; I sinned against light and knowledge; I knew better, Chaplain, I knew better, for my conscience troubled me; it was God's Spirit striving with me, — yes, I knew better, for I once loved Jesus. O Jesus, have mercy on a poor sinner!'

"' Hear God's own answer to your question,' said I. "If any man sin, we have an Advocate with the Father, Jesus Christ the righteous; and He is the propitiation for our sins, and not for ours only, but also for the sins of the whole world." "God so loved the world that He gave His only-begotten Son, that whosoever believeth in him might not perish, but have everlasting life." Now, these words are as much addressed to you as if there were not another sinner upon earth. Take them as God's own words to yourself, and remember that that dear Savior whom you say that you once served, loves you yet, loves you now, and is yearning over you with the deepest sympathy. He waits to take away the heavy burden from your heart, and give you joy and peace in believing. Just come back as a poor wanderer, weary and helpless; and remember you are coming to your own God and Savior, who knows just what you need, and how you feel, and is more willing to receive you and forgive you than you are to return to him.'

"' O, if I was just as happy as I once was! but now I'm here wounded and dying — and O, this awful pain — what will I do — what will I do — Jesus, Jesus, what will I do!' he exclaimed in the deepest agony of body and mind.

"' Believe on the Lord Jesus Christ, cast your poor troubled soul upon the Savior, just place yourself as a poor helpless sinner in His hands, and you will be saved,' said I, trying to lead his mind to the one only source of comfort.

"The agony of this poor boy was terrible. His pitiful groans sunk into my very heart, and made me feel as if I was entirely powerless to do him good.

"Sometimes it was difficult to tell whether his bodily or mental anguish was greater. Frequently the deep, agonizing groan of bodily pain would end in a most pathetic cry for mercy, or a child-like petition to be received into the favor of his heavenly Father. Sometimes he turned upon me such a pitiful, helpless look, such a look as a drowning child might cast towards its mother; a look of unutterable meaning, but which plainly said, 'I'm dying, — won't you help me?' Seeing that to all appearance he was rapidly sinking, I urged him to accept the free offer of reconciliation to God through the atonement of Christ, and after again praying with him, I left him for a little time. An hour, perhaps, had elapsed, when I again was beside him. The first words he uttered were:

" 'I'm trying to come back to God, and I think that he will not cast me off; but I'm afraid.'

" 'I am going to ask you one question,' said I; 'but you must not answer it till you think over it. It is this: Do you think that God loves you?'

" He seemed to ponder the question a little, and then answered, —

" 'I think — I think He does.'

" 'Yes,' I said, 'He loves you dearly, and sympathizes with you in your great distress, and is so very anxious for your soul's salvation that He is waiting even now, this moment, to forgive you all your sins and make you happy in His love. Can you not take your own heavenly Father's word, that "whosoever believeth on the Lord Jesus Christ shall be saved!" Just trust in him; just throw yourself as you are, — a poor, helpless sinner, — into His hands, and you will be saved.'

" 'Is that all I'm to do?' said he, musingly; 'and yet what else can I do? Yes, yes; I think I see it all; I have been afraid to trust in the promises of God, I feel myself to be so unworthy; but now, Jesus, Savior, I come to thee, a poor, helpless sinner.

> "Here, Lord, I give myself to thee —
> 'Tis all that I can do."

Yes, Lord, it is all that I can do!'

" Then followed a scene I shall never forget to my dying day. It was night. The temporary hospital was in an old, dark, dingy house. The candle burned dimly, and seemed, by its flickering, uncertain light, to make the gloomy surroundings all the more gloomy. The poor mangled soldier boy lay rolling uneasily from side to side. Large drops of cold sweat stood like beads on his open brow. A quivering sensation seemed to pass through every nerve and fibre of his body; and there was a long, deep, shivering sigh, which told of the very extremity of mortal anguish. His large bright eye grew dim, and seemed as if looking up from a great depth; and that mysterious change of color and feature took place, which tells that the wheels of life are about to stand still. Suddenly he threw out his arms and clasped me tightly round the neck as I stooped over him, and exclaimed, 'What shall I do, O Chaplain, what shall I do?'

" 'Put your trust in Christ, your own Savior, who died for you,' I replied.

" 'I do believe in Jesus,' he said, 'and I think He will save me; yes, He will save me! But O, what is this? am I dying now? Tell me, am I dying?'

" 'Yes, you are dying, dear brother,' I answered; 'you will soon be in the spirit world. Is Jesus near you? Have you peace of mind?'

" 'It's all over now,' he whispered. 'God has, for Christ's sake, forgiven me, a poor sinner; and he will take me to himself. Good by, Chaplain; good by.'

" He fell into a kind of stupor, or what might be called an uneasy slumber, and I sat by his side waiting and watching. He dreamed. He seemed to be again at home, mingling with loved ones, for he whispered the name of mother. Then he seemed to be praying, as if, a child again, he knelt at a parent's knee and repeated his evening prayer. I stooped over him and listened attentively to every whisper. At last I caught a few disjointed sentences, as follows: 'Our Father — who art — this night — I lay me — down — O Jesus — my Savior — take me — to heaven. Hallowed be — thy name —' There was then a pause, and a deep sigh. The angel of death had come! The golden bowl was broken, and the wheel stood still at the cistern! Poor mangled sufferer! he had found Christ; and his dream of childhood's devotions gave place, we trust, to the brighter visions of glory and the songs of salvation!"

CONFEDERATE SONG OF FREEDOM.

BY EMILY M. WASHINGTON.

MARCH on, ye children of the brave —
Descendants of the free!
On to the hero's bloody grave,
  Or glorious liberty!
    On, on — with clashing sword and drum;
    The foe! — they come! they come! — strike home!
For more than safety, or for life, —
For more than mother, child, or wife,
    Strike home for Liberty!

Charge, charge! nor shed the pitying tear;
  Too long hath mercy plead!
Charge, charge! and share the hero's bier,
  Or strike the foeman dead!
    Charge, charge! for more than vital gains,
    Strike home, and rend the freeman's chains;
For more than safety, or for life, —
For more than mother, child, or wife,
    Strike home for Liberty!

Draw, draw — by every hope this hour
  That animates the brave!
Draw! — strike! — and rend the foeman's power,
  Or fill the patriot's grave!
    Strike — die — or conquer with the free!
    Strike home, strike home for Liberty!
For more than glory, safety, life, —
For more than mother, child, or wife,
    Strike home for Liberty!

COLONEL GILLEM was one day reprimanding one of his soldiers, who was slightly intoxicated at the time. After the Colonel had concluded, the soldier remarked, "Yez wuddint have occasion to talk to me so ef I had a pistol." The Colonel, much astonished, asked, "Well, sir, what would you do if you had a pistol?" "Why, I'd shoot — myself, sir."

"OUR RIGHTS." — The following conversation occurred at Normandy, Tennessee, between a Confederate prisoner, captured at Knoxville, and the correspondent of a Northern paper:

"Are you going to take the oath?"

"No; I'll rot in prison first."

"What are you fighting for?"

"Our rights."

"What are your rights?"

"Well," — hesitating, and attempting to clear his throat, — "well, I can't 'xactly tell yer; the fact is, I can't read; but there's them that *does* know."

A NEGRO'S PRAYER. — The following is a prayer offered by a colored man at a funeral, and reported by Dr. Calkins, Surgeon of a Mass. regiment:

"Massa Jesus, like de people ob de ole time, de Jews, we weep by de side ob de ribber, wid de strings ob de harp all broke; but we sing ob de broken heart, as dem people could not do. Hear us, King, in de present state ob our sorrow. You know, King Jesus, honey, we just got from de Red Sea, and wander in de wilderness, a poor, feeble portion ob de children ob Adam, feeble in body, feeble in mind, and need de help ob de good Almighty God. O, help us, if you please, to homes, for we's got no homes, Massa Jesus, but de shelter ob de oak tree in de daytime, and de shelter ob de cotton tent at night. Help us for our own good and de good of God's blessed Union people, dat want all people free, whatsomebber be de color. Massa Jesus, you know de deep tribulations ob our hearts, dat sickness is among us, dat our children is dyin' in de camp; and as we tote 'em from one place to tudder, and bury dem in de cold ground, to go in spirit to de God ob de people whar de soul hab no spot nor color. Great King ob Kings, and Doctor ob Doctors, and God ob battles! help us to be well; help us to be able to fight wid de Union sogers de battle for de Union; help us to fight for liberty, fight for de country, fight for our own homes, and our own free children, and our children's children. Fotch out, God ob battles, de big guns wid de big bustin' shells, and gib dem God-forsaken secesh, dat would carry to shame our wives and daughters. O, mighty Jesus! if you please, a right smart charge ob grape and canister; make 'em glad to stop de war and come back to shoes and de fatted calf, and de good tings ob de Union. No more murderin' brudder ob de Norf States. No more ragged, bare feet. No more slave-whippers and slave-sellers. No more faders ob yellow skins. No more meaner as meanest niggers."

A CLASSIC SOLDIER. — A Lieutenant in the Twelfth Indiana relates the following:

Being out on a scout with a squad of his men, and becoming fatigued, they stopped at a house to see if they could get some buttermilk to drink. In their squad was a young man who had been highly educated, but who had become dissipated before entering the army, and had the appearance of one very low in life. When they entered the house, there were two young ladies sitting in the room, very busily engaged in reading, and did not seem to take any notice of them whatever. After getting their buttermilk, the young man, supposed to be an ignoramus, walked to one of the ladies, and very politely asked her what book she was

reading. Thinking his question impertinent, she indignantly replied, "You would not know, if I should tell you." "That may be true," says he; "still, I would like very much if you would tell me." "Well," says she, "if you must know, I am reading Virgil." "Ah! Virgil! And how do you like it?" "Very well; but I have come to a hard, knotty sentence here, that I cannot translate." "Well, perhaps I can assist you about it, if you will allow me." "You assist me! It is Latin that I am reading!" "Very well, miss. Will you be so kind as to let me see if I cannot assist you with it?" Somewhat softened by his kind and gentlemanly manner, she handed him the book, when, to her utter astonishment, he translated the difficult sentence with great ease. She now addressed him politely. "Are you an officer, sir?" "O, no, miss; I am only a private. If I had had a little better education, I do not know but I might have been an officer in the Federal army." Surprised still more, she replied, "I am astonished! I thought I was a good Latin scholar. Here is a boy in the Federal army who can read Latin better than I can, and yet he says he is not well enough educated to be an officer. Why, sir, what kind of an army have you?" "Well, miss, we have a very intelligent army; one that knows what they are fighting about, and what they are fighting for. We have an army of men who will continue to fight until this wicked rebellion you intelligent Southerners have stirred up is crushed. Good by, miss."

CAPTURE ON MOSBY'S HORSE. — Captain J. S. Graham, of the Twenty-first New York cavalry, detailed the following:

"One hundred and fifty of the Twenty-first cavalry were sent out from Halltown, Va., on a three days' scout. At night they stopped about five miles above Berryville. Sergeant Wetherbee and Corporals Simpson and Van Antwerp went about a mile from the camp to a house to get supper. After eating, they concluded to stay there all night, and so put their horses in the stable. Having safely, as they thought, secured their animals, they sat down in the house by the fire to warm their feet and make themselves as comfortable as possible. Just then the door opened, and three men, with revolvers in hand, marched in and demanded a surrender. There was no alternative. Having disarmed their prisoners, the guerrillas took them to the stables to get their horses. While in the stable Van Antwerp noticed a hole in the floor, into which he dropped and concealed himself. Mosby (for he was the leader of the party) supposed that Van Antwerp had run away, and gave him no further thought. He took the other prisoners and hurried them away into the Loudon Mountains to a little place called Paris. Stopping at a house, Mosby dismounted, and told his prisoners to do likewise, and follow him into a house. Simpson dismounted, and while pretending to tie his horse, snatched a pistol from the holster on Mosby's saddle, shot the Lieutenant who stood on the

19

other side of the horse, mounted Mosby's horse, fired a shot at Mosby, and away he flew as fast as the horse could carry him. Mosby returned his fire, but without effect, and Simpson rode at full gallop towards the Shenandoah. Wetherbee, who had not dismounted, took advantage of the occasion to take the same course, and both got safely into the Federal camp, — Simpson with Mosby's famous gray horse."

THE CHARGE AT PORT HUDSON. — A soldier who participated in the storming of Port Hudson, on the 14th of June, 1863, gives the following account of that unfortunate affair: "I have been in many battles, but I never saw, and never wish to see, such a fire as that poured on us on June 14th. It was not terrible — it was HORRIBLE.

"Our division (Second) stormed about a mile from the Mississippi. We left our camp at twelve o'clock, midnight, on the 13th, and proceeded to the left, arriving just at daylight, where the balance of our brigade (Second) awaited us.

"Colonel Benedict arrived from opposite Port Hudson on the 12th, and our regiment was transferred from the First to the Second brigade, and he placed in command. The movement to the left took all by surprise; but we got in shape behind a piece of woods which concealed the enemy's works, and rested. The First brigade went in first, and we followed — the Third brigade being a reserve. I saw the First brigade file left and move on, but saw no more of it. When the order came to move on, we did so in 'column of company,' at full distance. Ask some good military man what he thinks of a brigade moving to a charge in that manner. The One Hundred and Sixty-second leading, the One Hundred and Seventy-fifth (Bryan's) after us; then the Forty-eighth Massachusetts, and Twenty-eighth Maine. We were in a road parallel to the enemy's works, and had to change direction to, or file left round the corner of the woods, and then started forward by a road leading up. The ground rose gradually, and away above, the rebel works were in plain sight. The moment we turned into the road, shot, shell, grape, and canister fell like hail, in, amongst, and around us. But on we went. A little higher, a new gun opened on us. Still farther they had a cross-fire on us — O! such a terrible one; but on we went, bending as, with sickening shrieks, the grape and canister swept over us. Sometimes it fell in and about us; but I paid no heed to it.

"After the first, my whole mind was given to the colors, and to keep my men around them; and they did it well. I wonder now, as I think of it, how I did so. I walked erect, though from the moment I saw how they had us, I was sure I would be killed. I had no thought (after a short prayer) but for my flag. I talked and shouted. I did all man could to keep my boys to their 'colors.' I tried to draw their attention from the enemy to it, as I knew we would advance more rapidly. The brave fellows stood by it, as the

half-score who fell attest. The 'color-bearer' fell, but the 'flag' did not. Half the guard fell, but the 'flag' was there. Ask (if I never come home) my Colonel or Lieutenant-Colonel if any one could have done better than I did that day. I do not fear their answer. When about three hundred yards from the works, I was struck. The pain was so intense that I could not go on. I turned to my Second Lieutenant, who was in command of company C, as he came up to me, and said: 'Never mind me, Jack; for God's sake, jump to the colors.' I don't recollect any more, till I heard Colonel B. say: 'Up, men, and forward.' I looked, and saw the rear regiments lying flat to escape the fire, and Colonel B. standing there, the shot striking all about him, and he never flinching. It was grand to see him. I wish I was of 'iron nerve,' as he is. When I heard him speak, I forgot all else, and, running forward, did not stop till at the very front and near the colors again. There, as did all the rest, I lay down, and soon learned the trouble. Within two hundred yards of the works was a ravine parallel with them, imperceptible till just on the edge of it, completely impassable by the fallen timber in it. Of course we could not move on. To stand up was certain death; so was retreat. Nought was left but to lie down with what scanty cover we could get. So we did lie down, in that hot, scorching sun. I fortunately got behind two small logs, which protected me on two sides, and lay there, scarcely daring to turn, for four hours, till my brain reeked and surged, and I thought I should go mad. Death would have been preferable to a continuance of such torture. Lots of poor fellows were shot as they were lying down, and to lie there and hear them groan and cry was awful. Just on the other side of the log lay the gallant Colonel Bryan, with both legs broken by shot. He talked of home, but bore it like a patriot. Near him was one of my own brave boys, with five balls in him. I dared not stir, my hand ached so, and it would have been death also. Well, the Colonel got out of pain sooner than some, for he died after two hours of intense agony. Bullets just grazed me as they passed over, and one entered the ground within an inch of my right eye. I could not go that. Our boys had run back occasionally, but got a volley as they did so from the rebels, who would curse them. I waited till our cannon fired a round at them, then up and ran across the road, and fell flat behind some low bush or weeds; and well I did. They saw my sword, and fired several volleys after me. As my hand was very lame, I crawled several rods back, then under a big log, got behind it, and, for the first time in five hours, sat up. I bathed my hand, and after a while made my way to the rear, got it dressed, and was on my way back, when I learned that the men were to work in, by one and twos; so I staid. I then learned of poor Bryan's fate, and one by one came the tidings of my own men, and when the word came of them I cried like a child. Some of them passed me on the way to have their wounds dressed, and blessed me as they passed by. When night came, the troops came in and line was formed, and a small one we had. The Major's body was brought in to be sent home, and my pet favorite, Sergeant Fred. Mitchell (who, as a favor to me, Colonel Benedict had made an acting Lieutenant — he was so good a soldier, and handsome and talented), the last I saw of him, was his sword flashing in the sunlight as he urged the men forward; but he was brought in with half his head torn off, and it was hard to recognize him. But God bless him! He was true, for his right hand grasped his sword firmly in death. I have it stored to be sent to his friends. Colonel B. and Lieutenant-Colonel B. came out safe. The Lieutenant-Colonel had been sick for some time, and this finished him. So I took command of the regiment, brought it to the mortar battery, and bivouacked for the night."

THE TRUE STORY ABOUT COLONEL DAHLGREN'S BODY. — It was not until the war was over, that all the facts of this somewhat mysterious case could be cleared up; and now it is apparent that a loyal Virginian, living near Richmond, rescued his corpse from its obscure and ignominious burial-place, and reinterred it in a place whence it could easily be recovered by his friends.

After having been stripped and plundered, by the roadside, near Richmond, two men were ordered to take the corpse away and bury it where none would ever know the spot, or be able to recover the remains. But a loyal Virginian, not far from whose house he had been shot, determined to watch their operations, and know the place of the grave.

It was midnight, and they took him, in the stillness and gloom, across the city, to the other side of the James River, and to the outer corner of an obscure burial-place, in the skirt of the forest, where common soldiers who had died in the hospitals had been interred. He could only observe them at a distance, and was able to recognize only the vicinity of the spot where they buried him. When he went there afterwards, he found three graves all fresh, and with no mark of any kind to indicate which was Dahlgren's.

Determined, however, not to abandon his efforts, he only waited a favorable time. Pickets were much more numerous and particular at night than during the day; and he accordingly determined to put a bold front on the enterprise. So, taking a small cart, he drove out in midday, and went directly over to the grave-yard, in the dress, and apparently on the errand, of a laborer. The first body he exhumed had a leg missing, and the hair, and eyes, and figure, answered to the description of Dahlgren. Laying him in the cart, he proceeded to dig up and lay over him quite a number of young peach trees, with dirt enough to cover the body, and with this very peaceful-looking and unsuspicious load he passed all the sentries, and through the streets of Richmond, without challenge. Arriving home, he dug another grave for his body in the corner of

his own door-yard, and only a few steps from his door. Here, in silent sympathy, and loyal regret at the death of the brave but unfortunate young soldier, his body, mutilated in battle, and insulted by the country's foes, was laid.

Not long after, a boat, with a flag of truce, went up the James, and requested of the Confederate authorities to know the place of his burial. A party was sent out to the cemetery where they had buried him, and to their great astonishment, the corpse was not there, and his unhappy friends had almost despaired of ever receiving his body back again to give it a Christian and a soldier's burial, when the above facts became known to an officer on General Meade's staff, and they were at once communicated to the Government.

About the same time, the Union army lines were advanced so near Richmond as to take in the farm of the loyal Virginian who had displayed such praiseworthy zeal in securing the remains from ignominy.

For a second time he was disinterred, and upon removal to Washington, the third time buried, being finally laid to rest, with full military honors, among those who loved and admired him in life, and bewailed his premature but glorious death.

THE SPIRIT OF ILLINOIS. — Governor Yates, of Illinois, received a letter from a town in the south part of the State, in which the writer complained that traitors in his town had cut down the American flag, and asked what ought to be done in the premises. The Governor promptly wrote him as follows: " Whenever you raise the flag on your own soil, or on the public property of the State or county, or at any public celebration, from honest love to that flag, and patriotic devotion to the country which it symbolizes, and any traitor dares to lay his unhallowed hand upon it to tear it down, then I say, shoot him down as you would a dog, and I will pardon you for the offence."

WHILE MR. BUCHANAN was President, the Pottstown Bank came into existence, and out of compliment to him the notes contained his portrait. But during the war, the bank received so many mutilated notes, with the words "traitor," "Judas Iscariot," &c., inscribed under the portrait, that it was resolved to call in all the notes bearing the likeness, and re-issue new ones.

THE DOCTOR KNOW'D WHAT HE GIV' HIM. — During the war, one of those lovely ladies, who devoted themselves to relieving the sufferings of the soldiers, was going through a ward of a crowded hospital. There she found two convalescent soldiers sawing and hammering, making such a noise that she felt it necessary to interfere in her gentle way.

" Why," she said, " what is this? — what are you doing? "

"What we doin'? Makin' a coffin — that's what."

"A coffin? indeed, and whom is it for?"

"Who for? that feller over there" — pointing behind him.

The lady looked, and saw a man lying on his white bed, yet alive, who seemed to be watching what was being done.

"Why," she said, in a low voice, "that man isn't dead. He is alive, and perhaps he won't die. You had better not go on."

"Go on! Yes, yes, we shall. The doctor he told us. He said, make the coffin; and I guess he know'd what he giv' him."

"GREENBACKS."

The following was written across the back of one of those bills.

GREEN be thy back upon thee!
　Thou pledge of happier days,
When bloody-handed treason
　No more its head shall raise;
But still, from Maine to Texas,
　The Stars and Stripes shall wave
O'er the hearts and homes of freemen,
　Nor mock one fettered slave.

Pledge — of the people's credit,
　To carry on the war,
By furnishing the sinews
　In a currency at par;
With cash enough left over,
　When they've cancelled every note,
To buy half the thrones of Europe,
　With the crowns tossed in to boot.

Pledge — to our buried fathers,
　That sons of patriot sires,
On Freedom's sacred altars,
　Relight their glorious fires —
That fortune, life, and honor
　To our country's cause we give;
Fortune and life may perish,
　Yet the Government shall live.

Pledge — to our unborn children,
　That, free from blot or stain,
The flag hauled down at Sumter
　Shall yet float free again;
And, cleansed from foul dishonor,
　And rebaptized in blood,
Wave o'er the land forever,
　To Freedom and to God!

SCENES AT FORT DONELSON. — The following incidents were given in a narrative sermon preached by Rev. Robert Collyer, at Chicago, a few days after the terrible battle at Fort Donelson:

"After leaving home our great desire was, of course, to get to Fort Donelson and to our work in the shortest possible time; and I am sure you will not thank me for a full account of Cairo, historical and descriptive. I will merely say, when you want to solicit a quiet place of retirement in the summer, do not even go to look at Cairo. I assure you, it will not suit. It is notable here only for being the first point where we meet with traces of the great conflict. The first I saw were three or four of those long boxes, that hold only and always the same treasure; these were shells nailed together by comrades in the camp, I suppose, to send some brave man home. As I went past one lying on the sidewalk in the dreary rain and mud, I read on a card the name of a gallant officer who had fallen in the fight; and as I stood for a moment to look at it, the soldier who had attended it came up, together with the brother of the dead man, who had been sent for to meet the body. It seemed there was some doubt whether this might not be some other of the half dozen who had been labelled at once, and the coffin must be opened before it was taken away.

"I glanced at the face of the living brother as he stood and gazed at the face of the dead; but I must not desecrate that sight by a description. He was his brother beloved, and he was dead; but he had fallen in a great battle, where treason bit the dust, and he was faithful unto death. He must have died instantly, for the wound was in a mortal place; and there was not one line or furrow to tell of a long agony, but a look like a quiet child, which told how the old confidence of Hebrew David, 'I shall be satisfied when I wake in thy likeness,' was verified in all the confusion of the battle. God's finger touched him, and he slept; and

'The great intelligences fair
　That range above our mortal state,
　In circle round the blessed gate,
Received and gave him welcome there.'

"One incident I remember, as we were detained at Cairo, that gave me a sense of how curiously the laughter and the tears of our lives are blended. I had hardly gone a square from that touching sight, when I came across a group of men gathered round a soldier wounded in the head. Nothing would satisfy them but to see the hurt; and the man, with perfect good nature, removed the bandage. It was a bullet wound, very near the centre of the forehead; and the man declared the ball had flattened, and fallen off. 'But,' said a simple man, eagerly, 'why didn't the ball go into your head?' 'Sir,' said the soldier, proudly, 'my head's too hard; a ball can't get through it!'

"A journey of one hundred and sixty miles up the Ohio and Cumberland Rivers brought us to Fort Donelson, and we got there at sunset. I went at once into the camp, and found there dear friends, who used to sit in those pews, and had stood fast through all the thickest battle. They gave us coffee, which they drank as if it were nectar, and we as if it were senna.

"A body of men drew up to see us, and demanded the inevitable 'few remarks;' and we told them, through our tears, how proud and thankful they had made us, and what great tides of gladness had risen for them in our city, and wherever the tidings of victory had run; and how our hands gave but a feeble pressure, our voices but a feeble echo of the mighty spirit that was everywhere reaching out to greet those that were safe, to comfort the suffering, and to sorrow for the dead.

"The 'own correspondents' of the newspapers describe Fort Donelson just as if a man should say that water is a fluid, or granite a solid. I have seen no printed description of it that will make a picture in the mind. I think there is a picture graven on some silent soul that will get itself printed some time. But it took years to get a word-picture of Dunbar, and it may take as long to get one of Donelson. If you take a bow and tighten the string until it is very much over-bent, and lay it down on a table, with the string towards you, it will give a faint idea of the breast-works — the river being to them what the cord is to the bow. At the right hand corner, where the bow and cord join, is the famous water battery, commanding a straight reach in the river of about a mile, where the gunboats must come up; and at the other end of the cord, up the river, lies the town of Dover.

"It was my good fortune to go over the entire ground with a number of our friends, and to wander here and there alone at rare moments besides. The day I spent there was like one of our sweetest May-days. As I stood in a bit of secluded woodland, in the still morning, the spring birds sang as sweetly, and flitted about as merrily, as if no tempest of fire, and smoke, and terror had ever driven them in mortal haste away. In one place where the battle had raged, I found a little bunch of sweet bergamont, that had just put out its brown-blue leaves, rejoicing in its first resurrection, and a bed of daffodils, ready to unfold their golden robes to the sun; and the green grass, in sunny places, was fair to see. But where great woods had cast their shadows, the necessities of attack and defence had made one haggard and almost universal ruin — trees cut down into all sorts of wild confusion, torn and splintered by cannon ball, trampled by horses and men, and crushed under the heavy wheels of artillery. One sad wreck covered all.

"Of course, it was not possible to cover all the ground, or to cut down all the trees. But here and there, where the defenders would sweep a pass, where our brave men must come, all was bared for the work of death; and where the battle had raged, the wreck was fearful.

"Our ever-busy mother Nature had already brought down great rains to wash the crimson stains from her bosom; and it was only in some blanket cast under the bushes, or some loose garment taken from a wounded man, that these most fearful sights were to be seen. But all over the field were strewn the implements of death, with garments, harness, shot and shell, dead horses, and the resting-places of dead men. Almost a week had passed since the battle, and most of the dead were buried. We heard of twos and threes, and in one case of eleven, still lying where they fell; and, as we rode down a lonely pass, we came to one waiting to be laid in the dust, and stopped for a moment to note the sad sight. Pray look out from my eyes at him, as he lies where he fell. You see by his garb that he is one of the rebel army, and, by the peculiar marks of that class, that he is a city rough. There is little about him to soften the grim picture that rises up before you, as he rests in perfect stillness by that fallen tree; but there is a shawl, coarse and homely, that must have belonged to some woman; and

'His hands are folded on his breast;
There is no other thing expressed,
But long disquiet merged in rest.'

"Will you still let me guide you through that scene as it comes up before me? That long mound, with pieces of board here and there, is a grave; and sixty-one of our brave fellows rest in it, side by side. Those pieces of board are the gravestones, and the chisel is a black lead pencil. The queer straggling letters tell you that the common soldier has done this, to preserve, for a few days at least, the memory of one who used to go out with him on the dangerous picket guard, and sit with him by the camp fire, and whisper to him, as they lay side by side in the tent through the still winter night, the hope he had before him when the war was over, or the trust in this comrade if he fell. There you see one large board, and in a beautiful flowing hand, 'John Olver, Thirty-first Illinois;' and you wonder for a moment whether the man who has so tried to surpass the rest was nursed at the same breast with John Olver, or whether John was a comrade, hearty and trusty beyond all price.

"And you will observe that the dead are buried in companies, every man in his own company, side by side; that the prisoners are sent out after the battle to bury their own dead; but that our own men will not permit them to bury a fellow-soldier of the Union, but every man in this sacred cause is held sacred even for the grave.

"And thus on the crest of a hill is the place where the dwellers in that little town have buried their dead since ever they came to live on the bank of the river. White marble and gray limestone, and decayed wooden monuments, tell who rests beneath. There stands a gray stone, cut with these home-made letters, that tell you how William N. Ross died on the 26th day of March, 1814, in the twenty-sixth year of his age; and right alongside are the graves, newly-made, of men who died last week in a strife which no wild imagining of this native man ever conceived possible in that quiet spot. Here, in the midst of the cemetery, the rebel officers have pitched their tents; for the place is one where a commander can see easily the greater part of the camp. Here is a tent where some woman has lived, for she has left a sewing-machine and a small churn; and not far away you see a hapless kitten shot dead; and everywhere things that make you shudder, and fill you with sadness over the wreck and ruin of war.

"Here you meet a man who has been in command, and stood fast; and when you say some simple word of praise to him in the name of all who love their country, he blushes and stammers like a woman, and tells you he tried to do his best; and when we get to Mound City, we shall find a man racked with pain, who will forget to suffer in telling how this brave man you have just spoken to, not only stood by his own regiment in a fierce storm of shot, but when he saw a regiment near his own giving back, because their officers showed the white feather, rode up to the regiment, hurled a mighty curse at those who were giving back, stood fast by the men in the thickest fight, and saved them; and, says the sick man, with tears in his eyes: 'I would rather be a private under him, than a captain under any other man!'

"I noticed one feature in this camp that I never saw before; the men do not swear and use profane words as they used to do. There is a little touch of seriousness about them. They are cheerful and hearty, and in a few days they will mostly fall back into the old bad habit so painful to hear; but they have been too near to the tremendous verities of hell and heaven on that battle-field, to turn them into small change for every-day use just yet. They have taken the eternal name for common purposes a thousand times; and we feel as if we could say with Paul, 'The times of this ignorance God passed by.' But on that fearful day, when judgment fires were all aflame, a voice said, 'Be still, and know that I am God;' and they are still under the shadow of that awful name.

"Now, friends, I can give you these hints and incidents, and many more if it were needful; but you must still be left without a picture of the battle-field, and I must hasten to the work we want to do. The little town of Dover was full of sick and wounded; and they, first of all, commanded our attention. I have seen too much of the soldier's life to expect much comfort for him; but we found even less than I expected among those who were huddled together there. There was no adequate comfort of any kind; many were laid on the floor; most were entirely unprovided with a change of linen, and not one had any proper nourishment. What we carried with us was welcome beyond all price. The policy of our commanders was to remove all the wounded on steamboats to Paducah, Mound City, and other places on the rivers; and it was a part of my duty, with several other gentleman acting as surgeons and nurses, to attend one hundred and fifty-eight wounded men from Fort Donelson to Mound City.

"I may not judge harshly of what should be done in a time of war like this in the West; it is very easy to be unfair. I will simply tell you that had it not been for the things sent up by the Sanitary Commission in the way of linen, and things sent by our citizens in the way of nourishment, I see no possibility by which those wounded men could have been lifted out of their blood-stained woollen garments, saturated with wet and mud, or could have had any food and drink, except corn-mush, hard bread, and the turbid water of the river.

"That long cabin of the steamboat is packed with wounded men, laid on each side, side by side, so close that you can hardly put one foot between the men to give them a drink, or to cool their fearful hurts. Most of us have been hurt badly at some time in our life, and remember what tender and constant care we needed, and got. If you will substitute a rather careless and clumsy man for the mother or wife who waited on you, and divide his time and attention among perhaps forty patients, you will be able to conceive something of what had been the condition of these poor travellers, but for the Chicago Committee.

"Here is one who has lost an arm, and there one who has lost a leg. This old man of sixty has been struck by a grape shot, and that boy of eighteen has been shot through the lung. Here a noble-looking man has lived through a fearful bullet wound just over the eye; and that poor German, who could never talk English so as to be readily understood, has been hit in the mouth, and has lost all hope of talking, except by signs.

"That man with a shattered foot talks in the old dialect I spoke when I was a child; and when I answer him in his own tongue, the words touch him like a sovereign medicine.

"The doctor comes to this young man, and says quietly, 'I think, my boy, I shall have to take your arm off;' and he cries out in a great agony, 'O dear doctor! do save my arm!' and the doctor tells him he will try a little longer, and when he has gone, the poor fellow says to me, 'What *shall* I do if I lose my arm? I have a poor old mother at home, and there is no one to do anything for her but me.'

"That man who has lost his arm is evidently sinking. As I lay wet linen on the poor stump, he tells me how 'he has a wife and two children at home, and he has always tried to do right, and to live a manly life.' The good, simple heart is clearly trying to balance its accounts, before it faces the great event which it feels to be not far distant. As I go past him, I see the face growing quieter; and at last good Mr. Williams, who has watched him to the end, tells me he put up his one hand, gently closed his own eyes, and then laid the hand across his breast and died.

"That boy in the corner, alone, suffers agony such as I may not tell. All day long we hear his cries of pain through half the length of the boat; far into the night, the tide of anguish pours over him; but at last the pain is all gone, and he calls one of our number to him, and says, 'I am going. I want you to please write a letter to my father; tell him I owe such a man two dollars and a half, and such a man owes me four dollars; and he must draw my pay, and keep it all for himself.' Then he lay silently a little while, and, as the nurse wet his lips, said, 'O, I should so like a drink out of my father's well!' and in a moment he had gone where angels gather immortality

'By Life's fair stream, fast by the throne of God.'

"And so all day long, with cooling water and soft linen, with morsels of food and sips of wine, with words of cheer and tender pity to every one, and most of all to those that were in the sorest need, we tried to do some small service for those that had done and suffered so much for us. Some are dead, and more will die, and some will live, and be strong men again; but I do not believe that one will forget our poor service in that terrible pain; while to us there came such a reward in the work as not one of us ever felt before, and we all felt that it was but a small fragment of the debt we owed to the brave men who had given life itself for our sacred cause.

"Two or three things came out of this journey to the battle-field that gave me some new thoughts and realizations. And first, in all honor, I realized more fully than you can do, that in those victories of which Fort Donelson is the greatest, we have reached not only the turning-point, as we hope, of this dreadful war, but we have plucked the first fruits of our Western civilization. I am not here to question for one moment the spirit and courage of our brothers in the East; the shade of Winthrop, noblest and knightliest man, the peer of Arthur for truth, of Richard for courage, and of Sidney for gentleness, would rise up to rebuke me. Ball's Bluff was worse than Balaklava as a criminal blunder, and equal to it in every quality of steady, hopeless courage. America will never breed a true man who will not weep as he reads the story of those hapless Harvard boys, whose clear eyes looked out at death steadily to the last, and who scorned to flinch.

"But here on our Western prairies, and in our backwoods, we have been raising a new generation of men, whose name we never mentioned, under new influences, whose bearing we did not understand; and the first time they could get a fair field and no favor, they sprang into the foremost soldiers in the land.

"Good elderly New England ministers, of our own faith, have made it a point to speak, in Eastern conventions, of our hopeless struggle with the semi-savagery of these mighty wildernesses. My dear doctor, that boy of eighteen was born in the prairies, and went to meetings where you would have gone crazy with the noise of the mighty prayers and psalms: and he got the conversion which you do not believe in, and was a sort of Methodist or Baptist; but he stood like one of Napoleon's Old Guard through all the battle; and when he was shot down, and could fight no longer, his mighty spirit dragged the broken tabernacle into the bushes, and there he prayed with all his might, not for himself, but that the God of battles would give us the victory. That rough-looking man was wounded twice with ghastly hurts, and twice went from the surgeon back to the fight, and only gave up when the third shot crippled him beyond remedy.

"'I saw those "Iowa Second" boys come on to charge the breastworks,' said our friend Colonel Webster to us. 'More than one regiment had been beaten back, and the fortunes of the day began to look very uncertain. They came on steadily, silently, through the storm of shot, closing up as their comrades fell; and without stopping to fire a single volley that might thin the ranks of the defenders, and make some gap by which they might pour into the fortress, they went down into the ditch, and clean over the defences, and there they staid in spite of all.'

"One quiet-looking officer saw his company sorely thinned in the beginning of the day; and that the cause might have one more arm, he took musket and ammunition from one who could use them no more, and fought at the head of his company, shot for shot, all day long; and, as a wounded soldier told me this through his pain, he added, 'I tell you, sir, if that man ever runs for an office, I'll vote for him, sure.'

"Secondly, from all these experiences, I have got a fresh conviction of the great mystery of the shedding of blood for salvation. We have been accustomed, especially in Unitarian churches, to consider Paul's ideas about blood-shedding as the fruit of his education under a sacrificial Judaism, and that, again, as a twin-sister of barbarism; but as I went over this battle-field, and thought on the dead heroes, and of all they died for, I kept repeating over each one, 'He gave his life a ransom for many;' and I wondered, when I thought of how we had all gone astray as a people, and how inevitable this war had become, in consequence, as the final test of the two great antagonisms, whether it may not be true in our national affairs, as in a more universal sense, 'without the shedding of blood there is no remission of sins.' And so, by consequence, every true hero fallen in this struggle for the right is also a savior to the nation and the race.

"Finally, I came to feel a more tender pity for the deluded men on the other side, and a more unutterable hatred of that vile thing that has made them what they are. On all sides I found young men with faces as sweet and ingenuous as the faces of our own children,—as open to sympathy, and, according to their light, as ready to give all they had for their cause.

"I felt like weeping to see children of our noble mother so bare, and poor, and sad; to see their little villages so different from those where the community is not tainted by the curse and proscription of human bondage; and I felt more deeply than ever before how, for the sake of those men, who, in spite of all, are our brothers, this horrible curse and delusion of slavery ought to be routed utterly out of the land."

WILLIAM REID, an old sailor and man-of-war's-man, who was on board the Owasco, was one of the heroes of the fight at Galveston. During the hottest moments of the battle between the Owasco and the rebel batteries, this man received a severe wound while in the act of loading his rifle. His two forefingers on his left hand were shot away, and the surgeon ordered him below; but he refused to go, and, tying his pocket handkerchief around his fingers, he remained on deck, and did good execution with his rifle. Not more than thirty minutes after, another shot struck him in his right shoulder, and the blood spirted out through his shirt. Master's Mate Arbana then ordered him to go below, and have the surgeon dress his wounds. The brave old fellow said: "No, sir; as long as there is any fighting to be done, I will stay on deck!"

After the engagement was over, the noble-hearted sailor had his wounds dressed and properly attended to. He remained on board the Owasco, and whenever they beat to general quarters, William Reid was at his post ready for orders. He was told one day by the captain to go below, as he was on the sick list, and his place was in the hospital. He was displeased with this remark, and replied: "No, captain, my eyes are good, and I can pull a lock-string as well as any on 'em." The lock-string is a lanyard connected with the cap that fires the gun.

JOHN BURNS, THE HERO OF GETTYSBURG. — The following thrilling narrative was related by B. D. Bevea, who spent several days on the battle-field in search of the body of Captain C. H. Flagg, who fell in that terrible fight:

"In the town of Gettysburg live an old couple by the name of Burns. The old man was in the war of 1812, and is now nearly seventy years of age; yet the frosts of many winters have not chilled his patriotism, nor diminished his love for the old flag under which he fought in his early days. When the rebels invaded the beautiful Cumberland Valley, and were marching on Gettysburg, old Burns concluded that it was time for every loyal man, young or old, to be up and doing all in his power to beat back the rebel foe, and, if possible, give them a quiet resting-place beneath the sod they were polluting with their unhallowed feet. The old hero took down an old State musket he had in his house, and commenced running bullets. The old lady saw what he was about, and wanted to know what in the world he was going to do. 'Ah,' said Burns, 'I thought some of the boys might want the old gun, and I am getting it ready for them.' The rebels came on. Old Burns kept his eye on the lookout until he saw the Stars and Stripes coming in, carried by our brave boys. This was more than the old fellow could stand. His patriotism got the better of his age and infirmity. Grabbing his musket, he started out. The old lady hallooed to him: 'Burns, where are you going?' 'O,' says Burns, 'I am going out to see what is going on.' He immediately went to a Wisconsin regiment, and asked them if they would take him in. They told him they would, and gave him three rousing cheers.

"The old musket was soon thrown aside, and a first-rate rifle given him, and twenty-five rounds of cartridges.

"The engagement between the two armies soon came on, and the old man fired eighteen of his twenty-five rounds, and says he killed three rebels to his certain knowledge. Our forces were compelled to fall back and leave our dead and wounded on the field; and Burns, having received three wounds, was left also, not being able to get away. There he lay in citizen's dress; and if the rebs found him in that condition, he knew death was his portion; so he concluded to try strategy as his only hope. Soon the rebs came up, and approached him, saying: 'Old man, what are you doing here?' 'I am lying here wounded, as you see,' he replied. 'Well, but what business have you to be here? and who wounded you? our troops, or yours?' 'I don't know who wounded me; but I only know that I am wounded, and in a bad fix.' 'Well, what were you doing here? — what was your business?' 'If you will hear my story, I will tell you. My old woman's health is very poor, and I was over across the country to get a girl to help her; and, coming back, before I knew where I was, I had got right into this fix, and here I am.' 'Where do you live?' inquired the rebels. 'Over in town, in such a small house.' They then picked him up, and carried him home, and left him. But they soon returned, as if suspecting he had been lying to them, and made him answer a great many questions; but he stuck to his old story, and they failed to make anything out of old Burns, and then left him for good.

"He says he shall always feel indebted to some of his neighbors for the last call; for he believes some one had informed them of him. Soon after they left, a bullet came into his room, and struck in the wall about six inches above where he lay on his sofa; but he don't know who fired it. His wounds proved to be only flesh wounds, and he is getting well, feels first-rate, and says he would like one more good chance to give them a rip."

THE BATTLE OF GETTYSBURG.

BY HOWARD GLYNDON.

THE days of June were nearly done;
The fields, with plenty overrun,
Were ripening 'neath the harvest sun,
    In fruitful Pennsylvania!

Sang birds and children, "All is well!"
When, sudden, over hill and dell,
The gloom of coming battle fell
    On peaceful Pennsylvania!

Through Maryland's historic land,
With boastful tongue, and spoiling hand,
They burst — a fierce and famished band —
    Right into Pennsylvania!

In Cumberland's romantic vale
Was heard the plundered farmer's wail,
And every mother's cheek was pale
    In blooming Pennsylvania!

With taunt and jeer, and shout and song,
Through rustic towns they passed along —
A confident and braggart throng —
    Through frightened Pennsylvania!

The tidings startled hill and glen;
Up sprang our hardy Northern men,
And there was speedy travel then,
    All into Pennsylvania!

The foe laughed out in open scorn ;
For "Union men were coward-born,"
And then — they wanted all the corn
    That grew in Pennsylvania !

.   .   .

It was the languid hour of noon,
When all the birds were out of tune,
And nature in a sultry swoon,
    In pleasant Pennsylvania ! —

When, sudden o'er the slumbering plain,
Red flashed the battle's fiery rain ;
The volleying cannon shook again
    The hills of Pennsylvania !

Beneath that curse of iron hail,
That threshed the plain with flashing flail,
Well might the stoutest soldier quail,
    In echoing Pennsylvania !

Then, like a sudden summer rain,
Storm-driven o'er the darkened plain,
They burst upon our ranks and main,
    In startled Pennsylvania !

We felt the old ancestral thrill,
From sire to son transmitted still,
And fought for Freedom with a will,
    In pleasant Pennsylvania !

The breathless shock — the maddened toil —
The sudden clinch — the sharp recoil —
And we were masters of the soil,
    In bloody Pennsylvania !

To westward fell the beaten foe ;
The growl of battle, hoarse and low,
Was heard anon, but dying slow,
    In ransomed Pennsylvania !

Sou'-westward, with the sinking sun,
The cloud of battle, dense and dun,
Flashed into fire — and all was won
    In joyful Pennsylvania !

But ah ! the heaps of loyal slain !
The bloody toil ! the bitter pain !
For those who shall not stand again
    In pleasant Pennsylvania !

Back, through the verdant valley lands,
East fled the foe, in frightened bands,
With broken swords, and empty hands,
    Out of fair Pennsylvania !

AN HEROIC OLD MAN. — A soldier of the Confederate army, writing from Missionary Ridge, in October, 1863, says : " I presume you know Father Challon, a Catholic priest of Mobile. Well, he has a brother, an old man of, perhaps, sixty years, who is a member of Captain Hurtel's company. This old man was in Kansas when the war broke out ; he immediately turned his steps homeward, and coming across a Louisiana regiment, he joined it as a private. General McCullough, with whom the regiment was, happening to notice this brave old man, and also seeing how cheerfully he bore the fatigues and dangers of camp and battle, offered him a staff appointment ; but Mr. Challon refused it, preferring to fight as a private in the ranks, until he could find some of the Mobile or Alabama troops. This was not effected, however, until he got to Corinth with Price's army. Soon after, he was transferred to the 24th Alabama regiment, company A, commanded by your fellow-citizen, A. Hurtel, where he has remained ever since, discharging his duties faithfully and well, so much so, indeed, that he was noticed by the General of the brigade, and other officers, with whom he was a great favorite ; and many was the time that he might have been noticed sitting around the General's fire, in free conversation with that officer, always eager for news, and when he obtained any that was good, would hurry off to impart it to his regiment. But for the incident.

" It was on the ever-memorable day of the 20th of September (battle of Chickamauga), that Mr. Challon took his place in the front ranks to attack the enemy in a strong position on a hill. Gallantly did all act on this occasion ; but conspicuous among those brave men was the subject of this anecdote. They rushed on, driving the enemy from his breastworks, capturing three pieces of artillery, &c. ; but the enfilade fire from the right and left was so very heavy that we were obliged to fall back. Here Mr. Challon fell with his thigh broken. Lieutenant Higley, passing by, and seeing his condition, tendered him assistance ; but the old man waved him off, telling him to go and whip the Yankees, and let him alone ; that he would take care of himself. We moved on, leaving the litter-bearers to take care of the dead and wounded ; but in a few moments the news reached us that the enemy had set fire to the woods by their guns, and that the wounded would all be burned to death.

" Several officers immediately volunteered to take a party, and rescue the sufferers. They hastened to the spot, and succeeded in saving all our men, but not until some of them had been scorched. Among these latter was my old friend, who was manfully battling with this new enemy. He had crawled some distance from the spot where he fell, and many of the surgeons think that he, in these efforts, broke his thigh entirely, that was only fractured in the first instance by the ball. The old man is still alive, and strong hopes are entertained of his recovery, his cheerfulness aiding in it. Many of the brigade have visited him. He is always cheerful, and says, ' No matter — the old man can die ; we whipped the rascals.' "

THE DEAD AT VICKSBURG. — They lay in all positions ; some with musket grasped as though still contending ; others with the cartridge in the fingers, just ready to put the deadly charge where it might meet the foe. All ferocity had gone. Noble patriots ! uninhabited tenements ! ye rest here now in security ! Your portals, whence the spirits fled, are as calm and pale as moonlight upon snow — as though no sweet love had ever woven for ye myrtle wreaths, nor death draped your hearts in ivy — as though mirth had never smiled, nor sorrow wept where all is now silent.

War with its dangers, earth with its perplexities, neglect and poverty with their pangs, slander with its barb, the dear heart-broken ones at home — all fail to call ye back to strife. A dark and fearful shadow has crept over the land, and gathered ye in its gloom. O the tears that will be shed! O the hearths that will be desolated! Eyes will look in vain for your return to the hearths that ye once gladdened, while Fame crowns ye with its laurels, and the land of the hereafter welcomes ye as "they who saved the land."

A remarkably sweet and youthful face was that of a rebel boy. Scarce eighteen, and as fair as a maiden, with quite small hands, long hair of the pale, golden hue that auburn changes to when much in the sun, and curling at the ends. He had on a shirt of coarse white cotton, and brown pants, well worn; while upon his feet were a woman's shoes of about the size known as "fours." Too delicate was his frame for war; perchance some mother's idol. His left side was torn by a shell, and his left shoulder shattered. Poor misguided boy! Hyacinth was scarce more delicately beautiful than he. Mayhap he had his Apollo, too.

Two men, who had caught at a fig tree to assist them up a steep embankment, lay dead at its feet, slain, in all probability, by an enfilade fire from their right; the branch at which they caught was still in their grasp. Some could not be recognized by their nearest friends. Several were headless — others were armless; but the manner of their death was always plain. The minie left its large, rather clear hole; the shell its horrid rent, the shrapnel and grape their clear, great gashes, as though one had thrust a giant's spear through the tender, quivering flesh.

In one trench lay two, grasping the same weapon — friend and foe. Across their hands fell a vine, the end upon the breast of the rebel, where it had fallen with them from an elevation above, the roots still damp with the fresh earth; upon it was a beautiful passion flower in full bloom, and two buds; the buds were stained with blood — the flower as bright as was the day when the morning stars sang together. On the faces of both was the calm that follows sleep — rather pale, perhaps, but seeming like him of old, of whom it was said, "He is not dead, but sleepeth." But ah, the crimson! All is not well where earth is stained with blood. In some places the dead were piled, literally, like sacks of grain upon the shore.

It is remarkable with what patience the fatally wounded, they who already stood upon the shore, bore their sufferings. Some knew that they could not recover, but bore it manfully. Sometimes a tear, and a low voice would say, "My sweet wife," or "Darling," "Mother," "God forgive" — a quiver, then all was over. Let us hope that friend and foe alike found favor in His sight where all is well.

Death is life's mystery — that undiscovered country whence none return — in no place so great and marvellous a study as here.

One would think that war would develop ferocity in hard natures; perhaps it does, but it is not shown in the faces of the dead. They enter the silent land with eyes open; a stare of surprise is in them; the lines of care are softened upon the brow, and the cheek, when untorn, shows determination, as though they slept where doubt is unknown, where all mystery is revealed, where the reason of our creation, to bear the myrtle leaf of joy or the habiliments of mourning, to reap the golden sheaves of content or gather the mildew of misery, is known.

They have been sent, rather than gone, to the garner where all shall be gathered.

This is the work of treason! This it is to unroof the temple of law and order, and let loose the demon of discord. A people more than prosperous have fallen upon evil times. Murder, arson, theft, all kinds of injustice, follow in the footsteps of war. Nor is the end yet. When shall spears and swords be beaten into ploughshares and pruning-hooks? "How long, O Lord?"

THE ESCAPE OF THE "PLANTER." — A correspondent on board the gunboat Onward, on duty in the port of Charleston, gives the following account of this important event:

"We have been anchored in the ship channel for some days, and have frequently seen a secesh steamer plying in and around the harbor. Well, this morning, about sunrise, I was awakened by the cry of 'All hands to quarters;' and before I could get out, the steward knocked vigorously on my door: 'All hands to quarters, sir! de ram is a coming, sir!' I don't recollect of ever dressing myself any quicker, and got out on deck in a hurry. Sure enough, we could see, through the mist and fog, a great black object moving rapidly, and steadily, right at our port quarter. Notwithstanding 'Merrimacs,' Iron Rams, Turtles, and death and destruction in all shapes, were instantly conjured up in the minds of all, yet every man worked with a determination and will that showed too plainly that be it a Ram, Turtle, or the old boy himself, he would meet with a warm reception. Springs were bent on, and the Onward was rapidly warping around so as to bring her broadside to bear on the steamer, that was still steadily approaching us; and when the guns were brought to bear, some of the men looked up at the Stars and Stripes, and muttered: 'You! if you run into us we will go down with colors flying.' Just as No. 3 port gun was being elevated, some one cried out, 'I see something that looks like a white flag;' and sure enough there was something flying on the steamer that would have been white by an application of soap and water. As she neared us, we looked in vain for the face of a white man. When they discovered that we did not fire on them, there was a rush of contrabands out on her deck, some dancing, some singing, whistling, jumping, and others looking towards Fort Sumter, shaking their fists, and muttering all sorts of maledictions on Fort Sumter and the '*heart of the South*' *generally.* As the steamer came under the stern of the Onward, a very ancient old darky stepped out of the crowd, and taking off his hat, said, 'Good morning, sir! I'se brought you some of dem old United States guns, sir!—from Fort Sumter, sir!' and all the others around him set up a yell — 'Hi! dat's so! yah!' and the antics and capers they cut could only be done by slaves, who, by a bold and successful move had gained their freedom — running a steamer out of a large city — passing the frowning battlements of Castle Pinckney, Forts Moultrie and Sumter. Had such a feat been performed by a white man, Congress would have passed a vote of thanks, and the public would have gone into ecstasies, and feted them. But to continue: As soon as she came up, Captain Nichols went alongside of her, and was joyously received on board. They all flocked around him, and asked eagerly, 'Has you got one of dem old flags, sir?' 'We'd like to see him, sir!' The boat's flag was hauled up, and bent on the halliards of the steamer, amidst the greatest excitement. The male contrabands again commenced dancing, singing, whistling, and cheering, and in a few moments out came five female contrabands and three children. As soon as the females came out, they commenced shouting — looking up to the old flag, 'Hi! yah! dat's him! dat's de same old fellow! I know'd him!' and one rather good-looking one, with a very young child, elevated her baby over her head, and said, 'Just look up dare, honey! it'll do you good, I knows it will;' and she held the infant close to her breast, and cut the 'pigeon wing,' with a vim, across the deck, and then shook her clothes like a hen in a rain-storm, and settled down the happiest looking creature the world ever saw.

"We learned from some of the most intelligent that they had been concocting this thing for three weeks. The leader in it was an old darky named Robert Small — they call him the 'Major.' The Major says they would have run two weeks ago with a large number of rifle cannon on board, but there was one fellow that they couldn't trust; so they were compelled to postpone it. They have done very well as it is, for they have brought off four long thirty-two pounders, one one hundred and twenty-eight pounder rifle cannon, and one small mortar, besides minie rifles, ammunition, derricks, and a lot of apparatus used for planting heavy guns in battery. One of the men has been on her for some time, in the capacity of an engineer, and another as pilot. The whole number on her is sixteen, viz.: eight men, five women, and three children.

"The old 'Major' said he thought he'd try it, any way; for if he staid there he'd get killed, and he couldn't more than get killed in making the attempt, and wound up by saying, 'I tells you what it is, sar! I was born under the old flag, and I'se gitting old, and I jist feel as though I'd like to die under it, and all we wants of you, gentlemen, is to let us live under de old flag — give us a little to start on, and we will earn our own living. We ain't no poor, lazy niggers.'

The steamer is now on her way to the Augusta, the flag-ship on this station, and as she passes by the different vessels, the crews man the rigging, and it would do your heart good to hear the hearty and prolonged cheers that greet her as she is passing through the fleet. I have forgotten to tell you that the steamer is the 'Planter.' She is armed with the thirty-twos and a howitzer, and is the same one we have seen so often. The other guns and apparatus were put on board the day before, to be transported to a new battery they are building."

INCIDENT OF STONE RIVER. — In the rebel charge upon McCook's right, the rebel Third Kentucky was advancing full upon one of the loyal Kentucky regiments. These two regiments were brought from the same county, and consequently were old friends and neighbors, and now about to meet for the first time as enemies. As soon as they came near enough for recognition, they mutually ceased firing, and began abusing, and cursing, and swearing at each other, calling each other the most outlandish names; and all this time the battle was roaring around them without much attention from either side. It was hard to tell which regiment would come off the victor in this wordy battle. As far as I could see, both sides were terrible at swearing; but this could not always last; by mutual consent they finally ceased cursing, and, grasping their muskets, charged into each other with the most unearthly yell ever heard on any field of battle. Muskets were clubbed, bayonet met bayonet, and in many instances, when old feuds made the belligerents crazy with passion, the musket was thrown away, and at it they went, pummelling, pulling, and gouging in rough-and-tumble style, and in a manner that any looker-on would consider a free fight. The rebels were getting rather the better of the fight, when the Twenty-third Kentucky succeeded in giving a flanking fire, when they retreated with quite a number of prisoners in their possession. The rebels had got fairly under way, when the Ninth Ohio came up on the double-quick, and charging on their now disordered ranks, succeeded in capturing all their prisoners, besides taking in return a great many of the rebels. As the late belligerents were conducted to the rear, they appeared to have forgotten their late animosity, and were now on the best terms imaginable, laughing, and chatting, and joking, and, as the rebels were well supplied with whiskey, the canteens were readily handed about from one to the other, until they all became as jolly as possible under the circumstances.

A MASONIC INCIDENT. — The day after the battle of Antietam, the Fifth New Hampshire formed the picket line along the edge of the cornfield where Richardson's division fought. The reserve was in one edge of the corn, and the pickets about middle way of the field concealed in the corn, as the sharpshooters of the enemy fired on all who undertook to walk around on the battle-field at that locality. Early in the morning one of the wounded rebels, who lay just outside the pickets, called one of the New Hampshire men, and handed him a little slip of paper, on which he had, evidently with great difficulty, succeeded in making some mystic signs in a circle with a bit of stick wet in blood. The soldier was begged to give it to some Freemason as soon as possible, and he took it to Colonel E. E. Cross, of his regiment. The Colonel was a Master Mason, but could not read the mystic token, it belonging to a higher degree. He therefore sent for Captain J. B. Perry, of the Fifth, who was a member of the thirty-second degree of Freemasonry, and showed him the letter. Captain Perry at once said there was a brother Mason in great peril, and must be rescued. Colonel Cross instantly sent for several brother Masons in the regiment, told the story, and in a few moments four "brothers of the mystic tie" were crawling stealthily through the corn to find the brother in distress. He was found, placed on a blanket, and at great risk drawn out of range of the rebel rifles, and then carried to the Fifth New Hampshire hospital. He proved to be First Lieutenant Edon of the Alabama volunteers, badly wounded in the thigh and breast. A few hours and he would have perished. Lieutenant Edon informed his brethren of another wounded Mason, who, when brought out, proved to be a Lieutenant Colonel of a Georgia regiment. These two wounded rebel officers received the same attention as the wounded officers of the Fifth, and a warm friendship was established between men who a few hours before were in mortal combat. This is one of the thousand instances in which the Masonic bond has proved a blessing to mankind.

AN AGREEABLE SURPRISE. — Three fathers went up the Cumberland River in the same boat, with three metallic coffins, to bring away the bodies of their sons who had fallen in the battle of Stone River. As they stepped ashore at Clarksville they met their boys jolly and hearty, with as little idea of going into burial cases as into a Southern convention.

INCIDENTS OF CURTIS' MARCH. — On the 16th of May, 1862, Elijah D. Jenkins, of Henry County, Illinois, was shot at Cotton Plant, Arkansas. The company to which he belonged attempted to take him with them, although in a dying state. Stopping at a house by the roadside, they carried him in. He suddenly grew pale, and, staring wildly around, said to his comrades, " Raise me up, boys; I want to give three cheers for the old flag," and instantly expired.

. . . . .

The battle of the 7th of July, near " Bayou Cache " — won against tremendous odds — resulted in the death of over a hundred and ten rebels and the utter demoralization of six Texan regiments. The army under General Curtis was

encamped at the junction of the Bayou Cache and Cache River, where his progress was delayed by a blockade of fallen timber. A road had been cut through this blockade on the evening of the 6th, and early next morning Colonel Hovey of the 33d Illinois regiment was ordered by General Steele to open the road on the opposite side of the Cache, make a reconnoissance in front down to the Clarendon road, along which the army were to march, and also to scour the woods thoroughly. Colonel Hovey detailed for this enterprise the following force : Colonel Harris of the 11th Wisconsin, with parts of four companies of his regiment, viz.: company D, Captain Jesse Miller ; company F, Lieutenant Chesebro ; company H, Captain Christie ; company G, Captain Patridge ; and also parts of four companies of the 33d Illinois, viz.: company E, Captain Elliott ; company K, Captain Nixon ; company F, Captain Lawton ; and company A, Captain Potter, who took charge ; and one small rifled steel gun, belonging to the First Indiana cavalry. The whole force numbered not over three hundred and fifty men. Colonel Hovey started about six A. M., with company D of the Eleventh Wisconsin ahead. Skirmishers were thrown out, and in this way they proceeded to the Hill plantation, at the forks of the road, four miles distant from camp. On the way some pickets were driven in. The main road here leads to Cotton Plant and Clarendon. The road to the left is a neighborhood road, while that turning to the side leads across the Cache, four miles distant, and thence to the Des Arc, on the White River. Detachments were sent forward on each of these roads to reconnoitre. Colonel Harris, with three companies of the Eleventh Wisconsin, and Captain Potter, with the small rifle piece, proceeded rapidly down the Des Arc road, having no cavalry. They passed a cornfield on the left, entered an open wood, and, reaching a turn in the road, at the same time rising up in elevation, they fell in with two Texan regiments of cavalry, with a regiment of conscript infantry drawn up on their right, ready to receive them. The rebels fired a murderous volley as soon as the nationals got into the snare, killing five of the men and wounding Colonel Harris and Captain Potter. The men returned the fire and fell back, the enemy being too preponderating in numbers to withstand with the little force. Captain Potter, though wounded, gave them a few rounds from his piece, and fell back, firing into the enemy's ranks. The rebels then made a charge, and the retreat became temporarily a panic. Colonel Hovey, hearing the firing, and judging the turn affairs were taking by the clouds of dust which rose and filled the air above the trees, took the remaining companies of the Thirty-third Illinois, and hastened to the scene of action. Some of the men first fired upon did not stop till they reached Hill's house, rushing past Captain Potter, who would unlimber his gun, fire a round, and then retire ; thus checking the advance of the rebels until Colonel Hovey came up. The latter had hardly time to place his men in ambush behind the fence, at the angle of the cornfield, when the rebels, coming furiously forward with loud yells, received a well-aimed fire from Colonel Hovey and his men. Twenty-five rebels were killed the first pop. They were checked. The column reeled, and staggered by this murderous fire, broke, and the men fled in confusion. At the same time a heavy column of the enemy was seen moving through the woods between Colonel Hovey's position and the Union camp. "Their intention was to get to the road on our rear," says a correspondent, "cut us off from our camp, and thus surround our brave men. But when they reached the road, and seeing the Wisconsin troops, which had fallen back, and, supposing them to be a reënforcement come to our aid, they abandoned their design, and returned. Thus what appeared to be disastrous at one time, turned to our advantage."

Colonel Hovey rallied the above companies, and, advancing one fourth of a mile, to a cotton gin, held the position over an hour.

At this time (about half past ten), Lieutenant-Colonel Wood came up with the second battalion of the First Indiana cavalry, bringing with him two steel rifled guns. This detachment had been ordered by General Curtis to proceed to the Bayou De Vue — fifteen miles from camp — with orders to save the bridge at that point from being destroyed by the enemy. The arrival of this reënforcement proved extremely opportune. Colonel Hovey was posted about a hundred and fifty yards from Colonel Hill's house on the Des Arc road, and the army was not in view. Coming up at full speed, having heard the firing, the First Indiana were welcomed with enthusiastic cheers from the brave little command of Colonel Hovey. The latter exclaimed, "There comes Colonel Wood; we are all right now, boys;" and, advancing to Colonel Wood, he said, "You'll find them (the enemy) down there, Colonel, thick enough; pitch into 'em." The cavalry, with shouts and yells, then plunged forward at a furious rate towards the rebels. The horses leaped a ditch four feet in width, which crossed their path, the bridge being torn up. One of the horses had a leg broken, and some of the men were pitched to the ground while making the perilous leap. Fortunately, none were seriously hurt. A few rails were piled into the ditch, and the steel rifled guns were passed over. A solitary rebel was now seen advancing to within one hundred yards of our front. He wheeled about and fled. The pieces, under charge of Lieutenant Baker, were unlimbered, and the cavalry brought into line of battle. The command was given: "Pieces by hand to the front; forward march." The cannoneers seized their pieces by hand, and advanced on the enemy; the latter being now discovered advancing, with extended wings, in the form of a V, the concave side facing towards our men. Their intention, it appeared evident, was to surround us. The rebels were dismounted, no horses being seen. Our pieces were loaded with canister, and, getting within point-blank range — some two hundred yards — we opened upon them with a terrible fire. The enemy halted,

and replied by a heavy volley from their cross-fire on the gunners. Several of the latter were wounded, but not disabled. The steel rifled guns now belched forth a continued round of firing; when the enemy, finding it too hot, fell back into the woods out of sight. The command was given again, "Pieces by hand to the front; forward march." Colonel Hovey himself caught hold of the trail of one of the guns, and exclaimed, "Let's push them forward, boys." Colonel Wood and Lieutenant Baker also took hold of the drag rope hooks, and assisted in moving the guns forward. On the guns were pushed, the cavalry under Major Clendenning following in line of battle, ready for the charge. Our men pressed on with enthusiastic ardor. Advancing in this way a quarter of a mile, the enemy were descried formed in the same mode as before. We got up to within one hundred yards, when they opened fire upon us. We returned the fire with canister from the little guns, with occasional carbine and pistol shots from the cannoneers. The fire proving too galling for the enemy, he again retreated, leaving a number of dead strewn on the ground. Thirteen dead rebels were biting the dust from the effects of our canister shots. Bowels and brains were scattered on the ground, and the blood besmeared the bushes in the vicinity.

The order was given by Colonel Wood to Major Clendenning to draw sabre and charge. Taking companies E and G, the Major shouted, "Come on, boys; it's our turn now;" and plunged down the road into the brush, where they were met by a tremendous volley poured in on them by the rebels. At the first fire the Major was wounded severely, receiving a ball through the left lung; and Captain Sloane, of company E, who was bravely charging in front, was instantly killed by a shot in the head. The Major, unmindful of his wound, still led on his men, and the latter poured in several volleys on the rebels from their carbines and pistols, unhorsing one and killing a number of the enemy. The rebels were staggered, and turning on their heels, fled in confusion. Our artillery followed close up, when the recall was sounded, and the cavalry fell back behind the pieces. Major Clendenning, in returning, fainted and fell from his horse, and was picked up by one of the men, who carried him off the field on his shoulders.

The pieces were then limbered up and pushed forward in pursuit, the cavalry keeping close in the rear. In this way we advanced three fourths of a mile, when small parties of the rebels were discovered, still retreating. The guns were again unlimbered, and a dozen shells were thrown after them, killing four, who were found at a long distance ahead in the road, soon afterwards, by the pursuing cavalry. Colonel Hovey now ordered the infantry to the front, intending to deploy them as skirmishers, with an extended front, and follow up the foe. A consultation was held by the officers, and it was decided to hold the ground already won, and wait further developments, as our force was getting too far from succor, in a country with which we were perfectly ignorant. The woods were thick, the force of the enemy unknown. We had driven the enemy three miles. After halting there two hours, and no enemy making his appearance, Lieutenant-Colonel Wood returned to the Clarendon road, and went to the Bayou du Vue to carry out his original intention. General Benton came up with his brigade and took command. In camp it was supposed that the fight took place on another road, and, consequently, General Benton's orders were to make a rapid reconnoissance down the Des Arc road. Bowen's howitzers were pushed forward down one road after the enemy. A shot was fired on the rebels and three men killed. Four kegs of powder were found concealed. The houses along the road were filled with rebel wounded, and the porches and door-steps were besmeared with blood from those which they carried away. They abandoned their camp and fled across the Cache River, destroying a bridge they had constructed with boats. The bank on the opposite side was also cut out very steep, so as to prevent pursuit from our cavalry.

The following incident occurred on the battle-field. At one time four out of six cannoneers serving one of the pieces were wounded at the same time. Sheafner, a German, clapped his hand to his left temple, and exclaimed, "Mine Got, I'm shot!" Sheppard placed his hand on his back, saying, "O Lord, I'm shot!" Then Lieutenant Dennaman brought his hand to his eye, saying, "I'm shot, too!" Charley Barge was hit in the neck. He only said, "I'm burnt." The simultaneous movement of the hands of the cannoneers to the parts injured, and the accompanying exclamations, were a little singular.

Riding leisurely along, General Curtis inquired of a contraband, whose broadly-spread mouth indicated satisfaction at our approach, "Where did those rascals go whom we thrashed up above here?"

Contraband inquired, "Dem as what run down dis way yester' night, sah? O, dem fellers was awful scared. One lot of 'em went down to de bayou, and one lot had done gone out on de Des Arc road, and de Colonel dat was wid 'em wanted 'em all to go de Des Arc track; but dem at de bayou told him right out dat dey would not do it; and just about den dey dat was on de Des Arc road had run up ag'in one ob your Cap'ns, and back all dey come to de bayou, where de oders was; and jes' as dey all went down in de swamp, up come your Cap'ns wid dem little guns, and commenced what you call a shellin' dem; and dat is de last account."

The above version was given off rapidly, in a high key, in the regular "Brudder Bones" style, and was highly applauded.

ROBERT CUMMINGS. — The reader will recollect the circumstance of a lad on board the Harriet Lane exhibiting unusual courage in the fight that took place on the deck of that vessel, ending in her capture, on the morning of January 1, 1863. Robert was engaged as a "messenger boy" on board the Harriet Lane, and won the

good will of her officers by his pluck, good humor, and vivacity. When the attack occurred, and the storm of bullets was pouring down upon the overmatched crew from the cotton bulwarks of the Neptune and Bayou City, as our wounded men were carried below, the lad picked up two of their fallen revolvers, and taking his place upon the quarter-deck, blazed away at the invaders, firing off every charge of both weapons, and then hurling them overboard. As the rebels clustered, thick as bees, on the cotton-bales, in the words of our informant, "every shot must have told." Robert was subsequently wounded in the hand by a musket bullet, when momentarily his spirit gave way. Surrendering with the rest, he shared the fortunes of the paroled officers, naturally becoming a great favorite with them.

NEGRO SONG OF MISSION RIDGE.

Ole massa he come dancin' out,
　And call de black uns roun',
　　　　Oh—O! Oh—O!
He feel so good he couldn't stan'
　Wid boff feet on de groun'.
　　　　Oh!—O—ee!

Say! don't you hear dem 'tillery guns
　You niggers? don't you hear?
　　　　Oh—O! Oh—O!
Ole Gen'ral Bragg's a mowin' down
　De Yankees ober dar!
　　　　Oh!—O—ee!

You Pomp, and Pete, and Dinah too,
　You'll catch it now, I swear,
　　　　Oh—O! Oh—O!
I'll whip you good for mixin' wid
　Dem Yanks when dey was here.
　　　　Oh!—O—ee!

Here comes our troops! in crowds on crowds!
　I knows dat red and gray.
　　　　Oh—O! Oh—O!
But, Lord! what makes dem hurry so,
　And frow dere guns away?
　　　　Oh!—O—ee!

Ole massa den keep boff feet still,
　And stared wid boff he eyes,
　　　　Oh—O! Oh—O!
Till he seed de blue-coats jes behin',
　Which cotch him wid surprise!
　　　　Oh!—O—ee!

Ole massa's busy duckin' 'bout
　In de swamps up to he knees.
　　　　Oh!—O! Oh—O!
While Dinah, Pomp, and Pete, dey look
　As if dey's mighty pleas'.
　　　　Oh!—O—ee!

WASHING DAY IN CAMP. — "This is 'washing day' with us," writes a soldier of the Forty-first Ohio regiment. "Washing day! You know at home what a terrible disturber of domestic comfort it is. My recollections of it are associated with cold feet, damp floors, meagre dinners, cross mothers, and birch rods. The servant girls and I used to fight more on washing days than on any other. Washing is as much a duty as fighting. Woe to the unlucky sloven that appears at Sunday morning inspection with dirty clothes, dirty hands, long hair, or untrimmed beard. We are expected to bathe all over once or twice a week. This requirement is one of the soldier's greatest blessings. At first, clothes washing was a difficult and tedious operation; but now there is not one of us that is not thoroughly initiated into the mysteries of washing, rinsing, and wringing. It is genuine satisfaction to see a fastidious youth, who, perhaps, has often found fault with his mother or sister on account of fancied imperfections in his linen, knee deep in water, worrying about some garment, in vain endeavors to wash it. Justice comes round at last. When I was a little brat I frequently used to throw down my bread and butter when it was not sugared to suit my whim. My mother would then say, ' You'll see the day, my boy, when you'll be glad to get that crust.' I have realized the truth of her words scores of times within the last year. Washing day with us has its amusements. On one occasion, last summer, while we were stationed at Murfreesboro', a party of about a hundred of us were washing at a large spring on the opposite side of the town from where we were encamped. Buell's army was, at that time, exceedingly short of supplies. But few of us had more than one shirt — some were not even that fortunate. It was a warm, pleasant day. We had removed our clothes, placed them in kettles, built fires, and were boiling them out, busying ourselves, meanwhile, in playing ' leap-frog,' ' tag,' ' blackman,' and divers other games, when lo! a party of rebel cavalry came thundering down upon us in pursuit of a forage train that had been sent out in the morning. What were we to do? We had no arms with us; our clothes were in boiling hot water; the enemy were drawing near, fearfully near. Jumping over the fence, the whole party of us scud right through the town for camp like so many wild Indians, as fast as our legs could carry us. The citizens, supposing we would all be captured, came out in great glee, shouting, ' Run, Yanks! run Yanks!' as we fled through the streets. We reached camp in safety, to the great astonishment and amusement of our comrades. It was a long time before we heard the last of that washing day. I asked one old black woman if she didn't blush when she saw us running through town. She replied, ' Why, de Lord God A'mi'ty bress ye, child — I couldn't blush for laughing.' "

ADVENTURE WITH AN ALLIGATOR. — A soldier writing from Louisiana gives the following interesting and exciting personal adventures :

" You must remember that this whole country is one vast swamp, thickly wooded with gum and cypress trees, and interlaced with bayous, which answer the purpose of roads. After attending to the pickets, I often indulge my spirit of adventure, and learn important facts about the country, by running up some small bayou on an exploring expedition. I presume you remember the old picture, in the Geography, of the Dismal Swamp : a little strip of water, trees meeting overhead; the fallen tree in the water with a huge alligator on it; the snakes here and there on bits of float wood; the pelican and cranes, and many other birds. This is a true picture. It is what I see every day. I do not notice the reptiles, except a large alligator comes within range of my pistol, and then, with almost certain aim, I send a ball whizzing into his eye, the only place where a ball will penetrate. The alligators are not very large, — few of them being over ten feet long. Some of the snakes are very large, measuring over fifteen feet in length; but the most common snake is the water moccason, usually about five feet long. Its bite is more fatal than the rattlesnake.

" Now that I am on the alligator chapter, I will tell you of an exciting adventure I had with one. I had always been anxious to obtain some portion of an alligator to carry home as a trophy. One day, as I was returning from one of the outposts, I put into Alligator Bayou. An alligator swimming shows but little bumps above water, the larger one at his eyes, the other at his nose; and it requires a marksman of no mean skill to hit it. I soon fell in with a number, and, picking out the largest, I fired. He turned on his back, his feet quivered in the air, his jaws opened, and he sank. I paddled to the spot, and brought his lordship to the surface. After a good deal of prying and pulling, I got him into the boat, turning his head to the bow. He had hardly struck the bottom of the boat, when his mouth and eyes opened with a start, and his tail swept from side to side with the force of a sledge hammer. In an instant I comprehended my situation. To jump out and swim for shore was to jump into the jaws of a dozen reptiles, and my only salvation was to keep out of the reach of his tail, the canoe being so narrow that he could not face me.

" At length, by throwing his head over the side of the boat, he got his head towards me, and made a charge with his jaws wide open. For once in my life I think I was thoroughly frightened. In an instant I plunged my paddle down his throat. His jaws closed on it like a vice, and he was quiet for a moment, and I had time to draw my pistol and send two balls into his head. He now lay quiet, but I saw that he was by no means dead, and I loaded my pistol, preparatory to another attack; but as he did not seem disposed to renew hostilities, I paddled swiftly down the stream, and landed at the first convenient place. I then paid my last respects to his alligatorship by sending another ball entirely through his head, and 'went on my way rejoicing.' I did not succeed in getting the desired trophy, for alligators are like snakes; 'their tails do not die until sundown,' and every time I touched him his tail would fly from side to side with such force as to endanger my bones. I think I shall never handle another alligator until his head and tail are cut off."

STORY OF PRESIDENT LINCOLN. — A personal friend said to him : " Mr. President, do you really expect to end this war during your administration ? "

" Can't say, can't say, sir. "

" But, Mr. Lincoln, what do you mean to do ? "

" Peg away, sir ; peg away. Keep pegging away ! "

INCIDENTS OF ALEXANDRIA. — On Sunday morning, August 3, 1862, that place was plundered by a band of seventy-five rebels. After they had searched and robbed the Union stores of all the arms and ammunition they could find, and destroyed a national flag found in the store of B. J. Kinney, Esq., they magnanimously paid their respects to the only five Union families in the place. The house of Mrs. H. A. Conway, a widow lady, and for years a resident of the place, was proposed to be the first one searched; but for the well-known reception her two daughters would have given the Vandals, Secesh deemed " discretion the better part of valor," and visited the house of Mr. J. Haller, where, by threats and vile oaths, they forced his daughter Julia to surrender a Union flag, which she had often been seen waving to the boats passing on the Mississippi.

Then mounting their horses, they rode to the houses of other Union families, giving insults, and acting in a manner that would disgrace a civilized people. When passing the residence of one Fitzpatrick, a secesh sympathizer, and in whose house had been made a rebel flag presented them, the drunken rabble, in their frenzy, dropped the captured Union flag, which they had been trailing in the street ; when Miss Banscie Conway, a young lady of seventeen, seeing it fall, ran and picked it up, and safely carried it off, amid the angry oaths of the rebel throng. When commanded to give it up, " No," she replied, " though you disgrace the name of men, with my life I'll defend the Stars and Stripes." On going into the house, she pinned the flag beneath her dress, and then bravely walked down the street, returning it to Miss Haller.

ADVENTURES OF SERGEANT EDWARDS. — In the charge made upon the rebels by company F, of the Seventeenth Indiana regiment, at the fight at Woodbury, Tenn., Sergeant William B. Edwards was amongst the foremost to dash in the enemy's midst, closely followed by four of his companions. In a moment, however, the Sergeant, without being aware of it, was separated from the rest, they taking another direction. The rebels were endeavoring, by a free use of the spur, to reach the mouth of a certain lane before they should be intercepted by another party of ours, who were coming from another quarter to cut them off.

Edwards fired off his gun, and, without knowing he was alone, galloped up to a Texan Ranger, who, with the rest, was in full retreat, and seizing hold of him, endeavored, by main strength, to drag him from the saddle. The rebel, who had a revolving rifle, turned fiercely around to shoot his assailant; but Edwards caught his gun, and, after a desperate struggle, both going at full gallop, succeeded in wresting it from him. It was then Edwards' turn to endeavor to shoot the Ranger. He elevated the piece and snapped it; but, from some injury the rifle had received, the hammer would not fairly strike the caps, and the gun could not be discharged. All this time Edwards had forgotten his own single-barrelled gun. He now perceived it in the hands of the Ranger. *They had exchanged pieces during the scuffle!*

Edwards dashed ahead. The Ranger had drawn his revolver. He fired it after his opponent, and the ball passed through his coat. Not another one of the retreating rebels attempted to molest him for some time. As he galloped by each one, he called upon him to surrender, still supposing that he was closely followed by his four companions, and, a little further back, by his entire party. The frightened rebels seemed to be under the same impression, and those that Edwards called upon immediately halted, waiting for whoever were to take them in charge to come up. This gave them time to look about, and to perceive that none of our soldiers were following. Some of them then climbed the fences and skedaddled in different directions, while the rest, gnashing their teeth with vexation and rage, dashed after Edwards.

Above the shouts of all the rest, the Sergeant could now hear behind him the voice of the Ranger with whom he had maintained so desperate a scuffle: " Shoot him ! shoot him ! why don't you shoot that d—d Yankee ? " Most of the rebels having blue overcoats on, they did not exactly know which was Edwards, and called back to the Ranger to say which one he meant. But the Sergeant had lost his hat in the mêlée, and the Ranger shouted, " The one without a hat ! " Several bullets were immediately sent whizzing round his ears ; but, fortunately, none of them took effect, and, a number of the rebels surrounding him, he surrendered, while a dozen revolvers were levelled at his head and heart. But he only gave himself up when he perceived that no other Union soldier was in sight.

Edwards remained a prisoner in the hands of the rebels four days. They were a portion of Morgan's old regiment.

All sorts of questions were put to the prisoner by his captors. One asked him if it were true that Lincoln had called out three millions of men. Another wanted to know if he indorsed the proclamation ; and, on his signifying that he did, an officer pulled out a copy of Vallandigham's speech, thrust it in his face, and asked him how he liked *that*. He found quite a number of officers who each had a copy of this infamous speech, which they were in the habit of quoting to confuse and confound our poor soldier boys who fell into their hands. The prayer of the patriot, as he grasps his rifle and kneels in the mud, the snow, or the blood of his murdered comrades, is : " Palsied be the tongue that uttered that accursed harangue !

Anathema upon the head of the wretch who dares put cunning falsehoods in the mouths of our country's enemies, that they may cast them in the teeth of the poor soldier, who has given up all — home, comfort, friends — that he may fight in that country's behalf!"

They robbed him of everything — overcoat, blankets, and even a lead pencil which he carried in his pocket.

Their living was rather scant. Each man drew, for a day's rations, half a pound of rusty bacon and a little corn meal. They did not depend altogether upon this supply, however, but regaled themselves with chickens, &c., stolen from the country people.

After he had been with them for four days, a corporal and a few men were detached from the principal party, in order to take Edwards and four conscripts, who had been found concealed in the woods, to McMinnville.

This squad stopped the first night at the house of a widow Beckwith, and partook of a comfortable supper at her expense. The night was rainy and dark, and Edwards determined, if possible, to effect his escape. Making a pretence of going into the back yard of the house, he was accompanied by the Corporal, gun in hand. After looking round a moment, Edwards stepped upon the porch, as if to go back into the house; and, while the eye of the reassured Corporal was taken off him, he made a leap from the porch into the darkness, and ran with all speed towards the bottom of the yard. The astonished Corporal hastily fired his gun, but the ball probably went far wide of the mark, as Edwards did not hear it. Indeed, such was his haste that he scarcely heard the report.

He could see nothing, so dense was the darkness; but as he ran he unluckily struck the yard fence in such a way that he tumbled sheer over it, and heels over head into a thick patch of briers on the other side. Gathering himself up, and getting out of the briers as best he could, — his head, face, and hands terribly scratched and torn, — he ran hastily on until he became certain that he was not pursued. Then he stopped to rest a while. After this he wandered about for nearly a week, travelling mostly by night, and concealing himself by day, several times passing in and out the rebel picket lines, sometimes within a few yards of them; he once wholly lost his way, and was put upon the track by a member of a poor Union family, and subsisted almost all this time upon an ear or two of raw corn. At last he came in sight of Union soldiers at the burnt bridge on Stone River, seven miles north of Murfreesboro', where he once more gained his freedom under the old flag.

COMEDY OF BATTLE. — A correspondent tells this incident of the fight at Murfreesboro':

"A cluster of mangled fellows were huddled about a field hospital waiting surgical attention. A big, brawny trooper, with a bullet in his left leg and another in his right arm, hobbled up, holding his wounded arm in his left hand. 'Doctor,' said

he, with much less piety than pain, 'the d—d rebs came pretty near hitting me.' Another fellow, blowing blood copiously from his nose, — the point of which had been shot off, — as a whale spouts sea-water, interposed, 'The d—d rascals' — sputter — 'come d—d near' — another blow and sputter — 'missin' me.'"

HOW GENERAL HOOKER TALKED TO A CAVALRY BRIGADIER. — Said he to a Brigadier of cavalry, "I know the South, and I know the North. In point of skill, of intelligence, and of pluck, the rebels will not compare with our men, if they are equally well led. Our soldiers are a better quality of men. They are better fed, better clothed, better armed, and infinitely better mounted; for the rebels are fully half mounted on mules, and their animals get but two rations of forage per week, while ours get seven. Now, with such soldiers, and such a cause as we have behind them — the best cause since the world began — we *ought* to be invincible, and by —, sir, we *shall* be! You have got to stop these disgraceful cavalry 'surprises.' I'll have no more of them. I give you full power over your officers, to arrest, cashier, shoot — whatever you will — only you must stop these 'surprises.' And, by —, sir, if you don't do it, I give you fair notice, I will relieve the whole of you, and take the command of the cavalry myself!"

THE SURRENDER OF VICKSBURG. — A correspondent gives the following interesting particulars of the surrender of the city:

"As melancholy a sight as ever man witnessed, for brave men conquered and humbled, no matter how vile the cause for which they fight, present always a sorrowful spectacle; and these foes of ours, traitors and enemies of liberty and civilization though they be, are brave, as many a hard-fought field can well attest. They marched out of their intrenchments by regiments upon the grassy declivity immediately outside their fort; they stacked their arms, hung their colors upon the centre, laid off their knapsacks, belts, cartridge-boxes, and cap-pouches, and thus shorn of the accoutrements of the soldier, returned inside their works, and thence down the Jackson road into the city. The men went through the ceremony with that downcast look so touching on a soldier's face; not a word was spoken; there was none of that gay badinage we are so much accustomed to hear from the ranks of regiments marching through our streets; the few words of command necessary were given by their own officers in that low tone of voice we hear used at funerals. Generals McPherson, Logan, and Forney, attended by their respective staffs, stood on the rebel breastworks overlooking the scene never before witnessed on this continent. The rebel troops, as to clothing, presented that varied appearance so familiar in the North from seeing prisoners, and were from Texas, Alabama, Mississippi, Louisiana, Georgia, and Missouri; the arms were mostly muskets and rifles of superior

20

excellence, and I saw but very few shot-guns, or indiscriminate weapons of any kind; it was plain that Pemberton had a splendidly-appointed army. Their flags were of a kind new to me, all I saw being cut in about the same dimensions as our regimental colors, all of the single color red, with a white cross in the centre.

"The ceremony of stacking arms occupied a little over an hour upon that part of the lines; and when it was concluded, the glittering cavalcade of officers, Federal and rebel, mounted and swept cityward on the full gallop, through such clouds of dust as I hope never to ride through again. A few minutes, fortunately, brought us to a halt at a house on the extreme outskirts of the city, built of stone, in the Southern fashion, with low roof and wide verandas, and almost hidden from view in an exuberance of tropical trees, and known as Forney's headquarters.

"And here were gathered all the notables of both armies. In a damask-cushioned armed rocking-chair sat Lieutenant-General Pemberton, the most discontented-looking man I ever saw. Presently there appeared in the midst of the throng a man small in stature, heavily set, stoop-shouldered, a broad face, covered with a short, sandy beard, habited in a plain suit of blue flannel, with the two stars upon his shoulder, denoting a Major-General in the United States army. He approached Pemberton and entered into conversation with him; there was no vacant chair near, but neither Pemberton nor any of his Generals offered him a seat; and thus for five minutes the conqueror stood talking to the vanquished seated, when Grant turned away into the house, and left Pemberton alone with his pride or his grief — it was hard to tell which. Grant has the most impassive of faces, and seldom, if ever, are his feelings photographed upon his countenance; but there was then, as he contemplated the result of his labors, the faintest possible trace of inward satisfaction peering out of his cold gray eyes. All this occupied less time than this recital of it; and meantime officers of both armies were commingled, conversing as sociably as if they had not been aiming at each other's lives a few hours before. Generals McPherson and Logan now turned back towards our camps to bring in the latter's division; and a party, specially detailed, galloped cityward, about a mile distant, for the purpose of hoisting the flag over the court-house.

"Lieutenant-Colonel William E. Strong, assisted by Sergeant B. F. Dugan, fourth company Ohio independent cavalry, and followed by a numerous throng of officers, soldiers, and civilians, ascended to the cupola of the court-house; and at half past eleven o'clock on the Fourth of July, 1863, flung out our banner of beauty and glory to the breeze."

A GALLANT MICHIGAN CAPTAIN. — During the retreat of the Confederates, after a cavalry skirmish near Corinth, Captain Botham, of the Third Michigan cavalry, who was finely mounted, pursued them; and with the cry, "Come on, boys!" gave his horse rein and spur, and quickly disappeared in the wood, through which their course lay. He was followed by two or three of the cavalry, Captain Sailor taking the same direction with his company. But Captain Botham, without hat, his face glowing with excitement, his sabre flashing aloft, outstripped all save the three men in question, and went flying after the frightened foe, now fairly on the Corinth road. The chivalry ran well, but the mudsills gained upon them every instant. The party numbered about fifty strong; and in the mad race they threw away their blankets, haversacks, and, in some instances, their revolvers, carbines, and sabres. Like all reconnoitring parties, they were all armed to the teeth. At the end of the first mile the Captain left both of his companions behind; and about the time the half of the second mile was accomplished he came up with the rear of the flying column, yelling at the top of his voice. By a single blow with his sabre he killed the first man he reached, the good blade cleaving his skull; but just at this time observing a road that led into a field on the right, in order to avoid a stretch of the highway that was very bad, he dashed into it, and by the manoeuvre headed off about thirty of the rebels, crying out to them to surrender, or he would cut them all down, at the same time swinging his sabre madly around his head. They drew rein at once, and there he stood alone with them, and in a loud voice bade them throw down their arms and surrender. Meantime, one half of them, when they found themselves headed off, turned down a road to the left. But their captor put a stop to this by swearing that if another man left he would shoot him dead in his saddle. The two cavalrymen who started with Captain Botham now came up and disarmed the prisoners. Upon counting them, the Captain found that he had bagged thirteen live secesh, single-handed and alone! Has the feat been beaten during the war? Thirteen of their cavalry taken by a single mudsill! Upon each of the prisoners was either a loaded pistol, a loaded carbine, or a sabre. They were never more completely panic-stricken. They were all safely brought to camp. Eight or ten others were also taken, and four or five killed and wounded. None of the Union men received a scratch, although several of their horses were wounded.

MRS. JOHN HART. — A soldier, belonging to the One Hundred and Forty-ninth New York regiment, in February, 1863, wrote as follows: "We have a woman in our regiment, who has marched with us through all our tedious and tiresome journeys, and shared all our tribulations without a murmur. Her name is Mrs. John Hart, of Syracuse. She is a stout Irish woman, with a good constitution, capable of enduring as much fatigue and labor as any man in the regiment, and withal, she is a kind-hearted, virtuous, and estimable lady, who performs many kind offices for the men, and is universally esteemed in the regiment. Her husband is a member of company E, and is a good soldier and an intelligent man. She came with the regiment to share his fortunes, and in all our troubles and exposures not a whimper of complaint has ever been heard from her lips.

"For some considerable time she was employed while in camp in mending and washing for the men; but since the arrival of Colonel Barnum, an officers' mess has been formed, with Mrs. Hart for cook and hostess; and well does she perform the duties of our camp household. Out of the simplest materials she sets a meal upon our table fit for a prince, and our sharpened appetites are abundantly satisfied. Her services in this department are invaluable, and it is difficult for us to understand how we could possibly dispense with them. In addition to her other duties, she is now acting as nurse for Colonel Barnum in his illness, and we all hope her motherly care will soon restore him to health and strength again."

ANECDOTE OF STONEWALL JACKSON. — The night after the battle of Fredericksburg a council of war was held by General Lee, to which all his Generals of divisions were invited. General Jackson slept throughout the proceedings, and upon being waked, and asked for his opinion, curtly said: "Drive 'em in the river; drive 'em in the river!"

CIVILITIES OF WAR. — A letter from the army of the Potomac, dated February 12, 1863, contains the following:

"The rebels recently rigged up a plank, with a sail and rudder attached, and on top placed a drawer, evidently taken from an old secretary, in which they put two Richmond papers, and on top a half plug of tobacco, with a written request for a New York Herald, and stating that 'they would come over and have a little chat,' if we would pledge faith. But this kind of intercourse is strictly forbidden on our part. The next day, after the Ninth army corps had left, the rebels hailed our pickets, and asked 'where the Ninth army corps had gone.'"

"I returned this morning from a visit to our pickets. Company I, One Hundred and Thirty-ninth Pennsylvania volunteers, has a very good location for standing post, but the 'Johnny Rebs' are perfectly docile. Night before last Harry Born, one of our boys, was busily engaged in singing a song entitled 'Fairy Bell,' and when the time came for the chorus, the four rebs on the post opposite struck up, drowning Harry's voice almost entirely."

INCIDENTS OF HELENA. — "Yesterday, in company with Captain Sherman, of the Second Wisconsin cavalry," says a writer in the Milwaukee News, "we rode by the negro graveyard in the rear of General Washburn's headquarters. Four darkies had just deposited on the ground a stout negro, dead as a door nail. His woolly head and dirty feet protruded from under the worn-out horse blanket, which served as a winding-sheet. One of the living was slowly digging a trench, the others stood watching.

"'Halloo, boys, what's the matter with *him*?'

"'He's dun gone dead, massa!' and they chuckled to think we could not guess why he was there.

"'What's the matter of him?'

"'Too much hard times, massa! De niggers can't stan' everyting.'

"'Niggers die pretty easy here — don't they?'

"'Yes, massa, dey get shut of theyselves right smart now — dem's hard times for niggers!'

"And so thought we, as they were left behind to conduct their funeral to a termination. In half an hour some thousand-dollar chap will be left to rot, and add richness to the soil, which will hereafter grow larger peaches than ever before.

"In the house of Dr. Grant, where I board, is an intelligent African girl, about twenty-four years old, owned by the doctor. The other morning, while she was sweeping up the hearth, said I:

"'Millie, are you a slave?'

"'Course I is — why?'

"'Why don't you run away, and be free?'

"'Umph — umph! Dis chile is too smart for dat. Dere is no fun in sleepin' in de mud, starvin' to death, and gittin' no medicine when you are sick.'

"'There are lots and lots of niggers in town who have run away — ain't there, Millie?'

"'Umph — umph — right smart lot of 'em.'

"'Well, Millie, ain't they better off than before they run away?'

"'Now, wat's de use of foolin'? You know better. Would you be better off without clothes, and a bed, and a house to sleep in, and somebody to look out for you, than if you had 'em all? De time was here when us niggers had our parties, and heaps of fun — and we had good clo'es, and was jis as good as anybody. Before dis war begun, a wagon-load of niggers didn't dun gone dead every day as dem does now. Dis chile knows somefin' yet, and dat is, to stick to missus.'

"'Well, Millie, cannot the niggers take care of themselves?'

"'Lord help you, no! About one in a hundred is smart enough to live, and de odders would dun gone dead right smart. Wat-wat-wat-wat de niggers know about buyin' stuff, and takin' care of demselves — dey never done 'em! De massa always buys for de niggers jes like as if dey was his own family, and wen dem is sick, he has 'em doctored up. Umph — umph! de white Yankee folks skin de last chicken out of de nigger 'fore it were hatched, if de nigger took care of demselves! Deed dey would!'

"'Well, Millie, you are a very sensible girl; stick to your home, and you will be better off.'

"'Deed I will. We've all dun gone got sick of Yankees long ago. Nebber had such thieves in town afore. Dey beat de niggers stealin', and some of de niggers steal right smart too, I reckon.'

"'What do they steal, Millie?'

"'Golly, dey steal all dey see, if two men don't

jes watch it all de time. We nebber had white folks in jail here till de army come, and now dey is in dar all de time.'

"'Don't you look on the white folks who come with the army as your friends?'

"'Umph—umph! Not now; dey is too wicked. Wat-wat-wat-wat dey care for niggers, when dey lets dem die here, and won't give dem nothin'. Niggers don't know much, but dey learn who am dar friends right smart!'

"And there is a world of truth in her ideas."

CAPTURE OF ARKANSAS POST.

ACCOUNT BY A HOOSIER WHO WAS THERE.

In storming and taking Arkansas Post the Sixteenth Indiana regiment has realized the exulting sense of being conquerors. Once defeated, almost annihilated, in Kentucky, a few days before compelled to retreat before the rebel stronghold of Mississippi, it knows now what it is, after a desperate fight, to charge upon fortifications, in a blinding tornado of shells, grape, canister, and musket balls, to be the first regiment inside of the intrenchments, and among the smoking ruins, dismantled casemates, and exploded cannon, to plant the glorious old flag on the stronghold of the traitor's fort.

On Friday, the 9th of January, 1863, the Mississippi squadron, returning from Vicksburg, sailed up White River, through the cut-off, and forty miles up the Arkansas. Late at night, when the soldiers were sleeping in the steamer's elegantly furnished cabin, the General opened his maps and gave us some idea of the morrow's work.

On Saturday morning the troops were disembarked, cannon dragged up the bank, wagons loaded with provisions, and an occasional feeling shot was fired from the gunboats. Messengers were galloping, and Generals with their staffs superintending the movements. There was a putting revolvers in order, donning fatigue suits, leaving hastily written letters behind.

At twelve o'clock the Sixteenth started. The long voyage, the terrible sixty miles' march in Louisiana in thirty-six hours, when we destroyed their Western Railroad, and the five days in the Chickasaw swamps before the enemy's works at Vicksburg, had sadly thinned their ranks. Many, almost exhausted with fever, dragged themselves into the ranks, determined to go with their regiment. Forward rode our General to where at such an hour a leader should be — the front. No doubt his heart thrilled with pride as he glanced along the regiments of his brigade. Young, tall, and handsome, his chivalric bearing and courteous manners have won the love of all who know him. A General at thirty, made so for gallant conduct at Shiloh, his after conduct proved that we were not mistaken in deeming him the beau-ideal of a hero. The brigade marched up along the river bank, and rested in an open field for a short time. Steele's division, mud to their knees, after having vainly tried to pass through the swamps and bayous, returned and took a new course.

It is now sunset, and we move forward past the outer rifle pits, from which the rebels had been driven this afternoon, on through the dense woods. Mud was everywhere; we no longer stopped to avoid deep places, but plunged right through. It is now dark, and the gunboats have opened on the fort, from which the one hundred and twenty-eight pounders are shaking the ground in thundering replies. It is not like looking upon a mountain's quiet grandeur, but rather, only tenfold more intense, like the lightning crashing at your feet, rending the oak in splinters. There is a blaze of light from the gunboats. As sight is quicker than sound, a moment's pause before the awful roar and scream of the monstrous missile flying through the air followed by a dull explosion. Seldom can you thus trace the journey of a single shot in the roar of a dozen guns. Now they are shelling the woods. One passes to the right, another strikes to the left of our regiment, killing one and wounding four or five in company B. Darkness, with its half-seen horrors, the cannon's awful roar, the screams of shell and crash of falling timber, the blood and smoke and groans of wounded men, make life seem so intense. In such an hour, into what nothingness sink common every-day affairs before such awful realities! The puffing gunboats drop slowly down the river, the fort fires two shells, and all is quiet.

Silently commands are given and obeyed: the men lie down where they had stood, in line of battle, on bush and in the mud. No fire is allowed. With their sixty rounds of ammunition they have brought but one blanket, which they wrap around them as a feeble protection against the winter cold. From out a broken slumber I am roused by a gun's report. A Corporal, in his sleep, has kicked the hammer of his gun, and his wife and little ones will sadly hear of a right hand shot off.

I could stand the cold no longer. In our rear were some huts, upon reaching which, I found men from different regiments gathered around sickly-looking fires, making coffee. An Eighth Missouri regiment man was telling how they hustled the rebels through the woods that afternoon; about sixty of the scamps had been captured, while a wounded one lay dying in the corner. Slowly the night dragged along, till we almost thought the morrow never would come.

Steele's division was passing silently, save with the hum which always marks the movements of large bodies of men, and the rumbling artillery wagons cutting through ruts. Brigade after brigade moves on to join the right.

With morning comes General Burbridge, telling us that Sherman would commence the attack on the right, while he intends that his brigade shall be the first to mount the breastworks on the left.

We are now within five hundred yards of the fort; we can see the buildings within its walls. The skirmishers who have been thrown in front have stirred up the hornets, who favor us with a few shells.

Some of those able-bodied young men — those contemptible cowards — who are lounging in school-rooms, and smirking behind counters, may think it a very light matter to storm the enemy's intrenchments ; but plain soldiers, who have stood on battle-fields before, and seen the flow of blood as it gushed from fountains in human hearts, deem it no disparagement to their manhood to think it a serious matter to meet the crashing rounds of grape and canister, and musket balls, as they lead the advance of a storming party.

The Colonel calls us up around him, and reads the order. Our army, with batteries placed in every available position, and the gunboats on the river, have completely encircled the fort. After the batteries have opened, Sherman is to commence the attack on the right, which is the signal for us to advance. The Sixteenth is to lead the advance, with the Sixtieth Indiana and the Eighty-third Ohio on our right and left. The gunboats are moving to the attack, though not a gun has yet been fired from our side.

The stillness grows irksome. All know full well the awful storm is coming. At length a huge roar from one of the gunboats, followed by a shot from one of the thirty-two pounders on the left, announces that the ball is opened. A shot from the battery on the right tells that Sherman has commenced. Fiercely the rebel guns answer back. Thicker and faster come the shells and solid shot, crossing in the air in curves from the circle of batteries around the devoted works. Not often could you trace the course of a single shot amid that incessant roar. Old soldiers say it was a cannonading only equalled by Donelson.

The rebel regiments had retired from our front within the protection of their works. The boys took off overcoats, blankets, haversacks, canteens, drew their coats down, and buckled their belts tightly around their waists. In charge of sick men were left letters, photographs, and articles of value. Officers unbuckled their swords and took guns. The McClellan exercise we had learned on the Potomac might be useful here. Cheering far to the right is heard. It is the signal. Every man was at his post, and blood was throbbing high, as heard and obeyed were the commands, "Attention, battalion — by the right of companies to the front — Forward!" On coming into the field, "By company into line — guide centre." Lieutenant-Colonel Orr shouted, "Now, men, fellow me." We looked from our own glorious banner to the traitorous red, white, and red, that floated full in view from the garrison staff. The mud was over ankle deep, but with Hoosier yells, onward right gallantly they went, like men whose blood was up, though met by a plunging storm of grape, canister, shells, and musket balls. The regiments on either side gave back, or, in the language of the General's report, "My right and left wavered, while my centre stood firm, though met by a perfect tornado of the enemy's missiles." We passed the house where two guns were posted, over the fence, into a little peach orchard. An exploding shell sent rails and men flying.

We are now within a hundred yards of their strongest work, and the order is given to lie down and fire. Many, killed or badly wounded, never discharged their guns the first time. Lieutenant-Colonel Orr is severely wounded in the head by a piece of one of the shells that go flying over us, while the grape and singing bullets made music around our ears not soon forgotten. The huge pivot gun is throwing canister, at least half a bushel at each discharge. One load killed and wounded men in three companies. But our men were not idle, and soon their showers of balls silenced the cannon that bore on us. A rebel captain of artillery told us he could not get his men to go near the guns. Still the ceaseless fire from our gunboats was vying with the land batteries in raining the iron storm upon the devoted works.

Here let me relate a little incident of personal experience, to show how the thing works. While lying on my side loading a gun, whack ! went something ; and I felt like the darky who, when shaking a coon off a tree, felt something drop that was not exactly a coon. A bullet had grazed the skin below my shoulder. It stunned me like hitting a man over the head with a club. Almost at the same instant, a piece of shell, hunting for its affinity, as A. Ward, Esq., would say, gently rolled against my leg.

I retired in good order to the rear, and meeting a negro with coffee, I was reënforced and enabled to return. Upon rejoining the company I was very proud to find each man at his place, the Lieutenant interlarding an oath after each discharge of his gun, and the Orderly, a dark, stern, resolute man, giving the boys worthy models for imitation.

The sun had sunk low in the west. The gunboats were still steadily puffing up towards the fort. Many who had fired away their sixty rounds of ammunition would coolly roll over the dead and wounded to get their cartridges. A Quaker lad came to me saying, very deliberately, "Captain, I am out of ammunition."

The gunboats sent solid shot through the four feet thickness of oak, and scattered in splinters the railroad iron with which the top was plated. Some shells, which made centre shots, had torn off the muzzles of their monstrous guns as they exploded.

Many of their guns were dismounted while the circle of our batteries was drawing closer in.

Among the most unpleasant things were the groans of the wounded. A Corporal in company D lay groaning with the brain oozing out of his head, as though death would never come to his relief. The stifling smell of powder, the cannon's awful roar, the explosion of shells, illuminating the smoke that hung in clouds, made it seem as if we beheld the opening of hell's fiery caverns.

At last a white flag is seen at the upper end of the breastworks; we rise up and commence cheering, but they pour in a murderous volley from the lower pits, and we drop down. Soon more white flags are seen on bayonets, and a man passes along the lower works waving the emblem of defeat. O, how the exulting shout of victory at that maddening hour of triumph rolled along the lines of the Union army. All start on a foot race for the fort.

General Burbridge, with a flag around his waist, was followed by Colonel Lucas, who, when Colonel Orr's riderless horse had come through the woods, had left his sick bed and rode out in time to be "in at the death."

The sullen rebels seemed a little startled as half a score of regiments came rushing pell-mell into their ruined works. After a four hours' fight the day was ours.

General Churchill, who had fought us at Richmond, gave his sword to Burbridge. Seven thousand one hundred and some odd prisoners, mostly Texans, besides a vast amount of company stores and arms, were captured. Wagons that once belonged to our regiment, and guns with our boys' names on them, are found here in Arkansas, that had been lost on the far-off Kentucky battle-field. It is worth going through a battle to celebrate its victory. Some of their dead, with arms cut off, heads and brains scattered, lay in the trenches. At one place a man's shoes were standing with his feet in them, while the body lay a rod away. I saw a pile of flesh and bones, which had lost all semblance of a human being. All distinctions of rank were forgotten; general and private shook hands; friends, rejoicing to find each other safe, embraced; and from the whole body of troops rang shouts of joy.

The regiment returned to the point from which the assault was made, and made coffee around blazing fires. Now came the saddest part — the *after the battle*. The red sun was sinking in the west, "like a banner bathed in slaughter." Ambulances were running to the hospitals, and men were gathering the dead and wounded. Heart-rending were the groans and labored breathing of many of the latter. Horses lay with white foam and blood oozing from their nostrils. Gazing upon such a scene, we feel the truth of those beautiful lines:

"There is something of pride in the perilous hour,
   Whate'er be the shape in which Death may lower;
Fame is there to say who bleeds,
And Honor's eye is on daring deeds;
But when all is past, it is humbling to tread
O'er the weltering field of the tombless dead."

Leaving to official reports to bestow praise upon those who hold command, let me mention one from among the humblest, as a name to be remembered — the flag-bearer of the 16th, Dick S. Tenant, a beardless student, fresh from college. He was a faithful guardian to his trust amid that blinding hail, and was among the first to mount and plant the banner of our fathers upon the conquered ramparts.

A SNOWBALL BATTLE. — A soldier of one of the New Jersey regiments writes as follows:

"You are probably aware that the Second brigade of this division consists of four Vermont regiments, besides the Twenty-sixth. During the late heavy fall of snow, the Vermonters twice made an attack on the encampment of the Twenty-sixth, sending a perfect shower of snow balls at the head of every luckless Jerseyman who made his appearance without his tent. The first attack was a complete surprise to us; but we essayed a sally from the camp, and drove the attacking party back to their reserves. Being heavily reënforced, they charged on us again, and after a desperate resistance we were driven back into camp, fighting resolutely from the shelter of our tents until darkness put an end to the contest. Our casualties were quite heavy, but those of the enemy, it is thought, exceeded ours. A few days afterwards the attack was renewed, but we took up a strong position on a hill in the rear of the camp, and repulsed every assault of the foe. The snow was crimsoned with the blood issuing from the olfactory organs of the Vermonters, and the appearance of the battle-field indicated the fierce nature of the contest. The enemy raised a flag of truce, an armistice of a few hours was concluded, and then ensued that novel spectacle of war — men, who but a few minutes previous were engaged in one of the most sanguinary battles of modern times, harmonizing and fraternizing with clasped hands.

"But the matter did not rest here. The night of the 24th had enveloped terra firma with its dusky shades. Many a waxen nose in the camps of the Second brigade snored sonorously, happily unconscious of its ruby discoloration on the morrow. Many an eye placidly closed in slumber was to be violently closed in battle ere the approach of another nightfall. And many a phrenological bump sparsely developed on the night in question was to be suddenly brought to an age of puberty on the approaching day. The eventful morning opened. Colonel Morrison sent a challenge to Colonel Seaver of the Third Vermont to engage in the open field at three o'clock P. M. The challenge was accepted, on the condition that the Fourth Vermont should be included with the Third. This was agreed to by the Colonel. Before the appointed time some of our men were detailed on fatigue duty, and at the time of the engagement we were only able to muster some three hundred men.

"Nothing daunted by the superiority of numbers, Colonel Morrison ordered Lieutenant McCleese, of company C (Captain Pemberton being sick), to fortify a small hill on our right, make as much ammunition as possible, and pile the snow-balls in pyramids. This arduous duty was hastily performed. It was a strong position, a swollen brook at its base answering the purpose of a moat — too strong, in fact, for the Vermonters, and they declined to attack us while occupying this miniature Chepultepec. Commissioners were appointed, and after a parley, the Twenty-sixth was marched across the brook, and formed in line of battle on the field fronting the Vermonters. The hills were covered with spectators, and the eagerness to witness the novel contest knew no bounds. Companies A and B were thrown out

as skirmishers. Company E occupied the right, C was given the centre, and H rested on the left. The Colonel dashed over the field in all directions, encouraging the men to stand fast, amid the blue wreaths curling from a 'brier wood' nonchalantly held in his left hand, and the Adjutant danced about on a spirited charger, apparently impatiently awaiting the hour of contest, the light of battle dilating within his eyes, and a quid of 'navy plug' reposing beneath his cheek. Lieutenant Woods, of the ambulance corps, and Lieutenant —— acted as mounted aids to the Colonel, while the 'Sergeant' and John K. Shaw, an aspiring Newark youth of eighteen, acted as perambulating aids. The line being formed and everything in readiness for the contest, a red flag was raised as a signal, and in a breath of time a strong body of the enemy drove in our skirmishers, and fiercely attacked our centre. At the same moment another strong force advanced against our right, but only as a feint; for they suddenly wheeled to the right, and joined their comrades in a furious charge on our centre. Major Morris ordered up company E from our right, but too late to be of any advantage, and they were completely cut off from the main body of our army. Although flanked and pressed in front by overwhelming numbers, our centre heroically contested the advance of the enemy. Animated by the presence of the Colonel, they fought like veterans, and the white snowballs eddied through the air like popping corn from a frying pan. But the enemy were madly surging upon us in superior force, and it was hardly within the power of human endurance to stand such a perfect *feu d'enfer* any longer. Gradually the centre fell back inch by inch, the line then wavered to and fro, and finally the men broke in confusion and rolled down the hill followed by the victorious Vermonters. In vain the Colonel breasted the torrent; in vain the Major urged the men to stand fast; in vain did Adjutant White, the chivalric De Bayard of the Twenty-sixth, implore the gods for aid.

"The boys never rallied. Lieutenant Woods made an attempt to rally them and form them in hollow square on the fortified hill to the right, but he was mistaken by the boys for a Vermonter, and unceremoniously pelted from their midst. But the Colonel was not totally deserted by his men. The Vermonters seized his horse by the bridle, and made a desperate attempt to take him prisoner. The fight at this point was terrific beyond description. The men fought hand to hand. Colonel Seaver, the Achilles of the day, dashed through the combatants, seized Colonel Morrison by the shoulder, and called upon him to surrender. But his demand was choked by the incessant patter of snow-balls on his 'physog.' Around the rival chieftains the men struggled fearfully; there was the auburn-haired Hodge, alias 'Wild Dutchman,' fighting manfully. There was the fierce Teuton Captain of company E, dropping the foe right and left at every swing of his arms; but all in vain. Amid the wild excitement consequent upon the shouting, the rearing, and

plunging of horses, the Colonel was drawn from his saddle and taken by the enemy. Most of his 'staff' followed him as prisoners. A desperate attempt was made to rescue him, but it proved of no avail. Major Morris fared no better. Adjutant White, however, made a bold attempt to retrieve the fortunes of the day. Dashing into the dense ranks of the foe, he seized the bridle of Colonel Stoughton's Bucephalus, and gallantly attempted the impossibility of capturing the Colonel, who was the acting Brigadier of the attacking party. But the Adjutant had 'caught a Tartar,' for the Vermonters rushed around him like the waves beating upon some lone rock in the ocean, and vainly clamored for his surrender. He fought like an Ajax mounted on a 'Black Bass,' retaining his position in the saddle by resting his knee against the pommel. This was at last observed by a shrewd Yankee, who dexterously slipped between the two horses, detached the supporting knee, and the Adjutant fell from his lofty position like a tornado-stricken oak. This fall disheartened the Twenty-sixth, and only detached parties of a dozen, scattered over the field, persisted in an obstinate resistance. The 'Sergeant' received a solid shot in the back of the head, and was borne to the rear a captive, and then

'The bugles sang truce.'

"Thus ended the great battle of Fairview; unequalled in desperateness, and the theme of many a future poet's cogitations. Our loss was very heavy, and we were severely defeated. The spectators, acting on the well-known principle of kicking a man when he is down, pitched into us most unmercifully when our centre was broken, and prevented us from re-forming in line of battle. The slaughter of the enemy was fearful, and the prowess of the Newark ball players and firemen was displayed on their battered visages. Colonel Stoughton was honored with a black eye, and the gallant Seaver fared but little better. The following is a fair recapitulation of the casualties on both sides:

"Bloody noses, fifty-three; bunged peepers, eighty-one; extraordinary phrenological developments, twenty-nine; shot in the neck after the engagement, unknown.

"The Vermonters fought with the determined energy characterizing them when engaging Jeff's myrmidons."

COOLNESS IN BATTLE. — In the report of Major-General Foster, of his expedition to Kinston, N. C., in the list of killed and wounded is the name of Ezra Wormouth. Ezra was wounded at Whitehall, while serving at one of the guns of Captain Jenny's battery, Third New York artillery. A ball struck his left wrist, shattering the bones, and cutting off his little finger. Amputation was rendered necessary immediately — so now, all that Ezra has left of his arm is four or five inches below the elbow. The noble fellow says "he has done all he can do to whip the enemy and crush the rebellion, and he is not sorry he ever enlisted, but is conscious of having done his duty, as all true men should." Does not that, and many other such sentiments which are uttered by men who have felt the sad effects of war, show who are true heroes?

Not fifteen minutes before Ezra was wounded, Thomas Johnson, of Oswego, N. Y., while serving at the same gun, was severely wounded in the left forearm and hand. Says Captain Jenny to him, "Johnson, you had better go to the rear, and have your wound dressed." Hear the reply: "No, Captain, I am going to work!" And work he did; but in a few minutes another ball took his right arm off. Turning to Captain Jenny, said he, "Now, Captain, I guess I'll quit!"

Numbers of such instances can be cited, especially that of a private in Company K (Captain Cole's), Third New York cavalry, who was shot down by a ball passing through his head, making nearly an inch hole. He immediately jumped up, and with true cavalry recklessness exclaimed, "Blast them! give 'em thunder, boys! I'll live to fight them yet!" And, sure enough, he did.

THE "THIRD ARTICLE" OF WAR. — A soldier correspondent writes the following from the camp of the Ohio volunteers, at Falmouth:

"Yesterday being Sunday, after the usual guard, picket, and inspection calls, the ensuing hour and a half was spent in hearing the Articles of War read. As Corporal Humphrey, of our company, was reading the aforesaid 'Articles,' we noticed that 'Eph' smiled 'out loud' several times, — attempting each time to disguise it by dryly coughing, — and after the inspection was over, we asked him what made him cough while in the ranks. 'Why,' said he, 'when the Corporal read "Article Third," about any non-commissioned officer or soldier who should use any profane oath or execration, should forfeit one sixth of a dollar, to be applied for the benefit of the sick soldiers of the command; and a commissioned officer should forfeit and pay, for each such offence, one dollar, to be applied in the same manner, I thought the "Article" was one of "Old Abe's jokes;" and that the Corporal had got to the place "where the laugh came in."' We told him that the Articles of War were no 'joke,' but that they were enacted by Congress for the government of all our armies.

"'Well,' said "Eph," 'if that is so, my opinion is that the sick soldiers of this army will "fare sumptuously every day," and as banks have what they call a "sinking fund," I think it would be well for Congress to provide the officers with a "swearing fund."' As he was speaking, 'Ike' plodded past in charge of the pickets of this division, and 'Eph' continued: 'Now, there goes "Ike" on picket, and he don't swear — only when he thinks it a "military necessity" — but I'll bet you a paper of "Fighting Joe smoking tobacco" that before he arrives at the Lacy House, over those hills and through all that mud, Article Three will get busted more than one hundred dollars worth; and if the members of Congress, who framed those Articles, were the picket that is going out with him, it would cost them more pay than they get in one season extra session, mileage and all.'

"During the day 'Eph' came into our quarters, and, taking from his pocket a little morocco covered book, said he would like to read a few lines from to-day's evening prayer — '22d day'— and accordingly read as follows:

". . 'Manassas is mine; Ephraim also is the strength of my head. . . Who will lead me into the strong city? . . Hast thou not forsaken me, O God? and wilt not thou, O God, go forth with our hosts? O, help us against the enemy, for vain is the help of man. Through God we shall do great acts; it is He that shall tread down our enemies.

"'Now,' remarked "Eph," 'my opinion is, David meant us. We have got Manassas; took it — "without loss" — over a year ago. But "who will lead us into the strong city"? Who will bring us into Richmond? "Fighting Joe" is here in command of the army, and "Eph" is here too, and I hope he may have the honor of following "Old Joe" into Richmond. I believe God is on our side; but my opinion is, we had better let those works, the enemy have erected on the other side, alone. The last time I was there I made up my mind General French was correct in his opinions. Said he to General Couch, "General, the men can't take those works." Said General Couch, "Brave men can do anything!" "Brave men can't stop a cannon-ball, —— ——," said old General French, at the same time busting Article Three; but out we went, and tried it all day. I saw over twenty men try to stop one cannon ball — brave men, too — but, poor fellows!' French was right; they could not do it. In fact, the ground was piled up with brave men, who looked as though they had tried very hard to stop some of those cannon balls, but were 'wearied out,' and had lain down to rest. Through God, brave men may do many, very many, great things; but in the providence of God, He has not so constituted man, that even, though he is brave, he can stop a cannon ball."

THE HOSPITAL.

Narrow beds by one another —
    White and low!
Through them softly, as in church-aisles,
    Nurses go —
For the hot lips ice-drops bring,
    Cold and clear;
Or white eyelids gently closing,
    For the bier.

Strong men, in a moment smitten
    Down from strength,
Brave men, now in anguish praying —
    Death at length,
Burns the night-lamp where the watchers,
    By the bed,
Write for many a waiting loved one,
    "He is dead!"

One lies there in utter weakness —
　　Shattered, faint —
But his brow wears calm befitting
　　Martyred saint ;
And although the lips must quiver,
　　They can smile, ,
As he says, "This will be over
　　In a while.

" As the old crusaders, weeping
　　In delight,
Knelt when Zion's holy city
　　Rose in sight,
So I fling aside my weapon,
　　From the din
To the quietness of heaven
　　Entering in.

" Standing in the solemn shadow
　　Of God's hand,
Love of glory fading from me,
　　Love of land,
I thank God that he has let me
　　Strike one blow
For this poor and helpless people,
　　Ere I go."

White and whiter grows the glory
　　On his brow ;
Does he see the towers of Zion
　　Rising now ?
Stands the doctor, weary, hurried,
　　By his bed :
" Here is room for one more wounded —
　　He is dead."

ARMY DISCIPLINE. — A writer in the Cincinnati Commercial relates the following anecdote of General A. J. Smith, who was in command of a division of General Grant's army of the Mississippi. It shows, characteristically, his style of treating with delinquent officers, whose shortcomings chance to come within his observation :

" As I, with my small command, was quartered on board the steamer Des Arc, which boat was at that time used as General A. J. Smith's headquarters, I necessarily became a witness to this (to lookers on) most amusing interlude :

" On our passage down from Arkansas Post to Young's Point, after our glorious victory at the former place, we had on board with us (for transportation) three companies of the —th Illinois volunteers. Now it happened that these men had rather neglected to clean their guns, which the sharp eye of the old veteran soon discovered. It was in the morning of our third day out — the wind was blowing terribly, and the weather unusually cold, rendering it very unpleasant to remain long on the hurricane roof — that the General came rushing into the cabin, where nearly all the officers were comfortably seated around a warm stove.

" 'Captain,' exclaimed the General, in no very mild tone, addressing himself to the commander of one of the companies aforesaid, ' have you had an inspection of arms this morning ?'

" 'No, General,' timidly replied the Captain, 'I have not.'

" 'Have you held an inspection of your company at any time since the battle of Arkansas Post ?' sharply asked the General.

" 'No, sir ; the weather has been so unpleasant, and I thought I would let my men rest a while,' hesitatingly replied the Captain, already nervous, through fear that something disagreeable was about to turn up.

" 'You thought you'd let them rest a while ? Indeed ! The d—l you did ! Who pays you, sir, for permitting your men to lie and rot in idleness, while such important duties remain unattended to ? What kind of condition are your men in, now, to defend this boat, or even the lives of your own men, in case we should be attacked by the enemy this moment. What the d—l are you in the service for, if you thus neglect your most important duty ?' fairly yelled the old General. And then starting menacingly towards the quaking Captain, said he imperatively : 'Mount, sir ! on that roof this moment, and call your men instantly into line, that I may examine their arms. And you,' resumed he, turning and addressing the lieutenants, who commanded the other companies, ' are fully as delinquent as the Captain. Sirs ! I must see your men into line within ten minutes.'

" It is scarcely necessary to state that the officers in question made the best of their time in drumming up their men, whom they found scattered in all parts of the boat. Finally, however, the companies referred to were duly paraded on the 'hurricane,' and an abridged form of inspection was gone through with. The General, finding their arms in bad condition, very naturally inflicted some severe talk, threatening condign punishment in case such neglect should be repeated.

" But during the time in which one of these companies was falling in, which operation was not executed with that degree of promptness on the part of the rank and file satisfactory to the Lieutenant commanding, that officer called out in a most imploring strain — ' Fall in, gentlemen ! Fall in lively, gentlemen !' That application of the word 'gentlemen' fell upon the ear of General Smith, who, turning quickly around, hastily inquired, ' Are you the Lieutenant in command of that company ?' addressing the individual who had given the command in such a polite manner.

" 'Yes, sir,' replied the trembling subaltern.

" 'Then, who the d—l are you calling gentlemen ?' cried the General. ' I am an old soldier,' continued he, approaching and looking more earnestly at the Lieutenant, ' but I must confess, sir, that I never before heard of the rank of gentlemen in the army. Soldiers, sir, are all supposed to be gentlemen, of course ; but hereafter, sir, when you address soldiers, remember to say soldiers, or men ; let us have no more of this " bowing and scraping," where it is your duty to " command." ' Then turning upon his heel, his eyes snapping with impatience, the old General gave vent in the following words : ' Gentlemen ! Gentlemen, forsooth ! And rusty guns ! Umph ! That's good ! But that is the way it goes in our army nowadays. Each man expects to run for some civil office, on his return from the war, and so great is his fear of giving offence to his men, and thus injure his popularity, that he permits them to neglect their most important duties; and to "trump all," he has to address his command with the word "gentlemen" prefixed in order to be obeyed! Alas, what militia.'"

ANECDOTES OF GENERAL KEARNY. — "I have never told you how popular the memory of Kearny is with all here," said a soldier — "Jersey Kearny, as some call him. 'What is that patch of red on your hat for?' I asked a young fellow one day. 'It is for Kearny, sir,' said he; and anybody could see he was proud of it.

"Stories are related by the dozen of the daring of Kearny in action. Among a party of a dozen officers, many of whom had fought under him in the battles on the Peninsula and Manassas, I heard a number of adventures related to which the narrators had been witnesses. In the midst of the most desperate battles, when the whole field was ablaze with fire and smoke, Kearny was in an ecstasy of delight, as he rode along his unbroken columns, cheering where the fight was thickest! 'You might hear the shrill voice of Kearny,' said Colonel Kiddoo, of a Pennsylvania regiment, 'ringing out, as he rode along the lines, "Gayly, men, gayly!"' I shall hear that voice of Kearny's till I die,' said the Colonel. But the old General's cheering was not always couched in the choicest terms; for, when a little doubt lowered over our arms, then Kearny would put on his whole armor, he would sink the rowels of his spurs into that wonderful horse he rode, and, flying along from right to left and from left to right, he would hail the line with, 'We are whipping them like h—l, like h—l we are whipping them!'

"He had lost the left arm, and he would often catch the rein in his teeth; his sword in his right hand, carried above his head. Nothing was too daring for him. Once he had cleared an immense log and ditch together, but one of his aids halted when he came to it. Kearny saw him hesitate, and spoke out, 'Jump it, you d—d ass! jump, I say, you d—d ass!' he often repeated.

"It is said that when Kearny fell, he had ridden furiously, and become suddenly surprised by a force of the enemy in a strip of woods. They had him entrapped, and sang out, 'Surrender, surrender!' 'Never, by G—d!' and Kearny, wheeling his horse, received the fatal bullet."

HOW WATERFORD WAS SAVED. — Just before the rebels evacuated the village of Waterford, near Leesburg, Virginia, they openly avowed they would burn it to the ground, as it was nothing more than a "cursed Quaker settlement." A noble-hearted Quaker woman, whose husband had been chased from his home by the rebels some months before, besought a gentleman of her faith to hasten over to Colonel Geary's camp, some eight miles away, and ask him to send a force to Waterford to prevent the threatened con-

flagration. He had a fine horse, but declined the duty, owing to the dangers of getting through the rebel pickets. "Lend me thy horse, then," she said. He declined again. "Then I will steal thy horse," she said, "and go myself." She forthwith directed a servant to take the horse to a neighboring wood, to which the owner made no resistance. Another servant took her side-saddle to the horse, when the heroine appeared, and, mounting the animal, rode off in open day right through the pickets, who did not stop her, strange to say. When she got to Geary's camp, she met her husband; and, being brought into presence of the Colonel, she made known the object of her mission, which was quickly complied with, and she rode back to Waterford at the head of a detachment, which got into the village just in time to see the rebel force leaving the opposite end of the town as fast as their heels could carry them. And thus this pretty little village was saved from conflagration by the resolute conduct of this Quaker lady.

THE ESCAPE OF JOHN MORGAN.

GENERAL JOHN MORGAN was honored with an ovation on the 7th of January, 1864, on his arrival at Richmond. The following is an account of his escape from the Ohio Penitentiary, and subsequent adventures:

"Their bedsteads were small iron stools, fastened to the wall with hinges. They could be hooked up, or allowed to stand on the floor; and, to prevent any suspicion, for several days before any work was attempted, they made it a habit to let them down, and sit at their doors and read. Captain Hines superintended the work, while General Morgan kept watch to divert the attention of the sentinel, whose duty it was to come round during the day, and observe if anything was going on. One day this fellow came in while Hokersmith was down under the floor, boring away, and, missing him, said, 'Where is Hokersmith?' The General replied, 'He is in my room sick;' and immediately pulled a document out of his pocket, and said to him, 'Here is a memorial I have drawn up to forward to the Government at Washington. What do you think of it?'

"The fellow, who, perhaps, could not read, being highly flattered at the General's condescension, took it, and very gravely looked at it for several moments before he vouchsafed any reply; then, handing it back, he expressed himself highly pleased with it. In the mean time, Hokersmith had been signalled, and came up, professing to feel 'very unwell.' This sentinel was the most difficult and dangerous obstacle in their progress, because there was no telling at what time he would enter during the day, and at night he came regularly every two hours to each cell, and inserted a light through the bars of their door, to see that they were quietly sleeping; and frequently, after he had completed his rounds, he would slip back in the dark, with a pair of India-rubber shoes on, to listen at their cells if anything was going on. The General says that he would almost invariably know of his presence by a certain magnetic shudder which it would produce; but, for fear that this acute sensibility might sometimes fail him, he broke up small particles of coal every morning, and sprinkled them before the cell-door, which would always announce his coming.

"Everything was now ready to begin the work; so, about the latter part of October, they began to bore. All were busy,— one making a rope-ladder, by tearing and twisting up strips of bed-ticking, another making bowie-knives, and another twisting up towels. They labored perseveringly for several days, and, after boring through nine inches of cement, and nine thicknesses of brick placed edgewise, they began to wonder when they should reach the soft earth. Suddenly a brick fell through. What could this mean? What infernal chamber had they reached? It was immediately entered; and, to their great astonishment and joy, it proved to be an air-chamber extending the whole length of the row of cells. Here was an unexpected interposition in their favor. Hitherto they had been obliged to conceal their rubbish in their bed-tickings, each day burning a proportionate quantity of straw. Now they had room enough for all they could dig. They at once commenced to tunnel at right angles with this air-chamber, to get through the foundation; and day after day they bored— day after day the blocks of granite were removed —and still the work before them seemed interminable.

"After twenty-three days of unremitting labor, and getting through a granite wall of six feet in thickness, they reached the soil. They tunnelled up for some distance, and light began to shine. How glorious was that light! It announced the fulfilment of their labors; and if Providence would only continue its favor, they would soon be free. This was the morning of the 26th day of November, 1863. The subsequent night, at twelve o'clock, was determined on as the hour at which they would attempt their liberty. Each moment that intervened was filled with dreadful anxiety and suspense, and each time the guard entered increased their apprehensions. The General says that he had prayed for rain; but the morning of the 27th dawned bright and beautiful. The evening came, and clouds began to gather. How they prayed for them to increase! If rain should only begin, their chances of detection would be greatly lessened. While these thoughts were passing through their minds, the keeper entered with a letter for General Morgan. He opened it, and what was his surprise —and I may say, wonder —to find it from a poor Irish woman of his acquaintance, in Kentucky, commencing: 'My dear Ginral —I feel certain you are going to try to git out of prison; but, for your sake, don't you try it, my dear Ginral. You will only be taken prisoner again, and made to suffer more than you do now.'

"The letter then went on to speak of his kindness to the poor when he lived at Lexington, and concluded by again exhorting him to trust in God, and wait his time. What could this mean? No human being on the outside had been informed of his intention to escape; and yet, just as all things were ready for him to make the attempt, here comes a letter from Winchester, Kentucky, advising him not to 'try it.' This letter had passed through the examining office of General Mason, and then through the hands of the lower officials. What if it should excite their suspicion, and cause them to exercise an increased vigilance? The situation, however, was desperate. Their fate could not be much worse, and they resolved to go. Nothing now remained to be done but for the General and Colonel Dick Morgan to change cells. The hour approached for them to be locked up. They changed coats, and each stood at the other's cell door with his back exposed, and pretended to be engaged in making up their beds. As the turnkey entered, they 'turned in,' and pulled their doors shut.

"Six, eight, ten o'clock came. How each pulse throbbed as they quietly awaited the approach of twelve! It came —the sentinel passed his round —all well. After waiting a few moments to see if he intended to slip back, the signal was given. All quietly slipped down into the air-chamber, first stuffing their flannel-shirts, and placing them in bed as they were accustomed to lie. As they moved quietly along through the dark recess to the terminus where they were to emerge from the earth, the General prepared to light a match. As the lurid glare fell upon their countenances, a scene was presented which can never be forgotten. There were crouched seven brave men who had resolved to be free. They were armed with bowie-knives made out of case-knives. Life, in their condition, was scarcely to be desired, and the moment for the desperate chance had arrived. Suppose, as they emerged from the ground, that the dog should give the alarm —they could but die.

"But few moments were spent in this kind of apprehension. The hour had arrived, and yet they came. Fortunately —yes, providentially— the night had suddenly grown dark and rainy, the dogs had retired to their kennels, and the sentinels had taken refuge under shelter. The inner wall, by the aid of the rope-ladder, was soon scaled, and now the outer one had to be attempted. Captain Taylor (who, by the way, is a nephew of Old Zach), being a very active man, by the assistance of his comrades reached the top of the gate, and was enabled to get the rope over the wall. When the top was gained, they found a rope extending all around, which the General immediately cut, as he suspected that it might lead into the Warden's room. This turned out to be correct. They then entered the sentry-box on the wall and changed their clothes, and let themselves down the wall. In sliding down, the General skinned his hand very badly, and all were more or less bruised. Once down, they separated —Taylor and Shelton going one way, Hokersmith, Bennett, and McGee another, and General Morgan and Captain Hines proceeding immediately towards the depot.

"The General had, by paying fifteen dollars in gold, succeeded in obtaining a paper which informed him of the schedule time of the different roads. The clock struck one, and he knew, by hurrying, he could reach the down-train for Cincinnati. He got there just as the train was moving off. He at once looked around to see if there were any soldiers on board, and espying a Union officer, he boldly walked up and took a seat beside him. He remarked to him, that 'as the night was damp and chilly, perhaps he would join him in a drink.' He did so, and the party soon became very agreeable to each other. The cars, in crossing the Scioto, have to pass within a short distance of the Penitentiary. As they passed, the officer remarked: 'There's the hotel at which Morgan and his officers are spending their leisure.' 'Yes,' replied the General, 'and I sincerely hope he will make up his mind to board there during the balance of the war, for he is a great nuisance.' When the train reached Xenia, it was detained by some accident more than an hour. Imagine his anxiety, as soldier after soldier would pass through the train, for fear that when the sentinel passed his round at two o'clock their absence might be discovered.

"The train was due in Cincinnati at six o'clock. This was the hour at which they were turned out of their cells, and, of course, their escape would be then discovered. In a few moments after it would be known all over the country. The train, having been detained at Xenia, was running very rapidly to make up the time. It was already past six o'clock. The General said to Captain Hines: 'It's after six o'clock; if we go to the depot, we are dead men. Now or never.' They went to the rear, and put on the brakes. 'Jump, Hines!' Off he went, and fell heels over head in the mud. Another severe turn of the brakes, and the General jumped. He was more successful, and lighted on his feet. There were some soldiers near, who remarked, 'What in h—l do you mean by jumping off the cars here?' The General replied: 'What in the d—l is the use of my going into town when I live here? and, besides, what business is it of yours?'

"They went immediately to the river. They found a skiff, but no oars. Soon a little boy came over, and appeared to be waiting. 'What are you waiting for?' said the General. 'I am waiting for my load.' 'What is the price of a load?' 'Two dollars.' 'Well, as we are tired and hungry, we will give you the two dollars, and you can put us over.' So over he took them. 'Where does Miss —— live?' 'Just a short distance from here.' 'Will you show me her house?' 'Yes, sir.' The house was reached, a fine breakfast was soon obtained, money and a horse furnished, a good woman's prayer bestowed, and off he went. From there, forward through Kentucky, everybody vied with each other as to who should show him the most attention — even to the negroes; and young ladies of refinement begged the honor to cook his meals.

"He remained in Kentucky some days, feeling perfectly safe, and sending into Louisville for many little things he wanted. Went to Bardstown, and found a Federal regiment had just arrived there, looking for him. Remained here and about for three or four days, and then struck out for Dixie; sometimes disguising himself as a Government cattle-contractor, and buying a large lot of cattle; at other times a Quartermaster, until he got to the Tennessee River. Here he found all means of transportation destroyed, and the bank strongly guarded; but with the assistance of about thirty others, who had recognized him, and joined him in spite of his remonstrances, he succeeded in making a raft, and he and Captain Hines crossed over. His escort, with heroic self-sacrifice, refused to cross until he was safely over. He then hired a negro to get his horse over, paying him twenty dollars for it. The river was so high that the horse came near drowning, and after more than one hour's struggling with the stream, was pulled out so exhausted as scarcely to be able to stand.

"The General threw a blanket on him and commenced to walk him, when suddenly, he says, he was seized with a presentiment that he would be attacked, and remarking to Captain Hines, 'We shall be attacked in twenty minutes,' commenced saddling his horse. He had hardly tied his girth when 'Bang! bang!' went the minie balls. He bounced his horse, and the noble animal, appearing to be inspired with new vigor, bounded off like a deer up the mountain. The last he saw of his poor fellows on the opposite side, they were disappearing up the river bank, fired upon by a whole regiment of Yankees. By this time it was dark, and also raining. He knew that a perfect cordon of pickets would surround the foot of the mountain, and if he remained there until morning he would be lost. So he determined to run the gantlet at once, and commenced to descend. As he neared the foot, leading his horse, he came almost in personal contact with a picket. His first impulse was to kill him, but finding him asleep, he determined to let him sleep on. He made his way to the house of a Union man that he knew lived near there, and went up and passed himself off as Captain Quartermaster of Hunt's regiment, who was on his way to Athens, Tenn., to procure supplies of sugar and coffee for the Union people of the country. The lady, who appeared to be asleep while this interview was taking place with her husband, at the mention of sugar and coffee, jumped out of bed in her night-clothes, and said: 'Thank God for that; for we ain't seen any rale coffee up here for God knows how long!' She was so delighted at the prospect, that she made up a fire and cooked them a good supper. Supper being over, the General remarked that he understood that some rebels had 'tried to cross the river this afternoon.' 'Yes,' said the woman 'but our men killed some on um, and driv the rest back.' 'Now,' said the General, 'I know that; but didn't some of them get over?' 'Yes,' was her reply, 'but they are on the mountain, and cannot get down without being killed, as every road is stopped up.' He then said to her: 'It is very important for me to get to Athens by to-morrow night, or I may lose that sugar and coffee; and I am afraid to go down any of these roads for fear my own men will kill me.'

"The fear of losing that sugar and coffee brought her again to an accommodating mood, and she replied: 'Why, Paul, can't you show the Captain through our farm, that road down by the field?' The General says: 'Of course, Paul, you can do it; and as the night is very cold, I will give you ten dollars (in gold) to help you along.' The gold, and the prospect of sugar and coffee, were too much for any poor man's nerves, and he yielded, and getting on a horse, he took them seven miles to the big road.

"From this time forward he had a series of adventures and escapes, all very wonderful, until he got near another river in Tennessee, when he resolved to go up to a house and find the way. Hines went to the house, while the General stood in the road. Hearing a body of cavalry come dashing up behind him, he quietly slipped to one side of the road, and it passed by without observing him. They went travelling after Hines, and, poor fellow! he has not been heard of since. How sad to think that he should be either captured or killed after so many brave efforts, not only in his own behalf, but also in that of the General; for the General says that it is owing chiefly to Hines's enterprise and skill that they made their escape.

"When he arrived at the river referred to above, he tried to get over, intending to stop that night with a good Southern man on the other side. He could not get over, and had to stop at the house of a Union man. The next morning he went to the house that he had sought the night previous, and found the track of the Yankees scarcely cold. They had been there all night, expecting that he would come there, and had murdered everybody who had attempted to reach the house, without hailing them. In pursuing this brutal course, they had killed three young men, neighbors of this gentleman, and went away, leaving their dead bodies on the ground.

"After he had crossed Okey's River, and got down into Middle Tennessee, he found it almost impossible to avoid recognition. At one time he passed some poor women, and one of them commenced clapping her hands, and said, 'O! I know who that is! I know who that is!' but, catching herself, she stopped short, and passed on with her companions.

"The General says that his escape was made entirely without assistance from any one on the outside, and, so far as he knows, also without their knowledge of his intention; that the announcement of his arrival in Toronto was one of those fortuitous coincidences that cannot be accounted for; that it assisted him materially, no doubt. In fact, he says that his 'wife's prayers' saved him, and, as this is the most agreeable way of explaining it, he is determined to believe it."

AN INCIDENT. — Among the excuses offered for exemptions, some are extremely ludicrous. In Smyth County, Va., we learn, one man on enrolling himself wrote opposite his name, "one leg too short." The next man that came in, noticing the excuse, and deeming it pretty good, thought he would make his better, and wrote opposite his name, "both legs too short"!

WIT WORTH PRESERVING. — The committee appointed to collect metal for cannon for General Beauregard's army, applied to a planter of Adams County, Miss., for his bell. Not having such an article, he mentioned it to his wife, when she very patriotically offered her brass kettle. The little ones rather demurred to the sacrifice, and one of them, with a sweet tooth, said, "La, pa, what will we do for preserves?" "My daughter," said the wag of a father, "our whole duty now is to *preserve* our country." The kettle was sent.

BUELL'S STRATEGY. — A soldier who was in the battle of Pittsburg gives the following account of General Buell's strategy in the field:

"On Monday morning, about ten o'clock, General Buell executed a manœuvre that reflects great credit on him as a commander. The rebels were advancing in great force to turn our left and capture our transports and supplies, when Buell, becoming aware of their intentions, made preparations to receive them. About half a mile above the landing are two large ridges, and between them he placed a brigade of infantry. The troops were ordered to lie down. He then ordered a lower battery to fire on the enemy and make a show of retreating in confusion to draw the rebels on. On came the rebels, pell-mell, yelling at the top of their voices, 'Bull's Run,' 'Bull's Run,' thinking, I suppose, to frighten us.

"As soon as the rebels came in range, the lower battery, agreeably to orders, opened fire, retreated, and took a position in rear of the upper battery. The rebels, seeing our men retreating, charged up the hill, and took possession of the battery. The rebels, in the mean time, were not aware of our troops being in the hollow below them. At this moment the signal was sounded, and the whole brigade rose to their feet, and poured a deadly fire of rifle balls into the ranks of the rebels, cutting them down by scores. At this favorable moment, also, the upper battery poured in a perfect storm of grape and canister shot. The rebels reeled and staggered like drunken men, and at last broke and fled in every direction, leaving the ground strewed with dead and dying."

INCIDENT OF FORT DONELSON. — One little incident will show what the rebels expected. Having exhibited such a large force, and completely surrounded the nationals, they thought it was about time for them to surrender, as many others had done; and they began to be out of patience at the men's foolish tenacity, as they termed it, and determined to make a charge upon the siege gun, which they hoped to capture and decide the contest. Two rebels, more venturesome than the rest, rode rapidly to the advance of the charging force, and ventured a little advice — yelling out, " You d—d fools you, don't you know when to surrender? Don't you see you are completely surrounded?" Our gallant little force at this point did not appreciate this admonition; but just then bang went the old gun, blowing Mr. Rebels and horses to atoms, repulsing the charge, and saving this point again. The men and horses were about fifteen feet from the gun when it went off, loaded with canister.

A CASE OF AFFECTION. — A soldier at La Grange, Tennessee, gives the following: "The women would rather we would take prisoners all the men on the plantation than one blind mule. A case of like *filial* affection I witnessed one time while our company was out picking up scattering members of Faulkner's guerrilla band. Coming up to a house where we had ascertained one of them lived, our Lieutenant inquired of the ' gude woman' of the house, the whereabouts of her lord. She hurriedly informed him that her husband was not at home. The Lieutenant knew he was, however, and set some of us to searching for Mr. Butternut, while others were looking about for anything else contraband. During the search, the woman noticed the boys catching a mule in the lot, and bursting into tears, sobbed piteously, ' O, dear, Mr. Lieutenant, they are taking my poor old mool! O, Mr. Lieutenant, good Mr. Lieutenant, for the love of God and your mother, if you ever had one, *don't* let 'em take my poor old mool!' To this appeal, Lieutenant Watson only asked again where she had concealed her husband. ' O, I'll show you where he is, but for God's sake spare me that poor old mool!' Her trembling husband was soon forthcoming, and mounting him upon the mule, we left the woman standing in the door wringing her hands and crying, not for her betrayed husband, but ' my poor old mool' — doubtless beginning to think this war was not so fine a thing as the country had supposed before it had followed them home to their hearthstones."

HEROISM AT FREDERICKSBURG. — Captain James H. Platt, Jr., of company B, Fourth Vermont regiment, having been ordered with his company to the right of the skirmish line, after having once expended nearly all its ammunition and been re-supplied, led his men out in front of a battery within three hundred yards, where they did noble execution till a charge of canister struck down half the company, killing four and wounding fourteen, when he ordered them back to reform, which they did, and retired in good order with the regiment just relieved. Yet not all, for calling some to his side, the humane Captain, a skilful physician, bound up the most dangerous wounds, thus prolonging at least several lives, and with the assistance he had summoned, bore away to the hospital, a mile distant, all who were unable to help themselves. This was done amid bullets flying like hail, yet, through a kind Providence, no one was harmed. As the gallant Captain said, " God would not let us suffer while in discharge of such a duty."

"WHILE GOD HE LEAVES ME REASON, GOD HE WILL LEAVE ME JIM." *

BY MARY H. C. BOOTH.

"SOLDIER, say, did you meet my Jimmy in the
    fight?
You'd know him by his manliness, and by his eyes'
    sweet light."
" I fought beside your gallant son — a brave, good
    fellow he;
Alas! he fell beneath the shot that should have
    taken me."

"And think you that my Jimmy cared about a
    little fall?
Why make a great ado of what he would not mind
    at all?
When Jimmy was a little boy, and played with
    Bobby Brown,
He always played the enemy, and Bob he shot him
    down.

"I've seen him fall a hundred times, the cunning
    little sprite;
He can't forget his boyish tricks though in an
    earnest fight.
But never mind about the fall; I want to hear of
    him;
Perhaps you've heard the Captain speak of what he
    thinks of Jim."

" I've often heard the Captain say Jim was a splendid lad,
The bravest and the handsomest of all the boys
    he had.
And here's a lock of Jimmy's hair, and here's a
    golden ring;
I found it tied around his neck upon a silken
    string."

The mother took the matted tress, she took the
    ring of gold,
But shook her head, and laughed aloud at what the
    soldier told.
"Soldier," said she, " where is my boy? where is
    my brave boy, Jim?
I gave the others all to God, but God he left me
    him.

" Hush, there is Uncle Abraham a-knocking at the
    door;
He calls for other mothers' sons, ' *Three hundred
    thousand more!*'
Be still, Old Uncle Abraham; 'twill do no good
    to call;
You think my house is full of boys; ah, Jimmy
    was my all."

* Words of a soldier's mother, who, on hearing that
her only son had fallen in battle, became hopelessly
insane, though continually declaring that his having
" fallen " was of no consequence.

A LAUGHABLE ADVENTURE. — The following story was related by Lieutenant J. H. Spencer, of the First Minnesota regiment:

"On the —th we moved towards Madison Court House, and when within two and one half miles of the town we came to Robson River, which was so high, from the recent rains, that we could not cross, there being no bridge. We camped for the night, and remained until the 20th. At three A. M. we crossed the river, and at daybreak the advance guard, which consisted of sixteen men, a guide and myself, charged through the town, and drove the enemy's pickets towards Gordonsville. On the south side of the town we found a horse hitched in front of a house, saddled and bridled, and covered with sweat. Our guide told us that the man who lived there was a strong 'secesh,' and I recognized the horse as one I had seen the day before, through my glass, mounted by a rebel scout. I ordered my men to surround the house, while I quietly knocked at the door. An elderly lady made her appearance. I asked her if Mr. Newton (the man's name) was at home. She said 'no, he had gone to Gordonsville; had been gone two days.' I asked her whose horse that was at the front gate. She did not know, but thought, perhaps, it belonged to the rebel pickets that had been stationed near the house. I told her that I thought so too, and that I should have to search the house, for I believed that some one was secreted in it. She begged of me not to do so, and assured me that no one was in the house but herself and daughter-in-law; that her daughter was very sick, and could not be disturbed. I told her that I would not disturb her or interfere with private property, unless in the discharge of my duties. I searched all the rooms but the one in which the sick lady was. I found two Enfield rifles, and one Colt's revolver, all loaded with ball cartridges. The old lady begged of me not to disturb her daughter — she was very sick. My modesty prompted me not to enter the room, but it was my duty to make a thorough search. I quietly opened the door, and looked in. The lady was in the bed, and apparently in great agony. I stepped into the room and looked carefully around into the closet and under the bed, but discovered nothing suspicious. I noticed, with some misgivings, that the lady took up more room in the bed than I thought was necessary, (unless she had on hoops). I turned down the bed clothes, and found — what? The identical soldier, Newton, who had 'been gone to Gordonsville two days!' He was snugly curled up on the back side of the bed, and it seemed that he had gone to bed in something of a hurry, for he had on all his clothes, even his cap and boots. His wife also seemed to recover very rapidly from her illness. I shall never forget the expression that was depicted upon Newton's countenance. I posted my pickets and returned with my prisoner to camp."

A RABBIT IN BATTLE. — A full-grown rabbit had hid itself away in the copse of a fence, which separated two fields near the centre and most ex-posed portion of the battle-ground. Rabbits are wont to spend the day almost motionless, and in seeming dreamy meditation. This one could have had but little thought — if rabbits think — when choosing its place of retreat at early dawn, that ere it was eventide there would be such an unwonted and ruthless disturbance.

During all the preparations for battle made around its lair during the forenoon, it nevertheless remained quiet. Early, however, in the afternoon, when the rage of battle had fairly begun, and shot and shell were falling thick and fast in all directions, a shell chanced to burst so near the rabbit's hiding-place that he evidently considered it unsafe to tarry longer. So, frightened almost to death, out he sprang into the open field, and ran hither and thither, with vain hope of finding a safe retreat. Whichever way it ran, cannons were thundering out their smoke and fire, regiments of men were advancing or changing position, horses galloping here and there, shells bursting, and solid shot tearing up the ground. Sometimes it would squat down and lie perfectly still, when some new and sudden danger would again start it into motion. Once more it would stop, and raise itself as high as possible on its hind legs, and look all round for some place of possible retreat. At length that part of the field seemed open which lay in the direction opposite from where the battle raged most fiercely. Thither it accordingly ran with all its remaining speed.

Unobserved by it, however, a regiment was in that direction held in reserve, and, like Wellington's at Waterloo, was lying flat on the ground, in order to escape the flying bullets. Ere the rabbit seemed aware, it had jumped into the midst of these men. It could go no farther, but presently nestled down beside a soldier, and tried to hide itself under his arm. As the man spread the skirt of his coat over the trembling fugitive, in order to insure it all the protection in his power to bestow, he no doubt feelingly remembered how much himself then needed some higher protection, under the shadow of whose arm might be hidden his own defenceless head from the fast multiplying missiles of death scattered in all directions.

It was not long, however, before the regiment was ordered up and forward. From the protection and safety granted, the timid creature had evidently acquired confidence in man — as the boys are wont to say, "had been tamed." As the regiment moved forward to the front of the battle, it hopped along, tame, seemingly, as a kitten, close at the feet of the soldier who had bestowed the needed protection. Wherever the regiment went, during all the remaining part of that bloody day and terrible battle, the rabbit kept close beside its new friend. When night came on, and the rage of battle had ceased, it finally unmolested and quietly hopped away, in order to find some one of its old and familiar haunts.

AN IRISH GUNNER. — At the battle of Fredericksburg a large cannon was located quite a distance from the rebels, and so much so that it was not being fired. An Irishman came along and wanted to fire, but they told him it would only be a waste of ammunition. " But," said the Irishman, " be d—d if I don't pay for the ammunition if it don't hit 'em." Consent was given, and he loaded his gun, cutting his fuse from his own sense of distance, drawn from his unerring sight. Soon an officer was seen, with another on each side, when Pat sighted his gun, and let go. Down went the officer, smash went the shell, wounding or killing the other two; and thus, with equal precision, he continued to cut his fuse and fire as long as they remained on the ground.

NOTE FROM AN OFFICER'S JOURNAL. — " Near Chattanooga, Thursday, September 17. — To-day a young lady called with her mother at headquarters, and asked to see the ' old flag,' saying for two years they had been denied a sight of it. As it was unrolled before them, they burst into tears. In the door-yard of her home is a grave, and I will tell you how it came there — then wonder at her weeping if you will. While the rebels were in this place, and were enforcing the conscription, her father fled to the mountains. Sought out and captured by the rebel fiends, without the knowledge of his wife and daughter, by night they brought him to his home and hung him on the tree beneath which he now sleeps. Morning came, and two rebel soldiers called to tell them the husband and father was outside, wishing to see them. Going out, expecting to embrace him, what a sight met their eyes! Horror-stricken, they appealed to the men to aid them in giving him a decent burial, but to no purpose; and amid the jeers and brutal insults of the God-forsaken wretches, they themselves were compelled to cut him down, dig his grave, and bury him from their sight forever. What wonder that they wept when they saw the old banner of freedom waving over them? Is God just, and will he allow such men to triumph? Little indeed do those at home know of the persecutions, the tortures, agonies the Union people have endured. Until mine own eyes had seen it, I could not hold such belief against my fellow-man."

INCIDENTS OF GETTYSBURG. — The following incidents are taken from the diary of an English officer, who was present at the battle :

"General Hill told me that in the first battle, near Gettysburg, the Yankees had fought with a determination unusual to them. He pointed out a railway cutting, in which they had made a good stand; also a field, in the centre of which he had seen a man plant the regimental colors, round which the regiment had fought for some time with much obstinacy; and when, at last, it was obliged to retreat, the color-bearer retreated last of all, turning around every now and then to shake his fist at the advancing rebels. General Hill said he felt quite sorry when he saw this gallant Yankee meet his doom.

" In the first day's contest the rebels had about twenty thousand men in the field. In the second day's fight — 2d of July — General Lee is described as sitting most of the time ' quite alone on the stump of a tree.' What I especially remarked was, that during the whole time the firing continued, he only sent one message, and only received one report."

Of the preparations made for the third and decisive day's contest, the writer says :

" Pickett's division, which had just come up, was to bear the brunt in Longstreet's attack, together with Hill's, and Pettigrew in Hill's corps. Pickett's division was a weak one — under five thousand — owing to the absence of two brigades."

After the battle had opened, the writer proceeded to join General Longstreet :

" And although astonished to meet such vast numbers of wounded, I had not seen enough to give me any real idea of the extent of the mischief. When I got close up to General Longstreet I saw one of his regiments advancing through the woods in good order; so, thinking I was just in time to see the attack, I remarked to the General that I wouldn't have missed this for anything. Longstreet was seated at the top of a snake fence, and looking perfectly calm and unperturbed. He replied, laughing, ' The devil you wouldn't! *I would like to have missed it very much. We've attacked and been repulsed. Look there!*' For the first time I then had a view of the open space between the two positions, and saw it covered with Confederates slowly and sulkily returning towards us, under a heavy fire of artillery. But the fire where we were was not so bad as farther to the rear; for although the air seemed alive with shell, yet the greater number burst behind us.

" The General was making the best arrangements in his power to resist the threatened advance, by advancing some artillery, rallying the stragglers, &c. I remember seeing a General (Pettigrew, I think it was) come up to him, and report that ' he was unable to bring his men up again.' Longstreet turned upon him and replied, with some sarcasm, ' Very well; never mind, then, General; just let them remain where they are; the enemy's going to advance, and will spare you the trouble.'

" He asked for something to drink; I gave him some rum out of my silver flask, which I begged he would keep in remembrance of the occasion; he smiled, and, to my great satisfaction, accepted the memorial. He then went off to give some orders to McLaw's division.

" Soon afterwards, I joined General Lee, who had, in the mean while, come to the front, on becoming aware of the disaster. If Longstreet's conduct was admirable, that of General Lee was perfectly sublime. He was engaged in rallying and encouraging the broken troops, and was riding about a little in front of the wood, quite alone, the whole of his staff being engaged in a similar manner farther to the rear. His face, which is always placid and cheerful, did not show signs of the slightest disappointment, care, or annoyance; and he was addressing to every soldier he met a few words of encouragement, such as, 'All this will come right in the end; we'll talk it over afterwards; but, in the mean time, all good men must rally. We want all good and true men just now,' &c. He spoke to all the wounded men that passed him; and the slightly wounded he exhorted 'to bind up their hurts and take up a musket' in this emergency. Very few failed to answer his appeal; and I saw many badly wounded men take off their hats and cheer him.

"He said to me, 'This has been a sad day for us, Colonel — a sad day; but we can't expect always to gain victories.' He was also kind enough to advise me to get into some more sheltered position.

"Notwithstanding the misfortune which had so suddenly befallen him, General Lee seemed to observe everything, however trivial. When a mounted officer began beating his horse for shying at the bursting of a shell, he called out, 'Don't whip him, Captain — don't whip him; I've got just such another foolish horse myself, and whipping does no good.'

"I happened to see a man lying flat on his face in a small ditch, and I remarked that I didn't think he seemed dead. This drew General Lee's attention to the man, who commenced groaning dismally. Finding appeals to his patriotism of no avail, General Lee had him ignominiously set on his legs by some neighboring gunners.

"I saw General Wilcox (an officer who wears a short round jacket and a battered straw hat) come up to him and explain, almost crying, the state of his brigade. General Lee immediately shook hands with him, and said, cheerfully, 'Never mind, General — all this has been my fault; it is I that have lost this fight, and you must help me out of it in the best way you can.'

"In this manner I saw General Lee encourage and reanimate his somewhat dispirited troops, and magnanimously take upon his own shoulders the whole weight of the repulse."

LOYALTY IN EAST TENNESSEE. — A letter from a soldier in Burnside's army, written from Knoxville, says:

"I saw an old man from Jefferson County, in this State, who, although seventy-three years of age, came to join the army. He brought, as he terms them, his own crowd, of one hundred men, and another of eighty. He and forty of his company have been bushwhacking in the mountains for fourteen months.

"Seven or eight regiments are under way, several of which will be full this week. Morristown, Greenville, and Jonesboro' have, I learn, each a regiment nearly full.

"When we were at Morristown, and getting on the cars for Greenville, an old countryman from back some twenty miles came riding into town. As he did not know we were there, he looked at the brigade a while with astonishment. When the state of things began to flash upon him, he asked if we 'weren't the blue-bellied Yankees;' and, as soon as he was satisfied, he went almost crazy, shouting, 'Glory to God, they have come at last;' then, sinking his heels into his horse's sides, he went galloping through the town, waving his hat and shouting away, 'Glory to God, they've come at last!'

"It was not long, however, before he was back, and coaxing some of the boys to go home with him. He said 'it weren't only twenty miles;' if they would go home with him, 'he know'd the old woman would go crazy.' He said she had been 'saving thirteen jars of apple butter ever since last summer, for the Yankees to eat.' When our boys told him there would be a fight at the saltworks, and that that was our destination, he wanted to borrow a gun and go along, saying the rule of the rebels was over now, and his had come, and he was 'arter revenge like a four-year-old.'"

WHOSE FATHER WAS HE? — After the battle of Gettysburg a Union soldier was found in a secluded spot on the field, where, wounded, he had laid himself down to die. In his hands, tightly clasped, was an ambrotype containing the portraits of three small children, and upon this picture his eyes, set in death, rested. The last object upon which the dying father looked was the image of his children, and, as he silently gazed upon them, his soul passed away. How touching! how solemn! What pen can describe the emotions of this patriot father as he gazed upon these children, so soon to be made orphans! Wounded and alone, the din of battle still sounding in his ears, he lies down to die. His last thoughts and prayers are for his family. He has finished his work on earth; his last battle has been fought; he has freely given his life to his country; and now, while his life's blood is ebbing, he clasps in his hands the image of his children, and, commending them to the God of the fatherless, rests his last lingering look upon them.

FIGHTING BY THE DAY. — At the siege of Lexington, Missouri, an old Texan, dressed in buckskin and armed with a long rifle, used to go up to the works every morning about seven o'clock, carrying his dinner in a tin pail. Taking a good position, he banged away at the Federals till noon, then rested an hour, ate his dinner; after which he resumed operations till six P. M., when he returned home to supper and a night's sleep. The next day, a little before seven, saw him, dinner and rifle in hand, trudging up street to begin again his regular day's work, — and in this style he continued till the surrender.

INCIDENT OF LINN CREEK, MISSOURI. — During the hottest of the conflict, Lieutenant Montgomery, son of the captain of that name, found himself without a sabre, having lost it when he discharged both of his revolvers, and having nothing with which to reload, and no other weapon of defence, he "pitched in" with his fist. One of the prisoners brought in showed unmis-

21

takable marks of violence from this source. At the close of the fight, Captain Switzler became separated from his company, and soon afterwards found himself set upon by three of the rebels, who, with their guns, were intent on taking his life by means of clubbing him, their guns being unloaded. As each approached, the Captain struck him a blow with the side of his sabre, ordering him to surrender. He succeeded in defending himself in this way until young Montgomery came to his assistance, when all three of the rebels were taken prisoners.

A THRILLING NARRATIVE. — Rev. H. D. Fisher, a well-known minister of the Methodist Episcopal Church, gives the following thrilling account of his escape from death during the Lawrence massacre:

"Many miraculous escapes from the assassin's hand were made: none perhaps more so than in my own case. For the last eighteen months I have been marked by the rebels for death, because I have been ordered by various Generals to provide 'homes for refugees,' and find work for them to do to support themselves and families. Now, three times I have signally escaped their hands. God has saved my life as by fire. When Quantrell and his gang came into our town almost all were yet in their beds. My wife and second boy were up, and I in bed, because I had been sick with the quinsy. The enemy yelled and fired a signal. I sprang out, and my other children and myself clothed ourselves as quick as possible.

"I took the two oldest boys and started to run for the hill, as we were completely defenceless and unguarded. I ran a short distance, and felt as if I should be killed. I returned to my house, where I had left my wife with Joel, seven years old, and Frank, six months old, and thought to hide in our cellar. I told Willie, twelve years old, and Eddie, ten years old, to run for life, and I would hide. I had scarcely found a spot in which to secrete myself, when four murderers entered my house and demanded of my wife, with horrid oaths, where that husband of hers was, who was hid in the cellar. She replied, 'The cellar is open; you can go and see for yourselves. My husband started over the hill with the children.' They demanded a light to search. My wife gave them a lighted lamp, and they came, light and revolvers in hand, swearing to kill at first sight. They came within eight feet of where I lay, but my wife's self-possession in giving the light had disconcerted them, and they left without seeing me. They fired our house in four places, but my wife, by almost superhuman efforts, and with baby in arms, extinguished the fire. Soon after three others came, and asked for me. But she said, 'Do you think he is such a fool as to stay here? They have already hunted for him; but, thank God, they did not find him.' They then completed their work of pillage and robbery, and fired the house in five places, threatening to kill her if she attempted to extinguish it again. One

stood, revolver in hand, to execute the threat if it was attempted. The fire burned furiously. The roof fell in, then the upper story, and then the lower floor; but a space about six by twelve feet was by a great effort kept perfectly deluged by water by my wife, to save me from burning alive. I remained thus concealed as long as I could live in such peril.

"At length, and while the murderers were still at my front door and around my lot, watching for their prey, my wife succeeded, thank God, in covering me with an old dress and a piece of carpet, and thus getting me out into the garden, and to the refuge of a little weeping willow covered with 'morning glory' vines, where I was secured from their fiendish gaze and saved from their hellish thirst for my blood. I still expected to be discovered and shot dead. But a neighbor woman, who had come to our help, aided my wife in throwing a few things saved from the fire around the little tree where I lay, so as to cover me more securely. Our house and all our clothes — except a few old and broken garments (not a full suit of anything for one of us) and some carpet — with beds, books, and everything to eat or read, were consumed over us or before our eyes. But what of that? I live! Through God's mercy I live!"

THE TWIN BROTHERS. — That fact is stranger than fiction, is exemplified in the following true story of two brothers, twins, which occurred during the memorable siege of Port Hudson. Passing, one day, through the streets of that little town, we noticed two corpses lying upon the gallery of the carpenter's shop, awaiting their turn for the boxes, dignified with the title of coffins, to consign them to their last resting-place. They were bodies of tall stature, stout and well built, betokening the hardy backwoodsmen of the Southwest. Over the face of each was thrown a cloth, through which the blood was oozing, showing that they had received their death wounds through the head. It was no uncommon sight, during the siege, to see death in every form, from the body pierced by the single bullet, to the one shattered to atoms by the cannon ball or mortar shell. Yet there was something in the appearance of those bodies which riveted our attention: we indulged the inquiry as to who they were. A rough, grizzly Confederate soldier was sitting by their side, whose arm, tied up, showed that, for the present, he was unfit for active service. The tears were trickling down his cheeks as he gazed mournfully upon the dead before him, while his quivering lip told, better than words, that they had been more to him than simple comrades of the tent and field.

He related their story in a few words. "They were my sons," said he, "and were twins. One of them joined at the same time I did. We came here with General Beale, and have done our duty to the best of our knowledge, and, I believe, to the satisfaction of our officers.

"This morning, sir, while at the breastworks, one of my boys, in order to get good aim at the sharpshooters outside, thoughtlessly raised himself too high, when a rifle ball pierced his brain, and he fell dead at my feet. His brother, seeing him fall, sprang forward to pick him up, but, in so doing, exposed himself above the line of defences, when he too received a ball through the brain, and he fell dead upon the still quivering corpse of his brother. As they came into the world, so they went out of it — together. In removing their bodies from the breastworks, I got this wound, which has shattered my arm. Would that I had died with them, sir, for I have no one to love now upon this earth."

"And their mother — your wife?"

"Died, sir, in giving them birth."

One coffin received the remains of the twins, and, a few days after, while sitting in front of his tent, an exploding shell gave a death wound to their heart-broken father.

AMENITIES OF PICKET DUTY. — "Our regiment (the First Delaware) was on picket, and confronting the enemy. 'Barney,' our Sergeant-Major, — who, by the way, is quite an institution, — espied a cow, which had just escaped from the rebel lines, with a reb in hot pursuit, both coming towards neutral territory. 'Barney,' seizing his sword, rushed towards the scene. Secesh, seeing the advance, halted. Imagine his surprise, when 'Barney' ran up to the cow, and, waving his sword, gave her a gentle poke with it, and started her towards our lines. The rebel, astonished at the audacity, cried out: 'Halloo, you Yank! bring that cow back here! She belongs to us.' 'Barney,' flourishing his sword, stopped, and looked back towards him, and responded: 'Who are you *cursing*, you darned rebel? The animal has seceded!' Giving the cow another reminder with his sword that she was needed in our *bivouac*, he brought her in triumphantly, — several of the rebs, who had been drawn out by the colloquy, laughing at the signal discomfiture of their companion in arms. 'Barney,' having milked the cow, and obtained about a gallon and a half of the lacteal fluid, — enough to supply the entire picket reserve, — turned her back towards the rebel lines, and cried out to the defeated Johnny that he might have the beast now — that he didn't need her any longer. The last seen of her, she was wending her way slowly to the enemy in quest of her calf, which was tied to a tree. This, to say the least, was a handsome piece of strategy; to say nothing of the milk, it was a *coup de main*."

SCENES IN THE SOUTH-WEST. — The following narrative of a recruiting expedition into Arkansas was given by Engineer L. G. Bennett, who left St. Louis in April, 1863, in company with William M. Fishback, who was authorized by General Curtis to raise a regiment among the loyal Arkansians: "The party started for Cassville, Missouri, intending to make that place their point of departure for the journey to the mountains.

"The road to Cassville is intersected several times by a limpid stream, called Flat Creek. It was very high, from the recent rains. On the road, four 'great strapping girls' were overtaken, who were footing it from Newton County to Cassville. The girls sometimes kept up with, and occasionally outstripped, his ambulance. Occasionally the vehicle would get the start on a level stretch of road, and the girls would fall behind. Coming up to a deep ford, the Colonel, with gallant intentions, halted his ambulance, until the girls came up, and politely offered to convey them to the opposite bank in his ambulance. 'O, no; we never ride,' said one; and they leaped into the boiling current, and, although the creek was 'waist deep,' they soon emerged, dripping, on the opposite bank, leaving the very modest Colonel completely nonplused by the adventurous "Amazons. The damsels were soon half a mile in advance, singing:

" ' O, did you see my sister? '

"On arriving at Cassville, intelligence was received that Fayetteville, our advanced post in Arkansas, was ordered to be abandoned, and that the Federal troops were on the retrograde march to Missouri. This information put a damper on recruiting prospects in that section, and the party returned to Springfield.

"It was resolved to penetrate Arkansas by way of Forsyth, on the White River, and a rather formidable company was made up, consisting of a number of Kansas officers, 'regular dare-devils,' and a few Arkansas fugitives, numbering eighteen in all — armed to the teeth — under command of Colonel Fishback.

"The White River was reached by the recruiting party about a mile above Forsyth. The river was swollen by the recent rains, and the prospect of crossing seemed dubious. The region was in possession of the rebels, and infested with secesh sympathizers. It was getting towards night. A butternut individual was discovered on the opposite shore.

"After hailing the stranger, and parleying some time with him, it was agreed that one of the party should cross, and perfect arrangements. Kelley, a bold, adroit man, volunteered to go over, and a boy paddled over in a 'dug-out' to get him. Kelley and the boy started in the 'dug-out' to cross, but before they reached the other side, three more men appeared on the opposite bank, with muskets and revolvers ready cocked. Their movements were closely watched, and our men rested their rifles across logs, and, with steady aim, intended to blaze away in case any hostile move should be made on Kelley. The latter was allowed to land, and had a long conference, in which he represented that his party were bushwhackers, who had been chased by the Federal authorities out of Missouri, and were on their way south. This artful story was credited, and the boat permitted to bring over the balance of the party — which had to be done one at a time — making some eighteen round trips. It was, consequently, late in the night before all had got over. In swimming their horses, four were drowned.

"The men who so readily assisted in ferrying the party across the river turned out to be among the worst class of bushwhackers in that region.

"One was Hendrick, who had hung and shot a number of loyal men in Ozark and Stone Counties, Missouri. Another, named Bird, was also a noted desperado, being a horse thief and a murderer. He and his gang had 'cleaned out' every loyal family on Bull and Swan Creeks, in Taney County, Missouri, utterly depopulating that section for miles around.

"On taking leave of these desperadoes next morning, the kindest wishes for the success of our party were expressed. A list of rebel leaders was also given, where the party would be welcomed, and receive assistance in their journey throughout the country.

"Proceeding three miles further, up popped a picket from the side of the road, who, ordering the party to halt, demanded who they were and their destination. The ever-prompt Kelley was sent forward, and, after a brief explanation, made all things satisfactory to the picket. The picket said he was from St. Louis, and was among forty prisoners who escaped from the guard-house at Springfield, one dark and rainy night. He was asked why he was stationed in that out of the way place, and replied that pickets were stationed in these places to kill the 'Mountain Feds,' as they were called, who were in the habit of fleeing from Arkansas to Missouri. He informed the party that ten more pickets were concealed in the brush. His credulity was so far overcome that he gave the party the rebel pass-word. It consisted in whistling three times like a quail. He said by making that noise they would not be molested when they ran across any of their men. If any one was seen in the act of firing, he said, just whistle the signal as directed, and the fire-locks would drop instantly. Kelley soon became a proficient in making the desired signal.

"The bald tops of the hills were clothed with a light verdure, sprinkled with flowers. They descended from the hill country into a long piece of woods. The last picket had given the locality of the pickets, and in order to avoid a strongly posted picket guard some fourteen miles ahead, the travellers held a council and resolved to leave the main travelled road. By this detour they intended to circumvent the picket guard. On leaving the main road they got among the hills again, and after travelling a whole day, ascending and descending the hills, they emerged at night on the road and found they had advanced but five miles.

"The next morning the blankets were tied to the saddles, and the party, mounting their horses, determined to keep the road and run the risk of encountering the pickets. When they got in sight of the latter, instead of meeting with opposition, the cowardly pickets mounted their steeds and precipitately fled to Carrolton, the county seat of Carrol County, sixteen miles distant. The pickets spread the alarm that the Missouri en-

rolled militia was coming in full force. They followed the terrified pickets, and camped within eight miles of Carrolton, procuring a few ears of corn, which was parched for supper.

"In order to avoid the rebel bands, who were patrolling the country, it became necessary, much of the time, to travel in the woods, over mountains, and through rocky ravines, away from the 'settlements.' Ignorance of the geography of the country kept the party so long on the way that their scanty supply of hard tack was exhausted. Hogs and cattle were plenty, and one of the party, a Rocky Mountain hunter, exercised his agility in lassoing a fat steer, without exposing their position by a shot.

"The Colonel one day came up to a cabin, and inquired of the butternut owner if he had any corn bread to spare. 'No,' said Butternut, 'don't raise much of nothin' down yere; the crap's poor.' Casting a glance over into a small enclosure, bristling with weeds, the Colonel thought he discovered something resembling onions. Inquiry was made of the man if he had onions to spare, and he answered he 'reckoned not.' Presently his barefooted better-half, who had been listening, said, 'Pap, I reckon it's injuns he's arter.' 'O,' said Butternut, 'if it's injuns you're arter, I 'low we kin spare you a heap on 'em.' And the Colonel returned to camp with an abundant supply of 'injuns' to regale his half-famished command.

"Not far from Carrolton was found one Lewis, a most wicked rebel, who, with an 'oath' and 'protection papers' in his pocket, obtained from Colonel Weir, of the Tenth Kansas, boasted that he had all along made it his business to hunt and help to hang and rob Union men, or oblige them to flee from the country. Under the idea that the party were Southern men, he piloted them eight miles on the way.

"On the top of Gaither Mountain were several droves of horses belonging to the secesh residing on Crooked Creek. Some of the party were much better mounted when they left the top of the mountain.

"Arriving at Jasper, in Newton County, the party considered themselves safe, as the people among the mountains are mostly loyal. Captain Vanderpool, of the First Arkansas infantry, was in the neighborhood, with a number of armed recruits. He had had several encounters with the rebels, and defeated them every time. It was judged best not to confine recruiting operations to one neighborhood. Accordingly a portion went about thirty miles east, in Pope County, on the border of Searcy and Conway Counties.

"An expedition was planned to a saltpetre cave in Searcy County, which was being worked by the rebels, who manufactured at the rate of one hundred barrels per day. The ubiquitous Kelley, at the head of twelve men, cautiously approached the cave, surprised and captured the guard, destroyed all the machinery, kettles, vats, arches, &c., pertaining to the works, and, with his prisoners and a number of captured horses, returned without a single misfortune to any of his party.

This little adventure so won the confidence of the mountaineers, that they thought there was no such man as Kelley and the Kansas jayhawkers.

"Volunteers came flocking in by the score, and in ten days a company of ninety-six was formed, with William Brashears, an Arkansian, as Captain, Kelley as First Lieutenant, and Joseph Brown as Second Lieutenant. Other expeditions were planned, many horses, guns, and prisoners taken, and much property recovered which had been captured from Union men.

"Word finally came that an expedition of three hundred rebels was coming from Dover, the county seat of Pope County, to break up Brashears' company. The boys retired to a favorable position among the mountains, and for two days awaited their coming. At length word was brought from what was deemed a reliable source that the rebels had returned.

"Captain Brashears, having business at home, and not suspecting danger, with only four men in his company, was proceeding to the transaction of his business, when suddenly he fell among the entire secesh force. They chased him over a mile, wounding him several times, and finally killing him.

"One of Captain Brashears' companions made his escape, another was killed, and two others, brothers, were captured and hung, after enduring many tortures and fiendish barbarities, disgraceful even to savage Indians, and too repulsive to be related. The neighboring women were not even permitted to bury their dead bodies without being threatened and insulted.

"Mention has already been made that Captain Vanderpool was recruiting in the neighborhood of Jasper. One morning, the citizens of Jasper were surprised to find a force of two hundred rebels, under Captains Mitchell, Love, and Sisel, in their midst, and four or five of Vanderpool's recruits were captured. The Captain was in the immediate neighborhood, but his men were scattered, and it was impossible immediately to collect them. Eighteen, however, were near at hand; with this handful, he did not hesitate to attack them. Approaching the lower part of the town, and covering the men behind rocks, fences, and trees, a hot and destructive fire was poured upon the enemy, and they were glad to seek the cover of the neighboring hills. But Vanderpool's men beginning to collect, a retreat was ordered. At the crossing of Hudson Creek, our boys gave them a few more rounds, scattering them in every direction, and leaving their dead behind. Our party met with no loss, except the prisoners captured early in the morning.

"An expedition was planned to make a raid in the direction of Clarksville and the Arkansas River, and about sixty men were collected for the enterprise. Two of Bennett's recruiting officers resided south of the Arkansas, and aimed to get in their own neighborhoods, where their chances for recruiting were more flattering. In this scout, Vanderpool promised to aid them to the river, and accordingly all who had not already gone to Pope County joined the expedition. After

scouting two days among the mountains and deep valleys, which had alternately been devastated by the rebels and 'Mountain Feds,' and where nothing but the most abject poverty and wretchedness existed, our party struck the valley of Mulberry Creek, in Johnson County, which had not been visited by a military force since the war. Large fields of corn and plenty abounded on every side. The inhabitants were mostly of the rebel persuasion. No armed force was met with. A number of horses, a few guns and ammunition, were captured, and also four prisoners. A large force prevented them from going to Clarksville. The two recruiting officers crossed the river, but nothing has been heard from them since.

"The acquaintance was formed of Captain Samuel Farmer, who resides near the head of Mulberry Creek. Some of the party had been but a few minutes at his house, when some of his smaller children went to his hiding-place in the woods, and informed him that a party of Federals was at the house. The Captain soon made his appearance, and with tears of joy bade them welcome, saying that anything he had was free. Such demonstrations of friendship deterred the boys from meddling with even his bees, and the old fellow had to take the lead in opening two of his best hives of honey for the boys. Corn bread and bacon were served liberally, and for the first time since the scout the boys got enough to eat.

"The Captain said he was an early settler in Arkansas, and for many years had represented Johnson County in the State Senate. At the breaking out of the secession troubles, he had taken an open stand in favor of the Union, and in the elections preliminary to the Convention, had steadily voted against secession. By the action of the Convention (not the people), the State finally drifted with the Southern tide. Military companies were everywhere raised for the South, and, quite early, one in Mr. Farmer's own neighborhood. He had served in the Mexican and Florida wars, and more recently in the Indian war in California and Oregon, and his military experience and qualities were well known. At once, every device which rebel ingenuity could invent was brought to bear to force him into the service. Flattery, threats, promises of high positions, and the personal influence of Governor Rector, in a measure overcame his scruples, and he was made Major of Hill's Fifteenth Arkansas regiment. The work of drilling and preparing the regiment for duty devolved entirely upon him.

"During Price's occupation of Springfield, in the winter of 1861-2, his regiment was stationed at Elm Springs, under McCulloch. Price's rapid retreat before General Curtis called for help from McCulloch, and he with other forces met the retreating Missourian at Sugar Creek, where a stand was resolved upon. All remember the result of that skirmish, in which the Federal cavalry, under Carr, Ellis, and Bowen, charged so vigorously among the rebel horse, foot, and artillery as to again set them in a headlong flight. The impetuous charge of the Federal squadron of cavalry in a measure removed from Farmer's eyes the scales which Lexington, Wilson Creek, and Bull Run had placed over them. He saw that the arm of the national government was not yet palsied, but was capable of dealing to traitors powerful blows. At Cross Hollows, Price, who outranked McCulloch, determined to make a stand. To this the latter was opposed, and so serious was the quarrel between the two leaders that a council of war was called the settle the difficulties and adopt a policy.

"Farmer was the only one of that council who sided with McCulloch. He admitted the strength of the position, provided Curtis was foolish enough to attack in front, but stated that the topography of the country was such that their position could be easily turned, and predicted that the next thing the Federals would be on their (the rebels') flank. Sure enough, the next day Sigel was at Osage Springs, threatening Price's flank and rear; and nothing was left for them to do but resume the skedaddle to the Boston Mountains, where McCulloch wished to remain and receive Curtis' attack. But here Van Dorn assumed the chief command, which soon culminated in the battle of Pea Ridge. At this battle Colonel Hill and his Lieutenant-Colonel early ran away from the fight, taking a small part of the regiment with them. But Major Farmer kept the remainder in their places, and was drawn up in line but a few rods from the field, and but a few paces from where Ben McCulloch was killed. He was the first man to aid him after he was shot.

"About ten minutes before McCulloch fell, they were together reconnoitring the Federal position. The Thirty-sixth Illinois formed in line for a charge; and when the breeze unfolded the Stars and Stripes to view, Major Farmer's old love for the flag returned, and turning to McCulloch, he said that 'this was the last battle and the last time he should ever raise his hand against that flag.' The scene, and such surrounding circumstances, in the midst of the thunders of a great battle, an expression from one he highly esteemed, affected even McCulloch, and he asserted that it was a trying ordeal for him to fight against that once-honored flag. He was among the last to leave the field at Elkhorn, at the rebels' final retreat.

"Farmer, shortly after, tendered his resignation, which, after many delays, was granted, and he returned to his home. Shortly after the conscript law was put in force, and at a public meeting in his neighborhood he denounced the measure with all his powers. Though not daring openly to avow himself a Union man, yet he predicted that such arbitrary measures would soon drive the people of Arkansas to rebel against the rebellion. He compared the helpless condition of Arkansas, after the battle of Pea Ridge, to the 'valley of dry bones; and his conviction that a wind would blow from the North, and that bone would seek its bone, and the whole become a living mass.' How truly has this come to pass in the present uprising of the people of Arkansas, and the development of a Union sentiment there! 'Bone is seeking its bone' all over the South.

"Three of his sons came within reach of the conscription act, and to avoid it they sought safety among the neighboring crags of the mountains and woods. They were hunted like wolves, and one of them shot down by the rebel home guard; and though this occurrence was near a year ago, he was still almost helpless from the effect of the shot. The father and sons, however, by hiding in the woods, had thus far escaped the provisions of the act, and hailed us as his dearest friends and benefactors. He stated that there were a large number in the neighboring mountains who were hunted the same as he.

"The Captain was advised to form a company, and join the Federal army, and that, if he ever expected Arkansas to be free, and restored to the Union, he must help to do it. He could not expect others to do that which more intimately concerned him. Said he, 'Will the Federals receive me after the part I have taken against them?' Having been satisfied in regard to this, he avowed his intention to immediately raise a company. He was given the necessary instructions, and when next heard from, the company numbered over sixty, with himself as captain, with others equally as loyal, as lieutenants. When last heard from, his company numbered one hundred and three men.

"Nearly every day after the formation of his company, expeditions were planned and executed against the secessionists for arms, ammunition, and horses, for his men. At one time a few of his boys entered Clarksville, captured a rifle from one Basham, which cost one hundred and fifty dollars; also a horse, valued at one thousand dollars. This Basham was a noted secessionist, and had been a Lieutenant-Governor of the State. On another occasion, Lieutenant Middleton, with but one companion, came suddenly upon a Captain Birch and three soldiers, and demanded their surrender. Birch, in reply, ordered Middleton to surrender. Both parties prepared for a fight, but after a long parley, Birch and his men surrendered. Captain Birch was armed with a splendid Sharp's cavalry rifle, and all were mounted on good horses. Middleton would scarcely take a thousand dollars for his rifle.

"One day Captain Farmer was alone at a blacksmith's shop, getting his horse shod for the journey, and not dreaming of rebels in many miles of him. He heard a rustling in a neighboring cornfield, but paid no attention to it, until suddenly he was fired on by forty men. The bullets cut his clothes, and tore up the gravel all around him, but he was not hurt. He dashed into a neighboring thicket, losing his hat in his flight. Shots were poured after him, and a number of rebels pursued, among whom was Captain Birch, whom he had kindly treated, and released but a few days before, after promising upon honor not to molest the Union people again. Captain Farmer had a rifle and a pistol with him, but the rifle missed fire, but with his pistol he scratched the

Captain in the face, and cut his ear nearly free from his head.

"Of course, the forty beat a hasty retreat, forgetting even to take off the Captain's horse. They rejoined the other portion of their band, consisting, in all, of one hundred and fifty men. The Captain soon met seven of his boys, and gave the alarm. While he went to collect the remainder, the seven secreted themselves in a cornfield, and fired into the whole secesh crowd as they passed along, killing two and wounding one. The secesh prepared to make a charge into the corn, but another round from their hidden foe put the whole crowd to flight, leaving five dead and two wounded in the road. The seven, among whom were two of Farmer's sons, chased the rebels to Clarksville.

"The mountainous districts of Arkansas are its loyal portions. Particularly is this so in the Boston range, which extends from near Batesville to an unlimited distance westward. Its gorges, caves, and thickets form a safe retreat from danger, and beswarm with loyal men, objects of rebel cruelty and persecution.

"To cross these mountain ranges, or ascend the isolated peaks, is a most laborious undertaking. With difficulty one clambers up the steep sides, while a loose rock occasionally tumbles with a crash into a chasm below. The summits are often surrounded by a perpendicular wall of rock, with only an occasional opening up the natural steps by which they are attained.

"From these commanding eminences is had the most singular and romantic view which imagination can paint. To some this rough scenery would be enchantingly sublime. On either side of narrow valleys, mountains piled up almost to the clouds, exhibiting a variegated view of huge rocks, crags, caverns, and peaks, and the whole covered by a thick, almost impenetrable wilderness.

"These are the fortresses of the hardy mountaineers, from which they bid defiance to the surrounding rebel hordes, and often sweep down upon them like an eagle on its prey.

"Nearly every crag and ravine among the Boston Mountains have echoed the sharp crack of the rifle, used in deadly conflict between the contending factions which divide the people of Arkansas. The mountains are the fortresses of the Union men, and woe be to the rebel who shows himself in these haunts. The Union man who ventures into the surrounding country is caught and hung to the first limb. A rebel raid was made up the valley of Hudson's Creek 'for the purpose of cleaning out Vanderpool and his cursed Feds,' under the command of Love and Sisel. As they proceeded up the valley, two or three unsuspecting Federal recruits were caught and hung.

"But Vanderpool was not idle. Hastily collecting about sixty or seventy of his men, he made an attack on them at Huston's. The rapid fire of the huntsmen's rifles resounded among the mountains, and both parties fought with the determination to conquer or die. But our men found themselves between two fires from the barn and house,

and being largely outnumbered, were obliged to fall back. But Lieutenant Cross was determined not to give up the unequal contest, and collecting a few brave spirits, charged almost among the enemy. He paid for his temerity with his life, for he fell pierced with a score of balls. The survivors fled; but no opportunity was lost to now and then drop a stray shot among the rebels, until their situation became so dangerous that they retreated into Carroll county, burying eight of their dead in a field adjoining the house, and carrying off a large number of wounded.

"Our loss was one killed and four slightly wounded. But by the death of Lieutenant Cross the mountaineers lost their bravest and best friend. He knew no fear, and his only fault was rashness. None had such influence over the men to prevent them from the same excesses as the rebels, as he. After his death Vanderpool's recruits lost much of the discipline which the Lieutenant had enforced. His death added another to the large list of widows and orphans who can trace their bereavement directly to this cruel, heartless war.

"Mrs. Cross came with the recruiting party to Springfield, for the purpose of getting the pay due him for many months' faithful services; but met with little success. Many of the heartless officers who have the management of much of the army business, can, and often do, manage to strip the ignorant, but deserving, Arkansas widow or soldier of all or much of their hard earnings — oftentimes costing blood and life.

"About the 1st of July, it was determined, with the recruits on hand, to fight their way out, if necessary, to the Federal lines; and all were ordered to rendezvous on Hudson's Creek, about four miles above Jasper. But a bareheaded female express rider, mounted on a bare-backed horse, reeking with sweat, announced that Sisel, with a hundred men, was on Big Creek, eight miles distant, committing depredations on the Union inhabitants. About one hundred of our men were mounted and off in an instant. It was thought best to go over the mountain, to the head of the creek, and then down it and meet him, as he was reported to be moving up the stream. This required a circuit of twenty miles; and when we reached the settlement on Big Creek, we found the bird had flown, retracing his course down the creek. We followed on until midnight, when horses and men were completely worn down. They had travelled forty miles since two o'clock.

"They finally struck the Buffalo Creek, or River, and camped on the farm of one Jackey Adair. 'Uncle Jackey' was an old man, was quite wealthy, and a most bitter rebel. His hogs and corn-cribs paid the penalty of this; and, during the two days at his place, man or beast lacked not for something to eat. Here Mr. Bennett had a severe attack of the pleurisy. It became necessary for the men to go to other portions of the State, and he was left with 'Uncle Jackey,' who was informed that his life would pay the forfeit for any harm which befell his patient. The old gentleman promised to do the best he could.

"Before daylight the pursuit was resumed, and

at sunrise the spot was reached where Sisel had camped during the night. Of course he was gone, and out of reach. The jaded steeds were turned in another direction, to Shinn's tanyard, to get something for man and horse to eat. Here were caught two persons, who said Sisel did not leave his camp for the night until early sunrise. Had it been known they were so close upon him, there would have been either a fight or a foot-race. It was now too late.

"The next morning, before daylight, the house was surrounded by Sisel's whole gang, and the old man was rudely asked in what room Mr. B. was. Never did man plead for another as 'Uncle Jackey' pleaded for his patient. He knew he would be killed if he was found, and being a personal friend of Sisel, he finally persuaded him to leave. They did not even take the rifle or revolver. In the mean time, Vanderpool had heard of Sisel's movements, and early in the morning was back at 'Uncle Jackey's.' The way that the rebels had gone being pointed out, a reconnoitring party was sent out, headed by Lieutenant Fesperman, a man as brave and rash as Lieutenant Cross. They had followed the rebel trail about a mile in the woods, when, from an ambush, they were fired upon, and Lieutenant Fesperman and another were dangerously wounded. The remainder fled in confusion.

"The rebels came from their covert and shot Fesperman, wounded as he was, through the head, killing him instantly. Vanderpool soon came up, and the rebels fled. The burial of Fesperman, and the care of the wounded man, occupied them until afternoon. After this, the rebels made no more raids among the mountains, and were much afraid of the 'Mountain Feds,' even at their places of resort. It was believed that our own and Vanderpool's men numbered eight hundred, and that we had a natural fort in the mountains from which no force could drive us.

"On their return to the Federal lines, the party were not molested until after passing Huntsville. Guerrillas had threatened to fire upon them from every point; but strong flanking parties on either side prevented this, and the only loss from them was one horse, while several regular soldiers and a few guerrillas were captured.

"At Fayetteville was found a small party of Federal soldiers, about fifty in number, mostly convalescents from the hospitals, on their way to their commands, with a number of recruiting officers for Phelps' Second Arkansas cavalry. Our party numbered about four hundred, and the column had not all entered the town when a sharp firing was heard in the western suburbs, which was ascertained to be an attack of Ingraham, a guerrilla Captain, upon the pickets, who, after exchanging a few shots, were driven in. Receiving orders to conduct the unarmed men (which included near half our number) to a place of safety, Mr. Bennett directed them to march out upon the telegraph road, in the direction of Cassville, until out of danger. The firing coming nearer towards the centre of the town, a sort of panic seized Vanderpool's men, and they hastily retreated to the eastern portion of the town. By the exertions of Vanderpool and a few others, a stand was here made, but the rebel shots soon began to whistle around them, and our mountaineers again took to flight. The officers in charge of the detachment of regular soldiers were somewhat under the influence of liquor, and they, too, participated in the panic and flight, in confusion, up the telegraph road. Lieutenant Kelley had command of the rear guard of our column, but so rapid had been Vanderpool's flight from the town as to leave him alone with a small detachment of his company. He, too, fell back on the telegraph road.

"By the exertions of Captain Farmer, Kelley, Mr. Bennett, and one or two of the officers in charge of the convalescents, the flight was stopped, order soon restored, and Kelley prepared to make a charge upon the rebels, who now had entire possession of the town. Hastily collecting about twenty men, he bore down upon the rebel flank just as the last shots were being exchanged with Vanderpool. The rebels, thinking this to be a Federal reinforcement, designed to cut off their retreat, fired one volley, and then hastily fled, thus presenting the novel spectacle of two contending parties fleeing from each other. Lieutenant Kelley was severely wounded by the last fire of the rebels, a rifle shot entering above the knee, and coming out of his back, which prevented his pursuing the flying rebels.

"They left three of their number dead, and seven so seriously wounded as to be left behind. Others of their number, less dangerously wounded, made their escape. Our loss was but two wounded, including Lieutenant Kelley. In numbers, the rebels were only about eighty, while our armed force was at least near three hundred. Had the rebels known our strength, they would not have made the attack. They supposed there were none to contend with but the small party of convalescents and recruiting officers, who entered the town the evening before.

"The fight following so closely upon our entering the town, and there being no difference between the dress of the 'Mountain Feds' and the rebels, led the former to suppose the whole was a rebel scheme to capture them. Hence their rapid flight up the telegraph road. But Kelley's daring charge undeceived them, and they were no longer afraid of us. About sixty of our own and Vanderpool's recruits were so frightened as not to stop their flight until they reached Cassville. Vanderpool, with the remainder, after about three hours, came back to the town. It was resolved to hold the place for a time at least, and if the rebels wished to attack us again, to retrieve what had been lost in the first encounter.

"The country around Fayetteville had been made desolate by both armies, which had alternately occupied it. There was but one small field of corn for many miles from town, and it was difficult subsisting the horses. Bushwhackers swarmed around, firing upon and annoying the Federal foraging and scouting parties. In a few days, Captains Robb and Worthington, with two companies of the First Arkansas cavalry, came down from Cassville. Not having orders to hold the place, it was determined to abandon it, after retaining possession only a week.

"Captain Vanderpool, with his recruits for the First infantry, and the convalescents, about one hundred and seventy-five, went to his regiment at Fort Gibson, while Captains Robb and Worthington, with the recruits and a large number of citizens, who were moving north, took the telegraph road for Cassville.

"While Mr. Bennett was at Fayetteville, having some leisure, he wrote the details of his trip in a letter to his wife, which he read to Lieutenant Kelley, at his solicitation, while the Lieutenant was lying sick in bed. A native Arkansian, who was an attentive listener to the narrative, broke out:

"'Major, you must have been to school a right smart.'

"The unsophisticated native was informed that, like all the people of the North, he had enjoyed the advantage of some schooling.

"'Wall, you know a heap. That letter to your wife reads just like a book.'

"It was late in the day before the march northward was resumed. Ten miles were made the first day. The next morning Captain Robb's and Lieutenant Kelley's companies (now under Captain Farmer,) numbering near one hundred men, were ordered to proceed to the Elm Spring road, and endeavor to catch some bushwhackers, who, it was reported, infested it, and join the main command at Cross Hollows.

"At the same time, Lieutenant Odlin, with forty men, were sent to the rear of a mountain on the right of the road in search of guerrillas, this being a favorite haunt of theirs. Captain Worthington with the remainder, now reduced to about fifty armed men, and all our unarmed rabble and women and children, proceeded up the telegraph road. They had proceeded but two or three miles when a heavy volley was poured upon them from the brush. The unarmed crowd fled in every direction, but Captain Worthington, with his men, for a few minutes bravely held the ground and returned the enemy's fire. But the Captain being wounded, and a large number of horses and men being killed and wounded, they, too, finally retreated.

"Captain Robb's command was nearly four miles away when the firing commenced. 'To the rescue, boys,' was his brief order; and Mr. Bennett's party went flying through the woods in the direction of the firing. The rebels were preparing to charge upon the train and capture the fugitives, when Captain Robb appeared in sight. The clatter of hoofs, the shouts of the men, and the immense cloud of dust we raised, led the enemy to suppose the party were a large and unlooked-for reinforcement coming from an opposite direction, and they fled precipitately to the woods.

"It was ascertained that the rebels numbered four hundred, commanded by Colonel Hunter. Captain Odlin encountered them in their retreat,

and with his thirty charged among them, killing a few; but seeing their overwhelming numbers pouring around him, he prudently retreated with the loss of one prisoner. In this fight we lost three killed and quite a number wounded, besides a number that were missing, that we could not ascertain what had become of them. Twelve dead horses belonging to our men were counted. This was considered a defeat for the Federals. In fact, our men were so separated that victory was impossible.

"The most disgraceful part of the whole affair was the leaving of our dead unburied, and three of the wounded behind. The only excuse for this was, that the enemy was expected to either renew the attack there, or make a circuit around and attack the party at Cross Hollows, and it was necessary to proceed as fast as possible. We were left in possession of the battle-field, and there can be no reasonable excuse for this negligence on our part. Camped that night in Cross-Timbers Hollow, but a few miles from Keetsville, being molested no more on the march."

THE STARS AND STRIPES.

BY JAMES T. FIELDS.

RALLY round the flag, boys—
  Give it to the breeze!
That's the banner we love
  On the land and seas.

Brave hearts are under it;
  Let the *traitors* brag;
Gallant lads, fire away!
  And fight for the flag.

Their flag is but a rag,—
  Ours is the *true* one;
Up with the Stars and Stripes!
  Down with the new one!

Let our colors fly, boys—
  Guard them day and night;
For victory is liberty,
  And God will bless the right.

A HOSPITAL INCIDENT. — A brother from the Christian Commission, while going the rounds among the wounded, approached the bed of a soldier suffering from a severe wound in the leg.

"Ah, my dear brother, war is a dreadful thing," said the preacher.

"If you had my leg, you'd think so; but I had the satisfaction of killing a few of them d—d rebels before they knocked me down," said the soldier.

"Yes, but you must remember that the rebels are not our only enemy. Satan is our greatest enemy — he is the enemy of our souls," said the preacher.

"Satan is a pretty bad fellow, but he can't give us worse than we got at Chickamauga," replied the soldier, writhing under the pain of his wound.

"We must pray for our souls' salvation, brother."

"No, I'll pray for my leg's salvation first, till

I get another crack at them hounds," pointing to Lookout Mountain, "and then I'll pray for my soul," said the soldier.

The preacher left, convinced that the case was a hopeless one.

A SUBSTITUTE WANTED. — Chief Engineer Dean, of the fire department, called at the office where I make shoes for a living, and handed me a big white envelope, notifying me that I was drafted, and must report myself for examination at Lawrence on the 18th day of August.

Now I consider it the duty of every citizen to give his life, if need be, for the defence of his country; so, on the morning of the eventful 18th, I put on a clean shirt and my Sunday clothes, and started for Lawrence, to see if I could get exempted.

Lawrence, as all know, is situated on the Merrimac River, and its principal productions are mud, dust, and factory girls. The city proper, at least that part I saw, consisted of a long, narrow entry, up one flight of stairs, adorned overhead with a frescoing of gas meters, and carpeted with worn-out tobacco quids, and furnished with one chair, two settees, and as many huge, square packing cases, marked "Q. M. D." Scattered around this palatial entrance-hall were some forty or fifty conscripts, looking very much as if they expected to be exempted by old age before the young man with a ferocious mustache should notify them of their turn. Most of them were doomed to disappointment; for, while they counted the hours of delay, a door would suddenly open, and the tall young man would single out one man, and march him through the open doorway, to be seen no more.

By and by — that is, after several hours' waiting — my turn came.

"John Smith!" shouted the doorkeeper.

"That's me," says I. With a cheer from the crowd, I entered a large, square room, where two persons sat writing at a table, and the third, evidently the surgeon, was examining a man in the last stages of nudity.

One of the writers at the table, a young man, with curly eyes and blue hair, nodded to me, and dipping his pen in the ink, commenced :

"John Smith, what's your name?"

"John Smith," says I.

"Where was you born?"

"Podunk, Maine."

"What did your great grandfather die of?"

"Darned if I know," says I.

"Call it hapentoo," says he; "and your grandfather, too?"

"I don't care what you call it," says I, for I was a little riled by his nonsensical question.

"Did you ever have boils?"

"Not a boil."

"Or fits?"

"Nary fit."

"Nor delirium tremens?"

"No, sir-ee!"

"Or rickets?"

"I'll ricket you," for I thought he meant something else.

"Did you ever have the measles?" says he.

Here I took off my coat.

"Or the itch?"

"Yes, sir," said I, "that fist"—and I shoved a very large brown one within three inches of his nose — "has been itching for the last ten minutes to knock your pesky head off, you little, mean, low-lived, contemptible whelp, you."

"My dear sir," said the mild-spoken, gentlemanly surgeon, laying his hand on my arm; "calm yourself, I pray. Don't let your angry passions rise, but take off your clothes, so I can see what you are made of."

So I suppressed my anger, and withdrawing to a corner, I hung my clothes upon the floor, and presented myself for examination, clad only with the covering nature had given me, except about a square inch of court plaster on my right shin, where I had fallen over a chair, the night before, feeling for a match.

"Young man," said the surgeon, looking me straight in the eye, "you have got the myopia."

"Hey?"

"You have got the myopia."

"Yes, sir," said I, "and a good one, too — a little Bininger, with a drop of Stoughton, makes an excellent eye-opener, of a morning."

"And there seems to be an amaurotic tendency of the right eye, accompanied with ophthalmia."

"Pshaw!" says I.

"And that white spot in the left eye betokens a cataract."

"I guess you mean in the ear," says I, "'cause I went in swimming this morning, and got an all-fired big bubble in my left ear;" and here I jumped up and down, two or three times, on my left foot, but to no purpose. As soon as I stopped, he mounted a chair, and commenced feeling the top of my head.

"Was your family ever troubled with epilepsy?" says he.

"Only two of the boys," says I; "and when they catch them, my wife always goes at them with a fine tooth comb the first thing."

Jumping off the chair, he hit me a lick in the ribs that nearly knocked me over; and before I had time to remonstrate, his arms were around my neck, and his head pressed against my bosom the same way that Sophia Ann does, when she wants me to buy a new bonnet or dress.

"Just what I thought," said he, "tuberculosis and hemoptysis, combined with a defect in the scapular membrane and incipient phthisis."

"Heaven!" says I, "what's that?"

"And cardiac disease."

"No?" said I.

"And pericarditis!"

"Thunder!" said I.

"Stop talking! Now count after me — one!"

"One!" said I, more than half dead with fright.

"Asthma! Two."

"Two!" I yelled.

"Exostosis of the right fistula! Three!"

"Three!" I gasped.

"Coxalgia! Four!"

"Murder!" said I. "Four!"

"Confirmed duodenum of the right ventricle! Five!"

"O, doctor! dear doctor! ain't you most through? I feel faint."

"Through? No; not half through. Why, my friend, Pandora's box was nothing to your chest. You have sphinxiana, and gloriosis, and conchologia, and persiflage, and —"

Here my knees trembled so, I leaned against the table for support.

"And a permanent luxation of the anterior lobe of the right phalanx."

My only answer was a deprecatory gesture.

"And scrofulous diathesis and omnipoditis."

I sank to the floor in utter despair.

"Eluration!" he yelled, — for he saw I was going fast, — "and maxillarium, and —"

. . . .

When I woke to consciousness again, I found myself in a puddle of water, an empty bucket near by, and the surgeon astride my chest, shouting something in my ear, of which, however, I could hear nothing.

I smiled feebly in acknowledgment of his attentions. At a sign from him, two attendants drew near, and having lifted him into a chair, — for he was absolutely black in the face with the violence of his exertions, — they hoisted me to a perpendicular, and the examination proceeded.

But I will not harass your feelings by repeating the heart-rending details. Suffice it to say, that I was afflicted with gastritis, emphysemation, marcidity, empyema, obesity, condyle of the humerus, pilicose veins, hernia in both great toes, and hemorrhoids in the left heel, besides lots of other diseases, whose names I cannot remember. Finally, after a rigid examination of my toe-nails in search of eruptive lesions, he arose to his feet, drew a long breath, wiped the perspiration from his face with a stray newspaper, and commenced.

"Young man," said he, — and his eyes glistened with delight as he spoke, — "you are really the most interesting subject I ever met with. Really a most wonderful case! I don't know when I have enjoyed a half hour so thoroughly. Why, sir, with the exception of two, or at most three, you have symptoms of every disease in the medical dictionary. Please let me embrace you again, just to see if I can detect exicosis of the viscous membrane. Well, — no," he continued, with a slightly disappointed air, as he released me, "I don't seem to find it, exactly; but would you mind coming round to my boarding-house, after tea, so that I can spend the evening auscultating after it?"

He was so anxious to find that particular symptom, that I was sorry to refuse him; but I had promised Sophia Ann that I would be home to tea, and knew she would worry if I staid; so I was obliged to decline. Seeing there was a lady in the case, he very politely excused me — very much to my relief.

"Well, good by, my friend," said he, as I took my hat to go; "I wish it was so you could go to the war; I would have you in my hospital in less than a month, and then I could examine you at my leisure. I am positive a little exposure would bring on those two symptoms I spoke of, and then what a magnificent subject you would be! How I should like to dissect you! But then, perhaps you don't like it; and if you don't, I don't know as I blame you for wishing to preserve your wonderful organization as long as possible; so you just go into the next room, and Captain Herrick will give you a furlough to go home and provide a substitute, or pay your commutation fee. Boy, call the next on the list."

"But, sir," said I, aghast at his concluding remarks, "you don't pretend to accept me as able-bodied?"

"Really, my friend," said he, "the fact is, you have so many diseases that I actually don't know which to specify. It won't do to say cranial disease, when it's your heart that's affected; and if I mention your heart, what's the use of your having the consumption? But I know Dr. Coggswell will be glad to get your commutation fee; or if you will bring up a likely substitute, I shall be delighted to examine him; and some day, when we are both at liberty, I shall be most happy to have you call upon me. Hold! just unbutton your coat, for a moment; I must find that exico—"

But here I broke from his grasp, and stopping in the next room only long enough to procure my furlough, I started for the railway station, and never looked behind until I was safe in the arms of Sophia Ann and my dear children.

And now can anybody tell me where I can find a good substitute, warranted diseased in the head, heart, lungs, and legs, or all of them? To such a man I will give three hundred dollars down; or, if he prefer, at the rate of five dollars apiece for each symptom; and I promise him, in behalf of our Uncle Samuel, food and clothing for three years, together with medical attendance in proportion to the number and malignity of his diseases.

CAPTURE OF A SECESSION FLAG. — The commander of Camp Herron, Mo., in November, 1861, having learned that a certain very fine secession flag, that had waved defiantly from a flagstaff in the village of Manchester, twenty miles distant, until the successes of the Union forces caused its supporters to conclude that, for the present, "discretion would be the better part of valor," was still being very carefully preserved, its possessors boasting that they would soon be enabled to rehoist it, determined upon its capture.

On the 15th inst., he directed First Lieutenant H. C. Bull, of company C, of the Ninth Iowa regiment, to take charge of the expedition, and to detail fifteen good men for the purpose, which detail the Lieutenant made from company C.

They left camp by the cars at half past five P. M., landing at Merrimac, three miles from Manchester, proceeding from thence to Manchester on foot, and surrounded the house of Squire B., who had been foremost in the secession movement of that strong secession town, and was reported to be in possession of the flag.

The Squire protested against the imputation, declaring that the flag was not in his possession, and that he knew not of its whereabouts. His lady acknowledged that she had for a time kept it secreted in a box in the garden; but as it was likely to become injured, she took it out, dried it in the sun, when it was taken away by some ladies, who lived a *long* distance in the country, whose names she refused to give. Finally, after a thorough but fruitless search of the house, after the Lieutenant had placed her husband under arrest, and he was being started for headquarters, the lady, probably hoping to save her husband, acknowledged that it was taken by a Mrs. S., who resided a mile and a half in the country,— not such a terrible long distance, after all. Her husband was then sent to Merrimac, escorted by four soldiers, and the remainder, conducted by the gallant Lieutenant, started to visit the residence of Mrs. S., in search of the flag. The distance to the lady's residence was soon travelled, the house surrounded, and the flag demanded of Mrs. S., who proved to be a very intelligent lady, and was surrounded by a very interesting family. The lady replied to the demand that she would like to see the person that stated that she took the flag from Squire B.'s; that as to its whereabouts she had nothing to say; that the Lieutenant could search her house, and if he could find anything that looked like a flag, he was welcome to it. Accordingly, a thorough search was made, in which the lady and her daughter aided, but no flag was to be found. The lady then thanked the officer for the gentlemanly manner in which the search had been conducted, and added that she trusted he was satisfied. He replied he was quite certain that she had the flag, and that it would have been far better for her to have yielded it; but as she did not, as unpleasant as the task was, he should arrest her and take her to headquarters at Pacific City. Two men were then despatched for a carriage with which to convey the lady to Merrimac, and from thence the lady was informed that she would be sent by railroad. She accordingly made preparations to go; but after about an hour had elapsed in waiting for the carriage, the lady again demanded the name of the informants, and when told that it was Mrs. B., and that Squire B. was already under arrest, she then asked whether any indignity would have been offered to her had the flag been found in her possession, to which the courteous Lieutenant replied, "Certainly not, madam; our object with Squire B. was his arrest, and the capture of the flag; but with you, our object was the flag."

"Will you pledge your *honor*," said she, "that if I surrender the flag I shall not be arrested, nor my family disturbed?" When replied to in the affirmative, she added, "I wish you to understand, sir, that no fear of arrest or trouble would ever have made me surrender that flag; but Squire B.'s family induced me to take that flag to save their family from trouble, saying that it should be a sacred trust, known only to ourselves, and I, consequently, surrender it."

She then went to a bed that had been fruitlessly searched, took from it a quilt, and with the aid of her daughters proceeded to open the edges of the quilt, and cut the stitches through the body of it, and pulled off the top, when, behold! there lay the mammoth flag next to the cotton, being carefully stretched twice and nearly a half across the quilt. When taken out and spread, it proved to be a magnificent flag, over twenty-one feet in length, and nearly nine feet in width, with fifteen stars, to represent the prospective Southern Confederacy.

"Recollect," said the lady to Lieutenant Bull, "that you did not find it yourself, and when you wish detectives, you had better employ ladies." She also added, that she gave up the flag unwillingly. The daughter remarked that she had slept under it, and that she *loved* it, and that fifteen stars were not so terribly disunion, in her estimation, after all.

THE BATTLE-CRY OF FREEDOM.

Yes, we'll rally round the flag, boys,
　　We'll rally once again,
Shouting the battle-cry of Freedom;
We will rally from the hill-side,
　　We will rally from the plain,
Shouting the battle-cry of Freedom.

Chorus.

The Union forever! Hurrah, boys, hurrah!
Down with the traitors, up with the Stars;
While we rally round the flag, boys,
　　Rally once again,
Shouting the battle-cry of Freedom.

We are springing to the call
　　Of our brothers gone before,
Shouting the battle-cry of Freedom;
And we'll fill the vacant ranks
　　With a million freemen more,
Shouting the battle-cry of Freedom.
　　The Union forever, &c.

We will welcome to our number
　　The loyal, true, and brave,
Shouting the battle-cry of Freedom;
And although he may be poor
　　He shall never be a slave,
Shouting the battle-cry of Freedom.
　　The Union forever, &c.

We are springing to the call,
　　From the East and from the West,
Shouting the battle-cry of Freedom;
And we'll hurl the rebel crew
　　From the land we love the best,
Shouting the battle-cry of Freedom.
　　The Union forever, &c.

We are marching to the field, boys,
　　Going to the fight,
Shouting the battle-cry of Freedom;
And we'll bear the glorious Stars
　　Of the Union and the Right,
Shouting the battle-cry of Freedom.
　　The Union forever, &c.

We'll meet the rebel host, boys,
　With fearless hearts and true,
Shouting the battle-cry of Freedom;
And we'll show what Uncle Sam
　Has for loyal men to do,
Shouting the battle-cry of Freedom.
　The Union forever, &c.

If we fall amid the fray, boys,
　We will face them to the last,
Shouting the battle-cry of Freedom;
And our comrades brave shall hear us,
　As we are rushing past,
Shouting the battle-cry of Freedom.
　The Union forever, &c.

Yes, for Liberty and Union
　We are springing to the fight,
Shouting the battle-cry of Freedom;
And the victory shall be ours,
　Forever rising in our might,
Shouting the battle-cry of Freedom.
　The Union forever, &c

BATTLE OF GETTYSBURG.

BY SAMUEL WILKESON.

HEADQUARTERS ARMY OF POTOMAC,
　　　Saturday Night, July 4.

How can I write the history of a battle when my eyes are immovably fastened upon a central figure of transcendingly absorbing interest — the dead body of my oldest born son, caused by a shell in a position where the battery he commanded should never have been sent, and abandoned to die in a building where surgeons dared not to stay?

The battle of Gettysburg! I am told that it commenced on the 1st of July, a mile north of the town, between two weak brigades of infantry and some doomed artillery and the whole force of the rebel army. Among other costs of this error was the death of Reynolds. Its value was priceless, however, though priceless was the young and the old blood with which it was bought. The error put us on the defensive, and gave us the choice of position. From the moment that our artillery and infantry rolled back through the main street of Gettysburg, and rolled out of the town to the circle of eminences south of it, we were not to attack, but to be attacked. The risks, the difficulties, and the disadvantages of the coming battle were the enemy's. Ours were the heights for artillery; ours the short, inside lines for manœuvring and reënforcing; ours the cover of stone walls, fences, and the crests of hills.

The ground upon which we were driven to accept battle was wonderfully favorable to us. A popular description of it would be to say that it was in form an elongated and somewhat sharpened horse-shoe, with the toe to Gettysburg and the heel to the south.

Lee's plan of battle was simple. He massed his troops upon the east side of this shoe of position, and thundered on it obstinately to break it. The shelling of our batteries from the nearest overlooking hill, and the unflinching courage and complete discipline of the army of the Potomac, repelled the attack. It was renewed at the point of the shoe — renewed desperately at its southwest heel — renewed on its western side with an effort consecrated to success by Ewell's earnest oaths, and on which the fate of the invasion of Pennsylvania was fully put at stake. Only a perfect infantry and an artillery educated in the midst of charges of hostile brigades could possibly have sustained this assault. Hancock's corps did sustain it, and has covered itself with immortal honors by its constancy and courage. The total wreck of Cushing's battery — the list of its killed and wounded — the losses of officers, men, and horses Cowen sustained — and the marvellous outspread upon the board of death of dead soldiers and dead animals — of dead soldiers in blue and dead soldiers in gray — more marvellous to me than anything I have ever seen in war — are a ghastly and shocking testimony to the terrible fighting of the Second corps that none will gainsay. That corps will ever have the distinction of breaking the pride and power of the rebel invasion.

For such details as I have the heart for. The battle commenced at daylight, on the east side of the horse-shoe position, exactly opposite to that which Ewell had sworn to crush through. Musketry-firing preceded the rising of the sun. A thick wood veiled this fight, but out of its leafy darkness arose the smoke — and the surging and swelling of the fire, from intermittent to continuous and crushing, told of the wise tactics of the rebels in attacking in force and changing their troops. Seemingly the attack of the day was to be made through that wood. The demonstration was protracted — absolutely it was preparative. There was no artillery fire accompanying the musketry, but shrewd officers on our western front mentioned, with the gravity due to the fact, that the rebels had the day before fallen trees at intervals upon the edge of the wood they occupied in face of our position. These were breastworks for the protection of artillerymen.

Suddenly, and about ten in the forenoon, the firing on the east side, and everywhere about our lines, ceased. A silence as of deep sleep fell upon the field of battle. Our army cooked, ate, and slumbered. The rebel army moved one hundred and twenty guns to the west, and massed there Longstreet's corps and Hill's corps, to hurl them upon the really weakest point of our entire position.

Eleven o'clock — twelve o'clock — one o'clock. In the shadow cast by the tiny farm-house, sixteen by twenty, which Gen. Meade had made his headquarters, lay wearied staff officers and tired journalists. There was not wanting to the peacefulness of the scene the singing of a bird, which had a nest in a peach tree within the tiny yard of the whitewashed cottage. In the midst of its warbling, a shell screamed over the house, instantly followed by another, and another, and in a moment the air was full of the most complete artillery prelude to an infantry battle that was ever exhibited. Every size and form of shell, known to British and to American gunnery, shrieked, whirled, moaned, whistled, and wrathfully fluttered over our ground. As many as six in a second, constantly two in a second, bursting and screaming over and around the headquarters, made a very hell of fire that amazed the oldest officers. They burst in the yard — burst next to the fence on both sides, garnished as usual with the hitched horses of aids and orderlies. The fastened animals reared and plunged with terror. Then one fell, then another — sixteen lay dead and mangled before the fire ceased. Still fastened by their halters, which gave the expression of their being wickedly tied up to die painfully, these brute victims of a cruel war touched all hearts. Through the midst of the storm of screaming and exploding shells, an ambulance, driven by its frenzied conductor at full speed, presented to all of us the marvellous spectacle of a horse going rapidly on three legs. A hinder one had been shot off at the hock. A shell tore up the little step of the Headquarters Cottage, and ripped bags of oats as with a knife. Another soon carried off one of its two pillars. Soon a spherical case burst opposite the open door — another ripped through the low garret. The remaining pillar went almost immediately to the howl of a fixed shot that Whitworth must have made. During this fire, the horses at twenty and thirty feet distant were receiving their death, and soldiers in Federal blue were torn to pieces in the road, and died with the peculiar yells that blend the extorted cry of pain with horror and despair. Not an orderly — not an ambulance — not a straggler, was to be seen upon the plain swept by this tempest of orchestral death, thirty minutes after it commenced. Were not one hundred and twenty pieces of artillery trying to cut from the field every battery we had in position to resist their purposed infantry attack, and to sweep away the slight defences behind which our infantry were waiting? Forty minutes — fifty minutes — counted on watches that ran, O, so languidly! Shells through the two lower rooms! A shell into the chimney that fortunately did not explode. Shells in the yard. The air thicker and fuller, and more deafening with the howling and whirling of these infernal missiles. The chief of staff struck. Seth Williams, loved and respected through the army, separated from instant death by two inches of space vertically measured. An aid bored with a fragment of iron through the bone of the arm. Another cut with an exploded piece of case shot. And the time measured on the sluggish watches was one hour and forty minutes.

Then there was a lull, and we knew that the rebel infantry were charging. And splendidly they did this work — the highest and severest test of the stuff that soldiers are made of. Hill's division, in line of battle, came first on the double-quick, their muskets at the "right-shoulder-shift." Longstreet's came as the support, at the usual distance, with war cries and a savage insolence, as yet untutored by defeat. They rushed in perfect order across the open field up to the very muzzles of the guns, which tore lanes through them as they came. But they met men who were their equals in spirit, and their superiors in tenacity. There never was better fighting, since Thermopylæ, than was done yesterday by our infantry and artillery. The rebels were over our defences. They had cleaned cannoneers and horses from one of the guns, and were whirling it around to use upon us. The bayonet drove them back. But so hard pressed was this brave infantry, that at one time, from the exhaustion of their ammunition, every battery upon the principal crest of attack was silent, except Cowen's. His service of grape and canister was awful. It enabled our line, outnumbered two to one, first to beat back Longstreet, and then to charge upon him, and take a great number of his men and himself prisoners. Strange sight! So terrible was our musketry and artillery fire, that when Armistead's brigade was checked in its charge, and stood reeling, all of its men dropped their muskets, and crawled on their hands and knees underneath the stream of shot till close to our troops, where they made signs of surrendering. They passed through our ranks scarcely noticed, and slowly went down the slope to the road in the rear. Before they got there, the grand charge of Ewell, solemnly sworn to and carefully prepared, had failed.

The rebels retreated to their lines, and opened anew the storm of shell and shot from their one hundred and twenty guns. Those who remained at the riddled headquarters will never forget the crouching, and dodging, and running of the butternut-colored captives when they got under this, their friends' fire. It was appalling to as good soldiers even as they were.

What remains to say of the fight? It straggled surlily over the middle of the horse-shoe on the west, grew big and angry on the heel at the south-west, lasted there till eight o'clock in the evening, when the fighting Sixth corps went joyously by as a reënforcement through a wood bright with coffee pots on the fire.

My pen is heavy. O, you dead, who at Gettysburg have baptized with your blood the second birth of Freedom in America, how you are to be envied! I rise from a grave whose wet clay I have passionately kissed, and I look up and see Christ spanning this battle-field with his feet, and reaching fraternal and loving up to heaven. His right hand opens the gates of Paradise, — with his left he sweetly beckons to these mutilated, bloody, swollen forms to ascend.

INCIDENT OF NASHVILLE. — The Sixty-ninth Illinois regiment, after marching in column through the principal streets of Nashville, cheering for the Union, came to a halt and in line of battle in front of the St. Cloud Hotel, where Governor Andy Johnson was stopping, and offered three cheers for the "Union, the Constitution, and the enforcement of the laws;" whereupon Governor Andy Johnson appeared, hat in hand,

and made a very little war speech. While these things were going on, a pretty young lady, expensively and tastily dressed, promenading the street, was put to the inconvenience of having to pass round the right wing of the battalion, which blocked up two streets. As she swept along, she turned up her pretty nose (as is their custom) at a manly, soldierly appearing Corporal in company D. The Corporal promptly stepped out of ranks, caused three soldiers to do the same, and invited the young lady to pass through the interval. She accepted the invitation, but, in passing through the lines, gave the Corporal a "withering glance," as Reynolds would have it, and said to him, "You had better all of you go home." "O, no," answered the Corporal, "we like your country, your climate, your people." "Our *people!*" the young lady exclaimed, sucking in a good supply of breath; "are you not ashamed to drive our poor men from their homes and their families?" "But we don't want to drive them away," said the Corporal, "if they will only have any sense — we don't want their niggers — don't want to free them — have too many niggers North now — all we want is to keep together the old government, and to keep up the old flag, and that we are going to do."

A TRUE KENTUCKIAN. — The Provost Marshal of the Eighth District of Kentucky, having called upon those whom he had enrolled to show cause for exemption, — if cause there were, — was waited on by a large crowd, nearly all of whom were rebels, many of them having served several months in the rebel army, but considered themselves unfit for the hardships of the tented field. Hereupon, the Provost Marshal was favored with the following letter:

RICHMOND, Ky., December 17, 1863.

Captain Robert Hays, Provost Marshal Eighth District, London, Kentucky:

DEAR SIR: I have seen your advertisement giving the people desiring exemption from the coming draft an opportunity to lay in their complaints, &c. Now, sir, I have never had the honor of your acquaintance, but I can refer you, for the truth of what I am about to say, to my worthy friend, James D. Foster, surgeon, and a member of your honorable Board. My complaints are as follows, viz.:

I have no broken limbs. I have no chronic diseases, such as inflammatory rheumatism, chronic inflammation of the stomach, phthisic, white swelling, &c. I am not blind in either eye. I am not knock-kneed. I am not bandy shanked. I am not bow-legged. I have no bad teeth, and can bite off a cartridge. I stand straight on my pastern joints. I have never been drilled in the Southern army, and never been so fortunate as to belong to the sympathizing party in Madison. I have no impediment in my speech. I am neither near-sighted nor far-sighted. I can hear well; I can hear the ring of a musket as well as the ring of a silver dollar. In short, I am sound in wind and limb.

I am about twenty-eight years old. I am a housekeeper, and have a wife (a good Union woman), and no children living. I am a citizen of Madison County, Kentucky, from which you want two hundred and thirty-nine soldiers. I am as brave as any man who is no braver than I am. One of my legs is as long as the other, and both are long enough to run well. I am for the "last man and the last dollar," "nigger or no nigger;" especially the last man. If you have a good musket marked "U. S.," send it down here, and I am ready to bear it in defence of the Union. I am no foreigner, and claim all the papers that entitle me to "go in." WILLARD DAVIS.

AT ISLAND NUMBER TEN, Major Corse, Inspector-General on General Pope's staff, discovered a crowd of secessionists in a cornfield. As soon as he was seen by them, they hid themselves amongst the corn, and the Major, being alone, naturally feared that he himself would be taken prisoner instead of making them his captives. There was nothing to be done, however, but to put a bold face on the matter; so he took down the rail fence surrounding the field, rode in among them, and ordered them to march into the road, and stack arms there. This order was obeyed, and the Major's feelings were considerably relieved when a guard came along with other prisoners, to whom he very willingly transferred those he had taken, and went on his way rejoicing. Secretary Scott and Adjutant-General Butler found themselves at one time in a similar position; they, too, trusting to the justness of their cause, commanded the rebels to surrender. This they did, and these two officers brought into camp one hundred and fifty-three prisoners of their own manufacture.

THE VERMONT BRIGADE. — The following description of this noted brigade was written by "one who did not belong to it, and who never was in Vermont." It will be seen, by the tenor of the article, that the writer is no flatterer, although the relation of the truth constitutes his production complimentary to the gallant "Green Mountain boys:"

"They were honest farmers turned vagabonds. They were simple countrymen changed into heroes. They were quiet townsmen that had become rovers. They stole ancient horses and bony cows on the march. They pillaged moderately in other things. They swept the dairies, and they stripped the orchards for miles where they travelled. They chased rabbits when they went into camp, after long marches, and they yelled like wild Indians when neighboring camps were silent through fatigue. They were ill disciplined and familiar with their officers. They swaggered in a cool, impudent way, and looked down with a patronizing Yankee coolness upon all regiments that were better drilled, and upon that part of the army generally that did not belong to the Vermont brigade. They were strangely proud, not of themselves individually, but of the brigade collectively; for they knew perfectly well they were the best fighters in the known world. They were long of limb, and could outmarch the army. They were individually self-reliant and skilful in the use of arms; and they honestly believed that the Vermont brigade could not be beaten by all the combined armies of the rebellion.

"They were veterans in fighting qualities almost from their first skirmish. This was at Lee's Mills. They crossed a narrow dam under a fire, made the attack they were instructed to make, and came back, wading deep in the water, with a steadiness that surprised the army. They were an incorrigible, irregular, noisy set of rascals. They were much sworn at during their four years of service; yet they were at all times a pet brigade. There were but two things they would do — march and fight; and these they did in a manner peculiarly their own. They had a long, slow, swinging stride on the march, which distanced everything that followed them. They had a quiet, attentive, earnest, individual way of fighting that made them terrific in battle. Each man knew that his neighbor in the ranks was not going to run away; and he knew, also, that he himself intended to remain where he was. Accordingly none of the attention of the line was directed from the important duty of loading and firing, rapidly and carefully. When moving into action, and while hotly engaged, they made queer, quaint jokes, and enjoyed them greatly. They crowed like cocks, they ba-a-ed like sheep, they neighed like horses, they bellowed like bulls, they barked like dogs, and they counterfeited, with excellent effect, the indescribable music of the mule. When, perchance, they held a picket line in a forest, it seemed as if Noah's ark had gone to pieces there.

"In every engagement in which this brigade took part, it was complimented for gallant conduct. One of the most remarkable of these performances, however, has never appeared in print, nor has it been noticed in the reports. After the battle of Gettysburg, when Lee's army was in the vicinity of Hagerstown and the Antietam, the Vermont brigade was deployed as a skirmishing line, covering a point of nearly three miles. The enemy were in force in front, near Beaver Creek. The Sixth corps was held in readiness in rear of the skirmish line, anticipating a general engagement. The enemy had evidently determined to attack. At last his line of battle came forward. The batteries opened at once, and the skirmishers delivered their fire. Our troops were on the alert, and stood watching for the skirmishers to come in, and waiting to receive the coming assault. But the skirmishers would not come in; and when the firing died away, it appeared that the Vermonters thus deployed as a skirmish line had actually repulsed a full line of battle attack. Twice afterwards the enemy advanced to carry the position, and were each time again driven back by this perverse skirmish line. The Vermonters, it is true, were strongly posted in a wood, and each man fired from behind a tree. But then everybody knows that the etiquette in such matters is for a skirmish line to come in so soon as they are satisfied that the enemy means business. These simple-minded patriots from the Green Mountains, however, adopted a rule of their own on this occasion; and the enemy, disgusted with such stupidity, retired across the Beaver Creek.

"When the Vermonters led the column on a march, their quick movements had to be regulated from corps or division headquarters, to avoid gaps in the column as it followed them. If a rapid or forced march were required, it was a common thing for Sedgwick to say, with a quiet smile, 'Put the Vermonters at the head of the column to-day, and keep everything well closed up.'

"After the riots in New York, when it was found necessary to send troops to the city to prevent a recurrence of the outbreak, the Vermont brigade was specially named by the War Department for this duty. Within two hours after the receipt of the despatch, the command was en route for the city. They occupied the public squares here for some time, enjoyed themselves not wisely, nor yet virtuously; and returned to the army of the Potomac sadly demoralized in all but the two great essential qualities of fighting and marching. It was a fortunate thing for the New York mob that it avoided a conflict with the New England troops at that time.

"Upon the return of the brigade to the field they quietly held on to their old routine of life, and maintained to the close of the war the splendid reputation they had won at the very outset.

"There were many regiments equal to the Vermont regiments in actual battle, and some that, like the Fifth New York volunteers, not only equalled them in fighting qualities, but greatly surpassed them in drill, discipline, and appearance on parade. As a brigade, however, they were undoubtedly the best brigade in the army of the Potomac, for they not only fought as well as it was possible to fight, but they could outmarch, with the utmost ease, any other organization in the army.

"It was the intention of the writer only to refer to this brigade, as furnishing the best type of the American soldier; but this article has grown beyond its intended limit, and we have, therefore, not the space to examine into the causes of this superiority. Two, however, may be briefly stated. First, that the regiments from Vermont were brigaded together. This rule, strange to say, seemed to work well only in regard to the smaller States, like Vermont and New Jersey. Second, the fact that Vermont, during the first year of the war, recruited for her regiments, and kept them full. Regimental and company officers, knowing that their ranks would be filled up, discharged men freely, and thus managed to get rid of their weak and worthless soldiers. For these reasons the Vermonters were good men. They were fortunate, moreover, in having such commanders as General W. F. Smith and General W. T. H. Brooks. It naturally resulted from this combination of circumstances that they became a great power in battle, and earned a reputation of which every man and woman in Vermont may well be proud."

SPIRITUALISM AT THE WHITE HOUSE. — A correspondent at Washington, in the spring of 1863, narrated the following story:

"A few evenings since, Abraham Lincoln, President of the United States, was induced to give a spiritual *soirée* in the crimson room at the White House, to test the wonderful alleged supernatural powers of Mr. Charles E. Shockle. It was my good fortune, as a friend of the medium, to be present, the party consisting of the President, Mrs. Lincoln, Mr. Welles, Mr. Stanton, Mr. L——, of New York, and Mr. F——, of Philadelphia. We took our seats in the circle about eight o'clock, but the President was called away, shortly after the manifestations commenced, and the spirits, which had apparently assembled to convince him of their power, gave visible tokens of their displeasure at the President's absence, by pinching Mr. Stanton's ears, and twitching Mr. Welles' beard. He soon returned, but it was some time before harmony was restored, for the mishaps to the secretaries caused such bursts of laughter that the influence was very unpropitious. For some half hour the demonstrations were of a physical character — tables were moved, and the picture of Henry Clay, which hangs on the wall, was swayed more than a foot, and two candelabras, presented by the Dey of Algiers to President Adams, were twice raised nearly to the ceiling.

"It was nearly nine o'clock before Shockle was fully under spiritual influence; and so powerful were the subsequent manifestations, that twice, during the evening, restoratives were applied, for he was much weakened; and though I took no notes, I shall endeavor to give you as faithful an account as possible of what took place.

"Loud rappings, about nine o'clock, were heard directly beneath the President's feet, and Mr. Shockle stated that an Indian desired to communicate.

"'Well, sir,' said the President, 'I should be happy to hear what his Indian majesty has to say. We have recently had a visitation from our red brethren, and it was the only delegation, black, white, or blue, which did not volunteer some advice about the conduct of the war.'

"The medium then called for pencil and paper, and they were laid upon the table in sight of all. A handkerchief was then taken from Mr. Stanton, and the materials were carefully concealed from sight. In less space of time than it has required for me to write this, knocks were heard, and the paper was uncovered. To the surprise of all present, it read as follows:

"'Haste makes waste, but delays cause vexations. Give vitality by energy. Use every means to subdue. Proclamations are useless; make a bold front, and fight the enemy; leave traitors at home to the care of loyal men. Less note of preparation, less parade and policy talk, and more action. HENRY KNOX.'

"'That is not Indian talk, Mr. Shockle,' said the President. 'Who is Henry Knox?'

"I suggested to the medium to ask who General Knox was; and before the words were from my lips, the medium spoke in a strange voice: 'The first Secretary of War.'

"'O, yes, General Knox,' said the President, who, turning to the Secretary, said : 'Stanton, that message is for you; it is from your predecessor.'

"Mr. Stanton made no reply.

"'I should like to ask General Knox,' said the President, 'if it is within the scope of his ability, to tell us when this rebellion will be put down.'

"In the same manner as before, this message was received:

"'Washington, Lafayette, Franklin, Wilberforce, Napoleon, and myself, have held frequent consultations on this point. There is something which our spiritual eyes cannot detect, which appears well formed. Evil has come at times by removal of men from high positions, and there are those in retirement, whose abilities should be made useful to hasten the end. Napoleon says, concentrate your forces upon one point; Lafayette thinks that the rebellion will die of exhaustion; Franklin sees the end approaching, as the South must give up for want of mechanical ability to compete against Northern mechanics. Wilberforce sees hope only in a negro army.
KNOX.'

"'Well,' exclaimed the President, 'opinions differ among the saints as well as among the sinners. They don't seem to understand running the machines among the celestials much better than we do. Their talk and advice sound very much like the talk of my cabinet — don't you think so, Mr. Welles?'

"'Well, I don't know — I will think the matter over, and see what conclusion to arrive at.'

"Heavy raps were heard, and the alphabet was called for, when, 'That's what's the matter,' was spelt out.

"There was a shout of laughter, and Mr. Welles stroked his beard.

"'That means, Mr. Welles,' said the President, 'that you are apt to be long-winded, and think the nearest way home is the longest way round. Short cuts in war times. I wish the spirits could tell us how to catch the Alabama.'

"The lights, which had been partially lowered, almost instantaneously became so dim that I could not see sufficiently to distinguish the features of any one in the room, and on the large mirror over the mantel-piece there appeared the most beautiful, though supernatural, picture ever beheld. It represented a sea view, the Alabama with all steam up, flying from the pursuit of another large steamer. Two merchantmen, in the distance, were seen, partially destroyed by fire. The picture changed, and the Alabama was seen at anchor under the shadow of an English fort — from which an English flag was waving. The Alabama was floating idly, not a soul on board, and no signs of life visible about her. The picture vanished, and in letters of purple appeared: 'The English people demanded this of England's aristocracy.'

"'So England is to seize the Alabama, finally,' said the President. 'It may be possible; but, Mr. Welles, don't let one gunboat or monitor less be built.'

"The spirits called for the alphabet, and again 'That what's the matter,' was spelt out.

"'I see, I see,' said the President. 'Mother England thinks that what's sauce for the goose may be sauce for the gander. It may be tit-tat, too, hereafter. But it is not very complimentary to our navy, anyhow.'

"'We've done our best, Mr. President,' said Mr. Welles. 'I'm maturing a plan which, when perfected, I think, if it works well, will be a perfect trap for the Alabama.'

"'Well, Mr. Shockle,' remarked the President, 'I have seen strange things, and heard rather odd remarks; but nothing which convinces me, except the pictures, that there is anything very heavenly about all this. I should like, if possible, to hear what Judge Douglas says about this war.'

"'I'll try to get his spirit,' said Mr. Shockle; 'but it sometimes happens, as it did to-night in the case of the Indian, that though first impressed by one spirit, I yield to another more powerful. If perfect silence is maintained, I will see if we cannot induce General Knox to send for Mr. Douglas.'

"Three raps were given, signifying assent to the proposition. Perfect silence was maintained, and after an interval of perhaps three minutes, Mr. Shockle rose quickly from his chair, and stood up behind it, resting his left arm on the back, his right thrust into his bosom. In a voice, such as no one could mistake, who had ever heard Mr. Douglas, he spoke. I shall not pretend to quote the language. It was eloquent and choice. He urged the President to throw aside all advisers who hesitate about the policy to be pursued, and to listen to the wishes of the people, who would sustain him at all points, if his aim was, as he believed it was, to restore the Union. He said there were Burrs and Blennerhassets living, but that they would wither before the popular approval which would follow one or two victories, such as he thought must take place ere long. The turning-point in this war will be the proper use of these victories. If wicked men, in the first hours of success, think it time to devote their attention to party, the war will be prolonged; but if victory is followed up by energetic action, all will be well.

"'I believe that,' said the President, 'whether it comes from spirit or human.'

"Mr. Shockle was much prostrated after this, and at Mrs. Lincoln's request, it was thought best to adjourn the seance."

SEVENTY-SIX AND SIXTY-FOUR. — Among a large number of articles sent to the Sanitary Commission was a good and patriotic old lady's last tribute, to be laid on the altar of her country, bearing the following inscription:

"These socks were spun and knit by Mrs. Zeruah Clapp, ninety-six years old, whose hands,

in youth, were engaged in moulding bullets in the Revolutionary War." — *Chestertown, New York.*

GENERAL LEE'S WOOING.

"My Maryland! My Maryland!"

My MARYLAND! My Maryland!
Among thy hills of blue
I wander far, I wander wide,
A lover bold and true;
I sound my horn upon the hills,
I sound it in the vale;
But echo only answers it —
An echo like a wail.

My Maryland! My Maryland!
I bring thee presents fine —
A dazzling sword with jewelled hilt,
A flask of Bourbon wine;
I bring thee sheets of ghostly white,
To dress thy bridal bed,
With curtains of the purple eve,
And garlands gory red.

My Maryland! My Maryland!
Sweet land upon the shore,
Bring out thy stalwart yeomanry,
Make clean the threshing-floor.
My ready wains lie stretching far
Across the fertile plain,
And I among the reapers stand
To gather in the grain.

My Maryland! My Maryland!
I fondly wait to see
Thy banner flaunting in the breeze,
Beneath the trysting tree;
While all my gallant company
Of gentlemen, with spurs,
Come tramping, tramping o'er the hills,
And tramping through the furze.

My Maryland! My Maryland!
I feel the leaden rain!
I see the wingéd messenger
Come hurling to my brain!
If feathered with thy golden hair,
'Tis feathered not in vain;
I spurn the hand that loosed the shaft,
And curse thee in my pain.

My Maryland! My Maryland!
Alas the ruthless day
That sees my gallant buttonwoods
Ride galloping away!
And ruthless for my chivalry,
Proud gentlemen, with spurs,
Whose bones lie stark upon the hills,
And stark among the furze.

AN ANECDOTE OF COLONEL HUGH McNEIL. — During the battle of South Mountain the rebels held a very strong position. They were posted in the mountain pass, and had infantry on the heights on every side. Our men were compelled to carry the place by storm. The position seemed impregnable; large craggy rocks protected the enemy on every side, while our men were exposed to a galling fire.

A band of rebels occupied a ledge on the extreme right, as the Colonel approached with a few of his men. The unseen force poured upon them a volley. McNeil, on the instant, gave the command:

"Pour your fire upon those rocks!"

The Bucktails hesitated; it was not an order that they had been accustomed to receive; they had always picked their men.

"Fire!" thundered the Colonel; "I tell you to fire at those rocks!"

The men obeyed. For some time an irregular fire was kept up, the Bucktails sheltering themselves, as best they could, behind trees and rocks. On a sudden McNeil caught sight of two rebels peering through an opening in the works to get an aim. The eyes of the men followed their commander, and half a dozen rifles were levelled in that direction.

"Wait a minute," said the Colonel; "I will try my hand. There is nothing like killing two birds with one stone."

The two rebels were not in line, but one stood a little distance back of the other, while just in front of the foremost was a slanting rock. Colonel McNeil seized a rifle, raised it, glanced a moment along the polished barrel; a report followed, and both the rebels disappeared. At that moment a loud cheer a little distance beyond rent the air.

"All is right now," cried the Colonel; "charge the rascals."

The men sprang up among the rocks in an instant. The affrighted rebels turned to run, but encountered another body of the Bucktails, and were obliged to surrender. Not a man of them escaped. Every one saw the object of the Colonel's order to fire at random among the rocks. He had sent the party around to their rear, and meant thus to attract their attention. It was a perfect success.

The two rebels by the opening in the ledge were found lying there stiff and cold. Colonel McNeil's bullet had struck the slanting rock in front of them, glanced, and passed through both their heads. There it lay beside them, flattened. The Colonel picked it up, and put it in his pocket.

INCIDENTS OF SHERMAN'S MARCH. — A correspondent who accompanied the army of General Sherman gives the following:

"I entered a house. The hostess was standing in a small room with closed door, looking through a small aperture, and crying: 'O! don't kill me. I am *afeard* of you.' I assured her my profound respect for her sex had always led me to treat them with the most tender kindness. 'O, yes,' she said, 'but — but you Yankees have been *recommended* to us to be a very bad and murdersome set of people!'

"In another hut I saw two women and seven small children, the oldest not more than nine years of age. They looked forlorn and hopeless. It seemed to me that death would be a relief to them all. Though they had not eaten a mouthful for three days, both women were smoking. A child was lying on the bed. I saw, by its burning cheek, that it was very ill. I said, 'Is your child sick?' 'Yes,' she replied, and seemed, by her indifference, to have even lost a mother's love. I procured one of our surgeons; he examined the child, and said, 'Dying of starvation.' Before I left, the doctor had ordered provisions from the Commissary, for which he paid out of his own funds. There are some kind men left yet. The husbands of these women were in the rebel army. The authorities make no provision for the poor. It is hard to see the suffering here endured by these harmless, illiterate people.

"One cause of their sufferings is the necessity of taking something in the way of provisions. If the supplies of forage are not up, the boys will take the corn, and other things, too. I saw one fellow attacking a beehive which had been left behind. The bees were worse than rebels. He was repulsed. But, on making the second attack, he drew a large grain sack over his head and shoulders, donned his buckskin gauntlets, took the enemy, and divided the spoils. It is laughable to see the German soldiers out foraging. It is not unfrequently that an ancient hen is seen swinging from the pommel of a saddle, and a brood of young chickens following the horse."

BRAVERY OF CAPTAIN HESS. — On the 19th of May, 1864, at Milford Station, on the Virginia Central Railroad, F. W. Hess, senior Captain of the Third Pennsylvania cavalry, with a detachment of the First Pennsylvania cavalry, was ordered to take some rifle pits defending the enemy's position, at a bridge over the Matapony River. Dismounting his men, he led them over a field, about three hundred yards, without cover of any kind from the enemy's bullets. The number of men at Captain Hess' disposal was less than one hundred, armed with Sharp's carbines and pistols. The pits were taken in the most gallant style; and in them were captured six officers and fifty enlisted men of the 11th Virginia infantry. Captain Horton, their commanding officer, as he gave up his sword to Captain Hess, said, "Sir, you are a brave man!" The loss in this charge was six killed and eight wounded. By the exploit the bridge was uncovered, and the passage of the river secured. Captain Hess and his men were warmly commended for their gallantry by General Torbert, and measures have been taken to obtain for the Captain the vacant Majority of his regiment. Captain Hess belonged in McConnellsburg, Fulton County, Penn.

CAPTURING A GUN. — There was an old chap in the Berdan Sharpshooters, near Yorktown, known as "Old Seth." He was quite a character, and a crack shot — one of the best shots in the regiment. His "instrument," as he termed it, was one of the heaviest telescopic rifles. One night at roll-call, "Old Seth" was *non est.* This was somewhat unusual, as the old chap was always up to time. A Sergeant went out to hunt him up, he being somewhat fearful that the old man had been hit. After perambulating around in the advance of the picket line, he heard a low "halloo." "Who's there?" inquired the Sergeant. "It's me," responded Seth, "and I've captured a secesh gun." "Bring it in," said the Sergeant. "Can't do it," exclaimed Seth.

It soon became apparent to the Sergeant that "Old Seth" had the exact range of one of the enemy's heaviest guns, and they could not load it for fear of being picked off by him. Again the old man shouted: "Fetch me a couple of haversacks full of grub, as this is my gun, and the cussed varmints shan't fire it again while the scrimmage lasts." This was done, and the old patriot kept good watch over that gun. In fact it was a "captured gun."

AMENITIES OF WAR. — The following extracts from letters written by a general officer in the Union army exhibit some of the pleasures of active service:

"CAMP PIERREPOINT, Va., December 19, 1861.

"MY DEAR L.: . . . . .

" . Nine P. M. — I had written the foregoing before breakfast, when I was interrupted by the return of one of my 'guides,' or scouts, who had just come in from a night ride beyond our lines.

"He informed me that the enemy had, two days before, thrown forward his pickets to within four or five miles of my advance guard, and had carried off two good Union men living within a mile of the advance, and had threatened others. This party had of course retired as soon as they had completed their work of revenge on such of their fellow-citizens as they suspected of entertaining feelings favorable to the Union party. Not knowing whether their rallying point was west or south of the railroad, I at once sent a squadron of the First cavalry, with two guides, who knew the country well, to make an extended circuit, to pick up any small parties prowling near my advanced cavalry picket, and to collect such information from the natives respecting larger bodies, as they might possess. They have just returned, and Major —— reports having obtained reliable information of a strong body of cavalry on the Centreville road below Dranesville, and a rumor of a large force expected to-morrow, with a heavy wagon train, to sweep the country around Dranesville of forage. I shall move a brigade in that direction at daylight, to be followed by a second at eight A. M., and I shall, by a rapid ride, join them as soon as the morning business will let me. My watch (near twelve M.) reminds me that I must soon lie down, as I want to get a good sleep before day; but before I close my letter, I must tell you of an amusing occurrence of this morning.

"What think you of being formally called upon to give my name to a new-born son of Mars?

"But without further prelude let me inform you that about noon, as I was quietly sitting in my office writing on official matters, the orderly in waiting opened the door and reported that a soldier asked to be admitted to speak to me on urgent business. The many wants of the private soldier were at the moment engrossing my thoughts, and were in fact the purport of my communication then being addressed to general headquarters; therefore I said, 'Let him come in.' A man of middle size, with a beaming smile overspreading his whole countenance, approached the table and apologized for interrupting me, saying, 'General, I will not detain you a minute; but I have just received a letter from my wife; she tells me she has a son four days old, and I have come to ask permission to name the boy after yourself.' 'What is your own name, my man?' I asked. 'Thomas H. Walker' was the reply.

"'You have a very good name; why not call the child after yourself?'

"He replied, a little embarrassed, 'The company won't let me, sir: the men say he must be named after the General; and I have come to ask you to write your name on a piece of paper, in full, for I mean to give him the whole of it.'

"Seeing the affair was of a desperate character, I thought the wisest course was to despatch it at once; so, tearing off a slip of paper, I began to write, when private Walker remarked, 'General, you may, if you please, send a couple of necklaces — one for the wife, and one for the old woman, her mother!' 'O ho!' says I to myself; 'now comes the gist of the matter; and as I pushed the paper towards him, I said, 'Here is the name, Walker; but where the necklaces are to come from I can't exactly say.' 'Ah! that's easy enough said,' put in Walker; 'I can get them at the store across the road, opposite to the General's quarters.' 'And what,' I asked, 'are the necklaces to cost?' 'Thirty-seven and a half cents apiece,' was the demure reply.

"Much relieved by this information, for I thought I was in for, at least, twenty dollars, I handed the man a gold dollar. Receiving the money with a low bow, he again spoke: 'If the orderly would let me pass in again, I should like to show them to the General.' 'Then tell the orderly to let you pass,' I said, and resumed my writing. Already the affair had passed from my mind, when the orderly again opened the door, with 'Walker again, sir.' 'Send him in;' and in came he, if possible, more beaming than before, and carrying a package about six inches in diameter, nicely tied up in brown paper, which he presented to me. It felt very soft, and was securely bound. 'Will the General please to look at them?' 'Upon my word, Walker, if I undo them, I shall never be able to do them up again.' 'Never mind, sir; you undo them, and I'll do them up again.' So, without further parley, I gave the string a jerk; the knot parted suddenly, and out rolled at full length upon the floor, one end remaining under my hands, not two 'necklaces,' but two gayly-colored silk and worsted 'neck-scarfs,' about six feet long, and six inches wide. The surprise was immense, and an almost irresistible fit of a strong sense of the ludicrous seized me. I did manage to restrain it, as

Walker exclaimed, 'Ain't they beautiful?' I looked at the honest face on the other side of the table, and I could not laugh at him. After a pause, I observed him wipe the palm of his right hand upon the leg of his pantaloons, and then, extending his fingers to their full length, he placed a silver quarter of a dollar upon the centre of the palm, and said: 'Here is the change, sir.' 'And what are you going to do with that, my man?' I asked. He replied very seriously, 'I don't know, sir — what do you think, yourself?' After a moment's reflection, I said, 'Suppose you buy a pair of red woollen socks for the boy.' His eyes brightened, and he said, with vehemence, 'I'll do it, General, for I expect he's a BUSTER; anyhow, General, when the company hears this, they'll have a *bust-out*, certain!' With that, private Walker, who had been in service about three months, and still retained the native honesty and simplicity which he had brought from the western wilds of Pennsylvania, gathered up his necklaces, and bowed himself from my presence.

"Good night; it is time for me to lie down.

"Friday Evening, December 20, 10 o'clock P. M.

"Dear L.: As I did not close my letter last night, I will add a postscript, to let you know that I met the enemy to-day at Dranesville, and thrashed him soundly. His force was about three thousand, infantry and cavalry, and one battery of artillery; ours about the same — that is, one brigade, the Rifles and Easton's battery, four pieces.

"General J. E. B. Stuart was in command of the rebel force, and had with him one hundred wagons, which the prisoners I have just examined inform me were sent home, pretty well filled with wounded soldiers, instead of plundered forage. His loss must have been heavy, as he left forty-three killed and severely wounded on the field. The First and Second brigades of my division did not arrive on the ground in time to participate in the affair. Our men fought very handsomely, and so, in fact, did the rebels. As I had moved out without special authority from general headquarters, and had brought with me only the day's rations, I resolved to return to my camp, after collecting the wounded of the enemy, and placing them in the keeping of the people of the town, where they were attended to, and their wounds dressed by our own surgeons. Such as I had ambulances for, in addition to what were required for our own wounded, I brought in. Our loss I cannot yet state accurately; it will not reach more than sixty, killed and wounded. I reached camp, with all my men in good condition, about one hour ago.

"I will write you more particularly to-morrow, if I have the time.

"Good night, my dear L.   G. A. Mc——."

INCIDENT OF HAGERSTOWN. — A young lady, living near Hagerstown, had an American flag around her body, and a party of rebels appeared, and demanded it. She refused to give it up, when the brave Southrons drew pistols, and threatened to shoot her if she did not deliver it up at once. She then took it off, and said, that rather than suffer violence, she would present it to them, and hoped they would not say they captured it from our soldiers. She also said she hoped they would meet before long, and under different circumstances. They took their departure, and soon after stopped at a hotel, where, it seems, the landlord regaled them bountifully with liquor. On leaving this place, and before proceeding far, they were surprised at being ordered to halt and surrender, by a party of our cavalry, who had got wind of their proceedings, which they did, and were led back to where the young lady lived, from whom they had taken the flag. "Ah!" said she, "back already? Why, I did not expect to see you so soon, although I was confident you would pay us a visit before long. Now, I will thank you to return me the flag I presented you, as I am satisfied it would become soiled if it remained in your hands." It was handed over without reply, the party feeling as cheap as though they had been caught at sheep stealing.

AN AFFECTING INCIDENT. — The following touching incident occurred in one of the hospitals at St. Louis:

"In another ward I saw a Tennesseean, whose cheek presented the pallor of death. I walked up to his bedside. His hand was trying to grasp some object, that, in his fitful delirium, was pictured on his dying imagination. His lips feebly uttered the word 'Catherine.' I took his hand in mine; his eyes, that were rolled upward in their sockets, wandered around until he was able to fix their gaze on me. 'Do you say something?' said I, tenderly. He motioned to me to put my ear down. 'O my wife — Catherine — my children!' His breathing was short — his voice very faint. 'How many children have you?' said I. He held up his four fingers. 'What is your name?' said I. 'William C. Brandon,' replied he. 'Where are you from?' I asked. 'Dodsville, Jackson County, Tennessee.' I was revolving in my mind if there would be an opportunity to forward intelligence of him to his family, when he said, 'Will you write to Catherine? Tell her I — I thought of her and the children; I — I prayed for them — O God! O God!' I assured him I would endeavor to fulfil his request. I then talked to him about a Redeemer, and after a while he seemed happier. His looks spoke what words could not."

ENDURANCE OF COLORED TROOPS. — General Wistar, commanding at Yorktown, in December, 1863, sent one of the colored regiments on a raid through Matthews County, Virginia, accompanied by a white cavalry regiment. The black troops marched a distance of sixty miles in forty hours, and endured the fatigues of a tramp considerably easier than the mounted white men.

CHICKAMAUGA, "THE STREAM OF DEATH!"

CHICKAMAUGA! Chickamauga!
O'er thy dark and turbid wave
Rolls the death-cry of the daring,
Rings the war-shout of the brave;
Round thy shore the red fires flashing,
Startling shot and screaming shell—
Chickamauga, stream of battle,
Who thy fearful tale shall tell?

Olden memories of horror,
Sown by scourge of deadly plague,
Long had clothed thy circling forests
With a terror vast and vague;
Now to gather fiercer vigor
From the phantoms grim with gore,
Hurried by war's wilder carnage
To their graves on thy lone shore.

Long, with hearts subdued and saddened,
As th' oppressor's hosts moved on,
Fell the arms of Freedom backward,
Till our hopes had almost flown;
Till outspoke stern Valor's fiat—
"Here th' invading wave shall stay;
Here shall cease the foe's proud progress;
Here be crushed his grand array!"

Then, their eager hearts all throbbing
Backward flashed each battle-flag
Of the veteran corps of Longstreet,
And the sturdy troops of Bragg;
Fierce upon the foeman turning,
All their pent-up wrath breaks out
In the furious battle-clangor,
And the frenzied battle-shout.

Roll thy dark waves, Chickamauga;
Trembles all thy ghastly shore,
With the rude shock of the onset,
And the tumult's horrid roar:
As the Southern battle-giants
Hurl their bolts of death along,
Breckinridge, the iron-hearted,
Cheatham, chivalric and strong;—

Polk and Preston, gallant Buckner,
Hill and Hindman, strong in might;
Cleburne, flower of manly valor;
Hood, the Ajax of the fight;
Benning, bold and hardy warrior;
Fearless, resolute Kershaw,
Mingle battle-yell and death-bolt,
Volley fierce and wild hurrah!

At the volleys bleed their bodies,
At the fierce shout shrink their souls,
While their fiery wave of vengeance
On their quailing column rolls;
And the parched throats of the stricken
Breathe for air the roaring flame,
Horrors of that hell foretasted,
Who shall ever dare to name?

Borne by those who, stiff and mangled,
Paid, upon that bloody field,
Direful, cringing, awe-struck homage
To the sword our heroes wield;
And who felt, by fiery trial,
That the men who will be free,
Though in conflict baffled often,
Ever will unconquered be!

Learned, though long unchecked they spoil us,
Dealing desolation round,
Marking with the tracks of ruin
Many a rod of Southern ground.
Yet, whatever course they follow,
Somewhere in their pathway flows,
Dark and deep, a Chickamauga,
Stream of death to vandal foes!

They have found it darkly flowing
By Manassas' famous plain,
And by rushing Shenandoah
Met the tide of woe again:
Chickahominy! immortal,
By the long, ensanguined flight,
Rappahannock, glorious river,
Twice renowned for matchless fight.

Heed the story, dastard spoilers,
Mark the tale these waters tell,
Ponder well your fearful lesson,
And the doom that there befell:
Learn to shun the Southern vengeance,
Sworn upon the votive sword,
"Every stream a Chickamauga
To the vile, invading horde!"

IN AUGUST, 1862, Colonel Holcomb of the First Indiana volunteers sent a long letter to General Butler's headquarters at New Orleans, detailing an account of a disturbance in his camp, and stating at the close. that he had been obliged to shoot one of the mutineers. General Butler read the paper carefully, indorsed it, "Shoot another," and sent it back to the Colonel.

"HOME. SWEET HOME."—War, terrible as it is, has its little stanzas of poetry, its chapters of romance, but lost and forgotten in the heavy thunders and sterner duties of the battle.

One of those incidents that make their way straight to the heart is related as having occurred before the two days at Pittsburg Landing.

Thursday evening preceding the battle was as lovely as spring and moonlight could make it. On that night the band of the Lead Mine regiment were serenading General McClernand at his headquarters, within cannon shot of the Landing. And when the band poured out upon the still night the air "Home, Sweet Home," the camps were hushed. In one of them a poor fellow lay in a tent ill with fever. As the well-remembered tune fell upon his ear, he turned his face with a groan to the canvas wall and died with the dying strain. And so he found "Sweet Home."

SNOW BIRD AND OWASSO. — An Indian tradition is thus related by a soldier in camp at the Green River Bridge:

"The site of our camp seems dedicated to blood-shedding from time immemorial. The spot is rife with stories and legends of the noble tribe of 'Harper' Indians, who once held undisputed possession of the soil. One of their tales runs thus: Their chief, notorious for his cruelty and ungovernable passions, became smitten with a young white lady, whom he had captured some time previous. In the legend she is described as having been surpassingly beautiful. She very naturally did not reciprocate his brutal and unsought affection, but smiled with favor on a young and handsome warrior, whose deeds of daring and innumerable virtues caused him to be loved by all the tribe, with the single exception of the 'Black Chief.' More than once had his protecting arm shielded 'Snow Bird' from the wiles of the base-minded chieftain.

"On a calm, lovely night, while the beautiful girl was paddling slowly up and down the stream, musing with her thoughts, she was startled by the voice of her persecutor calling from the bank. After vainly importuning her to row to the shore and take him in the boat, the enraged chief sprang into the water and struck out for the boat. The frightened maiden seized the oars, plied them swiftly and with a skilful hand; swiftly the frail vessel darted over the sparkling waters, but not less swiftly did the powerful chief, aroused to renewed strength by his raging passion, follow, till the exhausted girl, wearied with almost superhuman exertions, was compelled to drop the oars. With a fiendish smile he grasped the prow of the boat and climbed into it. Gazing calmly on the terrified girl, he complimented her rowing, and ordered her to again take up the oars, and bade her row to a spot still farther from their encampment, still known as the 'Black Pool.' Fearing to refuse, with trembling hand and fast-beating heart she obeyed. Arriving at the spot designated, the chief demanded her hand in marriage. After vainly pressing his suit, using entreaties and threats, the enraged villain then attempted force. With strength almost equal to his own did she endeavor to protect what is dearer than life to a woman — her maiden virtue. Drawing a small dagger she had concealed on her person, she furiously struck at him, inflicting a severe wound on his arm, disabling it. The infuriated fiend now seized an oar and struck the agonized girl a furious blow, which threw her from the boat. The helpless maiden seized the side of the boat to keep from drowning, and, with prayers, tears, and entreaties, begged the heartless wretch to spare her life; but her only answer was another blow from the hands of her enemy. She loosed her hold and sank, but arose to the surface in a moment, when the blood-stained murderer again struck her, this time with his tomahawk, burying it in her brain. She sank, with a shriek fearful to hear in that lonely spot, to rise no more.

"On the return of the chief to their camp, he met Owasso, the lover of Snow Bird, who had just returned from a protracted hunt. He had searched the entire encampment, also, her favorite haunts, without finding any trace of her, till he at last, becoming alarmed, sought Black Chief, and demanded to know her whereabouts. The chief, with a smile beaming with scorn and hatred, answered: 'Snow Bird sleeps at the bottom of the Black Pool.' 'What! murdered, and by thy hand?' 'Ay! by my hand.' 'Fiend! can it be that he, the Great Spirit, is just, and let you live after such a horrid deed? But I'll not be so merciful.' With these words Owasso sprang upon him. The contest was fierce and deadly. Owasso at length, completely exhausted by the superior strength of his adversary, gathered all his strength, and succeeded in wrenching the knife — having lost his own in the struggle — from the grasp of his foe, and plunged both blade and hilt deep in the throat of his enemy. As soon as he found his foe was dead, he, with great exertion, drew the knife from the chief's throat, and raising himself on his knees, he raised the dripping blade towards heaven and cried out, 'Snow Bird, I have revenged thee, and will now follow thee,' saying which, he rose to his feet and rushed to the cliff overhanging the place where she had been so cruelly murdered. Without a word, merely casting round his head, taking a farewell glance at his once happy home, he plunged forward knife in hand — a splash, a gurgle, and the brave Owasso was never seen more.

"Tradition says that Snow Bird and Owasso are often seen in a spirit boat rowing calmly and silently along the river, always disappearing at the fatal spot, the Black Pool, and that the form of Owasso is often seen flitting round the top of the cliff from which he made the fatal leap.

"Our stockade is built on the point of the cliff. So you see we are camped in a romantic spot. It was built, under the supervision of a 'regular' engineer, during the latter part of 1862, and burned by the notorious horse thief, John H. Morgan, on the 1st of January last. It is needless to speak of the glorious defence of the place on the 4th of July. It will ever be one of the brightest jewels in the wreath of fame that Michigan's brave sons have woven for her since the beginning of this war."

GENERAL PORTER'S RECONNOISSANCE. — "The exciting event of the day," wrote a correspondent on the 11th of April, 1862, "has been a balloon reconnoissance by General Fitz-John Porter on a scale of rather larger magnitude than was intended. At five o'clock in the morning General Porter took place in Professor Lowe's balloon. He supposed the usual number of ropes were attached to it, whereas there was only one, and a place in this, as was afterwards ascertained, had been burned by vitriol, used in generating gas. Taking his seat in the car, unaccompanied by any one, the rope was let out to nearly its full length, — the length is about nine hundred yards, — when suddenly snap went the cord, and up went the balloon. This was an unexpected part of the programme. The men below looked up with astonishment, and the General looked down with equal bewilderment.

"'Open the valve,' shouted one of the men below.

"'I'll manage it,' responded the General.

"Up went the balloon, higher, higher. It rose with great rapidity; its huge form lessened as it wildly mounted into the regions of the upper air; it became a speck in the sky. The wind was taking it in the direction of the enemy's territory. By this time every staff officer and hundreds of others were looking at the moving speck. It is impossible to describe the anxiety felt and expressed for the fate of him, the central object of thought, in that far away moving speck, every moment becoming less visible. It is seen to move in our direction; the countenances of our men brighten with hope. It passes over our heads. Soon it begins to descend, but with a rapidity that arouses renewed apprehension. Quickly a squad of cavalry, led by Captain Locke, Lieutenant McQuade, of the General's staff, plunge spurs into their horses, and dash away in the direction of the descending balloon. The rest of the story is as I received it from the General's own lips. While the rope was being played out, he adjusted his glass in readiness for his proposed view of the enemy's territory. A sudden bound of the balloon told him in a moment that the rope had given way. He dropped his glass, heard the call, 'Open the valve,' made the response given above, and set about looking for the valve. He was sensible of being flighty (the General loves a pun as well as the next one), but was not at all nervous. He saw the wind had taken him over the line of the rebel intrenchments. Having no wish to drop in among them, he let the valve take care of itself, and proceeded to take advantage of his position to note the aspect of rebel objects below. Crowds of soldiers rushed from the woods, and he heard their shouts distinctly. Luckily he was above the reach of their bullets; so he was not afraid on this score. The map of the country was distinctly discernible. He saw Yorktown and its works, York River and its windings, and Norfolk and its smoking chimneys. A counter current of air struck the balloon, and its course was reversed. Its retreat from over Rebeldom was rapid. He opened the valve, the gas escaped, and down he came. He could not say how fast he came down, but it was with a rapidity he would not care to have repeated. The car struck the top of a shelter tent, — under which, luckily, no one happened to be at the time, — knocked the tent into pi, and left him enveloped in a mass of collapsed oil silk. He crawled out, and found himself in the middle of a camp, not one hundred rods from General McClellan's headquarters.

" 'I came mounted, you see,' was his remark to General Burns, who was about the first man by his side. He gave the details of his aerial voyage to General Burns, who, seeing the opportunity of getting off a joke, could not lose the opportunity.

" 'You are a suspicious character,' remarked Burns.

" 'How so?' asked Porter.

" 'In the space of half an hour you have been taken up by a balloon, and arrested by a shelter tent.'

" 'And you have come down safe, I see,' broke in Captain Locke, before the laughter at General Burns' duet of puns; 'I came with this cavalry company to look you up.'

" 'You ought to have sent flying artillery after me,' rejoined Porter."

A WOMAN'S SACRIFICE. — The following eloquent and touching tribute to the memory of Miss Cutler, a volunteer army nurse, who died at Newbern, of disease contracted while in the performance of her duties, is from a private letter written by T. H. Squire, Surgeon, Eighty-ninth New York volunteers:

"The daughter of Dr. Cutler, Twenty-first Massachusetts, of which I have spoken in a previous letter, died a few days ago, at Newbern, of typhoid fever. Her remains were brought back to this island, and buried to-day. Who will write her epitaph in befitting verse? She was the friend of the sick and wounded soldiers, educated, accomplished, young, beautiful, affectionate, patriotic, pious, and self-sacrificing. In her death in the van of the army, a woman pure and lovely has been laid as a victim upon the altar of Liberty. She died away from home: a father, whom she loved, stood by her; but his duties to the wounded prevented him from accompanying her remains to their temporary resting-place on this beautiful island. Sacred be the spot where her remains now lie! Ye winds that whisper in the pines, breathe her a requiem! Ye grapes and mistletoe that climb upon the trees, and droop from overhanging boughs, bend down and kiss her lonely grave! Bay, myrtle, and magnolia, distil your fragrance around the tomb; in life her gentle virtues breathed a like perfume! Dear girl, I would that I had power to hand thy name down to all coming time!'"

HARDEE THROWN IN THE SHADE. — A well-known Confederate Major-General was stopping for a while in a Georgia village, which circumstance coming to the knowledge of the "Home Guard" of that vicinity, the Captain resolved to give the General an opportunity of witnessing the "revolutions" of his superb corps. In due time, Captain ——'s company, having "fell in," were discovered by the General in front of his quarters, in the execution of his command, "In two ranks, git," &c. During the exhibition, by some dexterous double-quick movement among militia officers, the Captain, much to his surprise and chagrin, found the company in a "fix," best described, I reckon, as a "solid circle." In stentorophonic tones he called them to "halt!" The General became interested, and drew near, in order to see in what way things would be righted. The Captain, in his confusion, turned his head to one side, like a duck when she sees the shadow of a hawk flit past, and seemed to be in the deepest thought. At last an idea seemed to strike him; a ray of intelligence mantled his face, and straightening himself up, he turned to the company, and cried out: "Company, disentangle to the front, march."

The company was "straightened," and the General gave it as his opinion that it was the best command he had ever heard given.

AN INCIDENT BY THE WAY. — When a love for the old flag does exist in Dixie, it is clear, warm, and earnest. It gushes out sometimes in the most unexpected places, like a spring in a desert; and many a time have Federal prisoners been startled into tears at finding a loyal heart beating close beside them, when they had only looked for taunt and treason. A body of Federal prisoners had reached Rome, en route for Richmond. Weary, famished, thirsting, they were herded like cattle in the street, under the burning sun — a public show. It was a gala day in that modern Rome. The women, magnificently arrayed, came out and pelted them with balls of cotton, and with such sneers and taunts as, "So you have come to Rome — have you, you Yankees? How do you like your welcome?" and then more cotton and more words. The crowds and the hours came and went, but the mockery did not intermit, and our poor fellows were half out of heart.

My informant, Major P., faint and ill, had stepped back a pace or two, and leaned against a post, when he was lightly touched upon the arm. As he looked around, mentally nerving himself for some more ingenious insult, a fine-looking, well-dressed boy of twelve stood at his elbow, his frank face turned up to the Major's. "And he, too?" thought the officer.

With a furtive glance at a rebel guard, who stood with his back to them, the lad, pulling the Major's skirt, and catching his breath, boy-fashion, said, "Are you from New England?" "I was born in Massachusetts," was the reply. "So was my mother," returned the boy, brightening up; "she was a New England girl, and she was what you call a 'school-ma'am,' up North; she married my father, and I'm their boy; but how she does love New England, and the Yankees, and the old United States! and so do I."

The Major was touched, as well he might be; and his heart warmed to the boy as to a young brother; and he took out his knife, severed a button from his coat, and handed it to him for a remembrance. "O, I've got half a dozen just like it. See here!" and he took from his pocket a little string of them — gifts of other boys in blue.

"My mother would like to see you," he added, "and I'll go and tell her."

"What are you doing here?" growled the guard, suddenly wheeling round upon him; and the boy slipped away into the crowd, and was gone. Not more than half an hour elapsed before a lovely lady, accompanied by the little patriot, passed slowly down the sidewalk next to the curb-stone. She did not pause, she did not speak; if she smiled at all, it was faintly; but she handed to one and another of the prisoners bank notes as she went. As they neared the Major, the boy gave him a significant look, as much as to say, "That's my New England mother." The eyes of the elegant lady and the poor, weary officer

met for an instant, and she passed away like a vision, out of sight. Who will not join with me in fervently breathing two beatitudes : God bless the young Georgian, and blessed forever be the Northern schoolma'am? — D. F. Taylor.

"GOOD SHOOTING." — The color-bearer of the Tenth Tennessee (Irish) having been shot down in the battle of Chickamauga, the Colonel ordered one of the privates to take the colors. Pat, who was loading at the time, replied : "By the holy St. Patrick, Colonel, there's so much good shooting here, I haven't a minute's time to waste fooling with that thing."

GAINING THE CREST OF ROCKY FACE. — After the evacuation of Tunnel Hill, Georgia, by the rebels, the Fourth corps (Howard's) passed to the right of the place, confronting them on Rocky-face Ridge.

On Sunday, the 8th of May, 1864, a detachment of Harker's brigade was ordered on a reconnoissance to the northern extremity of the ridge. The balance of the brigade being held in reserve at the base, Colonel Opdyke, with his five hundred Ohio (One Hundred and Twenty-fifth) Tigers was ordered forward, with a guide, to develop the enemy on the ridge, and, if possible, gain a position there. Skirmishing commenced at the base, and increased in severity as our men ascended. But up they went, the skirmishers dodging from tree to tree, and from rock to rock, to escape the bullets that were showered upon them from the crest. The sides of the ridge were so steep and rocky that the men were obliged to cling to the trees and jutting cliffs to help themselves along. Field officers were obliged to dismount and lead their horses, and even then could only proceed with great difficulty. Twice the men were ordered to lie down and rest, in order to cool themselves, as the day was exceedingly warm, and the exercise severe.

Simultaneously with the second order to halt, the cry rung out from the rocks above us, "We have gained the crest! — WE HAVE GAINED THE CREST!!!" The announcement seemed to electrify the men, and with a shout that rent the air, they sprang forward like tigers, and in a moment the entire regiment rested on the summit of the ridge. Stopping a moment to breathe, they were again ordered to advance, which they did with a determined bravery that defied the sneaking enemy that skulked from rock to rock, improving every obstacle to embarrass them. Having driven the enemy more than half a mile, the men were ordered to throw up stone-works for temporary security, until further orders were received from the rear. The reply came in these words — "You have accomplished all, and more than was expected. Take a strong position and await orders."

The Sixty-fifth Ohio infantry, and shortly afterwards the remainder of the brigade, came to the support of the One Hundred and Twenty-fifth.

INCIDENTS OF THE BATTLE OF RESACA, GA. — *May 18.* — " I have just been over that portion of the battle-field where the Twentieth corps repulsed the enemy yesterday, and the sight presented is enough to make the heart of one long accustomed to war ache. The ambulance corps, so complete in all its details, is gathering in the wounded, and the groans of the sufferers are grating to the ear. All the rebel dead and wounded are left in our hands to be cared for. The ground is thickly strewn with the victims in about equal proportions, excepting at those places where desperate charges were made upon our line, when the enemy came out of his breastworks; there the rebels largely predominate. There, within a few yards of me, a wounded rebel is stopping the blood that endeavors to make its exit through a ghastly grape wound in the leg of a Union soldier; while over yonder, beneath an oak, a wounded Federal is in the act of giving water from his canteen to an enemy who fell beside him, and whose life-blood discolors the garments of both. After the shock of battle has passed, the helpless inhabitants of the rifle pits and trenches are no longer enemies. A common sympathy seems to inspire them, and they are once more friends and brothers — children of one Father.

"On the field, yesterday, on the left, near Tilton, where our cavalry engaged the enemy, a beautiful garden, clothed in all the loveliness that rare plants and southern flowers could give it, attracted my attention, and I was drawn to it. The house had been deserted by its owners, and the smiling magnolias and roses seemed to stand guard over the deserted premises. I entered through an open gate, stooped to pluck a rose from the bush, when I discovered one of the enemy's pickets lying partially covered by the grass and bushes — dead. He was a noble-looking man, and upon his countenance there seemed to rest the remnant of a smile. The right hand clasped a rose, which he was in the act of severing from its stem when he received the messenger of death. In the afternoon the cavalry dug a narrow grave, and, with Federal soldiers for pall-bearers, and the beautiful flowers for mourners, he was laid to rest, the rose still clasped in his stiffened hand. Nothing was found to identify him, and in that lonely grave his life's history lies entombed. No sister's tears will baptize the grave among the roses where the dead picket sleeps."

GENERAL TERRY AND COLONEL OLMSTED. — Major Gardiner, of the Seventh Connecticut regiment, tells this characteristic story of General Terry, the late Colonel of his regiment:

"After Fort Pulaski had been placed in General Terry's charge, and as its rebel commander, Colonel Olmsted, was about to be sent North as a prisoner of war, General Terry, appreciating the embarrassments to which he might be subjected, told him that as it was not probable that he was supplied with current money, and as Confederate money was valueless except as a curiosity, he desired that he would accept of a sum that might free him from temporary inconvenience, and presented him with fifty dollars in good money. The offer was gratefully accepted, of course, with suitable acknowledgments of the generosity which prompted it.

AN HEROIC SAILOR. — In the record of the war, not the least interesting features are the heroic deeds of the humble men who compose the rank and file of the army and navy. Instances of individual heroism and self-sacrifice present themselves in abundance, and furnish a rich harvest of materials for the annalist and historian. One of the most conspicuous of these is the case of the gallant tar, John Davis, whose courage in the attack on Elizabeth City, N. C., is made the subject of special mention by his immediate commander and by Commodore Goldsborough, who thus unite to make manifest the bond of true chivalry which binds together all brave men, however widely separated their station. The following is the story of this brave sailor:

"Lieutenant J. C. Chapin, commanding United States steamer Valley City, off Roanoke Island, writes to Commodore Goldsborough under date of February 25th, noticing a magnanimous act of bravery by John Davis, gunner's mate on board his vessel, at the taking of Elizabeth City. He says John Davis was at his station, during the action, in the magazine issuing powder, when a shell from the enemy's battery penetrated into the magazine, and exploded outside of it. He threw himself over a barrel of powder, protecting it with his own body from the fire, while at the same time passing out the powder for the guns. Commodore Goldsborough, in transmitting this letter to the Navy Department, says: 'It affords me infinite pleasure to forward this communication to the Navy Department, to whose especial consideration I beg leave to recommend the gallant and noble sailor alluded to;' and he adds in a postscript: 'Davis actually seated himself on the barrel, the top being out, and in this position he remained until the flames were extinguished.'"

The Navy Department promptly rewarded John Davis, the brave sailor who so courageously protected from the flames a barrel of gunpowder on the steamer Valley City during the attack upon Elizabeth City. He was a gunner's mate, receiving a salary of twenty-five dollars per month, or three hundred dollars per year. The evidence of his bravery was received at the Navy Department on the evening of the 10th instant, and on the next day Secretary Welles sent him the following letter, appointing him a gunner, an office which carries with it a salary of one thousand dollars per year, and is a life appointment, the salary increasing by length of service to one thousand four hundred and fifty dollars:

"NAVY DEPARTMENT, March 11, 1862.

"SIR: Your commanding officer and the Flag-Officer of the Northern Atlantic Blockading Squadron, have brought to the notice of the Department your courage and presence of mind, displayed on the 10th ultimo, in protecting with your person a barrel of gunpowder from the flames.

"As a mark of appreciation of your bravery, you are hereby appointed an acting-gunner in the navy of the United States from this date.

"Enclosed herewith is a blank oath of office, which, having executed, you will return to the Department, accompanied by your letter of acceptance.

"If, after you have served six months at sea, you shall furnish the Department with satisfactory testimonials from your commanding officer, a warrant will be issued to you, bearing the same date of this acting appointment.

"I am, respectfully, your obedient servant, GIDEON WELLES."

A JOAN D'ARC. — A marauding band of rebels in Kentucky, on their way to Mount Sterling, stopped at the house of a Mr. Oldom, and, he being absent at the time, plundered him of all his horses, and among them a valuable one belonging to his daughter Cornelia. She resisted the outrage as long as she could, but finding all her efforts in vain, she sprang upon another horse, and started post haste towards the town to give the alarm. Her first animal gave out, when she seized another, and meeting the messenger from Middleton, she sent him as fast as his horse could carry him to convey the necessary warning to Mount Sterling, where he arrived most opportunely. Miss Oldom then retraced her way towards home, taking with her a double-barrelled shot-gun. She found a pair of saddle-bags on the road, belonging to a rebel officer, which contained a pair of revolvers, and soon she came up with the advancing marauders, and ordered them to halt. Perceiving that one of the thieves rode her horse, she ordered him to surrender her horse; this he refused, and finding that persuasion would not gain her ends, she levelled the shot-gun at the rider, commanded him, as Damon did the traveller, "down from his horse," and threatened to fire if he did not comply. Her indomitable spirit at last prevailed, and the robbers, seeing something in her eye that spoke a terrible menace, surrendered her favorite steed. When she had regained his back, and patted him on the neck, he gave a neigh of mingled triumph and recognition, and she turned his head homeward and cantered off as leisurely as if she were taking her morning exercise.

THE BALLAD OF ISHMAEL DAY.

ONE summer morning a daring band
Of rebels rode into Maryland,
   Over the prosperous peaceful farms,
   Sending terror and strange alarms,
   The clatter of hoofs and the clang of arms.

Fresh from the South, where the hungry pine,
They ate like Pharaoh's starving kine;
   They swept the land like devouring surge,
   And left their path, to its farthest verge,
   Bare as the track of the locust-scourge.

"The rebels are coming," far and near
Rang the tidings of dread and fear;
   Some paled, and cowered, and sought to hide;
   Some stood erect in their fearless pride;
   And women shuddered, and children cried.

But others — vipers in human form,
Stinging the bosom that kept them warm —
   Welcomed with triumph the thievish band,
   Hurried to offer the friendly hand,
   As the rebels rode into Maryland, —

Made them merry with food and wine,
Clad them in garments rich and fine, —
   For rags and hunger to make amends, —
   Flattered them, praised them with selfish ends:
   "Leave us scathless, for we are friends!"

Could traitors trust a traitor? No!
Little they favored friend or foe,
   But gathered the cattle the farms across,
   Flinging back, with a scornful toss —
   "If ye are friends, ye can bear the loss!"

Flushed with triumph, and wine, and prey,
They neared the dwelling of Ishmael Day,
   A sturdy veteran, gray and old,
   With heart of a patriot, firm and bold,
   Strong and steadfast — unbribed, unsold.

And Ishmael Day, his brave head bare,
His white locks tossed by the morning air,
   Fearless of danger, or death, or scars,
   Went out to raise, by the farm-yard bars,
   The dear old flag of the Stripes and Stars.

Proudly, steadily, up it flew,
Gorgeous with crimson, and white, and blue:
   His withered hand, as he shook it freer,
   May have trembled, but not with fear,
   While, shouting, the rebels drew more near.

"Halt!" They had seen the hated sign
Floating free from old Ishmael's line —
   "Lower that rag!" was their wrathful cry.
   "Never!" rung Ishmael Day's reply;
   "Fire, if it please you — I can but die!"

One, with a loud, defiant laugh,
Left his comrades, and neared the staff.
   "Down!" — came the fearless patriot's cry —
   "Dare to lower that flag, and die!
   One must bleed for it — you or I!"

But caring not for the stern command,
He drew the halliards with daring hand;
   Ping! went the rifle-ball — down he came
   Under the flag he had tried to shame —
   Old Ishmael Day took careful aim!

Seventy winters and three had shed
Their snowy glories on Ishmael's head;
   But though cheeks may wither, and locks grow gray,
   His fame shall be fresh, and young alway —
   Honor be to old Ishmael Day!

ALIENATIONS OF WAR. — The war produced strange alienations. Two Kentuckians, father and son, were on a railroad train in Indiana. The father was a rebel prisoner; the son was a Fedcral guard on the platform of the car. The old man, seeing his son, presumed to take more liberty than the rule allowed, and put his head outside the door. His son hastily advanced, piece at the shoulder, with a sharp "Get back there, you old rebel!"

INCIDENTS OF THE PENINSULA. — During the first day's skirmish near Lee's Mills, two soldiers, one from Maine, the other from Georgia, posted themselves each behind a tree, and indulged in sundry shots, without effect on either side, at the same time keeping up a lively chat. Finally, that getting a little tedious, Georgia calls out to Maine, "Give me a show," meaning step out, and give an opportunity to hit. Maine, in response, pokes out his head a few inches, and Georgia cracks away, and misses. "Too high," says Maine. "Now give me a show." Georgia pokes out her head, and Maine blazes away. "Too low," sings Georgia. In this way the two alternated several times, without hitting. Finally, Maine sends a ball so as to graze the tree within an inch or two of the ear of Georgia. "Cease firing," shouts Georgia. "Cease it is," responds Maine. "Look here," says one, "we have carried on this business long enough for one day. 'Spose we adjourn for rations?" "Agreed," says the other. And so the two marched away in different directions, one whistling "Yankee Doodle," the other "Dixie."

"While coming home from a scout," says a soldier at Yorktown, "we called at a house, and found a couple of ladies, quite young, and one as handsome as a Hebe. They were secesh to the 'backbone,' and had each a lover in the rebel army; one of them was at Yorktown, and only left the day before, to pick his way back along the York River, and carry such information as he had gotten from us. The young lady showed us his photograph, a good-looking Lieutenant, and hoped we should meet him face to face, that he might leave us for dead. 'O,' said she, 'if all the Yankees were one man, and I had a sword here, I should like to cut his throat!'

"And she said it with a vim, too. We told her we would take good care of young Lieutenant White, and see that Miss Florill had an opportunity to change her name after the battle was over, hoping for an invitation to the wedding; and as she had called me the 'Divine,' chaplain of the regiment, I proposed to marry them.

"'Never,' said she. 'I hope he will come home dead before you shall take Yorktown. I would wade in blood up to my knees to bury his body.'

"She spoke of poison in a glass of water we drank, but I replied that 'one look of her angel face, one smile from her lovely features, would be an antidote to the rankest poison.' 'Yes,' she replied, 'and to your hatred of the South too?'

"The flirtation nearly made her in favor of Union, and us the more so. But we had not gone far when we observed a company of soldiers approaching, who brought with them the lover a corpse upon a litter, returning to his sweetheart. He had been shot, while trying to avoid the quick eye of our sharpshooters, near a house upon the York River shore, where his father had resided, and where a negro informed the soldiers that his mother and sister were at the house where we had been in conversation with the ladies, one of whom was his sister, and our soldiers had, after receiving orders, carried him to be buried.

"We did not mar the sorrow of the relatives by stopping to witness the reception of the body."

"MILITARY NECESSITY." — A knot of newspaper correspondents in the department of the Rappahannock took formal possession of certain rebel premises, and adopted the following declaratory resolutions:

"1. Resolved, That the house belonged to the Federal Government by reason of its owner's secession and abandonment, and not to the officers who occupied it. That we were equally children of Uncle Sam, and that, inasmuch as Uncle Sam has repudiated primogeniture from his first start out in life, all his children were entitled to share alike, at present and in prospective, and that the house was ours to use, as much as the officers. That we, therefore, should take possession of any unoccupied portion of it. That the dining-room was unoccupied for the night, and that there we should take up our lodgings.

"2. Resolved, Of all the appliances of comfort that we could find unappropriated, ditto. That we should take some wood, enough to keep a roaring fire all night, to warm our feet by.

"3. Resolved, Of everything to eat, ditto; provided that we could get cook's consent, acknowledging valid authority over the matter in him, derived from his skill and labor in making it eatable.

"4. Resolved, That we do all these things as a military necessity, and in strict conformity to, and most devoted regard for, the constitution of the doers."

A BRAVE PENNSYLVANIAN. — At the battle and capture of Port Gibson, Sergeant Charles Bruner, a Pennsylvanian, of Northampton County, with a squad of fifty men of the Twenty-third regiment Wisconsin volunteers, was the first to enter the fort. The flag-sergeant being wounded, Sergeant Bruner seized the colors, and, amid cheers and a rain of bullets, planted the Stars and Stripes upon the ramparts.

Again, at Champion Hill, the Twenty-third was about breaking, when Sergeant Bruner took the colors in his hand, and cried, "Boys, follow! don't flinch from your duty!" and on they went, following their brave color-bearer; and the intrenchment was taken.

Again, at the battle of Big Black, company B, of the Twenty-third Wisconsin, got orders from General Grant to plant a cannon, and try to silence a battery, which was bravely done; when the cannon was dismantled, Captain and First Lieutenant were gone and wounded. Sergeant Bruner again cheered on his men, and in a hand-to-hand fight the enemy were routed. The Sergeant was made prisoner twice; but his captors were soon put *hors du combat* by his brave followers, who would die for their gallant Sergeant, and now Captain. The rebels were driven back, with lost colors.

Singular to say, Sergeant Bruner has led on his men in more than thirteen battles, always in front, yet he has never been wounded. He captured with his own hands three rebel flags, which he handed over to General Grant.

Sergeant Bruner, the only Pennsylvanian in that regiment, does the old Keystone State great honor.

BRAVERY AT LEE'S MILLS. — Among the incidents of the fight at Lee's Mills, Virginia, on the 16th of April, 1862, was the recovery from a fever of Sergeant Fletcher, of company E, Third Vermont, on the sick list, and excused from duty, and the use he made of his temporary health. He crossed the stream and went through the fight; then, on his return, was among those who went back and rescued the wounded. On his return to camp, he went into hospital and resumed his fever, with aggravation.

John Harrington, a beardless orphan boy of seventeen, unarmed, went over and rescued out of the rifle pit a disabled comrade.

Lieutenant Whittemore commanded company E, which is without a Captain for some reason. This officer, with his revolver, covered Harrington in his hazardous expedition, and killed several rebels who aimed their pieces at the boy. His most intimate friend in the company, private Vance, had been killed in the rifle-pit. Whittemore, enraged with sorrow, burst into tears, and seizing the dead soldier's musket, stood over him, and threatened death to any who should retreat; and then stooping down, he took cartridge after cartridge from his friend's box, and killed his man with every fire — raging with a divine fury the while.

Among the phenomena of the fight was the condition of the uniform of Captain Bennett, of company K, of the Third Vermont. It had eight bullet holes in it — one through the collar of his coat, one through the right coat-sleeve, one through his pantaloons below the left knee, one through both pantaloons and drawers above the right knee, and four through the skirts of his coat. There was not a scratch upon this man's skin.

ROSECRANS AND THE CONFEDERATE CAPTAIN. — The following interview took place, during the progress of the battle of Chickamauga, between General Rosecrans and a Captain Rice, of the First Texas regiment. The Captain was made prisoner on Saturday afternoon, and taken immediately to Rosecrans, who was two hundred and fifty yards in the rear of the portion of his army which was engaged by Hood's division. Rosecrans appeared, dressed in black breeches, white vest, and plain blouse, and was surrounded by a gorgeous staff. The General is short and thickset, with smooth face, rosy cheeks and lips, brilliant black eyes, and is very handsome. He is exceedingly affable and pleasant in conversation. On the approach of Captain R., he dismounted, tapped him familiarly on the shoulder, and said, "Let us step aside and talk a little." Seated on a fallen tree, some thirty yards from the staff, the General, *à la* genuine Yankee, picked up a stick and commenced whittling, and the following conversation ensued:

Rosecrans. Where are your lines?

Rice. General, it has cost me a great deal of trouble to find your lines; if you take the same amount of trouble, you will find ours.

Rose. (Wincing slightly.) What brigade do you belong to?

Rice. Robertson's.

Rose. What division?

Rice. I don't know.

Rose. What corps?

Rice. I don't know.

Rose. Do you belong to Bragg's army?

Rice. O, yes, sir.

Rosecrans looked at him, and smiled at his ingenuous manner, so perfectly open and candid the Captain seemed, then again commenced, blandly:

Rose. How many of Longstreet's men got here?

Rice. About forty-five thousand.

Rose. Is Longstreet in command?

Rice. O, no, sir! General Bragg is in command.

Rose. Captain, you don't seem to know much, for a man whose appearance seems to indicate so much intelligence.

Rice. Well, General, if you are not satisfied with my information, I will volunteer some. We are going to whip you most tremendously in this fight.

Rose. Why?

Rice. Because you are not ready to fight.

Rose. Were you ready?

Rice. Yes; we were ready.

Rose. How do you know we were not ready?

Rice. You sent a brigade to burn a bridge. General Bragg sent a brigade to drive yours back. You were forced to reënforce; then General Bragg reënforced, and forced you into an engagement.

Rose. I find you know more than I thought you did. You can go to the rear. — *Southern paper.*

HOW AN AMPUTATION IS PERFORMED. — Imagine yourself in the hospital of the Sixth corps after a battle. There lies a soldier, whose thigh has been mangled by a shell; and, although he may not know it, the limb will have to be amputated to save his life. Two Surgeons have already pronounced this decision; but, according to the present formation of a hospital in this camp, no one Surgeon, nor two, can order an amputation, even of a finger. The opinion of five, at least, and sometimes more, including the division Surgeon, always a man of superior skill and experience, must first be consulted, and then, if there is an agreement, depend upon it, the operation is necessary. This did not use to be, in the earlier months of the war; but it is so now. Suppose that the amputation has been decided upon; the man, who is a rebel, and an Irishman, with strong nerve and frame, is approached by one of the Surgeons, and told that he will now be attended to, and whatever is best will be done for him. They cannot examine his wound thoroughly where he lies, so he is tenderly lifted on to a rough table. A rebel Surgeon is among the number present. The man, as I have said, has strong nerve, and is not reduced by loss of blood. So, then, the decision is communicated to him that he must lose his leg. While the operating Surgeon is examining, and they are talking to the poor fellow, chloroform is being administered to him through a sponge. The first sensations of this sovereign balm are like those pleasant ones produced by a few glasses of whiskey, and the Irishman begins to think he is on a spree, and throws out his arms and legs, and talks funnily. The inhalation goes on, and the beating of the pulse is watched; and when it is ascertained that he is totally oblivious to all feeling, the instruments are produced, and the operation commences. Down goes the knife into the flesh, but there is no tremor or indication of pain. The patient is dreaming of the battle out of which he has just come. Hear him, for he's got his rifle pointed over the earthworks at our advancing line of battle: "Arrah, now they come! Give it to 'em! Down goes my man! Load up, load up quick! for there they are again! Hi! hi! hi! Up they come! Now for another shot!" Such are a sample of the exclamations the Celt makes, in his own brogue, while the Surgeons are cutting, and carving, and sawing away. The leg is off, and carried away; the arteries are tied up, and the skin is neatly sewed over the stump. The effect of the chloroform is relaxed; and when the patient opens his eyes, a short time afterwards, he sees a clean white bandage where his ghastly wound had been, and his lost limb is removed. He feels much easier, and drinks an ounce and a half of good whiskey with gusto. This is a real instance of amputation, and the chief characteristics of the description will answer every one.

ANECDOTE OF GENERAL SHERMAN. — On the arrival of General Sherman at Savannah, he saw a large number of British flags displayed from buildings, and had a curiosity to know how many British Consuls there were there. He soon ascertained that these flags were on buildings where cotton had been stored away, and at once ordered it to be seized. Soon after that, while the General was busily engaged at headquarters, a pompous gentleman walked in, apparently in great haste, and inquired if he was General Sherman. Having received an affirmative reply, the pompous gentleman remarked, "that when he left his residence, United States troops were engaged in removing his cotton from it, when it was protected by the British flag."

"Stop, sir!" said General Sherman; "not your cotton, sir, but my cotton, — in the name of the United States Government, sir. I have noticed," continued General Sherman, "a great

many British flags all about here, protecting cotton. I have seized it all, in the name of my Government."

"But, sir," said the Consul, indignantly, "there is scarcely any cotton in Savannah that does not belong to me."

"There is not a pound of cotton here, sir, that does not belong to me, for the United States," responded Sherman.

"Well, sir," said the Consul, swelling himself up with the dignity of his office, and reddening in the face; "my Government shall hear of this. I shall report your conduct to my Government, sir!"

"Ah! pray, who are you, sir?" said the General.

"Consul to Her British Majesty, sir!"

"O! indeed!" responded the General. "I hope you will report me to your Government. You will please say to your Government, for me, that I have been fighting the English Government all the way from the Ohio River to Vicksburg, and thence to this point. At every step I have encountered British arms, British munitions of war, and British goods of every description — at every step — sir. I have met them, sir, in all shapes; and now, sir, I find you claiming all the cotton, sir. I intend to call upon my Government to order me to Nassau at once."

"What do you propose to do there?" asked the Consul, somewhat taken aback.

"I would," replied the General, "take with me a quantity of picks and shovels, and throw that cursed sand-hill into the sea, sir; and then I would pay for it, sir — if necessary! Good day, sir."

ONE OF GOD'S NOBLEMEN. — A flat-boat full of soldiers, a few of whom were African, attempted to land at Rodman's Point, on the coast of North Carolina.

The rebels were awaiting their approach in ambuscade, and reserved their fire till the end of the boat was resting on the shore, and then opened a deadly fire. Life could only be saved by lying flat on the boat's bottom; and if they remained inactive long, the whole boat-load would be captured. One of the negro soldiers, who saw the situation, and the vital importance of getting the boat off, as well as the imminent danger of the attempt, said: "Somebody got to die to get us all out dis 'ere, and it mought jus' as well be me as anybody!"

He then deliberately rose up, stepped on shore, and pushed the boat off. As she swung clear, and the men crouching in the bottom were saved, the body of the noble African fell forward into the end of the boat, pierced by five bullets.

STORIES OF WAR. — A Chaplain, on the eve of a battle, bade the soldiers of his corps fight bravely, for those who fell "would sup in heaven," and thereupon himself marched to the rear, replying, when called to stop, "that for his part he never took suppers." A kindred anecdote is related of a militia colonel in the last war with Great Britain. Addressing his soldiers, on the eve of an engagement, he told them to "press where they saw his white plume wave," adding that, "if by any accident the regiment was overpowered and driven off the field, and should need further orders after the battle, they would find him (the Colonel) behind Simon Norris' barn, in the town of Buxton."

HALF AN HOUR AMONG THE REBELS. — The sun was shining down in a style that would have done honor to the sweltering regions of the tropics. Beneath its torrid beams several hundred rebels, who had taken the oath of allegiance to their native country, trudged their way from the Delaware Wharf to the depot, in West Philadelphia, where they awaited transportation. Among the motley crowd were a number possessing natural intelligence, although uneducated. From the excessive heat, they might have supposed they were already in the "Sunny South," and that under such a high temperature it would be impossible for Northerners to be the coldhearted barbarians they had been represented to be. The repentants presented a varied picture for philosophical contemplation. Some of them were decidedly sullen, and at times exhibited a morose disposition. Others seemed to regard matters and things as they found them, with a degree of philosophy entirely creditable. Numbers were loquacious, and their speech indicated the peculiarities of various localities of our country. Among that crowd was a tall individual, with grayish-blue eyes, sunken cheek, sallow complexion, and long, yellowish hair, dangling down his neck. He seemed possessed of natural intelligence, but was deficient in point of education. In his speech he was remarkably profane.

Among the spectators was a gentleman remarkable for the emphatic style in which he enforces argument on the different topics of the day. He eyed the crowd of rebels for some time, mingled among them, and finally singled out the tall, yellow-haired individual, above alluded to, for a little especial conversation.

"You're a South Carolinian, I suppose?" said the spectator.

"That's my native country," replied the repentant rebel.

"Your native country; were you born there?"

"Waal, I was."

"Then the whole country is your native country, and not simply South Carolina," responded the gentleman.

"Waal, I don't know about that ar, stranger; you fellows have licked us like ——"

"Don't say that, sir, for you are entirely mistaken," replied the interlocutor.

"Waal, I don't know what you call a lickin'; if we didn't get it, then I don't know what a lickin' is; why, sir, we're tore out, root and branch, and smashed down like Virginny tobacco in a press."

"Now, let me tell you," responded the dialogist, "the North has only brought you fellows back into the Union; the North did not invade the South merely to thrash you; the North took the good old flag of the Union there, and asked you to come under its protection; you refused, and the North went at you, and, after pretty hard fighting, have brought you under that flag again. This is all the North has done. The North said that the Union should not be divided, and this doctrine is fully maintained by American arms and American valor."

By this time the argument began to increase in interest; other rebels gathered around, and attentively listened; they looked upon the strange gentleman as though a sort of demigod had paid them a visit, and felt that words of wisdom were dropping from his lips.

"Guess that are leader must be a Congressman," said one rebel to another, aside.

"He's one on 'em, eny how," said another; "but he don't look like an abolitioner."

"No, I guess he arn't one on 'em critters, no how," responded a third; "but he talks pooty."

"I like them ar sentiments, and when I get to Red River I'll express 'em as me own," said a rough-looking customer with bushy whiskers.

"Well," continued the gentleman, "now don't return to your homes with any false notion about the people of the North. They are your friends; they will assist you if you will only show a disposition to assist yourselves in industrial pursuits. You must go to work, love the good old flag, and, if necessary, you must fight for it, and not against it."

"By ——, stranger, you speak like a man; we never will fight against the old flag."

"Nor the Union?"

"No, sir, never; we are for the Union against all enemies; we've been enemies to ourselves."

"You have been misled by false teachers, and you must guard against them; you must think for yourself; but never array yourself against that good old flag. [Here he pointed to one floating from the staff on the depot.] You must put all your Jeff Davises down under your feet, and not permit them to trample you in the dust."

"That's so, by ——," chimed in several. "D—— Jeff Davis; if the Government don't hang him, we will, if we can only get a chance."

It really seemed that these men would have instantly hung Jeff Davis, or any admirers of the "stern statesman," had an opportunity been given them. By the time the dialogue was concluded the rebels gave unmistakable evidence of the change that had come over the spirit of their dreams, by actually giving three cheers for the United States, and death to Jeff Davis.

SPEECH IN THE MISSISSIPPI CONVENTION OF THE "GENTLEMAN FROM JONES." — "I am a mossy-back, sir, and I stand here to-day to represent the county of Jones. People said that the county of Jones seceded from Mississippi. Yes, sir, we did secede from the Confederacy, and, sir, we fought them like dogs; we killed them like devils; we buried them like asses! Yea, like asses, sir. My own people down there in the county of Jones did, in their sovereign capacity, secede, and did become mossy-backs. We did fight them like dogs and kill them like hellions—like hellions, I say, sir! But I didn't come here to gas, sir; and I surrender my rights to the floor, sir, expressing only the one sentiment, that I stand up for the county of Jones in general. Yes, sir, I am for Jones all the time. In my suffering county the wails of three hundred and eighty widowed women and shirt-tail children are ascending before the God of right, and appealing in tears to the powers appointed for relief."

THE LAWRENCE MASSACRE.—A survivor of the terrible scenes at Lawrence relates the following incidents: Early on the morning of the massacre, young Collamore, son of Mayor Collamore, a youth of eighteen, started from Lawrence for a farm which was owned by his father, to shoot some birds for a sick brother. He had cleared the limits of the city and come to a cross road, when, upon looking up, he saw, within a dozen paces, the advance guard of Quantrel, comprising about twenty or thirty men. He kept on and passed them, when they ordered him to halt. He turned and came towards them, scarcely suspecting that they were foes, when the ruffians aimed at him and fired. Providentially not a ball hit him, although several grazed his person, one of them actually cutting off one of his eyelashes. Seeing that the young man was unscathed, one of the ruffians, with a blasphemous denunciation of his comrades for their inexpertness, rode up to him, and, taking deliberate aim, fired, with the intention of lodging a ball in his abdomen. Young Collamore was cool and collected in this trying moment, and turning himself so as to disturb his assailant's aim, just as the rifle was discharged rolled from his horse, exclaiming—"I am killed!" The shot took effect in the fleshy part of the thigh. The young man was perfectly conscious, but lay entirely still, feigning death. Several others of the band rode up and discharged their pistols or rifles point blank at him, but he never flinched, and fortunately was not again hit. The advance guard passed on, and Collamore then attempted to drag himself to a house in the neighborhood, occupied by an Irishman, which had been spared through the intercessions of some Irishmen who were among the guerrillas. While doing this he saw the main body of Quantrel's gang approaching. He hastened his steps, using his gun as a crutch, and just reached the house in time to throw himself into a cellar window, when some of the gang rode up in full chase. They shot a man who showed himself at a window, but did not discover Collamore, who finally escaped, although he lay for several hours in the cellar before the people in the house could venture to his relief. The young man owes his life to his

nerve and his presence of mind. He is now with friends in this city. His wound is a severe one, and may cripple him for life, as the ball has not yet been extracted.

When the band of Quantrel entered the town, but few of the inhabitants had arisen, and their work was the more speedy and certain. Quantrel himself visited the house of Mayor Collamore, against whom the ruffians had a peculiar spite because of his energy in thwarting their designs of invasion. Mrs. Collamore, aroused by the sound of fire-arms, got up and went to the window, when she saw some of the ruffians chasing an unarmed man in the yard of a house near by. They shot him repeatedly, even after he was mortally wounded. Shocked at this scene, and at once comprehending the danger, she aroused her husband, whose first impulse was to get his pistols and resist. But Mrs. Collamore urged her husband to conceal himself, and suggested a hayrick in the rear of the house. But before he could get out of the house it was surrounded, and the ruffians were thundering at the door. Mrs. Collamore then suggested the well, and hastened her husband to the well-room. Mr. Collamore hesitated before entering the well, expressing apprehensions for his wife; but she implored him to seek his own safety, assuring him that there could be no danger to a defenceless woman. He went into the well, and the boards having been replaced, Mrs. Collamore went to the door. She was confronted by Quantrel himself, who inquired for her husband. She replied, calmly and composedly looking him in the face, that he had gone east. With a fearful oath, the ruffian strode past her, and went directly to the chamber of Mr. Collamore, being evidently well acquainted with the premises. Disappointed, he instituted a search, though not very thorough, for the cellar was not visited; and not finding the object of his vengeance, he demanded of Mrs. Collamore the money that was in the house. She gave him what she had, but he insisted that there was more. Mrs. Collamore remembering that one of the children had about five dollars in specie, gave that to Quantrel, which seemed to satisfy the ruffian. He rummaged the drawers, but did not touch the silver belonging to Mrs. Collamore, or Mr. Collamore's signet ring.

One of the children, eight years old, held up to him a ten cent piece, and said, with child-like simplicity, "I will give you that if you won't kill me." The ruffian turned on his heel with the exclamation, "P'shaw! what do you suppose I want of that? He threatened the life of another of the children, a boy of fifteen; but Mrs. Collamore implored him to spare him. She remarked, with a presentiment that her oldest boy was killed, "He is my all. You have doubtless killed his brother, who went out gunning this morning, and must have met your band." A smile of fearful malignity passed over the countenance of the ruffian, as he signified his knowledge of the circumstance, and turned away.

After plundering the house, Quantrel set it on fire, and when Mrs. Collamore attempted to quench the flames, threatened her life. When the ruffians had left, and while the house was burning, Mrs. Collamore went to the well and called to her husband, who answered " yes " to the inquiry if he was safe. But when the danger was entirely passed, on going to the well he was found to be dead. He is supposed to have been suffocated by the smoke.

The anguish of the wife, bereft of a tender and affectionate husband, and left houseless and homeless, was yet to be intensified by anxiety for the safety of her children. She found a temporary shelter, to which her oldest son was conveyed for medical treatment. Two days subsequent to the massacre an alarm was started at midnight, that Quantrel was returning to complete the work of destruction. The panic-stricken inhabitants fled to the woods, deserting the city and all of their property, many of them having nothing but their night garments. Mrs. Collamore sent her children and their nurse to a place of safety, but would not leave her wounded son. With the help of a young minister she procured a buggy, and putting him into it with great difficulty, dragged him with superhuman strength to the river bank.

It was dark and rainy; but the shelterless exiles — mostly women and children — scarcely dared to speak above a whisper, lest the murderous ruffians should be upon them. The terrors of that night of fear and foreboding will never be effaced from the memory of the people of Lawrence. It turned out that there was no truth in the reports of the return of Quantrel.

The work of the ruffian band was carried on in the most erratic manner. Many buildings were studiously protected. Jim Lane's house was burned down; but so was the house of Mrs. Jenkins, whose husband, it will be recollected, was murdered by Lane. Many who were known to be opposed to jayhawking were murdered. Governor Robinson's house was spared. It has been said that it was protected by a squad of soldiers across the river. But other houses were burned, which were nearer to these soldiers, and the ruffians breakfasted in a house which was between Ex-Governor Robinson's and the river. Ex-Governor Shannon's property was spared, and at the request of Mrs. Shannon a guard was furnished for his office.

Some few of the band showed a merciful spirit, but most of them seemed actuated by the most fiendish malice, and thirsted for blood, with which they were certainly sated. They were not content with wounding unarmed men, but shot at them until life was extinct. No massacre in the history of our country has been more fearful, or attended with incidents more cruel.

The people of Leavenworth opened their hearts and their houses to the sufferers, who speak in the highest terms of their generosity. Mrs. Collamore, particularly, found there many who remembered and appreciated her noble husband, and warmly expresses her gratitude to them for their kindness to herself and her children. There is much destitution and suffering among the people of Lawrence, which only the liberal benevolence of the rest can relieve, and we hope that the appeals which have been made in their behalf will meet with a prompt response.

THOUGHTS OF HOME. — " Let me tell you of a little incident that happened to me this morning," said a soldier in Louisiana. " I had been out all day on the skirmish line; all was still; I had not heard the singing of a bullet for some time. I was sitting on the ground, with my rifle across my knees, thinking of home and friends far away — wondering what the future had in store for me, and if I should ever see that home again. As I sat thus, a little bird, called the Baltimore oriole, perched himself on a bush so close to me that I might have touched him with my rifle, and commenced singing. The voice of this bird is much like that of our robin, and he is about the same size, though his color is different, being a dark red. The poor little fellow had been driven away through the day by the shower of bullets that visited that quarter, but had returned at night to visit his home, and seemed now to be returning thanks to God for his safe return. And so, thought I, my case may be like the little bird. After this struggle is over, I, too, may return to friends and home. I accepted the omen, thanked God for his watchful care over me, and, with renewed courage and hope, pressed on."

AN ADVENTURE. — A "Silent Observer" of company B, of the Fourth Pennsylvania regiment, gives the following narrative of an adventure in West Virginia, in the spring of 1864: —

"The person I am going to write about is a regular harum-scarum individual, and is never with his regiment except he is on duty; he is always travelling about the country (or I should say scouting around), and there is little that he does not know, and few places he can't find. But, as regards his duty, I am made to understand that he never shirks anything that is right, though sometimes he growls when he imagines he is imposed upon, but it is generally soon over: this much I can say, he is a good and I believe brave soldier. I will give you the narrative as I got it from him at New Creek. He said : 'After I got out to our pickets, I thought I would stay there all night, and in the morning go on. I remained there about two hours, when the Fourteenth Virginia infantry came along; so I concluded to go with them as far as they went. I started, and went with them to Burlington; here they stopped and camped. I was told by some of the men of another regiment, that our men did no fighting there, but had gone on to Moorsfield; so I concluded to go on after the regiment. The next morning I went on with some wagons as far as the junction of the Romney and Moorsfield road. I staid there until about half past eleven o'clock A. M. While I was there, an ambulance came along, and, as I ascertained that it was going near my regiment, I concluded to go with it. I got in, and, on inquiring, I found it belonged to the Second regiment Maryland Home Brigade.

23

"'We had proceeded along the road towards Moorsfield about five miles when I observed five men come out of the mountains about fifty yards from the road, and, as they drew near us, I discovered them to be rebels. There was no time to jump out, and run away, nor to use arms; for they had us surrounded in a jiffy, and it would have been madness anyhow, as there was only one gun between us, and that was not ready for use. Let me state here that the regiment was not more than five or six miles ahead of us, and there were cavalry passing that road all the time. The rebels came on us with pointed pistols, and ordered us to surrender. We had no choice; so we gave up. They asked us to give them all the arms from the ambulance. I gave them my gun and equipments, and then we were ordered to drive up a by-road about one hundred yards from the main road on the right going to Moorsfield. After they had taken the horses from the ambulance, they run it down a hill, and cut some of the spokes. They then took the things which they could carry, and mounted us on the horses, and took us up in the mountains to the left of the road about a quarter of a mile. After we got there, they searched us, and took everything that they thought dangerous. My companion's pocket knife and gloves were taken from him, and my canteen and a piece of emery paper I had were taken from me. And they asked us if we had any money, but we had nary red. They told us that they had been sent there to intercept our despatches, and pick up all stragglers. I made very light of being a prisoner, and told them I did not care, as I was under arrest, and expected to get a court-martial for desertion, and perhaps be sent to a fort for one or two years. I laughed, and seemed so contented, that they did not think I would try to escape; my companion was downhearted and discontented, and all his energy had left him.

"'We had been up there about half an hour, when the lookout reported a cavalryman coming down the road, and as they supposed him to be a despatch-bearer, a reb started down the mountain after him. I whispered to my companion to grab the rebel guard, and I would help him. The guard was a very strong man, and I knew if we intended to do anything, we must surprise him, and make quick work of it. The guard was very anxious to see his comrades take a Yankee despatch-bearer, and did not pay much attention to us. I suppose he thought it foolishness for us to attempt to escape. He had a short rifle, and no revolver, nor sabre. As my companion was the stoutest, he was to take his gun. The rebel guard then immediately took us in sight of the road, to show us the fun of taking a Yankee. The rebels surrounded the cavalryman before he knew it, and soon disarmed him. I got behind the rebel guard, and my companion on the side his rifle was on, and just as the four rebels with their prisoners got to the foot of the mountain, my companion grasped the gun, and I grasped the rebel; I put my hand over his mouth, and threw one arm around his neck, at the same time throwing his

head back; my companion wrenched the gun from him, and then gave him a punch in the bread-basket with the muzzle, which made him "holler" blue murder, and I told him to hit him on the head. But he was too slow, and before I could throw him down he forced himself away from me, and went stumbling down the mountain towards his comrades, who were then within one hundred yards of me. My companion had gone, and was about thirty yards from me; and thinking it was time for me to get away, I darted off; and after running up and down the mountain for about four miles with my companion, we discovered the rebels trying to outflank us. My companion threw away the rifle which he had carried until then; we then separated; he threw himself down behind a log, and I kept on for about one mile; then I started for the road. At the time I separated from my companion the rebels were only about fifty yards from him, and one hundred and fifty yards from me; but the fog prevented them from seeing him, and the bushes them from seeing me. After I got down in the field I saw a man coming through it, and as I knew he was not armed, and as I saw harness on the horse, I determined to seek aid from him. I went up to him, and hailed him with, "Hold on there, mister!" When I had got close to him I said: "Look here, stranger; I want you to tell me the truth; are you a Union man or a secesh?" He said: "I am a Union man!" "Well," said I, "then you must help me." I told him I must ride on his horse a little way; he told me to mount behind him. After doing so he took me across the creek and across the fence about three hundred yards, and then told me which way to go. I followed his directions, and soon came into our lines.'"

FREEDOM OF SPEECH. — A letter-writer in Alabama says: "Our minister nearly got himself into a scrape the other day; and whether he is 'a bit of a wag,' or a very careless fellow, or an 'abolition traitor,' is now the topic of discussion with us. At the meeting on Fast Day he gave out Dr. Watts' hymn, commencing —

'And are we wretches yet alive;
And do we yet rebel?
'Tis wondrous, 'tis amazing grace,
That we are out of hell.'"

"LYMAN BEECHER ADAMS." — While the Thirty-eighth Ohio regiment was home on furlough, a man hailing from Dayton, but represented as formerly from Rhode Island, desirous of distinguishing himself in the field, proposed to be mustered into the service of the United States as a volunteer in that regiment. Being apparently sound in body and mind, and responding to the name of Lyman Beecher Adams (which bespoke, more than individual assurances, a patriotic ancestry), he was promptly received into the good faith and fellowship of the veterans of the regiment. With such a name, and hailing from the little State of

Rhode Island, so fruitful in loyal progress, who could demand any further voucher or guarantee of his genuine character? He underwent the ceremonies attending his initiation into the volunteer service, accepted his allotted bounty, and started for the seat of war, sharing, for a season, with his companions in arms many of the fatigues and exposures incident to army life, and, during his passage with us, continually repeated mentally the sentiment of the negro melody:

"I'm gwine 'long down to Georgia — I hain't got long to stay."

Shortly after the arrival of the regiment at Ringgold, Georgia, it was sent out upon picket duty, and Lyman Beecher Adams was expected to, and did (willingly, of course), enter upon this rather unpleasant branch of the service; and being a true soldier, did not feign sickness, or attempt to shirk from any duties. Taking advantage of this, his first experience on picket duty, he concluded to absent himself from the next roll call, and, with rifle, cartridge-box, and person, entered into the rebel lines.

A few days thereafter, a party of rebel officers, with a flag of truce, having some communication with General Grant, appeared before the Union lines, and were met by others from the army. During the interchange of civilities common to such occasions, a rebel officer stated that he was requested by the *late Lyman Beecher Adams* to present his compliments to the Thirty-eighth Ohio regiment, and to tender his grateful acknowledgments for their kindness in delivering him from the land of his captivity to the bosom of his friends.

A brief summary of this story is this: Lyman Beecher Adams was a rebel Captain under John Morgan, and having escaped from Johnson's Island, was generously provided by his enemies with a dead-head ticket to Dixie. The joke is — To be relished exclusively by rebels. The moral — New recruits should sometimes, previous to being accepted, furnish proper credentials.

AN INCIDENT OF THE HOSPITAL. — "One of the patients was a mere boy, not more than seventeen years old. I think you would have described him as a *little* boy, and altogether unfit for military service. But he was brave-hearted, and of a pleasant countenance. He was first sick of the measles, and had been exposed to the cold and rain during our march to Decatur Junction; now he suffered under an attack of pneumonia; his mind wandered, and there was no hope of his recovery. Our hospital steward, a noble, warm-hearted man, whom all the men love, came in, and as he passed along the ward the little sufferer asked, in a plaintive, child-like voice, to be taken in his lap. The steward tenderly raised him in his arms, and began to soothe him with loving words. Such words and acts find their way even to maddened brains.

"'Mayn't I kiss you? I want some one to love,' asked the grateful heart of the patient.

"Consent was given, with a smothered, sobbing voice; the dying boy kissed him lovingly, and then grew tranquil as a babe. No doubt, I thought, he was again, in thought and feeling, at home, enclosed in the arms that had clasped him a thousand times. I don't know, but I think the steward will treasure that kiss in his memory, as worldly men do ancestral jewels, and in the end find it written to his credit in heaven."

HOW A CAPTAIN WAS CAPTURED. — "I was officer of the guard, on as bright a July day as ever dawned on creation; and though it was oppressively warm, as early as guard mounting, eight o'clock, yet that interesting ceremony had passed off magnificently, and I was preparing to go the grand rounds immediately after the call for the second relief, when Lieutenant H., the old officer of the guard, sent his respects, with an earnest request for me to call on him at his marquée for special consultation. 'H—l is brewing at post number twelve,' said he, as he took me by the hand, 'and this fellow will tell you what he saw there; and you may rely upon trouble there before to-morrow.' 'An' I saw nothing at all, at all, but a ghost, sure,' said the Irish soldier; 'it came out of the hill forenent the old graveyard, shook its fist at me as it passed, and went into the bush towards the fort.'

"'How did it look?' inquired H.

"'Look? indade, how should it look, but like a woman draped in white, with eyes of fire?'

"An hour after, I was carefully searching the ground in the vicinity of post number twelve, when my ears were saluted with the well-known cry of, 'Buy any pies 'n' cakes? — all clean and new; twenty-five cents for the pies, two cakes for a penny.'

"'Where is your pass, my good lady, if you are a camp follower; and why are you here among the rocks and bushes, if you wish to sell your marketing?' said G.

"'I am the honest wife of Pat Maloney, of the Fourteenth Maryland, and sthopped here to rest me weary limbs afther coming five miles down from me home in the hill, your honor!'

"'Very likely,' said I; 'but you will please march down to the camp, and submit to a slight inspection of your basket and papers, if you have any.'

"'I have no papers, sir; and why should you put a loyal woman, and a wife of a Union soldier, to this trouble, bad luck till ye?'

"'You will not be harmed, madam. If you are a loyal woman, as you say, you will see the propriety of so doing.'

"Cakes and pies, sure enough, but no papers; and I began to believe that there was no connection between her and Pat's 'ghost;' but why should she wear a pair of men's boots?

"'Och, these were the boots me husband wore before he 'listed, sure!'

"And so the Captain, somewhat given to gallantry, volunteered to accompany her to her friends, two miles towards her 'home in the hill,' where she was to give positive proof that she was 'neither a spy nor a ghost.' And away they went, a single soldier only accompanying them, amid the ill-suppressed laughter of the regiment.

"Noon, one o'clock, two o'clock, and no tidings of the Captain! What was to be done? A squadron of cavalry was ordered to dash up the hill, reconnoitre, and report. And then time wore heavily away for an hour, when the cavalry charged into camp and up to headquarters, when instantly the long roll was beat, and in five minutes the regiment was under arms in line of battle. A perfect silence ensued, and the Adjutant read the following note:

"'Colonel D.: I am willing to exchange the pies, cakes, and basket for the soldier and the d—d fool Captain whom I caught with crinoline. Pedlers and ghosts are at a premium in these parts just now. Yours, in *haste*,
"'BLAND, First Lieutenant C. S. A.'

"The soldier's musket was found four miles from camp, with the note from the *woman Lieutenant* sticking on the point of the bayonet; and so the Captain was captured."

ANECDOTE OF PHILIPPA. — Among the troops in Western Virginia, stories about the Philippa affair formed a staple of conversation. Here is one of the best:

A certain Indiana company, almost worn out with marching, was straggling along, with very little regard to order. Hurrying up to his men, the Captain shouted, "Close up, boys! D—n you, close up! If the enemy were to fire on you when you're straggling along that way, they couldn't hit a d—n one of you! Close up!" And the boys closed up immediately.

SHE REGRETTED IT. — In the early part of the war, an elderly lady, who attended a meeting of the First Vermont regiment, arose, full of enthusiasm, and said she thanked God that she was able to do something for her country; her two sons, all she possessed in the world, were in the regiment; and the only thing she had to regret was, that she could not have known it twenty years ago — she would have furnished more.

"BROKE THE CONNECTION." — In the battle of Champion Hills, a Colonel was mounted on a horse which did not like the whistling of bullets and bursting of shells which showered about him. The Colonel, who was one of those officers always found in advance of his regiment, held a different opinion from his horse; so he called Sam, the negro servant, to take the animal back, and bring the "Morgan," that could stand fire. Sam, who was in sympathy with the disgraced charger, gladly obeyed; but on his way back with the Morgan, a shell dropped in the field right before him, and burst, sending the mud and stones in every direction. This was too much for Sam, and he broke for the rear, not to be seen again

for several days. One of the officers, finding him not wholly recovered from his fear, at this time, of his irate master, said: "Why don't you go back to the Colonel? He was angry, but you may return; you know he was always friendly to you." "Dat ar am all berry true," replied Sam, with an inimitable expression of countenance, and a significant gesture of the hand; "de Colonal and I were berry good friends, but de fac is, dat ar shell broke de connection."

INCIDENTS OF KNOXVILLE. — "After thirteen days of menace and siege," says a correspondent, "the enemy gathered his forces, and struck the mighty blow that was to have broken our lines, demolished our defences, and captured Knoxville. It was an utter and disastrous failure. In justice to our enemy, it is conceded by all, that more desperate valor, daring gallantry, or obstinate courage, has not been recorded during the war. They contended against the impossible. The men who opposed them were as brave, as well trained on the same bloody fields of Virginia, as they, and, having as large a stake, had the advantages of an impregnable position. The enterprise was a bold one, the plan masterly, and the attempt vigorous. Success would have given the enemy possession of the key to all our works on the west side of the town, if not the town itself. But Fort Sanders lost, our position in Knoxville would be more precarious. But they failed. We do not know if Longstreet has done his worst; but it is evident that he expected to have exploited a brilliant and decisive *coup de guerre*. He was thirteen days deciding upon it. He waited until reënforced by the forces of General Jones, Mudwall Jackson, Carter, and Cerro Gordo Williams. He selected three brigades of picked regiments, and determined upon a night attack, always the most dangerous and bloody, but if successful, the most decisive. It is evident that he played a tremendous odds to insure success, and every man in those doomed brigades advanced to the storming of Fort Sanders with that confident courage that usually commands it. To resist him were part of the Seventy-ninth New York in the front, four companies of the One Hundredth Pennsylvania on the right, and four companies of the Second Michigan on the left. No part of the fort is complete. One bastion on the north-west angle, and a parapet on the west side, only are up. Temporary traverses were made by cotton bales, and also two salients from which guns could sweep the ditches on the north and west. Spirited skirmishing commenced on the right of the position at ten o'clock P. M. on Saturday. The vigor and persistence of it evidently foreshadowed something more serious behind, and such became the feeling of all the immense audience within our lines, who listened to the continuous and unceasing crash of musketry, hour after hour, to one, two, and three o'clock A. M. Many an anxious heart that night beat high with hope and fear for their rebel friends without, and many a tearful and timid prayer went up to the God of battles for the safety of friends within. All felt that an eventful moment was at hand, for weal or woe, in the destinies of East Tennessee and her brave defenders. The enemy dashed upon the left of our position several times, as if in confident bravado, and finally drove our skirmishers from the advanced rifle pits, and occupied them about daylight Sunday morning. Our men rallied, and as determinedly regained them, driving the rebels back in turn. Suddenly an avalanche of men was hurled upon the disputed rifle pits ; our skirmishers were forced back, and covered by our guns from the fort by our retreating men. Two storming brigades were enabled to approach within one hundred yards of the bastion. It was their intention, probably, to draw out our boys, and then attempt to return with them and enter the works. In this they were foiled. Our skirmishers fell in on the left, and the rebel storming party advanced directly upon the bastion. Then ensued a scene of carnage and horror which has but few parallels in the annals of warfare. Balaklava was scarcely more terrible. Stunned for a moment by the torrent of canister and lead poured upon them by Buckley's First Rhode battery and our line of musketry, on they came. Again and again the deadly missiles shattered their torn and mangled columns. Their march was over dead and wounded comrades; yet still they faltered not, but onward, still onward : whole ranks stumbled over wires stretched from stump to stump, and fell amid the dead and dying ; yet still over their prostrate bodies marched the doomed heroes of that forlorn hope.

"At last the ditch was reached, and the slaughter became butchery, as if on a wager of death against mortality. Benjamin's guns on the salients swept the ditch as the tornado would the corn. The earth was sated with blood — men waded in blood, and struggled up the scarp, and slipping in blood fell back to join their mangled predecessors in the gory mud below. The shouts of the foiled and infuriate rebels, the groans of the dying and shrieks of the wounded, arose above the din of the cannon. Benjamin lighted shell and threw them over the parapet, and artillerymen followed his example. One rebel climbed the parapet and planted the flag of the Thirteenth Mississippi regiment on the summit; but the rebel shout that greeted its appearance had scarce left the lips that framed it when man and flag were in the ditch below, pierced by a dozen balls. Another rebel repeated the feat, and joined his comrade. A third essayed to bear off the flag, and was cloven with an axe. One man entered an embrasure, and was blown to fragments; two more were cut down in another, but not one entered the fort. The three veteran regiments of the Ninth army corps stood up to the work before them unflinching and glorious to a man. The heroes of a dozen campaigns from the Potomac to Vicksburg, they found themselves for the third time arrayed for trial of courage and endurance with the flower of the Southern army, — the picked men of Longstreet's boasted veterans,

— and saw the sun rise, on that chill Sunday morning in November, on an entire brigade annihilated, and two more severely punished. Even the dead outnumbered us, for not more than three hundred of our force participated in the defence of Fort Sanders. Benjamin, of the Third United States artillery, and Buckley, of the First Rhode Island battery, were foremost in acts of daring and gallantry. General Ferraro, who has never left the fort since Longstreet's appearance before it, to whose skill and foresight much of the admirable dispositions for defence was due, was in command, and right nobly has he earned his star. His coolness, energy, and skill are subjects of universal encomium.

"The dead and wounded were left on the field, and the ghastly horrors were rendered sickening by the vain cries of hundreds for water and help. In full view from the embrasures the ground was covered with dead, wounded, and dying. Forty-eight were heaped up in the ditch before the bastion; thirteen in another place, almost within reach of those who, though late their foes, would have willingly heeded their anguished shrieks for water; yet none dared go to their assistance. The humanity of General Burnside was not proof against so direct an appeal, and he at once sent in a flag of truce, offering an armistice until five o'clock P. M., for the purpose of burying their dead and caring for their wounded."

A REVIVAL IN FORT SUMTER. — Rev. A. B. Stephens, chaplain of the Eleventh South Carolina regiment, wrote in September, 1863 : "We now constitute the garrison of Fort Sumter. On the last fast day I began a meeting which has been going on and increasing in interest all the while, till now God has honored us with a gracious revival of religion among the soldiery of this command. A few months ago but two officers in the regiment were members of the church; now but few more than that number are not professors of religion. About two hundred have joined the church, and a larger number have been converted, and are now happy in the love of God. It would do your soul good to visit the old fort, battered and scarred as it is, and hear the soldiers make the tattered walls ring with the high praise of the living God. No camp-meeting that I have ever attended can come near it."

ADMIRATION OF STONEWALL JACKSON. — "I was much amused," said a correspondent, "at the rebel prisoners' account of Stonewall Jackson's admission into heaven. They were strong admirers of General Jackson, and especially of the great success of his flank movements. 'The day after his death,' said they, 'two angels came down from heaven to carry General Jackson back with them. They searched all through the camp, but could not find him. They went to the prayer-meeting, to the hospital, and to every other place where they thought themselves likely to find him, but in vain. Finally they were forced to return without him. What was their surprise to find that he had just executed a splendid flank movement, and got into heaven before them!'"

INCIDENTS OF PITTSBURG LANDING. — One of the soldiers who was in the battle happened to be inordinately fond of card-playing. During the fight he had three of his fingers shot off. Holding up his mangled member, he gazed at it with a look of ineffable sorrow, and exclaimed, as a big tear stole into the corner of his eye: "I shall never be able to hold *a full hand* again!"

An incident somewhat curious occurred in General McClernand's quarters. When the rebels were driven back on Monday, and he regained his position, on entering his tent a figure in rebel costume was sitting in a chair, the head resting on a table, as if its owner was dozing, very much in the style that sleepy clerks do after a hard day's work. A slight shake to waken the apparent sleeper, and the body of a corpse fell upon the floor. Wounded in a manner that must have caused him excruciating pain when lying down, he had crawled into the chair and died.

Private John Ferguson, company K, Sixty-fifth Ohio, who was killed in the second day's battle, was accompanied to camp by a young Newfoundland dog, who persistently followed him from the time of his enlistment, and from camp to camp, to the moment of his death. Two days after the battle the faithful dog was found lying upon the inanimate breast of his master; nor would he consent to leave the spot until the remains were buried.

McCLELLAN'S SOLILOQUY.

BY A DAUGHTER OF GEORGIA..

ADVANCE, or not advance; that is the question!
Whether 'tis better in the mind to suffer
The jeers and howlings of outrageous Congressmen,
Or to take arms against a host of rebels,
And, by opposing, beat them? — To fight — to win —
No more; and by a victory, to say we end
This war, and all the thousand dreadful shocks
The flesh's exposed to — 'tis a consummation
Devoutly to be wished. To fight, to win,
To beat! perchance be beaten; — ay, there's the rub;
After a great defeat, what would ensue!
When we have shuffled off the battle-field,
Must give us pause; there's the respect
That makes calamity a great defeat.
But shall I bear the scorn of all the North,
The "outward" pressure, and Old Abe's reviling,
The pangs of being scoffed at for this long delay,
The turning out of office (ay, perchance,
When I myself might now my greatness make
With a great battle)? I'd not longer bear
To drill and practise troops behind intrenchments,
But that the fear of meeting with the foe
On dread Manassas, from whose plains
Few of us would return — puzzles my will,
And makes me rather bear the evils I have,
Than fly to others which are greater far.
These Southerners make cowards of us all.

SCENES ON THE HOSPITAL BOAT. — "The steamer arrived at our wharf from Pittsburg Landing," says a correspondent, "with hundreds of the sick and wounded.

"As we first entered the cabin, we were struck by the pallid and ghastly face of one of the poor fellows stretched upon the floor at our feet. As we passed him, he faintly begged for water. He breathed with great labor, and was suffering, as the doctor told us, with some internal injury. Half an hour later we saw him again, the doctor bending over him, and trying to get him to tell his name. It was with great difficulty he articulated.

"'Tell me now, quietly and slowly; don't be in a hurry,' said the doctor, in the kindest tones.

"'Company —, First Ohio cavalry,' he struggled out.

"'And what is your name?'

"'H-i-r-a-m H-e-n-k-e-f-e-r!'

"The doctor hurried back to record his name, and as we returned, we were startled to find him dead! his body straightened by the last throe, and his fixed eyes staring coldly and vacantly upward.

"'Poor boy!' murmured the doctor, as he reached down, and gathering up his blanket, cast it over his body and face.

. . . .

"Limbs are being amputated, and the stillness of the hour is disturbed by the groans of the suffering victims. Sounds of distress are heard from the upper cabin and from below. Estes, of Utica, has had his leg amputated; he cannot live. Another undergoes the same operation. Two men are being trepanned, and instances almost innumerable occur where men are having bullets extracted, and their wounds dressed. The rebel wounded are being as well taken care of as our own. Caseaux, of the Orleans Guard, of Louisiana, has a painful wound in the groin; he is being cared for by an Ohioan of venerable appearance, named Dodd. The Orleanian's appetite, it seems, is not lost, for he enjoys his wholesome repast with apparent relish. Next to him is a Mobilian, formerly from Philadelphia, named Davis; he is badly wounded in two places, but keeps his spirits up remarkably well. The philanthropic Dodd next turns his attention to him. Davis is unable to feed himself; but Dodd helps him by tablespoonfuls from a tin can filled with wholesome beef soup. Dodd has evidently said something to Davis that is understood by Caseaux, who says he understands 'very little English,' although a member of the wealthy and highly educated family of Caseaux, of New Orleans, which has already borne a somewhat conspicuous place in the annals of the present war. Caseaux actually laughs. Dodd has said that 'he wished they were feeding beef soup to one another all over the Union.' In a state-room near by lies young Walker, of Mobile, — not he of Nicaragua, — but he who was of the rebel army, who says that his side was confident of victory at the last battle; that 'the Federal wounded are well taken care of by the

Confederates; and that in Mobile the ladies even extended to them hospitalities, furnishing them with hats, shoes, and other clothing.'

"When one of the wounded rebels, a French creole, was brought on board, in answer to all questions about his position, the battle, the Southern situation, &c., his invariable answer was: '*Non comprends vous, Monsieur.* Me no understand Anglaise.'

"After a few hours had elapsed, and the nurse had been busily engaged in serving hot soup to other wounded soldiers, one of them approached our Frenchman and said, in pure Western patois, 'Hello, mister, won't you have some soup?' 'Yes, sir-ee! by damn!' There was no difficulty in making him understand after that."

HARDEE OUTDONE. — A militia captain in North Carolina was marching his company "by the front," when he found himself in front of a gate through which he desired to go. Here was a dilemma. The front of the company was much wider than the opening of the gate, and unless some change should be made in the order of march, part of his men would go full tilt against the fence. Our hero belabored his brain for the proper command; but the words, "By the right flank — file left — march," obstinately refused to come to his help. He extricated himself from the difficulty in a way which showed his possession of the ready wit of an accomplished guerrilla. With a bold voice he shouted, "Company, halt — break ranks — march; form on the other side of the fence!"

GOVERNOR SMITH'S TACTICS. — A Confederate correspondent relates the following at the expense of Governor Smith, of Virginia: "At the first battle of Manassas he rode up to his regiment (he was then a Colonel) at a critical point of the conflict, and, rising in his stirrups, shouted — "Boys, I don't know what orders to give you, but String 'em! String 'em!"

PLEASANT DREAMS. — A soldier of the Sixteenth New York artillery tells the following: Sometimes the boat does not bring our bread from Yorktown, and some laughable scenes ensue among the men for the want of it. In the next tent to us the following funny scene occurred the other morning. One of the men went to his haversack for a piece of bread he had left there the night before, and found it was missing, and accused the others of stealing it; but they all stoutly denied it except one. "Arrah, drink yer coffee," said he, "and I'll tell ye about a dhream I had last night." "An' what has your dhrame to do with my loaf?" said the loser of the bread. "Hould on, bedad, till you hear it," cried the other.

"You see, I dhreamed Captain Sheibner bucked and gagged me; an' put me in the guard-house, the spalpeen, for twenty-four hours. An' I was very hungry. Well! a beautiful lady came to me,

and released me, an' sint me to my tint. 'You'll find bread in the haversack,' says she.

"Well?" said the loser of the bread. "Well," said Pat, "I got up in my sleep an' ate your loaf." The roar of laughter that followed drowned the complaint of the loser, who, to use his own words, "had to dhrink dhry coffee that morning."

BRAVERY AT OLUSTEE. — Color-Sergeant James Cox, of the Forty-seventh New York regiment, at the battle of Olustee, Fla., although he had received a ball in the body (hardly an inch from the heart, as it was ascertained), and another in his thigh, never let the fact be known, but remained bare-headed, facing the enemy, advancing and then slowly falling back with the colors, as ordered from time to time. Once, when struck, he fell; but the colors were instantly grasped by Orderly Sergeant Michael Roden, of company B, who likewise conducted himself nobly all through. The enemy never saw Sergeant Cox's back, and he stuck by his flag until we left the field, when Sergeant Roden had the honor of carrying it home.

A THRILLING SCENE. — During the passage of the fleet conveying the Sixteenth army corps to Vicksburg in the winter of 1864, the following scene occurred: "Our transport being in the advance," said a correspondent, "we backed out from Memphis this morning, and steamed southward. One after another followed, with their hurricane and boiler decks covered, yea, blackened with their patriotic human life. Banners were flying, and the air was rent, as cheer after cheer went up, mingled with the always inspiring fife and drum. Countenances indicated cheerful, hearty, but solemn earnestness. The martial music ceased. I jumped upon the wheel-house, and at the top of my voice called for the 'Battle Cry of Freedom.' Souls and voices unused to song sung this morning. We dropped past Fort Pickering; the high bluffs were lined with colored troops. How they cheered, how they shouted, and waved hats and handkerchiefs! In the song we poured forth

'And although he may be poor, he shall never be a slave,
Shouting the battle cry of Freedom:'

the winds wafted it on shore, and again and again went up the glad acclaim. 'Coronation' was called for.

'All hail the power of Jesus' name'

was never more appropriately sung. The excellent Christian Colonel of the One Hundred and Seventeenth was urged to speak. He declined, saying to me, 'Your lungs are adapted to the open air.' I could not help add a few words as the historic moments were passing. At the close, with hat in hand, and leading a hatless auditory, we reverently approached into the King of kings' audience chamber. We thanked and praised Him, and begged of Him to be with our transport, the fleet, and expedition."

"God Save the South." — This is the title of a national Confederate anthem, composed by Professor C. G. De Coniel, of Richmond ; words by Captain Ernest Halpin, of the C. S. A. The great prolificness of the Southern press in the production of music is one of the best indications that, amidst all the horrors and devastations of this cruel war, the people of the South have remained uncontaminated by its demoralizing influence, and still preserve, in all its former purity, their love for "the true, the beautiful, the good." As a means of civilization, — an element of spiritual life, — it would be difficult to overrate the importance and interest which attach to music. It is the language of the soul ; and its peculiar function is to facilitate the development of the emotional language of our nature, and to call into exercise those sympathies which prepare us for the enjoyment of the higher sphere of happiness which our Creator has allotted to us. The vague feelings of inexpressible felicity which music arouses, the indefinite impressions of an unknown ideal life which it calls up, may be considered as prophetic of our future state. The strange capacity which all have for being affected by melody and harmony, may be taken to imply both that it is within the possibilities of our nature to realize those intenser delights they dimly suggest, and that they are in some way concerned in the realization of them.

"'Tis the golden key
That opes the palace of eternity."

It has long been conceded that a martial strain will urge a man into the front ranks of battle sooner than an argument, and a fine anthem excite his devotion more certainly than a logical discourse. As has been truly said, the sentiment of the age has written itself in music. Its wild intelligence, its keen analysis, its revolutionary spirit, its restlessness, and its humanity, may be traced in the rich combinations of Rossini, in the grand symphonies of Beethoven, in the pleading tenderness of Bellini, and in the mingled war-notes and sentiment of Verdi. We should, therefore, hail with delight the active life which seems to animate the composers and singers of our country. It is a clear demonstration that the spirit of the people is not broken, notwithstanding all the outrages and horrors to which they have been subjected by the remorseless foe. As long as they can tune their voices to the rich melody of song, so long will the spirit of patriotism remain unsubdued in their hearts.

Among the many good pieces that have been published, we know of none superior, if equal, to the one under consideration, by Professor De Coniel. It is what we have long wished for — a national anthem, breathing a spirit of patriotism and devotion suited to our troublous times. The pure and simple religious feeling which pervades the poetry of this piece is beautifully interpreted by, and carried home to, the heart, in the deep pathos and majestic tones of the music. The sentiments of the anthem are perfectly in accordance with the religious feeling and faith of our people. Our hope of success, in this dreadful struggle, has not been in our own strength, but in the mighty arm of Him "who weigheth the earth in a balance," and "before whom all nations are as nothing." As a national anthem, we know nothing to compare with this in sublimity. The opening stanza is peculiarly grand ; while the minor key of the words,

"God be our shield,
At home, or on the field ;
Stretch thine arm over us,
Strengthen and save,"

must, we think, send a thrill of deep emotion, and find a responsive chord in the heart of every one not dead to "the concord of sweet sounds." There are several very fine passages in the last two stanzas ; but we do not deem it proper here to enter into a critical review of the pieces, as all who delight in song will examine and judge for themselves. We had the pleasure of hearing the anthem sung, the other evening, by a fair friend, whose soul seemed to enter into and realize the beauty and spirit of the music, and can truly say, with the poet, —

"And when the stream of sound
Which overflowed the soul had passed away,
A consciousness survived those it had left
Dispirited upon the silent shore
Of memory, images and gentle thoughts,
Which cannot die, and will not be destroyed."

To sing this anthem properly, requires a voice of great depth, compass, flexibility, and tone ; and those who may have heard it rendered by *amateurs* deficient in these, were, no doubt, disappointed in their expectations as to its merits. One of the most interesting and profitable exercises our "fair daughters of song" can engage in, will be the mastery of this anthem. In it they will find ample scope for all of their vocal and artistic talents ; and we confidently believe that when it shall be fully known, it will rival in popularity the celebrated national anthems of France and England. — *Southern paper.*

First American Flag over Richmond. — The crowning event of the rebellion was undoubtedly the capture of Richmond by the loyal or Federal forces. The most striking incident of this achievement was the reëstablishment of the United States or American flag in the rebel capital, over the rebel capitol, in which the rebel Congress met and deliberated, and a traitor convention passed the ordinance of secession, which they vainly hoped would carry Virginia forever out of the Union. The details of this interesting event are as follows:

The one division of the Twenty-fifth and one of the Twenty-fourth corps composing that portion of the army of the James which lay on the extreme right of Grant's army of investment, occupied positions within seven miles of the beleaguered rebel stronghold. From an adjacent hill Richmond was as plainly to be discerned as Port Ewing from the hills above Barrytown.

This corps was commanded by Major-General Godfrey Weitzel. His chief of the staff was Brigadier-General George F. Shepley, formerly military Governor of New Orleans, and lately of Norfolk. His Aid-de-camp, Lieutenant Johnston L. de Peyster, had been transferred with his chief to the staff of General Weitzel, and thus became Aid-de-camp to the latter. Lieutenant de Peyster belonged to the 13th New York artillery, and was, as is well known, from Tivoli, Red Hook, Dutchess County, New York.

The night of the 2d and 3d April was one of intense anxiety and expectation in the army of the James. Throughout the previous day they could hear the tremendous roar of the terrible battle in which their comrades were engaged, far away across the river upon the extreme left and around Petersburg, and they knew that the next morning, early, they were to play their dangerous part by assaulting the rebel works in their front in order to capture Richmond itself.

About two A. M., April 3, Lieutenant de Peyster, hearing tremendous explosions, and seeing a vast blaze in the direction of Richmond, mounted the wooden signal tower, about seventy feet high, at General Weitzel's headquarters, and reported that he could discern a great fire towards Richmond. He could not decide, however, that the city was burning. Efforts were at once made to capture a rebel picket. About three A. M. they were successful. A prisoner, of the Thirty-seventh Virginia artillery, reported that he neither knew where his general nor his command were. This led General Shepley to believe the rebels were evacuating Richmond. About half past three A. M., a deserter came in and announced that the city was being abandoned. At four A. M. a negro drove into the Federal lines in a buggy, and confirmed the glorious news. Joy and exultation at once absorbed every other feeling, and orders were immediately given for the troops to move. This was about six A. M. Brevet Brigadier-General Draper's colored brigade led the advance along a road strewn with all kinds of abandoned munitions of war, and amid the roar of bursting shells, which was terrific. On either side small red flags indicated the position of buried torpedoes between the two lines of abatis in Weitzel's immediate front. These warning indications the rebels had not had time to remove. This fortunate incident preserved many lives, as the space was very narrow between the explosives.

The rebel defences seemed almost impregnable. Every elevation along the road was defended by fieldworks, and very strong forts. Two lines of abatis and three lines of rifle pits and earthworks, one within the other, defended every avenue of attack and point of advantage. The first and second lines were connected by regular lines of redans and works — the third, near the city and commanding it, disconnected. If our troops should have had to carry the defences by storm, the loss would have been fearful, since the contest would have been constantly renewed, because the rebels, as fast as one line of defences was occupied, would only have had to fall back into another to recommence the butchery of the assailants under every advantage to themselves.

Brigadier-General Shepley had brought with him, from Norfolk, a storm flag, which had formerly belonged to the Twelfth Maine volunteers. Of this regiment he had been originally Colonel. This flag had floated triumphantly over the St. Charles Hotel at New Orleans. This latter building was the headquarters of General Butler, to whom General Shepley had acted as chief of staff. Shepley had previously, in sport, made the remark that the flag referred to would do to float over Richmond, and that he hoped to see it there. Lieutenant de Peyster, who heard this, asked the General "if he would allow him to raise it for him." Shepley said, "Yes, if you bring it with you, and take care of it, you shall raise it in Richmond." As the Twenty-fifth corps left their lines to advance towards Richmond, the aid asked his General if he recollected his promise about the flag. "Yes, go to my tent and get the flag, and carry it on your saddle; I will send you to raise it if we get in."

April 3, six A. M., General Weitzel and his staff, together more than thirty officers, each having an orderly following in the rear, galloped on through the wrecks of the retreating rebels and the columns of the advancing Federals. As soon as they entered the suburbs of the rebel capital, the shouts of welcome broke forth. Meanwhile, several arsenals, stored with shells, were burning. The explosions of the missiles mingled into one continuous roar. Even as they drew near the capitol itself, the populace rushed into the streets to hail their deliverers, or shake hands with them. In fact, their whole line of march within the suburbs was thronged with men, women, and boys, colored and white, all shouting welcome. The excitement was intense. Old men, gray, and scarred with many battles, acted the part of boys, hurrahing and yelling at the top of their voices. Meanwhile, the male negroes were bowing down to the ground, and the sable matrons chorusing with all their strength of lungs, "Bress de Lord! de year ob jubilee hab come!"

When near the foot of Shockoe Hill, the high, abrupt elevation, whose front is crowned by the capitol, Lieutenant de Peyster spurred on through the promiscuous throng up to the capitol itself. This building, the most conspicuous object in Richmond, owes everything to its size and position, since neither the architecture nor the material corresponds with the site and proportions. The front, with its Ionic colonnade, looked down upon the business part of the city, which was all ablaze. The rear faced the fashionable quarter of Richmond, an elevated plain, considered the most eligible locality for private residences. The capitol had two flag-staffs, one at either end of the roof. Upon the front one an enormous rebel flag had been displayed, which, when not extended by the wind, trailed down to the steps below. This had been torn down, and had been partially rent into thousands of pieces, to be preserved as mementoes of the occasion. Upon the staff in the rear, in full sight of the domiciles of the rebel magnates and sympathizers, "the first real American flag" was raised by Lieutenant de Peyster.

That flag, which had been consigned to his care for that very purpose, which he had carried into the city buckled to his saddle, which had floated in like triumph over the Crescent City of the South, the first real American flag hoisted over the rebel capitol, was raised by a Dutchess County officer, aged eighteen, in the presence of Captain Langdon, chief of artillery to the staff of Major-General Weitzel. As it rose aloft, displayed itself, and steadily streamed out in the strong gale, which was filling the air with fiery flakes from the adjacent conflagration, it was hailed with deafening shouts by the redeemed populace, who swarmed the open space below and around.

A short time before this real flag-raising, Major Atherton H. Stevens, of the Fourth Massachusetts cavalry, and Major E. Graves, of General Weitzel's staff, had elevated, or hoisted, two cavalry guidons, small swallow-tailed flags, with the staffs to which they were attached. These were so small that they were scarcely visible, if visible at all, from the streets below. Moreover, it should be remembered that there is a vast difference, as to honor and possession, between planting these, and hoisting a United States flag; the true emblem and act of occupation and triumph. Therefore, as conceded, to Lieutenant de Peyster belongs the historic glory of being the first to run up "the first real American flag," selected and carried in by him for that very purpose, over the chief building of a city preëminently the stronghold and seat of life of the rebellion.

That this hoisting the flag was not attended with great peril, detracts in no manner whatever from the merit of the achievement, inasmuch as, when it occurred, a letter dated "March 28, in the Field," had already been received in New York, stating that Lieutenant de Peyster was pledged to his General, if Richmond were taken, "to put a certain flag on the house of Jefferson Davis, or on the rebel capitol, or perish in the attempt." Everything was perfectly prepared for an intended assault when General Shepley and his Aid discovered that the works which they were ready to storm had been abandoned.

Having, amid gale, tumult, and triumph, drank upon the roof to the success of our arms, the young Aid-de-camp went down into the private room of Jefferson Davis in the custom-house, at the foot of the hill, and thence wrote a letter describing the entrance of the loyal army, which reached New York the same day (April 6) on which the Commercial Advertiser published a telegram from its own correspondent, stating that "to Lieutenant G. [should be J.] L. Dupeyster and to General Shepley belongs the honor of hoisting our flag on the capitol" of Richmond. This was corroborated by the correspondent of the New York Herald, dated "Herald Rooms, Richmond, Virginia, April 11, three P. M." Published 13, A. M.

Lieutenant de Peyster was subsequently quartered in the residence of Jefferson Davis. He describes the house as a perfect gem, as to interior arrangements, although the exterior was altogether unattractive. The furniture was magnificent — rosewood the predominant material. Large pier glasses were to be found in every room. Some of the mirrors were enormous. The floors were covered with splendid carpets, so thick that the foot actually sunk into their rich material. All this lavish expenditure was made in accordance with the acts of the Rebel or Confederate Congress, while the people were naked and starving, and their army in want of shoes.

At the age of sixteen, Lieutenant de Peyster greatly assisted in raising a company for the regiment of Colonel Cowles. Almost all the recruits from the northern district of the town of Red Hook and adjacent, were due to his exertions and the contributions of his relations and connections.

Although he was actually in command for a few days, it was by some trickery he lost the fruit of his labors. Colonel Cowles expressed a very high opinion of him as an officer, and regretted that he could not retain him. In the spring of 1864 he was mustered into the Thirteenth New York artillery, and appointed Post Adjutant to Major Hassler's Battalion. Thence he was transferred to the staff of Brigadier-General Shepley, Military Governor of Norfolk, afterwards chief of staff to General Weitzel before Richmond, and first loyal Military Governor of the rebel capital.

On the 28th of June, Lieutenant de Peyster received official notice that His Excellency, Governor Fenton, in pursuance of the extraordinary power vested in him by the Legislature the last winter, had breveted him a "Lieutenant-Colonel for his meritorious conduct as a New York volunteer in the service of the United States, and for raising the first national ensign over the capitol in Richmond, Virginia, after the insurgents were driven therefrom."

———

WOMEN OF THE SOUTH. — A letter from Lincoln County, Tennessee, written in July, 1861, says:

"I witnessed many a scene in this rural district, which the gay ladies of our fashionable cities may well ponder on, with the reflection of surprise, of how little they know of the hardships which their sex are forced to undergo to sustain and support their families, while their husbands and brothers are absent fighting the battles of our country. On the small farms throughout this section all is life, activity, and industry. Many a woman, who never before held a plough, is now seen in the cornfield; many a young girl, who would have blushed at the thought of handling a plough-line, now naturally and unconsciously cries, 'Gee up!' to Dobbin, to the silvery tones of which the good brute readily responds, as if a pleasure to comply with so gentle a command. Many a Ruth, as of old, is seen to-day binding and gleaning in the wheat-fields; but, alas! no Boaz is there to console or to comfort. The picture of the rural soldier's home is at this time but a picture of primitive life. Throughout the country, at every farm-house and cottage, the regular sound of the loom, as the shuttle flies to and fro, with the whirl of the spinning-wheel, is heard, telling of home industry. Cotton fabrics, of neat, pretty figures, the production of home manufactory, are now almost wholly worn in Tennessee, instead of calicoes.. But it is a sad thought, that while these exertions of thriving industry are being made for the support of the soldier's family, his little cottage home, of which he nightly dreams, is to be abandoned and left unprotected by the falling back of our troops, and subject to the pillage and plunder of the vandal infidels. Such, at least, I fear will be the case in the Counties of Bedford and Coffee, from which we have fallen back."

THE ATTACK ON THE SEWARDS. — The following account of the sensations experienced at the time of their attempted assassination by Payne, was given by Mr. Secretary Seward and his son Frederick:

"Mr. Frederick Seward said, that on stepping from his bed-room into the passage, and seeing the assassin, he merely wondered what he was doing there, and called him to account. On his resisting the fellow's endeavor to pass into Mr. Seward's room, the assassin drew a revolver, which he presented at Mr. Frederick Seward's head. What followed, it must be remembered, took place in a few seconds. Mr. Frederick Seward's first thought was, 'That's a navy revolver.'

"The man pulled the trigger, but it only snapped; and his intended victim thought, 'That cap missed fire.'

"His next sensation was that of confusion; and being upon the floor, resting upon his arm, which, like his father's jaw, was barely recovered from a bad fracture, — the assassin had felled him to the floor with the butt of the pistol, — he put his hand to his head, and finding a hole there, he thought, 'That cap did not miss fire after all.'

"Then he became insensible, and remained so for two days or more. His first indication of returning consciousness was the question, 'Have you not got the ball out?' after which he fell off again into a comatose condition, which was of long continuance.

"On the very afternoon of the day when Mr. Lincoln was assassinated, Mr. Frederick Seward, who was Assistant Secretary of State, had asked his father what preparation should be made for the presentation of Sir Frederick Bruce, which was to take place the next day. Mr. Seward gave him the points of a reply to be made to Sir Frederick, and he laid the outline of the speech upon the President's table, and, as I have previously informed my readers, Mr. Lincoln that afternoon wrote out the reply, adopting Mr. Seward's suggestions, and thus preparing the reception of the British Minister by President Johnson, which was regarded at the time by the people to whose representative it was addressed as so friendly, and fair, and dignified.

"Mr. Frederick Seward's first inquiry, after he came fully to his senses, which was a long time

after the assassination, was, 'Has Sir Frederick Bruce been presented?' He thought that only one night had passed, since he knew not what had happened to him, and his mind took up matters just where it had left them.

"Mr. Seward's mental experience during his supposed assassination was in its nature so like that of his son, that it raises the question whether this absence of consternation and observation of minute particulars is not common in circumstances of unexpected and not fully apprehended peril. Mr. Seward was lying upon his side, close to the edge of the bed, with his head resting in a frame, which had been made to give him ease and protect his broken jaw from pressure.

"He was trying to keep awake, having been seized upon by a sick man's fancy — it was, if he slept he would wake up with lockjaw. He was brought to full consciousness by the scuffle in the passage-way, followed by the entrance of the assassin, and the cry of Miss Seward, 'O, he will kill my father!' But he saw nothing of his assailant until a hand appeared above his face, and then his thought was, 'What handsome cloth that overcoat is made of!' The assassin's face then appeared, and the helpless statesman only thought, 'What a handsome man!' (Payne was a fine-looking fellow.)

"Then came a sensation as of rain striking him smartly upon one side of his face and neck, then quickly the same upon the other side, but he felt no severe pain. This was the assassin's knife. The blood spouted; he thought, 'My time has come,' and falling from the bed to the floor, fainted. His first sensation of returning consciousness was, that he was drinking tea, and that it 'tasted good.' Mrs. Seward was giving him tea with a spoon. He heard low voices around him, asking and replying as to whether it would be possible for him to recover. He could not speak, but his eyes showed his consciousness, and that he desired to speak. They brought him a porcelain tablet, on which he managed to write, 'Give me some tea; I shall get well.' And from that moment he has slowly but steadily recovered his health and strength."

HISTORY OF A TORPEDO BOAT. — General Dabney H. Maury, in his report of the defence of Mobile, narrates the following eventful history of a torpedo boat:

"It was built of boiler iron, was about thirty-five feet long, and was manned by a crew of nine men, eight of whom worked the propeller by hand. The ninth steered the boat and regulated her movements below the surface of the water. She could be submerged at pleasure to any desired depth, or could be propelled upon the surface. In smooth, still water her movements were exactly controlled, and her speed was about four knots. It was intended that she should approach any vessel lying at anchor, pass under her keel, and drag a floating torpedo, which would explode on striking the side or bottom of the ship attacked.

"She could remain submerged more than half an hour without inconvenience to her crew.

"Soon after her arrival in Charleston, Lieutenant Payne, of the Confederate navy, with eight others, volunteered to attack the Federal fleet with her. While preparing for their expedition, the swell of a passing steamer caused the boat to sink suddenly, and all hands, except Lieutenant Payne, who was standing in the open hatchway, perished. She was soon raised and again made ready for service. Lieutenant Payne again volunteered to command her. While lying near Fort Sumter she capsized, and again sunk in deep water, drowning all hands, except her commander and two others.

"Being again raised and prepared for action, Mr. Aunley, one of the constructors, made an experimental cruise in her in Cooper River. While submerged at great depth, from some unknown cause, she became unmanageable, and remained for many days on the bottom of the river with her crew of nine dead men.

"A fourth time was the boat raised, and Lieutenant Dixon, of Mobile, of the Twenty-first volunteers, with eight others, went out of Charleston harbor in her, and attacked and sunk the Federal steamer Housatonic.

"Her mission at last accomplished, she disappeared forever with her crew. Nothing is known of their fate, but it is believed they went down with the enemy."

How I Enlisted. — A soldier of the Second regiment of Ohio cavalry writes: "On New Year's day, 1864, as our regiment was lying in line of battle beyond Mossy Creek, in East Tennessee, the proposition to reënlist as veteran volunteers was submitted to that grim organization. Peter Longstreet's ragged but plucky skirmish line was a stone's throw in front, with a forward tendency; snow was on the hills; the Second Ohio cavaliers had drawn no rations from Uncle Sam in fifteen days, and not an average of one eighth ration during the preceding four months; their diaphragms were devoid of burden; they had not 'lived in tents' for an eighth-month; the supply of pone and cerulean hog was failing in that land, and zero was biting at the noses of the cavaliers. Amid all these favorable surroundings the cavaliers said, 'Go to, let us have more of this good thing; give unto us yet thirty and six moons of this goodly service.' Thus the thing was done. Under such circumstances our veteran volunteers enlisted.

"While the cavaliers were signing their names to the enlistment roll, at the rate of a hundred per hour, a ludicrous memory of a former enlistment came to us. Two days after Sumter fell, on a bright April morning, big church full of indignant sovereigns and enthusiastic women; organ thundered, band crashed out 'Hail Columbia;' impromptu banners wagged briskly, and the air was redolent of patriotism. Music ceased. Speeches followed. Roll was opened, and volunteers called for. Five hundred pairs of starry eyes waited to illume the path of the first volunteer. Five hundred pairs of little white hands were nervous to begin clapping at the advent of the first masculine sacrifice. He came, and Emperors have had poorer receptions. He was apotheosized. More followed. The pressure increased. I cowered in my pew, imagining that every woman of sense, and every girl of beauty, was saying to herself, 'Why don't he go?' I reasoned with myself, but the clapping and waving of white kerchiefs made me dizzy. With a mighty effort, I made a resolution. I mentally bade adieu to all terrestrial matters. I buried from view all relatives nearer than second cousins, drew the veil of forgetfulness over the dear form of Julia, and most of my outstanding debts, made up my mind to be shot for my country, and began to stride up the aisle. What a path to a graveyard! The male audience yelled — the female audience waved kerchiefs with unexampled energy, and they were perfumed with divine odors. I saw nothing but a dancing sea of snow-white foam, interspersed with smiling stars. I heard nothing but an undefined roar — to me an echo from eternity, to which I regarded myself as rapidly going. I scrawled my name on the elongated foolscap, and thus added my two hundred pounds to the growing hecatomb. I was a volunteer! That night I dreamed of battles. Next day, twenty-seven Testaments, thirteen 'housewifes,' eleven pin-cushions, and thirty-eight rolls of bandages, were left at my boarding-house, each with a touching note from the fair donors. Such was three months' soldiering 'in the brave days of old.' Then we were green — how sadly veteran we are now!"

The Ride of the Wounded Brigade. — B. F. Taylor, the army correspondent of the Chicago Journal, wrote thus, from the army of the Cumberland, of a night's ride of the wounded brigade, after the battle of Chickamauga: "They were loaded upon the train; two platform cars were packed with them, forty on a car. Seven boxes were so packed you could not set your foot down among them as they lay. The roofs of the cars were tiled with them; and away we pounded, all day, all night, into the next morning, and then Nashville. Half of the boys had not a shred of a blanket, and it rained steadily, pitilessly. What do you think of platform cars for a triumphal procession wherein to bear wounded heroes to the tune of 'The soldier's return from the war?' Well, what I would come at is this: the stores of the Sanitary Commission, and the gifts of such ladies as are now, I believe, making your city a Bethel — a place of angels — kept the boys' hearts up through all those weary, drizzling hours. It is midnight, and the attendants are going through the train with coffee, graced with milk and sugar — think of that! — two fresh, white, crisp crackers apiece, and a little taste of fruit. Did your hands prepare it, dear lady? I hope so, for the little balance in your favor is set down in the ledger of God.

"But here they come with a canteen; will you

go with them? Climb through that window into a car black as the Hole of Calcutta. But mind where you step; the floor is one layer deep with wounded soldiers. As you swing the lantern round, bandages show white and ghastly everywhere; bandages, bandages, and now and then a rusty spot of blood. What worn-out, faded faces look up at you! They rouse like wounded creatures hunted down to their lairs as you come. The tin cups, extended in all sorts of hands but plump, strong ones, tinkle all around you. You are fairly girdled with a tin-cup horizon. How the dull, faint faces brighten as those cups are filled! On we go, out at one window, in at another, stepping gingerly among mangled limbs. We reach the platform cars, creaking with their drenched, chilled, bruised burdens; and I must tell you — it's a shame, though — that one poor fellow among them lay with a tattered blanket pinned around him; he was literally *sans culotte!* 'How is this?' I said. 'Haven't got my descriptive list — that's what's the matter,' was the reply.

"Double allowance all around to the occupants of the platforms, and we retrace our steps to the rear of the train. You should have heard the ghost of a cheer that rose and fluttered like a feeble bird, as we went back. It was the most touching vote of thanks ever offered; there was a little flash up of talk for a minute, and all subsided into silence and darkness again. Wearily wore the hours, and heavily hammered the train. At intervals the guard traversed the roofs of the cars, and pulled in the worn-out boys that had jarred down to the edges — pulled them in to the middle of the cars without waking them! Occasionally one slips over the eaves, I am told, and is miserably crushed. What a homeward march is all this to set a tune to.

"By some error in apportionment there was not quite coffee enough for all on deck, and two slips of boys on the roof of the car where I occupied a corner were left without a drop. Whenever we stopped — and that was two hours there and three hours here, waiting for this and for that; there was no hurry, you know, and the side-door was slid back in its groove — I saw two hungry faces stretched down over the car's edge, and heard two feeble voices crying, 'We have had nothing up here since yesterday noon, we two — there are only us two boys — *please* give us something. Haven't you got any hard tack?' I heard that pitiful appeal to the officers in charge, and saw those faces till they haunted me, and to-day I remember those plaintive tones as if I were hearing a dirge.

"I felt in my pockets and haversack for a cracker, but found nothing. I really hated myself for having eaten my dinner, and not saved it for them. A further search was rewarded with six crackers from the Chicago Mechanical Bakers', and watching my chance when Pete's back was turned, — the cook, and a smutty autocrat was Pete in his way, — I took a sly dip with a basin into the coffee-boiler. As the car gave a lurch in the right direction I called from the window,

'Boys!' I heard them crawling to the edge, and handed up the midnight supper. 'Bully for you!' they said, and I saw them no more. When the train reached Nashville, and I clambered down to solid ground again, I looked up at the roof; it was bare. God grant the boys are with their mothers to-night. And how do you like the Ride of the Wounded Brigade?"

OHIO AT STONE RIVER. — On the memorable 31st of December, at Stone River, after the right wing was broken, the centre driven back, and destruction was holding wide its jaws to crush the Union army, to a few regiments of the gallant Crittenden's left wing was reserved the distinguished honor of turning back the tide of adverse battle. For three horrible hours, while Bragg was massing his victorious and exultant columns, and hurling them successively upon Crittenden's position with reckless desperation, that in the moment of expected triumph lavishes oceans of blood and ages of life to make the final victory, the 26th Ohio, under Major Squires, held its ground from first to last, and amid the tempest of confusion around, and the deluge of death pouring upon it, completely run over by more than one entire regiment, that had been shivered by the shock on its right and front, itself still firm as a rock, a very breakwater against the tide of ruin, three times saw the solid masses of the enemy stagger, recoil, and break up within short pistol range of its bayonets, and flee from the horrible slaughter. On this field the 26th Ohio was baptized in blood. When the struggle was over, one third of the command lay dead and bleeding on the ground they fought over."

"OUT RAKING OYSTERS." — A correspondent at Brandy Station, Va., records the following: "On our late reconnoissance, a new recruit, belonging to the Third Michigan regiment, and who had not been in any 'forward movement' before, asked an old soldier, one of his comrades, 'Where are we going?' 'Out reconnoitring,' replied the vet. 'Out raking oysters?' exclaimed the recruit, with astonishment. 'Good heavens! what does the General want to take the whole corps out to rake oysters for? I should think a brigade could rake all the oysters he wanted to eat!' I rather guessed at the time that he thought it an awful long distance to where the oysters were. We did not get quite to the spot where the raking was taking place, and believe there were not many found; but the 'shells' were around us at one time pretty thick, and our recruit had a taste of them for the first time."

ANECDOTE OF PRESIDENT LINCOLN. — The President's stories grew better and better as he grew older. One of the best was told to a visitor who congratulated him on the almost certain purpose on the part of the people to reëlect him for another term of four years. Mr. Lincoln replied that he had been told this frequently before, and that when it was first mentioned to him he was reminded of a farmer in Illinois who determined to try his own hand at blasting. After successfully boring and filling in with powder, he failed in his effort to make the powder go off; and after discussing with a looker-on the cause for this, and failing to detect anything wrong in the powder, the farmer suddenly came to the conclusion that it would not go off because it had been shot before.

SONG OF THE SOLDIERS.

BY CHARLES G. HALPINE.

AIR : "*Jamie's on the Stormy Sea.*"

COMRADES known in marches many,
Comrades tried in dangers many,
Comrades bound by memories many,
　　Brothers ever let us be.
Wounds or sickness may divide us,
Marching orders may divide us,
But whatever fate betide us,
　　Brothers of the heart are we.

Comrades known by faith the clearest,
Tried when death was near and nearest,
Bound we are by ties the dearest,
　　Brothers evermore to be :
And, if spared, and growing older,
Shoulder still in line with shoulder,
And with hearts no thrill the colder,
　　Brothers ever we shall be.

By communion of the banner,
Crimson, white and starry banner,
By the baptism of the banner
　　Children of one church are we.
Creed nor faction can divide us,
Race nor language can divide us,
Still, whatever fate betide us,
　　Children of the flag are we !

A HERO AT GETTYSBURG. — First Lieutenant Bayard Wilkeson, son of Samuel Wilkeson of the New York Tribune,[*] commanding Battery G, Fourth United States artillery, was killed in the extreme front of the first day's battle, while pouring grape and canister into Ewell's advancing columns. He was but nineteen years old. Before he was eighteen he was recommended for promotion as Captain, by General Peck, for gallantry in the battle of the "Deserted House," on the Blackwater. His battery was considered the model one of the Eleventh corps, and was assigned the advance in the order of march. He actually fought his battery after his leg was shot off. In his devotion to his command, which was proverbial in the army, he ordered the four men who carried him a short distance off the field, to leave him and go back to their pieces. This generous heroism insured his loss. Immediately after, the advance was routed and driven in disorder into and through Gettysburg, and the brave artillery

[*] See account of the battle of Gettysburg, by Mr. Wilkeson, *ante.*

officer fell into the hands of the rebels and died for want of amputation.

THE COMMISSIONS. — A soldier correspondent at Stevenson, Alabama, writes : " The Sanitary and Christian Commissions are the means, in God's hand, of accomplishing an infinite amount of good. I know the soldiers are directly benefited by the essentials and 'goodies' prepared by the devoted mothers and loving sisters of our dear 'dear men in blue.' The trouble is, too many of them want the identical cookie his mother made."

BRAVERY AT CHICKAMAUGA. — A writer relates the following instances of heroic conduct at the battle of Chickamauga : " Commendatory articles, touching the acts and bearing of different persons and officers in the late battle of Chickamauga, appearing, have led me, for the first time in my life, to volunteer an item or two for the public eye. My notices here are unsolicited and gratuitous, without the knowledge or consent of either of those of whom I design to speak. Disinterested spectators are generally allowed to be unbiassed. Thus situated, I shall write freely, and leave the consequences to take care of themselves ; naming some three or four, who, occupying subaltern positions, are almost wholly unnoticed by the paid contributors of the press. Let the record be made with fidelity, and an enlightened public will give a just verdict. First, I would name the noble Harrison, Colonel of the Thirty-ninth mounted infantry, an Achilles, baptized in blood at Shiloh, and Stone River, with his full regiment of veterans, with a Vulcan's armor (the dreaded sight-shotted Spencer rifles), the only gun known worthy to grace the hands of such soldiers. Henceforth may our Government give her brave boys no other small arm for the field. Late in the afternoon of Sunday, when the mighty numbers of the enemy were carrying everything before them, and sweeping round to the road leading to Chattanooga, the only outlet to a large portion of our beleaguered army, he met them there. Enthusiastic with success, and confident through superiority of numbers, the foe charged desperately on his steady lines ; a continued sheet of flame burst upon them. Unaccustomed to such swift and fatal volleys, they calculate on a cessation to load, and rush on, only to see their front ranks fall almost to the last man, and still the livid lightning was unabated. Mortal man cannot face such sweeping fires. Backward they rush, impetuously, and the ground is held ; the way remains open ; the flanking columns were here hurled back upon their centre, resulting in safety to many teams and thousands of our disorganized troops. Such was the worth of Thomas J. Harrison, the quiet and noble American officer.

" Next in order stands the energetic German, General Turchin, whose decisive will saved General Reynolds', General Brannan's, and a part of General Palmer's divisions from almost certain capture. Late on Sunday afternoon, when some were talking of a surrender, being almost surrounded, General Turchin was called upon to give an opinion as to the best plan of action. 'What, surrender?' said he, 'No, sir; never! I shoost takes my prigade, and *cuts* my way right out. When I tells my men to sharge, dey sharges right through. I tells, sir, we never surrender!' Speaking and acting with increasing vehemence, and a determination as irresistible as it was prompt, silencing all opposition, which was, indeed, useless, and seemed out of the question, and, true to his promise, he did take his 'prigade" and burst through the closing lines of the enemy, with an irresistibility equalled only by his energy and indomitable will, amid one of the most terrific storms of shot and shell, and whistling bullets, that has, perhaps, ever burst upon a moving column of men without checking them. Such was, and is, General Turchin. Though possibly he be not a Ulysses in the council, he is an Ajax in the '*sharge*.' When our columns were just put in motion for this desperate charge, the ready thought of a Provost Marshal was most opportune, and its effects perfectly electrical. It was Lieutenant S. Fortner, who, taking off his hat, and waving it, as for a triumph, shouted: 'A cheer, boys, as we take on the double-quick. Huzza for General Thomas and victory!' One long and deafening shout rose above the thunder of the battle, along those dusty lines. How tame is language! how utterly futile the attempt to tell the thrilling interests of such a scene at such a moment! There I saw Assistant Dewey, of the One Hundred and First Indiana, on foot, and still with his regiment, the only surgeon of the divisions, then, who remained unflinchingly with his command through every storm of those two bloody days, and through the chilly night, where they rested in line of battle, and where he found and relieved, as far as possible, the suffering of some seventeen or eighteen wounded left in an old house, and lost sight of by their commands. The Twenty-fourth and Thirty-sixth Ohio and Thirty-sixth Indiana were represented in this dismal hut, moaning and asking for water. Assistance is ordered, water procured; a lonely ride of miles is at once taken to order ambulances for their removal, a promise extorted for their early appearance on the ground; returns to the lines; a sleepless, lingering, frosty night slowly wears away; ambulances have not come. As daylight approaches, coffee is procured, and the sufferers eagerly partake, while cheering hopes are given that the conveyances will soon come; all is made safe. The ambulances do come just in time to get off before battle opens — a terrible carnage sweeps that spot — the house is burned away. Who can appreciate services like these, unless they, too, have suffered such necessities? Some have gone to their long rest, here in the hospital. But to our subject. Quietly he passes through the terrific storm, halting briefly to bandage a bleeding arm for a comrade, and to give a little water from his canteen to even a pleading enemy, wounded and helpless. On scathless he passes, protected by unseen hands. A Confucius on the

billows of Mars — a blending of patriotism and philanthropy. The blood-stained laurels of conquering heroes pale before those which heaven-born charity wreathes. Such are a few incidents among many as brave and noble, no doubt; and, in recalling and recording, we do not forget those not here cited, least of all, we do not — we could not — forget the great Agamemnon of the army, our noble commander, General Thomas, the angel of our safety." — *Nashville Press*.

A NIGHT SCENE AT FREDERICKSBURG. — The following graphic story was told by "Carleton," the accomplished correspondent:

"FREDERICKSBURG, May 17, 1864.

"The day is past. The cool night has come, refreshing the fevered cheek, cooling the throbbing pulse, and soothing the aching wounds of the thousands congregated in this city. I have made it in part a day of observation, visiting the hospitals, and conversing with patients and nurses; and now, wearied, worn, with nerves unstrung by sickening sights, I make an attempt to sketch the scenes of the day.

"The city is a vast hospital; churches, all public buildings, private dwellings, stores, chambers, attics, basements, — all are occupied by patients, or are attended by medical officers, or by those who have come to take care of the wounded. All day long the trains of ambulances have been arriving from the field hospitals. There are but few wounded left at the front, — those only whom to move would be certain death. Those able to bear removal have been sent in, that the army may move on to finish its appointed work.

"A red flag is flung out at the Sanitary Commission rooms — a white one at the rooms of the Christian Commission. There are three hundred volunteer nurses in attendance. The Sanitary Commission have fourteen wagons bringing supplies from Belle Plain. The Christian Commission has less transportation facilities, but in devotion, in hard work, in patient effort, it is the compeer of its more bountifully supplied neighbor. The nurses are divided into details, — some for day service, some for night work. Each State has its relief committee.

"Governor Smith, of Vermont, is here; Senator Sprague, of Rhode Island; Senator Sherman, of Ohio; Senator Pomeroy, of Kansas; Ex-Mayors Bunton and Smyth, of Manchester, N. H.; Ex-Mayor Fay, of Chelsea; Rev. Mr. Means, of Roxbury; and scores of men, aside from the Commissions' nurses, doing what they can to relieve the necessities, and alleviate the sufferings, of the wounded.

"How patient the brave fellows are! Not a word of complaint, but thanks for the slightest favor. There has been a lack of crutches. This morning I saw a soldier of a California regiment, an old soldier who fought with the lamented Baker at Ball's Bluff, and who has been in more than twenty battles, and who, till Thursday last, has escaped unharmed, hobbling about with the arms of a settee nailed to strips of board. His regiment went home to-day, its three years of service having expired. It was but a score or two of weather-beaten, battle-scarred veterans. The disabled comrade could hardly keep back the tear as he saw them pass down the street. 'Few of us left. The bones of the boys are on every battle-field where the army of the Potomac has fought,' said he.

"There was a sound of the pick and spade in the churchyard, a heaving up of new earth — a digging of trenches, not for defence against the enemy, but the preparation of the last resting-place of departed heroes. There they lie — a dozen of them — each wrapped in his blanket — the last bivouac! For them there is no more war — no charges into the thick, leaden rain-drops — no more hurrahs — no more cheering of the dear old flag, bearing it onward to victory. They have fallen, but the victory is theirs, theirs the roll of eternal honor. One by one — side by side — men from Massachusetts, and from Pennsylvania, and from Wisconsin — from all the States, resting in one common grave. Peace to them — blessings on those whom they have left behind!

"Go into the hospitals, — armless, legless men, wounds of every description. Men on the hard floor, on the hard seats of church pews, lying in one position all day, unable to stir till the nurse going the rounds comes to their aid. They must wait till their food comes. Some must be fed with a spoon, as if they were little children.

"'O that we could get some straw for the brave fellows,' said Rev. Mr. Kimball, of the Christian Commission. He had wandered about town, searching for the article. 'There is none to be had. We shall have to send to Washington for it.'

"'Straw! I remember two stacks, four miles out on the Spottsylvania road. I saw them last night as I galloped in from the front.'

"Armed with a requisition from the Provost Marshal to seize two stacks of straw, with two wagons driven by intelligent contrabands, four Christian Commission delegates, and away we went across the battle-field of December — fording Hazel Run — gained the heights, and reached the straw stacks, owned by Rev. Mr. Owen.

"'By whose authority do you take my property?'

"'The Provost Marshal's, sir.'

"Rev. Mr. Kimball was on the stack pitching it down. I was pitching it in, and the young men were stowing it away.

"'Are you going to pay me for it?'

"'You must see the Provost Marshal, sir. If you are a loyal man, and will take the oath of allegiance, doubtless you will get your pay.'

"'It is pretty hard. My children are just ready to starve. I have nothing for them to eat, and you come to take my property without paying for it.'

"'Yes, sir; war is hard. You must remember, sir, that there are thousands of wounded men — *your* wounded as well as ours. If your children

are on the point of starving, those men are on the point of dying. We must have the straw for them. What we don't take to-night we will get in the morning. Meanwhile, sir, if anybody attempts to take it, please say to them that it is for the hospital, and they can't have it.'

"Thus with wagons stuffed we leave Rev. Mr. Owen, and return to make glad the hearts of several thousand men. O, how they thank us!

"'Did you get it for me? God bless you, sir!'

"It is evening. Thousands of soldiers, just arrived from Washington, have passed through the town to take their places in the front. The hills all around are white with innumerable tents and thousands of wagons.

"A band is playing lively airs to cheer the wounded in the hospitals. I have been looking in to see the sufferers. Two or three have gone. They will need no more attention. A surgeon is at work upon a ghastly wound, taking up the arteries. An attendant is pouring cold water upon a swollen limb. In the Episcopal Church a nurse is bolstering up a wounded officer in the area behind the altar. Men are lying in the pews, on the seats, on the floor, on boards on the top of the pews.

"Two candles in the spacious building throw their feeble rays into the dark recesses, faintly disclosing the recumbent forms. There is heavy, stifled breathing, as of constant effort to suppress involuntary cries extorted by acutest pain. Hard it is to see them suffer and not be able to relieve them.

"Passing into the street, you see a group of women, talking about *our* wounded — rebel wounded who are receiving their especial attention. The Provost Marshal's patrol is going its rounds to preserve order.

"Starting down the street, you reach the rooms of the Christian Commission. Some of the men are writing, some eating their rations, some dispensing supplies. Passing through their rooms, you gain the grounds in the rear — a beautiful garden once — not unattractive now. The air is redolent with honeysuckle and locust blossoms. The pennifolia is unfolding its delicate milk-white petals — roses are opening their tinted leaves.

"Fifty men are gathered round a summer-house — warm-hearted men — who have been all day in the hospitals. Their hearts have been wrung by the scenes of suffering, in the exercise of Christian charity imitating the example of the Redeemer of men. They have given bread for the body and food for the soul. They have given cups of cold water in the name of Jesus, and prayed with those departing to the silent land. The moonlight shimmers through the leaves of the locust.

"The little congregation breaks into singing —

'Come, thou fount of every blessing.'

"After the hymn, a chaplain says: 'Brethren, I had service this afternoon in the First division hospital of the Second corps. The surgeon in charge, before prayer, asked all who desired to be prayed for to raise their hands; and nearly every man who had a hand raised it. Let us remember them in our prayers to-night.'

"A man in the summer-house — so far off that I cannot distinguish him in the shadow — says: 'There is manifestly a spirit of prayer among the soldiers of the Second division of the Sixth corps hospital. Every man there raised his hand for prayers!'

"Similar remarks are made by others, and then there are earnest prayers offered that God will bless them, relieve their sufferings, give them patience, restore them to health; that He will remember the widow and fatherless far away — that Jesus may be their Friend.

"Ah! this night scene! There was an allusion, by one who prayed, to the garden scene of Gethsemane — the blood of the Son of God, and in connection with the blood shed for our country. You who are far away can understand but little of the reality of these scenes. Friends, everywhere, you have given again and again, but continue to give — you cannot repay these brave defenders of our country. Give as God has prospered you, and great shall be your reward. — Faint, feeble, tame, lifeless is this attempt to portray the scenes of a day at Fredericksburg. Picture it as you may, and you will fall short of the reality."

THE EAGLE OF CORINTH.*

Did you hear of the fight at Corinth,
  How we whipped out Price and Van Dorn?
Ah! that day we earned our rations
(Our cause was God's and the Nation's,
  Or we'd have come out forlorn!) —
A long and a terrible day!
And, at last, when night grew gray,
  By the hundred there they lay
  (Heavy sleepers, you'd say) —
    That wouldn't wake on the morn.

Our staff was bare of a flag;
We didn't carry a rag
  In those brave marching days:
Ah! no; but a finer thing!
With never a cord or string, —
An eagle, of ruffled wing,
  And an eye of awful gaze!

The grape, it rattled like hail;
The minies were dropping like rain,
  The first of a thunder-shower —
  The wads were blowing like chaff
(There was pounding, like floor and flail,
  All the front of our line!)
So we stood it, hour after hour —
  But our eagle, he felt fine!
    'Twould have made you cheer and laugh,
To see, through that iron gale,
  How the old fellow'd swoop and sail
Above the racket and roar —
To right and to left he'd soar,
But ever came back, without fail,
  And perched on his standard staff.

All that day, I tell you true,
  They had pressed us, steady and fair,
Till we fought in street and square
(The affair, you might think, looked blue) —
But we knew we had them there!
Our works and batteries were few;
Every gun, they'd have sworn, they knew —
But, you see, there was one or two
  We had fixed for them, unaware.

They reckon they've got us now!
  For the next half hour 'twill be warm —
Ay, ay, look yonder! — I vow,
If they weren't secesh, how I'd love them!
  Only see how grandly they form
(Our eagle whirling above them)
  To take Robinette by storm!
They're timing! — it can't be long —
Now for the nub of the fight!
  (You may guess that we held our breath).
By the Lord, 'tis a splendid sight!
  A column, two thousand strong,
    Marching square to the death!

On they came, in solid column;
  For once, no whooping nor yell
(Ah! I dare say they felt solemn) —
Front and flank — grape and shell
  Our batteries pounded away!
And the minies hummed to remind 'em
  They had started on no child's play!
Steady they kept a going,
But a grim wake settled behind 'em —
  From the edge of the abatis
  (Where our dead and dying lay,
  Under fence and fallen tree),
Up to Robinette, all the way
  The dreadful swath kept growing!
    'Twas butternut, flecked with gray.

Now for it, at Robinette!
Muzzle to muzzle we met
  (Not a breath of bluster or brag,
  Not a lisp for quarter or favor) —
Three times, there, by Robinette,
  With a rush, their feet they set
On the logs of our parapet,
  And waved their bit of a flag —
    What could be finer or braver!

But our cross-fire stunned them in flank;
They melted, rank after rank —
  (O'er them, with terrible poise,
  Our bird did circle and wheel!)
Their whole line began to waver —
Now for the bayonet, boys!
  On them with the cold steel!

Ah! well — you know how it ended —
  We did for them, there and then;
But their pluck throughout was splendid.

---

*"The finest thing I ever saw was a live American eagle, carried by the Eighth Iowa in the place of a flag. He would fly off over the enemy during the hottest of the fight, then would return and seat himself upon his pole, clap his pinions, shake his head, and start again. Many and hearty were the cheers that arose from our lines as the old fellow would sail around, first to the right, then to the left, and always return to his post, regardless of the storm of leaden hail that was around him. Something seemed to tell us that that battle was to result in our favor; and when the order was given to charge, every man went at them with fixed bayonets, and the enemy scattered in all directions, leaving us in possession of the battle-field." — *Letter from Chester D. Howe, company E, Twelfth Illinois volunteers.*

24

(As I said before, I could love them!)
They stood, to the last, like men —
Only a handful of them
    Found the way back again.

Red as blood o'er the town,
The angry sun went down,
    Firing flag-staff and vane —
And our eagle — as for him,
There, all ruffled and grim,
He sat, o'erlooking the slain!

Next morning you'd have wondered
    How we had to drive the spade!
There, in great trenches and holes
    (Ah! God rest their poor souls!)
We piled some fifteen hundred,
    Where that last charge was made!

Sad enough, I must say!
    No mother to mourn and search,
No priest to bless or to pray —
We buried them where they lay,
    Without a rite of the church —
But our eagle all that day
    Stood solemn and still on his perch.

'Tis many a stormy day
    Since, out of the cold, bleak North,
Our great war eagle sailed forth
To swoop o'er battle and fray.
Many and many a day
    O'er charge and storm hath he wheeled —
Foray and foughten-field —
    Tramp, and volley, and rattle! —
Over crimson trench and turf,
Over climbing clouds of surf,
Through tempest and cannon-rack,
Have his terrible pinions whirled —
    (A thousand fields of battle!
    A million leagues of foam!)
But our bird shall yet come back,
He shall soar to his eyrie home —
And his thunderous wings be furled,
In the gaze of a gladdened world,
    On the nation's loftiest dome.
                   H. H. B.

A HEROIC CHAPLAIN. — Rev. F. Denison, the Chaplain of the Third Rhode Island heavy artillery, is the hero of the following incident:

Acting as aid to a commander of cavalry, who was out on a scouting or reconnoitring expedition from Port Royal, the Chaplain, with only his unarmed colored servant, became separated, in the darkness, from his companions, when coming suddenly upon a body of six armed rebels, and finding escape impossible, with wonderful presence of mind he instantly leaped from his horse directly among them, drew his sword, and ordered them to surrender, threatening them with instant death unless they fired off their guns and submitted unconditionally to his demand, which, in their moment of surprise, they concluded to do, and were at once marched in triumph to the Union camp, a distance of two miles, by the redoubtable Chaplain and his colored servant.

A RAID FROM PETERSBURG. — Martin Reichenbacher, a Sergeant in the Second artillery, regular troops, in a letter to a friend, relates the following: "Yesterday (December 2, 1864) we returned from one of the most successful raids the cavalry ever made. It was as follows: On the 30th of November, we received orders to be in full marching order, which were most promptly obeyed. On the morning of the 1st of December, about four o'clock, we broke camp, taking what is known as the Lee's Mill road, running in a south-westerly direction from a point on the Norfolk Railroad, where our camp is. The same day, about eleven o'clock, we suddenly found ourselves near the Stony Creek Station, on the Weldon Railroad, where the rebels were known to have large quantities of stores, and much valuable lumber, guarded, as they imagined, very well indeed by fortifications and earthworks of various descriptions, with a considerable garrison and some heavy guns, they not in the least thinking that we would be so bold as to go twenty-five miles, that being the distance, with cavalry, and attack, whip them handsomely, and carry off and destroy all the property in that vicinity, besides demolishing the depot and sawmills which were close by. When the harm was done, they must have felt very much ashamed, for, in addition to all I have mentioned, we captured a great number of prisoners — say over two hundred. This, it will be remembered, was the cavalry force that accomplished this, the battery which I belong to being included, as we took part in the fight. When the rebels saw all their buildings in flames, they formed and made a most desperate charge on our line of battle, our battery occupying a position in the centre. We received them very warmly, in every sense of the word, with fire, shot, and shell, as the cavalrymen say. When asked how the battery fire acts, the reply is generally, 'The ten-pound checks the rebels do not appreciate that you fire from those bull-dogs;" and true, on most every occasion, a charge is successfully checked by our battery, as it was this time. When the rebels found us prepared, and they handsomely repulsed, our men rent the air with cheers, and our battery received considerable of a large share of them. I again commanded a section of ten-pounder rifle guns. Finally, we fell back in good order, and safely arrived in camp with our prisoners, and trophies of the battle-field, consisting of wagons, horses, mules, and many useful articles, too numerous to mention. It is, in our military circles, pronounced a most brilliant success."

HOW THE OFFICERS LOST THEIR BOOTS. — During the winter of 1863-4 a division of Federal cavalry encamped in the vicinity of Huntsville, Ala., for the purpose of keeping down guerrillas and encouraging whatever Union sentiment might happen to generate there under the humane system of General George Crook, who was commander of the division. The railroad was not in running order, and the nearest point from which to procure supplies was nearly a hundred miles distant. In consequence of the limited transportation a sufficient quantity of Government stores could not be obtained, and the exigencies of the situation compelled the men to resort to illegitimate means to supply the demand. Among other articles, boots and shoes were decidedly scarce, and when a soldier lay down at night he would sleep with his boots on, if he had any; for it required a hard exercise of faith to believe that he would find them in the morning if left in a place less secure. Every dwelling and out-house in the town and surrounding country was ransacked and compelled to pay tribute to the feet of the Yankee invaders, and even then the supply did not begin to equal the demand. The contrabands, as they came into our lines, would involuntarily swap their boots and shoes with our men, and as a general thing would get the worst of the bargain. Picket duty in general is not pleasant, but at that time was very desirable, for the men invariably came into camp better shod than when they went out, though in most cases they had great difficulty in getting their feet into the stirrups, from the largeness of the brogans lately worn by the negroes. It was not an uncommon occurrence to see the adopted Union citizens of the place in their stocking feet when they ventured out at night, exchanging their boots for the well-ventilated ones of the Federal troopers.

On the occasion of a review it was noticed by some of the men of the 4th U. S. cavalry that General Crook and staff had little reason to complain of the article which they so much needed. On returning to camp a plan was devised to relieve the General and his officers of their boots. A young man named Adams procured some female apparel in a negro shanty, and having rubbed his face slightly with burnt cork, proceeded at night to the hotel where the General and his staff were quartered. Adams, besides his wild and frolicsome disposition, was young, well formed, and a little under the medium height. It was not his first adventure of the kind; and in his new guise, he presented the appearance of a tall finely-formed mulatto girl of interesting attractions. Proceeding to the officer's room, he inquired if they wanted their boots blacked. Whether they required blacking or not, he had little difficulty in getting all the boots he could stuff in a corn sack, very considerately numbering each pair to prevent mistakes. He received injunction to hurry up, and in some cases got paid in advance. About the time Adams had returned to camp and divided the spoils among his friends the officers began to suspect that the female bootblack was bestowing unusual pains on their boots, and had they not been confined to their stocking feet, would no doubt have ventured down stairs to look her up. As each officer was unaware of the visit of the fair mulatto to any one else but himself, they individually consoled themselves with the assurance that their boots would be found at the door in the morning. How each one supplied himself with another pair is probably unknown to any but himself and the sutlers. But

Adams and his friends wore their boots quietly, none being suspected of the theft but the vagrant negroes about town, in whose employ the wench was supposed to be engaged. — *The Citizen.*

THE MEN OF THE CUMBERLAND.

BY THE AUTHOR OF "THE NEW PRIEST."

This ship went down on the 9th of March, under Lieutenant George M. Morris, with her flag flying, and her guns firing (while the water was closing over them) at the iron monster, Virginia, which had cut two yawning holes in her side.

CHEER! cheer! for our noble Yankee tars,
　That fought the ship Cumberland!
Not a sigh for these, with their maims and scars,
　Or their dead that lie off the strand!

Who whines of the ghastly gash and wound,
　Or the horrible deaths of war?
Where, where should a brave man's death be found,
　And what is a true heart for?

Cheer! cheer! for these men! Ah! they knew when
　Was the time for true hearts to die!
How their flag sank, apeak, will flush the brave cheek,
　While this earth shall hang in the sky!

In the bubbling waves they fired their last,
　Where sputtered the burning wad;
And fast at their post, as their guns were fast,
　Went a hundred and more before God!

Not a man of all but had stood to be shot
　(So the flag might fly), or to drown;
The sea saved some, for it came to their lot,
　And some with their ship went down!

Then cheer for these men! they want not gold;
　But give them their ship once more,
And the flag that yet hangs in wet and cold
　O'er their dead by that faithless shore.

Our sunken ship we'll yet weigh up,
　And we'll raise our deep-drowned brave,
Or we'll drain those Roads till a baby's cup
　May puddle their last shoal wave.

And we'll tell in tale, and sing in song,
　How the Cumberland was fought
By men who knew that all else was wrong
　But to die when a sailor ought.

PASSING TO THE FRONT. — It so happened in the course of human events, that a goodly number of delegates to the Christian Commission at Chattanooga found themselves landed at Bridgeport without any visible means of further conveyance. Anxious to make their way through to Chattanooga immediately, they tried all round the tented village for something — anything that would carry them over the mountain, and finally, through the intervention of Providence, succeeded in securing *one* very diminutive female specimen of the asinine species. Here then was a quandary. Who, *and how many*, should ride? After some miscellaneous discussion on this point, it was finally agreed that the distinguished honor should be conferred on a Bostonian brother alone, the fit of whose boots and quality of whose cloth being, no doubt, taken into consideration ; for be it known that a walk of forty miles on the roads of that country, and sleeping out by the wayside, were calculated to take the nap off of French goods.

Well, they started, the "hub" man astride of the little personification of injured innocence, and the rest with a Government train. Their journey was without accident or incident worthy of mention until they had rounded the top of Wallen's Ridge and were coming down the side — which, by the way, is very declivous — when, all of a sudden, the thing the Eastern delegate was riding got mulish, stopped, and the parson went on — tilted square over its head, his feet unfortunately held tight by the stirrups. As soon as his brethren, who were a little way behind, heard of the disaster, they rushed to his relief, and found the position thus : The quadruped was standing stock still, and so was brother A., varying, however, from the usual manner in this, that the end which custom has established as proper for men to have up, when appearing in company, was in his case just the opposite. He was, in fact, standing on his hands — a slight improvement on the Nebuchadnezzar style — his feet yet fast in the stirrups, and sticking up either side of the beast's neck, very much after the fashion of a goose yoke ; meanwhile he was earnestly calling for help, but holding still for life. From this undignified and no less unpleasant situation his brethren very soon relieved him, and all were rejoiced to learn that, with the exception of a few scratches on his hands — and a few specks of mud — each the size of a man's hat — on his clothes, he was uninjured.

But, favorable as it turned out, the mishap did not pass so easily from the mind of the Puritan brother. He went on to Chattanooga, but an unbroken cloud seemed to rest on his countenance, and after a few days, no doubt full of trouble, he bent his steps towards the Monumental City; where desperate adventures and hair-breadth escapes are not looked upon as mere matters of amusement or subjects for joke.

AMONG the curiosities of army life is this : Dress eighty or a hundred thousand men pretty nearly alike, and everybody resembles his neighbor, and nobody looks like himself. Take those men and sprinkle "a half section," as they say in Illinois, pretty thickly with them, put them under the big umbrellas of the camps, chink a little town full of them till every house swarms like a hive in June, set them all in the usual motion of army life, and then begin to look for your "next best friend," and I wish you joy of your journey ; you might better be "Japhet in search of his father." Perhaps you may remember having passed a familiar friend who was reclining in the chair with his face upturned, as is the fashion of those who come under the barber's hands —

passed without recognizing him. Of course it was the unwonted position that gave him the look of a stranger ; the shadows fell in new places, and the effect was a new impression. You would be struck with this in looking down upon the faces turned towards heaven after a battle, either on the field or in the hospital ; the light falls squarely down ; no shadows under the brow, no shading beneath the chin, and the whole face so clears up, softens and grows delicate, that you may be looking upon a friend and not know it. Death generally impairs the beauty of women, but it sometimes makes homely men wonderfully handsome.

A SOUTHERN MARTYR. — When the secret history of current events at the South is brought to light, there will be revelations of sacrifice and suffering for loyalty to the Union that will show that the age of heroism has not wholly gone by. A letter from a lady in Charleston, of undoubted authenticity, gives an account of a martyr to loyalty whose name will be honored in the history that is to be written of the great events of this age, though now concealed from motives of prudence :

"Poor F—— is dead ; before the fall of Sumter he exerted all his influence, using both pen and voice against the rebellion, until he was thrown into prison. At first he was treated as an ordinary criminal awaiting trial ; but after the battle of Manassas, the Confederates seemed drunk with triumph at their victory, and mad with rage over the vast number of victims who fell in their ranks. I wrote you with what pomp this city mourned her dead ; amid it all, when the Confederate host seemed like to win, F—— was offered freedom and promotion if he would espouse the Confederate cause. His military and scientific attainments were considerable, which made them anxious for his services. 'I have sworn allegiance to the Union,' said he, 'and am not one to break my pledge.' When tempted with promotion if he could be prevailed upon to enlist beneath their banner, he said, 'You cannot buy my loyalty. I love Carolina and the South ; but I love my country better.' Finding him faithful to the flag he loved, he was made to feel the power of his enemies. He was cast into a miserable, damp, ill-ventilated cell, and fed on coarse fare ; half the time neglected by his drunken keeper. His property was confiscated, and his wife and children beggared. Poor fellow ! he sank beneath his troubles, and was soon removed from the persecution of his oppressors. The day before his death he said to his wife : 'Mary, you are beggared because I would not prove disloyal.' 'God be thanked for your fidelity!' replied the wife. 'They have taken your wealth and life, but could not stain your honor, and our children shall boast of an unspotted name. My husband, rejoice in your truth.' She returned to her friends after his death, openly declaring her proudest boast should be, her husband died a martyr to his patriotism. Who shall say the day of heroism has passed?"

PETS IN THE ARMY. — They have the strangest pets in the army, that nobody would dream of "taking to" at home, and yet they are little touches of the gentler nature that give you so much cordial feeling when you see them. One of the boys has carried a red squirrel through "thick and thin" over a thousand miles. "Bun" eats hard tack like a veteran, and has the freedom of the tent. Another's affections overflow upon a slow-winking, unspeculative little owl, captured in Arkansas, and bearing a name with a classical smack to it — Minerva. A third gives his heart to a young Cumberland Mountain bear; but chief among camp pets are dogs. Riding on the saddle-bow, tucked into a baggage wagon, mounted on a knapsack, growling under a gun, are dogs brought to a premature end as to ears and tails, and yellow at that; pug-nosed, square-headed brutes, sleek terriers, delicate morsels of spaniels, "Tray, Blanche, Sweetheart, little dogs and all." A dog, like a horse, comes to love the rattle and crash of musket and cannon. There was one in an Illinois regiment, and regarded as belonging to it, though his name might not be on the muster-roll, that chases half-spent shot as a kitten frolics with a ball of worsted. He has been under fire and twice wounded, and left the tip of his tail at the battle of Stone River. Woe to the man that shall wantonly kill him. But I was especially interested in the fortunes of a little white spaniel that messed with a battery and delighted in the name of "Dot." No matter what was up, that fellow's silken coat must be washed every day; and there was need of it, for when the battery was on the march, they just plunged him into the sponge-bucket — not the tidiest chamber imaginable — that swings like its more peaceful cousin, the tar-bucket, under the rear axle of the gun-carriage — plumped him into that, clapped on the cover, and Dot was good for an inside passage. One day the battery crossed a stream and the water came well up to the guns. Nobody thought of Dot, and when all across, a gunner looked into the bucket; it was full of water, and Dot was as dead as a little dirty door mat. — *B. F. Taylor.*

A CURIOUS STORY. — The Southern papers told a curious story about a ghostly army that was seen down there. Nobody has pretended to give a solution of the mystery; but it was wisely suggested that it was an optical illusion. Here is the story :

"A remakable phenomenon was witnessed a few miles west of Lewisburg, Greenbrier County, Va., on the 1st of October, 1863, about three o'clock P. M., by Mr. Moses Dwyer, who happened to be seated in his porch at the time, as well as by others at or near the house.

"The weather was quite hot and dry; not a cloud could be seen; no wind even ruffled the foliage on the surrounding trees. All things being propitious, the grand panorama began to move. Just over and through the tops of the trees on the adjacent hills, to the south, immense numbers of rolls, resembling cotton or smoke, apparently of the size and shape of doors, seemed to be passing rapidly through the air, yet in beautiful order and regularity. The rolls seemed to be tinged on the edge with light green, so as to resemble a border of deep fringe. There were apparently thousands of them ; they were perhaps an hour in getting by. After they had passed over and out of sight, the scene was changed from the air above to the earth beneath, and became more intensely interesting to the spectators who were witnessing the panorama from different standpoints.

"In the deep valley beneath, thousands upon thousands of (apparently) human beings (men) came in view, travelling in the same direction as the rolls, marching in good order, some thirty or forty in depth, moving rapidly — 'double-quick' — and commenced ascending the almost insurmountable hills opposite, and had the stoop peculiar to men ascending a steep mountain. There seemed to be a great variety in the size of the men ; some were very large, whilst others were quite small. Their arms, legs, and heads could be distinctly seen in motion. They seemed to observe strict military discipline, and there were no stragglers.

"There was uniformity of dress ; white blouses or shirts, with white pants; they were without guns, swords, or anything that indicated 'men of war.' On they came through the valley and over the steep road, crossing the road, and finally passing out of sight, in a direction due north from those who were looking on.

"The gentleman who witnessed this is a man with whom you were once acquainted, Mr. Editor, and as truthful a man as we have in this country, as little liable to be carried away by 'fanciful speculations' as any man living. Four others (respectable ladies) and a servant girl witnessed this strange phenomenon.

"On the 14th instant the same scene, almost identical, was seen by eight or ten of the Confederate pickets at Runger's Mill, and by many of the citizens in that neighborhood ; this is about four miles east of Percy's. It was about an hour passing."

THE CHICKAMAUGA BATTLE-FIELD. — A Southern writer gives the following description :

"As it grows darker, we observe a bright light about one mile in front of us ; which our guide informs us is the burning of their second line of works, which the Yankees fired before leaving. 'You will see some awful sights if you go there,' remarked he. Ere long,

'The pale moon rose up slowly, and calmly she looked down
On the red sands of the battle-field with bloody corses strewn.'

"And wending our way among the grand old oaks of the forest, now scarred and withered by the strife enacted beneath them, and picking our way among the dead bodies of men and horses, we at length reached the works constructed by the enemy on Saturday night, and defended with such obstinacy on Sunday. Notwithstanding I have seen some dozen battle-fields during the war, I have never seen anything to compare with the horrors of the scene presented here. As I stated before, the enemy had set fire to their works when forced to leave them, and the fire had communicated to the forests and lit up the scene far and wide. The dead and wounded lay in heaps, literally piled upon each other, and in many instances the fire had burned them to a cinder, and many of the wounded had their clothes burned off, and their bodies were a perfect blister. The cries of these poor, wretched creatures were awful to hear, and many implored us to kill them and put them out of their misery.

"Upon examining their haversacks, nothing was found but corn bread, and several told me that they had been eating for five days without food or water, and that their leaders did not care for them after they had received a wound. It was a scene long to be remembered — the groups of dead men and horses, and writhing forms of the wounded there in that dreary forest, only seen by the scattered moonbeams as they stole through the branches, and the flickering fire light, as it crept slowly but steadily up to where they lay, and the fearful cries of those who watched its advance, unable to drag their broken limbs beyond the reach of the destroyer; and then the distorted and upturned faces of those whose bodies were lying amidst the grim shadows which fell around, conspicuous among which was the shadow of death. All the pompous pageantry of the scene was gone, and nought remained of all the glory lost and won upon that bloody field save the wretched forms of those who no more will spring forward at the call to arms."

THE BATTLE OF FREDERICKTON. — The victory of the national troops at Frederickton, next to their own bravery and daring, may be ascribed to the agency of an old negro, who informed them of the ambuscade by Jeff Thompson, into which, if they had fallen, a terrible slaughter would have followed. The agency of this negro is described as follows:

"I saw but two white men in the town as we marched through. No one came out to meet our advance. This was a little mysterious and ominous. The negroes told us that the troops had left by the south road, indicating the direction by pointing. While we were sleeping, a Lieutenant was walking a little south of the town, accompanied by an old darky, who said, 'Heap of men, massa, out souf in de timber dar.' 'Guess not; you are mistaken.' 'No mistake, massa.' The Lieutenant thought enough of the remark to mention it to a Major near by, who also remarked, 'It must be a great mistake.' The old darky had followed up, and, hearing the reply, said, 'No mistake, no mistake.' The Major thought he would go with the news to Colonel Carlin, who also thought it a mistake; but, concluding it best not to be fooled, he sent a man to reconnoitre. The timber referred to lies about a mile south of the town, and skirts both sides of the road by which the enemy were said to have left. The scout found the timber all alive with armed men — infantry and cavalry. The old darky had betrayed them, and their trick was all revealed, viz., to get us into an ambush while following them.

"The man galloped back with the information. The soldiers were roused up, ordered into line, and in less than ten minutes our whole brigade was ready to march, and most of the regiments were in motion. The artillerymen had got a twenty-four-pounder out ready to shell the timber; also a six-pounder was placed. The enemy, seeing himself found out, prepared to make the most of it. He had judged well where our cannon would be placed, and had artillery bearing directly on those points. When I first waked up, I heard the report of a six-pounder. 'Hallo! guess they're cleaning out their guns.' This roused all, and, before we had got our traps on, several guns had sounded, and now they bellowed thick and fast. 'A fight, boys! They're at it!' rung along the line.

"The enemy had begun the firing, and performed well, their second shot having smashed a wheel on our six-pounder. Thus the battle began. Not ten minutes had yet elapsed since the time the scout had returned."

COLONEL MOSBY OUTWITTED. — On the 25th of March, 1864, Captain E. B. Gere, of the Griswold Light Cavalry, was sent out from the Union camp, with one hundred and twenty-five men, to the neighborhoods of Berryville and Winchester, Va., on a scout, and encamped at Millwood, some six or eight miles from the former place. After the men had got their fires built, Sergeant Weatherbee, of company B, Corporal Simpson, of company H, and a private, went some two miles from camp to get supper at a farm-house, and while waiting for the long-delayed tea, were surprised to find several revolvers suddenly advance into the room, behind each pair of which was either Colonel Mosby, a rebel Captain, or a Lieutenant, all rather determined men, with "shoot in their eyes," who demanded the immediate surrender of the aforesaid Yankees. The aim being wicked, the three Twenty-firsters saw they were "under a cloud," and so quietly gave up the contest.

Colonel Mosby was much elated with his good fortune, and required his prisoners to follow him supperless on his rounds to his headquarters at Paris; the private, however, while pretending to get his horse, hid himself in the hay and escaped, Mosby not daring to wait and hunt him up.

On the way to Paris the Colonel amused himself by constantly taunting his prisoners with questions. "Were they with Major Cole when he thrashed him at Upperville?" "Were they with Major Sullivan, of the First Veterans, when his men ran away and left him?" "How did they fancy his gray nag? — he took that from a Yankee Lieutenant." "Didn't the Yanks dread him and his men more than they did the regular rebel cavalry?" "How did they" (the prisoners) "like his style of fighting?" and a hundred such remarks, that indicated the man as being more of a vain braggart than a hero.

He was, in the mean time, engaged in gathering his men with the avowed intention of attacking Capt. Gere's force at daylight, and, if possible, of cutting it to pieces. His followers live in the farm-houses of Loudon, Clarke, and Jefferson Counties, and are either rebel soldiers or Union citizens, as the case may require. He would ride up to a house, call Joe or Jake, and tell them that he wanted them at such an hour at the *usual* place — to go and tell Jim or Mose. *Almost every farm turned out somebody in answer to his call,* proving that these men, with the certified oath of allegiance in their pockets, and with passes allowing them to come in and go out of our lines at will, are not only in sympathy with the enemy, but are themselves *perjured rebels.*

When they arrived at Paris, Colonel Mosby dismounted and stepped into the house where he had his headquarters, leaving his pistols in the holsters. The Lieutenant, with drawn revolver, watched the prisoners, while the Captain endeavored to find an orderly to take the horses. Corporal Simpson, who had been marking the road for future use, and had been long looking for it, saw his chance, and pretended to tie his horse, but really putting his foot into the stirrup of Mosby's saddle, and laying hold of one of the overlooked pistols. The Lieutenant, detecting the move, fired at him, when S. shot him through the heart with the weapon he had secured. The Captain turned round and fired, and Colonel Mosby came to the door to see "what all that —— row was about," just in time to hear a bullet whiz unpleasantly close to his head, that S. fired at him, "just for luck," as he and his comrade left — yelling back: "*Colonel Mosby, how do you like our style of fighting? We belong to the Twenty-first New York.*" And away they went, leaving Colonel Mosby dismounted, and outwitted of his best horse, saddle, pistols, and overcoat, two Yankee prisoners, and with at least one vacancy among his commissioned officers. Corporal Simpson rode twelve miles to the camp, closely followed by the Sergeant, and gave Captain Gere such notice of the enemy's intentions that they thought best not to pitch in at the appointed time.

OBEDIENCE TO ORDERS. — When Stonewall Jackson was ordered from the valley of Western Virginia to take part in the operations of General Lee against the national troops threatening Richmond, General Whiting's division was sent to join him. In this division was the celebrated Texas brigade of General Hood. These men had never seen Jackson, and knew him only by reputation. As the movement was of the highest importance, it was necessary to keep it as secret as possible. Orders were accordingly issued to the men to refuse to give information of any kind to civilians on the route, and to answer all questions with, "I don't know."

On the second day of the march, General Jackson saw two of Hood's men leave the ranks and start for a cherry tree in the neighboring field. Riding up to them, he demanded, sternly, —

"Where are you going?"

"I don't know," replied one of the men, coolly, not knowing to whom he was speaking.

"What is your name?"

"I don't know."

"What regiment do you belong to?"

"I don't know."

"What does this mean?" asked the General, turning to the other man, who stood by silently.

"Why, you see," replied the soldier, "Old Stonewall gave orders yesterday that we are not to know anything until after the next fight, and we mean to obey him."

The General smiled — he rarely laughed — and sent the men back to their regiment.

AFTER THE FIGHT.

ONE of the boys lies dead in his tent,
  All alone.
Soldier, go in, go in,
And smooth back his hair,
And close the dead eyes,
  So dreamily blue,
  That are staring straight through
The night, towards the skies,
  Where his soul has gone!

Ay, and we made a desperate charge
  Through the smoke,
And the terrible roar, for the guns
That had growled all day
From the rebel right —
  Rank after rank,
  On our wearied flank,
Had gone down in the fight,
  When those cannons spoke.

Scorching hot, from their grinning jaws,
  With a shout,
Came the whirling shot
And the bursting shell,
And the air grew gray
  With the drifting smoke,
  That quivered and broke
And heaved and fell,
  When the roar burst out.

And Death rode over the battle-field,
  Through the storm,
Like the withering breath of a curse ;
And his voice rang out,
With a shrill report,
  When the rifles flashed
  And the bayonet gashed
The quivering heart,
  And the knife struck home.

Up through the smoke and the driving shot,
  And the strife,
Ring the bugle-notes sounding a charge ;
And the spurs strike deep,
And away we plunge,
  With a deafening shout,
  And our swords are out,
For the ghastly lunge
  At the foeman's life.

Still are the guns for a space, as though
    Without breath ;
And our men go gallantly down,
    With unbroken ranks,
And a shout for the " Stars."
    There's a swift, bright flash
    From the guns, and a crash,
And the red earth jars
    'Neath the thunder of death.

And many a brave boy fell when that fire
    Burst out.
Yet we hurled the foe heavily back,
    In the fierce, wild fight,
And the victory was won ;
    But the dead lay white
    In the ghastly light,
As the sinking sun
    Looked in on the rout.

This one came from the fight with a ball
    In his side ;
And he sleeps so peacefully now
That we'll leave him to rest
By our camp on the hill.
    Yet never will come,
    To the loved ones at home,
Who watch for him still,
    The Soldier who died.

THOMAS' GREAT FIGHT. — The following graphic description of the contest at Chickamauga was written by a correspondent of the Cincinnati Gazette, on Monday, September 21, 1863, the day after the second day's operations.

"As soon as the sun was fairly risen, I mounted my horse, intending to ride to the extreme left of our line, and thence proceed from it to right, so as to get as accurate an idea of it as possible before the real work of the day should commence. Riding about a mile, I saw troops coming into the road from the woods to the east of it, and had I not perceived through my glass that they were habited in blue, should have judged from the direction whence they came, that they were a portion of the rebel army. Suddenly I saw a courier shoot out from the crowd, and coming towards me hatless and with frantic speed.

"As he came, a dozen rifle cracks from the woods skirting a cornfield along which he was riding, informed me that hostile demonstrations of some kind were being made in our immediate vicinity. I halted until the courier came up. He delivered his despatches to another horseman, who immediately started with them towards the head-quarters of General Thomas. I then asked the hatless courier what troops those were ahead. He informed me they were two brigades (Colonel Mitchell's and Colonel McCook's) of General Gordon's corps, who had been skirmishing the day before in the neighborhood of Roid's Bridge and of Ringgold, as I have already described. They had come to form a junction with the main army, had halted, and were waiting for orders.

"'Are you going back to them now?' I inquired of the courier.

"'I am,' he replied, 'but it is hazardous business; for the woods just on the other side of that cornfield are lined with rebel sharpshooters, who fire at any one passing along the road ; just now they fired quite a volley at me as I came through.'

"As I wished to reach these troops of General Granger's in order to learn from them what they had been doing the day before, this answer was a little discouraging. Nevertheless, my curiosity finally prevailed over my apprehensions, and myself and the courier started back upon a full gallop. Of course the sharpshooters paid us their respects, and more than one bullet whistled uncomfortably close to our ears while we were running this dangerous gantlet. But fortunately none of them hit either of us, although one cut the hair from my horse's mane.

"Scarcely had I reached our troops in safety when an order from General Rosecrans, which had reached General Granger by another route, directed the two brigades to fall back at once to Rossville, get a supply of rations for the three days, and hold themselves in readiness to march at a moment's notice. As the close proximity of the rebels rendered it somewhat difficult just then to reach General Bird's men, who were nearest to me on the right, I 'fell back' with General Granger's troops, and remained in the vicinity of Rossville until the sound of battle in the direction whence I had come attracted my attention. A wild gallop back to the left immediately ensued. I was accompanied in the ride by a member of the Corps of Topographical Engineers, attached to General Rosecrans' headquarters, and a citizen who had accompanied him in the morning on an excursion undertaken for the purpose of gaining knowledge of the surrounding country.

"All three of us agreed that it was a hazardous experiment to attempt making our way back to the army, the nearest portion of which was distant half a dozen miles. But the citizen wanted to get back, the engineer said he ought to be back, and my own duties in that direction were absolutely imperative. So off we started.

"Here comes a single soldier, covered with dust and sweat. Let us question him.

"'Where do you belong?' 'To the regular brigade.'

"'Has it been engaged this morning?' 'I should think it had.'

"'With what result?' 'It was nearly all cut to pieces.'

"'What regiment is yours?' 'The Sixteenth United States infantry.'

"'Did it suffer much?' 'Only thirty or forty of its members are left.'

"Here is a man with an arm roughly bandaged and very bloody. The blood has dried upon it, and hangs to it in great black clots. 'Who are you?' 'Private ——, of the Thirty-eighth Indiana.' 'What news have you?' 'Bad news enough.' 'Has your regiment been in the fight?' 'If it has not, no one has.' 'With what result?' 'One third of its number are killed and wounded.' 'Were you whipped?' 'Our brigade was left unsupported, overpowered by numbers, and compelled for a time to give way.' 'Is Colonel Scribner safe?' 'So far as I know, he is.'

"Another with a ghastly wound in the head has upon his jacket the red stripes which show him to be an artilleryman. 'Whose battery do you belong to?' 'Gunither's.' 'Why, that is the regular battery belonging to General King's brigade; what has it been doing?' 'It has been taken by the enemy.' 'Can it be possible?' 'It is, but I have heard since that it was retaken.' 'How came it lost?' 'The infantry supports gave way, and the horses being nearly all killed, of course, the guns were captured.'

"The stream grew stronger and stronger. Stragglers were run over by wagons dashing back towards the rear. Ambulances, filled with wounded, came in long procession from towards where the battle was raging. Men with wounds of every imaginable description, not affecting their locomotion, came staggering by on foot, and scores even of those who had been shot in their lower limbs, hobbled slowly on through blinding masses of dust, which at times concealed everything from view.

"The brigade commanded by Colonel B. F. Scribner, Thirty-eighth Indiana, one of the very first in the army, was left particularly exposed, as its right flank had been somewhat too far advanced where it had taken position in the morning. Almost before its pickets were driven in, it found itself literally surrounded by thrice its numbers, who came on with their infernal yells, pouring volley after volley of deadly bullets into the very bosom of this gallant brigade. For a moment it was thrown into confusion, and that moment sufficed to place the rebels upon its front, flanks, and rear. But it was not destined to surrender. The Second, Thirty-third, and Ninety-fourth Ohio, the Thirty-eighth Indiana, the Tenth Wisconsin, and Loomis' battery are composed of the best material in their respective States, and their commander, Scribner, had succeeded in infusing into them his own magnanimous and gallant spirit. Gathering together their broken ranks under the infernal fire which every instant mowed them down, and following their heroic leader, they charged the dense legions surrounding them, and like a whirlwind in a forest, tore their way through.

"But, alas! the guns of the immortal First Michigan battery were left behind — those black, stern-looking rifle cannon, each one of which I had come to regard with a feeling of almost reverential awe, because upon a dozen battle-fields I had seen them flinging destruction into the ranks of traitors, and never knew them once turned against a legion of my country's enemies which they did not scatter like leaves before the blast. Even in the opinion of the rebels themselves, Loomis had made these guns invincible. They were commanded now by a young man who, possessing naturally the noblest qualities, had thoroughly learned the lessons of his teacher, and promised to prove a most worthy successor, even to Loomis himself — Lieutenant Van Pelt. Van Pelt loved his pieces with the same unselfish devotion which he manifested for his life. In the desperate conflict which broke around Scribner's brigade, he managed the battery with much dexterity and coolness, and for some moments rocked the very trees over the heads of the rebels by the fiery blasts from his guns. But his horses were shot down. Many of his artillerists were killed or wounded. The infantry supporting him had been compelled to turn and cut their way through the enemy, and a horde of traitors rushed to the muzzles of the now harmless pieces. Van Pelt, almost alone, stationed himself in front of them, and drew his sword. 'Scoundrels,' said he, 'dare not touch these guns!' The miserable barbarians, unable to appreciate true heroism, brutally murdered him where he stood. The history of the war furnishes not an incident more touching, more sublime, than the death of Lieutenant Van Pelt.

"All the guns of the battery, save one, fell into the enemy's hands.

"Along the entire line of the left and centre there were similar instances of heroism, only two or three of which I have time to mention.

"At one time the guns of the Fourth Indiana battery (Captain Bush) were all in the hands of the enemy, but were retaken subsequently, by a simultaneous charge of the infantry and artillerymen. This battery is attached to General Starkweather's brigade.

"During the fierce assault upon the First division, the Second Ohio, being in confusion, was rallied by General Baird in person, and led back to a most effective charge.

"Major-General J. J. Reynolds, who combines the chivalrous courage of an olden knight with the cool, calm ability of a Turenne, had time, not only to keep his own division in effective order, but to give his generous assistance to the forces around him. A tremendous onslaught of the enemy broke General Palmer's lines, and scattered several of his regiments in wild dismay towards the rear. Amongst these was the Sixth Ohio, which, in charge of the fine-spirited Anderson, had, up to that moment, nobly maintained its ground. General Reynolds, perceiving the danger, quick as lightning threw himself amongst the brave but broken Guthries.

"'Boys,' he shouted, 'are you the soldiers of the Sixth Ohio who fought with me at Cheat Mountain? You never turned your backs upon traitors in Virginia; will you do it here?'

"'No, no,' they screamed almost frantically; 'lead us back, lead us back!'

"From every quarter came rushing up the scattered fragments of the regiment; with magic swiftness they re-formed the ranks; with General Reynolds at their head, they charged the insolent enemy, and, after a moment's struggle, every rebel in front of them, not killed or wounded, was in confused retreat.

"The rebels had been manoeuvring all day on Friday about the position at Gordon's Mill, and seeing its great strength, had menaced our left flank, doubtless with the express purpose of compelling General Rosecrans to abandon it. As the left must be protected at all hazards, their plan partially succeeded, and the immense transfer of Thomas from right to left on Friday night, so far suited their designs. But it rendered our own left so strong that it became impossible for the rebels to turn it, as they had all along hoped and intended to do. The attempt, on our part, to hold Gordon's Mill after this transfer, perhaps, occasioned too great a lengthening of our lines, and consequently too little solidity. True, it seemed every way adapted to prevent the enemy from flanking us upon the right; but the simple withdrawal of our right wing to Mission Ridge, allowing it to rest there, would have fully secured that flank, enabled us to bid defiance to the rebels in that direction, greatly contracted our front, and released, for immediate service on Saturday, the splendid divisions of Negley and Wood. The entire distance over which the line extended was little short of three and a half miles.

"It was between ten and eleven when Croton's brigade, of Brannan's division, going down to ford the creek, just opposite their position, encountered the enemy, who was advancing in force, and, after a gallant combat, was driven back. Reënforcements immediately coming up from the remainder of Brannan's division, the rebels were, in turn, driven pell-mell towards the ford. Another fierce charge, by a largely increased force of the enemy, pushed back the whole of Brannan's division, involving General Baird, who at once became fiercely engaged. The regulars, outflanked, after the withdrawal of Brannan's men, fought like tigers, but rolled back and over Scribner's brigade (the right of which, being rather too far advanced, was crumpled up, and the brigade literally surrounded), until, by unparalleled gallantry, it cut its way through. The storm, rolling from left to right, fell next upon Johnston, and almost simultaneously upon Reynolds, who both fought with desperate valor, wavering at times, but again regaining their firmness, — giving back a little, but again advancing, — until the troops of Brannan and Baird, rallied by their able leaders, and by the personal exertions of Thomas himself, whose courage was as conspicuous as his coolness, came up once more to the work.

"Then the order was issued for the entire line to advance; and nothing in history exceeds in grandeur the charge of that powerful corps. Longstreet's men from Virginia were directly opposed to the troops of Thomas; and although they fought with stubborn determination, they could not for an instant check the slow and stately march of our battalions. In vain they rallied and re-rallied; in vain they formed double lines, which fired simultaneously; in vain they wheeled their cannons into a score of new positions. Thomas moved resistlessly on. Much of our artillery lost in the morning was recaptured. Seven pieces were taken from the enemy. They had been pushed already three quarters of a mile, and Longstreet was threatened with actual annihilation, when a new danger caused Thomas to halt.

"While our left was so remorselessly driving the rebels, Polk and Hill, collecting their chosen legions, threw them, with great impetuosity, upon Palmer and Van Cleve, in order to effect a diversion in favor of Longstreet. An obstinate contest ensued, but the overpowering numbers of the enemy speedily broke to pieces large portions of our two divisions, especially Van Cleve's. In fact, the rout of this part of our line was becoming as complete as that of the enemy's right, when Davis, who had been marching up as rapidly as possible to intersect with Van Cleve's left, arrived upon the ground, went in most gallantly, and, for a time, restored in that locality the fortunes of the day. But the enemy, knowing that all depended upon his effecting a diversion in favor of the defeated Longstreet, massed nearly the whole of his available force, hurled it upon Van Cleve, and Davis drove the former to the left and the latter to the right, and entered boldly the opening thus made. It was just at this juncture that Thomas' troops, whose attention had been called to the extreme danger of our centre, began to return. Reynolds immediately sent the heroic Wilder to the assistance of Davis, and the celebrated brigade of mounted infantry at first scattered the enemy in terror before them. But the persevering rebels rallying again, and charging in fresh numbers, even Wilder began to fall slowly back. General Sheridan, who had been following after Davis, now came up, and led Colonel Bradley's brigade into the fight. It held its own nobly, until the rebels, in large force, getting possession of a piece of timber near its flank, opened upon it an enfilading fire, which compelled it to give way.

"But now new actors appeared upon the scene. Wood and Negley, who had gallantly repelled the assaults of the enemy at Owen's Ford (assaults intended as a feint to conceal the design of the rebels against our left), came up to the rescue. Their troops went to work with a will. The progress of the enemy against Davis, Van Cleve, and Sheridan was speedily checked. Reynolds, returning from the pursuit of Longstreet, assisted in rallying the broken battalions of Palmer. Thousands of our scattered troops reorganized almost of their own accord. Baird, Brannan, and Johnston resumed their places. A consuming fire swept all along our front. The rebels retired everywhere before it; and before sunset our line was again in battle array upon almost precisely the ground held that morning.

"The morrow came. No sound of crackling musketry, or roaring cannon, or bursting shell disturbed the peacefulness of that Sabbath morning. The Sabbath! Yes, it was the blessed day of rest — rest given in mercy by kind Heaven to ungrateful man. Will the battle be renewed to-day? If so, it will be by the action of the enemy, for General Rosecrans does not willingly fight on the Sabbath. The first hour after sunrise passed. 'Surely,' said our officers and soldiers, 'there will be no fight, for if the enemy had intended to attack us, he would, following his usual tactics, have fallen upon us at daybreak.'

"Two hours more had gone by, and some dropping musketry began to be heard along the various parts of our lines. Finally, at about ten o'clock there were several fierce volleys, and the loud booming of half a dozen pieces of artillery announcing that the enemy had again, as on the day before, assaulted our left.

"And now that the battle has begun, let us glance one moment at the contending forces. On one side is our old army which fought at Stone River, reënforced by two divisions (Brannan's and Reynolds' corps,) and Starkweather's brigade of Baird's division. But counterbalancing these to some extent, Post's brigade of Davis' division, and Wagner's of Wood's, were both absent. We might or might not also rely for assistance upon Steadman's division of General Granger's corps.

"Opposed to these was the old army of the Tennessee, which Bragg had so long commanded, Longstreet's formidable corps from Virginia, one half of Johnston's army from Mississippi, Buckner's division from East Tennessee, Dabney Maury's division from Mobile, Brigadier-General Lee's command from Atlanta, and from twelve to fifteen thousand fresh troops in the service of the State of Georgia — in all, amounting to at least seventy-five thousand men. The Union army confronting them was certainly not more than fifty-five thousand strong.

"The fight upon the extreme left commenced by a desperate assault of the enemy upon General John Beatty's brigade of Negley's division. The brigade, as well as its famous leader, stood their ground nobly, but being somewhat isolated from the remainder of the line, finally retired. It will be remembered that the other brigades of Negley's division were posted much farther to the right. A desire to reunite the two portions of his command induced General Rosecrans to send General Wood to take General Negley's place in line until the latter should effect the reunion of his brigades. Wood proceeded immediately to execute the order, filling up the gap as Negley retired. The rebels, understanding the movement of Negley's to be a retreat, immediately advanced their skirmishers, not only here, but all along the left, and the fighting at once became terrific, as I have described. The rebels, however, soon ceased to attack General Wood's front, and for a time appeared to devote their entire attention to General Thomas. I went down to the extreme left of General Wood's position about this time, and looking thence into some cornfields, could see the desperate efforts of the enemy to break the lines of Brannan and Reynolds. The soldiers of these two noble divisions were lying behind rude breastworks of logs and rails constructed the night before. Their artillery in the rear fired over their heads, and it really seemed as if that long line of defence was some immense serpent, instinct with hideous life, and breathing continually from his huge, rough sides volumes of smoke and flame. Colonel Vanderveer, Thirty-fifth Ohio, of Brannan's division, was fighting here with a brigade second to but few in the service. The Colonel himself is a true hero, and the command and the commander are worthy of each other. Here also was the brave

and able Turchin, with a brigade composed principally of Ohio troops, who won for themselves and the State that sent them forth immortal honor during the conflicts of that day.

"Again and again the rebel lines, advancing from the cover of the woods into the open cornfields, charged with impetuous fury and terrific yells towards the breastworks of logs and rails; but each time the fiery blasts from our batteries and battalions swept over and around them, and their ranks were crumbled and swept away as a bank of loose clay washed by a rushing flood. But as fast as one line fell off another appeared, rushing sternly on over the dead and bleeding bodies of their fallen comrades. Longstreet's corps was seeking to regain its lost laurels of yesterday. D. H. Hill, at the head of Hardee's old corps, was lending them the assistance of a division, and Buckner's troops were throwing their weight into the scale. Thomas fought only with his forces of Saturday weakened by Saturday's heavy losses. It was an unequal contest, and a pang of agony shot through my heart as I saw our exhausted veterans begin to waver. To waver in the face of the charging, shouting, thundering host which confronted them, was to lose all; and the next moment wave after wave of the rebel sea came surging down towards the breastworks, dashing madly against and over the barrier, and greedily swallowing up its defenders, with all their matériel. Never was resistance more stubborn and determined, but never was attack prosecuted with more devilish pertinacity.

"Meantime, as General Reynolds was so sorely pressed, General Wood was ordered to march instantly by the left flank, pass Brannan, and go to his relief. Davis and Sheridan were to shift over to the left, and thus close up the line. As the occasion was urgent, General Wood drew in his skirmishers with considerable haste, and the rebels, for the second time mistaking a withdrawal for a flight, pressed forward like a torrent, and poured into the ranks of General Wood a storm of musket balls, canister, and grape. Moving upon the double-quick, the men endeavored for a time to keep their files in order, but as that pitiless storm of lead and iron continued to be hurled against them, the regiments began to spread out like a fan, wider and wider, until finally they were torn to flinters. This was especially the case with the brigade commanded by Colonel Buell. The undaunted Wood, with Harker's brigade, comparatively intact, passed on to his destination.

"Here was the great turning-point in the battle. Here, indeed, the battle was lost.

"Davis, coming up to fill the vacancy occasioned by Wood's withdrawal, was caught upon the left flank by the fiery rebel torrent now pouring through the opening and pushed off towards the right in utter disorder, like a door which is swung back upon its hinges, and shattered by the same blow. Van Cleve and what remained of Palmer were struck upon the other side, and shivered as a sapling by a thunderbolt. Even the personal exertions of Rosecrans himself, who, with drawn sword, and at the head of his devoted staff, endeavored to check the rout, were ineffectual.

"After that fatal break our line of battle was not again re-formed during the day.

"It was about half past twelve, when, hearing a heavy cannonade open upon the right, I galloped over in that direction to see what it might mean. A longitudinal gap in Mission Ridge admits the Rossville road into Chattanooga valley, and skirts along a large cornfield at the mouth of the gap. Looking across the cornfield from the gap, you see thick woods upon the other side. The cornfield itself is a sort of 'cove' in the ridge; and here were numbers of all sorts of army vehicles mingled with the debris of dismantled and discomfited batteries. Fragments of Davis' flying squadrons had also lodged in this field.

"While I stood gazing upon this scene from the summit of the ridge, some rebel skirmishers appeared in the skirts of the woods opposite the gap I have mentioned, and flung perhaps a dozen musket balls into the field. Instantly men, animals, vehicles, became a mass of struggling, cursing, shouting, frightened life. Everything and everybody appeared to dash headlong for the narrow gap, and men, horses, mules, ambulances, baggage wagons, ammunition wagons, artillery carriages, and caissons were rolled and tumbled together in a confused, inextricable, and finally motionless mass, completely blocking up the mouth of the gaps. Nearly all this booty subsequently fell into the hands of the enemy. Sickened and disgusted with the spectacle, I turned away to watch the operations of General Thomas' corps, upon which alone depended the safety of the army.

"General Thomas had withdrawn his men almost entirely from the valley, and taken up a position on the side of Mission Ridge. His left still rested upon the Lafayette road, and his right upon the ridge near the gap I have already spoken of. Here were collected the shattered remains of the powerful corps which had so long breasted the fierce assaults of the enemy in the forenoon.

"Not long was the new line of battle permitted to remain idle. Cannon bellowed against it; missiles of every kind were hurled against it; shells burst above it; rifle balls went tearing through it; but still it remained firm.

"It was certain, however, as truth itself, that unless assistance should reach it from some quarter, and that right speedily, it must at length succumb, for the rebel leaders, emboldened by the rout of McCook and Crittenden, were gathering their hosts to hurl them in a last mighty effort against the feeble band that confronted them. Whence should that succor come?

"Suddenly a vast cloud of dust was seen to rise above the trees away to the left, and a few minutes afterwards long lines of men emerged from the woods, crossed the Lafayette road, and began advancing towards us over the fields. Their discipline seemed very perfect, and it was an imposing pageant when, as they came, their banners fluttered above their heads, and their glittering arms flashed back the sunlight through the thick clouds of dust.

"Captain Johnson, of General Negley's staff, who, on being severed from his own division, had immediately reported to General Thomas for duty, had already, at great personal risk, ascertained that the advancing battalions were infantry; and now the question arose, was it our own or the enemy's. Hope and fear alternately agitated our bosoms, until at last, looking through our glasses, we could clearly distinguish the red and blue, with the white crescent! It was the battle flag of General Granger, and the troops we saw were two brigades, Mitchell's and Whitaker's, of Steadman's strong division.

"As soon as General Granger had reported to General Thomas for duty, he was sent by the latter to bring over an ammunition train from the Rossville road. The train had fallen into the hands of the enemy; but the march in search of it brought Steadman at once into contact with the rebels, and a desperate conflict immediately ensued. It was now that the brilliant courage of Colonel John G. Mitchell, commanding one of General Steadman's brigades, became conspicuous. Now General Whitaker had an opportunity of baptizing in glory the star recently placed upon his shoulder; and now the troops of the reserve corps, comparatively unused to battle, had an opportunity of testing their mettle. Nobly did all pass through the ordeal; and although once thrown into confusion by the concentrated fire from a score of rebel regiments and half as many batteries, they *rallied under the fire*, and drove the enemy from a hill almost as formidable as that which formed the key of General Thomas' position. The rebels made one desperate endeavor to retake this position, but were bloodily repulsed; and almost for the first time since the fight began there was a lull in the fearful storm.

"An hour passed by, and it became evident that Bragg would not be foiled in his attempt to annihilate our gallant army without another effort. Polk's corps, assisted by the Georgia State troops, by Dabney Maury's division, and by various detached fragments of the rebel army, were to try their hands upon the heroic band, who, as the forlorn hope of the army, still held the hill. Our feeble ranks were gathered up. The thinned battalions were brought closer together. The dozen pieces of artillery were planted to sweep all approaches to the hill; and each man, looking at his neighbor, vowed, some mentally and others audibly, to die right there, if it were necessary, for their country, for freedom, and for mankind!

"All along the woods skirting the cleared fields at the south-eastern foot of the hill, in the hollows and ravines to the right, and away to the left, upon and beyond the Lafayette road, the rebel legions were seen gathering for the onset.

"Just before the storm broke, the brave and high-souled Garfield was perceived making his way to the headquarters of General Thomas. He had come to be present at the final contest; and in order to do so had ridden all the way from Chattanooga, passing through a fiery ordeal upon the road. His horse was shot under him, and his orderly was killed by his side. Still he had come through, he scarcely knew how; and here he was, to inspire fresh courage into the hearts of the brave soldiers who were holding the enemy at bay, to bring them words of greeting from General Rosecrans, and to inform them that the latter was reorganizing the scattered troops, and as fast as possible would hurry them forward to their relief.

"The fight around the hill now raged with terror inexperienced before, even upon this terrible day. Our soldiers were formed in two lines, and as each marched up to the crest and fired a deadly volley at the advancing foe, it fell back a little way, the men lay down upon the ground to load their guns, and the second line advanced to take their place. These, too, in their turn, retired; and thus the line kept marching back and forth, and delivering their withering volleys till the very brain grew dizzy as it watched them. And all the time not a man wavered. Every motion was executed with as much precision as though the troops were on a holiday parade, notwithstanding the flower of the rebel army was swarming around the foot of the hill, and a score of cannon was thundering from three sides upon it. Every attempt of the enemy to scale it was repulsed; and the gallant Harker looked with pride upon his lines, standing or lying just where they were when the fight began.

"But our troops are no longer satisfied with the defensive. General Turchin, at the head of his brigade, charged into the rebel lines, and cut his way out again, bringing with him three hundred prisoners. Other portions of this brave band followed Turchin's example, until the legions of the enemy were fairly driven back to the ground they occupied previous to commencing the last fight. Thus did twelve or fifteen thousand men, animated by heroic impulses and inspired by worthy leaders, save from destruction the army of the Cumberland. Let the nation honor them as they deserve!

"At night General Thomas fell back to Rossville, four miles from Chattanooga, around and in which city the army lies to-night.

"Our losses have been most severe, and can scarcely fall short of one thousand seven hundred killed, and eight thousand wounded. Colonel Barnett tells me that our loss in artillery will not fall short of fifty pieces. Our deficiency in transportation and baggage cannot now be estimated."

THE BRIER-WOOD PIPE.

BY CHARLES DAWSON SHANLY.

HA! Bully for me, again, when my turn for picket is over;
And now for a smoke, as I lie, with the moonlight, out in the clover.
My pipe, it's only a knot from the root of the brier-wood tree;
But it turns my heart to the northward — Harry gave it to me.

And I'm but a rough, at best — bred up to the row and the riot;
But a softness comes over my heart when all are asleep and quiet.
For many a time in the night strange things appear to my eye,
As the breath from my brier-wood pipe sails up between me and the sky.
Last night a beautiful spirit arose with the wisping smoke;
O, I shook, but my heart felt good as it spread out its hands and spoke,
Saying, "I am the soul of the brier; we grew at the root of a tree
Where lovers would come in the twilight, two ever, for company;
Where lovers would come in the morning, ever but two, together,
When the flowers were full in their blow, the birds in their song and feather;
Where lovers would come in the noon-time, loitering, never but two,
Looking in each other's eyes, like the pigeons that kiss and coo.
And O, the honeyed words that came when the lips were parted,
And the passion that glowed in eyes, and the lightning looks that darted.
Enough: love dwells in the pipe, so ever it glows with fire!
I am the soul of the bush, and spirits call me 'sweet-brier.'"

That's what the brier-wood said, as nigh as my tongue can tell;
And the words went straight to my heart, like the stroke of the fire bell!
To-night I lie in the clover watching the blossomy smoke;
I'm glad the boys are asleep, for I ain't in the humor to joke.
I lie in the hefty clover: between me and the moon
The smoke from my pipe arises: my heart will be quiet soon.
My thoughts are back in the city. I'm everything I've been.
I hear the bell from the tower, I run with the swift machine.
I see the red shirts crowding around the engine-house door;
The foreman's hail through the trumpet comes with a sullen roar.
The reel in the Bowery dance-house, the row in the beer saloon,
Where I put in my licks at Big Paul, come between me and the moon.
I hear the drum and the bugle, the tramp of the cowskin boots;
We are marching to the capital, the Fire Zouave recruits!
White handkerchiefs move before me: O, but the sight is pretty!
On the white marble steps, as we march through the heart of the city.
Bright eyes and clasping arms, and lips that bid us good hap,
And the splendid lady who gave me the Havelock for my cap.
O, up from my pipe-cloud rises, between me and the moon,
A beautiful white-robed lady: my heart will be quiet soon.

The lovely golden-haired lady ever in dreams I see,
Who gave me the snow-white Havelock — but what
  does she care for me?
Look at my grimy features : mountains between us
  stand —
I with my sledge-hammer knuckles, she with her
  jewelled hand!
What care I? The day that's dawning may see me,
  when all is over,
With the red stream of my life-blood staining the
  hefty clover.
Hark! the reveille sounding out on the morning
  air!
Devils are we for the battle — will there be angels
  there?
Kiss me again, sweet-brier! The touch of your lips
  to mine
Brings back the white-robed lady, with hair like the
  golden wine!

PRESIDENT LINCOLN'S INAUGURATION, MARCH 4, 1865. — The days of omens and presages are past. The Roman warriors and sages were frequently influenced, in the most important acts, by the feeding of the sacred chickens, the flight of a flock of birds, or the quivering of the flesh of a victim.

The appearances of nature which take place at the time of great historical events are often long remembered, and subsequent occurrences reflect upon them a striking and painful emphasis.

This is true of the following incident, which was witnessed, at the second inauguration of President Lincoln, by the editor of this volume. The 4th of March, 1865, as commonly happens in the latitude of Washington, was one of those fitful March days when cloud and sunshine chase each other, in vivid alternation, across the landscape. The editor was standing, with Hon. S. B. Colby, Register of the Treasury, on the Senate portico of the Capitol, in the midst of the vast and expectant throng, who were awaiting, with suppressed enthusiasm, the stepping out of that tall, familiar figure that had for four years moved at the head of our public affairs. He who now sits in the Executive chair had just made that famous speech in which the plebeian extraction of a great number of the prominent men of America was so distinctly brought forward. All eyes were now turned in one direction; and at this instant the gaunt figure, surmounted by the kindly face, was seen moving forward to the place where the Chief Justice of the United States was waiting to administer the sacred oath of office.

At this moment a bar of bright sunlight, bursting through the rifts of a flying cloud, rested for a moment upon the head of Lincoln, and surrounded it as with a halo, which was greeted with murmurs of admiration, and exclamations of delight, from thousands of lips. It lasted but an instant. The deep shadow of a storm-cloud swept across the Capitol, and the vast crowd by which it was surrounded; and that head, which a moment before had been bright with an unnatural lustre, was shrouded now in gloom.

A month had hardly passed before hundreds who saw the phenomenon were wondering whether the tragedy of April had not been dimly prefigured in the flying clouds of that fitful day in March.

INCIDENT OF THE SOUTHERN SERVICE. — Von Borcke, chief of staff to General J. E. B. Stuart, in his reminiscences of the war, relates the following incident:

"During the night, there came a telegram for General Stuart, which I opened, with his other despatches, and found to contain the most painful intelligence. It announced the death of little Flora, our chief's lovely and dearly-loved daughter, five years of age — the favorite of her father and of his military family. This sweet child had been dangerously ill for some time, and more than once had Mrs. Stuart summoned her husband to Flora's bedside; but she received only the response of the true soldier: 'My duty to my country must be performed before I can give way to the feelings of a father.' I went at once to acquaint my General with the terrible tidings; and when I had awakened him, perceiving, from the grave expression of my features, that something had gone wrong, he said, 'What is it, Major? Are the Yankees advancing?' I handed him the telegram without a word. He read it, and, the tenderness of the father's heart overcoming the firmness of the warrior, he threw his arms around my neck, and wept bitter tears upon my breast. My dear General never recovered from this cruel blow. Many a time afterwards, during our rides together, he would speak to me of his lost child. Light blue flowers recalled her to him. In the glancing sunbeams he caught the golden tinge of her hair; and whenever he saw a child with such eyes and hair, he could not help tenderly embracing it. He thought of her even on his death-bed, when, drawing me towards him, he whispered, 'My dear friend, I shall soon be with little Flora again!'"

INCIDENTS OF GETTYSBURG. — A soldier who participated in the battle relates the following: "Let me mention something which is, after all, the real occasion for the writing of this letter. I have a Bible taken from the knapsack of a dead rebel which has a history. On the first cover of the Bible (which fastens with a clasp) is the name of 'Miss Almira Alice Wilson, Presqu'Isle, August 18, '52 or '62' — I cannot clearly see which. On the first leaf is the name of 'Moses C. Ames, or Amors.' Upon the opposite page is the name of 'Wm. M. Nichols, company F, 21st regiment, Georgia V. I., May 27, 1863.' Upon the last leaf and cover is written, 'William Martin Nichols' Book; picked up on the battle-field near Chancellorsville, May 31, 1863.' To which I have added, 'Taken from the knapsack of a dead rebel at Warehouse Hospital, Gettysburg, July, 1863.' My theory is this: Miss Wilson gave the Bible to

Moses Ames; Ames, like a loyal son of Maine, enlisted and fought at Chancellorsville. Either killed, wounded, or a prisoner, his knapsack was rifled by a Georgian named Nichols. Nichols in turn was wounded and captured at Gettysburg, where he dies, and the Bible falls into the hands of a nurse from Maine, who is anxious to restore it to the original owner.

"Among the wounded in the battle were several Germans, from a German regiment, and when one of them died the boys proposed the German chaplain should officiate at the funeral. Accordingly a grave was dug, and the body, attended by many comrades, was borne to its last resting-place. Arriving there the German chaplain began:

"'Mine frens, dis ish de *first time* dis man has *died*.' Observing a titter among his audience, he began again in a tone of Christian severity:

"'Mine frens, I say, dis ish de *first* time dis man has died.' Human nature could bear no more, and the boys shouted. Indignant at the disrespect shown him as a minister, the chaplain turned round, pointed to the open grave, and simply saying, 'Stick him in,' marched away. Remember I do not vouch for the story, but I laughed over it till I cried when I heard it told."

A MARCH IN TENNESSEE. — J. P. Glezen, in the story of a march from Montgomery to London, Tennessee, relates the following incidents: "A tramp in these mountains at this time (October, 1863) affords few things calculated to cheer the hearts of soldiers. The ravages of war have made desolation more desolate, and rendered the poor inhabitants more destitute. In some neighborhoods we occasionally passed houses that were tenanted and fields that were cultivated. Sometimes, however, we would march all day without seeing a field or even a garden, in cultivation, or a house that was occupied. Unoccupied cabins and uncultivated fields are the unmistakable evidences of the fidelity and patriotism of their former occupants and owners. The doors and windows of dwellings have been broken in, fences have been burned, and ragweeds and briers have taken the place of corn and grain. Now and then the stacks of chimneys and the charred ruins of some dwelling mark the spot where there once lived a man who revered the flag of the Union, and honored the government of our fathers; and for this his dwelling has been consumed by the torch of some merciless incendiary, and his family have been driven from a comfortable home, to seek refuge in a lonely cavern among the rocks. The inhabitants themselves, who ventured out to the road from the different by-paths to see us pass, looked as poor as the country they live in, and a majority of them appeared nearly as destitute of intelligence as their country is of forage. At one place three women came to the road to get a peep at the 'Yanks.' They were all barefooted, and each had a pipe in her mouth, a baby in her arms, and a sharp-nosed dog following her. But they generally appear to be clever people, and they will, no doubt, feel sorry when they receive the painful intelligence of the death of Andrew Jackson. We occasionally fell in with brave mountaineers, armed and mounted, who, being animated with the love of liberty that characterized the early inhabitants of the mountains of Switzerland and the Highlands of Scotland, have formed confederate bands to punish their tormentors and strike down their cruel invaders.

"Near the town of Montgomery is an extensive cave in the mountains, called Beatty's Cave. In that rich valley, Beatty, the leader of those mountain patriots, is intrenched and fortified, and thousands of acres are there cultivated in corn and other grain for their subsistence.

"Before the late advance of our army, Beatty kept pickets constantly posted to warn him of the approach of the enemy, and whenever a rebel force was discovered in the vicinity, the sound of Beatty's horn, the signal of alarm, was simultaneously responded to by a hundred other horns amongst the neighboring hills, when the members of the Union League would start for Beatty's cave for safety and defence. At one time the rebel cavalry, fifteen hundred strong, made an assault on Beatty at this cave, whom he repulsed with desperate slaughter. When the pen of the historian shall have faithfully recorded the chivalrous deeds of 'Tinker Beatty,' he will be regarded by his countrymen as the 'William Tell' of the Cumberland Mountains."

RIP VAN WINKLE IN VIRGINIA. — When the Union troops under McClellan and Rosecrans, in the summer of 1861, were penetrating the mountain region of West Virginia, as they marched through a quiet nook on the side of Laurel Ridge, they saw a venerable matron standing in the door of a log cabin.

One of the men fell into conversation with her, and found her views on the issues of the day were not very well defined. At length he said:

"You'll not refuse to hurrah for Old Abe, will you, old lady?"

"Who's Old Abe?" asked the dame, growing more astonished every minute.

"Abraham Lincoln, President of the United States."

"Why, hain't Genrul Washington President?"

"No! he's been dead for more than sixty years."

"Genrul Washington dead?" she repeated in blank amazement.

Then, rushing into the cabin, she called, "Yeou, Sam! — "

"Well, what is it, mother?" said a voice within.

In a moment she reappeared with a boy of fifty, whom the men afterwards learned was her son.

"Only to think, Sam," she cried excitedly, "Genrul Washington's dead. Sakes alive! I wonder what's going to happen next."

THE SLEEPING SENTINEL.

BY FRANCIS DE HAES JANVIER.

[The incidents woven into the following beautiful verses relate to William Scott, a young soldier from Vermont, who, while on duty as a sentinel at night, fell asleep, and, having been condemned to die, was pardoned by the President. They form a brief record of his life at home and in the field, and of his glorious death in defence of the Union.]

'Twas in the sultry summer-time, as war's red records show,
When patriot armies rose to meet a fratricidal foe;
When from the North, and East, and West, like the upheaving sea,
Swept forth Columbia's sons, to make our country truly free.

Within a prison's dismal walls, where shadows veiled decay,
In fetters, on a heap of straw, a youthful soldier lay;
Heart-broken, hopeless, and forlorn, with short and feverish breath,
He waited but th' appointed hour to die a culprit's death.

Yet, but a few brief weeks before, untroubled with a care,
He roamed at will, and freely drew his native mountain air —
Where sparkling streams leap mossy rocks, from many a woodland font,
And waving elms and grassy slopes give beauty to Vermont; —

Where, dwelling in a humble cot, a tiller of the soil,
Encircled by a mother's love, he shared a father's toil —
Till, borne upon the wailing winds, his suffering country's cry
Fired his young heart with fervent zeal, for her to live or die.

Then left he all : — a few fond tears, by firmness half concealed,
A blessing, and a parting prayer, and he was in the field —
The field of strife, whose dews are blood, whose breezes war's hot breath,
Whose fruits are garnered in the grave, whose husbandman is death !

Without a murmur he endured a service new and hard ;
But, wearied with a toilsome march, it chanced one night, on guard,
He sank, exhausted, at his post, and the gray morning found
His prostrate form — a sentinel asleep upon the ground !

So, in the silence of the night, aweary on the sod,
Sank the disciples, watching near the suffering Son of God ;
Yet Jesus, with compassion moved, beheld their heavy eyes,
And, though betrayed to ruthless foes, forgiving, bade them rise !

But God is love — and finite minds can faintly comprehend
How gentle Mercy, in His rule, may with stern Justice blend ;
And this poor soldier, seized and bound, found none to justify,
While war's inexorable law decreed that he must die.

———

'Twas night. — In a secluded room, with measured tread and slow,
A statesman of commanding mien paced gravely to and fro.
Oppressed, he pondered on a land by civil discord rent ;
On brothers armed in deadly strife : — it was the President !

The woes of thirty millions filled his burdened heart with grief ;
Embattled hosts, on land and sea, acknowledged him their chief ;
And yet, amid the din of war, he heard the plaintive cry
Of that poor soldier, as he lay in prison, doomed to die !

———

'Twas morning. — On a tented field, and through the heated haze,
Flashed back, from lines of burnished arms, the sun's effulgent blaze ;
While, from a sombre prison-house, seen slowly to emerge,
A sad procession, o'er the sward, moved to a muffled dirge.

And in the midst, with faltering step, and pale and anxious face,
In manacles, between two guards, a soldier had his place.
A youth — led out to die ; — and yet it was not death, but shame,
That smote his gallant heart with dread, and shook his manly frame !

Still on, before the marshalled ranks, the train pursued its way
Up to the designated spot, whereon a coffin lay —
His coffin ! And, with reeling brain, despairing, desolate —
He took his station by its side, abandoned to his fate !

Then came across his wavering sight strange pictures in the air :
He saw his distant mountain home ; he saw his parents there ;
He saw them bowed with hopeless grief, through fast declining years ;
He saw a nameless grave ; and then, the vision closed — in tears !

Yet once again. In double file, advancing, then, he saw
Twelve comrades, sternly set apart to execute the law —
But saw no more : — his senses swam — deep darkness settled round —
And, shuddering, he awaited now the fatal volley's sound !

Then suddenly was heard the noise of steeds and
    wheels approach, —
And, rolling through a cloud of dust, appeared a
    stately coach.
On, past the guards, and through the field, its rapid
    course was bent,
Till, halting, 'mid the lines was seen the nation's
    President !

He came to save that stricken soul, now waking
    from despair ;
And from a thousand voices rose a shout which
    rent the air !
The pardoned soldier understood the tones of ju-
    bilee,
And, bounding from his fetters, blessed the hand
    that made him free !

'Twas Spring. — Within a verdant vale, where
    Warwick's crystal tide
Reflected, o'er its peaceful breast, fair fields on
    either side :
Where birds and flowers combined to cheer a syl-
    van solitude,
Two threatening armies, face to face, in fierce defi-
    ance stood !

Two threatening armies ! One invoked by injured
    Liberty —
Which bore above its patriot ranks the symbol of
    the Free ;
And one, a rebel horde, beneath a flaunting flag of
    bars,
A fragment, torn by traitorous hands from Free-
    dom's Stripes and Stars !

A sudden burst of smoke and flame, from many a
    thundering gun,
Proclaimed, along the echoing hills, the conflict had
    begun ;
While shot and shell athwart the stream with fiend-
    ish fury sped,
To strew among the living lines the dying and the
    dead !

Then, louder than the roaring storm, pealed forth
    the stern command,
"Charge ! soldiers, charge !" and, at the word,
    with shouts, a fearless band,
Two hundred heroes from Vermont, rushed on-
    ward, through the flood,
And upward, o'er the rising ground, they marked
    their way in blood !

The smitten foe before them fled, in terror, from
    his post —
While, unsustained, two hundred stood, to battle
    with a host !
Then, turning, as the rallying ranks, with murder-
    ous fire replied,
They bore the fallen o'er the field, and through
    the purple tide !

The fallen ! And the first who fell in that unequal
    strife
Was he whom Mercy sped to save when Justice
    claimed his life —
The pardoned soldier ! And, while yet the con-
    flict raged around —
While yet his life-blood ebbed away through every
    gaping wound —

25

While yet his voice grew tremulous, and death be-
    dimmed his eye —
He called his comrades to attest he had not feared
    to die !
And, in his last expiring breath, a prayer to heaven
    was sent,
That God, with his unfailing grace, would bless
    our President !

ON THE BATTLE-FIELD. — A correspondent
of a Southern paper gives the following description of the feelings of a soldier for the first time
on a battle-field :

"No person who was not upon the ground,
and an eye-witness of the stirring scenes which
there transpired, can begin to comprehend from
a description the terrible realities of a battle ;
and even those who participated are competent
to speak only of their own personal experience.
Where friends and foes are falling by scores, and
every species of missile is flying through the air,
threatening each instant to send one into eternity, little time is afforded for more observation or
reflection than is required for personal safety.

"The scene is one of the most exciting and
exhilarating that can be conceived. Imagine a
regiment passing you at ' double-quick,' the men
cheering with enthusiasm, their teeth set, their eyes
flashing, and the whole in a frenzy of resolution.
You accompany them to the field. They halt.
And aid-de-camp passes to or from the commanding General. The clear voices of officers ring
along the line in tones of passionate eloquence,
their words hot, thrilling, and elastic. The word
is given to march, and the body moves into
action. For the first time in your life you listen
to the whizzing of iron. Grape and canister fly
into the ranks, bombshells burst overhead, and
the fragments fly all around you. A friend falls ;
perhaps a dozen or twenty of your comrades lie
wounded or dying at your feet ; a strange, involuntary shrinking steals over you, which it is impossible to resist. You feel inclined neither to
advance nor recede, but are spell-bound by the
contending emotions of the moral and physical
man. The cheek blanches, the lip quivers, and
the eye almost hesitates to look upon the scene.

"In this attitude you may, perhaps, be ordered
to stand an hour inactive, havoc meanwhile marking its footsteps with blood on every side. Finally
the order is given to advance, to fire, or to charge.
And now, what a metamorphosis ! With your
first shot you become a new man. Personal
safety is your least concern. Fear has no existence in your bosom. Hesitation gives way to an
uncontrollable desire to rush into the thickest
of the fight. The dead and dying around you,
if they receive a passing thought, only serve to
stimulate you to revenge. You become cool and
deliberate, and watch the effect of bullets, the
shower of bursting shells, the passage of cannon-
balls as they rake their murderous channels
through your ranks, the plunging of wounded
horses, the agonies of the dying, and the clash
of contending arms, which follows the dashing

charge with a feeling so calloused by surrounding circumstances that your soul seems dead to every sympathizing and selfish thought.

"Such is the spirit which carries the soldier through the field of battle. But when the excitement has passed, when the roll of musketry has ceased, the noisy voices of the cannons are stilled, the dusky pall of sulphurous smoke has risen from the field, and you stroll over the theatre of carnage, hearing the groans of the wounded, discovering here, shattered almost beyond recognition, the form of some dear friend whom only an hour before you met in the full flush of life and happiness, there another perforated by a bullet, a third with a limb shot away, a fourth with his face disfigured, a fifth almost torn to fragments, a sixth a headless corpse, the ground ploughed up and stained with blood, human brains splashed around, limbs without bodies and bodies without limbs scattered here and there, and the same picture duplicated scores of times, — then you begin to realize the horrors of war, and experience a reaction of nature. The heart opens its floodgates, humanity asserts herself again, and you begin to feel.

"Friend and foe alike now receive your kindest ministerings. The enemy, whom, but a short time before, full of hate, you were doing all in your power to kill, you now endeavor to save. You supply him with water to quench his thirst, with food to sustain his strength, and with sympathizing words to soothe his troubled mind. All that is human or charitable in your nature now rises to the surface, and you are animated by that spirit of mercy 'which blesseth him that gives and him that takes.' A battle-field is eminently a place that tries men's souls."

THE FIGHT AT KELLEY'S ISLAND. — Colonel Wallace had been accustomed to send his mounted scouts to different posts along the several approaches to Cumberland. There were only thirteen of the scouts ; but they were picked men, who, from such practice, had become accustomed to their peculiar duty. The following are their names and companies:

Company A — D. B. Hay, E. H. Backer. Company B — Ed. Burkett, J. C. Hollenback. Company C — Tim. Grover, James Hollowell. Company D — Thos. Brazier. Company E — Geo. W. Huebargar. Company F — Lewis Farley. Company H — Frank Harrison. Company I — P. M. Dunlap. Company K — Robt. Dunlap, E. P. Thomas. On the 27th of June, 1861, the Colonel found it impossible to get reliable information of the enemy. Uniting the scouts in a body, he gave them in charge of Corporal D. B. Hay, with directions to proceed to a little town on the pike from Cumberland to Romney, named Frankfort, and ascertain if rebel troops were there.

Hay was sharp, cunning, and bold — the very man for the business. Filling their canteens and haversacks, the brave men strapped their rifles on their backs, and started on their mission. Their horses were of the class now known as condemned. Hay's was the only good one. He had some reputation as a racer, and went by the name of "Silverheels." His rider had captured him in a scuffle a few days before, and prized him highly as a trophy. All the rest had been impressed into the service, and now made sad profert of their ribs by way of protest against their usage.

A rumor passed through the camp that morning that Hay was going to fight before he returned. His procedure was certainly that of a man in search of one. He took the turnpike to Romney, and never drew rein, until, from a little eminence, he looked down into the straggling village of Frankfort. The street was full of infantry. The horses picketed about indicated a large body of cavalry. Most men would have been anxious, after that sight, to return to camp as quickly as possible. Not so Hay and his comrades. Sitting on their horses, they coolly made up their estimate of the enemy's number, and when they were perfectly agreed on the point, turned about, and rode leisurely away. On the return, they took another road very much broken, and which, threading among the hills, after many devious windings, finally brought up to the track of the Baltimore and Ohio Railroad. The taking of this road was a mere freak of fancy. It was by no means the shortest to camp, nor was its exploration of any probable use ; yet it led to a fight ; and if the scouts had known that beforehand, it is not likely they would have changed their course. Three or four miles from Frankfort, while descending a mountain side, after turning a sharp elbow in the road, the men came suddenly upon a party of rebel cavalry. Each instinctively drew his bridle rein, and for an instant halted. Rapidly they commenced counting.

"Forty-one of them, boys!" cried Hay, turning in his saddle. "What do you say? Will you stand by me?"

"Go in, Dave," was the unanimous vote.

It took but a moment to unsling their rifles.

"Are you ready?" asked Hay.

"All ready," they replied.

"Come on, then," shouted the leader. "The best horse gets the first man!"

With the last word they were off.

It happened the rebels themselves were going in the same direction. They were also somewhat below them in the descent of the road. With his usual shrewdness, and quick as thought, Hay grasped his advantage of position. An abrupt declivity on the left of the narrow road made it impossible for the enemy to form line. Neither could the rebels turn and charge up hill. They must go on to escape. If they stopped, "Silverheels" would go through like a thunderbolt.

The rebels heard the shout, and, in surprise, halted and took a look. The sight, under ordinary circumstances, would have been interesting to them. Not seventy-five yards behind, they saw Hay and his party galloping down the decline at break-neck speed ; their glance rested briefly on the little jackets, and big gray breeches, on the short, brown rifles shaken menacingly over the scarlet-tipped caps, and on the straining horses; their ears recognized the yell of pursuit; and then they staid not on their order of going. What they said, and whether they counted the assailants, we know not; but they began a retreat that soon took the form of a promiscuous fox chase, except that the shouts, which momentarily neared them, had little likeness to the joyous halloo of hunters.

Hay led the pursuit; Farley was next; the others followed as best they could; not one hung back. It is to be doubted whether in his best days "Silverheels" had made better time. A short distance from the foot of the hill he overtook the rebels. Just before the collision, Hay rose in his stirrups, and fired his rifle into the party. He was so close that to miss would have been an accident. Swinging the weapon round his head, he hurled it at the nearest man, and the next moment, with drawn pistol, plunged furiously amidst them. They closed around him. The pistol shooting became sharp and quick. Hay received one wound, and then another, but for each one he killed a man. When his revolver was empty, he drew his sabre bayonet. The rebel Captain gave him from behind a heavy cut on the head. Still he sat on his horse, and, though weakened by the blow, and half blind with blood, he laid out right and left. He fared illy enough, but it would have been worse, had not Farley then come up, and pitched loyally into the *mêlée*. Close at his heels, but singly or doubly, according to the speed of their horses, rode all the rest. The rebel Captain was shot before he could repeat his sabre blow. Farley was dismounted by the shock of the collision. He clinched a foeman in like situation; a struggle ensued; he was thrown, but his antagonist was knocked down by young Hollowell before he could use his victory. Farley caught another horse. The eager onset relieved Hay, and again started the rebels, who, in their flight, took to the railroad. Not a moment was allowed them to turn upon their pursuers. Over the track helter-skelter they went. Suddenly they came to a burnt culvert. It was too late to dodge it: over or into it they had to go. Eight men were killed in the attempt to cross it. Hay, in close pursuit, saw the leap just as it was unavoidable. "Silverheels" in his turn cleared the culvert, but fell dead a few yards beyond. The chase ended there. When his comrades crossed over, they found Hay sitting by his horse crying like a child, on account of his death.

The scouts then proceeded to collect the spoils. When they were all in, the net proceeds of the victory were seventeen horses, with their equipments, and eleven dead rebels — three on the hill-side and eight in the culvert. Hay remounted himself, and started with the party for Cumberland. It may be imagined with what satisfaction the brave victors pictured to each other their triumphal entry into camp. After going a few miles Hay became so faint from loss of blood that he had to be taken out of his saddle. The dilemma in which they found themselves was settled by sending two of their number to a farm-house for a wagon; meantime they laid their leader in the shade, and brought water for him from the river. While they were thus nursing him back to strength, a fire was suddenly opened upon them from a hill on the left. This was a surprise, but their coolness did not desert them. Hay bade them put him on a horse, and leave him to take care of himself. They complied: clinging painfully to the saddle, he forded the Potomac and was safe. The others could probably have saved themselves, but in a foolish effort to save their horses, they lost the opportunity. Farley then became leader. "Let the horses go, and give the rebels thunder," was his simple, emphatic order.

The fire thickening on them was then returned. Years before Farley had lost one of his eyes; the sound one, however, was now admirably used. He saw the rebels were trying to surround the party, and would succeed if better cover was not soon found. Behind them ran Patterson's Creek. The ground on its opposite shore was scarcely higher than that which they occupied, but it was covered with rocks washed naked by the flowing stream. Farley saw that to get there would be a good exchange.

"It's a pretty slim chance, boys," he coolly said, "but it won't do to give in or stay here. Let's make a rush for the big rocks yonder, and get the creek between them and us."

The rush was made; under a sharp fire they crossed the creek, and took shelter behind the boulders. Ten of them were there, but, to use their own language, they were all "sound as new fifty-cent pieces, and not whipped by a long sight."

Peeping over the rocks, they counted over seventy rebels on foot making at full speed for the creek, evidently with the intention of crossing it. Each one felt that the crisis had come.

"Look out now, and don't waste a cartridge. Recollect they are scarce," said Thomas.

"Yes, and recollect Buena Vista," said Hollowell.

The first rebel entered the creek before a gun was fired, so perfectly calm were those ten men. Then crack, crack, in quick succession, went the rifles, scarcely a bullet failing in its mark. The assailants recoiled, ran back, and finding cover as best they could, began the exciting play of sharpshooters. This practice continued for more than an hour. The sun went down on it. About that time, a small party of horsemen galloped down the road, and hitching their horses, joined the enemy. One of the new comers made himself conspicuous by refusing to take to the ground. Walking about, as if in contempt of the minies which were sent whistling round him, he gave directions which resulted in another sudden dash for the creek. Again the rifle went crack, crack, in quick succession, and with the same fatal consequence: but this time the rebels had a leader; men were seen to fall in the water, but there was no second recoil; the obstructions were cleared in the face of the rifles, and with much cursing and shouting the attacking party closed in upon the Zouaves.

The fight was hand-to-hand. No amount of courage could be effective against the great odds at such close quarters. Nevertheless, all that was possible was done. Night was rapidly closing upon the scene; over the rocks, and through the tangled thicket, and in the fading twilight, the struggle for revenge and life went on. There was heroism on both sides; that of the Zouaves was matchless, because it was in no small degree the prompting of despair.

Farley found himself again engaged with the leader of the rebels, a man of as much strength as courage. Hollowell saved his life at the cost of his rifle, but snatching the dead man's pistols, he resumed the fight. The pistols were brought into camp, and next morning presented to the young hero by the Colonel.

Thomas killed two by rifle shots; while loading a third time, he was struck by a pistol ball on the side of the temple, and fell senseless. A man in the act of striking him with a sabre was shot through by Grover, and died on Thomas. It was dark when Thomas recovered. Hearing no sound of fighting, he pushed the dead body from him, secured his rifle, and hid himself in vines and bushes. In a little while the rebels came to remove the dead. He saw them carry thirteen bodies across the creek. In searching the island they found Hollenback, who had been shot through the body. Thomas heard the exclamation announcing the discovery.

"Here's a Yankee!" was the shout.

"Kill him, kill him!" arose on all sides.

"Come, get out of this!" said a strong voice.

"I can't, I'm shot," feebly protested Hollenback.

Yet they made him rise, and wade the creek. When all was still, Thomas escaped by wading and swimming the Potomac.

Baker and Dunlap, of company I, the men sent for the wagon, hearing the second engagement, galloped with all speed to camp, and reported. The regiment was on drill when they arrived. Fifty men, under Major Robinson, were instantly detailed to go to the rescue. When the detachment reached the edge of the town it was swelled to two hundred: the guards found it impossible to keep the Zouaves in the lines. The relief travelled fast, but arrived too late. The island was deserted. Pistols, broken guns, dead horses, and rocks stained with blood, told the story.

The detail returned late in the night. Early next morning, two companies, under Major Robinson, were sent down to search for some of the missing men and property, and bury such dead as they might find. In the afternoon the Major came back with some trophies, eight horses, and poor Hollenback. He had found Hollenback lying on a farmer's porch, dead, but warm and bleeding, with a bullet hole and a bayonet thrust through his body. The woman of the house told Major Robinson how he died.

"The man wasn't dead when they brought him here," she said; "but a little while ago, when they heard you coming, they set him on a horse to take him off with them; but he fainted: he couldn't stand it. A man then stuck a bayonet into his back."

The Major glanced at the porch, and observed blood on the floor.

"Did they bring anybody else here, madam?" he asked.

"O, yes! I reckon they did. Me and my man came out while they were at work, and we counted twenty-three men laid out, side by side, on the porch there. Two or three of them were wounded. I heard some one say that they had brought some of the dead men down the railroad. Ashby was one of the wounded."

The Ashby alluded to was a brother of the Colonel Ashby of Black Horse Cavalry renown. He afterwards died of his wounds.

By five o'clock the day after the fight the scouts were all in camp. They straggled in one by one. Citizens and soldiers turned out to receive them. Never did returning heroes have more sympathizing and admiring audiences. Thomas showed the kiss of the bullet on his temple. Baker wore the cap of a rebel — his own had been shot off his head. Dunlop had three bullet holes through his shirt. Hollowell exhibited his captured pistols and broken rifle. Farley yet retained the handle of his sabre bayonet, shivered in the fray. Several of the men testified to his killing six enemies with his own hand. Not a man but had some proofs of the engagement, such as torn clothes and bruised body. But Hay was the hero. Three ghastly wounds entitled him to the honor.

The final escape of each had been in the same manner. Finding themselves overpowered and separated, each one, at the first opportunity, had abandoned the battle ground, which proved to be Kelley's Island, at the mouth of Patterson's Creek, and plunging into the river, succeeded in crossing it. The enemy followed to the canal, on the northern side.

Hollenback was buried in the cemetery. A more solemn funeral never took place in the old town. The sorrow was universal. Loyal men thought:

> "To every man upon this earth
> Death cometh soon or late;
> And where can man die better
> Than facing fearful odds,
> For the ashes of his fathers,
> And the temples of his Gods!"

Indiana's Roll of Honor.

INCIDENT OF CHICKAMAUGA. — On the first day of the engagement, Captain Ogan, of company K, Fourteenth Ohio regiment, was taken prisoner by the rebels. As they were approaching their lines, the idea of practising a little finesse, or military stratagem, suggested itself; so, pretending to be highly gratified with the idea of being a prisoner, he told his captors that this was what he wanted — that he had long been anxious to get out of the war, and was well satisfied with that mode of getting out. "But," said he, "you are taking me right back into the Federal lines." They, supposing they had become confused in the heat and hurry of the movement, turned around, and carried him back within the Federal lines, when it became his turn to reciprocate by capturing his captors, and commanding them to deliver up their arms, which they did in a very gracious manner, taking their places among the rebel prisoners.

General Steedman won great praise for his gallantry on the field. His horse was shot from under him, and in the fall his hand became seriously injured. Upon rising, he discovered some of his men straggling from his division, when he commenced pelting them with stones, driving them back to their work — concluding that if words would not do, he would try the virtues of harder material. For a long time he held the Union colors in his own hand, in the heat of the conflict.

Colonel P. P. Baldwin, of the Sixth Indiana, commanding a brigade, fell from his horse in the earlier part of the engagement, badly wounded. He had seized a flag, which had fallen from the hands of one of his slain Color-Sergeants, and, waving it aloft, amid the confusion, shot, and shell of the enemy, was gallantly leading his brigade to meet a charge of the enemy, when he fell, wounded, between the two lines.

THE LITTLE DRUMMER.

A SOLDIER'S STORY.

BY R. H. STODDARD.

I.

'Tis of a little drummer,
  The story I shall tell,
Of how he marched to battle,
  And all that there befell,
Out in the West with Lyon
  (For once the name was true),
For whom the little drummer beat
  His *rat-tat-too.*

II.

Our army rose at midnight,
  Ten thousand men as one,
Each slinging on his knapsack,
  And snatching up his gun:
"*Forward!*" and off they started,
  As all good soldiers do,
When the little drummer beats for them
  The *rat-tat-too.*

III.

Across a rolling country,
  Where the mist began to rise,
Past many a blackened farm-house,
  Till the sun was in the skies,
Then we met the rebel pickets,
  Who skirmished and withdrew,
While the little drummer beat and beat
  The *rat-tat-too.*

IV.

Along the wooded hollows
  The line of battle ran;
Our centre poured a volley,
  And the fight at once began;
For the rebels answered shouting,
  And a shower of bullets flew;
But still the little drummer beat
  His *rat-tat-too.*

V.

He stood among his comrades,
  As they quickly formed the line,
And when they raised their muskets
  He watched the barrels shine!
When the volley rang, he started!
  For war to him was new;
But still the little drummer beat
  His *rat-tat-too.*

VI.

It was a sight to see them,
  That early autumn day,
Our soldiers in their blue coats,
  And the rebel ranks in gray:
The smoke that rolled between them,
  The balls that whistled through,
And the little drummer as he beat
  His *rat-tat-too!*

VII.

His comrades dropped around him —
  By fives and tens they fell,
Some pierced by minie bullets,
  Some torn by shot and shell;
They played against our cannon,
  And a caisson's splinters flew;
But still the little drummer beat
  His *rat-tat-too!*

VIII.

The right, the left, the centre —
  The fight was everywhere;
They pushed us here — we wavered —
  We drove and broke them there.
The gray-backs fixed their bayonets,
  And charged the coats of blue,
But still the little drummer beat
  His *rat-tat-too!*

IX.

"Where is our little drummer?"
  His nearest comrades say,
When the dreadful fight is over,
  And the smoke has cleared away.
As the rebel corps was scattering
  He urged them to pursue,
So furiously he beat and beat
  The *rat-tat-too!*

X.

He stood no more among them,
  For a bullet, as it sped,
Had glanced and struck his ankle,
  And stretched him with the dead!
He crawled behind a cannon,
  And pale and paler grew:
But still the little drummer beat
  His *rat-tat-too!*

XI.

They bore him to the surgeon;
A busy man was he:
"A drummer boy — what ails him?"
His comrades answered, "See!"
As they took him from the stretcher,
A heavy breath he drew,
And his little fingers strove to beat
The *rat-tat-too!*

XII.

The ball had spent its fury:
"A scratch," the surgeon said,
As he wound the snowy bandage
Which the lint was staining red!
"I must leave you now, old fellow."
"O, take me back with you,
For I know the men are missing me,
And the *rat-tat-too!*"

XIII.

Upon his comrade's shoulder
They lifted him so grand,
With his dusty drum before him,
And his drumsticks in his hand!
To the fiery front of battle,
That nearer, nearer drew —
And evermore he beat and beat
His *rat-tat-too!*

XIV.

The wounded as he passed them
Looked up and gave a cheer:
And one in dying blessed him,
Between a smile and tear!
And the gray-backs — they are flying
Before the coats of blue,
For whom the little drummer beats
His *rat-tat-too!*

XV.

When the west was red with sunset,
The last pursuit was o'er,
Brave Lyon rode the foremost,
And looked the name he bore!
And before him on his saddle,
As a weary child would do,
Sat the little drummer fast asleep,
With his *rat-tat-too.*

SOUTHERN SNOWBALLING. — The author of "Memoirs of the Confederate War," Van Borcke, gives the following account of a snowball engagement in General Lee's army: "We were enlivened by snowball fights, which commenced as skirmishes near our headquarters, but extended over the neighboring camps, and assumed the aspect of general engagements. In front of our headquarters, beyond an open field of about half a mile square, Hood's division lay encamped in a piece of wood; in our immediate rear stretched the tents and huts of a part of M'Law's division. Between these two bodies of troops animated little skirmishes frequently occurred whenever there was snow enough on the ground to furnish the ammunition; but on the morning of the 4th, an extensive expedition having been undertaken by several hundred of M'Law's men against Hood's encampments, and the occupants of those finding themselves considerably disturbed thereby, suddenly the whole of the division advanced in line of battle, with flying colors, the officers leading the men, as if in real action, to avenge the insult. The assailants fell back rapidly before this overwhelming host, but only to secure a strong position, from which, with reënforcements, they might resume the offensive. The alarm of their first repulse having been borne with the swiftness of the wind to their comrades, sharpshooters in large numbers were posted behind the cedar bushes that skirt the Telegraph Road, and hundreds of hands were actively employed in erecting a long and high snow wall in front of their extended lines. The struggle had now the appearance of a regular battle, with its charges and counter-charges; the wild enthusiasm of the men and the noble emulation of the officers finding expression in loud commands and yet louder cheering, while the air was darkened with the snowballs as the current of the fight moved to and fro over the well-contested field. Nearer and nearer it came towards our headquarters, and it was soon evident to us that the hottest part of the engagement would take place on our neutral territory. Fruitless were the efforts of Stuart and myself to assert and maintain the neutrality of our camp, utterly idle the hoisting of a white flag: the advancing columns pressed forward in complete disregard of our signs and our outspoken remonstrances. Clouds of snowballs passed across the face of the sun, and ere long the overwhelming wave of the conflict rolled pitilessly over us. Yielding to the unavoidable necessity which forbade our keeping aloof from the contest, Stuart and I had taken position, in order to obtain a view over the field of battle, on a big box, containing ordnance stores, in front of the General's tent, where we soon became so much interested in the result, and so carried away by the excitement of the moment, that we found ourselves calling out to the men to hold their ground, and urging them again and again to the attack, while many a stray snowball, and many a well-directed one, took effect upon our exposed persons. But all the gallant resistance of M'Law's men was unavailing. Hood's lines pressed resistlessly forward, carrying everything before them, taking the formidable fortifications, and driving M'Law's division out of the encampments. Suddenly, at this juncture, we heard loud shouting on the right, where two of Anderson's brigades had come up as reënforcements. The men of M'Law's division, acquiring new confidence from this support, rallied, and in turn drove, by a united charge, the victorious foe in headlong flight back to their own camps and woods. Thus ended the battle for the day, unhappily with serious results to some of the combatants, for one of Hood's men had his leg broken, one of M'Law's men lost an eye, and there were other chance wounds on both sides. This sham-fight gave ample proof of the excellent spirits of our troops, who, in the wet, wintry weather, many of them without blankets, some without shoes, regardless of their exposure and of the scarcity of provisions, still maintained their good humor, and were ever ready for any sort of sport or fun that offered itself to them."

"THE GALLANT SIXTY-NINTH." — Two gallant sons of Erin, being just discharged from the service, were rejoicing over the event with a "wee taste of the cratur'," when one, who felt all the glory of his own noble race, suddenly raised his glass above, and said, "Arrah, Mike, here's to the gallant ould Sixty-ninth: *The last in the field and the first to leave!*" "Tut, tut, man," said Mike, "you don't mane that." "Don't mane it, is it? Then what do I mane?" "You mane," said Mike, and he raised his glass high, and looked lovingly at it, "Here's to the gallant ould Sixty-ninth — *equal to none!*" And so they drank.

THE DEATH OF COLONEL ELLSWORTH. — On the evening of the 23d of May, 1861, there was a feverish flush and ill-suppressed anxiety among the political and military circles of the Federal capital. It was generally understood, though not announced, that some very important military movement was on foot, and that an "enterprise" of great pith and moment would in a few hours, perhaps, agitate the whole American people.

Yet, as the night advanced, the excitement wore away, and the city of magnificent distances fell into its usual tranquillity.

Not so, however, at the camp along the Potomac, and especially at the quarters of the Fire Zouaves.

This splendid and dashing regiment had come out from New York a month before, and had electrified that city and the less excitable citizens of Washington by the splendor of their costume, the perfection of their drill, and the fine figure and well-known martial qualities of their leader, Colonel Ellsworth. Their brethren of the fire companies in New York had turned out en masse to escort them to the steamer, and after twenty days in Washington, they had now received marching orders, and their quiet camp was to-night to realize all that poets ever wrote of the wild and romantic scenery of war.

The night was uncommonly still and clear, and the moon was so bright that the line of white cones marking their camp could be distinctly seen from the other side of the broad Potomac.

As the visitor approached, sounds of bustle filled the air, and the rustle of arms and the tramp of the men on drill were now and then drowned in the powerful chorus of manly voices rolling out upon the night air the great national songs of Columbia.

It was felt by all that the hour of bloodshed was now come. Aside from the four men killed by the explosion of a gun at Sumter, and the killing of Ladd and Whitney by the Baltimore mob, no lives had as yet been offered up; the crimson current had not begun to flow.

Yet all felt that some one must be the first victim — that ere many days, or hours perhaps, the sacred soil of Virginia would be wet with the blood of the first contestants in the mighty struggle. Yet who could have foreseen that the fine, youthful, vigorous, manly figure of the Colonel, whom we now see moving about among the men that idolized him, would be the first to be pierced by rebel balls — that he was to be the proto-martyr of the holy cause.

It is midnight now, and the men that were a little while ago singing "Columbia, the gem of the ocean," with all the fervor they could bring to it, are still in their tents. The knapsacks are packed. The guns are oiled and polished. Ammunition is in the cartridge boxes and cooked rations in the haversacks. They are ready to start at a drum tap.

Though it is past midnight, Colonel Ellsworth is still at his table, in his tent, completing the official arrangements that remained, and carefully instructing his subordinates as to the line of conduct proper in this or that emergency.

An hour later, and he is done, and not now occupied with the rough plans of brave exploits. A sadder and a tenderer task occupies the young soldier's pen. He writes those last words to his parents: "To-night, thinking over the probabilities of the morrow, and the occurrences of the past, I am perfectly content to accept whatever my fortune may be, confident that He who noteth even the fall of a sparrow will have some purpose even in the fate of one like me. My darling and ever-loved parents, good by!" Other, and perhaps still more tender and touching adieus are dashed off with rapid pen and full heart ere the young figure leaves the table, and wraps his army blanket around him for an hour of sleep.

A little after two o'clock, the encampment began to show signs of activity again. Captain Dahlgren, the commander of the navy yard, came to announce that all was ready for transportation. The men marched forward in line, and were drawn up by companies along the beach.

The night air along the water side is chill, and some of the men were wrapped from head to foot in great red blankets. Most were clad in their gray jackets and trowsers, and embroidered caps. These vivid costumes of the men — the lines of tents, glowing from the lights within like huge lanterns — the glittering rows of bayonets and gun-barrels — the woods and hills in the distance — the placid river in front — and, to add historic significance, the dome of the Capitol towering sublime and calm in the still moonlight, — all these combined to form a picture which was not effaced from the memory of those who saw it by the long succession of darker and bloodier scenes which followed.

The embarkation was rapidly conducted, and, just as dawn light began to break over hill and river, the last of the regiment was aboard, and the boats steamed slowly down the river.

Armed resistance to any invasion of the "sacred soil" of Virginia was confidently expected. So much ferocious talk had poured from the Richmond press that it was fair to suppose that every wharf would have its Leonidas, and every street-crossing be defended by a Horatius Cocles.

But the rebel strategy was different. Johnson's head was cool, and his judgment sound. He saw that Alexandria was no point for serious resistance, and when the Pawnee sent a yawl filled with armed marines, and proposed terms of submission, the Confederates had consented to vacate within a specified time.

About five o'clock the Zouaves landed, and Colonel Ellsworth gave rapid directions for tearing up some of the rails at the railroad station, and then turned his attention to the means of destroying all communication southward by the telegraph — a step which he regarded as very important.

As he started away to execute this duty in person, with the dash and enthusiasm peculiar to his youth and his ardent nature, he took as his guard but a small squad of men from the first company, with Sergeant Brownell at their head. Mr. Wisner, the Military Secretary of the regiment, Mr. Dodge, the Chaplain, and a journalist of the New York Tribune, went with him.

The little group, amounting to about ten men in all, walked rapidly through the quiet streets, and were about turning a corner to go in the direction of the telegraph office, when the Colonel saw flaunting from the top of a hotel a rebel flag, which had long been visible from the balconies of the President's house in Washington.

He immediately sent back the Sergeant with an order for the first company of the regiment to advance and join him.

Here was the first instance of the rashness of youthful enthusiasm on the part of Colonel Ellsworth. He did not wait for the arrival of the company, but passed rapidly on to the tavern, which he entered, and accosted the first man he saw with the question — "What sort of a flag is that hanging over the roof of this house?" The man seemed a good deal alarmed, and said he knew nothing about it, as he was only a boarder there. Without calling for the proprietor of the house, or making any demand for the removal of the obnoxious emblem, Colonel Ellsworth ran up stairs, and reached the topmost story, where by means of a ladder he clambered to the roof, and borrowing Mr. Wisner's knife, cut the small rope, and pulled the flag away from the mast from which it floated.

This was the work of but a few moments, and the party now turned to descend from the roof. Brownell went first, and Colonel Ellsworth close behind him carrying the flag. As Brownell reached the first landing-place or entry after a descent of a dozen or more steps, a man stepped quickly out from a dimly-lighted passage, and without noticing the private levelled a double-barrelled shot-gun full at Colonel Ellsworth's breast. Brownell made a quick pass to throw up the muzzle of the piece, but the fellow's hand was firm, and his aim was not diverted.

Another second and the load of one barrel, either slugs or buckshot, went crashing through the vitals of Colonel Ellsworth, and killed him instantly. He was on the third step from the bottom when he received the shot, and fell forward with that horrible, headlong weight and heavy *thud* upon the floor of the passage which might have been expected from death so sudden.

The assailant now turned like a flash, and brought the other barrel to bear on Brownell. But the Zouave was this time too quick for him, and struck the piece so the load passed over his head and through a door behind him. The next instant the contents of his own rifle were discharged full in Jackson's face, and following up the ball with the bayonet, he lunged it through his body, and pushed it down the second flight of steps.

The three reports followed each other with as much rapidity as the successive loads of a revolver can be discharged, and the frightful consequences were seen in the bodies of two men, Ellsworth and Jackson, who lay each at the foot of a flight of stairs, dead and weltering in a pool of blood.

The body of Colonel Ellsworth was taken up and laid on a bed in an adjoining room. The blood was wiped from his clammy and marble but manly features, and the rebel flag, on account of which two men had so suddenly passed into eternity, lay soiled with blood across his feet.

In a few moments Jackson's wife came out from a room on the second floor, and saw the body of her husband lying dead in the passage in a pool of blood. She flung her arms into the air, cried wildly, and seemed utterly abandoned to desolation and agony. She offered no reproaches, nor seemed conscious of the crowd of strange soldiers around. No one could witness such agonizing grief and horror without emotion.

The only remark which seemed for a moment to arrest her attention was an assurance on the part of some of the Union soldiers that her children should not be molested.

The dead body of the Colonel of the Zouaves was now carried sadly away on a litter of muskets, and the thrilling story of that morning's bloody work went over the wires in all directions. Colonel Ellsworth throughout one section, being lamented as the first costly sacrifice laid on the altar of loyalty, and Jackson as much praised throughout the South for the prompt audacity with which he had avenged the first insult to rebel bunting.

HEROISM OF THE "M. D's." — The mule driver of the army abolishes the step between the sublime and ridiculous by making the ridiculous sublime. There, for instance, emerging from the leafy curtain of woods on the thither side of the creek, comes mule team No. 1, thundering with locked wheels — "*quadrupedante sonitu*" — down the abrupt declivity. The treacherous causeways of brush and mud give way under the weight; the ponderous wagon, blocked by the log corduroy, careens on the sinking wheels, and topples quivering on the brink of a disastrous upset into the Stygian creek, where the water is deep and the mud fathomless. Not Hercules could lift the embedded wain from the engorging rut. The spectators, gathered in the leafy galleries of the surrounding bluffs, and in the muddy pit of the river bank, shriek at the imminent catastrophe. All but the imperturbable M. D. are appalled at the impending overthrow. For M. D., seated on his stalwart wheeler, like a king upon his throne, a quiet glance behind and before suffices to reveal the nature of the exigency. There is a majestic repose in his features, and a placid confidence in his own powers, as he urgently waves away the proffered help, which stamps him the master of the situation. In that moment, grim and dingy though he be, the M. D. is sublime; he rises to the classic grandeur of the calm heroic, like the famous "statue on the gates of Altorf."

A hush of thrilled and awful expectation falls upon the audience. The M. D. speaks one low cabalistic word. The single guiding line in his left hand throbs like a nerve with the electric quiver of his potent will, and flaps the flanks of his leaders. In that single word and motion of the guiding rein he has organized and concentrated the sextuple power of his muscular motives in one simultaneous impulse. There is a zigzag tug and twist to the right and left, and almost before you know it the enormous wagon is lifted from the abysmal mud, and is rolling triumphantly over the shaking bridge. Already the mighty hybrids are clambering and straining up the steep ascent.

This is the real crisis of the play. To go back is to go to the devil; but the M. D., rising to the magnitude of the emergency, unfolds new and awful powers. The hero becomes a fury. His placid eye flashes with a fierce and wrathful fire. From the statuesque calm of his severe but dirty visage bursts a terrific storm of stunning curses. His huge whip, till now unused, writhes and cracks like a thunderbolt over the backs of his imperturbable mules. They go on. They falter and pause half way up the steep ascent. The wheels go back, and all seems lost. Ajax and Telamon, and all the Titans, spring to the wheels, to avert the threatened retrogression down to Styx.

But ordinary human agencies avail nothing, till the *deus ex machina* appears on the off side, in the person of the wagon master, with a monstrous and horrific thong. There is another, wilder, louder, fiercer tempest of imprecations on the heads, eyes, hearts of the dumb beasts, and a double crash of lashing thunderbolts from front to rear. Onward and upward rolls the wagon up and over the hills; the miracle is achieved, and the mules are browsing on the level plain above as if nothing uncommon had happened. This, a hundred times repeated with a hundred variations, such as the idiosyncrasy of the actor or the circumstances inspire, with an occasional breakdown and upset, and all the comic by-play of comment and jest, stands, for the day, in place of politics and war — of Charleston and Chattanooga. — *St. Paul Press.*

THE MAUL.

BY MARY E. NEALY.

I saw a boy in a black-jack wood,
　With a tall, lank, awkward "figger,"
Striking away with his heavy maul,
　By the side of a young slave "nigger."
And he said to himself, "I'll maul away,
　And cleave a path before me;
I'll hew *all* 'black-jacks' out of my way,
　'Till the Star of Fame shines o'er me."

I saw him again on a broad swift stream;
　But the maul this time was a paddle,
And I watched the tiny rainbow's gleam,
　As he made the waves skedaddle.
And he said, "I'll paddle away, away,
　Till space shall flee before me;
And I yet shall live to see the day
　When the Star of Fame shines o'er me."

I saw him again, with his musty books,
　A-pondering Coke and Story;
And little there was in his homely looks
　To tell of his future glory.
But he said, "I'll master, I know I will,
　The difficult task before me;
I'll maul my way through the hard world still,
　Till the Star of Fame shines o'er me."

I saw him again, when he rose to cope,
　Hand to hand, with the "Western Giant;"
His eye lit up with a beam of hope,
　On his sinewy strength reliant.
"I'll fight him," he said, "with the maul of Truth,
　Till he shrink and quail before me,
Till he stand abashed in astonished ruth,
　While the Star of Fame shines o'er me."

I saw him again in the White House chair,
　A-writing the Proclamation;
And the pen he used was the heaviest maul
　In this rail-mauling nation.
And he said, "'Tis the only way to make
　The traitors flee before us;
While the light it sheds will leave a wake
　That will shine when the sod grows o'er us."

I saw him again but the other night,
　And he shook my hand in greeting;
And little he thought how soon I'd write,
　And tell the world of our meeting.
The hand I clasped has swung the maul,
　And my own has written its story.
But never, I ween, could any hand
　Write half of its toil and glory.

DRAKE DE KAY'S EXPLOIT. — This dashing soldier was one day out on James River, doing some corsair work in one of the Cumberland's launches.

Some distance to leeward he saw his persistent foe, the Teaser, but kept on his course with "a wet sheet and a flowing sea." But all at once she whirled, and getting into the blaze of the afternoon sun, steamed down on Drake.

As quickly, Drake had his helm hard up, and soon his five oars were out, and the launch head on for shore. Bang! went the Teaser's bow rifled gun. De Kay shouted back in derision, and fired his revolver. The chase now assumed a desperate interest. At every puff of smoke from the Teaser's bow, De Kay put down his helm a little, and threw the launch out of range. Nice seamanship, a quick eye, and a cool head, carried him through, though shot and shell from the Teaser were screaming and splashing all around him. But Drake was irrepressible, and kept up an audacious pantomime of defiance, till his launch touched the river bank.

He was not many seconds in pulling out the plug from the boat's bottom, tumbling out his five men, the oars, mast, and sail, and ordering them to run for the bluff. Nor was the Teaser any longer in dropping a launch, getting a dozen men and as many muskets into her, and pushing off in pursuit.

Drake saw the approaching danger, and planned his defence.

Running to a picket fence close by, he tore off six pickets, and gave one to each of the men, who drew up in formidable order on the edge of the bluff, and had their launch apparently covered by an array of six deadly gun-barrels.

The launch of the Teaser passed, viewed the situation through a double-barrelled sea-glass, and, thinking discretion the better part of valor, turned, and De Kay's launch was saved by the formidable bristle of the pickets' battery.

SHELLING, AND HOW SHELLS ARE DODGED. — A correspondent, writing from Morris Island, says : "At night we can see the path of a shell through its journey, lighted as it is by a burning fuse. When the range is two miles, the track of a shell from a mortar describes very near half the arc of a circle. On leaving the mortar, it gracefully moves on, climbing up and up into the heavens till it is nearly or quite a mile above the earth, and then it glides along for a moment, apparently in a horizontal line ; but quickly you see that the little fiery orb is on the home stretch, describing the other segment of the circle.

"A shell from a Parrott rifle-gun, in going two and a half miles, deviates from a straight line not quite as much as a shell from a mortar. But in passing over this space, considerable time is required. The report travels much faster than the shot. A shell from a mortar makes the distance of two miles in about thirty seconds, and from a Parrott gun in about half that time. The flash of a gun at night, and the white smoke by day, indicate the moment of discharge, and fifteen or twenty seconds give an abundance of time to find a cover in a splinter proof, behind a trench, or something else. It is wise and soldierly to do so, but many pay no attention to those hissing, screaming, flying, in the day-time invisible devils, except to crack jokes at their expense ; and occasionally one pays with his life for this foolhardiness."

A SCENE IN WAR. — Chaplain Quint relates the following painful episode in war :

"It was a military execution. The person thus punished belonged to the Third Maryland. His crime was *desertion*. It was his second offence. For the first he had been sentenced only to three months' labor and loss of pay ; for the second, death !

"While the army was passing through Frederick, Maryland, he had got out of camp. His regiment passed on, and he went to Baltimore. Arrested there, he was returned to the army, was convicted, and was sentenced.

"On Tuesday his sentence was formally read to him. He was to be shot to death with musketry on the next Friday, between the hours of noon and four P. M. But he had learned the decision on the Sunday before.

"There is no Chaplain to the Third Maryland regiment. But Chaplain Welsh, of the Fifth Connecticut, in the same brigade, ministered to him in spiritual matters faithfully, and like himself, day by day. At last it fell to me to see him, and to be with him during most of his remaining hours. But what could be done, in the way of instruction, had been done by Mr. Welsh, and for it the man was grateful.

"The day of his execution was wet and gloomy. I found him in the morning in the midst of the provost guard. He was sitting on a bag of grain, leaning against a tree, while a sentry, with fixed bayonet, stood behind, never turning away from him, and never to turn away, save as another took his place, until the end. Useless seemed the watch, for arms and feet had been secured, though not painfully, since the sentence was read.

"The captain of the guard had humanely done all he could, and it was partly by his request that I was there. A Chaplain could minister where others could not be allowed.

"The rain fell silently on him. The hours of his life were numbered — even the minutes. He was to meet death, not in the shock and excitement of battle ; not as a martyr for his country ; not in disease ; but in full health, and as a criminal.

"I have seen many a man die, and have tried to perform the sacred duties of my station. I have never had so painful a task as that, because of these circumstances. Willingly, gladly, he conversed, heard, and answered. What he said is, of course, not a matter for publicity ; for the interviews of a minister with the one with whom he has official relations are sacred everywhere. Yet, while painful is such a work, it has its bright side, because of the 'exceeding great and precious promises' it is one's privilege to tell.

"When the time came for removal to the place of execution, he entered an ambulance, a Chaplain accompanying him. Next, in another ambulance, was the coffin. Before, behind, and on either side, a guard. Half a mile of this sad journey brought him to within a short distance of the spot. Then leaving the ambulance, he walked to the place selected. The rain had stopped. The sun was shining on the dark lines of the whole division drawn up on three sides of a hollow square. With guard in front and rear, he passed with steady step through an opening left in the head of the square, still with the Chaplain, and to the open side. There was a grave just dug, and in front of it was his coffin placed. He sat upon his coffin; his feet were re-confined, to allow of which he lifted them voluntarily, and his eyes were bandaged.

"In front of him, the firing party, of two from each regiment, were then drawn up, — half held as reserve, — during which there was still a little time for words with his Chaplain. The General stood by, and the Provost Marshal read the sentence, and shook hands with the condemned. Then a prayer was offered, amid uncovered heads and solemn faces. A last hand-shake with the Chaplain, which he had twice requested; a few words from him to the Chaplain,; a lingering pressure by the hand of the condemned; his lips moving with a prayer-sentence which he had been taught, and on which his thoughts had dwelt before, and he was left alone.

"The word of command was immediately given. He fell over instantly, unconscious. A record of wounds was made by the Surgeons. The troops filed by his grave on the banks of the swollen stream, and then passed off, under cover of the woods, as they had come, to avoid being seen by the enemy. And so, twenty years old, and with only a mother and sister, he was left there. The sun was soon covered with clouds, and the rain poured down on his solitary grave."

INCIDENTS IN TENNESSEE. — The scenes during the march of General Burnside into Tennessee were myriad and peculiarly affecting. "We had not extended our march far into the State," wrote a soldier, "before we had evidence of the prevalence of the most intense loyalty, and, in consequence, the most severe suffering. We had previously seen nothing like it. It is unconditional, and without regard to any of those questions of policy which have been so damaging to the unity of the Union men in Kentucky, and of which the masses here are blissfully ignorant. They kindle into rapture at the sight of our advancing columns, and are moved to tears at the sight of the Stars and Stripes, that 'banner of beauty and glory,' which symbolizes the institutions of our country. We were hailed with tears of joy and with shouts of rapture as their deliverers and defenders. Notwithstanding the many vacant, deserted houses, the many exiles from their homes, which have resulted in so extensive a depletion of population, there were groups of men, women, and children at every turn to greet us with expressions of joy and gratitude, and to tell of wrongs and sufferings which were calculated to touch the hardest heart and to make the ear to tingle.

"Never, perhaps, have patriotism and wrath been so combined, gratitude and vengeance so commingled in expression, as by this loyal, downtrodden, and long-suffering people. It would be impossible to narrate the numerous incidents of interest in this connection of which we were witnesses. One or two may serve as illustrations of their unrestrained and rustic manner in the expression of their feelings.

"On the day we left Montgomery, the head of our column was startled by the voice of an aged woman, shouting 'Glory to God in the highest!' whilst, with streaming eyes, she expressed her gratitude that she had lived to see the deliverers of her State, and, with clasped hands, as she pursued our advancing commands, she prayed most fervently that the God of battles would be with us, to prosper, and defend, and preserve us. Her petitions were ever and anon interrupted by the narration of her suffering, which was made only the more telling by the presence of her husband, who limped behind her, as he leaned with one hand upon a staff, whilst the other rested upon the thigh of his wounded leg, which was made to support more than its wonted share of his body, he having been severely wounded in the other leg by some dastardly, prowling rebel, by which he was made a cripple for life. She would appeal to him for the confirmation of the truth of her statements in regard to their sufferings, and then point him to our soldiery as those who would avenge his wrongs and be his future security and defence. At one time, being near Major-General Hartsuff, whom she readily recognized as chief in command, she made him the subject of her petition, which he acknowledged by respectfully lifting his hat from his head and holding it in his hand the while. Taking the scene altogether, it was an interesting and moving exhibition of patriotism, gratitude, and keen sense of wrongs endured, which, in her esteem, called for vengeance.

"A scene somewhat similar occurred the same day, by another family and group of friends, who, amid shouts of welcome to the 'Yankees,' extended the warm hand of friendly greeting to the soldiers, as they passed, until the eyes of an old lady rested upon a prisoner in our custody, whom she recognized as the despoiler of her peace and home. She told him of the wrongs she and hers had suffered at his hands; how he had driven her husband and herself from their home; how he had hunted her son like a wild animal through the mountains, until he was driven from the State. She upbraided him with his thefts and murders, imploring us in the name of everything sacred not to release him.

.   .   .   .   .   .

"Our *entrée* into Knoxville was a grand ovation. The people of the surrounding country flocked in crowds to welcome us, and the city presented very much the appearance of an Independence Day. No pen can do justice to the scene, and my heart melts as I call it to mind. Old, gray-haired men and women, the middle-aged, and even little prattling children were perfectly frantic with joy. We had a large number of men from this section in our army, who had been away from their homes for two years; and to see the re-union of these brave fellows with those they love better than life would melt the hardest heart.

"I saw one woman, with two little girls, standing on the sidewalk, and watching intently as the column passed. Presently a browned and weather-beaten soldier rode out from the ranks, and the scene that followed more than paid me for the two years of toil and hardship that I have passed in the army. It was his wife and little ones, whom he had not seen, and from whom he had not heard but once, for twenty-eight months. This was but one of many similar instances. It was a common thing, after we got into this vicinity, to see numbers of soldiers riding along in the ranks with one, two, and sometimes three little boys and girls on the horse with them.

"One of the most thrilling scenes I ever had the pleasure to witness occurred on our arrival here. Generals Burnside, Carter, and Shackleford took up their quarters at the fine house of a noted rebel who had left the place, and were followed there by an immense concourse of citizens clamorous for a speech. General Carter was first called out, he being an East Tennessean. He was followed by Generals Burnside and Shackleford, and the excitement and enthusiasm of the crowd gained with every word. Meanwhile I had taken my way around to the rear of the house, and had got upon the roof of the balcony, and as General Shackleford finished his speech I unfurled our large garrison flag, and threw it over the balcony. It was caught by the breeze, and as its beautiful folds streamed out upon the air, the people could no longer contain themselves. Shout after shout rent the air. Old men and gray-haired matrons took each other by the hand, and laughed, shook, and cried, all at the same time. Young men and maidens were uproarious, and little children were 'clean gone crazy.' I looked into the house and saw Generals Burnside, Carter, and Shackleford shaking hands, while tears rolled down their cheeks as if they 'couldn't help it.' Some one sang out — 'Get under it, get under it' — and it seemed as if the crowd would trample each other under foot in their wild endeavors to do so. I never saw anything like it in my life, and felt some as I imagine the old Patriarch must have felt when he wanted to 'depart in peace.' You may think from the way I write there are no rebels here. There are a few, probably one tenth of the population, but they look as if they 'enjoyed very poor health.'"

HOW BRECKINRIDGE ESCAPED. — After Johnston's surrender, the rebel Secretary of War and Ex-Vice-President of the United States made his way to Florida, and with a few companions secured a little launch, in which they coasted down towards the Cedar Keys, and eventually got across to Cuba.

From the mouth of Indian Inlet they had worked down the coast some fifty or sixty miles, when they beached their boat to hunt for turtle eggs and other provisions.

At this time a United States war vessel was running down south between the shore and the Florida Reef, when the commander observed the party, and despatched a boat to ascertain who they were and what they were doing there.

The approach of the boat, filled with the boys in blue, made some stir among the egg-hunters; but "Breck," as the papers familiarly called him in 1856, is quite a strategist in his way, and decided to put a bold front on the affair and play a bluff game. Taylor Wood, a grandson of old "Rough and Ready," took two men, and, the others having retired to the cover of the palmettoes, launched the boat, and went out to meet the advancing party. As he approached, an officer in the stern seat of the gig, revolver in hand, challenged him, and put the usual marine questions.

Taylor was at once the roughest long-shore wrecker and fisherman that ever lived in Florida. "His men were all paroled soldiers; they had to live somehow, and till they could find something better, were glad to get turtle's eggs, and shell-fish driven on shore; they thought they might get down to Indian Key or Key West; had a boat-load of papers, if he wanted to see them."

The ready boys pulled out their parole papers, which were found all right. "The folks on shore were all of the same sort, had the same papers, and were trying to cook dinner if they could find some eggs or clams. Pr'aps the cap'n would like to go ashore; he would be perfectly welcome to the best they had, and their papers too." After a little more good-natured talk, the officer pronounced that satisfactory dictum "all right," told his oarsmen to "give to," and away shot the gig to the steamer, greatly to the relief of the distinguished fugitive, who was anxiously watching the interview from behind a shellbark.

That evening the party left the shore with a few dozen eggs, a little bread, and a few small clams. In thirty-six hours they reached the banks, having spoken one ship and obtained a supply of fresh water. On the morning of the ninth day, after leaving the coast of Florida, they reached Cardenas, where they were received by the people and the authorities with great kindness.

THE ZOUAVE AND THE MULE. — A soldier in the army of the Potomac relates the following: I was riding from Brandy Station to Stevensburg in company with Colonel A., of the Michigan —— regiment, and had reached a point opposite General P.'s headquarters, when we were overtaken by a couple of soldiers mounted on two decidedly un-Rarey-fied mules. The boys had evidently been up to the sutler's, for they were a trifle topheavy. The road crosses a considerable creek, which the mules seemed to hold in strong aversion. Nevertheless, through the persuasive eloquence of two heavy sticks, they were urged on to the middle of the stream, and then they flatly refused to advance. The boys tried all the expedients at hand, but it was "no go;" and when, at length, one of them caught the tail of the other's mule in his hand, and attempted to twist a forward movement out of him, the refractory animal reared, whirled to one side, kicked and snorted, and depositing his rider in the dirty drink, he started on a keen run back towards the corral. Zouave gathered himself up, and seeing that he could not overtake his frightened steed, he only followed with sundry expletives and imprecations not found in the Westminster Catechism. Colonel A., by the way, is a very pious man, and he took it upon himself to chide the exasperated and unfortunate "vet" for using such unchristian-like language; but the soldier would have his joke: so, shaking what water he could out of his red pants, he waded to a dry spot on shore, and muttered that it was "damned hard if a feller couldn't cuss a mule." But soon appreciating the ludicrousness of his condition, he turned to the Colonel, and offered to lay a bet that that was the first time he ever saw a mule tear (muleteer) shed. It was some time before either the Colonel or myself was able to see the *pungency* of the joke; but it came to us after a while, and it helped amazingly to dry up the mud between there and Strasburg."

AN INCIDENT OF THE GREAT BETHEL FIGHT. — Orderly Sergeant Goodfellow, of Colonel Allen's regiment, was mortally wounded in the breast. He handed his musket to a comrade, and several flocked around him. "O," said he, "I guess I've got to go;" and he placed his hand upon the wound. "O, don't mind me, boys," he continued; "go on with the fight; don't stop for me!" and pressing away those who attempted to support him, he sank down upon the ground. Just at that instant his Colonel passed; and looking up to him, he gasped, "Good by, Colonel!" Colonel Allen turned ghastly white as he observed it. He bit his lips, too much moved to speak, and rushed on to avenge his death.

INCIDENTS OF CHICKAMAUGA. — A division Surgeon relates the following: He was riding across a field where the battle had raged fiercely, but just swept on, and was making his way slowly among the drifts of friends and foes, — the blue and the gray together, — when a wounded Federal soldier asked for water. The Surgeon gave him the draught, when a voice from a gray heap near by said, "Won't you give *me* one too, Doctor?" "Certainly I will;" and he was just raising the rebel, and bringing round the canteen slung under his arm to put it to his lips, when a cannon shot from a rebel battery struck the earth on one side; a second bounded by on the other. The man looked up in the Surgeon's face with a smile, "I'm afraid they mean *us*, Doctor." At that instant, a third shot *hit the target*, and a headless trunk fell from the supporting arm. There was another dead rebel. Of truth they *did* "mean us," and the Surgeon hastened away.

Shells are queerly behaved things, often harmless against all probabilities, and when you think they must be deadly, only patching thunder. If a shell passes you by only a few feet before it bursts, you are pretty sure to be good for the next one that comes, since each fragment takes away its share of the motion and flies on. If a shell shows symptoms of "making a landing" just in front of you, your best route would seem to be towards and past the shell; but how rapidly one could run *in that direction* I have no means of knowing, having never seen the man that tried it. A solid shot is the most deceptive of projectiles. It may seem to move lazily, to be almost dead; but so long as it moves at all, beware of it. Just before the battle an artilleryman received his discharge for disability; but delaying for some reason his northward journey, he was yet with his battery on the eve of the engagement, and true to his instincts, took his old place beside his horse, and was just preparing to mount, when a solid shot came ricocheting across the field, bounded up and struck him in the lower part of the body. Crying out, "I've got the first ticket, boys!" he sank down, and only added, with that strange dread of a *little* hurt a terribly wounded man almost always seems to feel, "lay me down by a tree where they won't run over me." They complied with his request, hastened into position, and saw him no more. The poor fellow's discharge was confirmed by Heaven. Now, that fatal ball, having finished its work there, leaped lazily on, and pushed out the skirt of the artillerist's coat, as a hand would move a curtain, without rending it!

THE SOUTHERN WAGON.

COME, all ye sons of freedom, and join our Southern band;
We're going to fight the enemy, and drive them from our land.
Justice is our motto, Providence our guide;
So jump in the wagon, and we'll all take a ride.

Chorus.

O, wait for the wagon,
The dissolution;
The South is our wagon,
And we'll all take a ride.

Secession is our watchword; our rights we all demand;
And to defend our firesides we pledge our hearts and hand.
Jeff Davis is our President, with Stephens by his side;
Brave Beauregard, our General, will join us in the ride.

Our wagon is plenty big enough, the running-gear is good;
It's stuffed around with cotton, and made of Southern wood;
Carolina is our driver, with Georgia by her side;
Virginia will hold her flag up, and we'll all take a ride.

There are Tennessee and Texas also in the ring;
They wouldn't have a government where cotton wasn't king.
Alabama and Florida have long ago replied;
Mississippi and Louisiana are anxious for the ride.

Missouri, North Carolina, and Arkansas are slow;
They must hurry, or we'll leave them, and then
    what will they do?
There's Old Kentucky and Maryland won't make
    up their mind;
So I reckon, after all, we'll take them up behind.

The Tennessee boys are in the field, eager for the
    fray;
They can whip the Yankee boys three to one, they
    say;
And when they get in conflict, with Davis by their
    side,
They'll pitch into the Yankee boys, and then you'll
    see them slide.

Our cause is just and holy, our men are brave and
    true;
We'll whip the Lincoln cutthroats, is all we have
    to do.
God bless our noble army; in him we all confide;
So jump into the wagon, and we'll all take a ride.

THE FIRST UNION VOLUNTEER. — Two days after the fall of Sumter, the Governor of Pennsylvania called for three companies of militia from the Counties of Mifflin, Schuylkill, and Berks. On the 16th April, John T. Hunter, of Philadelphia, telegraphed his application, and was enlisted for three months with the Logan Guard, of Lewiston, Mifflin County, and was afterwards a member of the Nineteenth Pennsylvania volunteers.

ADVENTURES OF A SPY. — Dan. R. Cole, a Sergeant in company D, Third Indiana cavalry, was sent by General Hooker, on the 1st of March, 1863, to Fredericksburg, as a spy.

He crossed the Rappahannock below the Federal lines, and went into Fredericksburg, looking for work, as a mechanic, in the shops. He found them mostly closed, and obtained from General Lee a pass to go to Richmond, where he went in company with some rebel citizens, and remained several days, obtaining much important information.

But when he wished to leave, he met with difficulty in getting a pass, but fell in with a company of political prisoners, who were leaving at night, and passing as one of them, was conducted to Washington under guard. Here he ran from the guards, and reported at the war office with his information.

A YANKEE SAILOR RESORTS TO STRATEGY. — The United States brig "Bohio" was cruising in the Gulf of Mexico in the spring of 1862, when the crew saw a schooner in the horizon, and hoisted the Spanish ensign. But when she changed it for the Stars and Stripes, the schooner took alarm and stood off. The brig put on sail and chased her, but she was a smart sailer, and kept out of the way. The Bohio then run out her guns and fired two shots at the schooner, of which she took no notice.

The captain then ordered the sails to be wet down, and then began to come up with her. At last he resorted to strategy, and rigged a "smoke-stack" amidships, and built a fire, and had " steam on."

As soon as the schooner saw this she gave it up, thinking she was chased by a steamer, and must be overtaken. The captain of the Bohio now boarded her, and found her a blockade-runner, with a cargo of coffee and soap worth fifty thousand dollars. He took her in at the Southwest Pass, and she became a prize, her officers having learned, by a forcible example, that appearances are sometimes deceptive.

THE FIRST FATAL SHOT. — However indifferent men become to human life, they have the most vivid and minute remembrance of the first man they brought down with a deliberate aim.

In the instant of time preceding the fatal shot, the fashion of features, color of eyes and hair, and even the expression of face, are all painted, by the vivid sympathies of the instant, in a picture that remains forever photographed on the brain.

"My first man," said an artilleryman, "I saw but twenty seconds; but I shall remember him forever. I was standing by my gun, when a rebel infantry soldier rushed up and made a lunge with his bayonet at one of the horses. I whipped out my revolver, and took him through the breast. He tossed up his arms, gave me the strangest look in the world, and fell forward upon his face. He had blue eyes, brown, curling hair, a dark mustache, and a handsome face. I thought, the instant I shot, that I should have loved that man if I had known him. I tell you what, this war is terrible business!"

SOUTH CAROLINA VS. NORTH CAROLINA. — Sisterly affection between these two adjacent sovereignties does not appear to be very warm, nor have the events of the civil war done much to draw them together, judging from the following journal of a North Carolina traveller, written in the fall of 1863:

"After spending a day or two in the neat and quiet village of Franklin, I went directly to Walhalla, South Carolina, through Rayburn County, Georgia. At Walhalla I took the train to Columbia, South Carolina, where I arrived at six o'clock P. M. I procured an omnibus to carry me to the Congaree House; on arriving at which, I said to the negro who carried me up from the depot, 'What's the fare, boy?' 'One dollar, sah.' I pulled out a one dollar North Carolina treasury note, and presented it to the negro; on taking which, he exclaimed, 'O, dis no good — no good, sah; dis is North Ca'liner money; North Ca'liner money no good here, sah!' I paid the negro in other money.

"I thought but little of the circumstance, until I saw, the same evening, a North Carolina soldier attempt to purchase some bread with North Carolina money, which he could not do. This was the first time I learned that North Carolina soldiers could not buy something to eat with North Carolina money, however hungry they may be, while passing through the State of South Carolina. I do not know whether this disposition to receive North Carolina in this *dashing* State is general, or not. If it is, it is the duty of the people of North Carolina to refuse South Carolina treasury notes — keep their *shins* out of our State.

"After spending one night in Columbia, I left for Augusta. On the way down, three South Carolina gentlemen occupied the seats immediately opposite me. I overheard one of them, whom the other gentleman called Major : 'I really think North Carolina is the tail end of the Confederacy, and Tennessee is but little behind her — both these States are rotten to the core — neither of them is possessed of any national pride." The other two South Carolina gentlemen concurred in the opinion. I felt indignant at the remark, and as the gentlemen presented the appearance of respectability, I felt inclined to resent the insult offered to my native State — so, after apologizing to the gentlemen for interrupting their conversation, I answered their majesties :

"'Sir, what are your reasons for making such a remark about North Carolina?'

"'Well, I have a reason for thinking so.'

"'Sir, I claim at least the privilege of asking what that reason is.'

"'Why do you claim such a right?'

"'Because, sir, I am a North Carolinian, *to the manor born*, and feel insulted at your opprobrious remark.'

"The South Carolina Major coughed, spit, cleared his throat, and repeated the operation; and, after a rather lengthy pause, during which his *accomplices* seemed not a little confused, at length said :

"'Your State is for reconstruction!'

"I felt still more indignant, and rather tartly replied : 'I ask your pardon, sir; but that is positively false. There is not one man in North Carolina who is in favor of reconstruction. I feel confident you have a greater proportion of reconstructionists in South Carolina than we have.'

"My antagonist seemed a little confused, but gathered courage and retorted: 'North Carolina has never furnished the proportion of troops, nor have her troops won the distinction on the battlefield that South Carolina troops have.'

"In reply to this very ungenerous charge, I referred the Palmetto worshippers to the fact that it was a North Carolinian who fired the first gun of the war; that a North Carolina regiment won the first victory (at Bethel); that a North Carolina regiment (Colonel Fisher's) captured the first Yankee battery; that North Carolina troops had won distinguished laurels at Manassas, at the Seven Pines, during the 'Seven Days' Fight' before Richmond (in which they lost half as many troops as all the other States together), at the second battle of Manassas, at Sharpsburg, Fredericksburg, Chancellorsville, Gettysburg, — indeed, wherever her troops have been called into action. This gentleman only replied that he was not familiar with what North Carolina had done. I told him I hoped he would never again be guilty of making such an ungenerous remark about a State and a people of which he was so ignorant."

SHERIDAN'S RIDE.

BY T. BUCHANAN READ.

Up from the South, at break of day,
Bringing to Winchester fresh dismay,
The affrighted air with a shudder bore,
Like a herald in haste, to the chieftain's door,
The terrible grumble and rumble and roar,
Telling the battle was on once more,
And Sheridan twenty miles away.

And wider still those billows of war
Thundered along the horizon's bar,
And louder yet into Winchester rolled
The roar of that red sea, uncontrolled,
Making the blood of the listener cold
As he thought of the stake in that fiery fray,
And Sheridan twenty miles away.

But there is a road to Winchester town,
A good, broad highway, leading down ;
And there, through the flush of the morning light,
A steed, as black as the steeds of night,
Was seen to pass as with eagle flight:
As if he knew the terrible need,
He stretched away with his utmost speed,
Hill rose and fell; but his heart was gay,
With Sheridan fifteen miles away.

Still sprung from those swift hoofs, thundering south,
The dust, like the smoke from the cannon's mouth,
Or the trail of a comet, sweeping faster and faster,
Foreboding to traitors the doom of disaster ;
The heart of the steed, and the heart of the master
Were beating, like prisoners assaulting their walls,
Impatient to be where the battle-field calls.
Every nerve of the charger was strained to full play,
With Sheridan only ten miles away.

Under his spurning feet the road
Like an arrowy Alpine river flowed ;
And the landscape sped away behind
Like an ocean flying before the wind ;
And the steed, like a bark fed with furnace ire,
Swept on with his wild eyes full of fire.
But lo! he is nearing his heart's desire ;
He is snuffing the smoke of the roaring fray,
With Sheridan only five miles away.

The first that the General saw were the groups
Of stragglers, and then the retreating troops.
What was done — what to do — a glance told him both ;
Then, striking his spurs, with a terrible oath,
He dashed down the line 'mid a storm of huzzas,
And the wave of retreat checked its course there, because
The sight of the master compelled it to pause.
With foam and with dust the black charger was gray,
By the flash of his eye, and his red nostrils' play,
He seemed to the whole great army to say:
"I have brought you Sheridan, all the way
From Winchester down, to save you the day!"

Hurrah, hurrah, for Sheridan!
Hurrah, hurrah, for horse and man!
And when their statues are placed on high,
Under the dome of the Union sky —
The American soldiers' Temple of Fame, —
There, with the glorious General's name,
Be it said, in letters both bold and bright:
    "Here is the steed that saved the day
By carrying Sheridan into the fight,
    From Winchester, twenty miles away!"

INCIDENTS OF CAVALRY SERVICE. — When, on the 30th of June, 1863, the rear of General Kilpatrick's cavalry division was attacked in the town of Hanover, Pennsylvania, the first charge fell upon a remnant of the Eighteenth Pennsylvania cavalry. This command was somewhat scattered, and the rebels, passing through it, came upon the private ambulance of Dr. Wood, chief Surgeon of the division. Two soldiers, named Spaulding and Forsyth, occupied this vehicle — both hospital attendants. As the enemy approached, they made a vigorous attack upon the covering of the wagon with their swords — cutting a dozen or more holes in the top — when Spaulding, who was sick, suggested to Forsyth, who was driving, that he (Spaulding) should drive, and the other drive off the assailants with a six-shooter one of the party had. This arrangement was carried into effect; the enemy were driven away, and the worthy Surgeon's traps were saved to the service.

In the same battle, Folger, a private in company H, Fifth New York cavalry, performed an act of great coolness and daring. He got mixed up some way in the charge upon the Eighteenth Pennsylvania cavalry. Not having time to reload his carbine, he picked up a loaded one some person had dropped, shot a horse upon which the rebel Colonel Payne was riding, the rider falling into a tan-vat, and it was with difficulty Folger saved him from drowning. Just at the moment the Colonel was safely out of the vat, his orderly rode up, and, presenting a pistol to Folger, ordered him to surrender. Folger hesitated, but looking up the street and seeing the advance of the Fifth in the celebrated charge made at that time, suddenly seized upon his unloaded carbine, and aiming it at Mr. Orderly, in no very complimentary terms, ordered him to surrender or he would blow his brains out. The orderly, completely taken by surprise at this turn of affairs, surrendered without making any resistance, so that young Folger, by the display of a little coolness and daring in extremes, not only saved himself from capture, but captured a Colonel and a private from the ranks of the enemy during the heat of battle.

A FLAG-RAISING IN KENTUCKY. — In the fall of 1861, just before Grant made those masterly movements by which the upper end of the Mississippi Valley was open to the Union arms, some of his troops were quartered at Camp McAulay, near Paducah, Kentucky. They were commanded by Brigadier-General Smith. Some of his troops, particularly the Eleventh Indiana regi-

ment, did not agree with him in his toleration of the emblems and expressions of disunion.

A family named Woolfolk, living near the camp, had not only failed to exhibit any Union flag, but on several occasions had waved a little rebel flag from the chamber window, greatly to the disgust of the loyal boys of the Eleventh Indiana. One afternoon, therefore, a party of officers procured a beautiful flag, bearing the "Stars and Stripes," and headed by Adjutant Macauley, waited on the aforesaid family, reminded them of their late "suspicious" doings, and politely, but firmly, stated their intention of "placing the American flag upon their house." The lady requested them to wait until her husband (he being then absent) returned. To this they consented, not wishing to violate the domestic sanctity of any citizen. In the mean time one of the ladies wended her way over to Brigadier-General Smith's headquarters, and asked him to protect them from the "sacrilegious (?) outrage that was about to be committed upon their premises." In a few moments, here and just as the husband of the lady returned, here came Brigadier-General Charles F. Smith bearing down, and in thundering tones demanded "by whose authority this was being done." Adjutant Macauley respectfully informed him "that it was being done by no constituted authority; but it was the wish of the Indiana Eleventh that the flag should be raised." General Smith replied, "I care not what the Indiana Eleventh wants; I'm commander of this post, by —. Disperse to your quarters!" The officers then came back, and their non-success was soon known all through the regiment. General Smith's conduct was regarded with indignation by the Zouaves, and from a murmur of indignation there soon arose a mighty hurricane. The idea that our flag should not be permitted to wave from any place occupied by us was more than they could tolerate. Soon the excitement became too intense to be easily quelled. With one thought and one mind the men all declared that that flag should be raised upon that traitor's house, General Smith's orders to the contrary notwithstanding; "and woe to the man, no matter who, that should dare to pull it down." The flag was again brought forth, and headed by the band, the whole regiment "broke guard," marched to the aforesaid rebel's premises, and there distinctly informed him that "the Stars and Stripes must be immediately planted over his house."

The man Woolfolk made his appearance, and tried to smooth matters over by making a set speech. "He was loyal to the State of Kentucky, and so long as the State was loyal to the Union, that long was he also a loyal citizen. A secession flag had not been in his house since the advent of our troops. As to my private sentiments, I am answerable to my God."

Adjutant Macauley answered him — "That as Kentucky was loyal to the Union, and as the flag was emblematical of the Union, he should have no objection to its floating from the roof."

"You have the power and the means; you can do it then," was the reply.

The roof was scaled, and the flag was waved from it. Three times three cheers and several "tigers" were given. The band played all the national "hims," and warmly were they greeted, we assure you.

General Wallace, who had entered the crowd unobserved, here mounted a stand.

"Boys, the flag is there; your work is done; go home!" was all he said. That was sufficient.

CHAPLAINS. — The graphic correspondent, B. F. Taylor, in a letter from the army of the Cumberland, gives the following:

"'But how about the Chaplains?' you ask; and though an ungrateful business, I will be frank to tell you. I have met three dozen men, whose symbol is the cross, and of that number, two should have been in the ranks, two in the rear, one keeping the temperance pledge, one obeying the third commandment — to be brief about it, five repenting, and eight getting common sense. The rest were efficient, faithful men. Not one Chaplain in fifty, perhaps, lacks the paving-stones of good intentions, but the complex complaint that carries off the greatest number is ignorance of human nature, and want of common sense. Four cardinal questions, I think, will exhaust the qualifications for a chaplaincy: Is he religiously fit? Is he physically fit? Is he acquainted with the animal, 'man?' Does he possess honest horse sense? Let me give two or three illustrative pictures from life. Chaplain A has a *puttering* demon; he is forever not letting things alone. Passing a group of boys, he hears one oath, stops short in his boots, hurls a commandment at the author, hears another and reproves it, receives a whole volley, and retreats, pained and discomfited. Now, Mr. A is a good man, anxious to do his duty; but that habit of his, that darting about camp like a 'devil's darning needle,' with a stereotype reproof in his eye, and a pellet of rebuke on the tip of his tongue, bolts every heart against him. Chaplain B preaches a sermon — regular army fare, too — on Sunday, buttons his coat up snugly under his chin all the other days of the week, draws a thousand dollars, and is content. Chaplain C never forgets that he is C 'with the rank of Captain,' perfumes like a civet cat, never saw the inside of a dog-tent, never quite considered the rank and file fellow-beings. Of the three, the boys hate the first, despise the second, and d—n the third.

"'Demoralize' has become about as common a thing in the army as a bayonet, though the boys do not always get the word right. One of them — 'one of 'em,' in a couple of senses — was talking of himself one night. 'Maybe you wouldn't think it, but I used to be a regular, straight-laced sort of a fellow; but since I joined the army I have got damnably *decomposed!*' Now, a drunken General and a 'decomposed' Chaplain are about as useless lumber as can cumber an army.

"There is Chaplain D, well equipped with heart, but with no head 'to speak of,' and with the purest intentions, a perfect provocative to evil. It was next to impossible for a man to put the best side out when he was by; a curious two-footed diachylum plaster, he drew everybody's infirmities to the surface. I think the regiment grew daily worse and worse, and where *he* was, words were sure to be the dirtiest, jokes the coarsest, deeds the most unseemly. The day before the battle of Chickamauga, the regiment had signed, almost to a man, a paper inviting him to resign; but on the days of the battle he threw off his coat, and carried water to the men all day. In the hottest places there was Chaplain D, water here, water there, assisting the wounded, aiding the Surgeons, a very minister of mercy. I need not add that the 'invitation' lighted the fire under somebody's coffee-kettle on Monday night. The Chaplain had struck the right vein at last; the boys had found something to respect and to love in him, and the clergyman's future usefulness was insured. The bond between Chaplain and men was sealed on that field with honest blood, and will hold good until doomsday.

"One noble Illinois Chaplain, who died in the harness, used to go out at night, lantern in hand, among the blended heaps of the battle-field, and as he went, you could hear his clear, kind voice, 'Any wounded here?' and so he made the terrible rounds. That man was idolized in life and bewailed in death. Old Jacob Trout, a Chaplain of the Revolution, and who preached, if I remember right, a five minute sermon before the battle of Brandywine, was the type of the man that soldiers love to honor. His faith was in 'the sword of the Lord and of Gideon,' but his work was with the musket of Jacob Trout. I do not mean to say that the Chaplain should step out from the little group of non-combatants that belong to a regiment, but I do say, that he must establish one point of contact, quicken one throb of kindred feeling between the men and himself, or his vocation is as empty of all blessings and honor as the old wine flasks of Herculaneum. No man can honestly misunderstand what I have written. The Chaplaincy, at best, is an office difficult and thankless. It demands the best men you have to fill it well and worthily — men whose very presence and bearing put soldiers 'upon their honor;'" and it is safe to say that he who is fit to be a Chaplain is fit to rule a people. How nobly many of them have labored in the army of the Cumberland, I need not testify; ministers of mercy, right-hand men of the Surgeons, and the Nightingales, bearers of the cup of cold water and the word of good cheer; the strong regiment may be the Colonel's, but the wounded brigade is the Chaplain's. To mingle with the men, and share in their frolics, as well as their sorrows, without losing self-respect; to be with them, and yet not of them; to get at their hearts without letting them know it, — these are indeed tasks most delicate and difficult, requiring a tact a man must be born with, and a good, honest sense that can never be derived from Gill's 'Body of Divinity.' How do you like Chaplain

S., I asked of a group of Illinois boys, one day. 'We'll *freeze* to him, every time,' was the characteristic reply; and not unanticipated, for I had seen him dressing a wound, helping out a blundering boy, whose fingers were all thumbs, with his letter to ' the girl he left behind him,' playing ball, running a race, as well as heard him making a prayer and preaching a sermon. The Surgeon and the Chaplain are co-workers. I said the former should report to the women, and I half believe that the Chaplain should do likewise."

A NOBLE RICHMOND GIRL. — Early in the war, S. R. McCullough entered the ranks of the First Wisconsin regiment, and soon after became its hospital steward. At the disastrous battle of Chickamauga, in company with three thousand others, he was taken prisoner, and passed through Atlanta, on his way to Richmond. Here, he says, the loyalty of a great number of the Southern women was distinctly proved; more than a hundred came to the cars where the prisoners were confined, and handed them blankets and other clothing, within which were rolled greenbacks, varying in amount from two to ten dollars. Similar demonstrations took place at various other points along the route; and at Richmond he found a friend indeed in a pretty looking young lady, to whose agency he and a comrade owe their escape. She did the planning, and part of the execution; they the remainder. This young lady met young McCullough, and sent to the hospital for him a pretty bag, containing about a pound of tobacco. It occurred to McCullough that there might be something besides tobacco in it; and sure enough, at the bottom of the bag was a slip of paper, containing substantially these words: " Would you be free? Then be prepared to act — meet me to-morrow at ——." The meeting took place. In a few hasty words her plan was unfolded; a day for its attempt was agreed upon, and the parties separated without attracting the attention of the guard.

A subsequent note, conveyed in like manner, told him he might arrange for a single comrade; that necessary clothes would be provided, and gave short, but specific directions for the future. The to him important day approaches; he can think of no way to pass the guard but to feign sickness and death. It is adopted, and on *the* day four of his fellow-prisoners carry him between blankets to the " dead house " beyond the guard, but within the high fenced enclosure, where he lies, " dead as a nit," from midday till dusk, all the time fearing that some troublesome guard might peep in, or *a real dead one* be brought, and his deception disclosed; but neither happened. At length he raised up and listened; then made a short reconnoissance barefooted, and finding all right, returned, put on his traps, and sallied forth. Meanwhile, a sham fight was gotten up in another part of the enclosure among a lot of prisoners, to quell which drew the guard from their legitimate line, during which the comrade passed beyond to a designated negro hut,

where he was safely stowed away till little pebble stones thrown against it by McCullough told him to come forth. The two proceeded to scale the high fence by one clambering upon the shoulders of the other, thus reaching the top, then drawing up his comrade. After a while they reached the place appointed by the lady (not far distant), and had been there but a few moments when she joined them, directed that they follow her at such a distance only as to be able to keep in view a white handkerchief which she carried in her hand. They did follow her for twenty-five blocks, when she led them into a house, which proved to be that of her father. Up to this time her father did not know a word of her doings; but still he received the rescued men cordially, and at once set to work to get them safely off. He procured two passes for them, for which he paid twenty-five hundred dollars in Confederate currency. In a few days, disencumbered of everything that could by possibility expose them if examined, the good man furnished them a carriage; and with his blessing and that of his family, they set forth for the Federal lines, which they reached on the 23d of December, 1863. Once, on the road, they were stopped and examined by Confederate detectives, but there being no apparent reasons for their detention, were allowed to proceed.

ANECDOTES OF JUDGE CHASE. — During the visit of Chief Justice Chase to New Orleans he received many elegant attentions.

An evening party was given him by a relative in Jackson Street, where Miss Chase, his accomplished daughter, was the cynosure of all eyes. The Chief Justice, who has very little official stiffness, indulged during the evening in many a delightful anecdote, some of which were far more interesting than reports of the Supreme Court.

"While at Key West," said the Chief Justice, "I fell in with an intelligent contraband, who, after eying me intently for a while, approached me with a broad grin, and said:

"'Ise — Ise seen you somewhere, massa.'

"Thinking this smiling recognition worth something, I pulled out a greenback, which the negro recognized better than your humble servant, and with a still broader grin, sputtered out:

"'O, I know you now, massa, I know you now; you'se Old Greenbacks.'" Whereupon the Chief Justice also smiled with a smile of satisfaction, and told another.

"One summer, during my administration, when the Treasury was more than usually low, I had occasion to visit a body of troops that had not been paid off for a long time. Among the men was one with whom I had some acquaintance, but who did not seem to recognize me, whereupon I introduced myself.

"'O, yes, Mr. Chase, Secretary of the Treasury. I recollect,' he said; 'but it is so long since we have seen your picture that I had almost forgotten you."

THE KENTUCKY PARTISAN.

BY PAUL H. HAYNE.

HATH the wily Swamp Fox
　Come again to earth?
Hath the soul of Sumter
　Owned a second birth?
From the Western hill-slopes
　Starts a hero-form,
Stalwart, like the oak tree,
　Tameless, like the storm!
His an eye of lightning!
　His a heart of steel!
Flashing deadly vengeance,
　Thrilled with fiery zeal!
Hound him down, ye minions!
　Seize him — if ye can;
But woe worth the hireling knave
Who meets him, man to man!

Well done, gallant Morgan!
　Strike with might and main,
Till the fair fields redden
　With a gory rain;
Smite them by the roadside,
　Smite them in the wood,
By the lonely valley,
　And the purpling flood;
'Neath the mystic starlight,
　'Neath the glare of day,
Harass, sting, affright them,
　Scatter them, and slay; —
Beard, who durst, our chieftain!
　Blind him — if ye can, —
But woe worth the Hessian thief
Who meets him, man to man!

There's a lurid purpose
　Brooding in his breast,
Born of solemn passion
　And a deep unrest:
For our ruined homesteads
　And our ravaged land,
For our women outraged
　By the dastard hand,
For our thousand sorrows
　And our untold shame,
For our blighted harvests,
　For our towns aflame —
He has sworn, (and recks not
　Who may cross his path) —
That the foe shall feel him
　In his torrid wrath —
That, while will and spirit
　Hold one spark of life,
Blood shall stain his broadsword,
　Blood shall wet his knife: —
On! ye Hessian horsemen!
　Crush him — if ye can!
But woe worth your stanchest slave
Who meets him, man to man!

'Tis no time for pleasure!
　Doff the silken vest!
Up, my men, and follow
　Marion of the West!
Strike with him for freedom!
　Strike with main and might,
'Neath the noonday splendor,
　'Neath the gloom of night;

Strike by rock and roadside,
　Strike in wold and wood;
By the shadowy valley,
　By the purpling flood;
On! where Morgan's war-horse
　Thunders in the van!
God! who would not gladly die
Beside that glorious man?

Hath the wily Swamp Fox
　Come again to earth?
Hath the soul of Sumter
　Owned a second birth?
From the Western hill-slopes
　Starts a hero-form,
Stalwart, like an oak tree,
　Restless, like the storm!
His an eye of lightning!
　His a heart of steel!
Flashing deadly vengeance,
　Thrilled with fiery zeal!
Hound him down, ye robbers!
　Slay him — if ye can!
But woe worth the hireling knave
Who meets him, man to man!

THE EXECUTION OF A SPY. — When a man meets death with true courage, our sympathies are drawn towards him, no matter what may have been his crimes. And no military duty is more painful than the execution of a spy, especially when his bearing is manly, and he displays sentiments of honor and magnanimity at the foot of the scaffold.

The following account gives the particulars of an event of this character which took place at Pulaski, about eighty miles south of Nashville, Tennessee, in December, 1863.

On Friday the citizens and soldiers of Pulaski witnessed one of those painful executions of stern justice which makes war so terrible, and, though sanctioned by the usages of war, is no more than men in the service of their country expose themselves to every day.

Samuel Davis, of General Coleman's scouts, having been found within the Federal lines with despatches and mails destined for the enemy, was tried on the charge of being a spy, and, being found guilty, was condemned to be hung between the hours of ten o'clock A. M. and six o'clock P. M., on Friday, November 27, 1863.

The prisoner was apprised of his sentence by Captain Armstrong, local Provost Marshal, and though somewhat surprised at the sentence of death, did not manifest any outward signs of agitation. Chaplain Young, of the Eighty-first Ohio infantry, visited the prisoner, and administered spiritual consolation.

The prisoner expressed himself resigned to his fate and perfectly prepared to die. He exhibited a firmness unusual for one of his age, and up to the last showed a lively interest in the news of the day, expressing regret when told of the defeat of Bragg. The scaffold for the execution of the prisoner was built upon the ridge east of the town, near the seminary — a position which could be seen from any part of the town. At precisely ten o'clock A. M., the prisoner was taken from his cell, his hands tied behind him, and, accompanied by the Chaplain of the Eighty-first Ohio, was placed in a wagon, seated upon his coffin, and conveyed to the scaffold. Provost Marshal Armstrong conducted the proceedings. At precisely five minutes past ten o'clock the wagon containing the prisoner and the guards entered the hollow square formed by the troops, in the centre of which was the scaffold. The prisoner then stepped from the wagon, and seated himself upon a bench at the foot of the scaffold. He displayed great firmness, glancing casually at his coffin as it was taken from the wagon. Turning to Captain Armstrong, he inquired how long he had to live, and was told he had just fifteen minutes; he then remarked, "We would have to fight the rest of the battles alone."

Captain Armstrong — "I am sorry to be compelled to perform this painful duty."

Prisoner, with a smile — "It does not hurt me, Captain. I am innocent, though I am prepared to die, and do not think hard of it."

Captain Chickasaw then asked the prisoner if it would not have been better for him to have accepted the offer of life upon the disclosure of facts in his possession; when the prisoner answered, with much indignation:

"Do you suppose I would betray a friend? No, sir! I would die a thousand times first!"

He was then questioned upon other matters, but refused to give any information which could be of service.

The prisoner then mounted the scaffold, accompanied by the Chaplain, James Young, whom he requested to pray with him at his execution.

The prisoner then stepped upon the trap, the rope was adjusted about his neck, and the cap drawn over his head. In a moment the trap was sprung, and the prisoner fell suspended in the air. For a few moments he struggled with his hands and feet. This was succeeded by a slight quivering of the body, which ceased at three and a half minutes from the time he fell. After being suspended seventeen and a half minutes, the officiating Surgeon (D. W. Vayles, Sixty-sixth Indiana) pronounced the prisoner dead, and he was cut down and placed in his coffin. It was supposed, from the protracted animation which the prisoner exhibited, that the fall had not broken his neck, and that he died by strangulation; but upon subsequent examination his neck was found to be completely broken.

So fell one whom the fate of war cut down in early youth, and who exhibited traits of character which, under other circumstances, might have made him a valuable friend and member of society.

THE FIGHT IN HAMPTON ROADS. — On Saturday, the 8th March, 1862, about noon, the United States frigate Cumberland lay off in the roads at Newport News, about three hundred yards from shore, the Congress being two hundred yards south of her. The morning was mild and pleasant, and the day had opened without any noteworthy incident.

Soon after eleven o'clock a dark-looking object was seen coming round Craney Island through Norfolk Channel, and making straight for the two Union war vessels. It was instantly recognized as the Merrimac. The officers of the Cumberland and of the Congress had been on the lookout for her for some time, and were as well prepared for the impending fight as wooden vessels could be.

As the strange-looking craft came ploughing through the water right onward towards the port bow of the Cumberland, she resembled a huge, half submerged crocodile. Her sides seemed of solid iron, except where the guns pointed from the narrow ports, and rose slantingly from the water like the roof of a house, or the arched back of a tortoise. Probably the entire height of the apex from the water's edge was ten perpendicular feet. At her prow could be seen the iron ram projecting straight forward somewhat above the water's edge, and apparently a mass of iron. Small boats were slung or fastened to her sides, and the rebel flag from one staff, and a pennant to another at the stern. There was a smoke-stack near her middle; but no side-wheels or machinery was visible, and all exposed parts of the formidable craft were heavily coated with iron.

Immediately on the appearing of the Merrimac, both Union vessels made ready for action. All hands were ordered to places, and the Cumberland was swung across the channel, so her broadside would bear on the hostile craft. The armament she could use against the Merrimac was about eleven nine and ten-inch Dahlgren guns, and two pivot guns of the same make. The enemy came on at the rate of four or five knots an hour. When within a mile, the Cumberland opened on her with her pivot guns, and soon after with broadsides. Still she came on, the balls bounding from her sides like India rubber, making apparently no impression except to cut away the flag-staff.

The Merrimac passed the Congress, discharging a broadside at her, one shell from which killed and disabled every man at Gun No. 10 but one, and made directly for the Cumberland, which she struck on the port bow just starboard of the main chains, knocking a hole in the side near the water line as large as the head of a hogshead, and driving the vessel back upon her anchors with great force. The water at once commenced pouring into the hold, and rose so rapidly as to reach in five minutes the sick-bay on the berth-deck. Almost at the moment of the collision the Merrimac discharged from her forward gun an eleven-inch shell. This shell raked the whole gun-deck, killing ten men at Gun No. 1, among whom was Master Mate John Harrington, and cutting off both arms and legs of Quarter-Gunner Wood. The water rushed in from the hole made below, and in five minutes the ship began to sink by the head. Shell and solid shot from the Cumberland were rained on the Merrimac as she passed ahead, but the most glanced harmlessly from the incline of her iron-plated bomb-roof.

As the Merrimac rounded to and came up, she again raked the Cumberland with heavy fire. At this fire sixteen men at Gun No. 10 were killed or wounded, and were all subsequently carried down in the sinking ship.

Advancing with increased momentum, the Merrimac struck the Cumberland on the starboard side, smashing her upper works and cutting another hole below the water-line.

The ship now began rapidly to settle, and the scene became most horrible. The cockpit was filled with the wounded, whom it was impossible to bring up. The forward magazine was under water, but powder was still supplied from the after magazine, and the firing kept steadily up by men who knew that the ship was sinking under them. They worked desperately and unremittingly, and amid the din and horror of the conflict gave cheers for their flag and the Union, which were joined in by the wounded. The decks were slippery with blood, and arms and legs and chunks of flesh were strewed about. The Merrimac lay off at easy point-blank range, discharging her broadsides alternately at the Cumberland and the Congress. The water by this time had reached the after magazine of the Cumberland. The men, however, kept at work, and several cases of powder were passed up, and the guns kept in play. Several men in the after shell-room lingered there too long in their eagerness to pass up shell, and were drowned.

The water had at this time reached the berth or main gun-deck, and it was felt hopeless and useless to continue the fight longer. The word was given for each man to save himself; but after this order Gun No. 7 was fired, when the adjoining Gun, No. 6, was actually under water. This last shot was fired by an active little fellow named Matthew Tenney, whose courage had been conspicuous throughout the action. As his port was left open by the recoil of the gun, he jumped to scramble out; but the water rushed in with so much force that he was washed back and drowned. When the order was given to cease firing, and to look out for their safety in the best way possible, numbers scampered through the port-holes, whilst others reached the spar-deck by the companionways. Some were unable to get out by either of these means, and were carried down by the rapidly sinking ship. Of those who reached the upper deck, some swam off to the tugs that came out from Newport News.

The Cumberland sank in water nearly to her cross-trees. She went down with her flag still flying — a memento of the bravest, most daring, and yet most hopeless defence that has ever been made by any vessel belonging to any navy in the world. The men fought with a courage that could not be excelled. There was no flinching, no thought of surrender.

The whole number lost of the Cumberland's crew was one hundred and twenty.

The Cumberland being thoroughly demolished, the Merrimac left her — not, to the credit of the rebels it ought to be stated, firing either at the men clinging to the rigging, or at the small boats on the propeller Whildin, which were busily employed rescuing the survivors of her crew — and proceeded to attack the Congress. The officers of the Congress, seeing the fate of the Cumberland, and aware that she also would be sunk if she remained within reach of the iron beak of the Merrimac, had got all sail on the ship, with the intention of running her ashore. The tug-boat Zouave also came out and made fast to the Cumberland, and assisted in towing her ashore.

The Merrimac then surged up, gave the Congress a broadside, receiving one in return, and getting astern, raked the ship fore and aft. This fire was terribly destructive, a shell killing every man at one of the guns except one. Coming again broadside to the Congress, the Merrimac ranged slowly backward and forward, at less than one hundred yards distant, and fired broadside after broadside into the Congress. The latter vessel replied manfully and obstinately, every gun that could be brought to bear being discharged rapidly, but with little effect upon the iron monster. Some of the balls caused splinters of iron to fly from her mailed roof, and one shot, entering a port-hole, dismounted a gun. The guns of the Merrimac appeared to be specially trained on the after magazine of the Congress, and shot after shot entered that part of the ship.

Thus slowly drifting down with the current and again steaming up, the Merrimac continued for an hour to fire into her opponent. Several times the Congress was on fire, but the flames were kept down. Finally the ship was on fire in so many places, and the flames gathering such force, that it was hopeless and suicidal to keep up the defence any longer. The national flag was sorrowfully hauled down, and a white flag hoisted at the peak.

After it was hoisted the Merrimac continued to fire, perhaps not discovering the white flag, but soon after ceased firing.

A small rebel tug that had followed the Merrimac out of Norfolk, then came alongside the Congress, and a young officer gained the gun-deck through a port-hole, announced that he came on board to take command, and ordered the officers on board the tug.

The officers of the Congress refused to go on board, hoping from the nearness to the shore that they would be able to reach it, and unwilling to become prisoners whilst the least chance of escape remained. Some of the men, supposed to number about forty, thinking the tug was one of our vessels, rushed on board. At this moment the members of an Indiana regiment, at Newport News, brought a Parrott gun down to the beach and opened fire upon the rebel tug. The tug hastily put off, and the Merrimac again opened fire upon the Congress. The fire not being returned from the ship, the Merrimac commenced shelling the woods and camps at Newport News, fortunately, however, without doing much damage, only one or two casualties occurring.

By the time all were ashore, it was seven o'clock in the evening, and the Congress was in a bright sheet of flame, fore and aft. She continued to burn until twelve o'clock at night, her guns, which were loaded and trained, going off as they became heated. A shell from one struck a sloop at Newport News, and blew her up. At twelve o'clock the fire reached her magazines, and with a tremendous concussion her charred remains blew up. There were some five tons of gunpowder in her magazine.

After sinking the Cumberland and firing the Congress, the Merrimac, with the Yorktown and Jamestown, stood off in the direction of the steam-frigate Minnesota, which had been for some hours aground, about three miles below Newport News. This was about five o'clock on Saturday evening. The rebel commander of the Merrimac, either fearing the greater strength of the Minnesota, or wishing, as it afterwards appeared, to capture this splendid ship without doing serious damage to her, did not attempt to run the Minnesota down, as he had run down the Cumberland. He stood off about a mile distant, and with the Yorktown and Jamestown threw shell and shot at the frigate. The Minnesota, though, from being aground, unable to manœuvre, or bring all her guns to bear, was fought splendidly. She threw a shell at the Yorktown, which set her on fire, and she was towed off by her consort, the Jamestown. From the reappearance of the Yorktown next day, the fire must have been suppressed without serious damage. The after cabins of the Minnesota were torn away, in order to bring two of her large guns to bear from her stern ports, the position in which she was lying enabling the rebels to attack her there with impunity. She received two serious shots: one, an eleven-inch shell, entered near the waist, passed through the chief engineer's room, knocking both rooms into ruins, and wounding several men. Another shot went clear through the chain plate, and another passed through the mainmast. Six of the crew were killed outright on board the Minnesota, and nineteen wounded. The men, though fighting at great disadvantage, stuck manfully to their guns, and exhibited a spirit that would have enabled them to compete successfully with any ordinary vessel.

About nightfall, the Merrimac, satisfied with her afternoon's work of death and destruction, steamed in under Sewall's Point. The day thus closed most dismally for the Union side, and with the most gloomy apprehensions of what would occur the next day. The Minnesota was at the mercy of the Merrimac; and there appeared no reason why the iron monster might not clear the Roads of the fleet, destroy all the stores and warehouses on the beach, drive the troops into the Fortress, and command Hampton Roads against any number of wooden vessels the Government might send there. Saturday was a terribly dismal night at Fortress Monroe.

About nine o'clock, Ericsson's battery, the Monitor, arrived at the Roads; and upon her performance was felt that the safety of their position in a great measure depended. Never was a greater hope placed upon apparently more insignificant means; but never was a great hope more triumphantly fulfilled. The Monitor was the reverse

of formidable, lying low on the water, with a plain structure amidships, a small pilot-house forward, a diminutive smoke-pipe aft: at a mile's distance she might be taken for a raft, with an army ambulance amidships.

When Lieutenant Worden was informed of what had occurred, though his crew were suffering from exposure and loss of rest from a stormy voyage around from New York, he at once made preparations for taking part in whatever might occur next day.

Before daylight on Sunday morning, the Monitor moved up, and took a position alongside the Minnesota, lying between the latter ship and the Fortress, where she could not be seen by the rebels, but was ready, with steam up, to slip out.

Up to this time, on Sunday, the rebels gave no indication of what were their further designs. The Merrimac lay up towards Craney Island, in view, but motionless. At one o'clock she was observed in motion, and came out, followed by the Yorktown and Jamestown, both crowded with troops. The object of the leniency towards the Minnesota on the previous evening thus became evident. It was the hope of the rebels to bring the ships aboard the Minnesota, overpower her crew by the force of numbers, and capture both vessel and men.

As the rebel flotilla came out from Sewall's Point, the Monitor stood out boldly towards them. It is doubtful if the rebels knew what to make of the strange-looking battery, or if they despised it. Even the Yorktown kept on approaching, until a thirteen-inch shell from the Monitor sent her to the right about. The Merrimac and the Monitor kept on approaching each other, the latter waiting until she would choose her distance, and the former apparently not knowing what to make of her funny-looking antagonist. The first shot from the Monitor was fired when about one hundred yards distant from the Merrimac, and this distance was subsequently reduced to fifty yards, and at no time during the furious cannonading that ensued were the vessels more than two hundred yards apart.

It is impossible to reproduce the animated descriptions given of this grand contest between two vessels of such formidable offensive and defensive powers. The scene was in plain view from Fortress Monroe, and in the main facts all the spectators agree. At first the fight was very furious, and the guns of the Monitor were fired rapidly. As she carried but two guns, whilst the Merrimac had eight, of course she received two or three shots for every one she gave. Finding that her antagonist was much more formidable than she looked, the Merrimac attempted to run her down. The superior speed and quicker turning qualities of the Monitor enabled her to avoid these shocks, and to give the Merrimac, as she passed, a shot. Once the Merrimac struck her near amidships, but only to prove that the battery could not be run down nor shot down. She spun round like a top; and as she got her bearing again, sent one of her formidable missiles into her huge opponent. The officers of the Monitor, at this time, had gained such confidence in the impregnability of their battery, that they no longer fired at random, nor hastily. The fight then assumed its most interesting aspects. The Monitor ran round the Merrimac repeatedly, probing her sides, seeking for weak points, and reserving her fire with coolness, until she had the right spot and the exact range, and made her experiments accordingly. In this way the Merrimac received three shots, which seriously damaged her. Neither of these shots rebounded at all, but cut their way clear through iron and wood into the ship. Soon after receiving the third shot, the Merrimac turned towards Sewall's Point, and made off at full speed.

The Monitor followed the Merrimac until she got well inside Sewall's Point, and then returned to the Minnesota.

The Merrimac then took the Patrick Henry and Jamestown in tow, and proceeded to Norfolk. In making the plunge at the Monitor, she had lost her enormous iron beak and damaged her machinery, and was leaking considerably.

Thus ended the most terrific naval engagement of the war. The havoc made by the Merrimac among the wooden vessels of the Federal navy was appalling; but the providential arrival of the Monitor robbed the rebel craft of its terrors, and the destruction of that one Saturday afternoon in March was the last serious mischief she ever did.

A SQUARE MEAL. — One of the Wisconsin boys, on the reception at the return of the Fifth regiment of that State, said: "This is the first square meal I've had since I left home." Being asked what a square meal was, he replied, "Four cups of coffee, all the ham I can eat, with bread, butter, pies, cakes, pickles, and cheese in proportion, with ladies smiling to inspire the appetite."

ANECDOTE OF PRESIDENT LINCOLN. — It will be remembered that an extra session of Congress was called in July following Mr. Lincoln's inauguration. In the message then sent in, speaking of secession, and the measures taken by the Southern leaders to bring it about, there occurs the following remark: "With rebellion thus sugar-coated, they have been drugging the public mind of their section for more than thirty years, until at length they have brought many good men to a willingness to take up arms against the Government," &c. Mr. Defries, the Government printer, told me that, when the message was being printed, he was a good deal disturbed by the use of the term "sugar-coated," and finally went to the President about it. Their relations to each other being of the most intimate character, he told Mr. Lincoln frankly that he ought to remember that a message to Congress was a different affair from a speech at a mass meeting in Illinois; that the message became a part of history, and should be written accordingly.

"What is the matter now?" inquired the President.

"Why," said Mr. Defrees, "you have used an undignified expression in the message;" and then, reading the paragraph aloud, he added, "I would alter the structure of that, if I were you."

"Defrees," replied Mr. Lincoln, "that word expresses precisely my idea, and I am not going to change it. The time will never come, in this country, when the people won't know exactly what *sugar-coated* means!"

THE COMMON SOLDIER.

NOBODY cared, when he went to war,
But the woman who cried on his shoulder;
Nobody decked him with immortelles:
He was only a common soldier.

Nobody packed in a dainty trunk
Folded raiment and officer's fare:
A knapsack held all the new recruit
Might own, or love, or eat, or wear.

Nobody gave him a good-by fête,
With sparkling jest and flower-crowned wine:
Two or three friends on the sidewalk stood
Watching for Jones, the fourth in line.

Nobody cared how the battle went
With the man who fought till the bullet sped
Through the coat undecked with leaf or star
On a common soldier left for dead.

The cool rain bathed the fevered wound,
And the kind clouds wept the livelong night:
A pitying lotion Nature gave,
Till help might come with morning light —

Such help as the knife of the surgeon gives,
Cleaving the gallant arm from shoulder;
And another name swells the pension-list
For the meagre pay of a common soldier.

See, over yonder all day he stands —
An empty sleeve in the soft wind sways,
As he holds his lonely left hand out
For charity at the crossing ways.

And this is how, with bitter shame,
He begs his bread and hardly lives;
So wearily ekes out the sum
A proud and grateful country gives.

What matter how he served the guns
When plume and sash were over yonder?
What matter though he bore the flag
Through blinding smoke and battle thunder?

What matter that a wife and child
Cry softly for that good arm rent?
And wonder why that random shot
To him, their own beloved, was sent?

O patriot hearts, wipe out this stain;
Give jewelled cup and sword no more;
But let no common soldier blush
To own the loyal blue he wore.

Shout long and loud for victory won
By chief and leader stanch and true;
But don't forget the boys that fought —
Shout for the common soldier too.

AN INCIDENT OF THE WILDERNESS. — During one of the battles on the left of Grant's army, in 1865, a son in one of the New York regiments met his father in one of the rebel regiments, and took him prisoner. It was an actual occurrence, vouched for upon good authority, and the manner of it was this. Just before the war commenced, the son left his home, and went to the State of New York; he enlisted in the Federal service, and went down into General Grant's army, and for gallantry in action was promoted to a Lieutenancy. The father was in the ranks yet. On the day of the battle, while charging the rebel works on the left, this son, by some curious happening of providence, came directly upon his father on the other side. "Hold!" he cried, hastily, as he noticed his father was levelling his gun upon him; "don't you know whom you are firing at?" During the four years of his service, this son had grown so much that the father did not know him. "Well," says he, "I am your son, and you are my prisoner." The father looked up, came quickly to a recognition of his offspring, and went to the rear. The head of the family was once a shoemaker in the city of Petersburg.

A PATRIOTIC ARTIST. — A correspondent who visited the studio of Powers, at Florence, says:

"Though courted and petted by the English, who have been among his best patrons, Powers has always been true to his country — loyal to the core. I was reminded of a little incident which occurred a few months before, when he was in his studio, and an English lady, or some one of secession proclivities, asked him if he had ever executed a bust of Jefferson Davis. 'No, madam,' said he, his bright eye flashing with fire, 'I hope that before long, an artist of another profession than mine may have the pleasure of executing him.' We spoke of the readiness of the English to be on our side, now that success had crowned our arms. 'Ah,' said he, 'I know not which is the more annoying, when you are trying to get a heavy load up hill, to have some one hitch on his horse behind and pull you back, or when you are going down hill, to have him put on his horses before, and dash away with all fury, to the risk of upsetting your load and breaking your neck.'"

A NIGHT IN MISSOURI. — Until I began to follow the camp, I had never known, save by auricular evidence, of those unpoetical insects known as fleas; but one night in Syracuse, Mo., "our mess" experienced the cruelty and savageness of the diminutive foes of man, to our bodies' extremest dissatisfaction. We were all lounging in the tent, reading, undreaming of enemies of any kind, when we all became restless, and the interest of our books began seriously to diminish. There were various manual applications to various parts of the body, multifarious shiftings of position, accompanied with emphatic expletives that sounded marvellously like oaths.

"What is the matter?" was asked by one of us to the other. "What renders you so uneasy?" "Heaven knows," was the answer; "but I itch like Satan."

"My body is on fire," observed one.

"I wonder," said another, "if I have contracted a loathsome disease."

"Confound it! what ails me?"

"And me?" "And me?" "And me?" was echoed from my companions.

One hand became insufficient to allay the irritation of our corporeality. Both hands became requisite to the task, and our volumes were necessarily laid aside. No one yet appeared aware of the cause of his suffering. If we were not all in Tophet, no one could deny we had gone to the old Scratch. We seemed to be laboring under an uncontrollable nervous complaint. We threw our hands about wildly. We seized our flesh rudely, and rubbed our clothes until they nearly ignited from friction. One of the quartet could stand it no longer. He threw off his coat and vest spasmodically, and even his undergarments, and solemnly exclaimed:

"Flee from the wrath to come!"

The mystery was explained, the enigma solved. The martyr's person was covered with small black spots, that disappeared and reappeared in the same instant.

To be practically expressive, he was covered with fleas.

The rest of us followed his example, and converted ourselves into model artists.

We were all covered with fleas.

Fleas were everywhere. Tent, straw, books, blankets, valises, saddles, swarmed with them.

The air scintillated with their blackness.

We rushed out of the tent.

They were there in myriads.

The moonlight fell in checkered beams through their innumerable skippings.

They made a terrible charge, as of a forlorn hope, and drove us back.

We roared with anger and with pain, and loud curses made the atmosphere assume a violet hue.

Three of the flea-besieged caught up canteens of whiskey and brandy, and poured the contents over their persons and down their throats; scratching meanwhile like a thousand cats of the Thomas persuasion, and leaping about like dancing dervishes. The more the fleas bit, the more the victims drank; and I, having no taste for liquor, began to envy them, as, in their increasing intoxication, they seemed to enjoy themselves after a sardonic fashion. The fleas redoubled their ferocity on me, and I surrendered at discretion, and at last became resigned to their attacks, until, a few minutes after, a storm that had been gathering burst with fierce lightning, heavy thunder, and torrents of rain.

A happy idea seized me.

I caught up my saddle and bridle, and placed them on my sable steed, "Festus," which stood neighing to the tempest, a few feet from the camp. I mounted the fleet-footed horse, and, nude as the Apollo Belvedere, cried, "Go," to the restive animal; and off we sped, to the amazement of the sentinels, through the darkness and the storm. Every few moments the lightning blazed around us with a lurid sheen, as we went like the wind through the tempestuous night.

"Festus" enjoyed it, as did his rider; and six swift-speeding miles were passed ere I drew the rein upon the neck of the panting beast, covered with white flecks of foam.

I paused, and felt that the fleas had been left behind. The pelting rain and rushing blast had been too much for them, while the exercise had made my attireless body glow into a pleasant warmth. "Festus" galloped back, and soon I was in the tent, rolled so closely in the blanket that no new attack of the fleas could reach me. My companions, overcome with their exertions, sufferings, and potations, had lain down; but the fleas were still upon them, and they rolled and tossed more than a rural tragedian in the tent scene of "Richard the Third." They were asleep, and yet they moaned piteously, and scratched with demoniac violence. In spite of my pity for the poor fellows, I could not refrain from laughing.

With the earliest dawn I awoke, and the tent was vacant.

Horrid thought!

Had the fleas carried them off?

I went out to search for them, and, after diligent quest, found them still in Nature's garb, distributed miscellaneously about the encampment. In their physical torture they had unconsciously rolled out of the tent. One lay in an adjacent ditch, a second under an artillery wagon, and the third was convulsively grasping the earth, as if he were endeavoring to dig his own grave; believing, no doubt, that in the tomb neither Fortune nor fleas could ever harm him more. The unfortunate two were covered with crimson spots, and looked as if recovering from the small-pox. I pulled them, still stupid from their spiritual excess, into the tent again, and covered them with blankets, though they swore incoherently as I did so, evidently believing that some giant flea was dragging them to perdition.

When they were fully aroused, they fell to scratching again most violently, but knew not what had occurred until they had recalled the events of the previous night. They then blasphemed afresh, and unanimously consigned the entire race of fleas to the bottomless pit. The fleas still tried to bite, but could find no new places, and my companions had grown accustomed to them.

They felt no uneasiness for the coming night; they were aware that the new fleas would retire from a field so completely occupied, and that the domesticated creatures were in sufficient force to rout all invaders.

So ended that memorable Noche Triste, an exemplification of the scriptural declaration:

"The wicked flee when no man pursueth."

SERVILE INSURRECTIONS. — In the first year of the war the people of the South in many places felt that they were standing over a smouldering volcano. It was feared, and by many believed, that a general servile insurrection would take place simultaneously with the advance of the Union forces, and that Southern society would be crushed to pieces by the combined action of hostile pressure from without and terrible commotions within.

In fact, disturbances of this kind did take place in various parts of the South, and when they were quieted and the mutineers were arrested there followed scenes of horrid torture and sickening executions which have had no equal on the continent, except in the Indian wars. The following account of an insurrection in South Carolina and the executions that followed it is from a private letter written from Charleston in the fall of 1861:

"No general insurrection has taken place, though several revolts have been attempted; *two quite recently, and in these cases whole families were murdered before the slaves were subdued.* Then came retaliation of the most fearful character. At any time where servants assail or murder white persons, speedy and severe punishment is administered; but now they do not wait for the action of the law. Lynch law prevails. In these revolts, which occurred in the interior of the State, most of the servants who participated were either shot in the conflict or as soon as captured, and two of them were burned to death.

"To say they were burned to death seems a simple sentence, devoid of any special horror; but the scene, as described to me by a witness, was too dreadful for mortal eyes. Imagine the poor wretches, red with the blood of their masters, cowering in the hands of those from whom they need not look for pity; not even for time to repent of deeds which exclude them from hope hereafter. They are dogged and defiant towards their captors, until their doom is pronounced — a fate of which they have a special horror. Dragged to the place of execution, within sight of their own houses, surrounded by their fellow-servants, who are compelled to witness the sight, they are bound to strong trees, with great heaps of pine knots piled close around their persons. Directly the torch is applied, and the inflammable pine bursts into a vivid flame. When the blaze reaches the bodies, and the sensitive flesh peels and crackles, their cries are too fearful to be heard by human ears. Nor is the torment soon over. The flames scorch the upper part of the bodies, producing exquisite agony, but slowly burn into the vitals, until the wretched sufferers go to judgment with all their crimes upon their heads.

"I undertook to say the apprehension of servile insurrection lost its power when, as time passed, all seemed peaceful; so we easily fell back into dreams of security until these events aroused us to watchfulness. This news is suppressed as far as possible, and kept entirely from the papers, for the negroes hear what is published, if they do not read it, and such examples might produce disastrous consequences."

A SAILOR'S STORY. — On the 10th of April, 1862, a month after the great naval fight in Hampton Roads, there was a grand reception in New York of the surviving heroes of the Congress and the Cumberland.

In the course of the evening Mr. Willard, one of the sailors on the Congress, gave, in his vigorous way, an account of the action, as follows:

"Gentlemen and ladies: I am not acquainted with this kind of speaking. I am not used to it. I have been too long in a man-of-war. I enlisted in a man-of-war when I was thirteen years of age. (I am now forty.) I have been in one ever since. We had been a long time in the Congress, waiting for the Merrimac, with the Cumberland. I claim a timber-head in both ships. I belonged to the Cumberland in the destroying of the navy yard and the ships at Norfolk. On the 8th of March, when the Merrimac came out, we were as tickled as a boy would be with his father coming home with a new kite for him. [Loud laughter and applause.] She fired a gun at us. It went clean through the ship, and killed nobody. The next one was a shell. It came in at a port-hole, killed six men, and exploded and killed nine more. The next one killed ten. Then she went down to the Cumberland. She had an old grudge against her, and she took her hog-fashion, as I should say. [Great laughter.] The Cumberland fought her as long as she could. She fired her spar-deck guns at her after her gun-deck was under water; but the shot had no more effect than peas. She sunk the Cumberland in about seven fathoms of water. You know what a fathom is — six feet. We lay in nine fathoms; and it would not do to sink in that. We slipped our cable, and ran into shallower water to get our broadside on the Merrimac, but we got her bows on. That gave them a chance to rake us as they did. The commander opened a little port-hole and said: 'Smith, will you surrender the ship?' Says he, 'No, not as long as I have got a gun, or a man to man it.' They fired a broadside. The men moved the dead bodies away, and manned the guns again. They fired another broadside, and dismounted both the guns, and killed the crews. When they first went by us, they set us afire by a shell exploding near the magazine. (I know where the magazine is — you folks don't.) Last broadside she killed our commander, Mr. Smith, our sailing-master, and the pilot. We had no chance at all. We were on the spar-deck — most of us — the other steamers firing at us, and we dodging the shot. No chance to dodge down below, because you could not see the shot till they were inside of the ship. We had no chance, and we surrendered. The rebel officers — we knowed 'em all — all old playmates, shipmates — came home in the Germantown with them — all old playmates, but rascals now. She left us, and she went toward Norfolk to get out of the way. She returned in the morning to have what I'd call

a 'fandango' with the Minnesota; and the first thing she knowed, the little bumble-bee, the Monitor, was there, and she went back. I have no more to say, people; but there is the flag that the fathers of our country left us, and, by the powers of God above us, we'll — "

The brave sailor's closing sentence was broken off by long and repeated cheers from the audience.

ANECDOTE OF PRESIDENT LINCOLN. — President Lincoln, having been applied to to pardon a repentant slave-trader who had been sentenced to prison, answered the applicant: "My friend, if this man had been guilty of the worst murder that can be conceived of, I might, perhaps, have pardoned him. You know the weakness of my nature — always open to the appeals of repentance or of grief; and with such a touching letter, and such recommendations, I could not resist. But any man who would go to Africa and snatch from a mother her children, to sell them into interminable bondage, merely for the sake of pecuniary gain, shall never receive pardon from me."

TAKING THE OATH. — A very shrewd, sensible man in Maury County, Tennessee, who had been a strong Union man until the Yankees got there, but who, after that, became equally as strong a Southerner, went to Columbia one day, and was brought before General Negley. "Well," said General Negley, "Mr. B., you must take the oath before you go home."

"Very well," said B.; "just have it boxed up, General, and I'll take it out."

"O," said General Negley, "you don't understand me; you must take the oath to support the Government of the United States."

"Why, General," said friend B., "I have a wife and several children, and it's as much as I can do to support them. I am a poor man, and I can't think of supporting the *whole United States* — that's rather too much."

By this time Negley became rather impatient. "Here," said he, handing B. the printed oath, "read it for yourself."

"I can't read," said B.

"Well, then," said Negley, turning to the Provost Marshal, "give him a pass anyhow; he has no sense."

And thus he went home without taking the oath, and the Yankee General was outwitted.

GET OFF THAT STUMP. — Among the paroled rebel soldiers who were sent to Cairo was a man a little over seven and a half feet in height. He started out with the Missouri troops at the commencement of the war, and stuck to them until the "dog was dead," and never received a scratch. Soon after he was mustered into the rebel service, the regiment to which he belonged appeared before the Colonel on dress parade, and the Colonel, who prided himself on the fine appearance and good size of his men, cast his eyes along the line with a smile of self-satisfaction, until they rested on the towering form of the tall Missourian, when he knit his brows, and called out fiercely in thunder tones, "Get off that stump, you impertinent scoundrel, or I'll order you under arrest." The soldiers looked at each other, wondering what the Colonel meant, but no one moved. Finding his authority treated with disrespect, he fairly boiled with rage, and advancing to the soldier, he exclaimed, "What in the devil are you standing on?" The soldier respectfully replied, "On my feet, Colonel." The Colonel was completely taken back, as he surveyed this tall specimen of humanity from head to foot in blank amazement; he mumbled an apology for his rude remarks, and hastened away, leaving his men convulsed with laughter. "Get off that stump" became a by-word with the Missouri rebels, and it will, no doubt, live as long as the long Missourian.

THE CAPTURE OF JEFFERSON DAVIS. — An officer who accompanied Davis in his flight from Richmond, and who was present at his capture, gives the following account of that affair:

"Davis ran his risks and took his chances, fully conscious of imminent danger, yet powerless, from physical weariness, to do all he designed doing against the danger. When the musketry firing was heard in the morning, at 'dim gray dawn,' it was supposed to be between the rebel marauders and Mr. Davis' few camp defenders. Under this impression he hurriedly put on his boots, and prepared to go out for the purpose of interposing, saying:

" 'They will at least as yet respect me.'

"As he got to the tent door thus hastily equipped, and with this good intention of preventing an effusion of blood by an appeal in the name of a fading, but not wholly faded authority, he saw a few cavalry ride up the road and deploy in front.

" 'Ha, Federals!' was his exclamation.

" 'Then you are captured,' cried Mrs. Davis, with emotion.

"In a moment she caught an idea — a woman's idea — and as quickly as women in an emergency execute their designs, it was done. He slept in a wrapper — a loose one. It was yet around him. This she fastened ere he was aware of it, and then, bidding him adieu, urged him to go to the spring, a short distance off, where his horses and arms were. Strange as it may seem, there was not even a pistol in the tent. Davis felt that his only course was to reach his horse and arms, and complied. As he was leaving the door, followed by a servant with a water-bucket, Miss Howell flung a shawl over his head. There was no time to remove it without exposure and embarrassment, and as he had not far to go, he ran the chance exactly as it was devised for him. In these two articles consisted the woman's attire of which so much nonsense has been spoken and written, and under these circumstances, and in this way, was Jefferson Davis going forth to perfect his escape.

"But it was too late for any effort to reach his horses, and the Confederate President was at last a prisoner in the hands of the United States."

BOB, THE "BULLY BOY." — Among the sharp boys in Sherman's army, on the grand march, was a graduate of the common schools of Northern Ohio — the only son of a widowed mother. The fond mother had no word from her son from the time the army left Chattanooga till it reached Atlanta. She waited for tidings with much anxiety, watching daily the newspaper reports. At length, several days after the taking of Atlanta had been announced, a letter was brought her, which read as follows:

"ATLANTA.

"DEAR MOTHER: Bully boy all right.
"BOB."

In due time, Sherman marched from Atlanta to Savannah. There was a fight behind Savannah. The widowed mother read in the newspapers that the company to which her boy belonged was in that fight. With almost sleepless anxiety she waited for news from him. One day she received a note which read thus:

"SAVANNAH.

"DEAR MOTHER: Bully boy got a hole in his hide — not bad.   BOB."

In the march of events, Sherman's men reached Washington, were mustered out, and the company to which "Bob" belonged went to the capital of Ohio. Here "Bob" had his final, honorable discharge, and when he had made it "all right" with the paymaster, and was again a citizen, he sent the following telegram:

"COLUMBUS.

"DEAR MOTHER: Bully boy home to-morrow.
"BOB."

When asked by a friend, to whom the infrequency and brevity of his epistles home had been mentioned, why he did not write oftener, and at greater length, he answered:

"Bully boy's got his haversack full. Keep it all to tell by word of mouth. Won't he have a good time talking up the old lady?"

THE FIRST REBEL ADMIRAL. — Harry Maury was a dashing young Southron, a nephew of the Lieutenant of National Observatory memory. He had been educated for the navy, and was only thoroughly alive in scenes of adventure and peril. He rushed into Walker's Nicaragua expedition as if it had been a schoolboy frolic; and his escapade of capturing the revenue cutter Susan, with all on board, officers and men, and running her off to the West Indies, without compass or pilot, and making his way back by the corks he left in his wake, are yet fresh in the memory.

In January, 1861, this young "Harry" mounted one six-pound gun upon his bit of a pleasure yacht, laid in three hams and five barrels of whiskey for stores, anchored off Fort Morgan, in Mobile Bay, trained a pump-log against the fortress, took observations with a table-leg, sent a summons to surrender, and thus inaugurated the Confederate navy.

Subsequently he led an Alabama regiment, was badly wounded, captured, and exchanged, and now, disabled either for mischief or for frolic, lingers out a painful life somewhere in Dixie.

So much for the first Admiral of the rebel Armada. — *B. F. Taylor.*

WANTED TO "GET OUT." — The following story was told by a correspondent, at the depot of Prisoners of War, at Johnson's Island :

"Last night, a number of prisoners made a futile attempt to escape by digging under the fence. They commenced a mine under the floor of a building next to the wall, and four succeeded in getting through, making their exit on the side of the fence. But fortunately the fifth was a size larger than he imagined himself to be, and stuck in the mud, as the boys say. He succeeded in getting his head through, but somehow got his arms in such a position that he could not move, being evidently under much excitement, and anxious to make his escape with all possible speed.

"In the mean time, his comrades, who had made their escape, were anxious that he should accompany them on their imaginary journey South ; and after undergoing a severe operation of hairpulling — as that was the only hold they could get — he declined going any farther at that time. And after bidding his more fortunate comrades to take a lock of his extricated hair with them to his sweetheart in Dixie, he bade them farewell ; and they left him in this ludicrous position, perfectly disgusted.

"But now arose the second difficulty : his friends on the inside thought that he was intruding upon their rights, and informed him that if he did not intend to go any farther it was very impolite to stop up the hole with his precious self, and keep them from going too. After much persuading, by way of pulling at his legs, and again pushing, of no avail, they, too, abandoned the enterprise of extricating the poor, miserable wretch. But what this unlucky being lacked in the organ of size he made up in the organ of endurance, for he actually remained in this tight place from nine o'clock in the evening until half past five in the morning. It was raining nearly the whole night, and was uncomfortably cold. The first that was discovered of him was by the sentinel, who heard a suppressed voice, saying :

" 'I want to get out o' this.'

"Sentinel — 'Where are you ?'

"Rebel — 'Here, under the fence. I want to get out !'

"Sentinel — 'Well, get out, or I'll shoot you.'

"Rebel — 'I am fast ! Don't shoot ! I am fast !'

"The Corporal of the guard was called, who brought a light, and, sure enough, there was a rebel planted, with his head protruding out of the solid earth.

"It was agreed among the boys, that with the addition of a head-board, with his name inscribed on it, 'Captain Pole, who stuck in the hole,' he would be buried decently enough. But after consulting the officer of the guard they concluded to dig him out. The ludicrous appearance he presented created great merriment ; muddy, dripping, half foundered, forth he came, wringing himself as he went, 'with the look of a "wetdown" rooster in a fall rain storm.' He said he was the first who attempted to escape, but no reliance was placed on his statement, and pickets were sent out, and those prisoners who were out were discovered in the back part of the island building a raft, and were brought in and secured."

AN INCIDENT OF FAIR OAKS. — On the dark nights that followed the first and the disastrous day at Fair Oaks, hundreds of soldiers remember with what fierce enthusiasm Meagher and his Irish brigade pressed forward over the dead and dying. Then early the following morning there came the wild shout, the rush, the clash, the dead stillness, and then the yell of victorious Erin.

In the midst of that red battle scene there occurred one of those touching incidents in which this unhappy civil war has abounded.

Among General Meagher's men was one O'Neill, a soldierly appearing fellow, aged, perhaps, thirty, dark complexioned, robust, and undoubtedly full of pluck. On that terrible Sabbath morning a portion of the Irish brigade swept over the railroad and into an adjacent swamp, full of dead horrors, for there was one scene of the previous day's struggle. A rebel Lieutenant, at the head of those who remained of his company, dashed madly on the Irish line of steel, which stood firm as the rock of Cashel ; and the impotent, insurrectionary wave was repelled with a reactionary shock that scattered it like spray. Forty rebels lay dead and wounded ; and foremost among them all the young Lieutenant, a bullet having shattered his left knee. Of course he fell into our hands a prisoner, and with his companions was thereafter soon carried to the rear. This young man — long hair, dark eyes, straight and soldierly — was admired for his bearing, which was that of a proud foe, foiled, but not vanquished. There was a halt near the station, where the O'Neill alluded to above then was, as a temporary guard over some other prisoners. As he gazed at the wounded rebel officer, a visible change overspread his features. He asked one of his superiors if he might speak to the Lieutenant. His joy knew no bounds when he learned that this was Phil O'Neill, C. S. A., a younger brother, of whom the family had had no tidings for fifteen years. He had lived as a clerk in Savannah, had enlisted as a private, for good conduct had been promoted, and was at length a prisoner. The young Confederate, when fully aware of this interesting discovery, again wept tears of joy, and the scene was one never to be forgotten. The romantic circumstance was made known to General Meagher, to whom the Lieutenant was introduced, and for whom the General did everything in his power. Though the captured officer would not fight on our side, he would not be exchanged, and went North, where, in a brief period, he took the oath of allegiance. His brother was killed while butting under Burnside against the stone wall at Fredericksburg, and *his evergreen sprig was nearest to the enemy.*

SPEECH OF MRS. BOOTH. — On the 3d of April, 1864, the widow of Major Booth, who was killed in the barbarous attack on Fort Pillow, arrived at Fort Pickering, below Memphis, Tennessee. Colonel Jackson, of the Sixth United States heavy artillery, had his regiment formed into line for her reception. In front of its centre stood fourteen men, as fine, brave fellows as tread the earth. They were the remnant of the first battalion of the regiment now drawn up — all who had escaped the fiendish scenes of Fort Pillow — scenes that have stamped the deepest blackness on the infamous brow of treason.

Mrs. Booth came forward. In her hand she bore a flag, red and clotted with human blood. She took a position in front of the fourteen heroes, so lately under her deceased husband's command.

The ranks before her observed a silence that was full of solemnity. Many a hardy face showed by twitching lids and humid eyes how the sight of the bereaved lady touched bosoms that could meet steel, and drew on the fountain of tears that had remained dry even amid the piteous sights witnessed on the battle-field after a fierce action.

Turning to the men before her, she said:

"Boys, I have just come from a visit to the hospital of Mound City. There I saw your comrades, wounded at the bloody struggle in Fort Pillow. There I found this flag — you recognize it. One of your comrades saved it from the insulting touch of traitors at Fort Pillow!

"I have given to my country all I had to give — my husband — such a gift! Yet I have freely given him for freedom and my country.

"After my husband's cold remains, the next dearest object left me in the world is this flag — the flag that waved in proud defiance over the works of Fort Pillow!

"Soldiers: this flag I give to you, knowing that you will ever remember the last words of my noble husband: 'Never surrender the flag to traitors.'"

Colonel Jackson then received from her hand, on behalf of his command, the blood-stained flag. He called upon the regiment to receive it as such a gift ought to be received. At that call he and every man of the regiment fell upon their knees, and, solemnly appealing to the God of battles, each one swore to avenge their brave and fallen comrades, and never — never to surrender the flag to traitors!

The scene was one never surpassed in emotional incident. Beside the swift-rolling waters of the Mississippi — within the enclosure that bristled with the death-dealing cannon — knelt these rough soldiers, whose bosoms were heaving with emotion, and on many of whose cheeks quivered a tear they tried to hide, though it did honor to their manly natures. Beside them stood in her grief the widow of the loved officer they had lost, and above them was held the bloody flag — that eloquent record of crime which has capped the climax of rebellion, and which will bring a reckoning so fearful.

In a few pointed words, Colonel Alexander pledged himself and his command to discharge to the uttermost the solemn obligation of justice they had that day taken.

Colonel Kappan followed him, expressing himself in favor of such retaliatory acts of justice as the laws of warfare required, in a case of such fiendish and wicked cruelty.

ADVENTURE OF A LONG ISLAND GIRL. — A Western journalist relates this story of a young woman's adventures: "Miss Fanny Wilson is a native of Williamsburg, Long Island. About four years ago, or one year prior to the war, she came West, visiting a relative who resided at La Fayette, Indiana. While here her leisure moments were frequently employed in communicating, by affectionate epistles, with one to whom her heart had been given, and her hand had been promised, before leaving her native city — a young man from New Jersey. After a residence of about one year with her Western relative, and just as the war was beginning to prove a reality, Fanny, in company with a certain Miss Nelly Graves, who had also come from the East, and there left a lover, set out upon her return to her home and family. While on their way thither, the two young ladies concocted a scheme, the romantic nature of which was doubtless its most attractive feature.

"The call for troops having been issued, and the several States coming quickly forward with their first brave boys, it so happened that those two youths whose hearts had been exchanged for those of the pair who now were on their happy way towards them, enlisted in a certain and the same regiment. Having obtained cognizance of this fact, Fanny and her companion conceived the idea of assuming the uniform, enlisting in the service, and following their lovers to the field. Soon their plans were matured and carried into effect. A sufficient change having been made in their personal appearance, their hair having been cut, and themselves reclothed to suit their wish, they sought the locality of the chosen regiment, offered their services, were accepted, and mustered in. In another company from their town, of the same regiment (the Twenty-fourth New-Jersey), were their patriotic lovers, 'known, though all unknowing.' On parade, in the drill, they were together — they obeyed the same command. In the quick evolutions of the field, they came as close as they had in other days, even on the floor of the dancing-school; and yet — so says Fanny — the facts of the case were not made known.

"But the Twenty-fourth, by the fate of war, was ordered before Vicksburg, having already served through the first campaign in Western Virginia; and here, alas for Fanny! she was to suffer by one blow. Here her brave lover was wounded. She sought his cot, watched over him, and half revealed her true nature in her devotion and gentleness. She nursed him faithfully and long, but he died. Next after this, by the reverse of fortune, Fanny herself and her companion were both thrown upon their hospital cots, exhausted, sick. With others, both wounded and debilitated, they were sent to Cairo. Their attendants were more constant and more scrutinizing. Suspicion was first had; the discovery of Fanny's and Nelly's true sex was made. Of course, the next event in their romantic history was a dismissal from the service. But not until her health had improved sufficiently, was Fanny dismissed from the sick-ward of the hospital. This happened, however, a week or two after her sex had become known. Nelly, who up to this time had shared the fate of her companion, was now no longer allowed to do so; her illness became serious, she was detained in the hospital, and Fanny and she parted — their histories no longer being linked. Nelly we can tell no further of; but Fanny, having again entered society in her true position, what became of her?

"We now see her on the stage of a theatre at Cairo, Illinois, serving an engagement as ballet girl. But this lasts but a few nights. She turns up in Memphis, even as a soldier again. But she has changed her branch of the service; Fanny has now become a private in the Third Illinois cavalry. Only two weeks has she been enlisted, when, to her surprise, while riding through the street with a fellow-soldier, she is stopped by a guard, and arrested for being 'a woman in men's clothing.' She is taken to the office of the detective police, and questioned until no doubt can remain as to her identity — not proving herself, as suspected, a rebel spy, but a Federal soldier. An appropriate wardrobe is procured her, and her word is given that she will not again attempt a disguise. And here we leave her. Fanny is a young lady of about nineteen years; of a fair face, though somewhat tanned; of a rather masculine voice, and a mind sprightly and somewhat educated — being very easily able to pass herself off for a boy of about seventeen or eighteen."

COTTON-DOODLE.

Written by a lady on hearing that Yankee Doodle had been hissed in New Orleans.

Hurrah for brave King Cotton!
    The Southerners are singing;
From Carolina to the Gulf
    The echo's loudly ringing;
In every heart a feeling stirs
    'Gainst Northern abolition!
Something is heard of compromise,
    But nothing of submission.

Cotton-doodle, boys, hurrah!
    We've sent old Yankee hissing;
And when we get our Southern rights,
    I guess he'll turn up missing!

His poet, Lowell, is singing
    'Gainst "sacred compromises;"
Prays, "God confound the dastard word,"
    At which his "gall arises."
No wonder that he hates it,
    He surely has good reason,
He broke the faith of Seventy-six,
    And it proclaims his treason.

Cotton-doodle, boys, hurrah!

He does not love the negro;
    That's but a pretext hollow
To hide his greedy longing
    For the "almighty dollar."
Where was his tender conscience,
    When for "blood-stained gold"
His Narraganset captives
    Were into slavery sold?

Cotton-doodle, boys, hurrah!

'Gainst nullifying tariffs
    He raised a mighty din,
And loudly talked in Thirty-two
    Of Carolina's sin;
But now appeals from Congress
    To the "higher law" of Heaven!
'Twas horrible in one, you know,
    But God-like in eleven!

Cotton-doodle, boys, hurrah!

Thank God, his day is passing!
    He can no longer vex us;
For, State by State, we'll firmly stand,
    From Maryland to Texas.
King Cotton is a monarch
    Who'll conquer abolition,
And set his foot upon the neck
    Of treason and sedition.

Cotton-doodle, boys, hurrah!
    We've sent old Yankee hissing;
And when we get our Southern rights,
    I guess he'll turn up missing!

"ALEX. HAYES." — A soldier of Gettysburg, a few days after the battle, wrote:

"I wish you could have seen a picture, just at the close of last Friday's battle, on the left of our centre, of which his splendid figure formed a prominent part. Our little brigade, which had been lying on Cemetery Hill, was ordered over to the position that was so valiantly but unsuccessfully charged by Pickett's rebel division. We hurried there through a storm of shot and shell, but only arrived in time to see the grand finale, the *tableaux vivants*, and, alas, *mourants*, at the close of the drama. The enemy's batteries were still playing briskly, and their sharpshooters kept up a lively fire, but their infantry, slain and wounded and routed, were pouring into our lines throughout their whole extent. Then enter Alex. Hayes, Brigadier-General United States Army, the brave American soldier. Six feet or more in height, and as many inches the length of his mighty mustache, erect and smiling, lightly holding well in hand his horse — the third within a half hour, a noble animal, his flanks be spattered with blood, tied to his streaming tail a rebel flag that drags ignominiously in the mud — he dashes along our lines, now rushing out into the open field, a mark for a hundred sharpshooters, but never touched, now quietly cantering back to our lines to be welcomed with a storm of cheers. I reckon him the grandest view of my life. I bar not Niagara. It was the arch spirit of glorious Victory wildly triumphing over the fallen foe.

"The night after, I met General Hayes again. After the fight of Friday afternoon, we held the battle-field, our skirmishers forming a line on the outer edge of it. This field was strewn with rebel wounded. It was impossible for us to bring them in Friday night; every apology for a hospital being crowded, our own wounded, in many cases, lying out all night. But Saturday morning bandsmen were sent out with litters to bring in the poor fellows, *and were fired upon by the rebel sharpshooters so briskly that it was impossible to help them.* Stories similar to this I had often heard, but never believed. This came under my own observation. So all day Saturday the poor fellows lay there, praying for death. When night fell, another officer of my regiment and myself got a few volunteers to go out with us, thinking there might be some who could creep into our lines, supported, on either side, by one of us. May God preserve me from such a position again! We could do almost nothing. Of a thousand wounded men, we found one whom four of us carried into our lines in a blanket. Other poor souls would think they might accomplish it, but, at the slightest change of position, would fall back, screaming in awful agony. Litters we had none. Then appeared General Alex. Hayes in another light, less of the bravado, perhaps, not less of the hero. He sent out two companies, who cleared the rebel sharpshooters from a position they held in a ruined building, busied himself in procuring litters and bearers, and before morning many of the poor fellows were safe within our lines. It is not my good fortune to be personally acquainted with this General Alex. Hayes; but I wish every one, as far as I can effect it, to honor him as the bravest of soldiers, and love him as the best-hearted of men. A true chevalier he must be, *sans peur et sans reproche.*"

THE FALL OF LEXINGTON, MO.

COLONEL MULLIGAN'S OWN STORY.

"On the 10th of September, 1861," said Colonel Mulligan, in his speech at Detroit, "a letter arrived from Colonel Peabody, saying that he was retreating from Warrensburg, twenty-five miles distant, and that Price was pursuing him with ten thousand men. A few hours afterwards, Colonel Peabody, with the Thirteenth Missouri, entered Lexington. We then had two thousand seven hundred and eighty men in garrison, and forty rounds of cartridges. At noon of the 11th we commenced throwing up our first intrenchments. In six hours afterwards, the enemy opened their fire. Colonel Peabody was ordered out to meet them. The camp then presented a lively scene; officers were hurrying hither and thither, drawing the troops in line and giving orders, and the commander was riding with his staff to the bridge to encourage his men and to plant his artillery. Two six-pounders were planted to oppose the enemy, and placed in charge of Captain Dan Quirk, who remained at his post till daybreak. It was a night of fearful anxiety. None knew at what moment the enemy would be upon the little band, and the hours passed in silence and anxious waiting. So it continued until morning, when the Chaplain rushed into headquarters, saying that the enemy were pushing forward. Two companies of the Missouri Thirteenth were ordered out, and the Colonel, with the aid of his glass, saw General Price urging his men to the fight. They were met by Company K, of the Irish brigade, under Captain Quirk, who held them in check until Captain Dillon's company, of the Missouri Thirteenth, drove them back, and burned the bridge. That closed our work before breakfast. Immediately six companies of the Missouri Thirteenth and two companies of Illinois cavalry were despatched in search of the retreating enemy. They engaged them in a cornfield, fought with them gallantly, and harassed them to such an extent as to delay their progress, in order to give time for constructing intrenchments around the camp on College Hill. This had the desired effect, and we succeeded in throwing up earthworks three or four feet in height. This consumed the night, and was continued during the next day, the outposts still opposing the enemy, and keeping them back as far as possible.

"At three o'clock in the afternoon of the 12th, the engagement opened with artillery. A volley of grape shot was thrown among the officers, who stood in front of the breastworks. The guns within the intrenchments immediately replied with a vigor which converted the scene into one of the wildest description. The gunners were inexperienced, and the firing was bad. We had five six-pounders, and the musketry was firing at every angle. Those who were not shooting at the moon were shooting above it. The men were ordered to cease firing, and they were arranged in ranks, kneeling, the front rank shooting and the others loading. The artillery was served with more care, and within an hour a shot from one of our guns dismounted their largest piece, a twelve-pounder, and exploded a powder caisson. This achievement was received with shouts of exultation by the beleaguered garrison. The enemy retired a distance of three miles. At seven o'clock the engagement had ceased, and Lexington was ours again.

"Next morning General Parsons, with ten thousand men at his back, sent in a flag of truce to a little garrison of two thousand seven hundred men, asking permission to enter the town and bury his dead, claiming that when the noble Lyon went down, his corpse had fallen into his hands, and he had granted every privilege to the Federal officers sent after it. It was not necessary to adduce this as a reason why he should be permitted to perform an act which humanity would dictate. The request was willingly granted, and we cheerfully assisted in burying the fallen foe.

"On Friday the work of throwing up intrenchments went on. It rained all day, and the men stood knee deep in the mud, building them. Troops were sent out for forage, and returned with large quantities of provisions and fodder. On Friday, Saturday, and Sunday, we stole seven days' provisions for two thousand seven hundred men. We had found no provisions at Lexington, and were compelled to get our rations as best we could. A quantity of powder was obtained, and then large cisterns were filled with water. The men made cartridges in the cellar of the college building, and cast one hundred and fifty rounds of shot for the guns, at the founderies of Lexington. During the little respite the evening gave us, we cast our shot, made our cartridges, and stole our own provisions. We had stacks of forage, plenty of hams, bacon, &c., and felt that good times were in store for us. All this time, our pickets were constantly engaged with the enemy, and we were well aware that ten thousand men were threatening us, and knew that the struggle was to be a desperate one. Earthworks had been raised breast-high, enclosing an area of fifteen to eighteen acres, and surrounded by a ditch. Outside of this was a circle of twenty-one mines, and still farther down were pits to embarrass the progress of the enemy.

"During the night of the 17th, we were getting ready for the defence, and heard the sounds of preparation in the camp of the enemy for the attack on the morrow. Father Butler went around among the men and blessed them, and they reverently uncovered their heads and received his benediction. At nine o'clock on the morning of the 18th, the drums beat to arms, and the terrible struggle commenced. The enemy's force had been increased to twenty-eight thousand men and thirteen pieces of artillery. They came as one dark, moving mass — men armed to the teeth; as far as the eye could reach, men, men, men, were visible. They planted two batteries in front, one on the left, one on the right, and one in the rear, and opened with a terrible fire, which was answered with the utmost bravery and determination. Our spies had informed us that the rebels intended to make one grand rout, and bury us in the trenches of Lexington. The batteries opened at nine o'clock, and for three days they never ceased to pour deadly shot upon us. About noon the hospital was taken. It was situated on the left, outside of the intrenchments. I had taken for granted that it was not necessary to build fortifications around the sick man's couch. I had thought that, among civilized nations, the soldier sickened and wounded in the service of his country, would, at least, be sacred. But I was inexperienced, and had yet to learn that such was not the case with the rebels. They besieged the hospital, took it, and from the balcony and roof their sharpshooters poured a deadly fire within our intrenchments. It contained our chaplain and surgeon, and one hundred and twenty wounded men. It could not be allowed to remain in the possession of the enemy.

A company of the Missouri Thirteenth was ordered forward to retake the hospital. They started on their errand, but stopped at the breastworks, 'going not out because it was bad to go out.' A company of the Missouri Fourteenth was sent forward, but it also shrank from the task, and refused to move outside the intrenchments. The Montgomery Guards, Captain Gleason, of the Irish brigade, were then brought out. The commander admonished them that the others had failed, and with a brief exhortation to uphold the name they bore, gave the word to 'charge.' The distance was eight hundred yards. They started out from the intrenchment, first quick, then double-quick, then on a run, then faster. The enemy poured a deadly shower of bullets upon them; but on they went, a wild line of steel, and what is better than steel, human will. They stormed up the slope to the hospital door, and with irresistible bravery drove the enemy before them, and hurled them far down the hill beyond. At the head of those brave fellows, pale as marble, but not pale from fear, stood the gallant officer, Captain Gleason. He said, 'Come on, my brave boys,' and in they rushed. But when their brave captain returned, it was with a shot through the cheek and another through the arm, and with but fifty of the eighty he had led forth. The hospital was in their possession. This charge was one of the most brilliant and reckless in all history, and to Captain Gleason belongs the glory. Each side felt, after this charge, that a clever thing had been done; and the fire of the enemy lagged. We were in a terrible situation. Towards night the fire increased, and in the evening word came from the rebels that if the garrison did not surrender before the next day, they would hoist the black flag at their cannon and give us no quarter. Word was sent back that 'when we asked for quarter it would be time to settle that.' It was a terrible thing to see those brave fellows mangled, and with no skilful hands to bind their gaping wounds. Our surgeon was held with the enemy, against all rules of war, and that, too, when we had released a surgeon of theirs on his mere pledge that he was such. Captain Moriarty went into the hospital, and with nothing but a razor, acted the part of a surgeon. We could not be without a chaplain or a surgeon any longer. There was in our ranks a Lieutenant Hickey, a rollicking, jolly fellow, who was despatched from the hospital with orders to procure the surgeon and chaplain at all hazards. Forty minutes later and the brave lieutenant was borne by severely wounded. As he was borne past I heard him exclaim, 'God have mercy on my little ones!' And God did hear his prayers, for the gay Lieutenant is up, as rollicking as ever, and is now forming his brigade to return to the field.

"On the morning of the 19th the firing was resumed, and continued all day. We recovered our surgeon and chaplain. The day was signalized by a fierce bayonet charge upon a regiment of the enemy, which served to show them that our men were not yet completely worried out. The officers had told them to hold out until the 19th, when they would certainly be reënforced. Through that day our little garrison stood with straining eyes, watching to see if some friendly flag was bearing aid to them — with straining ear, awaiting the sound of a friendly cannonade. But no reënforcements appeared, and, with the energy of despair, they determined to do their duty at all hazards. The 19th was a horrid day. Our water cisterns had been drained, and we dared not leave the crown of the hill, and make our intrenchments on the bank of the river, for the enemy could have planted his cannon on the hill and buried us. The day was burning hot, and the men bit their cartridges; their lips were parched and blistered. But not a word of murmuring. The night of the 19th two wells were ordered to be dug. We took a ravine, and expected to reach water in about thirty hours. During the night, I passed around the field, smoothed back the clotted hair, and by the light of the moon, shining through the trees, recognized here and there the countenances of my brave men who had fallen. Some were my favorites in days gone past, who had stood by me in these hours of terror, and had fallen on the hard fought field. Sadly we buried them in the trenches.

"The morning of the 20th broke; but no reënforcements appeared, and still the men fought on. The rebels had constructed movable breastworks of hemp bales, rolled them up the hill, and advanced their batteries in a manner to command the fortification. Heated shot were fired at them, but they had taken the precaution to soak the bales in the Missouri. The attack was urged with renewed vigor, and, during the forenoon, the outer breastworks were taken by a charge of the rebels in force. The whole line was broken, and the enemy rushed in upon us. Captain Fitzgerald, whom I had known in my younger days, and whom we had been accustomed to call by the familiar name of 'Saxy,' was then ordered to oppose his company to the assailants. As I gave the order, 'Saxy, go in,' the gallant Fitzgerald, at the head of company I, with a wild yell rushed in upon the enemy. The commander sent for a company on which he could rely; the firing suddenly ceased, and when the smoke rose from the field, I observed the Michigan company, under their gallant young commander, Captain Patrick McDermott, charging the enemy and driving them back. Many of our good fellows were lying dead, our cartridges had failed, and it was evident that the fight would soon cease. It was now three o'clock, and all on a sudden an orderly came, saying that the enemy had sent a flag of truce. With the flag came the following note from General Price:

"'Colonel: What has caused the cessation of the fight?'

"The Colonel returned it with the following reply written on the back: —

"'General: I hardly know, unless you have surrendered.'

"He took pains to assure me, however, that such was not the case. I learned soon after that the Home Guard had hoisted the white flag. The Lieutenant who had thus hoisted the white flag

27

was threatened with instant death unless he pulled it down. The men all said, 'We have no cartridges, and a vast horde of the enemy is about us.' They were told to go to the line and stand there, and use the charge at the muzzle of their guns, or perish there. They grasped their weapons the fiercer, turned calmly about, and stood firmly at their posts. And there they stood without a murmur, praying, as they never prayed before, that the rebel horde would show themselves at the earthworks. An officer remarked, 'This is butchery.' The conviction became general, and a council of war was held. And when, finally, the white flag was raised, Adjutant Cosgrove, of your city, shed bitter tears. The place was given up, upon what conditions, to this day I hardly know or care. The enemy came pouring in. One foppish officer, dressed in the gaudiest uniform of his rank, strutted up and down through the camp, stopped before our men, took out a pair of handcuffs, and holding them up, said, 'Do you know what these are for?' We were placed in file, and a figure on horseback, looking much like 'Death on the pale horse,' led us through the streets of Lexington. As we passed, the secession ladies of Lexington came from their houses, and from the fence tops jeered at us. We were then taken to a hotel with no rations and no proprietor. After we had boarded there for some time, we started with General Price, on the morning of the 30th, for 'the land of Dixie.'"

THE RIVER FIGHT.

BY H. H. BROWNELL.

Do you know of the dreary land,
    If land such region may seem,
Where 'tis neither sea nor strand,
Ocean nor good dry land,
    But the nightmare marsh of a dream?
Where the Mighty River his death-road takes,
'Mid pools and windings that coil like snakes,
A hundred leagues of bayous and lakes,
    To die in the great Gulf Stream?

No coast-line clear and true,
Granite and deep-sea blue,
    On that dismal shore you pass,
Surf-worn boulder or sandy beach, —
But ooze-flats as far as the eye can reach,
    With shallows of water-grass;
Reedy savannas, vast and dun,
Lying dead in the dim March sun;
Huge rotting trunks and roots that lie
Like the blackened bones of shapes gone by,
    And miles of sunken morass.

No lovely, delicate thing
    Of life o'er the waste is seen;
But the cayman, couched by his weedy spring,
    And the pelican, bird unclean,
Or the buzzard, flapping with heavy wing,
    Like an evil ghost o'er the desolate scene.

Ah! many a weary day
With our leader there we lay,
    In the sultry haze and smoke,
Tugging our ships o'er the bar,
Till the spring was wasted far,

Till his brave heart almost broke.
For the sullen river seemed
As if our intent he dreamed, —
  All his sallow mouths did spew and choke.

But ere April fully passed,
All ground over at last,
And we knew the die was cast —
Knew the day drew nigh
To dare to the end one stormy deed,
Might save the land at her sorest need,
  Or on the old deck to die!

Anchored we lay, — and a morn the more,
To his captains and all his men
Thus wrote our old Commodore —
  (He wasn't Admiral then):

"GENERAL ORDERS.

" Send your to'gallant-masts down,
  Rig in each flying jib-boom !·
  Clear all ahead for the loom
Of traitor fortress and town,
Or traitor fleet bearing down.

  "In with your canvas high;
  We shall want no sail to fly !
Topsail, foresail, spanker, and jib
(With the heart of oak in the oaken rib), ∖
  Shall serve us to win or die !

  "Trim every sail by the head,
  (So shall you spare the lead,)
Lest, if she ground, your ship swing round,
  Bows in shore, for a wreck.
See your grapnels all clear with pains,
And a solid kedge in your port main-chains,
  With a whip to the main yard :
  Drop it heavy and hard
  When you grapple a traitor deck !

" On forecastle and on poop
  Mount guns, as best you may deem.
If possible, rouse them up
  (For still you must bow the stream).
Also hoist and secure with stops
Howitzers firmly in your tops,
  To fire on the foe a-beam.

" Look well to your pumps and hose ;
  Have water-tubs fore and aft,
  For quenching flame in your craft,
  And the gun-crews' fiery thirst.
See planks with felt fitted close,
  To plug every shot-hole tight.
  Stand ready to meet the worst !
For, if I have reckoned aright,
They will serve us shot, both cold and hot,
  Freely enough to-night.

" Mark well each signal I make
(Our life-long service at stake,
  And honor that must not lag) —
Whate'er the peril and awe,
In the battle's fiercest flaw,
Let never one ship withdraw
  Till the orders come from the flag !"

Would you hear of the River Fight ?
It was two of a soft spring night ;
  God's stars looked down on all ;
And all was clear and bright

But the low fog's clinging breath :
Up the River of Death
  Sailed the Great Admiral.

On our high poop-deck he stood,
  And round him ranged the men
Who have made their birthright good
  Of manhood once and again —
Lords of helm and of sail,
Tried in tempest and gale,
  Bronzed in battle and wreck.
Bell and Bailey grandly led
Each his line of the Blue and Red ;
Wainwright stood by our starboard rail ;
  Thornton fought the deck.

And I mind me of more than they,
  Of the youthful, steadfast ones,
  That have shown them worthy sons
Of the seamen passed away.
Tyson conned our helm that day ;
  Watson stood by his guns.

What thought our Admiral then,
Looking down on his men ?
  Since the terrible day
  (Day of renown and tears),
When at anchor the Essex lay,
  Holding her foes at bay, —
When a boy by Porter's side he stood,
Till deck and plank-shear were dyed with blood :
  'Tis half a hundred years, —
  Half a hundred years to a day !

Who could fail with him ?
Who reckon of life or limb ?
  Not a pulse but beat the higher !
There had you seen, by the starlight dim,
Five hundred faces strong and grim :
  The Flag is going under fire !
Right up by the fort, with her helm hard a-port,
  The Hartford is going under fire !

The way to our work was plain.
Caldwell had broken the chain,
(Two hulks swung down amain
  Soon as 'twas sundered).
Under the night's dark blue,
Steering steady and true,
Ship after ship went through,
Till, as we hove in view,
  "Jackson" out-thundered.

Back echoed "Philip !" Ah ! then
Could you have seen our men,
  How they sprung, in the dim night haze,
To their work of toil and of clamor !
How the boarders, with sponge and rammer,
And their captains, with cord and hammer,
  Kept every muzzle ablaze.
How the guns, as with cheer and shout
Our tackle-men hurled them out,
  Brought up on the water-ways !

First, as we fired at their flash,
  'Twas lightning and black eclipse,
With a bellowing roll and crash.
But soon, upon either bow,
What with forts, and fire-rafts, and ships
(The whole fleet was hard at it, now),
All pounding away ! — and Porter
Still thundering with shell and mortar —
  'Twas the mighty sound and form !

(Such you see in the far South,
After long heat and drought,
  As day draws nigh to even,
Arching from north to south,
  Blinding the tropic sun,
  The great black bow comes on,
Till the thunder-veil is riven —
  When all is crash and levin,
And the cannonade of heaven
  Rolls down the Amazon !)

But, as we worked along higher,
  Just where the river enlarges,
Down came a pyramid of fire —
  It was one of your long coal barges.
  (We had often had the like before.)
'Twas coming down on us to larboard,
  Well in with the eastern shore ;
And our pilot, to let it pass round,
  (You may guess we never stopped to sound),
Giving us a rank sheer to starboard,
  Ran the flag hard and fast aground !

'Twas nigh abreast of the Upper Fort ;
  And straightway a rascal Ram
  (She was shaped like the Devil's dam)
Puffed away for us, with a snort,
  And shoved it, with spiteful strength,
Right alongside of us to port.
  It was all of our ship's length —
A huge crackling Cradle of the Pit !
  Pitch-pine knots to the brim,
  Belching flame red and grim —
What a roar came up from it !

Well, for a little it looked bad :
  But these things are, somehow, shorter
In the acting than in the telling ;
There was no singing out or yelling,
  Or any fussing and fretting,
  No stampede, in short ;
But there we were, my lad,
  All afire on our port quarter
Hammocks ablaze in the netting,
  Flame spouting in at every port,
Our Fourth Cutter burning at the davit
  (No chance to lower away and save it).

In a twinkling, the flames had risen
Half way to main-top and mizzen,
  Darting up the shrouds like snakes !
  Ah, how we clanked at the brakes,
  And the deep steaming-pumps throbbed under,
Sending a ceaseless flow !
Our top-men, a dauntless crowd,
Swarmed in rigging and shroud :
  There ('twas a wonder)
The burning ratlines and strands
They quenched with their bare hard hands ;
  But the great guns below
  Never silenced their thunder !

At last, by backing and sounding,
When we were clear of grounding,
  And under headway once more,
The whole rebel fleet came rounding
  The point. If we had it hot before.
  'Twas now, from shore to shore,
One long, loud thundering roar,
Such crashing, splintering, and pounding,
  And smashing as you never heard before !

But that we fought foul wrong to wreck,
  And to save the land we loved so well,
You might have deemed our long gun-deck
  Two hundred feet of hell !

For above all was battle,
Broadside, and blaze, and rattle,
  Smoke and thunder alone.
(But, down in the sick-bay,
Where our wounded and dying lay,
  There was scarce a sob or a moan.)
And at last, when the dim day broke,
And the sullen sun awoke,
  Drearily blinking
O'er the haze and the cannon smoke,
That ever such morning dulls, —
There were thirteen traitor hulls
  On fire and sinking !

Now, up the river ! — through mad Chalmette
Sputters a vain resistance yet.
Small helm we gave her, our course to steer, —
  'Twas nicer work than you well would dream,
With cant and sheer to keep her clear
  Of the burning wrecks that cumbered the stream.

The Louisiana, hurled on high,
Mounts in thunder to meet the sky !
Then down to the depths of the turbid flood, —
Fifty fathom of rebel mud !
The Mississippi comes floating down
A mighty bonfire, from off the town ;
And along the river, on stocks and ways,
A half-hatched devil's brood is ablaze, —
The great Anglo-Norman is all in flames
  (Hark to the roar of her tumbling frames),
And the smaller fry that Treason would spawn
Are lighting Algiers like an angry dawn !

From stem to stern, how the pirates burn,
  Fired by the furious hands that built !
So to ashes forever turn
  The suicide wrecks of wrong and guilt !

But as we neared the city,
  By field and vast plantation,
  (Ah, millstone of our nation !)
With wonder and with pity,
  What crowds we there espied
Of dark and wistful faces,
Mute in their toiling places,
  Strangely and sadly eyed !
  Haply, 'mid doubt and fear,
  Deeming deliverance near.
  (One gave the ghost of a cheer !)

And on that dolorous strand,
  To greet the victor brave
One flag did welcome wave, —
Raised, ah me ! by a wretched hand,
All outworn on our cruel land, —
  The withered hand of a slave !

But all along the Levee,
  In a dark and drenching rain,
(By this 'twas pouring heavy),
  Stood a fierce and sullen train.
A strange and frenzied time !
  There were scowling rage and pain,
  Curses, howls, and hisses,
  Out of Hate's black abysses, —
Their courage and their crime
  All in vain — all in vain !

For, from the hour that the Rebel Stream,
With the Crescent City lying abeam,
  Shuddered under our keel,
Smit to the heart with self-struck sting,
Slavery died in her scorpion-ring,
  And Murder fell on his steel!
'Tis well to do and dare;
But ever may grateful prayer
Follow, as aye it ought,
When the good fight is fought,
  When the true deed is done!
Aloft in heaven's pure light
(Deep azure crossed on white),
Our fair Church pennant waves
O'er a thousand thankful braves,
  Bareheaded in God's bright sun!

Lord of mercy and frown,
  Ruling o'er sea and shore,
Send us such scene once more!
  All in line of battle,
When the black ships bear down
On tyrant fort and town,
  'Mid cannon cloud and rattle;
And the great guns once more
Thunder back the roar
Of the traitor walls ashore,
And the traitor flags come down!

NOTES FROM THE SADDLE.

FROM THE "COURIER." *

STILL pushing on! Still watching the warm, white clouds, and the fields, green with the winter grain. Still weaving of way-side flowers a simple garland to fling in through the open gates of Janus, while our fancies wander homeward, as the youth of the Roman Republic loved to do in those early days of struggle and victory. The birds chatter in great flocks among the trees, and say, mockingly, "Go South with us." The hoarse brooks, intoxicated with the dissipation of plenty, go roaring along, tumbling over the stones, and making crooked paths over the meadow. Alas! how poor! for yesterday they were covered with the first and oldest resource of leaves, dark as Tempe, but now quite stripped bare, are driven along, tormented and complaining, out of the gardens into the waste. Only the wild flowers along the ravines hold their beauty, peeping out timidly between the gnarled roots of the leaning chestnuts, or smiling under some broad fern, like an Eastern lady behind her fan. To be sure, a few vines hang gracefully over gray limbs, and trail tenderly, as if to hide the poor bushes, which once called their foliage their own, and would not own how much they depended on the frail stem that clung to them for protection.

But refinement is not weakness, and pride is not strength, and storm brings the judgment. Then we look over the swelling river with its turbid current, into Virginia, where the masses of trees, and the clumps of shrubbery, and the open glades, reveal, after these same summer experiences, their own individuality. Golden and leaden,

* Boston Courier, November 23, 1861.

purple and silver, with here and there a flash of green across the softer shades, as if the glorious clouds, just at sunset, heavy with quiet, chastened grief, had drooped too low, and could not sail away when the sun crept down behind the hills. And we weave our garland, conqueror of times and seasons, while the wind scatters the treasures of the forest about, and throws the leaves before our horses' feet, gilded with the golden sky and soft sun of the Indian summer until musing of changing scenes, of the fate of those who wander along life's way, and the city of unfading rest, we find that the leaves have fallen even from our garland, and like one of old, weeping in the midst of triumph, only the thorns remain to us!

But this is not so very sad, if, as a friend remarks quietly, we are ourselves to leave so soon. Seaward and Southward is now the cry, and we long for our orders. On every hill, by every way, are the deserted camps of those who have moved before us. It is a singular feeling which creeps over you, as you sit and look into these same camping grounds. If it is sad to do anything for the last time, how much more to stand where there has been so much activity for the last time. Here are the streets laid out in order, where your feet seem to intrude, the trenches still full of water; the outlines and walls of tents and rude coverings of trees; the posts still waiting for the horse; the ovens, which, weary of their weight, have fallen; the broken jars and bones which are the skeletons of past feasts! Here was the place called "home," here the guard tent, and there the place of sport, and beyond the scene of worship. It is Pompeii over again, with its pavements and houses, its walls and posts, with dwellings and theatres and temples! A deserted city, or, if you wish to believe it, a city whose inhabitants may return at any moment to ask why you have taken such liberty in your inquisitiveness. The fire-places are full of water. The wood lies cut beside the cold embers. The grain still waits under the trees for the horses, or springs up in a carpet of green, to show you that nothing is lost; and even the fruit of opportunities which we throw aside, others may reap when we are gone. The fashionable line of trees, and the arbors, where every one sat under the pine and fir tree, lean away from the last storm. It is easy to see by the worn ground over what hills the sentry marched, or by what trees the way towards the spring passed. But now only the crows sail away before you, and shout from the tree tops their inhospitable complaints.

By this stake a rope passed to another, not twenty feet away, that the cavalry horses might be fastened. Just beyond stood some staff horse, and there a wagon. Pieces of torn caps, and boxes, and knapsacks, and broad shoes broken out at the sides, which I venture to say Cinderella could not have worn — and little rubber blankets, which served as coverings of miniature tents in this deserted village, under which Evangeline never could have plied the distaff, and fragments of envelopes, lie scattered about. But all this desolation may have happened long ago. The leaf retains the marks of its fibres, along which poured the tide of life, long after it is dead. Does not the print of the face remain on the walls of the theatre of Herculaneum, though the actor passed away at the first part, when the fiery deluge surprised the attendants and drowned the applauses of the audience, and caught him just fleeing, unhappy man! So this forsaken camp, with its impress of the mind, our fancy tells us, may have been peopled by a host of olden time, and haunted for three generations. And as we ride on in the moonlight, the old oaks throw their shadow over the straw and trenches, sighing like the tempest, and urging us on, as it did the poor Wandering Jew.

They "found the man by the way;" so they told me, with a tone which said, "He is only a stranger." The horses were feeding by the roadside, with their harness still on, and the reins fallen under their feet. From the top of the heavy army wagon the white canvas had been pushed slightly back, and two empty bags lay within. Upon these was an old man. His uncombed beard was gray, and his long, tangled hair hung in masses on his shoulders. His features were sharp with poverty, and his thin, bony hands were hard with labor. By his words we knew that he was from the West; but we could tell nothing more. He was past the years of service, but of an iron constitution, which never gives way to such accidents as years until it is broken. He was very meanly dressed, quite in rags, with a soiled cap and dirty flannel shirt. His hands were thrown wildly over his head, and his eyes rolled with unnatural brightness. We spoke to him, but he did not reply — only kept driving his horses, who, unused to the strange tone, were still at work on the green grass which sprang up under the wooden fence. He had evidently staid in his seat until overcome with the fever, and then, unknown and uncared for, had fallen backward into the wagon. They carried him to the hospital. Two days he grew thinner and more weak. Sometimes the light of intelligence seemed to rekindle; but it was the lightning in the tempest, a moment bright, only to leave the clouds more dark. It was late at night when I last saw him. A storm was raging through the trees, and shaking the thin canvas of the tent. By a single candle two men were busy over some vials in one corner, and at the opposite end the two rows of silent forms, wrapped in coarse blankets, with faces which looked sallow and ghostly, seemed like some tomb. They sent for me because they thought he showed signs of reason, and his mind grew more steady as the bark of life touched on the shores of eternity. It was too late. As he had lived, so he must die, by himself, without a man who knew him. At once I saw it was too late; yet I leaned breathlessly forward to listen to his answer, as one man kneeled by the bedside of the dying man.

"Have you friends?" Said he, "My money is not paid — what will they do?" "Have you a wife?" He looked up a moment, and then began to talk about his pay. "What is your name?" He gave no answer. Whether he had friends or a family we could not tell. His very name was unknown, and he was dying. His long limbs trembled. His voice grew less strong. A group of pale faces, half seen in the flickering light about. There was a prayer, an awful silence. The old man grew quiet, and only one trembling voice wrestled with the pattering of the rain and the moaning of the trees overhead. He hardly breathed. It was almost midnight. The next morning I heard that another had fallen by the way in the onward march of the army. He had nothing to leave. No one ever heard of his home or friends. In the broad West are doubtless some that think of him. How slowly will they believe that he is lost — hoping against hope, in silence taking comfort! There are strange unwritten histories in camp, there are patient, unseen offerings, and they consecrate the cause by their silent tenderness.

We happened in the town of Rockville on election day. Little boys strutted about with white tickets in their breasts, full of secession. Here and there a blue Union vote could be seen, as it was slyly slipped from pocket to pocket. A little electioneering was done by the more influential; but the most contented themselves with clinching their fists behind their backs and talking in gusts, which died away and rose again, like the fitful storm. The Court House is of brick, of two stories height, and quite imposing for this miserable place. It is situated in the centre of the town, on a green lawn, which is enclosed by a neat iron fence. The soldiers were stationed opposite, and the sentries kept a quiet lookout across the street. Three men stood in the window to receive the votes, white and blue. From every street they came pouring in, — some on "hunters," some on "cobs." A father is held on by his boy, who sits behind. A great wagon, with votes and whiskey, stops the throng, and sends them on their way rejoicing. An old farmer mounts his ample plough-horse, and goes trotting on, his brains quite lost in a sombre black hat of unknown date, and a coat with bright buttons, that might have served his ancestor at a fourth remove. There is a motley throng of long-haired, sallow, misanthropic beings, eager to save their feelings or their country, as the case may be. Everything moves quietly, despite some long-limbed boys with tanned faces and black eyes. Evidently they have grown too fast. Their short pants, and sharp voices, and restless gestures, seem to demand a quarrel. They are walking about, as if to say, "Who dares to blow this straw of a vote off my shoulder?" but in the spirit of the dignified Government whose cause is at stake, the better educated representatives of liberty say, "It is but hollow, and very light. We will keep you quiet. The wind will take care of the straw."

Close by the way stands the jail. The little jailer, grown thin and old, approaches the gate with the importance of St. Peter, moving his keys and admiring his lock, whose only value is its antiquity. It turns with a gloomy sound. On the right hang a few slave fetters, and within, another door opens into a yard. It is not thirty paces long, or twenty wide. The pile of wet wood in the corner mocks comfort, and the rain, grown stained and dirty, gathers timidly in the corner, trying to escape. A door opens from the yard into a passage lighted by two grated windows on the right. Our eyes grow familiar with darkness, as from the two cells opposite — long, and wide, and quite dark, only as a fire kindling in the great chimney lights it — come a dozen heavy hearts. They are all manacled — some by the hands, some by the feet. Some are even chained to the floor. The iron, as they move, sounds gloomy enough. Their faces look like despair. They are slaves who liked their freedom. "Let them be quiet for a while — their time is coming!" said my friend to the jailer; and I heard their hands clasped in joy as they bent down over the floor. It was a wild scene. The flames danced over the wooden walls and polished floor, making the whitewashed chimney gleam with a mockery of neatness. A few rags were on the floor, and moving about were these dark shadows, clanking their chains, and moving their great eyes in wonder. They had been taken without free papers, and are supposed to be fugitives. None care to claim them, or perhaps they do not know where they are; and so they stay and drag along the hours, as if they too were chained, and sit in the sullen sun, which gleams as if it had lost its spirit as it came through the bars. How fresh and free seemed everything as we came out again into the street!

Like all the other roads, the way from Washington is terribly rough. In the centre is the most stony road imaginable. On either side is the most muddy, and full of holes, ever conceived of. It begins to rain, and to get inside is a matter of necessity. Every stone shakes the carriage. It is impossible to sit upright. On one side and the other, on trunks and mail-bags and wooden partitions, on stools and saddles and tables, roll our poor head and arms and body. There is no relief. Four hours in the rain under torture. How faint and hungry the violent exercise makes one! How chilly, too! And now the horses stop. We are fording a stream. The driver shouts, then the lash descends. It is useless. The driver will not get out of the carriage, nor will they get out of the brook. Some one comes to our relief. With a spring they clear the brook, and begin to climb the hill. Again they stop. Whip and reins are alike useless. The front leader turns, and the tall pole horse, a foot higher than his little mate, shakes his head. Urge him, and he stands on his feet and looks over the hill for some Hercules to assist. It is a "no go." The driver, in despair, gets three men to assist. They pull the wagon, but not the horses. "Try waiting." And three clouds, drop by drop, roll down the manes of the horses. "Fury!" and the men, out of patience, jump out humming the ditty, "If I had a donkey," &c. Now the rails are broken, sticks are stripped and worn out, whips are like oat straws. Go? Of course not. Here is a final effort. All shout and pound together. I put my face up to the little hole in front, and shout lustily; I who had frightened so many by my noise. The wagon runs back; out plunges the passenger into the mud and rain, through the side, fearful of going over. "Once more it has started," says the mocking wagoner; and that tall, large-boned horse rears, and then sits down on the pole. There is a smash, and we are fixed. All are in despair. Night is coming on. Six hours find us eighteen miles from Washington! Another wagon is sent for. We must wait.

Fortunately a little ruined cottage is left standing beside the road. Shivering and wet, the coarse shelter seems delightful. I always sigh as I enter a deserted building. There are so many sad and pleasant things which must have been done there, yet no one cares for it. Now I draw back. A few rough men are seated on a wooden bench playing cards. They are not soldiers; who can they be? A little fire flickers in an enormous chimney, which seems ready to fall. Out beyond are rooms stripped of their roof and sides. The wind and rain drive me nearer. A few guns are hung upon the wall, and a great bed of straw is pushed into one corner. There are boxes to sit upon, and by the fire is a kettle boiling, the only sign of comfort. I cannot understand what the men were talking about, but by their gestures they seemed very angry. At any rate, through the chimney I looked up and saw the heavy clouds with despair. I pity the very rat who looks out through the broken chimney at me. How lonely a place! Pieces of board were nailed over the window, and the light came in through the door, which certainly would not swing many times more. A broken door step, a green lawn reaching away to a large stream, a ruined house, and an intensely disagreeable road are all I see. The dingy rafters at least keep off the rain, and the floor is dry, but it is not pleasant to spend the night in such company. It is growing dark.

At length a wagon with five mules waits for me — an army wagon, a heavy, tough wagon, without the slightest suspicion of springs. It starts furiously. I only remember, in the darkness, a battery of artillery go by, a camp fire, and then stopping to arrange the harness. The terrible noise of the wagon drowns the cracking of whips, and the shouts of the drivers who rode the mules. I thought I should not survive the terrible jar; it was a torment. Had I not a coach and five, outriders, a carriage for thirty, four led horses? What was left to desire for a Bourbon?

The mules stopped at length; and, tired as I was, I felt happy to plod through the deep mud, and wade the pools, amid the darkness of the forest and a furious storm. I had quiet, at least, though the sound still rang in my ears, and the feverish flush of the terrible exercise remained on the cheeks.

Have we not been long enough on the way? The sun does not always shine, and it is not perpetual summer in camp. Doubtless, when we look back on the campaign, there will be more lights than shadows; and under the direction of a hand more skilful than our own, a beautiful pattern will be wrought of the many-colored threads, which we may look upon in the halls of our memory, as one looks upon the tapestries of the Vatican — once a mystery and rarity to the artisan, but a simple unity to the mind of Raphael, who walked with him by the way.

YANKEES — HYENAS. — "Justinian," a correspondent of the Southern Literary Messenger, sends the following to that periodical :

"The comparison so well made by President Davis, in his recent speech, of Yankees to Hyenas, had been frequently suggested to my mind, not only from the fiendish and felonious character of both animals, but from having referred to the derivation of the term Yankee, or Yanhee, as given in 'Aubury's Travels in America,' in the year 1791. That author asserts that Yankee, or Yanhe, is derived from the Cherokee word Eanke, or Eanhe, which signifies, in that language, coward, and was applied by the Virginians to the people of the North for not arming and joining them to resist the assaults of the Cherokees in the year 1780. If, then, the true orthography of the word Yankee be Yanhe, it may be assimilated to the word Hyena, by the simple rule of transposition, as follows : In the term Yanhe, the letters are the same — the y in hyena being the second, the a being fifth, the n being the fourth, the h being the first, and the e being the third. I therefore think that we are fully authorized in denominating the Yankees as Hyenas."

FEMALE BUSHWHACKERS. — The women of the South are the goads that prick the men to action. I should have said first that there are female as well as male bushwhackers. When a woman takes one of these creatures to her home or heart, as the case may be, she becomes a partner to his guilt, according to the common law. She thus recognizes his vocation, and applauds him in his robberies. She is the receiver, and the receiver is as bad as the thief. All the country is infested by these guerrillas and bushwhackers; they have certain haunts, where they make their headquarters and store away their plunder. These haunts are invariably presided over by that creature (God help her, after all) of modern growth, and the offspring of the miseries of war — the "war widow." They are, without exception, bitter and inveterate secesh. Usually, indeed in all cases, ignorant and wholly uneducated, they are entirely controlled by passion. Being in destitute circumstances, and lonely, they gladly become the accomplices of the herd of robbers prowling about. I am not to be understood as saying that all the women of the South who unfortunately have lost their husbands in this war, are of the class known as "war widows." Far be it from me. I have found many such women as intelligent, refined, and pure as any I have ever known. But everybody knows, or is supposed to know, what the real "war widow" is, and it is of her I write. She

makes a good home bushwhacker; aids and abets freely and voluntarily in all the depredations of her warring accomplice. She feeds and clothes him, secretes him when hunted down, encourages him in his bad work, and does all she can (and women are all-powerful for good or evil) to make him a reckless and depraved outlaw. There is a certain sort of superstitious poetry of innocence attached to woman's being, which has been handed down to us from the time Adam beheld the beautiful image of Eve in the clear, crystal water. While I would regret to despoil woman of any of the romance of her nature, I must say that, as far as regards women bushwhackers, there is nothing in their natures except poetical depravity — a license in licentious liberty, which mars and blackens her nature. As liars, they cannot be excelled in the universe. Actually, they would lie anything or anybody out of existence. And they do it with such brazen impudence — such a shameless air of innocence. Their little hearts are awfully corrupt. While out with scouting parties, I have repeatedly asked for various kinds of information from these frail creatures, and, looking into my face as innocent as an unwooed maiden, they have told lie upon lie, yes, mountains of them. Their moral perception of right and wrong is very blunt, while their perceptive faculties are quite acute in judging of the relative value of a ring, a blanket, a watch, or other article brought them by their bushwhacking lords. — "Dr. Adonis," in the Louisville Journal.

THE BATTLE OF DUNKSBURG. — The following amusing account of a battle that occurred in the wilds of Missouri has not yet taken its appropriate place in the history of the rebellion :

"The village of Dunksburg is situated in the north-east corner of Pettis County, Missouri, and very near the stream known as the Black Water. In the south-east part of Lafayette County, and immediately in the neighborhood of Dunksburg, there is a large German settlement. From the very commencement of the present troubles in Missouri, the Germans have been loyal to the Government, and as they were the first against whom the vengeance of the secessionists was directed, they were the first to take up arms in the defence of their adopted country, and a small company of some forty or fifty banded themselves together for the purposes of self-defence, making the church at Dunksburg their temporary headquarters. Late one afternoon they were notified of the approach of a considerable body of rebels from Pettis and Saline Counties, and they prudently determined to retreat from the position they held in the church, believing that they would be unable to defend it against greatly superior numbers.

"The attacking party, not aware that the Germans had retreated, advanced cautiously, under cover of night, and by a dexterous movement succeeded in surrounding the church, and at a signal agreed on, immediately commenced a heavy fire upon the building, which being only weather-boarded with thin pine or poplar plank, offered scarcely any resistance to the bullets which were rapidly discharged from rifles and shot guns, and which, passing through and through the house, killed and wounded many of the assailants. Unprepared for what they mistook for a vigorous defence on the part of the Germans, after considerable loss in killed and wounded, they retreated to their camp a short distance off; but dissatisfied with the result, and believing it entirely in their power to capture the small force which had peppered them so severely, they determined to return to the charge, and to carry the church at the point of the bayonet.

"The same precaution was used in making their advances for the second attack, and they completely surrounded the building before the word was given to fire. Greatly to their astonishment, at the first volley many of their men were killed, and being in close proximity to the building, several were seriously wounded by splinters, which were scattered in every direction by the balls passing through the house. The fire was so destructive that no time was lost in forcing the doors of the building, with the purpose of making a finish of all the Dutch inside; but greatly to their disappointment and mortification, they discovered that there was not a single Dutchman anywhere about the house, and that they had been guilty of the extreme folly of shooting each other. Thus ended the battle of Dunksburg — an event long to be remembered by the peaceful inhabitants of that quiet village, which has thus become famous among the bloody localities of Missouri."

THE OLD RIFLEMAN.

BY FRANK TICKNOR, M. D.

Now, bring me out my buckskin suit,
　My pouch and powder too;
We'll see if seventy-six can shoot
　As sixteen used to do.

Old Bess, we've kept our barrels bright,
　Our triggers quick and true —
As far, if not as *fine* a sight,
　As long ago we drew.

And pick me out a trusty flint —
　A real white and blue;
Perhaps 'twill win the *other* tint
　Before the hunt is through.

Give boys your brass percussion caps;
　Old "shut-pan" suits as well:
There's something in the *sparks*, — perhaps
　There's something in the smell.

We've seen the red-coat Briton bleed;
　The red-skin Indian too;
We never thought to draw a bead
　On Yankee-doodle-doo.

But, Bessie, bless your dear old heart,
　Those days are mostly done;
And now we must revive the art
　Of shooting on the run.

If Doodle must be meddling, why,
　There's only this to do —
Select the black spot in his eye,
　And let the daylight through.

And if he doesn't like the way
　That Bess presents the view,
He'll, may be, change his mind, and stay
　Where the good Doodles do, —

Where Lincoln lives — the man, you know,
　Who kissed the Testament;
To keep the Constitution? No,
　To keep the Government!

We'll hunt for Lincoln, Bess, old tool,
　And take him half and half;
We'll aim to *hit* him, if a fool,
　And *miss* him, if a calf.

We'll teach these shot-gun boys the tricks
　By which a war is won;
Especially, how Seventy-six
　Took Tories on the run.

THE DRUMMER-BOY OF THE EIGHTH MICHIGAN. — Charles Howard Gardner was a school-boy thirteen and a half years old, in the city of Flint, Michigan, when the war commenced. His father was connected with a military organization of long standing, and under the first call for seventy-five thousand troops, immediately left for the defence of the national capital. Soon there came a second call for three hundred thousand more, when Charlie's teacher, S. C. Guild, a most exemplary young man, soon to enter the ministry, joined the army. Between Charlie and him there existed a very ardent attachment, and Captain Guild seconded Charlie's earnest entreaties that he might go with him as a drummer. He had been famous from his babyhood for his musical ability, and had acquired a good deal of merited notoriety for his skilful handling of the drumsticks. "If I can go to the war with my drum, and thus take the place of a man who can handle a musket," was Charlie's persistent plea, "I think it is my duty to go, especially as you, mother, do not greatly need me at home." So, reluctantly, the poor mother, who had surrendered her husband, consented that her boy should join the Eighth Michigan infantry.

The regiment was ordered to Port Royal, and on their way thither, Charlie met his father in Washington. As they were returning from the navy yard, where they had been for their arms, he saw his father a little way off, and forgetting military rule, he broke from the ranks, and with child-like joy ran to his father's arms. It was their last earthly meeting, as the November following Mr. Gardner died of typhoid fever at Alexandria. Charlie's letters to his mother after this bereavement, written from Port Royal, are exceedingly touching, and remarkably thoughtful for a boy not yet fourteen. "I am near broken-hearted," he writes: "I try to be cheerful, but it is of no use; my mind continually runs in the direction of home, a fresh gush of tears comes to my eyes, and I have to weep. But, mother, if this is so hard for me, what must it be for you? Don't take it *too much* to heart, for remember that you have me left, and I will do my best to help you. I shall send you all my money hereafter, for I do not really need money here."

This promise he fulfilled to the letter. Always cheerful, he was a great favorite with the officers and men, for whom he never did a favor but they would compel him to receive some small compensation in return. These small gains he carefully husbanded, and increased them by peddling papers and periodicals, making enough for his little extra expenses, and invariably, on every pay-day, he sent his money to his widowed mother. None of the vices of the camp clung to him, and amid the profane, and drunken, and vulgar, he moved, without assoiling the whiteness of his young soul. His teacher and Captain guarded him like a father; he shared his bed and board with Charlie, and the two loved one another with an affection so unusual that it was everywhere the subject of comment.

By and by we hear of the fearless little fellow, small beyond his years, on the battle-field with the surgeon, where the grape and canister were falling like hail around them, pressing forward to the front, during an engagement, with the hospital flag in his hand, to aid in the care of the wounded. Only a peremptory order from a superior officer was able to turn him back to the rear; and there, when the wounded were brought in, he worked all night and the next day, carrying water, and bandages, and lint, and lighting up the sorrowfulness of the hour by his boyish but unfailing kindness. Never was he more serviceable than during a battle. At the terrible battle of James' Island, in an assault on the fort, his beloved Captain, always foremost in the fight, had climbed to the parapet of the fort, when a shot struck him, and he fell backward, and was seen no more. Now was Charlie indeed bereaved — his teacher, captain, friend, father, lover, dead on the battle-field, and even the poor satisfaction denied his friends of burying his remains. His letters, after this event, are one long wail of sorrow — he could not be comforted; and yet, always thoughtful for others, he writes: " *O, how I pity his poor mother!*"

Months passed, and the Eighth Michigan was ordered to Vicksburg, to reënforce Grant, who had beleaguered that doomed city. Battle after battle ensued — *nineteen of them* — in all of which Charlie more or less participated, often escaping death as by a miracle. Something of the fierce life led by this regiment may be inferred from the fact that one thousand six hundred and fifty-three men have enlisted in it since it first took the field; of these, only four hundred survive to-day, all but eight of whom have just reënlisted. Through all battles, all marches, all reconnoissances, all campaigns, Charlie kept with the regiment, crossing the mountains with them to Knoxville, in Burnside's corps, on rations of three ears of corn per day, and then for weeks shut up in that city, besieged by Longstreet's

force, and subsisting on quarter rations. Yet not one word of complaint ever came from the patriot boy, not one word of regret, only an earnest desire to remain in the service till the end of the war.

At last there came a letter from the surgeon. During the siege of Knoxville, Charlie had been wounded for the first time. A chance shot, that passed through the window of the house in which he was, struck him on the shoulder, and entered the lung. " He has been in a very dangerous condition," wrote the surgeon, " but he is now fast recovering. He is a universal pet, and is well cared for in the officers' quarters." The next tidings were more joyful. The regiment were on their way to Detroit, on a thirty days' furlough, and would remain to recruit. Now the telegraph notified those interested that they were in Louisville — then in Indianapolis — in Michigan City — at last in Detroit.

With a happy heart the good mother telegraphed to have her boy sent to Chicago as soon as possible; and then she watched the arrival of the trains. " He will be here to-night — he will be here to-morrow," she said; and every summons to the door she was sure was her Charlie. Everything was in readiness for the darling — his room — his clothes — the supper-table set with the luxuries he loved — and there sat mother, sister, and brother, waiting for him. A knock at the door — all start — all rush — 'tis Charlie! No, only a telegram. God help the poor broken hearts, as they read it — " *The regiment has arrived, but Charlie is dead!*" And this was all.

A SHELL ON BOARD SHIP. — A shell from a rifled cannon must be a very nice visitor to " drop in " to a small party, if we may judge from the exploits of one which struck the United States steamer Massachusetts, off Ship Island, and which a writer who was on board describes as follows :

" During the action I think we hit her, the Florida, four times, and I know she hit us once with a sixty-eight pound rifle shell (that is the way we got the exact size of her rifled gun). The shell entered on our starboard quarter, just above the iron part of the hull; it came through the side angling aft (as we were a little abaft her beam when it struck us), and took the deck in the passage way between two state-rooms, and completely cut off eighteen of the deck planks, and then struck a beam, which canted it up a little, so that it took the steam-heating pipes under our dining-table, cutting off five of them, and tearing our dining-table all to pieces — then went through the state-room, bulkhead, and ceiling of the ship on the opposite side, and struck one of the outside timbers, and broke every plank abreast of it short off, from the spar to the gun deck : it then fell down on to the cabin deck and exploded, knocking four state-rooms into one, breaking all the glass and crockery ware, shattering the cabin very badly, breaking up the furniture, and setting fire to the ship; but we had three streams of water upon the fire at very short notice, and put it out before it did any damage — keeping up our chase as though nothing had happened."

A letter from the Surgeon of the Massachusetts, Dr. John H. Mackie, gives information that he was the only person wounded by this destructive visitor. He was struck by a splinter on the shin.

A COLORED HERO. — During the thickest of the fight at Belmont, the body servant of General McClernand, a mulatto named William Stains, exhibited conspicuous courage. He was close by the General during the whole engagement, cheering the soldiers, and swearing that he would shoot the first man that showed the white feather. Many of the soldiers laughed heartily at the fighting negro, while the bullets flew about like hail.

In the course of the fight a captain of one of the companies was struck by a spent ball, which disabled him from walking. The mulatto boy, who was mounted, rode up to him, and shouted out, "Captain, if you can fight any longer for the old Stars and Stripes, take my horse and lead your men." He then dismounted and helped the wounded officer into his saddle, and as he was walking away, a rebel dragoon rushed forward at the officer to take him prisoner. The negro drew his revolver, and put a ball through the rebel's head, scattering his brains over the horse's neck.

PASSING THE BATTERIES. — The world knows how Vicksburg was taken. After four months of ineffectual but constant labor to flank it on the north, and to cut a canal across the bend so as to divert the river from its course, Grant suddenly projected a new and brilliant line of strategy, which was crowned with success.

That was to march his army down past the stronghold, on the Louisiana shore, run six or eight boats by the batteries and take them down twenty-five miles to Bruinsburg, just below Jeff Davis' Plantation, and act as ferry-boats in taking the army across. Then his problem was to march north, cut the roads between Vicksburg and Jackson, and establish a base of supplies on the Yazoo River, and forcing the army of Pemberton back into the "Gibraltar of the South," surround it, and either storm or starve it into surrender. This was the plan that succeeded.

But the most hazardous part of this enterprise was to run the batteries. Volunteers, however, for this dangerous service, were numerous, and among others three army correspondents of leading New York papers were on board — Mr. Richardson of the Tribune, Mr. Browne of the Herald, and Mr. Colburn of the World.

These knights-errant of the quill have each given to the world their story. But the narrative of Mr. Colburn, especially what relates to the passing of the batteries, is not surpassed by either of the others in thrilling interest.

"It was ten o'clock on a beautiful moonlight night," says Mr. C., "even for those latitudes, when we cast loose at Milliken's Bend, and our little tug snorted down the river accompanied by the transport A. D. Hine.

"Our adieus said, we quietly chatted, and finished a solitary bottle of dry Catawba which some good friends had sent on board for our comfort. We had on board, as a guard, fifteen sharpshooters from the Forty-seventh Ohio, under Captain Ward, Surgeon Davidson, the tug's crew of eight, four persons on their way to join their regiments, and our party of three, all volunteers.

"I should here mention, as illustrating the temper of that army, that when fourteen volunteers were called for, the whole regiment stepped forward. Company A was selected, and still there was a squabble to go. Fourteen were then marked off; a fifteenth begged permission of the Colonel, and one actually paid a premium of five dollars to his comrade for the privilege of going on this hazardous service. The barges were covered with tiers of hay in order to protect the tug, but the hay was deemed almost unnecessary, and so put on quite loosely, and the ends of the boat were quite exposed.

"At midnight we came in sight of Vicksburg. At half past twelve, as we were steaming across the upper side of the point, the rebel pickets on the Louisiana shore began to fire upon us; their shots, however, did no damage.

"At quarter before one a rocket shot up from the upper batteries. There was no need of such a warning, for the boats might be seen almost as clearly as by sunlight, and the loud puff of our exhaust pipe gave ample warning when we were three miles distant.

"At five minutes past one the first shot was fired, and struck so near as to leave us in doubt whether the barges were hit. A lull of a few minutes, then another, closely followed by a round. It kept up in this way as we were rounding the bend, the shots all seeming to come very near to us, but few striking, as we could perceive by the momentary throb of the hull when struck.

"With the exception of Captain Ward, the pilots, engineers, and firemen, the rest of us were posted along the barges, on the alert for an attempt at boarding.

"By reference to a map of the locality, it will be seen that the river forms a kind of loop in front of Vicksburg; so that we had to run a portion of the distance by, and then turn under fire, and run the whole line back again. In this way we were exposed to a fire from the starboard side, then from the bow, and, when fairly in front of the batteries, from all three directions to a concentrated fire.

"At first there were efforts to peer from behind the rampart of hay bales and duck on perceiving the flash of the rebel guns; but soon the shots were so rapid, and from points so widely apart, that that exciting amusement was dropped. The screaming of the shells as they went over us, the splashing and spray, were for a time subjects of jesting and imitation, when a shell burst three feet over our heads with a stunning report.

"Twenty minutes (long minutes those) under fire, and nobody hurt!

"The barges still floating, and the little propeller making eight miles an hour. We had already passed the upper batteries, and were congratulating ourselves on our good luck, the guns pouring broadsides at us with amazing noise, as we were but four hundred yards from the guns, and it seemed in the clear air as if we were right in front of the muzzles. Several shots struck the barges very heavily; still there was no stoppage. It must have been about a quarter before two, when all the roar of the guns was drowned in one terrific report, as if a magazine had burst under us.

"My first thought was that the powder had been stowed on the barges, and had ignited; but, on clambering up among smoke and flames, I could see indeed nothing like a tug. She had exploded, and the white hot cinders were thrown up in a spouting shower, while steam and smoke enveloped the barges like a pall.

"Almost at the same minute the batteries commenced a vengeful, and, as it seemed to me, a savage fire upon us, faster and faster. The shells burst all round and above us for a few moments with a stunning and blinding effect. The coals had set fire to the hay bales in several places; the bursting shells had aided in the work. In vain did we trample upon them, and throw them overboard, burning our hands, feet, and clothing in the effort. No buckets were to be found. They had been blown away. On looking down between the barges, there hung the fragments of the tug by the tow ropes. The little craft, being nearly all boiler, had been shattered to atoms, as we learned afterwards, by a ten-inch shell.

"The rebels then set up a hideous yell from the bluffs, as if in mockery at our crippled condition. The batteries kept on firing, the blazing hay lighting up the river. We were then slowly drifting with the current past the front of the city. Our disaster happened right abreast of the court-house, when we had passed more than half the batteries, and under the fire of them all.

"As soon as we could clearly see through the blinding smoke, we found Mr. Browne standing bareheaded on the topmost bale, as if he were a defiant target for the rebel gunners. Captain Ward had been blown forward thirty feet from the tug into the river, and two of his men were engaged in fishing him up. The wounded and scalded men were crying for help, answered only by an occasional shell or malicious cheer.

"After a few moments of hasty and rather informal consultation, it was deemed best to quit the barges, as the flames were crowding us very closely. Bales of hay were then tumbled off into the river, and the wounded placed upon them.

"The heat now became intense. Mr. Browne and myself remained till all were off, and then, with but one bale for the two, stripped for the plunge. Just as we were ready, a solid shot whistled between us, and ploughed into the water under Mr. Richardson's feet, overturning him from his bale, and producing a fountain of spray where he had sunk.

"Our eyes were gladdened at his return to the surface unhurt.

"We leaped into the muddy flood and buffeted the waves for some minutes — with a sense of relief from the insupportable heat. Junius followed, and together we commenced swimming for the Louisiana shore, supposing that our pickets occupied it.

"We had been in the water for half an hour perhaps, when the sound of the stroke of oars reached us, and presently a yawl pulled round the barges. Our first emotions were pleasant enough, but they were all destroyed when we saw the gray clothing of the boatmen. They scooped us in by the time we had drifted two miles below the city, and with some roughness impressed upon us the fact that we were prisoners. Dripping and shivering, we were marched up to the city and taken before the Provost Marshal and registered."

WILLIE JOHNSON, thirteen years old, of St. Johnsbury, a drummer boy in company D, Third Vermont regiment, received a medal for his heroic conduct in the seven days' fight before Richmond. On the retreat, when strong men threw away their guns, knapsacks, and blankets, that they might have less weight to carry, this little fellow kept his drum, and brought it safely to Harrison's Landing, where he had the honor of drumming for division parade, being the only drummer who brought his drum from the field. When these facts were reported to the War Department by the division commander, Willie was presented with the star medal of honor by Secretary Stanton in person.

STORY OF THE DRAFT. — The enrolling officer of ——— district, was very active and thorough in the performance of his duties. One day he went to the house of a countryman, and finding none of the male members at home, he made inquiry of an old woman about the name and age of the "males" of the family. After naming several, the old lady stopped. "Is there any more?" asked the officer. "No," replied the woman, "none except Billy Bray." "Billy Bray? Where is he?" "He was at the barn a moment ago," said the old lady. Out went the officer, but he could not find the man. Coming back, the worthy officer questioned the old lady as to the age of Billy, and went away, after enrolling his name among those to be drafted. The time of drafting came, and among those on whom the draft fell was Billy Bray. No one knew him. Where did he live? The officer who enrolled him was called upon to produce the conscript: and lo and behold, Billy Bray was a jackass! and stands now on the list of drafted men as forming one of the quota of Maryland.

A BEAUTIFUL INCIDENT. — A Washington correspondent mentions the following incident as showing the kindness of heart of President Lincoln:

At the reception this afternoon, at the President's house, many persons present noticed three little girls, poorly dressed, the children of some mechanic or laboring man, who had followed the visitors into the house to gratify their curiosity. They passed round from room to room, and were hastening through the reception room with some trepidation, when the President called to them, "Little girls! are you going to pass me without shaking hands?" Then he bent his tall, awkward form down, and shook each little girl warmly by the hand. Everybody in the apartment was spell-bound by the incident, so simple in itself, yet revealing so much of Mr. Lincoln's character. His heart overflows with kindness, he possesses deep anti-slavery convictions, and he never takes a backward step, even if he does sometimes hesitate long before taking one in advance.

"THAT DEAR OLD FLAG." — Perhaps no man, since the days of Falstaff and the Merry Wives of Windsor was ever more tormented by women than was General Butler, after the issue of his famous "Order, No. 28," directed to the women of New Orleans. The secesh crinoline from that time forward delighted to tease, vex, and irritate him. Numberless were the pretexts they would get up to go and call on him, and extract impatient or angry retorts from him, which they would retail to their friends afterwards, with the greatest gusto. "To take the oath," was with them the height of infamy; nevertheless, there were found men, who not willingly only, but gladly renewed their fealty to the United States Government. Of these, one man, who had always been known as a Union man, but whose wife was intensely Southern in her views and feelings, promptly came forward and "took the oath." It was not long before she became acquainted with the hideous fact, and she determined upon some sort of revenge. A magnificent looking woman she was, and of elegant and commanding manner. Attiring herself in the most elaborate and becoming style and costume, she waited upon the General, gave her husband's name, and was received with eminent distinction and courtesy. After exchanging a few elegant and gracious compliments with the General and his staff, and attracting the attention of every one in the room, she proceeded to unfold the object of her visit.

"General," said she, "some of my friends have taken the oath; my husband has taken the oath;" and clasping her hands upon her breast, and rolling her eyes heavenward, she exclaimed in tones that Mrs. Siddons, even, might have envied, "I have come down to swear allegiance to that dear flag." The denouement was as irresistible as it was unexpected. Bursts of laughter rung through the presence-chamber, and Butler, seeing that he was sold, retorted angrily, "We don't want your oath, madam; go home and take care of your house and your family; that's the proper place for women."

A LOUD OUTCRY. — General Sherman, before starting on that great campaign, passed some part of the winter of 1863–4 in Huntsville, Alabama.

As this community had been from the first intensely and bitterly disloyal, he did not regard them as entitled to any special leniency or protection. Houses vacated by fugitive rebels were generally taken for quarters by his officers, and the expression of open and defiant disloyalty was checked by the bayonet. This natural result of the success of the Union arms is commented on and described in the following terms by a Huntsville correspondent of a Southern paper, signing himself "Exile:"

"It is but a short time since I left Huntsville, Alabama. The iron hand of despotism is upon the people; not perhaps as roughly, nor as grossly, as two years ago, when the impotent Mitchel commanded there; nevertheless, the hand is iron, and thumb-screws are in it, which daily are tightened, slowly, but surely, a little more and a little more. The people, as a body, are true to our cause, and the principles involved in it; yet there are a few, four or five at the most, who are not only untrue, but vilely and fetidly dishonorable in their conduct towards men who are honorable, and whose degradation to their unholy level is a prime object in their movement. It would do no good to name them; the absentees, refugees, and exiles from Huntsville know them; but personal wrongs inflicted by these men tempt strongly to name, and hold the wretches up to a just and blasting reprobation. A few days ago, a body of gentlemen, unexceptionable in character, and conservative by age, were exiled upon a fourteen hours' order to leave, because they refused to take an oath of allegiance to a Government they abhor in their inner souls. The promptness and alacrity with which they obeyed the order appeared to chagrin the domestic traitors, and rather exasperate the enemy in possession of the place. This is evidenced by a change of policy after the departure of the gentlemen alluded to, because the grace with which they left, indicated that it was no trial at all to their faith or spirit of martyrdom, if you choose so to call it. They — the officers in charge — have determined not to make any more exiles, by sending the recusants of the oath South; they will, henceforth, be ordered North, and buried in Northern bastiles. Already they have immured one heroic old soul, William McDowell, in the penitentiary in Nashville. They intend to murder him, and in this way — but, thank Heaven, they have elected one, who, God willing, will be up to the emergency. If his country calls on him for the sacrifice, I know no man (and I know him well) who will more cheerfully, more heroically, make it. As another indication of Yankee barbarism, brutality, cruel and relentless, I will mention an incident, all the more cruel because it involved not wounds of the body, not torture of the nerve and flesh, but terrific convulsions of the soul itself, and the more painful because that soul, or rather those souls, are up to the highest standard of moral perfection, and susceptible of keenest torture. The venerable Ex-Governor Chapman received an order, on the 19th of January, to leave his house and family at nine o'clock A. M. on the 20th; and when in the arms of his family, bidding adieu to the loved ones, on whom the winds of heaven had never blown roughly, — at that painful moment, as if to sound the depths of their own depravity, and the unknown depths of sensitive souls, a Yankee order was thrust into his hands, requiring wife and daughters to vacate their premises by two o'clock P. M. the same day, not allowing any article to be removed; and a guard was placed to carry out the order. The circumstances, with the fortitude manifested, presented to me a spectacle of moral grandeur occasionally read of — rarely witnessed. Whilst speaking of the heroism of the old Governor, I will mention an incident that occurred in an interview between him and the Yankee Colonel commanding the post. The Governor, knowing he would be compelled to leave in a day or so, to secure some of the commonest claims of humanity towards his family during his absence, approached the Colonel, who replied: 'Governor Chapman — I believe that is your name.' 'Yes, sir.' 'Did you not, in a public speech, in Huntsville, say, that to secure secession, you would sacrifice your property and your life?' After a moment's hesitation, the venerable man replied, with emphasis, 'No, sir. To the best of my recollection, Colonel, I have made no public speech since the revolution commenced. I was in Europe at the time. You know my principles, Colonel, from the conversations I have had with you; and though I do not recollect any such "speech," or expression, my principles, as you very well know, lead in that direction. And, lest you might suppose I would desire to evade consequences and responsibilities attachable to such principles,' rising to the full height of person and dignity, 'I will say it *now*, and *more* — not only will I sacrifice myself and property, but, sir, wife and children, to the preservation of our holy cause.' The statement of these honorable incidents runs out this to great length; but I will state a fact or two: 'Greenbacks' are two and a half for one in gold in Huntsville and Nashville; and though the money quotations in Northern papers place them one hundred and fifty-nine to one hundred and sixty, the truth is, two months ago, in New York, in Wall Street, no 'operation' could be performed at less rate than two for one. The Yankee troops in Huntsville, whose term of service has expired, are converting their 'greenbacks' into Confederate currency to take home. I state this for an incontrovertible *fact*. Not in one instance only, but I witnessed several of the same. The streets are becoming foul; the groves and woodland around the town being swept away, all the lesser houses about the town are being torn down to floor and weather-board winter quarters for them. Every house in the city has been surveyed for occupation by them — not in a desultory manner, but regularly and systematically. It is the duty of an officer, one Lieutenant Cliff, to assign these quarters; thus, according to rank or personal standing (if any) at home, are they placed in palaces of average respectability in appearance. Colonel G. P. Birney's mansion is assigned as headquarters for General Sherman & Co. A regular system of operating is thus instituted, and as an entering wedge to confiscation, this is the object of this procedure. But, through all, the people are true and devoted. I would mention more, but already I have written at too much length. You may rely on the women — God bless them — in North Alabama. I do know, however, one or two disgraceful and unpatriotic exceptions."

———

THE HOUSE THAT JEFF BUILT. — The Hartford Post published the following history of the celebrated edifice erected by J. Davis, Esq., as authentic. It was written for the purpose of giving infant politicians a clear, concise, and truthful description of the habitation, and the fortunes and misfortunes, and doings of the inmates:

"I. THE SOUTHERN CONFEDERACY. — This is the house that Jeff built.

"II. THE ETHIOPIAN. — This is the malt that lay in the house that Jeff built.

"III. THE UNDERGROUND RAILROAD. — This is the rat that ate the malt that lay in the house that Jeff built.

"IV. THE FUGITIVE SLAVE LAW. — This is the cat that killed the rat that ate the malt that lay in the house that Jeff built.

"V. THE PERSONAL LIBERTY BILL. — This is the dog that worried the cat that killed the rat that ate the malt that lay in the house that Jeff built.

"VI. CHIEF JUSTICE TANEY. — This is the cow with crumpled horn that tossed the dog that worried the cat that killed the rat that ate the malt that lay in the house that Jeff built.

"VII. JAMES BUCHANAN. — This is the maiden all forlorn that milked the cow with crumpled horn that tossed the dog that worried the cat that killed the rat that ate the malt that lay in the house that Jeff built.

"VIII. C. CESH. — This is the man all tattered and torn that married the maiden all forlorn that milked the cow with crumpled horn that tossed the dog that worried the cat that killed the rat that ate the malt that lay in the house that Jeff built.

"IX. PLUNDER. — This is the priest all shaven and shorn that married the man all tattered and torn to the maiden all forlorn that milked the cow with crumpled horn that tossed the dog that worried the cat that killed the rat that ate the malt that lay in the house that Jeff built."

———

EPIGRAM.

WHILST Butler plays his silly pranks,
And closes up New Orleans' banks,
Our Stonewall Jackson, with more cunning,
Keeps Yankee Banks forever running.

FRIENDS IN SCOTLAND. — When the news of the fall of Vicksburg and General Lee's retreat reached the village of Bankfoot, in Perthshire, the friends of the North got quite jubilant. A banner was hastily painted with the motto on one side, "Vicksburg is taken;" on the reverse, "God speed the North." A floral device on a large scale was also extemporized, and at eight o'clock a procession set out through the village, accompanied by the music band. At the close of the procession the political lions of the place and the members of the band repaired to the inn, where President Lincoln and his successful Generals' healths were drunk with rounds of cheers, and then all went peaceably and gladly to their homes.

AT PORT ROYAL.

BY JOHN GREENLEAF WHITTIER.

THE tent-lights glimmer on the land,
  The ship-lights on the sea;
The night-wind smooths with drifting sand
  Our track on lone Tybee.

At last our grating keels outslide,
  Our good boats forward swing;
And while we ride the land-locked tide,
  Our negroes row and sing.

For dear the bondman holds his gifts
  Of music and of song —
The gold that kindly Nature sifts
  Among his sands of wrong; —

The power to make his toiling days
  And poor home-comforts please;
The quaint relief of mirth that plays
  With sorrow's minor keys.

Another glow than sunset's fire
  Has filled the West with light,
Where field and garner, barn and byre
  Are blazing through the night.

The land is wild with fear and hate;
  The rout runs mad and fast;
From hand to hand, from gate to gate,
  The flaming brand is passed.

The lurid glow falls strong across
  Dark faces broad with smiles:
Not theirs the terror, hate, and loss
  That fire yon blazing piles.

With oar-strokes timing to their song,
  They weave in simple lays
The pathos of remembered wrong,
  The hope of better days; —

The triumph-note that Miriam sung,
  The joy of uncaged birds:
Softening with Afric's mellow tongue
  Their broken Saxon words.

SONG OF THE NEGRO BOATMEN.

O, praise an' tanks! De Lord he come
  To set de people free;
An' massa tink it day ob doom,
  An' we ob jubilee.

De Lord, dat heap de Red Sea waves,
  He jus' as 'trong as den;
He say de word: we las' night slaves,
  To-day de Lord's free men!
    De yam will grow, de cotton blow,
      We'll hab de rice and corn;
    O nebber you fear, if nebber you hear
      De driver blow his horn!

Ole massa on he trabbles gone;
  He leaf de land behind:
De Lord's breff blow him furder on,
  Like corn shuck in de wind.
We own de hoe, we own de plough,
  We own de hands dat hold;
We sell de pig, we sell de cow,
  But nebber chile be sold.
    De yam will grow, de cotton blow,
      We'll hab de rice an' corn;
    O nebber you fear, if nebber you hear
      De driver blow his horn!

We pray de Lord; he gib us signs
  Dat some day we be free;
De norf wind tell it to de pines,
  De wild-duck to de sea;
We tink it when de church-bell ring,
  We dream it in de dream;
De rice-bird mean it when he sing,
  De eagle when he scream.
    De yam will grow, de cotton blow,
      We'll hab de rice an' corn;
    O nebber you fear, if nebber you hear
      De driver blow his horn!

We know de promise nebber fail,
  An' nebber lie de word;
So, like de 'postles in de jail,
  We waited for de Lord;
An' now he open ebery door,
  An' trow away de key;
He tink we lub him so before,
  We lub him better free.
    De yam will grow, de cotton blow,
      He'll gib de rice an' corn;
    O nebber you fear, if nebber you hear
      De driver blow his horn!

So sing our dusky gondoliers;
  And with a secret pain,
And smiles that seem akin to tears,
  We hear the wild refrain.

We dare not share the negro's trust,
  Nor yet his hope deny;
We only know that God is just,
  And every wrong shall die.

Rude seems the song; each swarthy face,
  Flame-lighted, ruder still;
We start to think that hapless race
  Must shape our good or ill; —

That laws of changeless justice bind
  Oppressor with oppressed;
And close as sin and suffering joined,
  We march to fate abreast.

Sing on, poor hearts! your chant shall be
  Our sign of blight or bloom, —
The Vala-song of Liberty,
  Or death-rune of our doom!

INCIDENT OF LOOKOUT VALLEY. — "An un-recorded incident of the midnight fight between Hooker's and Longstreet's forces in Lookout Valley, ten days ago, has come to my knowledge, and deserves to have a place on the record," says a correspondent. "A short time subsequent to this magnificent charge on the enemy in their breastworks by General Geary's brigade, General Howard, taking with him a small escort of cavalry, started for that part of the field where General Geary was supposed to be. He had not gone far when he came up with a body of infantry. 'What cavalry is that?' was the hail. 'All right,' responded General Howard, at the same time calling out, 'What men are those?' 'Long-street's,' was the reply. 'All right; come here,' said General Howard. The men approached. 'Have we whipped those fellows?' asked General Howard, in a manner to keep up the deception. 'No, d—n them; they were too much for us, and drove us from our rifle pits like devils. We're whipped ourselves.' By this time the rebels had gathered nearer. 'Lay down your arms,' de-manded General Howard in a stern voice. The men surrendered. Taking his prisoners in charge, General Howard proceeded on his way. He had not gone far before another party of rebel infantry called out, 'What cavalry is that?' 'All right,' was the response again of General Howard, as he proceeded. On approaching the position oc-cupied by Geary, that officer had observed the advancing horsemen and infantry, as he supposed the prisoners to be, and supposing them to be rebels, he had ordered his guns to be loaded with canister, and in a moment more would have given the intrepid Howard and his little forces the ben-efit of it. But the General who had successfully deceived the enemy found a way to make himself known to friends, and so escaped a reception of that kind."

A RAID. — A correspondent at Washington wrote: "Owing to Mosby's depredations, the word 'raid' is worked into almost every expres-sion. I have in my employ a contraband, of double-dyed blackness, called John. I went out to my barn one morning, and, noticing that his face was wet with perspiration, remarked that he 'looked pretty warm.' 'Yes, massa,' was his re-ply, 'Ise had a pretty big raid on my muscle dis mornin', an' Ise mos' done gone.'"

FEMININE WRATH. — In the fall of 1863, after the great national successes at Vicksburg, Chat-tanooga, and Gettysburg, the President of the United States appointed a day of Thanksgiving to God for the victories that had crowned the national arms.

The Bulletin, a Union paper published in Mem-phis, Tennessee, made a simple announcement of the fact, and remarked that there were many, no doubt, in that city who would heartily join in celebrating the day. This suggestion drew upon the editor's head the following glowing and defiant philippic from the pen of one of the fair citizens of Memphis:

"EDITOR BULLETIN: You call attention to Lin-coln's appointment of a day of Thanksgiving for the successes which have blessed our cause, and you hope the day will be properly observed. By 'our cause' you mean the Union cause. I won-der how you think the people of Memphis can thank God for the successes of the Union Aboli-tion cause. You pretend to think that a great Union sentiment has sprung up in Memphis, be-cause you say that upwards of eleven thousand persons have taken the oath of allegiance. Let me tell you, if they have taken it, they did not do it of their own free will, and they don't feel bound by it; they had to take it under a military despotism, and don't feel bound to regard any oath forced upon them in that way. Do you be-lieve that any preacher in Memphis will appoint services in his church at Lincoln's dictation? Let one dare to try it, and see how his congregation will stand it. They know better. They know full well that the people of Memphis give thanks over Union disasters with sincere hearts, but don't rejoice at Union victories, as they call them. The women of Memphis will stick to the Confed-erate cause, like Ruth clung to her mother-in-law, and say to it, 'Where thou goest I will go, where thou livest I will live, where thou diest I will die, and there will I be buried.' But where are your great successes? Your own papers say that Lee brought off a train of captured spoils twelve miles long, and that Morgan destroyed seven or eight millions of dollars' worth, before all Ohio and Indiana could stop him. Pretty dear success, this. Still I won't rejoice over it at Lincoln's dictation. But wait till President Da-vis' day comes round. Perhaps by that time Meade may get another whipping, and if you don't see rejoicing and thanksgiving then, you may well believe that you and your officious local fail to see half that exists in Memphis. Now you won't publish this, perhaps, because it don't suit you. You can say the reason is, because I don't put my real name to it. You can do as you please about it. I choose to sign it.

MARY LEE THORNE.

RELENTLESS CONSCRIPTION. — The rebel con-script act, which was enforced on and after the 20th April, 1862, brought dismay to thousands of Southern families. A large portion of the rebel army, at that time, was composed of men who had enlisted for twelve and three months, and whose time would expire in May, when their re-turn was eagerly and anxiously anticipated by their families, for many of whom no pecuniary provision had been made after the expiration of the time enlisted for. One of the regiments un-der Bragg's command at this time was composed of men from East Tennessee, most of them poor and leaving at home small provision for their wives and children. Of this regiment, one com-pany, at the expiration of the twelve months of their enlistment, laid down their arms, and demanded permission to return to their families. By threat and argument, most of them were induced to return to duty; but three or four held out, declaring that they would insist on their right to go home; but all these, save one, were at last convinced that there was no alternative but death or obedience, and, at whatever sacrifice of feeling, concluded to shoulder arms again, and return to duty. One man, however, firmer than the rest, and who was continually haunted by the memory of his destitute family at home, steadily refused obedience to the new and terrible law. He said he had fought faithfully and willingly for his country, but his time had expired, and he demanded, *as a right*, that he should go home and make proper provision for the support of his family, when he promised to return and become a voluntary conscript. Argument, persuasion, threat, imprisonment were powerless to move him from this position. At last he was tried by court-martial for mutiny, and sentenced to be shot on the following day. He received his sentence with perfect coolness, declaring that he was right, and if they chose to shoot him, they might do so. His case elicited universal sympathy, and Bragg was persuaded, by the entreaties of some of his officers, to extend the condemned man three days of grace. He was allowed the liberty of the camp, and every argument used to persuade him to get away, which he could easily do. "No," he replied to all such suggestions; he had done nothing wrong, and he would not sneak away, as though he were guilty. He wished nothing unjust or wrong; his family at home were starving; his first duty was to provide for them. The three days passed; and the Crescent regiment, which was enlisted for three months, and which was, perhaps, as anxious to return home as any other in the field, was detailed to complete the tragedy. The army was drawn up, enclosing the Crescent regiment, for fear, it was said, they should refuse to obey orders. The doomed man was brought out, and marched, with a firm step, to his stand beside the coffin prepared to receive his dead body. At the appointed moment he bared his breast, gave the signal to fire, and fell, in the same moment, upon his coffin, a lifeless corpse. A squad of men were immediately detailed to bury him, and the army was marched back to camp. The unfortunate regiment, which was chosen as the instrument of this terrible despotism, was sickened by the sight, as though there had been administered to them the most powerful emetic; and from that time on, upon the name of Braxton Bragg were heaped curses, both loud and deep; but open mutiny was effectually suppressed.

RECOLLECTIONS OF JOHN B. FLOYD. — A "Soldier" of the South contributed the following story to a Confederate journal:

Having recently read a notice of the death of General Floyd, my thoughts went back to the days of Fort Donelson, and the period immediately following that disaster to our arms. Having taken a humble part in those affairs, and having been an eye-witness to the part acted in it by General Floyd, it has suggested itself that a few thoughts thereon would not be inappropriate. I first saw General Floyd, at Nashville, in January, 1862. He was then on his way to join General A. S. Johnston, whose headquarters were at Bowling Green, on Green River, Kentucky. General Floyd had his command with him, the same that served with him in West Virginia. It was then supposed that the great battle of the war would take place at or near Bowling Green, which would decide the question whether Kentucky was ours or belonged to the Federals. General Buell commanded the Federal forces, which occupied the line of Green River, and his army was rapidly reënforced, until, on the 1st of February, 1862, it numbered one hundred thousand men. It was given out that General Johnston's army was also one hundred thousand strong, and that the line of Green River would be held. A line of defence had been drawn from Bowling Green westward to Columbus, on the Mississippi, embracing Forts Henry, on the Tennessee River, and Donelson, on the Cumberland. The latter place was selected by Governor Harris, of Tennessee, on account of the natural strength of the position, and because it was the key of Nashville. This point was strongly fortified. Most of the heavy guns were mounted under the supervision of General Buckner, who took command of the post in January, 1862. Thus, on the 1st of February, 1862, the people who were south of this military line felt perfectly secure from the horrors of invasion, fully confident that the tide of war would roll towards the Ohio, instead of south, on the Cumberland and Tennessee. With the accomplished Sidney Johnston, commanding an army one hundred thousand strong, in Central Kentucky, and the people of that gallant State rising in arms, it was believed that the enemy would be beaten, and his flying cohorts driven out of the State. Such was the feeling of the people of Tennessee and Southern Kentucky on the 1st of February, 1862. Fatal security! It lost us an empire, not yet recovered.

Early in February General Gideon J. Pillow assumed command of the forces at Fort Donelson. He was the universal choice of the people of Tennessee for that position. On arriving at the fort he commenced work with his usual energy. It was under his direction that the rifle pits were dug, earthworks thrown up, timber and undergrowth cut down, and guns mounted, to prepare for a land attack from the enemy. His presence seemed to inspire every man with confidence, and he infused new energy into every laggard. I think it was on the 12th of February that General Floyd arrived at the fort, from Bowling Green, and assumed command of all the forces. He immediately examined the earthworks and defences, and pronounced everything that had been done "good." For a day or two previous the gunboats of the enemy had been hovering about the point below, and everything was in preparation to give them a warm reception. The scouts brought in word that the enemy was landing a large force below the point, and it then became apparent that the ditching and digging were not labor lost. Our entire force, all told, amounted to thirteen thousand men. The fight was commenced by the enemy's gunboats on Thursday, the 13th, and continued through three days. From prisoners, which were taken on Friday, we learned that the enemy's land force was thirty thousand strong, and that they were being daily reënforced with fresh troops. The history of the three days' fight is well known. I do not desire to enter into an account of each day's fight; suffice it to say that the enemy was repulsed at all points with great slaughter, and that he gained no material advantage until Saturday evening, when, by the loss of a battery, our line was bent back, and we stood in great danger of being flanked. During the three days' fight the gunboats had made no impression on the fort, while the fort had disabled two of the gunboats, and injured, to some extent, a third. No boat could stand a fire from heavy guns mounted on a bluff one hundred feet above the river. The terrible plunging fire of solid shot was certain destruction to all below. In Saturday's fight we were so overwhelmed by numbers that we were forced to give back.

Our line of defence once lost, we were then at a great disadvantage. The weather was terrible. It had been sleeting and snowing for two days and nights, and was bitter cold. Several of the men had frozen to death in the trenches. The rifle pits were knee-deep in water and ice. Many of the men had not tasted food for two days. Some were physically exhausted from hunger, loss of sleep, and cold. More than three fourths of the whole command were raw troops, and had never faced an enemy before. Some murmuring was heard among the men, such as, "We can't fight forever; if Johnston don't send us reënforcements we ought to leave here." In this state of affairs a council of war was held late on Saturday evening. It was admitted that the place could not be held without reënforcements. General Pillow believed that reënforcements would yet arrive, and he was in favor of commencing a vigorous attack on the enemy next morning (Sunday), to regain our former line, and hold that position at all hazards until help came. He said that he had promised Governor Harris that he would hold that place at all hazards and defend the capital, and he was in favor of holding it. General Floyd said that no more aid would come; that he had brought the last available man that General Johnston could spare; that he had but twenty-five thousand men left; and that he thought it best to make a vigorous attack on the enemy next morning, and, under cover of the attack, to retire the whole command. To this General Buckner made some objection, but finally he assented to it. It was admitted by all that the place could not be longer held without reënforcements, and after General Floyd's statement it was seen that it was impossible to be reënforced. The plan of General Floyd was assented to by Generals Buckner and Pillow, and it was deter-

mined to commence the attack on Sunday morning at daylight.

Some time later in the night another meeting of general officers was held, I understood at the request of General Buckner, at which he stated that the men were physically worn out and incapable of fighting any more, and that he was in favor of surrendering; that they were entirely surrounded by the enemy, and that even if they succeeded in cutting their way out, that there was not sufficient river transportation to convey the troops to Nashville; that an attack next morning would end only in a wanton destruction of life, and that he could not see any benefit that would result from it. General Pillow spoke in favor of the attack next morning. He thought the men capable of another effort, and he spoke eloquently against a surrender, which would dim all the glory that had been achieved. He eulogized the troops; said they were not lacking in strength or spirit; that they were capable of one more effort, and that effort should be made; that he would never surrender to the enemy. General Floyd said he was opposed to surrendering; that he could not and would not surrender; that he knew the men were worn out, yet he thought almost the entire command could be saved by a vigorous attack next morning. General Buckner replied that the men were exhausted, and could fight no more, and that he would stay with his men. General Floyd said, "I cannot surrender; I pass the command over to you, General Pillow." General Pillow said, "Nor can I surrender; I pass the command to General Buckner." General Buckner said, "I accept the command." On these facts becoming known to the men, all was commotion. Many prepared to leave at once. It was given out that all that wanted to could now leave, as the way to Nashville was open. Many crossed the river, and went on foot on to Nashville. Colonel Forrest, of the Tennessee cavalry, now General Forrest, said that he would form a rear guard of his command, and protect all who would come out. Many availed themselves of this offer, and Colonel Forrest kept his word. General Floyd brought out almost his entire command, which had come with him from Virginia. General Pillow was instrumental in bringing several of the men out. He made personal appeals to many of the officers commanding Tennessee troops not to remain, which was responded to. It is my opinion that the entire command could have been saved had General Floyd's plan been adopted. As it was, more than four thousand men left the fort and the trenches on that night, and arrived safe at Nashville. All left who chose to, and those who remained chose to remain. Indeed, many left the fort after it had been surrendered, on Sunday, and walked all the way to Nashville. Eleven members of a Texas regiment came into camp at Murfreesboro', thirteen days after the surrender, having left the fort on Monday morning after the surrender. The report that the fort was surrounded by the enemy was a mistake. It was not even invested on Sunday evening, as our men were continually leaving the

28

fort from morning until night on that day. About six thousand men remained with General Buckner, and he surrendered these with the fort on Sunday, the 16th of February. Our loss in killed, wounded, and missing was not more than one thousand. The loss of the enemy was immense; it could not have been less than six thousand in killed and wounded. The ground on the slope in front of the rifle pits was literally covered with his dead and dying. Never were troops handled better than ours were at Fort Donelson. Never did men fight with greater resolution. The force brought against them was immensely superior in men and munitions of war, and for three days they held out, fighting each day fresh troops, and repulsing them with terrible slaughter. That the victory was not ours is not the fault of those who fought on that ensanguined field. Had five thousand fresh troops arrived on Saturday evening the victory would have been ours.

I now desire to state a few facts in relation to the surrender, not for the purpose of doing any injustice to the living, but to do justice to the dead. In stating these facts I do not wish to draw any invidious distinction between the troops from the different States who fought at Fort Donelson. They all fought well, and they all deserve well of their country. As long as success seemed possible, the different State troops vied with each other in bravery and gallantry. When success seemed impossible, then murmurs were heard, and there was dissatisfaction expressed at the non-arrival of reënforcements. When the question was mooted, whether the garrison "fall back" or surrender, loud disclaimers were heard against the former. It was said, "Are we to leave our homes and families, and fall back fighting for other States? No; we have fought enough; we will surrender and go home."

The troops that fought at Fort Donelson were volunteers, many of them "home guards," who had left their homes, as they thought, to fight at Fort Donelson, and then go home. They had no idea, if unsuccessful there, to "fall back" and fight indefinitely. These men fought bravely as long as there was a show of victory; but when the dark hour came, and the question was surrender or fall back, they preferred the former. There were many such at Fort Donelson. It was said that these men had some weight in influencing General Buckner to remain. If true, it is no argument against his humanity, honor, or patriotism. On the contrary, he deserves credit for remaining with his men, to share their fortunes, good or evil. There was another class of men at Fort Donelson, who were not from any particular State, but from all the States there represented, who had determined never to surrender — who preferred death to surrender. The head and front of this class was General Floyd. When he said, "I cannot surrender," there was a deep meaning in it. He had been Secretary of War under the Buchanan administration. He had sent the arms belonging to the Government South, and the whole North howled like demons over it. He had been denounced by the whole abolition tribe,

from Seward to Garrison. They all, from Lincoln to the lowest minion, hated, with a venomous hatred, John B. Floyd. Therefore he could not surrender. To that noble old man it would have been too deep a humiliation. Had he surrendered, the vile Northern rabble would have hooted and howled at his heels, from the Ohio to the St. Lawrence. He would have been hawked at by the Yankee owls in every city and village through which he passed. Therefore General Floyd "could not surrender." Did he do wrong, then, in leaving Fort Donelson, and saving all that he could of the garrison? I think not. He did right in saving a part, if he could not save the whole. He was willing to make the effort to save all, but in this he was opposed; he then did the next best thing, — he saved all he could. It was said by one high in authority, that he could not understand how seven thousand men could surrender with arms in their hands. How, then, could it be conceived that twelve thousand men could surrender with arms in their hands, which would have been the case had General Floyd remained at Fort Donelson.

When it was known on the march from Murfreesboro' to Decatur that the President had suspended General Floyd for the part he took at Fort Donelson, a feeling of regret pervaded the army. It was supposed that his suspension would be of short duration. Men of common sense could not see wherein he had done wrong. He had the sympathies of the whole army, and all hoped that he would soon be reinstated by the President. But he never was. He was too proud

"To bow the supple hinges of the knee
That thrift might follow fawning,"

and he went down to the grave with the censure of the President upon him. What a pity it could not have been otherwise! General Buckner was promoted for the part he acted at Fort Donelson, and he deserved it. General Pillow was reinstated in his command, but General Floyd was left to go down to the grave with this foul censure clinging to him to the last. Why was this? Did the good of the cause require that it should be so? Let us suppose that, in refusing to surrender at Fort Donelson, he committed a wrong. Did the good of the country require that he should never be forgiven? If General Floyd committed a wrong, General Pillow was guilty of a like offence. General Pillow was reinstated in his command. Why was not the same justice rendered towards General Floyd? The writer of this is a friend and ardent admirer of President Davis. He has full confidence in his patriotism, integrity, and ability; but he is constrained to say that the old patriot, who has gone down to his grave, was wronged at his hands. A more patriotic man than John B. Floyd did not live in the limits of this Confederacy. He was brave and able, honest and sagacious, kind and courteous to those under him, and one of the truest men I ever knew. Those who served under him at Fort Donelson, who saw him sharing the dangers and perils of his men, his face and breast bared to the

MAJ.GEN. SHERIDAN

pitiless storm, with the icicles hanging to his gray beard; those who heard his words of cheer and comfort to the doubtful and desponding will never forget him. And again at Nashville, after the fall of Donelson, restoring order out of chaos, quieting the fears of the timid, putting down the lawlessness of the rabble, and saving the property of the Government. Before the arrival of the Federals at Nashville he had removed to a place of safety more than a million dollars worth of Government stores, which would otherwise have been destroyed in the general panic. He also saved the State of Tennessee many hundreds of thousands of dollars by his timely arrival at the capital.

Such was John B. Floyd. This imperfect, but impartial sketch is but a poor tribute to the man. The future historian will do him justice. He was a noble, chivalrous, patriotic Virginian; but his heart was large enough to hold his whole country. It can be said of him —

"This was the noblest Roman of them all!
                        The elements
So mixed in him that Nature might stand up
And say to all the world, THIS WAS A MAN."

A DINNER PARTY BROKEN UP. — In April, 1863, the 17th of the month, a party of somewhat crestfallen but defiant rebel officers were dining at the plantation of a great slave-owner on the Mississippi River, about half way between Vicksburg and Port Hudson. There was a commissary captain, a surgeon, the governor of rebel Louisiana, and others of greater or less rank in secession circles.

The planter's wines had been long ago consumed, but he had a demijohn of Louisiana rum, to which his guests were welcome, and everything which the large and admirably cultivated plantation garden could supply graced the table.

Strong opinions were expressed that no boat on the Mississippi could live ten minutes under the fire of the Vicksburg batteries — that yellow fever would soon appear in Grant's army at Milliken's Bend, that the South would hold that portion of the Mississippi Valley against all opposition; and fearful accounts were related of Yankee cowardice, Yankee barbarism and atrocity, with strong determinations "never to submit or yield."

In the midst of all this bravery one of the gentlemen was summoned to the door by a courier, who had an important communication from the General commanding at Vicksburg, and also another from the commander at Port Hudson.

One telegram read, "Five gunboats passed last night: notify all boats and river batteries." The other, from below, was, "Hartford and two others coming up: look out." He stepped back and read them to the company.

If a ten-inch shell had exploded, the change would not have been greater. First there was a blank pause. Then one said, "It's all up with us, gentlemen; if five have passed, twenty will

pass, and the Valley is gone." — "Colonel, will you order my horse?" "Colonel, I will have mine at the same time."

In ten minutes the party had broken up, and were scattering in every direction, some for Shreveport, others for Mobile; and the boom of the guns on the Hartford as she came sweeping around the bend of the river was the knell of all their high-blown hopes and sanguine boasts.

SHERIDAN'S EARLY ORDERS.

I.

PHIL SHERIDAN down in the valley made
    A rule the "rebs" to soften:
'Twas — " Out with the blade,
    Away with the spade;
Fight EARLY, and fight often! "

II.

But "often" was not quite often enough
    To have things done up rarely;
So he wrote, and said,
    "Have *this* order read:"
'Twas, " Boys, fight late and EARLY."

III.

But "late" and "often" give too many rests
    To clear the valley fairly;
"They are not bad tests,"
    Thought Phil — " but the best's
To whip the enemy, EARLY."

IV.

So he says, "No matter for hour or date:
    To use the foe up squarely,
Fight him early, late —
    When we thrash him straight,
They'll admit we whipp'd him, EARLY."

ANECDOTE OF PRESIDENT LINCOLN. — A gentleman called on the President, and solicited a pass for Richmond. "Well," said the President, "I would be very happy to oblige you, if my passes were respected; but the fact is, sir, I have, within the last two years, given passes to two hundred and fifty thousand men to go to Richmond, and not one has got there yet."

GENERAL ROSSER ON THE BORDER. — In the winter of 1863-4, the two opposing armies in Virginia lay on the upper branches of the Rapidan, not far from Culpepper and Brandy Station, sixty miles south of the Potomac. As General Meade had all his supplies to bring in wagons from Alexandria, the possible plunder that might reward an enterprising raid in the country between the Union army and the Potomac was a strong bait to Southern enterprise. There were, consequently, two or three of these expeditions during the winter, of which the most successful in the way of plunder was that of the rebel General Rosser, who, next to Stuart and Forrest, won the greatest name among the Confederates as a cavalry officer. The following story of his exploit that winter was prepared by a correspondent of a Richmond paper:

"The foray made by Early, Fitz Lee, and Rosser, about the 1st of January, proving rather unsuccessful, it was ordered that General Early, with one brigade of infantry (General Thomas'), Rosser's brigade of cavalry, and McCallahan's battery, should make another effort towards relieving the border of its Yankees and cattle. Information had been received that a large supply train would start from New Creek to Petersburg on a certain day; and, moreover, it was necessary that we should hold Petersburg in order to make our search for cattle successful. The plan of operation having been decided upon, General Early, with Thomas' brigade of infantry, crossed by Orkney Springs, General Rosser's brigade, with McCallahan's battery, at Brook's Gap, forming a junction at Mathias' on the 31st, and entering Moorefield on the 1st of February. That night our picket on the Petersburg road, through negligence, was captured by a scouting party of the enemy that advanced within half a mile of General Early's headquarters without becoming aware of our presence. General Rosser, in order to prevent communication between Petersburg and the expected train, sent out Baylor's squadron of the Twelfth Virginia cavalry, with a guide, to intercept couriers passing from one point to another. The brigade moved off about ten A. M. on the road crossing the mountain, and intersecting the Petersburg and New Creek road about five miles above Williamsport.

"As we were approaching the top of the mountain, our advance guard was checked by an infantry picket of the enemy, about two hundred strong, which had been engaged in obstructing the road. They moved off rapidly and safely; for pursuit was impracticable, in consequence of the thorough blockade the enemy had constructed by throwing heavy timber across the road for a distance of three miles, and digging away the road itself for some distance. These obstacles, by means of axes and picks in the hands of eager and determined men, were speedily removed, and in a few moments the Yankees were again in sight, in rapid rout for the Petersburg road. The Twelfth, moving down on them, speedily checked them up, but was unable to inflict any injury on account of the enemy's position, who had lost no time in ensconcing himself in the thick growth on the side of the mountain. At this crisis, however, Baylor's squadron, misled, through the ignorance of their guide, came up in the rear of the enemy, and speedily dislodged him. General Rosser, following with his cavalry and battery, turned towards Williamsport, and came up within sight of the enemy about two miles below, just as the Yankee picket met their main column. The Yankees were eleven hundred strong, under Colonel Snyder. Confident of easy victory, they had parked their train, and were prepared to receive us. General Rosser, dismounting detachments from the Eleventh, Seventh, Twelfth, and White's battalion, in all about three hundred

guns, placing his battery in position, and throwing forward the remaining squadron of the Seventh under Major Myers, to charge the enemy when an opportunity offered, sent Lieutenant-Colonel Massie, with the rest of the Twelfth Virginia, to make a demonstration in the enemy's rear, intercept communication, and blockade the road, and commenced the attack. Here was presented a sight novel and suggestive — dismounted cavalry, with short-range guns, attacking more than three times their number of infantry, prepared both by time and position to receive them. Here the genius that has placed General Rosser, at twenty-five, in a position unsurpassed in our military annals, the genius that has won the admiration of his men, and is rapidly filling, in their hearts, the place left void by the death of Ashby, was fully manifested. Pressing rapidly upon the enemy, he drove them from one position to another, until, having fairly uncovered their train, the appearance of our cavalry in their rear excited an agitation in their ranks which the effective charge of Major Myers quickly fomented into a panic; the enemy sought safety in the neighboring mountain. Meantime General Early was moving on Petersburg, and, in order to coöperate with him, the pursuit was abandoned, and attention turned to the captured train — ninety-four wagons, four hundred and fifty mules, flour, bacon, salt, molasses, sugar, coffee, beans, rice, overcoats, and blankets, with three or four sutlers' wagons, loaded with all manner of eatables and wearables.

"'Quod nunc describere longum est,' were the fruits of victory! Moving back towards Petersburg, we encamped for the night about ten miles from that place. Oysters, sardines, canned fruits, brandy peaches, cheese, crackers, &c., comprised our 'homely fare.' We learned next day, while on the march, that Colonel Thorburn, commanding at Petersburg, had 'vamosed the ranche' during the night, and was then on his way towards New Creek. On reaching Petersburg we found the camps deserted, but the huts and tents still standing, and apparently but few things had been burned. Everything bore marks of haste, confusion, and flight; large quantities of clothing, blankets, overcoats, and provisions were secured, and two large sutlers' establishments unearthed and promptly despatched. In a short time General Early, with Thomas' brigade, came up, chagrin and disappointment depicted in their visages, deprived of their expected glory by Yankee prudence, and of their anticipated plunder by cavalry promptness. As the only means of relieving their furore and assuaging their grief, they were generously permitted to burn the Yankee quarters and dig down their earthworks. After a conference with General Early, General Rosser moved again towards Burlington, and reached there next day by twelve M., driving in and bagging the Yankee picket. Halting here, we threatened, by our position, both New Creek and Cumberland; and information received during the day showed that at the former place we were painfully expected. We moved that night five miles below, in the direction of Cumberland, and encamped for the night on the farm of the Hon. James Karscaddan, senator, from that district, in the august council of 'West Virginia.' Passing through Frankfort next day, we struck the Baltimore and Ohio Railroad at Patterson's Creek Station. Lieutenant-Colonel White, with his memorable battalion, being in front, charged the camp, riding over the infantry picket; he surprised the guard of forty men, killed and wounded several, and captured the rest. Here we destroyed effectually two large railroad bridges, two canal locks and bridges, besides destroying the railroad houses and telegraph wires, and relieving a large Yankee storehouse of its contents. I neglected to mention that Colonel Marshall, with the Seventh, had been previously sent to hold the Mechanicsburg Gap, three miles from Romney, and that Colonel Massie, with the Twelfth, had been left at Frankfort to collect cattle. It was important that he should return the same day. Leaving the railroad, he reached Frankfort, and learned that Averill was in Romney, and had started to Springfield, and was, consequently, apprised of our whereabouts. At the same time we received information from Colonel Marshall that he had been compelled to abandon the Gap near Romney. Things certainly did wear a sombre hue. But General Rosser, with a sagacity amounting almost to intuition, divined their schemes, and prepared to thwart them. Pushing on with his command, cattle, and prisoners, he reached Sheetz's Mills about ten A. M., and took the road that intersects the north-western grade, between Burlington and Romney, the enemy holding both places. Moving towards Moorefield, he encamped about twenty miles from there, reaching there next morning, the enemy occupying our camps shortly after we left.

"Everything was ready for an early start homeward next day. But lo! Averill, mystified by our movements, and thrown completely off the scent, appeared next morning before our camps, and threatened immolation. With the Christian fortitude that characterizes true martyrs, we awaited our fate — awaited long and patiently, but waited in vain. Yankee Generals rode to the front, flourished their flags, and retired; Yankee reconnoitrers rode up on high hills, reconnoitred, and rode down again; Yankee skirmishers expended much private strategy in securing safe positions, and desperately held them. Wearied with waiting, we moved off, and as we reached the summit of the mountain, looking back down the valley, we saw, with such emotions as Gulliver experienced when the Lilliputian army marched between his legs, these valiant defenders of the Constitution drawn up in formidable lines, determined 'to do or fly.' We reached camp on the 6th, with twelve hundred cattle, and the captures already enumerated. Our casualties are, Lieutenant Howell, Seventh, lost an arm; Captain Richardson, Eleventh, shot through the leg; the gallant Lieutenant Baylor, slightly in the arm; Mr. John H. Buck, of the brigade staff, in the leg."

THE PRESENT CRISIS.

BY JAMES RUSSELL LOWELL.

WHEN a deed is done for Freedom, through the
        broad earth's aching breast
Runs a thrill of joy prophetic, trembling on from
        east to west;
And the slave, where'er he cowers, feels the soul
        within him climb
To the awful verge of manhood, as the energy sub-
        lime
Of a century bursts full-blossomed on the thorny
        stem of Time.

Through the walls of hut and palace shoots the in-
        stantaneous throe,
When the travail of the Ages wrings earth's sys-
        tems to and fro;
At the birth of each new Era, with a recognizing
        start,
Nation wildly looks on nation, standing with mute
        lips apart,
And glad Truth's yet mightier man-child leaps be-
        neath the Future's heart.

For mankind are one in spirit, and an instinct
        bears along,
Round the earth's electric circle, the swift flash of
        right or wrong;
Whether conscious or unconscious, yet humanity's
        vast frame,
Through its ocean-sundered fibres, feels the gush
        of joy or shame;
In the gain or loss of one race, all the rest have
        equal claim.

Once, to every man and nation, comes the moment
        to decide,
In the strife of Truth with Falsehood, for the good
        or evil side;
Some great cause, God's *new* Messiah, offering each
        the bloom or blight,
Parts the goats upon the left hand, and the sheep
        upon the right,
And the choice goes by forever 'twixt that darkness
        and that light.

Hast thou chosen, O my people, on whose party
        thou shalt stand,
Ere the Doom from its worn sandals shakes the
        dust against our land?
Though the cause of Evil prosper, yet 'tis Truth
        alone is strong;
And albeit she wander outcast now, I see around
        her throng
Troops of beautiful, tall angels, to enshield her
        from all wrong.

We see dimly, in the Present, what is small and
        what is great;
Slow of faith, how weak an arm may turn the iron
        helm of Fate;
But the soul is still oracular — amid the market's
        din,
List the ominous stern whisper from the Delphic
        cave within —
"They enslave their children's children who make
        compromise with Sin!"

Slavery, the earth-born Cyclops, fellest of the
    giant brood,
Sons of brutish Force and Darkness, who have
    drenched the earth with blood,
Famished in his self-made desert, blinded by our
    purer day,
Gropes in yet unblasted regions for his miserable
    prey:
Shall we guide his gory fingers where our helpless
    children play?

'Tis as easy to be heroes, as to sit the idle slaves
Of a legendary virtue carved upon our fathers'
    graves:
Worshippers of light ancestral make the present light
    a crime.
Was the Mayflower launched by cowards? —
    steered by men behind *their* time?
Turn those tracks towards Past, or Future, that
    make Plymouth Rock sublime?

They were men of *present* valor — stalwart old
    iconoclasts;
Unconvinced by axe or gibbet that all virtue was
    the Past's;
But we make *their* truth *our* falsehood, thinking
    that has made *us* free,
Hoarding it in mouldy parchments, while our ten-
    der spirits flee
The rude grasp of that great Impulse which drove
    them across the sea.

New occasions teach new duties! Time makes an-
    cient good uncouth;
They must upward still, and onward, who would
    keep abreast of Truth;
Lo, before us gleam her camp fires! we *ourselves*
    must Pilgrims be,
Launch *our* Mayflower, and steer boldly through
    the desperate winter sea,
Nor attempt the Future's portal with the Past's
    blood-rusted key.

A SIGHT ON THE BATTLE-FIELD. — A soldier who fought on the bloody field of Shiloh,
in describing the sights of that Golgotha, says
that no spectacle was more appalling than one he
witnessed just as the defeated army of Beauregard commenced its retreat upon Corinth.

The enclosures of that country are all the old
Virginia snake fence, in the angle of which a
person may sit and be supported on each side.
In such an angle, and with his feet braced against
a little tree, sat a man apparently in middle life,
bolt upright, and gazing at a locket in his hand.

Approaching nearer he was shocked to find
him stone dead and rigid; his stiffened feet so
braced against the tree that he could not fall forward, and the fence supporting each side of the
corpse.

The dead man's eyes were open, and fixed, with
a horrible stony stare, on the daguerreotype,
which was clinched in both hands.

In a hasty glance over his shoulder the soldier
saw the figures of a woman, and a child standing
beside her; the wife and daughter, no doubt,
of the dead man, upon which the eyes of the
husband and father had not, even in death, ceased
to gaze.

A WAR PICTURE. — Chickamauga was fought
the 20th September, 1863, and Lookout Mountain a little more than a month after. During
that interval the two antagonist armies lay within cannon shot of each other — the Union force
in Chattanooga, the rebel on Lookout Mountain
and Missionary Ridge.

The panorama presented from the top of Lookout Mountain, aside from its rare beauty as a
landscape, combined more of the wild and romantic scenery of war than any other combination of
picturesque elements made during the whole war.

A correspondent of the Richmond Sentinel
wrote the following admirable sketch of what he
saw from the mountain top, and in the rebel camp
and hospitals:

"When setting out for the West from your
city a few weeks ago, a friend said to me at parting, 'If you write from the West, be sure and
give us the truth.' Having been accustomed to
look upon 'News from the West' with the same
suspicion, I promised to exercise due caution.

"Judge of my chagrin when the first message I
sent by telegraph, on getting to Atlanta, turned
out to be false. Arriving a few days after the
fight, a rumor that Chattanooga had been evacuated by the Yankees, was very current. I did
not believe it. It happened, however, during the
day, that I was introduced to a gentleman of high
position among the railroad men of the town,
and, on inquiry, I was informed that the report
was true; that General Bragg had telegraphed
for a train to leave next morning for that point,
via Cleveland, and that the train would certainly
go. These data even my cautious friend in
your city would have regarded as satisfactory. I
have no doubt but that such a message was
received, and the General, for the second time,
at least, in his life, telegraphed too soon.

"I have seen about fifteen hundred of our
wounded, and have also been to the battle-field.
The wounded I saw were among the worst cases.
They had been sent down to the (then) terminus
of the railroad, on Chickamauga River, — many
of them after being operated upon, and many
others where further attempts would be made to
save the limb. Some of these poor fellows were
terribly hurt. Many were wounded in two and
three places — sometimes by the same ball.
Though suffering much for food and attention,
they were in remarkably good spirits. It would
sicken many of your readers were I to describe
minutely the sufferings of these men — exposed,
first, for four days upon the field, and in the field
hospitals; then hauled in heavy army wagons
over a rocky road for twelve miles, and afterwards to lie upon straw; some in the open air,
and others under sheds, for two and three days
more, with but one blanket to cover with, and
none to lie upon. Nothing that I have seen since
the war began has so deeply impressed me with
the horrors of this strife as frequent visits to this
hospital at Chickamauga. God forbid that such
a spectacle may be witnessed again in this Confederacy! I did not visit the entire battle-field,
but only that part of it where the strife was most
deadly. It being a week after the fight, I saw

only about fifteen unburied Yankees and two Confederates, and about twenty dead horses — nine lying upon a space thirty feet square. They had belonged to one of our batteries which attempted to go into action within one hundred and twenty yards of a Yankee battery — the latter being masked. The chief evidences of a severe engagement were the number of bullet marks on the trees. The ground on which this severe conflict took place was a beautiful wood, with but little undergrowth.

"I never saw a more beautiful place for skirmishing, and I have understood from men in the fight that the Yankees favored this mode of warfare greatly, the men taking to the trees. But our boys dashed upon them and drove them from this cover. I had heard that the battle-ground was like that of Seven Pines, but that part I visited had no such resemblance. It was open and gently undulating. Here and there you would find a small, cleared field. Very little artillery was used, though some correspondents say the 'roar was deafening.' It has been also said that the enemy were driven from behind 'strong breastworks' on Sunday. The works I saw were mean, consisting of old logs, badly thrown together. I saw in one collection thirty-three pieces of captured artillery, and nineteen thousand muskets, in very good order. These latter will be of great service in arming the exchanged Vicksburg prisoners. But before closing I must tell you of a little affair in which Longstreet's artillery took a part. Chattanooga, as you know, lies in a deep fold of the Tennessee River. In front of the town, and three miles east of it, Missionary Ridge runs from north to south, completely investing the town in this direction. On the west of the town Lookout Mountain, with its immense rocky 'lookout' peak, approaches within three miles, and rests upon the river, which winds beneath its base. The Yankee line (the right wing of it) rests about three fourths of a mile from the base of the mountain. Our pickets occupy the base. The river makes a second fold just here, and in it is 'Moccason Ridge,' on the opposite side, where the Yankees have several casemated batteries, which guard their right flank. When on the mountain this ridge is just beneath you, say twelve hundred yards, but separated by the river. From this mountain you have one of the grandest views, at present, I ever beheld. You see the river far beneath you in six separate and distinct places, like six lakes. You see the mountains of Alabama and Georgia and Tennessee in the distance, and just at your feet you see Chattanooga and the Yankee army, and in front of it you see the 'Star' fort, and also two formidable forts on the left wing, north of the town. You see their whole line of rifle pits, from north to south. Along the base of Missionary Ridge the Confederate tents are seen forming a beautiful crescent; and perched high upon the top of this ridge, overlooking this grand basin, you see four or five white tents, where General Bragg has his headquarters. Our army is strongly fortified upon the rising ground along the base of the ridge. I

have ridden three miles along these fortifications, and think they are the best of the kind I ever saw. Now for the little affair I spoke of. Colonel E. P. Alexander, General Longstreet's active and skilful Chief of Artillery, hoped he might be able to shell Chattanooga, or the enemy's camps, from this mountain, and three nights ago twenty long-ranged rifle pieces were brought up, after great difficulty. It was necessary to bring them up at night, because the mountain road is in many places commanded by the batteries on Moccason Ridge. We used mules in getting our heaviest pieces up. They pull with more steadiness than horses. Every gun was located behind some huge rock, so as to protect the cannoneers from the cross-fire of the 'Ridge.' The firing was begun by some guns upon the right in General Polk's corps. Only one gun in that quarter (twenty-four pound rifle gun) could reach the enemy's lines. At one P. M., order was given to open the rifles from the mountain. Parker's battery, being highest up the mountain, opened first, and then down among the rocky soils of the mountain. Jordan's, Woolfolk's, and other batteries spoke out in thunder tones. The reverberations were truly grand. Old Moccason turned loose upon us with great fury; but 'munitions of rocks' secured us. All their guns being securely casemated, we could do them little or no injury; so we paid little or no attention to them. Colonel Alexander, with his glass and signal flag, took position higher up in the mountain, and watched the shots. Most of our fuses (nine tenths of them, indeed) were of no account, and hence there was great difficulty to see where our shot struck, only a few exploding. The Yankees in their rifle pits made themselves remarkably small. They swarmed before the firing began, but soon disappeared from sight. We fired slowly, every cannoneer mounting the rocks and watching the shot. After sinking the trail of the guns, so as to give an elevation of twenty-one degrees, the shots continued to fall short of the camps and the principal works of the enemy, and the order was given to cease firing. It has been reported we killed and wounded a few men in the advanced works. Last night at nine, four shots, at regular intervals and for special reasons, were fired at the town, and it was amusing to see the fires in the camps go out. The pickets, poor fellows, were the first to extinguish their little lights, which, like a thread of bright beads, encircled the great breast of the army. We have spent two nights upon the mountain. It is hard to say which is the most beautiful — the scene by night, when thousands of camp fires show the different lines of both armies with a dark, broad band between them, called 'neutral ground,' and when the picket by his little fire looks suspiciously into this dark *terra incognita* the livelong night, or the view after sunrise before the fog rises, when the valley northward and eastward as far as the eye can reach looks like one great ocean. The tops of the trees of Missionary Ridge, in the east, are seen above the great waste of waters, and here and there in the great distance some mountain peak rears its head. I have seen celebrated pictures of Noah's deluge, but nothing comparable to this.

"The view by clear daylight is also very grand and beautiful. The Yankees and their lines are seen with great distinctness, and appear so near that you think you could almost throw a stone into their camps. You see every wagon that moves, and every horse carried to water. What will be done next I would not tell if I knew. Something decisive can and ought to be done, and done soon too. Bragg has a fine army, and is able to whip Rosecrans in a fair field. Longstreet's men say these Western Yankees do not fight like the Eastern Yankees. There is no difference of opinion on this subject, I find. May God give wisdom, and soon crown our efforts with great and complete success."

ANECDOTE OF PRESIDENT LINCOLN. — Mr. Lincoln's practical shrewdness is exemplified in the following anecdote, which is sufficiently characteristic:

In the purlieus of the Capitol at Washington, the story goes that, after the death of Chief Justice Taney, and before the appointment of Mr. Chase in his stead, a committee of citizens from the Philadelphia Union League, with a distinguished journalist at their head as chairman, proceeded to Washington, for the purpose of laying before the President the reason why, in their opinion, Mr. Chase should be appointed to the vacancy on the bench. They took with them a memorial addressed to the President, which was read to him by one of the committee. After listening to the memorial, the President said to them, in a very deliberate manner: "Will you do me the favor to leave that paper with me? I want it in order that, if I appoint Mr. Chase, I may show the friends of the other persons for whom the office is solicited, by how powerful an influence, and by what strong personal recommendations, the claims of Mr. Chase were supported."

The committee listened with great satisfaction, and were about to depart, thinking that Mr. Chase was sure of the appointment, when they perceived that Mr. Lincoln had not finished what he intended to say. "And I want the paper, also," continued he, after a pause, "in order that, if I should appoint any other person, I may show his friends how powerful an influence, and what strong recommendations, I was obliged to disregard in appointing him." The committee departed as wise as they came.

A GOOD RUSE. — While the rebels were near Georgetown, Kentucky, in 1862, a resident of Lexington put on secesh clothes and rode to the house of Mrs. Johnston, widow of the late "Provisional Governor," and when at the gate met a little son of John C. Breckinridge, who said:

"Yes, I am Champ Ferguson."

"You are one of Morgan's men."

"Well, let me call aunt (Mrs. Johnston); she will do anything she can for you."

In a moment Mrs. Johnston appeared.

"You are the celebrated Mr. Ferguson; welcome here."

A dinner was prepared, of which the individual partook with great relish. When he was about to remount, Mrs. Johnston said:

"Your horse is jaded; I'll give you a better one to drive the Yankee's from the State."

A contraband was called, and one of the finest horses brought out, on which the pretended secesh returned to Lexington rejoicing.

THE DOG OF THE REGIMENT.

"IF I were a poet, like you, my friend,"
　Said a bronzed old Sergeant, speaking to me,
"I would make a rhyme on this mastiff here;
　For a right good Union dog is he,
Although he was born on 'secesh' soil,
　And his master fought in the rebel ranks.
If you'll do it, I'll tell you his history,
　And give you in pay, why — a soldier's thanks.

"Well, the way we came across him was this:
　We were on the march, and 'twas getting late
When we reached a farm-house, deserted by all
　Save this mastiff here, who stood at the gate.
Thin and gaunt as a wolf was he,
　And a piteous whine he gave 'twixt the bars;
But, bless you! if he didn't jump for joy
　When he saw our flag with the Stripes and Stars.

"Next day, when we started again on the march,
　With us went Jack, without word or call,
Stopping for rest at the order to 'halt,'
　And taking his rations along with us all,
Never straggling, but keeping his place in line,
　Far to the right, and close beside me;
And I don't care where the other is found,
　There never was better drilled dog than he.

"He always went with us into the fight,
　And the thicker the bullets fell around,
And the louder the rattling musketry rolled,
　Louder and fiercer his bark would sound;
And once, when wounded, and left for dead,
　After a bloody and desperate fight,
Poor Jack, as faithful as friend can be,
　Lay by my side on the field all night.

"And so, when our regiment home returned,
　We brought him along with us, as you see;
And Jack and I being much attached,
　The boys seemed to think he belonged to me.
And here he has lived with me ever since;
　Right pleased with his quarters, too, he seems.
There are no more battles for brave old Jack,
　And no more marches except in dreams.

"But the best of all times for the old dog is
　When the thunder mutters along the sky,
Then he wakes the echoes around with his bark,
　Thinking the enemy surely is nigh.
Now I've told you his history, write him a rhyme,
　Some day poor Jack in his grave must rest, —
And of all the rhymes of this cruel war
　Which your brain has made, let his be the best."

A PROVIDENTIAL DELIVERANCE. — It is well known that Major Anderson was an earnest suppliant for divine guidance in all the perplexities of his position in Charleston harbor. He recognizes many instances of direct answers to his prayers during the long and anxious weeks in which he upheld the honor of his country's flag. The following incident is narrated by a contributor to the Christian Intelligencer:

"Permit me to give an unpublished fact in respect to the hero of Fort Sumter. It was narrated by the General himself, in the following words. Said he: 'A remarkable circumstance occurred at the surrender of Fort Sumter, which I can only attribute to a kind Providence. On abandoning Fort Moultrie, we, of course, took what ammunition we could with us. Sumter was a new and unfinished fort. It had two magazines, but neither was completed. A Lieutenant came to me for orders as to which he should put the ammunition into. Thinking there was no choice, or, perhaps, not having any special reason, I assigned the one to be occupied. I afterwards discovered that the one so taken was the most exposed. In a word, it was a moral certainty, that if I had first examined the two, I should not have ordered the occupancy of the one I did. In the bombardment, hot shot was freely used. Judge of our feelings at the surrender, when it was found that a red-hot cannon ball was lying at the bottom of the unused magazine. So that, had I selected that one, the entire garrison must have been blown into eternity!' It would be well if our public men generally observed the precept: 'In all thy ways acknowledge Him.'"

THE STAR BRIGADE AT CHICKAMAUGA. — The Southern war-writers have said much of the courage and prowess displayed by their arms in the last great battle won by the Confederates, and, no doubt, the praises bestowed upon McNair's brigade, of Hood's division, were won by the most gallant and soldierly qualities on that hard-fought field.

The war correspondent of one of the Montgomery papers has given a vivid description of the part they bore in the two days' battles.

"The band of heroes," he writes, "composing this brigade, consists of the First, Second, and Fourth Arkansas dismounted cavalry, the Twenty-first and Thirty-first Arkansas infantry, the Fourth Arkansas battalion, and the Thirty-ninth North Carolina, under Colonel Coleman. In the command the North Carolinians were better known as the 'Tar heels,' perhaps from their tenacity of purpose as well as their having been enlisted in the piny woods of the old North State.

"On Saturday, the first day of the battle of Chickamauga, at noon, this brigade was ordered to support General Gregg's command, then sorely pressed, on the left of Hood's division. Gregg was holding his position with great difficulty against tremendous odds. When ordered to advance, McNair's brigade rushed over Gregg's column, the Thirty-ninth North Carolina and the Twenty-fifth Arkansas being led by Colonel Coleman. The Yankees gave way, but in good order, and were driven not less than three fourths of a mile. General Gregg pronounced this charge one of the most brilliant achievements of the day. A Yankee regiment, which encountered the Thirty-ninth North Carolina and Twenty-fifth Arkansas, was almost annihilated. These two skeleton regiments halted once to await support; but not receiving it, they advanced through the woods into the open country, where their own weakness and the strength of the Federal lines became apparent. Coleman's command, having exhausted their ammunition, withdrew to Gregg's line of battle, and encamped for the night.

"In the great battle of Sunday, McNair's brigade were on the left, next to Hood's division. At half past nine they were lying behind an imperfect breastwork of fallen trees. A strong column of the enemy advanced upon them. They were received with a destructive fire, and falling back, were charged by McNair's brigade, and driven in confusion over two lines of breastworks into the open fields. On an eminence, two lines of Yankee batteries commanded the open space. Just before his men entered this broad field, General McNair was wounded. The gallant Colonel Harper, of the First Arkansas, was killed, and the command of the brigade devolved upon Colonel Coleman. The brigade now diverged to the right, and, under the leadership of the gallant North Carolinian, captured both the batteries. Eight of the pieces were at once taken to the rear, and two others were afterwards removed. General Bragg gave Colonel Coleman an order for three of these guns to attach to his command.

"These batteries were supported by a very strong Federal force; — but McNair's brigade charged so rapidly, loading and firing as they went, that the Yankees were surprised and routed. The assault was ferocious, and the victory complete.

"The Federal artillerists fought infinitely better than their infantry supports, actually throwing shell and shot with their hands into the faces of our men when they could no longer load their pieces. The two batteries captured were about one hundred yards apart, and when the guns were captured, our men were compelled to move off with the utmost rapidity.

"Colonel Coleman was the first to place his hand upon a Federal field piece, and the banner of the Thirty-ninth North Carolina was the first unfurled above them, cheer after cheer announcing the triumph of our gallant men; and then came the hurried withdrawal of the guns from their place in the Federal lines.

"Lieutenant-Colonel Reynolds and Adjutant J. D. Hardin were just behind Colonel Coleman when he reached the Federal guns. Hardin was shot through the neck in the afternoon. When the brigade again fell back to our lines, and had obtained supplies and ammunition, it was again ordered forward to a height on the left, to support Robinson's battery on the Lookout Valley road.

With Johnson's brigade and Hindman's division on the right, and Manigault's on the left, Colonel Coleman advanced to the closing fight of the day.

"By successive charges the enemy were driven slowly, but steadily, from the chain of hills which formed his position, and the battle closed. Two hours more of daylight, and this portion of Rosecrans' army would have been annihilated.

"Captain Culpepper, belonging to this brigade, displayed great skill and heroism. The loss of the brigade in killed and wounded was about forty per cent. The Thirty-ninth North Carolina entered the fight with two hundred and thirty-eight men, and lost over one hundred. Of the whole brigade there are left about eight hundred men. Colonel Coleman's coat was pierced by a ball, but he is unharmed.

"The gallant Captain Moore was killed, and Colonel Huffshedler, of the Twenty-fifth Arkansas, was pierced by five balls, yet not killed."

ORDERS HIS OWN EXECUTION.—During the siege at Yorktown, a correspondent, who was watching its progress, related the following incident: "Last night an officer was shot by one of his own men. The officer, Captain A. R. Wood, had posted his last picket and left him with this order: 'Shoot the first man who approaches from the direction of the rebels, without waiting to ask for the countersign.' It was quite dark, and the officer left the picket and lost his way, wandering from our 'lines' instead of to them. He soon discovered his mistake, and turned back. He approached the soldier to whom he had given the decisive order. In the shadow the faithful and quick-sighted private saw the dark figure stealing towards him: in an instant he raised his piece, and shot his own Captain through the side. The wound was mortal; and thus it turned out that the officer had given the orders for his own execution. Such are the chances of war. Picket service here is most perilous; and, considering that the safety of the whole army depends on the faithfulness with which this duty is performed, one cannot wonder that those detailed for it are so ready to execute the commands of their superiors."

LET US LOVE OUR FLAG.—"As I sat by the bed of a sick soldier, I saw on his arm what appeared to me to be our national flag.

"'You have the American flag on your arm?' I said to him, inquiringly.

"'Yes, ma'am,' he replied, and began to pull up his shirt sleeve that I might see it more distinctly. 'That was put in when I was nine years old; I fainted several times while it was being done, but I would have it there.'

"I looked at his arm. There was the Goddess of Liberty, bearing in her hand our Star-spangled Banner. The red stripes had been put on in vermilion.

"'That is a mark the rebels would not like,' I remarked to him.

"I always supposed if I should be taken prisoner I should be murdered, because of this mark; but I was determined to fight for the flag that protected me. It protected me when I came to this country, seven years old, and under it I have had my living ever since. I want to die under its folds.'

"'You die for your country just as truly as if you died on the battle-field, and I thank you for what you have done for us,' I said to the poor fellow, who was suffering from heart disease and dropsy, and who is liable every moment to be taken from this fighting world.

"'Do you ever regret that you volunteered?'

"'Never. I have done what I could, and am willing to die in this way.'

"The young Irishman seemed to have a true attachment to the flag of his adopted country. He has given his life for it. How is it with ourselves? Do we really love it, and prize it as we should? Is it the symbol of progress, of political and religious freedom? We should cherish it as we cherish God's best gifts to us, and we should be willing, if need be, to die for it. We must teach our children to love it, to consider its safety superior to their own, and to be willing to make any sacrifice which it requires. We must pray for it, and teach our children to pray for it. Let us not be too much tried by the self-denials and privations that war is bringing upon us. Let us bear it nobly and uncomplainingly, with hearts full of steadfast faith and trust in God, and let us grow strong in patriotism, as were our grandmothers before us. They left us a precious legacy. Shall we leave one of less value to our children?"

THE CHARGE AT SPRINGFIELD, MO.—This brilliant exploit of Fremont's Body Guard, under the leadership of Major Zagonyi, and the "Prairie Scouts" of Major Frank Ward, forms one of the most interesting chapters in the history of the war.

"The foe were advised of the intended attack. When Major Wright was brought into their camp, they were preparing to defend their position. As appears from the confession of prisoners, they had twenty-two hundred men, of whom four hundred were cavalry, the rest being infantry, armed with shot guns, American rifles, and revolvers. Twelve hundred of their foot were posted along the edge of the wood upon the crest of the hill. The cavalry was stationed upon the extreme left, on top of a spur of the hill, and in front of a patch of timber. Sharpshooters were concealed behind the trees close to the fence alongside the lane, and a small number in some underbrush near the foot of the hill. Another detachment guarded their train, holding possession of the county fair ground, which was surrounded by a high board fence.

"This position was unassailable by cavalry from the road, the only point of attack being down the lane on the right; and the enemy were so disposed as to command this approach perfectly. The lane was a blind one, being closed, after passing the brook, by fences and ploughed land;

it was in fact a *cul-de-sac*. If the infantry should stand, nothing could save the rash assailants. There are horsemen sufficient to sweep the little band before them, as helplessly as the withered forest-leaves in the grasp of the autumn winds; there are deadly marksmen lying behind the trees upon the heights, and lurking in the long grass upon the lowlands; while a long line of foot stand upon the summit of the slope, who, only stepping a few paces back into the forest, may defy the boldest riders. Yet down this narrow lane, leading into the very jaws of death, came the three hundred.

"On the prairie, at the edge of the woodland, in which he knew his wily foe lay hidden, Zagonyi halted his command. He spurred along the line. With eager glance he scanned each horse and rider. To his officers he gave the simple order, 'Follow me! do as I do!' and then, drawing up in front of his men, with a voice tremulous and shrill with emotion, he spoke:

"'Fellow-soldiers, comrades, brothers! This is your first battle. For our three hundred, the enemy are two thousand. If any of you are sick, or tired by the long march, or if any think the number is too great, now is the time to turn back.' He paused — no one was sick or tired. 'We must not retreat. Our honor, the honor of our General and our country, tell us to go on. I will lead you. We have been called holiday soldiers for the pavements of St. Louis; to-day we will show that we are soldiers for the battle. Your watchword shall be — "*The Union and Fremont!*" Draw sabre! By the right flank — quick trot — march!'

"Bright swords flashed in the sunshine, a passionate shout burst from every lip, and with one accord, the trot passing into a gallop, the compact column swept on in its deadly purpose. Most of them were boys. A few weeks before, they had left their homes. Those who were cool enough to note it say that ruddy cheeks grew pale, and fiery eyes were dimmed with tears. Who shall tell what thoughts, what visions of peaceful cottages nestling among the groves of Kentucky, or shining upon the banks of the Ohio and the Illinois — what sad recollections of tearful farewells, of tender, loving faces, filled their minds during those fearful moments of suspense? No word was spoken. With lips compressed, firmly clinching their sword-hilts, with quick tramp of hoofs and clang of steel, honor leading and glory awaiting them, the young soldiers flew forward, each brave rider and each straining steed members of one huge creature, enormous, terrible, irresistible.

> 'Twere worth ten years of peaceful life,
> One glance at their array.'

"They pass the fair ground. They are at the corner of the lane where the wood begins. It runs close to the fence on their left for a hundred yards, and beyond it they see white tents gleaming. They are half way past the forest, when, sharp and loud, a volley of musketry bursts upon the head of the column; horses stagger, riders reel and fall, but the troop presses forward undismayed. The farther corner of the wood is reached, and Zagonyi beholds the terrible array. Amazed, he involuntarily checks his horse. The rebels are not surprised. There to his left they stand crowning the height, foot and horse ready to ingulf him, if he shall be rash enough to go on. The road he is following declines rapidly. There is but one thing to do — run the gantlet, gain the cover of the hill, and charge up the steep. These thoughts pass quicker than they can be told. He waves his sabre over his head, and shouting, 'Forward! follow me! quick trot! gallop!' he dashes headlong down the stony road. The first company, and most of the second, follow. From the left a thousand muzzles belch forth a hissing flood of bullets; the poor fellows clutch wildly at the air and fall from their saddles, and maddened horses throw themselves against the fences. Their speed is not for an instant checked; farther down the hill they fly, like wasps driven by the leaden storm. Sharp volleys pour out of the underbrush at the left, clearing wide gaps through their ranks. They leap the brook, take down the fence, and draw up under shelter of the hill. Zagonyi looks around him, and to his horror sees that only a fourth of his men are with him. He cries, 'They do not come — we are lost!' and frantically waves his sabre.

"He has not long to wait. The delay of the rest of the Guard was not from hesitation. When Captain Foley reached the lower corner of the wood, and saw the enemy's line, he thought a flank attack might be advantageously made. He ordered some men to dismount, and take down the fence. This was done under a severe fire. Several men fell, and he found the wood so dense that it could not be penetrated. Looking down the hill, he saw the flash of Zagonyi's sabre, and at once gave the order, 'Forward!' At the same time, Lieutenant Kennedy, a stalwart Kentuckian, shouted, 'Come on, boys! remember Old Kentucky!' and the third company of the Guard, fire on every side of them — from behind trees, from under the fences — with thundering strides and loud cheers, poured down the slope, and rushed to the side of Zagonyi. They have lost seventy dead and wounded men, and the carcasses of horses are strewn along the lane. Kennedy is wounded in the arm, and lies upon the stones, his faithful charger standing motionless beside him. Lieutenant Goff received a wound in the thigh; he kept his seat, and cried out, 'The devils have hit me, but I will give it to them yet!'

"The remnant of the Guard are now in the field under the hill, and from the shape of the ground the rebel fire sweeps with the roar of a whirlwind over their heads. Here we will leave them for a moment, and trace the fortunes of the Prairie Scouts.

"When Foley brought his troop to a halt, Captain Fairbanks, at the head of the first company of Scouts, was at the point where the first volley of musketry had been received. The narrow lane was crowded by a dense mass of struggling horses, and filled with the tumult of battle. Captain Fairbanks says, — and he is corroborated by several of his men who were near, — that at this moment an officer of the Guard rode up to him, and said, 'They are flying; take your men down that lane, and cut off their retreat' — pointing to the lane at the left. Captain Fairbanks was not able to identify the person who gave this order. It certainly did not come from Zagonyi, who was several hundred yards farther on. Captain Fairbanks executed the order, followed by the second company of Prairie Scouts, under Captain Kehoe. When this movement was made, Captain Naughton, with the Third Irish dragoons, had not reached the corner of the lane. He came up at a gallop, and was about to follow Fairbanks, when he saw a Guardsman who pointed in the direction in which Zagonyi had gone. He took this for an order, and obeyed it. When he reached the gap in the fence, made by Foley, not seeing anything of the Guard, he supposed they had passed through at that place, and gallantly attempted to follow. Thirteen men fell in a few minutes. He was shot in the arm, and dismounted. Lieutenant Connolly spurred into the underbrush, and received two balls through the lungs, and one in the left shoulder. The dragoons, at the outset not more than fifty strong, were broken, and, dispirited by the loss of their officers, retired. A Sergeant rallied a few, and brought them up to the gap again, and they were again driven back. Five of the boldest passed down the hill, joined Zagonyi, and were conspicuous for their valor during the rest of the day. Fairbanks and Kehoe, having gained the rear and left of the enemy's position, made two or three assaults upon detached parties of the foe, but did not join in the main attack.

"I now return to the Guard. It is forming under the shelter of the hill. In front, with a gentle inclination, rises a grassy slope, broken by occasional tree-stumps. A line of fire upon the summit marks the position of the rebel infantry, and nearer, and on the top of a lower eminence to the right, stand their horse. Up to this time no Guardsman has struck a blow; but blue-coats and bay horses lie thick along the bloody lane. Their time has come. Lieutenant Maythenyi, with thirty men, is ordered to attack the cavalry. With sabres flashing over their heads, the little band of heroes spring towards their tremendous foe. Right upon the centre they charge. The dense mass opens, the blue-coats force their way in, and the whole rebel squadron scatter in disgraceful flight through the cornfields in the rear. The bays follow them, sabring the fugitives. Days after, the enemy's horses lay thick among the uncut corn.

"Zagonyi holds his main body until Maythenyi disappears in the cloud of rebel cavalry; then his voice rises through the air: 'In open order — charge!' The line opens out to give play to their sword-arm. Steeds respond to the ardor of their riders, and quick as thought, with thrilling cheers, the noble hearts rush into the leaden torrent which pours down the incline.

With unabated fire the gallant fellows press through. Their fierce onset is not even checked. The foe do not wait for them — they waver, break, and fly. The Guardsmen spur into the midst of the rout, and their fast-falling swords work a terrible revenge. Some of the boldest of the Southrons retreat into the woods, and continue a murderous fire from behind trees and thickets. Seven Guard horses fall upon a space not more than twenty feet square. As his steed sinks under him, one of the officers is caught around the shoulders by a grape-vine, and hangs dangling in the air until he is cut down by his friends.

"The rebel foot are flying in furious haste from the field. Some take refuge in the fair ground, some hurry into the cornfields, but the greater part run along the edge of the wood, swarm over the fence into the road, and hasten to the village. The Guardsmen follow. Zagonyi leads them. Over the loudest roar of battle rings his clarion voice — 'Come on, Old Kentuck! I'm with you!' And the flash of his sword-blade tells his men where to go. As he approaches a barn, a man steps from behind the door and lowers his rifle; but before it has reached a level, Zagonyi's sabre point descends upon his head, and his life-blood leaps to the very top of the huge barn-door.

"The conflict now raged through the village — in the public square, and along the streets. Up and down the Guards ride in squads of three or four, and wherever they see a group of the enemy, charge upon and scatter them. It is hand-to-hand. No one but has a share in the fray.

"There was at least one soldier in the Southern ranks. A young officer, superbly mounted, charges alone upon a large body of the Guard. He passes through the line unscathed, killing one man. He wheels, charges back, and again breaks through, killing another man. A third time he rushes upon the Federal line; a score of sabre-points confronts him; clouds of bullets fly around him; but he pushes on until he reaches Zagonyi: he presses his pistol so close to the Major's side, that he feels it, and draws convulsively back; the bullet passes through the front of Zagonyi's coat, who, at the instant, runs the daring rebel through the body; he falls, and the men, thinking their commander hurt, kill him with a dozen wounds.

"'He was a brave man,' said Zagonyi afterwards, 'and I did wish to make him prisoner.'

"Meanwhile it has grown dark. The foe have left the village, and the battle has ceased. The assembly is sounded, and the Guard gathers in the *Plaza.* Not more than eighty mounted men appear; the rest are killed, wounded, or unhorsed. At this time one of the most characteristic incidents of the affair took place.

"Just before the charge, Zagonyi directed one of his buglers, a Frenchman, to sound a signal. The bugler did not seem to pay any attention to the order, but darted off with Lieutenant Maythenyi. A few moments afterwards he was observed in another part of the field vigorously pursuing the flying infantry. His active form was always seen in the thickest of the fight. When the line was formed in the *Plaza*, Zagonyi noticed the bugler, and approaching him, said: ' In the midst of battle you disobeyed my order. You are unworthy to be a member of the Guard. I dismiss you.' The bugler showed his bugle to his indignant commander — the mouth-piece of the instrument was shot away. He said : ' The mouth was shoot off. I could not bugle viz mon bugle, and so I bugle viz mon pistol and sabre.' It is unnecessary to add, the brave Frenchman was not dismissed.

"I must not forget to mention Sergeant Hunter, of the Kentucky company. His soldierly figure never failed to attract the eye in the ranks of the Guard. He had served in the regular cavalry, and the Body Guard had profited greatly from his skill as a drill-master. He lost three horses in the fight. As soon as one was killed, he caught another from the rebels ; the third horse taken by him in this way he rode into St. Louis.

"The Sergeant slew five men. 'I won't speak of those I shot,' said he ; 'another may have hit them ; but those I touched with my sabre I am sure of, because I felt them.'

"At the beginning of the charge, he came to the extreme right, and took position next to Zagonyi, whom he followed closely through the battle. The Major, seeing him, said :

"'Why are you here, Sergeant Hunter? Your place is with your company on the left.' 'I kind o' wanted to be in the front,' was the answer.

"'What could I say to such a man?' exclaimed Zagonyi, speaking of the matter afterwards.

"There was hardly a horse or rider among the survivors that did not bring away some mark of the fray. I saw one animal with no less than seven wounds, none of them serious. Scabbards were bent, clothes and caps pierced, pistols injured. I saw one pistol from which the sight had been cut as neatly as it could have been done by machinery. A piece of board a few inches long was cut from a fence on the field, in which there were thirty-one shot-holes.

"It was now nine o'clock. The wounded had been carried to the hospital. The dismounted troopers were placed in charge of them — in the double capacity of nurses and guards. Zagonyi expected the foe to return every minute. It seemed like madness to try and hold the town with his small force, exhausted by the long march and desperate fight. He therefore left Springfield, and retired before morning twenty-five miles on the Bolivar road.

"Captain Fairbanks did not see his commander after leaving the column in the lane, at the commencement of the engagement. About dusk he repaired to the prairie, and remained there within a mile of the village until midnight, when he followed Zagonyi, rejoining him in the morning.

"I will now return to Major White. During the conflict upon the hill, he was in the forest, near the front of the rebel line. Here his horse was shot under him. Captain Wroton kept careful watch over him. When the flight began he hurried White away, and, accompanied by a squad of eleven men, took him ten miles into the country. They stopped at a farm-house for the night. White discovered that their host was a Union man. His parole having expired, he took advantage of the momentary absence of his captor to speak to the farmer, telling him who he was, and asking him to send for assistance.

"The countryman mounted his son upon his swiftest horse, and sent him for succor. The party lay down by the fire, White being placed in the midst. The rebels were soon asleep, but there was no sleep for the Major. He listened anxiously for the footsteps of his rescuers. After long, weary hours, he heard the tramp of horses. He arose, and walking on tiptoe, cautiously stepping over his sleeping guard, he reached the door, and silently unfastened it. The Union men rushed into the room, and took the astonished Wroton and his followers prisoners. At daybreak White rode into Springfield, at the head of his captives and a motley band of Home Guard. He found the Federals still in possession of the place. As the officer of highest rank, he took command. His garrison consisted of twenty-four men. He stationed twenty-two of them as pickets in the outskirts of the village, and held the other two as a *reserve*. At noon the enemy sent a flag of truce, and asked permission to bury their dead. Major White received the flag with proper ceremony, but said that General Siegel was in command, and the request would have to be referred to him. Siegel was then forty miles away. In a short time, a written communication, purporting to come from General Siegel, saying that the rebels might send a party, under certain restrictions, to bury their dead. White drew in some of his pickets, stationed them about the field, and under their surveillance, the Southern dead were buried.

"The loss of the enemy, as reported by some of their working party, was one hundred and sixteen killed. The number of wounded could not be ascertained. After the conflict had drifted away from the hill-side, some of the foe had returned to the field, taken away their wounded, and robbed our dead. The loss of the Guard was fifty-three, out of one hundred and forty-eight actually engaged, twelve men having been left by Zagonyi in charge of his train. The Prairie Scouts reported a loss of thirty-one out of one hundred and thirty : half of these belonged to the Irish Dragoons. In a neighboring field an Irishman was found stark and stiff, still clinging to the hilt of his sword, which was thrust through the body of a rebel who lay beside him. Within a few feet a second rebel lay, shot through the head. — *Major Dorsheimer*.

LETTERS FROM SOLDIERS. — One of the agents of the Sanitary Commission in Washington said : "As an evidence of the literary capacity of our soldiers, I may mention that our boys are to-day stamping over ten thousand letters I brought up from the front, from soldiers wounded but slightly, or not at all, telling their friends of their condition after the fights."

THE DEAD CAVALIER — GENERAL J. E. B. STUART.

BY J. MARSHALL HANNA.

THE drums came back muffled, that, beating aloud,
  Went out in the morning all thrill to the fight,
For the hero lies dead in his battle-flag shroud,
  And his steed is led groomed without rider to-
    night.
Then beat the drums muffled, and play the fife low,
  And march on the *cortége* to cadences slow.

Who saw him that morning as gayly he rode
  At the front of his troopers, who filed proudly af-
    ter him,
Thought to look on to-night the visage that showed
  The pale death relapse, and the eye sunk and
    dim?
Then toll the bell sadly, solemnly toll;
  A hero is passing to glory's last goal.

Come, stand by the corpse, look down on that face,
  Mark where the bullet burst its way through,
See where the death-pang left its last trace
  As the lead messenger struck, unerring and true.
Then, hushed, gather round; let our tears be like
    rain;
  A truer cavalier we shall ne'er see again.

Ah! the story he wrote with the point of his sword,
  How it thrilled through the cities, how it stirred
    up the land!
Who can forget how the hireling horde
  Ran blating for mercy when he did command?
At the North though they mock, and rejoice at his
    fall,
  With grief-laden flowers will we cover his pall.

O, how like the besom of fate in their rear
  Came the wave of his plume and the flash of his
    blade,
When, bursting from covert, to his troopers' wild
    cheer,
  The bugle it sounded the charge in the raid.
Now his plume is at rest, his sword in its sheath,
  And the hand that should grasp it is nerveless
    in death.

Make his grave where he fought, nigh the field
    where he fell,
  In blossoming Hollywood, under the hill,
In sight of the hearth-stones he defended so well,
  That his spirit may be guardian sentinel still,
And there let a finger of marble disclose
  The spot where he lies — point the skies where
    he rose.

EXPERIENCE ON A GUNBOAT. — A pilot on the gunboat Louisiana, the most formidable and effective of any which Farragut encountered in his battle at the forts below New Orleans, came stealthily creeping into the city two or three days after its occupation by Butler.

He was covered with mud from head to foot. His clothes were hanging in tatters; his face and hands swollen by the poison of mosquitoes and blistered by the fierce rays of an almost tropical sun, and he had eaten nothing for three days and nights but a few green berries, which he found in the swamps.

Only a week before he had left New Orleans on that gunboat in perfect health, and hoping for a speedy and easy victory over the Federal fleet.

He described his three days' experience on the vessel before she was blown up as the nearest approach to a sojourn in the infernal regions of anything he had ever experienced or thought possible in this world.

Shut up in a stifling atmosphere of hot gunpowder smoke, with the incessant clatter and thunder and hiss of shells and round shot just over his head, pounding against the plating of railroad iron, with the tide of battle turning against them, and the chances for success, and finally for escape with life, growing less and less every hour, it is not strange that in referring to it he exclaimed, "I thought I was in hell."

When all hope of victory was gone, and the Admiral had passed the forts, the commanding officer of the Louisiana determined to blow her up rather than to allow her to fall into the hands of the Federals. She was run ashore on the right bank, about fifty miles below the city. The officers and crew, escaping to the shore, betook themselves to the swamp for concealment.

Here they waded, sometimes up to their necks in water, sometimes coming in where the land was higher, and then striking out into deep swamp again. At Chalmette, Jackson's old battle-ground, they went far into the swamp in order to flank the fortifications there erected; and finally most of them reached the city in the miserable plight above described.

The pilot was among the earliest of those who professed themselves ready to take the oath.

A LITERAL TRANSLATION. — As the Twenty-fourth Massachusetts regiment was about leaving Washington, N. C., in 1862, an incident occurred which reflected credit upon the acumen of one of its officers. A pretty mulatto slave girl, belonging to a citizen of the town, had been acting as house servant to Lieutenant Turner, and when marching orders were received, expressed great anxiety to go with the regiment to Newbern, and escape bondage. She took refuge on board one of the steamers on which the Twenty-fourth had embarked; but just before the time for starting, her owner appeared with an order, which read as follows:

"John Doe has permission to search for his slave girl Henrietta, and will be protected in so doing."

This he presented to Quartermaster William V. Hutchings, and demanded the girl. Mr. Hutchings, seeing the trepidation and anxiety manifested in the countenance of Henrietta, asked her, "Are you willing to return to your master?" "O, no, sir!" she said; please don't give me up to him!" "Let me see that order, sir," said he to the owner; and reading it aloud, he remarked, "This gives you authority to *search* for your girl; you have searched for her, and there she is. You are to be protected in making your search; you have been protected. This gives you no authority to take her against her will. She does not wish to return to you, and you can't take her. And now, the sooner you get off this boat, the better it will be for your skin." As he said this with the determination of a man who was not to be trifled with, the discomfited owner beat a precipitate retreat, amid the jeers and shouts of the bystanders.

THE PRESIDENT'S CHOICE. — During a conversation on the approaching election, in 1864, a gentleman remarked to President Lincoln that nothing could defeat him but Grant's capture of Richmond, to be followed by his nomination at Chicago and acceptance. "Well," said the President, "I feel very much like the man who said he didn't want to die particularly, but if he had got to die, that was precisely the disease he would like to die of."

THE TRAITOR'S "COAT-OF-ARMS." — Joseph Schofield — an Englishman by birth, but an adopted citizen of the United States, residing in Iowa, who justly boasted of having two sons in the army, one of whom had reënlisted to fight for the flag of his country — sent his annual subscription to the Scientific American, for another year, and closed his letter with the following pungent remarks:

"The traitor's 'coat-of-arms' consists of a flea, a fly, a magpie, and a side of bacon. Explanation: A flea will bite either the quick or the dead; so will a traitor. A fly 'blows,' corrupts, and contaminates, all it comes in contact with; so will a traitor. A magpie is always chattering, talking, and lying; so is a traitor. A side of bacon is never 'cured' till it is hung; neither is a traitor."

WHISKEY IN CAMP. — When the war first broke out, Bragg was in command of about ten thousand troops, stationed at Pensacola. He remained there for more than a year, until Grant drew all eyes away from the Southern border by his vigorous and successful campaign in the upper Mississippi Valley.

Bragg made the long semicircular shore bristle with sand batteries, that bore upon the defiant and loyal Fort Pickens, but his infantry had nothing to do. Month after month passed, and they neither attacked nor were attacked. The true point of strategy and of interest was elsewhere. Bragg soon found scope for his peculiar genius in keeping up the morals of his army.

The war has not developed a more vigilant police officer than Braxton Bragg: yet his abilities in that line were taxed to their utmost to check the gross drunkenness that prevailed in his camp; for "Satan finds some mischief still for idle hands to do," and the soldiers employed their time and talents in circumventing his strict general order excluding intoxicating drinks from the camp, or any place within the distance of ten miles in every direction.

About a mile back of his main force, in the woods, lay a long, narrow lake. It would take a soldier seven or eight hours to walk around to the other side, but a good swimmer could reach it in twenty minutes' time.

During the hot months of that long, dull summer the men discovered a commendable zeal for personal cleanliness. Every evening the lake was alive with swimmers, for in the South swimming and horsemanship are accomplishments equally necessary and universal. Yet Bragg's inspectors found some mysterious and constant connection between swimming and intoxication. The best swimmers were often quarrelsome and noisy, and found their way into the guard-house for drunkenness. But with all his vigilance, the mystery was no nearer solution than at first — how the men got their whiskey.

There was a puzzle, too, among the butchers. There arose an astonishing demand for bladders among the soldiers. Whenever a beef was killed, half a dozen eager fellows stood by and bid against each other for this part of the animal. Bragg heard of this, but he could see no connection between it and the solution of the whiskey question; and he never learned the secret till the army had left Pensacola, and the disclosure could do no harm.

A poor, inoffensive fisherman lived on the opposite side of the lake. Some of the men swam across, made his acquaintance, and persuaded him to open an account with a liquor dealer in Mobile, saying he would lose nothing by the operation, and might make a great deal. He accordingly kept himself well supplied with the genuine article, and had the satisfaction every evening of seeing platoons of naked customers come swimming across the lake, with bladders around their necks, which they filled from his barrel, and paid for in hard money, which they brought over in their mouths.

Emboldened by their success in smuggling by the bladder full, they managed at length to get a barrel of the coveted liquor across the lake. But they were like the man who bought the elephant. They did not know what to do with it. At length a genius brighter than the rest hit upon a happy expedient. The spring where most of their drinking water was obtained, rose from a sandy soil, in which a pit could be easily excavated. In the darkness of a rainy night this was done, and the barrel buried close to the spring. Of course, nothing could be more natural than that soldiers in the month of August, and in that latitude, should go often to the spring. But the water seemed to have a strange effect upon them. After leaning over to quaff from the cooling fountain, they grew chatty, then boisterous, noisy, and quarrelsome, and ended the day in the guard-house.

There was no solving the mystery, till, at last, just as they all left Pensacola, they told Bragg's orderly how the whiskey barrel was buried close by the spring, and they kept just a straw convenient, so that when they seemed to be drinking from the spring, they were, in fact, sucking from the whiskey barrel.

THE ANCIENT MARINER.

IT was an ancient mariner,
  And thus he spake to me :
"Twice twenty year or more I've sailed
  Upon the salt, salt sea."

More stronger of salt the sea must be
  Than XX all of malt,
When such an ancient sailor-man
  Must call it doubly salt.

"Twice twenty year I've sailed," he said,
  "Upon the salt, salt sea,
And many strange and fearful things
  Have happened unto me."

"Avast, thou ancient mariner !
  Thou smellest much of tar;
Besides, I've got a telegram,
  With good news from the war."

"Twice twenty year I've sailed," he said,
  "Upon the salt, salt sea;
The knowledge I have gained, my boy,
  Were worth a mint to thee."

"Hands off, thou ancient mariner !
  And let my flipper drop ;
We've glorious news from Grant to-day,
  And stocks are rushing up.

"The hour is now, the Board has met,
  And I am 'in the ring;'
Eric is flying like a kite,
  And I may hold the string.

"I must be off, thou ancient man,
  To call on Jones & Tuttle ;"
"I knew Jack Bunsby well," quoth he,
  "And sailed with Cap'n Cuttle."

He placed his chair beside my own,
  That ancient marinere;
And then he called for brandy neat,
  And I for lager beer.

He gave to me for my repast
  Salt-horse and pine-wood cracker ;
And rammed into his starboard cheek
  Some stuff he called terbacker.

Then thrice he winked his larboard eye
  Right solemnly at me,
And thus commenced his wondrous tale :
  "There was a man," quoth he —

"Twice twenty year, or more, I've sailed,
  Upon the salt, salt sea ;
But never have I chanced to meet
  With such a man as he.

"He's older than the hills, they say,
  This old, old marinere ;
Or just about the age of Airth —
  Say seven thousand year.

"He's older than Methusaler,
  Or any man before ;
They say he piloted the craft
  That carried Father Noar.

"Our great Rail-splitter dug him up —
  He split the solid stone,
And there he found this ancient man
  A sittink all alone.

"Our Uncle Abe is fond, you know,
  Of jolly jokes and sells,
But never cracked a harder joke,
  Than this same Gidyun Welles.

"Quoth Abraham, 'From rebel ram
  Here's just the man to save ye.'
And so he made old Daddy Welles
  The ruler of our navy.

"From Richmond town the ram came down,
  To Hampton Roads it crept,
And still old Daddy Gidyun
  He slept, and slept, and slept.

"It stove our splendid frigates' sides,
  And slew our gallant tars,
While Welles was dreamink ancient dreams
  Of masts, and ropes, and spars.

"Old England sent a steamer out —
  A clipper-ship, and new, sir ;
A pirate ship some called the craft,
  And some a rebel cruiser.

"She burned and sank our merchant-ships
  All o'er the ocean wide,
And Daddy Welles's 'creeping things'
  Owdaciously defied.

"That boat had such a jolly time,
  That England scoffed and laughed,
And sent upon the briny deep
  Some more swift-sailing craft.

"Our flag was driven from the sea,
  Our commerce, sir, was floored,
And still old Daddy Welles he slept,
  And snored, and snored, and snored."

"Avast, thou sailor-man !" I said,
  "For all athirst am I ;
So salty is this throat of mine,
  That I shall surely die."

"Come hither, then, thou waiter-boy,"
  The mariner he said.
"Bring us some beer and brandy neat,
  Before I punch thy head."

The cups were set, our lips were wet,
  And then again began
To tell his mournful, bitter tale,
  That ancient sailor-man.

"In vain the people raved and swore,
  In vain the merchants wailed :
Old Welles sent out his 'creeping things,'
  But still the pirates sailed.

"The 'creeping things' beset the coast
  Of all the rebel land ;
But nightly still the boats slipped in,
  With goods called contraband.

"Another man this ancient man
  Employed to do his talks ;
A sly, and slippery, cunning chap —
  I think they called him Fox.

"So, while this ancient man slept well,
  His head upon a hawser;
This sly and slippery cunning chap
  Was mate, all hands, and boss, sir.

"And while our ships were burned and sunk,
  And commerce went to pot,
He squandered millions of our cash —
  I want to know for what.

"Thou knowest, broker of the stocks,
  How great has been the cost;
Thou knowest well what wondrous wealth
  Beneath the sea is lost.

"At times the thunder of our guns
  Awakes this ancient bore;
He claims the credit of the work,
  And falls asleep once more."

"I know, thou antique sailor-man,"
  I said, "of Welles and Fox;
But what has that to do with me,
  Or with the price of stocks?"

"That Old Man of the Sea," he said,
  "About our necks has hung,
And though we sought to shake him off,
  Has clung, and clung, and clung.

"Must we be bothered four more years
  By dozes and by dreams?
And can't we swop such horses off,
  Even in crossing streams?"

"O, think, thou broker of the stocks,
  What fate must yet be ours,
If we must still be swayed and spoiled
  By dull and drowsy powers!"

I left that ancient mariner,
  Swift to the Board I ran;
But stocks were down, and I was then
  A wiser, poorer man.
     Anthracite Hill (of the Board of Brokers).

INCIDENT OF CORINTH. — A correspondent who visited Corinth after the evacuation in 1862 writes as follows:

"Among the few inhabitants found in Corinth was an elderly female, decidedly rebellious in her disposition, having all the prominent facial symptoms of the most abhorrent freak of nature — an ill-tempered woman. An Illinois soldier advanced towards her as she stood on the doorstep of her residence, and addressed her thus:

"'Well, misses, them ere fellers got away, eh? Wish we'd caught 'em. We'd gin 'em the wust whippin' they ever got. Which way did the d—d hounds go, anyhow?'

"Lady (indignant) — 'I reckon you don't know who you're talking to. I've got a son in the Southern army, and he ain't no d—d hound. He's a gentleman, sir.'

"Soldier — 'Well, I've heard a good deal about secesh gentlemen, but I never saw one. Gen-tlemen don't steal, as a general thing; but these fellers live by stealin'.'

"Lady (whose nose takes an upward tendency) — 'They never stole nothin' from you, I guess. What did you ever lose by them, I'd like to know?'

"Soldier — 'Lose! why the cussed thieves stole three undershirts and two pair of drawers from me at Pittsburg. They stole all our sutler's goods, and all the officers' clothes in our regiment. I'll know my shirts, and if I catch 'em on any butternut, I'll finish him, sure. But you see, misses, I don't want to talk saucy to a woman. I just called to ask you if you had any fresh bread to sell.'

"Lady — 'No, hain't. I ain't no baker, and don't keep no bake shop, neither. I guess you'll have to go North for fresh bread.'

"Soldier — 'Well, it's no use gittin' mad about it. I've got money to pay for what I buy. I intend to go North, after a while, when we whip these run-away fellers, but not before. If they hadn't run off, secesh would have been played out in a week. I guess it's played out anyhow, eh?'

"Exit lady unceremoniously, slamming the door, through which she disappears."

ROUGH SKETCH OF PRESIDENT LINCOLN. — Senator Sherman of Ohio, in a speech at Sandusky in the fall of 1864, drew this rough but accurate outline of the lamented President's character:

"I know Old Abe; and I tell you there is not, at this hour, a more patriotic, or a truer man living than that man, Abraham Lincoln. Some say he is an imbecile; but he not only held his own in his debates with Douglas, whose power is admitted, and whom I considered the ablest intellect in the United States Senate, but got a little the better of him. He has been deliberate and slow, but when he puts his foot down, it is with the determination and certainty with which our generals take their steps; and, like them, when he takes a city he never gives it up. This firm old man is noble and kind-hearted. He is a child of the people. Go to him with a story of woe, and he will weep like a child. This man, so condemned, works more hours than any other President that ever occupied the chair. His solicitude for the public welfare is never-ceasing. I differed from him at first myself, but at last felt and believed that he was right, and shall vote for this brave, true, patriotic, kind-hearted man. All his faults and mistakes you have seen. All his virtues you never can know. His patience in labor is wonderful. He works far harder than any man in Erie County. At the head of this great nation — look at it! He has all the bills to sign passed by Congress. No one can be appointed to any office without his approval. No one can be punished without the judgment receives his signature, and no one pardoned without his hand. This man — always right, always just — we propose to reëlect now to the Presidency."

29

LETTER OF GENERAL SEDGWICK. — The following letter from Major-General John Sedgwick to Adjutant-General E. D. Townsend, is characteristic of the brave and honorable soldier who wrote it. It was written in December, 1863, at the time it was proposed to change and consolidate the army of the Potomac.

"MY DEAR TOWNSEND: There is a change proposed in the organization of this army — reducing the number of corps to three. Whether I am to be retained as one of the commanders, I do not know; but I write this to ask you, when the matter is brought up in Washington, to retain the number of this corps — the Sixth. It is entirely harmonious, and a great deal of *esprit du corps* is in it. I do not believe there is a regiment in it that would leave willingly. Another reason is — since its organization there has never been a regiment added or detached. This is not the case with the other corps. The Third has been made up of the odds and ends from several armies, and this is partly true of the First; and every corps (the Sixth excepted) has had several regiments assigned to it, from time to time.

" I am afraid the First, Second, and Third will be retained, when I should like to see the Second, Third, and Sixth.

" I am sure you will assist me in this matter, if in your power; at all events, I rely upon you in letting me know when the subject comes up."

THE WOOD OF CHANCELLORSVILLE.

BY DELIA R. GERMAN.

THE ripe red berries of the wintergreen
　　Lure me to pause a while
In this deep, tangled wood. I stop and lean
　　Down where these wild flowers smile,
　　And rest me in this shade ; for many a mile,
Through lane and dusty street,
I've walked with weary, weary feet ;
And now I tarry 'mid this woodland scene,
　'Mong ferns and mosses sweet.

Here all around me blows
　　The pale primrose.
I wonder if the gentle blossom knows
The feeling at my heart — the solemn grief
　　So whelming and so deep
That it disdains relief,
　　And will not let me weep.
I wonder that the woodbine thrives and grows,
And is indifferent to the nation's woes.
For while these mornings shine, these blossoms
　　bloom,
Impious rebellion wraps the land in gloom.

Nature, thou art unkind,
Unsympathizing, blind !
Yon lichen, clinging to th' o'erhanging rock,
　　Is happy, and each blade of grass,
　　O'er which unconsciously I pass,
Smiles in my face, and seems to mock
　　Me with its joy. Alas ! I cannot find
　　One charm in bounteous nature, while the wind
That blows upon my cheek bears on each gust
The groans of my poor country, bleeding in the
　　dust.

The air is musical with notes
That gush from winged warblers' throats,
And in the leafy trees
I hear the drowsy hum of bees.
　　Prone from the blinding sky
　　Dance rainbow-tinted sunbeams, thick with
　　　motes,
　　Daisies are shining, and the butterfly
Wavers from flower to flower ; yet in this wood
The ruthless foeman stood,
And every turf is drenched with human blood.

O heartless flowers !
　　O trees, clad in your robes of glistering sheen,
　　Put off this canopy of gorgeous green !
These are the hours
For mourning, not for gladness. While this smart
Of treason dire gashes the Nation's heart,
Let birds refuse to sing,
And flowers to bloom upon the lap of spring.
Let Nature's face itself with tears o'erflow,
In deepest anguish for a people's woe.

While rank rebellion stands
With blood of martyrs on his impious hands ;
While slavery, and chains,
　　And cruelty, and direst hate,
　　Uplift their heads within th' afflicted state,
And freeze the blood in every patriot's veins, —
Let these old woodlands fair
Grow black with gloom, and from its thunder-lair
Let lightning leap, and scorch th' accursed air,
Until the suffering earth,
Of treason sick, shall spew the monster forth,
And each regenerate sod
Be consecrate anew to Freedom and to God !

FORREST ON FORT PILLOW. — A letter written by Bryan McAllister at Meridian, Mississippi, on the 13th of May, 1865, contains the following:

"Before the large chimney-place of a small cabin-room, surrounded by a group of Confederate officers and men, the room dimly lighted by a small tallow candle, I first saw Lieutenant-General N. B. Forrest, commanding a corps of cavalry in the rebel army. Forrest is a man of fine appearance, about six feet in height, having dark, piercing hazel eyes, carefully trimmed mustache, and chin-whiskers dark as night, finely cut-features, and iron-gray hair. His form is lithe, plainly indicating great physical power and activity. He was neatly dressed in citizen's clothes of some gray mixture — the only indication of military service being the usual number of small staff-buttons on his vest. I should have marked him as a prominent man had I seen him on Broadway; and when I was told that he was the 'Forrest of Fort Pillow,' I devoted my whole attention to him, and give you the result of our conversation. My first impression of the man was rather favorable than otherwise. Except a guard of some hundred Federal soldiers, more than half a mile away, I was, with the exception of another person, the only Yankee in the room, and, being dressed in citizen's clothes, was never suspected, except by the landlord.

"'General,' said I, 'I little expected to be seated by this fire with you.'

" ' Why so ? '

" ' Well, because your name has been in the mouth of nearly every person for a long time.'

" ' Yes,' said he, displaying the finest set of teeth that I think I have ever seen ; ' I have waked up the Yankees everywhere, lately.'

" ' Now that you have time, General, do you think you will ever put upon paper the true account of the Fort Pillow affair ? '

" ' Well,' said he, ' the Yankees ought to know. They sent down their best men to investigate the affair.'

" ' But are we to believe their report, General ? '

" ' Yes, if we are to believe anything a nigger says. When I went into the war, I meant to fight. Fighting means killing. I have lost twenty-nine horses in the war, and have killed a man each time. The other day I was a horse ahead ; but at Selma they surrounded me, and I killed two, jumped my horse over a one-horse wagon, and got away.'

" I began to think I had some idea of the man at last. He continued :

" ' My Provost-Marshal's book will show that I have taken thirty-one thousand prisoners during the war. At Fort Pillow I sent in a flag of truce, and demanded an unconditional surrender, or I would not answer for my men. This they refused. I sent them another note, giving them one hour to determine. This they refused. I could see, on the river, boats loaded with troops. They sent back, asking for an hour more. I gave them twenty minutes. I sat on my horse during the whole time.

" ' The fort was filled with niggers and deserters from our army — men who lived side by side with my men. I waited five minutes after the time, and then blew my bugle for the charge. In twenty minutes my men were over the works, and the firing had ceased. The citizens and Yankees had broken in the heads of whiskey and lager-beer barrels, and were all drunk. They kept up firing all the time, as they went down the hill. Hundreds of them rushed to the river, and tried to swim to the gunboats, and my men shot them down. The Mississippi River was red with their blood for three hundred yards. During all this, their flag was still flying, and I rushed over the works and cut the halyards, and let it down, and stopped the fight. Many of the Yankees were in tents in front, and they were in their way, as they concealed my men, and some of them set them on fire. If any were burned to death, it was in those tents.

" ' They have a living witness in Captain Young, their Quartermaster, who is still alive ; and I will leave it to any prisoner I have ever taken if I have not treated them well.' ' You have made some rapid marches, General,' said I. ' Yes,' said he, ' I have five thousand men that can whip any ten thousand in the world. Sturgis came out to whip me once, and was ten thousand strong. I marched off as if I was going to Georgia, and fell upon the head of his column when he least expected me, and, with two thousand three hundred men, killed over three thousand, captured as many more, with all the trains and mules, and drove him back. I meant to kill every man in Federal uniform, unless he gave up.' He spoke of capturing a fort from Colonel Crawford, in Athens, Alabama, garrisoned by one thousand five hundred men. Said he : ' I took him out and showed him my forces, — some brigades two or three times, — and one battery I kept marching around all the time. My men dismounted, leaving every fourth man to hold the horses, and formed the rest in front as infantry ; and the darn fool gave up without firing a shot.'

" Speaking of Streight's capture, he said it was almost a shame. ' My men rode among them and shot them down like cattle. They were mounted on sharp-edged saddles, and were worn out, and I killed several of them myself. Didn't hardly know what to do with them.' But the heart sickens at the infamous conduct of this butcher. He is one of the few men that are general ' blowers,' and yet will fight. Forrest is a thorough bravo — a desperate man in every respect. He was a negro-trader before the war, and in ' personal affairs,' as he calls them, had killed several men.

" He had a body guard of one hundred and fifty picked men. These he placed in the rear, with orders to shoot any one that turned back. I have spoken to numbers of Confederate officers, and they speak of him with disgust, though all admit his bravery and fitness for the cavalry service. He has two brothers living, one of whom is spoken of as being a greater butcher than the Lieutenant-General. He is a man without education or refinement, married, I believe, to a very pretty wife. Any one would call him handsome.

" Any one hearing him talk would call him a braggadocio. As for myself, I would believe one half he said, and only dispute with him with my finger upon the trigger of my pistol. When I told him I was a Yankee, and late upon a prominent General's staff, he looked about him, and among his staff, for corroborative proof. Volleys of this, ready prepared, poured forth upon his order. My not being a short-hand writer necessarily deprived me of the pleasure of a further contribution to this true story.

" Two young Kentuckians were walking along the road, when Forrest came up ; he called them deserters, and deliberately shot them. It appears that these young men were upon legitimate duty, and one of them under military age. The fathers of these youths are upon Forrest's track, sworn to kill him. Poetic justice requires that he should meet with a violent death. Probably one hundred men have fallen by his hand. He says ' the war is played out ; ' that, where he lives, there are plenty of fish ; and that he is going to take a tent along, and don't want to see any one for twelve months."

A ROMANTIC INCIDENT. — Governor Curtin, of Pennsylvania, while sojourning in Philadelphia, was called upon by a young woman, who, when she was introduced, expressed her great joy at seeing the Governor, at the same time imprinting a kiss upon his forehead.

"Madam," said he, "to whom am I indebted for this unexpected salutation?"

"Sir, do you not know me?"

"Take a chair," said the Governor, at the same time extending one of the handsomest in the parlor.

"Shortly after the battle of Antietam, you were upon that bloody field," said she to the Governor.

"I was," replied the Governor.

"You administered to the wants of the wounded and the dying."

"It was my duty as a feeling man."

"You did your duty well. Heaven alone will reward you, sir, for in this life there is no reward adequately expressive of your deserts. You, sir, imparted consolation and revived the hopes of a dying soldier of the Twenty-eighth Ohio. He was badly wounded in the arm; you lifted him into an ambulance, and the blood dripping from him stained your hands and your clothing. That soldier was as dear to me as life itself.

"A husband?" said the Governor. "No, sir."

"A brother perhaps?" "No, sir."

"A father?" "No, sir."

"A son?" "No, sir."

"A lover?" "No, sir."

"If not a husband, father, brother, son, or lover, who, then, could it be?" said the Governor, at length breaking the silence: 'this is an enigma to me. Please explain more about the gallant soldier of Ohio."

"Well, sir, that soldier gave you a ring. C. E. D. were the letters engraved on the interior. That is the ring now upon your little finger. He told you to wear it, and carefully have you done so."

The Governor pulled the ring off, and sure enough the letters were there.

"The finger that used to wear that ring will never wear it any more. The hand is dead, but the soldier still lives."

The Governor was now more interested than ever.

"Well, madam," said he, "tell me all about it. Is this ring yours? Was it given to you by a soldier whom you loved?"

"I loved him as I loved my life; but he never returned that love. He had more love for his country than for me; I honor him for it. That soldier who placed that little ring upon your finger stands before you." So saying the strange lady arose from her chair, and stood before the Governor.

The scene that now ensued we leave to the imagination of the reader. A happy hour passed. The girl who had thus introduced herself was Catharine E. Davidson, of Sheffield, Ohio. She was engaged to be married, but her future husband responded to the call of the President, and she followed him by joining another regiment. He was killed in the same battle where she fell wounded. She is alone in the world, her father and mother having departed this life years ago. She was the soldier of the Twenty-eighth Ohio

who had placed the ring upon the finger of Governor Curtin, for the kind attention given her upon the bloody field of Antietam.

INCIDENTS OF LEESBURG. — A Southern letter writer gives the following incidents of the battle of Ball's Bluff, called by the Confederates the battle of Leesburg:

"One personal encounter is worthy of record. As Captain Jones, of company B, Seventeenth Mississippi, was passing through the woods at the head of his men, he met another party headed by an officer. The two halting instantly upon discovering their close proximity, Jones exclaimed, "For God Almighty's sake, tell me quick — friends or enemies — who are you?' The other replied, 'We are friends,' and at the same time advanced. A little boy named Joseph Ware, who was behind the Mississippian, instantly cried out, 'Captain, they are not friends; don't you see they have not guns like ours. They are Yankees: let me shoot.' Again Jones exclaimed, 'Who are you? Speak quick, for I can't keep my men from firing.' 'I'll let you know who we are, you d——d rebel,' said the Yankee officer, — for such he was, — and suiting the action to the word, he sprang upon and seized Captain Jones by the collar. For a second or two a scuffle ensued between the officers, when the latter broke loose. At the same instant one of the Mississippians dashed out the Yankee's brains with the butt of his musket.'

"Frequently the ladies are in the habit of visiting the prisoners, but oftener from curiosity than sympathy. Another incident is told of an encounter between several of them and an Irishman.

"It had become a matter of habit with the fair ones to open conversation with the very natural inquiry, 'Where are you wounded?' and accordingly, when a party of three or four, the other day, approached our cell, they launched out in the usual way. Paddy made believe that he didn't hear distinctly, and replied, 'Pretty well, I thank yez.' 'Where were you wounded?' again fired away one of the ladies. 'Faith, I'm not badly hurt, at all. I'll be thravelling to Richmond in a wake,' replied Pat, with a peculiarly distressing look, as if he was in a tight place. Thinking that he was deaf, one of the old ladies in the background put her mouth down to his ear, and shouted again, 'We want to know where you are hurt.'

"Pat, evidently finding that if the bombardment continued much longer he would have to strike his flag anyhow, concluded to do so at once, and accordingly, with a face as rosy as a boiled lobster, and with an angry kind of energy, he replied: 'Sure, leddies, it's not dafe that I am; but, since you are determined to know where I have been wounded, it's on my sate. The bullet entered behind ov me breeches. Plase to excuse me feelings and ax me no more questions.'

"I leave it to you to imagine the blushing consternation of the inquisitors and sudden locomotion of the crinoline out of the front door."

ANECDOTE OF PRESIDENT LINCOLN. — The following transpired at the Executive Mansion in Washington. Its moral will be appreciated by all thoughtful men. Some gentlemen were present from the West, excited and troubled about the commissions or omissions of the Administration. The President heard them patiently, and then replied : "Gentlemen, suppose all the property you were worth was in gold, and you had put it in the hands of Blondin to carry across the Niagara River on a rope; would you shake the cable, or keep shouting out to him — Blondin, stand up a little straighter — Blondin, stoop a little more — go a little faster — lean a little more to the north — lean a little more to the south? No, you would hold your breath as well as your tongue, and keep your hands off until he was safe over. The Government are carrying an immense weight. Untold treasures are in their hands. They are doing the very best they can. Don't badger them. Keep silence, and we'll get you safe across." This simple illustration answered the complaints of half an hour, and not only silenced but charmed the audience.

AN INCIDENT. — As the fleet of transports of the great expedition for the reduction of the forts at Hilton Head was passing down the Chesapeake Bay on that beautiful day in October, 1861, a large bald eagle came sweeping out from the shore of Maryland, and, soaring high in air over the fleet, finally alighted on the masthead of the Atlantic, the headquarters of the army. In an instant all eyes were on him, and conjecture was busy as to whether he were a loyal bird come to give his blessing at parting, or a secession rooster, intent on spying out the nation's strength. "We gave the bird the benefit of the doubt," said one present ; "an officer peremptorily stayed the hand of a soldier who would have shot him, and we accepted the omen as auguring the full success of our enterprise."

THE FIGHT AT BRANDY STATION. — "We were lying at Warrenton Junction, making ourselves as comfortable as possible after the raid, when, on the morning of the 8th of June, 1863, the whole division was ordered out in the very lightest marching order. That night we lay close to Kelly's Ford in column of battalions, the men holding their horses as they slept, and no fires being lighted.

"At four o'clock on the morning of the 9th we were again in motion, and got across the ford without interruption or discovery. Yorke, with the third squadron, was in advance, and as we moved he managed so well that he bagged every picket on the road. Thus we had got almost upon the rebel camp before we were discovered. We rode right into Jones' brigade, the First New Jersey and First Pennsylvania charging together ; and before they had recovered from the alarm we had a hundred and fifty prisoners. The rebels were then forming upon the hill-side by the station, and they had a battery playing upon us like fun. Martin's New York battery, on our side, galloped into position, and began to answer them. Then Wyndham formed his whole brigade for a charge, except a squadron of the First Maryland, left to support the battery. Our boys went in splendidly, keeping well together, and making straight for the rebel battery on the hill behind the station. Wyndham himself rode on the right, and Broderick charged more towards the left, and with a yell we were on them. We were only two hundred and eighty strong, and in front of us was White's battalion of five hundred. No matter for that. Wyndham and Broderick were leading, and they were not accustomed to count odds. As we dashed fiercely into them, sabre in hand, they broke like a wave on the bows of a ship, and over and through them we rode, sabring as we went. We could not stop to take prisoners, for there in front of us was the Twelfth Virginia, six hundred men, riding down to support White. By Jove, sir, that was a charge !

"They came up splendidly, looking steadier than we did ourselves after the shock of the first charge. I do not know whether Wyndham was still with us, or if he had gone to another regiment ; but there was Broderick, looking full of fight, his blue eyes in a blaze, and his sabre clinched, riding well in front. At them we went again, and some of them this time met us fairly. I saw Broderick's sabre go through a man, and the rebel gave a convulsive leap out of his saddle, falling senseless to the ground. It seemed but an instant before the rebels were scattered in every direction, trying now and then to rally in small parties, but never daring to await our approach. Now there were the guns plain before us, the drivers yelling at their horses, and trying to limber up. We caught one gun before they could move it, and were dashing after the others, when I heard Broderick shouting in a stormy voice. I tell you, it was a startling sight. The fragments of White's battalion had gathered together towards the left of the field, and were charging in our rear. The First Maryland was there, and Broderick was shouting at them, in what their Colonel considered a 'very ungentlemanly manner,' to move forward to the charge. At the same time two fresh regiments, the Eleventh Virginia and another, were coming down on our front. Instead of dashing at White's men, the First Maryland wavered and broke, and then we were charged at the same time front and rear. We had to let the guns go, and gather together as well as possible to cut ourselves out. Gallantly our fellows met the attack. We were broken, of course, by the mere weight of the attacking force ; but, breaking them up too, the whole field was covered with small squads of fighting men. I saw Broderick ride in with a cheer and open a way for the men. His horse went down in the mêlée ; but little Wood, the bugler of company

G, sprang down and gave him his animal, setting off himself to catch another.

"A rebel rode at the bugler, and succeeded in getting away his arms before help came. As Wood still went after a horse another fellow rode at him. The boy happened at that moment to see a carbine where it had been dropped after firing. He picked up the empty weapon, aimed it at the horseman, made him dismount, give up his arms, and start for the rear. Then he went in again. Lucas, Hobensack, Brooks, and Beekman charged with twelve men into White's battalion. Fighting hand to hand, they cut their way through, but left nine of the men on the ground behind them. Hughes was left almost alone in a crowd, but brought himself and the men with him safe through. Major Shelmire was last seen lying across the dead body of a rebel cavalryman. None of us thought anything of two to one odds, as long as we had a chance to ride at them. It was only when we got so entangled that we had to fight hand to hand that their numbers told heavily. It was in such a place that I lost sight of Broderick. The troop of horse that he was riding was not strong enough to ride through a knot of men, so that he had to fight them. He struck one so heavily that he was stunned by the blow, but his horse was still in the way; swerving to one side, he escaped a blow from another, and, warding off the thrust of a third, managed to take him with his point across the forehead. Just as he did so, however, his sabre, getting tangled with the rebel's, was jerked from his hand. Drawing his pistol, he fired into the crowd, and put spurs to his horse. The bullet hit a horse in front of him, which fell. His own charger rode at it, but stumbled, and as it did Broderick himself fell, from a shot fired within arm's length of him and a sabre stroke upon his side.

"I saw all this as a man sees things at such times, and am not positive even that it all occurred as I thought I saw it; for I was in the midst of confusion, and only caught things around by passing glimpses. You see I was myself having as much as I could do. The crowd with whom Broderick was engaged was a little distance from me; and I had just wheeled to ride up to his help when two fellows put at me. The first one fired at me and missed. Before he could again cock his revolver I succeeded in closing with him. My sabre took him just in the neck, and must have cut the jugular. The blood gushed out in a black-looking stream; he gave a horrible yell and fell over the side of his horse, which galloped away. Then I gathered up my reins, spurred my horse, and went at the other one. I was riding that old black horse that used to belong to the signal sergeant, and it was in fine condition. As I drove in the spurs it gave a leap high in the air. That plunge saved my life. The rebel had a steady aim at me; but the ball went through the black horse's brain. His feet never touched ground again. With a terrible convulsive contraction of all his muscles, the black turned over in the air, and fell on his head and side stone dead, pitching me twenty feet. I

alighted on my pistol, the butt forcing itself far into my side; my sabre sprung out of my hand, and I lay with arms and legs all abroad, stretched out like a dead man. Everybody had something else to do than to attend to me, and there I lay where I had fallen.

"It seemed to me to have been an age before I began painfully to come to myself; but it could not have been many minutes. Every nerve was shaking; there was a terrible pain in my head, and a numbness in my side, which was even worse. Fighting was still going on around me, and my first impulse was to get hold of my sword. I crawled to it, and sank down as I grasped it once more. That was only for a moment, for a rebel soldier, seeing me move, rode at me. The presence of danger roused me, and I managed to get to my horse, behind which I sank, resting my pistol on the saddle, and so contriving to get an aim. As soon as the man saw that, he turned off without attacking me. I was now able to stand and walk; so, holding my pistol in one hand and my sabre in the other, I made my way across the fields to where our battery was posted, scaring some with my pistol and shooting others. Nobody managed to hit me through the whole fight. When I got up to the battery I found Wood there. He sang out to me to wait and he would get me a horse.

"One of the men, who had just taken one, was going past; so Wood stopped him and got it for me. Just at that moment White's battalion and some other troops came charging at the battery. The squadron of the First Maryland, who were supporting it, met the charge well as far as their numbers went, but were, of course, flanked on both sides by the heavy odds. All of our men who were free came swarming up the hill, and the cavalry were fighting over and around the guns. In spite of the confusion, and even while their comrades at the same piece were being sabred, the men at that battery kept to their duty. They did not even look up or around, but kept up their fire with unwavering steadiness. There was one rebel, on a splendid horse, who sabred three gunners while I was chasing him. He wheeled in and out — would dart away and then come sweeping back and cut down another man in a manner that seemed almost supernatural. We at last succeeded in driving him away, but we could not catch or shoot him, and he got off without a scratch.

"In the mean time the fight was going on elsewhere. Kilpatrick's brigade charged on our right. The Second New York did not behave as well as it has sometimes done since, and the loss of it weakened us a great deal. The Tenth New York, though, went in well, and the First Maine did splendidly, as it always does. In spite of their superior numbers (Stuart had a day or two before reviewed thirty thousand cavalry at Culpepper, according to the accounts of rebel officers) we beat them heavily, and would have routed them completely if Duffie's brigade had come up. He, however, was engaged with two or three hundred men on the left; the aid-de-camp sent to him with orders was wounded and taken prisoner, and he is not the sort of man to find out the critical point in a fight of his own accord.

"So now, they bringing up still more reserves, and a whole division of theirs coming on the field, we began to fall back. We had used them up so severely that they could not press us very close, except in the neighborhood of where the Second New York charged. There some of our men had as much as they could do to get out, and the battery had to leave three of its guns. We formed in the woods between a quarter and half a mile of the field; another moved back to cover the left of Buford, who was in retreat towards Beverly Ford. Hart and Wynkoop tried hard to cover the guns that were lost; but they had too few men, and so had to leave them. The rebels were terribly punished. By their own confession they lost three times as many as we did. In our regiment almost every soldier must have settled his man. Sergeant Craig, of company K, I believe, killed three. Slate, of the above company, also went above the average. But we lost terribly. Sixty enlisted men of the First New Jersey were killed, wounded, or missing. Colonel Wyndham was wounded, but kept his saddle; Lieutenant-Colonel Broderick and Major Shelmire were killed; Lieutenant Brooks was wounded; Captain Sawyer and Lieutenant Crocker were taken prisoners; and I, as you see, have had to come in at last and refit."

THE CAVALRY CHARGE.

BY EDMUND C. STEDMAN.

Our good steeds snuff the evening air,
  Our pulses with their purpose tingle;
The foeman's fires are twinkling there;
  He leaps to hear our sabres jingle!
    Halt!
Each carbine sent its whizzing ball:
Now, cling! clang! Forward, all,
  Into the fight!

Dash on beneath the smoking dome:
  Through level lightnings gallop nearer!
One look to Heaven! No thoughts of home;
  The guidons that we bear are dearer.
    Charge!
Cling! clang! Forward, all!
Heaven help those whose horses fall —
  Cut left and right!

They flee before our fierce attack!
  They fall! they spread in broken surges.
Now, comrades, bear our wounded back,
  And leave the foeman to his dirges.
    Wheel!
The bugles sound the swift recall:
Cling! clang! Backward, all!
  Home, and good-night!

FREEDOM OF SPEECH. — An editor of a Western journal narrates the following: "At D—— dwells a rabid secessionist, we are sorry to say,

for the honor of the town. This man, it seems, is a person of substance, having considerable means invested in Southern State stocks. He has a dog 'Shep,' as intelligent and obedient as his master is bigoted and dunder-headed. 'Tis sometimes said the master is only tolerated on the dog's account, as the quadruped is much the more respected of the two.

"One day Mr. Secesh was holding forth on the right of speech, the freedom of the press, and all that kind of thing, averring that every man had a right to say what he pleased, where he pleased, and when he pleased, and no one had a right to molest him or make him afraid. Just then a big bull dog walked past the door. He was a tremendously savage dog, the terror of all the canines in town, and able to clean out and chaw up fourteen dozen such dogs as 'Shep.' A young fellow, who had listened to the man's stuff long enough, determined to give him a practical illustration of his own doctrine: so he sprang towards the door, and pointing towards the big dog, said, 'Lick him, Shep! Seize him, Shep! Pitch into him, and lick him. Seize him, Shep!' Obedient to the lightest command, the faithful dog started as he was bidden, and but for his master's interference would have been badly torn.

"Full of wrath, he turned to the young man who had incited his dog to fight the bull dog, and said, 'What did you do that for, you rascal? Set Shep on to a dog that would tear him to pieces?'

"'O, I was only exercising your freedom of speech. It's nobody's business what I say to any dog.' The way the thing was done created an immense laugh, and effectually dried up the rebel gentleman. He hadn't a word to say."

CONSERVATIVE CHORUS.

Abraham, spare the South,
  Touch not a single slave;
Nor e'en by word of mouth
  Disturb the thing, we crave.
'Twas our forefathers' hand
  That Slavery begot;
There, Abraham, let it stand;
  Thine acts shall harm it not.

INCIDENTS OF BELMONT. — Major Bledsoe Harmon, of the Confederate army, relates the following incidents of the battle at Belmont:

"During the battle many incidents occurred, many acts of heroism were performed, that will be told only when the war shall have ended, and when the patriot has returned to his home to enjoy the fruits of the independence his valor has helped to win. Then, beside the hearth-stone, tales of chivalry and daring will be told, and handed down from father to son to the remotest generations.

"Among the many acts of heroism told of those engaged, is that of a mere youth, a little boy who was attached to Tappan's Arkansas regiment, and carried two mimic flags, one in each hand.

The regiment was driven to the water's edge, and the enemy poured in a terrific volley, killing many of them, who fell into the river, and such as were not instantly killed met a watery grave. Among those struck was the little boy who bore the flags. Giving one last hurrah, which was cut short by the ebbing flood of his young life, he waved the flags over his head, tottered into the river, and was seen no more. The incident was witnessed by a whole regiment that was crossing the river at the time, and not one member of it but shed a tear at the sight.

"When General Pillow's brigade first discovered the enemy, Colonel Pickett's regiment was ordered to charge. They commenced it at double-quick, when they were met by a withering volley, which prostrated about forty of the men. Of those wounded was Lieutenant Jesse Tate, who was struck in the knee, and fell. Colonel Pickett's horse was shot in three different places, and killed under him. Major J. C. Cole's horse was shot dead. Lieutenant Hiram Tilman, although a prominent mark and in the thickest of the fight, encouraging on his men, escaped unhurt. Colonel Pickett acted like a veteran. Cool and undismayed, he saw his men fall beside him; but the carnage seemed to inspire him to greater deeds. In fact, the utmost gallantry was displayed by all the field and commissioned officers and men in the regiment.

"Perhaps the most unflinching determination and courage upon the part of the men in Colonel Pickett's regiment was displayed by Captain J. D. Layton, of the Liberty Guards. In the first charge, while standing in front of his men, who were loading and firing as fast as possible, he received a severe wound just beneath his left arm, the ball lodging in his body. His sword fell from his grasp, but he quickly recovered it, and, notwithstanding the severity of his hurt, fought the battle through; nor did he leave his men until he saw that his wounded were properly cared for at night. Such acts entitle a man to the name of hero.

"The gallant conduct of Captain Frazier, also of Pickett's regiment, is highly spoken of. We must not omit Captain Dashiell, whose praises are sounded by all. James B. Hatcher, a not very old nor remarkably large young gentleman, who was in the battle as an amateur fighter, succeeded in 'surrounding' a Lincolnite twice his size, and disarmed him of his gun and knife, besides one of the Roman sabres he had captured from one of our men in Watson's battery. The last-named weapon he carried home with him, but was not permitted to take away the rest.

"Captain J. Welby Armstrong was struck full in the breast by two six-pounder canister shots, and of course death was instantaneous.

"From Columbus the fight could be witnessed with ease. As our men retired to the river for ammunition, gallantly contesting every inch of ground, the Federals in pursuit could be seen bayoneting the wounded left upon the field. Not only this, they set fire to the tents used as hospitals, and many of the poor fellows confined in them were consumed by the flames. These acts of barbarity did not lessen the already awakened vengeance of our men, and we hear it stated that the most ample retaliation was made."

A BELLIGERENT WOMAN. — At Branchville, S. C., in the days when the Confederate rule was strictest, a lady presented herself at the platform of a passenger car going to Charleston, where a guard with fixed bayonet was standing, and desired to enter.

The guard told her it was contrary to orders, and raised his piece in a position that indicated clearly that he meant to obey instructions. She ordered him to lower his musket. He refused.

She then drew a revolver, and pointing it at him, threatened to shoot if he did not let her pass. With some surprise he demanded: "Are you a man in woman's clothes?" "No," was the reply, "I am a woman." "Then come in," said the sentinel, "for hang me if I fight a woman, or be killed by one. You can't be classed with non-combatants, and they are the only persons I am ordered to keep out of this car." So she was classed as a "belligerent power," and allowed to pass.

THE MARCH TO NASHVILLE. — A soldier-writer, on the march to Nashville, in the autumn of 1862, narrates the following: "I engaged in a pleasant two hours' chat with General Rousseau, and found him an agreeable and entertaining conversationist. There is no compromise in him, except *in the Union*. He holds that a *rebel* has no rights under our Constitution. Eight or ten of the gentry called on him near Mitchellville, and commenced using treasonable language. The General peremptorily ordered them to cease, as he had heard all he wanted of such talk.

"'Well, but, General, I understand you are a Kentuckian; you don't go in for any abolition document like Lincoln has just issued, do you?'

"'No matter, sir, what I like; *you* have no right to complain.'

"'Why, you don't approve of their stealing our negroes, do you?'

"'I approve, sir, of anything my Government does to put down the rebellion; and anything *you love* I hate.'

"'Well, why don't you take our houses and lands?'

"'Well, sir, if we wanted them, I go in for that, too; take everything you have, and drive you to the dominions of Jeff Davis, whom you love so much; and, so far as lies in my power, I will drive every one of you beyond our lines, according to all rules of war, where you cannot do us injury as spies. Yes, sir, I would send you all to Jeff Davis, or hell.'

"Soon after the above, a tattered specimen of gawky ignorance entered the General's tent.

"'Well, sir,' said the General, 'what will you have?'

"'I kem over here for pertection.'

"'Are you a Union man? However,' continued he, 'you are *all* Union men now; it is scarcely worth asking the question.'

"'Well, General,' said the Tennesseean, 'I'm not an aberlitionist; I don't go in for —'

"'O, go to my Adjutant, Captain Pohrman. I'm tired of such evasions. If you deserve protection, you shall have it; if not, you must accept the consequences of the calamity you have aided in bringing upon your own head.'

"I heard a good story told of a joke played off by a secession wag, a short time since, upon General Negley. A whiskey-drinking, facetious joker, residing in the town of Goolctsville, a strong sccesh hole, in which there never was but one Union man, *and he died.* Well, this wag wagered a gallon of whiskey that he could go into Nashville, and go all over the city, notwithstanding the strictness of General Negley's orders; further, that he would see Negley personally, and talk with him. The bet was taken, and this fellow, whose name is Paul, well known in Nashville as a violent sccessionist, the next day took a flag of truce, rode into the city, saw crowds of his friends, rode up to the headquarters of General Negley, and demanded the surrender of the city, stating that he was Assistant Adjutant Paul, and that there was an immense quantity of troops ready to enforce the demand. General Negley refused to entertain the thought of a surrender, and Paul *returned to Goolets-ville, having won his bet.*

"General Negley found it out when too late. It wouldn't do to try that game again in Nashville."

ANECDOTE OF PRESIDENT LINCOLN. — Some one was smoking in the presence of the President, and complimented him on having no vices, neither drinking nor smoking. "That is a doubtful compliment," answered the President. "I recollect once being outside a stage in Illinois,' and a man sitting by me offered me a cigar. I told him I had no vices. He said nothing, smoked for some time, and then grunted out, "It's my experience that folks who have no vices have plaguy few virtues."

A SOLDIER'S LAST LETTER. — John Moseley, a youth who fell at Gettysburg on the Southern side, wrote the following touching but manly letter, from his death-bed, to his parents in Alabama:

"BATTLE-FIELD, GETTYSBURG, July 4, 1863.

"DEAR MOTHER: I am here a prisoner of war, and mortally wounded. I can live but a few hours, at farthest. I was shot fifty yards from the enemy's line. They have been exceedingly kind to me. I have no doubt as to the final result of this battle, and I hope I may live long enough to hear the shouts of victory before I die. I am very weak. Do not mourn my loss. I had hoped to have been spared; but a righteous God has ordered it otherwise, and I feel prepared to trust my case in his hands. Farewell to you all! Pray that God may receive my soul.

"Your unfortunate son,   JOHN."

AN INCIDENT OF ANTIETAM. — One of the correspondents who was with the division of General Sturgis at the battle of Antietam gives the following account of the part taken by that division in the contest:

"Our division, under General Sturgis, were on the extreme left, and were not placed in line until about five o'clock P. M., when a double-quick movement took place, and the whole division started like Bengal tigers let loose for prey. They ran through a galling fire of shot and shell until they were within reach of the enemy's musketry, when a heavy fire opened on us, which General Nagle (commanding our brigade) saw at once would decimate the brigade, and so the order came to charge bayonets. Promptly the glistening steel was placed in position; and here one of the most brilliant bayonet charges took place that has been seen during the war. The brigade had to charge up hill, over stone walls and other obstructions, and met the enemy at great disadvantage. The Massachusetts Thirty-fifth regiment was put in order of battle, and did great execution at the first onset. In General Nagle's brigade and Sturgis' division was also the Ninth regiment New Hampshire volunteers, Colonel Fellows, one of the most experienced Colonels in the army. It was a handsome sight to see him put his regiment into action. When the clear, sonorous print came from Colonel Fellows, 'Charge bayonets!' every eye gleamed in the 'Bloody Ninth,' as the brigade now call the regiment. Every man threw away his knapsack, blanket, and haversack, and leaped over a stone wall six feet high with a yell that fairly sent terror through the rebel ranks opposite. With eyes gleaming with joy and determination, and every bayonet fixed, they charged up the hill and through the cornfield at double-quick with a yell of perfect triumph. Colonel Fellows and Lieutenant-Colonel Titus astonished the old veterans in the service by the manner in which they brought the Ninth New Hampshire volunteers into the action. It was a grand and magnificent sight, and one seldom seen in battle. The rebels fled before them, and every rebel regiment broke and ran. General Reno fell beside the Ninth New Hampshire volunteers and the Thirty-fifth Massachusetts about dark, just in the moment of victory."

AN IMPRESSIVE SCENE. — A most interesting and eloquent episode occurred at Trinity Church, Washington, in May, 1861. The rector, Rev. Dr. Butler, began his sermon with the remark that the discourse he was about to deliver was preached by himself here twelve years ago, and he should repeat it verbatim. It was a lucid and effective argument to prove that the popular idea of government among us is held in a too loose and secular estimation; while the fact is, that, however carelessly we may regard it, as merely a contract with ministerial agents, and however inadequate our respect for law and constituted authorities, it is a divine institution.

The peroration was powerful. Said the reverend gentleman: "Twelve years ago, after I had finished this course, I met the lamented Daniel Webster just outside the church. He said to me, 'Sir, you are right; it is the true doctrine.' In this view, my brethren, I see in the awakened strength of the Government the glittering sword of almighty vengeance suspended over its enemies. In this view alone do I descry the only hope for my glorious, my beloved country;" and, at these words, the tears streaming down the preacher's face, in a voice choked with inexpressible emotion, he raised his eyes towards Heaven, and, hesitating to receive utterance, he concluded, in faltering, though articulate, tones, "*Esto perpetua.*" The effect was electrical; all eyes were suffused with tears, and the quiet of the sanctuary was broken only by sobs and weeping.

INCIDENTS OF BEAUFORT. — A soldier, who was present at the capture of Beaufort, South Carolina, relates the following:

"A black fellow was reported to our Colonel, and taken to general headquarters. He was very communicative. 'Massa,' he inquired, 'is Abe Lincoln here?' He seemed at fault when informed he had not come. It seems he was present during the bombardment, and nearer than he liked to be. 'What did it look like?' asked Colonel L. 'It looked as if de fire and brimstone was comin' down, and de yearth was agwine up.' The sand that flew as every discharge came down filled the description perfectly.

"One of these negroes reports that when Major Lee, the Confederate commander, finished the fort, he said, profanely, 'The devil couldn't take it — God Almighty himself couldn't take it.' On the day of the battle, when his black body servant got out his horse for him, and saw him mounted, and they both ran together for their lives to get out of range of the merciless storm of shot and shell falling around them, the negro said, 'O massa, God Almighty come, and de Yankees come wid him,' — seeming to imply that such a union of forces had not been contemplated when his master had concluded upon the impregnability of his fortifications."

A BRAVE WOMAN. — Mrs. John F. Phelps is the wife of the Colonel of a loyal Missouri regiment, and resided at a point about one mile and a half from Springfield. On the afternoon after the battle of Wilson's Creek, it was noised that the rebels had determined to cut out the heart of General Lyon, and preserve it as a trophy over the United States army. Mrs. Phelps, learning of this outrage on the slain General, armed herself, as she was accustomed to do for some time, in order to preserve her life and the lives of her family from the murderous assaults of the secessionists. Thus armed, she drove to Price's camp by nightfall, and there, all alone, guarded the body of General Lyon. When ordered by the rebels to give up the body, she positively refused, and declared they must cut out her heart before they could get the heart of the General. There, all alone, she stood guard during the whole night, with her arms in readiness to defend her charge, regardless of her own life, — thus fearlessly passing the dreary night amidst the associations of the dead, the wounded, and the bloodthirsty men who were awaiting an opportunity to obtain the coveted heart of the noble Lyon.

After daylight, having made arrangements in reference to her precious charge, she repaired to her home, and sent a colored servant with a wagon and two horses to bring the remains of General Lyon to her residence, in order to burial in her garden or on her farm, with all the respect in her power towards the commander of the loyal army. But as the wagon had not returned in due time, she drove again to Price's camp, found her wagon had been seized for the use of the rebel army, and her servant confined in it and gagged. As the horses had been unhitched from the wagon, with her own hands she again hitched them. When resistance was again offered to her course she fearlessly declared she would deal death with her revolver to any one who molested her. About the time she had released the servant, and got her precious treasure in the wagon, resistance was again threatened. She then pressed her way to the presence of General Price, who, at her pressing instance, ordered her to have the body of the slain General, without further interruption.

Having thus obtained her cherished object, more dear to her than life, she accompanied it to her residence, and there interred it in the best manner she could. And all this was done in the absence of her loyal husband, who, in consequence of his duties as Colonel, could not be present to accompany his noble wife in performing this work of loyalty and humanity.

A CONTRABAND'S DESCRIPTION. — A letter from a soldier at Newport News relates the following incident, giving a slave woman's account of the capture of the rebel batteries on General McClellan's advance upon Yorktown: "The attack on the batteries cannot be better described than in the words of an old contraband whom I fell in with, while on a scout to Young's Mills, the day after its capture. She was secesh, and took us to belong to the same race. On asking her if there was much fighting at the battery, she replied: 'Why, lordy, you won't blebe me, massa, but de Yankee he fire jes one round, den commence hollering like de debbel, and frew rite ober de breastworks; but dey couldn't ketch our folks (secesh), dey run so fast.' The nigger explained in thirty-seven words what a 'special correspondent' would have found impossible, probably, in half a column."

SECESSION CATECHISED. — Colonel Tom Ford, of the Thirty-second Ohio regiment, while at New Creek, Virginia, in June, 1862, engaged in conversation with an old resident, who had taken a seat on the bench beside him.

"Have you lived long about here?" inquired the Colonel.

"Yes," said the old man, "I have lived in this (Hampshire) county all my life."

"I suppose, then," said the Colonel, "you know all about how secession commenced here, who commenced it, and how it has been carried on."

"Yes," again said the old man, "and I will tell you how I tried to expose it at the start to the people. My opinion did not pass for much at the time, as I owned no big farm nor any niggers, but I think it would pass for something now."

"Well, how was it?" inquired the Colonel.

"Colonel Parsons was one of the main getters up of it. He advertised to make a speech over in Romney, after the ordinance passed, and I and several of my neighbors went over to hear him speak. Just as he was about to commence, I took the liberty, as I was an old acquaintance of the Colonel's, to ask him a question. So I said: 'Colonel Parsons, we have come over here to-night to hear you make your speech in favor of secession; and before you begin, I want you to tell me and my friends here one thing.' 'What is it?' said the Colonel. 'Why, I want you to make a speech to-night, without ever mentioning the nigger once. Me and my friends, who own no niggers, want to know why we should be secessionists. Will you please tell us, Colonel, why men who own no niggers should be secessionists?'

"Well, what did Colonel Parsons say?" asked Colonel Ford of the old man.

"Why, he came the nearest to saying nothing that ever I saw," said the old man. "At last he said that he wouldn't speak on such terms; that he was going to speak on the whole subject."

"Well, what did you say then?" asked Colonel Ford.

"I said," continued the old man, "'Now, Colonel Parsons, you know that aside from the nigger there is nothing in this secession; and you ought to know that all the slaves that now live in the country, live in the slave States, and that you will not increase their number a single one by secession, but on the contrary that you will bring about the escape of hundreds of them, before you get through with the job you are undertaking!'"

"Well, how did Colonel Parsons take your talk?" asked Colonel Ford.

"Why," said he, "he got mad, like all the secessionists did in those days, when Union men opposed them — told me I was an abolitionist, and that the South was going to have her rights. And now, hasn't it come out as I told Colonel Parsons?" asked the old man. "Hasn't the South lost more niggers since this war commenced than she ever lost in the whole time before? and isn't she in a fair way to lose them all? And here," said he, "we people who have always lived by our own work have had to bear the ruin that these pride-swelled nigger aristocrats have brought upon us. I have had to bear it, and my Union friends who were with me that night have had to bear it. And all for what? Why, because these nigger-owners wanted to break up a government in which people like me, who owned no niggers, and had to work for a living, were on an equality with them. I tell you," continued the old man, "I owe them nothing but curses and war, and they are getting plenty of the first now, from hundreds of their miserable dupes around here, and plenty of the other from the Federal Government."

Colonel Ford, getting up and taking the old man by the hand, said that he had to acknowledge that much as he had heard against secession, he had never heard it as completely and strongly expressed in so few words before.

PICKET CONVERSATION. — In the summer of 1862, the national pickets at the Mechanicsville Bridge, Virginia, had a conversation with the rebel pickets, and under a newspaper flag of truce, exchanged the Baltimore Clipper for the Richmond Examiner. The colloquy was substantially as follows:

Rebel. (Waving his hat.) Three cheers for General Jackson!

Union Soldier. (Also waving his hat.) Three cheers for Burnside!

[It had been ascertained that the rebels were North Carolinians.]

Rebel. Have you any Baltimore Clippers?

Union. Ye-as; do you wish to *swap?*

Rebel. How'll yer trade fur the Examiner?

Union. Even, and you do the *toting.*

Rebel. Come over yer, all on yer!

Union. I'll come half way.

[Meanwhile both parties had dropped their guns, and with papers waving, passed down to the bridge.]

Union. How do you like soldiering?

Rebel. We've enlisted for life.

Union. Then you don't expect to live long?

Rebel. You whipped us at Hanover, but yer wouldn't if O'Brien Branch wasn't drunk. We give you just the best flogging yer ever had tha' at Fair Oaks. Tuk one hundred yer guns, all yer ammition, and everything, and two thousand prisoners.

Union. And we drove you back to Richmond, and had to bury your dead. We whipped you awfully.

Rebel. And General McClellan was wounded, and two of yer Generals killed. Yer all going back to Yorktown, ain't yer? We are coming over your side to-morrow.

Union. How many troops you got over there?

Rebel. Fifty thousand right yerabouts!

Union. How many had you at Fair Oaks?

Rebel. Yer had near two hundred thousand, and we but sixty thousand, but we whipped you.

The Unionist was less communicative than inquisitive, but thinking it hardly proper to continue the conversation, bade the rebel good day, and retraced his steps. But the rebel still kept his place, notwithstanding he was requested to face back, until a bullet and a flash, and quick report, suddenly hastened his steps.

BROTHER JONATHAN'S LAMENT FOR SISTER CAROLINE.*

BY OLIVER WENDELL HOLMES.

SHE has gone, — she has left us in passion and
  pride, —
Our stormy-browed sister, so long at our side!
She has torn her own star from our firmament's
  glow,
And turned on her brother the face of a foe!

O Caroline, Caroline, child of the sun,
We can never forget that our hearts have been
  one, —
Our foreheads both sprinkled in Liberty's name,
From the fountain of blood with the finger of flame!

You were always too ready to fire at a touch;
But we said, "She is hasty, — she does not mean
  much."
We have scowled when you uttered some turbulent
  threat;
But Friendship still whispered, "Forgive and forget!"

Has our love all died out? Have its altars grown
  cold?
Has the curse come at last which the fathers fore-
  told?
Then Nature must teach us the strength of the chain
That her petulant children would sever in vain.

They may fight till the buzzards are gorged with
  their spoil,
Till the harvest grows black as it rots in the soil,
Till the wolves and the catamounts troop from their
  caves,
And the shark tracks the pirate, the lord of the
  waves.

In vain is the strife! When its fury is past,
Their fortunes must flow in one channel at last,
As the torrents that rush from the mountains of
  snow
Roll mingled in peace through the valleys below.

Our Union is river, lake, ocean, and sky:
Man breaks not the medal when God cuts the die!
Though darkened with sulphur, though cloven with
  steel,
The blue arch will brighten, the waters will heal!.

O Caroline, Caroline, child of the sun,
There are battles with Fate that can never be won!
The star-flowering banner must never be furled,
For its blossoms of light are the hope of the world!

Go, then, our rash sister! afar and aloof, —
Run wild in the sunshine, away from our roof;
But when your heart aches and your feet have
  grown sore,
Remember the pathway that leads to our door!

HEROISM OF A BOY. — The following very interesting incident is related in connection with
the attack by the United States gunboat Galena

* Written upon the announcement of the passage
of the "Ordinance of Secession," on the 20th of December, 1860, by the Convention of South Carolina,
the first State which attempted to secede.

upon Fort Darling: A youth, about thirteen years
old, who was in the service of Lieutenant Nau-
man, as a messenger boy, seeing one of the powder boys wounded, immediately volunteered to
take his place. The services of the young volunteer were accepted, and he set to work with a
spirit to fill his new position, rendering great assistance to the officers and crew. The poor little
fellow's career of glory was destined to be short-
lived. Only a few hours later, while engaged in
carrying a quantity of powder, a shell came tearing along, burst right over the boy, and killed
him in an instant. The poor little fellow's sufferings were soon over; but the sight was too much
for many of the rough Jack Tars, down whose
bronzed cheeks the big tears rolled in abundance.
The boy's name was James Weber.

COLONEL RIKER, of the Anderson Zouaves,
was killed at the battle of Fair Oaks. He was
shot in the right side, while turning around to
cheer on his men, the ball coming out in front.
Riker rode upon a white horse, and was a prominent figure for the enemy's marksmen. He had,
previous to going into action, a presentiment that
he was to meet his death. He gave to Lieutenant
Bradley, his aid, some tokens of love for the
friends at home, and went bravely into the fight.
When the fatal shot was fired, he had just turned
around to the Zouaves, who were hemmed in, and
cried out, "Boys, we are surrounded — give them
cold steel now." Suddenly dropping from his
horse, the gallant spirit had fled forever.

AN INCIDENT OF MOBILE. — A letter writer relates the following recollections of the wounded at
Mobile: "They all bore their sufferings with the
most unexampled heroism. One, a Captain from
Wisconsin, shot through the back so that he could
not be turned, and scarcely taken up on his bed,
breathed only as he could catch a breath, while
an attendant fanned him. I awoke during the
night, and found the attendant, weary, had fallen
asleep. I took the fan and sat by him. 'Thank
you, you are kind; it is so hot;' and he looked
up, so heroic in his agony, and not one word of
complaint. Arrived at New Orleans, where he
could and would have been carefully and kindly
cared for, he died, and his last words were: 'Tell
the boys not to shrink, not to flinch. Fight on
— it will soon be over.' Poor fellow; young and
brave, it is too soon over with thee!

"Another. Passing through the cabin,
the wounded stretched on each side of me, on mat-
tresses ranged in rows on the floor, I saw — will
you believe it? — one man who had had his leg
amputated but three days before, braced up
with pillows and playing a violin, while a comrade, with one of his arms shot off, was playing
the castanets with the other. There's pluck for
you."

A CATHOLIC PRIEST'S WAR SPEECH. — The
Sunday after President Lincoln's proclamation

calling for seventy-five thousand troops, Father Creedon, the priest of the Catholic Church at Auburn, New York, preached a war sermon, as did other clergymen in Auburn. The other sermons were said to be up to the times, but Father Creedon's was conceded to be the most pertinent. He said, substantially:

"I wish every man who can leave his family to enlist. This is the first country the Irishman ever had that he could call his own country. The flag of the Stars and Stripes is the only flag he can fight under and defend as his own flag. Now, in the time of the nation's peril, let every Irishman show that he is worthy to be part of this great and glorious nation. Now, when the American flag is bombarded and struck down by traitors, let every Irishman show that he is true to the flag which always protects him. I wish every Irishman who hears me to enlist if he can. There are two classes whom I most despise — cowards and traitors; and those who can enlist, and do not, are either one or the other."

THE CHARGE AT ANTIETAM BRIDGE. — There have been many deeds of heroism recounted of the troops engaged in the battle of Antietam; but those of the Second Maryland infantry have been overlooked, though equal to any achieved by their fathers in the Revolution.

The Second Maryland was the heroic regiment of that bloody field, so prolific in heroes. It belonged to the corps of the gallant Burnside, had been with them at Newbern, and now the duty of storming the *tête du pont*, at Antietam Creek, had devolved upon it; and never did veterans move forward with steadier step to a more perilous enterprise, or one in which the chances of surviving it were so fearfully few. All the bluster, bravado, and recklessness, supposed to be the distinguishing characteristics of *l'enfant perdu* of Baltimore had given place to a sober and solemn gravity, in keeping with the awful struggle that was impending. There was no noise, no cheering in the ranks; but, on the other hand, there was no wavering or faltering, as they moved sternly and silently forward into the conflict. The measured and heavy tread of the battalion, falling in dull cadence on the ear, was the only sound audible as it entered the head of the bridge. Suddenly the enemy's cannon opened at short range, pouring upon it a tempest of round shot and shell, sweeping away whole files, and ploughing bloody furrows through the ranks. But it faltered not. At the sharp, short order of the officers, "Close up, boys," the bloody gaps were filled, and the heroic battalion pressed on. Standard-bearer after standard-bearer went down before the iron hurricane; but scarcely was he down when the standard, wrenched from his dying grasp, was borne aloft by his nearest comrade in the strife.

The way over the bridge was filled with corpses. Most of the officers had fallen. Captain Wilson, of a family that had sent five brothers to the war, for the moment commanding the regiment, had gone down, pierced through the middle of his forehead by a minie ball. Captain Martin, succeeding him, fell mortally wounded; but there was no check, no faltering or sign of confusion or hesitation. With their heads bent, their shoulders a little forward, at the charge step, they moved steadily on, until the bridge was cleared, and the way opened to the regiments in the rear. It was only when the bridge was won, and room obtained to deploy the column, that the old, lusty Maryland cheer which more than eighty years before had been heard at Brandywine, at Guilford and Eutaw, rang out on the sulphureous air of that dread September day, attesting that those who sent it were the legitimate sons of sires who had fought for freedom, and won immortal fame under Howard and Williams. They are no more forever the despised "Plug Uglies" of Baltimore, but a "new Maryland line," indomitable as the "old," baptized anew in fire and blood, which has washed away all former transgressions.

A great thing had been done by these daring men — a second bridge of Lodi had been carried; but no Napoleon was there to take advantage of the brave and glorious deed. It will, nevertheless, live in history as a deed of pride and glory, achieved by the soldiers of noble old Maryland, in a war to put down treason, in which every art had been used by the traitors to induce her to take a part.

WAR SPIRIT OF A SOLDIER. — It was immediately after the battle of the Hatchie. The dead in that terrible conflict had been laid beneath the mould, while the wounded had been brought to the church-building, or placed in the spacious apartments of wealthy disloyalists of Bolivar. Among the number of unfortunates was William C. Nowlon, a Sergeant in company G, of the Third Iowa infantry. His leg has been so badly shattered and torn by a musket shot as to render an amputation unavoidable. He was informed of such a necessity; but not a murmur or word of complaint escaped his lips; nor did the intelligence seem to cast over his face the least perceptible shade of seriousness. The table was prepared — the instruments were placed conveniently, and everything was put in readiness for the operation. He was brought out upon the veranda, and placed upon the table — his poor, shattered, torn, and half fleshless leg dangling around as if only an extraneous and senseless appendage. There was no sighing, no flinching, no drawing back or holding in. There was not a simple feeling of dumb resignation, nor yet of brute indifference, but a *soldierly* submission — an heroic submission, without a question or a sigh. He indulged freely in conversation respecting the operation, until the chloroform was applied. From the waking and rational state he glided into the anæsthetic without the convulsive motion of a single muscle, and without the utterance of a single incoherent sentence, but glided into it as the innocent and weary child glides into the sweet embrace of a healthful and restoring sleep. The operation was performed; the arteries all ligatured, the stump cleansed, and the last suture just in that instant applied. During the entire operation he had scarcely moved a muscle. Just at this time the large body of prisoners taken in the engagement were marched up the street, and were nearing the house where the maimed and bleeding soldier lay. The streets were all thronged by soldiery, and hundreds of them rushed to get a near sight of the vanquished, while they rent the heavens with their loud huzzas. A full regiment preceded the column of prisoners; and when just opposite, the band struck up in force the inspiring air of "Hail Columbia." In a moment, upon the very instant, the color mounted to his face! He opened his eyes half wonderingly, and raised his head from the pillow with the steadiness and dignity of a god! The scenes of the conflict came back to him, and he thought that his noble regiment was again breasting towards the enemy through a shower of shot and shell. His brave comrades, he deemed, were falling one by one around him, just as they had done in that dreadful hour of fratricide and carnage. The spirit of the time came over him, and his features assumed an air of bold, fierce, fiery, and unyielding determination, and he broke forth into exclamations the most terrible and appalling I had ever listened to in all my life.

"Louder with the music! louder! louder! louder! Burst the heavens with your strains! Sweeter! softer! sweeter! Charm the blessed angels from the very courts of heaven! Victory! victory! Onward! onward! No flagging! no flinching! No faltering! Fill up! fill up! Step forward! press forward! Your comrades' graves! The fresh graves of your slain! Remember the graves of your comrades! Blue Mills! Blue Mills! Shelbina! Shelbina! Hager Wood! Shiloh! Shiloh! For God's sake, onward! Onward, in heaven's name! onward! onward! onward! See the devils waver! See them run! See! see! see them fly! fly! *fly!*"

During the outburst of passion, his countenance kindled and grew purple, till his look seemed that of diabolism! Such a fury marked his lineaments that I instinctively drew back. But there was "method in his madness." He only erred in mistaking time, and in misplacing himself, and in misplacing his position; facts which the martial music and the "pomp and circumstance of war," in the public streets, would have a natural tendency towards producing. In the very middle of his fury he seemed suddenly to comprehend his mistake. He ceased abruptly, his whole frame in a tremor of emotion. He looked around upon the faces present, and without a word, quietly laid down his head. He grew meditative as he seemed to realize a full sense of his unhappy situation. At length his eyes gradually filled with tears, and his lips grew slightly tremulous. He quietly remarked, "Well, boys, good by, good by; I should do but sorry fighting on a wooden leg." He again relapsed into silence, and was shortly afterwards carried away to his room.

HEROISM OF THE MAINE SEVENTH. — At the battle of Antietam, Captain J. W. Walcott, of the First Maryland regiment, was stationed on a ridge near the bridge over the river. In front of him some hundred yards rose another ridge, along which ran a stone wall parallel with his position. His pieces were trained obliquely, firing at objects off one side from the last-named ridge. Meantime the enemy's sharpshooters crept up to the stone wall and opened fire on his gunners; in a very few minutes one of his pieces was bereft of all his men, and the regularity of the service of the others much impeded. Still he held his ground with the obstinacy that characterized all our troops on that eventful day.

Just then, when he was thinking on the necessity for changing his line of fire, he saw a battalion of some two hundred men, bearing regimental colors and the Stars and Stripes, moving laterally along the hollow intervening between him and the foe.

They deployed rapidly, and went up the opposite hill, towards the stone wall, at a charge, with wild hurrahs. Suddenly the stone wall became alive with rebels; it seemed as if a thousand traitors sprang from behind the cover of the wall, and poured a devouring, deadly discharge full into the bosoms of the charging Union battalion. Half of the battalion fell on the spot, and the rest hurriedly retired before the pursuing rebels.

Meantime Captain Walcott had turned his whole battery in that direction, and the single gun that had lost its men he manned with teamsters and others, and himself took charge of it, aiming and firing. From all his pieces he now poured grape, canister, and shell into the rebel column, while the enemy's sharpshooters from the stone wall still sent their messengers of death at his battery; but under the fire from his pieces the enemy's column wavered; it halted, it broke and fled. The shattered Union battalion in the valley had formed again, and now, with scarcely a hundred men, swept up the hill once more, drove the lingering foe from the stone wall, and sent volley after volley after the rebels, while the shells from Walcott's guns swept far beyond the ridge into the groves among which the traitors were retreating.

The little Union battalion that thus so daringly mounted the hill a second time under cover of Walcott's fire, was the remnant of Colonel Mason's Seventh Maine regiment.

THE FIRST MASSACHUSETTS MAN IN THE WAR. — Colonel Edward W. Hinks, in a letter to the Editor of the Boston Journal, November 17, 1865, makes the following statement: "The particulars given in the article headed 'The first Massachusetts man in the war,' which was copied from the Newburyport Herald into the Journal of this morning, are not strictly in accordance with the facts; and with your indulgence I will attempt — without detracting from the noble record of Captain Bartlett, who for a time served with credit under my command, and who gallantly yielded up his young life upon the bloody field of Antietam — to vindicate the truth of history.

"On Monday, April 15, 1861, at quarter past two o'clock, in reply to an offer of my services made in the morning of that day, I received from Governor Andrew a verbal command to summon the companies of the Eighth regiment, by his authority, to rendezvous at Faneuil Hall at the earliest possible hour. Leaving Boston on the half past two o'clock train, I proceeded to Lynn, and personally notified the commanding officers of the two companies in that city, and from thence telegraphed to Captain Bartlett, at Newburyport, and Captain Centre, of Gloucester, and then drove to Beverly, and summoned the company there, and from thence hastened to Marblehead, where I personally notified the commanding officers of the three Marblehead companies. I found Captain Martin in his slaughter-house with the carcass of a hog just killed and in readiness for the 'scald.' On communicating to the Captain my orders, I advised him to immediately cause the bells of the town to be rung, and to get all the recruits he could. Taking his coat from a peg, he seemed for a moment to hesitate about leaving his business unfinished, and then turning to me, and exclaiming, ' *Dom* the hog,' put the garment on, with his arms yet stained with blood and his shirt sleeves but half rolled down, and with me left the premises to rally his company.

"On Tuesday, April 16, I was directed to remain on duty at Faneuil Hall, and during the forenoon the following named companies arrived there, and reported for duty, to wit:

"1. Companies C, Eighth regiment, forty muskets, Captain Knott V. Martin, and H, Eighth regiment, twenty-six guns, Captain Francis Boardman, both of Marblehead, which place they left at half past seven o'clock A. M., and arrived in Boston at about nine o'clock.

"2. Company D, Fourth regiment, thirty-two muskets, Sergeant H. F. Wales, of Randolph, left home at nine o'clock, and arrived at about ten A. M.

"3. Company B, Eighth regiment, forty muskets, Captain Richard Phillips, of Marblehead, left home at nine o'clock, and arrived in Faneuil Hall about eleven A. M.

"4. Companies D, Eighth regiment, sixty-five muskets, Captain George F. Newhall, and F, Eighth regiment, seventy muskets, Captain James Hudson, both of Lynn, left home at quarter past nine o'clock, and reached Faneuil Hall a little after eleven o'clock, accompanied by Lieutenant-Colonel Timothy Monroe, subsequently Colonel of the Eighth regiment.

"At about twelve o'clock several companies, belonging to different regiments, arrived at Faneuil Hall; and among them was Company A, Eighth regiment, nineteen muskets, Captain A. W. Bartlett, of Newburyport, which company, as I then understood, and have since been informed, left Newburyport at about nine o'clock A. M., and I think that Company E, Eighth regiment, Captain Porter, of Beverly, arrived at about the same time, and that Company G, Captain Centre, of Gloucester, also arrived early in the afternoon of the same day.

"The several companies of the Eighth regiment were recruited during Tuesday and Wednesday, April 16 and 17, to an average of about eighty men.

"The above is substantially a true record, as will appear by reference to the files of the Journal of that date, and is prompted only by a desire to do justice to Captain Martin and the patriotic men of Marblehead, who, on the outbreak of the rebellion, were the first to leave home, the first to arrive in Boston, and subsequently, under my command, the first to leave the yard of the Naval Academy of Annapolis, to seize the depot and railroad, and to repair and relay the track in the march through Maryland to relieve the beleaguered capital of the nation."

THE HERO OF CORINTH. — Private Orrin B. Gould, of company G, Twenty-seventh Ohio, was the hero of the battle of Corinth. The following letter to Governor Tod, from Colonel John W. Fuller, commanding the Ohio Brigade, embodies a history of young Gould's resplendent conduct.

HEADQUARTERS, FIRST BRIGADE, SECOND
DIVISION, ARMY OF THE MISSISSIPPI,
NEAR RIPLEY, MISS., Oct. 9, 1862.

To the Governor of Ohio :

SIR : I have the honor of forwarding to your Excellency the "Battle-Flag" of the Ninth Texas regiment, which was captured by a private of the Twenty-Seventh Ohio infantry, at the battle of Corinth, Oct. 4, 1862.

The rebels, in four close columns, were pressing with gallantry, amounting to recklessness, upon the Ohio brigade, with the evident intention of breaking our lines, when the terrible and incessant fire of our men drove them back in the utmost confusion.

The Sixth Texas bore down upon the left centre of the 27th Ohio, with this flag at the head of their column, and advanced to within six or eight yards of our lines, when Orrin B. Gould, a private of company G, shot down the color-bearer, and rushed forward for the rebel flag. A rebel officer shouted to his men to " save the colors," and at the same moment put a bullet into the breast of Gould ; but the young hero was not to be intimidated. With the flagstaff in his hand and the bullet in his breast, he returned to his regiment, waving the former defiantly in the faces of the enemy.

After the battle, when visiting the hospitals, I found young Gould stretched upon a cot, evidently in great pain. Upon seeing me, his pale face was instantly radiant with smiles, and pointing to his wound, he said, " Colonel, I don't care for this, since I got their flag."

I have the honor to be, your Excellency's obedient servant, JOHN W. FULLER.
Colonel Twenty-seventh Ohio, commanding
First Brigade, Second Division.

Hon. DAVID TOD, Governor of Ohio.

AMBIGUITY. — As the Seventeenth regiment of Massachusetts was marching through Accomac County, Va., with the Stars and Stripes floating above them, a wayside looker-on was heard to say — " I hope it will rain everywhere it goes." There was an instantaneous wish to immolate the author of so inclement an aspiration. They immediately took him to account for it, calling him a " secesh." "Thunder! no, I ain't," said he. "Didn't you say you hoped it might rain wherever it went?" he was asked. "Yes, and so I do; I want it to rule everywhere." They immediately let him go, as the fault was in the dictionary, that made two words to sound alike.

ANECDOTE OF A CONTRABAND. — A Captain in one of the Maine regiments at Port Royal had a colored servant named Tally, who talked very bravely when spoken to about joining the colored brigade. To test his courage, the Captain told him that he was about to visit the main land, and asked Tally if he would go with him and help fight the rebels. Tally, after scratching his head and rubbing his shins a few moments, replied, "Dun know 'bout dat, boss; I'se ober on de main a short spell ago, an' trus' de Lord ter get me ober here, an' he dun it; but I dun dare risk him again, boss."

BROWNLOW passed a high eulogy on General Zollicoffer. Brownlow, who knew him intimately for twenty-five years, says: " He was a man who never wronged an individual out of a cent in his life; never told a lie in his life; as brave a man personally as Andrew Jackson ever was; and the only mean thing I ever knew him to do was to join the Southern Confederacy."

WORTHY OF RECORD. — A letter from an officer who was with Burnside's expedition at the battle of Camden, North Carolina, says:
"I met Colonel Robie, of Binghamton, during the battle, with his cap stuck on the back part of his head, looking the happiest man I ever saw. I remember meeting him as he was leading the centre of the regiment over a heavy ditch, with sword drawn, and hearing him speak to and encourage the boys on. Just then a tremendous volley was poured into the rebel nest. 'That's it!—a good one!' he cried. They returned a perfect shower of grape and canister, tearing through and over us. Colonel Robie's countenance was beaming, and turning to the men, he called out, 'Come on, my children, I'll die with you! Press on, my boys! Now is the time to show yourselves!' And as a rifled shell goes singing by his head, he cries, in his joy, 'Ye gods! isn't this a handsome fight?'"

THE DYING PATRIOT. — A correspondent mentions the following incident of the bombardment of Fort Henry:
"Of course the Essex was thenceforth unmanageable, and slowly drifted down the main channel, and was soon after met by a steamer, which towed her down to the place occupied by the boats before starting. The last ball took effect in the Essex about fifteen minutes before the rebel flag came down, and, consequently, she failed to be in at the death. One of the scalded men, being told by the physician, as they were drifting down, that he could not live, asked how the fight went on. 'They have surrendered,' was the reply. 'Glory to God!' said he, in a feeble voice, and at the same time trying to wave his hand. 'Glory to God!' he repeated; 'I can die now, and don't care!' In a few moments he was dead."

AN INCIDENT OF KIRKSVILLE. — When Colonel McNeil's forces approached within cannon shot of the place, it was apparently deserted. Not a soul could be seen in the streets or about the place. This fact, together with the previous information received, that Porter had drawn up his men west of the town, convinced Colonel McNeil that a trap had been set for him. He inquired of Lieutenant-Colonel Shaffer, of Merrill's Horse, if he would furnish a squad of ten volunteers from his detachment to reconnoitre the town. The number at once came forward, and under command of a Lieutenant they approached the place, — at first at a moderate pace; then, increasing in speed, they dashed boldly and directly into the town. No sooner had they come into musket range, than from every door and window, and from behind every fence, chimney, and building upon the route, poured a fearful tornado of bullets. The leaden messengers of death whizzed around the heroic ten like falling hail. But on they went. Death had no terrors for them. In breathless anxiety the whole army gazed after them as they rapidly receded from sight, accompanied by an incessant roar of guns. On they dashed through the principal streets of the town, straight through, coming out on the open ground on the west side!

Here they were beyond the range of the rebel rifles; they were now, however, between the rebels in the town and the rebels on the west. To return in safety, they must execute a wide circuit to the north or south. But did they choose this method? Nay. But turning southward one street, they plunged once more into the deadly storm — this time in a new street, where the rifles had not been unloaded during their first passage. Forward they went, following their brave leader, fearless and undaunted, straight through the street, back to the army.

One killed, one wounded, and one horse killed, were the only injuries sustained. Nothing short of an almost direct interposition of Providence prevented the death of every rider and horse. A feat of more brilliant, heroic, and sublime daring has not marked the history of the war.

GOOD FOR THE AGUE. — A Southern paper gave the following novel treatment for curing chills:

"It is stated that a soldier of a Mississippi regiment at Pensacola went to his tent and blankets, the other day, to fight through an ague. A bottle of hot water to his feet not being convenient, some of his comrades went out and picked up one of the numerous shells Colonel Brown sent over during the bombardment, heated it at the fire, and put it to bed with the sick man's feet. Unhappily, the shell had lost its cap, but had not exploded. The heat of the camp fire accomplished what Lincoln pyrotechny had failed in, to wit, an explosion. The tent was blown to pieces, and some of the men a little hurt and greatly astonished."

DISCIPLINE. — A captain, in one of the —— regiments, who had been drinking quite freely, met a private of his company in the same condition. The captain ordered him to "halt," and endeavoring in vain to assume a firm position on his feet, and to talk with dignified severity, exclaimed, "Private Smith, I'll give you t'l (hic) four o'clock to gissober in." "Cap'n," replied the soldier, "as you're (hic) — sight drunkerniam, I'll give you t'l five o'clock to gissober in."

A BEAUTIFUL INCIDENT. — There are bright spots in the darkness of war. Deeds of mercy by an enemy shed lustre on our common humanity. They have been commemorated in the heroic song of Homer, and have been eagerly caught and honored in every age by the human heart.

The following was written by a lady of Stockbridge, Massachusetts, and commemorates an incident very touching and beautiful, which rests upon the best authority, and which ought to be known :

"Colonel Mulligan refused his parole at Lexington, and his wife resolved to share his captivity. Accordingly she left her infant, fourteen months old, in the care of one of the strongest secessionist women in the town. That woman assumed the charge of the little child, and dressed it in the captured American flag."

BEAUREGARD'S BELLS. — At East Boston, Massachusetts, on the 29th of July, 1862, four hundred and eighteen bells, sent to that place by Major-General Butler, were sold at public auction. These bells were sent in to New Orleans by Southerners, in response to Beauregard's call for brass with which to fabricate cannon for use against Union men. When Butler captured New Orleans, these fell into his hands, and Boston became the recipient of the trophies.

There were bells from church spires that had called the lords of the manor to Sabbath prayers; bells from plantation sheds that once summoned the sable bondmen to unrequited labor; school bells, and steamboat bells, and factory bells, large and small; many of them in the best order and of the finest tones.

These four hundred bells bore upon them a Southern tribute to Northern labor. There were no ancient bells, no bells of historic worth, no old Spanish or French relics — those the Southerners had kept, and contributed instead the products of Northern skill. With only a dozen exceptions, the bells had upon their rims or tops the names of Northern makers — of the Buckeye Works of Cincinnati, the Allaire Works of New York, of Fulton Foundery, Pittsburg, and of the founders of Troy, of Louisville, and other places. How suggestive is all this, and what an added interest it gives to the poet's words !

O, swing them merrily to and fro ;
They'll not boom with a traitorous blow.

Shaped into cannon, not one — they lie
Eloquent tokens of victory.

Sing out, O bells, on the summer wind ;
Farragut's name with thy music twined.

The Crescent slips from the serpent's hold,
Though bound in many an angry fold.

Oft ye have pealed for the bridal morn,
Tolled for souls into mystery born,

Roused, on plantation, master and slave ;
Yet, ye were doomed, till won by the Brave.

O, ring ere long for the shout of peace ;
Jubilant ring when this strife shall cease.

Ring out Rebellion, dark as a pall ;
Ring for Stars and Stripes floating o'er all.

Laugh out on the Northern winds, I pray ;
Peal out, for this is your marriage day.

Wedded to Freedom, 'mid hills and dells,
Ye are no longer Beauregard's bells.

Previous to the sale, Mr. N. A. Thompson, the auctioneer, made a most eloquent and patriotic speech, which was warmly applauded, showing how deeply in earnest the South were in this war, as was instanced in the bells before us, and calling for an equal earnestness on our part, if we would hope to preserve our country in its integrity.

CHRISTMAS WITH THE SLAVES. — A letter writer at Port Royal, South Carolina, gives the following account of the way in which the slaves kept the first Christmas after the Proclamation of Emancipation :

"Christmas Eve was celebrated by the colored people at General Drayton's plantation. About half past eleven o'clock a bell was rung, and precisely at twelve a pine fire was kindled in front of the cabin where the meeting was to be held. They called the festival a serenade to Jesus. One of the leaders, of which there were three, was dressed in a red coat with brass buttons, wearing white gloves. The females wore turbans made of cotton handkerchiefs. All ages were represented, from the child of one year to the old man of ninety.

"The first exercise consisted in singing hymns

and spiritual songs, among which were those beginning, 'Salvation! O, the joyful sound;' 'The voice of free grace;' 'Come, humble sinner, in whose breast;' 'O, poor sinner, can't stand de fire, can't stand de fire in dat great day;' and a Christmas song containing a medley of everything the fruitful mind of the leader could suggest, with the refrain, 'We'll wait till Jesus comes.' One of the leaders lined the hymns, and though none of them could read, it was remarkable with what correctness they gave the words. Their Scripture quotations were also correct and appropriate, not only having the exact words, but naming the chapter and verse where they could be found.

"After singing for some time, a prayer-meeting was held. The prayers were fervent and powerful, and when an allusion would be made to the soldiers who had come from their distant homes, in the North country, to 'help and save de poor slave, and, like Jesus, bring dem good tidings of great joy,' a shout went up that sent its notes on the still night air to the distant pickets in the surrounding pines. When asked, as they could not read, how they could quote the Scriptures, they replied: 'We have ears, massa, and when de preacher give out his texts, den we remembers and says dem over and over till we never forgets dem; dat's de way, massa, we poor people learns de Word of God.'

"The next exercise consisted of speaking and singing, at intervals. While one was speaking, another would take a blazing pine torch from the fire, and hold it up, so that all might see the speaker. At two o'clock, a recess was had, and all were invited to partake of coffee, which luxury they can now purchase without any difficulty, as they have plenty of money, obtained of the soldiers for vegetables and poultry.

"After this came what they called the shouting exercise. It was introduced by the beating of time by three or four, with the feet. Soon the whole company formed into a circle, and commenced jumping and singing to the time and tune of

'Say, brothers, will you meet me,
Say, brothers, will you meet me,
Say, brothers, will you meet me,
On Canaan's happy shore?'

This was continued until the most fertile imagination was exhausted, embracing an invitation to sisters, soldiers, preachers, &c., to meet them on Canaan's happy shore.

"Never did these poor slaves celebrate a Christmas Eve under such circumstances before. Whatever may be their future, they are now, 'to all intents, purposes, and constructions whatever,' free; that they may 'choose it rather' is beyond question more certain."

FIGHTING MINISTERS. — The editor of a religious newspaper says that a Louisiana clergyman, writing over his own name, remarks:

"I am one of five ministers, of three different denominations, in a single company, armed for the defence of our rights and liberties, three of whom

are between fifty and sixty years old. And I tell you in candor, and in the fear of God, that if you or any of the *brethren* who have urged on this diabolical war, come on with the invading army, I would slay you with as hearty a good-will, and with as clear a conscience, as I would the midnight assassin.

"In the name of God, I conjure you, *let us alone*. I speak the spontaneous sentiment of every Southern heart — man, woman, and child. *We will never submit*. We will shed the last drop of blood in defence of our rights. You are my enemy, and I am yours."

INCIDENTS OF FORT DONELSON. — "On the two battle-grounds the scenes were fearful. The snow was so thoroughly saturated with blood, that it seemed like red mud as you walked around in it. Men writhing in agony, with their feet, arms, or legs torn off, many begging to be killed, and one poor fellow was delirious, who laughed hideously as he pointed to a mutilated stump, which an hour ago had been his arm. One old man, dressed in homespun, with hair white as snow, was sitting, moaning feebly, against a wall. A fragment of shell had struck him upon the head, bruising off his scalp as if detached from the skull by a knife, and causing it to hang suspended from the forehead over his face. Instances of suffering were on every hand, and added to the revolting horrors of the two fields. A young Southern officer, who gave his name as Charles C. Seymour, of Memphis, was found on the side of a ravine. A ball had passed through his breast, and he had a finger upon the wound, vainly endeavoring to stop the life which was issuing out. He gave to one of us a little square block of dark wood, set in a frame of gold, and requested it to be sent to his mother in Memphis. Some event long past, a hidden history perhaps, was connected with the strange memento."

A UNION MAN. — During the combined expedition of General Sherman and Admiral Porter, up the Sunflower River, Steele's Bayou, and the Black Bayou, which failed in its purpose, Admiral Porter's guide was a negro, the same who carried the despatch to General Sherman through the rebel lines. When the national forces arrived in the midst of the rebel lines, a scouting party came suddenly upon a house which belonged to the sheriff of the county from whom the negro had escaped. He ordered his old servant to get his horse, as the Yankees were coming. "Couldn't tink of it — wouldn't do it for a tousand dollars. Ise a Union man, now, massa." The horse was not got, but the sheriff was.

THE MISSILES AT ANTIETAM. — Broken railroad iron and blacksmiths' tools, hammers, chisels, &c., were fired from rebel cannon. Some of these missiles made a peculiar noise, resembling "which away, which away," by which the national troops came to distinguish them from the regular shot and shell, and as they heard them approaching, would cry, "Turkey! turkey coming!" and fall flat to avoid them. An artillerist, a German, when he saw the tools falling around him, exclaimed, "My Got! we shall have the blacksmith's shop to come next!"

DIRGE

FOR ONE WHO FELL IN BATTLE.

Room for a soldier! lay him in the clover;
He loved the fields, and they shall be his cover;
Make his mound with hers who called him once her
    lover;
    Where the rain may rain upon it,
    Where the sun may shine upon it,
    Where the lamb hath lain upon it,
    And the bee will dine upon it.

Bear him to no dismal tomb under city churches;
Take him to the fragrant fields, by the silver
    birches,
Where the whip-poor-will will mourn, where the
    oriole perches;
    Make his mound with sunshine on it,
    Where the bee will dine upon it,
    Where the lamb hath lain upon it,
    And the rain will rain upon it.

Busy as the busy bee, his rest should be the clover;
Gentle as the lamb was he, and the fern should be
    his cover;
Fern and rosemary shall grow my soldier's pillow
    over;
    Where the rain may rain upon it,
    Where the sun may shine upon it,
    Where the lamb hath lain upon it,
    And the bee will dine upon it.

Sunshine in his heart, the rain would come full
    often
Out of those tender eyes which ever more did
    soften;
He never could look cold till we saw him in his
    coffin.
    Make his mound with sunshine on it,
    Where the wind may sigh upon it,
    Where the moon may stream upon it,
    And memory shall dream upon it.

"Captain," or "Colonel," — whatever invocation
Suit our hymn the best, no matter for thy station, —
On thy grave the rain shall fall from the eyes of a
    mighty nation!
    Long as the sun doth shine upon it
    Shall grow the goodly pine upon it,
    Long as the stars do gleam upon it
    Shall memory come to dream upon it.

INCIDENT OF DRANESVILLE. — During a skirmish near Dranesville, Virginia, Colonel Jackson, of the Ninth Pennsylvania regiment, left his negro servant in charge of his horse, while he advanced towards the enemy. Seeing two rebels, who had discharged their muskets, approaching him, the boy drew his carbine and threatened to shoot them if they did not surrender at once. This they did, and marched before him to the camp.

A CONTRABAND INCIDENT. — A correspondent, writing from Munfordville, Kentucky, gives the following:

"While on the other side of the river my attention was attracted to a quiet group coming up the hill. First were two intelligent-looking contrabands, next a little 'go-cart,' drawn by a mule, in which was a female slave and about a dozen little negroes, carefully wrapped in sundry and divers coats. An Uncle Tom sort of a chap, with a Miss Dinah, brought up the rear. As they came by I addressed Tom:

"'Well, Uncle, where did your party come from?'

"'We's from de town, dar, sah.'

"'And where are you going?'

"'Gwine home, sah.'

"'Then you do not live in the village?'

"'No; we lib right ober yonder, 'bout a mile; de secesh druv us from home.'

"'Ah! well, now stop a minute, and tell me all about it.'

"'Dat I do, sure, massa. Jim [to the leader of the mule cart], you go on wid de wagon, an' I kotch you fore you gits home. Now, I tells you, massa, all about 'um. My massa am Union, an' so is all de niggers. Yesterday, massa wor away in de town, an' de firs' 'ting we know, 'long come two or free hundred ob dem seceshers, on horses, an' lookin' like cutfroats. Golly, but de gals wor scared. Jus' right back ob us wor de Union soldiers — God bless [reverentially], for dey keep de secesh from killin' nigger. De gals know dat, an' when dey see de secesh comin' dey pitch de little nigger in de go-cart, an' den we all broke for de Union soldiers.'

"'So you are not afraid of the Union soldiers?'

"'God bless you, massa, nebber. Nigger gets ahind dem Union soldiers, secesh nebber gets 'um. Secesh steal nigger — Union man nebber steal 'um. Dat's a fac', massa.'

"And, with a smile on his face, the clever old darky bade me good morning, and trotted on after the go-cart."

BORDER SCOUTS. — Among the most active and daring of the Union scouts in the Southwest were four young men, known as the Norrises and Breedins. Acquainted with every crossroad and by-way, they scoured the country for a radius of seventy-miles south and east of Fort Scott. Their very names were a terror to secession, and every plan that ingenuity could devise was resorted to to effect their destruction. At one time the younger Norris was wounded in a skirmish, near Shanghai, in which six, out of a party of twelve, under Lieutenant Lewis, met with a similar fate while contending against treble their number of the enemy. He was soon in the saddle again, however, and ready for the field. These men formerly lived in Golden Grove, Missouri, fifteen miles beyond Lamar, in the direction of Greenfield. The elder Breedin had a wife and family living there; and being anxious to visit them, he took with him a party of six well-armed and determined men, and went down. Their arrival in the settlement became known to some of his secession neighbors, and a plan was instantly set on foot to "take them in." On the third night, being apprehensive of an attack, they assembled at a house in the settlement, where, after making all necessary preparations, they betook themselves to sleep. About two o'clock they were awakened by the approach of the enemy, and quietly took their places behind the fence surrounding the house, ready to give the foe a warm reception. The secession force approached to within thirty yards, halted, and most of them dismounted for the attack. "Now," said the Captain, "creep up cautiously, and when I fire the signal gun, make a rush for the house and surround it." Breedin and his comrades lay quietly in their corners until the enemy were within a few yards of them, when they delivered their fire with terrible effect, just as the secesh Captain was about to fire his "signal gun." A prisoner, whom the attacking party had with them, shouted as he heard the discharge, "Gentlemen, there's a good many signal guns there." For a few minutes the skirmish was a hot one, when four of the men, having emptied all their rifles and pistols, and fearing that they might be surrounded, retired past the house into the timber, and made their way to Fort Scott, on foot, leaving Breedin, Carpenter, and Jones still at the fence fighting. Jones had nothing but a musket, but he made every shot tell. Carpenter, a boy of eighteen or nineteen years, had left his revolver in the house. After firing his Sharpe's rifle, he threw it down, ran into the house, got his revolver, and coolly closing the door after him, returned to his post at the fence. Astonished at the telling and rapid fire from the fence, the enemy became panic-stricken, and rushing to their horses with loud cries of "We're whipped," "We can't stand the minies," &c., fled in utter confusion on the Greenfield road, leaving two dead and six wounded — two of whom afterwards died on the field. They continued their flight about three miles, when the Captain succeeded in stopping a few of them; but the barking of some dogs started them again, and no more halts were made until they reached Greenfield. A messenger was immediately sent to Price for a regiment of troops to come and drive Breedin out of the country.

Eight horses were left by the enemy in their flight; these were captured by Breedin and his companions, and after scouring the country two days longer, they returned to Fort Scott, bringing two prisoners, the eight secession horses, and the horses left by their own party. The distance is about seventy miles. The secession party, by their own account, numbered not less than one hundred and thirty men.

WHAT ARE TRUMPS?

BY JAMES R. RANDALL.*

Not Diamonds! treason breaks bedight
Beyond their leprosy of light,
And all that's chivalric and fair
Is gorgoned by their stony glare.
Not Diamonds! for the glut of gain
Is but the Diamond's frosty brain,
Bespread in golden beads of rain.
Kentucky feels the golden gust enow;
It galleth her bewildered brow.
My Maryland! ah, where art thou?
No! Freedom is not won with them.
Down, Diamond! down, perfidious gem!

Not Hearts! — let's keep our Hearts at home;
They'll wreck us 'mid the battle-foam.
We want no Hearts to marshal forth
Against the Vikings of the North.
No! we will make reverberate
The death-dirge of the fools of Fate.
Hearts, ye have ever thugged and swirled
The hurly-burlies of the world!
If Sherman comes to cut our throats,
What then? Why, send his horses oats!
Pooh, pooh! he did not couch the blow
Which laid poor Beaufort sacked below.
The darkies did it all; just so!
If Grant swoops down o'er Belmont plain,
And cumbers bluff and wood with slain, —
Good fellow! Swill him with champagne!
Hearts, ye would gild the robber's bier!
Down! down! ye are betrayers here!

Not Spades! we are but too expert
In technicalities of dirt.
Scarp, redan, bastion, and lunette
But make our native valor fret.
If Courage imps an cyrle pitch,
Dear Courage, you must dig a ditch.
With bloody signs the welkin's big —
Portentous symbols! we must dig!
Sangrado, M. D., famed in Seville,
Dosed generations to the Devil.
He killed, like any Pottowatomie,
With tepid water and phlebotomy.
He knew his shocking thaumaturgy
Was death to laymen and to clergy.
But then the Doctor wrote, with travail,
A tome, to prove, above all cavil,
That his curriculum — his plan —
Was Gilead's balm to damaged man;
And not by any hook or crook
Would old Sangrado snub his book.
O, "burn the books," and down mud-lumps!
We scoop our graves when Spades are trumps!

* Mr. Randall's poetry is too curiously phrased to please the lover of plain, pure English; but his tribute to the King of Trumps — nay, the very Ace of all the Face Cards in the Pack of War — is so well-timed, and so full of sensible suggestions to the dirt-diggers, dilly-dalliers, delayers, defensive policists, and do-nothing-ites of the West Point school, that we are glad to insert it in our Table. Price may be snubbed by the powers that be; but the poets will immortalize him. He may be defeated; but the people will love him, exalt him, honor him, and wear him forever in their heart of hearts, because he dared to do. — *Southern paper.*

Yes, Clubs! One's inspiration jumps,
And cuts a caper! Clubs and trumps!
Di'monds will not appease the dead
That shake beneath the brigand's tread,
Under the sands of Hilton Head.
Lo! Carolina is ablaze!
Bold beauty! loveliest of our days!
Her fruitful fields one scorching pyre —
She's shrined the very Queen of Fire!
Hearts! would ye give invaders tears?
Clubs are the Hearts for buccaneers.
Spades! would ye nest them in the earth,
Rotting the spring's emblossomed birth?
No! let the buzzard kiss his kind,
As they bloat in the nostrils of the wind;
Each corpse "a black flag," mightier far
Than the rags that token the hell of war!

Lo! for a trump to beat them all —
A trump beyond a system's thrall.
Advance, thou worthiest and best —
Our grim old Scipio of the West!
Thou wast not suckled in the schools;
But thou canst conquer in spite of rules.
'Gainst thee Red-Tape is all aglow;
But mark his legions! how they go,
Hounding the haunches of the foe!
With havoc still the clouds are dun
That crouched o'er fallen Lexington;
Yet cleaves his ever-sheathless blade
'Yond Osage and the Gasconade,
Soon will the thunder of his bands
Boom through the lusty prairie lands,
Thick with the lightning of their brands.
On, hero! for the Southern heart
Knows thee and loves thee as thou art!
Thou Trump of Trumps! anointed thrice! —
Our Sword and Buckler — *Sterling Price!*

THE STORY OF ANTIETAM.

By George W. Smalley.

Battle-Field of Antietam, }
Wednesday Evening, Sept. 17, 1862. }

Fierce and desperate battle between two hundred thousand men has raged since daylight, yet night closes on an uncertain field. It is the greatest fight since Waterloo, all over the field contested with an obstinacy equal even to Waterloo. If not wholly a victory to-night, I believe it is the prelude to a victory to-morrow. But what can be foretold of the future of a fight in which from five in the morning till seven at night the best troops of the continent have fought without decisive result?

After the brilliant victory near Middletown, General McClellan pushed forward his army rapidly, and reached Keedysville with three corps on Monday night. That march has already been described. On the day following the two armies faced each other idly until night. Artillery was busy at intervals, once in the morning opening with spirit, and continuing for half an hour with vigor, till the rebel battery, as usual, was silenced.

McClellan was on the hill where Benjamin's battery was stationed, and found himself suddenly under a rather heavy fire. It was still uncertain whether the rebels were retreating or reënforcing. Their batteries would remain in position in either case; and as they had withdrawn nearly all their troops from view, there was only the doubtful indication of columns of dust to the rear.

On the evening of Tuesday, Hooker was ordered to cross the Antietam Creek with his corps, and, feeling the left of the enemy, to be ready to attack next morning. During the day of apparent inactivity, McClellan, it may be supposed, had been maturing his plan of battle, of which Hooker's movement was one development.

The position on either side was peculiar. When Richardson advanced on Monday, he found the enemy deployed and displayed in force on a crescent-shaped ridge, the outline of which followed more or less exactly the course of Antietam Creek. Their lines were then forming, and the revelation of force in front of the ground which they really intended to hold, was probably meant to delay our attack until their arrangements to receive it were complete.

During that day they kept their troops exposed, and did not move them even to avoid the artillery-fire, which must have been occasionally annoying. Next morning the lines and columns which had darkened cornfields and hill-crests had been withdrawn. Broken and wooded ground behind the sheltering hills concealed the rebel masses. What from our front looked like only a narrow summit fringed with woods was a broad tableland of forest and ravine; cover for troops everywhere, nowhere easy access for an enemy. The smoothly sloping surface in front and the sweeping crescent of slowly mingling lines was all a delusion. It was all a rebel stronghold beyond.

Under the base of these hills runs the deep stream called Antietam Creek, fordable only at distant points. Three bridges cross it; one on the Hagerstown road, one on the Sharpsburg pike, one to the left in a deep recess of steeply-falling hills. Hooker passed the first to reach the ford by which he crossed, and it was held by Pleasanton with a reserve of cavalry during the battle. The second was close under the rebel centre, and no way important to yesterday's fight. At the third Burnside attacked, and finally crossed. Between the first and third lay most of the battle-lines. They stretched four miles from right to left.

Unaided attack in front was impossible. McClellan's forces lay behind low, disconnected ridges in front of the rebel summits, all, or nearly all, unwooded. They gave some cover for artillery, and guns were therefore massed on the centre. The enemy had the Shepherdstown road, and the Hagerstown and Williamsport road, both open to him in rear for retreat. Along one or the other, if beaten, he must fly. This, among other reasons, determined, perhaps, the plan of battle which McClellan finally resolved upon. The plan was generally as follows: Hooker was to cross on the right, establish himself on the enemy's left if possible, flanking his position, and to open the fight. Sumner, Franklin, and Mansfield were to send their forces also to the right, co-operating with and sustaining Hooker's attack, while advancing also nearer the centre. The heavy work in the centre was left mostly to the batteries, Porter massing his infantry supports in the hollows. On the left, Burnside was to carry the bridge already referred to, advancing then by a road which enters the pike at Sharpsburg, turning at once the rebel flank, and destroying his line of retreat. Porter and Sykes were held in reserve. It is obvious that the complete success of a plan contemplating widely divergent movements of separate corps, must largely depend on accurate timing — that the attacks should be simultaneous, and not successive.

Hooker moved Tuesday afternoon at four, crossing the creek at a ford above the bridge and well to the right, without opposition. Fronting southwest, his line advanced not quite on the rebel flank, but overlapping and threatening it. Turning off from the road after passing the stream, he sent forward cavalry skirmishers straight into the woods and over the fields beyond. Rebel pickets withdrew slowly before them, firing scattering and harmless shots. Turning again to the left, the cavalry went down on the rebel flank, coming suddenly close to a battery which met them with unexpected grape and canister. It being the nature of cavalry to retire before batteries, this company loyally followed the law of its being, and came swiftly back without pursuit.

Artillery was sent to the front, infantry was rapidly deployed, and skirmishers went out in front and on either flank. The corps moved forward compactly. Hooker, as usual, reconnoitring in person. They came at last to an open grass-sown field enclosed on two sides with woods, protected on the right by a hill, and entered through a cornfield in the rear. Skirmishers penetrating these woods were instantly met by rebel shots, but held their ground, and, as soon as supported, advanced and cleared the timber. Beyond, on the left and in front, volleys of musketry opened heavily, and a battle seemed to have begun a little sooner than it was expected.

General Hooker formed his lines with precision and without hesitation. Rickett's division went into the woods on the left in force. Meade, with the Pennsylvania reserves, formed in the centre. Doubleday was sent out on the right, planting his guns on the hill, and opening at once on a rebel battery that began to enfilade the central line. It was already dark, and the rebel position could only be discovered by the flashes of their guns. They pushed forward boldly on the right, after losing ground on the other flank, but made no attempt to regain their hold on the woods. The fight flashed, and glimmered, and faded, and finally went out in the dark.

Hooker had found out what he wanted to know. When the firing ceased, the hostile lines lay close to each other — their pickets so near that six rebels were captured during the night. It was inevitable that the fight should recommence at daylight. Neither side had suffered considerable loss; it was a skirmish, not a battle. "We are through for to-night, gentlemen," remarked the General; "but to-morrow we fight the battle that will decide the fate of the republic."

Not long after the firing ceased, it sprang up again on the left. General Hooker, who had taken his headquarters in a barn, which had been nearly the focus of the rebel artillery, was out at once. First came rapid and unusually frequent picket-shots, then several heavy volleys. The General listened a moment, and smiled grimly. "We have no troops there. The rebels are shooting each other. It is Fair Oaks over again." So everybody lay down again, but all the night through there were frequent alarms.

McClellan had been informed of the night's work, and of the certainties awaiting the dawn. Sumner was ordered to move his corps at once, and was expected to be on the ground at daylight. From the extent of the rebel lines developed in the evening, it was plain that they had gathered their whole army behind the heights, and were waiting for the shock.

The battle began with the dawn. Morning found both armies just as they had slept, almost close enough to look into each other's eyes. The left of Meade's reserves and the right of Ricketts' line became engaged at nearly the same moment, one with artillery, the other with infantry. A battery was almost immediately pushed forward beyond the central woods, over a ploughed field, near the top of the slope where the cornfield began. On this open field, in the corn beyond, and in the woods, which stretched forward into the broad fields, like a promontory into the ocean, were the hardest and deadliest struggles of the day.

For half an hour after the battle had grown to its full strength, the line of fire swayed neither way. Hooker's men were fully up to their work. They saw their General everywhere in front, never away from the fire; and all the troops believed in their commander, and fought with a will. Two thirds of them were the same men who, under McDowell, had broken at Manassas.

The half hour passed; the rebels began to give way a little — only a little; but at the first indication of a receding fire, Forward, was the word, and on went the line with a cheer and a rush. Back across the cornfield, leaving dead and wounded behind them, over the fence, and across the road, and then back again into the dark woods, which closed around them, went the retreating rebels.

Meade and his Pennsylvanians followed hard and fast — followed till they came within easy range of the woods, among which they saw their beaten enemy disappearing — followed still, with another cheer, and flung themselves against the cover.

But out of those gloomy woods came suddenly and heavily terrible volleys — volleys which smote, and bent, and broke in a moment that eager front, and hurled them swiftly back for half the distance they had won. Not swiftly, nor in panic, any farther. Closing up their shattered lines, they came slowly away; a regiment where a brigade had been; hardly a brigade where a whole division had been victorious. They had met at the woods the first volleys of musketry from fresh troops — had met them and returned them till their line had yielded and gone down before the weight of fire, and till their ammunition was exhausted.

In ten minutes the fortune of the day seemed to have changed; it was the rebels now who were advancing, pouring out of the woods in endless lines, sweeping through the cornfield from which their comrades had just fled. Hooker sent in his nearest brigade to meet them, but it could not do the work. He called for another. There was nothing close enough, unless he took it from his right. His right might be in danger if it was weakened; but his centre was already threatened with annihilation. Not hesitating one moment, he sent to Doubleday, "Give me your best brigade instantly."

The best brigade came down the hill to the right on the run, went through the timber in front, through a storm of shot and bursting shell, and crashing limbs, over the open field beyond, and straight into the cornfield, passing, as they went, the fragments of three brigades shattered by the rebel fire, and streaming to the rear. They passed by Hooker, whose eyes lighted as he saw these veteran troops, led by a soldier whom he knew he could trust. "I think they will hold it," he said.

General Hartsuff took his troops very steadily, but, now that they were under fire, not hurriedly, up the hill from which the cornfield begins to descend, and formed them on the crest. Not a man who was not in full view — not one who bent before the storm. Firing at first in volleys, they fired then at will with wonderful rapidity and effect. The whole line crowned the hill, and stood out darkly against the sky, but lighted and shrouded ever in flame and smoke. They were the Twelfth and Thirteenth Massachusetts, and another regiment which I cannot remember — old troops all of them.

There for half an hour they held the ridge, unyielding in purpose, exhaustless in courage. There were gaps in the line, but it nowhere bent. Their General was severely wounded early in the fight, but they fought on. Their supports did not come — they determined to win without them. They began to go down the hill and into the corn; they did not stop to think that their ammunition was nearly gone; they were there to win that field, and they won it. The rebel line for the second time fled through the corn and into the woods. I cannot tell how few of Hartsuff's brigade were left when the work was done; but it was done. There was no more gallant, determined, heroic fighting in all this desperate day. General Hartsuff is very severely wounded; but I do not believe he counts his success too dearly purchased.

The crisis of the fight at this point had arrived. Ricketts' division, vainly endeavoring to advance, and exhausted by the effort, had fallen back. Part of Mansfield's corps was ordered in to their relief; but Mansfield's troops came back again

and their General was mortally wounded. The left nevertheless was too extended to be turned, and too strong to be broken. Ricketts sent word he could not advance, but could hold his ground. Doubleday had kept his guns at work on the right, and had finally silenced a rebel battery that for half an hour had poured in a galling enfilading fire along Hooker's central line. There were woods in front of Doubleday's hill which the rebels held, but so long as those guns pointed towards them they did not care to attack.

With his left, then, able to take care of itself, with his right impregnable, with two brigades of Mansfield still fresh and coming rapidly up, and with his centre a second time victorious, General Hooker determined to advance. Orders were sent to Crawford and Gordon — the two Mansfield brigades — to move forward at once, the batteries in the centre were ordered to advance; the whole line was called on, and the General himself went forward.

To the right of the cornfield and beyond it was a point of woods. Once carried and firmly held, it was the key of the position. Hooker determined to take it. He rode out in front of his farthest troops on a hill to examine the ground for a battery. At the top he dismounted and went forward on foot, completed his reconnoissance, returned, and remounted. The musketry fire from the point of woods was all the while extremely hot. As he put his foot in the stirrup a fresh volley of rifle bullets came whizzing by. The tall, soldierly figure of the General, the white horse which he rode, the elevated place where he was, all made him a most dangerously conspicuous mark. So he had been all day, riding often without a staff officer or an orderly near him, — all sent off on urgent duty, — visible everywhere on the field. The rebel bullets had followed him all day, but they had not hit him, and he would not regard them.

Remounting on this hill, he had not ridden five steps when he was struck in the foot by a ball. Three men were shot down at the same moment by his side. The air was alive with bullets. He kept on his horse a few minutes, though the wound was severe and excessively painful, and would not dismount till he had given his last order to advance. He was himself in the very front. Swaying unsteadily on his horse, he turned in his seat to look about him. "There is a regiment to the right. Order it forward! Crawford and Gordon are coming up. Tell them to carry those woods and hold them — and it is our fight!"

It was found that the bullet had passed completely through his foot. The surgeon, who examined it on the spot, could give no opinion whether bones were broken; but it was afterwards ascertained that though grazed they were not fractured. Of course the severity of the wound made it impossible for him to keep the field, which he believed already won, so far as it belonged to him to win it. It was nine o'clock. The fight had been furious since five. A large part of his command was broken, but with his right still untouched, and with Crawford's and Gordon's brigades just up, above all, with the advance of the whole central line, which the men had heard ordered with cheers, and with a regiment already on the edge of the woods he wanted, he might well leave the field, thinking the battle was won — that *his* battle was won, for I am writing only about the attack on the rebel left.

I see no reason why I should disguise my admiration of General Hooker's bravery and soldierly ability. Remaining nearly all the morning on the right, I could not help seeing the sagacity and promptness of his movements, how completely his troops were kept in hand, how devotedly they trusted him, how keen was his insight into the battle, how every opportunity was seized, and every reverse was checked and turned into another success. I say this the more unreservedly, because I have no personal relation whatever with him, never saw him till the day before the fight, and don't like his politics or opinions in general. But what are politics in such a battle?

Sumner arrived just as Hooker was leaving, and assumed command. Crawford and Gordon had gone into the woods, and were holding them stoutly against heavy odds. As I rode over towards the left I met Sumner at the head of his column, advancing rapidly through the timber, opposite where Crawford was fighting. The veteran General was riding alone in the forest, far ahead of his leading brigade, his hat off, his gray hair, and beard, and mustache strangely contrasting with the fire in his eyes and his martial air, as he hurried on to where the bullets were thickest.

Sedgwick's division was in advance, moving forward to support Crawford and Gordon. Rebel reënforcements were approaching also, and the struggle for the roads was again to be renewed. Sumner sent forward two divisions — Richardson and French — on the left. Sedgwick, moving in column of divisions through the woods in rear, deployed and advanced in line over the cornfield. There was a broad interval between him and the nearest division, and he saw that if the rebel line were complete, his own division was in immediate danger of being flanked. But his orders were to advance, and those are the orders which a soldier — and Sedgwick is every inch a soldier — loves best to hear.

To extend his own front as far as possible, he ordered the Thirty-fourth New York to move by the left flank. The manœuvre was attempted under a fire of the greatest intensity, and the regiment broke. At the same moment, the enemy, perceiving their advantage, came round on that flank. Crawford was obliged to give way on the right, and his troops, pouring in confusion through the ranks of Sedgwick's advance brigade, threw it into disorder, and back on the second and third lines. The enemy advanced, their fire increasing.

General Sedgwick was three times wounded, in the shoulder, leg, and wrist, but he persisted in remaining on the field so long as there was a chance of saving it. His Adjutant-General, Major Sedgwick, bravely rallying and trying to re-form

the troops, was shot through the body, the bullet lodging in the spine, and fell from his horse. Severe as the wound is, it is probably not mortal. Lieutenant Howe, of General Sedgwick's staff, endeavored vainly to rally the Thirty-fourth New York. They were badly cut up, and would not stand. Half their officers were killed or wounded, their colors shot to pieces, the color-sergeant killed, every one of the color-guard wounded. Only thirty-two were afterwards got together.

The Fifteenth Massachusetts went into action with seventeen officers and nearly six hundred men. Nine officers were killed or wounded, and some of the latter are prisoners. Captain Simons, Captain Saunders of the sharpshooters, Lieutenant Derby, and Lieutenant Berry are killed. Captain Bartlett and Captain Jocelyn, Lieutenant Spurr, Lieutenant Gale, and Lieutenant Bradley are wounded. One hundred and thirty-four men were the only remains that could be collected of this splendid regiment.

General Dana was wounded. General Howard, who took command of the division after General Sedgwick was disabled, exerted himself to restore order; but it could not be done there. General Sumner ordered the line to be re-formed. The test was too severe for volunteer troops under such a fire. Sumner himself attempted to arrest the disorder, but to little purpose. Lieutenant-Colonel Revere and Captain Audenried, of his staff, were wounded severely, but not dangerously. It was impossible to hold the position. General Sumner withdrew the division to the rear, and once more the cornfield was abandoned to the enemy.

French sent word he could hold his ground. Richardson, while gallantly leading a regiment under a heavy fire, was severely wounded in the shoulder. General Meagher was wounded at the head of his brigade. The loss in general officers was becoming frightful.

At one o'clock affairs on the right had a gloomy look. Hooker's troops were greatly exhausted, and their General away from the field. Mansfield's were no better. Sumner's command had lost heavily, but two of his divisions were still comparatively fresh. Artillery was yet playing vigorously in front, though the ammunition of many of the batteries was entirely exhausted, and they had been compelled to retire.

Doubleday held the right inflexibly. Sumner's headquarters were now in the narrow field where, the night before, Hooker had begun the fight. All that had been gained in front had been lost. The enemy's batteries, which, if advanced and served vigorously, might have made sad work with the closely-massed troops, were fortunately either partially disabled or short of ammunition. Sumner was confident that he could hold his own, but another advance was out of the question. The enemy, on the other hand, seemed to be too much exhausted to attack.

At this crisis Franklin came up with fresh troops and formed on the left. Slocum, commanding one division of the corps, was sent forward along the slopes lying under the first ranges of the rebel hills, while Smith, with the other division, was ordered to retake the cornfields and woods which all day had been so hotly contested. It was done in the handsomest style. His Maine and Vermont regiments, and the rest, went forward on the run, and cheering as they went, swept like an avalanche through the cornfields, fell upon the woods, cleared them in ten minutes, and held them. They were not again retaken.

The field and its ghastly harvest which the Reaper had gathered in those fatal hours remained finally with us. Four times it had been lost and won. The dead are strewn so thickly that as you ride over it you cannot guide your horse's steps too carefully. Pale and bloody faces are everywhere upturned. They are sad and terrible; but there is nothing which makes one's heart beat so quickly as the imploring look of sorely wounded men, who beckon wearily for help which you cannot stay to give.

General Smith's attack was so sudden that his success was accomplished with no great loss. He had gained a point, however, which compelled him to expect every moment an attack, and to hold which, if the enemy again brought up reserves, would task his best energies and best troops. But the long strife, the heavy losses, incessant fighting over the same ground repeatedly lost and won inch by inch, and more than all, perhaps, the fear of Burnside on the left and Porter in front, held the enemy in check. For two or three hours there was a lull even in the cannonade on the right, which hitherto had been incessant. McClellan had been over on the field after Sumner's repulse, but had speedily returned to his headquarters. Sumner again sent word that he was able to hold his position, but could not advance with his own corps.

Meantime where was Burnside, and what was he doing? On the right, where I had spent the day until two o'clock, little was known of the general fortunes of the field. We had heard Porter's guns in the centre, but nothing from Burnside on the left. The distance was, perhaps, too great to distinguish the sound of his artillery from Porter's. There was no immediate prospect of more fighting on the right, and I left the field which all day long had seen the most obstinate contest of the war, and rode over to McClellan's headquarters. The different battle-fields were shut out from each other's view, but all partially visible from the central hill, which General McClellan had occupied during the day. But I was more than ever impressed, on returning, with the completely deceitful appearance of the ground the rebels had chosen, when viewed from the front.

Hooker's and Sumner's struggle had been carried on over an uneven and wooded surface, their own line of battle extending in a semicircle not less than a mile and a half. Perhaps a better notion of their position can be got by considering their right, centre, and left as forming three sides of a square. So long, therefore, as either wing was driven back, the centre became exposed to a very dangerous enfilading fire, and

the farther the centre was advanced the worse off it was, unless the lines on its side and rear were firmly held. This formation resulted originally from the efforts of the enemy to turn both flanks. Hooker at the very outset threw his column so far into the heart of the rebel lines that they were compelled to threaten him on the flank to secure their own centre.

Nothing of all this was perceptible from the hills in front. Some directions of the rebel lines had been disclosed by the smoke of their guns, but the whole interior formation of the country beyond the hills was completely concealed. When McClellan arranged his order of battle, it must have been upon information, or have been left to his corps and division commanders to discover for themselves.

Up to three o'clock Burnside had made little progress. His attack on the bridge had been successful, but the delay had been so great that to the observer it appeared as if McClellan's plans must have been seriously disarranged. It is impossible not to suppose that the attacks on right and left were meant in a measure to correspond, for otherwise the enemy had only to repel Hooker on the one hand, then transfer his troops, and push them against Burnside.

Here was the difference between Smith and Burnside. The former did his work at once, and lost all his men at once — that is, all whom he lost at all; Burnside seems to have attacked cautiously in order to save his men, and sending successively insufficient forces against a position of strength, distributed his loss over a greater period of time, but yet lost none the less in the end.

Finally, at four o'clock, McClellan sent simultaneous orders to Burnside and Franklin — to the former to advance and carry the batteries in his front at all hazards and at any cost; to the latter to carry the woods next in front of him to the left, which the rebels still held. The order to Franklin, however, was practically countermanded, in consequence of a message from General Sumner that, if Franklin went on and was repulsed, his own corps was not yet sufficiently reorganized to be depended on as a reserve. Franklin, thereupon, was directed to run no risk of losing his present position, and, instead of sending his infantry into the woods, contented himself with advancing his batteries over the breadth of the fields in front, supporting them with heavy columns of infantry, and attacking with energy the rebel batteries immediately opposed to him. His movement was a success, so far as it went, the batteries maintaining their new ground, and sensibly affecting the steadiness of the rebel fire. That being once accomplished, and all hazard of the right being again forced back having been dispelled, the movement of Burnside became at once the turning-point of success, and the fate of the day depended on him.

How extraordinary the situation was may be judged from a moment's consideration of the facts. It is understood that from the outset

Burnside's attack was expected to be decisive, as it certainly must have been if things went well elsewhere, and if he succeeded in establishing himself on the Sharpsburg road in the rebel rear. Yet Hooker and Sumner and Franklin and Mansfield were all sent to the right three miles away, while Porter seems to have done double duty with his single corps in front, both supporting the batteries and holding himself in reserve. With all this immense force on the right, but sixteen thousand men were given to Burnside for the decisive movement of the day.

Still more unfortunate in its results was the total failure of these separate attacks on the right and left to sustain, or in any manner coöperate with, each other. Burnside hesitated for hours in front of the bridge, which should have been carried at once by a *coup de main*. Meantime Hooker had been fighting for four hours, with various fortune, but final success. Sumner had come up too late to join in the decisive attack which his earlier arrival would probably have converted into a complete success ; and Franklin reached the scene only when Sumner had been repulsed. Probably before his arrival the rebels had transferred a considerable number of troops to their right to meet the attack of Burnside, the direction of which was then suspected or developed.

Attacking first with one regiment, then with two, and delaying both for artillery, Burnside was not over the bridge before two o'clock — perhaps not till three. He advanced slowly up the slopes in his front, his batteries in rear covering, to some extent, the movements of the infantry. A desperate fight was going on in a deep ravine on his right ; the rebel batteries were in full play, and apparently very annoying and destructive, while heavy columns of rebel troops were plainly visible, advancing, as if careless of concealment, along the road and over the hills in the direction of Burnside's forces. It was at this point of time that McClellan sent him the order above given.

Burnside obeyed it most gallantly. Getting his troops well in hand, and sending a portion of his artillery to the front, he advanced with rapidity and the most determined vigor straight up the hill in front, on top of which the rebels had maintained their most dangerous battery. The movement was in plain view of McClellan's position ; and as Franklin, on the other side, sent his batteries into the field about the same time, the battle seemed to open in all directions with greater activity than ever.

The fight in the ravine was in full progress, the batteries in the centre were firing with new vigor, Franklin was blazing away on the right, and every hill-top, ridge, and woods along the whole line was crested and veiled with white clouds of smoke. All day had been clear and bright since the early cloudy morning ; and now this whole magnificent, unequalled scene shone with the splendor of an afternoon September sun. Four miles of battle, its glory all visible, its horrors all hidden, the fate of the republic hanging on the hour — could any one be insensible of its grandeur ?

There are two hills on the left of the road, the farthest the lowest. The rebels have batteries on both. Burnside is ordered to carry the nearest to him, which is the farthest from the road. His guns, opening first from this new position in front, soon entirely controlled and silenced the enemy's artillery. The infantry came on at once, advancing rapidly and steadily, their long, dark lines and broad masses plainly visible without a glass as they moved over the green hill-side.

The next moment the road in which the rebel battery was planted was canopied with clouds of dust swiftly descending into the valley. Underneath was a tumult of wagons, guns, horses, and men, flying at speed down the road. Blue flashes of smoke burst now and then among them ; a horse or a man, or half a dozen, went down, and then the whirlwind swept on.

The hill was carried ; but could it be held ? The rebel columns, before seen moving to the left, increase their pace. The guns on the hill above send an angry tempest of shell down among Burnside's guns and men. He has formed his columns apparently in the near angles of two fields bordering the road — high ground about them everywhere except in rear.

In another moment a rebel battle-line appears on the brow of the ridge above them, moves swiftly down in the most perfect order, and though met by incessant discharges of musketry, of which we plainly see the flashes, does not fire a gun. White spaces show where men are falling, but they close up instantly, and still the line advances. The brigades of Burnside are in heavy column ; they will not give way before a bayonet charge in line, and the rebels think twice before they dash into those hostile masses.

There is a halt ; the rebel left gives way, and scatters over the field ; the rest stand fast and fire. More infantry comes up ; Burnside is outnumbered, flanked, compelled to yield the hill he took so bravely. His position is no longer one of attack ; he defends himself with unfaltering firmness, but he sends to McClellan for help.

McClellan's glass for the last half hour has seldom been turned away from the left. He sees clearly enough that Burnside is pressed — needs no messenger to tell him that. His face grows darker with anxious thought. Looking down into the valley where fifteen thousand troops are lying, he turns a half-questioning look on Fitz-John Porter, who stands by his side, gravely scanning the field. They are Porter's troops below, are fresh, and only impatient to share in this fight. But Porter slowly shakes his head, and one may believe that the same thought is passing through the minds of both generals. " They are the only reserves of the army ; they cannot be spared."

McClellan remounts his horse, and with Porter and a dozen officers of his staff rides away to the left in Burnside's direction. Sykes meets them on the road — a good soldier, whose opinion is worth taking. The three Generals talk briefly together. It is easy to see that the moment has come when everything may turn on one order given or withheld, when the history of the battle is only to be written in thoughts and purposes and words of the General.

Burnside's messenger rides up. His message is: "I want troops and guns. If you do not send them, I cannot hold my position half an hour." McClellan's only answer for the moment is a glance at the western sky. Then he turns and speaks very slowly: "Tell General Burnside this is the battle of the war. He must hold his ground till dark at any cost. I will send him Miller's battery. I can do nothing more. I have no infantry." Then, as the messenger was riding away, he called him back. "Tell him if he *cannot* hold his ground, then the bridge, to the last man!— always the bridge! If the bridge is lost, all is lost."

The sun is already down; not half an hour of daylight is left. Till Burnside's message came it had seemed plain to every one that the battle could not be finished to-day. None suspected how near was the peril of defeat, of sudden attack on exhausted forces — how vital to the safety of the army and the nation were those fifteen thousand waiting troops of Fitz-John Porter in the hollow. But the rebels halted instead of pushing on; their vindictive cannonade died away as the light faded. Before it was quite dark the battle was over. Only a solitary gun of Burnside's thundered against the enemy, and presently this also ceased, and the field was still.

The peril came very near; but it has passed, and in spite of the peril, at the close the day was partly a success; not a victory, but an advantage, had been gained. Hooker, Sumner, and Franklin held all the ground they had gained, and Burnside still held the bridge and his position beyond. Everything was favorable for a renewal of the fight in the morning.

———

THE BIBLE IN WAR. — At the meeting of the Christian Commission in Philadelphia, January 28, 1864, the following occurred in the address of the Rev. Dr. Taylor:

"Nothing has more touched my soul than when I heard of that poor rebel dying, stretched out upon one of the battle-fields of the Peninsula, with the Bible open beneath his hand, and his skeleton fingers pressed upon the words, 'Yea, though I walk through the valley of the shadow of death, I will fear no evil, for Thou art with me; Thy rod and Thy staff, they comfort me.' Oftentimes, sir, this Bible has been the only gravestone that has marked the resting-place of many an unknown soldier. Many could be known in no other way than by their Testaments in their pockets, saturated with their patriot blood; and sometimes the story of domestic grief has been uttered first in the solemn, silent sentences of that precious Word. I could tell you of an officer's wife from New England receiving a box from her husband in the army South, and when she came to open it, there was nothing there to tell why it was sent. There were the clothes, and the sword, and many little relics he had carried in his bosom. There was no letter there to tell the story; but there was the Bible! When it was opened, there were found, heavily underscored, simply these words: 'Woman, why weepest thou?' and, 'Why should it be thought an incredible thing with you that God should raise the dead?' That was all; but it was enough. It was the story of death!— it was the note of resurrection!"

———

"E PLURIBUS UNUM."

BY JOHN PIERPONT.

I.

THE harp of the minstrel with melody rings
    When the Muses have taught him to touch and
        to tune it ;
But though it may have a full octave of strings,
    To both maker and minstrel the harp is a unit.
        So the power that creates
        Our republic of States,
    Into harmony brings them at different dates;
And the thirteen or thirty, the Union once done,
Are "E Pluribus Unum" — of many made one.

II.

The science that weighs in her balance the spheres,
    And has watched them since first the Chaldean
        began it,
Now and then, as she counts them and measures
        their years,
    Brings into our system and names a new planet.
        Yet the old and new stars —
        Venus, Neptune, and Mars,
    As they drive round the sun their invisible cars,
Whether faster or slower their races they run —
Are "E Pluribus Unum" — of many made one.

III.

Of that system of spheres should but one fly the
        track,
    Or with others conspire for a general dispersion,
By the great central orb they would all be brought
        back,
    And held each in her place by a wholesome co-
        ercion.
        Should one daughter of light
        Be indulged in her flight,
    They would all be ingulfed by old Chaos and
        Night :
So must none of our sisters be suffered to run,
For, "E Pluribus Unum," we all go if one.

IV.

Let the demon of discord our melody mar,
    Or treason's red hand rend our Union asunder,
Break one string from our harp, or extinguish one
        star,
    The whole system's ablaze with its lightning and
        thunder.
        Let the discord be hushed !
        Let the traitors be crushed,
    Though "Legion" their name, all with victory
        flushed !
For aye must our *motto* stand, fronting the sun :
"E Pluribus Unum" — *though many we're* ONE.

ADVENTURES OF AN IOWA BOY. — Among the most remarkable adventures perpetrated during the war, is that related of Charles H. Smith, a private of the Fourth Iowa cavalry, which is as follows:

He started with his regiment on Colonel Winslow's expedition to Grenada, and was captured by the rebels at that place. He remained their prisoner for four days, walking in that time a distance of eighty miles in a state of semi-starvation. One evening they halted about sundown, and put up for the night in an old school-house, situated ten miles west of West Point, on the road leading from West Point to Grenada. The school-house had a door on each side, a chimney in one end, and a window without frame or shutter in the other. They barricaded the window with a desk convenient, barred the eastern door, and stationed a guard in the other.

When it had come sleeping time the Yankees — six in all — were allotted that portion next the chimney, while the Butternuts — twenty in number — occupied the other end; a line was designated across which no one must pass. Charlie lay down without removing any of his clothes, intending to lie awake and watch for an opportunity to escape, but weariness of body overcame the resolution, and he fell asleep. But he awakened between one and two o'clock, and saw the guard sitting in the door smoking his pipe and conversing with the corporal of the guard, who was sitting by the fire outside. Slipping off his boots, and gathering his hat, haversack, and canteen, he crept over the sleeping "chivalry" up on to the desk, and let himself quietly down and out at the window, reaching *terra firma* in safety. A splendid horse was tied to a tree at the end of the house, six or seven feet from where his doughty master and several companions were sleeping. A saddle and bridle were found on the window after considerable feeling around, which a few moments sufficed to put in their place, a moment more to lead the horse thirty yards and mount him. Six days sufficed to place him inside the Yankee lines at Lagrange, Tennessee, nearly two hundred miles being travelled in that time. In passing through the Confederacy he avoided all towns and stations at which troops were quartered, though with all his precaution he several times came near running into their camps, only escaping by the greatest good fortune. He met small squads of shot-gun gentlemen nearly every day. To these and to the citizens he passed himself off for a paroled prisoner belonging to McCulloch's command (Second Missouri), and going home to see his old mother for the first time since the war broke out. Charlie considered the capture of the horse a capital joke. Its proprietor belonged to the Fifteenth Mississippi regiment, and was home on a furlough.

BURNSIDE AT THE BRIDGE. — An eye-witness gives the following account of the fight at Antietam Bridge:

"The bridge across Antietam Creek, which General Burnside was ordered to take, and which was so stubbornly held by the rebels, is situated in a deep ravine. The face of the hill on the opposite side of the bridge is too steep to be ascended by a horse, and must be literally climbed to be surmounted by man. The roadway from the bridge turns abruptly to the right and left, and rises the hill along its side very gradually. The rebel infantry at first occupied the bridge itself, and the bank of the creek on our side, and a rebel battery was posted on the opposite hill directly above the bridge, so as to play upon our infantry as it approached the bridge, either from directly before it or from our right of the bridge. Some trees intervened on our left of the bridge immediately down upon the creek, but the approach down the hill on our side was bare in all directions, and exposed to the view of the enemy's gunners. The bridge is a stone arched and stone parapeted structure, a strong, rough, country bridge.

"The rebel prisoners state the number stationed to hold the bridge against us at from one hundred and fifty to three hundred infantry. It is hardly credible that a point to which any importance was attached on either side should be intrusted to so small a force; and the incredibility is heightened by the havoc that was made among at least four of our regiments; yet I am inclined to believe that a not much higher figure than the last would cover the actual number. I think there was not more than one regiment assigned to that duty; and as regiments go in armies that have been over a year in service, it did not probably number more than five hundred men; the chance is less. I notice that both our officers and men engaged in that contest are totally wanting in their usual claim of superior numbers against them — a claim commonly enough true whenever they have found much difficulty in making head against the foe, and, in fact, seem to concur in repeating what the rebels state, and there significantly letting the matter drop. On our part, Burnside had a couple of batteries on a hill on our left of the bridge at something less than a right angle with it, and a very little to our right of the bridge was another battery on another point of the same range of hills, just opposite to the enemy's battery. The parapets formed excellent breastworks against our batteries on either hand, and were protection against our small arms from the same direction. The creek was fordable hereabout — it has rained since — in several places; some of them, however, necessitating waist-deep wading. It was attempted to cross in this manner, as well as by the bridge. The Second Indiana, who was first ordered to the attack, did not get down to the water. That regiment and the Sixth New Hampshire were repulsed, but not until they had made some impression on the rebel defence, and left it weaker against succeeding regiments. The Fifty-first Pennsylvania was the first to cross. The Fifty-first New York supported its Pennsylvania namesake, or numbersake, and was close with it, but a little less forward. The bridge itself was not the only part of the creek defended against our attempt to cross. Our left was resisted all along its banks for many rods above and below. The enemy selected this as the front of this part of his line for its strong natural defences, and also having reference to the line of woods a mile or so in his rear for a hiding-place and an intrenchment, in case he was driven back in spite of his best *bona fide* efforts to stand firm ; or having reference to the woods as his real battle-line, into which he hoped to decoy us in pursuit of whatever success we might obtain, either in spite of him or in pursuance of his strategy. The bridge is no more noticeable than any other portion of the creek on our left wing, excepting that its stone parapets added so much artificial defence to the natural defence of the abrupt and rough line of hill and wood along the stream. The movement for the capture of this line of position was commenced between ten and eleven in the morning, and it was not crowned with success, throughout, until between three and four in the afternoon ; but the wonder is that it was taken at all. It was while crossing this creek, up to his waist in water, that Captain Griswold received his death-wound. His regiment (Connecticut Eleventh) was one of the regiments under General Rodman that attempted to, and finally succeeded after several hours' fighting, in crossing, half a mile or so below the bridge. Our cannonading on our left so far exceeded the anticipations of our Generals in rapidity and duration (it will do now to say), that General Burnside exhausted all his ammunition for some of his guns before the day was fairly done. As for the rebels, they probably could not have fought a general battle at all, and would not have made a stand, but for their immense acquisitions at Harper's Ferry. Whatever of mourning this battle has caused in the hundreds and thousands of families in the land for those who may never return to them ; whatever of discomfort they may suffer from the death or disabled condition of ten thousand husbands and fathers ; whatever of these, and a train of evils, may flow from this greatest and bloodiest of the battles of this unparalleled, preposterous revolution, it is all immediately chargeable to the surrender of Harper's Ferry.

" It is strange what a difference there is in the composition of human bodies, with reference to the rapidity that change goes on after death. Several bodies of rebels strewed the ground on the bank, in the vicinity of the bridge. They fought behind trees, and fence-rail and stone-heap barricades, as many a bullet mark in all these defences amply attested ; but all that availed not to avert death from these poor creatures. They had been dead at least forty-eight hours when I looked at them. Almost all of them had become discolored in the face and much swollen ; but there was one young man with his face so lifelike, and even his eye so bright, it seemed almost impossible that he could be dead. It was the loveliest looking corpse I ever beheld. He was a young man, not twenty-five, the soft, unshaved, brown beard hardly asserting yet the fulness of

its owner's manhood. The features were too small, and the character of the face of too small and delicate an order, to answer the requirements of masculine beauty. In death his eye was the clearest blue, and would not part with its surpassingly gentle, amiable, good, and charming expression. The face was like a piece of wax, only that it surpassed any piece of wax-work.

" One other young man, beardless, yet but of a brawnier type, furnished another example of slow decomposition. His face was not quite as lifelike ; still one could easily fancy him alive to see him anywhere else than on the field of carnage ; and strange, his face wore an expression of mirth, as if he had just witnessed something amusing. A painful sight especially was the body of a rebel who had evidently died of his wounds, after lingering long enough at least to apply a handkerchief to his thigh himself, as a tourniquet to stop the bleeding. His comrades were obliged to leave him, and our surgeons and men had so much else to do that they could not attend to him in time. Perhaps nothing would have saved him ; but perhaps, again, a little surgical aid was all he needed. How long he dragged out his lessening pulse in pain no one can tell.

" Subsequently, I visited the ground intervening between our pickets and the pickets of the enemy, after the fight was done. It was the ground over which our troops had driven the enemy, but which they failed to hold ; and it had since been jealously watched by both parties, each prohibiting the other from entering upon it even to care for his wounded or to bury his dead, if the skirmishing sharpshooters of either could prevent it. Numerous shots were exchanged yesterday between them in this spirit ; but to-day the rebel skirmishers had left ours sole occupants of the field, and we civilians even felt free and safe to wander over the entire battle-ground without restriction. Our men have been engaged to-day in looking up their dead comrades, and possibly here and there a surviving wounded one, over this inhibited district, and this afternoon your correspondent visited it himself. Had I seen it before jotting down my observations just concluded, it is questionable whether I should have had the spirit of charity enough to mention the rebels, living or dead, for anything but malediction.

" One field especially was thickly strewn with our dead, in which the Hawkins Zouaves (Ninth New York volunteers) were largely represented. Several members of the One Hundred and Third New York lay there also. Away across the fields, for a mile within the enemy's battle-line, our gallant soldiers had charged and chased the chivalry, but afterward had been obliged to retire before the enemy's batteries, leaving their fallen comrades on the ground. Every dead man's feet I saw were robbed of their shoes, and there were instances of our heroic boys being stripped of their pantaloons. Their arms and accoutrements were invariably taken, of course. On the other hand — I record it with a sense of relief from disgust at my kind — the enemy's dead within our reach lay just as they fell, untouched, excepting as their names might be sought after on their clothes, or the buttons might be cut off by the soldiers for trophies or remembrancers of the field. God only knows what some of our poor men have suffered before they died. It is to be hoped that none, or few, at worst, died lingering deaths.

"Some of the rebel missiles are military curiosities. One of the Hawkins Zouaves showed me a great big striped white marble that had hit him after it was spent from a cannon. Another soldier, a cultivated young man, known to literary friends of mine, told me of a comrade picking up the sheet-iron plate of a door-lock, all rolled up, keyhole perfect in it, no mistake, which had fallen near him from a rebel cannon. The key had probably been sent in another direction.

"A nervous, big-headed, little-bodied, amiable-faced rebel lay in the same barn with Dr. Bowen and the others named. He told me his name, but I reserve it. He said he was worn out and sick, and when his army moved to retire across the Potomac he fell out, on a natural pretext enough, and lay down to rest. His own regiment passed on and left him. He then moved farther out of sight, and lay down in some straw, and finally went into that barn, when our troops had advanced far enough to protect him. He hoped he should not be exchanged. He wanted to be paroled, so that he *could not* fight any more. He said he would not continue with the army another four months for ten thousand dollars. He joined it by conscription in North Carolina, where he resides."

COMPENSATIONS OF WAR. — In the address of the Rev. Dr. Eddy, at the meeting of the Christian Commission, in January, 1864, the following passages occur:

"This hour has its compensations. It has originated some of the noblest, grandest charities. It has inspired the purest patriotism that earth has ever seen; and it has developed piety in many places, resplendent as the noonday sun. I remember hearing of the interview you [addressing Mr. George H. Stuart, the president] had with a patriotic woman of the city of Philadelphia, on whom you called to make known the work of the Christian Commission. Her grandson, wrapped in the Stars and Stripes as his shroud, had just been brought to her, and as the clergyman endeavored to offer to her the consolations of religion, did she mourn in bitterness the loss of that child? did she mourn because he had done and suffered so much for his country? O, no! 'I have given,' she says, 'two sons, Commodore Ellet, of the Navy, and Brigadier-General Ellet, of the Marine Brigade, and four grandsons, to the country.' And was this all? No; but, 'If I had twenty sons, I'd give them all for my country and theirs, for it *must* be preserved; (applause) and if I was twenty years younger, I would go myself, woman though I am!' (Protracted applause.)

"Out of this war comes piety as well as patriotism. We have not been accustomed to look to the camp and the battle-field for religion; but, strange as it may seem, we are to-day turning from our cities to the camps and battle-fields for revivals of religion, and for the noblest forms of gospel evangelization. Never, since the Star of Bethlehem went marching up the skies, has a nobler, grander, holier sight been seen than that at Shiloh, so often quoted. When that terrible day was done, and the sun had gone to rest, and the two armies had rolled back to prepare for another bloody struggle, all was still and silent, save the moans of the wounded and the groans of the dying. By and by there peered through a rift in the clouds a single, solitary star, and it caught the eye of a dying soldier. It awakened the holiest memories of his heart, and he began to sing, —

'When, marshalled on the nightly plain,
The glittering hosts bestud the sky,
One star alone, of all the train,
Can fix a dying soldier's eye,' —

and ere he had reached the end of the first verse, another voice had taken up the strain, and another, and another, and another, until that gory field resounded with salvation's holiest notes, and that solitary star that had shone alone, was joined by all the glittering sisterhood of heaven, and the countless constellations of the skies sent back the melody of that bleeding soldier's song!"

UNACQUAINTED WITH THE ROPES. — Western officers were proverbial for shocking bad uniforms, and, in a majority of instances, it was rather difficult to distinguish them from the privates. Among this class was a brigadier-general named James Morgan, who looked more like a wagon-master than a soldier. On a certain occasion, a new recruit had just arrived in camp, lost a few articles, and was inquiring around among the "Vets" in hopes of finding them. An old soldier, fond of his sport, told the recruit the only thief in the brigade was in Jim Morgan's tent. The recruit immediately started for "Jim's" quarters, and poking his head in, asked:

"Does Jim Morgan live here?"

"Yes," was the reply, "my name is James Morgan."

"Then I want you to hand over those books you stole from me!"

"I have none of your books, my man."

"It's an infernal lie," indignantly exclaimed the recruit. "The boys say you are the only thief in the camp; turn out them books, or I'll grind your carcass into apple sass."

The General relished the joke much, but observing the sinewy recruit peeling off his coat, informed him of his relations to the brigade, and the recruit walked off, merely remarking: "Wall, blast me if I'd take you for a Brigadier. Excuse me, General, I don't know the ropes yet."

GENEROSITY. — A sick soldier on his way to his home in Georgia, while passing through the streets of Selma, Alabama, weary with his long march, seated himself beside the pavement to rest. His pale face and emaciated frame elicited much sympathy from the passers by, and a proposition was started to raise a purse for his benefit. But before there was time to carry it into effect, a gentleman stepped up to the poor sick soldier, and with the remark, " I will give him something to help him along," handed him a one hundred dollar note. Such acts are as certainly applauded by men as they are approved of Heaven. — *Southern paper.*

JEFF DAVIS ON HIS ELECTION AS PRESIDENT FOR SIX YEARS.*

BY LUCIUS MANLIUS SARGENT.

SATAN was chained a thousand years,
  We learn from Revelation,
That he might not, as it appears,
  Longer "deceive the nation."
'Tis hard to say, between the two,
  Which is the greater evil,
Six years of liberty for you —
  A thousand for the devil!
'Tis passing strange if you've no fears
Of being hanged within six years!

A hundred thousand rebels' ears
  Would not one half repay
The widows' and the orphans' tears
  Shed for the slain to-day:
The blood of all those gallant braves,
  Whom Southern traitors slew,
Cries sternly, from their loyal graves,
  For vengeance upon you ;
And if you're not prepared to die
The death of Haman, fly, Jeff, fly !

Fly, traitor, to some lonely niche,
  Far, far beyond the billow ;
Thy grave an ill-constructed ditch,
  Thy sexton General Pillow.
There may you turn to rottenness,
  By mortal unannoyed,
Your ashes undisturbed, unless
  Your grave is known by Floyd.
He'll surely trouble your repose,
And come to steal your burial-clothes.

EPITAPH.

Pause for an instant, loyal reader.
Here lies Jeff, the great seceder.
Above, he always lied, you know,
And now the traitor lies below.
His bow was furnished with two strings :
He flattered crowds, and fawned on kings ;
Repaid his country's care with evil,
And prayed to God, and served the devil.
The South could whip the Yankee nation,
So he proposed humiliation !
Their blessings were so everlasting,
'Twas just the time for prayer and fasting !
The record may be searched in vain,
From West Point Benedict to Cain,
To find a more atrocious knave,
Unless in Cæsar Borgia's grave.

* November 9, 1861.

THE STORY OF ULRIC DAHLGREN. — The month of March, 1864, is memorable in Richmond for one of the grandest Union raids that, up to that time, had menaced the Confederate capital — a raid which was the immediate precursor of General Grant's famous campaign from the Wilderness to James River.

The history of this raid is too familiar to the minds of all our readers to make necessary any recapitulation of it, even if it comported with our space. It is known that Colonel Dahlgren, after the attack on Richmond on Tuesday, the 1st of March, did not succeed in forming a junction with General Kilpatrick, and while pushing through King and Queen County, towards Gloucester Point, was killed on the night of Wednesday, March 2, near Walkerton. It is also known that his body was brought to Richmond ; but what disposition was made of it by the Confederate authorities was kept a mystery at the time, and the facts, even to this day, have never been published. We purpose to give them to the public for the first time, vouching for their entire authenticity.*

When intelligence was received in Richmond of the death of Colonel Dahlgren, messengers were despatched to bring the remains to the city for identification. They reached the city on Monday, March 7, by the York River Railroad, and lay, during that day at the depot, where they were examined by large numbers of persons. His death had been caused by a gun-shot wound in the head. The little finger of one hand had been cut off on the field where he fell by some one anxious to secure, with the least trouble, a valuable diamond ring. That night the body was carried to General Elzy's office, in Belvin's block ; and the next day, having been placed in a common pine coffin, of the kind then used for the burial of soldiers, — which, in turn, was placed in a box, — was transferred to Oakwood Cemetery, a mile east of the city. The hearse used on this occasion was a four-mule street wagon, and the attendants consisted of a Confederate officer of inferior rank and two soldiers. Arriving at Oakwood, which was the burial-place of all soldiers who died at Chimborazo, Howard's Grove, and other hospitals in the eastern portion of the city and suburbs, the negro grave-diggers and other attendants about the cemetery were driven off and ordered to absent themselves until notified that they might return. One of the negroes, now living in the city, having his curiosity excited, secreted himself in the woods near by, determined to see what was to be done. The two soldiers dug a grave, placed the box in it, and covered it up. They then shouted to recall the attendants of the cemetery, and, getting into the wagon, returned to the city.

The only circumstance in the proceedings that struck the negro as unusual, was the mystery observed, and the circumstance of the box, — no corpse ever having been brought there before, except in a pine coffin ; but, there having been a great deal of talk as to what was to be done

* See page 291, ante.

with the body of Colonel Dahlgren, he at once decided that this could be no other than the corpse of that officer. He, however, kept his opinion to himself at the time.

The question, What has been done with the body of Dahlgren? was the subject of inquiry and conversation for many days in Richmond, to be revived from time to time up to the day of the evacuation. And there were many stories on the subject — that it had been burnt, sunk in the river, &c. A city paper of that day announced, with a solemn and knowing air, that it would never be found until the trump of doom should sound. A number of Union men of the city, believing it possible that it might be recovered, were anxious to secure and preserve it for the family of the deceased. Prominent among them was Mr. F. W. E. Lohman, a grocer, doing business near the New Market. Mr. Lohman at at once began his inquiries and investigations, — which, in the then state of popular feeling, it was necessary to conduct with great caution, — and determined, at whatever cost and risk, to ascertain its fate. After nearly a month's patient and untiring inquiry, he, with the assistance of Mr. Martin Meredith Lipscomb, whose business it was to attend the interment of all the Union prisoners who died at this post, made the acquaintance of the negro grave-digger, whom we have mentioned as being the sole spectator of the burial of Colonel Dahlgren. They found him at Oakwood, pursuing his regular business. When first approached on the subject, the negro was very much alarmed, and protested he would have nothing to do with the matter. But after repeated assurance by Mr. Lipscomb, whom he knew well, that he might rely upon Mr. Lohman, and that no harm should befall him, he consented, on Mr. Lohman's giving him a hundred dollar note, to point out the grave. This he did by walking near and casting a stone upon it, while Lohman and Lipscomb stood at a distance. He was afraid to employ any other method, lest he might excite the suspicion of the superintendent of the cemetery, or some of the attendants. The grave lay among thousands of those of Confederate soldiers. Subsequently, after a great deal of persuasion, and the promise of a liberal reward, the negro agreed to meet Mr. Lohman at the cemetery on the night of the 6th April, at ten o'clock, and exhume the body.

The appointed night having arrived, Mr. Lohman, his brother, John A. Lohman, and Mr. Lipscomb, started for the cemetery in a cart drawn by a mule. The night was dark and stormy, and well suited to conceal their movements. The party left the city at nine o'clock, and reached their destination about ten, and there found waiting for them the grave-digger and two assistants. The negroes, being assured that all was right, began their work of exhumation, the three white men remaining with the cart outside the enclosure of the cemetery. The heavens were hung with their deepest black; no object ten feet distant could be distinguished, and no sounds broke upon the loneliness of the place, save the howling of the winds and the chopping of the resurrectionist's spade. Once the mule, snuffing the tainted air of the city of the dead, attempted to break away, but was quickly quieted by a firm hand.

In twenty minutes from the time the negroes began their work they approached the cart, bearing between them the coffin, which, being badly made, fell to pieces as they rested it on the ground. It was then discovered that the body had not decomposed in any perceptible degree. Mr. Lohman satisfied himself of the identity of the corpse by passing his hand over it. The little finger, torn off to secure the jewel it bore, and the leg, lost in battle, were missing. He paid the negro with whom he had contracted fifteen hundred dollars, and placing the body in the cart, the party started on their return. The mule, alarmed as animals frequently are when drawing a dead body for the first time, became difficult of management, and, with the darkness of the night, made the first part of the expedition one of no little peril. More than one hour was spent in reaching the gas lights of the city on Church Hill. It was part of the plan to convey the body to the house of William S. Rowlett, a Union man, living on Chelsea Hill, a half mile north-east of the city, there to remain until a metallic case could be procured for it. From Church Hill, Mr. Lohman drove down Broad Street to Seventeenth Street, thence up Seventeenth Street to its northern terminus, and thence up the hill to Mr. Rowlett's, reaching the last place at two o'clock on the morning of the 7th of April. Here the body was wrapped in a blanket, and Mr. Lohman came to the city in search of a coffin, which he obtained by the aid of Mr. Lipscomb. On his way into the city from Rowlett's, Lohman notified a number of persons of Union sentiments, among whom were several ladies, where the body had been placed, and they hurried out to see it. Several of these persons had seen Colonel Dahlgren while he was exposed at the York River Railroad depot, and immediately recognized the body as his. The metallic coffin having been procured, and the body placed in it, the two Lohmans, at noon on the 7th, set out with it, concealed in a wagon loaded with young fruit trees, for the farm of Robert Orricks, a Union man, living in Henrico, two miles from Hungary Station.

At four o'clock that evening they reached Orricks', and buried the body under an apple tree, in a field, avoiding the graveyard for fear of exciting inquiry, which might lead to discovery.

The rest of this story may be told in a few words. Orricks, some months after the second burial of Colonel Dahlgren, succeeded in getting through the Confederate lines, and, seeking an interview with Commodore Dahlgren, informed him of what had been done to secure the body of his son. The corpse of the soldier lay in this its second grave until the evacuation of Richmond, when, an order having been sent for it by the War Department, it was again disinterred by the two Lohmans, and sent to Washington.

It has been our object to lift the veil of mystery from an obscure and interesting event. In doing so, we have confined ourselves to facts strictly relative to the secret fate of Colonel Dahlgren's body from the time of its arrival in Richmond, which, until after the capture of the city, remained, to all except the few individuals named by us in the course of our narrative, one of the most impenetrable mysteries of the war. Many Confederate officials knew that the body had been deposited at Oakwood, but they were ignorant to the last that it had ever been removed. It has at length found its last earthly resting-place. — *Richmond Republic.*

AN EVEN CHANCE. — "Travelling in the County of Sevier, Arkansas," says an editor, " the stage was stopped on some trifling business at a house where lived one of the merriest and prettiest of the beautiful damsels of that highly favored country. She came out to the stage looking as fresh as Hebe, and we, having known her before, and presuming on the privileges of a *paterfamilias*, asked her if it were possible she had not married yet ?

" 'No, sir,' she answered ; ' and what's more than that, I don't intend to, until the very last one of the volunteers gets back. I mean to wait, and let them have an even chance.' "

PRICE'S APPEAL TO MISSOURI.

BY M. JEFF. THOMPSON.

Missouri ! Missouri ! Awake from thy slumbers:
Canst thou not hear the hammer that rivets thy chains ?
Can't the death-shriek of fathers, the wail of thy mothers,
The tears of thy daughters, arouse thee again ?
Come ! rise in thy might, shake the dewdrops of morning
From thy limbs, and walk forth as a lion to war,
For fanatics are forging bonds stronger than iron,
To bind thee forever to a conqueror's car.

Can thy slumbering senses be so callous and dead
That even in dreams thou canst hear not nor see
That the chains they are striking from Afric's black sons
Are being welded again to be placed upon thee ?
Canst thou not see through the world the finger of scorn
Is pointed at those who submissively stand
Beneath the foul yoke, while their brothers are striking
For the freedom and glory of our dearly loved land ?

O, rise in thy might ; drive the "Huns" from thy borders,
And stand by thy Southern sons in the fight ;
Pour forth all thy men to help them to battle
For Freedom, for Glory, for Justice, for Right !
Let thy watch-fires glow, and thy bugles blast high
O'er thy mountains and valleys, o'er woodland and lea.
Then the glad shout shall ring o'er thy prairies and streams,
" Hail ! brothers, hail ! Missouri is free ! "

A NEGRO from Williamsburg, who went into Fortress Monroe in company with one of the Union chaplains, says that,' before the national troops left Williamsburg, the slaves in that vicinity were told to beware of the " horrible Yankees, who had very small bodies, but great large heads, with front teeth like horses, and were known to eat human flesh." Upon being asked whether the slaves believed this, he replied : " Dun'no ; reckon not, massa. Dem Yankees has got no horns, but fights like de debble ! "

MAJOR WINTHROP, killed at Great Bethel, was shot by a negro. The writer says : " I have it from a member of the Wythe Rifles, of Hampton, Virginia, who was present at the fight, and saw Winthrop fall, that he was shot by a negro at the suggestion and command of the Captain of the Rifles, who said to him substantially : ' These Yankees will take you to Cuba, and sell you. If you wish to stay with your wife and children, drive them out of Virginia.' The negro fired, and, unconsciously to him, there fell one of the earliest and best friends of the race to which he belonged."

THE ESCAPE OF J. P. BENJAMIN. — A correspondent at Havana relates the following story of the escape of the Confederate Secretary of State, Judah P. Benjamin :

Early in May he separated from the President (Davis) near Washington, Georgia, for the purpose of making his way to Nassau and Havana from some point on the Florida coast. He was to attend to some public business at these ports, and then to rejoin the President in the trans-Mississippi via Matamoras and Texas. He travelled directly south, through Georgia and Florida, on horseback, disguised as a farmer in search of lands on which to settle, and passed through the country without exciting suspicion or attracting attention, until he reached the lower side of the Peninsula of Florida. He was informed that no boats were to be found on the eastern coast, and went thence to the Gulf shore, where after a month's delay he succeeded in getting a ship's yawl-boat and two men who were willing to risk their lives upon the sea in it. The open boat was about fifteen feet in length, in which they coasted the Peninsula until they reached one of the keys of the Florida Reef, where they succeeded in procuring a boat somewhat larger, but still an open boat, in which they put to sea to cross the Gulf Stream, and fortunately reached the Bimines upon the Banks, after a passage of sixty hours. On Monday, the 10th of July, after an unsuccessful attempt to reach Nassau, in which he was baffled by head winds and heavy weather, he put back to the Bimines. On the 13th he took passage from the Bimines for Nassau in a small sloop of nine tons burden, loaded with sponges, and on Friday, the 14th, this sloop foundered at sea, when thirty miles distant from the nearest land. The vessel went down so rapidly that he, with the colored men who formed the crew, had barely time to jump into a skiff in tow of the sloop before she sank. In this boat, with a light mast, sails, and compass, and their only provisions a pot of boiled rice, which the negroes had cooked for their breakfast, — in this leaky and overloaded boat, and having but one oar, they made for land, and, as the weather was calm and a vessel in sight, by dint of energetic sculling, they reached the light-house vessel at five P. M., and were cordially received, by Captain Stewart, on board the Georgia, Her Britannic Majesty's light-house yacht, and were warmly and most cordially entertained. This vessel was on an official tour of light-house inspection upon the banks, and at the request of Mr. Benjamin, returned him once more to the Bimines. There Mr. Benjamin chartered another vessel on the 25th of July, and arrived at Nassau, Friday, the 21st. On Saturday, the 22d, he sailed on board the good schooner Britannia, and arrived at Havana on the 25th, safe and sound.

His whole trip occupied the best part of three months, out of which thirty days were passed at sea in miserable open boats; at least, twenty-two days in the smallest crafts that float.

AN INCIDENT AT CHATTANOOGA. — Stepping to my door one evening, to take a view of the varied life of Market Street, I saw a refreshing spectacle. Coming down the centre of that broad thoroughfare, with musket at right shoulder shift, head bent slightly forward, and the step and air of a veteran, was a negro boy of about twenty years, wearing the army blue. Following behind, crowding close up around, and in a line extending far behind him, were about two hundred officers and soldiers of the so-called Confederate States army. On passed the colored Sergeant — such was his rank — and onward crowded and followed the late Southern warriors. Not another guard about them, not another menacing bayonet in sight. The gleam of the negro's bayonet told them of rations and quarters ahead, and of danger behind. I saw him pass on with his charge, never looking behind him, yet losing none, until he handed them over to the authorities at the military prison, from which they were next day paroled. — *Letter from a Soldier.*

GENERAL LOGAN AND THE IRISHMAN. — Just before the capture of Savannah, General Logan, with two or three of his staff, entered the depot at Chicago one fine morning, to take the cars east, on his way to rejoin his command. The General, being a short distance in advance of the others, stepped upon the platform of a car, and was about to enter it, but was stopped by an Irishman with:

"Ye'll not be goin' in there."

"Why not, sir?" asked the General.

"Because them's a leddies' caer, and no gentleman'll be goin' in there without a leddy. There's wan sate in that caer over there, ef yees want it," at the same time pointing to it.

"Yes," replied the General, "I see there is one seat, but what shall I do with my staff?"

"O, bother yer staff!" was the petulant reply. "Go you and take the sate, and stick yer staff out of the windy."

TAKING THE OATH. — At Richmond, Virginia, a modest young country girl, on applying for rations to one of the relief agents, was asked if she had ever taken the oath. "No, indeed, sir," was her terrified reply; "I never swore in all my life." "But you must take the oath, my good girl," said the agent, "or I cannot give you the rations." "No, indeed, I can't, sir," said the girl; "mother always taught me never to swear." The agent mildly persisted, and the maiden as pertinaciously refused all attempts at persuasion, until, overcome at last by the dreadful conflict between necessity and her high sense of moral duty, she stammered out with downcast lids, "Well, sir, if you will make me do such a horrid, wicked thing, then d—n the Yankees!"

REMINISCENCES OF PRESIDENT LINCOLN. — "It was not our good fortune to know much, personally, of the late President," says the editor of the Lowell Citizen. "In fact, the only time we ever saw him was on the occasion of a business visit to Washington, in the last days of March, just before the fall of Richmond. Our special errand related to an unfinished matter already in his hands, and, a moment's attention to it being all that was required, we made our way to the White House, fully resolved not to be intrusive, nor to worry him with impertinent matters, of which he had already more than enough. Our card was passed in, and we awaited our chances in the anteroom, with a dozen comers, perhaps, among whom were recognized senators and members of the 'popular branch.' One of the latter, coming from the President's own State, gave us a hint that this waiting for 'an audience' was a decided uncertainty, often resulting in hope deferred. Our friend added that he had been himself waiting and watching for his chance nearly three weeks. His case was simply that of a widow's son, who had deserted, and who was therefore liable to be shot.

"The mother was half distracted with grief, and her petition for pardon was to be urged. Presently walked in, with nimble step, a middle-sized, well-built, stern-visaged man, with his budget of papers, and who, as if at home, was immediately ushered into the President's room. That was Secretary Stanton. The waiting gentlemen, who recognized the Secretary of War, here gave knowing winks of discouragement, as much as to say, 'It's an all-night business; Stanton has important despatches from the front.' But a half hour sufficed, and, when the Secretary passed out, the gray-haired messenger, whose open, pleasant Irish countenance has been familiar to callers at the White House since it was occupied by President Jackson, notified the gentlemen in waiting — the Illinois member was now, unluckily, not among them — that the President would now see them all at once; and all were ushered in. This was our first and only view of Abraham Lincoln face to face. His countenance bore that open, benignant outline we had expected; but what struck us especially was its cheerful, wide-awake expressiveness, which we had never met with in the pictures of our beloved chief. The secret of this may have been that he had just been hearing good news from Grant — for such was the fact.

"But our chief purpose in this sketch is to describe, in brief, the bearing of the President in this short interview. After saluting his little circle of callers, they were seated, and attended to in turn. First in order was a citizen of Washington, praying for pardon in the case of a deserting soldier.

"'Well,' said the President, after carefully reading the paper, 'it is only natural for one to want pardon; but I must in such a case have a responsible name that I *know*. I don't know you. Do you live in the city?' 'Yes.' 'Do you know the Mayor?' 'Yes.' 'Well, bring me his name, and I'll let the boy off.' The soldier was pardoned.

"Next came a well-developed man of French accent, from New Orleans. He was evidently a diffident person, not knowing precisely how to state his case; but the burden of it was, that he was a real-estate holder in New Orleans, and since the advent of military rulers there, he could not collect his rents, which were his living. 'Your case, my friend,' said the President, 'may be a hard one, but it might have been worse. If, with your musket, you had taken your chance with our boys before Richmond, you might have found your bed before now. But the point is, what would you have me do for you? I have much to do, and the courts have been opened to relieve me in this regard.' The applicant, still embarrassed, said, 'I am not in the habit of appearing before big men.' 'And for that matter,' it was quickly responded, 'you have no need to change your habit, for you are not before very big men now;' playfully adding, 'I can't go into the collection business.' The New Orleans man was finally satisfied that a President cannot do everything that ought to be done to redress individual grievances. These instances, though not specially remarkable in themselves, serve to set off in a strong light those traits of character which shed such a radiance over the life of Mr. Lincoln. He studied intently the grievances of the humblest. There was no appearance of affected dignity on account of the high post which he filled. He had a fellow-feeling for his countrymen — a love for justice — above all, a true fear of God — a sacred regard for the rights of all. These were our first-sight impressions of Abraham Lincoln. They are likely to be lasting."

A VERSE OF WELCOME. — A clergyman in Illinois wrote an ode of welcome for a returning regiment. The first verse ran thus:

"And O, come home, thou wondrous man,
    Who never said, 'I can't' —
We wait, we look, we long for you:
    Come back, Ulysses Grant!"

THE SOUTHERN CROSS.

BY ST. GEORGE TUCKER.

O, SAY, can you see, through the gloom and the storm,
    More bright for the darkness, that pure constellation?
Like the symbol of love and redemption its form,
    As it points to the haven of hope for the nation.
How radiant each star! as they beacon afar,
Giving promise of peace, or assurance in war;
'Tis the Cross of the South, which shall ever remain
To light us to Freedom and Glory again.

How peaceful and blest was America's soil,
    Till betrayed by the guile of the Puritan demon,
Which lurks under Virtue, and springs from its coil,
    To fasten its fangs in the life-blood of freemen!
Then loudly appeal to each heart that can feel,
And crush the foul viper 'neath Liberty's heel;
And the Cross of the South shall forever remain
To light us to Freedom and Glory again.

'Tis the emblem of peace, 'tis the day-star of hope,
    Like the sacred Labarum, which guided the Roman:
From the shores of the Gulf to the Delaware's slope,
    'Tis the trust of the free, and the terror of foemen.
Fling its folds to the air, while we boldly declare
The rights we demand, or the deeds that we dare;
And the Cross of the South shall forever remain
To light us to Freedom and Glory again.

But, if peace should be hopeless, and justice denied,
    And war's bloody vulture should flap his black pinions,
Then gladly to arms! while we hurl, in our pride,
    Defiance to tyrants, and death to their minions,
With our front to the field, swearing never to yield,
Or return like the Spartan in death on our shield;
And the Cross of the South shall triumphantly wave
As the flag of the free, or the pall of the brave.

A PATRIOTIC FAMILY. — John Fon Rodd is a German, and a son of William Henry Fon Rodd, Esq., of Butztown, Pa. The father is eighty-nine years of age, and has lost *nine sons* in the war for the Union. Eight of these were killed in battle, and the other died of starvation in the rebel pens at Salisbury. While a prisoner, the son last referred to actually *ate his right hand*, so great was his hunger. John, from whom we have obtained our information, is the *tenth* and youngest of the brothers, and he bears the scars of *eight wounds* received in battle. He, too, was for a time a prisoner at Salisbury, and was only released at the close of the war. His recital of the treatment of the starving prisoners fully confirms all the accounts that have heretofore been published of the Southern barbarism under which our men suffered. Upon inquiry, we learn from other sources, that Henry William Fon Rodd, the father of the *ten heroes*, has for many years been one of the most highly respected citizens of Butztown. Is there another man in the world who has sacrificed more sons upon the altar of our country than this aged German? — *Harrisburg Telegraph.*

FAITHFUL UNTO DEATH. — In the year 1861, when the first call for troops was made, James Hendrick, a young man of eighteen, resolved to leave his father's roof, in Wisconsin, and go forth to battle for the flag. At the time mentioned he was attached to a young girl of nearly the same age as himself, whose parents were rated among the "rich ones" in that section of the country. Her name was Ellen Goodridge. Previous to leaving for the seat of war he informed her of his intentions, promising to return in a few months. After the first battle of Bull Run his regiment was ordered to Washington, and receiving a Lieutenant's commission, Hendrick resolved to enter the service for three years, and wrote to his parents and sweetheart to that effect. The news was received by the girl with foreboding, and she resolved to accompany him. She immediately acquainted her parents with her resolve, who, in reply, turned her from the house, and bade her never come back.

She went, and finding out her lover's regiment, obtained permission to do the cooking at the Colonel's headquarters. She followed the regiment through the battles of Gettysburg, Antietam, Fredericksburg, the Wilderness, Cold Harbor, Petersburg, and Richmond, and in the intervening time went out with young Hendrick in many skirmishes and raids, in one of which she was wounded in the arm, the ball making a very bad flesh wound. After Lee surrendered, the object of her choice was taken deathly sick, and was forwarded in an ambulance to Washington, where he was placed in the hospital. Here, again, her noble heart showed itself. She watched over him, bathed his fevered brow, read to him, wrote home letters for him, and finally, with a broken heart, closed his eyes in death. The day before his death an Episcopal minister joined the two in marriage — he dying with a painful disease, and she nearly crazed with the thought that, after four long years of suffering, he for whom she had given up home, friends, everything dear on earth, and for whom she had braved every danger, was going to another world.

GOVERNOR ANDREW AS A WAG AND A PATRIOT. — Military necessity prevented two young lovers from joining hands in marriage. The soldier was four times prevented from getting his leave of absence. The War Department did not find it consistent with its duty to permit the lady and her brother to go to the distant front to have the rite duly solemnized, so that the wife might share the lot of the husband.

At last an appeal was made to the heart of His Excellency the Governor of Massachusetts, and with the success that attends such an appeal when official obligation allows the indulgence of his kindly sensibilities and gentle sympathies. The letter of his fair correspondent moved the Executive and the man, and he at once forwarded it to Washington with the following indorsement, which succeeded in smoothing the course of true love, and melting Mars to tenderness. This was not the first or only instance in which the Governor brought about other unions, in the midst of his endeavors to preserve the Union of the States.

"*To the Hon. E. M. Stanton, Secretary of War :*

"This case appeals to all our sympathies as patriots and as gentlemen, and I appeal to the chivalry of the Department of War, which presides over more heroes than Homer ever dreamed of, and better and braver than his Muse ever sung — I pray you to grant this request of my fair correspondent, and generations will rise up and call us blessed. J. A. A."

UNCLE SAM EVERYWHERE. — A soldier of a Pennsylvania regiment, who was wounded at the battle of Chancellorsville, and left on the field, afterwards related his adventures to the Colonel. When the tide of battle had swept past the spot where he lay, a rebel soldier came to him, and took away his canteen, haversack, musket, and accoutrements, and finally demanded his coat and shoes. At this the Pennsylvanian at first demurred, but was forced to submit. Thereupon ensued a conversation :

"Where do you belong?" asked the rebel.

"To Pennsylvania," was the reply.

"And what are you doing down here in Virginia?"

"Vell, I comes down here to fight," said the unlucky Buck County man.

"To fight, eh?" said the Virginian; "why don't you fight in your own State, if you want to fight : what business have you here in Virginia?"

The question might have been a poser for some, but the brave Dutchman replied :

"Vel, I fights mit Uncle Sam, and Uncle Sam he goes efryvere."

GENERAL GRANT'S WAR HORSE. — The General was peculiarly proud of his stud, but particularly so of his war charger. To the few friends to whom he unbends he took great delight in exhibiting his horses. A friend was with Grant one day, and the conversation turned upon horses. "Perhaps," said the General, "you would like to see the horse I have ridden during all the campaigns that I have commanded." The General ordered his horse to be brought out. To the surprise of the gentleman, the animal seemed no more than a lady's palfrey. Small, slender, with agile limbs, black as a coal, an eye like a hawk, intelligent, but mild, with the unmistakable "lick" on each side of the mane, not unlike the "cowlick" on a boy's head, looking, for all the world, like a family pet for women and children. The visitor uttered his astonishment by saying: "Beautiful, but no endurance." "Endurance!" said General Grant; "this animal exceeds any horse flesh I ever saw for endurance. I have taken this horse out at daylight, and kept in the saddle till dark, and he came in as fresh when I returned as when I saddled him in the morning. Gold could not buy him. He was imported from a rare breed by Jeff Davis himself. He was taken from Jeff Davis' plantation." This conversation was held just before Davis was caught. "I suppose," said the visitor, "you would exchange this horse for Jeff Davis?" "You have said it," said the General. "I would exchange it for the rebel chief, but for nothing else under heaven."

THE PRESIDENT AND AN OHIO BOY. — A correspondent, describing the throng of visitors who crowded President Johnson's office, said:

"Among those favored with an interview was high private G. Van Zant, of the Seventy-ninth Ohio, thirteen years old, a clean-faced and bright-eyed youth, who has made the entire campaign from Atlanta with the regiment, acting part of the time as drummer-boy, and part as Orderly to General Ward. 'Well, my son,' said the President, 'what do you want? A Brevet, I suppose. Brevet Corporal? how will that do?' 'No, sir, I don't care for rank. I have a pony brought all the way through, and they are going to take him from me, and I want to take him home and keep him.' 'You shall have him'— and writing an order for transportation, directed the officers to let him have the pony. 'Now I am all right again;' and with a 'Thank you,' he left the President."

WANDERERS. — A large number of Ex-Confederate officers and soldiers were wandering about the Northern cities in a disconsolate sort of way, their "occupation gone."

A gentleman met one of them in the street. They had known each other in the old days, and the following conversation ensued:

Confederate Colonel — "Halloa, Jones! how are you?"

Union Gentleman — "Is that you, Harry? What are you doing here? You've no business here; I'll have you arrested."

Confederate — (throwing his arms wildly in the air) — "Great heavens! where am I to go? There's no North, no South, no East, no West, for me; where am I to go? I'm subjugated, whipped, conquered — anything you please. I'm a deuced sight better Union man than you. I'm for Andy Johnson, Lloyd Garrison, Wendell Phillips; am in favor of the abolition of slavery, and that sort of thing."

Union — "Well! I'll have you arrested, anyhow. You're a rebel!"

Confederate — "Arrested! Look a here — (pulling out a package of papers) — there's twenty oaths I've taken, besides being paroled.

Why, I've sworn myself into another Tophet to get out of that infernal Confederacy. Here's my brother, who has always been a Union man, and now furnishes me with the funds for speculation South. I am going down to Savannah to see if I can't buy my farm back again. Good by!"

INCIDENTS OF ANTIETAM. — My confrère and myself were within a few yards of Hooker. It was a very hot place. We could not distinguish the "ping" of the individual bullets, but their combined and mingled hum was like the din of a great Lowell factory. Solid shot and shell came shrieking through the air, but over our heads, as we were on the extreme front.

Hooker — commonplace before — the moment he heard the guns, loomed up into gigantic stature. His eye gleamed with the grand anger of battle. He seemed to know exactly what to do, to feel that he was master of the situation, and to impress every one else with the fact. Turning to one of his staff, and pointing to a spot near us, he said:

"Go, and tell Captain —— to bring his battery and plant it there at once!"

The Lieutenant rode away. After giving one or two further orders with great clearness, rapidity, and precision, Hooker's eye turned again to that mass of rebel infantry in the woods, and he said to another officer, with great emphasis:

"Go, and tell Captain —— to bring his battery here instantly!"

Sending more messages to the various divisions and batteries, only a single member of the staff remained. Once more scanning the woods with his eager eye, Hooker directed the aid:

"Go, and tell Captain —— to bring that battery here without one second's delay. Why, my God, how he can pour it into their infantry!"

By this time several of the body-guard had fallen from their saddles. Our horses plunged wildly. A shell ploughed the ground under my rearing steed, and another exploded near Mr. Smalley, throwing great clouds of dust over both of us. Hooker leaped his white horse over a low fence into an adjacent orchard, whither we gladly followed. Though we did not move more than thirty yards, it took us comparatively out of range.

The desired battery, stimulated by three successive messages, came up, with smoking horses, at a full run, was unlimbered in the twinkling of an eye, and began to pour shots into the enemy, who were also suffering severely from our infantry discharges. It was not many seconds before they began to waver. Through the rifting smoke, we could see their line sway to and fro; then it broke like a thaw in a great river. Hooker rose up in his saddle, and, in a voice of suppressed thunder, exclaimed:

"There they go, . . . Forward!"

Our whole line moved on. It was now nearly dark. Having shared the experience of "Fighting Joe Hooker" quite long enough, I turned towards the rear. Fresh troops were pressing forward, and stragglers were ranged in long lines behind rocks and trees.

Riding slowly along a grassy slope, as I supposed quite out of range, my meditations were disturbed by a cannon ball, whose rush of air fanned my face, and made my horse shrink and rear almost upright. The next moment came another behind me, and by the great blaze of a fire of rails, which the soldiers had built, I saw it *ricochet* down the slope, like a foot-ball, and pass right through a column of our troops in blue, who were marching steadily forward. The gap which it made was immediately closed up.

Men with litters were groping through the darkness, bearing the wounded back to the ambulances.

At nine o'clock I wandered to a farm-house occupied by some of our pickets. We dared not light candles, as it was within range of the enemy. The family had left. I tied my horse to an apple tree, and lay down upon the parlor floor, with my saddle for a pillow. At intervals during the night, we heard the popping of musketry, and at the first glimpse of dawn the picket officer shook me by the arm.

"My friend," said he, "you had better go away as soon as you can; this place is getting rather hot for civilians."

I rode around through the field, for shot and shell were already screaming up the narrow lane.

Thus commenced the long, hotly-contested battle of Antietam. Our line was three miles in length, with Hooker on the right, Burnside on the left, and a great gap in the middle, occupied only by artillery; while Fitz-John Porter, with his fine corps, was held in reserve. From dawn until nearly dark, the two great armies wrestled like athletes, straining every muscle, losing here, gaining there, and at many points fighting the same ground over and over again. It was a fierce, sturdy, indecisive conflict.

Five thousand spectators viewed the struggle from a hill comparatively out of range. Not more than three persons were struck there during the day. McClellan and his staff occupied another ridge half a mile in the rear.

"By Heaven! it was a goodly sight to see,
For one who had no friend or brother there."

No one who looked upon that wonderful panorama can describe or forget it. Every hill and valley, every cornfield, grove, and cluster of trees, was fiercely fought for.

The artillery was unceasing; we could often count more than sixty guns to the minute. It was like thunder; and the musketry sounded like the patter of rain-drops in an April shower. On the great field were riderless horses and scattering men, clouds of dirt from solid shot and exploding shells, long, dark lines of infantry swaying to and fro, with columns of smoke rising from their muskets, red flashes and white puffs from the batteries — with the sun shining brightly on all this scene of tumult, and beyond it, upon the dark, rich woods, and the clear blue mountains south of the Potomac. — *A. D. Richardson.*

A SPUNKY PRISONER. — A Captain of one of the New York companies said he was exceedingly anxious to be exchanged and return home; but if he thought such exchange would enure to the benefit of the Confederate States, and lead to their recognition by foreign powers, he would refuse it. He preferred rather that both sides should shoot or hang all the prisoners that should be taken, and he would willingly stand his chance with the rest. — *Southern paper.*

AT THE FRONT. — On the day of President Lincoln's funeral, a bronzed and weather-beaten soldier, anxious to obtain a better view of the procession, happened to step before a party of ladies and gentlemen. One of the gentlemen nudged him on the elbow, at the same time observing, "Excuse me, sir, but you are right in front of us." Bowing handsomely in return, the soldier replied, "That is nothing remarkable for me, sir; I have been in front of you for three years." So these iron men, marching with the nonchalance of veterans, are the men who have stood in "front of us for three years."

NOBLE SOUTHERN WOMEN. — Much has been written about Spartan women of old, — much about the noble Roman matron, — much about our excellent "foremothers of the Revolution;" but it has been reserved for the women of our Sunny South to blend the virtues of these heroines all in one, and present to the world the brightest example of firmness, courage, and patriotism. Look at the hundreds of women all over our land — delicate ones, who have been reared in the lap of luxury; who have heretofore been shielded from every rough blast; women who, a year ago, were lingering over the ivory keys of their pianos, or discussing with their dressmakers the shade of silk which became their complexion best; and see how they have risen, without a dissenting voice, to meet the exigencies of the times. "What shall I wear?" is now a question seldom asked. The only attention that dress demands is the consideration, "Will it be a piece of economy to purchase this or that?" and daily we hear the remark, "I want homespun dresses, — they are the best for us now." Instead of finding our women at the piano, or on the fashionable promenade, we find them busy at their looms, busy at their wheels, busy making soldiers' uniforms, busy making bandages, busy in hospitals, busy girding up their sons, their husbands, and their fathers for the battle-field. Tell me, are they not a noble race? Luxury has not enervated them; adversity has not depressed them. There was once a French queen, who, surrounding herself by her maids of honor, wrought, day after day, on delicate tapestry, with which the churches in her realm were afterwards hung. It was thought to be an act of great virtue in her. The fact was registered upon the page of history; and she has been held up to her sex as a "shining example." But she did not, as the wife of our Governor has done, set herself down to sew on heavy woollen goods for soldiers; she did not throw aside the silken robe and the golden chain, and apply herself, day after day, with unwearied assiduity, over stiff fabrics, which make the shoulders and the fingers alike ache. Nearly all the bandages that were used on the bloody field of Manassas, between the 21st and 23d of July, 1861, were made and forwarded by two Georgia women, Mrs. Robert Hardaway and her sister, who reside near Columbus. Southern matrons are indeed the jewels of our land. — *Southern Field and Fireside.*

UNITED STATES NATIONAL ANTHEM.

BY WILLIAM ROSS WALLACE.

God of the Free! upon Thy breath
Our Flag is for the Right unrolled
As broad and brave as when its Stars
First lit the hallowed time of old.

For Duty still its folds shall fly,
For Honor still its glories burn,
Where Truth, Religion, Valor, guard
The patriot's sword and martyr's urn.

No tyrant's impious step is ours;
No lust of power on nations rolled:
Our Flag—for *friends*, a starry sky;
For *traitors*, storm in every fold.

O, thus we'll keep our Nation's life,
Nor fear the bolt by despots hurled;
The blood of all the world is here,
And they who strike us strike the world!

God of the Free! our Nation bless
In its strong manhood as its birth,
And make its life a Star of Hope
For all the struggling of the earth.

Then shout beside thine Oak, O North!
O South, wave answer with thy Palm!
And in our Union's heritage
Together sing the Nation's Psalm!

THE COLORED SCHOOL AT DANVILLE. — A correspondent relates the following in a letter from Danville, North Carolina: A negro school had been established here in one of the hospital buildings for the benefit of the junior portion of the colored population. This morning I paid it a visit, and found that it numbered some two hundred and fifty scholars, and that there has been, until recently, a night school, with an attendance of about two hundred and sixty. The present teacher is a member of the Eighth Pennsylvania cavalry, who has been detailed for the duty. I could not help feeling amused at his style of teaching. An orthography class, consisting of two members, was reciting as I entered. The teacher was seated behind a square pine table. The pupils were in front of it, reclining on it with their elbows, and leaning half way across. One of them was a tall, listless-looking girl of about thirteen; her wool was gathered into sections and twisted into "pig tails," two of which were tied

under the chin, while the seams that marked the several partings looked like rivers winding through a cane-brake. In her hand she held a peach-tree switch, one end of which she chewed with commendable assiduity. "Goat," shouted the teacher. "Dat's not de word," said the girl; "I jest done spelled dat." "Well, boat, then; spell *that.* Say, you boys on those back benches, are you going to keep quiet there, *hey?* Look at your *books*, now, and don't stare at *me.* Sit up there, *you!* 'Moat, mo-o-a-t, moat.'. Say, you, there, better raise yourselves up on them seats, else you'll *git* raised purty soon. Stop that noise, there, you boys, or I'll give you a dose of hickory oil."

The next recitation was by a class of small children, spelling on cards. "Where's that pinter of mine?" demands the teacher. "It's done broke, sah," shouted half a dozen piccaninnies. "Who broke it?" (in a stentorian voice.) Silence is the only response. "Can none on you tell me who broke it? It'll be a dear break for them, if I find 'em out; I'll try how this hickory will break over their backs."

These illustrations are sufficient to show that the colored school at Danville is conducted in a style now nearly obsolete in more favored localities.

LUCKY AND UNLUCKY. — A young man from Worcester, Massachusetts, a private in the Fifty-seventh regiment, in the battle of Cold Harbor, was hit by a ball in the chin, which badly fractured the bone, and tore out several teeth. Another ball hit the right shoulder, fractured the shoulder-blade, and remains undiscovered. The third ball passed through his abdomen, and brought him to the ground. His companions dragged him to a hole. where his body and head could not be seen by the enemy; but his legs being exposed, one ball passed through the calf of his leg, another cut a deep groove through his shin, another cut through the top of the instep, and another carried away the next to the great toe. He lay in the hole all day, and was then taken prisoner, and starved for several months; yet this young man returned to Worcester erect and in good health, and not perceptibly lame. His name is E. P. Rockwood.

INCIDENTS OF THE SOUTH. — "A Southerner" relates the following amusing affairs:

"A certain General of brigade, who was mortally wounded at Gettysburg, and who died within our lines, was rather fond of the good whiskey for which the Old Dominion is famous. He rarely appeared on parade without being well fortified with a fair potion of it. As soon as the business of the parade was ended, it was his custom to dismount, and proceed to the front of the line, and dare any officer or man who thought he could whip him, to come out and fight him, accompanying his challenge with a volley of drunken abuse of the whole command. After keeping up this display for some time, without finding any one willing to accept his invitation, he would dismiss the parade, and return to his quarters very well pleased with the proceeding.

"With a favorite General the men took many liberties, and this very popularity seemed to destroy the deference usually paid to such high officers. A laughable occurrence of this kind took place during the retreat of the Confederates from Yorktown, in 1862.

"Just after the battle of Williamsburg, General Magruder and his staff stopped at the house of a widow lady on the road, and engaged dinner. Soon after their arrival a Louisiana soldier came up, and accosted the landlady with:

"'Madam, can I get dinner?'

"'Yes, sir,' was the reply; 'but as I am preparing dinner for General Magruder and staff, and have not room at my table for more, you will have to wait for a second table.'

"'Very well, ma'am. Thank you,' said the soldier, taking his seat in a position to command a view of the dining-room. Watching the movements of the servants, he waited until the feast was on the table, and while his hostess proceeded to the parlor to announce dinner to her distinguished guests, he entered the dining-room, and, seating himself at the table, awaited further developments, trusting to his impudence to get him out of the scrape.

"Upon the entrance of the party of officers, there was found to be seats for all but one, and one politely returned to the parlor to wait. The General took a seat next to the soldier, and, after the first course was finished, turned to him, and asked:

"'Sir, have you any idea with whom you are dining?'

"'No,' coolly replied the soldier; 'I used to be very particular on that score; but since I turned soldier, I don't care whom I eat with, so that the victuals are clean.'

"The joke was so good that Magruder laughed heartily at it, and even paid for the soldier's dinner, and sent him on his way."

AMONG THE REBELS. — Camp Dennison, about twenty miles from Cincinnati, Ohio, says a correspondent writing in the summer of 1862, was the first in that State, and very soon after the beginning of the war assumed the proportions of a military city. Of late it has been used only for the sick and wounded, a few regiments being under instructions there. Since, however, the new call for troops, it has been again full of activity and interest.

Among those who have been devoting much labor to both the physical and spiritual wants of the sufferers there, the Reverend Mr. Clayton, an earnest Methodist, formerly of the Bethel in this city, has been prominent. All the sufferers there have learned to look for his visits with anxiety. In the language of the Dutch doctor there, the general opinion is, "If preacher Clayton ain't a Christian, then t'ain't vort a tam to be a Christian."

Few things are more interesting than the results of his visits through the various wards, but I shall confine myself to some notes I have of conversations of his with wounded rebels, of whom we have thirty-four there. They are all from somewhere in the south-west, and have all applied to the Government for permission to take the oath, and be released thereon.

One of the most interesting cases was a youth, whose heart was evidently busy doing poetic justice to the Yankees he had been taught to hate, though he still was anxious about Southern rights. Mr. Clayton talked to him for some time concerning religious matters, and the young man at last broke in by saying, "We've talked about religion long enough; now let's talk politics." There was a peculiar Southernism about his look and tone that excited a smile all around. "Well," replied Mr. Clayton, "I'm not much on politics; I'd rather not talk about them; tell me how you felt when you were wounded." "Thought it would be a sharp pain, sir, but it wasn't; I was wounded in the legs, and it was just like being knocked off my pins by a strong blow from a log of wood. Fell flat on my belly, and my knees drew themselves up under my chin. Made sure I was dead, but thought it didn't make much difference, for I saw our men retreating, and knew the Yankees would get me and kill me sure; always told, sir, the Yankees had horns. Well, there I lay; and up came a Colonel leading his men — he was in front, sir; he jumped down from his horse, and ran to me, drawing something from his belt; so I gave up; but it wasn't a pistol, sir" — and here the boy's eyes moistened — "it was a canteen! He put it to my lips. I drank. He jumped on his horse again, and said, 'Charge, boys; they're fleeing!' Then some soldiers on foot came towards me, and I thought they were not all like that officer, and I gave up again. But, sir, they said, 'Comrade, get up.' They lifted me up, and said, 'Put your arms around our necks, and we'll lead you away from these bullets;' and these were the 'damned Yankees!' I tell you, sir, no man ever hugged his sweetheart more friendly than I hugged these Yankees' necks."

After a few more remarks the youth showed a determination to "talk politics," and asked Mr. Clayton, "What are you fighting for?" Mr. Clayton calmly, and in good humor, gave him his ideas of the issue, and in ending asked him what they were fighting for. "To hold property, sir," replied the youth — "our slave property." "How many slaves did you have?" "None." "And you?" to the next. "None." He then went around to all the thirty-four rebels, and but one was found who had owned a slave. "Now," said Mr. Clayton, "where are the men who have these slaves which they are so afraid of losing?" Here a man named McClellan, who has since died, rose up on his cot, and stretching out his thin hand, said, in a sepulchral voice, "They are at home enjoying themselves, and have sent us to die for them and theirs." And to this the echoes around the room were, "That's so; that's God's truth."

Lying near this one is an Irishman. "Well, sir," says the genial Mr. Clayton, "what's the matter with you?" "Wounded, sir; slight wound in the groin — worse one in the heel." "Where were you wounded?" "Pittsburg Landing, sir." "What part of the battle?" "Second fire of the last round, sir." "What, Monday? Why, it was rather hard, wasn't it, to fight two days and then get hurt at the very last?" "Devil a two days did I fight at all, sir." "Why, how was that?" "Why, you see, sir, I didn't know what I was fighting for, and I didn't want to blow a fellow-creature's brains out without knowing what I was blowing 'em out for — d'ye see? No more did I want a fellow-creature to blow my brains out without knowing what they was blown out for; so, sir, I just snaked away, sir. But on Monday they found me, sir, and drummed me in." He was from Texas.

The only man among these who has held slaves is a man named, if I remember, Staten; he is not only very anxious to take the oath, but prays fervently that our Government will bring peace by taking away the negroes from the Southerners. "I'm willing never to see mine again," said he, "and rely on it, it is the only way to bring peace, the only way."

WHAT SHALL WE DO FOR JEFF DAVIS?

WEAVE him a mantle of burning shame!
Stamp on his forehead that dreadful name
Which deeds like his inscribe in blood —
A *Traitor* to man! a *Traitor* to God!

Plait him a crown of the flower that comes
In the ashes that lie o'er buried homes!
Let his sceptre be the smoking brand
Which his fiat sent throughout the land!

Let his pæans be the bitter cries
From millions of anguished hearts that rise,
Both day and night, to that listening ear
Which ever stoops their plaints to hear.

'Mid the ruin dire his hands have wrought,
Let him find the *Throne* he long has sought,
While starving crowds, in hoarse notes ring,
Not Cotton, but grim old *Death* is king!

QUALITIES OF PRESIDENT LINCOLN. — The most marked characteristic of Mr. Lincoln's manner was his simplicity and artlessness. This immediately impressed itself upon the observation of those who met him for the first time, and each successive interview deepened the impression. People seemed delighted to find in the ruler of the nation freedom from pomposity and affectation, mingled with a certain simple dignity that never forsook him. Though pressed with the weight of responsibility resting upon him as President of the United States, he shrank from assuming any of the honors, or even titles, of the position. After years of intimate acquaintance with Mr. Lincoln, the writer cannot now recall a single instance in which he spoke of himself as President, or used that title of himself, except when acting in an official capacity. He always spoke of his position and office vaguely, as "this place," "here," or other modest phrases. Once, speaking of the room in the Capitol used by the Presidents of the United States during the close of a session of Congress, he said, "That room, you know, that they call " — dropping his voice and hesitating — "the President's room." To an intimate friend who addressed him always by his own proper title, he said, "Now call me Lincoln, and I'll promise not to tell of the breach of etiquette — if you won't — and I shall have a resting spell from Mister Lincoln."

With all his simplicity and unacquaintance with courtly manners, his native dignity never forsook him in the presence of critical or polished strangers; but mixed with his angularities and *bonhomie* was something which spoke the fine fibre of the man; and, while his sovereign disregard of courtly conventionalities was somewhat ludicrous, his native sweetness and straightforwardness of manner served to disarm criticism, and impress the visitor that he was before a man pure, self-poised, collected, and strong in unconscious strength. Of him an accomplished foreigner, whose knowledge of the courts was more perfect than that of the English language, said, "He seems to me one grand *gentilhomme* in disguise."

THREE WEEKS AT GETTYSBURG. — This eloquent and earnest sketch was written by an accomplished lady of New York, to whom the entire loyal people of the country are personally indebted for her devotion in her labors for the Sanitary Commission during the war:

"What we did at Gettysburg, for the three weeks we were there, you will want to know. 'We' are Mrs. —— and myself, who, happening to be on hand at the right moment, gladly fell in with the proposition to do what we could at the Sanitary Commission Lodge after the battle. There were, of course, the agents of the Commission, already on the field, distributing supplies to the hospitals, and working night and day among the wounded. I cannot pretend to tell you what was done by all the big wheels of the concern, but only how two of the smallest ones went round, and what turned up in the going.

"Twenty-four hours we were in making the journey between Baltimore and Gettysburg, places only four hours apart in ordinary running time; and this will give you some idea of the difficulty there was of bringing up supplies when the fighting was over, and the delays in transporting wounded. Coming towards the town at this crawling rate, we passed some fields where the fences were down, and the ground slightly tossed up. 'That's where Kilpatrick's cavalrymen fought the rebels,' some one said; 'and close by that barn a rebel soldier was found day before yesterday, sitting dead;' no one to help, poor soul, 'near the whole city full.' The railroad bridge, broken up by the enemy, Government had not rebuilt as yet, and we stopped two miles from the town, to find that, as usual, just where the Government had left off, the Commission had come in. There stood their temporary lodge and kitchen, and here, hobbling out of their tents, came the wounded men who had made their way down from the corps hospital, expecting to leave at once in the return cars.

"This is the way the thing was managed at first: The surgeons, left in care of the wounded three or four miles out from the town, went up and down among the men in the morning, and said, 'Any of you boys who can make your way to the cars, can go to Baltimore.' So off start all who think they feel well enough, anything being better than the 'hospitals,' so called, for the first few days after a battle. Once the men have the surgeon's permission to go, they are off; and there may be an interval of a day, or two days, should any of them be too weak to reach the train in time, during which these poor fellows belong to no one, the hospital at one end, the railroad at the other, with far more than chance of falling through between the two. The Sanitary Commission knew this would be so of necessity, and, coming in, made a connecting link between these two ends.

"For the first few days the worst cases only came down in ambulances from the hospitals; hundreds of fellows hobbled along as best they could, in heat and dust, for hours, slowly toiling, and many hired farmers' wagons, as hard as the farmers' fists themselves, and were jolted down to the railroad, at three or four dollars the man. Think of the disappointment of a soldier, sick, body and heart, to find, at the end of this miserable journey, that his effort to get away, into which he had put all his remaining stock of strength, was useless; that 'the cars had gone,' or 'the cars were full;' that while he was coming others had stepped down before him, and that he must turn all the weary way back again, or sleep on the roadside till the next train 'to-morrow.' Think what this would have been, and you are ready to appreciate the relief and comfort that was. No men were turned back. You fed and you sheltered them just when no one else could have done so; and out of the boxes and barrels of good and nourishing things, which you, people at home, had supplied, we took all that was needed. Some of you sent a stove (that is, the money to get it), some of you the beef stock, some of you the milk and fresh bread; and all of you would have been thankful that you had done so, could you have seen the refreshment and comfort received through these things.

"As soon as the men hobbled up to the tents, good hot soup was given all round; and that over, their wounds were dressed, — for the gentlemen of the Commission are cooks, or surgeons as occasion demands, — and, finally, with their blankets spread over the straw, the men stretched themselves out, and were happy and contented till morning, and the next train.

"On the day that the railroad bridge was repaired we moved up to the depot, close by the town, and had things in perfect order; a first-rate camping ground, in a large field directly by the track, with unlimited supply of delicious, cool water. Here we set up two stoves, with four large boilers, always kept full of soup and coffee, watched by four or five black men, who did the cooking under our direction, and sang (not under our direction) at the tops of their voices all day,

'O darkies, hab you seen my massa.'

'When this cruel war is over.'

Then we had three large hospital tents, holding about thirty-five each, a large camp-meeting supply tent, where barrels of goods were stored, and our own smaller tent fitted up with tables, where jelly-pots and bottles of all kinds of good sirups, blackberry and black currant, stood in rows. Barrels were ranged round the tent walls; shirts, drawers, dressing-gowns, socks, and slippers (I wish we had had more of the latter), rags and bandages, each in its own place on one side; on the other, boxes of tea, coffee, soft crackers, tamarinds, cherry brandy, &c. Over the kitchen, and over this small supply tent, we women rather reigned, and filled up our wants by requisitions on the Commission's depot. By this time there had arrived a 'delegation' of just the right kind from Canandaigua, New York, with surgeon, dressers, and attendants, bringing a first-rate supply of necessaries and comforts for the wounded, which they handed over to the Commission.

"Twice a day the trains left for Baltimore or Harrisburg, and twice a day we fed all the wounded who arrived for them. Things were systematized now, and the men came down in long ambulance trains to the cars; baggage cars they were, fitted with straw for the wounded to lie on, and broken open at either end to let in the air. A Government surgeon was always present to attend to the careful lifting of the soldiers from ambulance to car. Many of the men could get along very nicely, holding one foot up, and taking great jumps on their crutches. The latter were a great comfort; we had a nice supply at the Lodge, and they travelled up and down from the tents to the cars daily. Only occasionally did we dare let a pair go on with some very lame soldier, who begged for them; we needed them to help the new arrivals each day, and trusted to the men being supplied at the hospitals at the journey's end. Pads and crutches are a standing want — pads particularly. We manufactured them out of the rags we had, stuffed with sawdust from brandy boxes; and with half a sheet, and some soft straw, Mrs. —— made a poor dying boy as easy as his sufferings would permit. Poor young fellow! he was so grateful to her for washing, and feeding, and comforting him! He was too ill to bear the journey, and went from our tent to the church hospital, and from the church to his grave, which would have been coffinless but for the care of ——, for the Quartermaster's Department was overtaxed, and for many days our dead were simply wrapped in their blankets and put into the earth. It is a soldierly way, after all, of lying wrapped in the old war-worn blanket, — the little dust returned to dust.

"When the surgeons had the wounded all

placed, with as much comfort as seemed possible under the circumstances, on board the train, our detail of men would go from car to car, with soup made of beef-stock or fresh meat, full of potatoes, turnips, cabbage, and rice, with fresh bread and coffee, and, when stimulants were needed, with ale, milk punch, or brandy. Water pails were in great demand for use in the cars on the journey, and also empty bottles, to take the place of canteens. All our whiskey and brandy bottles were washed and filled up at the spring, and the boys went off, carefully hugging their extemporized canteens, from which they would wet their wounds, or refresh themselves, till the journey ended. I do not think that a man of the sixteen thousand, who were transported during our stay, went from Gettysburg without a good meal — rebels and Unionists together, they all had it — and were pleased and satisfied. 'Have you friends in the army, madam?' a rebel soldier, lying on the floor of the car, said to me, as I gave him some milk. 'Yes; my brother is on ——'s staff.' 'I thought so, ma'am. You can always tell; when people are good to soldiers they are sure to have friends in the army.' 'We are rebels, you know, ma'am,' another said; 'do you treat rebels so?' It was strange to see the good brotherly feeling come over the soldiers — our own and the rebels, when side by side they lay in our tents. 'Hallo, boys! this is the pleasantest way to meet, — isn't it? We are better friends when we are as close as this, than a little farther off.' And then they would go over the battles together — 'We were here,' and 'You were there,' in the friendliest way.

"After each train of cars, daily, for the three weeks we were in Gettysburg, trains of ambulances arrived too late — men who must spend the day with us until the five P. M. cars went, and men too late for the five P. M. train, who must spend the night till the ten A. M. cars went. All the men who came in this way, under our own immediate and particular attention, were given the best we had of care and food. The surgeon in charge of our camp, with his most faithful dresser and attendants, looked after all their wounds, which were often in a most shocking state, particularly among the rebels. Every evening and morning they were dressed. Often the men would say, 'That feels good. I haven't had my wound so well dressed since I was hurt.' Something cool to drink is the first thing asked for, after the long, dusty drive, and pailfuls of tamarinds and water — 'a beautiful drink,' the men used to say — disappeared rapidly among them.

"After the men's wounds were attended to, we went round giving them clean clothes; had basins and soap and towels; and followed these with socks, slippers, shirts, drawers, and those coveted dressing-gowns. Such pride as they felt in them — comparing colors, and smiling all over as they lay in clean and comfortable rows ready for supper, 'on dress parade,' they used to say. And then the milk, particularly if it were boiled and had a little whiskey and sugar, and the bread, with butter on it, and jelly on the butter — how

good it all was, and how lucky we felt ourselves in having the immense satisfaction of distributing these things, which all of you, hard at work in villages and cities, were getting ready and sending off, in faith.

"Canandaigua sent cologne with its other supplies, which went right to the noses and hearts of the men. 'That is good, now;' 'I'll take some of that;' 'worth a penny a sniff;' 'that kinder gives one life;' and so on, all round the tents, as we tipped the bottles up on the clean handkerchiefs some one had sent, and when they were gone, over squares of cotton, on which the perfume took the place of hem, — 'just as good, ma'am.' We varied our dinners with custard and baked rice puddings, scrambled eggs, codfish hash, corn starch, and always as much soft bread, tea, coffee, or milk as they wanted. Two Massachusetts boys I especially remember, for the satisfaction with which they ate their pudding. I carried a second plateful up to the cars, after they had been put in, and fed one of them till he was sure he had had enough. Young fellows they were, lying side by side, one with a right and one with a left arm gone.

"The Gettysburg women were kind and faithful to the wounded and their friends, and the town was full to overflowing of both. The first day, when Mrs. —— and I reached the place, we literally begged our bread from door to door; but the kind woman who at last gave us dinner would take no pay for it. 'No, ma'am, I shouldn't wish to have that sin on my soul when the war is over.' She, as well as others, had fed the strangers flocking into town daily; sometimes over fifty of them for each meal, and all for love, and nothing for reward; and one night we forced a reluctant confession from our hostess that she was meaning to sleep on the floor that we might have a bed — her whole house being full. Of course we couldn't allow this self-sacrifice, and hunted up some other place to stay in. We did her no good, however, for we afterwards found that the bed was given up that night to some other stranger who arrived late and tired: 'An old lady, you know, and I couldn't let an old lady sleep on the floor.' Such acts of kindness and self-denial were almost entirely confined to the women.

"Few good things can be said of the Gettysburg farmers, and I only use Scripture language in calling them 'evil beasts.' One of this kind came creeping into our camp three weeks after the battle. He lived five miles only from the town, and had 'never seen a rebel.' He heard we had some of them, and came down to see them. 'Boys,' we said, marching him into the tent, which happened to be full of rebels that day waiting for the train, 'boys, here's a man who never saw a rebel in his life, and wants to look at you;' and there he stood with his mouth wide open, and there they lay in rows, laughing at him, stupid old Dutchman. 'And why haven't you seen a rebel?' Mrs. —— said; 'why didn't you take your gun and help to drive them out of your town?' 'A feller might'er got hit' — which reply was quite too much for the rebels;

they roared with laughter at him, up and down the tent. One woman we saw, who was by no means Dutch, and whose pluck helped to redeem the other sex. She lived in a little house close up by the field where the hardest fighting was done, a red-cheeked, strong, country girl. 'Were you frightened when the shells began flying?' 'Well, no; you see we was all a baking bread round here for the soldiers, and had our dough a rising. The neighbors they ran into their cellars, but I couldn't leave my bread. When the first shell came in at the window, and crashed through the room, an officer came and said, "You had better get out of this," but I told him I could not leave my bread, and I stood working it till the third shell came through, and then I went down cellar, but (triumphantly) I left my bread in the oven.' 'And why didn't you go before?' 'O, you see, if I had, the rebels would have come in and daubed the dough all over the place.' And here she had stood, at the risk of unwelcome plums in her loaves, while great holes, which we saw, were made by shot and shell through and through the room in which she was working.

"The streets of Gettysburg were filled with the battle. People thought and talked of nothing else; even the children showed their little spites by calling to each other, 'Here, you rebel!' and mere scraps of boys amused themselves with percussion caps and hammers. Hundreds of old muskets were piled on the pavements, the men who shouldered them a week before lying underground now, or helping to fill the long trains of ambulances on their way from the field. The private houses of the town were, many of them, hospitals; the little red flags hung from the upper windows.

"Besides our own men at the Lodge, we all had soldiers scattered about whom we could help from our supplies; and nice little puddings and jellies, or an occasional chicken, were a great treat to men condemned by their wounds to stay in Gettysburg, and obliged to live on what the empty town could provide. There was a Colonel in a shoe shop, a Captain just up the street, and a private round the corner (whose young sister had possessed herself of him, overcoming the military rules in some way, and carrying him off to a little room, all by himself, where I found her doing her best with very little). She came afterwards to our tent, and got for him clean clothes and good food, and all he wanted, and was perfectly happy in being his cook, washerwoman, medical cadet, and nurse. Besides such as these, we occasionally carried from our supplies something to the churches, which were filled with sick and wounded, and where men were dying, — men whose strong patience it was very hard to bear, — dying with thoughts of the old home far away, saying, as last words for the woman watching there, and waiting with a patience equal in its strength, 'Tell her I love her!'

"Late one afternoon — too late for the cars — a train of ambulances arrived at our lodge with over one hundred wounded rebels to be cared for through the night. Only one among them seemed too weak and faint to take anything. He was badly hurt and failing. I went to him after his wound was dressed, and found him lying on his blanket, stretched over the straw — a fair-haired, blue-eyed young Lieutenant — a face innocent enough for one of our own New England boys. I could not think of him as a rebel. He was too near heaven for that. He wanted nothing — had not been willing to eat for days, his comrades said — but I coaxed him to try a little milk gruel, flavored nicely with lemon and brandy; and one of the satisfactions of our three weeks is the remembrance of the empty cup I took away afterwards, and his perfect enjoyment of that supper. 'It was so good — the best thing he had had since he was wounded;' and he thanked me so much, and talked about his 'good supper' for hours. Poor creature! he had had no care, and it was a surprise and pleasure to find himself thought of; so, in a pleased, child-like way, he talked about it till midnight, the attendant told me, — as long as he spoke of anything; for at midnight the change came, and from that time he only thought of the old days before he was a soldier, when he sang hymns in his father's church. He sang them now again, in a clear, sweet voice: 'Lord, have mercy upon me;' and then songs without words — a sort of low intoning. His father was a Lutheran clergyman in South Carolina, one of the rebels told us in the morning, when we went into the tent to find him sliding out of our care. All day long we watched him — sometimes fighting his battles over — oftener singing his Lutheran chants — till in at the tent door, close to which he lay, looked a rebel soldier, just arrived with other prisoners. He started when he saw the Lieutenant, and, quickly kneeling down by him, called, 'Henry! Henry!'— but Henry was looking at some one a great way off, and could not hear him.

"'Do you know this soldier?' we said.

"'O, yes, ma'am! and his brother is wounded, and a prisoner, too, in the cars now.'

"Two or three men started after him, found him, and half carried him from the cars to our tent. 'Henry' did not know him, though, and he threw himself down by his side on the straw, and for the rest of the day lay in a sort of apathy, without speaking, except to assure himself that he could stay with his brother without the risk of being separated from his fellow-prisoners.

"And there the brothers lay, and there we, strangers, sat watching, and listening to the strong, clear voice, singing, 'Lord, have mercy upon me.' The Lord had mercy, and at sunset I put my hand on the Lieutenant's heart to find it still!

"All night the brother lay close against the coffin, and in the morning he went away with his comrades, leaving us to bury Henry, having 'confidence,' but first thanking us for what we had done, and giving us all that he had to show his gratitude — the palmetto ornament from his brother's cap, and a button from his coat.

"Dr. W. read the burial service that morning at the grave, and —— wrote his name on the little head-board: 'Lieutenant Rauch, Fourteenth Régiment South Carolina Volunteers.'

"In the field where we buried him, a number of colored freedmen, working for Government, on the railroad, had their camp, and every night they took their recreation, after the heavy work of the day was over, in prayer meetings. Such an 'inferior race,' you know! We went over one night and listened for an hour, while they sang, collected under the fly of a tent, a table in the middle, where the leader sat, and benches all round the sides for the congregation, — men only, — all very black and very earnest. They prayed with all their souls, as only black men and slaves can, for themselves and for the dear white people, who had come over to the meeting, and for 'Massa Lincoln,' for whom they seemed to have a reverential affection, some of them a sort of worship, which confused Father Abraham and Massa Abraham in one general call for blessings. Whatever else they asked for, they must have strength and comfort and blessing for 'Massa Lincoln.' Very little care was taken of these poor men. Those who were ill, during our stay, were looked after by one of the officers of the Commission. They were grateful for every little thing. Mrs. —— went into the town and hunted up several dozen bright handkerchiefs, hemmed them, and sent them over to be distributed the next night after meeting. They were put on the table in the tent, and one by one the men came up to get them. Purple, and blue, and yellow, the handkerchiefs were, and the desire of every man's heart fastened itself on a yellow one; they politely made way for each other, one man standing back to let another pass up first, although he ran the risk of seeing the particular pumpkin color that riveted his eyes taken from before them. When the distribution was over, each man tied his head up in his handkerchief and sang one more hymn, keeping time all round, with blue and purple and yellow nods, and thanking and blessing the white people, in 'their basket and in their store,' as much as if the cotton handkerchiefs had all been gold leaf. One man came over to our tent next day to say: 'Missus, was it you who sent me that present? I never had anything so beautiful in all my life before;' and he only had a blue one, too.

"Among our wounded soldiers, one night, came an elderly man, sick, wounded, and crazy, singing and talking about home. We did what we could for him, and pleased him greatly with a present of a red flannel shirt, drawers, and red calico dressing-gown, all of which he needed, and in which he dressed himself up, and then wrote a letter to his wife, made it into a little book with gingham covers, and gave it to one of the gentlemen to mail for him. The next morning he was sent on with the company from the Lodge, and that evening two tired women came into our camp — his wife and sister, who hurried on from their home to meet him, arriving just too late. Fortunately we had the queer little gingham book to identify him by, and when some one said, 'It is the man, you know, who screamed so,' the poor wife was certain about him. He had been crazy before the war, but not for two years, now, she said. He had been fretting for home since he was hurt, and when the doctor told him there was no chance of being sent there, he lost heart, and wrote to his wife to come and carry him away. It seemed almost hopeless for two lone women, who had never been out of their own little town, to succeed in finding a soldier among so many, sent in so many different directions; but we helped them as we could, and started them on their journey the next morning, back on their track, to use their common sense and Yankee privilege of questioning.

"A week after, Mrs. —— had a letter, full of gratitude, and saying that the husband was found and secured for home. That same night we had in our tents two fathers, with their wounded sons, and a nice old German mother with her boy. She had come in from Wisconsin, and brought with her a patch-work bed-quilt for her son, thinking he might have lost his blanket; and there he lay, all covered up in his quilt, looking so home-like, and feeling so too, no doubt, with his good old mother close at his side. She seemed bright and happy — had three sons in the army, one had been killed, this one wounded — yet she was so pleased with the tents, and the care she saw taken there of the soldiers, that while taking her tea from a barrel-head as table, she said, 'Indeed, if she was a man, she'd be a soldier too, right off.'

"For this temporary sheltering and feeding of all these wounded men, Government could make no provision. There was nothing for them, if too late for the cars, except the open field and hunger, in preparation for their fatiguing journey. It is expected, when the cars are ready, that the men will be promptly sent to meet them; and Government cannot provide for mistakes and delays; so that, but for the Sanitary Commission's Lodge and comfortable supplies, for which the wounded are indebted to the hard workers at home, men badly hurt must have suffered night and day while waiting for the 'next train.' We had, on an average, sixty of such men each night, for three weeks, under our care; sometimes one hundred, sometimes only thirty; and with the 'delegation,' and the help of other gentlemen volunteers, who all worked devotedly for the men, the whole thing was a great success; and you, and all of us, can't help being thankful that we had a share, however small, in making it so. Sixteen thousand good meals were given; hundreds of men kept through the day, and twelve hundred sheltered at night, their wounds dressed, their supper and breakfast secured, rebels and all. You will not, I am sure, regret that these most wretched men, these 'enemies,' 'sick, and in prison,' were helped and cared for, through your supplies, though certainly they were not in your minds when you packed your barrels and boxes. The clothing we reserved for our own men, except, now and then, when a shivering rebel needed it; but in feeding them, we could make no distinction. It was curious to see, among our workers at the Lodge, the disgust and horror felt for rebels giving place to the kindest feeling for wounded men.

"Our three weeks were coming to an end; the work of transporting the wounded was nearly over; twice daily we had filled and emptied our tents, and twice fed the trains before the long journey. The men came in slowly at the last, a Lieutenant, all the way from Oregon, being among the very latest. He came down from the corps hospitals (now greatly improved), having lost one foot, poor fellow, dressed in a full suit of the Commission's cotton clothes, just as bright and as cheerful as the first man, and all the men that we received, had been. We never heard a complaint. 'Would he like a little nice soup?' 'Well, no, thank you, ma'am;' hesitating and polite. 'You have a long ride before you, and had better take a little; I'll just bring it, and you can try.' So the good thick soup came. He took a very little in the spoon to please me, and afterwards the whole cupful to please himself. He 'did not think it was this kind of soup I meant. He had some in camp, and did not think he cared for any more; his "cook" was a very small boy, though, who just put some meat in a little water, and stirred it round.' 'Would you like a handkerchief?' and I produced our last one, with a hem and cologne too. 'O, yes; that is what I need; I have lost mine, and was just borrowing this gentleman's.' So the Lieutenant, the last man, was made comfortable, thanks to all of you, though he had but one foot to carry him on his long journey home.

"Four thousand soldiers, too badly hurt to be moved, were still left in Gettysburg, cared for kindly and well at the large new Government hospital, with a Sanitary Commission attachment. Our work was over, our tents were struck, and we came away after a flourish of trumpets from two military bands, who filed down to our door, and gave us a farewell — 'Red, white, and blue.' "

FAREWELL TO BROTHER JONATHAN.*

BY CAROLINE.

FAREWELL! we must part; we have turned from
  the land
Of our cold-hearted brother with tyrannous hand,
Who assumed all our rights as a favor to grant,
And whose smile ever covered the sting of a taunt;

Who breathed on the fame he was bound to defend, —
Still the craftiest foe, 'neath the guise of a friend, —
Who believed that our bosoms would bleed at a
  touch,
Yet could never believe he could goad them too
  much;

Whose conscience affects to be scared with our sin,
Yet is plastic to take all its benefits in;
The mote in our eye so enormous has grown,
That he never perceives there's a beam in his own.

* A reply to "Brother Jonathan's Farewell to Sister Caroline." See ante.

O, Jonathan, Jonathan! vassal of pelf,
Self-righteous, self-glorious, yes, every inch self,
Your loyalty now is all bluster and boast,
But was dumb when the foemen invaded our coast.

In vain did your country appeal to you then;
You coldly refused her your money and men;
Your trade interrupted, you slunk from her wars,
And preferred British gold to the Stripes and the
  Stars!

Then our generous blood was as water poured
  forth,
And the sons of the South were the shields of the
  North;
Nor our patriot ardor one moment gave o'er,
Till the foe you had fed we had driven from the
  shore!

Long years we have suffered opprobrium and
  wrong,
But we clung to your side with affection so strong,
That at last, in mere wanton aggression, you broke
All the ties of our hearts with one murderous
  stroke.

We are tired of contest for what is our own;
We are sick of a strife that could never be done;
Thus our love has died out, and its altars are dark,
Not Prometheus' self could rekindle the spark.

O, Jonathan, Jonathan! deadly the sin
Of your tigerish thirst for the blood of your kin;
And shameful the spirit that gloats over wives
And maidens despoiled of their honor and lives!

Your palaces rise from the fruits of our toil;
Your millions are fed from the wealth of our soil;
The balm of our air brings the health to your
  cheek,
And our hearts are aglow with the welcome we
  speak.

O brother! beware how you seek us again,
Lest you brand on your forehead the signet of
  Cain;
That blood and that crime on your conscience must
  sit:
We may fall — we may perish — but never submit!

The pathway that leads to the Pharisee's door
We remember, indeed, but we tread it no more;
Preferring to turn, with the Publican's faith,
To the path through the valley and shadow of
  death!

A SANITARY INCIDENT. — A member of one of the Hospital Aid Societies called upon an elderly widow lady, and, stating the object of her mission, was responded to in the following words: "It is but little I can do for you, but I have an old sheet that has been used but very little, although it was woven with my own hands more than sixty years ago, which, if torn up properly, will make excellent bandages. The amount of the gift is not much, but it is my desire that this relic of my earlier days shall be used for that purpose." Although the day of the spinning-wheel and hand-loom has vanished, yet how clearly one is reminded of old revolutionary times, when our mothers part with some trivial article which they have so long treasured, that it may bind up the bleeding wounds of our brave comrades in battle.

THE CHRISTIAN SOLDIER. — After the battle of Gettysburg, a soldier lay in a house by the roadside, dying. A Major-General drove up to the door. His orderly took his horse. He got off, went in, and sat down by the dying man's side. Taking out a little book, he read from it, "Let not your heart be troubled : ye believe in God, believe also in me : in my Father's house are many mansions." He then knelt down and offered up a prayer to God for that dying soldier. Arising from his knees, he bent over and kissed him, and said, with loving accents, "Captain G——, we shall meet in heaven." He then rode off. That General was Major-General Howard, of Maine!

A LETTER FROM FLORIDA. — The following letter from a gentleman of high standing, and decidedly the most able lawyer in Florida, humorous and unguarded as it is, casts much light on the state of feeling and condition of things in the South in the latter part of the year 1861 :

"JACKSONVILLE, FLA., Oct. 16, 1861.

"MOST HIGH, MOST MIGHTY, AND MOST PUISSANT ANTIPODE: Sometimes a vessel manages to run over from Savannah or elsewhere to Nassau, New Providence, and with the expectation that one will be going from thence in a few days, I think proper to try and report myself. If therefore this should ever reach you, be pleased to understand that I and all my household are well. Notwithstanding the whole South seems to be turned into a military camp, I have been of late, and still am, much occupied in professional matters, and I write this under the influence of whip and spur, for I am to be off to-morrow morning to St. Augustine to attend the Confederate court, where divers cases and questions of prize, sequestration, &c., must be discussed and disposed of; and as there is now not a solitary lawyer remaining there, no, not even ——, there is no library, and I must select my books and authorities, and lug them along, for in these days of distrust and conceit, no court is going to believe the law is so and so, merely because I say so. It must be read from a book, printed paper, bound in sheep or calf, manufactured by asses; becomes an oracle, and reason, principle, and common sense are silenced and laughed out of countenance. Well, I am in a hurry, but I write you a line to say God bless you. I hope you and Mrs. —— are well, and I want to propose to you, if this d—d war continues, to go out to Nassau this winter to avoid the cold; and if you will, I will promise positively to go over from here and visit you. Now do it. The British steamers, you know, between Havana and New York, stop at Nassau twice a month; and I need not tell you how much more comfortable they are in every way than an American steamer. Pray take my advice for once; and do another thing; write me when you get this, and as often as you may find time, and enclose your letter for me to Mrs. ——, Nassau, New Providence. She, Mrs. ——, with all her family, removed there last winter; and she will always know when any vessel is leaving there for any part of the Southern coast, especially Florida, and will forward any letters to me.

"The last I heard from you was yours of the 16th July, enclosed to Mr. Reed. How many times, and when, I wrote you I have no recollection, and whether any of them got through nobody knows. Your kind solicitude for me moved me greatly; but it should not, for it was only the expression of a warm and generous friendship which I knew you entertained for me as well before as then. Alas! I have nothing to offer you. All that I could, at any time, was, indifferent accommodations, with a better climate than you had at home. Fate, Providence, or the devil, interfered last year, and retained you in arctic quarters. Now take my advice: take the reins into your own hands, or let Mrs. —— have them, which is, perhaps, still better, and pack up early, and go out to Nassau. I don't know much about the place; but I do know the climate is warm there; and, moreover, it is English, and according to my experience it is more safe, comfortable, respectable, and quiet among the English, wherever they govern, than with any other people on the earth. And, although that is a matter of little consequence, I presume living in Nassau is cheap. I should like to live there a while, however, just for economy's sake. Pray, have you any idea of our prices here? Pork fifty dollars per barrel; butter fifty cents per pound; lard forty cents. I have paid these prices this day. Soap also thirty-five cents per pound; and, in short, pretty much everything else in the same ratio, except, perhaps, flour. But we don't seem to mind it — except that it seems to me it makes us hungry, for I can swear we eat more than we ever did in peaceable times. We have raised this season abundant crops of all kinds of provisions in the South. This is attributed to Providence; but I understand He has done the same thing for our enemies. His position, therefore, is not very well defined. Although I am well satisfied, if the real truth could be got at, He is on our side, still I am inclined to think that the making of our crop for this year He left pretty much to our niggers. I mean to say, that if it hadn't been for the niggers, I don't think much of a crop would have been made.

"Well, I cannot tell you how much I wish that you and Mrs. —— could come and pass the winter with us. We could go boating (when there was no wind). We could go down to the bar, or to Indian River, or to Cedar Keys, and eat oysters, and do, in fact, whatever we pleased. As it is, I don't believe this war can last till spring; now mark my word. It can't last, and there is no reason on earth why it should. No matter — you and I cannot now discuss it; but the fact is, it cannot in my judgment last."

BARBARA FRITCHIE.*

BY JOHN G. WHITTIER.

Up from the meadows rich with corn,
Clear in the cool September morn,

The clustered spires of Frederick stand
Green-walled by the hills of Maryland.

Round about them orchards sweep,
Apple and peach tree fruited deep,

Fair as the garden of the Lord,
To the eyes of the famished rebel horde,

On that pleasant morn of the early fall
When Lee marched over the mountain wall,

Over the mountains winding down,
Horse and foot, into Frederick town.

Forty flags with their silver stars,
Forty flags with their crimson bars,

Flapped in the morning wind: the sun
Of noon looked down and saw not one.

Up rose Barbara Fritchie then,
Bowed with her fourscore years and ten;

Bravest of all in Frederick town,
She took up the flag the men hauled down;

In her attic-window the staff she set,
To show that one heart was loyal yet.

Up the street came the rebel tread,
Stonewall Jackson riding ahead.

Under his slouched hat left and right
He glanced: the old flag met his sight.

"Halt!" — the dust-brown ranks stood fast.
"Fire!"— out blazed the rifle-blast.

It shivered the window, pane, and sash;
It rent the banner with seam and gash.

Quick, as it fell, from the broken staff
Dame Barbara snatched the silken scarf;

She leaned far out on the window sill,
And shook it forth with a royal will.

"Shoot, if you must, this old gray head,
But spare your country's flag," she said.

A shade of sadness, a blush of shame,
Over the face of the leader came;

The nobler nature within him stirred
To life at that woman's deed and word:

"Who touches a hair of yon gray head
Dies like a dog! March on!" he said.

All day long through Frederick street
Sounded the tread of marching feet.

All day long that free flag tost
Over the heads of the rebel host.

* The incident upon which this ballad is founded took place literally as it is told by the poet upon the occupation of Frederick, in Maryland, on the second march northward of the insurgent forces.

Ever its torn folds rose and fell
On the loyal winds that loved it well;

And through the hill-gaps sunset light
Shone over it with a warm good night.

Barbara Fritchie's work is o'er,
And the rebel rides on his raids no more.

Honor to her! and let a tear
Fall for her sake on Stonewall's bier.

Over Barbara Fritchie's grave,
Flag of Freedom and Union, wave!

Peace and order and beauty draw
Round thy symbol of light and law;

And ever the stars above look down
On thy stars below in Frederick town!

INCIDENT OF SHERMAN'S MARCH. — General Howard, in a speech at the celebration of the Christian Commission, related the following little occurrence after the battle of Chattanooga. "My corps, with Sherman's," said he. "had been in pursuit of the enemy three ...ys. We had marched nearly one hundred and twenty miles, and then marched back again. The result of it was, that our clothes and our shoes were worn out; the men had scarcely any blankets to cover them, or pants to wear. They were toiling along on their journey home. Just as we had passed through the mountain ridge, the division commander, thinking that the men had marched far enough for one day, put them comfortably into camp, told them to make their coffee, and then sent word to me to know if they had permission to remain there during the night. It was raining hard, very hard. It was a severe storm. But I knew the position was an improper one. It was not the fulfilment of my orders. I sent back word, 'No; march forward to Tungston's Station. March!' It was dark — i' was cold — it was stormy. The poor men had ' be turned out once more, to march. Notwithstanding their labor, notwithstanding their toil and fatigue, they marched. 'What did they do? how did they take it?' do you ask? They took it as I hope you will take my speech. They went singing, singing, singing along the route — noble, patient fellows! — without a complaining word."

PUT IT IN GOLD LETTERS. — A few days after the fight at Skerry, near Charleston, Kanawha, Virginia, two or three Yankee officers visited the house of a Mr. Fry, who had been driven from his home by the enemy. A daughter of Mr. Fry saw them approaching through the gate, and confronted them in the porch, with a demand to know their business. They stated they were looking for secession flags, and heard there were some there.

"Brave men," said she in scorn, "take flags on the field of battle — cowards only hunt them at the houses of defenceless women. Mine is in the hands of our brave volunteers; go and take it from them." — *Southern paper.*

A TRUE EXPERIENCE.

BY FRANK CAHILL.

I HAD thoroughly made up my mind to enlist. The bounty may have tempted me; my young affections may have been blighted; or, which is the most likely case, a friend of mine, then a Lieutenant-Colonel, commanding a regiment, may have written me to come out, as promotion was speedy and sure.

I knew if I told any of my friends of my determination to enlist, they would endeavor to persuade me from it; so I kept it a profound secret from all — at least all save two; and how I came to tell them will be explained in due time.

I had a just appreciation of glory, and knew exactly what it meant, viz., hard fare, much discomfort, and the chances of being shot. So I shivered on the brink of Uncle Sam's servitude, hesitating to take the final plunge.

Visiting one of my friends at his place of business, I told him in the most mysterious manner that I wanted to talk to him on a most important matter.

"Hold on a few minutes," said he. "I shall be through directly."

I thought those few minutes were the longest I had ever experienced, so anxious was I to make known my intention of enlisting. At last I heard the sharp click of the clasps of his ledger, which he placed in the safe, turned the key, put that in his pocket, changed his coat, — his hat was already on, — and said he was ready.

I mentally determined to defer telling him till later in the evening.

Talking of almost everything but soldiering, we walked about the streets for hours, occasionally stopping at a wayside inn to refresh.

At last Smith — for that was my friend's name — said : "What do you want to see me about? I must be going; my wife is expecting me."

"O, nothing," I replied; "I just wanted to see you, and have a little talk; that was all."

But Smith knew better. He could tell by my face that this was not all; so we continued our perambulations, and occasional halts for refreshments.

Ten o'clock came, and I was no nearer telling him my intention. I was so sure he would dissuade me from it. Smith said he must really go; it was getting so late. He shook me by the hand, at the corner of his block, and left me.

"Smith," I cried, calling after him; "one moment. I may not see you again. I'm — I'm going to enlist."

"Are you?" was all he said, not at all startled by my announcement. "I should have done the same thing myself long ago, if I were not married."

"My county bounty," I continued, "I will send to you."

"All right; I'll take care of it."

"And if anything happens to me — " here my voice became somewhat emotional — "give it to your little girl, and tell her to sometimes think of me."

"There'll be no occasion to tell her that. You'll come back safe enough. Write often, and let me know how you are getting along."

"I will do so. Good by;" and I held out my hand.

"Good by," he responded, shaking it. "I wish I was single, so I could accompany you."

"Don't tell anybody where I have gone."

"Of course not, if you wish me not to;" and he was away.

The next morning I proceeded to the recruiting office in the City Hall Park, New York, for the express purpose of enlisting. But somehow or other the bustle and confusion in Mr. Orison Blunt's recruiting office unnerved me, and I thought a little walk would do me good.

My little walk meant a tramp to Central Park and back, and occupied some three or four hours. When I returned it was past three : much to my regret, the office was closed, and I had to wait till the following morning.

This annoyed me exceedingly; when I found it impossible to be enlisted that day, I was the more anxious to become a wearer of the army blue, and left highly irate at the policy that closed a recruiting station at such an early hour in the day, thus preventing any number of brave defenders rushing to the protection of their country.

"It is an outrage upon the nation," I said, "and I will write to the papers about the matter."

But I didn't.

Having left my boarding-house a day or two before, that night I slept at Tammany Hall, and had serious thoughts of lying on the floor, instead of on the bed, so as to accustom myself to the hardships of the tented field. After trying the floor for a few minutes I concluded that the bed was the more comfortable; so into it I turned.

At the time I enlisted, fifteen dollars hand money was given to all who brought a recruit. Laboring under the impression I should prefer a friend receiving the money, rather than a stranger, I hunted one up, and told him I wished to put fifteen dollars in his pocket.

"You're just the man I wanted to see," said he; "but how?"

"I am going to enlist."

"You don't tell me! My gracious!" exclaimed Jim, opening his eyes with astonishment. "Let us have a drink."

"What I want you to do, is to take me over to the recruiting office and receive fifteen dollars hand money."

"I can't do that, old fellow."

"Why not?"

"Well, you may get killed," asserted Jim, in the most matter-of-fact way.

"That's true," I somewhat ruefully agreed.

"If you were to, and I had taken any money for your enlistment, I should never forgive myself. It would be like receiving compensation for your death."

32

"But some one will have to get it."

"That some one will not be me. So it's no use talking any more about it."

I tried to reason him into it; but it was of no use. Jim was determined. So, after enjoining him to secrecy, we shook hands and parted, he much the sadder man of the two.

Immediately on leaving Jim, I went to the recruiting office, and made known my desire to enlist. "But," said I, "I have no one to receive the hand money. As I have brought myself, I suppose it will be paid to me."

"No. You can't enlist yourself; you'll have to get somebody to bring you here."

"But I haven't any one to bring me."

"We can't help that; you can't be enlisted, then."

"That appears to me to be a strange proceeding. The Government wants soldiers; I offer myself, and you won't accept me."

The officer beckoned to a policeman, who at once advanced, and requested me to move on. I did so.

As I was leaving the building, a clean-shaven, mild-spoken, gentlemanly-looking man approached me, and asked if I wanted to enlist.

I answered in the affirmative.

"Then I'll make out your papers, and put you through in no time."

He was as good as his word. In a few minutes he had recorded my age, height, occupation, and personal description, handing me over to the examining Surgeon when he had done so.

This last-named personage told me to strip myself, which I speedily did. He then put me through my paces, as though I were a horse he wished to purchase. First, he went to the farther end of the room, and taking up a pack of playing cards, selected one. Holding it up, he asked, —

"What card is this?"

"The nine of clubs."

"And this?"

"The ten of hearts."

"Right. Now come here."

I went to him, and he pounded me on the chest and bade me cough; he made me run, walk, stretch my legs as far apart as I possibly could, put my hands as high above my head as they could reach, and strike out in the most approved shoulder-hitting fashion.

Just as he was about to pass me, he espied a small varicose vein in my left leg; so he hesitated.

"That's nothing," said the clean-shaven, mild-spoken gentleman, who was interested in me to the extent of fifteen dollars.

"I don't know about that. Wait a moment; and he left the room, but quickly returned, followed by another Surgeon, who pronounced my varicose vein as nothing; so I passed.

He then led the way to the muster-in officer, who told me to place my left hand on a Bible that lay upon the table, and hold up my right hand. He then recited something, which was just as intelligible to me as,

"Mumble, mumble, mumble, mumble. So help you God."

I nodded. That nod made me a soldier for three years or during the war.

Having been paid my county bounty of three hundred dollars, I was placed on a sort of revolving niche and turned into another room, where some twenty-five or thirty other recruits, who had preceded me, were in waiting. Many of them were engaged playing cards, already gambling away the bounty they had just received.

I was taken in charge by a couple of men, who furnished me with a uniform, a knapsack, a haversack, a tin plate and cup, and knife, fork, and spoon. Bringing me in debtor to the United States Government to the amount of twenty-seven dollars and twenty-six cents.

About four o'clock a detachment of men belonging to the Invalid corps came to escort us to the Provost Marshal's office, situated on Broadway, between Thirty-sixth and Thirty-seventh Streets.

Arriving there, — forty-two of us in all, — we were placed in a filthily bare room on the third floor, measuring about seventeen feet long and fourteen feet wide. The windows were barred, and the invalid soldier who kept guard over us, with a cocked navy revolver in his hand, sternly forbade any one approaching them. One man, a little intoxicated, who insisted on looking out, he threatened to shoot.

We were kept confined in this room until nearly three o'clock the following day. There were no seats; neither was there sufficient room to lie down. Sleep was out of the question. Though, it is true, I did once drop into a fitful doze, in which I was strangely mixed up with the hold of a slave ship and the Black Hole of Calcutta.

Coffee, bread, and meat, wholesome and good, were given the men, which they threw at one another and trampled under foot. They had too much money in their pockets to eat such plebeian food as beef. So they bribed the Sergeant of the guard to procure them ham and eggs, and such like delicacies, from a neighboring restaurant.

Whiskey, too, was in great request. The demand far exceeded the supply, for the risk to procure it was great, and the price high — ten, fifteen, even twenty dollars being paid for a bottle.

Much to my relief, we were at last driven out of this room like so many wild beasts, and conveyed to Riker's Island.

When I enlisted, Hart's Island, with its commodious and clean barracks, was not the rendezvous for troops.

I was kept on Riker's Island for six weeks, — though I made several appeals to be sent to my regiment, — doing nothing, eating the bread of idleness, not even being taught the common rudiments of drill, subjected to the mean and petty extortions of the non-commissioned officers, and treated, as a rule, like an ill-bred dog.

Twenty-three of us were the occupants of one Sibley tent; the necessary caloric was provided through the means of a small stove — value three dollars. This stove was the property of the Government. The sergeant who had our street in charge came one day, and took it away. We remonstrated; he told us we could get it back by paying a dollar each — total, twenty-three dollars. As it was bitter cold weather, we were only too glad to do so. Such swindling was commonly practised.

"The men belonging to the army of the Cumberland leave the day after to-morrow."

This announcement, while it elated, also depressed me. I had been wire-pulling for a pass to visit the city; now I was ordered away without that wish being consummated.

However, as luck would have it, my pass was handed to me that same morning; so by the first boat I returned to the city.

On my departure this time, I took leave of all my friends. One of them, as I kissed her good by, gave symptoms of a tear or two; but changing her mind, she gave a little laugh, and looking up in my face, said:

"O, you'll come back. You're too homely to get shot."

This remark may have been truthful; it was anything but flattering.

SYMPATHIES. — An impromptu toast given in a saloon in New York, in June, 1861, by a loyal Canadian — present several Americans and Nova Scotians:

"May the Rose of England never blow,
  The Thistle of Scotland never grow,
May the Harp of Ireland never play,
  Till the Stars and Stripes have won the day."

DURING the battle of Tranter's Creek, N. C., Lieutenant Avery, of the Marine Artillery, thought he discovered rifle shots coming from the leafy boughs of a tall elm, not very far distant from the field of battle. He accordingly filled his howitzer with grape, and elevated it with a very satisfactory result, tumbling half a score of the rebels to the ground.

AN INCIDENT OF DRANESVILLE. — After the prisoners were taken into the cavalry camp of the nationals, an inquisitive young man, a member of a Wisconsin regiment, who wished to get a glimpse of them, went to the guard-house in which they were confined, where he immediately laid eyes on an overcoat which looked familiar to him. He walked up to the prisoner, turned up the collar, and found the name of his brother sewed in the cloth. The young man became so enraged, that he would have immediately taken the life of the prisoner, had not the guards been there to prevent him. It appeared that his brother was in the fight at Bull Run, where he was killed, and this miserable secessionist had robbed him of his clothing. The bullet-hole in the coat had been sewed up so as to prevent it from tearing any further.

AT GETTYSBURG.

LIKE a furnace of fire blazed the midsummer sun
  When to saddle we leaped at the order,
Spurred on by the boom of the deep-throated gun,
  That told of the foe on our border.
A mist in our rear lay Antietam's dark plain,
  And thoughts of its carnage came o'er us;
But smiling before us surged fields of ripe grain,
  And we swore none should reap it before us.

That night, with the Ensign who rode by my side,
  On the camp's dreary edge I stood picket;
Our ears intent, lest every wind-rustle should hide
  A spy's stealthy tread in the thicket;
And there, while we watched the first arrows of dawn
  Through the veil of the rising mist's quiver,
He told how the foeman had closed in upon
  His home by the Tennessee River.

He spoke of a sire in his weakness cut down,
  With last breath the traitor flag scorning
(And his brow at the memory grew dark with a frown
  That paled the red light of the morning).
For days he had followed the cowardly band;
  And when one lagged to forage or trifle,
Had seared in his forehead the deep minie brand,
  And scored a fresh notch on his rifle.

"But one of the rangers had cheated his fate —
  For him he would search the world over."
Such cool-plotting passion, such keenness of hate,
  Ne'er saw I in woman-scorned lover.
O, who would have thought that beneath those dark curls
  Lurked vengeance as sure as death-rattle?
Or fancied those dreamy eyes — soft as a girl's —
  Could light with the fury of battle?

To horse! pealed the bugle, while grape-shot and shell
  Overhead through the forest were crashing.
A cheer for the flag! and the summer light fell
  On the blades from a thousand sheaths flashing.
As mad ocean waves to the storm-revel flock,
  So on we dashed, heedless of dangers;
A moment our long line surged back at the shock
  Then swept through the ranks of the Rangers.

I looked for our Ensign: ahead of his troop,
  Pressing on through the conflict infernal,
His torn flag furled round him in festoon and loop,
  He spurred to the side of his Colonel.
And his clear voice rang out, as I saw his bright sword
  Through shako and gaudy plume shiver,
With, "This for the last of the murderous horde!"
  And, "This for the home by the river!"

At evening, returned from pursuit of the foe,
  By a shell-shattered caisson we found him;
And we buried him there in the sunset glow,
  With the dear old flag knotted around him.
Yet how could we mourn, when every proud strain
  Told of foemen hurled back in disorder!
When we knew that the North reaped her rich harvest grain
  Unharmed by a foe on her border!

A STRANGE INCIDENT. — Nine or ten years ago, a citizen of one of the towns in the eastern part of Massachusetts was unjustly suspected of a crime which the statute cannot easily reach, but which deservedly brings upon him guilty of it the indignation of upright men. There were circumstances which gave color to the suspicion, and the unfortunate gentleman suffered the misery of loss of friends, business, and reputation. His sensitive nature could not face these trials, and he fell into a condition of body and mind which alarmed his family. At length, having invested his property where it could be easily managed by his wife, he suddenly disappeared, leaving her a comfortable home and the care of two boys, ten and twelve years old. The first fear that he had sought a violent death was partly dispelled by the orderly arrangement of his affairs, and the discovery that a daguerreotype of the family group was missing from the parlor table. Not much effort was made to trace the fugitive. When, afterwards, facts were developed which established his innocence of the crime charged, it was found impossible to communicate with him; and as the publication of the story in the columns of several widely-circulated journals failed to recall him, he was generally supposed to be dead.

At the outbreak of the present civil war, his eldest son, now a young man, was induced by a friend, a captain in a Western regiment, to enlist in his company. He carried himself well through campaigns in Missouri and Tennessee, and after the capture of Fort Donelson was rewarded with a First Lieutenant's commission. At the battles of Murfreesboro' he was wounded in the left arm, but so slightly that he was still able to take charge of a squad of wounded prisoners. While performing this duty, he became aware that one of them, a middle-aged man, with a full, heavy beard, was looking at him with fixed attention. The day after the fight, as the officer was passing, the soldier gave the military salute, and said:

"A word with you, if you please, sir. You remind me of an old friend. Are you from New England?"

"I am."

"From Massachusetts?"

"Yes."

"And your name?"

The young Lieutenant told his name, and why he came to serve in a Western regiment.

"I thought so," said the other, and turning away, he was silent. Although his curiosity was much excited by the soldier's manner, the officer forbore to question him, and withdrew. But in the afternoon he took occasion to renew the conversation, and expressed the interest awakened in him by the incident of the morning.

"I knew your father," said the prisoner. "Is he well?"

"We have not seen him for years. We think he is dead."

Then followed such an explanation of the circumstances of his disappearance as the young man could give. He had never known the precise nature of the charges against his father, but was able to make it quite clear that his innocence had been established.

"I knew your mother, also," continued the soldier. "I was in love with her when she married your father."

"I have a letter from her, dated ten days ago. My brother is a nine months' man at New Orleans."

After a little desultory conversation the soldier took from under his coat a leather wallet, and disclosed a daguerreotype case. The hasp was gone, and the corners were rounded by wear.

"Will you oblige me," he said, "by looking at this alone in your tent?" Agitated almost beyond control, the young officer took the case and hurried away. He had seen the picture before! It represented a man and a woman, sitting side by side, with a boy at the knee of each.

The romantic story moved the commander of the division to grant the youth a furlough; and both father and son reached home soon after.

THE LITTLE FLAG-BEARER. — Among the many acts of heroism told of those engaged in the fight up the Arkansas River is that of a mere youth, a little boy, who was attached to Tappan's Arkansas regiment, and carried two mimic flags, one in each hand. The regiment was driven to the water's edge, and the enemy poured in a terrific volley, killing many of them, who fell into the river; and such as were not instantly killed met a watery grave. Among those struck was the little boy, who bore the flags. Giving one last hurrah, which was cut short by the ebbing flood of his young life, he waved the flags over his head, tottered into the river, and was seen no more. The incident, says the narrator, was witnessed by a whole regiment that was crossing the river at the time, and not one member of it but shed a tear at the sight.

COFFEE FOR THE SOUTHERNERS. — "The time is coming when every woman should do her duty in this struggle for our country's independence," said a "wife and mother" in Richmond, in May, 1861. "There are many things her hands can do which will as materially aid our cause as if she were a soldier with musket in hand. The battle will be brought right to our doors. Let every woman, then, in this city, who possesses the ability, prepare coffee, bread, and whatever else she may have to give, for our dear loved ones, who offer their precious bodies a wall of defence for our homes.

"One third pure coffee, the rest wheat or rye, rightly prepared, will furnish a strengthening drink which will add greatly to their comfort. Let the coffee be browned a little, then add the wheat or rye, toasting them together. In this way the taste of the coffee is imparted to the grain. Grind or pound well. To one measure of coffee add eight of boiling water. Let it boil well, stirring it down until the entire mass disappears, when it will look clear. Add a little cold water, let it stand until it settles, and you have quite nice coffee.

"Now, will not every woman at once toast her coffee, grind it, and have it ready for use? Surely all the milk carts, molasses barrels on carts, and any conveyance one may think of, can carry it to some places designated; when some persons, whose business it shall be, may portion it out. If a regiment were detailed for this business it would do good service. Let no one begrudge her little mite of coffee. There are some persons who have not the material, but who would gladly prepare it. Let, then, her more fortunate neighbor, who can spare of her little, pass it over to willing hands, longing to do something for our noble cause. Bid the men go — 'be courageous and fear not.'"

THE FEAT OF THE "ARKANSAS." — A correspondent states that after the ram Arkansas had successfully run the blockade of the national vessels and arrived off Vicksburg, she was boarded by General Van Dorn, who approached her commander, Captain Brown, and the following conversation was had:

General — "Captain Brown, allow me to congratulate you on your success in reaching us."

Captain Brown — "Thank you, General; it was a desperate undertaking; but I knew what my vessel was made of."

General — "I hardly expected that you would come through without making them more conscious of your superiority. It seems to me you might have sunk or disabled half a dozen of them. Why under heaven didn't you try it on?"

Captain Brown — "General Van Dorn, I have accomplished what no naval officer in the Confederate service would have dared attempt, and what no one conversant with naval warfare would have supposed possible. The bare achievement of getting this vessel through that fleet is glory enough for one day."

General — "Fie! fie! Captain, that's all very well; you've done well, but might have done better. Get up steam again, and run up and try them a turn. When you have sunk six or eight of their turtles, you can come back and let the people cheer you."

Captain Brown — "Sir, I know what I have done. Nor do I propose to risk the reputation I've won by encountering that fleet again, especially now that they have all got steam up and are prepared to meet me. I shall not risk my laurels by renewing the contest to-day."

General — "I can see no reason why you should not go out again. They'll hardly expect you now; and if they do, you know your vessel is a match for them. You hear my orders to go."

Captain Brown — "General Van Dorn, this boat is without a commander. I shall forward my resignation to Richmond immediately. In the mean time please consider the vessel in your possession. You are at liberty to send her out under any commander you can find here to take her out, or you may take her out yourself."

The General turned away chagrined and mortified. Captain Brown also left the boat almost immediately, and, although urgently requested to withdraw his resignation, obstinately refused to do so. Lieutenant Stevens was left in command, and it was under his direction that the second and last chapter in her career was enacted.

READING IN THE ARMY. — George H. Stuart, the President of the Christian Commission, in a speech at the anniversary of that noble institution related the following interesting incident: "There is a very large distribution of reading matter. The question sometimes arises, 'Is it all read?' You cannot, my friends, have any conception of the avidity with which these publications are received and read, and treasured up. Thousands of them are sent back, after being well worn, to their homes, the soldier writing his name upon them, thus marking them with the evidence of his value of the possession. I have visited many of the hospitals, and some of the camps, and distributed many of these religious books, and I can testify that from the beginning until now I have never met a man who refused my books, save only one, and he was from my own city of Philadelphia. I do not believe in being conquered. I do not give up anything if it is practicable, and can be effected. But here was a case for me. The man told me that he was an infidel, that he did not believe in my books, that he did not need them. Said he, 'I am from Philadelphia; I live at such a number Callowhill Street; if you will go there you will find out my character, and that I am as good a man as you are.' 'I trust a great deal better,' said I. But the case did seem a difficult one. 'Stuart,' said a friend to whom I related the incident, 'you are beaten for once.' 'No,' I replied, 'I am not done with that man yet.' I approached him a short time afterwards, and he said to me, 'What is the book you wanted to give me?' It was a selection from the Scriptures called Cromwell's Bible. 'O,' said he, 'I don't want your Bible; I've no need of it; I'm a good enough man without it;' and with a motion of supreme indifference he turned his head. Said I, 'My friend, I'm from Philadelphia, too; I know where you live, can find the exact house. On next Sunday evening, if God spares my life, I expect to speak for the Christian Commission in the Church of the Epiphany.' He looked at me with an inquisitive air — 'And what are you going to say?' 'I am going to tell the people that I had been distributing tracts all day all through the hospitals and camps I had visited, and that I found but one man who refused to take them, and he was from Philadelphia.' 'Well, what more are you going to say?' the man asked with a steady gaze, apparently defying my attempts to move him. 'Well, I'll tell them that I commenced my tract distribution this morning at the White House, in Washington, and the first gentleman I offered one of these little books to was one Abraham Lincoln; that he rose from his chair, read the title, expressed great pleasure in receiving it, and promised to read it; but that I came to one of his cooks, here in these quarters, and he was so exceedingly good that he didn't need a copy of the Word of God, and wouldn't have one!' 'Well,' said the man, completely conquered, 'if the President can take one I suppose I can,' as he reached out his hand and received it."

INCIDENT OF FAIR OAKS.—Edmund Q. Andrews, of the Fortieth New York regiment, was wounded at the battle of Fair Oaks, while in the act of taking aim at a rebel soldier. The ball entered the left side, striking a daguerreotype (on iron) of his wife, which he carried in his vest pocket, completely demolishing the picture, and cutting off the top of the bowl of a wooden pipe, which was also in his pocket. The ball then continued its course, entered the flesh, and, passing across the pit of his stomach, came out of his side.

The sudden and strong concussion of the ball doubled him up, and it was a long time before he was able to regain his breath. As soon as he again found himself capable of standing on his feet, he raised his musket, and fired at the man who had shot him, when he once more fell upon the ground from pain and exhaustion.

Soon after, he discovered that the enemy were approaching him, when he managed to crawl off the field on his hands and knees. He remarked that he "thought he made good time, considering he was not used to walking on all fours."

A THOUGHT.

FALLING leaves and falling men !
　When the snows of winter fall,
And the winds of winter blow,
　Will be woven Nature's pall.

Let us, then, forsake our dead ;
　For the dead will surely wait
While we rush upon the foe,
　Eager for the hero's fate.

Leaves will come upon the trees ;
　Spring will show the happy race ;
Mothers will give birth to sons —
　Loyal souls to fill our place.

Wherefore should we rest and rush ?
　Soldiers, we must fight and save
Freedom now, and give our foes
　All their country should — a grave !

THINGS ABOUT GENERAL GRANT.—Rev. J. L. Crane, the chaplain of the regiment of which Lieutenant-General Grant was Colonel, gives the following interesting reminiscences of his private and military character :

"Grant," he says, "is about five feet ten inches in height, and will weigh one hundred and forty or forty-five pounds. He has a countenance indicative of reserve, and an indomitable will, and persistent purpose.

"In dress he is indifferent and careless, making no pretensions to *style* or fashionable military display. Had he continued Colonel till now, I think his uniform would have lasted till this day ; for he never used it except on dress parade, and then seemed to regard it a good deal as David did Saul's armor.

"'His body is a vial of intense existence ;' and yet when a stranger would see him in a crowd he would never think of asking his name. He is no dissembler. He is a sincere, thinking, *real* man.

"He is always cheerful. No toil, cold, heat, hunger, fatigue, or want of money depresses him. He does his work at the time, and he requires all under his command to be equally prompt. I was walking over the camp with him one morning after breakfast. It was usual for each company to call the roll at a given hour. It was now probably a half hour after the time for that duty. The Colonel was quietly smoking his old meerschaum, and talking and walking along, when he noticed a company drawn up in line and the roll being called. He instantly drew his pipe from his mouth and exclaimed, 'Captain, this is no time for calling the roll. Order your men to their quarters immediately.' The command was instantly obeyed, and the Colonel resumed his smoking and walked on, conversing as quietly as if nothing had happened. For this violation of discipline those men went without rations that day, except what they gathered up privately from among their friends of other companies. Such a breach of order was never witnessed in the regiment afterwards while he was its Colonel. This promptness is one of Grant's characteristics, and it is one of the secrets of his success.

"On one of our marches, when passing through one of these small towns where the grocery is the principal establishment, some of the lovers of intoxication had broken away from our lines and filled their canteens with whiskey, and were soon reeling and ungovernable under its influence. While apparently stopping the regiment for rest, Grant passed quietly along and took each canteen, and wherever he detected the fatal odor, emptied the liquor on the ground with as much nonchalance as he would empty his pipe, and had the offenders tied behind the baggage wagons till they had sobered into soldierly propriety. On this point his orders were imperative : no whiskey nor intoxicating beverages were allowed in his camp.

"In the afternoon of a very hot day in July, 1861, while the regiment was stationed in the town of Mexico, Missouri, I had gone to the cars as they were passing, and procured the daily paper, and seated myself in the shadow of my tent to read the news. In the telegraphic column I soon came to the announcement that Grant, with several others, was made Brigadier-General. In a few minutes he came walking that way, and I called to him :

"'Colonel, I have some news here that will interest you.'

"'What have you, Chaplain ?'

"'I see that you are made Brigadier-General.'

"He seated himself by my side and remarked :

"'Well, sir, I had no suspicion of it. It never came from any request of mine. That's some of Washburne's work. I knew Washburne in Galena. He was a strong Republican, and I was a Democrat, and I thought from *that* he never liked me very well. Hence we never had more than a business or street acquaintance. But when the war broke out I found he had induced Governor Yates to appoint me mustering officer of the Illinois volunteers, and after that had something to do in having me commissioned Colonel of the Twenty-first regiment; and I suppose this is some of his work.'

"And he very leisurely rose up and pulled his black felt hat a little nearer his eyes, and made a few extra passes at his whiskers, and walked away with as much apparent unconcern as if some one had merely told him that his new suit of clothes was finished.

"Grant belongs to no church, yet he entertains and expresses the highest esteem for all the enterprises that tend to promote religion. When at home he generally attended the Methodist Episcopal Church. While he was Colonel of the Twenty-first regiment, he gave every encouragement and facility for securing a prompt and uniform observance of religious services, and was generally found in the audience listening to preaching.

"Shortly after I came into the regiment our mess were one day taking their usual seats around the dinner table, when he remarked:

"'Chaplain, when I was at home, and ministers were stopping at my house, I always invited them to ask a blessing at the table. I suppose a blessing is as much needed here as at home; and if it is agreeable with your views, I should be glad to have you ask a blessing every time we sit down to eat.'"

A GENTLEMAN, about whose Teutonic origin there could be but one opinion, was passing along the street, when he came to a halt before one of the huge posters, announcing the coming of the Panorama of Paradise Lost. He read this line, "A Rebellion in Heaven," when he broke forth as follows: "A Rebellion in Heaven: mine Got! that lasts not long now — Onkel Abe ish tare."

ADVENTURES OF AN IRISHMAN. — Sitting in a rainy tent at Centreville, I overheard the following fragment of a conversation between a party of Irish soldiers, which, for richness and raciness, Charles Lever would have immortalized himself by frescoing in one of his inimitable stories. The company were detailing their experiences, "hairbreadth escapes by flood and field," spinning Munchausian yarns and cracking wonderful jokes, when one Pat Mullooney, a genuine son of the sod, broke in with an account of his adventures during the battle of Bull Run. I give you the ebullition entire, though half its fun and force are lost by its transfer to paper:

"Ye see, gintlemin," said Pat ("God forgeve me for calling such spalpeens out uv yer names"),

"that time whin the ould Major came down like a flyin' divil on his chisnut mare with his illigant sword, that, be jabers, is like a scythe blade, a wavin' about his hid, and yelled to us to come on, and charge the bloody Yankees, be gorra, it was to Washington we thought we were goin' all the way, and the divil a time we were to stop at all, at all, on the road, not aven for a dhrap of wather.

"Well, sure enough, the ould feller wint in himself, and I after him, not thinking about anything at all, but jist goin' on. I jumped over a mite of a fence as tight as a toad, and took to the wather [Bull Run] like a duck; and whin I got to the middle of the strame I looked around, and the divil resave the one uv yez near me, I was alone intirely sure. Thin I thought, big fools as ye all are, that I was a bigger wan for not shtaying in the woods, like the rist of yez, and waiting for the spalpeens to come over. But as I was out there, I thought to meself, I'll take a look at how things is, how things is beyant, and p'raps I'll have a crack o' me goon. But divil uv a thing could I say. Jist as I was makin' up me mind to return to ye all, a big Yankee, who looked as if he was seventeen feet high, livilled his musket at me and fired. The bullet whistled by me ear wid a shrake worse than Tim Flangan's fife.

"'Bad luck to ye, ye thafe o' the wurrld,' says I, 'what are ye thrying to shoot me fur? sure I niver done nothing to yez;' and thin I aimed shtraight betwane his eyes, and fired at him; but the murtherin' ball didn't tuch a hair uv his head that I mist. 'Be gorra,' sez I to meself, 'now I'll take ye a prisoner, anyhow;' and I put meself across the river as hard as iver I could. I joomped up the bank, and lookin' mighty fierce at 'im, I said, 'Surrender, ye divil, or I'll blow yer brains out.' The fun uv it was, I'd forgot, in me charge upon the spalpeen, to load me goon at all, at all, and the bloody thafe must av knew it, for he made at me wid his bay'net, like a two-legged locomotive. By the powers but I was frightened. As he was coming down, lapin' several fate at a time, says I to meself, 'Pat, me boy, mind yer eye; now's yer time to kape wide awake, or you'll have a gimlet hole through yer valuable bow'lls, and Biddy Mullooney will be a widder.' Bad luck to the drillin', sure it's meself forgot to come to the charge. So I tuk me goon by the middle, just as ye wud hould a good ould-fashioned black-thorn shillaly, and balanced meself fur 'im. As he come down, the divil take me if I knew how to git that bay'net point out o' the way. I twirled me musket aroun' me head till me fingers ached; but suddenly, bliss all the Hooly Saints fur it, a root tuk the fut uv the bloody-minded rascal, and he went a sprawlin' on the turf, lookin' as pretty a lether X as ye iver signed to yer name; at the same time that his bay'net shtruck a fut in the ground, I gin a yell, and was on him before a pig could grunt, and put me fut on his neck. 'Surrender, ye divil,' said I; but the divil a word did he spake.

"I thought I had his throat too tight, an' I let him go, to give him a fair chance to utther his sentiments. What d'ye think the spalpeen thried to do? Sure it was to git his musket out uv the ground an' shtruck me wid it agin. But shtill I didn't want to hurt the baste; so I jist hit 'im a little crack in the head wid the butt o' me goon, an' broke his jaw. Then he became quiet, an' I made 'im take his musket and cross the crake, when I druv 'im to the hospital, an' the divil uv a dacenter, betther-behaved feller ye niver saw afther that. He laid in bed six wakes, and didn't spake nary word. That's what I did at Bull Run. Who'll give me a poteen o' whiskey?"

CAMP LIFE.

DESCRIBED BY A SOLDIER.

FEW can realize the real character of camp life, until they have tried its stern realities, until they forsake their brick and wooden walls for those of cotton. At home, where men only hear the roar of the storm, as its tones are muffled by the comfortable protections around them, and know of the rain only as it patters on the window panes, they can realize very little what it is to have the walls and roof of their dwellings shake, and quiver, and crack like the report of musketry, and not only hear the cold blast without, but feel it creeping in at many openings it is quite impossible to close. At home, locks and bars keep away intruders, and we lie down and sleep in stillness and safety. In camp, our locks are made of rope, and no other means are needed to open our doors than to untie a knot. Here, wake at what hour you may, and you hear the dull tread of the sentry, or are startled by the sharp challenge which he gives to some luckless wight, whose necessities have called him abroad at an unseasonable hour. At home, the wakeful cock, or speaking bell from the neighboring steeple, tells you of the early dawn, and that the time has come to begin the duties of the rising day. Here, the sharp twang and roll of the martial drum start you into wakefulness, and make you feel the full reality of the strange and awful scenes which have been pressed upon the land by this most unnatural rebellion. At our fireside we hear only the peaceful hum of agriculture, or the arts; but here none of those things are seen or heard; their place is taken by the shrill tones of the fife, the stirring notes of the bugle, as its blasts reverberate among the hills, the almost constant roll of the drum, the firing of musketry, and the roar of cannon. These, with the long ranks of martial men passing from point to point, the tread of horsemen, and the sharp, quick voice of those in command, are scenes all new and strange to our land of peace and thriftful enterprise. All these are scenes most intimately connected with camp life.

Every plain is covered with tents, nearly every eminence with fortifications, bristling with cannon. An evening or two since, we saw several regiments on their respective grounds, at what is styled "dress parade;" the day had been cloudy;

just at this moment the sun looked brightly through a rift in the clouds, and threw a flood of brightness over the scene. Each regiment was formed in two lines, drawn with military precision. As the light fell upon their thousand glittering bayonets, they presented above their heads a line of the most spotless white; then, as they changed the position of the weapon to a charge, the line changed from above the dark mass of men to their front, the rays of the sun, in the mean time, glancing from each weapon, and quivering in the quarter of a circle formed in the movement, until it settled again into one long, bright line of spotless white, the whole forming one of the most fairy scenes on which the eye could rest. One finds it hard to believe that such a scene, so much like the moving of the wing of that angel who is clothed in light, is really the solemn waving of the wing of the angel of death.

When leaving home, some of our friends said to us, "Tell us of the camp, and how you live there." There is some difficulty in doing this. If our friends were at our elbow, asking us questions about what they were curious to know, then we could answer them; as it is, we will do the best we can to meet their wishes.

Every camp should have a parade ground. This forms the front. Beginning with this, and going backwards, you have the tents of the men, each company having their tents arranged in lines facing on a street where the company forms, preparatory to marching on to the parade ground, and where they also meet for roll call, which occurs three times each day — at sunrise, at sunset, and at eight in the evening. Next, after the tents of the men, come those of the commissioned officers of the companies. These face on a street which runs at right angles with the company streets. In this broad aisle the men do their cooking and have their company fires. Here they meet of evenings to smoke, and talk, and sing. Still back of these are the tents of the Colonel and staff. This is composed of the Colonel, Lieutenant-Colonel, Major, Adjutant, Quartermaster, Chaplain, and Surgeons, the tent of the Colonel forming the centre. The flag-staff is at the edge of the parade ground, immediately in front of the Colonel's tent. In the rear of the whole may be found the Quartermaster, Commissary, and Sutler's departments.

When the ground has been marked off, the men proceed to pitch their tents, which, when raised and spread, are fastened to their places by cords and stakes; then a shallow trench is usually dug around each, to carry away the water which may drip from the roof. The dirt from this trench is sometimes thrown into the middle of the tent to raise the ground, thus avoiding the collection of water under the cloth. When this is done, the occupant gets some boards for a floor, if he can; if this cannot be, he uses the ground. He makes his bed by putting some stakes in the ground, on which he makes a platform, spreads it over with some boughs of evergreen or straw, rolls himself in his blanket, and sleeps sweetly, dreaming, it may be, of home and glory.

The soldier generally cooks his rations in the open air. Then sitting in his tent, or under the shade of some neighboring tree, with his plate upon his lap, he enjoys, with a soldier's zest, his frugal meal.

The signal for retiring is given by the drum — the ever-present drum. And when the morning breaks, again the roll of the stirring drum shakes sleep from his drowsy eyelids, and calls him forth, with his musket and his belt, to duty and to drill.

Each day the Colonel selects an officer, who is styled the officer of the day. He is known by his wearing his sash over his shoulder, the ordinary way of wearing it being around the waist. He has charge of the guard and the police of the camp. The guard is detailed for twenty-four hours by the Adjutant, each sentry being changed once in two hours. The guard entirely surrounds the camp, so that no one can leave, or come on the ground, without their notice and permission. Then when you retire to rest, you may be assured that these men are encamped round about you, and that they will be faithful; for if found asleep on his post, the sentry may be shot, or such other penalty as the court martial may inflict.

Such is the camp life of our noble soldiery. Near half a million of our fellow-citizens are daily meeting these fatigues for the weal of our nation. Let the whole church pray for them.

THE FREEDMAN'S SONG.

De Lord He make us free indeed
In His own time an' way;
We plant de rice an' cotton seed,
An' see de sprout some day;
We know it come, but not de why —
De Lord know more dan we;
We 'spected freedom by an' by,
An' now we all are free.
　　Praise de Lord! Praise de Lord!
　　　For now we all are free.

De Norf is on de side ob right,
An' full of men, dey say;
An' dere, when poor man work, at night
He sure to get his pay;
De Lord, He glad dey are so good,
An' make dem bery strong;
An' when dey called to gib deir blood,
Dey all come right along.
　　Praise de Lord! Praise de Lord!
　　　Dey all come right along.

Deir blue coats cover all de groun',
An' make it like de sky;
An' ebery grayback loafin' roun',
He tink it time to fly;
We not afraid; we bring de child,
An' stan' beside de door;
An' O, we hug it bery wild,
An' keep it ebermore.
　　Praise de Lord! Praise de Lord!
　　　We keep it ebermore.

De massa's come back from his tramp;
'Pears he is broken quite;
He takes de basket to de camp
For rations ebery night;

Dey fought him when he loud an' strong,
Dey feed him when he low;
Dey say dey will forgive de wrong,
An' bid him 'pent an' go.
　　Praise de Lord! Praise de Lord!
　　　Dey bid him 'pent an' go.

De rice is higher far dis year,
De cotton taller grow;
De lowest corn-silk on de ear
Is higher dan de hoe;
De Lord He lift up eberyting
'Cept rebel in his grabe;
De negro bress de Lord an' sing
He is no longer slabe.
　　Praise de Lord! Praise de Lord!
　　　De negro no more slabe.

THE STORY OF PRAIRIE GROVE.

EARLY in the month of December, General Blunt, commanding the Union forces in Arkansas, was encamped at Cane Hill, in the north-western part of the State, not far from Van Buren, and a few miles north of the Boston Mountain.

Across that mountain, twenty days before, he had driven Marmaduke, who commanded all the irregular and roving bands of horsemen that infested that part of the State.

His own force was about ten thousand strong. One hundred and twenty miles north of him, in Missouri, General Herron was encamped with a force about six thousand strong. On the 3d of December, he learned that all the rebel force in Arkansas had been assembled on the south side of the Mountain, and amounted to some twenty or twenty-five thousand, commanded by Hindman, a prominent rebel politician, who had now become a prominent rebel General. The position, numbers, and commanders of the Union armies were well known to him, and his plan of operations was obvious, and apparently very dangerous to the Union cause in Arkansas. If he should advance at once across Boston Mountain, fall upon Blunt with double his force, there was a flattering probability that he would crush him. Then continuing his march north, he proposed to launch his flushed columns at Herron, and wiping him out, leave no organized and adequate force between him and St. Louis. Flushed with these anticipations, and confident by a few days' fighting to make himself the hero of the Trans-Mississippi Department, he advanced with confidence against Blunt, and crossed Boston Mountain. Blunt saw his whole danger, and grasped his enemy's plan. Couriers were at once despatched to Herron to come with all haste to his relief, as the enemy, with numbers double his own, was advancing upon him from the South. Nobly and with the promptitude of a true soldier did Herron respond to the summons. The annals of the war hardly furnish an instance of swifter movement. On the noon of Wednesday, the 3d, he broke camp at Springfield, Missouri, and headed his column for the Arkansas line.

In three days he had marched one hundred and ten miles, and was in the vicinity of Fayetteville, and near the enemy. Hindman had in some manner contrived to steal a march on Blunt, and had passed him on his left flank, and was making for Herron as rapidly as possible. This startling intelligence reached Blunt about ten o'clock on the morning of the 7th, and he of course made his movements with the utmost rapidity to meet this new phase of affairs. Herron meanwhile, pushing on south as rapidly as possible, expected to form a junction with Blunt, and had no idea that he should be the first to engage the enemy. He was about eight miles south of Fayetteville, when his cavalry came dashing back in great disorder, having met the enemy advancing in great numbers. He rallied them and led them on against the foe, at the same time hurrying forward his artillery and his infantry. By ten o'clock he found himself on the north bank of Illinois Creek, the enemy on the other side strongly posted on a long ridge with magnificent positions for his batteries.

From a prisoner he learned that Hindman was on the ridge with his whole force, and expected to whip him out before Blunt, who was ten miles distant, could come up. There were but two courses for Herron. One was to retreat at once, give up his trains to the enemy, and abandon Blunt to his fate, without the power to assist him. The other was to move promptly across the creek, engage the enemy, and hope that Blunt, hearing the cannon, would make all haste to his relief. He was too good a soldier to hesitate as to which horn of this dilemma to take, and riding forward to view the ground, decided at once on a plan of operations.

Under a steady artillery fire from the enemy he crossed the creek, got all his guns in position, and threw out his infantry in line of battle. Finding his batteries were telling upon the enemy's line, he moved up the infantry, and in a few minutes the whole of his left wing was engaged. The battle, commencing thus on the part of General Herron, lasted some three hours, till the middle of the afternoon, his force holding their original position, but suffering terribly under the galling fire and frequent charges of the enemy, who made two vigorous efforts to turn his left by massing his forces on that wing.

It was now past three o'clock, and nothing from Blunt. All of Herron's force had been engaged, and some of his regiments were badly cut up. He told all his officers they must hold out till night; and there was no thought of anything else, though the case seemed a tough one. At four o'clock a battery opened on his extreme right. The shell came over and fell among his skirmish line. What could it mean? The fire soon grew hotter, and presently the ground was trembling with the heavy cannonade of seventy pieces, all actively worked. The roar of the first discharge had hardly died away, when a thrilling cheer went up from the whole of Herron's line. Relief had come at last. It was Blunt's guns thundering on the right. He had heard the sound of the battle, and his men, leaving the main road, had taken a straight shoot through fields of thorn

brush, and over fences and ditches, until Blunt found himself coming directly upon the enemy's left wing. Halting only to place his batteries, he at once opened fire, and from four o'clock till dark the battle raged along the whole of the now extended line, from Herron's left to Blunt's right. It was one of the loveliest days that ever beamed on a field of blood. In that mellow climate December often gives a day as clear and warm as the loveliest of an Indian summer.

As Hindman saw his plan had failed, he fought with desperation.

His line was covered with a small growth of timber, and occupied a moderate elevation, which commanded an open country in front, called Prairie Grove.

He had the advantage in position, as well as numbers. Again and again the Union infantry would charge into the woods, and drive the rebels; and then, again, they would rally and charge, driving the Union force back into the open prairie. Thus back and forth the battle wavered, till the sun set through lurid smoke, and darkness settled upon the scene. Blunt then ordered his forces to withdraw in good order.

Hindman, considering this a repulse, ordered a general charge all along the line. Expecting this, Blunt had stationed his artillery, and the pieces were loaded with grape and canister. The rebel line advanced to within sixty yards, when the fifty Federal cannon opened all along the line — a fire before which nothing human could stand.

A few desperate regiments rallied after the first discharge, and rushed almost to the cannon's mouth; but a second discharge tore the bleeding lines into flying fragments, and they ran howling into the cover of the forest from which they had emerged.

This closed the day. The Federal army bivouacked on their arms, expecting a renewal of the contest at daylight. But Hindman now thought discretion was the better part of valor, and taking his men's blankets to muffle his artillery wheels, he stole away so quietly, under cover of night, that by morning he had placed Boston Mountain between Blunt and the greater part of his force.

Never was a reverse more complete. On the morning of the 7th, he had the Union force divided, and was confident that he could whip each division separately. As some of his officers expressed it in the elegant vernacular of the South-west, "He would chaw up Herron for his breakfast, and then turn and gobble up Blunt at dinner." He had not calculated upon such obstinate resistance from one, nor such swift marching from the other.

Midnight saw his defeated and bleeding column, stealthily, and with muffled cannon wheels, moving away through the gorges of Boston Mountain.

———

DESOLATIONS OF WAR. — A Federal cavalryman, writing from the vicinity of Fredericksburg, where Burnside was encamped in December, 1862, gives the following account of the utter desolation that overtook so many of the old Virginia families, and the promptness with which even the kindest slaveholders were deserted by the negroes upon the advent of the Union armies:

"While on a scout after my breakfast on Saturday morning last, I galloped up to a fine-looking house, and as no one appeared, I shouted loudly for some one to come forth. I knew by the smoke from the chimney that it had an occupant; and directly an aged lady made her appearance, and I was invited to dismount and enter the house, which invitation I gladly accepted, and visions of hot corn cake, bacon and eggs, flitted before my fancy. These are no trifles to a hungry soldier, though of little interest to you, or your readers, perhaps. Not a soul was in sight or hearing but this poor old lady, every slave, out of one hundred and sixty-five, having left her. Though the owner of thirty-five hundred acres of beautiful cleared land, she was, she said, 'the most unhappy wretch on earth.' Of all her slaves, not one could be induced to remain with her. Even those she loved as her own children, and reared as tenderly, were the first to desert her, though offered their freedom and liberal wages. The tears trickled down her furrowed cheeks, and her gray head was bowed in anguish, as she told me the story of her last year's experience; and I shed a sympathizing tear with her, and with a saddened heart mounted my horse and rode away, my appetite for hot corn cake and fried bacon having failed me. So it is with hundreds of others; but of all the tales I have listened to, this affected me most."

EXPLOITS OF A FORAGING PARTY. — A soldier in the Fifty-sixth New York volunteers was engaged in one of those excursions — partly military and partly predatory — which characterized the earlier years of the war. Just after his first exploits in that line in the winter of 1862, he wrote home to his father the following account from Yorktown, Virginia:

"In order to make my promise good to you, I will now endeavor to pen you a short sketch of our expedition to Gloucester Court House.

"On the morning of the 11th of December, our regiment was drawn up in line at daylight, and a few minutes after, we started towards the fort. There was but little said by any of us as we marched along, keeping step to the beat of the drum. Every man's mind was busy; for none of us knew where we were to go. Some thought we were going to join Burnside's army; others, that we were going to Richmond direct; and none liked the idea of leaving our cheerful quarters for the fierce and bloody fight, and the hardships of a winter campaign.

"Well, we trudged along, entered the fort, and went down to the river, where we found a boat waiting to take us over to Gloucester Point. We found out, soon after crossing the river, that we were to go to Gloucester Court House to drive out some rebels, who, it was said, were fortifying themselves there. We started a little after seven, and one hour later, had passed the outer pickets, and were fairly in Secessia. The people were surprised at the display we made. There had never been any soldiers through there before us. The darkies were overjoyed at our coming, and kindly gave us all the eggs, milk, and hoe-cake we wanted. The country we passed through was a rich one. No army had been there to destroy their crops and cattle, and they possessed abundance.

"At three P. M. we entered the town. Our cavalry had driven off a few stray rebels, and we took peaceable possession. There was no visible evidence of the rebels' intending to fortify the town. Not knowing but that we might be attacked during the night, General Naglee had the battery planted in a good position, a strong picket posted, and issued orders to have every man ready to fall in at a minute's notice.

"Our regiment lay on their arms all night on the roadside. We suffered some from cold. The boys could not stand that; so they commenced prowling about the place for plunder. There was soon a great uproar among the fowls. Chickens cackled, geese and ducks quacked, and turkeys gobbled; but 'twas no use. It was too near Christmas to give them a chance for their lives. Consequently they lost their heads and feathers, and soon found themselves boiling in the camp-kettles.

"A good old Secesh dominie, living in the upper part of the town, heard a great racket in the neighborhood of his hennery. He poked his head out of the window to see what was going on. He saw three or four blue-jackets. One was lugging off a skip of honey.

"'Stop! stop! I command you!' roared out the old fellow.

"His wife (who, no doubt, had been in Richmond, and learned the military) told him to call, 'Corporal of the guard.' He did so, when a fellow jumped into the yard, saying he was a Corporal, and wanted to know what was the matter. Dominie told him how he had been robbed, and asked him to take care of his honey.

"'To be sure I will,' says the willing Corporal; and he picks up a skip, and starts off with it.

"'But where are you going with that skip?' says dominie.

"'O, I am going to take care of it for you,' says Bogus; and off he goes.

"The dominie hauls in his head, and the boys haul in the rest of his honey and fowls.

"At noon we pitched our camp in a gentleman's door-yard. We did nothing more to-day, and had a bully night's rest. Next morning the General gave orders for the Fifty-sixth to go out foraging. Captain Smith headed the party, numbering forty or fifty. We started for the plantation of a Mr. Field, a strong secessionist. On arriving at his house the Captain halted and fronted us, and then went up to Field and told him that we wanted some of his stock for Government use. He told the Captain to help himself to what he wanted. The Captain then divided the squad into two equal parts, one to capture and bring in stock, the other party to act as reserve and guard. Well, this fun lasted about an hour, and I caught but one old setting hen, and my sides ached with laughter. The ground was thickly strewn with dead poultry, for the boys soon learned to kill their birds, and they now set about picking them up. The Captain started twenty men back to camp with the plunder. The rest of us went to another house, but luckily for somebody, it was deserted. Farther on was to be seen another house. The first glance, on arriving at the place, told us that these folks were poor. Captain went to speak to an old woman, who came to the door. I went to the negro quarters, and found by inquiry, that the old lady had long been a widow, that she was very poor, and had three sons in the rebel army. One had been killed in the battle before Richmond. The boys now commenced a war on the poultry, and I was determined that all the fowls should be spared to the old lady. There she stood in the door with clasped hands, her gray hair looking out from underneath the wide border of her cap. A pretty little girl of five or six years (a grandchild), with golden hair in curls, stood near, clinging to the old lady's skirt, and trying to get her in and shut the door. The boys were bent on having the poultry, and as Captain Smith had not forbidden it, they took everything. Here I did one of the meanest acts that I ever did in all my life. It was this: after trying to save the old lady's property, I caught a duck and wrung its neck before her eyes. Never shall I forget the look she gave me. She thought me to be her only friend before this; but now I, too, had proved an enemy. O, how her heart sunk within her! She sank down into a chair, and gave herself up to the loudest lamentations. I can reconcile myself to take property from rich secessionists for the Government, but now I am down on robbing poor people's hen-roosts."

OBEYING ORDERS. — While in front of Petersburg, General Butler received information that his favorite horse, "Almond Eye," had been accidentally killed by falling into a ravine. Upon the departure of his informant, he ordered an Irishman to go and skin him.

"What! Is Almond Eye dead?" asked Pat.

"What's that to you? Do as I bid you, and ask no questions."

Pat went about his business, and in an hour or two returned.

"Well, Pat, where have you been all this time?"

"Skinning the horse, yer honor."

"Does it take nearly two hours to perform such an operation?"

"No, yer honor; but then, you see, it tuck 'bout half an hour to catch him."

"Catch him! Fire and furies! Was he alive?"

"Yes, yer honor; and you know I could not skin him alive."

"Skin him alive! Did you kill him?"

"To be sure I did. You know I must obey orders, without asking any questions."

General Butler eyed his servant with such a malicious look, that Pat thought he meditated skinning an Irishman, in revenge for the death of his horse.

INCIDENTS OF THE CHRISTIAN COMMISSION. — At the meeting of this noble institution, at Washington, in February, 1864, the Rev. Robert J. Parvin, in stating the practical operations of the Commission on the battle-fields and in the hospitals, said:

"At Gettysburg, in the Fifth Corps Hospital, of which I had charge in the Christian Commission's work for a few weeks, I had many such home links fastened to the last hours of dying soldiers. I remember well a Captain of your own State, sir [addressing Mr. George H. Stuart, the President], of the 20th Maine volunteers, who was brought into that old barn, where were sixty-five of the worst cases in the whole corps. O, they were all sadly wounded. The brave fellow had some of his own men lying on the floor not far from him. He loved them with a father's love. As one after another they died around him, it worked so upon his mind, that he became a raving maniac, until it took four or five to hold him. With great difficulty we got him away from his men who were dying, — in a room by himself, — and he rallied, became a little better. The Surgeon went in to see him. He came out, and I passed in. The Surgeon had told me he could not live. If he had had a primary amputation, — an amputation, that is, on the field, — he might have recovered, but he could not now. I took him by the hand. His first words were, 'Chaplain' (for such they call us), 'what did the Surgeon say?' 'Why, Captain, you are in a critical case.' 'I know that, Chaplain, but does the Surgeon think I can live?' 'He thinks it is hardly possible that you will live, Captain.' 'My wife, Chaplain — have you heard from her since your message yesterday?' 'No, we have received no answer. The lines are in the hands of the Government, who needs them; perhaps that is the reason we cannot get an answer at once. We hope she will be here.' 'Does the Surgeon say I cannot live long, Chaplain?' 'Yes; but you are a Christian man, Captain Billings?' 'Yes, Chaplain, I have no fears. I left my place in the Sabbath school for my place in the army. My hope is in the Lord Jesus Christ. I have tried to serve him in the army, and he will not forsake me now. I would like to see my wife,' he continued, as his thoughts recurred to that dear one. 'Well, Captain, if you have anything to say, will you give the message to me?' He asked me to give her his knapsack and sword, and other little things that he mentioned; and if she came, the message he wished me to deliver; and then he seemed to dismiss all these things from his mind, as he lay there calm, peaceful, a dying man, as well as a dying soldier, and, above all, a dying Christian. 'Now,' said he at length, 'don't stay longer with me. Go and minister to the boys, and run in here as you can to read a few words of Scripture to me, and kneel down and pray with me.' After I had prayed with him, he said to me, 'Could you have my body embalmed and sent home? I lost my money on the field.' 'Certainly, Captain, it shall be done; give yourself no further thought about that.' Not another time did he refer to it, but he passed away a dying Christian, triumphing over all the horrors of war, over all the sad circumstances surrounding him. It was in the morning at eleven o'clock that he passed away. At five o'clock that afternoon his body was sent to the embalmers. At ten o'clock that night, as I was busy writing letters from memoranda taken through the day, a knock was heard at my door. 'Walk in,' I responded. In stepped a man, inquiring, 'Is Captain Billings, of the 20th Maine, here?' What a question for us to meet! But I thought of the home-link. 'Who are you?' I asked. *'I am his brother. I have his wife with me. I have buoyed her up this long way with the hope that we would find the Captain in good condition. WHERE IS HE, SIR?'* 'You have not brought the Captain's wife out here with you to-night?' The corps hospital was four miles from Gettysburg. 'No; I left her in town for to-night.' 'O, it is well; the body of your brother was sent to the embalmers at five o'clock this afternoon!' 'O! O!' said he, 'I cannot tell her! *I cannot tell her! I cannot trust myself to tell her, or even to see her again, to-night!'* The poor man seemed overcome. 'I cannot see her,' he continued; 'I have brought her on all the way to Gettysburg, and now you must, *you must* tell her all.' And so our duty was to see the wife, and deliver to her the messages and the tokens of the dying love of her husband, and speak to her words of comfort in the name of the Lord! His body was carried on to the State of Maine, to repose with those of his kindred there."

FEMALE PATRIOTISM. — A Southern officer relates the following: "Let me now tell the story of a Kentucky lady. It was related to me by one in whom implicit confidence can be placed. Some time ago the hirelings of Lincoln went to Cynthiana, Ky., in search of 'arms' and 'secessionists.' A gentleman whom I will call Smith was a strong Southern man, and feeling that he would be among the first to be arrested, hastened away at dead of night. He was a man of wealth and influence; but such was the precipitancy with which he left his home and his all, that he could carry nothing with him. He hurriedly escaped in his shirt sleeves to a widow's house in the neighborhood, with whom he was well acquainted, and stated his condition. The lady, who was herself wealthy, instantly and intuitively conceived a plan to relieve him. And what does the reader suppose that plan was? She ordered a horse to be saddled, took a servant behind her, went to Cynthiana, six miles distant, procured money for her friend, bought cloth, returned home, had the cloth cut and made into garments by the next morning, and started Smith off bright and early!"

Here, is another: General Marshall sent his Quartermaster here for the artillery destined for his command. There was not a sufficient number of horses to be bought in the ordinary way, and the Quartermaster was empowered to impress. He met with a lady on a splendid gray horse. She was visiting some of her friends during the Christmas, and was twenty miles from home. She was asked the price at which she would sell her horse. She replied it was the only horse she had, and she had refused two hundred dollars for him frequently. The Quartermaster informed her that one hundred and fifty was as much as the Government could give, and he thought that the horse was necessary to aid in the defence of the country. Her reply was characteristic of the ladies in this country. "Kentuckian, take him."

JOHN BROWN'S SONG.

JOHN BROWN's body lies a-mouldering in the grave;
John Brown's body lies a-mouldering in the grave;
John Brown's body lies a-mouldering in the grave;
His soul is marching on!

CHORUS.

Glory, halle — hallelujah!
Glory, halle — hallelujah!
Glory, halle — hallelujah!
His soul is marching on!

He's gone to be a soldier in the army of the Lord!
He's gone to be a soldier in the army of the Lord!
He's gone to be a soldier in the army of the Lord!
His soul is marching on!

Glory, halle — hallelujah! &c.

John Brown's knapsack is strapped upon his back!
John Brown's knapsack is strapped upon his back!
John Brown's knapsack is strapped upon his back!
His soul is marching on!

Glory, halle — hallelujah! &c.

The pet lambs and angels will meet him on the way,
The pet lambs and angels will meet him on the way,
The pet lambs and angels will meet him on the way,
As they go marching on!

Glory, halle — hallelujah! &c.

We'll hang Jeff Davis to a sour apple-tree!
We'll hang Jeff Davis to a sour apple-tree!
We'll hang Jeff Davis to a sour apple-tree!
As we go marching on!

Glory, halle — hallelujah! &c.

Now, three rousing cheers for the Union!
Now, three rousing cheers for the Union!
Now, three rousing cheers for the Union!
As we are marching on!

Glory, halle — hallelujah! &c.
Hip, hip, hip, hip, hurrah!

INCIDENTS OF FREDERICKSBURG. — The following are from letters of soldiers written soon after the repulse of Burnside: "One man showed himself a hero. On the top of a house, apparently undismayed by the shells and bullets crashing around, above, and below him, stood a signal officer all day long; he calmly looked through his glass, and signalled with his flags. Fortunately he escaped unhurt."

A Lieutenant tells the following : "On passing through a street of the town, while in the heat of the engagement, my horse suddenly reared, and I could distinctly hear the shell whizzing either directly in front or under his fore feet. Looking down, I saw an artillery driver, of whom I was just asking a question, picking himself out of the mud, the shell having passed through both of his horses: fortunately he was unhurt.

"'Be jabers, Liftinant, but that was a close call for you and me,' said he.

"I replied, 'Are you hurt?'

"'No, sir; I b'lieve Ise only scared.'"

PRESIDENT LINCOLN AND THE FARMER. — A Western farmer sought the President day after day until he procured the much desired audience. He had a plan for the successful prosecution of the war, to which Mr. Lincoln listened as patiently as he could. When he was through, he asked the opinion of the President upon his plan. "Well," said Mr. Lincoln, "I'll answer by telling you a story. You have heard of Mr. Blank, of Chicago? He was an immense loafer in his way — in fact, never did anything in his life. One day he got crazy over a great rise in the price of wheat, upon which many wheat speculators gained large fortunes. Blank started off one morning to one of the most successful of the wheat speculators, and with much enthusiasm laid before him a plan by which he (the said Blank) was certain of becoming independently rich. When he had finished, he asked the opinion of his hearer upon his plan of operations. The reply came as follows: 'My advice is that you stick to your business.' 'But,' asked Blank, 'what is my business?' 'I don't know, I am sure, what it is,' says the merchant; 'but whatever it is, I advise you to stick to it.' And now," said Mr. Lincoln, "I mean nothing offensive, for I know you mean well, but I think you had better stick to your business, and leave the war to those who have the responsibility of managing it."

UNCLE SAM IN VIRGINIA. — In the early part of the war, some four or five of the Union cavalry were out towards the Blackwater, on a scout. They called at a large, nice-looking farm-house, and asked the matron to get them some dinner. While they were eating, the old lady asked them if they knew a man in Suffolk called "Uncle Samuel." They told her they did, they were very well acquainted with him. She then said, "I did not know but they had played a Yankee trick on me. Some of your men came here a few days ago, and bought all my turkeys and chickens; and when they had them all put up, ready to take away, they told me to come down to Suffolk, and Uncle Sam would pay for them." The old lady said she had lived within ten miles of Suffolk all her life, and had never heard of

that man before. She asked if he was a Northern man, and belonged to the Northern army. The cavalry told her that he was a very generous old gentleman, and if she would come down to Suffolk, he would not only pay her for her poultry, but pay her for their dinner beside.

A COLONEL ON GUARD. — A Lieutenant in one of the Ohio regiments was making a detail of men to guard a lot of army stores captured from the enemy. He approached a crowd of men all wearing overcoats such as Uncle Sam gives his boys, and selected four or five for special duty. It happened that Lieutenant-Colonel Gazley, of the Thirty-seventh Indiana, was in the crowd, and was selected by the Lieutenant. This was fun for the Colonel, and without a word he shouldered his gun and went to his post of duty. Not long afterwards, the Lieutenant, going his rounds, discovered by the firelight the bugle upon Gazley's cap. He rather authoritatively inquired where he got that bugle. The Colonel said he "must have picked up an officer's cap somewhere," and the Lieutenant passed on.

The Colonel stood his turn all night long, and was found in the morning walking his post. Having laid off his overcoat, his shoulder-straps appeared very conspicuously in connection with the musket on his shoulder. As soon as the Lieutenant discovered a Colonel on guard, he approached him, and courteously inquired how he came to be there upon guard? "Well, sir, you placed me here." With no little agitation the Lieutenant inquired who he was. "My name is Carter Gazley, and I am Lieutenant-Colonel of the Thirty-seventh Indiana regiment." The Colonel was speedily "released," but the Lieutenant was not yet relieved from his embarrassment.

INCIDENTS OF GRIERSON'S RAID. — While several of the Union scouts were feeding their horses at the stables of a wealthy planter of secession proclivities, the proprietor looking on, apparently deeply interested in the proceeding, suddenly burst out with: "Well, boys, I can't say I have anything against you. I don't know but that, on the whole, I rather like you. You have not taken anything of mine except a little corn for your horses, and that you are welcome to. I have heard of you all over the country. You are doing the boldest thing ever done. But you'll be trapped, though; you'll be trapped, mark me."

At another place, where the men thought it advisable to represent themselves as Jackson's cavalry, a whole company was very graciously entertained by a strong secession lady, who insisted on whipping a negro because he did not bring the hoe-cakes fast enough.

On one occasion, seven of Colonel Grierson's scouts stopped at the house of a wealthy planter to feed their jaded horses. Upon ascertaining that he had been doing a little guerrilla business on his own account, our men encouraged him to the belief that, as they were the invincible Van

Dorn cavalry, they would soon catch the Yankees. The secession gentleman heartily approved of what he supposed to be their intentions, and enjoined upon them the necessity of making as rapid marches as possible. As the men had discovered two splendid carriage horses in the planter's stable, they thought, under the circumstances, they would be justified in making an exchange, which they accordingly proceeded to do. As they were taking the saddles from their own tired steeds, and placing them on the backs of the wealthy guerrilla's horses, the proprietor discovered them, and at once objected. He was met with the reply that, as he was anxious the Yankees should be speedily overtaken, those after them should have good horses. "All right, gentlemen," said the planter; "I will keep your animals until you return. I suppose you'll be back in two or three days, at the farthest. When you return, you'll find they have been well cared for."

The soldiers were sometimes asked where they got their blue coats. They always replied, if they were travelling under the name of Van Dorn's cavalry, that they took them at Holly Springs of the Yankees. This always excited great laughter among the secessionists. The scouts, however, usually wore the regular "secesh" uniforms.

A SOUTHERN CONUNDRUM. — Which action of the Confederates was the most liberal towards the Yankees, but which they disliked the most?

The battle of Manassas, where they received a Confederate *check*, on which they made a *run* on the Bull Run *banks*, and drew more metallic currency than they wanted.

DRIVING HOME THE COWS.

Out of the clover and blue-eyed grass,
  He turned them into the river-lane;
One after another he let them pass,
  Then fastened the meadow bars again.

Under the willows and over the hill,
  He patiently followed their sober pace;
The merry whistle for once was still,
  And something shadowed the sunny face.

Only a boy! and his father had said
  He never could let his youngest go:
Two already were lying dead
  Under the feet of the trampling foe.

But after the evening work was done,
  And the frogs were loud in the meadow-swamp,
Over his shoulder he slung his gun,
  And stealthily followed the foot-path damp, —

Across the clover and through the wheat,
  With resolute heart and purpose grim,
Though cold was the dew on his hurrying feet,
  And the blind bats flitting startled him.

Thrice since then had the lanes been white,
  And the orchards sweet with apple-bloom;
And now, when the cows came back at night,
  The feeble father drove them home.

For news had come to the lonely farm
  That three were lying where two had lain;
And the old man's tremulous, palsied arm
  Could never lean on a son's again.

The summer day grew cool and late;
  He went for the cows when the work was done;
But down the lane, as he opened the gate,
  He saw them coming, one by one, —

Brindle, Ebony, Speckle, and Bess,
  Shaking their horns in the evening wind,
Cropping the buttercups out of the grass —
  But who was it following close behind?

Loosely swang in the idle air
  The empty sleeve of army blue;
And worn and pale, from the crisping hair,
  Looked out a face that the father knew; —

For Southern prisons will sometimes yawn,
  And yield their dead unto life again; *
And the day that comes with a cloudy dawn
  In golden glory at last may wane.

The great tears sprang to their meeting eyes;
  For the heart must speak when the lips are dumb,
And under the silent evening skies
  Together they followed the cattle home.

THE CHRISTIAN COMMISSION. — The Rev. George J. Mingins, in an address delivered at the great meeting of the Christian Commission at Washington, on the 2d day of February, 1864, spoke as follows:

"When, in 1861, in the month of November, the various representatives of the Young Men's Christian Associations of the loyal North met together to organize this United States Christian Commission, they asked and answered one simple question. It was this: What can we, who are at home, surrounded by home comforts, the recipients of every blessing, living in peace with each other, who have the liberty of worshipping God beneath our own vine and fig tree, — what can we do for those brave men who have left their homes and all that is near and dear to them, to sacrifice and suffer, that we may be blessed with the blessings of peace and safety? This was the simple question. For this these meetings have been held. For this we are gathered to-night, that you may understand precisely the simple, practical workings of this Commission. They are held that the loyal people of the North may be aroused to a due sense of their own responsibility in this matter. We desire that every man and every woman belonging to the loyal North may look at this matter aright, and be prepared to do their duty, so that our national existence may be sustained, and we may go on, a brighter, grander,

* Yet there are twelve thousand nine hundred and nineteen graves of Union soldiers at the one rebel prison-pen of Andersonville; while from the comfortable quarters in which the rebel prisoners were kept, there went back into the rebel armies some of "the finest fighting material" the rebel Commissioner of Exchange ever saw.

nobler, truer nation in the future than we have been in the past.

"I have not the honor to be 'native to this manor born.' I first saw the light in good old Scotland. Her sunlight first slanted adown the hill-side into the valley where my mother's cot was nestled; and I am ready to confess, sir, that when this great and gigantic war burst over our land, I used to look on coldly, not understanding thoroughly the great principle which prompted men to leave their homes and carry their lives in their hands, that they might save the land of Washington; and when I used to see soldiers going to the war, I used to indulge in a sort of vain philosophy, that I know a great many men indulge in to-day. I used to say, 'Now, these men like to fight: I don't. Therefore they are right in going to fight, and I am right in staying at home.' Or I used to say, 'Now, these men want fame, they want a name, they want position. I am perfectly satisfied with what I have and what I am. It is right for them to battle for fame; it is right for me to live quietly in all humility.' And I used to fling around my shoulder the philosopher's robe, and stand unmoved, as I saw men passing before me, going to battle and to death, and quiet my conscience with this miserable philosophy, that will never stand before the intelligent, the great, and the noble, and that the very devil despises!

"A touching little incident, Mr. President, converted me from the error of my way; and if you will permit me, I will relate it, for, I confess, it was a great turning-point in my life; I feel it so now. I happened to be in attendance on a meeting or Synod in the city of Easton, at the time when our honorable Chief Magistrate called out seventy-five thousand men to beat back the foe that was plunging onward to desecrate this holy temple. I stood in the street, one day, and heard the sound of martial music. I saw the men marching down. I knew who they were the moment I saw them — sturdy yeomen, who had left the hills of Pennsylvania and poured along her valleys; who had left their fields, and looms, and benches, their wives and little ones, their homes, and all that they held dear, to stand in front of the foe that had risen up against us. When I saw them my old philosophy came up, because I must have something to comfort me, you know.

"Just then I saw a little girl standing on the doorstep. She was ten or twelve years of age, I should judge. As I looked in her face my attention was arrested. I thought I saw a deep cloud of sorrow come over and rest upon that little brow. She stood with her little hands clasped tightly, and her little face seemed pinched with very agony. And I thought, Well, now, what can be the matter with the child? I determined to watch her; so I took my stand near by. The sound of the music drew nearer and nearer. By and by the heavy tramp of men was heard. As they drew near to us, I saw that little form becoming more fixed and rigid; the little hands began to quiver, her neck was stretched out with eager intensity, and she stood with eyes fairly riveted upon the men as they came marching slowly by the door. At last I was startled with the penetrating little voice, as it cried out, 'O, that's him! that's him! It's pa! it's pa! He's going! he's going! He's gone!' and with loud sobbing she turned away and entered into the house.

"Now conscience, just at that time, asked me one or two very ugly questions. One question that it asked me was, 'Well, what was the matter with the child?' The answer was at hand. I knew that that man who had marched to defend the Union was her father; that he was her all; that he was her comfort, her joy, her support, her sustenance; and when that little one had given up that, she had given up the very sunlight of her little existence, literally her *all*. And then conscience asked me another question. It said, 'Well, sir, *what have* you *done for your country?*' I whispered, 'Well — but — but I don't *really* belong to the country!' 'Don't belong to the country?' said conscience; 'don't belong to the country? — then, you infernal scamp, get out of it! *Get out of it!* This is not the country for men who belong nowhere — it's somewhere else! Don't belong to it?' and then memory carried me back many a year, when I first landed upon these hospitable shores, a poor, unknown lad, when year after year I struggled, and at every step I took I met sunlight, and warm hearts, and generous natures; and all the high road to an honest and a true ambition opened up before me. And 'not belong to the country? Then quit it! and give up all you have received from it and have in it!' 'Well, but,' conscience interposed, 'you got a wife here.' 'Yes; and I would not give her up for a great deal.' I thought, 'No, I cannot quit it;' and then the blush of very shame mantled my cheek; and standing in that street in Easton, as I looked back at the silent, dumb door that had closed upon that brave and God-like little patriot, I determined that, though not 'native to the manor born,' I would allow no man living here to outdo me, so far as I had the ability, in upholding, and sustaining, and defending the nation that had been my generous and my noble benefactor.

"But conscience was not done with me yet. I walked down the street. I saw the same company of men drawn up in line. I saw an old woman who was pulling a thin shawl about her. Ah, she was one of the poor of the earth. She hurried on, eagerly, anxiously scanning the faces of the men as she came. At last she stopped before a great, tall, raw-boned fellow who was joking with his companions. 'Well, boys,' he said, 'we're going off — ar'n't we?' And they said, 'Yes, we are.' He had a little bundle, tied up with a red handkerchief, in his arm. 'When we get down there, maybe we won't give them fits, eh?' They said, 'Maybe we won't.' They seemed to be making the same mistake with some of us just about that time, for we none of us had an idea that such a terrible desolating shadow was rising up in our midst.

"Just then the old woman pushed her way through the crowd, and stood before this man.

His eyes dropped in a moment, and his face was covered with a flush, and as he turned his head he lifted his finger to his eyes, and shook it with a twirl — 'Now, mother, mother! You promised me that you wouldn't come out, didn't ye? Now you promised me. When I said "good by" to ye, mother, I told ye I didn't want you to come out here and unman me; and here you've done it! Now I wish you hadn't!' The old woman lifted her hands up, and putting them on the great high shoulders of her son, as the tears streamed down her furrowed cheeks, she said, 'O Jack, don't scold me; don't scold your poor old mother, Jack: you know ye're all I have, Jack; and I didn't come out to unman ye, I didn't come out to unman ye — I have come to say, God bless ye, Jack, God bless ye!' and folding the thin shawl over her bosom she went away. The big fellow drew the sleeve over his face, and bringing down his arm with a sort of vexed emphasis, as if to defy the emotion he could not control, turning to the men, he said, 'Hang it, boys, she's mother, you know!' There, I felt, will be a brave man in the field. He's a noble, a true fellow. Men who have a right and true appreciation of their country's cause are lovers of their home and of their mother. It is unnecessary to say that conscience had done its work faithfully with me that time!

"And now, when I heard, Mr. Chairman, that the Christian Commission designed to follow these men wherever they go, with their homes and the influences of the loved ones there, that it was to be, as you have heard, a home-link of the war, I could not but admire and support it. When this Christian Commission was organized, many said, 'Now I hope you will stick to your legitimate business.' Well, we say, 'Pray what is the legitimate business of the Christian Commission?' 'Well, it is the giving of tracts, and prayer-books, and Testaments, and all sorts of good books; it is preaching, and praying, and talking with the men, and it is not anything else.' Now, I was sent out by the worthy Chairman of this Christian Commission in May, 1861, to see if there was anything to do for an organization like this within the lines of the army; and in the second place, if there was, to see how we could do it. We found there was plenty to do; and I found that there was only one way of doing it, and that was by following the example set us by the Master. Now, I have not the slightest respect for, nor the slightest faith in, that Christianity that goes into the deepest cellar or into the highest garret, and beholds the poor, wretched beings there, dressed in rags, and shivering in the cold, and pitches a sermon at the poor things' heads. It is not the religion of my Lord and Master that does this. For I remember that when he stood upon the earth, his hands were always busy, and his great heart was always drawn out in sympathy for the poor and lowly; and he ministered to their bodies as well as to their souls. When the poor leper came to him, saying, 'Lord, if thou wilt thou canst make me clean,' he first healed the man's body, and then talked to him of his soul's welfare. However, in this work in the army we soon find out from the soldier himself the kind of religion he wants. The soldier is the best judge, after all, of this. One of our delegates, in the early history of the Commission, approached a soldier who seemed very tired and worn, and holding in his hand a tract, he said, extending it to him, 'My good friend, will you have a tract?' 'No, but I'll have a cracker!' was the quick reply; and the delegate said, 'Pardon me, I did not know you were hungry, my good fellow, or I would not have offered you the tract first;' and putting his hand in his satchel, he pulled out a nice Boston cracker, and said, 'Take this; and if that is not sufficient, if you will wait ten minutes, till I run over to the Christian Commission's tent, I will bring you as much as you want.' The fellow's eyes brightened; he was moved; and he said, 'Well, stranger, excuse me; I didn't want to be impertinent, but I tell you I was hungry, that's a fact; and when you offered me that tract, I thought I would much rather have a cracker, and I said so. But give me the tract, too, stranger; give it to me. I promise you I will read it, and keep it; for if this is the kind of religion you men of the Christian Commission bring down to the soldiers in the army, it's just what they want.' And from the first time that its delegates have set out for the lines of the army, up to this present time, the universal testimony — I say it boldly — of every man who has come in contact with the Christian Commission, has been, 'THAT IT'S JUST THE VERY THING FOR THE ARMY.'

"The Rev. Mr. Parvin has given you some idea as to how the Commission's delegate goes to work. Out of these twelve hundred delegates every man has acted upon the simple principle of the organization, that it is the duty of every man to do something for his country. I suppose I have what you may consider a curious definition of patriotism. I believe that the word 'patriot' means 'one who is willing to *make sacrifices* for his country.' But you know there are 'many men of different minds,' and I have met some who would come down to the breakfast table at the hotel, with the luxuries of life spread out before them, and with their newspapers in hand, very complacently lean back, and with pompous air bolt out an oath from their unclean throats, 'By George, I told you so; the Government is going to smash; it is a wreck already!' and they would grumble and growl, and yet think themselves true patriots; indeed, if you doubted their patriotism they would become excessively angry! I may be mistaken, but the only patriotism it is right to acknowledge, in my opinion, in presenting this cause before the people of the North, is this: that whether this war be right or wrong, every man is bound to do what he can to relieve the sufferings of those men who are fighting for him, to bind up their broken bodies, and pour the oil of soothing upon the weak and weary wounded soldiers.

"You may ask me, How are these ministrations of delegates received by the soldiers? I have been out several times as delegate, and I testify that I have always been received most kindly by them. I met with but one exception. He was an Irishman. I do not say this to cast any reflection upon our Irish fellow-citizens; for I remember well when I stood at the battle-field of Antietam, that I was pointed out a ditch which lay full of the rebel dead, and when I asked, 'Whose work is this?' I was answered, 'The Irish brigade, sir!' and I said then, 'God bless them!' and so I say now, if that is the way they do! (Applause.) And I say, God bless all whom America has received from foreign countries, and made them sons; and may he confound all who, walking and living in the sunlight of its prosperity, defile her with curses and trample upon the bosom that has nourished them.

"Well, notwithstanding that, this was a very tough old Irishman, I assure you. It was at a time when a great many were sick, at Yorktown, with the typhoid fever and chronic dysentery — men who had marched, and marched, and dug and delved, and marched again, until they were completely broken down. A great many of them had no clean shirts on — for they had worn them long. I had got a large supply, and was going through the tent, giving them to the poor fellows. And here let me illustrate the Commission's proceeding in such cases. When word came that the men wanted shirts, we did not go back to the tent and hold a council of war over it. One did not rise and say, 'Now, do you think that man has a shirt? Do you really think it?' And after considering a while, and discussing the point, they conclude he has not. 'Well, do you think we had better give him one?' is asked; and it is agreed that it would be advisable to do so. 'I propose, then, that we give him a shirt,' says one. 'Is it seconded?' 'It is.' 'It is moved and seconded that this man have a shirt. All in favor, say ay.' They say ay, and the shirt is procured. 'But,' says one, 'how long have you been here, my friend?' 'Seven weeks.' 'O, then, you must give the man the shirt, because you are the senior officer here!' And at last the poor man gets the needed garment.

"No, no; it is nothing like this that the Commission goes to work. I had gone to the needy men and distributed what I had. I came to this Irishman. 'My dear friend,' said I, 'how are you? You seem to be an old man.' 'Shure and I am an ould mon, sir!' 'Well, how came you here, in the army, old as you are?' 'Och, sir, I'm not only an ould mon, but an ould soldier, too, I'd have ye know.' He had been twenty years in the British service in the East Indies, and had fought America's foes in Mexico. 'Yes, sir,' he continued, 'I'm ould, and I know it; but I'm not too ould to shoulder a musket and hit a rap for the ould flag yet!' (Applause.) 'You're a brave fellow,' said I, 'and I've brought these things to make you comfortable,' as I held out to him a shirt and drawers. He looked at me. Said he, 'What, thim things?' 'Yes, I want to give them to you to wear.' 'Well, I don't want them!' 'You do want them.' 'Well, I don't!' and he looked at me and then at the goods, and said somewhat

sharply as I urged them again, 'Niver mind, sir, I don't want them, and I tell ye, I won't have them!' 'Why?' 'Shure,' said he, 'do ye take me for an object of charity?' That was a kind of poser. I looked at him. 'No, sir,' said I, 'I do not take you for an object of charity, and I don't want you to look upon me as a dispenser of charity, either, for I am not.' 'Well, what are you, thin?' 'I am a delegate of the United States Christian Commission. I have left my home and my church, and I have come down here to serve the brave fellows. I have washed their feet, and have dressed them, and done everything that a nurse could do, for the sick and suffering men here. I came as a delegate from the loyal North, bearing the thank-offerings of mothers, and wives, and sisters, to you, brave defenders of the Stars and Stripes.' And I thought, surely, after such a speech as that, I would get hold of the old fellow's heart. But he looked at me and said, '*Any how, I won't have thim!*' (Laughter.) I felt really wounded. I did not at all like it. I have told you he was an Irishman, and I happened to be a Scotchman, and somehow you scarcely ever see an Irishman and Scotchman meet without there is a row. I couldn't help it, but it is so, that I didn't like the idea of that old Irishman's bluffing me off so. I was determined not to be conquered. I meant to try further; and when a Scotchman means to try a thing, he will come very near doing it. (Laughter.) I didn't forget my obligations, however, the cause I was serving, and that I was a Christian man. I didn't talk any further then, but determined to *prove* by my acts, my deeds, that I had come down to do this old man and his fellows good. So day after day I went about my work, nursing, giving medicines, cleaning up the tent, and doing anything and everything that I could.

"One day, as I went in, a soldier said, 'There's good news to-day, chaplain.' 'Ah, what is it?' 'The paymaster's come.' 'Well, that *is* good news.' 'Yes, but not to me, chaplain.' 'How is that?' 'I've not got my descriptive list, and if a fellow's not got that, the paymaster may come and go, and he's none the better off for it.' 'Well, why don't you get it?' 'I can't write, chaplain; I am suffering from chronic rheumatism.' 'Shall I write for you?' 'If you only would, chaplain!' I hauled out paper and pencil, asked the number of his regiment, name of his Captain, his company, &c., and sent a simple request that the descriptive list might be remitted to that point. When I had done this I found a good many who wanted their lists, and I went on writing them until I came to the cot next to the old Irishman's. It was occupied by another Irishman. I said to him, 'My friend, have you your descriptive list?' 'No.' 'Shall I write to your Captain for it?' 'If you please;' and I began to write. I noticed the old Irishman stretching over, all attention, listening to what I was saying. I spoke now and then a word meant for him, though I affected not to notice him. After I had written the request, I said to the young man, 'Shall I read it to you?' 'If you please, sir;' and I read aloud the simple note.

When I had done the old Irishman broke out with, 'Upon my sowl, sir, you write the natest letther for a descriptive list that I ever heard in my life! Shure, and a man would think ye had been a soldier all your days, you do write so nate a letther for a descriptive list!' I turned around and said, 'Have you got yours?' 'An' I haven't, sir.' 'Do you want it?' 'To be shure I do,' he said, flaring up; 'an' that's a queer question to ax a man, does he want his descriptive list, does he want his pay to buy some little delicacies to send home to the ould woman and the childer! I do want it, an' if you will lend us the shtroke of your pen, chaplain, you'll oblige us.' I sat down and wrote the letter, and when I had done, said, 'Now, boys, give me your letters, and I'll have them post-paid and sent for you.'

"When I returned sad work awaited me, for a delegate meets shadows as well as sunshine in his work. In that tent were several of the brave sons of New England. One of Massachusetts' sons lay there dying. You could tell it by the pale face, the sunken eye, and the pale, quivering lip. Then came the delegate's work as the minister of Christ. This Christian Commission, Mr. Chairman, believes that men are immortal, and that all the patriotism on God's earth will not open the gates of eternal glory to any soul unless it be saved by the great mercy of God, through Jesus Christ, our Lord; and then trembling, remembering the terrible responsibility that rests upon the living minister standing by a dying man, we try to preach the gospel to him.

"I spoke to the dying boy of mother, of Jesus, of home, of heaven. O, mothers who are here to-night, let me say to you that whatever else a soldier forgets, he never, *never*, NEVER forgets his mother. And I will tell you, my friends, that is one of the things I have noticed in an American army that I believe is a great characteristic of the American heart, that it clings to home and mother. I have stood by the cot of a dying soldier, and stooping down to catch his last breath, have heard him whisper 'mother.' I remember passing over a battle-field and seeing a man just dying. His mind was wandering. His spirit was no longer on that bloody field; it was at his home, far away. I stood and looked upon the poor fellow. A smile passed over his face — a smile, O, of so much sweetness, as, looking up, he said, 'O mother, O mother! I am *so* glad you have come.' And he seemed as if she was there by his side. By and by he said again, 'Mother, it's cold, it's cold; won't you pull the blanket over me?' I stooped down and pulled the poor fellow's ragged blanket closer to his shivering form. And he smiled again. 'That will do, mother, that will do!' and he turned over and passed sweetly to his rest, and he was borne up to the presence of God on the wings of a pious mother's prayers.

"But to come to the case in the tent. After I had done all I could for the Massachusetts boy, and had shook his hand in parting, I turned to leave the tent, when just as I was going out of the door I happened to see the old Irishman. He looked very queerly. There was certainly something the matter with him. He was rubbing his hands through his hair, pulling his beard, and acting otherwise very strangely; but I didn't take much notice of him, as I had been so solemnly engaged. Then he came up to me, and clasping my hands, he said, 'Be me sowl, sir, you are no humbug, anyhow!' 'What do you mean?' I said. 'O,' said he, 'haven't I watched you as day by day ye've been going through the tent caring for the boys? Why, ye've been like a mother to iv'ry one of them. Thanks to ye, chaplain, thanks to ye, an' may God bless ye,' he repeated, as he again wrung my hand. 'And,' said he, 'ye do this all for nothing; the boys have been telling me about ye.' 'O,' said I, 'that's a mistake.' 'Well, now, how's that? They been tellin' me that ye were a Presbyterian minister, and that ye came away from yer home, down here, for the love ye had for the boys. But ye don't do it for nothing, eh? Who, thin, pays ye? the Government?' 'No. If it means to pay me, it would take a great deal more money than it can spare. I would not sell my experience to-day for any price.' 'Well, does the Commission pay ye?' 'No.' 'Well, thin, if the Government doesn't pay ye, and the Commission doesn't, *who does* pay ye?' I looked the man straight in the face, and I said, 'That honest, hearty grasp of the hand, and that hearty "God bless ye," is ample reward for all that I have done for you. Remember, my brave fellow, that you have suffered and sacrificed for me, and I couldn't do less for you now.' He was broken down. He bowed his head and wept, and then, taking me by the hand again, said, 'Shure, an' if that's the pay ye take, why, *God bless ye, God bless ye, God bless ye!* Ye'll be rich of the coin of me heart all your days.' And after a few moments' pause, he said, '*And now, chaplain, if ye will just give us the shirt and the drawers, I'll wear them till there's not a thread of them left!*' (Cheers and laughter.)

"This incident will illustrate how we approach the soldier, what we try to do for him, and how it is received by him. I have already occupied my full time; but if you will permit me, Mr. Chairman, I want to say a word as to the great work of the Commission, after all. It sends its stores and cares for the bodies of men because it is Christ-like to do it, and because it gives it the key to the men's hearts; and this is its grand aim, to benefit and save the soul — to teach the men that it is 'not all of life to live, nor all of death to die.'

"Let me say, first, that the soldiers are accessible to this work. A great many seem to believe that the moment they put on the uniform of their country, they are left at once free of all moral obligations; and I tell you that I have seen in this city of Washington more wretched wickedness amongst our soldiers than I ever saw down in the lines of the army. The men there will come out to hear the gospel. I have preached night after night, within four miles of this city, to soldier audiences larger, I am safe in saying, than I ever saw a minister of the gospel address on any special religious subject in any church in this country. And these men came voluntarily together. The Christian Commission have a chapel capable of holding a thousand men, within four miles of this city, and it is better attended, far better, I do not hesitate to say, than the majority of the churches here. And let me also say, though do not let it startle you when I tell you, that the soldiers are not only more accessible to the gospel than the young men are at home, but that there are more brought to Christ, more are converted to God, in our armies, than there are at home! I will say even more — that, humanly speaking, there is more likelihood of your son's becoming a soldier of the cross down in the lines of the army than there is at home. 'How do you make it out?' some may ask. I answer, because the prayers of the people of the North are centring on that mighty and majestic host; because there is no mother in the land who does not lift up holy hands unto God, and beseech that victory may perch upon the banner of this nation, and that her son may return to her home a child of the eternal God; because there is not a wife or a sister in the land but who asks that the shadow of the Almighty's wings may be flung over their loved ones who have left them.

"I know, Mr. Chairman, that we have all suffered in this war; but it seems to me that those who suffer most are the Christian fathers and mothers of the soldiers. In conclusion, just let me give you an instance of a mother's keen and deep-felt anxiety about the welfare of her boy. Over a year ago, I saw a scene in an out hospital, near my own, as I was looking through the veranda, which I shall never forget. On a couch lay a young man of twenty or twenty-two years, just hovering between time and eternity.

"Bending over his couch in an attitude of agony, O, how intense! stood a woman. Her pale face has seemed to haunt me ever since. Her eye was fixed upon her dying boy before her. Ever and anon she would stoop down, and her lip would quiver as she whispered over that dull ear; and then she would noiselessly slip away from his side to get him some little delicacy, and swiftly coming back, would gently, gently steal her arm under his head, and minister to him. Then she would lay the head softly back again upon the pillow, and folding her hands, would watch, watch, watch, O, how long! how anxiously!

"I entered the room. She motioned to me. I approached and told her who I was; that I was a delegate of the Christian Commission.

"'What is it you do, sir?'

"'I came down here as a minister of the ascended Jesus, to speak to sinners of the Lamb of God, that taketh away the sins of the world; to tell the living and the dying soldier that there is a holier, a brighter, better home above.'

"She put her hand in mine in a moment. 'O sir,' said she, 'I am so glad to see you!' and pointing to the cot, she said, 'Do you see that? do you see him, sir?'

"'Yes, I do.'

"'Well, that is Joseph. O, that is my Joseph — all I have, sir — all that God ever gave me, sir — my comfort, my joy, my support! — and he's dying, sir! — he's dying!'

"'O, my dear friend, it may not be so bad as you think. He may get better.'

"'Ah,' she replied, 'I wish you could comfort me; but the doctors, who have been so kind to me, tell me that he must die. Why, sir, a bullet went crashing through his lung. If you will come, I will show you, sir.'

"'No, I do not want to see it.'

"After a moment, she said, as if to herself, 'It's hard; isn't it? You know he's all I've got. I know that we must sacrifice for this war, and I know that many have given one son, and more; but they had somebody left behind to love them. But O! my Joseph! my Joseph! O sir, he came to me and said, "I must go, mother. My friends are going, and I cannot stay behind!" And he put his arms around my neck, and begged me so. "I will come back again, mother — O, yes, I will — all safe; and you will be proud of me, mother, and glad you let me go." And I said, "Well, go, Joseph, my son; and God bless you!" And ever since that day, I've been asking God to shield the widow's son, sir. But, sir, He has done what seemed well in His sight, and it is all well.'

"And she paused a moment. I could but witness that sacred grief in silence. She then turned to me with even deeper grief, as she said: 'And that is only half the sacrifice.' Ah, I knew what was coming — I feared it. 'O sir, if his country only asked his body, I could give it. Yes, I could give it; for I could take his poor, cold body home, and lay it to rest with his father; but O!'— and with a look of unutterable woe she said it —'O my God! I cannot give up his soul! O, save his soul for Christ's sake!'

"Then, turning more composedly to me, she continued: 'Joseph is not a Christian, sir. Won't you come and speak to him of Jesus?'—and she brought me to the bedside. I spoke to Joseph. He was conscious. I found that he was like hundreds and thousands of others who had gone up from their mothers' knees to war — had been tossed about by temptation, and at last had fallen into grievous sin. He said, 'Chaplain, I have been a wicked fellow. Is there any use in my hoping?'

"Then came the grand mission of the cross of Jesus. Ah! I sat in this gallery yesterday, and in the gallery of the Senate-house, and I heard the men of the nation standing up pleading for their country's good; and I was proud of them, and I thought, 'O that I could have such a position!'—when something whispered, 'Hush! thou hast a higher and a holier one!' and I felt it; and I felt, 'May God give me strength to fill it faithfully.' (Amen! amen!) O, how glorious was my commission to that dying man, that seeking soul! To tell him that Jesus was ready to save to the uttermost — that God had no pleasure in the death of him that dieth. I delivered my message. 'Will you pray for me, chaplain?' the dying boy asked. We knelt down, I on one side, and his mother on the other, and he stretched out his thin hand, and took one hand of mine, and one hand of his mother's, and I prayed for him. When I had done, he let go my hand, and took both his mother's in one hand, and covered them with the other, and looked up into her face as the tears streamed down, and said, 'Mother, mother dear!'

" 'Well, Joseph, what is it?'

" 'O mother, you know you will never take me home alive. *Now* I think, mother, of what you used to tell me long ago, when I was at home. Mother, this man says that God loves us all, that Jesus is willing to receive us all, that I need not be cast out, mother, that I may see you again. Mother, I am going to try to love Jesus; I am going to trust him.'

" I had never seen a tear upon that mother's face until Joseph uttered that sentence, and then the fountains of her soul seemed to be broken up. The tears rolled down her cheeks, as she clasped her hands, and said, 'Thank God! Thank God! Thank God! Now, Joseph, I can give you up. You are dying in the cause of your country, Joseph, and you're going home to Jesus. Thank God! Thank God!' And murmuring, 'Thank God!' as she kissed him, she pillowed her face upon his bosom heaving in death.

" Now, my friends, we owe a man in this Christian country two things. We owe our brave soldiers two things. We owe them food for the body and sympathy for the heart, and food for the soul. We owe them the message of Christ and him crucified, that they may be led to live godly and sober lives, to the honor and glory of God. To my mind, Mr. President, this war hath been conducted by the Great Jehovah. He hath unsheathed the sword of his might, and he hath been stripping off from us our hideous sins that have made us deformed and hateful in his sight, and he hath stood us upon the platform of the great truth of equal liberty to all his creatures! (Long and loud cheers and applause.) In my mind he is crying out from the hill-tops, and the mighty voice is resounding from one hill-top to the other, 'Ye are my people, and they who follow in my paths, and care for my words, shall never be destroyed, for the Word of the Lord hath declared it!' "

RATHER FUNNY. — A company of some thirty or forty Union men were trying to make their escape to Kentucky, to join the Northern army. They came to a creek which they were compelled to wade. Not wishing to get their clothes wet, they shelled off all to their shirts, and while in this condition they were surprised by a company of Jeff's cavalry boys, who were in hot pursuit of them. Being somewhat frightened, they fled in double-quick, making a " straight shirt sail " up hill and down hill, leaving their clothing in the possession of our boys, who, of course, took possession and appropriated the same. What became of the tories we are unable to say, but rather suppose they are in a poor condition for the cold weather.

THE HEART OF THE WAR.

PEACE in the clover-scented air,
  And stars within the dome,
And underneath, in dim repose,
  A plain New England home.
Within, a murmur of low tones
  And sighs from hearts oppressed,
Merging in prayer at last, that brings
  The balm of silent rest.

I've closed a hard day's work, Marty —
  The evening chores are done;
And you are weary with the house,
  And with the little one.
But he is sleeping sweetly now,
  With all our pretty brood;
So come and sit upon my knee,
  And it will do me good.

O Marty! I must tell you all
  The trouble in my heart,
And you must do the best you can
  To take and bear your part.
You've seen the shadow on my face,
  You've felt it day and night;
For it has filled our little home,
  And banished all its light.

I did not mean it should be so,
  And yet I might have known
That hearts that live as close as ours
  Can never keep their own.
But we are fallen on evil times,
  And, do whate'er I may,
My heart grows sad about the war,
  And sadder every day.

I think about it when I work,
  And when I try to rest,
And never more than when your head
  Is pillowed on my breast;
For then I see the camp-fires blaze,
  And sleeping men around,
Who turn their faces towards their homes,
  And dream upon the ground.

I think about the dear, brave boys,
  My mates in other years,
Who pine for home and those they love,
  Till I am choked with tears.
With shouts and cheers they marched away
  On glory's shining track,
But, ah! how long, how long they stay!
  How few of them come back!

One sleeps beside the Tennessee,
  And one beside the James,
And one fought on a gallant ship,
  And perished in its flames.
And some, struck down by fell disease,
  Are breathing out their life;
And others, maimed by cruel wounds,
  Have left the deadly strife.

Ah, Marty! Marty! only think
  Of all the boys have done
And suffered in this weary war!
  Brave heroes, every one!
O, often, often in the night,
  I hear their voices call:
" Come on and help us! Is it right
  That we should bear it all?"

And when I kneel and try to pray,
  My thoughts are never free,
But cling to those who toil and fight
  And die for you and me.
And when I pray for victory,
  It seems almost a sin
To fold my hands and ask for what
  I will not help to win.

O, do not cling to me and cry,
  For it will break my heart;
I'm sure you'd rather have me die
  Than not to bear my part.
You think that some should stay at home
  To care for those away;
But still I'm helpless to decide
  If I should go or stay.

For, Marty, all the soldiers love,
  And all are loved again;
And I am loved, and love, perhaps,
  No more than other men.
I cannot tell — I do not know —
  Which way my duty lies,
Or where the Lord would have me build
  My fire of sacrifice.

I feel — I know — I am not mean;
  And though I seem to boast,
I'm sure that I would give my life
  To those who need it most.
Perhaps the Spirit will reveal
  That which is fair and right;
So, Marty, let us humbly kneel
  And pray to Heaven for light.

Peace in the clover-scented air,
  And stars within the dome;
And, underneath, in dim repose,
  A plain New England home.
Within, a widow in her weeds,
  From whom all joy is flown,
Who kneels among her sleeping babes,
  And weeps and prays alone!

SCOUTING ADVENTURES. — The following story of hair-breadth 'scapes along the border is told by a Federal cavalryman, who was scouting in the winter of 1862:

"We had a scout, on Monday last, towards the Isle of Wight, and an exciting one it was. Four companies of our regiment were detailed to carry ballot-boxes to Smithfield, about twenty-two miles south of this place; and on our return to camp we were almost entrapped by a large force of rebels, who had crossed the Blackwater on a foraging expedition; but we escaped after a desperate chase of five miles, and a little hard fighting. Your correspondent, in company with a friend, came near taking their Christmas dinners in Richmond; but, thanks to the pluck of friend Rogers, and the speed of our noble horses, we escaped. We had become hungry from long fasting, and, mounting our chargers, we slipped out of our camping-grounds to look for a warm breakfast, and feed for our jaded horses. After riding two or three miles we came to a comfortable-looking farm-house, and requested the frightened hostess to provide us with the Virginian's favorite breakfast — corn-cake, bacon, and fried eggs. In a few minutes we were discussing these delicious dishes, forgetting, for the time, that we were in the heart of Rebeldom, and only three miles from the famous Blackwater, where a large force of rebel cavalry was known to be posted the day previous. We had finished our breakfast, and were quietly wending our way to the stable, where our horses had been taken, when our attention was drawn to the fair hostess, who appeared to be telegraphing to some unseen object in the pine swamp in the rear of the house. Not liking to be inquisitive yet desiring to know the meaning of these strange movements, we kept our eyes upon the thicket, and we soon had the sequel. Two forms were there, each signalling in opposite directions; and soon five rebels stepped out from the shaded grove, and came slowly and cautiously towards the house. But we were not idle. With quickened steps we went towards the stable, and reached it just in the nick of time. We had barely entered, when our ears were saluted by the crack of a rifle, and a yell that made even our horses shudder. One moment more, and we were in the saddle, bounding over fences, fallen trees, and deep trenches, while the speed of our noble horses was accelerated by an occasional shot from our pursuers; but not a hair was injured, and with a defiant shout we were about to leap the fence that separated us from the main road, when two rebels darted from behind the fence, and shouted to us: 'Surrender, you Yankee sons of ——' But Rogers' fight was up, and quickly drawing his sabre, he made a dash at the foremost of the two, and wounded him in the shoulder, while your correspondent unslung his trusty carbine, and as the rebel was in the act of discharging his rifle, took deliberate aim, and lifted his hat into the air. But we were not yet out of danger, for we had barely recovered our composure, ere we had a new danger to contend with. At least twenty rebels were in pursuit of us; and putting spurs to our horses, we dashed away towards our picket at full speed, and reached it fifty yards ahead of our pursuers, who, thinking 'discretion the better part of valor,' in their turn took to flight, and were soon hidden by the pine forest. We slipped into camp as quietly as we had left; but our foaming horses betrayed us, and the Colonel demanded an explanation, which we were compelled to give. He, thinking our position rather a dangerous one, ordered an immediate move towards camp, on a different road from that on which we had been riding; but we had not proceeded three miles before an attack was made on our advance guard, and learning from a prisoner we had taken that the rebels were in large force, the order to retreat was given; but we had gone but a short distance, when the whole rebel force of cavalry, nine hundred strong, came up with our rear, and attacked it. But they were kept at bay until the main body got out of range of their guns, and we returned to camp at a much more rapid pace than we left it, with only two slightly wounded; while the enemy's loss is known to be eight killed and as many wounded. This was the first 'skedaddle' I ever witnessed, and I sincerely hope it may be the last."

SUDDENLY WAKED UP. — "Some time ago there was published in this paper," says the Richmond Dispatch, "a revolutionary reminiscence, wherein allusion was made to the sufferings of General Greene's army, in the early struggle for independence, for the want of suitable clothing, which in many instances rendered the men unfit for service. It chanced that a copy of the paper fell into the hands of a wealthy citizen of Alabama, who had previously resisted all the appeals of patriotism to his purse. We don't know how it happened that he put such a novel interpretation upon the revolutionary article, but after he got through he exclaimed, 'By Jove! that will never do in the world!' So he collected together a considerable quantity of clothing and other articles requisite for the comfort of the soldier, and packing the whole securely, directed the box to 'General Greene, of the Confederate army,' and started it off to Richmond. It arrived here in due season, and as a matter of course the depot agent was puzzled to find 'General Greene;' but it was finally turned over to the military authorities, who distributed the contents where they were needed. Whether the Alabamian had been asleep ever since the revolutionary war or not, we don't undertake to say; but we give him credit for doing a good thing, even though we could not help laughing when we heard the story."

INCIDENTS OF THE BATTLE OF BELMONT. — A correspondent, giving an account of the burial of the Union dead upon the field of battle at Belmont, by a party which returned, after the battle, with a flag of truce, relates the following incidents:

"Our dead were mostly lying upon their backs, and everything taken from their bodies that could be of value to the enemy. The countenances of the dead were mostly expressive of rage. One or two features were expressive of fear. One poor fellow, after he was wounded, bethought himself to take a smoke. He was found in a sitting position, against a tree, dead, with his pipe in one hand, his knife in the other, and his tobacco on his breast.

"A young lad about sixteen was found lying across a log, just as he fell, grasping his musket in both hands.

"A wounded man, with both legs nearly shot off, was found in the woods, singing the Star-spangled Banner; but for this circumstance the surgeons say they would not have discovered him.

"A Captain of one of the regiments was looking at the prisoners captured at Belmont, and recognized one as his own brother."

AN ELOQUENT PERORATION. — Governor John A. Andrew, in his address to the Legislature of Massachusetts, Jan. 8, 1864, concluded as follows:

"The heart swells with unwonted emotion when we remember our sons and brothers, whose constant valor has sustained on the field, during nearly three years of war, the cause of our country, of civilization, and liberty. Our volunteers have represented Massachusetts, during the year just ended, on almost every field, and in every department of the army where our flag has been unfurled. At Chancellorsville, Gettysburg, Vicksburg, Port Hudson, and Fort Wagner; at Chickamauga, Knoxville, and Chattanooga, under Hooker, and Meade, and Banks, and Gillmore, and Rosecrans, and Burnside, and Grant; in every scene of danger and of duty, — along the Atlantic, and the Gulf; on the Tennessee, the Cumberland, the Mississippi, and the Rio Grande, under Du Pont, and Dahlgren, and Foote, and Farragut, and Porter, — the sons of Massachusetts have borne their part, and paid the debt of patriotism and valor. Ubiquitous as the stock they descend from, national in their opinions, and universal in their sympathies, they have fought, shoulder to shoulder, with men of all sections and of every extraction. On the ocean, on the rivers, on the land, on the heights where they thundered down from the clouds of Lookout Mountain the defiance of the skies, they have graven with their swords a record imperishable.

"The Muse herself demands the lapse of silent years to soften, by the influence of time, her too keen and poignant realization of the scenes of war — the pathos, the heroism, the fierce joy, the grief of battle. But during ages to come she will brood over their memory, and into the hearts of her consecrated priests will breathe the inspirations of lofty and undying beauty, sublimity, and truth, in all the glowing forms of speech, of literature, and plastic art. By the homely traditions of the fireside, by the head-stones in the churchyard consecrated to those whose forms repose far off in rude graves by the Rappahannock, or sleep beneath the sea, embalmed in the memories of succeeding generations of parents and children, the heroic dead will live on in immortal youth. By their names, their character, their service, their fate, their glory, they cannot fail:

'They never fail who die
In a great cause. The block may soak their gore;
Their heads may sodden in the sun, their limbs
Be strung to city gates and castle walls;
But still their spirit walks abroad. Though years
Elapse, and others share as dark a doom,
They but augment the deep and sweeping thoughts
Which overpower all others, and conduct
The world at last to freedom.'

"The edict of Nantes, maintaining the religious liberty of the Huguenots, gave lustre to the fame of Henry the Great, whose name will gild the pages of philosophic history after mankind may have forgotten the martial prowess and the white plume of Navarre. The great proclamation of liberty will lift the ruler who uttered it, our nation and our age, above all vulgar destiny.

"The bell which rang out the Declaration of Independence has found at last a voice articulate, to 'proclaim liberty throughout all the land and to all the inhabitants thereof.' It has been heard across oceans, and has modified the sentiments of cabinets and kings. The people of the old world have heard it, and their hearts stop to catch the last whisper of its echoes. The poor slave has heard it; and with bounding joy, tempered by the mystery of religion, he worships and adores. The waiting continent has heard it, and already foresees the fulfilled prophecy, when she will sit 'redeemed, regenerated, and disinthralled by the genius of universal emancipation.' "

THE SONG OF THE SOUTH.

BY CAPTAIN R. M. ANDERSON.*

ANOTHER star arisen, another flag unfurled;
Another name inscribed among the nations of the
   world;
Another mighty struggle 'gainst a tyrant's fell decree,
And again a burdened people have uprisen, and
   are free.

The spirit of the fathers in the children liveth
   yet, —
Liveth still the olden blood that hath dimmed the
   bayonet;
And the fathers fought for freedom, and the sons
   for freedom fight;
Their God was with their fathers, and is still the
   God of right.

Behold, the skies are darkened! a gloomy cloud
   hath lowered!
Shall it break in happy peacefulness, or spread its
   rage abroad?
Shall we have the smiles of friendship, or feel the
   fierce, foul blow,
And bare the red right hand of war to meet an insulting foe?

In peacefulness we wish to live, but not in slavish
   fear;
In peacefulness we dare not die, dishonored on our
   bier;
To our allies of the Northern land we offer heart
   and hand;
But if they scorn our friendship, then the banner
   and the brand.

Honor to the new-born nation! honor to the brave!
A country freed from thraldom, or a soldier's honored grave!
Every rock shall be a tombstone, every rivulet run
   red,
And the invader, should he conquer, find the conquered in the dead.

But victory shall follow where the sons of freedom
   go,
And the signal for the onset be the death-knell of
   the foe;
And hallowed be the sacred spot where they have
   bravely met,
And the star that rises yonder shall never, never set.

* Captain R. M. Anderson, of Louisville, Kentucky, offered his whole command, consisting of ninety rifles, to the Governor of South Carolina, stipulating that they would bear their own expenses in going to Charleston and returning to Kentucky. — *Southern Literary Messenger.*

THE REBELS OVER THE BORDER. — On the 16th of June, 1863, it was first known in Chambersburg, Pa., that Milroy had been defeated at Winchester, and that the rebel General Rhoads was advancing across the Potomac, and approaching the Pennsylvania line.

On the morning of Monday, June 17, the flood of rumors from the Potomac fully confirmed the advance of the rebels; and the citizens of Chambersburg and vicinity, feeling unable to resist the rebel columns, commenced to make prompt preparation for the movement of stealable property. Nearly every horse, good, bad, and indifferent, was started for the mountains as early on Monday as possible, and the negroes darkened the different roads northward for hours, loaded with household effects, sable babies, &c., and horses and wagons and cattle crowded every avenue to places of safety. About nine o'clock in the morning, the advance of Milroy's retreating wagon train dashed into town, attended by a few cavalry, and several affrighted wagon-masters, all of whom declared that the rebels were in hot pursuit; that a large portion of the train was captured, and that the enemy was about to enter Chambersburg. This startling information, coming from men in uniform, who had fought valiantly until the enemy had got nearly within sight of them, naturally gave a fresh impetus to the citizens, and the skedaddle commenced in magnificent earnestness and exquisite confusion. Men, women, and children, who seemed to think the rebels so many cannibals, rushed out on the turnpike, and generally kept on the leading thoroughfares, as if they were determined to be captured, if the rebels were anywhere within range and wanted them. The motley cavalcade rushed along for a few hours, when it seems to have occurred to some one to inquire whether the rebels were not some distance in the rear; and a few moments of reflection and dispassionate inquiry satisfied the people that the enemy could not be upon them for several hours at least. The railroad men were prompt and systematic in their efforts to prepare for another fire; and by noon all the portable property of the company was safely under control, to be hauled and moved at pleasure. The more thoughtful portion of the people, who felt it a duty to keep out of rebel hands, remained until the cutting of telegraph communication south, and the reports of reliable scouts rendered it advisable to give way to the guerrilla army of plunderers.

Greencastle, being but five miles north of the Maryland line, and in the direct route of the rebels, was naturally enough in the highest state of excitement on Sunday night and Monday morning. Exaggerated rumors had of course flooded them, and every half hour a stampede was made before the imagined rebel columns. Hon. John Rowe at last determined to reconnoitre; and he mounted a horse, and started out towards Hagerstown. A little distance beyond, he was captured by a squad of rebels, and held until the rebel cavalry leader, General Jenkins, came up. Jenkins asked Rowe his name, and was answered correctly.

He subsequently asked Mr. ——, who was with Rowe, what Rowe's name was, and upon being told that the name had been given to him correctly, he insisted that the Major had been an officer in the United States service. Mr. —— assured Jenkins that the Major had never been in the service, and he was satisfied. (Jenkins had evidently confounded Major Rowe with his son, the gallant Lieutenant-Colonel Rowe, of the One Hundred and Twenty-sixth.) Jenkins then asked Mr. —— whom he had voted for at the last Presidential election. He answered that he had voted for Lincoln. To which Jenkins gave the following chaste and classic reply — " Get off that horse, you d—d Abolitionist." The horse was surrendered, and the same question was propounded to Major Rowe, who answered that he had voted for Douglas, and had scratched every Breckinridge man off his ticket. Jenkins answered — " You can ride your horse as long as you like — I voted for Douglas myself." He then demanded to know what forces were in Greencastle, and what fortifications. Major Rowe told him that the town was defenceless; but Jenkins seemed to be cautious lest he might be caught in a trap. He advanced cautiously, reconnoitred all suspicious buildings, and finally, being fully satisfied that there was not a gun in position, and not a man under arms, he resolved upon capturing the town by a brilliant charge of cavalry. He accordingly divided his forces into two columns, charged upon the vacated streets, and reached the centre of the town without the loss of a man!

The rebels were evidently under the impression that forces would be thrown in their way at an early hour, and they pushed forward for Chambersburg. About eleven o'clock, on Monday night, they arrived at the southern end of the town, and the same intensely strategic movements exhibited at Greencastle were displayed here. Several were thrown forward cautiously to reconnoitre, and a few of the Union boys captured them and took their horses. This taste of war whetted the appetite of Jenkins, and he resolved to capture the town by a brilliant dash, without so much as a demand for surrender. He divided his forces into several columns — about two hundred in advance as a forlorn hope, to whom was assigned the desperate task of charging upon the empty and undefended streets, store-boxes, mortar-beds, &c., of the ancient village of Chambersburg.

Every precaution that strategy could invent was taken to prevent failure. Men were detailed to ride along the columns before the charge was made, bawling out as loudly as possible to plant artillery at different points, although the redoubtable Jenkins had not so much as a swivel in his army. The women and children having been sufficiently frightened by the threatened booming of artillery, and all things being in readiness, the forlorn hope advanced, and the most desperate charge ever known in the history of war — in Chambersburg at least — was made. Down the street came the iron clatter of hoofs like the tem-

post with a thousand thunderbolts; but the great plan had failed in one particular, and the column recoiled before it reached the Diamond. A mortar-bed on the street, in front of Mr. White's new building, had not been observed in the reconnoitring of the town, nor had willing sympathizers advised him of it. His force was hurled against it; down went some men, and bang went a gun. To strike a mortar-bed and have a gun fired at the same time, was more than the strategy of Jenkins had bargained for; and the charge was broken and fell back. A few moments of fearful suspense, and the mortar-bed was carefully reconnoitred, and the musket report was found to be an accidental discharge of a gun in the hands of one of his own men who had fallen. With a boldness and dash worthy of Jenkins, it was resolved to renew the attack without even the formality of a council of war. Again the steeds of war thundered down the street, and there being nothing in the way, overcame all opposition, and the borough of Chambersburg was under the rule of Jenkins. Having won it by the most determined and brilliant prowess, Jenkins resolved that he would be magnanimous, and would allow nothing to be taken from the people — excepting such articles as he and his men wanted.

Jenkins had doubtless read the papers in his day, and knew that there were green fields in the " Green Spot;" and what is rather remarkable, at midnight he could start for a forty-acre clover patch belonging to the editor of the Repository without so much as stopping to ask where the gate might be found. Not even a halt was called to find it; but the march was continued until the gate was reached, when the order, " File right " was given, and Jenkins was in clover. Happy fellow, thus to find luxuriant and extensive clover as if by instinct! By way of giving the devil his due, it must be said that, although there were over sixty acres of wheat, and eighty acres of corn and oats, in the same field, he protected it most carefully, and picketed his horses so that it could not be injured. And equal care was taken of all other property about the place, excepting half a dozen of the fattest Cotswold sheep, which were necessary, it seems, to furnish chops, &c., for his men. No fences were wantonly destroyed; poultry was not disturbed, nor did he compliment the blooded cattle so much as to test the quality of their steak and roasts. Some of his men cast a wistful eye upon the glistening trout in the spring; but they were protected by voluntary order, and save a few quarts of delicious strawberries gathered with every care, after first asking permission, nothing in the gardens or about the grounds was taken.

However earnest an enemy Jenkins may be, he don't seem to keep spite, but is capable of being very jolly and sociable when he is treated hospitably. For prudential reasons, the editor was *not* at home to do the honors at his own table; but Jenkins was not particular, nor was his appetite impaired thereby. He called upon the ladies of the house, shared their hospitality, behaved in all respects like a gentleman, and expressed very earnest regrets that he had not been able to make the personal acquaintance of the editor. We beg to say that we reciprocate the wish of the General, and shall be glad to make his acquaintance personally — "when this cruel war is over." Colonel French and Surgeon Bee spent much of their time with Mrs. McClure, and the former showed his appreciation of her hospitality by taking her revolver from her when he left. An order having been made for the citizens to surrender all the guns and pistols they had, Colonel French took the pistol of his hostess.

Horses seemed to be considered contraband of war, and were taken without the pretence of compensation: but other articles were deemed legitimate subjects of commerce even between enemies, and they were generally paid for after a fashion. True, the system of Jenkins would be considered a little informal in business circles; but it's his way, and the people agreed to it, perhaps to some extent because of the novelty, but mainly because of the necessity of the thing. But Jenkins was liberal — eminently liberal. He didn't stop to higgle about a few odd pennies in making a bargain. For instance, he took the drugs of Messrs. Miller, Spangler, Nixon, and Heyser, and told them to make out a bill, or, if they could not do that, to guess at the amount, and the bills were paid. Doubtless merchants and druggists would have preferred "greenbacks" to Confederate scrip that is never payable, and is worth just its weight in old paper; but Jenkins hadn't "greenbacks," and he had confederate scrip, and such as he had he gave unto them. Thus he dealt largely. To avoid the jealousies growing out of rivalry in business, he patronized all the merchants, and bought pretty much everything he could conveniently use and carry. Some people, with the antiquated ideas of business, might call it stealing, to take goods and pay for them in bogus money; but Jenkins calls it business, and for the time being what Jenkins called business, was business. In this way he robbed all the stores, drug shops, &c., more or less, and supplied himself with many articles of great value.

Jenkins, like most doctors, don't seem to have relished his own prescriptions. Several horses had been captured by some of the Union boys, and notice was given by the General commanding that they must be surrendered or the town would be destroyed. The city fathers, commonly known as the town council, were appealed to in order to avert the impending fate threatened. One of the horses, and some of the equipments, were found and returned, but there was still a balance in favor of Jenkins. It was finally adjusted by the council appropriating the sum of nine hundred dollars to pay the claim. Doubtless Jenkins hoped for nine hundred dollars in "greenbacks," but he had flooded the town with Confederate scrip, pronouncing it better than United States currency, and the council evidently believed him, and desiring to be accommodating with a conqueror, decided to favor him by the payment of his bill in Confederate scrip. It was so done, and Jenkins got just nine hundred dollars worth of nothing for his trouble. He took it, however, without a murmur, and doubtless considered it a clever joke.

Sore was the disappointment of Jenkins at the general exodus of horses. It limited his booty immensely. Fully five hundred had been taken from Chambersburg and vicinity to the mountains, and Jenkins' plunder was thus made just so much less. But he determined to make up for it by stealing all the arms in the town. He therefore issued an order requiring the citizens to bring him all the arms they had, public or private, within two hours; and search and terrible vengeance were threatened in case of disobedience. Many of the citizens complied with the order, and a committee was appointed to take a list of the persons presenting arms. Of course very many did not comply; but enough did so to avoid a general search, and probable sacking of the town. The arms were assorted — the indifferent destroyed, and the good taken along.

On the following day, a few of Milroy's cavalry, escaping from Martinsburg, were seen by the redoubtable Jenkins hovering in his front. Although but thirteen in number, and without the least appetite for a battle with his two thousand men, he took on a fright of huge proportions, and prepared to sell his command as dearly as possible. Like a prudent general, however, he provided fully for his retreat. The shrill blast of the bugle brought his men to arms with the utmost possible alacrity: his pickets were called in to swell the ranks; the horses and baggage, consisting principally of stolen goods, were sent to the rear, south of the town; the surgeon took forcible possession of all the buildings, houses, barns, sheds, &c., to be used as hospitals, and especially requested that their wounded should be humanely treated in case of their sudden retreat without being able to take them along.

The hero of two brilliant cavalry charges upon undefended towns was agitated beyond endurance at the prospect of a battle; and instead of charging upon a little squad of men, who were merely observing the course of his robberies, he stood trembling in battle array to receive the shock. No foe was nearer than the State capital, over fifty miles distant, and there the same scene was being presented. Jenkins in Chambersburg, and the militia at Harrisburg, were each momentarily expecting to be cut to pieces by the other. But these armies, alike terrible in their heroism, were spared the deadly clash of arms, inasmuch as even the most improved ordnance is not deemed fatal at a range of fifty miles. Both armies, as the usual reports go, "having accomplished their purpose, retired in good order."

As a rule, private houses were not sacked by Jenkins' forces; but there were some exceptions. The residences of Messrs. Dengler and Gipe, near Chambersburg, were both entered (the families being absent), and plundered of clothing, kettles, and other articles. Bureaus and cupboards were all emptied of their contents, and such articles as they wanted were taken.

A very few of the citizens exhibited the spirit of the genuine "sympathizers;" but Jenkins and his men in no instance treated them even with courtesy. That they made use of some such creatures to obtain information, cannot be doubted; but they spurned all attempts to claim their respect because of professed sympathy with their cause. To one who desired to make fair weather with Jenkins, by ardent professions of sympathy with the South, he answered: "Well, if you believe we are right, take your gun and join our ranks!" It is needless to say that the cowardly traitor did not obey. To another he said — "If we had such men as you in the South we would hang them!" They say, on all occasions, that there are but two modes of peace, — disunion or subjugation, — and they stoutly deny that the latter is possible.

General Jenkins was fully informed as to the movements of one of the prominent citizens of Chambersburg, and described the horse he rode, and added that there were people in Chambersburg sufficiently cowardly and treacherous to give such information of their neighbors. When it was suggested that such people should be sent within the rebel lines, he insisted that the South should not be made a Botany Bay for Northern scoundrels.

Quite a number of negroes, free and slave, — men, women, and children, — were captured by Jenkins, and started South to be sold into bondage. Many escaped in various ways, and the people of Greencastle captured the guard of one negro train, and discharged the negroes; but, perhaps, full fifty were got off to slavery. One negro effected his escape by shooting and seriously wounding his rebel guard. He forced the gun from the rebel and fired, wounding him in the head, and then skedaddled. Some of the men were bound with ropes, and the children were mounted in front or behind the rebels on their horses. By great exertions of several citizens, some of the negroes were discharged.

The southern border of the county was literally plundered of everything in the stock line, excepting such as could be secreted. But it was difficult to secrete stock, as the rebels spent a full week in the county, and leisurely hunted out horses and cattle without molestation. Among many unfortunate, perhaps the greatest sufferer was Ex-Sheriff Taylor, from whom the rebels captured a drove of fat cattle in Fulton County.

The route of Jenkins was through the most densely populated and wealthiest portion of the county. From this point he fell back to Greencastle and south of it; thence he proceeded to Mercersburg, from where a detachment crossed the Cove Mountain to McConnellsburg, and struck down the valley from there. The main body, however, was divided into plundering parties, and scoured the whole southern portion of the county, spending several days in and about Greencastle, and Waynesboro', and giving Welsh Run a pretty intimate visitation.

The rebels seemed omnipresent, according to reports. They were, on several occasions, after their departure, just about to reënter, and the panic-stricken made a corresponding exit at the other side. On Thursday, the 18th, they were reported within two miles in large force, and a general skedaddle took place; and again on Sunday, the 21st, they were reported coming with reënforcements. A few ran off, but most of the people, knowing that there was a military force to fall back upon between Chambersburg and Scotland, shouldered their guns and fell into ranks to give battle. Prominent among these was Rev. Mr. Niccolls, whose people missed a sermon in his determination to pop a few rebels.

One of the first acts done by the rebels was to march down to the railroad bridge at Scotland, and burn it. The warehouse of Mr. Criswell, and several cars, were spared upon satisfactory assurance that they were private property. As soon as the rebels fell back, the Railroad Company commenced to rebuild the bridge, and on Sunday evening, the 21st, trains passed over it again. The only other instance of firing property was the warehouse of Oaks & Linn. It was fired just as they left the town; but the citizens extinguished it.

General Jenkins received his education at Jefferson College, in Pennsylvania, in the same class with J. McDowell Sharpe, Esq., and gave promise of future usefulness and greatness. His downward career commenced when, in an evil hour, he became a member of Congress from Western Virginia, and from thence may be dated his decline and fall. From Congress he naturally enough turned fire-eater, secessionist, and guerrilla. He is of medium size, has a flat but good head, light brown hair, blue eyes, immense flowing beard of a sandy hue, and rather a pleasant face. He professes to cherish the utmost regard for the humanity of war, and seemed sensitive on the subject of his reputation as a humane military leader. He pointed to the raids of Union troops, who left, in many instances, wide-spread and total desolation on their tracks, and expressed the hope that henceforth the Union raids would do no more damage to citizens than he does. He takes horses, cattle, and articles necessary for the army, as both sides treat them as contraband of war, and help themselves on every occasion offered. He pointed with bitter triumph at the raid of Montgomery in South Carolina, and at the destruction of Jacksonville, Fla., and Jackson, Mississippi, by the national troops, and reminded the people that his actions were in accordance with civilized warfare, while those referred to of the Union troops were barbarous.

On Sunday, 28th, the Eighth New York militia arrived at Chambersburg, having marched from Shippensburg, and they were received with the wildest enthusiasm. Considering that they were on the border in advance of any Pennsylvania regiments, they merit, as they will receive, the lasting gratitude of every man in the border.

The old men of the town organized a company, headed by Hon. George Chambers, for the defence of the town. None were admitted under forty-five. On Monday every man capable of bearing arms had his gun, and was in some organization to resist the rebels.

The ladies of Chambersburg gave the rebels rather a jolly time while they were there. They did not imitate the wives and daughters of the chivalry by spitting in the faces of soldiers, poisoning their meat and drink, flaunting flags in their faces, and unsexing themselves generally ; but they did give them rather an unwelcome taste of their heroism and strategy. One lady took her chickens from the rebels after they had killed them, and dined sumptuously at home at least one day under rebel rule. Another arrested Dr. Todd in his insolence by informing him, in rather an earnest manner, that further searches in her house would result in the splitting of his head with her hatchet. The valiant doctor subsided. Another amused herself by running rebel deserters out of the lines dressed in hoops and calico : and generally the ladies resented the arrogance of the rebel hosts with such spirit and determination as to astound them. In many instances the ladies prevented the boldest thieving by resolutely resisting, and shaming the rebels out of their purpose. Those who were so fortunate as to return to Virginia must carry with them the liveliest appreciation of the heroism and intelligence of Pennsylvania ladies.

Some of the border State, and most of the more Southern rebels, had rather peculiar conceptions of the Pennsylvania Dutch. Quite a number were astonished to find the people speaking English, as they supposed that the prevalent language was the German. At first, when they attempted derisive remarks, they would imitate the broken English of the Germans ; and judging from Ewell's demand for twenty-five barrels of sourkrout at a season when it is unknown in any country, even the commanding officers must have considered the Chambersburg people as profoundly Dutch. It would require an intensely Dutch community to supply sourkrout in July. The farm buildings, and especially the large and fine barns all through the valley, at once excited their astonishment and admiration. Quite a number of officers visited the barn of the editor as a matter of curiosity, although there are many in the valley much larger and quite as well finished. The private soldiers generally concluded that it must be the church of some very large denomination in this community ; and the out-buildings about it, such as chicken-house, hog-pen, carriage-house, &c., were generally supposed to be servants' houses, and very neat ones !

Clean as General Lee has kept his record by his humane orders, his army did the most gigantic and systematic stealing. They stole everything they could possibly use, or hope to use ; and when their little remnant of shame compelled them to offer some apology for it, they invariably answered that the Union troops had done so, and much more, in their country. Every rebel who wanted to steal a chicken, or a hat, or a watch, insisted that he was a most generous and humane conqueror — that his home had been burned down over the heads of his family by the Yankees, while he generously spared their homes from the torch.

Never was an army more confident and jubilant than were the rebels while in Chambersburg, and the officers evidently appreciated the necessity of keeping their hopes up to the highest point. The Richmond papers were received almost daily during their stay, and the men were inspired by the sensation lies published representing rebel success in almost every portion of the South ; and the universal demand made by the rebel press for a general devastation of the North induced the soldiers to believe that as soon as their lodgment was made safe, they would be at liberty to occupy or sack houses at pleasure. One edition of the Richmond papers received at Chambersburg announced that General Johnson had defeated General Grant and raised the siege of Vicksburg. It was read to the army when on parade, and they cheered themselves hoarse over their imaginary triumph. They were inspired by every conceivable falsehood. Not a rebel in the ranks doubted that Lee had from a hundred and twenty-five thousand to a hundred and fifty thousand men, while he had not over eighty thousand, all told ; and they were all firmly convinced that they had eluded General Meade's army, and that it was in search of them in the valley of Shenandoah, while nothing but the militia stood between them and Harrisburg, Baltimore, and Washington. Their rather sudden retreat from York and Carlisle threw a shadow of doubt over their high expectations, and their confidence was not strengthened any by the defiant and jubilant tone of the Pennsylvania people, who confronted them at every step with the assurance that they were marching to defeat, and many to death.

The only private property destroyed by the order of an officer in the Cumberland Valley was the extensive iron works of Hon. Thaddeus Stevens, ten miles east of Chambersburg. They consisted of a large charcoal furnace, forge, rolling-mill, coal-house, shops, &c. On Tuesday, the 23d, a portion of Jenkins' cavalry came upon the works by an unfrequented mountain road from Hughes' works, and demanded the horses, and especially the two riding horses, which they described. They threatened that they would destroy the buildings if the horses were not given up. Mr. Sweeney, who had charge of the works, agreed to deliver up the riding horses if the property should be protected. This they agreed to ; but on going for the riding horses, they met the teamsters, and compelled them to produce all the horses and mules, nearly forty in all, with gears, harness, &c. They had evidently been minutely informed of the whereabouts of Mr. Stevens' horses, as they described them, and knew exactly where to go after them. The day after, General Early rode up to the works, accompanied by his staff, and avowed his intention to destroy them. Mr. Sweeney reminded him that he would inflict a much more serious injury upon some hundred poor laborers who worked there than upon Mr. Stevens. General Early replied that Mr. Stevens was "an enemy of the South, in favor of confiscating their property, and arming their negroes, and the property must be destroyed." He then placed a guard around it, and gave special instructions that it should not be destroyed until he gave the order. He seemed exceedingly fearful that he might miss the delightful spectacle of Mr. Stevens' works in flames. He then returned to Greenwood, where he had his headquarters, but returned the next day, and personally detailed Colonel French, of Jenkins' guerrillas, with his command, to illustrate Southern chivalry and humanity by applying the torch to the private property of Mr. Stevens because he was guilty of the crime of defending the Republic. The work of destruction was well done, and soon all the works were in ashes. The houses occupied by families were not fired. Some three thousand dollars worth of charcoal was destroyed, seven thousand pounds of bacon stolen, leaving the families of the laborers without food, in spite of the earnest representations made by Mr. Sweeney as to their necessitous condition.

When the rebel horde first entered the State, flushed with the hope of easy victories on the field, and boundless plunder in Harrisburg, Philadelphia, Baltimore, and Washington, they would yell insolently at every man or woman they met: "Well, Yank, how far to Harrisburg?" "How far to Baltimore?" "What's the charge at the Continental?" "How do you like our *return* to the Union?" "Which is the way to Washington?" "How do you like Lincoln's Devils?" These and similar inquiries were made with a degree of arrogance and confidence that clearly betokened their expectations to see, as conquerors, all the cities named during their stay. When, however, their shattered and bleeding columns commenced their retreat on Saturday, after battle, there was but one inquiry made, alike by officers and men: "*How far to the Potomac?*" "*How far to the Potomac?*" And thus their broken, decimated ranks straggled along the mountain passes, grasping for the last hope left them — the Potomac!

The only engagement, beyond the skirmishing of scouts in the Cumberland Valley, was at Carlisle. General Lee had recalled his troops from York, Carlisle, and other points north, to join him at Gettysburg. General Fitzhugh Lee, with his division of cavalry, had crossed from Hanover Station to join General Rhodes at Carlisle; but when he reached that point, he found General Smith in the town with several thousand Union troops. Lee was evidently disconcerted; and in order to lead General Smith to suppose that he had purposely advanced to engage him, and thus enable him to make his escape should Smith's force be very large, he at once demanded an immediate surrender of the town. This General Smith emphatically refused; and when a second demand for his surrender was sent him, he notified Lee that he would receive no more such communications from him. *Twenty minutes* were generously allowed by the son of the rebel Commander-in-Chief for women and children to get out of the town. Of course but few got away, as it was after night, and the chivalric Lee opened his guns upon the town. He threw nearly two hundred shells, most of which did not explode, and but little damage was done. Several houses were penetrated, but none of the citizens were injured. Lee then retreated to witness his father's Waterloo at Gettysburg. — *Franklin Repository.*

THE SONG OF THE CAMPS.

BY J. R. M.

Far away in the piny woods,
  Where the dews fall heavy and damp,
A soldier sat by the smouldering fire,
  And sang the song of the camp.

"It is not to be weary and worn,
  It is not to feel hunger and thirst,
It is not the forced march, nor the terrible fight,
  That seems to the soldier the worst;

"But to sit through the comfortless hours, —
  The lonely, dull hours that will come, —
With his head in his hands, and his eyes on the fire,
  And his thoughts on visions of home;

"To wonder how fares it with those
  Who mingled so late with his life, —
Is it well with my little children three?
  Is it well with my sickly wife?

"This night-air is chill, to be sure,
  But logs lie in plenty around;
How is it with *them* where wood is so dear,
  And the cash for it hard to be found?

"O, that north air cuts bitterly keen,
  And the ground is hard as a stone;
It would comfort me just to know that they sit
  By a fire as warm as my own.

"And have they enough to eat?
  My lads are growing boys,
And my girl is a little tender thing,
  With her mother's smile and voice.

"My wife she should have her tea,
  Or maybe a sup of beer;
It went to my heart to look on her face,
  So white, with a smile and a tear.

"Her form it is weak and thin, —
  She would gladly work if she could, —
But how can a woman have daily strength
  Who wants for daily food?

"My oldest boy *he* can cut wood,
  And Johnny can carry it in;
But then, how frozen their feet must be
  If their shoes are worn and thin!

"I hope they don't cry with the cold —
  Are there tears in my little girl's eyes?
O God! say *peace!* to these choking fears,
  Those fears in my heart that rise.

"Many rich folks are round them, I know,
  And their hearts are not hard nor cold;
They would give to my wife if they only knew,
  And my little one three years old.

"They would go, like God's angels fair,
  And enter the lowly door,
And make the sorrowful glad with gifts
  From their abundant store.

"In this blessed Christmas-time,
  When the great gift came to men,
They would show, by their gentle and generous
     deeds,
How He cometh in hearts again.

"And my sickly, patient wife,
  And my little children three,
Would be kindly warmed and fed and clothed
  As part of Christ's family.

"Well, I leave it all with God,
  For my sight is short and dim;
He cares for the falling sparrow;
  My dear ones are safe with Him."

So the soldier watched through the night,
  Through the dew-fall, heavy and damp;
And as he sat by the smouldering fire,
  He sang the song of the camp.

How "Pat" entrapped an Officer. — The Confederate pickets had stationed themselves on the road from Warrington, Virginia, through New Baltimore, a mile or two beyond the latter point. Seeing a mounted soldier approaching from below, they supposed him to be an enemy, and sent forward one of their number, an Irish boy, newly recruited, to blarney him within reach. Patrick sauntered along on his mission, and when met by the Federal soldier was asked to what service he belonged. "And it's Mister Linkin, sure," answered Pat, "for it's a good Union boy I am." The other responded that he was the same. "Come wid me, then," says Pat, "and I'll take ye to the camp and show you to the boys, and ye shall have something to eat." On they moved, till the Federalist came near enough to see the home-spun uniform of one of our men. This opened his eyes. He stopped, and said he had forgotten his pipe, and would go back for it. "Niver mind the pipe, man," said Pat; "sure and we'll give you a pipe." The Yankee, however, insisted that he must go back, and started to execute his purpose. "You are my prisoner!" said Pat, "and if you move a foot I'll kill ye!" The Yankee, however, resolved to take the chances of running the blockade, and had already gained some rods, when young Ireland fired upon him, killing him instantly. On examining the papers upon his person, he proved to be a Sergeant of a New York company. Accompanying the Sergeant rode a negro, who also led a third horse. All the horses were secured, but the negro escaped.

Farragut and his Son. — They were on the Mississippi, and Farragut's fleet was about to pass Port Hudson, which was then held by the Confederates. Farragut's son, a lad of about twelve, had been importuning his father that he might be sent to West Point, where the military cadets are educated. Old Farragut said: "I don't know how that would do; I am not sure whether you would stand fire." "O, yes, father, I could do that." "Very well, my boy, we'll try; come up with me here." The Admiral and his son went up together into the maintop; the old man had himself and the boy lashed to it, and in this way they passed Port Hudson. The boy never flinched, while the shot and shell were flying past him. "Very well, my boy, that will do; you shall go to West Point."

An Incident. — On the evening previous to the battle of Sunday, at Bull Run, two of the Minnesota boys took it into their heads to forage a little, for amusement as well as eatables. Striking out from their encampment into the forest, they followed a narrow road some distance, until, turning a bend, five secession pickets appeared not fifty yards distant. The parties discovered each other simultaneously, and at once levelled their rifles and fired. Two of the Confederates fell dead, and one of the Minnesotians, the other also falling, however, but with the design of trapping the other three, who at once came up, as they said, to "examine the d—d Yankees." Drawing his revolver, the Minnesotian found he had but two barrels loaded, and with these he shot two of the pickets. Springing to his feet, and snatching his sabre bayonet from his rifle, he lunged at the survivor, who proved to be a stalwart Lieutenant, armed only with a heavy sword. The superior skill of the Southerner was taxed to the utmost in parrying the vigorous thrusts and lunges of the brawny lumberman, and for several minutes the contest waged in silence, broken only by the rustle of the long grass by the roadside, and the clash of their weapons. Feigning fatigue, the Minnesotian fell back a few steps, and as his adversary closed upon him with a cat-like spring, he let his sabre come down on the head of his antagonist, and the game was up. Collecting the arms of the secessionists, he returned to the camp, where he obtained assistance, and buried the bodies of his companions and his foes in one grave.

Picture of Robert E. Lee — "General Lee is, almost without exception, the handsomest man of his age I ever saw," says an English writer, who passed some time with him in the field. "He is fifty-six years old, tall, broad-shouldered, very well made, well set up — a thorough soldier in appearance; and his manners are most courteous, and full of dignity. He is a perfect gentleman in every respect. I imagine no man has so few enemies, or is so universally esteemed. Throughout the South, all agree in pronouncing him to be as near perfection as a man can be. He has none of the small vices, such as smoking, drinking, chewing, or swearing; and his bitterest enemy never accused him of any of the greater ones. He generally wears a well-worn long gray jacket, a high black felt hat, and blue trousers tucked into his Wellington boots. I never saw him carry arms, and the only mark of his military rank are the three stars on his collar. He rides a handsome horse, which is extremely well groomed. He himself is very neat in his dress and person, and in the most arduous marches he always looks smart and clean.

"In the old army he was always considered one of its best officers, and at the outbreak of these troubles he was Lieutenant-Colonel of the Second cavalry. He was a rich man, but his fine estate was one of the first to fall into the enemy's hands. I believe he has not slept in a house since he has commanded the Virginian army, and he invariably declines all offers of hospitality, for fear the person offering it may afterwards get into trouble for having sheltered the rebel General. The relations between him and Longstreet are quite touching. They are almost always together. Longstreet's corps complain of this sometimes, as, they say, they seldom get a chance of detached service, which falls to the lot of Ewell. It is impossible to please Longstreet more than by praising Lee. I believe these two Generals to be as little ambitious, and as thoroughly unselfish, as any men in the world. Both long for a successful termination of the war, in order that they may retire into obscurity. Stonewall Jackson (until his death the third in command of their army) was just such another simple-minded servant of his country. It is understood that General Lee is a religious man, though not as demonstrative in that respect as Jackson; and, unlike his late brother in arms, he is a member of the Church of England. His only faults, so far as I can learn, arise from his excessive amiability."

MARCHING ALONG.

BY WILLIAM B. BRADBURY.

THE army is gathering from near and from far;
The trumpet is sounding the call for the war;
For Grant is our leader — he's gallant and strong;
We'll gird on our armor and be marching along!

CHORUS.

Marching along, we are marching along,
Gird on the armor and be marching along;
For Grant is our leader — he's gallant and strong;
For God and our country we are marching along!

The foe is before us in battle array,
But let us not waver, nor turn from the way!
The Lord is our strength, and the Union's our song;
With courage and faith we are marching along!

Marching along, &c.

Our wives and our children we leave in your care;
We feel you will help them with sorrow to bear;
'Tis hard thus to part, but we hope 'twon't be long;
We'll keep up our hearts as we're marching along!

Marching along, &c.

We sigh for our country — we mourn for our dead!
For them, now, our last drop of blood we will shed!
Our cause is the right one — our foe's is the wrong;
Then gladly we'll sing as we're marching along.

Marching along, &c.

The flag of our country is floating on high;
We'll stand by that flag till we conquer or die!
For Grant is our leader — he's gallant and strong;
We'll gird on our armor and be marching along!

Marching along, &c.

INCIDENT OF PRAIRIE GROVE. — The following is related by Lieutenant William S. Brooks, of the Nineteenth Iowa regiment: "The fight was most determined, and the slaughter immense. I was struck at four o'clock P. M., while we were being driven back from a too far advanced position. We were outflanked, and had to run three hundred yards over open ground, and exposed to a murderous fire from the right, left, and centre, or rear. Here we lost our Lieutenant-Colonel McFarland. We lost one half our regiment, and in company D more than half our effective men. I was hit at the commencement of the retreat, and was near being captured, as I could not run. When more than half way to our battery, our color-sergeant fell, and I received the colors. The pursuing rebel Colonel shouted: 'Blast them, take their colors!' This enraged me, and I hallooed back, 'You can't do it.' The cowardly scoundrels did not dare to close on me, but let go a volley, which left nine holes in the flag, and eighteen in my clothes. Four bullets passed through the cuff of my shirt sleeve, but they could not wound the hand that held the 'Old Flag.'"

A SOUTHERN ANECDOTE. — An English officer, who passed some time with the army of General Lee, writes the following, in the pages of Blackwood:

"As we were riding back to Hagerstown, we fell in with Colonel Wickham, who commands a brigade of Stuart's cavalry, in connection with whom the following story was told me:—

"It will be remembered that Virginia was one of the last States to secede, and did not do so until she had exhausted every effort to effect a compromise; and when she did so, the few Southern States that were still hesitating followed her example, and the war became inevitable.

"Matters were coming to a crisis, when the leading men of Virginia sent a deputation of three of their number to wait on the President, Mr. Lincoln. They tried to impress him with a sense of the gravity of the situation, and urgently entreated that he would do something to calm the excitement amongst the people, whose irritation at the threats of the Administration, and of the Northern States, was getting beyond control.

"It was just after the taking of Fort Sumter, and Lincoln's having called out seventy-five thousand men to coerce the South.

"'But what would you have me do?' said Mr. Lincoln.

"'Mr. President,' replied one of the deputation, 'I would beg you to lend me your finger and thumb for five minutes'— meaning, of course, that he wished to write something that should allay the prevailing excitement.

"But Mr. Lincoln did not choose to understand him. ' My finger and thumb!' he repeated, ' My finger and thumb! What would you do with them? Blow your nose?'

"The deputation retired in disgust, and Virginia seceded!"

CAMP JEWELRY. — "'Jewelry,' you think and wonder, and perhaps it may be worth an explanation," says B. F. Taylor, in one of his inimitable letters from the army of the Cumberland. "The Tennessee and Stone Rivers are strewn with shells of rare beauty and exquisite coloring; blue, green, pink, and pure, clear pearl. If you look in any boy's knapsack you will be quite sure to find a shell in it. Of these queer, broken, little chests of former life, the soldiers make rings, pins, hearts, arrows, chains, crosses; and to see the rough tools they use, and then note the elegance of form and finish in the things they make, would set the means and the results incredibly apart. With a flat stone for a polishing table, they grind down the shells, and then with knife and file shape little fancies that would not be out of place on a jeweller's velvet, and beautiful souvenirs of fields of battle. Every ring and heart has a bit of a story the maker is not reluctant to tell. This little touch of fine arts gives to camps a pleasant, home-like look; and I have seen many a soldier putting the final polish to a pearl trinket by the light of his inch of candle flaring from a bayonet, as earnest over his work as if the shell possessed the charm of Aladdin's lamp, and rubbing it would summon spirits potent if not gray."

A SOLDIER'S ADVENTURE. — William M. Hecker, a soldier belonging to one of the Indiana regiments, gives the following account of his adventures in returning from the expedition to Grenada, Mississippi, which destroyed such an immense quantity of Southern railroad stock, from which will be gathered a better understanding of what the soldiers had often to endure in service of which no mention is ever made, than from the elaborate lamentations of elegant writers. After the dash upon Grenada, and the destruction of the railroad track, he, with seventeen other men, under Lieutenant Shaddock, was sent out to gather up mules. Here his adventures begin, and he thus tells them:

"We gathered up a lot of mules, and when we got back to the road we were four hours behind the column, with about two hundred rebels between us. We had arrived to within six miles of Cold Water Springs before we knew of this. Here the rebels had a skirmish with the rear of our advance column, and we took a side road, intending to go around them and cross the river at another place. When we reached there, however, the bridge had been burned, the river was full of snags, very deep, and about five rods wide, with a few rebels on each side to guard it. We did not offer to hurt them; neither did they propose to molest us. I swam my horse across first, being the best swimmer. Many of the boys could not get their horses across, and called to me to help them. Charles Keatch and myself stripped off and ' went in,' and all the horses but one were soon over, and the men crossed on logs, about fifteen yards below. I swam back after the horse still remaining, but it would not come. As I was returning, about one hundred rebels charged up the other side, and fired at the boys on the side I was going to. They didn't see me until I attempted to climb up the bank. They then began yelling at a desperate rate, and fired twenty or thirty shots at me, the balls striking all around. I was an excellent mark for them. I got upon the bank, but could not get to my clothing or arms. I, however, saw a rifle lying near, and picked it up, and ran back about two rods, and stopped. The other boys had taken cover behind trees, and the Lieutenant ordered me to do the same. I told him I would not do it until I got my clothes; but the rebel bullets came so thick and fast that I was glad to get out of the way the best I could. I fired three good shots at them. Some of them went up and others down the river, until they got into such shape as to cross-fire on us. I was only about three steps from Hardu when he was shot in the breast. I started to go to him, but the balls came so thick I couldn't.

"The rest of the boys had got back about twenty rods by this time, and called to me to come in; so I shouldered my rifle and followed, and ran about a mile before I stopped. Here we were fired into, and ran another mile, and hid in some canebrakes, Keatch and I being stark naked. I left my horse and all my equipments, my arms, consisting of a five-shooting revolving rifle and a Colt's revolver, every bit of my clothing and big boots. One of the boys loaned me a pair of drawers, and another a blouse, and I tied a handkerchief over my head. We lay until dark, and then took a northerly course, directed by the stars. We ran within a quarter of a mile of a rebel camp, and had to back out; went through the woods, over bluffs, swamps, brier patches, and of all the times you ever heard of, this beat them. One time we got to a bluff where it was about twenty-five feet perpendicularly down. We let ourselves over by the grubs, and travelled nearly all night in the woods. About an hour before day we got within four miles of Hernando, having travelled eight miles, and lay down till daylight. There were now only ten of us together; some had arms, and some hadn't.

"After daylight the Lieutenant and I went out to find a road, so as to get the right start. We got separated from the rest of the boys, and, after hunting about an hour, gave up. We then lay down again (it was foggy). Then we took a due north course through the woods, and travelled until noon, when we became so weak that we could hardly go farther, as we had not eaten anything since the morning before. The Lieutenant here lay in the bushes, and I went up to an old log house, and told the old man there that I had been taken prisoner by the Yankees at Grenada, and had escaped from them the night before. He took pity on me, and a good meal was provided, which I ate with a good deal of satisfaction. I had a long talk with him, and cursed the Yankees up and down at a great rate. I was furnished with a quantity of food to eat on the road, which I gave to the Lieutenant, and also a hat to keep the sun from burning me. Boots and shoes he was minus of. We kept in the swamps all day.

"About sundown we arrived within eighteen miles of Germantown, and were entirely 'used up.' We stopped at the house of a half-way Union man, and got supper, and revived so as to go on eight miles farther. Here we gave out entirely, and lay down and rested until morning, and then started, and went within two miles of camp, and I gave out again. The Lieutenant made out to get in, and sent men and a horse out after me. I reached there a little before noon, my feet swollen nearly as big as half bushels, and all cut to pieces. I was so sore the next morning that I couldn't stir, but felt well every other way.

"The boys had all given us up, and, when I went in, said I was the hardest looking sight they ever beheld. They did everything they could for my comfort. Some of the boys said they were so glad of our safe arrival, they did not know whether to laugh or cry."

NEW ORLEANS WON BACK.

A LAY FOR OUR SAILORS.

BY ROBERT LOWELL.

[The opening words of the burden are a scrap of an old song caught up.]

CATCH. O, up in the morning, up in the morning,
　　　Up in the morning early!
　　There lay the town that our guns looked
　　　down,
　　　With its streets all dark and surly.

God made three youths to walk unscathed
　In the furnace seven times hot;
And when smoky flames our squadron bathed,
　Amid horrors of shell and shot,
Then, too, it was God that brought them through
　That death-crowded thoroughfare:
So now, at six bells, the church pennons flew,
　And the crews went all to prayer.
Thank God! thank God! our men won the fight,
　Against forts, and fleets, and flame:
Thank God! they have given our flag its right,
　In a town that brought it shame.

　　　O, up in the morning, up in the morning,
　　　Up in the morning early!
　　Our flag hung there, in the fresh, still air,
　　　With smoke floating soft and curly.

Ten days for the deep ships at the bar;
　Six days for the mortar-fleet,
That battered the great forts from afar;
　And then, to that deadly street!
A flash! Our strong ships snapped the boom
　To the fire-rafts and the forts,

To crush and crash, and flash and gloom,
　And iron beaks fumbling their ports.
From the dark came the raft, in flame and smoke;
　In the dark came the iron beak;
But our sailors' hearts were stouter than oak,
　And the false foe's iron weak.

　　　O, up in the morning, up in the morning,
　　　Up in the morning early!
　　Before they knew, they had burst safe
　　　through,
　　　And left the forts grim and burly.

Though it be brute's work, not man's, to tear
　Live limbs like shivered wood,
Yet, to dare, and to stand, and to take death for
　share,
Are as much as the angels could.
Our men towed the blazing rafts ashore;
　They battered the great rams down;
Scarce a wreck floated where was a fleet before,
　When our ships came up to the town.
There were miles of batteries yet to be dared,
　But they quenched these all, as in play;
Then with their yards squared, their guns' mouths
　bared,
　They held the great town at bay.

　　　O, up in the morning, up in the morning,
　　　Up in the morning early!
　　Our stout ships came through shell, shot,
　　　and flame,
　　　But the town will not always be surly;

For this Crescent City takes to its breast
　The Father of Waters' tide;
And here shall the wealth of our world, in the
　West,
　Meet wealth of the world beside:
Here the date-palm and the olive find
　A near and equal sun;
And a hundred broad, deep rivers wind
　To the summer-sea in one:
Here the Fall steals all old Winter's ice,
　And the Spring steals all his snow;
While he but smiles at their artifice,
　And like his own nature go.

　　　O, up in the morning, up in the morning,
　　　Up in the morning early!
　　May that flag float here till the earth's last
　　　year,
　　　With the lake mists fair and pearly.

LETTERS FROM HOME. — Occupation is a grand thing, and quite as important to the tone and heart of an army as hard bread and bacon. The monster against which Dr. Kane fought so successfully in the Arctic night, with theatre and frolic, wanders listlessly up and down our camps. Would you believe — and yet it is true — that many a poor fellow in this army of the Cumberland has literally *died to go home*; died of the terrible, unsatisfied longing, homesickness? that it lies at the heart of many a disease bearing a learned name? It is languor, debility, low fever, loss of appetite, sleeplessness, death; and yet, through all, it is only that sad thing they call Nostalgia. Who shall dare to say that the boy who "lays him down and dies," a-hungered and *starving* for home, does not fall as well and truly for his country's sake as if a rebel bullet had found his heart out? Against it the Surgeon combats in vain, for "who can minister to a mind diseased?"

The loved ones at home have something to answer for in this business, and it pains me to think that more than one man has let his life slip out of a grasp too weak to hold it, just because his dearest friends did not send him a prescription once a week — price three cents — a letter from home. Is some poor fellow sinking at heart because *you* do not write him? If there is, lay my letter down at once and write your own, and may He who sent a messenger all the way from Heaven to earth with glad tidings, forgive you for deferring a hope to some soldier boy. You would not wonder at my warmth had you *seen* that boy waiting and waiting, as I have, for one little word from somebody. Too proud to own, and yet too sincere to quite conceal it, he tries to strangle the thought of home, and goes into the battle, whence he never comes forth. Let me relate one incident. An Indiana soldier was struck in the breast at Chickamauga and fell. The bullet's errand was about done when it reached him; it pierced coat and underclothing, and there was force enough left in it to wound, if not to kill him; it had to work its way through a precious package of nine letters, indited by one dear heart, and traced by one dear hand; that done, the bullet's power expended, there it lay asleep against the soldier's breast! Have *you* been making such a shield, dear lady, for anybody? Take care that it does not lack *one* letter of being bullet-proof. — *B. F. Taylor.*

INCIDENTS OF CHICKAMAUGA. — Colonel John T. Wilder, of Indiana, who participated in the battle of Chickamauga, relates these incidents: "There was fearful slaughter of Longstreet's men at the time they were driving back the left wing of the nationals. This celebrated corps, as desperate soldiers as ever lived, attacking two divisions, Van Cleve's and Davis', to the right and a little in front of Wilder, separated them and pushed on through the open space, yelping — the rebel shout is a yelp, instead of a civilized hurrah — and confident of victory. A portion of them had to cross a small field, behind which, in the bordering woods, Wilder lay, and through which ran a ditch five or six feet deep, to carry off the water of an adjacent stream or swamp.

"As the rebels entered this field, in heavy masses, fully exposed, the mounted infantry, with their seven-shooting rifles, kept up a continuous blast of fire upon them, while Lilly, with his Indiana battery, hurled through them double-shotted canister from his ten-pounder rifles, at less than five hundred yards. The effect was awful. Every shot seemed to tell. The head of the column, as it was pushed on by those behind, appeared to melt away, or sink into the earth, for though continually moving it got no nearer. It broke at last, and fell back in great disorder. It was rallied and came on again, and with a desperate resolution pushed through the solid fire to

the ditch. Here all who could get in took shelter. Instantly Lilly wheeled two of his guns and poured right down the whole length of the ditch his horrible double canister. Hardly a man got out of it alive. 'At this point,' said Wilder, 'it actually seemed a pity to kill them so. They fell in heaps, and I had it in my heart to order the firing to cease, to end the awful sight.' But the merciless seven-shooters and canister would not stop, and again the boasted flower of Lee's army was crushed into a disorderly mob and driven off.

"When the firing ceased, one could have walked for two hundred yards down that ditch on dead rebels, without ever touching the ground."

ARMY DISCIPLINE. — A soldier of the Second regiment of Rhode Island, writing from Brandy Station, Virginia, says: "Military discipline, though neither novel nor interesting in the army, would present many scenes and incidents of curious interest to the uninitiated. Let us take a short walk through the regimental guard-houses of this brigade. At the first, which is that of the Second Rhode Island, we see one with his knapsack strapped on his back, and a stick of wood weighing, say forty pounds, on his shoulder. With these he walks a beat of twenty paces for ten hours. Crime, absent from duty without leave and without reasonable excuse. Another walks a similar beat, with knapsack and musket. He was corporal of guard, but was reduced to the position of private, and sentenced to walk his beat twelve hours, for sending a private to post his guard while he slept. We pass to another guard-house. Here we find a man bucked and gagged. Crime, drunkenness. The operation consists of putting a stick in the mouth, with a string passed from each end around the back of the head. The bucking process consists of tying the hands together securely, placing them over the knees, and running a stick through under the knees and over the arms. Still another has his hands tied together and fastened as far up a tree as he can conveniently reach. He also is gagged. These have three hours on, and one off for twelve hours. We pass to a third guard-house. Here is one who has skulked from duty. He has a large pile of stone to move some twenty feet, a task many times as arduous as the fatigue duty he shirked. Near by is a grave fresh dug and rounded up, with a head sticking out at one end. At his head stands a board prepared and marked in large letters:

HERE LIES

THE BODY OF

GEORGE MARS,

WHO FELL

DEAD (DRUNK)

Nov. 17th, 1863.

"Doubtless the good friends at home would think this severe, but it is deemed necessary for the discipline of the army, by military commanders at least."

GEN. JOS. E. JOHNSTON

THE FIGHT AT PORT HUDSON. — A citizen of New Orleans, who was on board the Richmond when she attempted, with the rest of Farragut's fleet, to pass the batteries at Port Hudson, furnishes the following interesting account of the fight:

"A minute after, *fizz* went a rocket from the opposite (west) bank of the river, and shot away up into the air, while another seemed to rush *across* the river. It was a signal that we were discovered; and in a few moments a sudden flash appeared on the dark shore, a little ahead of us, and *bang* went the first gun. Then another and another, in quick succession. It was now just twenty-two minutes past eleven.

"All at once the Hartford revealed herself just ahead of us, a flood of flame leaping from her side, and a great cloud of white smoke rolling up, followed by a roar like the loudest and sharpest thunder, which went rolling and echoing down the river. From that time her broadsides continued in quick succession. The mortar schooners, too, opened from their station below — a sullen bellow, and then a *shooting* star traversing the sky in a vast curve, and dropping on the bluff with a loud explosion.

"All was quiet and silent with us; but now shot and shell began to whiz overhead; and it was plain that we, too, were aimed at in the rapid fire of the enemy. Mr. Cummings said, with a firm, quiet voice, 'Point your guns two points forward of the beam; aim at every flash, and give them grape and canister as fast as you can. Fire coolly, and don't hurry. Now, give them the bow guns. Now, the whole broadside.' The blaze, and concussion, and crash of this last were terrific. It took me some minutes to comprehend that our fire, which was most startling to eye and ear, was friendly, and to enjoy and exult in it.

"The real terrors were those swift flashes on the shore, and the missiles that went crashing and hissing over and around us. The first effective shot that I *saw* was a shell, which burst in the side near me, and set it on fire; but this was soon extinguished. A twenty-pounder Parrott shot had, however, already entered near the after gun, worked by marines, killed two men, and knocked down, though with slight injuries, some twelve men — in fact, demolished a whole gun's crew. Showers of splinters from the rigging fell all over us. Our tremendous fire, however, seemed to silence the lower batteries, until our own smoke enwrapped the ship so that we could not see half its length, and had to cease firing to let the smoke clear away, for fear we should go ashore. This was done several times.

"Meanwhile we were slowly ranging up, *within a hundred yards* of the batteries (some think less), as I could plainly see by the flashes, and also by fires which the enemy had kindled on the bluff. The Hartford, revealed at times by her blazing guns; the ships following, pouring in their fire; the rapid and deadly fire from the shore; the coolness and yet ardor of all our people, officers and men, — all this is more than I can describe. At this time I went, at the Captain's request, to carry the word from Mr. Terry (second Lieutenant), who, with heroic coolness and great skill, was on the lookout forward, to the men at the wheel. Two or three minutes after I left there, a round shot took off Mr. Cummings' left leg, just above the ankle, knocking him off the bridge to the deck, and he was carried below. Captain Alden was also thrown down, but not hurt.

"We were now abreast of the upper battery, and nearly '*past* Port Hudson.' I called out, 'There is the low land above the bluff,' as I caught a glimpse of it, from the forecastle, by the flash of a gun. We were just heading around to turn the point, and go up the other reach out of fire, when a loud and sharp 'sh-h-h-h' was heard amidships, and a cloud of steam came pouring out of the steam-pipe, and up from the engine-room. The sight and sound of this evidently guided the enemy's fire, for it was concentrated upon us, and with redoubled rapidity. We were evidently also no longer making progress against the mighty current which sweeps around there, and were therefore a stationary target, within short musket range of their biggest guns. Besides, we could scarcely hear or see anything on the deck for the steam. A moment more, and we might have drifted ashore, and been torn to pieces by shot and shell; *surrender*, I am satisfied, we never should have done.

"'Starboard!' shouted Captain Alden, and we went about rapidly; and with the steerage-way which the Genesee was able to give us, we went swiftly down, passing all the batteries, under this terrific fire, and brought up at our old anchorage ground. The last I saw of the Hartford was by one of her own illuminations, as she sailed rapidly up the reach above Port Hudson, looking as stanch and stately as ever, from her water-line to her trucks, and with her cloak of battle-smoke thrown around her fighting side.

"It was only after we were disabled that I learned of Mr. Cummings' misfortune, and then from Captain Alden, who was greatly affected by it, more even than by his great disappointment. At his request I went below to see Mr. Cummings, and to carry him a most affectionate message. The mangled hero, awaiting amputation, asked me what we were doing; and when I told him we were nearly out of danger, having been disabled in our steam and compelled to drop back, he uttered a cry of disappointment. 'O,' said he, 'I would have given my other leg to have gone by.' A noble tar lying there, terribly wounded, and who died soon after, said, 'Mr. Cummings, don't give up the ship.' 'No, Howard,' said he, 'we won't give up the ship.' All the officers and men were greatly grieved at Mr. Cummings' wound.

"We had hardly let go the anchor when a light began to show above, increasing rapidly. We feared it was one of our consort ships, all of which we had hoped had passed up successfully. Conjectures were divided between the flag-ship, the Monongahela, and the Mississippi. Soon after a boat's crew of the Mississippi came on board, and reported her hopelessly aground and abandoned.

We still feared that the fire might be on another ship. But soon the flames got such headway that they revealed the form of that stanch and valiant old ship; and we also learned that the Monongahela had returned to her anchorage, while the flag-ship was doubtless safe above. After a while the Mississippi swung off, headed down stream, and sailed right towards us, blazing to the top of her masts, a glorious but mournful and even terrible sight, for we could not get out of her way. She soon, however, sheered off to our port, and swept down past, firing off her port guns only a little before she passed us; and so, amid exploding shells, she passed down the river out of sight, and blew up, away below, about five o'clock.

"It was half past one when we let go our anchor, so that we had been nearly two hours under fire; and it was some time before any one could compose himself to sleep, though I did get some three hours' rest. The next morning was devoted to cleaning up the soiled and blood-stained decks, taking care of the wounded, receiving our unlucky comrades of the Mississippi, a noble set of officers and men, with the heroic Captain Smith at their head, all worthy to be the shipmates of the 'Richmonds' (I could not say more), preparing the deck for burial, and *writing home.* A heavy rain delayed some of these things.

"The next morning (Monday), having sent off to the city our guests of the Mississippi, with Mr. Cummings (whose valuable life seemed about to be spared to us, to his family, to his country), the crew was mustered at nine. Captain Alden made a pithy speech to them of praise for their coolness, bravery, and fidelity, and then prayers were offered by the acting Chaplain, and thanksgiving for our deliverance. It was a most solemn and beautiful termination to these transactions. The dead being buried with all solemnity, repairs were at once commenced, and by the next day we had steam up, and were 'ready for any ordinary service.'"

REBEL ATTEMPT TO TAKE A TRAIN, AND HOW IT CAME OUT.*

BY DANIEL D. STEEL, COMPANY G, SEVENTY-EIGHTH NEW YORK STATE VETERAN VOLUNTEERS.

ATTENTION to these verses,
    And I will tell no lies;
'Tis how the rebels came to take
    The Yankees by surprise.
They came with empty haversacks,
    A victory for to gain;
They said they would draw our rations
    When they took our wagon train.

* About midnight of October 28, 1863, the rebels came off from Lookout Mountain into Lookout Valley, at Wauhatchie, Tennessee, to capture the Eleventh corps supply train; but, to their mortification and chagrin, it proved to be a part of the White Star division (Second division, Twelfth corps), who gave them a sound thrashing, and they fled back, helter-skelter, in dismay, into their lines, with considerable loss.

They came so close upon us,
    So slyly they did creep,
They thought they had surely caught
    The Yankee boys asleep.
They fired in upon us;
    They don't deny this tale;
But when they saw the "White Star,"
    Their appetites did fail.

They said they never saw the like
    Since ever they were born;
Before they would fight the White Star,
    They would go and live on corn.
Away they went on double-quick,
    Saying, "If we come again,
We will take our rations with us,
    For fear we will miss the train."

It was on the road these graybacks
    Their comrades they did meet;
Some wanted Yankee hard tack,
    While others wanted meat.
The Yankees would not give it up,
    As sure as we are born;
Methinks we heard the General say,
    We would have to live upon corn.

Had we have known what we know now,
    We would never went so far;
We never thought the Yankee train
    Was guarded by the Star.
Where is the rest of our boys?
    Why did they not come back?
They were taken sick upon the field,
    By receiving Yankee tack.

Now Geary says, "If that's their game,
    We'll go and drive them back;
We'll go and take their wagon train,
    And dine upon rebel tack.
We'll charge up Lookout Mountain, boys,
    Where they have made a stand to fight;
We'll take them when they are wide awake,
    And not go at night.

On November, the twenty-fourth,
    General Geary took in hand
To drive them off the mountain,
    Where they have made a stand.
He took with him a little force,
    Advanced upon the hill;
Said he, "My boys, we'll go and see
    How Hardee likes his drill."

They looked upon our little force,
    As it was drawing nigh;
They said, "I wonder if the Yanks
    Are coming up to die?"
They then got in their breastworks,
    They said they would have some fun;
For up the mountain they were sure
    The Yankees could not come.

They laid there in their breastworks,
    But little did they fear,
Until they saw the White Star
    Advancing in their rear;
It came so close upon them,
    It glittered like the gold,
Which sent a terror to their hearts,
    And made their blood run cold.

"Our breastworks are not made aright,"
 The Johnny Rebs did cry;
While on every side they heard the word,
 "Surrender, Rebs, or die!"
They left their shoes and stockings,
 Through bushes they did creep,
While stones and briers plenty
 Came in contact with their feet.

On Missionary Ridge they got,
 Determined not to run;
The Stars followed after them,
 And captured all their guns.
Now Johnny Rebs, they felt so bad,
 They knew not what to do;
They turned around to look for Bragg,
 But he had skedaddled too.

Now Johnny Rebs have gone so far,
 We cannot see their flag;
Jeff Davis says he'll have revenge,
 And lays it all to Bragg.
But when he comes he'll find the Star;
 We'll meet him hand to hand,
Determined they will not be whipped
 By any such a man.

Here's health to brave General Geary, boys,
 Likewise to General Green;
Success to the Veteran Volunteers,
 And Colonel Hamerstine.
We have showed the Rebs a Yankee trick,
 And will do the same again
When they come to catch us Yanks asleep,
 And take our wagon train.

ONE OF A HUNDRED. — A rural conscript appeared before a Board of Enrolment, and desired to be exempted forthwith, that he might return to his country home. "What are your claims?" demanded the Doctor. "*I'm entirely dependent upon my mother for support*," was the innocent reply. Whereupon, thus the Doctor, while a smile faintly illumined the face of the Board: "I am happy to assure you, my honest-hearted friend, that the government is prepared at once to relieve your mother of so unsuitable a burden, and assume your entire charge and expense during the next three years, without the slightest recourse to the maternal fount for support or succor." The young draftee appeared a little bewildered, and referred to the papers to ascertain what was the matter.

AN AFFECTIONATE HORSE. — Many instances have been given by travellers of the affection shown by the Arabian horses towards their masters; and so much, also, has been written to prove their sagacity, as to make one believe, at times, that they must be endowed with an instinct which approaches nearly, if not quite, to the reasoning faculty of a human being. We very much doubt if among the feats narrated of the horses of the East any can be found that exceeds in affectionate devotion the following incident, which was told by the soldier to whom it occurred.

The narrator, a young Irishman, like many others of his nation, joined, shortly after his arrival in America, Sheridan's brigade. It was in one of those forced marches when they had driven back the enemy, and had been in the saddle several consecutive days and nights, that this trooper availed himself of a temporary halt to slip from his saddle and stretch himself upon the turf — his horse, meanwhile, browsing in the immediate vicinity. He had slept for some little time, when he was suddenly awakened by the frantic pawing of his horse at his side. Fatigued by his long ride, he did not rouse at once, but lay in that partially conscious state which so frequently attends great physical prostration. Soon, however, the faithful animal, perceiving that its efforts had failed to accomplish their object, licked his face, and placing its mouth close to his ear, uttered a loud snort. Now thoroughly awake, he sprang up, and as the horse turned for him to mount, he saw, for the first time, that his comrades had all disappeared, and that the enemy were coming down upon him at full gallop. Once mounted, the faithful beast bore him with the speed of the wind safely from the danger, and soon placed him among his companions. "Thus," he added, with emotion, "the noble fellow saved me from captivity, and perhaps from death."

STORY OF THE "ALBEMARLE." — On the night of the 27th of October, 1864, a small steam launch left Albemarle Sound, on the coast of North Carolina, and entered the mouth of the Roanoke River.

So small that she looked more like a yawl than a war vessel, and with no signs of armament, there was nothing about her to excite suspicion or to awaken hope. Yet she had been prepared and fitted up, manned by a picked crew of volunteers, and furnished with a terrible engine of destruction, for the sole purpose of fighting and sinking the most formidable war-vessel, after the Merrimac, that rebel skill had been able to launch upon the Southern waters.

The Albemarle had come out from the recesses of Roanoke River in April, and for six months had been the champion of the Southern waters, and the terror of the North Carolina squadron.

Twice she had fought long pitched battles with some of the best war-vessels in the United States navy, and had come out almost unscathed from a fierce storm of hundred pound Parrotts, nine-inch solid shot, percussion shell, shrapnel, and all the formidable enginery of modern naval warfare.

Torpedoes had been sunk for her, and men had swum the river at midnight in the hope of bringing some secret and sufficiently destructive agent to bear upon her mailed sides. But she had so far escaped all open attacks, and all secret torpedo plots.

The little steam launch that was now stealing up to attack the iron-clad giant was commanded by Lieutenant Cushing, an officer who brought to naval adventure the headlong dash of the playground, combined with the coolness and skill of an admiral.

Of an age and appearance that seemed to indicate an enthusiast in boat-racing, rather than in fighting iron-clads, he had associated his name with some of the most brilliant exploits, and the most fearless and dashing adventures of the war.

Having on previous occasions gained the admiration of the department by his daring and adventurous heroism, he had been selected to command this picket-boat, and use her in applying to the Albemarle a torpedo of extraordinary power, which had been invented by chief engineer W. W. Wood, and whose arrangements and application were suggested by Rear-Admiral Gregory and his able assistants. During the summer of 1864, the gallant young officer had gone on to New York. Admiral Gregory had explained and illustrated the best manner of conducting this novel but formidable mode of attack, but the details had been left wholly to Lieutenant Cushing.

No service could be more fraught with danger. One discharge from the Whitworth guns of the Albemarle would shatter and pierce the little picket-boat, as certainly as a minie ball shot at an egg-shell. And the torpedo was an invention whose recoil might prove as fatal to the vessel which carried it as to that to which it was to be applied.

The distance from the mouth of the river to where the ram was moored was about eight miles. The stream was on an average two hundred yards wide, and lined with the enemy's pickets.

The launch succeeded in passing the pickets, and even the wreck of the Southfield, within twenty yards, without discovery, and the Lieutenant was not challenged till within hail of the lookout on the Albemarle.

One of the Shamrock's cutters, which he had in tow, was then cast off by Lieutenant Cushing, and ordered back down the river, while under a full head of steam he made directly for the enemy.

The rebels sprang their rattles, rang the bell, and commenced firing. The light of a fire burning on the shore showed the iron-clad made fast to the wharf, with a pen of logs around her about thirty feet from her side.

Passing close by her, the launch made a complete circle, and turning so as to strike her fairly, went into her, bows on. By this time the enemy's fire was very severe; but the Lieutenant returned it vigorously with grape. An instant more, and the launch had struck against the logs of the stockade, behind which her enemy was ensconced, breasting them in some feet, and her bows resting on them. A storm of bullets now swept the decks of the launch. Three pierced the clothing of Lieutenant Cushing, and one struck Frank Swan, an officer of the Otsego, who was standing close beside the commander, wounding him severely, and rendering his escape impossible.

Now, or not at all, must the torpedo be applied. The boom to which it was attached was lowered, and by a vigorous pull the deadly engine was swung under the overhang of the ram, and brought close beneath her mailed side.

Simultaneously with its explosion came a crashing bolt from one of the big guns of the Albemarle. An immense wave from the bursting of the torpedo came surging over the little launch, and in an instant she was filled with water and wholly disabled.

The enemy continued their fire at fifteen feet range, and twice demanded surrender. This was refused, and Cushing ordered his men to save themselves as best they could, while he, throwing off his coat and shoes, sprang overboard.

Frank Swan was too much hurt to follow him, and soon became a prisoner in the hands of the enemy.

Most of the party, of thirteen officers and men, were captured; some were drowned, and only one besides the Lieutenant made his escape. Cushing swam ashore, crept exhausted into the swamp, and the next day succeeded in capturing a skiff from the rebel pickets, in which he made his way to the Valley City.

On the 30th he commenced his report to Admiral Porter, with this proud sentence: "Sir, I have the honor to report that the rebel iron-clad Albemarle is at the bottom of the Roanoke River."

REMINISCENCES OF PRESIDENT LINCOLN. — A correspondent, writing from Springfield, gives the following incidents in the early career of Mr. Lincoln, obtained from his law partner, Mr. Herndon:

"Mr. Lincoln came to Sangamon County in 1831. He cut the timber for a canoe at the mouth of Spring Creek, on which he floated down to Sangamon town, seven miles north-west of Springfield. In April of that year he went to New Orleans on a flat-boat, and returned the following August. He was at this time fine and noble-looking, weighed two hundred and ten pounds, was six feet three or four inches in height, and of florid complexion. Going to the town of New Salem, the judges of election being minus one clerk, and impressed with the good appearance of the young man, chose him as the clerk of election.

"Mr. Herndon said that Mr. Lincoln approached more nearly the angelic nature than any person he ever saw, women not excepted. He had, he said, more of the angel-looking eye and face than he had ever seen. Yet he was not without passions. These in Lincoln were powerful; but they were held under control by a giant will. He was, said Mr. Herndon, a great animal, but a great angel was ingrafted upon it. He had a towering ambition, but that ambition was directed to the attainment of power with which to elevate man.

"He seems to have retained very vivid impressions of his mother's virtues, and a tender sense of his obligations to her. Familiarly he once said to his partner, 'Billy, all that I am I owe to my blessed mother.'

"Because of his transparent honesty, he was

taken as a clerk in a store by a man named Offutt. This Offutt reposed all confidence in him, and in no point was he deceived.

"He obtained the name of 'Honest Abe' as follows: A lady came to pay him for a dress she had purchased of him; and in computing the amount, he made it come to two dollars and thirty-seven and a half cents; whereas it was six and a half cents too much. In the evening, after business hours were over, he took the six cents to the woman and corrected the mistake. At another time, a lady came to buy a pound of tea. By mistake a half pound weight was placed in the scale. After Lincoln discovered the error, he closed the store about sunset, and took the half pound of tea with him to the lady.

"In addition to this business integrity, he was extremely humorous, sociable, and agreeable, becoming everybody's friend and nobody's enemy. By these qualities people came to know him thoroughly. He was taken into every man's house as one of his own household. From his nature, honesty, purity, &c., people termed him 'Honest Abe.'

"When he first came to Springfield, he was extremely poor, having not a shilling in his pocket, and with but a very scanty wardrobe. He would stop a while with one, and then with another, going from neighbor to neighbor, all esteeming it a favor to have him in their houses. At that time he had read well and thoroughly everything he had touched, including the Bible and Shakspeare, which were his leading books at the time of his death. He was, said Mr. Herndon, a good biblical scholar. When he was twenty-three years of age, he had read history and biography considerably, and he had mastered Burns when he was twenty-five.

"He never, while engaged in his profession, accumulated much property. He seemed not to have had much care to gather wealth. When he did a service professionally, he would charge accordingly as he estimated the value of the work done, and not according to the standard of other men's fees. If he regarded a service worth a dollar, he charged only that, although other men might charge twenty dollars for doing the same thing.

"His strict fidelity to principle was illustrated by his partner by the following incident: He said, when Mr. Lincoln collected any money belonging to the firm, he would always take half the amount received, and fold up the other half, write upon it the word 'Billy' (the name he familiarly called his partner), and lay it away in his pocket-book. One time Mr. Herndon said to him:

"'Why do you do that? Why not take the whole of the money, and use it?'

"'Because,' said Lincoln, 'I promised my mother never to use anybody's money. Should anything happen to me, that money would be known to be yours.'

"Mr. Herndon took me into the law office where Mr. Lincoln used to sit and toil. It is plain and unpretending. Indeed, everything about the man was indicative of the simplicity of his character. And yet, though so transparent and unassuming, he was sagacious. His friend told me that he was a man of profound policy. His neighbor, to whom I have referred, said he was a great thinker — that he was accustomed to think much on the affairs of the nation. Sometimes he would pass his friends on the street without a sign of recognition — lost in his deep musings. Again, as a neighbor approached him, he would cast up his eye, smile, and remark, 'I've been thinking,' and then proceed to unfold the subject of his thoughts.

"Assassination cast its shadow on the hearts of his friends as early as the Presidential election of 1860. Mr. Herndon told me that himself and two other friends guarded Mr. Lincoln to the polls in Springfield on that day to prevent a stiletto from being aimed at his heart. At length he fell, but not until his great work was done, and he was enthroned among the chiefest of the illustrious benefactors of humanity."

A YEAR AGO.

The grass was wet with glistening dew,
  In the clear blue sky the stars were glowing,
Mournfully cried the whip-poor-will,
  Softly the mild south wind was blowing.

He kissed me once, he kissed me thrice;
  "Sweet," said my love, "time fast is flowing;
My troopers wait — we will meet again,
  When the perfumed rose of June is blowing."

Sharply his sabre rang as he rode,
  In the still night-air loud echoes waking;
And oft he turned to wave adieu
  Where I stood with a heart that was well nigh
    breaking.

The watch-dog howled and clashed his chain;
  "Come back," I cried, in terror springing; —
Alas! I could but faintly hear,
  Far down the road, his horse-hoofs ringing.

The roses of June are withered and dead —
  Their shrivelled leaves on his grave are lying;
Once more cries sadly the whip-poor-will,
  And softly the mild south wind is sighing.
                                        Wolverine.

THE SIEGE OF CINCINNATI.

BY T. BUCHANAN READ.[*]

THE live man of the old Revolution, the daring Hotspur of those troublous days, was Anthony Wayne. The living man to-day of the great North-west is Lewis Wallace. With all the chivalric dash of the stormer of Stony Point, he has a cooler head, with a capacity for larger plans, and the steady nerve to execute whatever he conceives. When a difficulty rises in his path, the difficulty, no matter what its proportions, moves aside; he does not. When a river, like the Ohio at Cincinnati, intervenes between him and his field of operations, there is a sudden sound of

* Written in January, 1863.

saws and hammers at sunset, and the next morning beholds the magic spectacle of a great pontoon-bridge stretching between the shores of Freedom and Slavery, its planks resounding to the heavy tread of almost endless regiments and army wagons. Is a city like Cincinnati menaced by a hungry foe, striding on by forced marches?—that foe sees his path suddenly blocked by ten miles of fortifications, thoroughly manned and armed, and he finds it prudent, even with his twenty thousand veterans, to retreat faster than he came, strewing the road with whatever articles impede his haste. Some few incidents in the career of such a man, since he has taken the field, ought not to be uninteresting to those for whom he has fought so bravely; and we believe his services, when known, will be appreciated; otherwise we will come under the old ban against republics, that they are ungrateful.

While returning from New York, at the expiration of a short leave of absence, the first asked for since the beginning of the war, General Wallace was persuaded by Governor Morton to stump the State of Indiana in favor of voluntary enlistments, which at that time were progressing slowly. Wallace went to work in all earnestness. His idea was to obtain command of the new levies, drill them, and take them to the field; and this idea was circulated throughout the State. The result was, enlisting increased rapidly; the ardor for it rose shortly into a fever, and has not yet abated. Regiments are still forming, shedding additional lustre upon the name of patriotic Indiana.

General Wallace was thus engaged when the news was received from Morgan of the invasion of Kentucky by Kirby Smith. All eyes turned at once to Governor Morton, many of whose regiments were now ready to take the field, if they only had officers to lead them. Wallace came promptly to the Governor's assistance, and offered to take command of a regiment for the crisis. His offer was accepted, and he was sent to New Albany, where the Sixty-sixth Indiana was in camp. In twelve hours he mustered it, paid its bounty money, clothed and armed it, and marched it to Louisville. Brigadier-General Boyle was in command of Kentucky. Wallace, who is a Major-General, reported to him at the above-named city, and a peculiar scene occurred.

"General Boyle," said Wallace, "I report to you the Sixty-sixth Indiana regiment."

"Who commands it?" asked the General.

"I have that honor, sir," was the reply.

"You want orders, I suppose."

"Certainly."

"It is a difficult matter for me," said Boyle. "I have no right to order you."

"That difficulty is easily solved," Wallace replied, with characteristic promptness. "I come to report to you as a Colonel. I come to take orders as such."

General Boyle consulted with his Adjutant-General, and the result was *a request* that General Wallace would proceed to Lexington with his command. Here was exhibited the ready, self-sacrificing spirit of a true patriot; he did not stand and wait until he could find the position to which his high rank entitled him, but stepped into the place where he could best and quickest serve his country in her hour of peril.

While Wallace was still at the railway station, he received an order from General Boyle, putting him in command of all the forces in Lexington. Here was a golden opportunity for our young commander. What higher honor could be coveted than to relieve the brave Morgan, pent up as he was with his little army in the mountain gorges of the Cumberland? The idea fired the soul of Wallace, and he pushed on to Lexington. But here he was sadly disappointed. He found the forces waiting there inadequate to the task. Instead of an army, there were only three regiments. He telegraphed for more troops. Indiana and Ohio responded promptly and nobly. In three days he received and brigaded nine regiments, and started them towards the Gap.

No one but an experienced soldier, one who has indeed tried it, can conceive of the labor involved in such an undertaking. The material in his hands was, to say the best of it, magnificently *raw*. Officers, from Colonels to Corporals, brave though they might be as lions, knew literally nothing of military affairs. The men had not learned even to load their guns. Companies had to be led, like little children, by the hand, as it were, into their places in line of battle. There was no cavalry, no artillery. It happened, however, that guns, horses, and supplies, intended for Morgan at the Gap, were in depot at Lexington. Then Wallace began to catch a glimpse of dawn through the dark tangle of the wilderness. Some kind of order, prompt and immediate, must be forced out of this chaos; and it came, for the master spirit was there to arrange and compel. He mounted several hundred men, giving them rifles instead of sabres. He manned new guns, procuring harness and ammunition for them from Louisville. Where there were no caissons, he supplied wagons. But his regiments were not his sole reliance; he is a believer in riflemen, a fighting class of which Kentucky was full. These he summoned to his assistance, and was met by a ready and hearty response; they came trooping to him by hundreds. Among others, Garret Davis, United States Senator, led a company of Home Guards to Lexington. In this way, General Wallace composed, or rather improvised, a little army, and all without help, his staff being absent, mostly in Memphis.

"Kentucky has not been herself in this war," exclaimed General Wallace; "she must be aroused; and I propose to do it thoroughly."

"How will you do it?" asked a sceptic.

"Easily enough, sir. Kentucky has a host of great names. Kentuckians believe in great names. It is to this tune that the traitors have carried them to the field against us. I will take with me to the field all the men living, old and young, who have made those names great. Buckner took the young Crittendens and Clays; by Heaven, I'll take their fathers!"

"But they can't march."

"I'll haul them, then."

"They can be of no service in that way."

"But the magic of their names!" exclaimed Wallace. "What will the young Kentuckians say, when they hear John J. Crittenden, Leslie Coombs, Robert Breckinridge, Tom Clay, Garrett Davis, Judge Goodloe, and fathers of that kind, are going down to battle with me?"

The sceptics held their peace.

General Wallace now constituted a volunteer staff. Wadsworth, M. C. from Maysville district, was his Adjutant-General. Brand, Gratz, Goodloe, and young Tom Clay were his Aids. Old Tom Clay, John J. Crittenden, Leslie Coombs, Judge Goodloe, Garrett Davis, were all prepared and going, when General Wallace was suddenly relieved of his command by General Nelson.

Without instituting any comparison between these two Generals, it is enough to say that the supersedure of Wallace by Nelson at that moment was most unfortunate and untimely, as the sequel proved, fraught, as it was, with disastrous consequences. The circumstances were these:

Scott's rebel cavalry had whipped Metcalf's regiment of loyalists at Big Hill, some twelve or fifteen miles from Richmond, Kentucky, and followed to within four miles of that town, where they were stopped by Lenck's brigade of infantry. The affair was reported to Wallace, with the number and situation of the enemy. He at once took prompt measures to meet the exigence of the situation. He could throw Lenck's and Clay's brigades upon the rebel front; the brigade at Nicholasville could take them in flank by crossing the Kentucky River at Tait's Ford; while, by uniting Clay Smith's command with that of Jacob, then en route for Nicholasville, he could plant seventeen hundred cavalry in their rear between Big Hill and Mount Vernon.

The enemy at this time were at least twenty miles in advance of their supports, and a night's march would have readily placed the several forces mentioned in position to attack them by daylight. This was Wallace's plan — simple, feasible, and soldier-like. All his orders were given. A supply train, with extra ammunition and abundant rations, was in line on the road to Richmond. Clay's brigade was drawn up ready to move, and General Wallace's horse was saddled. He was writing a last order in reference to the city of Lexington in his absence, and directing the officer left in charge to forward regiments to him at Richmond as fast as they should arrive, when General Nelson came, and instantly took the command. Fifteen minutes more, and General Wallace would have been on the road to Richmond, to superintend the execution of his plan of attack. The supersedure was, of course, a bitter disappointment; yet he never grumbled or demurred in the least, but, like a true soldier who knows his duty, offered that evening to serve his successor in any capacity, a generosity which General Nelson declined. The well-conceived plan which Wallace had matured failed for the

simple reason, that, instead of marching to execute it that night, as common sense would seem to have dictated, Nelson did not leave Lexington until the next day at one o'clock; and at daylight, when the attack was to have been made, the rebel leader, Scott, discovered his danger, and wisely retreated, finding nobody in his rear. The result was, Nelson went to Richmond, and was defeated. It is possible that the same result might have followed Wallace; but by those competent to judge, it is thought otherwise.

He had a plan adapted to the troops he was leading, who, although very raw, would have been invincible behind breastworks, as American troops have always shown themselves to be. Wallace never intended arraying these inexperienced men in the open field against the veteran troops of the rebels. Neither did he intend they should dig. He had collected large quantities of intrenching tools, and was rapidly assembling a corps of negroes, nearly five hundred of whom he had already in waiting in Morgan's factory, all prepared to follow his column, armed with spades and picks. In Madison County he intended getting at least five hundred more. "I will march," he said, "like Cæsar in Gaul, and intrench my camp every night. If I am attacked at any time in too great numbers, I can drop back to my nearest works, and wait for reënforcements." Such was his plan; and those who know him believe firmly that he could have been at Cumberland Gap in time not only to succor our little army there, but to have prevented the destruction and evacuation of that very important post.

Wallace, finding himself thus suddenly superseded, his plans ignored, and his voluntary services bluffly refused, left Lexington for Cincinnati. While there, the battle of Richmond was fought, the disastrous results of which are still too fresh in the public mind to require repeating. Nelson, who did not arrive upon the field until the day was about lost, and only in time to use his sword against his own men in a fruitless endeavor to rally them, received a flesh wound, and hastened back the same night to Cincinnati, leaving many dead and wounded on the field, and thousands of our brave boys prisoners, to be paroled by the rebels. These are simple matters of record, and are not here set down in any spirit of prejudice, or to throw a shadow upon the memory of the misguided, unfortunate, but courageous Nelson.

At this juncture, General Wallace was again ordered to Lexington, this time by General Wright, a General whose gentlemanly bearing in all capacities makes him an ornament to the American army. Wallace was ordered thither to resume command of the forces; but on arriving at Paris, the order was countermanded, and he was sent back to take charge of the city of Cincinnati. Shrewdly suspecting that our forces would evacuate Lexington, he hastened to his new post. General Wright was at that time in Louisville. On his way back, Wallace was asked by one of his aids:

"Do you believe the enemy will come to Cincinnati?"

"Yes," was the reply. "Kirby Smith will first go to Frankfort. He must have that place, if possible, for the political effect it will have. If he gets it, he will surely come to Cincinnati. He is an idiot if he does not. Here is the material of war, — goods, groceries, salt, supplies, machinery, &c., — enough to re-stock the whole bogus Confederacy."

"What are you going to do? You have nothing to defend the city with."

"I will show you," was the reply.

Within the first half hour after his arrival in Cincinnati, General Wallace wrote and sent to the daily papers the following proclamation, which fully and clearly develops his whole plan:

"PROCLAMATION.

"The undersigned, by order of Major-General Wright, assumes command of Cincinnati, Covington, and Newport.

"It is but fair to inform the citizens, that an active, daring, and powerful enemy threatens them with every consequence of war; yet the cities must be defended, and their inhabitants must assist in the preparation.

"Patriotism, duty, honor, self-preservation, call them to the labor, and it must be performed equally by all classes.

"First. All business must be suspended at nine o'clock to-day. Every business house must be closed.

"Second. Under the direction of the Mayor, the citizens must, within an hour after the suspension of business (ten o'clock, A. M.), assemble in convenient public places, ready for orders. As soon as possible, they will then be assigned to their work.

"This labor ought to be that of love, and the undersigned trusts and believes it will be so. Anyhow, it must be done.

"The willing shall be properly credited; the unwilling promptly visited. The principle adopted is: Citizens for the labor, soldiers for the battle.

"Third. The ferry-boats will cease plying the river after four o'clock A. M., until further orders.

"Martial law is hereby proclaimed in the three cities; but until they can be relieved by the military, the injunctions of this proclamation will be executed by the police.

"LEWIS WALLACE,
"Major-General commanding."

Could anything be bolder, and more to the purpose? It placed Cincinnati under martial law. It totally suspended business, and sent every citizen, without distinction, to the ranks or into the trenches. "Citizens for labor, soldiers for battle," was the principle underlying the whole plan — a motto by which he reached every able-bodied man in the metropolis, and united the energies of forty thousand people — a motto original with himself, and for which he should have the credit.

Imagine the astonishment that seized the city, when, in the morning, this bold proclamation was read — a city unused to the din of war and its impediments. As yet there was no word of an advance of the enemy in the direction of Cincinnati. It was a question whether they would come or not. Thousands did not believe in the impending danger; yet the proclamation was obeyed to the letter, and this, too, when there was not a regiment to enforce it. The secret is easy of comprehension; it was the universal confidence reposed in the man who issued the order; and he was equally confident, not only in his own judgment, but in the people with whom he had to deal.

"If the enemy should not come after all this fuss," said one of the General's friends, "you will be ruined."

"Very well," he replied; "but they will come. And if they do not, it will be because this same fuss has caused them to think better of it."

The ten days ensuing will be forever memorable in the annals of the city of Cincinnati. The cheerful alacrity with which the people rose *en masse* to swell the ranks and crowd into the trenches was a sight worth seeing, and being seen, could not readily be forgotten.

Here were the representatives of all nations and classes. The sturdy German, the lithe and gay-hearted Irishman, went shoulder to shoulder in defence of their adopted country. The man of money, the man of law, the merchant, the artist, and the artisan, swelled the lines hastening to the scene of action, armed either with musket, pick, or spade. Added to these was seen Dickson's long and dusky brigade of colored men, cheerfully wending their way to labor on the fortifications, evidently holding it their especial right to put whatever impediments they could in the northward path of those whom they considered their own peculiar foe. But the pleasantest and most picturesque sight of those remarkable days was the almost endless stream of sturdy men who rushed to the rescue from the rural districts of the State. These were known as the "Squirrel Hunters." They came in files numbering thousands upon thousands, in all kinds of costumes, and armed with all kinds of fire-arms, but chiefly the deadly rifle, which they knew so well how to use. Old men, middle-aged men, young men, and often mere boys, like the "minute-men" of the old Revolution, they left the plough in the furrow, the flail on the half-threshed sheaves, the unfinished iron upon the anvil — in short, dropped all their peculiar avocations, and with their leathern pouches full of bullets, and their ox-horns full of powder, poured into the city by every highway and by-way in such numbers that it seemed as if the whole State of Ohio were peopled only with hunters, and that the spirit of Daniel Boone stood upon the hills opposite the town beckoning them into Kentucky. The pontoon bridge, which had been begun and completed between sundown and sundown, groaned day and night with the perpetual stream of life all setting southward. In three days there were ten miles of intrenchments lining the hills, making a semicircle from the river above the city to the banks of the river below; and these were thickly manned from end to end, and made terrible to the astonished enemy by black and frowning cannon. General Heath, with his twenty thousand rebel veterans, flushed with their late success at Richmond, drew up before these formidable preparations, and deemed it prudent to take the matter into serious consideration before making the attack.

Our men were eagerly awaiting their approach, thousands in rifle pits, and tens of thousands along the whole line of the fortifications, while our scouts and pickets were skirmishing with their outposts in the plains in front. Should the foe make a sudden dash, and carry any point of our lines, it was thought by some that nothing would prevent them from entering Cincinnati.

But for this, also, provision was made. The river about the city, above and below, was well protected by a flotilla of gunboats, improvised from the swarm of steamers which lay at the wharves. A storm of shot and shell, such as they had not dreamed of, would have played upon their advancing column, while our regiments, pouring down from the fortifications, would have fallen upon their rear. The shrewd leaders of the rebel army were probably kept well posted by traitors within our own lines in regard to the reception prepared for them, and, taking advantage of the darkness of night, and the violence of a thunder-storm, made a hasty and ruinous retreat. Wallace was anxious to follow them, and was confident of success, but was overruled by those higher in authority.

The address which he now published to the citizens of Cincinnati, Covington, and Newport, was manly and well-deserved. He says:

"For the present, at least, the enemy has fallen back, and your cities are safe. It is the time for acknowledgments. I beg leave to make you mine. When I assumed command, there was nothing to defend you with, except a few half-finished works and some dismounted guns; yet I was confident. The energies of a great city are boundless; they have only to be aroused, united, and directed. You were appealed to. The answer will never be forgotten. Paris may have seen something like it in her revolutionary days, but the cities of America never did. Be proud that you have given them an example so splendid. The most commercial of people, you submitted to a total suspension of business, and without a murmur adopted my principle, 'Citizens for labor, soldiers for battle.' In coming time, strangers, viewing the works on the hills of Newport and Covington, will ask, 'Who built these intrenchments?' You can answer, 'We built them.' If they ask, 'Who guarded them?' you can reply, 'We helped in thousands.' If they inquire the result, your answer will be, 'The enemy came and looked at them, and stole away in the night.' You have won much honor. Keep your organization ready to win more. Hereafter be always prepared to defend yourselves.

"LEWIS WALLACE, Major-General."

It can safely be claimed for our young General, that he was the moving spirit which inspired and directed the people, and thereby saved Cincinnati and the surrounding cities, and, in the very face of Heath and his victorious hordes from Richmond, organized a new and formidable army. That the citizens fully indorsed this, was well exemplified on the occasion of his leading back into the metropolis a number of her volunteer regiments when the danger was over. They lined the streets, crowded the doors and windows, and filled the air with shouts of applause in honor of the great work he had done.

In writing this notice of Wallace and the siege, we have had no intention to overlook the services of his co-laborers, especially those rendered to the West by the gallant Wright, who holds command of the department. The writer has attempted to give what came directly under his own observation, and what he believes to be the core of the matter, and consequently most interesting to the public.

CAPTAIN SEMMES, C. S. A. N.

June 19, 1864.

OUT of Cherbourg harbor, one clear
Sunday morning, the cavalier,
Captain Semmes, with his cap a-cock,
Sailed from the friendly Frenchman's dock.
Gayly along the rebel came,
Under the flag of the cross of shame;
Knight of the handcuff and bloody lash,
He twirled the point of his red mustache,
And swore, in English not over nice,
To sink our Yankee scum in a trice,
Or burn our ship, as the thing might be,
Where the eyes of Cherbourg all should see.
    "Heigh-ho! you don't say so!"
Whispered his friend, little Jean Crapeau.

Semmes has been a wolf of the deep
For many a day to harmless sheep;
Ships he scuttled, and robbed, and burned,
Watches pilfered, and pockets turned;
And all his plunder, bonds, and gold,
He left for his Gallic friend to hold.
A little over-prudent was he,
For a cavalier of high degree;
And Raphael Semmes don't sound, indeed,
As if it came of the purple seed;
But all the blood in his veins was blue,
And his clay was porcelain through and through.
    Heigh-ho! the Lord doth know
We are but dirt, and our blood's so-so.

What will the doughty Captain do
With his British ship, his British crew,
His gunners, trained in the "Excellent,"
The guns his cousin Blakeley sent,
His shot and shell at Woolwich made, —
What will he do with the whole parade?
Up to the top of his cliffs Crapeau
Had clambered to see the Sunday show;
And his brother Ball, in his fancy yacht,
Stood off and on towards the fated spot;
And right across the bold Captain's way
The Kearsarge steamed in her war array.
    "Heigh-ho!" said Semmes. "Let's blow
That craft to splinters before we go."

Semmes had heard, with his lip a-curl,
In Cherbourg, that some Northern churl,
Backed by a gang of onion-eaters,
Waited the noble negro-beaters.
Shop-keeping, peddling, vulgar knaves,
To stick their heads into open graves!
"'Sdeath! 'Swounds! 'Ods bodikins! Ha! what
　then?
Will they dare to fight with gentlemen?
O, had I my lance, and shield, and things,
With which I tilted at Sulphur Springs!
Or a troop of horse marines! Of course,
A knight is nothing without his horse."
　Heigh-ho! this seemed to show
Our hero's spirits were running low.

Straight out to sea the Kearsarge drew,
And Semmes, who followed all that flew,
Followed, perhaps by some mistake,
Close in his foeman's frothing wake;
But when three leagues were gained from shore,
Slowly and grimly the Yankee wore;
And our starry ensign leaped above,
Round which the wind, like a fluttering dove,
Cooed low, and the sunshine of God's day
Like an open blessing on it lay;
So we felt our friendless ship would fight
Full under the great Disposer's sight.
　Heigh-ho! 'tis well to know
Who looks on the deeds done here below.

Semmes led the waltz, and struck the tune:
Shots at the sea and at the moon
The swashing, wasteful cavalier
Scattered around him, far and near.
The saving Yankees squandered not
An ounce of powder or pound of shot.
They held their peace till the guns would tell,
Then out they burst like the mouths of hell.
Terrible, horrible! how they tore
The Alabama, until the gore
From her bursting scuppers smoked and streamed,
The dying groaned, and the wounded screamed.
　"Heigh-ho!" said Semmes; "let's show
The Yankees the heels we boast of so."

Seven times in that deadly round
Sped the ships to the cannon's sound.
The vulture, through the smoke and din,
Saw the eagle's circles narrowing in;
And every time her pivots roared
The fatal bomb-shells came straight aboard.
His helm was useless, his engine failed,
His powder was wet, his Britons quailed;
And in his course, like a warning hand,
Stretched forth the flag of his outraged land.
In vain he hoisted his sails to flee;
For each foot he sailed, his foe sailed three.
　Heigh-ho! "Why, here's a blow,"
Said Semmes, as he hauled his flag below.

Well was it for the cavalier,
That brother Bull was lying near.
His vessel with a haughty curl
Turned up her nose, and in the whirl
Of the white sea, stern foremost, tore
As if in scorn of the crew she bore.
Then the thrifty Briton launched his boat,
To pick up aught that might be afloat,
And, amongst other less precious spoil,
Fished swordless Semmes from his watery coil!

"Hide me!" the gallant cried in affright;
"Cover me up from the Yankee's sight."
　Heigh-ho! they laid him low,
With a bit of sail to hide his woe.

Safely they bore the chief aboard,
Leaving behind his fame and sword;
And then the Deerhound stole away,
Lest Winslow's guns might have a say;
Landed him in Southampton town,
Where heroes like him have hand renown,
Ever since Lawrence, Perry, and Hull,
Took hold of the horns of great John Bull.
Had I been Winslow, I say to you,
As the sea is green, the sky is blue,
Through the Deerhound I'd have sent a shot,
And John might have liked the thing or not!
　Heigh-ho! come soon or slow,
In the end we are bound to have a blow.

What said the Frenchman from his hill,
After the cannon shots were still?
What said the Briton from his deck,
Gazing down on the sunken wreck?
Something was said of guns like mortars,
And something of smooth-bores at close quarters;
Chain armor furnished a word or two,
But the end of all was, both looked blue.
They sighed again o'er the "Great Contention,"
But never hinted at "Intervention."
One thing they wished, which they dared not say—
"If the fight had but gone the other way!
　Heigh-ho! I told you so!
O, Semmes was a sorry fool to go!"

　　　　　　　　　George H. Boker.

———

BRAVE OFFICERS MAKE A BRAVE ARMY.—A correspondent, writing of the battle of Chickamauga, says: "The rebel forces from the East fought with a gallantry allied to desperation, and I do not wonder that our boys were proud to say, when asked to whom they were opposed, 'Longstreet's men.' The rebel fashion of coming out to battle is peculiar. Had you seen them streaming out of the woods, in long, gray lines, into the open field, you could have likened them to nothing better than to streams of turbid water pouring through a sieve. And writing of valor, let me say that the difference among regiments consists not more in the material of the rank and file than it does in the coolness, judgment, and bravery of the officers, and the *faith* the soldiers repose in them. That faith has a magic in it that tones men up, and makes more and nobler of them than there was before. It is the principle recognized by the great Frederick when he addressed his General— 'I send you against the enemy with sixty thousand men.' 'But, sire,' said the officer, 'there are only fifty thousand.' 'Ah, I counted *you* as ten thousand,' was the monarch's wise and quick reply. I have a splendid illustration of this in an incident which occurred on the Sunday at Chickamauga. It was near four o'clock on that blazing afternoon, when a part of General Steedman's division of the Reserve corps bowed their heads to the hurtling storm of lead, as if it had been rain, and betrayed signs of breaking. The line wavered like a great flag in a breath of wind. They were as splendid material as ever shouldered a musket; but then what could they do in such a blinding tempest! General Steedman rode up — a great, hearty man, broad-breasted, broad-shouldered, a face written all over with sturdy sense and stout courage; no lady's man, to make bouquets for snowy fingers, and sing, 'Meet me by moonlight alone,' like *some* Generals I could name, but realizing the ideal of my boyhood, when I read of the stout old Morgan of the Revolution. Well, up rode Steedman, took the flag from the color-bearer, glanced along the wavering front, and with that voice of his that could talk against a small rattle of musketry, cried out, 'Go back, boys, go back; but the flag can't go with you,' — grasped the staff, wheeled his horse, and rode on. Must I tell you that the column closed up, and grew firm, and moved resistlessly on like a great strong river, and swept down upon the foe, and made a record that shall live when their graves are as empty as the cave of Machpelah? They were, in a sense nobler than Shakspeare's, they were *themselves* again."

A NEW KNIGHT OF THE GARTER. — While the Seventh regiment of New York was passing through Philadelphia, a fine old Quaker lady, observing that one of the band was in a state of great embarrassment for the lack of a string with which to secure the mouth of his bag of provisions, observed quietly, "Friend, I would not give thee an implement of war, but thee shall have a string to preserve thy food." Then she turned partly away for an instant, and stooped down, to tie her shoe, apparently; but when she rose up she handed to the blushing blower of brass a neat green band, that a moment before had been doing duty as a—a—a—well, *garter*.

FORCE OF HABIT. — A Captain, who had been a railroad conductor before the war, was drilling a squad, and while marching them by flank, turned to speak to a friend for a moment. On looking again towards his squad, he saw they were in the act of "butting up" against a fence. In his hurry to halt them, he cried out, "Down brakes! Down brakes!"

A LOVER'S letter picked up at Laurel Hill Camp, Va., runs as follows: "I say agen deer Melindy weer fitin for our liburtis to dew gest as we pleas, and we wil fite fur them so long as goddlemity give us breth."

A PRACTICAL JOKE. — A gallant volunteer officer was searching the houses of citizens for arms, with a squad of men, and on arriving at the residence of an old gentleman named Hayes, was met in the hall by his daughter, — a beautiful, black-eyed girl of eighteen, — who appeared deeply agitated, and implored the Captain not to search the house. The officer was sternly immovable,

resolved to do his duty, and the more bent upon searching from the apparent dismay of the fair girl. "Indeed — indeed," she exclaimed, "we have only three guns in the house."

The Captain smiled incredulously. "Fetch them to me," said he, remembering the fate of poor Ellsworth. The young lady hurried up stairs, and returned with an old, rusty, double-barrelled shot gun that no prudent man would have ventured to load and discharge. "The others — the other two!" demanded the officer. "O sir, my brothers!" sobbed the girl. "I cannot take them from them!"

The Captain pushed her on one side. "Forward, men!" he shouted, falling into the rear himself. As the file of soldiers hastily mounted the stairs, the young lady clung to the skirts of the officer, who was the last to ascend, exclaiming wildly:

"But — but, sir, my brothers — you will not harm my brothers?"

The Captain shook her off somewhat ungallantly, and rushed up after the soldiers, who, by this time, reached the closed door of a chamber. After a pause, the men pushed open the door, and rushed in with bayonets fixed, when two juvenile Zouaves, of the ages of eight and ten years, fully armed and equipped with wooden guns, appeared drawn up in line before them. At the same moment the silvery laugh of the black-eyed beauty was heard on the stairs, echoed by a couple of chambermaids, who were peeping over the balusters from above. The officer beat a hasty retreat, without making a seizure of the two remaining guns.

LOVE, HATE, AND PIETY ON THE BATTLE-FIELD. — A Rhode Island soldier, utterly exhausted, stepped aside to rest a few moments under the shade. There he found a gasping and dying Southern soldier, and put his almost exhausted canteen to his parched lips. The dying soldier — an enthusiast in his cause — with high excitement gasped out: "Why do you come to fight us? We shall utterly annihilate you. We have ninety thousand men. You can never subjugate us. We have a series of batteries beyond which will destroy all the armies you can bring." The Rhode Island soldier proceeded to state — and how strange and how tremendously *real* the discussion *then* and *so!* — that the object of the war was not the subjugation of the South, but the preservation of the Union. "And now," said the manly fellow, "I have given you water from my canteen, when its drops are more precious than diamonds. If you had found me in this state, what would you have done?" The eyes of the dying man gleamed, as the soldier said, like those of a basilisk, and he replied, "I would have put my bayonet to your heart." In a few moments he went into eternity, and the Rhode Islander resumed his place on the battle-field.

But there were also instances of Christian feeling exhibited on the battle-field, one of which is very affecting. A wounded Federal soldier was hastily carried to a wood, and placed by the side of a dying Georgian. The Georgian, evidently a gentleman, said to him, as they lay bleeding side by side, "We came on this field enemies — let us part friends;" and extended to him his hand, which the other grasped with the reciprocal expression of friendly feeling. They were both Christian men, and they lay with clasped hands on that bloody field, until the hand of the noble Georgian was cold in death. How beautiful that scene, amid the horrors of the battle-field! Who shall say, in view of it, that because of this strife between the North and South, they can never again clasp hands in mutual friendship and esteem? Who shall say that the time shall not come, when, on some well-fought field, they who met as enemies shall part as friends, and peace and restoration and mutual esteem ensue?

Another incident was sublime, and shows how close Christ Jesus is to his people, wherever they may be. A strong, tall man from Maine received a minie ball directly in his breast; and with the outstretched arms and the upward leap which is said often to mark such a death, he exclaimed, "Lord Jesus, receive my spirit."

To the Women of the South. — The Memphis Appeal of April 21, 1861, contains the annexed communication:

"While the men in every part of the country are arming themselves and mustering in squadrons to resist the invasion and oppression threatening our beloved land, let us emulate the enthusiasm of our husbands, sons, and friends in the cause. Many of our daughters are already active in the service with their needles. Let the matrons of every city, village, and hamlet form themselves into societies, called by some appropriate name, pledged to take care of the sick and wounded soldiers of the Confederate army, whenever the changing drama of war shall bring them in their neighborhood; to take them, if necessary and practicable, to their own homes. Let the organizations be commenced at once, with officers appointed and known, to whom the officers of the military companies may communicate the wants of the soldiers, and call upon for aid when the time for action shall come; and Baltimore has taught us how soon it may come. I offer myself for the work. Will not some matron with more time take the lead, and allow me to serve in a subordinate capacity? Let the women of the entire South join and spread the organization till not a spot within the Southern borders shall be without its band of sisters, pledged to the work and ready for it; and thus shall every mother feel assured, in sending her sons to the field, that in time of need they shall have the tender care of some other mother, whose loved ones are in the patriot ranks at other points, and our soldiers feel sure that true hearts are near them wherever they may be.   Mary E. Pope."

Juvenile Patriotism. — In Manchester, New Hampshire, a little fellow just past his first decade stepped into his father's office, and said to one of the clerks, "I shall get my company full pretty soon; I have sworn in three to-day." "Sworn in," said the clerk; "how did you do it?" "I made them hold up their hands and say, 'Glory to God,'" said the incipient Captain.

The following is a counterpart for the above story. A six-year old Boston boy, who had become deeply imbued with the martial spirit, undertook to act as commander of a diminutive company in a New Hampshire town, where he was spending his vacation. He somewhat "astonished the natives" by the following order, given in a very excited tone: "Company! Enemy's coming! Forward, march! *Amen!*"

THE JAGUAR HUNT.

BY J. T. TROWBRIDGE.

The dark jaguar was abroad in the land;
His strength and his fierceness what foe could withstand?
The breath of his anger was hot on the air,
And the white lamb of peace he had dragged to his lair.

Then up rose the farmer; he summoned his sons:
"Now saddle your horses, now look to your guns!"
And he called to his hound, as he sprang from the ground
To the back of his black pawing steed with a bound.

O, their hearts, at the word, how they tingled and stirred!
They followed, all belted, and booted, and spurred.
"Buckle tight, boys!" said he, "for who gallops with me,
Such a hunt as was never before shall he see.

"This traitor, we know him! for when he was younger,
We flattered him, patted him, fed his fierce hunger:
But now far too long we have borne with the wrong,
For each morsel we tossed makes him savage and strong."

Then said one, "He must die!" And they took up the cry,
"For this last crime of his he must die! he must die!"
But the slow eldest-born sauntered sad and forlorn,
For his heart was at home on that fair hunting-morn.

"I remember," he said, "how this fine cub we track
Has carried me many a time on his back!"
And he called to his brothers, "Fight gently! be kind!"
And he kept the dread hound, Retribution, behind.

The dark jaguar, on a bough in the brake,
Crouched, silent and wily, and lithe as a snake:
They spied not their game, but, as onward they came,
Through the dense leafage gleamed two red eyeballs of flame.

Black-spotted, and mottled, and whiskered, and
    grim,
White-bellied, and yellow, he lay on the limb,
And so still that you saw but one tawny paw
Lightly reach through the leaves, and as softly
    withdraw.

Then shrilled his fierce cry, as the riders drew
    nigh,
And he shot from the bough like a bolt from the sky:
In the foremost he fastened his fangs as he fell,
While all the black jungle re-echoed his yell.

O, then there was carnage by field and by flood!
The green sod was crimsoned, the rivers ran blood,
The cornfields were trampled, and all in their track
The beautiful valley lay blasted and black.

Now the din of the conflict swells deadly and loud,
And the dust of the tumult rolls up like a cloud:
Then afar down the slope of the Southland recedes
The wild rapid clatter of galloping steeds.

With wide nostrils smoking, and flanks dripping
    gore,
The black stallion bore his bold rider before,
As onward they thundered through forest and glen,
A-hunting the stark jaguar to his den.

In April, sweet April, the chase was begun ;
It was April again when the hunting was done ;
The snows of four winters and four summers green
Lay red-streaked and trodden, and blighted be-
    tween.

Then the monster stretched all his grim length on
    the ground ;
His life-blood was wasting from many a wound ;
Ferocious and gory, and snarling he lay,
Amid heaps of the whitening bones of his prey.

Then up spoke the slow eldest son, and he said,
"All he needs now is just to be fostered and fed !
Give over the strife ! Brothers, put up the knife !
We will tame him, reclaim him, but not take his
    life !"

But the farmer flung back the false words in his
    face :
"He is none of my race who gives counsel so base!
Now let loose the hound !" And the hound was
    unbound,
And like lightning the heart of the traitor he found.

"So rapine and treason forever shall cease !"
And they wash the stained fleece of the pale lamb
    of peace ;
When, lo ! a strong angel stands wingèd and white
In a wondering raiment of ravishing light !

Peace is raised from the dead ! In the radiance
    shed
By the halo of glory that shines round her head,
Fair gardens shall bloom where the black jungle
    grew,
And all the glad valley shall blossom anew !

A PATRIOTIC MARYLAND LADY. — In making
the surveys for the intrenchments to be made
on the northern and eastern sides of the city of
Washington, the engineer officers came to a
lovely spot near Bladensburg. A pretty cottage
stood on the brow of the hill, surrounded on all
sides by shrubbery, grapevines, orchards, shade
trees, a superb lawn, a beautiful flower garden,
&c. It was, indeed, a little paradise. It was the
residence of a lady and her daughters, whose
husband was now away fighting in the service of
his country. The line of the intrenchments, as
surveyed, passed directly over this spot. The hill
commands the surrounding country for miles, and
therefore is the proper spot for a battery. But
the officers saw at a glance that if a battery was
erected there, it would be necessary to cut down
every tree in the orchard, to clear away all the
shrubbery, and to make the ditch for the parapet in the flower garden. In a word, the military works would completely demolish the place,
and render it a desert. The officers made several surveys, in hopes of finding some way in
which to avoid the necessity of occupying this
property at all. But in vain. There was no
other hill in the neighborhood that possessed the
necessary military qualifications. Calling upon
the lady, therefore, the officers explained, in the
most delicate manner, the object of their visit,
and the military necessity which doomed her
beautiful grounds to destruction. The lady listened in silence. Tears rose to her eyes. She
arose, walked to the open window, looked for a
moment upon the lovely scene, and then, turning
to the officers, said : "If it must be so, take it
freely. I hoped to live here in peace and quiet,
and never to leave this sweet spot, which my husband has beautified for years past. But if my
country demands it, take it freely. You have my
consent." Then offering refreshments to the officers, she said no more on the subject. In the
war of the revolution, in 1777, a lady of South
Carolina brought to General Marion the arrows
with which to set fire to her own house. But
surely the devoted patriotism of this Maryland
lady is deserving of no less praise. — *Washington Letter.*

VILLIAM AND HIS HAVELOCK. — The members
of the Mackerel Brigade, says the inimitable
Orpheus C. Kerr, now stationed on Arlington
Heights, to watch the movements of the Potomac, which is expected to rise shortly, desire me
to thank the ladies of America for supplies of
havelocks and other delicacies of the season just
received. The havelocks, my boy, are rather
roomy, and we took them for shirts at first ; and
the shirts are so narrow-minded that we took
them for havelocks. If the women of America
could manage to get a little less linen into the col-
lars of the latter, and a little more into the other
department of the graceful "garmint," there
would be fewer colds in this division of the
Grand Army. The havelocks, as I have said before, are roomy — very roomy, my boy. Villiam
Brown, of company G, put one on last night
when he went on sentry duty, and looked like a
broomstick in a pillow-case, for all the world.
When the officer came round, and caught sight
of Villiam in his havelock, he was struck dumb with
admiration for a moment. Then he ejaculated :

"What a splendid moonbeam!"

Villiam made a movement, and the Sergeant came up.

"What's that white object?" says the officer to the Sergeant. "Thunder!" roared the officer; "tell him to go to his tent, and take off that nightgown."

"You're mistaken," says the Sergeant; "the sentry is Villiam Brown, in his havelock, which was made by the women of America."

The officer was so justly exasperated at his mistake, that he went immediately to his head-quarters and took the oath three times running, with a little sugar.

The oath is very popular, my boy, and comes in bottles. I take it medicinally myself.

The shirts made by the ladies of America are noble articles, as far down as the collar, but would not do to use as an only garment. Captain Mortimer de Montague, of the skirmish squad, put one on when he went to the President's reception, and the collar stood up so high that he couldn't put his cap on, while the other department didn't reach quite to his waist. His appearance at the White House was picturesque and interesting, and as he entered the drawing-room, General Scott remarked very feelingly:

"Ah! here comes one of the wounded heroes."

"He's not wounded, General," remarked an officer standing by.

"Then why is his head bandaged up so?" asked the venerable veteran.

"O," says the officer, "that's only one of the shirts made by the patriotic women of America."

In about five minutes after this conversation I saw the venerable veteran and the wounded hero at the office taking the oath together.

A REBEL KILLED BY A WOMAN. A Union man by the name of Glover, residing in one of the counties west of Quincy, Illinois, owning a number of valuable horses, and having fear of their appropriation to rebel uses, concluded to place them in the hands of a company of Home Guards in the neighborhood for safe keeping. A day or two afterwards, while Glover was absent from home, a rebel called at his house to inquire for him. His wife was in the garden adjoining a cornfield, some distance from the house, when the rebel approached her, and made several inquiries, to which she gave no very satisfactory answers. He then insisted on being informed where Glover was, and, with revolver in hand, threatened instant death if not told. He also demanded of her to deliver up a valuable gun owned by Glover. The two started for the house through the cornfield, and on the way, Mrs. Glover succeeded, without being observed, in getting possession of a large corn knife that had been left in the field, and watching the opportunity, took a favorable moment for striking a blow, which she did most effectually, the knife severing the skull, and killing the rebel instantly. Mrs. Glover had a small child with her in the gar-den, which she left when starting for the house, intending to return for it immediately. Having despatched the rebel, she returned to the garden, when she discovered several other rebels in ambush, a short distance from her. She took her child, and being yet unperceived by them, sought a place of concealment until they should retire. They soon emerged from their hiding-place, and searching for their companion, they found his lifeless body where he had been stricken down, and bore it off, greatly to the relief of Mrs. Glover.

"CONFISCATE DE OLE 'OMAN!"—One of the Pike County boys at Louisiana (Missouri) found an old negro in the woods who had heard that secession property was to be confiscated, and therefore commenced by executing the order upon himself. He surrendered to the invader, and gave a history of himself, concluding by saying: "Gorry, massa! I'll brack your boots, brush your close, bring your water—do anything you want me, if you'll only confiscate de ole 'oman!"

A TOUCHING INCIDENT. — Just before the advance of the national army towards Richmond, General Sherman's brigade, consisting of the Thirteenth, Sixty-ninth, and Seventy-ninth New York, and the Second Wisconsin regiments, was encamped near Ball's Cross-Roads, not far from a church known as Ball's Church. In the church-yard is the grave of a little child belonging to a Union family by the name of Osborne. The grave is surrounded by a picket fence, upon which there was no inscription. This being observed by Captain Haggerty, of the Sixty-ninth, he went to the trouble of placing upon it a board bearing the age and name of the little one. In a few days the brigade marched for the fatal field of Bull Run, where the gallant Haggerty met a soldier's fate, while acting as Lieutenant-Colonel of his regiment. After the return of the troops to the Potomac, Ball's Cross-Roads and the Church were used as outposts, and quite a number of soldiers who were from time to time stationed in the neighborhood, placed additional inscriptions upon the fence commemorative of the departed officer. One of these read as follows: "Bull Run was where Haggerty was killed. Will they do as much for him as he did for this poor child?"

The incident was related by private B. F. Morgan, of company A, Thirteenth regiment. Mr. M. visited the spot afterwards, in company with the mother of the child, as her escort. She was greatly affected on seeing what had been done.

RATTLESNAKES VS. REBELS. — The best piece of satire upon the leniency observed by the authorities, in the early part of the war, in reference to rebels found committing depredations, is contained in the following story: Some of the soldiers belonging to General Cox's army, stationed in Kanawha, Virginia, caught a large rattlesnake, which manifested a most mischievous disposition, snapping and thrusting out its forked tongue at all who came near it. The boys at last got tired of the reptile, and as nobody wanted such a dangerous companion, the question arose, "What shall we do with him?" This question was propounded several times without an answer, when a half-drunken soldier, who was lying near, upon his back, rolled upon his side, and relieved his companions by quietly remarking: "D—n it! swear him, and let him go!"

ONLY ONE.

"There is no cloud in all the sky ;
  I hear the distant bugles play ;
You tremble, sister — so do I.
  Our soldiers both come home to-day."

"One cloud there is, Maud, on the blue ;
  'Tis but a rustic horn you hear.
I tremble ? — nay ! or if I do,
  It is not for myself I fear."

"Not for yourself? For whom, then, pray ?
  For whom *can* you have cause to feel ?
Those *are* the bugles, Anne, I say,
  And — ha ! I see the flash of steel !"

The sabres glitter in the sun ;
  The war-worn ranks ride slowly past ;
One soldier halts, — ah ! only one ! —
  And cries, "At last, beloved — at last ! "

His steed stands, wistful-eyed, apart,
  And looks upon the ripening grain ;
But who is to the rider's heart
  Thus pressed — again, and yet again ?

Alas ! one cloud still spans the sky ;
  And still the distant bugles play.
Poor Maud ! the ranks have long passed by ;
  But only One came home to-day !

PRACTICAL PATRIOTISM. — In the early part of the war, when patriotic merchants and manufacturers were sending their clerks and workmen to the field, with a promise to provide for the wants of their families, as well as to continue their salaries during their absence, a very enthusiastic landlady of New York offered to allow her boarders' bills to run on, as usual, should any of them desire to go for the defence of the nation.

A COSMOPOLITAN HIBERNIAN. — A son of the Emerald Isle, but not himself *green*, was *taken up* (for he was at the time *down*) near a rebel encampment, not far from Manassas Junction. In a word, Pat was taking a quiet nap in the shade, and was roused from his slumber by a scouting party. He wore no special uniform of either army, but looked more like a spy than an alligator, and on this was arrested.

"Who are you?" "What is your name?" and "Where are you from?" were the first questions put to him by the armed party.

Pat rubbed his eyes, scratched his head, and answered:

"Be me faith, gentlemen, them is ugly questions to answer, anyhow ; an' before I answer any o' them, I'd be afther axin' ye, by yer lave, the same thing."

"Well," said the leader, "we are of Scott's army, and belong to Washington."

"All right," said Pat ; "I know'd ye was gintlemen, for I am that same. Long life to General Scott."

"Aha!" replied the scout, "now, you rascal, you are our prisoner," and seized him by the shoulder.

"How is that," inquired Pat ; "are we not friends ?"

"No," was the answer. "We belong to General Beauregard's army."

"Then ye tould me a lie, me boys ; and thinkin' it might be so, I tould you another. And now tell me the truth, an' I'll tell the truth, too."

"Well, we belong to the State of South Carolina."

"So do I," promptly responded Pat, "and to all the other States uv the country, too ; and there, I'm thinkin', I bate the whole uv ye. Do ye think I would come all the way from Ireland to belong to one State, when I had a right to belong to the whole uv 'em?"

This logic was rather a stumper ; but they took him up, as before said, and carried him for further examination.

INCIDENTS OF YORKTOWN. — The following stories by an officer show the temper and spirit with which the advent of the Yankees was looked for by the negroes. A couple of officers were advancing some distance apart from their men, when they were hailed by an old negro woman standing in the door of her rude cabin. "Bless de Lord, bless de Lord," she exclaimed as loud as she could, "yer's come at last, yer's come at last ! I've looked for yer these many years, and now yer's come. Bless de Lord." Nothing could exceed the old woman's delight at seeing the Yankees. This means something, and how much ! In the childish delight of that old woman what a history is suggested. Long years she had waited to see this deliverance. Slave she was, and the slow years dragged their weary lengths past her youth, and still hope whispered that the hour would come when the bondage would be broken. At last it comes, when the spring of life is gone, and yet her aged lips are eloquent with joy.

* * * * *

The battery of which I spoke is in charge of the First Connecticut artillery, and is built in front of a large and stately brick mansion, which is surrounded by peach orchards. It is the property of Mrs. Farrenholt, whose son and husband are in the rebel army.

Mrs. Farrenholt is a lady somewhat advanced in years, very secesh in opinion, who has remained on her estate ; but she is now dwelling in a small house removed from the danger resulting from the guns of her own friends. The other day an officer belonging to the artillery corps had some little conversation with the lady, to the following effect:

Federal Officer. — Madam, good morning; I desire to purchase a horse from you.

Secesh Lady. — I require what horses I have to plough; I cannot spare one.

F. O. — (Referring to the shells from the enemy.) That will be quite unnecessary; your people are ploughing up your ground for you.

S. L. — Are they planting also?

F. O. — They haven't planted any of *us* yet. But as they have not concluded their work yet, I cannot tell you what they will do.

S. L. — Ah! well, if they plant any of your blue-coated comrades, I hope they wont *sprout.* Good morning.

The officer withdrew. Evidently the secesh lady thought Uncle Sam's sprouts were quite thick enough on her estate.

THE EFFECT OF MUSIC. — A correspondent, writing from the army of the Potomac, in June, 1862, says: " Speaking of the spirit of the men reminds me of an incident, both grand and beautiful, which took place in Butterfield's brigade. For months there has been a standing order against the playing of bands in camp, and in not one instance of the numerous late battles have our splendid bands been allowed to inspire the heart of the brave soldier by the strains of patriotic music. A great mistake, all will say. During the fight yesterday afternoon, an order came for Morell's division to repair to the hill near where the battle was going on, and act as a support for the reserve artillery. The men obeyed the order to fall in promptly, though the weather was scorching hot, and they had been four days without rest or sleep.

"A happy thought struck Captain Thomas J. Hoyt, of General Butterfield's staff, who saw that the men looked weary and exhausted. He immediately gathered all the regimental bands, placed them at the head of the brigade, and ordered them to play. They started the 'Star-spangled Banner;' and the first note had hardly been struck when the men caught the spirit, and cheer after cheer arose from regiment after regiment, and was borne away upon the bosom of the placid river. The band continued to play, and other regiments and other brigades caught the spirit, and the air resounded with tumultuous applause at the happy hit, until all the columns on that vast plain were vying with each other to do homage to the inspiriting strains of the band. After several tunes, Major Welch, of the Sixteenth Michigan, in a brief speech, proposed three cheers for the hero of the command, General Daniel Butterfield, which were given in magnificent style. To add to the enthusiasm, General McClellan happened to ride through the field just then, and was received with an outburst that fairly astonished him.

"The scene was continued, the brigade moved off with the band playing, and had there been a fight in the next field, the men would have gone into action on the double-quick to the tune of Yankee Doodle, if every one had known that death would be his fate."

INDEX.

Q

R

S

560 INDEX TO ANECDOTES, POETRY, AND INCIDENTS.